"It is exactly what is needed in our time"

"It is always refreshing to be made aware of the unceasing efforts of concerned Christian authorities to make God's Word understood by today's generation of believers and skeptics. *The Evidence Bible* is specially designed to reinforce the faith of our times by offering hard evidence and scientific proof for the thinking mind. A welcome addition to the literature of apologetics."

Dr. D. James Kennedy
Coral Ridge Ministries

"*The Evidence Bible* is jam-packed with vignettes tucked right in the text that will help you in witnessing to your friends and in answering their objections to the gospel. If you're looking for a Bible with sneakers on that can run with you into life, *The Evidence Bible* is for you."

Dr. Woodrow Kroll, President
Back to the Bible

"In some countries, handing a pastor a study Bible like *The Evidence Bible* with all its solid teaching is like sending the pastor to seminary training. I look forward to distributing many of these Bibles to pastors all over the world."

Mike Weygandt, Director of International Ministries
The Voice of the Martyrs

"Clearly the Holy Spirit led you as you brought this wonderful document together. I could not be more impressed . . . It is like having a loving, mature Christian elder standing by your shoulder as you read the Scriptures. It is exactly what is needed in our time."

James D. Stambaugh, Director
Billy Graham Center Museum

"Ray Comfort's teaching is right on."

Joni Eareckson Tada
Joni & Friends

"I don't know of an evangelist today who has a better grasp of how to communicate Christ to the totally secular mind of our day than Ray Comfort. He is fearless and genuine. *The Evidence Bible* is filled with practical and theological insights to help anyone effectively communicate the gospel of Christ to their lost friends."

David E. Clippard, Associate Executive Director
Baptist General Convention of Oklahoma

"Any thinking person should demand evidence when it comes to the most important of all matters—eternity. If you are one of those, *The Evidence Bible* will bring your search to an end. It might even spur you on to talk about Christ with someone who's looking for evidence."

Ron DiCianni

"I love *The Evidence Bible.* It should be a great help in drawing others to Christ."

Dr. Kent Hovind, Director
Creation Science Evangelism

"Ray Comfort . . . cuts to the core of a man's spiritual dilemma. As we pray for revival and wonder what God's waiting for, we need to seriously consider this message. To ignore it puts us in spiritual peril."

Terry Meeuwsen, Co-host
The 700 Club

"*The Evidence Bible* is full of the wisdom of great Christian men, including Billy Graham, John MacArthur, and Oswald Chambers, to help answer all the 'why' questions, whether from the new believer, someone who's just beginning to seek the truth, or someone who has been in the faith for several years."

Ron Wheeler
Cartoonworks

The EVIDENCE BIBLE

Irrefutable Evidence For The Thinking Mind

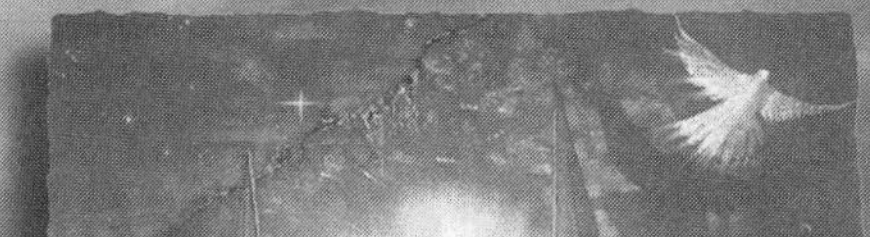

Compiled by
RAY COMFORT

Bridge-Logos *Publishers*

Gainesville, Florida 32614 USA

The Evidence Bible
Compiled by Ray Comfort

Published by:
Bridge-Logos Publishers
P.O. Box 141630
Gainesville, FL 32614, USA
www.bridgelogos.com

Edited by Lynn Copeland

Design and production by Genesis Group, Inc.
(www.genesiswebsite.com)

Printed in the United States of America

ISBN 0-88270-874-0

Information on Islam, Hinduism, Mormonism, and Buddhism is reprinted with permission by the North American Mission Board (www.namb.net/evangelism/iev) and may be reproduced in limited quantities for use by churches. Permission to reprint this material does not constitute an endorsement of Living Waters Publications or Bridge-Logos Publishers by the North American Missions Board or the Southern Baptist Convention.

The text used in this Bible is a "Comfort-able KJV"—a sensitively revised King James Version, in which archaic words have been simplified to make God's Word more understandable.

Scripture quotations designated Amplified are from *The Amplified Bible*, © 1965 by Zondervan Publishing House, Grand Rapids, Michigan.

Contents

List of Sketches

Springboards for Preaching and Witnessing

Principles of Growth for the New and Growing Christian

Points for Open-Air Preaching

In-depth Comments

Common Questions & Objections

God

Jesus Christ

The Bible

Sin

Scientific Facts in the Bible

Follow these linked verses to see all the Scientific Facts in the Bible:

Psalm 8:8; 19:5,6; 25:14; 33:6; 95:4,5; 102:25,26; 104:2; 104:19; 135:7; Luke 4:40; John 20:26; Acts 14:17; Heb. 11:3; 11:11

Would you like to send some of the material in this Bible to a friend or someone with whom you are sharing your faith? Simply go to **www.theevidencebible.com** and (without charge) cut and paste any of its vast resources. All we ask is that you include the words "From *The Evidence Bible* (Bridge-Logos)."

Preface

I HAVE OFTEN said that if you want to see the evangelism section in your local Christian book store, take your magnifying glass with you. Someone once put my claim to the test. When he entered a Christian book store and asked for the "evangelism section," the salesperson replied, "What's evangelism?"

Bill Bright, founder of Campus Crusade for Christ, stated that only 2 percent of today's church is actively involved in evangelism. I believe one great reason for this is that the Body of Christ hasn't been suitably equipped. What soldier is going to run into the heat of battle, facing modern warfare armed only with a feather duster? However, a soldier who is thoroughly equipped with state-of-the-art weapons and a bulletproof vest will find that his very weapons give him courage.

The Evidence Bible will equip the most timid of soldiers with the most powerful of weapons. As you read, you will learn how to trample underfoot grasshoppers that once seemed like daunting giants in the secular world. No longer will themes such as evolution, atheism, modernism, skepticism, and secular intellectualism intimidate you. The wisdom of this world stands on weak and shifting sand. *The Evidence Bible* will show you that, as a Christian, you stand on intellectually solid and immovable rock.

You will notice quotes from many well-known secular people. The apostle Paul, when he preached to the Athenians on Mars Hill, likewise cited secular Greek poets (Acts 17:28). Obviously, Paul wasn't endorsing their sinful lifestyle, nor was he promoting their poetry. He was simply using their words, familiar to his listeners, as a springboard for the gospel.

While *The Evidence Bible* is in essence a study Bible, it is also an evangelistic tool. If it is used merely to strengthen and encourage the faith of the Christian, it has missed its primary purpose. In 1999, I had the incredible experience of floating in the Dead Sea. It is true that it is impossible to sink into its waters, due to its high salt content and rich mineral deposits. The contemporary Body of Christ has become like the Dead Sea. The sea is "dead" because there is no outlet, and the Body of Christ (though rich in many ways) is evangelistically dead because it has stopped giving out what it has received. God forbid that *The Evidence Bible* should merely add more knowledge to the dead sea of contemporary Christianity.

Make sure that you give out what you take in. Become familiar with its commentary and its quotes. Take the Bible with you when you share your faith, and don't hesitate to read portions to the unsaved.

Much of the world doesn't realize how many great men and women of history believed and loved the Word of God. They are ignorant of its wealth of scientific and medical knowledge. Perhaps one simple quote from a famous person of the past may be enough to spark an interest in Holy Scripture. Perhaps God may use your words to bring the message of eternal life to those who are sitting in the shadow of death. There is no higher calling.

May God bless you for picking up this Bible, and may He use it to be a blessing to you and to this dying world.

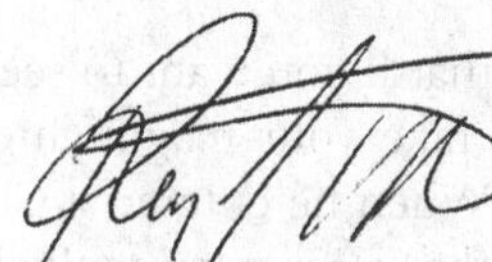

RAY COMFORT

HOW TO USE THIS BOOK

- *Meditate on evangelism verses:* **Shaded, italic verses** help give you the motivation to seek the lost.
- *Memorize evangelistic verses:* **Bold verses** are passages for you to use in witnessing and preaching.
- Look for **bold verse numbers** indicating that the verse has a corresponding comment nearby.
- Read **"Questions & Objections"** so you'll be ready to give a defense as you encounter these in witnessing.
- Follow **cross-references** to read more about a topic.
- Refer to the **Index** to look up topics of interest.

Acknowledgments

I AM VERY grateful to my friend Ron DiCianni for the use of his painting for our cover. Without a doubt, it is the resurrection of the Savior that provides the ultimate evidence of the truth of Christianity. All the quality quotes and powerful arguments about creation, the folly of evolution, etc., may not convince a man of the truth; however, an encounter with the resurrected Savior will. Jesus is still stopping Sauls on the Road to Damascus. He still gives light to those who are in darkness. The indwelling Savior makes a man a new creature in Christ. He gives him a new heart with new desires, making him love the things he once hated, and hate the things he once loved. When a man is born again he needs no more convincing. Knowing Jesus is an infallible proof: "To whom also he showed himself alive after his passion by many infallible proofs, being seen of them forty days" (Acts 1:3).

I am also grateful to my lifelong friend Richard Gunther for his fine cartoons, and to Alex Ruiz, Joe Potter, and Joel Hughs for their quality illustrations. My gratitude also goes to my beloved wife, Sue; my sons, Daniel and Jacob; Rachel and Emeal Zwayne; Ron Meade; Sarah Comfort; Felicia Woodson; Pastor Garry Ansdell; and to my good friend Mark Spence for their help.

My very special thanks to Lynn Copeland of the Genesis Group for her patience, her love of the truth, her concern for the lost, and for her wonderful editorial work. She made a sow's ear into a silk purse.

I am also indebted to Guy Morrell, the owner of Bridge-Logos Publishers. There are not too many Christian men in positions of importance who remember the reason that the Church exists. When the idea of this publication was first conceived, he was told by a respected source to be careful because "evangelism Bibles don't sell." Guy's response was, "That's why we *must* do it." He has a deep passion to see this world reached for Jesus Christ. I count it an honor to work with him and his staff at Bridge-Logos.

If you have any suggestions for future editions of *The Evidence Bible*, feel free to contact me: www.raycomfort.com.

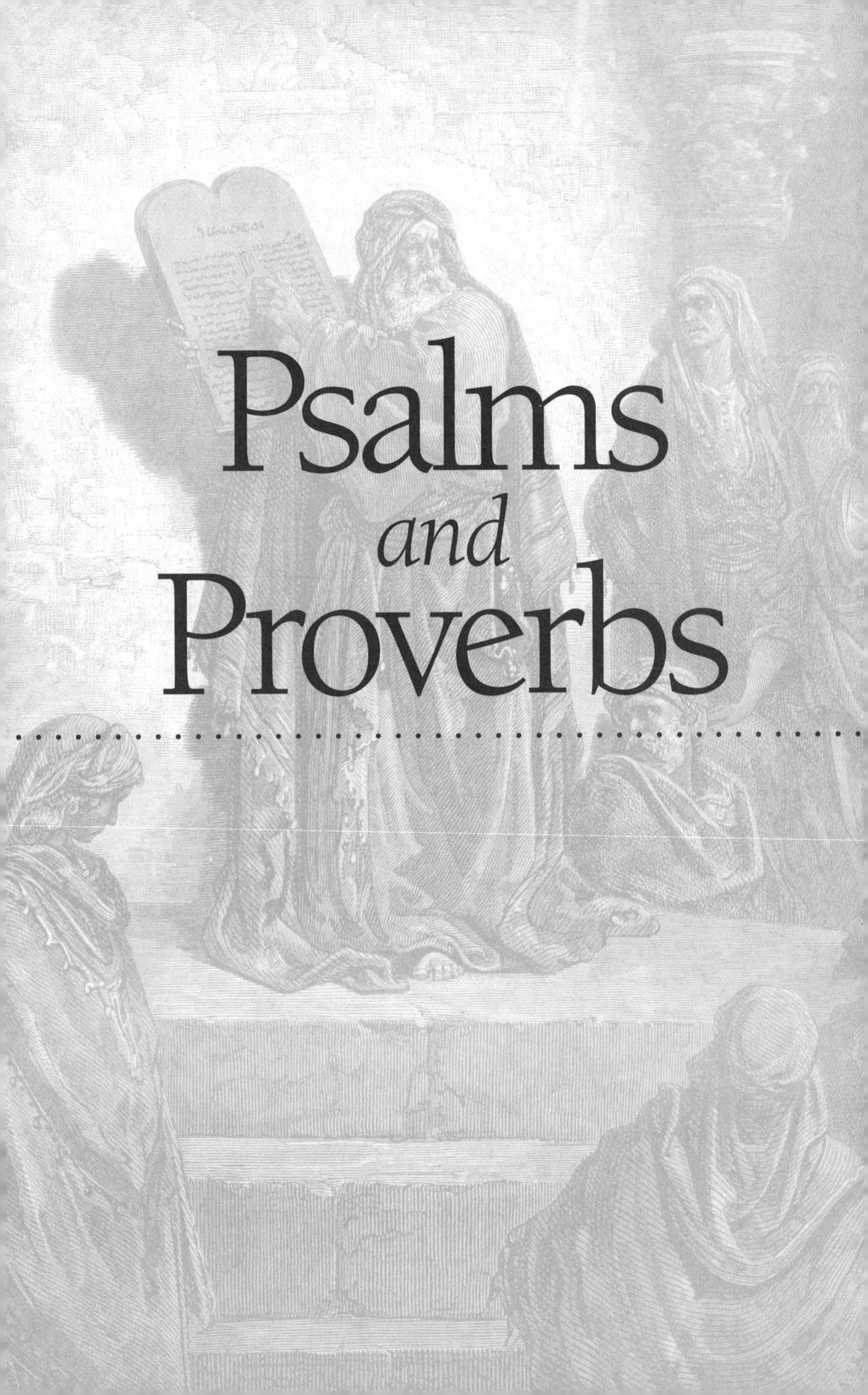

Psalms *and* Proverbs

Psalms

PSALM 1

BLESSED is the man that walks not in
the counsel of the ungodly, nor
stands in the way of sinners, nor sits in
the seat of the scornful.
2 But his delight is in the law of the
LORD; and in his law does he meditate
day and night.
3 And he shall be like a tree planted by
the rivers of water, that brings forth his
fruit in his season; his leaf also shall not
wither; and whatsoever he does shall prosper.
*4 The ungodly are not so: but are like the
chaff which the wind drives away.*
***5** Therefore the ungodly shall not stand in
the judgment, nor sinners in the congregation of the righteous.*
***6** For the LORD knows the way of the right-
eous: but the way of the ungodly shall perish.*

PSALM 2

WHY do the heathen rage, and the
people imagine a vain thing?
2 The kings of the earth set themselves,
and the rulers take counsel together,
against the LORD, and against his anointed, saying,
3 Let us break their bands asunder, and
cast away their cords from us.
4 He that sits in the heavens shall laugh:
the LORD shall have them in derision.
5 Then shall he speak unto them in his
wrath, and vex them in his sore displeasure.
6 Yet have I set my king upon my holy
hill of Zion.
7 I will declare the decree: the LORD has
said unto me, You are my Son; this day
have I begotten you.
8 Ask of me, and I shall give you the
heathen for your inheritance, and the uttermost parts of the earth for your possession.
9 You shall break them with a rod of iron;
you shall dash them in pieces like a potter's vessel.
**10 Be wise now therefore, O you kings:
be instructed, you judges of the earth.**
**11 Serve the LORD with fear, and rejoice
with trembling.**
**12 Kiss the Son, lest he be angry, and
you perish from the way, when his
wrath is kindled but a little. Blessed are**

1:1–3 Here is the biblical formula for success. The key to fruitfulness as a Christian is to meditate on God's Word every day, without fail. Have you ever gone one day when you have been too busy or have forgotten to read the Bible? Have you ever gone one day when you have been too busy or have forgotten to feed your stomach? Which comes first—your Bible or your belly? Be like Job, who "esteemed the words of His mouth more than [his] necessary food" (Job 23:12). Then whatever we do "shall prosper" (v. 3), including our evangelistic endeavors.

1:5 If the fate of the ungodly is our continual meditation, concern for their salvation will be our continual motivation.

QUESTIONS & OBJECTIONS

Q 1:6 *"Why are there so many denominations?"*

In the early 1500s, a German monk named Martin Luther was so conscious of his sins that he spent up to six hours in the confessional. Through study of the Scriptures he found that salvation didn't come through anything he did, but simply through trusting in the finished work of the cross of Jesus Christ. He listed the contradictions between what the Scriptures said and what his church taught, and nailed his "95 Theses" to the church door in Wittenberg, Germany.

Martin Luther became the first to "protest" against the Roman church, and thus he became the father of the Protestant church. Since that split, there have been many disagreements about how much water one should baptize with, how to sing what and why, who should govern who, etc., causing thousands of splinter groups. Many of these groups are convinced that they alone are right. These have become known as Protestant "denominations." Despite the confusion, these churches subscribe to certain foundational beliefs such as the deity, death, burial, and resurrection of Jesus Christ. The Bible says, "The foundation of God stands sure, having this seal, The Lord knows them that are his" (2 Timothy 2:19).

Thomas Jefferson once wrote of a preacher, *Richard Mote*, who "exclaimed aloud to his congregation that he did not believe there was a Quaker, Presbyterian, Methodist, or Baptist in heaven, having paused to give his hearers time to stare and to wonder. He added that, in heaven, God knew no distinctions."

all they that put their trust in him.

PSALM 3

LORD, how are they increased that trouble me! many are they that rise up against me.
2 Many there be which say of my soul, There is no help for him in God. Selah.
3 But you, O LORD, are a shield for me; my glory, and the lifter up of my head.
4 I cried unto the LORD with my voice, and he heard me out of his holy hill. Selah.
5 I laid me down and slept; I awaked; for the LORD sustained me.
6 I will not be afraid of ten thousands of people, that have set themselves against me round about.
7 Arise, O LORD; save me, O my God: for you have smitten all my enemies upon the cheek bone; you have broken the teeth of the ungodly.
8 Salvation belongs unto the LORD: your blessing is upon your people. Selah.

PSALM 4

HEAR me when I call, O God of my righteousness: you have enlarged me when I was in distress; have mercy

2:12 The warning of God's wrath. In 1969, twenty-four people decided to ignore warnings that Hurricane Camille was heading for Mississippi. They instead made up their minds that they were going to ride it out. Twenty-three of them died in the hurricane.

The cross is a warning of the fierce hurricane of God's wrath, which no one will "ride out" on Judgment Day. The only way to flee the coming wrath is to "kiss the Son"—to yield to the Lordship of the Savior, Jesus Christ. Those who put their trust in Him are blessed with forgiveness and eternal life.

3:8 Salvation belongs to the Lord. Scripture tells us that there are none who seek after God, and that no man can come to the Son unless the Father draws him (John 6:44). We have as much to do with our salvation as Lazarus had to do with his own raising from the dead. It is the Lord who quickens the believer. He makes us come alive, then we respond to His voice.

upon me, and hear my prayer.
2 O you sons of men, how long will you turn my glory into shame? how long will you love vanity, and seek after leasing? Selah.
3 But know that the LORD has set apart him that is godly for himself: the LORD will hear when I call unto him.
4 Stand in awe, and sin not: commune with your own heart upon your bed, and be still. Selah.
5 Offer the sacrifices of righteousness, and put your trust in the LORD.
6 There be many that say, Who will show us any good? LORD, lift up the light of your countenance upon us.
7 You have put gladness in my heart, more than in the time that their corn and their wine increased.
8 I will both lay me down in peace, and sleep: for you, LORD, only make me dwell in safety.

PSALM 5

GIVE ear to my words, O LORD, consider my meditation.
2 Hearken unto the voice of my cry, my King, and my God: for unto you will I pray.
3 My voice shall you hear in the morning, O LORD; in the morning will I direct my prayer unto you, and will look up.
4 For you are not a God that has pleasure in wickedness: neither shall evil dwell with you.
5 The foolish shall not stand in your sight: you hate all workers of iniquity.
6 You shall destroy them that speak leasing: the LORD will abhor the bloody and deceitful man.

THE FUNCTION OF THE LAW

5:5 "This Law, then, should be arrayed in all its majesty against selfishness and enmity of the sinner. All men know that they have sinned, but all are not convicted of the guilt and ill dessert of sin. But without this they cannot understand or appreciate the gospel method of salvation. Away with this milk-and-water preaching of a love of Christ that has no holiness or moral discrimination in it. Away with preaching a love of God that is not angry with sinners every day." *Charles Finney*

7 But as for me, I will come into your house in the multitude of your mercy: and in your fear will I worship toward your holy temple.
8 Lead me, O LORD, in your righteousness because of my enemies; make your way straight before my face.
9 For there is no faithfulness in their mouth; their inward part is very wickedness; their throat is an open sepulcher; they flatter with their tongue.
10 Destroy them, O God; let them fall by their own counsels; cast them out in the multitude of their transgressions; for they have rebelled against you.
11 But let all those that put their trust in you rejoice: let them ever shout for joy, because you defend them: let them also that love your name be joyful in you.
12 For you, LORD, will bless the righteous; with favor will you compass him as with a shield.

PSALM 6

O LORD, rebuke me not in your anger, neither chasten me in your hot dis-

5:5 Does God hate sinners? How can God hate sinners when John 3:16 says that He loves them? *Norman Geisler* and *Thomas Howe* write, "There is no contradiction in these statements. The difficulty arises when we wrongly assume that God hates in the same way men hate. Hatred in human beings is generally thought of in terms of strong emotional distaste or dislike for someone or something. However, in God, hate is a judicial act on the part of the righteous judge who separates the sinner from Himself" *(When Critics Ask)*. See Psalm 7:11–13 footnote.

5:9 Sinful man speaks from the abundance of his depraved heart. See Jeremiah 17:9; Mark 7:21–23; Romans 3:10–18.

pleasure.
2 Have mercy upon me, O LORD; for I am weak: O LORD, heal me; for my bones are vexed.
3 My soul is also sore vexed: but you, O LORD, how long?
4 Return, O LORD, deliver my soul: oh save me for your mercies' sake.
5 For in death there is no remembrance of you: in the grave who shall give you thanks?
6 I am weary with my groaning; all the night make I my bed to swim; I water my couch with my tears.
7 My eye is consumed because of grief; it waxes old because of all my enemies.
8 Depart from me, all you workers of iniquity; for the LORD has heard the voice of my weeping.
9 The LORD has heard my supplication; the LORD will receive my prayer.
10 Let all my enemies be ashamed and sore vexed: let them return and be ashamed suddenly.

PSALM 7

O LORD my God, in you do I put my trust: save me from all them that persecute me, and deliver me:
2 Lest he tear my soul like a lion, rending it in pieces, while there is none to deliver.
3 O LORD my God, If I have done this; if there be iniquity in my hands;
4 If I have rewarded evil unto him that was at peace with me; (yes, I have delivered him that without cause is my enemy:)
5 Let the enemy persecute my soul, and take it; yes, let him tread down my life upon the earth, and lay my honor in the dust. Selah.
6 Arise, O LORD, in your anger, lift up yourself because of the rage of my enemies: and awake for me to the judgment that you have commanded.
7 So shall the congregation of the people compass you about: for their sakes therefore return on high.
8 The LORD shall judge the people: judge me, O LORD, according to my righteousness, and according to my integrity that is in me.
9 Oh let the wickedness of the wicked come to an end; but establish the just: for the righteous God tries the hearts and reins.
10 My defense is of God, which saves the upright in heart.
11 God judges the righteous, and God is angry with the wicked every day.
12 If he turn not, he will whet his sword; he has bent his bow, and made it ready.
13 He has also prepared for him the instruments of death; he ordains his arrows against the persecutors.
14 Behold, he travails with iniquity, and has conceived mischief, and brought forth falsehood.
15 He made a pit, and digged it, and is fallen into the ditch which he made.
16 His mischief shall return upon his own head, and his violent dealing shall come down upon his own pate.
17 I will praise the LORD according to his righteousness: and will sing praise to the name of the LORD most high.

PSALM 8

O LORD, our Lord, how excellent is your name in all the earth! who have set your glory above the heavens.
2 Out of the mouth of babes and sucklings have you ordained strength because of your enemies, that you might still the enemy and the avenger.

7:11–13 This is the message we must bring to a sinful world. God is angry with the wicked every day. His wrath abides on them (John 3:36). Every time they sin, they are storing up for themselves wrath that will be revealed on the Day of Judgment (Romans 2:5). Unless they are convinced that there is wrath to come, they will not flee to the One who can deliver them from the wrath to come (1 Thessalonians 1:10). See 1 Timothy 1:8–10 footnote.

3 When I consider your heavens, the
work of your fingers, the moon and the
stars, which you have ordained;
4 What is man, that you are mindful of
him? and the son of man, that you visit
him?
5 For you have made him a little lower
than the angels, and have crowned him
with glory and honor.
6 You made him to have dominion over
the works of your hands; you have put
all things under his feet:
7 All sheep and oxen, yes, and the beasts
of the field;
8 The fowl of the air, and the fish of the
sea, and whatsoever passes through the
paths of the seas.
9 O LORD our Lord, how excellent is your
name in all the earth!

PSALM 9

I WILL praise you, O LORD, with my
whole heart; I will show forth all your
marvelous works.
2 I will be glad and rejoice in you: I will
sing praise to your name, O you most
High.
3 When my enemies are turned back,
they shall fall and perish at your presence.
4 For you have maintained my right and
my cause; you sat in the throne judging
right.
5 You have rebuked the heathen, you
have destroyed the wicked, you have put
out their name for ever and ever.
6 O you enemy, destructions are come to
a perpetual end: and you have destroyed
cities; their memorial is perished with
them.
7 But the LORD shall endure for ever: he
has prepared his throne for judgment.
8 And he shall judge the world in righteousness, he shall minister judgment to
the people in uprightness.
9 The LORD also will be a refuge for the
oppressed, a refuge in times of trouble.
10 And they that know your name will
put their trust in you: for you, LORD, have

8:5 "See what wickedness there is in the nature of man. How much are we beholden to the restraining grace of God! For, were it not for this, man, who was made but a little lower than angels, would make himself a great deal lower than the devils." *Matthew Henry*

8:6 Man's dominion. Man is not just an animal on the evolutionary food chain. God has given him dominion (authority) over all the animals (Genesis 1:28). He is intellectually superior to them and has *priority* over them—every animal is "under his feet" and may be brought into submission by him (James 3:7). Birds (parrots) can be taught to speak. With a crack of a whip lions will do what he says. Even killer whales obey his voice.

Man's dominion is obvious. Cows yield milk for his cereal, cheese for his hamburger, butter for his bread, yogurt to keep him healthy, and ice cream to delight his taste buds on hot days. The same cow gives him meat to keep him strong and leather to keep him warm. Sheep and goats also yield many of these same products. The chicken makes eggs for his breakfast and provides finger-licking meat for his dinner. The sea overflows with an incredible variety of fish for him to catch and eat. Dogs protect his property and herd his sheep. Elephants lift great weights for him. Camels carry him across deserts. The horse is perfectly designed to be ridden by him. See also Matthew 6:26 footnote.

8:8 Scientific facts in the Bible. The Bible says, "…and the fish of the sea, and whatsoever passes through the paths of the seas" (Psalm 8:8). What does the Bible mean by "paths of the seas"? Man discovered the existence of ocean currents in the 1850s, but the Bible declared the science of oceanography 2,800 years ago. *Matthew Maury* (1806–1873) is considered the father of oceanography. He noticed the expression "paths of the sea" in Psalm 8:8. "If God said there are paths in the sea," Maury said, "I am going to find them." Maury took God at His word and went looking for these paths. We are indebted to his discovery of the warm and cold continental currents. His book on oceanography remains a basic text on the subject and is still used in universities. Maury used the Bible as a guide to a scientific discovery; if only more would use the Bible as a guide in their personal lives.

not forsaken them that seek you.
11 Sing praises to the LORD, which dwells
in Zion: declare among the people his
doings.
12 When he makes inquisition for blood,
he remembers them: he forgets not the
cry of the humble.
13 Have mercy upon me, O LORD; consider my trouble which I suffer of them
that hate me, you that lift me up from the
gates of death:
14 That I may show forth all your praise
in the gates of the daughter of Zion: I will
rejoice in your salvation.
15 The heathen are sunk down in the pit
that they made: in the net which they hid
is their own foot taken.
16 The LORD is known by the judgment
which he executes: the wicked is snared
in the work of his own hands. Higgaion.
Selah.
17 The wicked shall be turned into hell,
and all the nations that forget God.
18 For the needy shall not always be forgotten: the expectation of the poor shall
not perish for ever.
19 Arise, O LORD; let not man prevail:
let the heathen be judged in your sight.
20 Put them in fear, O LORD: that the nations may know themselves to be but men.
Selah.

PSALM 10

WHY stand afar off, O LORD? why
hide yourself in times of trouble?
2 The wicked in his pride does persecute the poor: let them be taken in the
devices that they have imagined.
3 For the wicked boasts of his heart's
desire, and blesses the covetous, whom
the LORD abhors.
4 The wicked, through the pride of his
countenance, will not seek after God:
God is not in all his thoughts.
5 His ways are always grievous; your
judgments are far above out of his sight:
as for all his enemies, he puffs at them.
6 He has said in his heart, I shall not
be moved: for I shall never be in adver-
sity.
7 His mouth is full of cursing and deceit and fraud: under his tongue is mischief and vanity.
8 He sits in the lurking places of the villages: in the secret places does he murder the innocent: his eyes are privily set
against the poor.
9 He lies in wait secretly as a lion in his
den: he lies in wait to catch the poor: he
does catch the poor, when he draws him
into his net.
10 He crouches, and humbles himself,
that the poor may fall by his strong ones.
11 He has said in his heart, God has
forgotten: he hides his face; he will never
see it.
12 Arise, O LORD; O God, lift up your
hand: forget not the humble.
13 Wherefore does the wicked con-
temn God? he has said in his heart, You

9:8 See Acts 17:31.

9:17 How wrong it is for us to forget the One who gave us life. When nations, like individuals, forget God, they therefore die in their sins and reap His great wrath. See 1 John 1:9 footnote.

10:3–6,11,13 The thoughts of sinners. Scripture gives us insight into the thoughts of the unsaved: 1) His pride keeps him from seeking God. Any admittance of guilt is a blow to the pride of the human heart. 2) Because he's self-centered and self-sufficient, he feels no need to even consider God. 3) He thinks that he's in control of his life and that adversity will never come to him. 4) His willful ignorance leaves him without understanding of God's righteous judgments. 5) He believes that either God is blinded to his sinful lifestyle, or He has no sense of justice and will therefore not require any account for his lawlessness.

10:4 The reason that the proud don't seek after God is that they don't want to—they *will* not seek after God because they don't want to leave their sins. It's not that they cannot find Him, but that they *will* not.

will not require it.
14 You have seen it; for you behold mischief and spite, to requite it with your
hand: the poor commits himself unto you;
you are the helper of the fatherless.
15 Break the arm of the wicked and the
evil man: seek out his wickedness till you
find none.
16 The LORD is King for ever and ever:
the heathen are perished out of his land.
17 LORD, you have heard the desire of
the humble: you will prepare their heart,
you will cause your ear to hear:
18 To judge the fatherless and the oppressed, that the man of the earth may
no more oppress.

> All men who are eminently useful are made to feel their weakness in a supreme degree.
>
> **CHARLES SPURGEON**

PSALM 11

IN the LORD put I my trust: how say to
my soul, Flee as a bird to your mountain?
2 For, lo, the wicked bend their bow,
they make ready their arrow upon the
string, that they may privily shoot at the
upright in heart.
3 If the foundations be destroyed, what
can the righteous do?
4 The LORD is in his holy temple, the
LORD's throne is in heaven: his eyes behold, his eyelids try, the children of men.
5 The LORD tries the righteous: but the
wicked and him that loves violence his
soul hates.
6 Upon the wicked he shall rain snares,
fire and brimstone, and an horrible tempest: this shall be the portion of their cup.
7 For the righteous LORD loves righteousness; his countenance does behold
the upright.

PSALM 12

HELP, LORD; for the godly man ceases; for the faithful fail from among
the children of men.
2 They speak vanity every one with his
neighbor: with flattering lips and with a
double heart do they speak.
3 The LORD shall cut off all flattering lips,
and the tongue that speaks proud things:
4 Who have said, With our tongue will
we prevail; our lips are our own: who is
lord over us?
5 For the oppression of the poor, for the
sighing of the needy, now will I arise, says
the LORD; I will set him in safety from
him that puffs at him.
6 The words of the LORD are pure words:
as silver tried in a furnace of earth, purified seven times.
7 You shall keep them, O LORD, you shall
preserve them from this generation for
ever.
8 The wicked walk on every side, when
the vilest men are exalted.

PSALM 13

HOW long will you forget me, O
LORD? for ever? how long will you
hide your face from me?
2 How long shall I take counsel in my
soul, having sorrow in my heart daily?
how long shall my enemy be exalted over
me?
3 Consider and hear me, O LORD my
God: lighten my eyes, lest I sleep the sleep
of death;
4 Lest my enemy say, I have prevailed
against him; and those that trouble me
rejoice when I am moved.
5 But I have trusted in your mercy; my
heart shall rejoice in your salvation.

12:6,7 Men may list what they consider to be mistakes in the Bible. However, all Scripture is given by inspiration of God (2 Timothy 3:16); every word of the Lord is pure. Therefore any seeming "mistakes" are there because God has put them there, and they are therefore not mistakes. In time, we will find that the "mistakes" are actually ours. See Mark 15:26 footnote.

6 I will sing unto the LORD, because he
has dealt bountifully with me.

PSALM 14

**THE fool has said in his heart, There
is no God. They are corrupt, they
have done abominable works, there is
none that does good.**
**2 The LORD looked down from heaven
upon the children of men, to see if there
were any that did understand, and seek
God.**
**3 They are all gone aside, they are all
together become filthy: there is none
that does good, no, not one.**
4 Have all the workers of iniquity no
knowledge? who eat up my people as they
eat bread, and call not upon the LORD.
5 There were they in great fear: for God
is in the generation of the righteous.
6 You have shamed the counsel of the
poor, because the LORD is his refuge.
7 Oh that the salvation of Israel were
come out of Zion! when the LORD brings
back the captivity of his people, Jacob shall
rejoice, and Israel shall be glad.

PSALM 15

LORD, who shall abide in your tabernacle? who shall dwell in your holy
hill?
2 He that walks uprightly, and works
righteousness, and speaks the truth in his
heart.
3 He that backbites not with his tongue,
nor does evil to his neighbor, nor takes up
a reproach against his neighbor.
4 In whose eyes a vile person is contemned; but he honors them that fear the
LORD. He that swears to his own hurt,
and changes not.
5 He that puts not out his money to usury, nor takes reward against the innocent. He that does these things shall never
be moved.

PSALM 16

PRESERVE me, O God: for in you do
I put my trust.
2 O my soul, you have said unto the
LORD, You are my Lord: my goodness ex-
tends not to you;
3 But to the saints that are in the earth,
and to the excellent, in whom is all my
delight.
4 Their sorrows shall be multiplied that
hasten after another god: their drink offerings of blood will I not offer, nor take
up their names into my lips.
5 The LORD is the portion of my inheritance and of my cup: you maintain my lot.
6 The lines are fallen unto me in pleasant places; yes, I have a goodly heritage.
7 I will bless the LORD, who has given
me counsel: my reins also instruct me in
the night seasons.
8 I have set the LORD always before me:
because he is at my right hand, I shall

14:1 There is no such thing as an "atheist." He is a "fool." See Psalm 53:1 footnote.

14:1–3 Who is "good"? As far as the world is concerned, there are many people who do good. However, here is God's view of humanity: 1) All people are corrupt and do abominable things. 2) No one understands or seeks God. 3) All have turned away from God. 4) They have together become filthy. 5) There is no one who does good, not even one.

The world may consider it a good deed when a celebrity gives millions to charity. God, however, sees the motive for the act, which may be guilt for a past adulterous lifestyle. As long as the world is ignorant of God's Law (which Romans 7:12 says is "good"), it will have no idea of what "good" is.

15:1–5 This is the standard by which the Christian should live. We must walk in righteousness, speak the truth, keep our heart free from sin, keep our word, and be free from any corruption and covetousness. Those who fear God and want to be effective in their witness will gladly conform.

16:7 It is most profitable to arise from bed, pray, then allow your reins to instruct you in the night season. If you have allowed God to break your spirit, He is the one who has hold of the reins, and He will guide you in the way you should go. See Psalm 119:62.

not be moved.
9 Therefore my heart is glad, and my
glory rejoices: my flesh also shall rest in
hope.
10 For you will not leave my soul in
hell; neither will you suffer your Holy
One to see corruption.
11 You will show me the path of life: in
your presence is fullness of joy; at your
right hand there are pleasures for evermore.

. . . . . .

To learn the damage of gossip, see Proverbs 11:13 footnote.

. . . . . .

PSALM 17

HEAR the right, O LORD, attend unto
my cry, give ear unto my prayer,
that goes not out of feigned lips.
2 Let my sentence come forth from your
presence; let your eyes behold the things
that are equal.
3 You have proved my heart; you have
visited me in the night; you have tried
me, and shall find nothing; I am purposed
that my mouth shall not transgress.
4 Concerning the works of men, by the
word of your lips I have kept me from the
paths of the destroyer.
5 Hold up my goings in your paths, that
my footsteps slip not.
6 I have called upon you, for you will
hear me, O God: incline your ear unto me,
and hear my speech.
7 Show your marvelous lovingkindness,
O you that save by your right hand them
which put their trust in you from those
that rise up against them.
8 Keep me as the apple of the eye, hide
me under the shadow of your wings,
9 From the wicked that oppress me, from
my deadly enemies, who compass me
about.
10 They are enclosed in their own fat:
with their mouth they speak proudly.
11 They have now compassed us in our
steps: they have set their eyes bowing
down to the earth;
12 Like as a lion that is greedy of his
prey, and as it were a young lion lurking
in secret places.
13 Arise, O LORD, disappoint him, cast
him down: deliver my soul from the
wicked, which is your sword:
14 From men which are your hand, O
LORD, from men of the world, which have
their portion in this life, and whose belly
you fill with your hid treasure: they are
full of children, and leave the rest of their
substance to their babes.
15 As for me, I will behold your face in
righteousness: I shall be satisfied, when I
awake, with your likeness.

PSALM 18

I WILL love you, O LORD, my strength.
2 The LORD is my rock, and my fortress, and my deliverer; my God, my
strength, in whom I will trust; my buckler, and the horn of my salvation, and
my high tower.
3 I will call upon the LORD, who is worthy to be praised: so shall I be saved from
my enemies.
4 The sorrows of death compassed me,
and the floods of ungodly men made me
afraid.
5 The sorrows of hell compassed me
about: the snares of death prevented me.
6 In my distress I called upon the LORD,
and cried unto my God: he heard my voice
out of his temple, and my cry came before him, even into his ears.
7 Then the earth shook and trembled;
the foundations also of the hills moved
and were shaken, because he was wroth.
8 There went up a smoke out of his nostrils, and fire out of his mouth devoured:
coals were kindled by it.
9 He bowed the heavens also, and came
down: and darkness was under his feet.

16:10 Messianic prophecy: This was fulfilled in Acts 2:31.

10 And he rode upon a cherub, and did
fly: yes, he did fly upon the wings of the
wind.
11 He made darkness his secret place;
his pavilion round about him were dark
waters and thick clouds of the skies.
12 At the brightness that was before him
his thick clouds passed, hail stones and
coals of fire.
13 The LORD also thundered in the heavens, and the Highest gave his voice; hail
stones and coals of fire.
14 Yes, he sent out his arrows, and scattered them; and he shot out lightnings,
and discomfited them.
15 Then the channels of waters were
seen, and the foundations of the world
were discovered at your rebuke, O LORD,
at the blast of the breath of your nostrils.
16 He sent from above, he took me, he
drew me out of many waters.
17 He delivered me from my strong enemy, and from them which hated me:
for they were too strong for me.
18 They prevented me in the day of my
calamity: but the LORD was my stay.
19 He brought me forth also into a large
place; he delivered me, because he delighted in me.
20 The LORD rewarded me according to
my righteousness; according to the cleanness of my hands has he recompensed me.
21 For I have kept the ways of the LORD,
and have not wickedly departed from my
God.
22 For all his judgments were before me,
and I did not put away his statutes from
me.
23 I was also upright before him, and I
kept myself from my iniquity.
24 Therefore has the LORD recompensed
me according to my righteousness, according to the cleanness of my hands in his
eyesight.
25 With the merciful you will show yourself merciful; with an upright man you
will show yourself upright;
26 With the pure you will show yourself
pure; and with the froward you will show
yourself froward.
27 For you will save the afflicted people; but will bring down high looks.
28 For you will light my candle: the LORD
my God will enlighten my darkness.
29 For by you I have run through a troop;
and by my God have I leaped over a wall.
**30 As for God, his way is perfect: the
word of the LORD is tried: he is a buckler to all those that trust in him.**
31 For who is God save the LORD? or who
is a rock save our God?
32 It is God that girds me with strength,
and makes my way perfect.
33 He makes my feet like hinds' feet,
and sets me upon my high places.
34 He teaches my hands to war, so that
a bow of steel is broken by my arms.
35 You have also given me the shield of
your salvation: and your right hand has
held me up, and your gentleness has made
me great.
36 You have enlarged my steps under
me, that my feet did not slip.
37 I have pursued my enemies, and overtaken them: neither did I turn again till
they were consumed.
38 I have wounded them that they were
not able to rise: they are fallen under my
feet.
39 For you have girded me with strength
unto the battle: you have subdued under
me those that rose up against me.

18:30 A perfect God gave a perfect Law that demands that we live up to its perfection. He makes us perfect in Christ (Colossians 1:28). See verse 32.

18:39 We must run to the battle for the souls of men. Our aim is not to kill, but to make alive. Men have rushed into battle merely to obtain dirt. Many have given their lives to get back a hill in Vietnam, Korea, or Israel—a hill that may be returned to the enemy through peace negotiations twenty years later. Their costly efforts proved to be futile. Our labor, however, is not in vain (1 Corinthians 15:58).

QUESTIONS & OBJECTIONS

Q 19:1–4

"Doesn't the Big Bang theory disprove the Genesis account of creation?"

Try to think of any explosion that has produced order. Does a terrorist bomb create harmony? Big bangs cause chaos. How could a Big Bang produce a rose, apple trees, fish, sunsets, the seasons, hummingbirds, polar bears—thousands of birds and animals, each with its own eyes, nose, and mouth? A *child* can see that there is "grand design" in creation.

Try this interesting experiment: Empty your garage of every piece of metal, wood, paint, rubber and plastic. *Make sure there is nothing there.* Nothing. Then wait for ten years and see if a Mercedes evolves. Try it. If it doesn't appear, leave it for 20 years. If that doesn't work, try it for 100 years. Then try leaving it for 10,000 years.

Here's what will produce the necessary blind faith to make the evolutionary process believable: leave it for 250 million years.

"New scientific revelations about supernovas, black holes, quarks, and the big bang even suggest to some scientists that there is a 'grand design' in the universe." (*U.S. News & World Report*, March 31, 1997)

"The universe suddenly exploded into being... The big bang bears an uncanny resemblance to the Genesis command." *Jim Holt, Wall Street Journal* science writer

40 You have also given me the necks of my enemies; that I might destroy them that hate me.

41 They cried, but there was none to save them: even unto the LORD, but he answered them not.

42 Then did I beat them small as the dust before the wind: I did cast them out as the dirt in the streets.

43 You have delivered me from the strivings of the people; and you have made me the head of the heathen: a people whom I have not known shall serve me.

44 As soon as they hear of me, they shall obey me: the strangers shall submit themselves unto me.

45 The strangers shall fade away, and be afraid out of their close places.

46 The LORD lives and blessed be my rock; and let the God of my salvation be exalted.

47 It is God that avenges me, and subdues the people under me.

48 He delivers me from my enemies: yes, you lift me up above those that rise up against me: you have delivered me from the violent man.

49 Therefore will I give thanks unto you, O LORD, among the heathen, and sing praises unto your name.

50 Great deliverance gives he to his king; and show mercy to his anointed, to David, and to his seed for evermore.

PSALM 19

THE heavens declare the glory of God; and the firmament show his handiwork.

2 Day unto day utters speech, and night unto night show knowledge.

3 There is no speech nor language, where their voice is not heard.

4 Their line is gone out through all the earth, and their words to the end of the world. In them has he set a tabernacle for the sun,

19:1–4 Creation reveals the genius of God's creative hand. Men are without excuse when it comes to believing in God's existence. See Psalm 33:8 footnote and Romans 1:20.

5 Which is as a bridegroom coming out
of his chamber, and rejoices as a strong
man to run a race.
6 His going forth is from the end of the
heaven, and his circuit unto the ends of
it: and there is nothing hid from the heat
thereof.
7 The law of the LORD is perfect, con-
verting the soul: the testimony of the
LORD is sure, making wise the simple.
8 The statutes of the LORD are right, rejoicing the heart: the commandment of
the LORD is pure, enlightening the eyes.
9 The fear of the LORD is clean, enduring for ever: the judgments of the LORD
are true and righteous altogether.
10 More to be desired are they than
gold, yes, than much fine gold: sweeter
also than honey and the honeycomb.
11 Moreover by them is your servant
warned: and in keeping of them there is
great reward.
12 Who can understand his errors?
cleanse me from secret faults.
13 Keep back your servant also from
presumptuous sins; let them not have
dominion over me: then shall I be upright, and I shall be innocent from the
great transgression.
14 Let the words of my mouth, and the
meditation of my heart, be acceptable in
your sight, O LORD, my strength, and my
redeemer.

THE FUNCTION OF THE LAW

19:7–11 God's Law is perfect. It is His tool to convert the soul. When a sinner is confronted with God's holy Law, his conscience affirms its truth. The Law gives understanding to the unregenerate mind. It reveals God's absolutes and therefore produces the fear of God, leading to repentance. It is of great worth. It is sweet to the converted soul. Its function is to warn sinners of the wrath to come and lead them to shelter in the Savior.

"The law of the Lord...is of use to convert the soul, to bring us back to ourselves, to our God, to our duty; for it shows us our sinfulness and misery in our departures from God and the indispensable necessity of our return to Him.

"Those who would know sin must get the knowledge of the Law in its strictness, extent, and spiritual nature." *Matthew Henry*

PSALM 20

THE LORD hear you in the day of
trouble; the name of the God of Jacob
defend you;
2 Send you help from the sanctuary,
and strengthen you out of Zion;
3 Remember all your offerings, and accept your burnt sacrifice; Selah.
4 Grant you according to your own heart,
and fulfill all your counsel.
5 We will rejoice in your salvation, and

19:5,6 God's Law is like the sun. On Judgment Day it will arise with its burning heat and shine the brilliant light of eternal justice on the dark corners of the human heart. Nothing will be hidden from its consuming heat.

19:5,6 Scientific facts in the Bible. In speaking of the sun, the psalmist says that "his going forth is from the end of the heaven, and his circuit unto the ends of it: and there is nothing hid from the heat thereof." For many years critics scoffed at these verses, claiming that they taught the old false doctrine of geocentricity (i.e., the sun revolves around the earth). Scientists thought the sun was stationary. Then it was discovered in recent years that the sun is in fact moving through space at approximately 600,000 miles per hour. It is traveling through the heavens and has a "circuit" just as the Bible says. Its circuit is so large that it would take approximately 200 million years to complete one orbit.

19:7 God's Law does the following: 1) converts the soul; 2) makes wise the simple; 3) makes the heart rejoice; 4) enlightens the eyes; 5) produces the fear of the Lord; 6) reveals God's true and righteous judgments; 7) is more to be desired than gold; 8) is sweeter than honey; 9) warns us of God's wrath; 10) provides a great reward.

QUESTIONS & OBJECTIONS

22:1 ***"On the cross, Jesus cried, 'My God, why have You forsaken Me?' This proves He was a fake. God forsook Him."***

Jesus' words recorded in Matthew 27:46 and Mark 15:34 were the fulfillment of David's prophecy in Psalm 22:1. Verse 3 of this psalm then gives us insight into why God forsook Jesus on the cross: "But You are holy..." A holy Creator cannot have fellowship with sin. When Jesus was on the cross, the sin of the entire world was laid upon Him (Isaiah 53:6; 2 Corinthians 5:21), but Scripture says God is "of purer eyes than to behold evil, and cannot look on iniquity" (Habakkuk 1:13).

in the name of our God we will set up our banners: the LORD fulfill all your petitions.
6 Now know I that the LORD saves his anointed; he will hear him from his holy heaven with the saving strength of his right hand.
7 Some trust in chariots, and some in horses: but we will remember the name of the LORD our God.
8 They are brought down and fallen: but we are risen, and stand upright.
9 Save, LORD: let the king hear us when we call.

PSALM 21

THE king shall joy in your strength, O LORD; and in your salvation how greatly shall he rejoice!
2 You have given him his heart's desire, and have not withheld the request of his lips. Selah.
3 For you prevent him with the blessings of goodness: you set a crown of pure gold on his head.
4 He asked life of you, and you gave it him, even length of days for ever and ever.
5 His glory is great in your salvation: honor and majesty have you laid upon him.
6 For you have made him most blessed for ever: you have made him exceeding glad with your countenance.
7 For the king trusts in the LORD, and through the mercy of the most High he shall not be moved.
8 Your hand shall find out all your enemies: your right hand shall find out those that hate you.
9 You shall make them as a fiery oven in the time of your anger: the LORD shall swallow them up in his wrath, and the fire shall devour them.
10 Their fruit shall you destroy from the earth, and their seed from among the children of men.
11 For they intended evil against you: they imagined a mischievous device, which they are not able to perform.
12 Therefore shall you make them turn their back, when you shall make ready your arrows upon your strings against the face of them.
13 Be exalted, LORD, in your own strength: so will we sing and praise your power.

PSALM 22

MY God, my God, why have you forsaken me? why are you so far from helping me, and from the words of my roaring?
2 O my God, I cry in the day time, but you hear not; and in the night season,

21:9 "There's probably no concept in theology more repugnant to modern America than the idea of divine wrath." *R. C. Sproul*

and am not silent.
3 But you are holy, O you that inhabit
the praises of Israel.
4 Our fathers trusted in you: they trusted, and you did deliver them.
5 They cried unto you, and were delivered: they trusted in you, and were not
confounded.
6 But I am a worm, and no man; a reproach of men, and despised of the people.
7 All they that see me laugh me to scorn:
they shoot out the lip, they shake the head,
saying,
8 He trusted on the LORD that he would
deliver him: let him deliver him, seeing
he delighted in him.
9 But you are he that took me out of the
womb: you did make me hope when I
was upon my mother's breasts.
10 I was cast upon you from the womb:
you are my God from my mother's belly.
11 Be not far from me; for trouble is near;
for there is none to help.
12 Many bulls have compassed me: strong
bulls of Bashan have beset me round.
13 They gaped upon me with their
mouths, as a ravening and a roaring lion.
14 I am poured out like water, and all my
bones are out of joint: my heart is like wax;
it is melted in the midst of my bowels.
15 My strength is dried up like a potsherd; and my tongue cleaves to my jaws;
and you have brought me into the dust
of death.
16 For dogs have compassed me: the assembly of the wicked have enclosed me:
they pierced my hands and my feet.
17 I may tell all my bones: they look and

22:6–8 Christ's suffering on the cross. "Man, at the best, is a worm; but he [Jesus] became a worm, and no man. If he had not made himself a worm, he could not have been trampled upon as he was. The word signifies such a worm as was used in dyeing scarlet or purple, whence some make it an allusion to his bloody sufferings. See what abuses were put upon him. He was ridiculed as a foolish man, and one that not only deceived others, but himself too. Those that saw him hanging on the cross laughed him to scorn. So far were they from pitying him, or concerning themselves for him, that they added to his afflictions, with all the gestures and expressions of insolence upbraiding him with his fall. They make mouths at him, make merry over him, and make a jest of his sufferings: 'They shoot out the lip, they shake their head, saying, "This was he that said he trusted God would deliver him; now let him deliver him."'

"David was sometimes taunted for his confidence in God; but in the sufferings of Christ this was literally and exactly fulfilled. Those very gestures were used by those that reviled him (Matt. 27:39); they wagged their heads, nay, and so far did their malice make them forget themselves that they used the very words (v. 43), 'He trusted in God; let him deliver him.' Our Lord Jesus, having undertaken to satisfy for the dishonor we had done to God by our sins, did it by submitting to the lowest possible instance of ignominy and disgrace." *Matthew Henry, Commentary on the Whole Bible: New Modern Edition*

22:12–18 Messianic prophecy: This was clearly fulfilled in the crucifixion of Jesus of Nazareth. See John 19:28,37; Luke 23:35; and Matthew 27:35. Here is a graphic description of the Messiah on the cross:

- He was aware of their scorn (vv. 6,7).
- He could hear the mocking words (v. 8).
- He was praying (vv. 9–13).
- The strain of crucifixion pulled His bones out of joint (v. 14).
- Loss of blood made His heart feel as though it were melting (v. 14).
- His strength completely left Him (v. 15).
- Thirst caused his tongue to adhere to His mouth (v. 15).
- They pierced His hands and feet (v. 16).
- He could see them gambling for His clothes (v. 18).

stare upon me.
18 They part my garments among them,
and cast lots upon my vesture.
19 But be not far from me, O LORD: O my
strength, haste to help me.
20 Deliver my soul from the sword; my
darling from the power of the dog.
21 Save me from the lion's mouth: for
you have heard me from the horns of the
unicorns.
22 I will declare your name unto my
brethren: in the midst of the congregation will I praise you.
23 You that fear the LORD, praise him; all
you the seed of Jacob, glorify him; and
fear him, all you the seed of Israel.
24 For he has not despised nor abhorred
the affliction of the afflicted; neither has
he hid his face from him; but when he
cried unto him, he heard.
25 My praise shall be of you in the great
congregation: I will pay my vows before
them that fear him.
26 The meek shall eat and be satisfied:
they shall praise the LORD that seek him:
your heart shall live for ever.
27 All the ends of the world shall remember and turn unto the LORD: and all
the kindreds of the nations shall worship
before you.
28 For the kingdom is the LORD's: and
he is the governor among the nations.
29 All they that be fat upon earth shall
eat and worship: all they that go down to
the dust shall bow before him: and none
can keep alive his own soul.

"Those who will not be governed by God will be ruled by tyrants."

William Penn

22:14 When commenting on this verse, *Charles Spurgeon* said: "The placing of the cross in its socket had shaken Him with great violence, had strained all the ligaments, pained every nerve, and more or less dislocated all His bones. Burdened with His own weight, the august sufferer felt the strain increasing every moment of those six long hours. His sense of faintness and general weakness were overpowering; while to His own consciousness He became nothing but a mass of misery and swooning sickness...To us, sensations such as our Lord endured would have been insupportable, and kind unconsciousness would have come to our rescue; but in His case, He was wounded and *felt* the sword; He drained the cup and *tasted* every drop."

22:16 **Messianic prophecy:** This was fulfilled in Luke 24:39.

22:18 *Matthew Henry* wrote, "The shame of nakedness was the immediate consequence of sin [Genesis 3:7], and therefore our Lord Jesus was stripped of His clothes, when He was crucified, that the shame of our nakedness might not appear." (See Revelation 3:17,19; 16:15.)

22:18 **Messianic prophecy**: This was fulfilled in Mark 15:24.

22:28 "Men, in a word, must necessarily be controlled, either by a power within them, or by a power without them; either by the word of God, or by the strong arm of man; either by the Bible, or by the bayonet." *Robert Winthrop*

"We staked the whole future of American civilization, not upon the power of government, far from it. We have staked the future of all our political institutions upon the capacity of mankind for self government; upon the capacity of each and all of us to govern ourselves, to control ourselves according to the Commandments of God." *James Madison*

30 A seed shall serve him; it shall be accounted to the Lord for a generation.

31 They shall come, and shall declare his righteousness unto a people that shall be born, that he has done this.

PSALM 23

THE LORD is my shepherd; I shall not want.

2 He makes me to lie down in green pastures: he leads me beside the still waters.

3 He restores my soul: he leads me in the paths of righteousness for his name's sake.

4 Yes, though I walk through the valley of the shadow of death, I will fear no evil: for thou art with me; thy rod and thy staff they comfort me.

5 You prepare a table before me in the presence of my enemies: you anoint my head with oil; my cup runs over.

6 Surely goodness and mercy shall follow me all the days of my life: and I will dwell in the house of the LORD for ever.

PSALM 24

THE earth is the LORD's, and the fullness thereof; the world, and they that dwell therein.

2 **For he has founded it upon the seas, and established it upon the floods.**

3 **Who shall ascend into the hill of the LORD? or who shall stand in his holy place?**

4 He that has clean hands, and a pure heart; who has not lifted up his soul unto vanity, nor sworn deceitfully.

5 He shall receive the blessing from the LORD, and righteousness from the God of his salvation.

6 This is the generation of them that seek him, that seek your face, O Jacob. Selah.

7 Lift up your heads, O you gates; and be lift up, you everlasting doors; and the King of glory shall come in.

8 Who is this King of glory? The LORD strong and mighty, the LORD mighty in battle.

9 Lift up your heads, O you gates; even lift them up, you everlasting doors; and the King of glory shall come in.

10 Who is this King of glory? The LORD of hosts, he is the King of glory. Selah.

PSALM 25

UNTO you, O LORD, do I lift up my soul.

2 O my God, I trust in you: let me not be ashamed, let not my enemies triumph over me.

3 Yes, let none that wait on you be ashamed: let them be ashamed which transgress without cause.

4 Show me your ways, O LORD; teach me your paths.

5 Lead me in your truth, and teach me: for you are the God of my salvation; on you do I wait all the day.

6 Remember, O LORD, your tender mercies and your lovingkindnesses; for they have been ever of old.

7 Remember not the sins of my youth, nor my transgressions: according to your mercy remember me for your goodness' sake, O LORD.

8 Good and upright is the LORD: therefore will he teach sinners in the way.

9 The meek will he guide in judgment: and the meek will he teach his way.

23:1 See John 10:11 footnote.

23:4 This life is the valley of the shadow of death. The Scriptures describe all of humanity as sitting in darkness and the shadow of death, because they rebelled against the words of God (Psalm 107:10,11). The birth of the Savior gives "light to those who sit in darkness and the shadow of death" (Luke 1:79). The light of the gospel not only banishes the shadow of death, but the believer fears no evil because God is now for him, rather than against him.

24:1 No one truly "owns" anything. We are merely temporary custodians of that which God has entrusted to us. The entire earth and all who dwell in it belong to the Lord.

10 All the paths of the LORD are mercy
and truth unto such as keep his covenant and his testimonies.
11 For your name's sake, O LORD, pardon my iniquity; for it is great.
12 What man is he that fears the LORD?
him shall he teach in the way that he shall
choose.
13 His soul shall dwell at ease; and his
seed shall inherit the earth.
14 The secret of the LORD is with them
that fear him; and he will show them his
covenant.
15 My eyes are ever toward the LORD;
for he shall pluck my feet out of the net.
16 Turn you unto me, and have mercy
upon me; for I am desolate and afflicted.
17 The troubles of my heart are enlarged:
O bring me out of my distresses.
18 Look upon my affliction and my pain;
and forgive all my sins.
19 Consider my enemies; for they are

25:12–14 Look at what wonderful fruit comes from the fear of the Lord: God Himself will teach us. We will dwell in prosperity. Our descendants will be blessed, and we will be partakers of His incredible covenant.

25:14 *Samuel Morse,* famous for his invention of the telegraph, gave God the glory for his inventions. It's fitting that the first message he ever sent over the wire was taken from Scripture: "What hath God wrought!" (Numbers 23:23).

Morse, who graduated from Yale in 1810, wrote these words four years before he died: "The nearer I approach the end of my pilgrimage, the clearer is the evidence of the divine origin of the Bible. The grandeur and sublimity of God's remedy for fallen man are more appreciated and the future is illuminated with hope and joy."

25:14 Scientists who believe. "Most of the great scientists of the past who founded and developed the key disciplines of science were creationists. Note the following sampling:

Physics: Newton, Faraday, Maxwell, Kelvin
Chemistry: Boyle, Dalton, Pascal, Ramsay
Biology: Ray, Linnaeus, Mendel, Pasteur
Geology: Steno, Woodward, Brewster, Agassiz
Astronomy: Kepler, Galileo, Herschel, Maunder

"These men, as well as scores of others who could be mentioned, were creationists, not evolutionists, and their names are practically synonymous with the rise of modern science. To them, the scientific enterprise was a high calling, one dedicated to "thinking God's thoughts after Him." *Henry M. Morris* and *Gary E. Parker, What is Creation Science?*

"Science is the glimpse of God's purpose in nature. The very existence of the amazing world of the atom and radiation points to a purposeful creation, to the idea that there is a God and an intelligent purpose back of everything... An orderly universe testifies to the greatest statement ever uttered: 'In the beginning, God...'" *Arthur H. Compton*, winner of Nobel Prize in Physics

"The chief aim of all investigation of the external world should be to discover the rational order and harmony which has been imposed on it by God." *Johann Kepler*

"With regard to the origin of life, science... positively affirms creative power." *Lord Kelvin*

"All material things seem to have been composed of the hard and solid particles abovementioned, variously associated in the first creation by the counsel of an intelligent Agent. For it became Him who created them to set them in order. And if He did so, it's unphilosophical to seek for any other origin of the world, or to pretend that it might arise out of a chaos by the mere laws of nature." *Sir Isaac Newton*

"An increasing number of scientists, most particularly a growing number of evolutionists... argue that Darwinian evolutionary theory is no genuine scientific theory at all... Many of the critics have the highest intellectual credentials." *Michael Ruse*, "Darwin's Theory: An Exercise in Science," *New Scientist*

See also Psalm 33:8 footnote.

many; and they hate me with cruel hatred.
20 O keep my soul, and deliver me: let me not be ashamed; for I put my trust in you.
21 Let integrity and uprightness preserve me; for I wait on you.
22 Redeem Israel, O God, out of all his troubles.

PSALM 26

JUDGE me, O LORD; for I have walked in my integrity: I have trusted also in the LORD; therefore I shall not slide.
2 Examine me, O LORD, and prove me; try my reins and my heart.
3 For your lovingkindness is before my eyes: and I have walked in your truth.
4 I have not sat with vain persons, neither will I go in with dissemblers.
5 I have hated the congregation of evil doers; and will not sit with the wicked.
6 I will wash my hands in innocency: so will I compass your altar, O LORD:
7 That I may publish with the voice of thanksgiving, and tell of all your wondrous works.
8 LORD, I have loved the habitation of your house, and the place where your honor dwells.
9 Gather not my soul with sinners, nor my life with bloody men:
10 In whose hands is mischief, and their right hand is full of bribes.
11 But as for me, I will walk in my integrity: redeem me, and be merciful unto me.
12 My foot stands in an even place: in the congregations will I bless the LORD.

PSALM 27

THE LORD is my light and my salvation; whom shall I fear? the LORD is the strength of my life; of whom shall I be afraid?
2 When the wicked, even my enemies and my foes, came upon me to eat up my flesh, they stumbled and fell.
3 Though an host should encamp against me, my heart shall not fear: though war should rise against me, in this will I be confident.
4 One thing have I desired of the LORD, that will I seek after; that I may dwell in the house of the LORD all the days of my life, to behold the beauty of the LORD, and to enquire in his temple.
5 For in the time of trouble he shall hide me in his pavilion: in the secret of his tabernacle shall he hide me; he shall set me up upon a rock.

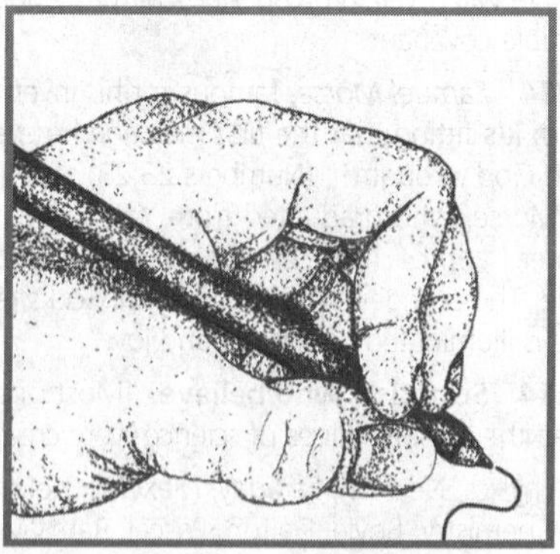

Who wrote the Bible—God or men? See 2 Peter 2:21 footnote.

6 And now shall my head be lifted up above my enemies round about me: therefore will I offer in his tabernacle sacrifices of joy; I will sing, yes, I will sing praises unto the LORD.
7 Hear, O LORD, when I cry with my voice: have mercy also upon me, and answer me.
8 When you said, Seek my face; my heart said unto you, Your face, LORD, will I seek.
9 Hide not your face far from me; put not your servant away in anger: you have been my help; leave me not, neither forsake me, O God of my salvation.
10 When my father and my mother forsake me, then the LORD will take me up.

27:12 Messianic prophecy: This was fulfilled in Matthew 26:60.

28:4,5 It is a fearful thing for sinners to be given exactly what they deserve.

11 Teach me your way, O LORD, and lead
me in a plain path, because of my enemies.
12 Deliver me not over unto the will of
my enemies: for false witnesses are risen
up against me, and such as breathe out
cruelty.
13 I had fainted, unless I had believed to
see the goodness of the LORD in the land
of the living.
14 Wait on the LORD: be of good courage,
and he shall strengthen your heart: wait,
I say, on the LORD.

PSALM 28

UNTO you will I cry, O LORD my
rock; be not silent to me: lest, if you
be silent to me, I become like them that
go down into the pit.
2 Hear the voice of my supplications,
when I cry unto you, when I lift up my
hands toward your holy oracle.
3 Draw me not away with the wicked,
and with the workers of iniquity, which
speak peace to their neighbors, but mischief is in their hearts.
4 Give them according to their deeds,
and according to the wickedness of their
endeavors: give them after the work of
their hands; render to them their desert.
5 Because they regard not the works of
the LORD, nor the operation of his hands,
he shall destroy them, and not build them
up.
6 Blessed be the LORD, because he has
heard the voice of my supplications.
7 The LORD is my strength and my shield;
my heart trusted in him, and I am helped:
therefore my heart greatly rejoices; and
with my song will I praise him.
8 The LORD is their strength, and he is
the saving strength of his anointed.
9 Save your people, and bless your inheritance: feed them also, and lift them up for
ever.

PSALM 29

GIVE unto the LORD, O you mighty,
give unto the LORD glory and
strength.
2 Give unto the LORD the glory due unto his name; worship the LORD in the beauty of holiness.
3 The voice of the LORD is upon the waters: the God of glory thunders: the LORD
is upon many waters.
4 The voice of the LORD is powerful; the
voice of the LORD is full of majesty.
5 The voice of the LORD breaks the cedars; yes, the LORD breaks the cedars of
Lebanon.
6 He makes them also to skip like a calf;
Lebanon and Sirion like a young unicorn.
7 The voice of the LORD divides the flames
of fire.
8 The voice of the LORD shakes the wilderness; the LORD shakes the wilderness
of Kadesh.
9 The voice of the LORD makes the hinds
to calve, and discovers the forests: and in
his temple does every one speak of his
glory.
10 The LORD sits upon the flood; yes, the
LORD sits King for ever.
11 The LORD will give strength unto his
people; the LORD will bless his people
with peace.

29:3–9 The voice of the Lord. It was the "voice of the Lord" (His Word) that brought creation into existence (see Genesis 1:3; John 1:1–3). God's voice then became flesh in the person of Jesus of Nazareth (John 1:14; 1 John 1:1–3). That's why Jesus said strange things about His voice: "Marvel not at this: for the hour is coming, in which all that are in the graves shall hear [My] voice" (John 5:28). He said, "The words that I speak to you, they are spirit, and they are life" (John 6:63). It was the voice of the Savior that brought Lazarus back to life (John 11:43), and it is His voice that will bring the dead out of their graves at the resurrection (John 5:28,29). His voice brings life.

This is just one example of a wonderfully unique aspect of the Bible. One can study a multitude of subjects in its different books, and find incredible continuity, despite the fact that the books were written thousands of years apart.

PSALM 30

I WILL extol you, O LORD; for you have lifted me up, and have not made my foes to rejoice over me.

2 O LORD my God, I cried unto you, and you have healed me.

3 O LORD, you have brought up my soul from the grave: you have kept me alive, that I should not go down to the pit.

4 Sing unto the LORD, O you saints of his, and give thanks at the remembrance of his holiness.

5 For his anger endures but a moment; in his favor is life: weeping may endure for a night, but joy comes in the morning.

6 And in my prosperity I said, I shall never be moved.

7 LORD, by your favor you have made my mountain to stand strong: you did hide your face, and I was troubled.

8 I cried to you, O LORD; and unto the LORD I made supplication.

9 What profit is there in my blood, when I go down to the pit? Shall the dust praise you? shall it declare your truth?

10 Hear, O LORD, and have mercy upon me: LORD, be my helper.

11 You have turned for me my mourning into dancing: you have put off my sackcloth, and girded me with gladness;

12 To the end that my glory may sing praise to you, and not be silent. O LORD my God, I will give thanks unto you for ever.

PSALM 31

IN you, O LORD, do I put my trust; let me never be ashamed: deliver me in your righteousness.

2 Bow down your ear to me; deliver me speedily: be my strong rock, for an house of defense to save me.

3 For you are my rock and my fortress; therefore for your name's sake lead me, and guide me.

4 Pull me out of the net that they have laid privily for me: for you are my strength.

5 Into your hand I commit my spirit: you have redeemed me, O LORD God of truth.

6 I have hated them that regard lying vanities: but I trust in the LORD.

7 I will be glad and rejoice in your mercy: for you have considered my trouble; you have known my soul in adversities;

8 And have not shut me up into the hand of the enemy: you have set my feet in a large room.

9 Have mercy upon me, O LORD, for I am in trouble: my eye is consumed with grief, yes, my soul and my belly.

10 For my life is spent with grief, and my years with sighing: my strength fails because of my iniquity, and my bones are consumed.

11 I was a reproach among all my enemies, but especially among my neighbors, and a fear to my acquaintance: they that did see me without fled from me.

12 I am forgotten as a dead man out of mind: I am like a broken vessel.

13 For I have heard the slander of many: fear was on every side: while they took counsel together against me, they devised to take away my life.

14 But I trusted in you, O LORD: I said, You are my God.

15 My times are in your hand: deliver me from the hand of my enemies, and from them that persecute me.

16 Make your face to shine upon your servant: save me for your mercies' sake.

17 Let me not be ashamed, O LORD; for I have called upon you: let the wicked be ashamed, and let them be silent in the grave.

18 Let the lying lips be put to silence; which speak grievous things proudly and contemptuously against the righteous.

19 *Oh how great is your goodness, which you have laid up for them that fear you; which you have wrought for them that trust*

31:19 Here is an amazing promise to those who are not ashamed to bear the reproach of the gospel.

QUESTIONS & OBJECTIONS

32:5

"What if someone says, 'I've broken every one of the Ten Commandments'?"

Do not take this statement to mean that the person has seen the gravity of his sinful state before God. He may say something like, "I'm a really *bad* person!" It is often used as a way of shrugging off conviction. Say to him, "Well let's take the time to go through them one by one and see if you have." As he is confronted with the righteous standard of God's Moral Law, pray that the Holy Spirit brings conviction of sin.

in you before the sons of men!

20 *You shall hide them in the secret of your presence from the pride of man: you shall keep them secretly in a pavilion from the strife of tongues.*

21 Blessed be the LORD: for he has showed me his marvelous kindness in a strong city.

22 For I said in my haste, I am cut off from before your eyes: nevertheless you heard the voice of my supplications when I cried unto you.

23 O love the LORD, all you his saints: for the LORD preserve the faithful, and plentifully reward the proud doer.

24 Be of good courage, and he shall strengthen your heart, all you that hope in the LORD.

PSALM 32

BLESSED is he whose transgression is forgiven, whose sin is covered.

2 Blessed is the man unto whom the LORD imputes not iniquity, and in whose spirit there is no guile.

3 When I kept silence, my bones waxed old through my roaring all the day long.

4 For day and night your hand was heavy upon me: my moisture is turned into the drought of summer. Selah.

5 I acknowledge my sin unto you, and my iniquity have I not hid. I said, I will confess my transgressions unto the LORD; and you forgave the iniquity of my sin. Selah.

6 For this shall every one that is godly pray unto you in a time when you may be found: surely in the floods of great waters they shall not come near unto him.

7 You are my hiding place; you shall preserve me from trouble; you shall compass me about with songs of deliverance. Selah.

8 I will instruct you and teach you in the way which you shall go: I will guide you with my eye.

9 Be not as the horse, or as the mule, which have no understanding: whose mouth must be held in with bit and bridle, lest they come near unto you.

10 Many sorrows shall be to the wicked: but he that trusts in the LORD, mercy shall compass him about.

11 Be glad in the LORD, and rejoice, you righteous: and shout for joy, all you that are upright in heart.

PSALM 33

REJOICE in the LORD, O you righteous: for praise is comely for the upright.

2 Praise the LORD with harp: sing unto

32:1,2 *Transgression* is violation of the Law. *Sin* is falling short of the Law's standard. *Iniquity* is lawlessness.

32:5 Contrition does not save us. Its outworking can be seen in these verses: we acknowledge our sin to God rather than justifying ourselves. No longer do we try to hide anything from God, but we confess our transgressions to Him.

him with the psaltery and an instrument
of ten strings.
3 Sing unto him a new song; play skill-
fully with a loud noise.
4 For the word of the LORD is right; and
all his works are done in truth.
5 He loves righteousness and judgment:
the earth is full of the goodness of the
LORD.
6 By the word of the LORD were the
heavens made; and all the host of them by
the breath of his mouth.
7 He gathers the waters of the sea together as an heap: he lays up the depth in
storehouses.
8 Let all the earth fear the LORD: let all the
inhabitants of the world stand in awe of
him.
9 For he spoke, and it was done; he commanded, and it stood fast.
10 The LORD brings the counsel of the
heathen to nought: he makes the devices
of the people of none effect.
11 The counsel of the LORD stands for
ever, the thoughts of his heart to all generations.
12 Blessed is the nation whose God is
the LORD; and the people whom he has
chosen for his own inheritance.
13 **The LORD looks from heaven; he**
beholds all the sons of men.
14 **From the place of his habitation he**
looks upon all the inhabitants of the
earth.
15 **He fashions their hearts alike; he**
considers all their works.
16 There is no king saved by the multitude of an host: a mighty man is not de-

32:9 Differences between men and animals. The Bible tells us that animals are created "without understanding." Human beings are different from animals. We are made in God's "image." As human beings, we are aware of our "being." God is "I AM," and we know that "we are." We have understanding that we exist.

Among other unique characteristics, we have an innate ability to appreciate God's creation. What animal gazes with awe at a sunset, or at the magnificence of the Grand Canyon? What animal obtains joy from the sounds of music or takes the time to form itself into an orchestra to create music? What animal among the beasts sets up court systems and apportions justice to its fellow creatures? We are moral beings.

While birds and other creatures have instincts to create (nests, etc.), we have the ability to uncover the hidden laws of electricity. We can utilize the law of aerodynamics to transport ourselves around the globe. We also have the God-given ability to appreciate the *value* of creation. We unearth the hidden treasures of gold, silver, diamonds, and oil and make use of them for our own benefit. Only humans have the unique ability to appreciate God for this incredible creation and to respond to His love.

33:6 Scientific facts in the Bible. The Scriptures say, "Thus the heavens and the earth were finished, and all the host of them" (Genesis 2:1). The original Hebrew uses the past definite tense for the verb "finished," indicating an action completed in the past, never again to occur. The creation was "finished"—once and for all. That is exactly what the First Law of Thermodynamics says. This law (often referred to as the Law of the Conservation of Energy and/or Mass) states that neither matter nor energy can be either created or destroyed. It was because of this Law that Sir Fred Hoyle's "Steady-State" (or "Continuous Creation") Theory was discarded. Hoyle stated that at points in the universe called "irtrons," matter (or energy) was constantly being created. But, the First Law states just the opposite. Indeed, there is no "creation" ongoing today. It is "finished" exactly as the Bible states.

33:8 Awe for the Creator. "Science can only be created by those who are thoroughly imbued with the aspiration toward truth and understanding. This source of feeling, however, springs from the sphere of religion. To this there also belongs the faith in the possibility that the regulations valid for the world of existence are rational, that is, comprehensible to reason. I cannot conceive of a genuine scientist without that profound faith." *Albert Einstein*

Sir John Frederick Herschel, an English astronomer who discovered over 500 stars, stated: "All

livered by much strength.
17 An horse is a vain thing for safety:
neither shall he deliver any by his great
strength.
18 Behold, the eye of the LORD is upon
them that fear him, upon them that hope
in his mercy;
19 To deliver their soul from death, and
to keep them alive in famine.
20 Our soul waits for the LORD: he is
our help and our shield.
21 For our heart shall rejoice in him,
because we have trusted in his holy name.
22 Let your mercy, O LORD, be upon us,
according as we hope in you.

PSALM 34

I WILL bless the LORD at all times: his
praise shall continually be in my mouth.
2 My soul shall make her boast in the
LORD: the humble shall hear thereof, and
be glad.
3 O magnify the LORD with me, and let
us exalt his name together.
4 I sought the LORD, and he heard me,
and delivered me from all my fears.
5 They looked unto him, and were lightened: and their faces were not ashamed.
6 This poor man cried, and the LORD
heard him, and saved him out of all his
troubles.
7 The angel of the LORD encamps round
about them that fear him, and delivers
them.
8 O taste and see that the LORD is good:
blessed is the man that trusts in him.
9 O fear the LORD, you his saints: for
there is no want to them that fear him.

human discoveries seem to be made only for the purpose of confirming more and more strongly the truths that come from on high and are contained in the Sacred Writings." His father, *Sir William Herschel*, also a renowned astronomer, insisted, "The undevout astronomer must be mad." See also Psalm 25:14 footnote.

"In antiquity and in what is called the Dark Ages, men did not know what they now know about humanity and the cosmos. They did not know the lock but they possessed they key, which is God. Now many have excellent descriptions of the lock, but they have lost the key. The proper solution is union between religion and science. We should be owners of the lock *and* the key. The fact is that as science advances, it discovers what was said thousands of years ago in the Bible." *Richard Wurmbrand, Proofs of God's Existence*

"Calvin said that the Bible—God's special revelation—was spectacles that we must put on if we are to correctly read the book of nature—God's revelation in creation. Unfortunately, between the beginning of science and our day, many scientists have discarded these glasses, and many distortions have followed." *D. James Kennedy* and *Jerry Newcombe, What if Jesus Had Never Been Born?*

33:12 The source of a nation's blessings. In Leviticus 26:1–13, God promises Israel many wonderful blessings if they would simply obey Him: The rain would come in due season; the land would yield its harvest and the trees would yield their fruit; their food would satisfy them; they would have peace and safety in the land (no violence), and they would prevail over their enemies. Truly, blessed is the nation whose God is the Lord.

"Suppose a nation in some distant region should take the Bible for their only law book, and every member should regulate his conduct by the precepts there exhibited! Every member would be obliged in conscience, to temperance, frugality, and industry; to justice, kindness, and charity towards his fellow men; and to piety, love, and reverence toward Almighty God...What a Eutopia, what a Paradise would this region be." *John Adams*

"If we abide by the principles taught in the Bible, our country will go on prospering and to prosper; but if we and our posterity neglect its instructions and authority, no man can tell how sudden a catastrophe may overwhelm us and bury all our glory in profound obscurity." *Daniel Webster*

34:2 The proud are not glad to hear a soul boast in the Lord. Try telling a proud unsaved person about an obvious answer to prayer, and watch him try to explain it away as coincidence. It is a humble heart that can hear a boast about God.

10 The young lions do lack, and suffer hunger: but they that seek the LORD shall not want any good thing.
11 Come, you children, hearken unto me: I will teach you the fear of the LORD.
12 What man is he that desires life, and loves many days, that he may see good?
13 Keep your tongue from evil, and your lips from speaking guile.
14 **Depart from evil, and do good; seek peace, and pursue it.**
15 **The eyes of the LORD are upon the righteous, and his ears are open unto their cry.**
16 **The face of the LORD is against them that do evil, to cut off the remembrance of them from the earth.**
17 The righteous cry, and the LORD hears, and delivers them out of all their troubles.
18 **The LORD is near unto them that are of a broken heart; and saves such as be of a contrite spirit.**
19 Many are the afflictions of the righteous: but the LORD delivers him out of them all.
20 He keeps all his bones: not one of them is broken.
21 Evil shall slay the wicked: and they that hate the righteous shall be desolate.
22 The LORD redeems the soul of his servants: and none of them that trust in him shall be desolate.

PSALM 35

PLEAD my cause, O LORD, with them that strive with me: fight against them that fight against me.
2 Take hold of shield and buckler, and stand up for my help.
3 Draw out also the spear, and stop the way against them that persecute me: say unto my soul, I am your salvation.
4 Let them be confounded and put to shame that seek after my soul: let them be turned back and brought to confusion that devise my hurt.
5 Let them be as chaff before the wind: and let the angel of the LORD chase them.
6 Let their way be dark and slippery: and let the angel of the LORD persecute them.
7 For without cause have they hid for me their net in a pit, which without cause they have digged for my soul.
8 Let destruction come upon him at unawares; and let his net that he has hid catch himself: into that very destruction let him fall.
9 And my soul shall be joyful in the LORD: it shall rejoice in his salvation.
10 All my bones shall say, LORD, who is like unto you, who delivers the poor from him that is too strong for him, yes, the poor and the needy from him that spoils him?
11 False witnesses did rise up; they laid to my charge things that I knew not.
12 They rewarded me evil for good to the spoiling of my soul.
13 But as for me, when they were sick, my clothing was sackcloth: I humbled my soul with fasting; and my prayer returned into my own bosom.
14 I behaved myself as though he had been my friend or brother: I bowed down heavily, as one that mourns for his mother.
15 But in my adversity they rejoiced, and gathered themselves together: yes, the abjects gathered themselves together against me, and I knew it not; they did tear me,

---

34:8 See John 17:3 footnote, "Experiential Faith."

34:8,9 The goodness of God cannot be separated from the fear of the Lord. Those who maintain that it is "the goodness of God" that leads to repentance, and therefore we need only speak of His goodness, need to study the context of Romans 2:3–11.

34:20 **Messianic prophecy:** This was fulfilled in John 19:33.

35:13 It is wise to make fasting a way of life. Missing a meal on a regular basis will help you to keep your appetite in check. It will also put a joyful thanksgiving in your heart every time you sit down to a meal.

and ceased not:
16 With hypocritical mockers in feasts,
they gnashed upon me with their teeth.
17 Lord, how long will you look on?
rescue my soul from their destructions,
my darling from the lions.
18 I will give you thanks in the great congregation: I will praise you among much
people.
19 Let not them that are my enemies
wrongfully rejoice over me: neither let
them wink with the eye that hate me without a cause.

> I remember two things: I am a great sinner and I have a great Savior; and I don't suppose an old slave trader needs to remember much more than that.
>
> **JOHN NEWTON**

20 For they speak not peace: but they
devise deceitful matters against them that
are quiet in the land.
21 Yes, they opened their mouth wide
against me, and said, Aha, aha, our eye has
seen it.
22 This you have seen, O LORD: keep not
silence: O Lord, be not far from me.
23 Stir up yourself, and awake to my
judgment, even unto my cause, my God
and my Lord.
24 Judge me, O LORD my God, according
to your righteousness; and let them not
rejoice over me.
25 Let them not say in their hearts, Ah,
so would we have it: let them not say,
We have swallowed him up.
26 Let them be ashamed and brought
to confusion together that rejoice at my
hurt: let them be clothed with shame and
dishonor that magnify themselves against
me.
27 Let them shout for joy, and be glad,
that favor my righteous cause: yes, let
them say continually, Let the LORD be
magnified, which has pleasure in the prosperity of his servant.
28 And my tongue shall speak of your
righteousness and of your praise all the
day long.

PSALM 36

*THE transgression of the wicked says
within my heart, that there is no fear
of God before his eyes.*
2 *For he flatters himself in his own eyes,
until his iniquity be found to be hateful.*
3 *The words of his mouth are iniquity and
deceit: he has left off to be wise, and to do
good.*
4 *He devises mischief upon his bed; he sets
himself in a way that is not good; he abhors
not evil.*
5 Your mercy, O LORD, is in the heavens;
and your faithfulness reaches unto the
clouds.
6 Your righteousness is like the great
mountains; your judgments are a great
deep: O LORD, you preserve man and beast.
7 How excellent is your lovingkindness,
O God! therefore the children of men
put their trust under the shadow of your
wings.
8 They shall be abundantly satisfied with
the fatness of your house; and you shall
make them drink of the river of your pleasures.
9 For with you is the fountain of life: in
your light shall we see light.
10 O continue your lovingkindness unto them that know you; and your righteousness to the upright in heart.
11 Let not the foot of pride come against
me, and let not the hand of the wicked
remove me.
12 There are the workers of iniquity fall-
en: they are cast down, and shall not be
able to rise.

PSALM 37

FRET not yourself because of evildoers, neither be envious against the
workers of iniquity.

36:2 "The greatest fault is to be conscious of none." *Thomas Carlyle*

2 For they shall soon be cut down like
the grass, and wither as the green herb.
3 Trust in the LORD, and do good; so shall
you dwell in the land, and verily you shall
be fed.
4 Delight yourself also in the LORD: and
he shall give you the desires of your heart.
5 Commit your way unto the LORD; trust
also in him; and he shall bring it to pass.
6 And he shall bring forth your righteousness as the light, and your judgment
as the noonday.
7 Rest in the LORD, and wait patiently
for him: fret not yourself because of him
who prospers in his way, because of the
man who brings wicked devices to pass.
8 Cease from anger, and forsake wrath:
fret not yourself in any wise to do evil.
9 For evildoers shall be cut off: but
those that wait upon the LORD, they shall
inherit the earth.
10 For yet a little while, and the wicked
shall not be: yes, you shall diligently
consider his place, and it shall not be.
11 But the meek shall inherit the earth;
and shall delight themselves in the abundance of peace.
12 The wicked plots against the just,
and gnashes upon him with his teeth.
13 The LORD shall laugh at him: for he
sees that his day is coming.
14 The wicked have drawn out the
sword, and have bent their bow, to cast
down the poor and needy, and to slay
such as be of upright conversation.
15 Their sword shall enter into their
own heart, and their bows shall be broken.
16 A little that a righteous man has is
better than the riches of many wicked.
17 For the arms of the wicked shall be
broken: but the LORD upholds the righteous.
18 The LORD knows the days of the upright: and their inheritance shall be for
ever.
19 They shall not be ashamed in the evil
time: and in the days of famine they shall
be satisfied.
20 But the wicked shall perish, and the
enemies of the LORD shall be as the fat of
lambs: they shall consume; into smoke
shall they consume away.
21 The wicked borrows, and pays not
again: but the righteous show mercy, and
gives.
22 For such as be blessed of him shall inherit the earth; and they that be cursed of
him shall be cut off.
23 The steps of a good man are ordered
by the LORD: and he delights in his way.
24 Though he fall, he shall not be utterly
cast down: for the LORD upholds him with
his hand.
25 I have been young, and now am old;
yet have I not seen the righteous forsak-
en, nor his seed begging bread.
26 He is ever merciful, and lends; and
his seed is blessed.
27 Depart from evil, and do good; and
dwell for evermore.
28 For the LORD loves judgment, and
forsakes not his saints; they are preserved
for ever: but the seed of the wicked shall
be cut off.
29 The righteous shall inherit the land,

37:4 Desires of the heart. What are our desires? What do we want most in life? Do we desire above all things to have a better paying job, a bigger house, thicker carpet, a superior car, and more money? Are we controlled by the lust of the flesh, the lust of the eyes, and the pride of life? Or have we been transformed from the way of this world by "the renewing of [our] mind" (Romans 12:2), that we may prove what is that good, and acceptable, and perfect will of God? Are our desires now in line with God's desires? Are we above all things "not willing that any should perish, but that all should come to repentance" (2 Peter 3:9)? If we delight ourselves in the Lord, the desires of our heart will match His—and those are the desires He will grant.

37:9 Does the reference to the wicked being "cut off" mean that they are annihilated? "If it did, then the Messiah would have been annihilated when He died, since the same word (*karath*) is used of the death of the Messiah (in Daniel 9:26)." *Norman Geisler* and *Thomas Howe, When Critics Ask* and dwell therein for ever.

30 *The mouth of the righteous speaks wisdom, and his tongue talks of judgment.*

31 *The law of his God is in his heart; none of his steps shall slide.*

32 The wicked watches the righteous, and seeks to slay him.

33 The LORD will not leave him in his hand, nor condemn him when he is judged.

34 Wait on the LORD, and keep his way, and he shall exalt you to inherit the land: when the wicked are cut off, you shall see it.

35 I have seen the wicked in great power, and spreading himself like a green bay tree.

36 Yet he passed away, and, lo, he was not: yes, I sought him, but he could not be found.

37 Mark the perfect man, and behold the upright: for the end of that man is peace.

38 But the transgressors shall be destroyed together: the end of the wicked shall be cut off.

39 But the salvation of the righteous is of the LORD: he is their strength in the time of trouble.

40 And the LORD shall help them, and deliver them: he shall deliver them from the wicked, and save them, because they trust in him.

PSALM 38

O LORD, rebuke me not in your wrath: neither chasten me in your hot displeasure.

2 For your arrows stick fast in me, and your hand presses me sore.

3 There is no soundness in my flesh because of your anger; neither is there any rest in my bones because of my sin.

4 For my iniquities are gone over my head: as an heavy burden they are too heavy for me.

5 My wounds stink and are corrupt because of my foolishness.

6 I am troubled; I am bowed down greatly; I go mourning all the day long.

7 For my loins are filled with a loathsome disease: and there is no soundness in my flesh.

8 I am feeble and sore broken: I have roared by reason of the disquietness of my heart.

9 Lord, all my desire is before you; and my groaning is not hid from you.

10 My heart pants, my strength fails me: as for the light of my eyes, it also is gone from me.

11 My lovers and my friends stand aloof from my sore; and my kinsmen stand afar off.

12 They also that seek after my life lay snares for me: and they that seek my hurt speak mischievous things, and imagine deceits all the day long.

13 But I, as a deaf man, heard not; and I was as a dumb man that opens not his mouth.

14 Thus I was as a man that hears not, and in whose mouth are no reproofs.

15 For in you, O LORD, do I hope: you will hear, O Lord my God.

16 For I said, Hear me, lest otherwise they should rejoice over me: when my foot slips, they magnify themselves against me.

17 For I am ready to halt, and my sorrow is continually before me.

18 For I will declare my iniquity; I will be sorry for my sin.

19 But my enemies are lively, and they are strong: and they that hate me wrong-

37:30,31 When we share the gospel, we speak the wisdom of God in Christ and of the justice of a holy God, revealed in a perfect Law.

38:11 The Bible's fascinating facts. If, down through the ages, scriptural principles had been applied during epidemics such as the Black Plague, millions of lives would have been saved. Long before man understood the principles of quarantine, the Bible spoke of the importance of isolating those who had a contagious disease and of disinfecting their houses. See Leviticus 13 and 14.

fully are multiplied.
20 They also that render evil for good
are my adversaries; because I follow the
thing that good is.
21 Forsake me not, O LORD: O my God,
be not far from me.
22 Make haste to help me, O Lord my
salvation.

PSALM 39

I SAID, I will take heed to my ways, that
I sin not with my tongue: I will keep
my mouth with a bridle, while the wicked
is before me.
2 I was dumb with silence, I held my
peace, even from good; and my sorrow
was stirred.
3 *My heart was hot within me, while I was*
musing the fire burned: then spoke I with
my tongue,
4 *LORD, make me to know my end, and the*
measure of my days, what it is: that I may
know how frail I am.
5 Behold, you have made my days as an
handbreadth; and my age is as nothing before you: verily every man at his best state
is altogether vanity. Selah.
6 Surely every man walks in a vain show:
surely they are disquieted in vain: he
heaps up riches, and knows not who shall
gather them.
7 And now, Lord, what wait I for? my
hope is in you.
8 Deliver me from all my transgressions:
make me not the reproach of the foolish.
9 I was dumb, I opened not my mouth;
because you did it.
10 Remove your stroke away from me: I
am consumed by the blow of your hand.
11 When you with rebukes do correct
man for iniquity, you make his beauty to
consume away like a moth: surely every
man is vanity. Selah.
12 Hear my prayer, O LORD, and give ear
unto my cry; hold not your peace at my
tears: for I am a stranger with you, and a
sojourner, as all my fathers were.
13 O spare me, that I may recover
strength, before I go hence, and be no
more.

PSALM 40

I WAITED patiently for the LORD; and he
inclined unto me, and heard my cry.
2 *He brought me up also out of an horri-*
ble pit, out of the miry clay, and set my feet
upon a rock, and established my goings.
3 *And he has put a new song in my mouth,*
even praise unto our God: many shall see
it, and fear, and shall trust in the LORD.
4 Blessed is that man that makes the LORD
his trust, and respects not the proud, nor
such as turn aside to lies.
5 Many, O LORD my God, are your wonderful works which you have done, and
your thoughts which are to us-ward: they
cannot be reckoned up in order unto
you: if I would declare and speak of them,
they are more than can be numbered.
6 Sacrifice and offering you did not desire; my ears have you opened: burnt offering and sin offering have you not required.
7 Then said I, Lo, I come: in the volume
of the book it is written of me,
8 *I delight to do your will, O my God: yes,*
your law is within my heart.
9 *I have preached righteousness in the*
great congregation: lo, I have not refrained
my lips, O LORD, you know.
10 I have not hid your righteousness
within my heart; I have declared your
faithfulness and your salvation: I have not
concealed your lovingkindness and your
truth from the great congregation.
11 Withhold not your tender mercies

40:7–9 This is a direct reference to the Messiah (see Hebrews 10:7). Jesus preached righteousness because God's Law was within His heart. When God's Law is written in our hearts, we will delight to do His will and will proclaim the good news of righteousness. We do this by preaching "the righteousness which is of the Law" (Romans 10:5). This will show men that they have sinned, and therefore need a Savior. See Romans 3:19,20.

from me, O LORD: let your lovingkindness
and your truth continually preserve me.
12 For innumerable evils have compassed me about: my iniquities have taken
hold upon me, so that I am not able to
look up; they are more than the hairs of
my head: therefore my heart fails me.
13 Be pleased, O LORD, to deliver me: O
LORD, make haste to help me.
14 Let them be ashamed and confounded together that seek after my soul to destroy it; let them be driven backward
and put to shame that wish me evil.
15 Let them be desolate for a reward of
their shame that say unto me, Aha, aha.
16 Let all those that seek you rejoice
and be glad in you: let such as love your
salvation say continually, The LORD be
magnified.
17 But I am poor and needy; yet the Lord
thinks upon me: you are my help and my
deliverer; make no tarrying, O my God.

PSALM 41

BLESSED is he that considers the poor:
the LORD will deliver him in time of
trouble.
2 The LORD will preserve him, and keep
him alive; and he shall be blessed upon
the earth: and you will not deliver him
unto the will of his enemies.
3 The LORD will strengthen him upon
the bed of languishing: you will make all
his bed in his sickness.
4 I said, LORD, be merciful unto me: heal
my soul; for I have sinned against you.
5 My enemies speak evil of me, When
shall he die, and his name perish?
6 And if he come to see me, he speaks
vanity: his heart gathers iniquity to itself;
when he goes abroad, he tells it.
7 All that hate me whisper together
against me: against me do they devise my
hurt.
8 An evil disease, say they, cleaves fast
unto him: and now that he lies he shall
rise up no more.
9 Yes, my own familiar friend, in whom
I trusted, which did eat of my bread, has
lifted up his heel against me.
10 But you, O LORD, be merciful unto
me, and raise me up, that I may requite
them.
11 By this I know that you favor me, because my enemy does not triumph over
me.
12 And as for me, you uphold me in my
integrity, and set me before your face for
ever.
13 Blessed be the LORD God of Israel from
everlasting, and to everlasting. Amen, and
Amen.

. . . . . .

Read how Spurgeon used the Law.
See Galatians 3:19 footnote.

. . . . . .

PSALM 42

AS the hart pants after the water brooks,
so pants my soul after you, O God.
2 My soul thirsts for God, for the living
God: when shall I come and appear before God?
3 My tears have been my meat day and
night, while they continually say unto
me, Where is your God?
4 When I remember these things, I pour
out my soul in me: for I had gone with
the multitude, I went with them to the
house of God, with the voice of joy and
praise, with a multitude that kept holy-
day.
5 Why are you cast down, O my soul?
and why are you disquieted in me? hope
in God: for I shall yet praise him for the
help of his countenance.

40:17 King David had great wealth and had his every need met, so he is speaking here in a spiritual sense. Describing himself as "poor and needy" shows he recognized his moral poverty and desperate need for God. See Luke 4:18 footnote.

41:9 Messianic prophecy: This was fulfilled in Mark 14:10.

41:4 *How to Confront Sinners*

When David sinned with Bathsheba, he broke *all* of the Ten Commandments. He coveted his neighbor's wife, lived a lie, stole her, committed adultery, murdered her husband, dishonored his parents, and thus broke the remaining four Commandments by dishonoring God. Therefore, the Lord sent Nathan the prophet to reprove him (2 Samuel 12:1–14).

There is great significance in the order in which the reproof came. Nathan gave David (the shepherd of Israel) a parable about something that David could understand—sheep. He began with the natural realm, rather than immediately exposing the king's sin. He told a story about a rich man who, instead of taking a sheep from his own flock, killed a poor man's pet lamb to feed a stranger.

David was indignant, and sat up on his high throne of self-righteousness. He revealed his knowledge of the Law by declaring that the guilty party must restore fourfold and must die for his crime. Nathan then exposed the king's sin of taking another man's "lamb," saying, "You are the man...Why have you despised the commandment of the Lord, to do evil in his sight?" When David cried, "I have sinned against the Lord," the prophet *then* gave him grace and said, "The Lord also has put away your sin; you shall not die."

Imagine if Nathan, fearful of rejection, changed things around a little, and instead told David, "God loves you and has a wonderful plan for your life. However, there is something that is keeping you from enjoying this wonderful plan; it is called 'sin.'"

Imagine if he had glossed over the *personal nature* of David's sin, with a general reference to *all* men having sinned and fallen short of the glory of God. David's reaction may have been, "What *sin* are you talking about?" rather than to admit his terrible transgression. Think of it —why should he cry, "I have sinned against the Lord" at the sound of *that* message? Instead, he may have, in a sincere desire to experience this "wonderful plan," admitted that he, like all men, had sinned and fallen short of the glory of God.

If David had not been made to *tremble* under the wrath of the Law, the prophet would have removed the very means of producing godly sorrow, which was so necessary for David's repentance. It is "godly sorrow" that produces repentance (2 Corinthians 7:10). It was the weight of David's guilt that caused him to cry out, "I have sinned against the Lord." The Law caused him to labor and become heavy laden; it made him hunger and thirst for righteousness. It enlightened him as to the *serious* nature of sin as far as God was concerned.

6 O my God, my soul is cast down within me: therefore will I remember you from the land of Jordan, and of the Hermonites, from the hill Mizar.

7 Deep calls unto deep at the noise of your waterspouts: all your waves and your billows are gone over me.

8 Yet the LORD will command his lovingkindness in the day time, and in the night his song shall be with me, and my prayer unto the God of my life.

9 I will say unto God my rock, Why have you forgotten me? why go I mourning because of the oppression of the enemy?

10 As with a sword in my bones, my enemies reproach me; while they say daily unto me, Where is your God?

11 Why are you cast down, O my soul? and why are you disquieted within me? hope in God: for I shall yet praise him, who is the health of my countenance, and my God.

PSALM 43

JUDGE me, O God, and plead my cause against an ungodly nation: O deliver me from the deceitful and unjust man.

2 For you are the God of my strength: why do you cast me off? why go I mourning because of the oppression of the enemy?

3 O send out your light and your truth: let them lead me; let them bring me unto your holy hill, and to your tabernacles.

4 Then will I go unto the altar of God,
unto God my exceeding joy: yes, upon
the harp will I praise you, O God my God.
5 Why are you cast down, O my soul?
and why are you disquieted within me?
hope in God: for I shall yet praise him,
who is the health of my countenance, and
my God.

PSALM 44

WE have heard with our ears, O God,
our fathers have told us, what work
you did in their days, in the times of old.
2 How you did drive out the heathen
with your hand, and plant them; how you
did afflict the people, and cast them out.
3 For they got not the land in possession by their own sword, neither did
their own arm save them: but your right
hand, and your arm, and the light of
your countenance, because you had a
favor unto them.
4 You are my King, O God: command
deliverances for Jacob.
5 Through you will we push down our
enemies: through your name will we tread
them under that rise up against us.
6 For I will not trust in my bow, neither
shall my sword save me.
7 But you have saved us from our enemies, and have put them to shame that
hated us.
8 In God we boast all the day long, and
praise your name for ever. Selah.
9 But you have cast off, and put us to
shame; and go not forth with our armies.
10 You make us to turn back from the
enemy: and they which hate us spoil for
themselves.
11 You have given us like sheep appointed for meat; and have scattered us
among the heathen.
12 You sell your people for nought, and
do not increase your wealth by their price.
13 You make us a reproach to our neighbors, a scorn and a derision to them that
are round about us.
14 You make us a byword among the
heathen, a shaking of the head among the
people.
15 My confusion is continually before
me, and the shame of my face has covered
me,
16 For the voice of him that reproaches
and blasphemes; by reason of the enemy
and avenger.
17 All this is come upon us; yet have we
not forgotten you, neither have we dealt
falsely in your covenant.
18 Our heart is not turned back, neither
have our steps declined from your way;
19 Though you have sore broken us in
the place of dragons, and covered us with
the shadow of death.
20 If we have forgotten the name of our
God, or stretched out our hands to a
strange god;
21 Shall not God search this out? for he
knows the secrets of the heart.
22 Yes, for your sake are we killed all the
day long; we are counted as sheep for the
slaughter.
23 Awake, why do you sleep, O Lord?
arise, cast us not off for ever.
24 Why do you hide your face, and forget our affliction and our oppression?
25 For our soul is bowed down to the
dust: our belly cleaves unto the earth.
26 Arise for our help, and redeem us
for your mercies' sake.

PSALM 45

MY heart is inditing a good matter: I
speak of the things which I have
made touching the king: my tongue is the
pen of a ready writer.

44:21 It is so easy to say, "God sees the heart." Think for a moment how incredible God must be to be able to search the thoughts of even one person. He sees the motives, the desires, and the deepest secrets. Sometimes our thoughts are so numerous that even we have trouble tracking them. Yet God sees the thoughts of every living person on this earth. This can either be a great comfort or a great terror, depending on whether or not our sins are forgiven.

2 You are fairer than the children of men:
grace is poured into your lips: therefore
God has blessed you for ever.
3 Gird your sword upon your thigh, O
most mighty, with your glory and your
majesty.
4 And in your majesty ride prosperous-
ly because of truth and meekness and
righteousness; and your right hand shall
teach you terrible things.
5 Your arrows are sharp in the heart of
the king's enemies; whereby the people fall
under you.
6 Your throne, O God, is for ever and
ever: the sceptre of your kingdom is a right
sceptre.

> A man can no more possess a private religion than he can possess a private sun and moon.
>
> **G. K. CHESTERTON**

7 You love righteousness, and hate
wickedness: therefore God, your God,
has anointed you with the oil of gladness
above your fellows.
8 All your garments smell of myrrh, and
aloes, and cassia, out of the ivory palaces,
whereby they have made you glad.
9 Kings' daughters were among your
honorable women: upon your right hand
did stand the queen in gold of Ophir.
10 Hearken, O daughter, and consider,
and incline your ear; forget also your own
people, and your father's house;
11 So shall the king greatly desire your
beauty: for he is your Lord; and worship
him.
12 And the daughter of Tyre shall be
there with a gift; even the rich among the
people shall entreat your favor.
13 The king's daughter is all glorious
within: her clothing is of wrought gold.
14 She shall be brought unto the king
in raiment of needlework: the virgins her
companions that follow her shall be
brought unto you.
15 With gladness and rejoicing shall they
be brought: they shall enter into the king's
palace.
16 Instead of your fathers shall be your
children, whom you may make princes in
all the earth.
17 I will make your name to be remembered in all generations: therefore shall the
people praise you for ever and ever.

PSALM 46

GOD is our refuge and strength, a very
present help in trouble.
2 Therefore will not we fear, though the
earth be removed, and though the mountains be carried into the midst of the sea;
3 Though the waters thereof roar and
be troubled, though the mountains shake
with the swelling thereof. Selah.
4 There is a river, the streams whereof
shall make glad the city of God, the holy
place of the tabernacles of the most High.
5 God is in the midst of her; she shall not
be moved: God shall help her, and that
right early.
6 The heathen raged, the kingdoms were
moved: he uttered his voice, the earth
melted.
7 The LORD of hosts is with us; the God
of Jacob is our refuge. Selah.
8 Come, behold the works of the LORD,
what desolations he has made in the earth.
9 He makes wars to cease unto the end
of the earth; he breaks the bow, and cuts
the spear in sunder; he burns the chariot
in the fire.
10 Be still, and know that I am God: I
will be exalted among the heathen, I will
be exalted in the earth.
11 The LORD of hosts is with us; the God
of Jacob is our refuge. Selah.

PSALM 47

O CLAP your hands, all you people;
shout unto God with the voice of
triumph.
2 For the LORD most high is terrible; he
is a great King over all the earth.
3 He shall subdue the people under us,
and the nations under our feet.
4 He shall choose our inheritance for us,

the excellency of Jacob whom he loved.
Selah.
5 God is gone up with a shout, the LORD
with the sound of a trumpet.
6 Sing praises to God, sing praises: sing
praises unto our King, sing praises.
7 For God is the King of all the earth:
sing praises with understanding.
8 God reigns over the heathen: God sits
upon the throne of his holiness.
9 The princes of the people are gathered
together, even the people of the God of
Abraham: for the shields of the earth belong unto God: he is greatly exalted.

PSALM 48

GREAT is the LORD, and greatly to be
praised in the city of our God, in the
mountain of his holiness.
2 Beautiful for situation, the joy of the
whole earth, is mount Zion, on the sides of
the north, the city of the great King.
3 God is known in her palaces for a refuge.
4 For, lo, the kings were assembled, they
passed by together.
5 They saw it, and so they marveled; they
were troubled, and hasted away.
6 Fear took hold upon them there, and
pain, as of a woman in travail.
7 You break the ships of Tarshish with an
east wind.
8 As we have heard, so have we seen in
the city of the LORD of hosts, in the city
of our God: God will establish it for ever.
Selah.
9 We have thought of your lovingkindness, O God, in the midst of your temple.
10 According to your name, O God, so
is your praise unto the ends of the earth:
your right hand is full of righteousness.
11 Let mount Zion rejoice, let the daughters of Judah be glad, because of your
judgments.
12 Walk about Zion, and go round about
her: tell the towers thereof.
13 Mark well her bulwarks, consider her
palaces; that you may tell it to the generation following.
14 For this God is our God for ever and
ever: he will be our guide even unto death.

PSALM 49

HEAR this, all you people; give ear,
all you inhabitants of the world:
2 Both low and high, rich and poor, together.
3 My mouth shall speak of wisdom; and
the meditation of my heart shall be of understanding.
4 I will incline my ear to a parable: I will
open my dark saying upon the harp.
5 Wherefore should I fear in the days of
evil, when the iniquity of my heels shall
compass me about?
6 *They that trust in their wealth, and boast*
themselves in the multitude of their riches;
7 *None of them can by any means redeem*
his brother, nor give to God a ransom for
him:
8 *(For the redemption of their soul is pre-*
cious, and it ceases for ever:)
9 *That he should still live for ever, and not*
see corruption.
10 *For he sees that wise men die, likewise*
the fool and the brutish person perish, and

49:7 Grief for the lost. Many of us have felt sorrow and grief over loved ones who don't know the salvation of God. If there was something we could do to save them, we would gladly do it. But often there is nothing we can do but pray—none of us can by any means redeem his brother or give God a ransom for him. We can however, trust God in the fact that One has already become a curse for Israel and for our loved ones. One has already provided the necessary redemption—He has paid the ransom for them. We inherit the promises of God through faith and patience, and therefore rest in the knowledge that God will answer our prayers for our loved ones.

But our zeal for the salvation of sinners shouldn't be limited to our loved ones. Salvation in the heart of the Christian should cause him to love his neighbor as he loves himself.

49:7,8 The blood of Jesus Christ was the precious cost of our redemption, something that humanity could not provide. See 1 Peter 1:18,19.

Questions & Objections

49:15 "When you're dead, you're dead."

What if you are wrong? What if God, Jesus, the prophets, the Jews, and Christians are right and you are wrong? If there is no afterlife, no Judgment Day, no heaven, and no hell, then God is unjust and each of the above is guilty of being a false witness. It means that Almighty God couldn't care less about the fact that a man rapes a woman, then cuts her throat and is never brought to justice. If you are right, and there is no ultimate justice, you won't even have the joy of saying, "I told you so." However, if you are wrong, you will lose your soul and end up eternally damned. You are playing Russian roulette with a fully loaded gun. See Hebrews 9:27 footnote.

leave their wealth to others.

11 *Their inward thought is, that their houses shall continue for ever, and their dwelling places to all generations; they call their lands after their own names.*

12 *Nevertheless man being in honor abides not: he is like the beasts that perish.*

13 *This their way is their folly: yet their posterity approve their sayings. Selah.*

14 *Like sheep they are laid in the grave; death shall feed on them; and the upright shall have dominion over them in the morning; and their beauty shall consume in the grave from their dwelling.*

15 But God will redeem my soul from the power of the grave: for he shall receive me. Selah.

16 Be not afraid when one is made rich, when the glory of his house is increased;

17 For when he dies he shall carry nothing away: his glory shall not descend after him.

18 Though while he lived he blessed his soul: and men will praise you, when you do well to yourself.

19 He shall go to the generation of his fathers; they shall never see light.

20 Man that is in honor, and understands not, is like the beasts that perish.

PSALM 50

THE mighty God, even the LORD, has spoken, and called the earth from the rising of the sun unto the going down thereof.

2 Out of Zion, the perfection of beauty, God has shined.

3 Our God shall come, and shall not keep silence: a fire shall devour before him, and it shall be very tempestuous round about him.

4 He shall call to the heavens from above, and to the earth, that he may judge his people.

5 Gather my saints together unto me; those that have made a covenant with me by sacrifice.

6 And the heavens shall declare his righteousness: for God is judge himself. Selah.

7 Hear, O my people, and I will speak; O Israel, and I will testify against you: I am God, even your God.

8 I will not reprove you for your sacrifices or your burnt offerings, to have been continually before me.

9 I will take no bullock out of your house, nor he goats out of your folds.

10 For every beast of the forest is mine, and the cattle upon a thousand hills.

11 I know all the fowls of the mountains: and the wild beasts of the field are mine.

12 If I were hungry, I would not tell you: for the world is mine, and the fullness thereof.

13 Will I eat the flesh of bulls, or drink the blood of goats?

49:17 "When we die we leave behind all that we have, and take with us all that we are." *Chapel of the Air*

14 Offer unto God thanksgiving; and pay your vows unto the most High:
15 **And call upon me in the day of trouble: I will deliver you, and you shall glorify me.**
16 But unto the wicked God says, What have you to do to declare my statutes, or that you should take my covenant in your mouth?
17 Seeing you hate instruction, and cast my words behind you.
18 When you saw a thief, then you consented with him, and have been partaker with adulterers.
19 You give your mouth to evil, and your tongue frames deceit.
20 You sit and speak against your brother; you slander your own mother's son.
21 These things have you done, and I kept silence; you thought that I was altogether such an one as yourself: but I will reprove you, and set them in order before your eyes.
22 **Now consider this, you that forget God, lest I tear you in pieces, and there be none to deliver.**
23 **Whoso offers praise glorifies me: and to him that orders his conversation aright will I show the salvation of God.**

PSALM 51

HAVE mercy upon me, O God, according to your lovingkindness: according unto the multitude of your tender mercies blot out my transgressions.
2 Wash me thoroughly from my iniquity, and cleanse me from my sin.
3 For I acknowledge my transgressions: and my sin is ever before me.
4 Against you, you only, have I sinned, and done this evil in your sight: that you might be justified when you speak, and be clear when you judge.
5 **Behold, I was shaped in iniquity; and in sin did my mother conceive me.**
6 Behold, you desire truth in the inward parts: and in the hidden part you shall make me to know wisdom.
7 Purge me with hyssop, and I shall be clean: wash me, and I shall be whiter than snow.
8 **Make me to hear joy and gladness; that the bones which you have broken may rejoice.**
9 **Hide your face from my sins, and blot out all my iniquities.**
10 Create in me a clean heart, O God; and renew a right spirit within me.
11 **Cast me not away from your presence; and take not your holy spirit from me.**
12 **Restore unto me the joy of your salvation; and uphold me with your free spirit.**
13 Then will I teach transgressors your

50:16 Verses 16–23 contain a fearful word for a godless world that delights in entertainment glorifying theft, violence, adultery, and hatred. They assume that heaven's silence is heaven's sanction. God threatens fearful wrath, then offers salvation to those who will listen. This is the biblical order of gospel proclamation—Law before grace.

51:1–4 When a sinner is ready for salvation, he exhibits personal responsibility for his sins. In these four verses David uses the words *me*, *my*, and *I* ten times in reference to his sins. See also Luke 15:21 footnote.

51:6 Civil law can search your house. It can search your car and even your person, but it cannot search the heart. Civil law cannot see human thoughts. God's Law, however, searches the inward parts. Like ten hungry bloodhounds, it chases the scent of injustice. It will pursue the guilty criminal until he is brought to justice. There is only one way for the ten ravenous hounds to leave the trail: sinners must cross over a "river." There is a river of blood that flows from Calvary's cross. Only the blood of Jesus Christ satisfies the Law's insatiable appetite for righteousness. See Hebrews 9:22.

51:7 "Direct my thoughts, words, and work. Wash away my sins in the immaculate Blood of the Lamb, and purge my heart by Thy Holy Spirit... Daily frame me more and more into the likeness of Thy Son Jesus Christ." *George Washington*, in his prayer book

51:6 *How to Use the Ten Commandments in Witnessing*

This should be done in a spirit of love and gentleness:

"Do you think you have kept the Ten Commandments? Have you ever told a lie (including 'white lies,' half-truths, exaggerations, etc.)? If you have, then you are a 'liar,' and you cannot enter the kingdom of God. Have you ever stolen (the value is irrelevant)? Then you are a thief. Jesus said that if you look with lust, you have committed adultery in your heart. If you hate someone, then you have committed murder in your heart. God requires truth 'in the inward parts'—He sees even the thought-life.

"Have you loved God above all else? Has He always been first in your affections? Have you made a 'god' to suit yourself (having your own beliefs about God)? That is called idolatry, and the Bible warns that no idolater will enter the kingdom of God. Have you ever used God's holy name to curse, or been greedy? Have you kept the Sabbath holy? Have you always implicitly honored your parents? Have you broken any of the Ten Commandments?

"Knowing that God has seen your thought-life and every deed done in darkness, will you be innocent or guilty on Judgment Day? You know you will be guilty. So, will you end up in heaven or hell?"

The Law brings individuals to a point of seeing that they have sinned against God—that His wrath abides on them. It causes them to see that their own "goodness" can't save them. It stops their mouth of justification (Romans 3:19), and prepares the heart for the good news of the gospel:

"The only thing you can do to be saved from His wrath is to repent and put your faith in the Savior, Jesus Christ. When He died on the cross, He took the punishment for our sins. He, once and for all, stepped into the Courtroom and completely paid the fine for us. Then He rose from the dead, defeating death. If you want to be saved from God's wrath, confess and forsake your sins, put your faith in Jesus for your eternal salvation, and you will pass from death into life. Then read the Bible daily and obey what you read (see John 14:21). God will never let you down."

ways; and sinners shall be converted unto you.
14 Deliver me from bloodguiltiness, O God, you God of my salvation: and my tongue shall sing aloud of your righteousness.
15 O Lord, open my lips; and my mouth shall show forth your praise.
16 For you desire not sacrifice; else would I give it: you delight not in burnt offering.
17 The sacrifices of God are a broken spirit: a broken and a contrite heart, O God, you will not despise.
18 Do good in your good pleasure unto Zion: build the walls of Jerusalem.
19 Then shall you be pleased with the sacrifices of righteousness, with burnt offering and whole burnt offering: then shall they offer bullocks upon your altar.

PSALM 52

WHY boast yourself in mischief, O mighty man? the goodness of God endures continually.
2 The tongue devises mischiefs; like a sharp razor, working deceitfully.
3 You love evil more than good; and lying rather than to speak righteousness. Selah.
4 You love all devouring words, O you deceitful tongue.

51:10 Those who confess and forsake their sins are given a clean heart in Christ, and the fruit of genuine salvation is a concern for the lost. See verse 13.

51:13–17 "Transgressors" are those who have transgressed the Moral Law. It is the "schoolmaster" (Galatians 3:24) that teaches them that they are sinners in the eyes of God (Romans 3:19,20). It is the Law that sings aloud of God's righteousness, breaks the human spirit, and gives the sinner reason to be contrite over sins in which he previously delighted. See Romans 7:13,24,25.

5 God shall likewise destroy you for ever,
he shall take you away, and pluck you out
of your dwelling place, and root you out
of the land of the living. Selah.
6 The righteous also shall see, and fear,
and shall laugh at him:
7 Lo, this is the man that made not God
his strength; but trusted in the abundance
of his riches, and strengthened himself in
his wickedness.
8 But I am like a green olive tree in the
house of God: I trust in the mercy of God
for ever and ever.
9 I will praise you for ever, because you
have done it: and I will wait on your name;
for it is good before your saints.

PSALM 53

**THE fool has said in his heart, There
is no God. Corrupt are they, and
have done abominable iniquity: there
is none that does good.
2 God looked down from heaven upon the children of men, to see if there
were any that did understand, that did
seek God.
3 Every one of them is gone back: they
are altogether become filthy; there is
none that does good, no, not one.**
4 Have the workers of iniquity no knowledge? who eat up my people as they eat
bread: they have not called upon God.
5 There were they in great fear, where no
fear was: for God has scattered the bones
of him that encamps against you: you have
put them to shame, because God has despised them.
6 Oh that the salvation of Israel were
come out of Zion! When God brings back
the captivity of his people, Jacob shall
rejoice, and Israel shall be glad.

PSALM 54

SAVE me, O God, by your name, and
judge me by your strength.
2 Hear my prayer, O God; give ear to
the words of my mouth.
3 For strangers are risen up against me,
and oppressors seek after my soul: they
have not set God before them. Selah.
4 Behold, God is my helper: the Lord is
with them that uphold my soul.
5 He shall reward evil unto my enemies:
cut them off in your truth.
6 I will freely sacrifice unto you: I will
praise your name, O LORD; for it is good.

52:7 The New Testament reminds us of this truth: We cannot love God *and* mammon (Luke 16:13).

53:1 Atheism. It is much more reasonable to believe that this publication had no printer than to believe that there is no God. Who in his right mind would ever believe that no one compiled its pages, no one produced the graphic art, and no one printed it. The publication happened by chance…from nothing. There was no paper, no ink, no cardboard, and no glue. The paper just came into being (from nothing), then trimmed itself into perfectly straight edges. All the words fell into place, forming coherent sentences, and then the graphic art appeared. The pages fell into numerical order, and finally the book bound itself.

The fact that there was a printer is axiomatic (self-evident), so it would be intellectually insulting to even begin to argue for the case of the printer's existence. For the same reason, the Bible does not enter into the case for God's existence. It simply begins by stating, "In the beginning God…" (Genesis 1:1). See Psalm 90:2 footnote.

"It takes no brains to be an atheist. Any stupid person can deny the existence of a supernatural power because man's physical senses cannot detect it. But there cannot be ignored the influence of conscience, the respect we feel for the Moral Law, the mystery of first life…or the marvelous order in which the universe moves about us on this earth. All these evidence the handiwork of the beneficent Deity…That Deity is the God of the Bible and Jesus Christ, His Son." *Dwight Eisenhower*

53:1–3 There are many "good" people from man's viewpoint. However, here is *God's* point of view. These verses leave no room for the self-righteous.

7 For he has delivered me out of all trouble: and my eye has seen his desire upon my enemies.

PSALM 55

GIVE ear to my prayer, O God; and hide not yourself from my supplication.
2 Attend unto me, and hear me: I mourn in my complaint, and make a noise;
3 Because of the voice of the enemy, because of the oppression of the wicked: for they cast iniquity upon me, and in wrath they hate me.
4 My heart is sore pained within me: and the terrors of death are fallen upon me.
5 Fearfulness and trembling are come upon me, and horror has overwhelmed me.
6 And I said, Oh that I had wings like a dove! for then would I fly away, and be at rest.
7 Lo, then would I wander far off, and remain in the wilderness. Selah.
8 I would hasten my escape from the windy storm and tempest.
9 Destroy, O Lord, and divide their tongues: for I have seen violence and strife in the city.
10 Day and night they go about it upon the walls thereof: mischief also and sorrow are in the midst of it.
11 Wickedness is in the midst thereof: deceit and guile depart not from her streets.
12 For it was not an enemy that reproached me; then I could have borne it: neither was it he that hated me that did magnify himself against me; then I would have hid myself from him:
13 But it was you, a man my equal, my guide, and my acquaintance.
14 We took sweet counsel together, and walked unto the house of God in company.
15 Let death seize upon them, and let them go down quick into hell: for wickedness is in their dwellings, and among them.
16 As for me, I will call upon God; and the LORD shall save me.
17 Evening, and morning, and at noon, will I pray, and cry aloud: and he shall hear my voice.
18 He has delivered my soul in peace from the battle that was against me: for there were many with me.
19 God shall hear, and afflict them, even he that abides of old. Selah. Because they have no changes, therefore they fear not God.

> Holy practice is the most decisive evidence of the reality of our repentance.
>
> **JONATHAN EDWARDS**

20 He has put forth his hands against such as be at peace with him: he has broken his covenant.
21 The words of his mouth were smoother than butter, but war was in his heart: his words were softer than oil, yet were they drawn swords.
22 Cast your burden upon the LORD, and he shall sustain you: he shall never suffer the righteous to be moved.
23 But you, O God, shall bring them down into the pit of destruction: bloody and deceitful men shall not live out half their days; but I will trust in you.

PSALM 56

BE merciful unto me, O God: for man would swallow me up; he fighting daily oppresses me.
2 My enemies would daily swallow me up: for they be many that fight against me, O you most High.
3 *What time I am afraid, I will trust in you.*
4 *In God I will praise his word, in God I have put my trust; I will not fear what flesh can do unto me.*

55:22 What an incredible promise—we have an anchor for the soul. See Matthew 6:25–34 for some of the ways the Lord sustains us.

QUESTIONS & OBJECTIONS

55:15

"I don't mind going to hell. All my friends will be there."

Obviously, those who flippantly say such things don't believe in the biblical concept of hell. Their understanding of the nature of God is erroneous. The slow-witted criminal thinks that the electric chair is a place to put up his feet for a while and relax.

It may be wise therefore to speak with him for a few moments about the *reasonableness* of a place called hell. Reason with him by saying, "If a judge in Florida turns a blind eye to the unlawful dealings of the Mafia, if he sees their murderous acts and deliberately turns the other way, is he a good or bad judge? He's obviously corrupt, and should be brought to justice himself. If he is a good judge, he will do everything within his power to bring those murderers to justice. He should make sure that they are justly punished.

"If Almighty God sees a man rape and strangle to death your sister or mother, do you think He should look the other way, or bring that murderer to justice? If He looks the other way, He's corrupt and should be brought to justice Himself. It makes sense then, that if God is good, He will do everything in His power to ensure justice is done. The Bible tells us that He *will* punish murderers, and the place of punishment—the prison God will send them to—is a place called hell.

"God should punish murderers and rapists. However, God is so good, he will also punish thieves, liars, adulterers, fornicators, and blasphemers. He will even punish those who *desired* to murder and rape but never took the opportunity. He warns that if we hate someone, we commit murder in our hearts. If we lust, we commit adultery in the heart, etc."

Then take the time to tell him of the *reality* of hell. Sinners like to picture hell as a fun, hedonistic, pleasure-filled place where they can engage in all the sensual sins that are forbidden here. But Jesus said that it is a place of torment, where the worm never dies and the fire is never quenched (Matthew 9:43,44). We tend to forget what pain is like when we don't have it. Can you begin to imagine how terrible it would be to be in agony, with no hope of relief?

Many human beings go insane if they are merely isolated for a long time from other people. Imagine how terrible it would be if God merely withdrew all the things we hold so dear—friendship, love, color, light, peace, joy, laughter, and security. Hell isn't just a place with an absence of God's blessings, it is punishment for sin. It is literal torment, forever. That's why the Bible warns that it is a fearful thing to fall into the hands of the living God.

God has given His Law to convince men of their sins, and unless a sinner is convinced that he has sinned against God, he won't see that hell is his eternal destiny. He may consider it a fit place for others, but not for himself. That's why we mustn't hesitate to open up the Law and show that each individual is personally responsible for sin, and that God's wrath abides on him because of it.

Ask him to consider why you would say such things to him if it wasn't true. Tell him to examine your motives. You are so concerned for his eternal welfare that you are prepared to risk offending him.

Then ask him if he would sell an eye for a million dollars. Would he sell *both* for ten million? No one in his right mind would. Our eyes are precious to us. How much more then is our eternal soul worth? (For a biblical description of hell, see Revelation 1:18 footnote.)

5 Every day they wrest my words: all their thoughts are against me for evil.

6 They gather themselves together, they hide themselves, they mark my steps, when they wait for my soul.

7 Shall they escape by iniquity? in your anger cast down the people, O God.

8 You tell my wanderings: put my tears into your bottle: are they not in your book?

9 When I cry unto you, then shall my enemies turn back: this I know; for God is for me.

10 In God will I praise his word: in the LORD will I praise his word.

11 In God have I put my trust: I will not be afraid what man can do unto me.
12 Your vows are upon me, O God: I will render praises unto you.
13 For you have delivered my soul from death: will not you deliver my feet from falling, that I may walk before God in the light of the living?

PSALM 57

BE merciful unto me, O God, be merciful unto me: for my soul trusts in you: yes, in the shadow of your wings will I make my refuge, until these calamities be overpast.
2 I will cry unto God most high; unto God that perform all things for me.
3 He shall send from heaven, and save me from the reproach of him that would swallow me up. Selah. God shall send forth his mercy and his truth.
4 My soul is among lions: and I lie even among them that are set on fire, even the sons of men, whose teeth are spears and arrows, and their tongue a sharp sword.
5 Be exalted, O God, above the heavens; let your glory be above all the earth.
6 They have prepared a net for my steps; my soul is bowed down: they have digged a pit before me, into the midst whereof they are fallen themselves. Selah.
7 My heart is fixed, O God, my heart is fixed: I will sing and give praise.
8 Awake up, my glory; awake, psaltery and harp: I myself will awake early.
9 I will praise you, O Lord, among the people: I will sing unto you among the nations.
10 For your mercy is great unto the heavens, and your truth unto the clouds.
11 Be exalted, O God, above the heavens: let your glory be above all the earth.

PSALM 58

DO you indeed speak righteousness, O congregation? do you judge uprightly, O you sons of men?
2 Yes, in heart you work wickedness; you weigh the violence of your hands in the earth.
3 The wicked are estranged from the womb: they go astray as soon as they be born, speaking lies.
4 Their poison is like the poison of a serpent: they are like the deaf adder that stops her ear;
5 Which will not hearken to the voice of charmers, charming never so wisely.
6 Break their teeth, O God, in their mouth: break out the great teeth of the young lions, O LORD.
7 Let them melt away as waters which run continually: when he bends his bow to shoot his arrows, let them be as cut in pieces.
8 As a snail which melts, let every one of them pass away: like the untimely birth of a woman, that they may not see the

---

56:11 The fear of man is the devil's paralyzing poison. Faith in God is the antidote. When the enemy feeds you the lie that you cannot share your faith, answer him with "I can do all things through Christ which strengthens me" (Philippians 4:13). Then put works with your faith—follow your convictions. Don't be concerned if you don't *feel* compassion for the lost. If a firefighter rescues someone from a burning building, he may have saved the person because he was motivated by compassion or because it was the job he had committed himself to do. His motive is of little concern to the person who has been pulled from the flames.

56:11 "Stop caring about what people think; begin to think about caring for people." *Emeal Zwayne*

58:6 Some have wondered how David could possibly be "a man after [God's] own heart" (Acts 13:22) when he exhibited such a vindictive attitude. However, he was merely pouring out his anger in prayer. Let it be a lesson to those of us who would like to seek vengeance—take it to God in prayer. Those who learn that secret prayer is the place to leave grievances will find that like David, they can then show mercy to those who have wronged them (see 1 Samuel 26:1–12).

sun.
9 Before your pots can feel the thorns,
he shall take them away as with a whirlwind, both living, and in his wrath.
10 The righteous shall rejoice when he
sees the vengeance: he shall wash his feet
in the blood of the wicked.
11 So that a man shall say, Verily there is
a reward for the righteous: verily he is a
God that judges in the earth.

PSALM 59

DELIVER me from my enemies, O
my God: defend me from them that
rise up against me.
2 Deliver me from the workers of iniquity, and save me from bloody men.
3 For, lo, they lie in wait for my soul:
the mighty are gathered against me; not
for my transgression, nor for my sin, O
LORD.
4 They run and prepare themselves without my fault: awake to help me, and behold.
5 You therefore, O LORD God of hosts,
the God of Israel, awake to visit all the
heathen: be not merciful to any wicked
transgressors. Selah.
6 They return at evening: they make a
noise like a dog, and go round about the
city.
7 Behold, they belch out with their
mouth: swords are in their lips: for who,
say they, does hear?
8 But you, O LORD, shall laugh at them;
you shall have all the heathen in derision.
9 Because of his strength will I wait upon you: for God is my defense.
10 The God of my mercy shall prevent
me: God shall let me see my desire upon
my enemies.
11 Slay them not, lest my people forget:
scatter them by your power; and bring
them down, O Lord our shield.
12 For the sin of their mouth and the
words of their lips let them even be taken
in their pride: and for cursing and lying
which they speak.
13 Consume them in wrath, consume
them, that they may not be: and let them
know that God rules in Jacob unto the
ends of the earth. Selah.
14 And at evening let them return; and
let them make a noise like a dog, and go
round about the city.
15 Let them wander up and down for
meat, and grudge if they be not satisfied.
16 But I will sing of your power; yes, I
will sing aloud of your mercy in the morning: for you have been my defense and
refuge in the day of my trouble.
17 Unto you, O my strength, will I sing:
for God is my defense, and the God of my
mercy.

To learn the beliefs of Hindus and how to witness to them, see page 546.

PSALM 60

O GOD, you have cast us off, you have
scattered us, you have been displeased; O turn yourself to us again.
2 You have made the earth to tremble;
you have broken it: heal the breaches
thereof; for it shakes.
3 You have showed your people hard
things: you have made us to drink the
wine of astonishment.
4 You have given a banner to them that
fear you, that it may be displayed because
of the truth. Selah.
5 That your beloved may be delivered;
save with your right hand, and hear me.
6 God has spoken in his holiness; I will
rejoice, I will divide Shechem, and mete
out the valley of Succoth.

7 Gilead is mine, and Manasseh is mine;
Ephraim also is the strength of my head;
Judah is my lawgiver;
8 Moab is my washpot; over Edom will
I cast out my shoe: Philistia, triumph because of me.
9 Who will bring me into the strong city?
who will lead me into Edom?
10 Will not you, O God, which had cast
us off? and you, O God, which did not go
out with our armies?
11 Give us help from trouble: for vain is
the help of man.
12 Through God we shall do valiantly: for
he it is that shall tread down our enemies.

PSALM 61

HEAR my cry, O God; attend unto my
prayer.
2 From the end of the earth will I cry unto you, when my heart is overwhelmed:
lead me to the rock that is higher than I.
3 For you have been a shelter for me,
and a strong tower from the enemy.
4 I will abide in your tabernacle for ever:
I will trust in the covert of your wings.
Selah.
5 For you, O God, have heard my vows:
you have given me the heritage of those
that fear your name.
6 You will prolong the king's life: and his
years as many generations.
7 He shall abide before God for ever: O
prepare mercy and truth, which may preserve him.
8 So will I sing praise unto your name for
ever, that I may daily perform my vows.

PSALM 62

TRULY my soul waits upon God: from
him comes my salvation.
2 He only is my rock and my salvation;
he is my defense; I shall not be greatly
moved.
3 How long will you imagine mischief
against a man? you shall be slain all of
you: as a bowing wall shall you be, and as
a tottering fence.
4 They only consult to cast him down
from his excellency: they delight in lies:
they bless with their mouth, but they curse
inwardly. Selah.
5 My soul, wait only upon God; for my
expectation is from him.
6 He only is my rock and my salvation:
he is my defense; I shall not be moved.
7 In God is my salvation and my glory:
the rock of my strength, and my refuge,
is in God.
8 **Trust in him at all times; you people, pour out your heart before him:
God is a refuge for us. Selah.**

> "The root of joy is gratefulness... It is not joy that makes us grateful; it is gratitude that makes us joyful."
>
> **DAVID STEINDL-RAST**

9 Surely men of low degree are vanity,
and men of high degree are a lie: to be laid
in the balance, they are altogether lighter
than vanity.
10 Trust not in oppression, and become
not vain in robbery: if riches increase, set
not your heart upon them.
11 God has spoken once; twice have I
heard this; that power belongs unto God.
12 Also unto you, O Lord, belongs mercy: for you render to every man according to his work.

PSALM 63

O GOD, you are my God; early will I
seek you: my soul thirsts for you, my
flesh longs for you in a dry and thirsty
land, where no water is;
2 To see your power and your glory, so
as I have seen you in the sanctuary.
3 Because your lovingkindness is better
than life, my lips shall praise you.
4 Thus will I bless you while I live: I
will lift up my hands in your name.
5 My soul shall be satisfied as with marrow and fatness; and my mouth shall
praise you with joyful lips:
6 When I remember you upon my bed,
and meditate on you in the night watches.
7 Because you have been my help, there-

"Worshipping God and the Lamb in the temple: God, for his benefaction in creating all things, and the Lamb, for his benefaction in redeeming us with his blood."

Isaac Newton

fore in the shadow of your wings will I rejoice.
8 My soul follows hard after you: your right hand upholds me.
9 But those that seek my soul, to destroy it, shall go into the lower parts of the earth.
10 They shall fall by the sword: they shall be a portion for foxes.
11 But the king shall rejoice in God; every one that swears by him shall glory: but the mouth of them that speak lies shall be stopped.

PSALM 64

HEAR my voice, O God, in my prayer: preserve my life from fear of the enemy.
2 Hide me from the secret counsel of the wicked; from the insurrection of the workers of iniquity:
3 Who whet their tongue like a sword, and bend their bows to shoot their arrows, even bitter words:
4 That they may shoot in secret at the perfect: suddenly do they shoot at him, and fear not.
5 They encourage themselves in an evil matter: they commune of laying snares privily; they say, Who shall see them?
6 They search out iniquities; they accomplish a diligent search: both the inward thought of every one of them, and the heart, is deep.
7 But God shall shoot at them with an arrow; suddenly shall they be wounded.
8 So they shall make their own tongue to fall upon themselves: all that see them shall flee away.
9 And all men shall fear, and shall declare the work of God; for they shall wisely consider of his doing.
10 The righteous shall be glad in the LORD, and shall trust in him; and all the upright in heart shall glory.

PSALM 65

PRAISE waits for you, O God, in Sion: and unto you shall the vow be performed.
2 O you that hearest prayer, unto you shall all flesh come.
3 Iniquities prevail against me: as for our transgressions, you shall purge them away.
4 Blessed is the man whom you choose, and cause to approach unto you, that he may dwell in your courts: we shall be satisfied with the goodness of your house, even of your holy temple.
5 By terrible things in righteousness will you answer us, O God of our salvation; who are the confidence of all the ends of the earth, and of them that are afar off upon the sea:
6 Which by his strength set fast the mountains; being girded with power:
7 Which still the noise of the seas, the noise of their waves, and the tumult of the people.
8 They also that dwell in the uttermost parts are afraid at your tokens: you make the outgoings of the morning and evening to rejoice.
9 You visit the earth, and water it: you greatly enrich it with the river of God, which is full of water: you prepare them corn, when you have so provided for it.
10 You water the ridges thereof abun-

dantly: you set the furrows thereof: you
make it soft with showers: you bless the
springing thereof.
11 You crown the year with your goodness; and your paths drop fatness.
12 They drop upon the pastures of the
wilderness: and the little hills rejoice on
every side.
13 The pastures are clothed with flocks;
the valleys also are covered over with corn;
they shout for joy, they also sing.

PSALM 66

MAKE a joyful noise unto God, all you
lands:
2 Sing forth the honor of his name: make
his praise glorious.
3 Say unto God, How terrible are you in
your works! through the greatness of your
power shall your enemies submit themselves unto you.
4 All the earth shall worship you, and
shall sing unto you; they shall sing to your
name. Selah.
5 Come and see the works of God: he is
terrible in his doing toward the children
of men.
6 He turned the sea into dry land: they
went through the flood on foot: there did
we rejoice in him.
7 He rules by his power for ever; his eyes
behold the nations: let not the rebellious
exalt themselves. Selah.
8 O bless our God, you people, and make
the voice of his praise to be heard:
9 Which hold our soul in life, and suffers
not our feet to be moved.
10 For you, O God, have proved us: you
have tried us, as silver is tried.
11 You brought us into the net; you laid
affliction upon our loins.
12 You have caused men to ride over our
heads; we went through fire and through
water: but you brought us out into a
wealthy place.
13 I will go into your house with burnt
offerings: I will pay you my vows,
14 Which my lips have uttered, and my
mouth has spoken, when I was in trouble.
15 I will offer unto you burnt sacrifices
of fatlings, with the incense of rams; I will
offer bullocks with goats. Selah.
16 Come and hear, all you that fear God,
and I will declare what he has done for
my soul.
17 I cried unto him with my mouth, and
he was extolled with my tongue.
18 If I regard iniquity in my heart, the
Lord will not hear me:
19 But verily God has heard me; he has
attended to the voice of my prayer.
20 Blessed be God, which has not turned
away my prayer, nor his mercy from me.

PSALM 67

GOD be merciful unto us, and bless
us; and cause his face to shine upon
us; Selah.
2 That your way may be known upon
earth, your saving health among all nations.
3 Let the people praise you, O God; let

66:10–12 We often blame tribulation on the enemy when God uses this very instrument to fulfill His will for our lives. God takes us through the fire, not to burn us, but to purify us. He takes us through the water, not to drown us, but to wash us. Understanding that the Lord chastens those He loves enables us to endure trials. The psalmist wrote, "It is good for me that I have been afflicted; that I might learn your statutes" (119:71). See also Hebrews 12:10–13.

66:15 Animal rights advocates who insist that "meat is murder" are misguided. God was the first to kill an animal (Genesis 3:21). In Exodus 12:5–8 God told Israel to kill and eat lambs. King Solomon sacrificed 22,000 oxen and 120,000 sheep when he dedicated the temple to God (1 Kings 8:63). When three angels appeared to Abraham, he killed a "tender and good" calf for them to eat (Genesis 18:7,8). In Genesis 27:7 we are told that Jacob ate venison (deer meat), which was his favorite food. Jesus ate the Passover lamb (Mark 14:12,18). In the parable of the prodigal son, the father rejoiced at his son's return by "killing the fatted calf" (which was eaten). See 1 Timothy 4:3,4 footnote.

all the people praise you.
4 O let the nations be glad and sing for
joy: for you shall judge the people righteously, and govern the nations upon earth.
Selah.
5 Let the people praise you, O God; let
all the people praise you.
6 Then shall the earth yield her increase;
and God, even our own God, shall bless
us.
7 God shall bless us; and all the ends of
the earth shall fear him.

· · · · · ·

Read a challenging letter from an atheist. See Romans 9:2,3 footnote.

· · · · · ·

PSALM 68

LET God arise, let his enemies be
scattered: let them also that hate him
flee before him.
2 As smoke is driven away, so drive them
away: as wax melts before the fire, so let
the wicked perish at the presence of God.
3 But let the righteous be glad; let them
rejoice before God: yes, let them exceedingly rejoice.
4 Sing unto God, sing praises to his name:
extol him that rides upon the heavens by
his name JAH, and rejoice before him.
5 A father of the fatherless, and a judge
of the widows, is God in his holy habitation.
6 God sets the solitary in families: he
brings out those which are bound with
chains: but the rebellious dwell in a dry
land.
7 O God, when you went forth before
your people, when you did march through
the wilderness; Selah:
8 The earth shook, the heavens also
dropped at the presence of God: even
Sinai itself was moved at the presence of
God, the God of Israel.
9 You, O God, did send a plentiful rain,
whereby you did confirm your inheritance, when it was weary.
10 Your congregation has dwelt therein:
you, O God, have prepared of your goodness for the poor.
11 The Lord gave the word: great was
the company of those that published it.
12 Kings of armies did flee apace: and
she that tarried at home divided the spoil.
13 Though you have lien among the
pots, yet shall you be as the wings of a
dove covered with silver, and her feathers
with yellow gold.
14 When the Almighty scattered kings
in it, it was white as snow in Salmon.
15 The hill of God is as the hill of Bashan; an high hill as the hill of Bashan.
16 Why do you leap, you high hills?
this is the hill which God desires to dwell
in; yes, the LORD will dwell in it for ever.
17 The chariots of God are twenty thousand, even thousands of angels: the Lord
is among them, as in Sinai, in the holy
place.
18 You have ascended on high, you have
led captivity captive: you have received
gifts for men; yes, for the rebellious also,
that the LORD God might dwell among
them.
19 Blessed be the Lord, who daily loads
us with benefits, even the God of our
salvation. Selah.
20 He that is our God is the God of salvation; and unto GOD the Lord belong
the issues from death.
21 But God shall wound the head of his
enemies, and the hairy scalp of such an

67:4 "It is the duty of all nations to acknowledge the Providence of Almighty God, to obey His will, to be grateful for His benefits, and humbly to implore His protection and favor." *George Washington*

"The foundations of our society and our government rest so much on the teachings of the Bible that it would be difficult to support them if faith in these teachings would cease to be practically universal in our country." *Calvin Coolidge*

one as goes on still in his trespasses.
22 The Lord said, I will bring again from Bashan, I will bring my people again from the depths of the sea:
23 That your foot may be dipped in the blood of your enemies, and the tongue of your dogs in the same.
24 They have seen your goings, O God; even the goings of my God, my King, in the sanctuary.
25 The singers went before, the players on instruments followed after; among them were the damsels playing with timbrels.
26 Bless God in the congregations, even the Lord, from the fountain of Israel.

> Beloved, we must win souls; we cannot live and see men damned.
> **CHARLES SPURGEON**

27 There is little Benjamin with their ruler, the princes of Judah and their council, the princes of Zebulun, and the princes of Naphtali.
28 Your God has commanded your strength: strengthen, O God, that which you have wrought for us.
29 Because of your temple at Jerusalem shall kings bring presents unto you.
30 Rebuke the company of spearmen, the multitude of the bulls, with the calves of the people, till every one submit himself with pieces of silver: scatter the people that delight in war.
31 Princes shall come out of Egypt; Ethiopia shall soon stretch out her hands unto God.
32 Sing unto God, you kingdoms of the earth; O sing praises unto the Lord; Selah:
33 To him that rides upon the heavens of heavens, which were of old; lo, he does send out his voice, and that a mighty voice.
34 Ascribe strength unto God: his excellency is over Israel, and his strength is in the clouds.
35 O God, you are terrible out of your holy places: the God of Israel is he that gives strength and power unto his people. Blessed be God.

PSALM 69

SAVE me, O God; for the waters are come in unto my soul.
2 I sink in deep mire, where there is no standing: I am come into deep waters, where the floods overflow me.
3 I am weary of my crying: my throat is dried: my eyes fail while I wait for my God.
4 They that hate me without a cause are more than the hairs of my head: they that would destroy me, being my enemies wrongfully, are mighty: then I restored that which I took not away.
5 O God, you know my foolishness; and my sins are not hid from you.
6 Let not them that wait on you, O Lord GOD of hosts, be ashamed for my sake: let not those that seek you be confounded for my sake, O God of Israel.
7 Because for your sake I have borne reproach; shame has covered my face.
8 I am become a stranger unto my brethren, and an alien unto my mother's children.
9 For the zeal of your house has eaten me up; and the reproaches of them that reproached you are fallen upon me.
10 When I wept, and chastened my soul with fasting, that was to my reproach.
11 I made sackcloth also my garment; and I became a proverb to them.
12 They that sit in the gate speak against me; and I was the song of the drunkards.
13 But as for me, my prayer is unto you, O LORD, in an acceptable time: O God, in the multitude of your mercy hear me, in the truth of your salvation.
14 Deliver me out of the mire, and let me not sink: let me be delivered from them that hate me, and out of the deep waters.

69:9 This is a direct reference to the Messiah. See John 2:17.

15 Let not the waterflood overflow me,
neither let the deep swallow me up, and
let not the pit shut her mouth upon me.
16 Hear me, O LORD; for your lovingkindness is good: turn unto me according
to the multitude of your tender mercies.
17 And hide not your face from your servant; for I am in trouble: hear me speedily.
18 Draw near unto my soul, and redeem
it: deliver me because of my enemies.
19 You have known my reproach, and
my shame, and my dishonor: my adversaries are all before you.
20 Reproach has broken my heart; and
I am full of heaviness: and I looked for
some to take pity, but there was none;
and for comforters, but I found none.
21 They gave me also gall for my meat;
and in my thirst they gave me vinegar to
drink.
22 Let their table become a snare before
them: and that which should have been
for their welfare, let it become a trap.
23 Let their eyes be darkened, that they
see not; and make their loins continually
to shake.
24 Pour out your indignation upon them,
and let your wrathful anger take hold of
them.
25 Let their habitation be desolate; and
let none dwell in their tents.
26 For they persecute him whom you
have smitten; and they talk to the grief of
those whom you have wounded.
27 Add iniquity unto their iniquity: and
let them not come into your righteousness.
28 Let them be blotted out of the book
of the living, and not be written with the
righteous.
29 But I am poor and sorrowful: let your
salvation, O God, set me up on high.
30 I will praise the name of God with a
song, and will magnify him with thanksgiving.
31 This also shall please the LORD better
than an ox or bullock that has horns and
hoofs.
32 The humble shall see this, and be
glad: and your heart shall live that seek
God.
33 For the LORD hears the poor, and despises not his prisoners.
34 Let the heaven and earth praise him,
the seas, and every thing that moves therein.
35 For God will save Zion, and will build
the cities of Judah: that they may dwell
there, and have it in possession.
36 The seed also of his servants shall inherit it: and they that love his name shall
dwell therein.

PSALM 70

MAKE haste, O God, to deliver me;
make haste to help me, O LORD.
2 Let them be ashamed and confounded
that seek after my soul: let them be turned
backward, and put to confusion, that desire my hurt.
3 Let them be turned back for a reward
of their shame that say, Aha, aha.
4 Let all those that seek you rejoice and
be glad in you: and let such as love your
salvation say continually, Let God be magnified.
5 But I am poor and needy: make haste
unto me, O God: you are my help and my
deliverer; O LORD, make no tarrying.

PSALM 71

IN you, O LORD, do I put my trust: let
me never be put to confusion.
2 Deliver me in your righteousness, and
cause me to escape: incline your ear unto me, and save me.
3 Be my strong habitation, whereunto I
may continually resort: you have given

69:21 Messianic prophecy: This was fulfilled in John 19:29.

70:3 An accusing world is quick to point out the slightest weakness in the Christian. If we become impatient, they say, "Aha…you're supposed to be a Christian." They are unaware that they will be judged by the same measure by which they judge. See Romans 2:1,3.

commandment to save me; for you are my
rock and my fortress.
4 Deliver me, O my God, out of the
hand of the wicked, out of the hand of
the unrighteous and cruel man.
5 For you are my hope, O Lord GOD:
you are my trust from my youth.
6 By you have I been held up from the
womb: you are he that took me out of my
mother's bowels: my praise shall be continually of you.
7 I am as a wonder unto many; but you
are my strong refuge.
8 Let my mouth be filled with your
praise and with your honor all the day.
9 Cast me not off in the time of old age;
forsake me not when my strength fails.
10 For my enemies speak against me;
and they that lay wait for my soul take
counsel together,
11 Saying, God has forsaken him: persecute and take him; for there is none to
deliver him.
12 O God, be not far from me: O my
God, make haste for my help.
13 Let them be confounded and consumed that are adversaries to my soul;
let them be covered with reproach and
dishonor that seek my hurt.
14 But I will hope continually, and will
yet praise you more and more.
15 My mouth shall show forth your
righteousness and your salvation all the
day; for I know not the numbers thereof.
16 I will go in the strength of the Lord
GOD: I will make mention of your righteousness, even of yours only.
17 O God, you have taught me from my
youth: and hitherto have I declared your
wondrous works.
18 Now also when I am old and grey-
headed, O God, forsake me not; until I
have showed your strength unto this generation, and your power to every one that
is to come.
19 Your righteousness also, O God, is
very high, who have done great things:
O God, who is like unto you!
20 You, who have showed me great and
sore troubles, shall quicken me again, and
shall bring me up again from the depths
of the earth.
21 You shall increase my greatness, and
comfort me on every side.
22 I will also praise you with the psaltery, even your truth, O my God: unto
you will I sing with the harp, O you Holy
One of Israel.
23 My lips shall greatly rejoice when I
sing unto you; and my soul, which you
have redeemed.
24 My tongue also shall talk of your
righteousness all the day long: for they
are confounded, for they are brought unto shame, that seek my hurt.

PSALM 72

GIVE the king your judgments, O
God, and your righteousness unto
the king's son.
2 He shall judge your people with righteousness, and your poor with judgment.
3 The mountains shall bring peace to
the people, and the little hills, by righteousness.
4 He shall judge the poor of the people,
he shall save the children of the needy,
and shall break in pieces the oppressor.
5 They shall fear you as long as the sun
and moon endure, throughout all generations.
6 He shall come down like rain upon the
mown grass: as showers that water the
earth.
7 In his days shall the righteous flourish;
and abundance of peace so long as the
moon endures.
8 He shall have dominion also from sea
to sea, and from the river unto the ends
of the earth.
9 They that dwell in the wilderness shall
bow before him; and his enemies shall
lick the dust.
10 The kings of Tarshish and of the isles
shall bring presents: the kings of Sheba
and Seba shall offer gifts.
11 Yes, all kings shall fall down before
him: all nations shall serve him.
12 For he shall deliver the needy when
he cries; the poor also, and him that has

no helper.
13 He shall spare the poor and needy, and shall save the souls of the needy.
14 He shall redeem their soul from deceit and violence: and precious shall their blood be in his sight.
15 And he shall live, and to him shall be given of the gold of Sheba: prayer also shall be made for him continually; and daily shall he be praised.
16 There shall be an handful of corn in the earth upon the top of the mountains; the fruit thereof shall shake like Lebanon: and they of the city shall flourish like grass of the earth.
17 His name shall endure for ever: his name shall be continued as long as the sun: and men shall be blessed in him: all nations shall call him blessed.
18 Blessed be the LORD God, the God of Israel, who only does wondrous things.
19 And blessed be his glorious name for ever: and let the whole earth be filled with his glory; Amen, and Amen.
20 The prayers of David the son of Jesse are ended.

PSALM 73

TRULY God is good to Israel, even to such as are of a clean heart.
2 But as for me, my feet were almost gone; my steps had well near slipped.
3 For I was envious at the foolish, when I saw the prosperity of the wicked.
4 For there are no bands in their death: but their strength is firm.
5 They are not in trouble as other men; neither are they plagued like other men.
6 Therefore pride compasses them about as a chain; violence covers them as a garment.
7 Their eyes stand out with fatness: they have more than heart could wish.
8 They are corrupt, and speak wickedly concerning oppression: they speak loftily.
9 They set their mouth against the heavens, and their tongue walks through the earth.
10 Therefore his people return hither: and waters of a full cup are wrung out to them.
11 And they say, How does God know? and is there knowledge in the most High?
12 Behold, these are the ungodly, who prosper in the world; they increase in riches.
13 Verily I have cleansed my heart in vain, and washed my hands in innocency.
14 For all the day long have I been plagued, and chastened every morning.
15 If I say, I will speak thus; behold, I should offend against the generation of your children.
16 When I thought to know this, it was too painful for me;
17 Until I went into the sanctuary of God; then understood I their end.
18 Surely you did set them in slippery places: you cast them down into destruction.
19 How are they brought into desolation, as in a moment! they are utterly consumed with terrors.
20 As a dream when one awakes; so, O Lord, when you awake, you shall despise their image.
21 Thus my heart was grieved, and I was pricked in my reins.

"No educated man can afford to be ignorant of the Bible."

Theodore Roosevelt

22 So foolish was I, and ignorant: I was as a beast before you.
23 Nevertheless I am continually with you: you have held me by my right hand.
24 You shall guide me with your counsel, and afterward receive me to glory.
25 Whom have I in heaven but you? and there is none upon earth that I desire beside you.
26 My flesh and my heart fails: but God is the strength of my heart, and my portion for ever.
27 For, lo, they that are far from you shall perish: you have destroyed all them that go a whoring from you.
28 But it is good for me to draw near to God: I have put my trust in the Lord GOD, that I may declare all your works.

PSALM 74

O GOD, why have you cast us off for ever? why does your anger smoke against the sheep of your pasture?
2 Remember your congregation, which you have purchased of old; the rod of your inheritance, which you have redeemed; this mount Zion, wherein you have dwelt.
3 Lift up your feet unto the perpetual desolations; even all that the enemy has done wickedly in the sanctuary.
4 Your enemies roar in the midst of your congregations; they set up their ensigns for signs.
5 A man was famous according as he had lifted up axes upon the thick trees.
6 But now they break down the carved work thereof at once with axes and hammers.
7 They have cast fire into your sanctuary, they have defiled by casting down the dwelling place of your name to the ground.
8 They said in their hearts, Let us destroy them together: they have burned up all the synagogues of God in the land.
9 We see not our signs: there is no more any prophet: neither is there among us any that knows how long.
10 O God, how long shall the adversary reproach? shall the enemy blaspheme your name for ever?
11 Why do you withdraw your hand, even your right hand? pluck it out of your bosom.
12 For God is my King of old, working salvation in the midst of the earth.
13 You did divide the sea by your strength: you brake the heads of the dragons in the waters.
14 You brake the heads of leviathan in pieces, and gave him to be meat to the people inhabiting the wilderness.
15 You did cleave the fountain and the flood: you dried up mighty rivers.
16 The day is Yours, the night also is yours: you have prepared the light and the sun.
17 You have set all the borders of the earth: you have made summer and winter.
18 Remember this, that the enemy has reproached, O LORD, and that the foolish people have blasphemed your name.
19 O deliver not the soul of your turtledove unto the multitude of the wicked: forget not the congregation of your poor for ever.
20 Have respect unto the covenant: for the dark places of the earth are full of the habitations of cruelty.
21 O let not the oppressed return ashamed: let the poor and needy praise your name.
22 Arise, O God, plead your own cause: remember how the foolish man reproaches you daily.
23 Forget not the voice of your enemies: the tumult of those that rise up against you increases continually.

PSALM 75

UNTO you, O God, do we give thanks, unto you do we give thanks: for that your name is near your wondrous

75:1 "It is a terrible thing, I found, to be grateful and have no one to thank, to be awed and have no one to worship." *Philip Yancey, What's So Amazing About Grace?*

works declare.
2 When I shall receive the congregation
I will judge uprightly.
3 The earth and all the inhabitants thereof are dissolved: I bear up the pillars of it.
Selah.
4 I said unto the fools, Deal not foolishly:
and to the wicked, Lift not up the horn:
5 Lift not up your horn on high: speak
not with a stiff neck.
6 For promotion comes neither from the
east, nor from the west, nor from the
south.
7 But God is the judge: he puts down
one, and sets up another.
8 For in the hand of the LORD there is a
cup, and the wine is red; it is full of mixture; and he pours out of the same: but
the dregs thereof, all the wicked of the
earth shall wring them out, and drink
them.
9 But I will declare for ever; I will sing
praises to the God of Jacob.
10 All the horns of the wicked also will
I cut off; but the horns of the righteous
shall be exalted.

PSALM 76

IN Judah is God known: his name is
great in Israel.
2 In Salem also is his tabernacle, and
his dwelling place in Zion.
3 There brake he the arrows of the bow,
the shield, and the sword, and the battle.
Selah.
4 You are more glorious and excellent
than the mountains of prey.
5 The stouthearted are spoiled, they have
slept their sleep: and none of the men of
might have found their hands.
6 At your rebuke, O God of Jacob, both
the chariot and horse are cast into a dead
sleep.
7 You, even you, are to be feared: and
who may stand in your sight when once
you are angry?
8 You did cause judgment to be heard
from heaven; the earth feared, and was
still,
9 When God arose to judgment, to save
all the meek of the earth. Selah.
10 Surely the wrath of man shall praise
you: the remainder of wrath shall you re-
strain.
11 Vow, and pay unto the LORD your
God: let all that be round about him bring
presents unto him that ought to be feared.
12 He shall cut off the spirit of princes:
he is terrible to the kings of the earth.

> There is no doctrine which I would more willingly remove from Christianity than the doctrine of hell, if it lay in my power. But it has the full support of Scripture and, especially, of our Lord's own words; it has always been held by the Christian Church, and it has the support of reason.
>
> **C. S. LEWIS**

PSALM 77

I CRIED unto God with my voice, even
unto God with my voice; and he gave
ear unto me.
2 In the day of my trouble I sought the
Lord: my sore ran in the night, and ceased
not: my soul refused to be comforted.
3 I remembered God, and was troubled:
I complained, and my spirit was overwhelmed. Selah.
4 You hold my eyes waking: I am so
troubled that I cannot speak.
5 I have considered the days of old, the
years of ancient times.
6 I call to remembrance my song in the
night: I commune with my own heart:
and my spirit made diligent search.
7 Will the Lord cast off for ever? and will
he be favorable no more?
8 Is his mercy clean gone for ever? does
his promise fail for evermore?
9 Has God forgotten to be gracious? has
he in anger shut up his tender mercies?
Selah.
10 And I said, This is my infirmity: but I
will remember the years of the right hand
of the most High.
11 I will remember the works of the

QUESTIONS & OBJECTIONS

76:8 "Could you be wrong in your claims about Judgment Day and the existence of hell?"

The existence of hell and the surety of the judgment are not the claims of fallible man. The Bible is the source of the claim, and it is utterly infallible.

When someone becomes a Christian, he is admitting that he was in the wrong, and that God is justified in His declarations that we have sinned against Him. However, let's surmise for a moment that there is no Judgment Day and no hell. That would mean that the Bible is a huge hoax, in which more than forty authors collaborated (over a period of 3,000 years) to produce a document revealing God's character as "just." They portrayed Him as a just judge, who warned that He would eventually punish murderers, rapists, liars, thieves, adulterers, etc. Each of those writers (who professed to be godly) therefore bore false witness, transgressing the very commandments they claimed to be true. It would mean that Jesus Christ was a liar, and that all the claims He made about the reality of judgment were therefore false. It would also mean that He gave His life in vain, as did multitudes of martyrs who have given their lives for the cause of Christ. Add to that the thought that if there is no ultimate justice, it means that the Creator of all things is unjust—that He sees murder and rape and couldn't care less, making Him worse than a corrupt human judge who refuses to bring criminals to justice.

Here's the good news, though, if there is no hell: You won't know a thing after you die. It will be the end. No heaven, no hell. Just nothing. You won't even realize that it's good news. Here's the bad news if the Bible is right and that there is eternal justice: You will find yourself standing before the judgment throne of a holy God, who has seen every sin you have ever committed. Think of it. A holy and perfect Creator has seen your thought-life and every secret sin you have ever committed. You have a multitude of sins, and God must by nature carry out justice. Ask Him to remind you of the sins of your youth. Ask Him to bring to remembrance your secret sexual sins, the lies, the gossip, and other idle words. You may have forgotten your past sins, but God hasn't. Hell will be your just desert (exactly what you deserve), and you will have no one to blame but yourself. This is the claim of the Bible. If you don't believe it, it is still true. It will still happen.

Yet, there is good news—incredibly good news. We deserve judgment, but God offers us mercy through the cross. He paid our fine so that we could leave the courtroom. He destroyed the power of the grave for all who obey Him. Simply obey the gospel, and live. By doing that you will find out for yourself that the gospel is indeed the "gospel truth." Jesus said that if you obey Him, you will know the truth, and the truth will make you free (see John 8:31,32). Get on your knees today, confess and forsake your sins. Tell God you are truly sorry, then trust the Savior as you would trust yourself to a parachute. Then you will find yourself in a terrible dilemma. You will know for certain that hell is a reality. When you get up the courage to warn people you care about, they will smile passively, and say, "Could you be wrong in your claims about Judgment Day and the existence of hell?"

LORD: surely I will remember your wonders of old.
12 I will meditate also of all your work, and talk of your doings.
13 Your way, O God, is in the sanctuary: who is so great a God as our God?
14 You are the God that does wonders: you have declared your strength among the people.
15 You have with your arm redeemed your people, the sons of Jacob and Joseph. Selah.
16 The waters saw you, O God, the waters saw you; they were afraid: the depths also were troubled.
17 The clouds poured out water: the

skies sent out a sound: your arrows also
went abroad.
18 The voice of your thunder was in the
heaven: the lightnings lightened the world:
the earth trembled and shook.
19 Your way is in the sea, and your path
in the great waters, and your footsteps are
not known.
20 You led your people like a flock by
the hand of Moses and Aaron.

PSALM 78

GIVE ear, O my people, to my law: incline your ears to the words of my
mouth.
2 I will open my mouth in a parable: I
will utter dark sayings of old:
3 Which we have heard and known, and
our fathers have told us.
4 We will not hide them from their children, showing to the generation to come
the praises of the LORD, and his strength,
and his wonderful works that he has done.
5 For he established a testimony in Jacob,
and appointed a law in Israel, which he
commanded our fathers, that they should
make them known to their children:
6 That the generation to come might
know them, even the children which
should be born; who should arise and
declare them to their children:
7 That they might set their hope in God,
and not forget the works of God, but
keep his commandments:
8 And might not be as their fathers, a
stubborn and rebellious generation; a
generation that set not their heart aright,
and whose spirit was not steadfast with
God.
9 The children of Ephraim, being armed,
and carrying bows, turned back in the
day of battle.
10 They kept not the covenant of God,
and refused to walk in his law;
11 And forgot his works, and his wonders that he had showed them.
12 Marvelous things did he in the sight
of their fathers, in the land of Egypt, in
the field of Zoan.
13 He divided the sea, and caused them
to pass through; and he made the waters
to stand as an heap.
14 In the daytime also he led them with
a cloud, and all the night with a light of
fire.
15 He clave the rocks in the wilderness,
and gave them drink as out of the great
depths.
16 He brought streams also out of the
rock, and caused waters to run down like
rivers.
17 And they sinned yet more against him
by provoking the most High in the wilderness.
18 And they tempted God in their heart
by asking meat for their lust.
19 Yes, they spoke against God; they
said, Can God furnish a table in the wilderness?
20 Behold, he smote the rock, that the
waters gushed out, and the streams overflowed; can he give bread also? can he
provide flesh for his people?
21 Therefore the LORD heard this, and
was wroth: so a fire was kindled against
Jacob, and anger also came up against

78:2 Messianic prophecy: Jesus fulfilled this in Matthew 13:34,35.

78:5,6 If you want to bring children to the Savior, teach them the Ten Commandments in light of New Testament revelation (lust is adultery, hatred is murder, etc.). Immediately after giving God's Moral Law (the Ten Commandments) to Israel, Moses said to teach them diligently. In Deuteronomy 6:6–9, he explains how to do that: speak of the Commandments when you sit with your children at home, as you go for walks together, at their bedtime, and when they get up (nighttime and morning devotions). Bind the Commandments on your hands, in front of your eyes, and at the entry of your house—in other words, do not forget them. Can you name the Ten Commandments? Can your children name them? See Exodus 20:1–17 and Deuteronomy 11:18–21.

To help your kids memorize the Ten Commandments, see page 456.

Israel;
22 Because they believed not in God, and
trusted not in his salvation:
23 Though he had commanded the
clouds from above, and opened the doors
of heaven,
24 And had rained down manna upon
them to eat, and had given them of the
corn of heaven.
25 Man did eat angels' food: he sent
them meat to the full.
26 He caused an east wind to blow in
the heaven: and by his power he brought
in the south wind.
27 He rained flesh also upon them as
dust, and feathered fowls like as the sand
of the sea:
28 And he let it fall in the midst of their
camp, round about their habitations.
29 So they did eat, and were well filled:
for he gave them their own desire;
30 They were not estranged from their
lust. But while their meat was yet in their
mouths,
31 The wrath of God came upon them,
and slew the fattest of them, and smote
down the chosen men of Israel.
32 For all this they sinned still, and believed not for his wondrous works.
33 Therefore their days did he consume
in vanity, and their years in trouble.
34 When he slew them, then they sought
him: and they returned and enquired early
after God.
35 And they remembered that God was
their rock, and the high God their redeemer.
36 Nevertheless they did flatter him with
their mouth, and they lied unto him with
their tongues.
37 For their heart was not right with him,
neither were they steadfast in his covenant.
38 But he, being full of compassion, forgave their iniquity, and destroyed them
not: yes, many a time turned he his anger
away, and did not stir up all his wrath.
39 For he remembered that they were
but flesh; a wind that passes away, and
comes not again.
40 How oft did they provoke him in the
wilderness, and grieve him in the desert!
41 Yes, they turned back and tempted
God, and limited the Holy One of Israel.
42 They remembered not his hand, nor
the day when he delivered them from
the enemy.
43 How he had wrought his signs in
Egypt, and his wonders in the field of
Zoan.
44 And had turned their rivers into blood;
and their floods, that they could not drink.
45 He sent divers sorts of flies among
them, which devoured them; and frogs,
which destroyed them.
46 He gave also their increase unto the
caterpillar, and their labor unto the locust.
47 He destroyed their vines with hail,
and their sycamore trees with frost.

> The beginning of anxiety is the end of faith, and the beginning of true faith is the end of anxiety.
>
> **GEORGE MUELLER**

48 He gave up their cattle also to the hail,
and their flocks to hot thunderbolts.
49 He cast upon them the fierceness of
his anger, wrath, and indignation, and
trouble, by sending evil angels among
them.
50 He made a way to his anger; he spared
not their soul from death, but gave their
life over to the pestilence;
51 And smote all the firstborn in Egypt;
the chief of their strength in the tabernacles of Ham:
52 But made his own people to go forth
like sheep, and guided them in the wilderness like a flock.
53 And he led them on safely, so that
they feared not: but the sea overwhelmed
their enemies.
54 And he brought them to the border
of his sanctuary, even to this mountain,
which his right hand had purchased.
55 He cast out the heathen also before
them, and divided them an inheritance
by line, and made the tribes of Israel to

dwell in their tents.
56 Yet they tempted and provoked the
most high God, and kept not his testimonies:
57 But turned back, and dealt unfaith-
fully like their fathers: they were turned
aside like a deceitful bow.
58 For they provoked him to anger with
their high places, and moved him to jealousy with their graven images.
59 When God heard this, he was wroth,
and greatly abhorred Israel:
60 So that he forsook the tabernacle of
Shiloh, the tent which he placed among
men;
61 And delivered his strength into captivity, and his glory into the enemy's hand.
62 He gave his people over also unto
the sword; and was wroth with his inheritance.
63 The fire consumed their young men;
and their maidens were not given to marriage.
64 Their priests fell by the sword; and
their widows made no lamentation.
65 Then the LORD awaked as one out of
sleep, and like a mighty man that shouts
by reason of wine.
66 And he smote his enemies in the hinder parts: he put them to a perpetual reproach.
67 Moreover he refused the tabernacle of
Joseph, and chose not the tribe of Ephraim:
68 But chose the tribe of Judah, the
mount Zion which he loved.
69 And he built his sanctuary like high
palaces, like the earth which he has established for ever.
70 He chose David also his servant, and
took him from the sheepfolds:
71 From following the ewes great with
young he brought him to feed Jacob his
people, and Israel his inheritance.
72 So he fed them according to the integrity of his heart; and guided them by
the skillfulness of his hands.

PSALM 79

O GOD, the heathen are come into
your inheritance; your holy temple
have they defiled; they have laid Jerusalem on heaps.
2 The dead bodies of your servants have
they given to be meat unto the fowls of
the heaven, the flesh of your saints unto
the beasts of the earth.
3 Their blood have they shed like water
round about Jerusalem; and there was
none to bury them.
4 We are become a reproach to our neighbors, a scorn and derision to them that are
round about us.
5 How long, LORD? will you be angry for
ever? shall your jealousy burn like fire?
6 Pour out your wrath upon the heathen
that have not known you, and upon the
kingdoms that have not called upon your
name.
7 For they have devoured Jacob, and laid
waste his dwelling place.
8 O remember not against us former iniquities: let your tender mercies speedily
prevent us: for we are brought very low.
9 Help us, O God of our salvation, for the
glory of your name: and deliver us, and
purge away our sins, for your name's sake.
10 Wherefore should the heathen say,
Where is their God? let him be known
among the heathen in our sight by the
revenging of the blood of your servants
which is shed.
11 Let the sighing of the prisoner come
before you; according to the greatness of
your power preserve those that are appointed to die;
12 And render unto our neighbors sevenfold into their bosom their reproach,
wherewith they have reproached you, O
Lord.
13 So we your people and sheep of your
pasture will give you thanks for ever: we
will show forth your praise to all generations.

PSALM 80

GIVE ear, O Shepherd of Israel, you
that lead Joseph like a flock; you that
dwell between the cherubims, shine forth.
2 Before Ephraim and Benjamin and Manasseh stir up your strength, and come

and save us.
3 Turn us again, O God, and cause your
face to shine; and we shall be saved.
4 O LORD God of hosts, how long will you
be angry against the prayer of your people?
5 You feed them with the bread of tears;
and give them tears to drink in great measure.
6 You make us a strife unto our neighbors: and our enemies laugh among themselves.
7 Turn us again, O God of hosts, and
cause your face to shine; and we shall be
saved.
8 You have brought a vine out of Egypt:
you have cast out the heathen, and planted it.

> Nothing worse can happen to a church than to be conformed to this world.
>
> **CHARLES SPURGEON**

9 You prepare room before it, and did
cause it to take deep root, and it filled the
land.
10 The hills were covered with the shadow of it, and the boughs thereof were
like the goodly cedars.
11 She sent out her boughs unto the sea,
and her branches unto the river.
12 Why have you then broken down her
hedges, so that all they which pass by the
way do pluck her?
13 The boar out of the wood does waste
it, and the wild beast of the field does devour it.
14 Return, we beseech you, O God of
hosts: look down from heaven, and behold, and visit this vine;
15 And the vineyard which your right
hand has planted, and the branch that you
made strong for yourself.
16 It is burned with fire, it is cut down:
they perish at the rebuke of your countenance.
17 Let your hand be upon the man of
your right hand, upon the son of man
whom you made strong for yourself.
18 So will not we go back from you:
quicken us, and we will call upon your
name.
19 Turn us again, O LORD God of hosts,
cause your face to shine; and we shall be
saved.

PSALM 81

SING aloud unto God our strength:
make a joyful noise unto the God of
Jacob.
2 Take a psalm, and bring hither the timbrel, the pleasant harp with the psaltery.
3 Blow up the trumpet in the new moon,
in the time appointed, on our solemn feast
day.
4 For this was a statute for Israel, and a
law of the God of Jacob.
5 This he ordained in Joseph for a testimony, when he went out through the land
of Egypt: where I heard a language that I
understood not.
6 I removed his shoulder from the burden: his hands were delivered from the
pots.
7 You call in trouble, and I delivered you;
I answered you in the secret place of thunder: I proved you at the waters of Meri-
bah. Selah.
8 Hear, O my people, and I will testify
unto you: O Israel, if you will hearken
unto me;
9 There shall no strange god be in you;
neither shall you worship any strange god.
10 I am the LORD your God, which
brought you out of the land of Egypt: open
your mouth wide, and I will fill it.
11 But my people would not hearken to
my voice; and Israel would none of me.
12 So I gave them up unto their own
hearts' lust: and they walked in their own
counsels.
13 Oh that my people had hearkened unto me, and Israel had walked in my ways!
14 I should soon have subdued their
enemies, and turned my hand against their
adversaries.
15 The haters of the LORD should have
submitted themselves unto him: but their
time should have endured for ever.

16 He should have fed them also with
the finest of the wheat: and with honey
out of the rock should I have satisfied you.

PSALM 82

GOD stands in the congregation of
the mighty; he judges among the
gods.
2 How long will you judge unjustly, and
accept the persons of the wicked? Selah.
3 Defend the poor and fatherless: do justice to the afflicted and needy.
4 Deliver the poor and needy: rid them
out of the hand of the wicked.
5 They know not, neither will they understand; they walk on in darkness: all the
foundations of the earth are out of course.
6 I have said, You are gods; and all of
you are children of the most High.
7 But you shall die like men, and fall like
one of the princes.
8 Arise, O God, judge the earth: for you
shall inherit all nations.

PSALM 83

KEEP not silence, O God: hold not
your peace, and be not still, O God.
2 For, lo, your enemies make a tumult:
and they that hate you have lifted up the
head.
3 They have taken crafty counsel against
your people, and consulted against your
hidden ones.
4 They have said, Come, and let us cut
them off from being a nation; that the
name of Israel may be no more in remembrance.
5 For they have consulted together with
one consent: they are confederate against
you:
6 The tabernacles of Edom, and the Ish-
maelites; of Moab, and the Hagarenes;
7 Gebal, and Ammon, and Amalek; the
Philistines with the inhabitants of Tyre;
8 Assur also is joined with them: they
have helped the children of Lot. Selah.
9 Do unto them as unto the Midianites;
as to Sisera, as to Jabin, at the brook of Ki-
son:
10 Which perished at Endor: they became as dung for the earth.
11 Make their nobles like Oreb, and like
Zeeb: yes, all their princes as Zebah, and
as Zalmunna:
12 Who said, Let us take to ourselves the
houses of God in possession.
13 O my God, make them like a wheel;
as the stubble before the wind.
14 As the fire burns a wood, and as the
flame sets the mountains on fire;
15 So persecute them with your tempest,
and make them afraid with your storm.
16 Fill their faces with shame; that they
may seek your name, O LORD.
17 Let them be confounded and troubled
for ever; yes, let them be put to shame,
and perish:
18 That men may know that you, whose
name alone is JEHOVAH, are the most
high over all the earth.

PSALM 84

HOW amiable are your tabernacles, O
LORD of hosts!
2 My soul longs, yes, even faints for the
courts of the LORD: my heart and my
flesh cries out for the living God.
3 Yes, the sparrow has found an house,
and the swallow a nest for herself, where
she may lay her young, even your altars,
O LORD of hosts, my King, and my God.
4 Blessed are they that dwell in your
house: they will be still praising you. Selah.
5 Blessed is the man whose strength is in
you; in whose heart are the ways of them.
6 Who passing through the valley of
Baca make it a well; the rain also fills the
pools.
7 They go from strength to strength, every
one of them in Zion appears before God.
8 O LORD God of hosts, hear my prayer:

82:7 "Every man must do two things alone: he must do his own believing, and he must do his own dying." *Martin Luther*

give ear, O God of Jacob. Selah.
9 Behold, O God our shield, and look upon the face of your anointed.
10 For a day in your courts is better than
a thousand. I had rather be a doorkeeper
in the house of my God, than to dwell in
the tents of wickedness.
11 For the LORD God is a sun and shield:
the LORD will give grace and glory: no good
thing will he withhold from them that
walk uprightly.
12 O LORD of hosts, blessed is the man
that trusts in you.

PSALM 85

LORD, you have been favorable unto
your land: you have brought back the
captivity of Jacob.
2 You have forgiven the iniquity of your
people, you have covered all their sin.
Selah.
3 You have taken away all your wrath:
you have turned yourself from the fierceness of your anger.
4 Turn us, O God of our salvation, and
cause your anger toward us to cease.
5 Will you be angry with us for ever?
will you draw out your anger to all generations?
6 Will you not revive us again: that your
people may rejoice in you?
7 Show us your mercy, O LORD, and
grant us your salvation.
8 I will hear what God the LORD will
speak: for he will speak peace unto his
people, and to his saints: but let them not
turn again to folly.
9 Surely his salvation is near them that
fear him; that glory may dwell in our land.
10 Mercy and truth are met together;
righteousness and peace have kissed each
other.
11 Truth shall spring out of the earth;
and righteousness shall look down from
heaven.
12 Yes, the LORD shall give that which is
good; and our land shall yield her increase.
13 Righteousness shall go before him;
and shall set us in the way of his steps.

PSALM 86

BOW down your ear, O LORD, hear me:
for I am poor and needy.
2 Preserve my soul; for I am holy: O you
my God, save your servant that trusts in
you.
3 Be merciful unto me, O Lord: for I cry
unto you daily.
4 Rejoice the soul of your servant: for
unto you, O Lord, do I lift up my soul.
5 For you, Lord, are good, and ready to
forgive; and plenteous in mercy unto all
them that call upon you.
6 Give ear, O LORD, unto my prayer; and
attend to the voice of my supplications.
7 In the day of my trouble I will call
upon you: for you will answer me.
8 Among the gods there is none like
unto you, O Lord; neither are there any
works like unto your works.
9 All nations whom you have made shall
come and worship before you, O Lord;
and shall glorify your name.
10 For you are great, and do wondrous
things: you are God alone.
11 Teach me your way, O LORD; I will
walk in your truth: unite my heart to fear
your name.
12 I will praise you, O Lord my God,
with all my heart: and I will glorify your
name for evermore.
13 For great is your mercy toward me:
and you have delivered my soul from the
lowest hell.
14 O God, the proud are risen against
me, and the assemblies of violent men
have sought after my soul; and have not
set you before them.
15 But you, O Lord, are a God full of
compassion, and gracious, long suffering,
and plenteous in mercy and truth.
16 O turn unto me, and have mercy upon me; give your strength unto your ser-

85:10 The cross of Calvary is where righteousness and peace kissed each other.

vant, and save the son of your handmaid.
17 Show me a token for good; that they
which hate me may see it, and be ashamed:
because you, LORD, have helped me, and
comforted me.

PSALM 87

HIS foundation is in the holy mountains.
2 The LORD loves the gates of Zion more
than all the dwellings of Jacob.
3 Glorious things are spoken of you, O
city of God. Selah.
4 I will make mention of Rahab and Babylon to them that know me: behold Philistia, and Tyre, with Ethiopia; this man
was born there.
5 And of Zion it shall be said, This and
that man was born in her: and the highest himself shall establish her.
6 The LORD shall count, when he writes
up the people, that this man was born
there. Selah.
7 As well the singers as the players on
instruments shall be there: all my springs
are in you.

PSALM 88

O LORD God of my salvation, I have
cried day and night before you:
2 Let my prayer come before you: incline your ear unto my cry;
3 For my soul is full of troubles: and my
life draws near unto the grave.
4 I am counted with them that go down
into the pit: I am as a man that has no
strength:
5 Free among the dead, like the slain that
lie in the grave, whom you remember no
more: and they are cut off from your hand.
6 You have laid me in the lowest pit, in
darkness, in the deeps.
7 Your wrath lies hard upon me, and you
have afflicted me with all your waves.
Selah.
8 You have put away my acquaintance far
from me; you have made me an abomination unto them: I am shut up, and I cannot come forth.
9 My eye mourns by reason of affliction: LORD, I have called daily upon you,
I have stretched out my hands unto you.
10 Will you show wonders to the dead?
shall the dead arise and praise you? Selah.
11 Shall your lovingkindness be declared
in the grave? or your faithfulness in destruction?
12 Shall your wonders be known in the
dark? and your righteousness in the land
of forgetfulness?
13 But unto you have I cried, O LORD;
and in the morning shall my prayer prevent you.
14 LORD, why cast off my soul? why hide
your face from me?
15 I am afflicted and ready to die from
my youth up: while I suffer your terrors
I am distracted.
16 Your fierce wrath goes over me; your
terrors have cut me off.
17 They came round about me daily like
water; they compassed me about together.
18 Lover and friend have you put far
from me, and my acquaintance into darkness.

PSALM 89

I WILL sing of the mercies of the LORD
for ever: with my mouth will I make
known your faithfulness to all generations.
2 For I have said, Mercy shall be built
up for ever: your faithfulness shall you
establish in the very heavens.
3 I have made a covenant with my chosen, I have sworn unto David my servant,
4 Your seed will I establish for ever, and
build up your throne to all generations.
Selah.
5 And the heavens shall praise your wonders, O LORD: your faithfulness also in
the congregation of the saints.
6 For who in the heaven can be com-

89:6 Nothing on this earth or in heaven compares to God. Even the regenerate mind can't begin to comprehend His infinite greatness.

QUESTIONS & OBJECTIONS

89:14

"Why does the Old Testament show a God of wrath and the New Testament a God of mercy?"

The God of the New Testament is the same as the God of the Old Testament. The Bible says that He *never* changes. He is just as merciful in the Old Testament as He is in the New Testament. Read Nehemiah 9 for a summary of how God mercifully forgave Israel, again and again, after they repeatedly sinned and turned their back on Him. The psalms often speak of God's mercy poured out on sinners.

He is also just as wrath-filled in the New Testament as He is in the Old. He killed a husband and wife in the Book of Acts, simply because they told one lie. Jesus warned that He was to be feared because He has the power to cast the body and soul into hell. The apostle Paul said that he persuaded men to come to the Savior because he knew the "terror of the Lord." Read the dreadful judgments of the New Testament's Book of Revelation. That will put the "fear of God" in you, which incidentally is "the beginning of wisdom."

Perhaps the most fearful display of His wrath is seen in the cross of Jesus Christ. His fury so came upon the Messiah that it seems God enshrouded the face of Jesus in darkness so that creation couldn't gaze upon His unspeakable agony. Whether we like it or not, our God is a consuming fire of holiness (Hebrews 12:29). He isn't going to change, so we had better... before the Day of Judgment. If we repent, God, in His mercy, will forgive us and grant us eternal life in heaven with Him.

pared unto the LORD? who among the sons of the mighty can be likened unto the LORD?

7 God is greatly to be feared in the assembly of the saints, and to be had in reverence of all them that are about him.

8 O LORD God of hosts, who is a strong LORD like unto you? or to your faithfulness round about you?

9 You rule the raging of the sea: when the waves thereof arise, you stillest them.

10 You have broken Rahab in pieces, as one that is slain; you have scattered your enemies with your strong arm.

11 The heavens are yours, the earth also is yours: as for the world and the fullness thereof, you have founded them.

12 The north and the south you have created them: Tabor and Hermon shall rejoice in your name.

13 You have a mighty arm: strong is your hand, and high is your right hand.

14 Justice and judgment are the habitation of your throne: mercy and truth shall go before your face.

15 Blessed is the people that know the joyful sound: they shall walk, O LORD, in the light of your countenance.

16 In your name shall they rejoice all the day: and in your righteousness shall they be exalted.

17 For you are the glory of their strength: and in your favor our horn shall be exalted.

18 For the LORD is our defense; and the Holy One of Israel is our king.

19 Then you spoke in vision to your holy one, and said, I have laid help upon one that is mighty; I have exalted one chosen out of the people.

20 I have found David my servant; with my holy oil have I anointed him:

21 With whom my hand shall be established: my arm also shall strengthen him.

22 The enemy shall not exact upon him; nor the son of wickedness afflict him.

23 And I will beat down his foes before his face, and plague them that hate him.

24 But my faithfulness and my mercy shall be with him: and in my name shall his horn be exalted.

25 I will set his hand also in the sea, and his right hand in the rivers.

Four Simple Laws

God is holy and just:

"For God shall bring every work into judgment, with every secret thing, whether it be good, or whether it be evil" *(Ecclesiastes 12:14).*

The wages of sin is death:

"Sin is the transgression of the Law" *(1 John 3:4).*

(See the Ten Commandments on page 336.)

God is rich in mercy:

"But God, who is rich in mercy, for his great love wherewith He loved us . . ." *(Ephesians 2:4).*

Eternal life is in Jesus Christ:

"For God so loved the world, that he gave his only begotten Son, that whosoever believes in him should not perish, but have everlasting life" *(John 3:16).*

"[God] now commands all men every where to repent: because he has appointed a day, in which he will judge the world in righteousness" *(Acts 17:30).*

A Model Prayer of Repentance

"God, please forgive me for sinning against You. I understand that, according to Your Law, I deserve to go to hell. However, You are not willing that I perish. Thank You that Jesus suffered and died for me and rose again on the third day. I now repent, and yield myself to Him to be my Lord and Savior. I will read Your Word daily and obey what I read. In Jesus' Name I pray. Amen."

QUESTIONS & OBJECTIONS

89:48

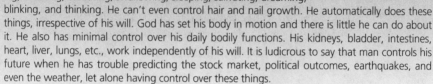

"Man is the master of his own destiny!"

If man is in total control of his future, then he should at least be in control of his own body. Instead, he is subject to involuntary yawning, sneezing, breathing, swallowing, sleeping, salivating, dreaming, blinking, and thinking. He can't even control hair and nail growth. He automatically does these things, irrespective of his will. God has set his body in motion and there is little he can do about it. He also has minimal control over his daily bodily functions. His kidneys, bladder, intestines, heart, liver, lungs, etc., work independently of his will. It is ludicrous to say that man controls his future when he has trouble predicting the stock market, political outcomes, earthquakes, and even the weather, let alone having control over these things.

26 He shall cry unto me, You are my father, my God, and the rock of my salvation.
27 Also I will make him my firstborn,
higher than the kings of the earth.
28 My mercy will I keep for him for evermore, and my covenant shall stand fast
with him.
29 His seed also will I make to endure for
ever, and his throne as the days of heaven.
30 If his children forsake my law, and
walk not in my judgments;
31 If they break my statutes, and keep
not my commandments;
32 Then will I visit their transgression
with the rod, and their iniquity with
stripes.
33 Nevertheless my lovingkindness will
I not utterly take from him, nor suffer
my faithfulness to fail.
34 My covenant will I not break, nor
alter the thing that is gone out of my lips.
35 Once have I sworn by my holiness
that I will not lie unto David.
36 His seed shall endure for ever, and
his throne as the sun before me.
37 It shall be established for ever as the
moon, and as a faithful witness in heaven.
Selah.
38 But you have cast off and abhorred,
you have been wroth with your anointed.
39 You have made void the covenant of
your servant: you have profaned his crown
by casting it to the ground.
40 You have broken down all his hedges;
you have brought his strong holds to
ruin.
41 All that pass by the way spoil him:
he is a reproach to his neighbors.
42 You have set up the right hand of his
adversaries; you have made all his enemies to rejoice.
43 You have also turned the edge of his
sword, and have not made him to stand
in the battle.
44 You have made his glory to cease, and
cast his throne down to the ground.
45 The days of his youth have you shortened: you have covered him with shame.
Selah.
46 How long, LORD? will you hide yourself for ever? shall your wrath burn like
fire?
47 Remember how short my time is:
wherefore have you made all men in vain?
48 What man is he that lives, and shall
not see death? shall he deliver his soul
from the hand of the grave? Selah.
49 Lord, where are your former lovingkindnesses, which you swore unto David
in your truth?
50 Remember, Lord, the reproach of your
servants; how I do bear in my bosom the
reproach of all the mighty people;

89:48 See James 4:14 footnote, "The Will to Live."

Questions & Objections

90:2 "Who made God?"

To one who examines the evidence, there can be no doubt that God exists. *Every* building has a builder. Everything made has a maker. The fact of the existence of the Creator is axiomatic (self-evident). That's why the Bible says, "The fool has said in his heart, 'There is no God'" (Psalm 14:1). The professing atheist denies the common sense given to him by God, and defends his belief by thinking that the question "Who made God?" can't be answered. This, he thinks, gives him license to deny the existence of God.

The question of who made God can be answered by simply looking at space and asking, "Does space have an end?" Obviously, it doesn't. If there is a brick wall with "The End" written on it, the question arises, "What is behind the brick wall?" Strain the mind though it may, we have to believe (have faith) that space has no beginning and no end. The same applies with God. He has no beginning and no end. He is eternal.

The Bible also informs us that time is a dimension that God created, into which man was subjected. It even tells us that one day time will no longer exist. That will be called "eternity." God Himself dwells outside of the dimension He created (2 Timothy 1:9, Titus 1:2). He dwells in eternity and is not subject to time. God spoke history before it came into being. He can move through time as a man flips through a history book. Because we live in the dimension of time, logic and reason demand that everything *must* have a beginning and an end. We can understand the concept of God's eternal nature the same way we understand the concept of space having no beginning and end—by faith. We simply *have* to believe they are so, even though such thoughts put a strain on our distinctly insufficient cerebrum.

51 Wherewith your enemies have reproached, O LORD; wherewith they have
reproached the footsteps of your anointed.
52 Blessed be the LORD for evermore.
Amen, and Amen.

PSALM 90

LORD, you have been our dwelling
place in all generations.
2 Before the mountains were brought
forth, or ever you had formed the earth
and the world, even from everlasting to
everlasting, you are God.
3 You turn man to destruction; and
say, Return, you children of men.
4 For a thousand years in your sight
are but as yesterday when it is past, and
as a watch in the night.
5 You carry them away as with a flood;
they are as a sleep: in the morning they

90:2 Microevolution vs. macroevolution. While we *do* see what's called "microevolution"—variations within species (different types of dogs, for instance)—we *don't* see any evidence of "macroevolution"—one species evolving into another species. Microevolution is observable, while macroevolution takes a tremendous leap of faith. If Christians had as much faith in God as atheists have in the theory of evolution, we would see revival. Like little children, atheists believe without a shred of evidence. *Ken Ham* writes, "Adaptation and natural selection are biological facts; amoeba-to-man evolution is not. Natural selection can only work on the genetic information present in a population of organisms—it cannot create new information. For example, since no known reptiles have genes for feathers, no amount of selection will produce a feathered reptile. Mutations in genes can only modify or eliminate existing structures, not create new ones" (*The Answers Book*).

Evolutionists claim that the appendix has no purpose—that it's left over from evolution. The truth is that the appendix is part of the human immune system. They also say that we have a tailbone (another leftover), proving that man is the product of evolution. The "tailbone" actually supports muscles that are necessary for daily bodily functions.

are like grass which grows up.
6 In the morning it flourishes, and grows up; in the evening it is cut down, and withers.
7 For we are consumed by your anger, and by your wrath are we troubled.
8 You have set our iniquities before you, our secret sins in the light of your countenance.
9 For all our days are passed away in your wrath: we spend our years as a tale that is told.
10 **The days of our years are threescore years and ten; and if by reason of strength they be fourscore years, yet is their strength labor and sorrow; for it is soon cut off, and we fly away.**

The average person dies at 70 years old.

IF YOU ARE:	YOU HAVE:
20 years old	2,500 weekends left
30 years old	2,000 weekends left
40 years old	1,500 weekends left
50 years old	1,000 weekends left
60 years old	500 weekends left

According to the U.S Census Bureau, 150,000 people die every 24 hours.

11 **Who knows the power of your anger? even according to your fear, so is your wrath.**
12 So teach us to number our days, that we may apply our hearts unto wisdom.
13 Return, O LORD, how long? and let it repent you concerning your servants.
14 O satisfy us early with your mercy; that we may rejoice and be glad all our days.
15 Make us glad according to the days wherein you have afflicted us, and the years wherein we have seen evil.
16 Let your work appear unto your servants, and your glory unto their children.
17 And let the beauty of the LORD our God be upon us: and establish the work of our hands upon us; yes, the work of our hands establish it.

PSALM 91

HE that dwells in the secret place of the most High shall abide under the shadow of the Almighty.
2 I will say of the LORD, He is my refuge and my fortress: my God; in him will I trust.
3 Surely he shall deliver you from the snare of the fowler, and from the noisome pestilence.
4 He shall cover you with his feathers, and under his wings shall you trust: his truth shall be your shield and buckler.
5 You shall not be afraid for the terror by night; nor for the arrow that flies by day;
6 Nor for the pestilence that walks in darkness; nor for the destruction that wastes at noonday.
7 A thousand shall fall at your side, and ten thousand at your right hand; but it shall not come near you.
8 Only with your eyes shall you behold

90:4 Time is God's creation. He Himself is not subject to the dimension of time. See 2 Peter 3:8 footnote.

90:7,8 The ungodly must be made to understand that every secret sin as well as sins of the heart are seen by God. He will bring every work to judgment, including every hidden thing, whether it is good or evil.

"When we merely say that we are bad, the 'wrath' of God seems a barbarous doctrine; as soon as we perceive our bad-ness, it appears inevitable, a mere corollary from God's goodness." *C. S. Lewis*

90:12 "Your days at the most cannot be very long, so use them to the best of your ability for the glory of God and the benefit of your generation. " *General William Booth*

91:1 This psalm is good medicine for those of us who sometimes feel sick with fear at the thought of evangelism. How can we not draw courage from such incredible promises?

and see the reward of the wicked.
9 Because you have made the LORD, which is my refuge, even the most High, your habitation;
10 There shall no evil befall you, neither shall any plague come near your dwelling.
11 For he shall give his angels charge over you, to keep you in all your ways.
12 They shall bear you up in their hands, lest you dash your foot against a stone.
13 You shall tread upon the lion and adder: the young lion and the dragon shall you trample under feet.
14 Because he has set his love upon me, therefore will I deliver him: I will set him on high, because he has known my name.
15 He shall call upon me, and I will answer him: I will be with him in trouble; I will deliver him, and honor him.
16 With long life will I satisfy him, and show him my salvation.

PSALM 92

IT is a good thing to give thanks unto the LORD, and to sing praises unto your name, O Most High:
2 To show forth your lovingkindness in the morning, and your faithfulness every night,
3 Upon an instrument of ten strings, and upon the psaltery; upon the harp with a solemn sound.
4 For you, LORD, have made me glad through your work: I will triumph in the works of your hands.
5 *O LORD, how great are your works! and your thoughts are very deep.*
6 *A brutish man knows not; neither does a fool understand this.*
7 When the wicked spring as the grass, and when all the workers of iniquity do flourish; it is that they shall be destroyed for ever:
8 But you, LORD, are most high for evermore.
9 For, lo, your enemies, O LORD, for, lo, your enemies shall perish; all the workers of iniquity shall be scattered.
10 But my horn shall you exalt like the horn of an unicorn: I shall be anointed with fresh oil.
11 My eye also shall see my desire on my enemies, and my ears shall hear my desire of the wicked that rise up against me.
12 The righteous shall flourish like the palm tree: he shall grow like a cedar in Lebanon.
13 Those that be planted in the house of the LORD shall flourish in the courts of our God.
14 They shall still bring forth fruit in old age; they shall be fat and flourishing;
15 To show that the LORD is upright: he is my rock, and there is no unrighteousness in him.

PSALM 93

THE LORD reigns, he is clothed with majesty; the LORD is clothed with

---

92:5,6 The unregenerate mind is able to see God's creation and not begin to comprehend how great God is. His understanding is darkened. He is alienated from the life of God through the ignorance that is in him (Ephesians 4:18). This ignorance is a willful blindness brought about by a hardened heart. See John 3:19,20 footnote.

92:13 "Most people think churches are like cafeterias; they pick and choose what they like! They feel the freedom to stay as long as there are no problems. But this does not agree at all with what the Bible teaches. You are not the one who chooses where you go to church. God does! The Bible does not say, 'God has set the members, each one of them, in the body *just as they please*.' Rather it says, 'But now God has set the members, each one of them, in the body *just as He pleased*' (1 Corinthians 12:18).

"Remember that, if you're in the place where God wants you, the devil will try to offend you to get you out. He wants to uproot men and women from the place where God plants them. If he can get you out, he has been successful. If you will not budge, even in the midst of great conflict, you will spoil his plans." *John Bevere, The Bait of Satan* strength, wherewith he has girded himself: the world also is established, that it cannot be moved.

2 Your throne is established of old: you are from everlasting.

3 The floods have lifted up, O LORD, the floods have lifted up their voice; the floods lift up their waves.

4 The LORD on high is mightier than the noise of many waters, yes, than the mighty waves of the sea.

5 Your testimonies are very sure: holiness becomes your house, O LORD, for ever.

PSALM 94

O LORD God, to whom vengeance belongs; O God, to whom vengeance belongs, show yourself.

2 Lift up yourself, you judge of the earth: render a reward to the proud.

3 LORD, how long shall the wicked, how long shall the wicked triumph?

4 How long shall they utter and speak hard things? and all the workers of iniquity boast themselves?

5 They break in pieces your people, O LORD, and afflict your heritage.

6 They slay the widow and the stranger, and murder the fatherless.

7 Yet they say, The LORD shall not see, neither shall the God of Jacob regard it.

8 Understand, you brutish among the people: and you fools, when will you be wise?

9 He that planted the ear, shall he not hear? he that formed the eye, shall he not see?

10 He that chastises the heathen, shall not he correct? he that teaches man knowledge, shall not he know?

11 **The LORD knows the thoughts of man, that they are vanity.**

12 Blessed is the man whom you chasten, O LORD, and teach him out of your law;

13 That you may give him rest from the days of adversity, until the pit be digged for the wicked.

14 For the LORD will not cast off his people, neither will he forsake his inheritance.

15 But judgment shall return unto righteousness: and all the upright in heart shall follow it.

16 *Who will rise up for me against the evildoers? or who will stand up for me against the workers of iniquity?*

17 *Unless the LORD had been my help, my soul had almost dwelt in silence.*

18 When I said, My foot slips; your mercy, O LORD, held me up.

19 In the multitude of my thoughts within me your comforts delight my soul.

20 Shall the throne of iniquity have fellowship with you, which frames mischief by a law?

21 They gather themselves together against the soul of the righteous, and condemn the innocent blood.

22 But the LORD is my defense; and my God is the rock of my refuge.

23 And he shall bring upon them their own iniquity, and shall cut them off in their own wickedness; yes, the LORD our God shall cut them off.

PSALM 95

O COME, let us sing unto the LORD: let us make a joyful noise to the rock of our salvation.

2 Let us come before his presence with thanksgiving, and make a joyful noise unto him with psalms.

3 For the LORD is a great God, and a great King above all gods.

94:1 "God is not disillusioned with us. He never had any illusions to begin with." *Luis Palau*

94:7–10 This is the great error of the ungodly. They don't consider the fact that if God can create an ear, He can therefore hear everything they say. If He can create an eye, He therefore can see everything they do.

94:12 Blessed is the man who is instructed out of God's Law. When God uses His Law to bring "the knowledge of sin," it acts as a "schoolmaster" (Galatians 3:24) to bring a sinner to the Savior.

4 In his hand are the deep places of the earth: the strength of the hills is his also.
5 The sea is his, and he made it: and his hands formed the dry land.
6 O come, let us worship and bow down: let us kneel before the LORD our maker.
7 For he is our God; and we are the people of his pasture, and the sheep of his hand. To day if you will hear his voice,
8 Harden not your heart, as in the provocation, and as in the day of temptation in the wilderness:
9 When your fathers tempted me, proved me, and saw my work.
10 Forty years long was I grieved with this generation, and said, It is a people that do err in their heart, and they have not known my ways:
11 Unto whom I swore in my wrath that they should not enter into my rest.

PSALM 96

O SING unto the LORD a new song: sing unto the LORD, all the earth.
2 Sing unto the LORD, bless his name; show forth his salvation from day to day.
3 Declare his glory among the heathen, his wonders among all people.
4 For the LORD is great, and greatly to be praised: he is to be feared above all gods.
5 For all the gods of the nations are idols: but the LORD made the heavens.
6 Honor and majesty are before him: strength and beauty are in his sanctuary.
7 Give unto the LORD, O you kindreds of the people, give unto the LORD glory and strength.
8 Give unto the LORD the glory due unto his name: bring an offering, and come into his courts.
9 O worship the LORD in the beauty of holiness: fear before him, all the earth.
10 Say among the heathen that the LORD reigns: the world also shall be established that it shall not be moved: he shall judge the people righteously.
11 *Let the heavens rejoice, and let the earth be glad; let the sea roar, and the fullness thereof.*
12 *Let the field be joyful, and all that is therein: then shall all the trees of the wood rejoice*
13 *Before the LORD: for he comes, for he comes to judge the earth: he shall judge the world with righteousness, and the people with his truth.*

PSALM 97

THE LORD reigns; let the earth rejoice; let the multitude of isles be glad thereof.
2 Clouds and darkness are round about him: righteousness and judgment are the habitation of his throne.
3 A fire goes before him, and burns up his enemies round about.
4 His lightnings enlightened the world: the earth saw, and trembled.
5 The hills melted like wax at the presence of the LORD, at the presence of the Lord of the whole earth.

95:4,5 Scientific facts in the Bible. Only in recent years has man discovered that there are mountains on the ocean floor. This was revealed in the Bible thousands of years ago. While deep in the ocean, Jonah cried, "I went down to the bottoms of the mountains…" (Jonah 2:6). The reason the Bible and true science harmonize is that they have the same author.

95:6 "I can safely say, on the authority of all that is revealed in the Word of God, that any man or woman on this earth who is bored and turned off by worship is not ready for heaven." *A. W. Tozer*

96:11–13 When a murderer is brought to justice, good people rejoice. Justice is sweet to the upright in heart. We are informed that the whole of creation rejoices because God is going to judge the world with righteousness and truth. This is what Paul preached in Acts 17:30,31, and it is what we must preach if we want the world to be saved.

97:2 Righteousness and justice are the very essence of God's character.

97:3–6 This is perhaps a reference to the giving of the Law on Mount Sinai (Exodus 19).

6 The heavens declare his righteousness,
and all the people see his glory.
7 Confounded be all they that serve grav-
en images, that boast themselves of idols:
worship him, all you gods.
8 Zion heard, and was glad; and the
daughters of Judah rejoiced because of
your judgments, O LORD.
9 For you, LORD, are high above all the
earth: you are exalted far above all gods.
10 You that love the LORD, hate evil: he
preserves the souls of his saints; he delivers them out of the hand of the wicked.
11 Light is sown for the righteous, and
gladness for the upright in heart.
12 Rejoice in the LORD, you righteous;
and give thanks at the remembrance of
his holiness.

. . . . . .

Is "hell-fire" preaching effective?
See Acts 24:25.

. . . . . .

PSALM 98

O SING unto the LORD a new song; for
he has done marvelous things: his
right hand, and his holy arm, has gotten
him the victory.
2 The LORD has made known his salvation: his righteousness has he openly
showed in the sight of the heathen.
3 He has remembered his mercy and his
truth toward the house of Israel: all the
ends of the earth have seen the salvation
of our God.
4 Make a joyful noise unto the LORD, all
the earth: make a loud noise, and rejoice,
and sing praise.
5 Sing unto the LORD with the harp; with
the harp, and the voice of a psalm.
6 With trumpets and sound of cornet
make a joyful noise before the LORD, the
King.
7 *Let the sea roar, and the fullness there-*
of; the world, and they that dwell therein.
8 *Let the floods clap their hands: let the*
hills be joyful together
9 *Before the LORD; for he comes to judge*
the earth: with righteousness shall he judge
the world, and the people with equity.

PSALM 99

THE LORD reigns; let the people tremble: he sits between the cherubims;
let the earth be moved.
2 The LORD is great in Zion; and he is
high above all the people.
3 Let them praise your great and terrible
name; for it is holy.
4 The king's strength also loves judgment;
you do establish equity, you execute judgment and righteousness in Jacob.
5 Exalt the LORD our God, and worship
at his footstool; for he is holy.
6 Moses and Aaron among his priests,
and Samuel among them that call upon
his name; they called upon the LORD, and
he answered them.
7 He spoke unto them in the cloudy pillar: they kept his testimonies, and the ordinance that he gave them.
8 You answered them, O LORD our God:
you were a God that forgave them, though
you took vengeance of their inventions.
9 Exalt the LORD our God, and worship at
his holy hill; for the LORD our God is holy.

PSALM 100

MAKE a joyful noise unto the LORD,
all you lands.
2 Serve the LORD with gladness: come
before his presence with singing.
3 Know that the LORD he is God: it is he
that has made us, and not we ourselves;
we are his people, and the sheep of his
pasture.

97:10 Do we truly hate evil, or do we secretly embrace lust and take pleasure in violent entertainment?

98:7–9 The whole of creation rejoices at the thought of God coming to judge the earth. Justice is a joy to the upright. See Psalm 96:11–13 footnote.

4 Enter into his gates with thanksgiving, and into his courts with praise: be thankful unto him, and bless his name.

5 For the LORD is good; his mercy is everlasting; and his truth endures to all generations.

PSALM 101

I WILL sing of mercy and judgment: unto you, O LORD, will I sing.

2 I will behave myself wisely in a perfect way. O when will you come unto me? I will walk within my house with a perfect heart.

3 I will set no wicked thing before my eyes: I hate the work of them that turn aside; it shall not cleave to me.

4 A froward heart shall depart from me: I will not know a wicked person.

5 Whoso privily slanders his neighbor, him will I cut off: him that has an high look and a proud heart will not I suffer.

6 My eyes shall be upon the faithful of the land, that they may dwell with me: he that walks in a perfect way, he shall serve me.

7 He that works deceit shall not dwell within my house: he that tells lies shall not tarry in my sight.

8 I will early destroy all the wicked of the land; that I may cut off all wicked doers from the city of the LORD.

PSALM 102

HEAR my prayer, O LORD, and let my cry come unto you.

2 Hide not your face from me in the day when I am in trouble; incline your ear unto me: in the day when I call answer me speedily.

3 For my days are consumed like smoke, and my bones are burned as an hearth.

4 My heart is smitten, and withered like grass; so that I forget to eat my bread.

5 By reason of the voice of my groaning my bones cleave to my skin.

6 I am like a pelican of the wilderness: I am like an owl of the desert.

7 I watch, and am as a sparrow alone upon the house top.

8 My enemies reproach me all the day; and they that are mad against me are sworn against me.

9 For I have eaten ashes like bread, and mingled my drink with weeping.

10 Because of your indignation and your wrath: for you have lifted me up, and cast me down.

11 My days are like a shadow that declines; and I am withered like grass.

12 But you, O LORD, shall endure for ever; and your remembrance unto all generations.

13 You shall arise, and have mercy upon Zion: for the time to favor her, yes, the set time, is come.

14 For your servants take pleasure in her stones, and favor the dust thereof.

15 So the heathen shall fear the name of the LORD, and all the kings of the earth your glory.

16 When the LORD shall build up Zion, he shall appear in his glory.

17 He will regard the prayer of the destitute, and not despise their prayer.

18 This shall be written for the generation to come: and the people which shall be created shall praise the LORD.

19 For he has looked down from the height of his sanctuary; from heaven did the LORD behold the earth;

20 To hear the groaning of the prisoner; to loose those that are appointed to death;

21 To declare the name of the LORD in Zion, and his praise in Jerusalem;

22 When the people are gathered together, and the kingdoms, to serve the LORD.

23 He weakened my strength in the way; he shortened my days.

24 I said, O my God, take me not away in the midst of my days: your years are throughout all generations.

25 Of old have you laid the foundation

101:1 Mercy and judgment met at the cross of Calvary. See Galatians 6:14.

of the earth: and the heavens are the work of your hands.

26 They shall perish, but you shall endure: yes, all of them shall wax old like a garment; as a vesture shall you change them, and they shall be changed:

27 But you are the same, and your years shall have no end.

28 The children of your servants shall continue, and their seed shall be established before you.

PSALM 103

BLESS the LORD, O my soul: and all that is within me, bless his holy name.

2 Bless the LORD, O my soul, and forget not all his benefits:

3 Who forgives all your iniquities; who heals all your diseases;

4 Who redeems your life from destruction; who crowns you with lovingkindness and tender mercies;

5 Who satisfies your mouth with good things; so that your youth is renewed like the eagle's.

6 The LORD executes righteousness and judgment for all that are oppressed.

7 He made known his ways unto Moses, his acts unto the children of Israel.

8 The LORD is merciful and gracious, slow to anger, and plenteous in mercy.

9 He will not always chide: neither will he keep his anger for ever.

10 He has not dealt with us after our sins; nor rewarded us according to our iniquities.

11 **For as the heaven is high above the earth, so great is his mercy toward them that fear him.**

12 **As far as the east is from the west, so far has he removed our transgressions from us.**

13 **Like as a father pities his children, so the LORD pities them that fear him.**

14 **For he knows our frame; he remembers that we are dust.**

15 **As for man, his days are as grass: as a flower of the field, so he flourishes.**

16 **For the wind passes over it, and it is gone; and the place thereof shall know it no more.**

17 But the mercy of the LORD is from everlasting to everlasting upon them that fear him, and his righteousness unto children's children;

18 To such as keep his covenant, and to those that remember his commandments to do them.

19 The LORD has prepared his throne in the heavens; and his kingdom rules over all.

20 Bless the LORD, you his angels, that excel in strength, that do his commandments, hearkening unto the voice of his word.

21 Bless the LORD, all his hosts; you ministers of his, that do his pleasure.

22 Bless the LORD, all his works in all places of his dominion: bless the LORD, O my soul.

PSALM 104

BLESS the LORD, O my soul. O LORD my God, you are very great; you are

---

102:25,26 Scientific facts in the Bible. Three different places in the Bible (Isaiah 51:6; Psalm 102:25,26; Hebrews 1:11) indicate that the earth is wearing out. This is what the Second Law of Thermodynamics (the Law of Increasing Entropy) states: that in all physical processes, every ordered system over time tends to become more disordered. Everything is running down and wearing out as energy is becoming less and less available for use. That means the universe will eventually "wear out" to the extent that (theoretically speaking) there will be a "heat death" and therefore no more energy available for use. This wasn't discovered by man until fairly recently, but the Bible states it in clear, succinct terms.

102:27 See Hebrews 13:8 footnote.

103:10 How true it is that God hasn't dealt with us according to our iniquities (vv. 10–18). He hasn't treated us as He treated Ananias and Sapphira (Acts 5:1–10). He has held back His just wrath and instead lavished us with mercy.

Questions & Objections

103:17 *"God couldn't forgive my sin."*

Those who think they are too sinful for God to accept them don't understand how merciful God is. The Bible says that He is "rich in mercy" (Ephesians 2:4). The Scriptures also tell us that "the mercy of the LORD is from everlasting to everlasting upon them that fear him" (Psalm 103:17). God was merciful to King David and forgave him when he committed adultery and murder. He forgave Moses when he committed murder. He also forgave Saul of Tarsus for murdering Christians (Acts 22:4). God promises to save "all" who call upon the name of Jesus (Romans 10:13). Those who think this promise isn't worth the paper it's written on are calling God a liar (see 1 John 5:10). Jesus shed His precious blood to pay for their sins. Wasn't it good enough for them? It was good enough for God. God *commands* them to repent. To offer any excuse is to remain in rebellion to His command—no matter how "noble" it may seem to say that they are too sinful.

clothed with honor and majesty.

2 Who covers yourself with light as with a garment: who stretches out the heavens like a curtain:

3 Who lays the beams of his chambers in the waters: who makes the clouds his chariot: who walks upon the wings of the wind:

4 Who makes his angels spirits; his ministers a flaming fire:

5 Who laid the foundations of the earth, that it should not be removed for ever.

6 You covered it with the deep as with a garment: the waters stood above the mountains.

7 At your rebuke they fled; at the voice of your thunder they hasted away.

8 They go up by the mountains; they go down by the valleys unto the place which you have founded for them.

9 You have set a bound that they may not pass over; that they turn not again to cover the earth.

10 He sends the springs into the valleys, which run among the hills.

11 They give drink to every beast of the field: the wild asses quench their thirst.

12 By them shall the fowls of the heaven have their habitation, which sing among the branches.

13 He waters the hills from his chambers: the earth is satisfied with the fruit of your works.

14 He causes the grass to grow for the cattle, and herb for the service of man: that he may bring forth food out of the earth;

15 And wine that makes glad the heart of man, and oil to make his face to shine, and bread which strengthens man's heart.

16 The trees of the LORD are full of sap; the cedars of Lebanon, which he has planted;

17 Where the birds make their nests: as for the stork, the fir trees are her house.

18 The high hills are a refuge for the wild goats; and the rocks for the conies.

19 He appointed the moon for seasons: the sun knows his going down.

20 You make darkness, and it is night: wherein all the beasts of the forest do creep forth.

21 The young lions roar after their prey, and seek their meat from God.

22 The sun arises, they gather themselves together, and lay them down in their dens.

23 Man goes forth unto his work and to his labor until the evening.

24 O LORD, how manifold are your works!

104:2 Scientific facts in the Bible. It is interesting to note that scientists are beginning to understand that the universe is expanding or stretching out. At least seven times in Scripture we are told that God *stretches* out the heavens like a curtain (Isaiah 40:22). See also Hebrews 11:3 footnote.

in wisdom have you made them all: the
earth is full of your riches.
25 So is this great and wide sea, wherein are things creeping innumerable, both
small and great beasts.
26 There go the ships: there is that leviathan, whom you have made to play therein.
27 These wait all upon you; that you
may give them their meat in due season.
28 That you give them they gather: you
open your hand, they are filled with good.
29 You hide your face, they are troubled:
you take away their breath, they die, and
return to their dust.
30 You send forth your spirit, they are
created: and you renew the face of the
earth.
31 The glory of the LORD shall endure
for ever: the LORD shall rejoice in his works.
32 He looks on the earth, and it trembles: he touches the hills, and they smoke.
33 I will sing unto the LORD as long as I
live: I will sing praise to my God while I
have my being.
34 My meditation of him shall be sweet:
I will be glad in the LORD.
35 Let the sinners be consumed out of
the earth, and let the wicked be no more.
Bless the LORD, O my soul. Praise the
LORD.

PSALM 105

O GIVE thanks unto the LORD; call upon his name: make known his deeds
among the people.
2 Sing unto him, sing psalms unto him:
talk of all his wondrous works.
3 Glory in his holy name: let the heart
of them rejoice that seek the LORD.
4 Seek the LORD, and his strength: seek
his face evermore.
5 Remember his marvelous works that
he has done; his wonders, and the judgments of his mouth;
6 O you seed of Abraham his servant,
you children of Jacob his chosen.
7 He is the LORD our God: his judgments
are in all the earth.
8 He has remembered his covenant for
ever, the word which he commanded to
a thousand generations.

104:19 Scientific facts in the Bible. God created the "lights" in the heavens "for signs, and for seasons, and for days and years" (Genesis 1:14). Through the marvels of astronomy we now understand that a year is the time required for the earth to travel once around the sun. The seasons are caused by the changing position of the earth in relation to the sun—"astronomers can tell exactly from the earth's motion around the sun when one season ends and the next one begins" (*Worldbook Multimedia Encyclopedia*). We also now understand that a "month [is] the time of one revolution of the moon around the earth with respect to the sun" (*Encyclopedia Britannica*). How could Moses (the accepted author of Genesis) have known 3,500 years ago that the "lights" of the sun and moon were the actual determining factors of the year's length, unless his words were inspired by God? (See also Psalm 136:7–9.)

104:24 The peppered moth: evolution comes unglued. "Almost all textbooks on evolution include the peppered moth as *the* classic example of evolution by natural selection. There are two types of peppered moths, a light-colored speckled variety and a dark variety. Most peppered moths in England were the light variety, which were camouflaged as they rested on tree trunks. The black variety stood out against the light bark and were easily seen and eaten by birds. But as the industrial revolution created pollution that covered tree trunks with soot, the dark variety was camouflaged better, so birds ate more of the light moths.

"The peppered moth story has been trumpeted since the 1950s as proof positive that evolution by natural selection is true. In 1978, one famous geneticist called the peppered moth 'the clearest case in which a conspicuous evolutionary process has actually been observed.'

"However, this 'clearest case' of purported Darwinian evolution by natural selection is not true! The nocturnal peppered moth does not rest on the trunks of trees during the day. In fact, despite over 40 years of intense field study, only two peppered moths have ever been seen naturally resting

9 Which covenant he made with Abraham, and his oath unto Isaac;
10 And confirmed the same unto Jacob for a law, and to Israel for an everlasting covenant:
11 Saying, Unto you will I give the land of Canaan, the lot of your inheritance:
12 When they were but a few men in number; yes, very few, and strangers in it.
13 When they went from one nation to another, from one kingdom to another people;
14 He suffered no man to do them wrong: yes, he reproved kings for their sakes;
15 Saying, Touch not my anointed, and do my prophets no harm.
16 Moreover he called for a famine upon the land: he brake the whole staff of bread.
17 He sent a man before them, even Joseph, who was sold for a servant:
18 Whose feet they hurt with fetters: he was laid in iron:
19 Until the time that his word came: the word of the LORD tried him.
20 The king sent and loosed him; even the ruler of the people, and let him go free.
21 He made him lord of his house, and ruler of all his substance:
22 To bind his princes at his pleasure; and teach his senators wisdom.
23 Israel also came into Egypt; and Jacob sojourned in the land of Ham.
24 And he increased his people greatly; and made them stronger than their enemies.
25 He turned their heart to hate his people, to deal subtly with his servants.
26 He sent Moses his servant; and Aaron whom he had chosen.
27 They showed his signs among them, and wonders in the land of Ham.
28 He sent darkness, and made it dark; and they rebelled not against his word.
29 He turned their waters into blood, and slew their fish.
30 Their land brought forth frogs in abundance, in the chambers of their kings.
31 He spoke, and there came divers sorts of flies, and lice in all their coasts.
32 He gave them hail for rain, and flaming fire in their land.

on tree trunks!

"So where did all the evolution textbook pictures of peppered moths on different colored tree trunks come from? They were all staged. The moths were glued, pinned, or placed onto tree trunks and their pictures taken. The scientists who used these pictures in their books to prove evolution *all* conveniently forgot to tell their readers this fact. If the *best* example of evolution is not true, how about all their *other* supposed examples? It makes you wonder, doesn't it?" *Mark Varney*

Evolutionary humor. It's humorous that evolutionists cite the peppered moth as their best example, enabling them to "watch evolution in action." Watch closely: Before the moth's environment changed, some of the moths were mostly white, some were mostly black. After their environment changed, some were mostly white, some were mostly black. No new color or variety came into being, yet we have supposedly just witnessed evolution.

Evolutionist *John Reader (Missing Links)* explains this biased interpretation: "Ever since Darwin's work..., preconceptions have led evidence by the nose." Harvard professor and evolutionist *Steven Jay Gould* admits this scientific bias, "Facts do not 'speak for themselves'; they are read in light of theory."

Even *Charles Darwin* concedes, "Alas, how frequent, how almost universal it is in an author to persuade himself of the truth of his own dogmas." Keep this in mind when scientists proclaim the theory of evolution as "fact."

105:17–19 If God is going to use you to reach the lost, be ready to be "tested." Your own family may turn against you. You may find yourself "laid in iron"—in a hardship in which there seems to be no escape. Don't get discouraged, and don't become passive in your evangelism. See 1 Peter 1:7 and "Closing Words of Comfort" in the appendix.

33 He smote their vines also and their fig
trees; and brake the trees of their coasts.
34 He spoke, and the locusts came, and
caterpillars, and that without number,
35 And did eat up all the herbs in their
land, and devoured the fruit of their
ground.
36 He smote also all the firstborn in their
land, the chief of all their strength.
37 He brought them forth also with silver and gold: and there was not one feeble person among their tribes.
38 Egypt was glad when they departed:
for the fear of them fell upon them.
39 He spread a cloud for a covering; and
fire to give light in the night.
40 The people asked, and he brought
quails, and satisfied them with the bread
of heaven.
41 He opened the rock, and the waters
gushed out; they ran in the dry places like
a river.
42 For he remembered his holy promise, and Abraham his servant.
43 And he brought forth his people with
joy, and his chosen with gladness:
44 And gave them the lands of the heathen: and they inherited the labor of the
people;
45 That they might observe his statutes,
and keep his laws. Praise the LORD.

PSALM 106

PRAISE the LORD. O give thanks unto
the LORD; for he is good: for his mercy endures for ever.
2 Who can utter the mighty acts of the
LORD? who can show forth all his praise?
3 Blessed are they that keep judgment,
and he that does righteousness at all
times.
4 Remember me, O LORD, with the favor
that you bear unto your people: O visit
me with your salvation;
5 That I may see the good of your chosen, that I may rejoice in the gladness of
your nation, that I may glory with your inheritance.
6 We have sinned with our fathers, we
have committed iniquity, we have done
wickedly.
7 Our fathers understood not your wonders in Egypt; they remembered not the
multitude of your mercies; but provoked
him at the sea, even at the Red sea.
8 Nevertheless he saved them for his
name's sake, that he might make his
mighty power to be known.
9 He rebuked the Red sea also, and it was
dried up: so he led them through the
depths, as through the wilderness.
10 And he saved them from the hand of
him that hated them, and redeemed them
from the hand of the enemy.
11 And the waters covered their enemies: there was not one of them left.
12 Then believed they his words; they
sang his praise.

> A little science estranges men from God, but much science leads them back to Him.
>
> **LOUIS PASTEUR**

13 They soon forgot his works; they
waited not for his counsel:
14 But lusted exceedingly in the wilderness, and tempted God in the desert.
15 And he gave them their request; but
sent leanness into their soul.
16 They envied Moses also in the camp,
and Aaron the saint of the LORD.
17 The earth opened and swallowed up
Dathan and covered the company of Abi-
ram.
18 And a fire was kindled in their company; the flame burned up the wicked.
19 They made a calf in Horeb, and worshipped the molten image.
20 Thus they changed their glory into
the similitude of an ox that eats grass.
21 They forgot God their savior, which
had done great things in Egypt;
22 Wondrous works in the land of Ham,
and terrible things by the Red sea.
23 Therefore he said that he would destroy them, had not Moses his chosen
stood before him in the breach, to turn

away his wrath, lest he should destroy
them.
24 Yes, they despised the pleasant land,
they believed not his word:
25 But murmured in their tents, and
hearkened not unto the voice of the LORD.
26 Therefore he lifted up his hand against
them, to overthrow them in the wilderness:
27 To overthrow their seed also among
the nations, and to scatter them in the
lands.
28 They joined themselves also unto Baal-
peor, and ate the sacrifices of the dead.
29 Thus they provoked him to anger with
their inventions: and the plague brake in
upon them.
30 Then stood up Phinehas, and executed
judgment: and so the plague was stayed.
31 And that was counted unto him for
righteousness unto all generations for
evermore.
32 They angered him also at the waters
of strife, so that it went ill with Moses for
their sakes:
33 Because they provoked his spirit, so
that he spoke unadvisedly with his lips.
34 They did not destroy the nations,
concerning whom the LORD commanded
them:
35 But were mingled among the heathen,
and learned their works.
36 And they served their idols: which
were a snare unto them.
37 Yes, they sacrificed their sons and
their daughters unto devils,
38 And shed innocent blood, even the
blood of their sons and of their daughters, whom they sacrificed unto the idols
of Canaan: and the land was polluted with
blood.
39 Thus were they defiled with their own
works, and went a whoring with their
own inventions.
40 Therefore was the wrath of the LORD
kindled against his people, insomuch that
he abhorred his own inheritance.
41 And he gave them into the hand of
the heathen; and they that hated them
ruled over them.
42 Their enemies also oppressed them,
and they were brought into subjection under their hand.
43 Many times did he deliver them; but
they provoked him with their counsel,
and were brought low for their iniquity.
44 Nevertheless he regarded their affliction, when he heard their cry:
45 And he remembered for them his
covenant, and repented according to the
multitude of his mercies.
46 He made them also to be pitied of all
those that carried them captives.
47 Save us, O LORD our God, and gather
us from among the heathen, to give thanks
unto your holy name, and to triumph in
your praise.
48 Blessed be the LORD God of Israel
from everlasting to everlasting: and let all
the people say, Amen. Praise the LORD.

106:35–39 Abortion—a result of idolatry. How can people believe in God and yet believe in the killing of children through abortion? Simply because they "serve idols." Idolatry is perhaps the greatest of all sins because it opens the door to unrestrained evil—"My god gives me the right to choose!" etc. It gives sinners license not only to tolerate sin, but to sanction it, fanned by demonic influence. Those who create a god in their own image feel at liberty to go "a whoring with their own inventions."

The following is typical of how easy it is to create your own god:

> Over the years, Ed and Joanne Liverani have found many reasons to summon God. But now, at middle age, they've boiled it down to one essential: "Not to get clobbered by life."
>
> So sometime in the past ten years the Liveranis began to build their own church, salvaging bits of their old religion that they liked and chucking the rest. The first to go were an angry, vengeful God and hell—"That's just something they say to scare you," Ed said. They kept Jesus, "because Jesus is big on love." *The Washington Post* (January 9, 2000)

PSALM 107

O GIVE thanks unto the LORD, for he
is good: for his mercy endures for
ever.
2 Let the redeemed of the LORD say so,
whom he has redeemed from the hand
of the enemy;
3 And gathered them out of the lands,
from the east, and from the west, from
the north, and from the south.
4 They wandered in the wilderness in a
solitary way; they found no city to dwell
in.
5 Hungry and thirsty, their soul fainted
in them.
6 Then they cried unto the LORD in their
trouble, and he delivered them out of
their distresses.
7 And he led them forth by the right way,
that they might go to a city of habitation.
8 Oh that men would praise the LORD for
his goodness, and for his wonderful works
to the children of men!
9 **For he satisfies the longing soul, and
fills the hungry soul with goodness.**
10 **Such as sit in darkness and in the
shadow of death, being bound in affliction and iron;**
11 **Because they rebelled against the
words of God, and contemned the counsel of the most High:**
12 **Therefore he brought down their
heart with labor; they fell down, and
there was none to help.**
13 **Then they cried unto the LORD in
their trouble, and he saved them out of
their distresses.**
14 **He brought them out of darkness
and the shadow of death, and brake
their bands in sunder.**
15 **Oh that men would praise the LORD
for his goodness, and for his wonderful works to the children of men!**
16 **For he has broken the gates of brass,
and cut the bars of iron in sunder.**
17 **Fools because of their transgression, and because of their iniquities, are
afflicted.**
18 **Their soul abhors all manner of
meat; and they draw near unto the gates
of death.**
19 **Then they cry unto the LORD in
their trouble, and he saves them out of
their distresses.**
20 He sent his word, and healed them,
and delivered them from their destructions.
21 Oh that men would praise the LORD
for his goodness, and for his wonderful
works to the children of men!
22 And let them sacrifice the sacrifices
of thanksgiving, and declare his works
with rejoicing.
23 They that go down to the sea in ships,
that do business in great waters;
24 These see the works of the LORD, and
his wonders in the deep.
25 For he commands, and raises the
stormy wind, which lifts up the waves
thereof.
26 They mount up to the heaven, they
go down again to the depths: their soul is

107:2 How can the redeemed not "say so"? We have been redeemed from the cold hand of death. See verse 14.

107:17 Self-inflicted misery. So much of the world's misery is self-inflicted: AIDS, alcoholism, obesity, guilt, drug addiction, nicotine addiction and its related diseases, etc. Look at the repercussions of adultery, revealed in this unsigned letter: "Eleven years ago, I walked out on a 12-year marriage. My wife was a good person, but for a long time she was under a lot of stress. Instead of helping her, I began an affair with her best friend. It was a disaster. This is what I gave up: 1) seeing my daughter grow up; 2) the respect of many long-time friends; 3) the enjoyment of living as a family; 4) a wife who was loyal, was appreciative and tried to make me happy. This is what I got: 1) two stepchildren who treated me like dirt; 2) a wife who didn't know how to make anything for dinner but reservations; 3) a wife whose only interest in me was how much money she could get; 4) a wife who made disparaging remarks about my family and ruined all my existing friendships; 5) finally, the best thing I got was a bitter, expensive divorce."

melted because of trouble.
27 They reel to and fro, and stagger like a drunken man, and are at their wit's end.
28 Then they cry unto the LORD in their trouble, and he brings them out of their distresses.
29 He makes the storm a calm, so that the waves thereof are still.
30 Then are they glad because they be quiet; so he brings them unto their desired haven.
31 Oh that men would praise the LORD for his goodness, and for his wonderful works to the children of men!
32 Let them exalt him also in the congregation of the people, and praise him in the assembly of the elders.
33 He turns rivers into a wilderness, and the watersprings into dry ground;
34 A fruitful land into barrenness, for the wickedness of them that dwell therein.
35 He turns the wilderness into a standing water, and dry ground into watersprings.
36 And there he makes the hungry to dwell, that they may prepare a city for habitation;
37 And sow the fields, and plant vineyards, which may yield fruits of increase.
38 He blesses them also, so that they are multiplied greatly; and suffers not their cattle to decrease.
39 Again, they are minished and brought low through oppression, affliction, and sorrow.
40 He pours contempt upon princes, and causes them to wander in the wilderness, where there is no way.
41 Yet sets he the poor on high from affliction, and makes him families like a flock.
42 The righteous shall see it, and rejoice: and all iniquity shall stop her mouth.
43 Whoso is wise, and will observe these things, even they shall understand the lovingkindness of the LORD.

PSALM 108

O GOD, my heart is fixed; I will sing and give praise, even with my glory.
2 Awake, psaltery and harp: I myself will awake early.
3 I will praise you, O LORD, among the people: and I will sing praises unto you among the nations.
4 For your mercy is great above the heavens: and your truth reaches unto the clouds.
5 Be exalted, O God, above the heavens: and your glory above all the earth;
6 That your beloved may be delivered: save with your right hand, and answer me.
7 God has spoken in his holiness; I will rejoice, I will divide Shechem, and mete out the valley of Succoth.
8 Gilead is mine; Manasseh is mine; Ephraim also is the strength of my head; Judah is my lawgiver;
9 Moab is my washpot; over Edom will I cast out my shoe; over Philistia will I triumph.
10 Who will bring me into the strong city? who will lead me into Edom?
11 Will not you, O God, who have cast us off? and will not you, O God, go forth with our hosts?
12 Give us help from trouble: for vain is the help of man.
13 Through God we shall do valiantly: for he it is that shall tread down our enemies.

PSALM 109

HOLD not your peace, O God of my praise;
2 For the mouth of the wicked and the mouth of the deceitful are opened against me: they have spoken against me with a lying tongue.
3 They compassed me about also with words of hatred; and fought against me without a cause.
4 For my love they are my adversaries: but I give myself unto prayer.

109:1–4 When the world turns against you because of your faith, and you find yourself in the valley of discouragement, climb up onto the high place of prayer.

QUESTIONS & OBJECTIONS

109:15 ***"God said He would blot out all remembrance of Amalek. The Bible itself disproves this statement by mentioning Amalek to this day."***

In Exodus 17:14, God told Moses to "write this for a memorial in a book..." Moses did that and God preserved the Book for 5,000 years, so skeptics would know that God keeps every promise He makes. The phrase "I will utterly put out the remembrance of Amalek from under heaven" means that he will blot them out as a nation from the earth. There are no descendants of the Amalekites on the earth. They don't exist.

5 And they have rewarded me evil for
good, and hatred for my love.
6 Set a wicked man over him: and let Satan stand at his right hand.
7 When he shall be judged, let him be
condemned: and let his prayer become sin.
8 Let his days be few; and let another
take his office.
9 Let his children be fatherless, and his
wife a widow.
10 Let his children be continually vaga-
bonds, and beg: let them seek their bread
also out of their desolate places.
11 Let the extortioner catch all that he
has; and let the strangers spoil his labor.
12 Let there be none to extend mercy
unto him: neither let there be any to
favor his fatherless children.
13 Let his posterity be cut off; and in
the generation following let their name
be blotted out.
14 Let the iniquity of his fathers be remembered with the LORD; and let not the
sin of his mother be blotted out.
15 Let them be before the LORD continually, that he may cut off the memory of
them from the earth.
16 Because that he remembered not to
show mercy, but persecuted the poor and
needy man, that he might even slay the
broken in heart.
17 As he loved cursing, so let it come
unto him: as he delighted not in blessing,
so let it be far from him.
18 As he clothed himself with cursing
like as with his garment, so let it come into his bowels like water, and like oil into
his bones.
19 Let it be unto him as the garment
which covers him, and for a girdle wherewith he is girded continually.
20 Let this be the reward of my adversaries from the LORD, and of them that
speak evil against my soul.
21 But do for me, O GOD the Lord, for
your name's sake: because your mercy is
good, deliver me.
22 For I am poor and needy, and my
heart is wounded within me.
23 I am gone like the shadow when it
declines: I am tossed up and down as the
locust.
24 My knees are weak through fasting;
and my flesh fails of fatness.
25 I became also a reproach unto them:
when they looked upon me they shook
their heads.
26 Help me, O LORD my God: O save me
according to your mercy:
27 That they may know that this is your
hand; that you, LORD, have done it.
28 Let them curse, but you bless: when
they arise, let them be ashamed; but let
your servant rejoice.
29 Let my adversaries be clothed with
shame, and let them cover themselves with
their own confusion, as with a mantle.
30 I will greatly praise the LORD with my

109:8 This is a direct reference to Judas Iscariot. See Acts 1:20.

mouth; yes, I will praise him among the
multitude.
31 For he shall stand at the right hand of
the poor, to save him from those that condemn his soul.

PSALM 110

THE LORD said unto my Lord, Sit at
my right hand, until I make your enemies your footstool.
2 The LORD shall send the rod of your
strength out of Zion: rule in the midst of
your enemies.
3 Your people shall be willing in the day
of your power, in the beauties of holiness
from the womb of the morning: you have
the dew of your youth.
4 The LORD has sworn, and will not repent, You are a priest for ever after the
order of Melchizedek.
5 The Lord at your right hand shall strike
through kings in the day of his wrath.
6 He shall judge among the heathen, he
shall fill the places with the dead bodies;
he shall wound the heads over many countries.
7 He shall drink of the brook in the way:
therefore shall he lift up the head.

PSALM 111

PRAISE the LORD. I will praise the LORD
with my whole heart, in the assembly
of the upright, and in the congregation.
2 The works of the LORD are great, sought
out of all them that have pleasure therein.
3 His work is honorable and glorious:
and his righteousness endures for ever.
4 He has made his wonderful works to
be remembered: the LORD is gracious and
full of compassion.
5 He has given meat unto them that fear
him: he will ever be mindful of his covenant.
6 He has showed his people the power
of his works, that he may give them the
heritage of the heathen.
7 The works of his hands are verity and
judgment; all his commandments are sure.
8 They stand fast for ever and ever, and
are done in truth and uprightness.
9 He sent redemption unto his people:
he has commanded his covenant for ever:
holy and reverend is his name.
10 The fear of the LORD is the beginning
of wisdom: a good understanding have
all they that do his commandments: his
praise endures for ever.

. . . . . .

For how to use the Law in evangelism, see Matthew 19:17–22 footnote.

. . . . . .

PSALM 112

PRAISE the LORD. Blessed is the man
that fears the LORD, that delights greatly in his commandments.
2 His seed shall be mighty upon earth:
the generation of the upright shall be
blessed.
3 Wealth and riches shall be in his house:
and his righteousness endures for ever.
4 Unto the upright there arises light in the
darkness: he is gracious, and full of compassion, and righteous.
5 A good man shows favor, and lends:
he will guide his affairs with discretion.
6 Surely he shall not be moved for ever:
the righteous shall be in everlasting remembrance.
7 He shall not be afraid of evil tidings: his
heart is fixed, trusting in the LORD.
8 His heart is established, he shall not
be afraid, until he see his desire upon his
enemies.
9 He has dispersed, he has given to the
poor; his righteousness endures for ever;

110 These verses speak of the coming Messiah. Hebrews 5:5,6 tells us that Jesus is our High Priest "after the order of Melchisedec" (v. 4), and John 5:22 says that God has committed all judgment to Jesus (v. 6). See also Hebrews 4:14; 7:22–26; Acts 10:42.

112:1 The apostle Paul is one who delighted in the Law of God. See Romans 7:22.

QUESTIONS & OBJECTIONS

115:4–9 ***"The First Commandment says, 'You shall have no other gods before Me.' That proves He isn't the only God!"***

That's true. Man has always made false gods. An old adage says, "God created man in His own image, and man has been returning the favor ever since." Hindus have millions of gods. Sometimes gods are made of wood or stone, other times man makes up a god in his mind. Whatever the case, making a god to suit yourself is called "idolatry," and is a transgression of both the First and Second of the Ten Commandments.

his horn shall be exalted with honor.

10 The wicked shall see it, and be grieved; he shall gnash with his teeth, and melt away: the desire of the wicked shall perish.

PSALM 113

PRAISE the LORD. Praise, O you servants of the LORD, praise the name of the LORD.

2 Blessed be the name of the LORD from this time forth and for evermore.

3 From the rising of the sun unto the going down of the same the LORD's name is to be praised.

4 The LORD is high above all nations, and his glory above the heavens.

5 Who is like unto the LORD our God, who dwells on high,

6 Who humbles himself to behold the things that are in heaven, and in the earth!

7 He raises up the poor out of the dust, and lifts the needy out of the dunghill;

8 That he may set him with princes, even with the princes of his people.

9 He makes the barren woman to keep house, and to be a joyful mother of children. Praise the LORD.

PSALM 114

WHEN Israel went out of Egypt, the house of Jacob from a people of strange language;

2 Judah was his sanctuary, and Israel his dominion.

3 The sea saw it, and fled: Jordan was driven back.

4 The mountains skipped like rams, and the little hills like lambs.

5 What ailed you, O you sea, that you fled? you Jordan, that you were driven back?

6 You mountains, that skipped like rams; and you little hills, like lambs?

7 Tremble, you earth, at the presence of the Lord, at the presence of the God of Jacob;

8 Who turned the rock into a standing water, the flint into a fountain of waters.

PSALM 115

NOT unto us, O LORD, not unto us, but unto your name give glory, for your mercy, and for your truth's sake.

2 Wherefore should the heathen say, Where is now their God?

3 But our God is in the heavens: he has done whatsoever he has pleased.

4 Their idols are silver and gold, the work of men's hands.

5 They have mouths, but they speak not: eyes have they, but they see not:

6 They have ears, but they hear not: noses have they, but they smell not:

7 They have hands, but they handle not: feet have they, but they walk not:

113:3 As the Declaration of Independence was being signed, *Samuel Adams* stated, "We have this day restored the Sovereign to Whom all men ought to be obedient. He reigns in heaven and from the rising to the setting of the sun, let His kingdom come."

neither speak they through their throat.
8 They that make them are like unto
them; so is every one that trusts in
them.
9 O Israel, trust in the LORD: he is their
help and their shield.
10 O house of Aaron, trust in the LORD:
he is their help and their shield.
11 You that fear the LORD, trust in the
LORD: he is their help and their shield.
12 The LORD has been mindful of us: he
will bless us; he will bless the house of
Israel; he will bless the house of Aaron.
13 He will bless them that fear the LORD,
both small and great.
14 The LORD shall increase you more
and more, you and your children.
15 You are blessed of the LORD which
made heaven and earth.
16 The heaven, even the heavens, are the
LORD's: but the earth has he given to the
children of men.
17 The dead praise not the LORD, neither
any that go down into silence.
18 But we will bless the LORD from this
time forth and for evermore. Praise the
LORD.

PSALM 116

I LOVE the LORD, because he has heard
my voice and my supplications.
2 Because he has inclined his ear unto
me, therefore will I call upon him as long
as I live.
3 The sorrows of death compassed me,
and the pains of hell gat hold upon me: I
found trouble and sorrow.
4 Then called I upon the name of the
LORD; O LORD, I beseech you, deliver my
soul.
5 Gracious is the LORD, and righteous;
yes, our God is merciful.
6 The LORD preserves the simple: I was
brought low, and he helped me.
7 Return unto your rest, O my soul; for
the LORD has dealt bountifully with you.
8 For you have delivered my soul from
death, my eyes from tears, and my feet
from falling.
9 I will walk before the LORD in the land
of the living.
10 I believed, therefore have I spoken: I
was greatly afflicted:
11 I said in my haste, All men are liars.
12 What shall I render unto the LORD for
all his benefits toward me?
13 I will take the cup of salvation, and
call upon the name of the LORD.
14 I will pay my vows unto the LORD
now in the presence of all his people.
15 Precious in the sight of the LORD is the
death of his saints.
16 O LORD, truly I am your servant; I am
your servant, and the son of your handmaid: you have loosed my bonds.
17 I will offer to you the sacrifice of
thanksgiving, and will call upon the name
of the LORD.
18 I will pay my vows unto the LORD now
in the presence of all his people.
19 In the courts of the LORD's house, in
the midst of you, O Jerusalem. Praise the
LORD.

PSALM 117

O PRAISE the LORD, all you nations:
praise him, all you people.
2 For his merciful kindness is great toward us: and the truth of the LORD endures for ever. Praise the LORD.

PSALM 118

O GIVE thanks unto the LORD; for he
is good: because his mercy endures
for ever.
2 Let Israel now say, that his mercy en-

116:11 "...20,000 middle and high-schoolers were surveyed by the Josephson Institute of Ethics—a nonprofit organization in Marina del Rey, Calif., devoted to character education. Ninety-two percent of the teenagers admitted having lied to their parents in the previous year, and 73 percent characterized themselves as 'serial liars,' meaning they told lies weekly. Despite these admissions, 91 percent of all respondents said they were 'satisfied with my own ethics and character.'" *Reader's Digest*, November 1999

dures for ever.
3 Let the house of Aaron now say, that
his mercy endures for ever.
4 Let them now that fear the LORD say,
that his mercy endures for ever.
5 I called upon the LORD in distress: the
LORD answered me, and set me in a large
place.
6 *The LORD is on my side; I will not fear:*
what can man do unto me?
7 *The LORD takes my part with them that*
help me: therefore shall I see my desire up-
on them that hate me.
8 *It is better to trust in the LORD than to put*
confidence in man.
9 *It is better to trust in the LORD than to put*
confidence in princes.
10 All nations compassed me about: but
in the name of the LORD will I destroy
them.
11 They compassed me about; yes, they
compassed me about: but in the name of
the LORD I will destroy them.
12 They compassed me about like bees:
they are quenched as the fire of thorns:
for in the name of the LORD I will destroy
them.
13 You have thrust sore at me that I might
fall: but the LORD helped me.
14 The LORD is my strength and song,
and is become my salvation.
15 The voice of rejoicing and salvation
is in the tabernacles of the righteous: the
right hand of the LORD does valiantly.
16 The right hand of the LORD is exalted:
the right hand of the LORD does valiantly.
17 I shall not die, but live, and declare
the works of the LORD.
18 The LORD has chastened me sore: but
he has not given me over unto death.
19 Open to me the gates of righteousness: I will go into them, and I will praise
the LORD:
20 This gate of the LORD, into which the
righteous shall enter.
21 I will praise you: for you have heard
me, and are become my salvation.
22 The stone which the builders refused
is become the head stone of the corner.
23 This is the LORD's doing; it is marvelous in our eyes.
24 This is the day which the LORD has
made; we will rejoice and be glad in it.
25 Save now, I beseech you, O LORD: O
LORD, I beseech you, send now prosperity.
26 Blessed be he that comes in the name
of the LORD: we have blessed you out of
the house of the LORD.
27 God is the LORD, which has showed
us light: bind the sacrifice with cords,
even unto the horns of the altar.
28 You are my God, and I will praise
you: you are my God, I will exalt you.
29 O give thanks unto the LORD; for he
is good: for his mercy endures for ever.

PSALM 119

BLESSED are the undefiled in the way,
who walk in the law of the LORD.
2 Blessed are they that keep his testimonies, and that seek him with the whole
heart.

118:6 Remember that courage isn't the absence of fear, but the conquering of it. If we really care for the lost, each of us must learn to push aside fear and replace it with faith in God. You do your part, and God will do His.

118:8 The middle of the Bible. Psalm 118 is the middle chapter of the entire Bible. Psalm 117 is the shortest chapter in the Bible. Psalm 119 is the longest chapter in the Bible. The Scriptures have 594 chapters before Psalm 118, and 594 chapters after Psalm 118. If you add up all the chapters except 118, you get a total of 1188 chapters. Psalm 118:8 is the middle verse of the entire Bible. It goes without saying that the central verse has an important message: "It is better to trust in the Lord than to put confidence in man."

118:22 This is a direct reference to the Messiah. See 1 Peter 2:7,8.

118:27 We must "bind" our bodies as living sacrifices on the altar of service for God (see Romans 12:1).

3 They also do no iniquity: they walk in
his ways.
4 You have commanded us to keep your
precepts diligently.
5 O that my ways were directed to keep
your statutes!
6 Then shall I not be ashamed, when I
have respect unto all your commandments.
7 I will praise you with uprightness of
heart, when I shall have learned your
righteous judgments.
8 I will keep your statutes: O forsake me
not utterly.
9 Wherewithal shall a young man cleanse
his way? by taking heed thereto according
to your word.
10 With my whole heart have I sought
you: O let me not wander from your commandments.
11 Your word have I hid in my heart,
that I might not sin against you.
12 Blessed are you, O LORD: teach me
your statutes.
13 With my lips have I declared all the
judgments of your mouth.
14 I have rejoiced in the way of your testimonies, as much as in all riches.
15 I will meditate in your precepts, and
have respect unto your ways.
16 I will delight myself in your statutes:
I will not forget your word.
17 Deal bountifully with your servant,
that I may live, and keep your word.
18 Open my eyes, that I may behold
wondrous things out of your law.
19 I am a stranger in the earth: hide not
your commandments from me.
20 My soul breaks for the longing that
it has unto your judgments at all times.
21 You have rebuked the proud that are
cursed, which do err from your commandments.
22 Remove from me reproach and contempt; for I have kept your testimonies.
23 Princes also did sit and speak against
me: but your servant did meditate in your
statutes.
24 Your testimonies also are my delight
and my counselors.
25 My soul cleaves unto the dust: quick-
en me according to your word.
26 I have declared my ways, and you
heard me: teach me your statutes.
27 Make me to understand the way of
your precepts: so shall I talk of your wondrous works.
28 My soul melts for heaviness: strength-
en me according unto your word.
29 Remove from me the way of lying:
and grant me your law graciously.
30 I have chosen the way of truth: your
judgments have I laid before me.
31 I have stuck unto your testimonies:
O LORD, put me not to shame.
32 I will run the way of your commandments, when you shall enlarge my heart.
33 Teach me, O LORD, the way of your
statutes; and I shall keep it unto the end.
34 Give me understanding, and I shall
keep your law; yes, I shall observe it with
my whole heart.
35 Make me to go in the path of your
commandments; for therein do I delight.
36 Incline my heart unto your testimonies, and not to covetousness.
37 Turn away my eyes from beholding

119:2 This wonderful psalm gives us insight into the rewards of meditating on God's Word. It reveals the great key to living a life of victory as a Christian. That key is to seek and serve Him with a "whole heart."

119:14 "I believe the Bible is the best gift God has given to man. All the good Savior gave to the world was communicated through this Book." *Abraham Lincoln*

119:16 "God's Word is our primary weapon in evangelism. It is not designed to destroy life, but to give it. It is not to be used to harm but like a surgeon's scalpel, to save. Just as a builder knows his tools and an artist knows his brushes and pens, we need to know the Bible." *Greg Laurie*

119:18 "Ignorance of the nature and design of the Law is at the bottom of most religious mistakes." *John Newton*

vanity; and quicken me in your way.
38 Establish your word unto your servant, who is devoted to your fear.
39 Turn away my reproach which I fear:
for your judgments are good.
40 Behold, I have longed after your precepts: quicken me in your righteousness.
41 Let your mercies come also unto me,
O LORD, even your salvation, according
to your word.
42 So shall I have wherewith to answer
him that reproaches me: for I trust in your
word.
43 And take not the word of truth utterly out of my mouth; for I have hoped
in your judgments.

> If you pick up a dog and make him prosperous, he will not bite you. This is the principal difference between a dog and a man.
>
> **MARK TWAIN**

44 So shall I keep your law continually
for ever and ever.
45 And I will walk at liberty: for I seek
your precepts.
46 I will speak of your testimonies also
before kings, and will not be ashamed.
47 And I will delight myself in your
commandments, which I have loved.
48 My hands also will I lift up unto your
commandments, which I have loved; and
I will meditate in your statutes.
49 Remember the word unto your servant, upon which you have caused me to
hope.
50 This is my comfort in my affliction:
for your word has quickened me.
51 The proud have had me greatly in derision: yet have I not declined from your
law.
52 I remembered your judgments of old,
O LORD; and have comforted myself.
53 Horror has taken hold upon me because of the wicked that forsake your law.
54 Your statutes have been my songs in
the house of my pilgrimage.
55 I have remembered your name, O
LORD, in the night, and have kept your
law.
56 This I had, because I kept your precepts.
57 You are my portion, O LORD: I have
said that I would keep your words.
58 I entreated your favor with my whole
heart: be merciful unto me according to
your word.
59 I thought on my ways, and turned
my feet unto your testimonies.
60 I made haste, and delayed not to keep
your commandments.
61 The bands of the wicked have robbed
me: but I have not forgotten your law.
62 At midnight I will rise to give thanks
unto you because of your righteous judgments.
63 I am a companion of all them that fear
you, and of them that keep your precepts.
64 The earth, O LORD, is full of your
mercy: teach me your statutes.
65 You have dealt well with your servant,
O LORD, according unto your word.
66 Teach me good judgment and knowledge: for I have believed your commandments.
67 Before I was afflicted I went astray:
but now have I kept your word.
68 You are good, and do good; teach me
your statutes.
69 The proud have forged a lie against
me: but I will keep your precepts with my
whole heart.
70 Their heart is as fat as grease; but I
delight in your law.
71 It is good for me that I have been afflicted; that I might learn your statutes.
72 The law of your mouth is better unto me than thousands of gold and silver.
73 Your hands have made me and fashioned me: give me understanding, that I

119:72 "A thorough knowledge of the Bible is worth more than a college education." *Theodore Roosevelt*

"Hold fast to the Bible as the sheet anchor of your liberties; write its precepts in your hearts, and practice them in your lives."

Ulysses S. Grant

may learn your commandments.
74 They that fear you will be glad when they see me; because I have hoped in your word.
75 I know, O LORD, that your judgments are right, and that you in faithfulness have afflicted me.
76 Let, I pray you, your merciful kindness be for my comfort, according to your word unto your servant.
77 Let your tender mercies come unto me, that I may live: for your law is my delight.
78 Let the proud be ashamed; for they dealt perversely with me without a cause: but I will meditate in your precepts.
79 Let those that fear you turn unto me, and those that have known your testimonies.
80 Let my heart be sound in your statutes; that I be not ashamed.
81 My soul faints for your salvation: but I hope in your word.
82 My eyes fail for your word, saying, When will you comfort me?
83 For I am become like a bottle in the smoke; yet do I not forget your statutes.
84 How many are the days of your servant? when will you execute judgment on them that persecute me?
85 The proud have digged pits for me, which are not after your law.
86 All your commandments are faithful: they persecute me wrongfully; help me.
87 They had almost consumed me upon earth; but I forsook not your precepts.
88 Quicken me after your lovingkindness; so shall I keep the testimony of your mouth.
89 For ever, O LORD, your word is settled in heaven.
90 Your faithfulness is unto all generations: you have established the earth, and it abides.
91 They continue this day according to your ordinances: for all are your servants.
92 Unless your law had been my delights, I should then have perished in my affliction.
93 I will never forget your precepts: for with them you have quickened me.
94 I am yours, save me: for I have sought your precepts.
95 The wicked have waited for me to destroy me: but I will consider your testimonies.
96 I have seen an end of all perfection: but your commandment is exceeding broad.
97 O how I love your law! it is my meditation all the day.
98 You through your commandments have made me wiser than my enemies: for they are ever with me.
99 I have more understanding than all my teachers: for your testimonies are my meditation.
100 I understand more than the ancients, because I keep your precepts.

119:97 "If there is anything in my thoughts or style to commend, the credit is due to my parents for instilling in me an early love of the Scriptures." *Daniel Webster*

101 I have refrained my feet from every
evil way, that I might keep your word.
102 I have not departed from your judgments: for you have taught me.
103 How sweet are your words unto my
taste! yes, sweeter than honey to my
mouth!
104 Through your precepts I get understanding: therefore I hate every false way.
105 Your word is a lamp unto my feet,
and a light unto my path.
106 I have sworn, and I will perform it,
that I will keep your righteous judgments.
107 I am afflicted very much: quicken
me, O LORD, according unto your word.
108 Accept, I beseech you, the freewill
offerings of my mouth, O LORD, and teach
me your judgments.
109 My soul is continually in my hand:
yet do I not forget your law.
110 The wicked have laid a snare for me:
yet I erred not from your precepts.
111 Your testimonies have I taken as an
heritage for ever: for they are the rejoicing
of my heart.
112 I have inclined my heart to perform
your statutes always, even unto the end.
113 I hate vain thoughts: but your law
do I love.
114 You are my hiding place and my
shield: I hope in your word.
115 Depart from me, you evildoers: for I
will keep the commandments of my God.
116 Uphold me according unto your
word, that I may live: and let me not be
ashamed of my hope.
117 Hold me up, and I shall be safe: and I
will have respect unto your statutes continually.
118 You have trodden down all them that
err from your statutes: for their deceit is
falsehood.
119 You put away all the wicked of the
earth like dross: therefore I love your testimonies.
120 My flesh trembles for fear of you;
and I am afraid of your judgments.
121 I have done judgment and justice:
leave me not to my oppressors.
122 Be surety for your servant for good:
let not the proud oppress me.
123 My eyes fail for your salvation, and
for the word of your righteousness.
124 Deal with your servant according unto your mercy, and teach me your statutes.
125 I am your servant; give me understanding, that I may know your testimonies.
126 It is time for you, LORD, to work: for
they have made void your law.
127 Therefore I love your commandments
above gold; yes, above fine gold.
128 Therefore I esteem all your precepts
concerning all things to be right; and I
hate every false way.
129 Your testimonies are wonderful:
therefore does my soul keep them.
130 The entrance of your words gives
light; it gives understanding unto the
simple.
131 I opened my mouth, and panted: for
I longed for your commandments.
132 Look upon me, and be merciful
unto me, as you used to do unto those that
love your name.
133 Order my steps in your word: and
let not any iniquity have dominion over
me.
134 Deliver me from the oppression of
man: so will I keep your precepts.
135 Make your face to shine upon your
servant; and teach me your statutes.

119:104 "But for this Book [the Bible], we could not know right from wrong...Take all you can of this Book upon reason, and the balance on faith, and you will live and die a happier man." *Abraham Lincoln*

119:128 This verse covers all of God's judgments over sinners—harsh though they may seem to our darkened minds.

119:133 Sin may beset the Christian, but those whose steps are in God's Word prevent sin from having dominion over them. See Romans 6:12–18. See also Galatians 5:16 comment.

119:105 *The Bible Stands Alone*

Compiled by Jordan and Justin Drake

In 1889 a schoolteacher told a ten-year-old boy, "You will never amount to very much." That boy was Albert Einstein. In 1954 a music manager told a young singer, "You ought to go back to driving a truck." That singer was Elvis Presley. In 1962 a record company told a group of singers, "We don't like your sound. Groups with guitars are definitely on their way out." They said that to the Beatles. Man is prone to make mistakes. Those who reject the Bible should take the time to look at the evidence before they come to a verdict.

1. It is unique in its continuity. If just 10 people today were picked who were from the same place, born around the same time, spoke the same language, and made about the same amount of money, and were asked to write on just one controversial subject, they would have trouble agreeing with each other. But the Bible stands alone. It was written over a period of 1,600 years by more than 40 writers from all walks of life. Some were fishermen; some were politicians. Others were generals or kings, shepherds or historians. They were from three different continents, and wrote in three different languages. They wrote on hundreds of controversial subjects yet they wrote with agreement and harmony. They wrote in dungeons, in temples, on beaches, and on hillsides, during peacetime and during war. Yet their words sound like they came from the same source. So even though 10 people today couldn't write on one controversial subject and agree, God picked 40 different people to write the Bible—and it stands the test of time.

2. It is unique in its circulation. The invention of the printing press in 1450 made it possible to print books in large quantities. The first book printed was the Bible. Since then, the Bible has been read by more people and printed more times than any other book in history. By 1930, over one billion Bibles had been distributed by Bible societies around the world. By 1977, Bible societies alone were printing over 200 million Bibles each year, and this doesn't include the rest of the Bible publishing companies. No one who is interested in knowing the truth can ignore such an important book.

3. It is unique in its translation. The Bible has been translated into over 1,400 languages. No other book even comes close.

4. It is unique in its survival. In ancient times, books were copied by hand onto manuscripts which were made from parchment and would decay over time. Ancient books are available today only because someone made copies of the originals to preserve them. For example, the original writings of Julius Caesar are no longer around. We know what he wrote only by the copies we have. Only 10 copies still exist, and they were made 1,000 years after he died. Only 600 copies of Homer's *The Iliad* exist, made 1,300 years after the originals were written. No other book has as many copies of the ancient manuscripts as the Bible. In fact, there are over 24,000 copies of New Testament manuscripts, some written within 35 years of the writer's death.

5. It is unique in withstanding attack. No other book has been so attacked throughout history as the Bible. In A.D. 300 the Roman emperor Diocletian ordered every Bible burned because he thought that by destroying the Scriptures he could destroy Christianity. Anyone caught with a Bible would be executed. But just 25 years later, the Roman emperor Constantine ordered that 50 perfect copies of the Bible be made at government expense. The French philosopher Voltaire, a skeptic who destroyed the faith of many people, boasted that within 100 years of his death, the Bible would disappear from the face of the earth. Voltaire died in 1728, but the Bible lives on. The irony of history is that 50 years after his death, the Geneva Bible Society moved into his former house and used his printing presses to print thousands of Bibles.

The Bible has also survived criticism. No book has been more attacked for its accuracy. And yet archeologists are proving every year that the Bible's detailed descriptions of historic events are correct. See Matthew 4:4 and 1 Peter 1:25 footnotes.

QUESTIONS & OBJECTIONS

119:160 ***"The Bible has changed down through the ages."***

No, it hasn't. God has preserved His Word. In the spring of 1947, the Dead Sea Scrolls were discovered. These manuscripts were copies of large portions of the Old Testament, a thousand years older than any other existing copies. Study of the scrolls has revealed that the Bible hasn't changed in content down through the ages as many skeptics had surmised. (See 1 Peter 1:25 footnote.)

Anyone can now obtain access to computer programs that give the original Hebrew and Greek words, and the only "changes" have been made for clarity. For example, the old English translation of 2 Corinthians 12:8 is "For this thing I besought the Lord thrice...," while a contemporary translation is "Concerning this thing I pleaded with the Lord three times..."

136 Rivers of waters run down my eyes, because they keep not your law.
137 Righteous are you, O LORD, and upright are your judgments.
138 Your testimonies that you have commanded are righteous and very faithful.
139 My zeal has consumed me, because my enemies have forgotten your words.
140 Your word is very pure: therefore your servant loves it.
141 I am small and despised: yet do not I forget your precepts.
142 Your righteousness is an everlasting righteousness, and your law is the truth.
143 Trouble and anguish have taken hold on me: yet your commandments are my delights.
144 The righteousness of your testimonies is everlasting: give me understanding, and I shall live.
145 I cried with my whole heart; hear me, O LORD: I will keep your statutes.
146 I cried unto you; save me, and I shall keep your testimonies.
147 I prevented the dawning of the morning, and cried: I hoped in your word.
148 My eyes prevent the night watches, that I might meditate in your word.
149 Hear my voice according unto your lovingkindness: O LORD, quicken me according to your judgment.
150 They draw near that follow after mischief: they are far from your law.
151 You are near, O LORD; and all your commandments are truth.
152 Concerning your testimonies, I have known of old that you have founded them for ever.
153 Consider my affliction, and deliver me: for I do not forget your law.
154 Plead my cause, and deliver me: quicken me according to your word.
155 Salvation is far from the wicked: for they seek not your statutes.
156 Great are your tender mercies, O LORD: quicken me according to your judgments.
157 Many are my persecutors and my enemies; yet do I not decline from your testimonies.
158 I beheld the transgressors, and was grieved; because they kept not your word.
159 Consider how I love your precepts: quicken me, O LORD, according to your lovingkindness.
160 Your word is true from the begin-

119:136 "And you, too, who are moral enough in your conversation, and regular in your attendance on the outward forms of religion, you who never weep over sinners, you who never pray for them, you who never speak to them, you who leave all that to your minister, and think you have nothing to do with it, the voice of your brother's blood crieth from the ground to heaven." *Charles Spurgeon*

SPRINGBOARDS FOR PREACHING AND WITNESSING

The Bible and All It Contains

119:162 A young man once received a letter from a lawyer stating that his grandmother had left him an inheritance. To his astonishment, it was $50,000 plus "my Bible and all it contains."

The youth was delighted to receive the money. However, he knew what the Bible contained, and because he wasn't into religion he didn't bother to open it. Instead, he put it on a high shelf.

He gambled the $50,000, and over the next fifty years he lived as a pauper, scraping for every meal. Finally he became so destitute, he had to move in with his relatives.

When he cleaned out his room, he reached up to get the dusty old Bible from the shelf. As he took it down, his trembling hands dropped it onto the floor, flinging it open to reveal a $100 bill between every page.

The man had lived as a pauper, simply because of his prejudice. He thought he knew what the Bible "contained."

ning: and every one of your righteous judgments endures for ever.
161 Princes have persecuted me without a cause: but my heart stands in awe of your word.
162 I rejoice at your word, as one that finds great spoil.
163 I hate and abhor lying: but your law do I love.
164 Seven times a day do I praise you because of your righteous judgments.
165 *Great peace have they which love your law: and nothing shall offend them.*
166 LORD, I have hoped for your salvation, and done your commandments.
167 My soul has kept your testimonies; and I love them exceedingly.
168 I have kept your precepts and your testimonies: for all my ways are before you.
169 Let my cry come near before you, O LORD: give me understanding according to your word.
170 Let my supplication come before you: deliver me according to your word.
171 My lips shall utter praise, when you have taught me your statutes.
172 My tongue shall speak of your word: for all your commandments are righteousness.
173 Let your hand help me; for I have chosen your precepts.
174 I have longed for your salvation, O LORD; and your law is my delight.
175 Let my soul live, and it shall praise you; and let your judgments help me.
176 I have gone astray like a lost sheep; seek your servant; for I do not forget your commandments.

PSALM 120

IN my distress I cried unto the LORD, and he heard me.
2 Deliver my soul, O LORD, from lying lips, and from a deceitful tongue.
3 What shall be given unto you? or what shall be done unto you, you false tongue?
4 Sharp arrows of the mighty, with coals of juniper.
5 Woe is me, that I sojourn in Mesech, that I dwell in the tents of Kedar!
6 My soul has long dwelt with him that hates peace.
7 I am for peace: but when I speak, they are for war.

PSALM 121

I WILL lift up my eyes unto the hills, from whence comes my help.
2 My help comes from the LORD, who made heaven and earth.
3 He will not suffer your foot to be moved: he that keeps you will not slumber.
4 Behold, he that keeps Israel shall neither slumber nor sleep.
5 The LORD is your keeper: the LORD is your shade upon your right hand.
6 The sun shall not smite you by day, nor the moon by night.

7 The LORD shall preserve you from all evil: he shall preserve your soul.
8 The LORD shall preserve your going out and your coming in from this time forth, and even for evermore.

PSALM 122

I WAS glad when they said unto me, Let us go into the house of the LORD.
2 Our feet shall stand within your gates, O Jerusalem.
3 Jerusalem is built as a city that is compact together:
4 Whither the tribes go up, the tribes of the LORD, unto the testimony of Israel, to give thanks unto the name of the LORD.
5 For there are set thrones of judgment, the thrones of the house of David.

> What health is to the heart, holiness is to the soul.
>
> **JOHN FLAVEL**

6 Pray for the peace of Jerusalem: they shall prosper that love you.
7 Peace be within your walls, and prosperity within your palaces.
8 For my brethren and companions' sakes, I will now say, Peace be within you.
9 Because of the house of the LORD our God I will seek your good.

PSALM 123

UNTO you lift I up my eyes, O you that dwells in the heavens.
2 Behold, as the eyes of servants look unto the hand of their masters, and as the eyes of a maiden unto the hand of her mistress; so our eyes wait upon the Lord our God, until that he have mercy upon us.
3 Have mercy upon us, O LORD, have mercy upon us: for we are exceedingly filled with contempt.
4 Our soul is exceedingly filled with the scorning of those that are at ease, and with the contempt of the proud.

PSALM 124

IF it had not been the LORD who was on our side, now may Israel say;
2 If it had not been the LORD who was on our side, when men rose up against us:
3 Then they had swallowed us up quick, when their wrath was kindled against us:
4 Then the waters had overwhelmed us, the stream had gone over our soul:
5 Then the proud waters had gone over our soul.
6 Blessed be the LORD, who has not given us as a prey to their teeth.
7 Our soul is escaped as a bird out of the snare of the fowlers: the snare is broken, and we are escaped.
8 Our help is in the name of the LORD, who made heaven and earth.

PSALM 125

THEY that trust in the LORD shall be as mount Zion, which cannot be removed, but abides for ever.
2 As the mountains are round about Jerusalem, so the LORD is round about his people from henceforth even for ever.
3 For the rod of the wicked shall not rest upon the lot of the righteous; lest the righteous put forth their hands unto iniquity.
4 Do good, O LORD, unto those that be good, and to them that are upright in their hearts.
5 As for such as turn aside unto their crooked ways, the LORD shall lead them forth with the workers of iniquity: but peace shall be upon Israel.

PSALM 126

WHEN the LORD turned again the captivity of Zion, we were like them

125:1 If we are "moved" by adversity, it is because we lack trust in the Lord. The amount of joy we retain in tribulation reveals the depth of our trust in God. The apostle Paul said, "I am exceeding joyful in all our tribulation" (2 Corinthians 7:4).

that dream.
2 Then was our mouth filled with laughter, and our tongue with singing: then said
they among the heathen, The LORD has
done great things for them.
3 The LORD has done great things for us;
whereof we are glad.
4 Turn again our captivity, O LORD, as
the streams in the south.
5 *They that sow in tears shall reap in joy.*
6 *He that goes forth and weeping, bearing
precious seed, shall doubtless come again
with rejoicing, bringing his sheaves with him.*

PSALM 127

EXCEPT the LORD build the house, they
labor in vain that build it: except the
LORD keep the city, the watchman wakes
but in vain.
2 It is vain for you to rise up early, to sit
up late, to eat the bread of sorrows: for so
he gives his beloved sleep.
3 Lo, children are an heritage of the LORD:
and the fruit of the womb is his reward.
4 As arrows are in the hand of a mighty
man; so are children of the youth.
5 Happy is the man that has his quiver
full of them: they shall not be ashamed,
but they shall speak with the enemies in
the gate.

PSALM 128

BLESSED is every one that fears the
LORD; that walks in his ways.
2 For you shall eat the labor of your
hands: happy shall you be, and it shall be
well with you.
3 Your wife shall be as a fruitful vine by
the sides of your house: your children like
olive plants round about your table.
4 Behold, that thus shall the man be
blessed that fears the LORD.
5 The LORD shall bless you out of Zion:
and you shall see the good of Jerusalem
all the days of your life.
6 Yes, you shall see your children's children, and peace upon Israel.

PSALM 129

MANY a time have they afflicted me
from my youth, may Israel now say:
2 Many a time have they afflicted me
from my youth: yet they have not prevailed against me.
3 The plowers plowed upon my back:
they made long their furrows.

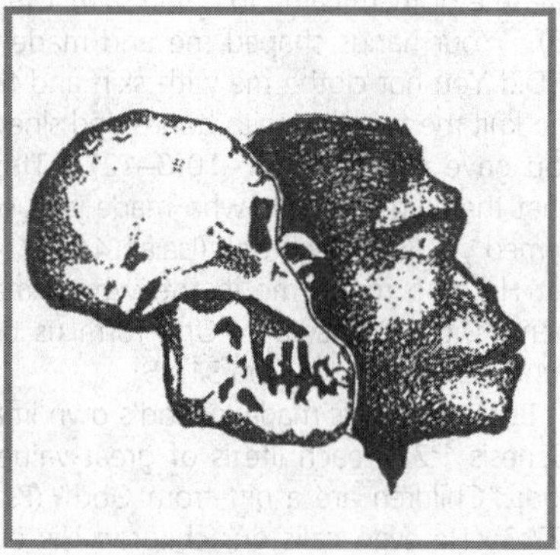

To see how the theory of evolution clashes with the facts, *see Acts 14:15 footnote.*

4 The LORD is righteous: he has cut asunder the cords of the wicked.
5 Let them all be confounded and turned
back that hate Zion.
6 Let them be as the grass upon the
housetops, which withers before it grows
up:
7 Wherewith the mower fills not his
hand; nor he that binds sheaves his bosom.
8 Neither do they which go by say, The

126:6 Sowing in tears. "But from whence shall I fetch my argument? With what shall I win them? Oh, that I could tell! I would write to them in tears, I would weep out every argument, I would empty my veins for ink, I would petition them on my knees. Oh how thankful I would be if they would be prevailed with to repent and turn!" *Joseph Alleine*

"Jesus Christ wept over Jerusalem, and you will have to weep over sinners if they are to be saved through you." *Charles Spurgeon*

127:3 *What God's Word Says About Abortion*

By Lynn Copeland

God speaks very clearly in the Bible on the value of unborn children.

God's Word says that He personally made each one of us, and has a plan for each life: "Before I formed you in the womb I knew you, before you were born I set you apart" (Jeremiah 1:5). "Even before I was born, God had chosen me to be His" (Galatians 1:15). "For You created my inmost being; You knit me together in my mother's womb...Your eyes saw my unformed body. All the days ordained for me were written in Your book before one of them came to be" (Psalm 139:13, 16). "Your hands shaped me and made me ...Did You not clothe me with skin and flesh and knit me together with bones and sinews? You gave me life" (Job 10:8–12). "This is what the Lord says—He who made you, who formed you in the womb" (Isaiah 44:2). "Did not He who made me in the womb make them? Did not the same One form us both within our mothers?" (Job 31:15).

Because man is made in God's own image (Genesis 1:27), each life is of great value to God: "Children are a gift from God" (Psalm 127:3). He even calls our children His own: "You took *your* sons and daughters whom you bore to Me and sacrificed them...You slaughtered *My* children" (Ezekiel 16:20,21).

The Bible says of our Creator, "In His hand is the life of every living thing and the breath of every human being" (Job 12:10). God, the giver of life, commands us not to take the life of an innocent person: "Do not shed innocent blood" (Jeremiah 7:6); "Cursed is the man who accepts a bribe to kill an innocent person" (Deuteronomy 27:25). "You shall not murder" (Exodus 20:13).

Taking the life of the unborn is clearly murder—"He didn't *kill* me in the womb, with my mother as my grave" (Jeremiah 20:17)—and God vowed to punish those who "ripped open the women with child" (Amos 1:13). The unborn child was granted equal protection in the law; if he lost his life, the one who caused his death must lose his own life: "If men who are fighting hit a pregnant woman and she gives birth prematurely but there is no serious injury, the offender must be fined... But if there is serious injury, you are to take life for life" (Exodus 21:22,23).

Life is a gift created by God, and is not to be taken away by abortion. God is "pro-choice," but He tells us clearly the only acceptable choice to make:

"I have set before you life and death, blessings and curses. Now choose life, so that you and your children may live" (Deuteronomy 30:19).

blessing of the LORD be upon you: we bless you in the name of the LORD.

PSALM 130

OUT of the depths have I cried unto you, O LORD.
2 Lord, hear my voice: let your ears be attentive to the voice of my supplications.
3 If you, LORD, should mark iniquities, O Lord, who shall stand?
4 But there is forgiveness with you, that you may be feared.
5 I wait for the LORD, my soul does wait, and in his word do I hope.
6 My soul waits for the Lord more than they that watch for the morning: I say, more than they that watch for the morning.
7 Let Israel hope in the LORD: for with the LORD there is mercy, and with him is plenteous redemption.
8 And he shall redeem Israel from all his iniquities.

130:1–4 Here is true contrition—a humble cry to God for mercy. Those who obtain the mercy of the cross and see the cost of redemption live their lives in the fear of the Lord, knowing that they were not redeemed with silver and gold, but with the precious blood of Christ. See 1 Peter 1:17–19.

PSALM 131

LORD, my heart is not haughty, nor my eyes lofty: neither do I exercise myself in great matters, or in things too high for me.
2 Surely I have behaved and quieted myself, as a child that is weaned of his mother: my soul is even as a weaned child.
3 Let Israel hope in the LORD from henceforth and for ever.

PSALM 132

LORD, remember David, and all his afflictions:
2 How he swore unto the LORD, and vowed unto the mighty God of Jacob;
3 Surely I will not come into the tabernacle of my house, nor go up into my bed;
4 I will not give sleep to my eyes, or slumber to my eyelids,
5 Until I find out a place for the LORD, an habitation for the mighty God of Jacob.

> There is no point on which men make greater mistakes than on the relation which exists between the Law and the gospel.
>
> **CHARLES SPURGEON**

6 Lo, we heard of it at Ephratah: we found it in the fields of the wood.
7 We will go into his tabernacles: we will worship at his footstool.
8 Arise, O LORD, into your rest; you, and the ark of your strength.
9 Let your priests be clothed with righteousness; and let your saints shout for joy.
10 For your servant David's sake turn not away the face of your anointed.
11 The LORD has sworn in truth unto David; he will not turn from it; Of the fruit of your body will I set upon your throne.
12 If your children will keep my covenant and my testimony that I shall teach them, their children shall also sit upon your throne for evermore.
13 For the LORD has chosen Zion; he has desired it for his habitation.
14 This is my rest for ever: here will I dwell; for I have desired it.
15 I will abundantly bless her provision: I will satisfy her poor with bread.
16 I will also clothe her priests with salvation: and her saints shall shout aloud for joy.
17 There will I make the horn of David to bud: I have ordained a lamp for my anointed.
18 His enemies will I clothe with shame: but upon himself shall his crown flourish.

PSALM 133

BEHOLD, how good and how pleasant it is for brethren to dwell together in unity!
2 It is like the precious ointment upon the head, that ran down upon the beard, even Aaron's beard: that went down to the skirts of his garments;
3 As the dew of Hermon, and as the dew that descended upon the mountains of Zion: for there the LORD commanded the blessing, even life for evermore.

PSALM 134

BEHOLD, bless the LORD, all you servants of the LORD, which by night stand in the house of the LORD.
2 Lift up your hands in the sanctuary, and bless the LORD.
3 The LORD that made heaven and earth bless you out of Zion.

PSALM 135

PRAISE the LORD. Praise the name of the LORD; praise him, O you servants of the LORD.

131:1 Beware of "intellectual Christianity." It is easy to become puffed up with a theology that forgets "the simplicity that is in Christ" (2 Corinthians 11:3). The measure of the quality of our Christian theology will be evidenced by the depth of our concern for the lost.

QUESTIONS & OBJECTIONS

135:14 ***"The Bible says 'God repented.' Doesn't that show He is capable of sin?"***

"Repent" means "to have a change of mind." When the Bible tells sinners to repent, it means to change their direction, to turn from their sins. God's "repenting" is when He turns away from His fierce anger toward sinners. He warns men of the consequences of their disobedience. If they repent (turn from their sins), He will "repent" by not pouring out His promised wrath on them. For instance, Jonah 3:8,9 says, "Let them turn every one from his evil way...Who can tell if God will turn and repent, and turn away from his fierce anger, that we perish not?" (See also Jeremiah 18:8.)

2 You that stand in the house of the LORD,
in the courts of the house of our God.
3 Praise the LORD; for the LORD is good:
sing praises unto his name; for it is pleasant.
4 For the LORD has chosen Jacob unto
himself, and Israel for his peculiar treasure.
5 For I know that the LORD is great, and
that our Lord is above all gods.
6 Whatsoever the LORD pleased, that did
he in heaven, and in earth, in the seas, and
all deep places.
7 He causes the vapors to ascend from
the ends of the earth; he makes lightnings
for the rain; he brings the wind out of his
treasuries.
8 Who smote the firstborn of Egypt, both
of man and beast.
9 Who sent tokens and wonders into the
midst of you, O Egypt, upon Pharaoh, and
upon all his servants.
10 Who smote great nations, and slew
mighty kings;
11 Sihon king of the Amorites, and Og
king of Bashan, and all the kingdoms of
Canaan:
12 And gave their land for an heritage,
an heritage unto Israel his people.
13 Your name, O LORD, endures for ever;
and your memorial, O LORD, throughout
all generations.
14 For the LORD will judge his people,
and he will repent himself concerning his
servants.
15 The idols of the heathen are silver and
gold, the work of men's hands.
16 They have mouths, but they speak
not; eyes have they, but they see not;
17 They have ears, but they hear not;
neither is there any breath in their mouths.
18 They that make them are like unto
them: so is every one that trusts in them.
19 Bless the LORD, O house of Israel: bless
the LORD, O house of Aaron:
20 Bless the LORD, O house of Levi: you
that fear the LORD, bless the LORD.
21 Blessed be the LORD out of Zion,
which dwells at Jerusalem. Praise the LORD.

135:7 Scientific facts in the Bible. The Scriptures inform us, "All the rivers run into the sea; yet the sea is not full; unto the place from whence the rivers come, there they return again" (Ecclesiastes 1:7). This statement alone may not seem profound. But, when considered with other biblical passages, it becomes all the more remarkable. For example, the Mississippi River dumps approximately 6 million gallons of water per second into the Gulf of Mexico. Where does all that water go? And that's just one of thousands of rivers.

The answer lies in the hydrologic cycle, so well brought out in the Bible. Ecclesiastes 11:3 states that "if the clouds be full of rain, they empty themselves upon the earth." Amos 9:6 tells us, "He...calls for the waters of the sea, and pours them out upon the face of the earth." The idea of a complete water cycle was not fully understood until the seventeenth century. However, more than 2,000 years prior to the discoveries of Pierre Perrault, Edme Mariotte, Edmund Halley, and others, the Scriptures clearly spoke of a water cycle.

QUESTIONS & OBJECTIONS

136:7–9 ***"How does the young-earth theory explain that we can see stars millions of light-years away? How would the light have reached us?"***

Since God made the sun, moon, and stars "to give light upon the earth" (Genesis 1:14–18), those lights would be immediately visible on earth. They fulfilled their purpose on the day God spoke them into being, because He "saw that it was good." No doubt God also made Adam as a fully-grown man—perhaps with the appearance of being 30 years old, even though he was only minutes old. Likewise, herbs and trees were already mature and fruit-bearing, to provide a ready supply of food. That would be the case with all of His creation.

PSALM 136

O GIVE thanks unto the LORD; for he
is good: for his mercy endures for
ever.
2 O give thanks unto the God of gods:
for his mercy endures for ever.
3 O give thanks to the Lord of lords: for
his mercy endures for ever.
4 To him who alone does great wonders: for his mercy endures for ever.
5 To him that by wisdom made the heavens: for his mercy endures for ever.
6 To him that stretched out the earth
above the waters: for his mercy endures
for ever.
7 To him that made great lights: for his
mercy endures for ever:
8 The sun to rule by day: for his mercy
endures for ever:
9 The moon and stars to rule by night:
for his mercy endures for ever.
10 To him that smote Egypt in their
firstborn: for his mercy endures for ever:
11 And brought out Israel from among
them: for his mercy endures for ever:
12 With a strong hand, and with a
stretched out arm: for his mercy endures
for ever.
13 To him which divided the Red sea
into parts: for his mercy endures for ever:
14 And made Israel to pass through the
midst of it: for his mercy endures for ever:
15 But overthrew Pharaoh and his host
in the Red sea: for his mercy endures for
ever.
16 To him which led his people through
the wilderness: for his mercy endures for
ever.
17 To him which smote great kings: for
his mercy endures for ever:
18 And slew famous kings: for his mercy endures for ever:
19 Sihon king of the Amorites: for his
mercy endures for ever:
20 And Og the king of Bashan: for his
mercy endures for ever:
21 And gave their land for an heritage:
for his mercy endures for ever:

136:4–6 Worshiping a faithful Creator. We should pray, "Open my eyes that I might continually see the genius of Your mind displayed in creation." If we could walk in such a spirit of illumination, we would walk around awestruck! We would continually worship God. We would be filled with such faith, we would see no problem too great for our God. As the revelation of His greatness astounds us, we would say, "Ah, Lord God! Behold You have made the heavens and the earth by Your great power and outstretched arm. There is nothing too hard for You!" (Jeremiah 32:17).

Such knowledge of His power and ability would cause us to have faith that produces joy, even at the edge of the Red Sea, even in the lion's *mouth.* We can look at the world with all its problems, sins, and pains, and know that with one small breath of Almighty God's Spirit, our nation can be saved. If the mere tip of the finger of God is for us, nothing can be against us.

22 Even an heritage unto Israel his servant: for his mercy endures for ever.
23 Who remembered us in our low estate: for his mercy endures for ever:
24 And has redeemed us from our enemies: for his mercy endures for ever.
25 Who gives food to all flesh: for his mercy endures for ever.
26 O give thanks unto the God of heaven: for his mercy endures for ever.

PSALM 137

BY the rivers of Babylon, there we sat down, yes, we wept, when we remembered Zion.
2 We hanged our harps upon the willows in the midst thereof.
3 For there they that carried us away captive required of us a song; and they that wasted us required of us mirth, saying, Sing us one of the songs of Zion.

> Is sin so luscious that you will burn in hell forever for it?
> **CHARLES SPURGEON**

4 How shall we sing the LORD's song in a strange land?
5 If I forget you, O Jerusalem, let my right hand forget her cunning.
6 If I do not remember you, let my tongue cleave to the roof of my mouth; if I prefer not Jerusalem above my chief joy.
7 Remember, O LORD, the children of Edom in the day of Jerusalem; who said, Rase it, rase it, even to the foundation thereof.
8 O daughter of Babylon, who are to be destroyed; happy shall he be, that rewards you as you have served us.
9 Happy shall he be, that takes and dashes your little ones against the stones.

PSALM 138

I WILL praise you with my whole heart: before the gods will I sing praise unto you.
2 I will worship toward your holy temple, and praise your name for your lovingkindness and for your truth: for you have magnified your word above all your name.
3 In the day when I cried you answered me, and strengthened me with strength in my soul.
4 All the kings of the earth shall praise you, O LORD, when they hear the words of your mouth.
5 Yes, they shall sing in the ways of the LORD: for great is the glory of the LORD.
6 Though the LORD be high, yet has he respect unto the lowly: but the proud he knows afar off.
7 Though I walk in the midst of trouble, you will revive me: you shall stretch forth your hand against the wrath of my enemies, and your right hand shall save me.
8 The LORD will perfect that which concerns me: your mercy, O LORD, endures for ever: forsake not the works of your own hands.

PSALM 139

O LORD, you have searched me, and known me.
2 You know my down sitting and my

139:2 God's presence. The ungodly are unaware of the immediate presence of a holy Creator. They think that God somehow becomes present when we bow our head in prayer or walk reverently into a lofty cathedral. In truth, our Creator is ever-present. He knows when we sit down and when we stand up (vv. 2–12). He searches our heart and sees our innermost thoughts. He knows every detail of our lives, including every whispered word.

The knowledge that a holy God sees every thought and deed is disconcerting to the guilty, but wonderfully comforting to the forgiven and saved soul (see v. 17). It is with this understanding that we should regularly cry with the psalmist, "Search me, O God, and know my heart: try me, and know my thoughts: and see if there be any wicked way in me, and lead me in the way of everlasting" (vv. 23,24).

uprising, you understand my thought afar off.
3 You compass my path and my lying down, and are acquainted with all my ways.
4 For there is not a word in my tongue, but, lo, O LORD, you know it altogether.
5 You have beset me behind and before, and laid your hand upon me.
6 Such knowledge is too wonderful for me; it is high, I cannot attain unto it.
7 Whither shall I go from your spirit? or whither shall I flee from your presence?
8 If I ascend up into heaven, you are there: if I make my bed in hell, behold, you are there.
9 If I take the wings of the morning, and dwell in the uttermost parts of the sea;
10 Even there shall your hand lead me, and your right hand shall hold me.
11 If I say, Surely the darkness shall cover me; even the night shall be light about me.
12 Yes, the darkness hides not from you; but the night shines as the day: the darkness and the light are both alike to you.
13 For you have possessed my reins: you have covered me in my mother's womb.
14 I will praise you; for I am fearfully and wonderfully made: marvelous are your works; and that my soul knows right well.
15 My substance was not hid from you, when I was made in secret, and curiously wrought in the lowest parts of the earth.
16 Your eyes did see my substance, yet being imperfect; and in your book all my members were written, which in continuance were fashioned, when as yet there was none of them.
17 How precious also are your thoughts unto me, O God! how great is the sum of them!
18 If I should count them, they are more in number than the sand: when I awake, I am still with you.
19 Surely you will slay the wicked, O God: depart from me therefore, you bloody men.
20 For they speak against you wickedly, and your enemies take your name in vain.
21 Do not I hate them, O LORD, that hate you? and am not I grieved with those that rise up against you?

139:14 We are wonderfully *made*. In his book *Darwin's Black Box*, biochemistry professor *Michael J. Behe*, an evolutionist, acknowledges a "powerful challenge to Darwinian evolution"—something he refers to as "irreducible complexity." He gives a simple example: the humble mousetrap. The mousetrap has five major components that make it functional. If any one of these components is missing, it will not function. It becomes worthless as a mousetrap.

Charles Darwin admitted, "If it could be demonstrated that any complex organ existed which could not possibly have been formed by numerous, successive, slight modifications, my theory would absolutely break down" *(The Origin of Species).*

If we just take the human eye, one small part of an incredibly complex creation, we will see this same principle of irreducible complexity. The eye cannot be reduced to anything less than what it is. It has thousands of co-equal functions to make it work. If we take away just one of those functions, the rest of the eye is worthless as an eye. How then did the eye evolve when all functions had to be present at once to give it any worth at all? We are indeed fearfully and wonderfully made.

"To suppose that the eye, with all its inimitable contrivances for adjusting the focus to different distances, for admitting different amounts of light, and for the correction of spherical and chromatic aberration, could have been formed by natural selection, seems, I freely confess, absurd in the highest degree." *Charles Darwin, The Origin of Species*

(No wonder—the focusing muscles in the eye move an estimated 100,000 times each day. The retina contains 137 million light-sensitive cells.)

139:16 *An Interesting Quiz…*

How would you respond in these situations?

1. A preacher and his wife are very, very poor. They already have 14 kids. Now she finds out she's pregnant with the 15th. They're living in tremendous poverty. Considering their poverty and the excessive world population, would you consider recommending she get an abortion?
2. The father is sick with sniffles, the mother has TB. Of their four children, the first is blind, the second has died, the third is deaf, the fourth has TB. She finds she's pregnant again. Given this extreme situation, would you consider recommending abortion?
3. A white man raped a 13-year-old black girl and she's now pregnant. If you were her parents, would you consider recommending abortion?
4. A teenage girl is pregnant. She's not married. Her fiancé is not the father of the baby, and he's upset. Would you recommend abortion?

In the first case, you would have killed John Wesley, one of the great evangelists in the 19th century.

In the second case, you would have killed Beethoven.

In the third case, you would have killed Ethel Waters, the great black gospel singer.

If you said yes to the fourth case, you would have declared the murder of Jesus Christ!

God is the author of life, and He has given every single individual supreme value. Each life—whether inside or outside the womb—should therefore be valued by us. God knows the plans He has for each individual and has written in His book all the days ordained for us before one of them came to be.

When we presume to know better than God who should be given life, we are putting ourselves in the place of God and are guilty of idolatry.

See also Psalm 127:3 footnote.

22 I hate them with perfect hatred: I
count them my enemies.
23 *Search me, O God, and know my heart:*
try me, and know my thoughts:
24 *And see if there be any wicked way in*
me, and lead me in the way everlasting.

PSALM 140

DELIVER me, O LORD, from the evil
man: preserve me from the violent
man;
2 Which imagine mischiefs in their heart;
continually are they gathered together for
war.
3 They have sharpened their tongues like
a serpent; adders' poison is under their
lips. Selah.
4 Keep me, O LORD, from the hands of
the wicked; preserve me from the violent
man; who have purposed to overthrow my
goings.
5 The proud have hid a snare for me, and
cords; they have spread a net by the wayside; they have set gins for me. Selah.
6 I said unto the LORD, You are my God:
hear the voice of my supplications, O LORD.
7 O GOD the Lord, the strength of my
salvation, you have covered my head in
the day of battle.
8 Grant not, O LORD, the desires of the
wicked: further not his wicked device; lest
they exalt themselves. Selah.
9 As for the head of those that compass
me about, let the mischief of their own lips
cover them.
10 Let burning coals fall upon them: let
them be cast into the fire; into deep pits,
that they rise not up again.
11 Let not an evil speaker be established
in the earth: evil shall hunt the violent man
to overthrow him.
12 I know that the LORD will maintain
the cause of the afflicted, and the right of
the poor.

140:2,3 "The heart is like a viper, hissing and spitting poison at God." *Jonathan Edwards*

13 Surely the righteous shall give thanks unto your name: the upright shall dwell in your presence.

PSALM 141

LORD, I cry unto you: make haste unto me; give ear unto my voice, when I cry unto you.

2 Let my prayer be set forth before you as incense; and the lifting up of my hands as the evening sacrifice.

3 Set a watch, O LORD, before my mouth; keep the door of my lips.

4 Incline not my heart to any evil thing, to practice wicked works with men that work iniquity: and let me not eat of their dainties.

5 Let the righteous smite me; it shall be a kindness: and let him reprove me; it shall be an excellent oil, which shall not break my head: for yet my prayer also shall be in their calamities.

6 When their judges are overthrown in stony places, they shall hear my words; for they are sweet.

7 Our bones are scattered at the grave's mouth, as when one cuts and cleaves wood upon the earth.

8 But my eyes are unto you, O GOD the Lord: in you is my trust; leave not my soul destitute.

9 Keep me from the snares which they have laid for me, and the gins of the workers of iniquity.

10 Let the wicked fall into their own nets, while I withal escape.

PSALM 142

I CRIED unto the LORD with my voice; with my voice unto the LORD did I make my supplication.

2 I poured out my complaint before him; I showed before him my trouble.

3 When my spirit was overwhelmed within me, then you knew my path. In the way wherein I walked have they privily laid a snare for me.

"I have always said, and always will say, that the studious perusal of the Sacred Volume will make better citizens, better fathers, and better husbands."

Thomas Jefferson

4 I looked on my right hand, and beheld, but there was no man that would know me: refuge failed me; no man cared for my soul.

5 I cried unto you, O LORD: I said, You are my refuge and my portion in the land of the living.

6 Attend unto my cry; for I am brought very low: deliver me from my persecutors; for they are stronger than I.

7 Bring my soul out of prison, that I may praise your name: the righteous shall compass me about; for you shall deal bountifully with me.

PSALM 143

HEAR my prayer, O LORD, give ear to my supplications: in your faithfulness answer me, and in your righteousness.

2 And enter not into judgment with your servant: for in your sight shall no man living be justified.

3 For the enemy has persecuted my soul;

141:5 This is a test of our humility. Are we prepared to submit ourselves to godly counsel?

THE FUNCTION OF THE LAW

143:2 "It is amazing for a soul to discover that God gave a law to be observed but that its observance is not even taken into account as a means of salvation. Then why was the law given? What good are moral standards? They were not given because God had the illusion that we could conform our lives to them. God knows that we are a degenerate race and that there is nothing good in our carnal nature.

"The law serves another purpose: to show us our sins. Man is confronted with a moral law that is just and good. His mind, while acknowledging that here is the truth, confesses at the same time that he does not live according to this law. And no matter how hard he tries, he realizes he does not reach the ideal. This is how he discovers he is a lost sinner.

"This is the great purpose of the law. It teaches us what sin is and it shows us how wrong we are, just as a mirror reveals to us how filthy we are and what needs cleansing. But just as a mirror does not and cannot wash us but only reveals our condition, so the law cannot correct us but only shows us what great sinners we are.

"The purpose of the law is to make you know your sin so that you will begin to pray with the psalmist, "Do not enter into judgment with Your servant, for in Your sight no one living is righteous (Psalm 143:2)."
Richard Wurmbrand

he has smitten my life down to the ground;
he has made me to dwell in darkness, as
those that have been long dead.
4 Therefore is my spirit overwhelmed
within me; my heart within me is desolate.
5 I remember the days of old; I meditate
on all your works; I muse on the work of
your hands.
6 I stretch forth my hands unto you: my
soul thirsts after you, as a thirsty land. Selah.
7 Hear me speedily, O LORD: my spirit
fails: hide not your face from me, lest I be
like unto them that go down into the pit.
8 Cause me to hear your lovingkindness
in the morning; for in you do I trust: cause
me to know the way wherein I should
walk; for I lift up my soul unto you.
9 Deliver me, O LORD, from my enemies:
I flee unto you to hide me.
10 Teach me to do your will; for you are
my God: your spirit is good; lead me into the land of uprightness.
11 Quicken me, O LORD, for your name's
sake: for your righteousness' sake bring
my soul out of trouble.
12 And of your mercy cut off my enemies, and destroy all them that afflict my
soul: for I am your servant.

PSALM 144

BLESSED be the LORD my strength
which teaches my hands to war, and
my fingers to fight:
2 My goodness, and my fortress; my high
tower, and my deliverer; my shield, and
he in whom I trust; who subdues my people under me.
3 *LORD, what is man, that you take knowledge of him! or the son of man, that you
make account of him!*
4 *Man is like to vanity: his days are as a
shadow that passes away.*
5 Bow your heavens, O LORD, and come
down: touch the mountains, and they shall
smoke.
6 Cast forth lightning, and scatter them:
shoot out your arrows, and destroy them.
7 Send your hand from above; rid me,
and deliver me out of great waters, from
the hand of strange children;
8 Whose mouth speaks vanity, and their
right hand is a right hand of falsehood.
9 I will sing a new song unto you, O
God: upon a psaltery and an instrument
of ten strings will I sing praises unto you.
10 It is he that gives salvation unto kings:

143:2 How fearful it would be stand in judgment and be judged by the standard of God's Law. See Galatians 2:16 for what God did so that we could live.

who delivers David his servant from the hurtful sword.
11 Rid me, and deliver me from the hand of strange children, whose mouth speaks vanity, and their right hand is a right hand of falsehood:
12 That our sons may be as plants grown up in their youth; that our daughters may be as corner stones, polished after the similitude of a palace:
13 That our garners may be full, affording all manner of store: that our sheep may bring forth thousands and ten thousands in our streets:
14 That our oxen may be strong to labor; that there be no breaking in, nor going out; that there be no complaining in our streets.
15 Happy is that people, that is in such a case: yes, happy is that people, whose God is the LORD.

PSALM 145

I WILL extol you, my God, O king; and I will bless your name for ever and ever.
2 Every day will I bless you; and I will praise your name for ever and ever.
3 Great is the LORD, and greatly to be praised; and his greatness is unsearchable.
4 One generation shall praise your works to another, and shall declare your mighty acts.
5 I will speak of the glorious honor of your majesty, and of your wondrous works.
6 And men shall speak of the might of your terrible acts: and I will declare your greatness.
7 They shall abundantly utter the memory of your great goodness, and shall sing of your righteousness.
8 The LORD is gracious, and full of compassion; slow to anger, and of great mercy.
9 The LORD is good to all: and his tender mercies are over all his works.
10 All your works shall praise you, O LORD; and your saints shall bless you.
11 They shall speak of the glory of your kingdom, and talk of your power;
12 To make known to the sons of men his mighty acts, and the glorious majesty of his kingdom.
13 Your kingdom is an everlasting kingdom, and your dominion endures throughout all generations.
14 The LORD upholds all that fall, and raises up all those that be bowed down.
15 The eyes of all wait upon you; and you give them their meat in due season.
16 You open your hand, and satisfy the desire of every living thing.

> I believe the holier a man becomes, the more he mourns over the unholiness which remains in him.
>
> CHARLES SPURGEON

17 The LORD is righteous in all his ways, and holy in all his works.
18 The LORD is near unto all them that call upon him, to all that call upon him in truth.
19 He will fulfill the desire of them that fear him: he also will hear their cry, and will save them.
20 The LORD preserves all them that love him: but all the wicked will he destroy.
21 My mouth shall speak the praise of the LORD: and let all flesh bless his holy name for ever and ever.

PSALM 146

PRAISE the LORD. Praise the LORD, O my soul.
2 While I live will I praise the LORD: I will sing praises unto my God while I have any being.
3 Put not your trust in princes, nor in

145:8 This is why we have the cross of Calvary. Nothing in man's character drew out God's love for us. It came simply because the Lord is gracious and full of compassion.

145:17,18 Notice the word "all" in these verses.

the son of man, in whom there is no help.
4 His breath goes forth, he returns to his
earth; in that very day his thoughts perish.
5 Happy is he that has the God of Jacob
for his help, whose hope is in the LORD his
God:
6 Which made heaven, and earth, the sea,
and all that therein is: which keeps truth
for ever:
7 Which executes judgment for the oppressed: which gives food to the hungry.
The LORD looses the prisoners:
8 The LORD opens the eyes of the blind:
the LORD raises them that are bowed down:
the LORD loves the righteous:
9 The LORD preserves the strangers; he
relieves the fatherless and widow: but the
way of the wicked he turns upside down.
10 The LORD shall reign for ever, even
your God, O Zion, unto all generations.
Praise the LORD.

PSALM 147

PRAISE the LORD: for it is good to sing
praises unto our God; for it is pleasant; and praise is comely.
2 The LORD does build up Jerusalem: he
gathers together the outcasts of Israel.
3 He heals the broken in heart, and binds
up their wounds.
4 He tells the number of the stars; he calls
them all by their names.
5 Great is our Lord, and of great power:
his understanding is infinite.
6 The LORD lifts up the meek: he casts
the wicked down to the ground.
7 Sing unto the LORD with thanksgiving;
sing praise upon the harp unto our God:
8 Who covers the heaven with clouds,
who prepares rain for the earth, who makes
grass to grow upon the mountains.
9 He gives to the beast his food, and to
the young ravens which cry.

> The church is like manure. Pile it up, and it stinks up the neighborhood. Spread it out, and it enriches the world.
>
> **LUIS PALAU**

10 **He delights not in the strength of
the horse: he takes not pleasure in the
legs of a man.**
11 **The LORD takes pleasure in them
that fear him, in those that hope in his
mercy.**
12 Praise the LORD, O Jerusalem; praise
your God, O Zion.
13 For he has strengthened the bars of
your gates; he has blessed your children
within you.

146:6 Evolution's circular reasoning. "At least six different radiometric dating methods are available. *The assumed age of the sample will dictate which dating method is used because each will give a different result.*

"For example: when dinosaur bones containing carbon are found, they are *not* carbon dated because the result would be only a few thousand years. Because this would not match the assumed age based on the geologic column, scientists use another method of dating to give an age closer to the desired result. All radiometric results that do not match the preassigned ages of the geologic column are discarded." *Dr. Kent Hovind*

"Contrary to what most scientists write, the fossil record does not support the Darwinian theory of evolution because it is this theory (there are several) which we use to interpret the fossil record. By doing so we are guilty of circular reasoning if we then say the fossil record supports this theory." *Ronald R. West*, Ph.D.

146:7–9 Here is the ministry of the Savior. Jesus fed the hungry, loosed the prisoners of sin and suffering, opened the eyes of the blind, and raised up those who were bowed down.

147:4 In Jeremiah 33:22, the Bible states that "the host of heaven cannot be numbered, neither the sand of the sea measured." When this was written, 2,500 years ago, no one knew how vast the stars were, since only about 1,100 were visible. Now we know that there are *billions* of stars, and that they *cannot* be numbered.

QUESTIONS & OBJECTIONS

147:9

"The Bible calls the hare a cud-chewing animal. As any veterinarian could tell you, this statement is false."

This statement is made in Leviticus 11:6, where the Hebrew literally means "raises up what has been swallowed." The rabbit does re-eat partially digested fecal pellets that come from a special pouch called the *caecum*. Bacteria in these pellets enrich the diet and provide nutrients to aid digestion. According to the *Encyclopedia Britannica*:

> "Some lagomorphs [rabbits and hares] are capable of re-ingesting moist and nutritionally rich fecal pellets, a practice considered comparable to cud-chewing in ruminants...The upper tooth rows are more widely separated than the lower rows, and chewing is done with a transverse movement."

14 He makes peace in your borders, and fills you with the finest of the wheat.
15 He sends forth his commandment upon earth: his word runs very swiftly.
16 He gives snow like wool: he scatters the hoarfrost like ashes.
17 He casts forth his ice like morsels: who can stand before his cold?
18 He sends out his word, and melts them: he causes his wind to blow, and the waters flow.
19 He showed his word unto Jacob, his statutes and his judgments unto Israel.
20 He has not dealt so with any nation: and as for his judgments, they have not known them. Praise the LORD.

PSALM 148

PRAISE the LORD. Praise the LORD from the heavens: praise him in the heights.
2 Praise him, all his angels: praise him, all his hosts.
3 Praise him, sun and moon: praise him, all stars of light.
4 Praise him, heavens of heavens, and waters that be above the heavens.
5 Let them praise the name of the LORD: for he commanded, and they were created.
6 He has also established them for ever and ever: he has made a decree which shall not pass.
7 Praise the LORD from the earth, dragons, and all deeps:
8 Fire, and hail; snow, and vapors; stormy wind fulfilling his word:
9 Mountains, and all hills; fruitful trees, and all cedars:
10 Beasts, and all cattle; creeping things, and flying fowl:
11 Kings of the earth, and all people; princes, and all judges of the earth:
12 Both young men, and maidens; old men, and children:
13 Let them praise the name of the LORD: for his name alone is excellent; his glory is above the earth and heaven.
14 He also exalts the horn of his people, the praise of all his saints; even of the children of Israel, a people near unto him. Praise the LORD.

. . . . . .

For the biblical way to present God's love, see Matthew 10:22 footnote.

. . . . . .

PSALM 149

PRAISE the LORD. Sing unto the LORD a new song, and his praise in the congregation of saints.
2 Let Israel rejoice in him that made him: let the children of Zion be joyful in their King.
3 Let them praise his name in the dance: let them sing praises unto him with the timbrel and harp.
4 For the LORD takes pleasure in his people: he will beautify the meek with salvation.

5 Let the saints be joyful in glory: let them
sing aloud upon their beds.
6 Let the high praises of God be in their
mouth, and a two-edged sword in their
hand;
7 To execute vengeance upon the heathen, and punishments upon the people;
8 To bind their kings with chains, and
their nobles with fetters of iron;
9 To execute upon them the judgment
written: this honor have all his saints.
Praise the LORD.

> Any man who declares children to be born perfect was never a father. Your child without evil? You without eyes, you mean!
>
> **CHARLES SPURGEON**

PSALM 150

PRAISE the LORD. Praise God in his
sanctuary: praise him in the firmament
of his power.
2 Praise him for his mighty acts: praise
him according to his excellent greatness.
3 Praise him with the sound of the trumpet: praise him with the psaltery and harp.
4 Praise him with the timbrel and dance:
praise him with stringed instruments and
organs.
5 Praise him upon the loud cymbals:
praise him upon the high sounding cymbals.
6 Let every thing that has breath praise
the LORD. Praise the LORD.

Bible Statistics

Number of books in the Bible: 66

Chapters: 1,189

Verses: 31,101

Words: 783,137

Letters: 3,566,480

Longest word (and name): Mahershalalhashbaz (Isaiah 8:1)

Longest verse: Esther 8:9 (78 words)

Shortest verse: John 11:35 (2 words: "Jesus wept")

Middle books: Micah and Nahum

Middle chapter: Psalm 118

Middle verse: Psalm 118:8

Shortest book (number of words): 3 John

Shortest chapter (number of words): Psalm 117

Longest book: Psalms (150 chapters)

Longest chapter: Psalm 119 (176 verses)

Number of times the word "God" appears: 3,358

Number of times the word "Lord" appears: 7,736

Number of different authors: Approximately 40

Number of languages the Bible has been translated into: more than 1,200

Number of new Bibles distributed (sold or given away) in the U.S.: about 168,000 per day

Proverbs

CHAPTER 1

THE proverbs of Solomon the son of David, king of Israel;
2 To know wisdom and instruction; to perceive the words of understanding;
3 To receive the instruction of wisdom, justice, and judgment, and equity;
4 To give subtlety to the simple, to the young man knowledge and discretion.
5 A wise man will hear, and will increase learning; and a man of understanding shall attain unto wise counsels:
6 To understand a proverb, and the interpretation; the words of the wise, and their dark sayings.
7 The fear of the LORD is the beginning of knowledge: but fools despise wisdom and instruction.
8 My son, hear the instruction of your father, and forsake not the law of your mother:
9 For they shall be an ornament of grace unto your head, and chains about your neck.
10 My son, if sinners entice you, consent not.
11 If they say, Come with us, let us lay wait for blood, let us lurk privily for the innocent without cause:
12 Let us swallow them up alive as the grave; and whole, as those that go down into the pit:
13 We shall find all precious substance, we shall fill our houses with spoil:
14 Cast in your lot among us; let us all have one purse:
15 My son, walk not in the way with them; refrain your foot from their path:
16 For their feet run to evil, and make haste to shed blood.
17 Surely in vain the net is spread in the sight of any bird.
18 And they lay wait for their own blood; they lurk privily for their own lives.
19 So are the ways of every one that is greedy of gain; which takes away the life of the owners thereof.
20 Wisdom cries without; she utters her voice in the streets:
21 She cries in the chief place of concourse, in the openings of the gates: in the city she utters her words, saying,
22 How long, you simple ones, will you love simplicity? and the scorners delight in their scorning, and fools hate knowledge?

1:2 It is wise to read a proverb for each day of the month. They were written that we might have wisdom, instruction, and understanding.

1:22,23 One just has to observe the gospel being preached in the open air to know the truth of these words. When presented with the knowledge of how to be saved from death and hell, the world delights in scorn. Yet despite their contempt, our Creator offers salvation to a God-hating humanity. He will make His words known to all who turn to His reproof.

23 Turn you at my reproof: behold, I will
pour out my spirit unto you, I will make
known my words unto you.
24 Because I have called, and you refused; I have stretched out my hand, and
no man regarded;
25 But you have set at nought all my
counsel, and would none of my reproof:
26 I also will laugh at your calamity; I will
mock when your fear comes;
27 When your fear comes as desolation,
and your destruction comes as a whirlwind; when distress and anguish comes
upon you.
28 Then shall they call upon me, but I
will not answer; they shall seek me early,
but they shall not find me:
29 For that they hated knowledge, and
did not choose the fear of the LORD:
30 They would none of my counsel: they
despised all my reproof.
31 Therefore shall they eat of the fruit
of their own way, and be filled with their
own devices.
32 For the turning away of the simple
shall slay them, and the prosperity of fools
shall destroy them.
33 But whoso hearkens unto me shall
dwell safely, and shall be quiet from fear
of evil.

CHAPTER 2

MY son, if you will receive my words,
and hide my commandments with
you;
2 So that you incline your ear unto wisdom, and apply your heart to understanding;
3 Yes, if you cry after knowledge, and lift
up your voice for understanding;
4 If you seek her as silver, and search for
her as for hidden treasures;
5 Then shall you understand the fear of
the LORD, and find the knowledge of God.
6 For the LORD gives wisdom: out of his
mouth comes knowledge and understanding.
7 He lays up sound wisdom for the righteous: he is a buckler to them that walk
uprightly.
8 He keeps the paths of judgment, and
preserves the way of his saints.
9 Then shall you understand righteousness, and judgment, and equity; yes, every
good path.
10 When wisdom enters into your heart,
and knowledge is pleasant unto your soul;
11 Discretion shall preserve you, understanding shall keep you:
12 To deliver you from the way of the
evil man, from the man that speaks froward things;
13 Who leave the paths of uprightness,
to walk in the ways of darkness;
14 Who rejoice to do evil, and delight in
the frowardness of the wicked;
15 Whose ways are crooked, and they
froward in their paths:
16 To deliver you from the strange woman, even from the stranger which flatters with her words;
17 Who forsakes the guide of her youth,
and forgets the covenant of her God.
18 For her house inclines unto death,
and her paths unto the dead.
19 None that go unto her return again,
neither take they hold of the paths of life.
20 That you may walk in the way of good
men, and keep the paths of the righteous.
21 For the upright shall dwell in the
land, and the perfect shall remain in it.
22 But the wicked shall be cut off from
the earth, and the transgressors shall be
rooted out of it.

2:1–5 The fear of the Lord. This is how to obtain the fear of the Lord, the most necessary virtue: 1) receive the Word of God; 2) hide His commandments within you; 3) incline your ear to wisdom; 4) apply your heart to understanding; 5) cry out for knowledge and discernment; 6) seek it as you would for silver or hidden treasures.

2:12 Wisdom, knowledge, discretion, and understanding will keep you from perversity and sexual sin. They give the blind light as to the end result of sin: see verse 18.

CHAPTER 3

MY son, forget not my law; but let
your heart keep my commandments:
2 For length of days, and long life, and
peace, shall they add to you.
3 Let not mercy and truth forsake you:
bind them about your neck; write them
upon the table of your heart:
4 So shall you find favor and good understanding in the sight of God and man.
**5 Trust in the LORD with all your heart;
and lean not unto your own understanding.**
**6 In all your ways acknowledge him,
and he shall direct your paths.**
7 Be not wise in your own eyes: fear the
LORD, and depart from evil.
8 It shall be health to your navel, and
marrow to your bones.
9 Honor the LORD with your substance,
and with the firstfruits of all your increase:
10 So shall your barns be filled with
plenty, and your presses shall burst out
with new wine.
11 My son, despise not the chastening
of the LORD; neither be weary of his correction:
12 For whom the LORD loves he corrects;
even as a father the son in whom he delights.
13 Happy is the man that finds wisdom,
and the man that gets understanding.
14 For the merchandise of it is better
than the merchandise of silver, and the
gain thereof than fine gold.
15 She is more precious than rubies:
and all the things you canst desire are not
to be compared unto her.
16 Length of days is in her right hand;
and in her left hand riches and honor.
17 Her ways are ways of pleasantness,
and all her paths are peace.
18 She is a tree of life to them that lay
hold upon her: and happy is every one
that retains her.
19 The LORD by wisdom has founded
the earth; by understanding has he established the heavens.
20 By his knowledge the depths are broken up, and the clouds drop down the
dew.
21 My son, let not them depart from your
eyes: keep sound wisdom and discretion:
22 So shall they be life unto your soul,
and grace to your neck.
23 Then shall you walk in your way
safely, and your foot shall not stumble.
24 When you lie down, you shall not
be afraid: yes, you shall lie down, and your
sleep shall be sweet.
25 Be not afraid of sudden fear, neither
of the desolation of the wicked, when it

3:1–3 The Law leads to mercy and truth. See John 1:17 and Galatians 3:24.

3:5 The world says the opposite—doubt the Word of God and have faith in yourself.

3:6 "It was the Lord who put it into my mind... I could feel His hand upon me... There is no question the inspiration was from the Holy Spirit because He comforted me with rays of marvelous illumination from the Holy Scriptures... No one should fear to undertake any task in the name of our Savior if it is just and if the intention is purely for His holy service. The gospel must still be preached to so many lands in such a short time. This is what convinces me." *Christopher Columbus* (from his diary, in reference to his discovery of "the New World")

3:19 "Slight variations in physical laws such as gravity or electromagnetism would make life impossible... The necessity to produce life lies at the center of the universe's whole machinery and design." *John Wheeler*, Princeton University professor of physics (*Reader's Digest*, Sept. 1986)

Even evolutionist *Stephen Hawking*, considered the best-known scientist since Albert Einstein, acknowledges "the universe and the laws of physics seem to have been specifically designed for us. If any one of about 40 physical qualities had more than slightly different values, life as we know it could not exist: Either atoms would not be stable, or they wouldn't combine into molecules, or the stars wouldn't form the heavier elements, or the universe would collapse before life could develop, and so on..." (*Austin American-Statesman*, October 19, 1997)

3:19 *Questions for Evolutionists*

by Dr. Kent Hovind

The test of any theory is whether or not it provides answers to basic questions. Some well-meaning but misguided people think evolution is a reasonable theory to explain man's questions about the universe. Evolution is not a good theory—it is just a pagan religion masquerading as science.

1. Where did the space for the universe come from?
2. Where did matter come from?
3. Where did the laws of the universe come from (gravity, inertia, etc.)?
4. How did matter get so perfectly organized?
5. Where did the energy come from to do all the organizing?
6. When, where, why, and how did life come from dead matter?
7. When, where, why, and how did life learn to reproduce itself?
8. With what did the first cell capable of sexual reproduction reproduce?
9. Why would any plant or animal want to reproduce more of its kind since this would only make more mouths to feed and decrease the chances of survival? (Does the individual have a drive to survive, or the species? How do you explain this?)
10. How can mutations (recombining of the genetic code) create any new, improved varieties? (Recombining English letters will never produce Chinese books.)
11. Is it possible that similarities in design between different animals prove a common Creator instead of a common ancestor?
12. Natural selection only works with the genetic information available and tends only to keep a species stable. How would you explain the increasing complexity in the genetic code that must have occurred if evolution were true?
13. When, where, why, and how did:

    a) Single-celled plants become multi-celled? (Where are the two- and three-celled intermediates?)

    b) Single-celled animals evolve?

    c) Fish change to amphibians?

    d) Amphibians change to reptiles?

    e) Reptiles change to birds? (The lungs, bones, eyes, reproductive organs, heart, method of locomotion, body covering, etc., are all very different!) How did the intermediate forms live?
14. When, where, why, how, and from what did:

    a) Whales evolve?

    b) Sea horses evolve?

    c) Bats evolve?

    d) Eyes evolve?

    e) Ears evolve?

    f) Hair, skin, feathers, scales, nails, claws, etc., evolve?
15. Which evolved first (how, and how long, did it work without the others)?

    a) The digestive system, the food to be digested, the appetite, the ability to find and eat the food, the digestive juices, or the body's resistance to its own digestive juice (stomach, intestines, etc.)?

    b) The drive to reproduce or the ability to reproduce?

    c) The lungs, the mucus lining to protect them, the throat, or the perfect mixture of gases to be breathed into the lungs?

    d) DNA or RNA to carry the DNA message to cell parts?

    e) The termite or the flagella in its intestines that actually digest the cellulose?

    f) The plants or the insects that live on and pollinate the plants?

    g) The bones, ligaments, tendons, blood supply, or muscles to move the bones?

    h) The nervous system, repair system, or hormone system?

    i) The immune system or the need for it?

comes.
26 For the LORD shall be your confidence,
and shall keep your foot from being taken.
27 Withhold not good from them to
whom it is due, when it is in the power
of your hand to do it.
28 Say not unto your neighbor, Go, and
come again, and tomorrow I will give;
when you have it by you.
29 Devise not evil against your neighbor, seeing he dwells securely by you.
30 Strive not with a man without cause,
if he has done you no harm.
31 Envy not the oppressor, and choose
none of his ways.
32 For the froward is abomination to
the LORD: but his secret is with the righteous.
33 The curse of the LORD is in the house
of the wicked: but he blesses the habitation of the just.
34 Surely he scorns the scorners: but he
gives grace unto the lowly.
35 The wise shall inherit glory: but shame
shall be the promotion of fools.

CHAPTER 4

HEAR, you children, the instruction
of a father, and attend to know understanding.
2 For I give you good doctrine, forsake
not my law.
3 For I was my father's son, tender and
only beloved in the sight of my mother.
4 He taught me also, and said unto me,
Let your heart retain my words: keep my
commandments, and live.
5 Get wisdom, get understanding: forget it not; neither decline from the words
of my mouth.
6 Forsake her not, and she shall preserve
you: love her, and she shall keep you.
7 Wisdom is the principal thing; therefore get wisdom: and with all your getting
get understanding.
8 Exalt her, and she shall promote you:
she shall bring you to honor, when you
do embrace her.

3:27,28 We must never lose sight of love for our neighbor. A good deed can be a stronger evangelistic witness than a thousand words. See Proverbs 27:10 footnote.

3:34 It has been said that the Italian dictator Mussolini, in his youth, stood on a high pinnacle and cried, "God, if you are there, strike me dead!" When God did not bow to his dictates, Mussolini concluded that there is no God. God did, however, answer his prayer some time later.

4:1–5 Training our children. We are responsible to God to train our children in the way they should go (Proverbs 22:6), and must constantly be on guard against humanism, atheism, relativism, evolution, and any other teaching that opposes the Christian worldview. (See also Ephesians 6:4 footnote.)

"I think that the most important factor moving us toward a secular society has been the educational factor. Our schools may not teach Johnny how to read properly, but the fact that Johnny is in school until he is sixteen tends toward the elimination of religious superstition. The average American child now acquires a high school education, and this militates against Adam and Eve and all other myths of alleged history." *P. Blanchard*, "Three Cheers for Our Secular State," *The Humanist*

"Education is thus a most powerful ally of humanism. What can a theistic Sunday school's meeting for an hour once a week and teaching only a fraction of the children, do to stem the tide of the five-day program of humanistic teaching?" *Humanism: A New Religion*, 1930

"Fundamental parents have no right to indoctrinate their children in their beliefs. We are preparing their children for the year 2000 and life in a global one-world society, and those children will not fit in." *Senator Paul Hoagland*, 1984

"Give me your four year olds, and in a generation I will build a socialist state." *Vladimir Lenin*

4:7 How do we get this "principal thing" that preserves and promotes? Primarily through prayer and Proverbs. Seek God and feed on this wealth of wisdom daily.

"I do not believe that any man can preach the gospel who does not preach the Law."

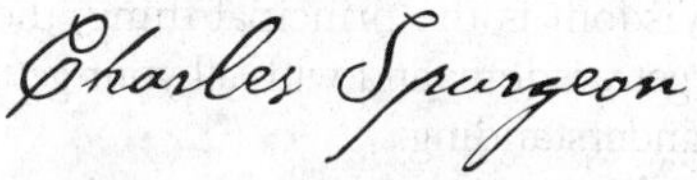

9 She shall give to your head an ornament of grace: a crown of glory shall she deliver to you.
10 Hear, O my son, and receive my sayings; and the years of your life shall be many.
11 I have taught you in the way of wisdom; I have led you in right paths.
12 When you go, your steps shall not be straitened; and when you run, you shall not stumble.
13 Take fast hold of instruction; let her not go: keep her; for she is your life.
14 Enter not into the path of the wicked, and go not in the way of evil men.
15 Avoid it, pass not by it, turn from it, and pass away.
16 For they sleep not, except they have done mischief; and their sleep is taken away, unless they cause some to fall.
17 For they eat the bread of wickedness, and drink the wine of violence.
18 **But the path of the just is as the shining light, that shines more and more unto the perfect day.**
19 **The way of the wicked is as darkness: they know not at what they stumble.**
20 My son, attend to my words; incline your ear unto my sayings.
21 Let them not depart from your eyes; keep them in the midst of your heart.
22 For they are life unto those that find them, and health to all their flesh.
23 Keep your heart with all diligence; for out of it are the issues of life.
24 Put away from you a froward mouth, and perverse lips put far from you.
25 Let your eyes look right on, and let your eyelids look straight before you.
26 Ponder the path of your feet, and let all your ways be established.
27 Turn not to the right hand nor to the left: remove your foot from evil.

CHAPTER 5

MY son, attend unto my wisdom, and bow your ear to my understanding:
2 That you may regard discretion, and that your lips may keep knowledge.
3 For the lips of a strange woman drop as an honeycomb, and her mouth is smoother than oil:
4 But her end is bitter as wormwood, sharp as a two-edged sword.
5 Her feet go down to death; her steps take hold on hell.
6 Lest you should ponder the path of life, her ways are moveable, that you can not know them.
7 Hear me now therefore, O you children, and depart not from the words of my mouth.
8 Remove your way far from her, and come not near the door of her house:
9 Lest you give your honor unto others, and your years unto the cruel:
10 Lest strangers be filled with your wealth; and your labors be in the house of a stranger;
11 And you mourn at the last, when your flesh and your body are consumed,
12 And say, How have I hated instruction, and my heart despised reproof;
13 And have not obeyed the voice of my teachers, nor inclined my ear to them that instructed me!
14 I was almost in all evil in the midst

of the congregation and assembly.
15 Drink waters out of your own cis-
tern, and running waters out of your own
well.
16 Let your fountains be dispersed abroad,
and rivers of waters in the streets.
17 Let them be only your own, and not
strangers' with you.
18 Let your fountain be blessed: and rejoice with the wife of your youth.
19 Let her be as the loving hind and
pleasant roe; let her breasts satisfy you at
all times; and be ravished always with her
love.
20 And why will you, my son, be ravished with a strange woman, and embrace
the bosom of a stranger?
21 **For the ways of man are before the
eyes of the LORD, and he ponders all his
goings.**
22 **His own iniquities shall take the
wicked himself, and he shall be held
with the cords of his sins.**
23 He shall die without instruction; and
in the greatness of his folly he shall go
astray.

CHAPTER 6

MY son, if you be surety for your
friend, if you have stricken your
hand with a stranger,
2 You are snared with the words of your
mouth, you are taken with the words of
your mouth.
3 Do this now, my son, and deliver yourself, when you are come into the hand of
your friend; go, humble yourself, and
make sure your friend.
4 Give not sleep to your eyes, nor slumber to your eyelids.
5 Deliver yourself as a roe from the hand
of the hunter, and as a bird from the hand
of the fowler.
6 Go to the ant, you sluggard; consider
her ways, and be wise:
7 Which having no guide, overseer, or
ruler,
8 Provides her meat in the summer, and
gathers her food in the harvest.
9 How long will you sleep, O sluggard?
when will you arise out of your sleep?
10 Yet a little sleep, a little slumber, a little folding of the hands to sleep:
11 So shall your poverty come as one
that travels, and your want as an armed
man.
12 A naughty person, a wicked man,
walks with a froward mouth.
13 He winks with his eyes, he speaks
with his feet, he teaches with his fingers;
14 Frowardness is in his heart, he devises mischief continually; he sows discord.
15 Therefore shall his calamity come suddenly; suddenly shall he be broken without remedy.
16 These six things does the LORD hate:
yes, seven are an abomination unto him:
17 A proud look, a lying tongue, and
hands that shed innocent blood,
18 An heart that devises wicked imaginations, feet that be swift in running to
mischief,
19 A false witness that speaks lies, and
he that sows discord among brethren.
20 My son, keep your father's command-

5:19 Biblical sexuality. It comes as a shock to the world that God's Word speaks so openly about sex. It is a gift of God given for both procreation and pleasure, within the bounds of marriage. Those who refuse to keep sexual intimacy within the bounds of the marriage bed will suffer the consequences of their actions (vv. 20–23). It is interesting to note that a man and a woman can have sexual relations thousands of times within their marriage with no fear of AIDS or any sexually transmitted diseases. See verse 11.

6:6–8 The ant is an example of the Christian who knows the will of God—to seek and save that which is lost. He understands that God isn't willing that any should perish, so he sets about the task of reaching the lost with the gospel. The ant doesn't need anyone telling him what to do. He just does it. See 1 Corinthians 15:58.

THE FUNCTION OF THE LAW

6:23 "The absence of God's holy Law from modern preaching is perhaps as responsible as any other factor for the evangelistic impotence of our churches and missions. Only by the light of the Law can the vermin of sin in the heart be exposed. Satan has effectively used a very clever device to silence the Law, which is needed as an instrument to bring perishing men to Christ.

"It is imperative that preachers of today learn how to declare the spiritual Law of God; for, until we learn how to wound consciences, we shall have no wounds to bind with gospel bandages." *Walter Chantry, Today's Gospel: Authentic or Synthetic?*

"The Law is the God-given light to illuminate the dark soul of man." *Mark A. Spence*

"Unless we see our shortcomings in the light of the Law and holiness of God, we do not see them as sin at all." *J. I. Packer*

ment, and forsake not the law of your mother:
21 Bind them continually upon your heart, and tie them about your neck.
22 When you go, it shall lead you; when you sleep, it shall keep you; and when you awake, it shall talk with you.
23 For the commandment is a lamp; and the law is light; and reproofs of instruction are the way of life:
24 To keep you from the evil woman, from the flattery of the tongue of a strange woman.
25 Lust not after her beauty in your heart; neither let her take you with her eyelids.
26 For by means of a whorish woman a man is brought to a piece of bread: and the adulteress will hunt for the precious life.
27 Can a man take fire in his bosom, and his clothes not be burned?
28 Can one go upon hot coals, and his feet not be burned?
29 So he that goes in to his neighbor's wife; whosoever touches her shall not be innocent.
30 Men do not despise a thief, if he steal to satisfy his soul when he is hungry;
31 But if he be found, he shall restore sevenfold; he shall give all the substance of his house.
32 But whoso commits adultery with a woman lacks understanding: he that does it destroys his own soul.
33 A wound and dishonor shall he get; and his reproach shall not be wiped away.
34 For jealousy is the rage of a man: therefore he will not spare in the day of vengeance.
35 He will not regard any ransom; neither will he rest content, though you give many gifts.

CHAPTER 7

MY son, keep my words, and lay up my commandments with you.
2 Keep my commandments, and live; and my law as the apple of your eye.
3 Bind them upon your fingers, write them upon the table of your heart.
4 Say unto wisdom, You are my sister; and call understanding your kinswoman:
5 That they may keep you from the strange woman, from the stranger which flatters with her words.
6 For at the window of my house I looked through my casement,
7 And beheld among the simple ones, I discerned among the youths, a young man void of understanding,
8 Passing through the street near her corner; and he went the way to her house,
9 In the twilight, in the evening, in the black and dark night:

6:23–30 Never fall into the trap of thinking that God's Law has no relevance for the Christian. Not only is it a schoolmaster to bring him to Christ (Galatians 3:24), but it leaves him with knowledge that will guide him for the rest of his life. We shouldn't disregard instruction of the schoolmaster after we graduate. The Ten Commandments will keep the Christian from fornication (v. 24), lust (v. 25), adultery (v. 29), and theft (v. 30).

10 And, behold, there met him a woman
with the attire of an harlot, and subtle of
heart.
11 (She is loud and stubborn; her feet
abide not in her house:
12 Now is she without, now in the streets,
and lies in wait at every corner.)
13 So she caught him, and kissed him,
and with an impudent face said unto him,
14 I have peace offerings with me; this
day have I paid my vows.
15 Therefore came I forth to meet you,
diligently to seek your face, and I have
found you.

> If you will not have death unto sin, you shall have sin unto death. There is no alternative. If you do not die to sin, you shall die for sin. If you do not slay sin, sin will slay you.
>
> **CHARLES SPURGEON**

16 I have decked my bed with coverings
of tapestry, with carved works, with fine
linen of Egypt.
17 I have perfumed my bed with myrrh,
aloes, and cinnamon.
18 Come, let us take our fill of love until
the morning: let us solace ourselves with
loves.
19 For the goodman is not at home, he
is gone a long journey:
20 He has taken a bag of money with
him, and will come home at the day appointed.
21 With her much fair speech she caused
him to yield, with the flattering of her lips
she forced him.
22 He goes after her straightway, as an
ox goes to the slaughter, or as a fool to the
correction of the stocks;
23 Till a dart strike through his liver; as
a bird hastens to the snare, and knows not
that it is for his life.
24 Hearken unto me now therefore, O
you children, and attend to the words of
my mouth.
25 Let not your heart decline to her ways,
go not astray in her paths.
26 For she has cast down many wounded: yes, many strong men have been slain
by her.
27 Her house is the way to hell, going
down to the chambers of death.

CHAPTER 8

DOES not wisdom cry? and understanding put forth her voice?
2 She stands in the top of high places,
by the way in the places of the paths.
3 She cries at the gates, at the entry of
the city, at the coming in at the doors.
4 Unto you, O men, I call; and my voice
is to the sons of man.
5 O you simple, understand wisdom:
and, you fools, be you of an understanding
heart.
6 Hear; for I will speak of excellent things;
and the opening of my lips shall be right
things.
7 For my mouth shall speak truth; and
wickedness is an abomination to my lips.
8 All the words of my mouth are in righteousness; there is nothing froward or perverse in them.
9 They are all plain to him that understands, and right to them that find knowledge.
10 Receive my instruction, and not silver;
and knowledge rather than choice gold.
11 For wisdom is better than rubies; and
all the things that may be desired are not
to be compared to it.
12 I wisdom dwell with prudence, and
find out knowledge of witty inventions.
13 The fear of the LORD is to hate evil:
pride, and arrogance, and the evil way,
and the froward mouth, do I hate.
14 Counsel is mine, and sound wisdom:
I am understanding; I have strength.
15 By me kings reign, and princes decree justice.
16 By me princes rule, and nobles, even
all the judges of the earth.
17 I love them that love me; and those
that seek me early shall find me.
18 Riches and honor are with me; yes,
durable riches and righteousness.

19 My fruit is better than gold, yes, than
fine gold; and my revenue than choice
silver.
20 I lead in the way of righteousness, in
the midst of the paths of judgment:
21 That I may cause those that love me
to inherit substance; and I will fill their
treasures.
22 The LORD possessed me in the beginning of his way, before his works of old.
23 I was set up from everlasting, from
the beginning, or ever the earth was.
24 When there were no depths, I was
brought forth; when there were no fountains abounding with water.
25 Before the mountains were settled,
before the hills was I brought forth:
26 While as yet he had not made the
earth, nor the fields, nor the highest part
of the dust of the world.
27 When he prepared the heavens, I was
there: when he set a compass upon the
face of the depth:
28 When he established the clouds
above: when he strengthened the fountains of the deep:
29 When he gave to the sea his decree,
that the waters should not pass his commandment: when he appointed the foundations of the earth:
30 Then I was by him, as one brought
up with him: and I was daily his delight,
rejoicing always before him;
31 Rejoicing in the habitable part of his
earth; and my delights were with the sons
of men.
32 Now therefore hearken unto me, O
you children: for blessed are they that
keep my ways.
33 Hear instruction, and be wise, and refuse it not.
34 Blessed is the man that hears me,
watching daily at my gates, waiting at the
posts of my doors.
35 For whoso finds me finds life, and
shall obtain favor of the LORD.
36 But he that sins against me wrongs
his own soul: all they that hate me love
death.

CHAPTER 9

WISDOM has built her house, she
has hewn out her seven pillars:
2 She has killed her beasts; she has
mingled her wine; she has also furnished
her table.
3 She has sent forth her maidens: she
cries upon the highest places of the city,
4 Whoso is simple, let him turn in hither: as for him that wants understanding,
she says to him,
5 Come, eat of my bread, and drink of
the wine which I have mingled.
6 Forsake the foolish, and live; and go in
the way of understanding.
7 He that reproves a scorner gets to himself shame: and he that rebukes a wicked
man gets himself a blot.
8 Reprove not a scorner, lest he hate
you: rebuke a wise man, and he will love
you.
9 Give instruction to a wise man, and he
will be yet wiser: teach a just man, and
he will increase in learning.

8:22 Jehovah's Witnesses. When Jehovah's Witnesses maintain that Jesus was "made" of the seed of David (that Jesus was *a* god "created" by Jehovah to die for our sins), they may point to Proverbs 8:22–35 for justification. However, the Bible is speaking here of "wisdom" (v. 12).

They also may refer to John 14:28 in which Jesus said, "I go to the Father: for my Father is greater than I," but they fail to show why Jesus said the Father was greater: "But we see Jesus, *who was made a little lower than the angels for the suffering of death,*...that he by the grace of God should taste death for every man" (Hebrews 2:9, emphasis added).

In Romans 1:3, the word used to refer to the incarnation ("made") is *ginomai*, which means "assembled." A body was prepared for God to manifest Himself in the flesh—"And without controversy great is the mystery of godliness: God was manifest in the flesh, justified in the Spirit, seen of angels, preached to the Gentiles, believed on in the world, received up into glory" (1 Timothy 3:16).

10 **The fear of the LORD is the beginning of wisdom: and the knowledge of the holy is understanding.**
11 For by me your days shall be multiplied, and the years of your life shall be increased.
12 If you be wise, you shall be wise for yourself: but if you scorn, you alone shall bear it.
13 A foolish woman is clamorous: she is simple, and knows nothing.
14 For she sits at the door of her house, on a seat in the high places of the city,
15 To call passengers who go right on their ways:
16 Whoso is simple, let him turn in hither: and as for him that wants understanding, she says to him,
17 Stolen waters are sweet, and bread eaten in secret is pleasant.
18 But he knows not that the dead are there; and that her guests are in the depths of hell.

. . . . . .

Will a sinner go to hell because he doesn't trust in Jesus? See John 16:9 footnote.

. . . . . .

CHAPTER 10

THE proverbs of Solomon. A wise son makes a glad father: but a foolish son is the heaviness of his mother.
2 Treasures of wickedness profit nothing: but righteousness delivers from death.
3 The LORD will not suffer the soul of the righteous to famish: but he casts away the substance of the wicked.
4 He becomes poor that deals with a slack hand: but the hand of the diligent makes rich.
5 He that gathers in summer is a wise son: but he that sleeps in harvest is a son that causes shame.
6 Blessings are upon the head of the just: but violence covers the mouth of the wicked.
7 The memory of the just is blessed: but the name of the wicked shall rot.
8 The wise in heart will receive commandments: but a prating fool shall fall.
9 He that walks uprightly walks surely: but he that perverts his ways shall be known.
10 He that winks with the eye causes sorrow: but a prating fool shall fall.
11 The mouth of a righteous man is a well of life: but violence covers the mouth of the wicked.
12 Hatred stirs up strifes: but love covers all sins.
13 In the lips of him that has understanding wisdom is found: but a rod is for the back of him that is void of understanding.
14 Wise men lay up knowledge: but the mouth of the foolish is near destruction.
15 The rich man's wealth is his strong city: the destruction of the poor is their poverty.
16 The labor of the righteous tends to life: the fruit of the wicked to sin.
17 He is in the way of life that keeps instruction: but he that refuses reproof errs.
18 He that hides hatred with lying lips, and he that utters a slander, is a fool.
19 In the multitude of words there wants not sin: but he that refrains his lips is wise.
20 The tongue of the just is as choice sil-

9:17 Our sinful hearts are so perverse that sin promises excitement. Despite the claim of modern evangelism that we can't find happiness until we come to Jesus, sin is indeed enticing and pleasurable, and can make a man or woman happy. See Jeremiah 12:1 and Hebrews 11:25.

10:2 All the money in the world will not turn the head of the Judge of the Universe. Money may buy a pardon from a civil court, but only righteousness will deliver the guilty from the wrath of Eternal Justice. See Proverbs 11:4.

10:7 Perhaps this is why not too many people name their children Adolf, Judas, or Jezebel.

ver: the heart of the wicked is little worth.
21 The lips of the righteous feed many: but fools die for want of wisdom.
22 The blessing of the LORD, it makes rich, and he adds no sorrow with it.
23 It is as sport to a fool to do mischief: but a man of understanding has wisdom.
24 The fear of the wicked, it shall come upon him: but the desire of the righteous shall be granted.
25 As the whirlwind passes, so is the wicked no more: but the righteous is an everlasting foundation.
26 As vinegar to the teeth, and as smoke to the eyes, so is the sluggard to them that send him.
27 The fear of the LORD prolongs days: but the years of the wicked shall be shortened.
28 The hope of the righteous shall be gladness: but the expectation of the wicked shall perish.
29 The way of the LORD is strength to the upright: but destruction shall be to the workers of iniquity.
30 The righteous shall never be removed: but the wicked shall not inhabit the earth.
31 The mouth of the just brings forth wisdom: but the froward tongue shall be cut out.
32 The lips of the righteous know what is acceptable: but the mouth of the wicked speaks frowardness.

CHAPTER 11

A FALSE balance is abomination to the LORD: but a just weight is his delight.
2 When pride comes, then comes shame: but with the lowly is wisdom.
3 The integrity of the upright shall guide them: but the perverseness of transgressors shall destroy them.
4 Riches profit not in the day of wrath: but righteousness delivers from death.
5 The righteousness of the perfect shall direct his way: but the wicked shall fall by his own wickedness.
6 The righteousness of the upright shall deliver them: but transgressors shall be taken in their own naughtiness.
7 When a wicked man dies, his expectation shall perish: and the hope of unjust men perishes.
8 The righteous is delivered out of trouble, and the wicked comes in his stead.
9 An hypocrite with his mouth destroys his neighbor: but through knowledge shall the just be delivered.
10 When it goes well with the righteous, the city rejoices: and when the wicked

---

10:32 Knowing what's acceptable. There is no record of David seeking God for His will before he confronted Goliath. How could this be? The Scriptures say, "In all your ways acknowledge him, and he shall direct your paths" (Proverbs 3:6). Shouldn't David have acknowledged the Lord in some way? No doubt, he did pray as he faced his enemy, but there is no proof that David asked God whether he should attack the giant Philistine. The reason for this is clear. The Bible tells us, "The lips of the righteous know what is acceptable." There are certain things that we know are not acceptable. If you saw an elderly woman fall to the ground, would you ask God whether or not you should help her up? Some things should be obvious to the godly. David took one look at the situation and saw that such a thing was completely unacceptable—that this "uncircumcised Philistine" was defying the armies of the Living God.

David could draw that conclusion because he had a relationship with God. His senses were "exercised to discern both good and evil" (Hebrews 5:14). He knew the Lord, and those who "know their God shall be strong, and do exploits" (Daniel 11:32).

11:1 We must never forget that God loves honesty in our dealings with others. See verse 3.

11:4 Riches in this life may buy a clever defense lawyer or turn a corrupt judge's head, but on the Day of Wrath the righteousness of Jesus Christ will be the only thing that will deliver the sinner from eternal death. See Revelation 6:15 footnote.

11:5–7 Notice the surety of these verses. They *shall* come to pass.

11:9 If we wouldn't say it in prayer, we shouldn't say it at all.

perish, there is shouting.
11 By the blessing of the upright the
city is exalted: but it is overthrown by the
mouth of the wicked.
12 He that is void of wisdom despises
his neighbor: but a man of understanding
holds his peace.
13 A talebearer reveals secrets: but he
that is of a faithful spirit conceals the
matter.
14 Where no counsel is, the people fall:
but in the multitude of counselors there
is safety.
15 He that is surety for a stranger shall
smart for it: and he that hates suretiship is
sure.
16 A gracious woman retains honor: and
strong men retain riches.
17 The merciful man does good to his
own soul: but he that is cruel troubles his
own flesh.
18 The wicked works a deceitful work:
but to him that sows righteousness shall
be a sure reward.
19 As righteousness tends to life: so he
that pursues evil pursues it to his own
death.
20 They that are of a froward heart are
abomination to the LORD: but such as are
upright in their way are his delight.
21 Though hand join in hand, the wicked shall not be unpunished: but the seed
of the righteous shall be delivered.
22 As a jewel of gold in a swine's snout,
so is a fair woman who is without discretion.
23 The desire of the righteous is only
good: but the expectation of the wicked
is wrath.
24 *There is that scatters, and yet increases; and there is that withholds more than is
meet, but it tends to poverty.*
25 *The liberal soul shall be made fat: and
he that waters shall be watered also himself.*
26 He that withholds corn, the people
shall curse him: but blessing shall be upon the head of him that sells it.
27 He that diligently seeks good pro-
cures favor: but he that seeks mischief, it
shall come unto him.
28 He that trusts in his riches shall fall;
but the righteous shall flourish as a branch.
29 He that troubles his own house shall
inherit the wind: and the fool shall be servant to the wise of heart.
30 *The fruit of the righteous is a tree of
life; and he that wins souls is wise.*
31 Behold, the righteous shall be recompensed in the earth: much more the wick-

11:13 The damage of gossip. A woman once spread some hot gossip about a local pastor. What he had supposedly done became common knowledge around town. Then she found that what she had heard wasn't true. She gallantly went to the pastor and asked for his forgiveness. The pastor forgave her, but then told her to take a pillow full of tiny feathers to a corner of the town, and in high winds, shake the feathers out. Then he told her to try to pick up every feather. He explained that the damage had already been done. She had destroyed his good reputation, and trying to repair the damage was like trying to pick up feathers in high winds.

The Bible says that there is life and death in the power of the tongue (Proverbs 18:21). Pray with the psalmist, "Set a watch, O LORD, before my mouth; keep the door of my lips" (Psalm 141:3). Remember the old saying, "He that gossips *to* you will gossip *about* you."

11:21 Though the entire world joins hands in a unity of spirit and says that there is no hell, it is still a reality. There *will* be a Judgment Day and justice will be done.

11:24 The wallet is the final frontier. There is nothing wrong with riches. However, those who have wealth must not trust in money (v. 28) and must be willing to share their prosperity with others. See 1 Timothy 6:17–19.

11:30 "Even if I were utterly selfish and had no care for anything but my own happiness, I would choose, if God allowed, to be a soul winner, for never did I know perfect, overflowing, unutterable happiness of the purest and most ennobling order till I first heard of one who had sought and found a Savior through my means." *Charles Spurgeon* ed and the sinner.

CHAPTER 12

WHOSO loves instruction loves knowledge: but he that hates reproof is brutish.
2 A good man obtains favor of the LORD: but a man of wicked devices will he condemn.
3 A man shall not be established by wickedness: but the root of the righteous shall not be moved.
4 A virtuous woman is a crown to her husband: but she that makes ashamed is as rottenness in his bones.
5 The thoughts of the righteous are right: but the counsels of the wicked are deceit.
6 The words of the wicked are to lie in wait for blood: but the mouth of the upright shall deliver them.
7 The wicked are overthrown, and are not: but the house of the righteous shall stand.
8 A man shall be commended according to his wisdom: but he that is of a perverse heart shall be despised.
9 He that is despised, and has a servant, is better than he that honors himself, and lacks bread.
10 A righteous man regards the life of his beast: but the tender mercies of the wicked are cruel.
11 He that tills his land shall be satisfied with bread: but he that follows vain persons is void of understanding.
12 The wicked desires the net of evil men: but the root of the righteous yields fruit.
13 The wicked is snared by the transgression of his lips: but the just shall come out of trouble.
14 A man shall be satisfied with good by the fruit of his mouth: and the recompense of a man's hands shall be rendered unto him.
15 The way of a fool is right in his own eyes: but he that hearkens unto counsel is wise.
16 A fool's wrath is presently known: but a prudent man covers shame.
17 He that speaks truth shows forth righteousness: but a false witness deceit.
18 There is that speaks like the piercings of a sword: but the tongue of the wise is health.
19 The lip of truth shall be established for ever: but a lying tongue is but for a moment.
20 Deceit is in the heart of them that imagine evil: but to the counselors of peace is joy.
21 There shall no evil happen to the just: but the wicked shall be filled with mischief.
22 Lying lips are abomination to the LORD: but they that deal truly are his

---

11:30 Lifestyle evangelism. Here's how to cultivate true lifestyle evangelism: 1) Pray that God uses you to reach the lost. 2) Ask for wisdom to use the time you have effectively for evangelism. Treat every day as though it were your last opportunity to share Christ. One day you will be right. 3) Study how to answer every man who asks you a reason for the hope that is in you (1 Peter 3:15; see Proverbs 16:23). 4) Find a "fishing hole" and go there regularly. Don't wait for sinners to approach you; go to them (Mark 16:15). 5) Use any anxiety as a catalyst to drive you to prayer and trust in God. Don't let the fear of man paralyze you (Philippians 1:28). You will realize the spiritual nature of fear after you conquer it. Confront it with the Word of God—"I can do all things through Christ who strengthens me" (Philippians 4:13). 6) Encourage others (by example and exhortation) into the task of evangelism.

12:15 This verse sums up the philosophy of a world that professes to be wise yet ignores the counsel of God's Word.

12:17 We are to follow the example of Jesus, who "preached righteousness in the great congregation" (see Psalm 40:6–10).

12:22 The ungodly try to justify themselves by saying that a "fib" or "white lie" never hurts anybody. Sin offends a holy God who demands retribution. See Proverbs 13:5.

delight.
23 A prudent man conceals knowledge:
but the heart of fools proclaims foolishness.
24 The hand of the diligent shall bear
rule: but the slothful shall be under tribute.
25 Heaviness in the heart of man makes
it stoop: but a good word makes it glad.
26 The righteous is more excellent than
his neighbor: but the way of the wicked
seduces them.
27 The slothful man roasts not that which
he took in hunting: but the substance of
a diligent man is precious.
28 In the way of righteousness is life: and
in the pathway thereof there is no death.

CHAPTER 13

A WISE son hears his father's instruction: but a scorner hears not rebuke.
2 A man shall eat good by the fruit of
his mouth: but the soul of the transgressors shall eat violence.
3 He that keeps his mouth keeps his life:
but he that opens wide his lips shall have
destruction.
4 The soul of the sluggard desires, and
has nothing: but the soul of the diligent
shall be made fat.
5 A righteous man hates lying: but a
wicked man is loathsome, and comes to
shame.
6 Righteousness keeps him that is upright in the way: but wickedness overthrows the sinner.
7 There is that makes himself rich, yet
has nothing: there is that makes himself
poor, yet has great riches.
8 The ransom of a man's life are his
riches: but the poor hears not rebuke.
9 The light of the righteous rejoices: but
the lamp of the wicked shall be put out.
10 Only by pride comes contention: but
with the well advised is wisdom.
11 Wealth gotten by vanity shall be di-
minished: but he that gathers by labor
shall increase.
12 Hope deferred makes the heart sick:
but when the desire comes, it is a tree of
life.
13 Whoso despises the word shall be
destroyed: but he that fears the commandment shall be rewarded.
14 The law of the wise is a fountain of
life, to depart from the snares of death.
15 Good understanding gives favor: but
the way of transgressors is hard.
16 Every prudent man deals with knowledge: but a fool lays open his folly.
17 A wicked messenger falls into mischief: but a faithful ambassador is health.
18 Poverty and shame shall be to him
that refuses instruction: but he that regards reproof shall be honored.
19 The desire accomplished is sweet to
the soul: but it is abomination to fools to
depart from evil.
20 He that walks with wise men shall
be wise: but a companion of fools shall be
destroyed.
21 Evil pursues sinners: but to the righteous good shall be repaid.
22 A good man leaves an inheritance to
his children's children: and the wealth of
the sinner is laid up for the just.
23 Much food is in the tillage of the poor:
but there is that is destroyed for want of
judgment.
24 He that spares his rod hates his son:
but he that loves him chastens him be-
times.

12:25 Are you worried and depressed about the future? Then read and believe the "good word" of God's Word. Nothing banishes fear like faith. Trusting in God's promises is like switching on a bright light in a dark room of gloom.

13:13 The Word will judge and condemn the guilty on the Last Day. Those who fear when they realize that they have sinned against God by transgressing His Law will be rewarded in the gospel. See Galatians 3:24.

13:19 Sinners love darkness; it is their security. See Proverbs 14:9; John 3:19,20.

SPRINGBOARDS FOR PREACHING AND WITNESSING

14:12

The Key

Back in the Old West, a number of men were upstairs in a boarding house amusing themselves with a game of cards when there was a cry from the street below of "Fire! Fire!" The men looked at one another in disbelief. One of the windows grew orange with the flames. "Wait!" said the dealer. "Let's just finish this hand; we've got plenty of time—I have a key to the back door." The men nodded in approval, then quickly picked up the dealt cards.

Precious minutes passed. One of the men became nervous as the flames licked through the now broken window. With darting eyes and a sweat-filled brow, he asked for the key. "Coward!" muttered the dealer as he tossed across the key. Each of them then rushed to the door and waited with bated breath as the key was placed into the lock. "It won't turn!" was the cry. "Let me have it!" said the dealer. As he tried in vain to turn the key, he whispered in horror, *"It's the wrong key!"*

25 The righteous eats to the satisfying of his soul: but the belly of the wicked shall want.

CHAPTER 14

EVERY wise woman builds her house: but the foolish plucks it down with her hands.

2 He that walks in his uprightness fears the LORD: but he that is perverse in his ways despises him.

3 In the mouth of the foolish is a rod of pride: but the lips of the wise shall preserve them.

4 Where no oxen are, the crib is clean: but much increase is by the strength of the ox.

5 A faithful witness will not lie: but a false witness will utter lies.

6 A scorner seeks wisdom, and finds it not: but knowledge is easy unto him that understands.

7 Go from the presence of a foolish man, when you perceive not in him the lips of knowledge.

8 The wisdom of the prudent is to understand his way: but the folly of fools is deceit.

9 **Fools make a mock at sin: but among the righteous there is favor.**

10 The heart knows his own bitterness; and a stranger does not intermeddle with his joy.

11 The house of the wicked shall be overthrown: but the tabernacle of the upright shall flourish.

12 There is a way which seems right unto a man, but the end thereof are the ways of death.

13 Even in laughter the heart is sorrowful; and the end of that mirth is heaviness.

14 The backslider in heart shall be filled with his own ways: and a good man shall be satisfied from himself.

15 The simple believes every word: but the prudent man looks well to his going.

16 A wise man fears, and departs from evil: but the fool rages, and is confident.

17 He that is soon angry deals foolishly: and a man of wicked devices is hated.

18 The simple inherit folly: but the prudent are crowned with knowledge.

19 The evil bow before the good; and the wicked at the gates of the righteous.

20 The poor is hated even of his own neighbor: but the rich has many friends.

21 He that despises his neighbor sins: but he that has mercy on the poor, happy

14:5 See verse 25.

14:14 False converts have no concern for God's will to reach the lost. Those who manage to find themselves in a pulpit will build their own kingdom rather than God's. See also Acts 20:30.

is he.
22 Do they not err that devise evil? but
mercy and truth shall be to them that devise good.
23 In all labor there is profit: but the
talk of the lips tends only to penury.
24 The crown of the wise is their riches:
but the foolishness of fools is folly.
25 A true witness delivers souls: but a
deceitful witness speaks lies.
26 In the fear of the LORD is strong confidence: and his children shall have a place
of refuge.
27 The fear of the LORD is a fountain of
life, to depart from the snares of death.
28 In the multitude of people is the
king's honor: but in the want of people
is the destruction of the prince.
29 He that is slow to wrath is of great
understanding: but he that is hasty of
spirit exalts folly.
30 A sound heart is the life of the flesh:
but envy the rottenness of the bones.
31 He that oppresses the poor reproaches
his Maker: but he that honors him has
mercy on the poor.
32 The wicked is driven away in his
wickedness: but the righteous has hope
in his death.
33 Wisdom rests in the heart of him
that has understanding: but that which
is in the midst of fools is made known.
**34 Righteousness exalts a nation: but
sin is a reproach to any people.**
35 The king's favor is toward a wise servant: but his wrath is against him that
causes shame.

CHAPTER 15

A SOFT answer turns away wrath: but
grievous words stir up anger.
2 The tongue of the wise uses knowledge aright: but the mouth of fools pours
out foolishness.
3 The eyes of the LORD are in every place,
beholding the evil and the good.
4 A wholesome tongue is a tree of life:
but perverseness therein is a breach in the
spirit.
5 A fool despises his father's instruction:
but he that regards reproof is prudent.
6 In the house of the righteous is much
treasure: but in the revenues of the wicked is trouble.
7 The lips of the wise disperse knowledge: but the heart of the foolish does
not so.
**8 The sacrifice of the wicked is an
abomination to the LORD: but the prayer
of the upright is his delight.**

14:25 A "witness" is not called upon to give an eloquent speech, but to merely testify to what he has seen and heard.

14:27 Here is a fountain from which most men refuse to drink. Their prejudicial minds think that its waters are bitter, when in truth they are incredibly sweet. The fear of the Lord helps men shake off that beast called "sin"—which is sucking from them their very life's blood.

14:34 "The moral principles and precepts contained in the Scriptures ought to form the basis of all our civil constitutions and laws. All the miseries and evils which men suffer from—vice, crime, ambition, injustice, oppression, slavery, and war—proceed from their despising or neglecting the precepts contained in the Bible." *Noah Webster*

15:1 Speak softly. This verse needs to be written on the hearts of all who preach the gospel, whether they share their faith with sinners one-on-one or preach open-air. If sinners become angry when you witness to them, speak softly. If you think you are about to be hit, ask the person his name to help diffuse the situation. Don't be afraid to gently change the subject, and don't wait to be a martyr. Jesus said to flee from a city that persecutes you (Matthew 10:23). Paul left one city in a basket (2 Corinthians 11:33). For other verses on the spirit in which we should share our faith, see Proverbs 16:32.

15:7 God's Law is what gives knowledge (see Romans 3:20,21). Those who are wise will tell sinners of its righteous requirements.

9 **The way of the wicked is an abomination unto the LORD: but he loves him
that follows after righteousness.**
10 Correction is grievous unto him that
forsakes the way: and he that hates reproof
shall die.
11 Hell and destruction are before the
LORD: how much more then the hearts of
the children of men?
12 A scorner loves not one that reproves
him: neither will he go unto the wise.
13 A merry heart makes a cheerful countenance: but by sorrow of the heart the
spirit is broken.
14 The heart of him that has understanding seeks knowledge: but the mouth of
fools feeds on foolishness.

> Never be afraid to try something new. Remember, amateurs built the ark; professionals built the Titanic.
>
> **UNKNOWN**

15 All the days of the afflicted are evil:
but he that is of a merry heart has a continual feast.
16 Better is little with the fear of the LORD
than great treasure and trouble therewith.
17 Better is a dinner of herbs where love
is, than a stalled ox and hatred therewith.
18 A wrathful man stirs up strife: but he
that is slow to anger appeases strife.
19 The way of the slothful man is as an
hedge of thorns: but the way of the righteous is made plain.
20 A wise son makes a glad father: but
a foolish man despises his mother.
21 Folly is joy to him that is destitute of
wisdom: but a man of understanding
walks uprightly.
22 Without counsel purposes are disap-
pointed: but in the multitude of counselors they are established.
23 A man has joy by the answer of his
mouth: and a word spoken in due season,
how good is it!
24 The way of life is above to the wise,
that he may depart from hell beneath.
25 The LORD will destroy the house of
the proud: but he will establish the border of the widow.
26 **The thoughts of the wicked are an
abomination to the LORD: but the words
of the pure are pleasant words.**
27 He that is greedy of gain troubles his
own house; but he that hates gifts shall
live.
28 *The heart of the righteous studies to
answer: but the mouth of the wicked pours
out evil things.*
29 **The LORD is far from the wicked:
but he hears the prayer of the righteous.**
30 The light of the eyes rejoices the heart:
and a good report makes the bones fat.
31 The ear that hears the reproof of life
abides among the wise.
32 He that refuses instruction despises
his own soul: but he that hears reproof
gets understanding.
33 The fear of the LORD is the instruction

15:8 When sinners think they are righteous because they give money, attend church, or live what they consider to be a virtuous life, it is an "abomination to the Lord." Even their thoughts are an abomination to Him (v. 26). This is because they stand guilty before Him. Their good works are provoked by a guilty conscience. Like a despicable criminal trying to pervert justice by offering the judge a bribe, they think their good deeds will outweigh their sins (see Hebrews 9:14).

"Good works, as they are called, in sinners are nothing but splendid sins." *Augustine*

15:15 Laughter is the enemy of legalism. Liberty and joy go hand in hand.

15:21 Use your time to further the gospel (see Ephesians 5:15,16). So much of today's entertainment is folly. If shallow entertainment gives us joy, it reveals our shallow understanding of the precious nature of time.

15:23 What a joy it is to direct a lost sinner to the Savior. The gospel is always in season. See 2 Timothy 4:2.

QUESTIONS & OBJECTIONS

16:10 ***"I have broken the Ten Commandments, but I do good things for people."***

Many people do similar things. They may steal from their employer or cheat on their taxes, then give to a charity or spend Thanksgiving helping at a soup kitchen. They think they are balancing the scales: they have done bad, and now they are doing good. However, the Bible reveals that the *motive* of guilty sinners is one of guilt (see Hebrews 9:14). They are attempting to bribe the Judge of the Universe. The Judge in this case will not be corrupted. He must punish all sinners. Good works cannot earn mercy; it comes purely by the grace of God. He will dismiss our iniquity only on the grounds of our faith in Jesus.

of wisdom; and before honor is humility.

CHAPTER 16

*THE preparations of the heart in man,
and the answer of the tongue, is from
the LORD.*
**2 All the ways of a man are clean in his
own eyes; but the LORD weighs the spirits.**
3 *Commit your works unto the LORD, and
your thoughts shall be established.*
4 The LORD has made all things for himself: yes, even the wicked for the day of
evil.
**5 Every one that is proud in heart is an
abomination to the LORD: though hand
join in hand, he shall not be unpunished.**
**6 By mercy and truth iniquity is purged:
and by the fear of the LORD men depart
from evil.**
7 *When a man's ways please the LORD, he
makes even his enemies to be at peace with
him.*
8 Better is a little with righteousness than
great revenues without right.
9 A man's heart devises his way: but the
LORD directs his steps.
10 A divine sentence is in the lips of the
king: his mouth transgresses not in judgment.
11 A just weight and balance are the
LORD's: all the weights of the bag are his
work.
12 It is an abomination to kings to commit wickedness: for the throne is established by righteousness.
13 Righteous lips are the delight of kings;
and they love him that speaks right.
14 The wrath of a king is as messengers
of death: but a wise man will pacify it.
15 In the light of the king's countenance

16:2 This is never so evident as when you ask a guilty sinner if he thinks he is a good person (see Proverbs 21:2; Luke 16:15). When the Law is used properly, it strips a man of self-righteousness. See Luke 18:18–23.

16:5 God resists those who are proud. Grace is only for the humble. Biblical evangelism is "Law to the proud; grace to the humble." With the Law, we break the hard heart. With the gospel, we heal the broken heart.

16:6 Men will not let go of their beloved sins unless the fear of the Lord grips their sin-loving hearts. Sinners are like a child whose eyes sparkle with delight as he holds a stick of lighted dynamite. He will not let go of it unless he is convinced that he is in terrible danger. The Law of God coupled with future punishment is the convincing agent that God has chosen to awaken the sinner. He must be told that God (who has the power to cast his soul into hell) will judge the world (on Judgment Day) in righteousness (by the perfect and righteous standard of His Law).

"Do I not destroy my enemies when I make them my friends?"

Abraham Lincoln

is life; and his favour is as a cloud of the latter rain.
16 How much better is it to get wisdom than gold! and to get understanding rather to be chosen than silver!
17 The highway of the upright is to depart from evil: he that keeps his way preserves his soul.
18 Pride goes before destruction, and an haughty spirit before a fall.
19 Better it is to be of an humble spirit with the lowly, than to divide the spoil with the proud.
20 He that handles a matter wisely shall find good: and whoso trusts in the LORD, happy is he.
21 The wise in heart shall be called prudent: and the sweetness of the lips increases learning.
22 Understanding is a wellspring of life unto him that has it: but the instruction of fools is folly.
23 *The heart of the wise teaches his mouth, and adds learning to his lips.*
24 Pleasant words are as an honeycomb, sweet to the soul, and health to the bones.
25 There is a way that seems right unto a man, but the end thereof are the ways of death.
26 He that labors labors for himself; for his mouth craves it of him.
27 An ungodly man digs up evil: and in his lips there is as a burning fire.
28 A froward man sows strife: and a whisperer separates chief friends.
29 A violent man entices his neighbor, and leads him into the way that is not good.
30 He shuts his eyes to devise froward things: moving his lips he brings evil to pass.
31 The hoary head is a crown of glory, if it be found in the way of righteousness.
32 *He that is slow to anger is better than the mighty; and he that rules his spirit than he that takes a city.*
33 The lot is cast into the lap; but the whole disposing thereof is of the LORD.

CHAPTER 17

BETTER is a dry morsel, and quietness therewith, than an house full of sacrifices with strife.
2 A wise servant shall have rule over a son that causes shame, and shall have part of the inheritance among the brethren.
3 The fining pot is for silver, and the furnace for gold: but the LORD tries the hearts.
4 A wicked doer gives heed to false lips; and a liar gives ear to a naughty tongue.
5 Whoso mocks the poor reproaches his Maker: and he that is glad at calamities

16:25 See Proverbs 12:15. The way of self-righteousness seems right to men. (See Proverbs 15:8 footnote.)

16:32 This is the spirit in which we should share our faith. See Luke 6:28.

"He who masters his passions is a king even while in chains. He who is ruled by his passions is a slave even while sitting on a throne." *Richard Wurmbrand*

shall not be unpunished.
6 Children's children are the crown of old men; and the glory of children are their fathers.
7 Excellent speech becomes not a fool: much less do lying lips a prince.
8 A gift is as a precious stone in the eyes of him that has it: whithersoever it turns, it prospers.
9 He that covers a transgression seeks love; but he that repeats a matter separates very friends.
10 A reproof enters more into a wise man than an hundred stripes into a fool.
11 An evil man seeks only rebellion: therefore a cruel messenger shall be sent against him.
12 Let a bear robbed of her whelps meet a man, rather than a fool in his folly.
13 Whoso rewards evil for good, evil shall not depart from his house.
14 The beginning of strife is as when one lets out water: therefore leave off contention, before it be meddled with.
15 He that justifies the wicked, and he that condemns the just, even they both are abomination to the LORD.
16 Wherefore is there a price in the hand of a fool to get wisdom, seeing he has no heart to it?
17 A friend loves at all times, and a brother is born for adversity.
18 A man void of understanding strikes hands, and becomes surety in the presence of his friend.
19 He loves transgression that loves strife: and he that exalts his gate seeks destruction.
20 He that has a froward heart finds no good: and he that has a perverse tongue falls into mischief.
21 He that begets a fool does it to his sorrow: and the father of a fool has no joy.
22 A merry heart does good like a medicine: but a broken spirit dries the bones.
23 A wicked man takes a gift out of the bosom to pervert the ways of judgment.
24 Wisdom is before him that has understanding; but the eyes of a fool are in the ends of the earth.
25 A foolish son is a grief to his father, and bitterness to her that bare him.
26 Also to punish the just is not good, nor to strike princes for equity.
27 He that has knowledge spares his words: and a man of understanding is of an excellent spirit.
28 Even a fool, when he holds his peace, is counted wise: and he that shuts his lips is esteemed a man of understanding.

CHAPTER 18

THROUGH desire a man, having separated himself, seeks and intermeddles with all wisdom.
2 A fool has no delight in understanding, but that his heart may discover itself.
3 When the wicked comes, then comes also contempt, and with ignominy reproach.
4 The words of a man's mouth are as deep waters, and the wellspring of wisdom as a flowing brook.
5 It is not good to accept the person of the wicked, to overthrow the righteous in judgment.

17:11 A rebellious heart is an open door to the demonic realm. This was the case with King Saul.

17:14 See Matthew 12:36 footnote.

17:22 Let the joy of the Lord be your strength. See Proverbs 15:15 footnote.

17:24 True riches are laid before us in the Word of God. Those who ignore these "exceedingly great and precious promises" (2 Peter 1:4) will never be content.

18:1 Never isolate yourself from other Christians. Those who are not in regular fellowship with other believers make themselves an easier target for the enemy. Satan is as a roaring lion, seeking to devour us (1 Peter 5:8). The first thing a lion does in stalking its prey is to isolate individual members from the herd. See Hebrews 10:25.

6 A fool's lips enter into contention, and his mouth calls for strokes.
7 A fool's mouth is his destruction, and his lips are the snare of his soul.
8 The words of a talebearer are as wounds, and they go down into the innermost parts of the belly.
9 He also that is slothful in his work is brother to him that is a great waster.
10 The name of the LORD is a strong tower: the righteous runs into it, and is safe.
11 The rich man's wealth is his strong city, and as an high wall in his own conceit.
12 **Before destruction the heart of man is haughty, and before honor is humility.**
13 *He that answers a matter before he hears it, it is folly and shame unto him.*
14 The spirit of a man will sustain his infirmity; but a wounded spirit who can bear?
15 The heart of the prudent gets knowledge; and the ear of the wise seeks knowledge.
16 A man's gift makes room for him, and brings him before great men.
17 He that is first in his own cause seems just; but his neighbor comes and searches him.
18 The lot causes contentions to cease, and parts between the mighty.
19 A brother offended is harder to be won than a strong city: and their contentions are like the bars of a castle.
20 A man's belly shall be satisfied with the fruit of his mouth; and with the increase of his lips shall he be filled.
21 Death and life are in the power of the tongue: and they that love it shall eat the fruit thereof.
22 Whoso finds a wife finds a good thing, and obtains favor of the LORD.
23 The poor uses entreaties; but the rich answers roughly.
24 A man that has friends must show himself friendly: and there is a friend that sticks closer than a brother.

CHAPTER 19

BETTER is the poor that walks in his integrity, than he that is perverse in his lips, and is a fool.
2 Also, that the soul be without knowledge, it is not good; and he that hastens with his feet sins.
3 The foolishness of man perverts his way: and his heart frets against the LORD.
4 Wealth makes many friends; but the poor is separated from his neighbor.
5 A false witness shall not be unpunished, and he that speaks lies shall not escape.
6 Many will entreat the favor of the prince: and every man is a friend to him that gives gifts.
7 All the brethren of the poor do hate him: how much more do his friends go far from him? he pursues them with words, yet they are wanting to him.
8 He that gets wisdom loves his own soul: he that keeps understanding shall find good.
9 **A false witness shall not be unpunished, and he that speaks lies shall perish.**
10 Delight is not seemly for a fool; much less for a servant to have rule over princes.

18:13 Be patient when sinners ramble. It is a discredit to our Christian witness to interrupt someone who is trying to tell us something, even though we have heard the empty argument many times before. Love will listen.

18:16 If you are wanting God to use you, He will open the doors in His time.

18:19 Make it a rule of life not to argue over petty doctrinal or prophetic interpretations. Strive to keep the unity of the Spirit. See Philippians 1:27.

19:3 See Romans 8:7.

19:5 Those who transgress the Ninth Commandment have a fearful fate. See Revelation 21:8.

11 *The discretion of a man defers his anger; and it is his glory to pass over a transgression.*

12 The king's wrath is as the roaring of a lion; but his favor is as dew upon the grass.

13 A foolish son is the calamity of his father: and the contentions of a wife are a continual dropping.

14 House and riches are the inheritance of fathers: and a prudent wife is from the LORD.

15 Slothfulness casts into a deep sleep; and an idle soul shall suffer hunger.

16 He that keeps the commandment keeps his own soul; but he that despises his ways shall die.

17 He that has pity upon the poor lends unto the LORD; and that which he has given will he pay him again.

18 Chasten your son while there is hope, and let not your soul spare for his crying.

19 A man of great wrath shall suffer punishment: for if you deliver him, yet you must do it again.

20 Hear counsel, and receive instruction, that you may be wise in your latter end.

21 There are many devices in a man's heart; nevertheless the counsel of the LORD, that shall stand.

22 The desire of a man is his kindness: and a poor man is better than a liar.

23 The fear of the LORD tends to life: and he that has it shall abide satisfied; he shall not be visited with evil.

24 A slothful man hides his hand in his bosom, and will not so much as bring it to his mouth again.

25 Smite a scorner, and the simple will beware: and reprove one that has understanding, and he will understand knowledge.

26 He that wastes his father, and chases away his mother, is a son that causes shame, and brings reproach.

27 Cease, my son, to hear the instruction that causes to err from the words of knowledge.

28 An ungodly witness scorns judgment: and the mouth of the wicked devours iniquity.

29 Judgments are prepared for scorners, and stripes for the back of fools.

CHAPTER 20

WINE is a mocker, strong drink is raging: and whosoever is deceived thereby is not wise.

2 The fear of a king is as the roaring of a lion: whoso provokes him to anger sins against his own soul.

3 It is an honor for a man to cease from

19:17 "We make a living by what we get, but we make a life by what we give." *Winston Churchill*

20:1 Alcohol is a poison. When someone is in-*toxic*-ated, he is "poisoned." The body protests with confused thinking, slurred speech, and impaired vision, memory, and judgment. The victim vomits. The next day his head throbs with pain, yet he still drinks the poison. Hundreds of thousands of innocent people have been maimed on the roads by drunk drivers, yet the world cannot bring itself to say, "Don't drink." It can only say, "Don't drink and drive." This is because alcohol is the only enemy man has succeeded in loving. It destroys his liver, heart, and kidneys. It gives him high blood pressure and causes blood vessels to burst in his skin. It leads him to beat his wife and abuse his kids. It will eventually destroy his ability to enjoy the intimacies of the marriage bed. Yet he still drinks.

He thinks alcohol is a "stimulant." In truth, it is a suppressant that reduces his inhibitions. It dulls the naggings of his conscience so that he can commit sexual and other sins that he couldn't indulge in while sober. A man who gives himself to the demon of alcohol becomes a slave to its addictive properties. It mocks him. It steals his dignity. It takes control of his will. Whoever is deceived by it (and there are millions) is not wise. See Proverbs 23:29–35.

20:3 It takes no skill to "argue" with sinners. We are called to reason—to plead with love and gentleness.

QUESTIONS & OBJECTIONS

20:9 ***"I used to be a liar and a thief, but that was years ago. Now I try to be a good person."***

Time doesn't forgive sin. If a man commits murder on Monday, but on Tuesday he is kind to others, he is still a murderer. If a man lies and steals, unless he comes to the Savior, his sins remain with him until he stands before God in judgment.

strife: but every fool will be meddling.

4 The sluggard will not plow by reason of the cold; therefore shall he beg in harvest, and have nothing.

5 Counsel in the heart of man is like deep water; but a man of understanding will draw it out.

6 Most men will proclaim every one his own goodness: but a faithful man who can find?

7 The just man walks in his integrity: his children are blessed after him.

8 A king that sits in the throne of judgment scatters away all evil with his eyes.

9 Who can say, I have made my heart clean, I am pure from my sin?

10 Divers weights, and divers measures, both of them are alike abomination to the LORD.

11 Even a child is known by his doings, whether his work be pure, and whether it be right.

12 The hearing ear, and the seeing eye, the LORD has made even both of them.

13 Love not sleep, lest you come to poverty; open your eyes, and you shall be satisfied with bread.

14 It is naught, it is naught, says the buyer: but when he is gone his way, then he boasts.

15 There is gold, and a multitude of rubies: but the lips of knowledge are a precious jewel.

16 Take his garment that is surety for a stranger: and take a pledge of him for a strange woman.

17 Bread of deceit is sweet to a man; but afterwards his mouth shall be filled with gravel.

18 Every purpose is established by counsel: and with good advice make war.

19 He that goes about as a talebearer reveals secrets: therefore meddle not with him that flatters with his lips.

20 Whoso curses his father or his mother, his lamp shall be put out in obscure darkness.

21 An inheritance may be gotten hastily at the beginning; but the end thereof shall not be blessed.

22 Say not, I will recompense evil; but wait on the LORD, and he shall save you.

23 Divers weights are an abomination unto the LORD; and a false balance is not good.

24 Man's goings are of the LORD; how

20:6 If you ask a man if he thinks he is a good person, he usually will say that he is. That's why we need to use the Law (which the Bible says in "good") to give him understanding about what "good" is (Romans 7:12). See Proverbs 21:2.

20:9 No man can do this. Only God can cleanse man's heart of sin and make him pure. See 1 John 1:9.

20:11 Those who deny the reality of the sinful nature haven't had children. See Proverbs 29:15 footnote.

20:12 See Psalm 94:7–11.

can a man then understand his own way?
25 It is a snare to the man who devours that which is holy, and after vows to make enquiry.
26 A wise king scatters the wicked, and brings the wheel over them.
27 The spirit of man is the candle of the LORD, searching all the inward parts of the belly.
28 Mercy and truth preserve the king: and his throne is upheld by mercy.
29 The glory of young men is their strength: and the beauty of old men is the grey head.
30 The blueness of a wound cleanses away evil: so do stripes the inward parts of the belly.

CHAPTER 21

THE king's heart is in the hand of the LORD, as the rivers of water: he turns it whithersoever he will.
2 Every way of a man is right in his own eyes: but the LORD ponders the hearts.
3 To do justice and judgment is more acceptable to the LORD than sacrifice.
4 An high look, and a proud heart, and the plowing of the wicked, is sin.
5 The thoughts of the diligent tend only to plenteousness; but of every one that is hasty only to want.
6 The getting of treasures by a lying tongue is a vanity tossed to and fro of them that seek death.
7 The robbery of the wicked shall destroy them; because they refuse to do judgment.
8 The way of man is froward and strange: but as for the pure, his work is right.
9 It is better to dwell in a corner of the housetop, than with a brawling woman in a wide house.
10 The soul of the wicked desires evil: his neighbor finds no favor in his eyes.
11 When the scorner is punished, the simple is made wise: and when the wise is instructed, he receives knowledge.
12 The righteous man wisely considers the house of the wicked: but God overthrows the wicked for their wickedness.
13 Whoso stops his ears at the cry of the poor, he also shall cry himself, but shall not be heard.
14 A gift in secret pacifies anger: and a reward in the bosom strong wrath.
15 It is joy to the just to do judgment: but destruction shall be to the workers of iniquity.
16 The man that wanders out of the way of understanding shall remain in the congregation of the dead.
17 He that loves pleasure shall be a poor man: he that loves wine and oil shall not

21:1 This is our great confidence when preaching to sinners. God has control of the hearts of men and women.

21:2 Right in his own eyes. Consider the way dogs cross the road. A dog will wander onto a freeway oblivious to the danger. His tail wags as he steps between cars without a second thought. Cars swerve. Tires squeal. The noise is deafening as vehicles smash into each other. The sleepy dog stops wagging his tail for a moment and looks at the pile of smoldering, broken cars on the freeway. His expression betrays his thoughts. His bone-burying brain doesn't realize for one moment that he is responsible for the disaster.

When man wanders onto the freeway of sin, his tail wags with delight. He thinks that this is what he was made for. His thoughts of any repercussions for his actions are shallow. His mind wanders into lust, then predictably he wanders onto the path of adultery. Suddenly a disaster sits before him. His marriage is shattered, his name is slurred, his children are twisted and scarred. But like the dumb dog, he doesn't realize for one moment that he is solely responsible for his sin.

This is why the perfect Law of God needs to be arrayed before his darkened eyes—to show him that his way is not right in the eyes of a perfect God.

21:6 It has been rightly said that taking the easy path is what makes men and rivers crooked.

21:10 Sinful men have no trouble seeing other people's sins.

be rich.
18 The wicked shall be a ransom for the righteous, and the transgressor for the upright.
19 It is better to dwell in the wilderness, than with a contentious and an angry woman.
20 There is treasure to be desired and oil in the dwelling of the wise; but a foolish man spends it up.
21 He that follows after righteousness and mercy finds life, righteousness, and honor.
22 A wise man scales the city of the mighty, and casts down the strength of the confidence thereof.
23 Whoso keeps his mouth and his tongue keeps his soul from troubles.
24 Proud and haughty scorner is his name, who deals in proud wrath.
25 The desire of the slothful kills him; for his hands refuse to labor.
26 He covets greedily all the day long: but the righteous gives and spares not.
27 The sacrifice of the wicked is abomination: how much more, when he brings it with a wicked mind?
28 A false witness shall perish: but the man that hears speaks constantly.
29 A wicked man hardens his face: but as for the upright, he directs his way.
30 There is no wisdom nor understanding nor counsel against the LORD.
31 The horse is prepared against the day of battle: but safety is of the LORD.

CHAPTER 22

A GOOD name is rather to be chosen than great riches, and loving favor rather than silver and gold.
2 The rich and poor meet together: the LORD is the maker of them all.
3 A prudent man foresees the evil, and hides himself: but the simple pass on, and are punished.
4 By humility and the fear of the LORD are riches, and honor, and life.
5 Thorns and snares are in the way of the froward: he that does keep his soul shall be far from them.
6 Train up a child in the way he should go: and when he is old, he will not depart from it.
7 The rich rules over the poor, and the borrower is servant to the lender.
8 He that sows iniquity shall reap vanity: and the rod of his anger shall fail.
9 He that has a bountiful eye shall be blessed; for he gives of his bread to the poor.
10 Cast out the scorner, and contention shall go out; yes, strife and reproach shall

---

21:23 Be slow to speak your personal opinions, and save yourself a great deal of trouble.

21:24 The proud, arrogant, and angry scorner gravitates to open-air preaching. These will be prevalent in the last days (2 Peter 3:3). The Scriptures reveal that the reason for their contention is that they are given to lust.

21:27 Mankind can never atone for his own sins and buy immortality by giving to charitable causes. Eternal life is a gift of God. See Romans 6:23; Ephesians 2:8,9.

22:1 We must guard our name, character, and reputation for the sake of the gospel. If men think evil of us, let it be only for the cause of righteousness.

22:4 Those who refuse to humble themselves will eventually lose their possessions, their dignity, and their very life. However, those who walk in humility of heart and obey God store up an eternal treasure in heaven. They will preserve their life and be honored by God Himself. See John 12:25.

22:6 Training our children. "Let the children . . . be carefully instructed in the principles and obligations of the Christian religion. This is the most essential part of education. The great enemy of the salvation of man, in my opinion, never invented a more effectual means of extirpating [removing] Christianity from the world than by persuading mankind that it was improper to read the Bible at schools." *Benjamin Rush* (See also Proverbs 4:1–5 and Ephesians 6:4 footnotes.)

cease.
11 He that loves pureness of heart, for the grace of his lips the king shall be his friend.
12 The eyes of the LORD preserve knowledge, and he overthrows the words of the transgressor.
13 The slothful man says, There is a lion without, I shall be slain in the streets.
14 The mouth of strange women is a deep pit: he that is abhorred of the LORD shall fall therein.
15 Foolishness is bound in the heart of a child; but the rod of correction shall drive it far from him.
16 He that oppresses the poor to increase his riches, and he that gives to the rich, shall surely come to want.
17 Bow down your ear, and hear the words of the wise, and apply your heart unto my knowledge.
18 For it is a pleasant thing if you keep them within you; they shall withal be fitted in your lips.
19 That your trust may be in the LORD, I have made known to you this day, even to you.
20 Have not I written to you excellent things in counsels and knowledge,
21 That I might make you know the certainty of the words of truth; that you might answer the words of truth to them that send unto you?
22 Rob not the poor, because he is poor: neither oppress the afflicted in the gate:
23 For the LORD will plead their cause, and spoil the soul of those that spoiled them.
24 Make no friendship with an angry man; and with a furious man you shall not go:
25 Lest you learn his ways, and get a snare to your soul.
26 Be not one of them that strike hands, or of them that are sureties for debts.
27 If you have nothing to pay, why should he take away your bed from under you?
28 Remove not the ancient landmark, which your fathers have set.
29 See a man diligent in his business? he shall stand before kings; he shall not stand before mean men.

CHAPTER 23

WHEN you sit to eat with a ruler, consider diligently what is before you:
2 And put a knife to your throat, if you be a man given to appetite.
3 Be not desirous of his dainties: for they are deceitful meat.
4 Labor not to be rich: cease from your own wisdom.
5 Will you set your eyes upon that which is not? for riches certainly make themselves wings; they fly away as an eagle toward heaven.
6 Eat not the bread of him that has an evil eye, neither desire his dainty meats:
7 For as he thinks in his heart, so is he: Eat and drink, says he to you; but his heart is not with you.
8 The morsel which you have eaten shall you vomit up, and lose your sweet words.
9 Speak not in the ears of a fool: for he will despise the wisdom of your words.
10 Remove not the old landmark; and enter not into the fields of the fatherless:
11 For their redeemer is mighty; he shall plead their cause with you.
12 Apply your heart unto instruction, and your ears to the words of knowledge.
13 Withhold not correction from the child: for if you beat him with the rod, he shall not die.
14 You shall beat him with the rod, and shall deliver his soul from hell.
15 My son, if your heart be wise, my heart shall rejoice, even mine.
16 Yes, my reins shall rejoice, when your

23:12 There is no greater way to do this than to read and meditate on God's Word every day. Say to yourself, "No Bible, no breakfast. No read, no feed." Put your Bible before your belly. See Psalm 1, and mediate on the promises for those who do this.

lips speak right things.
17 Let not your heart envy sinners: but be in the fear of the LORD all the day long.
18 For surely there is an end; and your expectation shall not be cut off.
19 Hear, my son, and be wise, and guide your heart in the way.
20 Be not among winebibbers; among riotous eaters of flesh:
21 For the drunkard and the glutton shall come to poverty: and drowsiness shall clothe a man with rags.
22 Hearken unto your father that begat you, and despise not your mother when she is old.
23 Buy the truth, and sell it not; also wisdom, and instruction, and understanding.
24 The father of the righteous shall greatly rejoice: and he that begets a wise child shall have joy of him.
25 Your father and your mother shall be glad, and she that bare you shall rejoice.
26 My son, give me your heart, and let your eyes observe my ways.
27 For a whore is a deep ditch; and a strange woman is a narrow pit.
28 She also lies in wait as for a prey, and increases the transgressors among men.
29 Who has woe? who has sorrow? who has contentions? who has babbling? who has wounds without cause? who has redness of eyes?
30 They that tarry long at the wine; they that go to seek mixed wine.
31 Look not upon the wine when it is red, when it gives his color in the cup, when it moves itself aright.
32 At the last it bites like a serpent, and stings like an adder.
33 Your eyes shall behold strange women, and your heart shall utter perverse things.
34 Yes, you shall be as he that lies down in the midst of the sea, or as he that lies upon the top of a mast.
35 They have stricken me, shall you say, and I was not sick; they have beaten me, and I felt it not: when shall I awake? I will seek it yet again.

CHAPTER 24

BE not envious against evil men, neither desire to be with them.
2 For their heart studies destruction, and their lips talk of mischief.
3 Through wisdom is an house built; and by understanding it is established:
4 And by knowledge shall the chambers be filled with all precious and pleasant riches.
5 A wise man is strong; yes, a man of knowledge increases strength.
6 For by wise counsel you shall make your war: and in multitude of counselors there is safety.
7 Wisdom is too high for a fool: he opens not his mouth in the gate.
8 He that devises to do evil shall be called a mischievous person.
9 The thought of foolishness is sin: and

23:17 See Psalm 73.

23:23 It is sad that so many Christian ministries demand money from their audience, often with the promise that God will bless them if they give. God knows the motives of the preacher, but the unsaved don't, and are therefore easily deceived by the practice. We should be careful never to give the impression that our motivation is the love of money.

23:24,25 This is the fruit of obedience to the Fifth Commandment.

23:29–35 See Proverbs 20:1 footnote.

24:3,4 Jesus Christ and His teachings are the only sure foundation. See Colossians 1:9; Matthew 7:24.

24:9 Never be discouraged when a man mocks you when you are preaching the gospel. Your love, gentleness, and reasonableness will be seen to contrast his foolishness.

the scorner is an abomination to men.
10 If you faint in the day of adversity, your strength is small.
11 If you forbear to deliver them that are drawn unto death, and those that are ready to be slain;
12 If you say, Behold, we knew it not; does not he that ponders the heart consider it? and he that keeps your soul, does not he know it? and shall not he render to every man according to his works?

> Nothing can damn a man but his own righteousness; nothing can save him but the righteousness of Christ.
>
> **CHARLES SPURGEON**

13 My son, eat honey, because it is good; and the honeycomb, which is sweet to your taste:
14 So shall the knowledge of wisdom be unto your soul: when you have found it, then there shall be a reward, and your expectation shall not be cut off.
15 Lay not wait, O wicked man, against the dwelling of the righteous; spoil not his resting place:
16 For a just man falls seven times, and rises up again: but the wicked shall fall into mischief.
17 Rejoice not when your enemy falls, and let not your heart be glad when he stumbles:
18 Lest the LORD see it, and it displease him, and he turn away his wrath from him.
19 Fret not thyself because of evil men, neither be envious at the wicked:
20 For there shall be no reward to the evil man; the candle of the wicked shall be put out.
21 My son, fear the LORD and the king: and meddle not with them that are given to change:
22 For their calamity shall rise suddenly; and who knows the ruin of them both?
23 These things also belong to the wise. It is not good to have respect of persons in judgment.
24 *He that says unto the wicked, You are righteous; him shall the people curse, nations shall abhor him:*
25 *But to them that rebuke him shall be delight, and a good blessing shall come upon them.*
26 *Every man shall kiss his lips that gives a right answer.*
27 Prepare your work without, and make it fit for thyself in the field; and afterwards build your house.
28 Be not a witness against your neighbor without cause; and deceive not with your lips.
29 Say not, I will do so to him as he has done to me: I will render to the man according to his work.
30 I went by the field of the slothful, and by the vineyard of the man void of understanding;
31 And, lo, it was all grown over with thorns, and nettles had covered the face thereof, and the stone wall thereof was broken down.
32 Then I saw, and considered it well: I looked upon it, and received instruction.
33 Yet a little sleep, a little slumber, a little folding of the hands to sleep:
34 So shall your poverty come as one that travels; and your want as an armed man.

CHAPTER 25

THESE are also proverbs of Solomon, which the men of Hezekiah king of

24:11,12 Surely these verses were written for those slothful servants who shun the task of evangelism. See Matthew 25:14–30.

24:25 We are to "preach the word; be instant in season, [and] out of season," and to "reprove, rebuke, exhort with all longsuffering and doctrine" (2 Timothy 4:2). Do this, and you will have the promise of the blessing of God.

Judah copied out.
2 It is the glory of God to conceal a thing:
but the honor of kings is to search out a
matter.
3 The heaven for height, and the earth for
depth, and the heart of kings is unsearchable.
4 Take away the dross from the silver,
and there shall come forth a vessel for the
finer.
5 Take away the wicked from before the
king, and his throne shall be established
in righteousness.
6 Put not forth yourself in the presence
of the king, and stand not in the place of
great men:
7 For better it is that it be said unto you,
Come up hither; than that you should be
put lower in the presence of the prince
whom your eyes have seen.
8 Go not forth hastily to strive, lest you
know not what to do in the end thereof,
when your neighbor has put you to shame.
9 Debate your cause with your neighbor
himself; and discover not a secret to another:
10 Lest he that hears it put you to shame,
and your infamy turn not away.
11 A word fitly spoken is like apples of
gold in pictures of silver.
12 As an earring of gold, and an ornament of fine gold, so is a wise reprover
upon an obedient ear.
13 As the cold of snow in the time of
harvest, so is a faithful messenger to them
that send him: for he refreshes the soul
of his masters.
14 Whoso boasts himself of a false gift
is like clouds and wind without rain.
15 By long forbearing is a prince persuaded, and a soft tongue breaks the bone.
16 Have you found honey? eat so much
as is sufficient for you, lest you be filled
therewith, and vomit it.
17 Withdraw your foot from your neighbor's house; lest he be weary of you, and
so hate you.
18 A man that bears false witness against
his neighbor is a maul, and a sword, and a
sharp arrow.
19 *Confidence in an unfaithful man in time
of trouble is like a broken tooth, and a foot
out of joint.*
20 As he that takes away a garment in
cold weather, and as vinegar upon nitre,
so is he that sings songs to an heavy heart.
21 If your enemy be hungry, give him
bread to eat; and if he be thirsty, give him
water to drink:
22 For you shall heap coals of fire upon
his head, and the LORD shall reward you.
23 The north wind drives away rain: so
does an angry countenance a backbiting
tongue.
24 It is better to dwell in the corner of
the housetop, than with a brawling woman and in a wide house.
25 As cold waters to a thirsty soul, so is
good news from a far country.
26 A righteous man falling down before
the wicked is as a troubled fountain, and
a corrupt spring.
27 It is not good to eat much honey: so
for men to search their own glory is not
glory.
28 He that has no rule over his own spirit is like a city that is broken down, and
without walls.

CHAPTER 26

AS snow in summer, and as rain in
harvest, so honor is not seemly for a
fool.
2 As the bird by wandering, as the swallow by flying, so the curse causeless shall
not come.
3 A whip for the horse, a bridle for the
ass, and a rod for the fool's back.

25:19 A broken tooth or a foot out of joint cause the most pain when they are put under pressure. How do we react when we are put under pressure to share our faith?

25:28 We allow the enemy entrance when we give the flesh free reign, having no self-control over our spirit.

4 Answer not a fool according to his folly, lest you also be like unto him.
5 Answer a fool according to his folly, lest he be wise in his own conceit.
6 He that sends a message by the hand of a fool cuts off the feet, and drinks damage.
7 The legs of the lame are not equal: so is a parable in the mouth of fools.
8 As he that binds a stone in a sling, so is he that gives honor to a fool.
9 As a thorn goes up into the hand of a drunkard, so is a parable in the mouths of fools.
10 The great God that formed all things both rewards the fool, and rewards transgressors.
11 As a dog returns to his vomit, so a fool returns to his folly.
12 See a man wise in his own conceit? there is more hope of a fool than of him.
13 The slothful man says, There is a lion in the way; a lion is in the streets.
14 As the door turns upon his hinges, so does the slothful upon his bed.
15 The slothful hides his hand in his bosom; it grieves him to bring it again to his mouth.
16 The sluggard is wiser in his own conceit than seven men that can render a reason.
17 He that passes by, and meddles with strife belonging not to him, is like one that takes a dog by the ears.
18 As a mad man who casts firebrands, arrows, and death,
19 So is the man that deceives his neighbor, and says, Am not I in sport?
20 Where no wood is, there the fire goes out: so where there is no talebearer, the strife ceases.
21 As coals are to burning coals, and wood to fire; so is a contentious man to kindle strife.
22 The words of a talebearer are as wounds, and they go down into the innermost parts of the belly.
23 Burning lips and a wicked heart are like a potsherd covered with silver dross.
24 He that hates dissembles with his lips, and lays up deceit within him;
25 When he speaks fair, believe him not: for there are seven abominations in his heart.
26 Whose hatred is covered by deceit, his wickedness shall be showed before the whole congregation.
27 Whoso digs a pit shall fall therein: and he that rolls a stone, it will return upon him.
28 A lying tongue hates those that are afflicted by it; and a flattering mouth works ruin.

CHAPTER 27

BOAST not yourself of tomorrow; for you know not what a day may bring forth.
2 *Let another man praise you, and not your own mouth; a stranger, and not your own lips.*
3 A stone is heavy, and the sand weighty; but a fool's wrath is heavier than them both.

26:10 The word "great" cannot describe how great God is. Worship takes over where words fail. Our God formed *all* things. They didn't evolve after a big bang.

26:12 New Age blasphemy. The inevitable result of man's darkened understanding is that he will think that he is God. His pride takes over his brain.

"We no longer feel ourselves to be guests in someone else's home and therefore obliged to make our behavior conform with a set of preexisting cosmic rules. It is our creation now. We make the rules. We establish the parameters of reality. We create the world, and because we do, we no longer feel beholden to outside forces. We no longer have to justify our behavior, for we are now the architects of the universe. We are responsible to nothing outside ourselves, for we are the kingdom, the power, and the glory forever and ever." *Jeremy Rifkin, Algeny*

26:17 This is wonderful guidance for the sincere Christian on what not to do. He who meddles will get hurt.

QUESTIONS & OBJECTIONS

27:10 *"How do I reach my neighbors with the gospel?"*

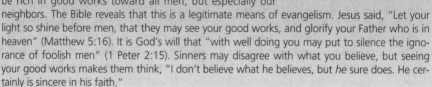

Neighbors are like family. We don't want to offend them unnecessarily, because we have to live with them. We need to be rich in good works toward all men, but especially our neighbors. The Bible reveals that this is a legitimate means of evangelism. Jesus said, "Let your light so shine before men, that they may see your good works, and glorify your Father who is in heaven" (Matthew 5:16). It is God's will that "with well doing you may put to silence the ignorance of foolish men" (1 Peter 2:15). Sinners may disagree with what you believe, but seeing your good works makes them think, "I don't believe what he believes, but *he* sure does. He certainly is sincere in his faith."

A friendly wave, a gift for no reason, fresh-baked goods, etc., can pave the way for evangelism. Offer to mow your neighbors' lawn or help do some painting. Volunteer to pick up their mail and newspapers while they're on vacation. Compliment them on their landscaping and ask for gardening tips. Invite them over for a barbecue or dessert. Pray for an opportunity to share the gospel, and be prepared for it when it comes.

4 Wrath is cruel, and anger is outrageous; but who is able to stand before envy?
5 *Open rebuke is better than secret love.*
6 Faithful are the wounds of a friend; but the kisses of an enemy are deceitful.
7 The full soul loathes an honeycomb; but to the hungry soul every bitter thing is sweet.
8 As a bird that wanders from her nest, so is a man that wanders from his place.
9 Ointment and perfume rejoice the heart: so does the sweetness of a man's friend by hearty counsel.
10 Your own friend, and your father's friend, forsake not; neither go into your brother's house in the day of your calamity: for better is a neighbor that is near than a brother far off.
11 My son, be wise, and make my heart glad, that I may answer him that reproaches me.
12 A prudent man foresees the evil, and hides himself; but the simple pass on, and are punished.
13 Take his garment that is surety for a stranger, and take a pledge of him for a strange woman.
14 He that blesses his friend with a loud voice, rising early in the morning, it shall be counted a curse to him.
15 A continual dropping in a very rainy day and a contentious woman are alike.
16 Whosoever hides her hides the wind, and the ointment of his right hand, which bewrays itself.
17 Iron sharpens iron; so a man sharpens the countenance of his friend.
18 Whoso keeps the fig tree shall eat the fruit thereof: so he that waits on his master shall be honored.
19 As in water face answers to face, so the heart of man to man.
20 Hell and destruction are never full; so the eyes of man are never satisfied.
21 As the fining pot for silver, and the furnace for gold; so is a man to his praise.

27:1 The only thing we can be sure of is the breath going into our lungs at this moment. We can't be sure of the next breath. That comes only by the permission of God. See James 4:13–16 and Luke 12:20 footnote.

27:5 We openly rebuke those in the world for their sin because we love them and are concerned for their eternal welfare.

22 Though you should bray a fool in a
mortar among wheat with a pestle, yet
will not his foolishness depart from him.
23 Be diligent to know the state of your
flocks, and look well to your herds.
24 For riches are not for ever: and does
the crown endure to every generation?
25 The hay appears, and the tender grass
show itself, and herbs of the mountains
are gathered.
26 The lambs are for your clothing, and
the goats are the price of the field.
27 And you shall have goats' milk enough
for your food, for the food of your household, and for the maintenance for your
maidens.

CHAPTER 28

THE wicked flee when no man pursues:
but the righteous are bold as a lion.
2 For the transgression of a land many
are the princes thereof: but by a man of
understanding and knowledge the state
thereof shall be prolonged.
3 A poor man that oppresses the poor is
like a sweeping rain which leaves no food.
4 *They that forsake the law praise the*
wicked: but such as keep the law contend
with them.
5 Evil men understand not judgment:
but they that seek the LORD understand
all things.
6 Better is the poor that walks in his uprightness, than he that is perverse in his
ways, though he be rich.
7 Whoso keeps the law is a wise son:
but he that is a companion of riotous
men shames his father.
8 He that by usury and unjust gain increases his substance, he shall gather it
for him that will pity the poor.
9 He that turns away his ear from hear-
ing the law, even his prayer shall be
abomination.
10 Whoso causes the righteous to go
astray in an evil way, he shall fall himself
into his own pit: but the upright shall
have good things in possession.
11 The rich man is wise in his own conceit; but the poor that has understanding
searches him out.
12 When righteous men do rejoice, there
is great glory: but when the wicked rise,
a man is hidden.

27:20 Men can never satisfy lust. It is an unquenchable inferno. The more it is given fuel, the more it continues to burn. Desire will make him crave sexual pleasure, money, fame, and power. He will continue to "want" until the Lord becomes his shepherd. See Psalm 23:1.

27:25 Marijuana advocates often point to Genesis 1:11 ("Let the earth bring forth grass") and other verses (Genesis 1:29; 3:18) to justify the smoking of what they refer to as "grass." They claim that God declared marijuana "good." However, He also made sand (which is good), but if we eat it by the spoonful we shouldn't complain if we get sick. Those who inhale the burning fumes of a weed shouldn't complain when it mentally impairs them. It is called "dope" for a reason.

28:4 When the Church forsakes the proclamation of God's Law, iniquity floods the land. *Daniel Webster* stated: "If truth is not diffused, error will be. If God and His Word are not known and received, the devil and his works will gain the ascendancy. If the evangelical volume does not reach every hamlet, the pages of a corrupt and licentious literature will.

"If the power of the gospel is not felt throughout the length and breadth of this land, anarchy and misrule, degradation and misery, corruption and darkness will reign without mitigation or end."

28:5 "God's justice stands forever against the sinner in utter severity. The vague and tenuous hope that God is too kind to punish the ungodly has become a deadly opiate for the consciences of millions. It hushes their fears and allows them to practice all pleasant forms of iniquity while death draws every day nearer and the command to repent goes unregarded. As responsible moral beings, we dare not so trifle with our eternal future." *A. W. Tozer, The Knowledge of the Holy*

28:9 If a professing Christian thinks that he can willfully serve sin by transgressing the Moral Law and still have peace with God, he is deceived.

13 He that covers his sins shall not prosper: but whoso confesses and forsakes them shall have mercy.
14 Happy is the man that fears always: but he that hardens his heart shall fall into mischief.
15 As a roaring lion, and a ranging bear; so is a wicked ruler over the poor people.
16 The prince that wants understanding is also a great oppressor: but he that hates covetousness shall prolong his days.
17 A man that does violence to the blood of any person shall flee to the pit; let no man stay him.
18 Whoso walks uprightly shall be saved: but he that is perverse in his ways shall fall at once.
19 He that tills his land shall have plenty of bread: but he that follows after vain persons shall have poverty enough.
20 A faithful man shall abound with blessings: but he that makes haste to be rich shall not be innocent.
21 To have respect of persons is not good: for for a piece of bread that man will transgress.
22 He that hastens to be rich has an evil eye, and considers not that poverty shall come upon him.
23 *He that rebukes a man afterwards shall find more favor than he that flatters with the tongue.*
24 Whoso robs his father or his mother, and says, It is no transgression; the same is the companion of a destroyer.
25 He that is of a proud heart stirs up strife: but he that puts his trust in the LORD shall be made fat.
26 He that trusts in his own heart is a fool: but whoso walks wisely, he shall be delivered.
27 He that gives unto the poor shall not lack: but he that hides his eyes shall have many a curse.
28 When the wicked rise, men hide themselves: but when they perish, the righteous increase.

CHAPTER 29

HE, that being often reproved hardens his neck, shall suddenly be destroyed, and that without remedy.
2 When the righteous are in authority, the people rejoice: but when the wicked bears rule, the people mourn.
3 Whoso loves wisdom rejoices his fa-

28:13 Sin cannot be covered from the eyes of a holy Creator. Biblical conversion not only comes from confessing sin to God, but also from forsaking sin. Those who do that and trust the Savior partake in the mercy of God.

Confessing our sins. "Whereas, it is the duty of nations as well as of men to own their dependence upon the overruling power if God, to confess their sins and transgressions in humble sorrow yet with assured hope that genuine repentance will lead to mercy and pardon, and to recognize the sublime truth, announced in the Holy Scriptures and proven by all history: that those nations only are blessed whose God is the Lord…

"We have been the recipients of the choicest bounties of Heaven. We have been preserved these many years in peace and prosperity. We have grown in numbers, wealth and power as no other nation has ever grown. But we have forgotten God. We have forgotten the gracious Hand which preserved us in peace, and multiplied and enriched and strengthened us; and we have vainly imagined, in the deceitfulness of our hearts, that all these blessings were produced by some superior wisdom and virtue of our own.

"Intoxicated with unbroken success, we have become too self-sufficient to feel the necessity of redeeming and preserving grace, too proud to pray to the God that made us!

"It behooves us then to humble ourselves before the offended Power, to confess our national sins and to pray for clemency and forgiveness." *Abraham Lincoln*, 1863, in declaring a day of national fasting, prayer, and humiliation

28:26 Never give in to the temptation to trust your feelings over God's promises. See Proverbs 3:5,6.

ther: but he that keeps company with harlots spends his substance.
4 The king by judgment establishes the land: but he that receives gifts overthrows it.
5 A man that flatters his neighbor spreads a net for his feet.
6 In the transgression of an evil man there is a snare: but the righteous does sing and rejoice.
7 The righteous considers the cause of the poor: but the wicked regards not to know it.
8 Scornful men bring a city into a snare: but wise men turn away wrath.
9 If a wise man contends with a foolish man, whether he rage or laugh, there is no rest.
10 The bloodthirsty hate the upright: but the just seek his soul.
11 A fool utters all his mind: but a wise man keeps it in till afterwards.
12 If a ruler hearken to lies, all his servants are wicked.
13 The poor and the deceitful man meet together: the LORD lightens both their eyes.
14 The king that faithfully judges the poor, his throne shall be established for ever.
15 The rod and reproof give wisdom: but a child left to himself brings his mother to shame.
16 When the wicked are multiplied, transgression increases: but the righteous shall see their fall.
17 Correct your son, and he shall give you rest; yes, he shall give delight unto your soul.
18 Where there is no vision, the people perish: but he that keeps the law, happy is he.
19 A servant will not be corrected by words: for though he understand he will not answer.
20 See a man that is hasty in his words? there is more hope of a fool than of him.
21 He that delicately brings up his servant from a child shall have him become his son at the length.
22 An angry man stirs up strife, and a furious man abounds in transgression.
23 A man's pride shall bring him low: but honor shall uphold the humble in spirit.
24 Whoso is partner with a thief hates his own soul: he hears cursing, and bewrays it not.
25 The fear of man brings a snare: but whoso puts his trust in the LORD shall be

29:1 It is a fearful thought that God would lose patience with those who harden their hearts against Him. Jesus spoke of a man to whom God said, "This night your soul shall be required of you" (Luke 12:20). It is prudent to warn sinners that God may lose patience with them and let death seize them, as He did with Ananias and Sapphira (Acts 5:1–10).

29:2 **Righteous authority.** When believers fulfill their responsibility to elect righteous leaders, the entire country benefits.

"In selecting men for office, let principle be your guide. Regard not the particular sect or denomination of the candidate—look to his character… It is alleged by men of loose principles, or defective views of the subject, that religion and morality are not necessary or important qualifications for political stations. But the Scriptures teach a different doctrine. They direct that rulers should be men who rule in the fear of God, able men, such as fear God, men of truth, hating covetousness…

"When a citizen gives his vote to a man of known immorality, he abuses his civic responsibility; he sacrifices not only his own interest, but that of his neighbor; he betrays the interest of his country." *Noah Webster*

29:9 It has been well said that a wise man will learn more from a fool's question than a fool will learn from a wise man's answer.

29:15 A child doesn't learn to do evil; he naturally knows how to be selfish and lie. However, he must be taught to share and truthful. See Proverbs 20:11.

29:25 See Psalm 56:11 footnote.

QUESTIONS & OBJECTIONS

30:5

"The fact that there are so many versions proves that the Bible has mistakes. Which one is right?"

True, there are many different versions of the Bible. There are versions in Chinese for the Chinese. There are versions in Russian for the Russian people. There are actually thousands of versions of the Bible—some are in modern languages, some in foreign languages, and some are in old English. Few, in the printing age, can claim that they don't have access to the Scriptures in their own language. However, each translation is based on the original biblical texts. See Psalm 119:105 footnote.

safe.
26 Many seek the ruler's favor; but every
man's judgment comes from the LORD.
27 *An unjust man is an abomination to*
the just: and he that is upright in the way is
abomination to the wicked.

CHAPTER 30

THE words of Agur the son of Jakeh,
even the prophecy: the man spoke
unto Ithiel, even unto Ithiel and Ucal,
2 Surely I am more brutish than any
man, and have not the understanding of
a man.
3 I neither learned wisdom, nor have
the knowledge of the holy.
4 Who has ascended up into heaven, or
descended? who has gathered the wind
in his fists? who has bound the waters in
a garment? who has established all the
ends of the earth? what is his name, and
what is his son's name, if you can tell?
5 Every word of God is pure: he is a
shield unto them that put their trust in
him.
6 Add not unto his words, lest he reprove you, and you be found a liar.
7 Two things have I required of you;
deny me them not before I die:
8 Remove far from me vanity and lies:
give me neither poverty nor riches; feed
me with food convenient for me:
9 Lest I be full, and deny you, and say,
Who is the Lord? or lest I be poor, and
steal, and take the name of my God in vain.
10 Accuse not a servant unto his master,
lest he curse you, and you be found guilty.
11 There is a generation that curses their
father, and does not bless their mother.
12 There is a generation that are pure
in their own eyes, and yet is not washed
from their filthiness.
13 There is a generation, O how lofty are
their eyes! and their eyelids are lifted up.
14 There is a generation, whose teeth are
as swords, and their jaw teeth as knives,
to devour the poor from off the earth, and
the needy from among men.

29:27 This is why the world hates the Christian. See John 15:18,19.

30:1,2 This is the foundational key to learning. See 1 Corinthians 1:21; 3:18.

30:4 His name is "I AM" and His Son's name is Jesus Christ. See Psalm 2:12.

30:5 *All* Scripture is given by inspiration of God (2 Timothy 3:16), and is His complete revelation to mankind. Many religions accept the words of Scripture, but consider them to be only part of the truth. Those who have added anything to God's Holy Word are in great error.

30:11,12 What better description do we have of this lawless generation? By transgressing the Fifth Commandment, it reaps the fearful consequences of disobedience and fails to receive the promise given in Ephesians 6:1–3. Because they have been left without the light of the Moral Law, they consider themselves pure and have therefore become a law to themselves.

15 The horseleach has two daughters, crying, Give, give. There are three things that are never satisfied, yes, four things say not, It is enough:
16 The grave; and the barren womb; the earth that is not filled with water; and the fire that says not, It is enough.
17 The eye that mocks at his father, and despises to obey his mother, the ravens of the valley shall pick it out, and the young eagles shall eat it.
18 There be three things which are too wonderful for me, yes, four which I know not:
19 The way of an eagle in the air; the way of a serpent upon a rock; the way of a ship in the midst of the sea; and the way of a man with a maid.
20 Such is the way of an adulterous woman; she eats and wipes her mouth, and says, I have done no wickedness.
21 For three things the earth is disquieted, and for four which it cannot bear:
22 For a servant when he reigns; and a fool when he is filled with meat;
23 For an odious woman when she is married; and an handmaid that is heir to her mistress.
24 There be four things which are little upon the earth, but they are exceeding wise:
25 The ants are a people not strong, yet they prepare their meat in the summer;
26 The conies are but a feeble folk, yet make they their houses in the rocks;
27 The locusts have no king, yet go they forth all of them by bands;
28 The spider takes hold with her hands, and is in kings' palaces.
29 There be three things which go well, yes, four are comely in going:
30 A lion which is strongest among beasts, and turns not away for any;
31 A greyhound; an he goat also; and a king, against whom there is no rising up.
32 If you have done foolishly in lifting up yourself, or if you have thought evil, lay your hand upon your mouth.
33 Surely the churning of milk brings forth butter, and the wringing of the nose brings forth blood: so the forcing of wrath brings forth strife.

CHAPTER 31

THE words of king Lemuel, the prophecy that his mother taught him.
2 What, my son? and what, the son of my womb? and what, the son of my vows?
3 Give not your strength unto women, nor your ways to that which destroys kings.
4 It is not for kings, O Lemuel, it is not for kings to drink wine; nor for princes strong drink:
5 Lest they drink, and forget the law, and pervert the judgment of any of the afflicted.
6 Give strong drink unto him that is ready to perish, and wine unto those that be of heavy hearts.
7 Let him drink, and forget his poverty, and remember his misery no more.
8 Open your mouth for the dumb in the cause of all such as are appointed to destruction.
9 Open your mouth, judge righteously, and plead the cause of the poor and needy.
10 Who can find a virtuous woman? for her price is far above rubies.

30:15,16 Perhaps one more can be added to this list of those who never say "It is enough"—the money-hungry television preacher. See 2 Peter 2:1–3.

30:20 Some people seem to have no conscience. In truth, they have a *seared* conscience (see 1 Timothy 4:2)—one that has become so hardened that it has lost its ability to function. A correct use of the Law will resurrect it. When you speak directly to the conscience of a hardened sinner by saying, "You *know* that it's wrong to steal, to lie, to commit adultery, etc.," the conscience affirms the truth of the Commandment. See Romans 2:15.

30:25–28 Here are four virtues needed to be an effective witness: initiative (1 Corinthians 15:58); wisdom (Matthew 7:24); unity (Philippians 1:27); and persistence (Acts 4:18–20).

QUESTIONS & OBJECTIONS

31:10

"Christianity oppresses women by making them submit to their husbands!"

The Bible does say, "Wives, submit yourselves to your own husbands, as to the Lord," but it also instructs, "Husbands, love your wives, even as Christ also loved the church, and gave Himself for it" (Ephesians 5:22,25). A man who understands that Jesus Christ sacrificed His life's blood for the Church will likewise love his wife sacrificially and passionately. He will honor her, respect her, protect, love, and cherish her as much as he does his own body, as he is instructed to do (Ephesians 5:28). He will never say or do anything to harm or demean her. It is in this atmosphere of love and security that a godly wife willingly submits herself to the protective arms of her husband. She does this not because he is better than she is, but simply because this is God's order for His creation.

A godless world rejects the God-given formula to make marriage work. It thinks it knows best, and suffers the heartbreaking consequences of destroyed marriages and ruined lives. The Christian ideal of marriage is not one of an authoritarian and chauvinistic male holding his cringing wife in submission like an obedient dog. It's the very opposite. While most of the great religions treat women as inferior to men, the Bible gives them a place of dignity, honor, and unspeakable worth, expressed so evidently in Proverbs 31.

11 The heart of her husband does safely trust in her, so that he shall have no need of spoil.
12 She will do him good and not evil all the days of her life.
13 She seeks wool, and flax, and works willingly with her hands.
14 She is like the merchants' ships; she brings her food from afar.
15 She rises also while it is yet night, and gives meat to her household, and a portion to her maidens.
16 She considers a field, and buys it: with the fruit of her hands she plants a vineyard.
17 She girds her loins with strength, and strengthens her arms.
18 She perceives that her merchandise is good: her candle goes not out by night.
19 She lays her hands to the spindle, and her hands hold the distaff.
20 She stretches out her hand to the poor; yes, she reaches forth her hands to the needy.
21 She is not afraid of the snow for her household: for all her household are clothed with scarlet.
22 She makes herself coverings of tapestry; her clothing is silk and purple.
23 Her husband is known in the gates, when he sits among the elders of the land.
24 She makes fine linen, and sells it; and delivers girdles unto the merchant.
25 Strength and honor are her clothing; and she shall rejoice in time to come.
26 She opens her mouth with wisdom; and in her tongue is the law of kindness.
27 She looks well to the ways of her household, and eats not the bread of idleness.
28 Her children arise up, and call her blessed; her husband also, and he praises her.
29 Many daughters have done virtuously, but you excel them all.
30 Favor is deceitful, and beauty is vain: but a woman that fears the LORD, she shall be praised.
31 Give her of the fruit of her hands; and let her own works praise her in the gates.

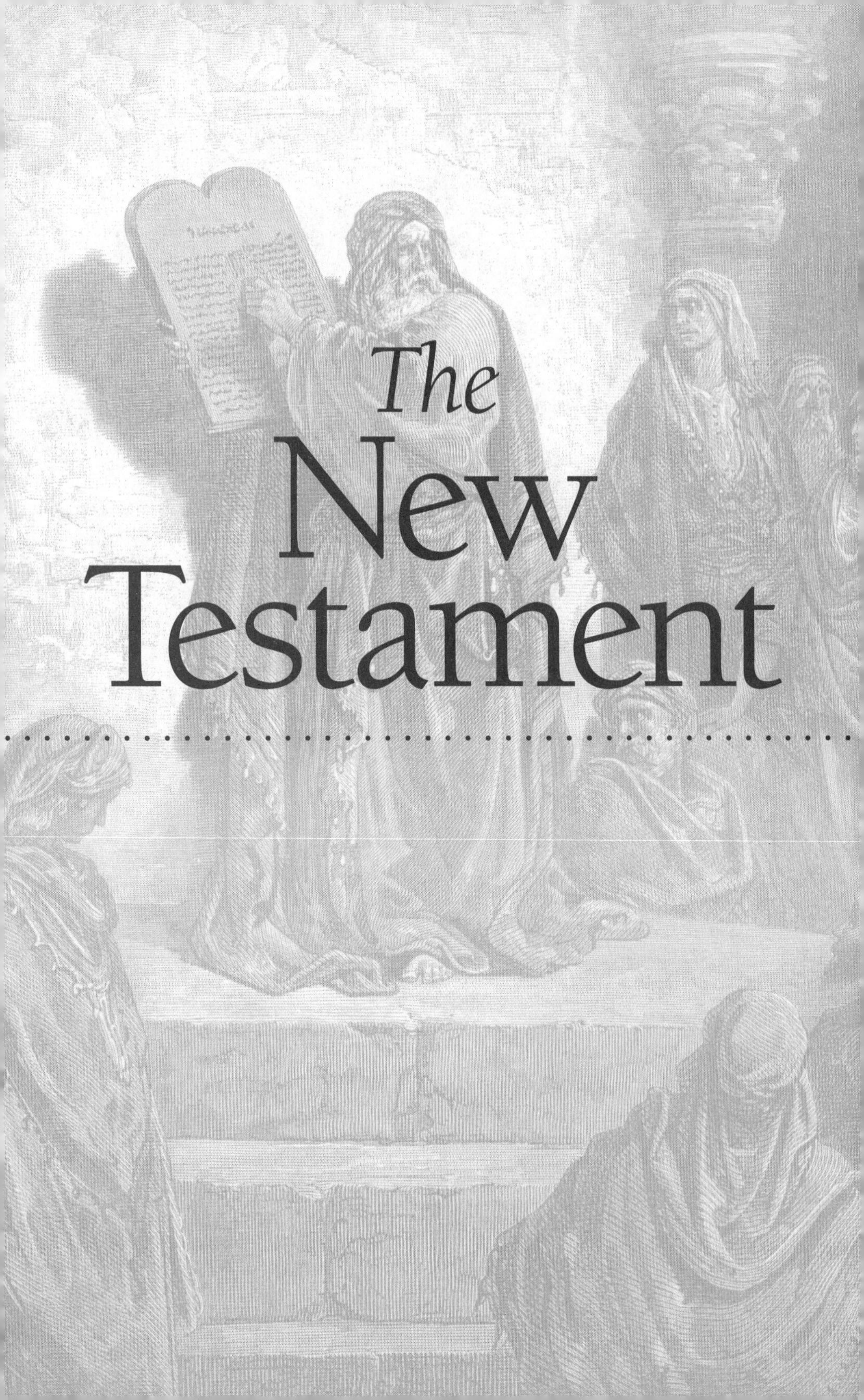

The New Testament

Matthew

CHAPTER 1

THE book of the generation of Jesus
Christ, the son of David, the son of
Abraham.
2 Abraham begat Isaac; and Isaac begat
Jacob; and Jacob begat Judas and his brethren;
3 And Judas begat Phares and Zara of
Thamar; and Phares begat Esrom; and Esrom begat Aram;
4 And Aram begat Aminadab; and Aminadab begat Naasson; and Naasson begat
Salmon;
5 And Salmon begat Booz of Rachab; and
Booz begat Obed of Ruth; and Obed begat Jesse;
6 And Jesse begat David the king; and David the king begat Solomon of her that
had been the wife of Urias;
7 And Solomon begat Roboam; and Roboam begat Abia; and Abia begat Asa;
8 And Asa begat Josaphat; and Josaphat
begat Joram; and Joram begat Ozias;
9 And Ozias begat Joatham; and Joatham
begat Achaz; and Achaz begat Ezekias;
10 And Ezekias begat Manasses; and
Manasses begat Amon; and Amon begat
Josias;
11 And Josias begat Jechonias and his
brethren, about the time they were carried
away to Babylon:
12 And after they were brought to Babylon, Jechonias begat Salathiel; and Salathiel begat Zorobabel;
13 And Zorobabel begat Abiud; and Abiud begat Eliakim; and Eliakim begat Azor;
14 And Azor begat Sadoc; and Sadoc begat Achim; and Achim begat Eliud;
15 And Eliud begat Eleazar; and Eleazar
begat Matthan; and Matthan begat Jacob;
16 And Jacob begat Joseph the husband
of Mary, of whom was born Jesus, who
is called Christ.
17 So all the generations from Abraham
to David are fourteen generations; and
from David until the carrying away into
Babylon are fourteen generations; and
from the carrying away into Babylon to
Christ are fourteen generations.
18 Now the birth of Jesus Christ was on
this wise: When as his mother Mary was
espoused to Joseph, before they came together, she was found with child of the
Holy Spirit.
19 Then Joseph her husband, being a
just man, and not willing to make her a
public example, was minded to put her
away privately.
20 But while he thought on these things,
behold, the angel of the Lord appeared to
him in a dream, saying, Joseph, you son
of David, fear not to take to you Mary your

1:1 Some point to the different genealogies of Jesus as "errors" in the Bible. However, Matthew gives the paternal genealogy of the Messiah (through His legal father), and Luke (3:23) gives His maternal genealogy (through His mother).

wife: for that which is conceived in her
is of the Holy Spirit.
21 And she shall bring forth a son, and
you shall call his name JESUS: for he shall
save his people from their sins.
22 Now all this was done, that it might
be fulfilled which was spoken of the Lord
by the prophet, saying,
23 Behold, a virgin shall be with child,
and shall bring forth a son, and they shall
call his name Emmanuel, which being interpreted is, God with us.
24 Then Joseph being raised from sleep
did as the angel of the Lord had bidden
him, and took to him his wife:
25 And knew her not till she had brought
forth her firstborn son: and he called his
name JESUS.

CHAPTER 2

NOW when Jesus was born in Bethlehem of Judea in the days of Herod the king, behold, there came wise men
from the east to Jerusalem,
2 Saying, Where is he that is born King
of the Jews? for we have seen his star in
the east, and are come to worship him.
3 When Herod the king had heard these
things, he was troubled, and all Jerusalem
with him.
4 And when he had gathered all the chief
priests and scribes of the people together,
he demanded of them where Christ should
be born.
5 And they said to him, In Bethlehem of
Judea: for thus it is written by the prophet,
6 And you Bethlehem, in the land of Judah, are not the least among the princes
of Judah: for out of you shall come a Governor, that shall rule my people Israel.
7 Then Herod, when he had privately
called the wise men, inquired of them diligently what time the star appeared.
8 And he sent them to Bethlehem, and
said, Go and search diligently for the
young child; and when you have found
him, bring me word again, that I may
come and worship him also.
9 When they had heard the king, they
departed; and, lo, the star, which they saw
in the east, went before them, till it came
and stood over where the young child was.
10 When they saw the star, they rejoiced
with exceeding great joy.
11 And when they were come into the
house, they saw the young child with Mary
his mother, and fell down, and worshipped him: and when they had opened
their treasures, they presented to him gifts;
gold, and frankincense, and myrrh.
12 And being warned of God in a dream
that they should not return to Herod, they
departed into their own country another
way.
13 And when they were departed, behold, the angel of the Lord appeared to Joseph in a dream, saying, Arise, and take
the young child and his mother, and flee
into Egypt, and be there until I bring you
word: for Herod will seek the young child
to destroy him.
14 When he arose, he took the young
child and his mother by night, and departed into Egypt:

1:20–23 Some say this was not a "virgin" but merely a "young maiden." Isaiah 7:14 says that God Himself will give a "sign." A young maiden becoming pregnant is not a sign from God, but an everyday occurrence. A *virgin* conceiving is a supernatural sign. See also Luke 1:31–35.

2:1 Wise men still seek Him. How is it that these wise men, who were not Jews, were aware of the birth of the "King of the Jews"? That they not only understood who He was, but desired to worship Him (v. 2) shows that God is able to reveal Himself to people in all lands and call them to Himself. These wise men "rejoiced with exceeding great joy" as God used a star to guide them to the Christ Child, then they "fell down and worshiped Him" (vv. 9–11). They made great personal and financial sacrifices to see this Child: they traveled a great distance, spent months away from their homes, and gave extravagant gifts to this newborn King.

Those who are wise today will listen for His voice, follow His guidance, and be willing to sacrifice everything for so great a privilege as meeting the King. See Philippians 3:8.

15 And was there until the death of Herod: that it might be fulfilled which was spoken of the Lord by the prophet, saying, Out of Egypt have I called my son.
16 Then Herod, when he saw that he was mocked of the wise men, was exceeding wroth, and sent forth, and slew all the children that were in Bethlehem, and in all the coasts thereof, from two years old and under, according to the time which he had diligently inquired of the wise men.
17 Then was fulfilled that which was spoken by Jeremiah the prophet, saying,
18 In Rama was there a voice heard, lamentation, and weeping, and great mourning, Rachel weeping for her children, and would not be comforted, because they are not.
19 But when Herod was dead, behold, an angel of the Lord appeared in a dream to Joseph in Egypt,
20 Saying, Arise, and take the young child and his mother, and go into the land of Israel: for they are dead which sought the young child's life.
21 And he arose, and took the young child and his mother, and came into the land of Israel.
22 But when he heard that Archelaus did reign in Judea in the room of his father Herod, he was afraid to go there: notwithstanding, being warned of God in a dream, he turned aside into the parts of Galilee:
23 And he came and dwelt in a city called Nazareth: that it might be fulfilled which was spoken by the prophets, He shall be called a Nazarene.

CHAPTER 3

IN those days came John the Baptist, preaching in the wilderness of Judea,
2 And saying, **Repent: for the kingdom of heaven is at hand.**
3 For this is he that was spoken of by the prophet Isaiah, saying, The voice of one crying in the wilderness, **Prepare the way of the Lord, make his paths straight.**

3:1 Open-air preaching. John the Baptist was an open-air preacher. Jesus was an open-air preacher. He preached the greatest sermon of all time, the "Sermon on the Mount" in the open-air. Peter preached in the open-air at Pentecost and Paul chose to stand on Mars Hill and preach open-air to the Athenians.

If we are serious about reaching this world, let us follow in the footsteps of Jesus and the apostles and preach where sinners gather. In thirty minutes, a good open-air preacher can reach more sinners than the average church does in twelve months.

Thank God that the disciples didn't stay in the upper room. They didn't carpet the building, pad the pews then put a notice outside the front door saying, "Tonight: Gospel outreach service, 7 P.M.—all welcome." They went into the open air.

The gospel is for the world, not the Church. One-third of the word "gospel" is "go." Two-thirds of "God" is "go"; but like King Og, we seem to have it backwards. We take sinners to meetings rather than meetings to sinners. The Church prefers to fish on dry land rather than get its feet wet. *Charles Finney* put his finger on the reason why: "It is the great business of every Christian to save souls. People complain that they do not know how to take hold of this matter. Why, the reason is plain enough; they have never studied it. They have never taken the proper pains to qualify themselves for the work. If you do not make it a matter of study, how you may successfully act in building up the kingdom of Christ, you are acting a very wicked and absurd part as a Christian."

He who loves his neighbor as himself will be concerned for his eternal welfare. He who couldn't care less that every day multitudes of living people are being swallowed by the jaws of hell has a heart of stone indeed.

3:2 Repentance—its necessity for salvation. The first word John the Baptist preached to Israel was "repent." However, it must be remembered that Israel had the Law and therefore had the "knowledge of sin" (Romans 7:7). Unregenerate humanity needs the Moral Law to show them what sin is (1 John 3:4). Without the knowledge that the "schoolmaster" brings, they remain in ignorance about sin's true nature and therefore their need for biblical repentance. See Luke 13:2.

4 And the same John had his raiment of camel's hair, and a leathern girdle about his loins; and his meat was locusts and wild honey.

5 Then went out to him Jerusalem, and all Judea, and all the region round about Jordan,

6 And were baptized of him in Jordan, confessing their sins.

7 But when he saw many of the Pharisees and Sadducees come to his baptism, he said to them, **O generation of vipers, who has warned you to flee from the wrath to come?**

8 **Bring forth therefore fruits meet for repentance:**

9 **And think not to say within yourselves, We have Abraham to our father: for I say to you, that God is able of these stones to raise up children to Abraham.**

10 And now also the axe is laid to the root of the trees: therefore every tree which brings not forth good fruit is hewn down, and cast into the fire.

11 I indeed baptize you with water to repentance: but he that comes after me is mightier than I, whose shoes I am not worthy to bear: he shall baptize you with the Holy Spirit, and with fire:

12 Whose fan is in his hand, and he will thoroughly purge his floor, and gather his wheat into the garner; but he will burn up the chaff with unquenchable fire.

13 Then came Jesus from Galilee to Jordan to John, to be baptized of him.

14 But John forbad him, saying, I have need to be baptized of you, and you come to me?

15 And Jesus answering said to him, Suffer it to be so now: for thus it becomes us to fulfil all righteousness. Then he suffered him.

16 And Jesus, when he was baptized, went up straightway out of the water: and, lo, the heavens were opened to him, and he saw the Spirit of God descending like a dove, and lighting upon him:

17 And lo a voice from heaven, saying, This is my beloved Son, in whom I am well pleased.

CHAPTER 4

THEN was Jesus led up of the Spirit into the wilderness to be tempted of the devil.

2 And when he had fasted forty days and forty nights, he was afterward an hungered.

3 And when the tempter came to him, he said, If you are the Son of God, command that these stones be made bread.

4 But he answered and said, It is written, Man shall not live by bread alone, but by every word that proceeds out of the mouth of God.

5 Then the devil took him up into the holy city, and set him on a pinnacle of the temple,

6 And said to him, If you are the Son of God, cast yourself down: for it is written, He shall give his angels charge concerning you: and in their hands they shall bear you up, lest at any time you dash your foot against a stone.

7 Jesus said to him, It is written again, You shall not tempt the Lord your God.

8 Again, the devil took him up into an exceeding high mountain, and showed him all the kingdoms of the world, and the glory of them;

9 And said to him, All these things will I give you, if you will fall down and worship me.

10 Then said Jesus to him, Get you hence, Satan: for it is written, You shall worship the Lord your God, and him only shall you serve.

11 Then the devil left him, and, behold, angels came and ministered to him.

12 Now when Jesus had heard that John was cast into prison, he departed into Galilee;

4:6 "The devil can cite Scripture for his purpose." *William Shakespeare*

4:9 The devil tempted Jesus to become a Satan worshiper.

4:4 *Archaeology and History Attest to the Reliability of the Bible*

By Richard M. Fales, Ph.D.

No other ancient book is questioned or maligned like the Bible. Critics looking for the flyspeck in the masterpiece allege that there was a long span between the time the events in the New Testament occurred and when they were recorded. They claim another gap exists archaeologically between the earliest copies made and the autographs of the New Testament. In reality, the alleged spaces and so-called gaps exist only in the minds of the critics.

Manuscript Evidence. Aristotle's *Ode to Poetics* was written between 384 and 322 B.C. The earliest copy of this work is dated A.D. 1100, and there are only forty-nine extant manuscripts. The gap between the original writing and the earliest copy is 1,400 years. There are only seven extant manuscripts of Plato's Tetralogies, written 427–347 B.C. The earliest copy is A.D. 900—a gap of over 1,200 years. What about the New Testament? Jesus was crucified in A.D. 30. The New Testament was written between A.D. 48 and 95. The oldest manuscripts date to the last quarter of the first century, and the second oldest A.D. 125. This gives us a narrow gap of thirty-five to forty years from the originals written by the apostles.

From the early centuries, we have some 5,300 Greek manuscripts of the New Testament. Altogether, including Syriac, Latin, Coptic, and Aramaic, we have a whopping 24,633 texts of the ancient New Testament to confirm the wording of the Scriptures. So the bottom line is, there was no great period between the events of the New Testament and the New Testament writings. Nor is there a great time lapse between the original writings and the oldest copies. With the great body of manuscript evidence, it can be proved, beyond a doubt, that the New Testament says exactly the same things today as it originally did nearly 2,000 years ago.

Corroborating Writings. Critics also charge that there are no ancient writings about Jesus outside the New Testament. This is another ridiculous claim. Writings confirming His birth, ministry, death, and resurrection include Flavius Josephus (A.D. 93), the Babylonian Talmud (A.D. 70–200), Pliny the Younger's letter to the Emperor Trajan (approx. A.D. 100), the Annals of Tacitus (A.D. 115–117), Mara Bar Serapion (sometime after A.D. 73), and Suetonius' *Life of Claudius* and *Life of Nero* (A.D. 120). Another point of contention arises when Bible critics have knowingly or unknowingly misled people by implying that Old and New Testament books were either excluded from or added into the canon of Scripture at the great ecumenical councils of A.D. 336, 382, 397, and 419. In fact, one result of these gatherings was to confirm the Church's belief that the books already in the Bible were divinely inspired. Therefore, the Church, at these meetings, neither added to nor took away from the books of the Bible. At that time, the thirty-nine Old Testament books had already been accepted, and the New Testament, as it was written, simply grew up with the ancient Church. Each document, being accepted as it was penned in the first century, was then passed on to Christians of the next century. So, this foolishness about the Roman Emperor Constantine dropping books from the Bible is simply uneducated rumor.

Fulfilled Prophecies. Prophecies from the Old and New Testaments that have been fulfilled also add credibility to the Bible. The Scriptures predicted the rise and fall of great empires like Greece and Rome (Daniel 2:39, 40), and foretold the destruction of cities like Tyre and Sidon (Isaiah 23). Tyre's demise is recorded by ancient historians, who tell how Alexander the Great lay siege to the city for seven months. King Nebuchadnezzar of Babylon had failed in a 13-year attempt to capture the seacoast city and completely destroy its inhabitants. During the siege of 573 B.C., much of the population of Tyre moved to its new island home approximately half a mile from the land city. Here it remained surrounded by walls as high as 150 feet until judgment fell in 332 B.C. with the arrival of Alexander the Great. In the seven-month siege, he fulfilled the remainder of the prophecies (Zechariah 9:4; Ezekiel 26:12) concerning the city at sea by completely destroying Tyre, killing 8,000 of its inhabitants and selling 30,000 of its population into slavery. To reach the island, he

(continued on next page)

(4:4 continued)
scraped up the dust and rubble of the old land city of Tyre, just like the Bible predicted, and cast them into the sea, building a 200-foot-wide causeway out to the island.

Alexander's death and the murder of his two sons was also foretold in the Scripture. Another startling prophecy was Jesus' detailed prediction of Jerusalem's destruction, and the further spreading of the Jewish diaspora throughout the world, which is recorded in Luke 21. In A.D. 70, not only was Jerusalem destroyed by Titus, the future emperor of Rome, but another prediction of Jesus Christ in Matthew 24:1,2 came to pass—the complete destruction of the temple of God.

Messianic Prophecies. In the Book of Daniel, the Bible prophesied the coming of the one and only Jewish Messiah prior to the temple's demise. The Old Testament prophets declared He would be born in Bethlehem (Micah 5:2) to a virgin (Isaiah 7:14), be betrayed for thirty pieces of silver (Zechariah 11:12,13), die by crucifixion (Psalm 22), and be buried in a rich man's tomb (Isaiah 53:9). There was only one person who fits all of the messianic prophecies of the Old Testament who lived before A.D. 70: Jesus of Nazareth, the Son of Mary.

Yes, the Bible is an amazing book. (See also 1 Peter 1:25 footnote.)

13 And leaving Nazareth, he came and dwelt in Capernaum, which is upon the sea coast, in the borders of Zabulon and Nephthalim:
14 That it might be fulfilled which was spoken by Isaiah the prophet, saying,
15 The land of Zabulon, and the land of Nephthalim, by the way of the sea, beyond Jordan, Galilee of the Gentiles;
16 The people which sat in darkness saw great light; and to them which sat in the region and shadow of death light is sprung up.
17 From that time Jesus began to preach, and to say, **Repent: for the kingdom of heaven is at hand.**
18 And Jesus, walking by the sea of Galilee, saw two brethren, Simon called Peter, and Andrew his brother, casting a net into the sea: for they were fishers.
19 *And he said to them, Follow me, and I will make you fishers of men.*
20 And they straightway left their nets, and followed him.
21 And going on from there, he saw other two brethren, James the son of Zebedee, and John his brother, in a ship with Zebedee their father, mending their nets; and he called them.
22 And they immediately left the ship and their father, and followed him.
23 And Jesus went about all Galilee, teaching in their synagogues, and preaching the gospel of the kingdom, and healing all manner of sickness and all manner of disease among the people.
24 And his fame went throughout all Syria: and they brought to him all sick people that were taken with divers diseases and torments, and those which were possessed with devils, and those which were lunatic, and those that had the palsy; and he healed them.
25 And there followed him great multitudes of people from Galilee, and from Decapolis, and from Jerusalem, and from Judea, and from beyond Jordan.

CHAPTER 5

AND seeing the multitudes, he went up into a mountain: and when he was set, his disciples came to him:
2 And he opened his mouth, and taught them, saying,

4:16 This life is the valley of the shadow of death. Sinners sit in darkness—waiting to die. The light of the Savior banishes the shadow of death.

4:17 Like John the Baptist, Jesus' first word in preaching to Israel was "repent." Israel already had the "knowledge of sin" (which only the Law can bring), but now they needed to repent—to turn from their sins as revealed by the Law.

5:1 *The Sermon on the Mount*

This sermon not only reveals God's divine nature, it puts into our hands the most powerful of evangelistic weapons. It is the greatest evangelistic sermon ever preached by the greatest evangelist who ever lived. The straightedge of God's Law reveals how crooked we are:

v. 3: The unregenerate heart isn't poor in spirit. It is proud, self-righteous, and boastful (every man is pure in his own eyes—Proverbs 16:2).

v. 4: The unsaved don't mourn over their sin; they love the darkness and hate the light (John 3:19).

v. 5: The ungodly are not meek and lowly of heart. Their sinful condition is described in Romans 3:13–18.

v. 6: Sinners don't hunger and thirst after righteousness. Instead, they drink iniquity like water (Job 15:16).

v. 7: The world is shallow in its ability to show true mercy. It is by nature cruel and vindictive (Genesis 6:5).

v. 8: The heart of the unregenerate is not pure; it is desperately wicked (Jeremiah 17:9).

Those who are born again manifest the fruit of the Spirit, live godly in Christ Jesus (vv. 3–9), and therefore suffer persecution (vv. 10–12). However, their purpose on earth is to be salt and light: to be a moral influence, and to bring the light to those who sit in the shadow of death (vv. 13–16).

Look now at how the Messiah expounds the Law and makes it "honorable" (Isaiah 42:21). He establishes that He didn't come to destroy the Law (v. 17); not even the smallest part of it will pass away (v. 18). It will be the divine standard of judgment (James 2:12; Romans 2:12; Acts 17:31). Those who teach it "shall be called great in the kingdom of heaven" (v. 19). The Law should be taught to sinners because it was made for them (1 Timothy 1:8–10), and is a "schoolmaster" that brings the "knowledge of sin" (Romans 3:19,20; 7:7). Its function is to destroy self-righteousness and bring sinners to the cross (Galatians 3:24).

The righteousness of the scribes and Pharisees was merely outward, but God requires truth in the inward parts (Psalm 51:6). Jesus shows this by unveiling the Law's *spiritual* nature (Romans 7:14). The Sixth Commandment forbids murder. However, Jesus shows that it also condemns anger "without cause," and even evil-speaking (vv. 21–26): "Every idle word that men shall speak, they shall give an account thereof in the day of judgment" (Matthew 12:36). The Seventh Commandment forbids adultery, but Jesus revealed that this also includes lust, and it even condemns divorce, except in the case of sexual sin of the spouse (vv. 27–32).

Jesus opens up the Ninth Commandment (vv. 33–37), and then shows that love is the spirit of the Law—"The end of the commandment is charity out of a pure heart..." (1 Timothy 1:5). This is summarized in what is commonly called the Golden Rule: "All things whatsoever you would that men should do to you, do you even so to them: *for this is the Law and the prophets*" (Matthew 7:12, emphasis added). "Owe no man any thing, but to love one another: for he that loves another has fulfilled the law. For this, You shall not commit adultery, You shall not kill, You shall not steal, You shall not bear false witness, You shall not covet; and if there be any other commandment, it is briefly comprehended in this saying, namely, You shall love your neighbor as yourself. Love works no ill to his neighbor: therefore love is the fulfilling of the law" (Romans 13:8–10).

When a sinner is born again he is able to do this (vv. 38–47). He now possesses "the divine nature" (2 Peter 1:4). In Christ he is made perfect and thus satisfies the demands of a "perfect" Law (Psalm 19:7; James 1:25). Without the righteousness of Christ he cannot be perfect as his Father in heaven is perfect (v. 48). The Law annihilated his self-righteousness leaving him undone and condemned. His only hope was in the cross of Jesus Christ. After his conversion, knowledge of the Law that brought him there keeps him at the foot of the cross.

John Wesley said, "Therefore I cannot spare the Law one moment, no more than I can spare Christ, seeing I now want it as much to keep me to Christ, as I ever wanted it to bring me to Him. Otherwise this 'evil heart of unbelief' would immediately 'depart from the living God.' Indeed each is continually sending me to the other—the Law to Christ, and Christ to the Law."

3 Blessed are the poor in spirit: for theirs is the kingdom of heaven.
4 Blessed are they that mourn: for they shall be comforted.
5 Blessed are the meek: for they shall inherit the earth.

> We have grasped the mystery of the atom and rejected the Sermon on the Mount…The world has achieved brilliance without conscience. Ours is a world of nuclear giants and ethical infants.
>
> GENERAL OMAR BRADLEY

6 Blessed are they which do hunger and thirst after righteousness: for they shall be filled.
7 Blessed are the merciful: for they shall obtain mercy.
8 Blessed are the pure in heart: for they shall see God.
9 Blessed are the peacemakers: for they shall be called the children of God.
10 Blessed are they which are persecuted for righteousness' sake: for theirs is the kingdom of heaven.
11 Blessed are you, when men shall revile you, and persecute you, and shall say all manner of evil against you falsely, for my sake.
12 Rejoice, and be exceeding glad: for great is your reward in heaven: for so persecuted they the prophets which were before you.
13 You are the salt of the earth: but if the salt has lost his savour, wherewith shall it be salted? it is thenceforth good for nothing, but to be cast out, and to be trodden under foot of men.
14 *You are the light of the world. A city that is set on an hill cannot be hid.*
15 *Neither do men light a candle, and put it under a bushel, but on a candlestick; and*

5:2 Sin, righteousness, and judgment. "The Sermon on the Mount is the greatest example we have of how to 'reprove the world of sin, of righteousness, and of judgment.' In Matthew chapter 5, Christ reproves the multitudes of sin by showing the essence of the Law. In chapter 6, He teaches on true righteousness, the essence of which is to cause men to glorify our Father which is in heaven, not to draw attention to ourselves. Then, in chapter 7, He teaches concerning judgment. He warns the multitudes that if they judge others as guilty for doing the same things they themselves are practicing, instead of pulling the log out of their own eye first, they are obviously hypocrites. If we will follow this method of preaching the gospel, then we can expect the Holy Spirit to help us. For Jesus Himself promised that this divine Helper would reprove the world of sin, of righteousness, and of judgment. He does this by causing our words to make saving impressions on the minds of men." *Joel Crumpton*

5:6 We should come to the Savior thirsting for *righteousness*, not *happiness* as modern evangelism maintains—"Riches profit not in the day of wrath: but *righteousness* delivers from death" (Proverbs 11:4, emphasis added).

5:7 Jesus didn't come to destroy the Law and the prophets, but to fulfill them (Matthew 5:17). It was our transgressions that necessitated the Savior. If we hadn't sinned, there would have been no need for a sacrifice. We broke the Law, and Jesus paid the fine. God loved the world with such passion that He sent His only Son to the cross of Calvary, so that we might trust in Him alone. In so doing, we would not perish under the wrath of His Law, but have everlasting life (John 3:16).

5:13 "The pulpit, not the media, is to be the most powerful voice in our land." *Bill Gothard*

5:14 Set on a hill. Some people say that religion is a personal thing and it should be kept to oneself. However, Jesus tells us that the gospel of salvation is the good news of everlasting life and is for this dying world. We should be set on a hill. We should be preaching on the housetops, lifting up our voice like a trumpet to show this people their transgression. The Bible tells us that God's Law is light (Proverbs 6:23). When the light of the Law and the glorious gospel of Christ shine together, they expose and banish the shadows of sin and death.

POINTS FOR OPEN-AIR PREACHING

5:10–12

Never Fear Hecklers

The best thing that can happen to an open-air meeting is to have a good heckler. Jesus gave us some of the greatest gems of Scripture because someone either made a statement or asked a question in an open-air setting. A good heckler can increase a crowd of 20 people to 200 in a matter of minutes. The air becomes electric. Suddenly, you have 200 people listening intently to how you will answer a heckler. All you have to do is remember the attributes of 2 Timothy 2:23–26: be patient, gentle, humble, etc. Don't worry if you can't answer a question. Just say, "I can't answer that, but I'll try to get the answer for you if you really want to know." With Bible "difficulties," I regularly fall back on the powerful statement of *Mark Twain*: "Most people are bothered by those passages of Scripture they don't understand, but for me I have always noticed that the passages that bother me are those I do understand."

A "good" heckler is one who will provoke your thoughts. He will stand up, speak up, then shut up so that you can preach. Occasionally, you will get hecklers who have the first two qualifications, but they just won't be quiet. If they will not let you get a word in, move your location. Most of the crowd will follow. Better to have 10 listeners who can hear than 200 who can't. If the heckler follows, move again... then the crowd will usually turn on him.

One ploy that often works with a heckler who is out solely to hinder the gospel is to wait until he is quiet and say to the crowd (making sure the heckler is listening also), "I want to show you how people are like sheep. When I move, watch this man follow me because he can't get a crowd by himself." His pride usually keeps him from following.

If you have a "mumbling heckler" who won't speak up, ignore him and talk over the top of him. This will usually get him angry enough to speak up and draw hearers. There is a fine line between him getting angry enough to draw a crowd, and hitting you; you will find it in time.

If you are fortunate enough to get a heckler, don't panic. Show him genuine respect, not only because he can double your crowd, but because the Bible says to honor all men, so you don't want to offend him unnecessarily. Ask the heckler his name, so that if you want to ask him a question and he is talking to someone, you don't have to say, "Hey you!"

Often, people will walk through the crowd so they can get close to you and will whisper something like, "I think you are a #@*!$!" Answer loud enough for the crowd to hear, "God bless you." Do it with a smile so that it looks as though the person has just whispered a word of encouragement to you. This will stop him from doing it again. The Bible says to bless those who curse you, and to do good to those who hate you.

Remember that you are not fighting against flesh and blood. Hecklers will stoop very low and be cutting and cruel in their remarks. If you have some physical disability, they will play on it. Try to smile back at them. Look past the words. If you are reviled for the name of Jesus, "rejoice, and be exceeding glad." Read Matthew 5:10–12 until it is written on the corridors of your mind.

The most angry hecklers are usually what we call "backsliders." These are actually false converts who never slid forward in the first place. They "asked Jesus into their heart" but never truly repented. Ask him, "Did you know the Lord?" (see Hebrews 8:11). If he answers "Yes," then he is admitting that he is willfully denying Him, and if he answers "No," then he was never a Christian in the first place—"This is eternal life, that they might know you, the only true God, and Jesus Christ, whom you have sent" (John 17:3). See 1 Corinthians 2:4 footnote.

it gives light to all that are in the house.
16 *Let your light so shine before men, that they may see your good works, and glorify your Father who is in heaven.*
17 Think not that I am come to destroy the law, or the prophets: I am not come
to destroy, but to fulfil.
18 For verily I say to you, Till heaven and earth pass, one jot or one tittle shall in no wise pass from the law, till all be fulfilled.
19 Whosoever therefore shall break one

SPIRITUAL NATURE OF THE LAW

5:22 "Herein is the Law of God above all other laws, that it is a spiritual law. Other laws may forbid compassing and imagining, which are treason in the heart, but cannot take cognizance thereof, unless there be some overt act; but the Law of God takes notice of the iniquity regarded in the heart, though it go no further." *Matthew Henry*

"The precepts of philosophy, and of the Hebrew code, laid hold of actions only. [Jesus] pushed His scrutinies into the heart of man, erected His tribunal in the region of his thoughts, and purified the waters at the fountain head." *Thomas Jefferson*

of these least commandments, and shall teach men so, he shall be called the least in the kingdom of heaven: but whosoever shall do and teach them, the same shall be called great in the kingdom of heaven.

20 For I say to you, That except your righteousness shall exceed the righteousness of the scribes and Pharisees, you shall in no case enter into the kingdom of heaven.

21 You have heard that it was said by them of old time, You shall not kill; and whosoever shall kill shall be in danger of the judgment:

22 But I say to you, That whosoever is angry with his brother without a cause shall be in danger of the judgment: and whosoever shall say to his brother, Raca, shall be in danger of the council: but whosoever shall say, You fool, shall be in danger of hell fire.

23 Therefore if you bring your gift to the altar, and there remember that your brother has anything against you;

24 Leave there your gift before the altar, and go your way; first be reconciled to your brother, and then come and offer your gift.

25 Agree with your adversary quickly, while you are in the way with him; lest at any time the adversary deliver you to the judge, and the judge deliver you to the officer, and you be cast into prison.

26 Verily I say to you, You shall by no means come out thence, till you have paid the uttermost farthing.

27 You have heard that it was said by them of old time, You shall not commit adultery:

28 But I say to you, That whosoever looks on a woman to lust after her has committed adultery with her already in his heart.

5:16 "If doing a good act in public will excite others to do more good, then 'Let your light shine to all.' Miss no opportunity to do good." *John Wesley*

5:20 Self-righteousness. These words would have astounded Jesus' hearers. If anyone was righteous, it was the scribes and Pharisees. Their hope of life from the Law was therefore shattered. That is what we must do: shatter the self-righteous beliefs of those poor souls who try to earn salvation. Jesus shows us how in the following verses by explaining that God requires truth even in the inward parts. He considers hatred to be murder (1 John 3:15). If we as much as have anger without cause, we are in danger of judgment (v. 22). If we have lust in our hearts, God considers us to be adulterers (v. 28). Sin is so serious, Jesus said that it would be better to be blind than to go to hell because of a lustful eye.

5:21,22 God sees the thought-life: He weighs our motives and judges the intent of the hearts: "Whoever hates his brother is a murderer" (1 John 3:15). See Matthew 5:27,28 footnote.

5:22 Hell: For verses warning of its reality, see Matthew 5:29,30.

5:27,28 God knows what's in the heart: "For God will bring every work into judgment, including every secret thing, whether good or evil" (Ecclesiastes 12:14). "But after your hardness and impenitent heart you treasure up to yourself wrath against the day of wrath and revelation of the righteous judgment of God; who will render to every man according to his deeds" (Romans 2:5,6). See Mark 7:20–23 footnote.

Questions & Objections

5:28

"What should I say if someone asks, 'Have you ever lusted?'"

An individual may challenge you on this issue while you're going through the Ten Commandments with him. Take care when answering. There is such a thing as being too candid. A U.S. president became synonymous with the word "lust" because he lacked discretion in answering this question. Soften your answer with, "I have broken *all* of the Ten Commandments in spirit, if not in letter." That will not only defuse the issue, but will give you opportunity to explain that we all have a sin nature and need God's forgiveness.

29 And if your right eye offend you, pluck it out, and cast it from you: for it is profitable for you that one of your members should perish, and not that your whole body should be cast into hell.

30 And if your right hand offend you, cut if off, and cast it from you: for it is profitable for you that one of your members should perish, and not that your whole body should be cast into hell.

31 It has been said, Whosoever shall put away his wife, let him give her a writing of divorcement:

32 But I say to you, That whosoever shall put away his wife, saving for the cause of fornication, causes her to commit adultery: and whosoever shall marry her that is divorced commits adultery.

33 Again, you have heard that it has been said by them of old time, You shall not forswear yourself, but shall perform to the Lord your oaths:

34 But I say to you, Swear not at all; neither by heaven; for it is God's throne:

35 Nor by the earth; for it is his footstool: neither by Jerusalem; for it is the city of the great King.

36 Neither shall you swear by your head, because you can not make one hair white or black.

37 But let your communication be, Yea, yea; Nay, nay: for whatsoever is more than these comes of evil.

38 You have heard that it has been said, An eye for an eye, and a tooth for a tooth:

39 But I say to you, That you resist not evil: but whosoever shall smite you on your right cheek, turn to him the other also.

40 And if any man will sue you at the law, and take away your coat, let him have your cloak also.

41 And whosoever shall compel you to go a mile, go with him two.

42 Give to him that asks you, and from him that would borrow of you turn not away.

43 You have heard that it has been said, You shall love your neighbour, and hate your enemy.

44 But I say to you, Love your enemies, bless them that curse you, do good to them that hate you, and pray for them which despitefully use you, and persecute you;

45 That you may be the children of your Father which is in heaven: for he makes his sun to rise on the evil and on the good, and sends rain on the just and on the unjust.

46 For if you love them which love you,

5:28 Men will often try to justify lust by saying that there's nothing wrong with looking at a pretty girl. True, the Bible doesn't condemn looking at a pretty girl; it condemns "lust." The conscience knows the difference.

5:29,30 Hell: For verses warning of its reality, see Matthew 10:28.

QUESTIONS & OBJECTIONS

5:38 ***"When the Bible says 'an eye for an eye,' it encourages us to take the law in our own hands by avenging wrongdoing."***

This verse is so often misquoted by the world. Many believe it is giving a license to take matters into our own hands and render evil for evil. In reality, it is referring to civil law concerning restitution. If someone steals your ox, he is to restore the ox. If someone steals and wrecks your car, he is to buy you another one... a car for a car, an eye for an eye, a tooth for a tooth.

The spirit of what Jesus is saying here is radically different from the "sue the shirt off the back of your neighbor" society in which we live.

what reward have you? do not even the
publicans the same?
47 And if you salute your brethren only,
what do you more than others? do not
even the publicans so?
48 Be therefore perfect, even as your Father which is in heaven is perfect.

CHAPTER 6

TAKE heed that you do not your alms
before men, to be seen of them: otherwise you have no reward of your Father
which is in heaven.
2 Therefore when you do your alms, do
not sound a trumpet before you, as the

5:44 There are several reasons why as Christians we should pray for those who persecute us: 1) we are commanded to; 2) prayer is an antidote against bitterness; and 3) it can lead to the salvation of the persecutor.

5:44 Capital punishment. Some maintain that this verse shows Jesus did not believe in capital punishment. However, just because we have love for an enemy doesn't give us the right to allow him to escape punishment for murder. The Bible says, "Let every soul be subject to the higher powers. For there is no power but of God: the powers that be are ordained of God. Whosoever therefore resists the power, resists the ordinance of God: and they that resist shall receive to themselves damnation... *But if you do that which is evil, be afraid; for he bears not the sword in vain: for he is the minister of God, a revenger to execute wrath upon him that does evil"* (Romans 13:1–4, emphasis added).

The Bible says that if I deliberately take a life, I should lose my own: "Whoso kills any person, the murderer shall be put to death by the mouth of witnesses: but one witness shall not testify against any person to cause him to die. Moreover you shall take no satisfaction for the life of a murderer, which is guilty of death: but he shall be surely put to death" (Numbers 35:30,31). Genesis 9:6 says, "Whoso sheds man's blood, by man shall his blood be shed: for in the image of God made he man." This shows the value that God places on human life. The seriousness of a crime is revealed in the punishment dealt to the criminal. It is interesting to note that when Oklahoma City bomber Timothy McVeigh requested the death penalty, 250 relatives of the victims he killed asked to watch his execution. Their desire to actually see justice done shows the value they place on the loved one they lost. Despite claims to the contrary, capital punishment does deter crime. The person executed will not do it again.

Still, there are respected Christian leaders whose conscience will not allow them to advocate capital punishment. This is understandable in light of the fact that innocent people fall through the cracks of a godless justice system. However, despite civil law's imperfections, we are told to be subject to the governing authorities.

It was God who instigated the death penalty in the beginning. The Judge of the Universe pronounced the death sentence upon all humanity when He said, "The soul that sins, it shall die" (Ezekiel 18:20).

hypocrites do in the synagogues and in
the streets, that they may have glory of
men. Verily I say to you, They have their
reward.
3 But when you do alms, let not your
left hand know what your right hand
does:
4 That your alms may be in secret: and
your Father which sees in secret himself
shall reward you openly.
5 And when you pray, you shall not be
as the hypocrites are: for they love to
pray standing in the synagogues and in
the corners of the streets, that they may
be seen of men. Verily I say to you, They
have their reward.
6 But you, when you pray, enter into
your closet, and when you have shut your
door, pray to your Father which is in secret; and your Father which sees in secret shall reward you openly.
7 But when you pray, use not vain repetitions, as the heathen do: for they think
that they shall be heard for their much
speaking.
8 Be not therefore like to them: for your
Father knows what things you have need
of, before you ask him.
9 After this manner therefore pray: Our
Father who is in heaven, Hallowed be
your name.
10 Your kingdom come. Your will be
done in earth, as it is in heaven.

> Before we can pray "Thy Kingdom come," we must be willing to pray "my kingdom go."
>
> **ALAN REDPATH**

11 Give us this day our daily bread.
12 And forgive us our debts, as we forgive our debtors.
13 And lead us not into temptation, but
deliver us from evil: For yours is the kingdom, and the power, and the glory, for
ever. Amen.
14 For if you forgive men their trespas-

5:48 Be perfect. Some believe Jesus didn't really mean "perfect" here, because that would require that we be "without defect, flawless." Instead, they think He was telling us to be "mature." If that were true, then He would be saying, "Be therefore mature, even as your Father which is in heaven is mature." However, calling God "mature" implies that He was once immature. Such a thought is contrary to Scripture. God never changes (Malachi 3:6); He has always been perfect and doesn't need to mature.

Throughout the Sermon on the Mount Jesus expounded the perfect Law of a perfect Creator. God's work is perfect (Deuteronomy 32:4), His way is perfect (Psalm 18:30), and His Law is perfect (Psalm 19:7; James 1:25). Jesus then climaxes His exposition with the demand of the Law—perfection in thought, word, and deed.

In magnifying the Law and making it honorable, He put righteousness beyond the reach of sinful humanity. He destroyed the vain hope that we can get right with a perfect Creator by our own imperfect efforts, i.e., by the works of the Law. (See Mark 7:5–13 footnote.)

Instead, we must seek righteousness by another means—through faith alone in the Savior (Romans 3:21,22). In doing so, Jesus was showing us the right use of the Law—as a "schoolmaster to bring us to Christ" (Galatians 3:24). This is what Jesus did with the rich young ruler. The young man asked, "Good Master, what good thing shall I do, that I may have eternal life?" (Matthew 19:16). Jesus corrected his misuse of the word "good," gave him five of the Ten Commandments, and then said, "If you will be perfect…" The young man's hope of "doing" something to be saved was dashed and he went away sorrowful. However, this is not a negative incident; it is positive when a sinner's vain hope is dashed. If he cannot find salvation "by the works of the Law," he may just seek it "by the hearing of faith" (Galatians 3:2). This is why we should use the Law when reasoning with the lost and press home its requirement of absolute perfection. (See James 2:10,11.) On hearing the demands of a perfect Law, it is not uncommon to hear a guilty sinner say, "Wow! Nobody's perfect." That's the point of the Law.

Our mission is to preach Christ and to warn sinners, "that we may present every man perfect in Christ Jesus" (Colossians 1:28).

PRINCIPLES OF GROWTH FOR THE NEW AND GROWING CHRISTIAN

6:9 *Prayer—"Wait for a Minute"*

God always answers prayer. Sometimes He says yes; sometimes He says no; and sometimes He says, "Wait for a minute." And since to the Lord a day is as a thousand years (2 Peter 3:8), that could mean a ten-year wait for us. So ask in faith, but rest in peace-filled patience.

Surveys show that more than 90% of Americans pray daily. No doubt they pray for health, wealth, happiness, etc. They also pray when grandma gets sick, and when grandma doesn't get better (or dies), many end up disillusioned or bitter. This is because they don't understand what the Bible says about prayer. It teaches, among other things, that our sin will keep God from even hearing our prayer (Psalm 66:18), and that if we pray with doubt, we will not get an answer (James 1:6,7).

Here's how to be heard:

- Pray with faith (Hebrews 11:6).
- Pray with clean hands and a pure heart (Psalm 24:3,4).
- Pray genuine heartfelt prayers, rather than vain repetitions (Matthew 6:7).
- Make sure you are praying to the God revealed in the Scriptures (Exodus 20:3–6).

1. How do you "pray with faith"? Someone once told me, "Ray, you're a man of great faith in God," thinking they were paying me a compliment. They weren't. What if I said to you, "I'm a man of great faith in my doctor"? It's a compliment to the doctor. If I have great faith in him, it means that I see him as being a man of integrity, a man of great ability—that he is trustworthy. I give "glory" to the man through my faith in him. The Bible says that Abraham "staggered not at the promise of God through unbelief; but was strong in faith, giving glory to God; and being fully persuaded that, what he had promised, he was able also to perform" (Romans 4:20,21). Abraham was a man of great faith in God. Remember, that is not a compliment to Abraham. He merely caught a glimpse of God's incredible ability, His impeccable integrity, and His wonderful faithfulness to keep every promise He makes. His faith gave "glory" to a faithful God.

As far as God is concerned, if you belong to Jesus, you are a VIP. You can boldly come before the throne of grace (Hebrews 4:16). You have access to the King *because you are the son or daughter of the King*. When you were a child, did you have to grovel to get your needs met by your mom or dad? I hope not.

So, when you pray, don't say, "Oh God, I *hope* you will supply my needs." Instead say something like, "Father, thank You that You keep *every* promise You make. Your Word says that You will supply *all* my needs according to Your riches in glory by Christ Jesus (Philippians 4:19). Therefore, I thank You that You will do this thing for my family. I ask this in the wonderful name of Jesus. Amen."

2. How do you get "clean hands and a pure heart"? Simply by confessing your sins to God through Jesus Christ, whose blood cleanses from all sin (1 John 1:7–9). God will not only forgive your every sin, He promises to *forget* them (Hebrews 8:12). He will even justify you based on the sacrifice of the Savior. This means He will count it as though you have never sinned in the first place. He will make you pure in His sight—sinless. He will even "purge" your conscience, so that you will no longer have a sense of guilt that you sinned. That's what it means to be "justified by faith." That's why you need to soak yourself in Holy Scripture; read the letters to the churches and see the wonderful things God has done for us through the cross of Calvary. If you don't bother to read the "will," you won't have any idea what has been given to you.

3. How do you pray "genuine heartfelt prayers"? Simply by keeping yourself in the love of God. If the love of God is in you, you will never pray hypocritical or selfish prayers. Just talk to your heavenly Father as candidly and intimately as a young child, nestled on Daddy's lap, would talk to his earthly father. How would you feel if every day your child pulled out a pre-written statement to dryly recite to you, rather than pouring out the events and emotions of that day? God wants to hear from your heart. When your prayer-life is pleasing to God, He will reward you openly (Matthew 6:6).

(continued)

(6:9 continued)

4. How do you know you're praying to "the God revealed in Scripture"? Study the Word. Don't accept the image of God portrayed by the world, even though it appeals to the natural mind. A kind, gentle Santa Claus figure, dispensing good things with no sense of justice or truth, appeals to guilty sinners. Look to the thunderings and lightnings of Mount Sinai. Gaze at Jesus on the cross of Calvary—hanging in unspeakable agony because of the justice of a holy God. Such thoughts tend to banish idolatry.

For the next principle of growth, see 2 Corinthians 4:4 footnote.

ses, your heavenly Father will also forgive you:
15 But if you forgive not men their trespasses, neither will your Father forgive your trespasses.
16 Moreover when you fast, be not, as the hypocrites, of a sad countenance: for they disfigure their faces, that they may appear to men to fast. Verily I say to you, They have their reward.
17 But you, when you fast, anoint your head, and wash your face;
18 That you appear not to men to fast, but to your Father which is in secret: and your Father, which sees in secret, shall reward you openly.
19 Lay not up for yourselves treasures upon earth, where moth and rust corrupts, and where thieves break through and steal:
20 But lay up for yourselves treasures in heaven, where neither moth nor rust corrupts, and where thieves do not break through nor steal:
21 For where your treasure is, there will your heart be also.
22 The light of the body is the eye: if therefore your eye be single, your whole body shall be full of light.
23 But if your eye be evil, your whole body shall be full of darkness. If therefore the light that is in you be darkness, how great is that darkness!
24 **No man can serve two masters: for either he will hate the one, and love the other; or else he will hold to the one, and despise the other. You cannot serve God and mammon.**
25 Therefore I say to you, Take no thought for your life, what you shall eat, or what you shall drink; nor yet for your body, what you shall put on. Is not the life more than meat, and the body than raiment?
26 Behold the fowls of the air: for they sow not, neither do they reap, nor gather into barns; yet your heavenly Father feeds them. Are you not much better than they?
27 Which of you by taking thought can add one cubit to his stature?
28 And why take thought for raiment? Consider the lilies of the field, how they grow; they toil not, neither do they spin:
29 And yet I say to you, That even Solomon in all his glory was not arrayed like one of these.
30 Wherefore, if God so clothe the grass of the field, which to day is, and tomorrow is cast into the oven, shall he not much more clothe you, O you of little faith?
31 Therefore take no thought, saying, What shall we eat? or, What shall we drink? or, Wherewithal shall we be clothed?
32 (For after all these things do the Gentiles seek:) for your heavenly Father knows that you have need of all these things.

6:12 See Proverbs 26:12 footnote.

6:26 Man is the pinnacle of God's earthly creation. He is not a mere part of the evolutionary process having to yield to the rights of animals. Jesus said that mankind is "much better" than birds and sheep (Matthew 12:12). He is to subdue the earth and have dominion over it (Genesis 1:28) by bringing its vast resources into submission. All were created for him by the infinite genius and loving hand of Almighty God. See also Psalm 8:6–8 footnote.

THE FUNCTION OF THE LAW

7:6 "Just as the world was not ready for the New Testament before it received the Old, just as the Jews were not prepared for the ministry of Christ until John the Baptist had gone before Him with his claimant call to repentance, so the unsaved are in no condition today for the gospel till the Law be applied to their hearts, for 'by the Law is the knowledge of sin.' It is a waste of time to sow seed on ground which has never been ploughed or spaded! To present the vicarious sacrifice of Christ to those whose dominant passion is to take fill of sin, is to give that which is holy to the dogs." *A. W. Pink*

33 But seek first the kingdom of God,
and his righteousness; and all these things
shall be added to you.
34 Take therefore no thought for the
morrow: for the morrow shall take thought
for the things of itself. Sufficient to the
day is the evil thereof.

CHAPTER 7

JUDGE not, that you be not judged.
2 For with what judgment you judge,
you shall be judged: and with what measure
you mete, it shall be measured to
you again.
3 And why behold the mote that is in
your brother's eye, but consider not the
beam that is in your own eye?
4 Or how will you say to your brother,
Let me pull out the mote out of your
eye; and, behold, a beam is in your own
eye?
5 You hypocrite, first cast out the beam
out of your own eye; and then shall you
see clearly to cast out the mote out of
your brother's eye.
6 Give not that which is holy to the dogs,
neither cast your pearls before swine,
lest they trample them under their feet,
and turn again and rend you.
7 *Ask, and it shall be given you; seek, and*
you shall find; knock, and it shall be opened
to you:
8 For every one that asks receives; and he
that seeks finds; and to him that knocks
it shall be opened.
9 Or what man is there of you, whom if
his son ask bread, will he give him a
stone?
10 Or if he ask a fish, will he give him a
serpent?
11 If you then, being evil, know how to
give good gifts to your children, how
much more shall your Father which is in
heaven give good things to them that ask
him?
12 Therefore all things whatsoever you
would that men should do to you, do you
even so to them: for this is the law and
the prophets.
13 Enter in at the strait gate: for wide is
the gate, and broad is the way, that leads

6:31–33 Seek first His kingdom. Think about how the Lord must feel when He sees us spending so much more energy satisfying and gratifying self while neglecting our commitments to Him. We spend so little time obeying His commandment to warn sinners to flee from the wrath to come. When we consider what He's done for us, our excuses fall short. It is as we seek *first* His kingdom that "all these things shall be added to you" (v. 33).

"The unmortified Christian and the heathen are of the same religion, and the deity they truly worship is the god of this world. What shall we eat? What shall we drink? What shall we wear? And how shall we pass away our time? Which way may we gather and perpetuate our names and families in the earth? It is a mournful reflection, but a truth which will not be denied, that these worldly lusts fill up a great part of the study, care and conversation of Christendom.

"The false notion that they may be children of God while in a state of disobedience to his holy commandments, and disciples of Jesus though they revolt from his cross, and members of his true church, which is without spot or wrinkle, notwithstanding their lives are full of spots and wrinkles, is of all other deceptions upon themselves the most pernicious to their eternal condition for they are at peace in sin and under a security in their transgression." *William Penn*

to destruction, and many there be which
go in thereat:
14 Because strait is the gate, and narrow
is the way, which leads to life, and few
there be that find it.
15 Beware of false prophets, which come
to you in sheep's clothing, but inwardly
they are ravening wolves.
16 You shall know them by their fruits.
Do men gather grapes of thorns, or figs
of thistles?
17 Even so every good tree brings forth
good fruit; but a corrupt tree brings forth
evil fruit.
18 A good tree cannot bring forth evil
fruit, neither can a corrupt tree bring forth
good fruit.
19 Every tree that brings not forth good
fruit is hewn down, and cast into the fire.
20 Wherefore by their fruits you shall
know them.
21 Not every one that says to me, Lord,
Lord, shall enter into the kingdom of heav-
en; but he that does the will of my Father
which is in heaven.
22 Many will say to me in that day, Lord,
Lord, have we not prophesied in your
name? and in your name have cast out
devils? and in your name done many wonderful works?
23 And then will I profess to them, I never knew you: depart from me, you that
work iniquity.
24 **Therefore whosoever hears these
sayings of mine, and does them, I will
liken him to a wise man, which built his
house upon a rock:**
25 **And the rain descended, and the
floods came, and the winds blew, and
beat upon that house; and it fell not: for
it was founded upon a rock.**

> The number one reason people don't share their faith is that their walk doesn't match their talk.
>
> **MARK CAHILL**

**26 And every one that hears these say-
ings of mine, and does them not, shall
be likened to a foolish man, which built
his house upon the sand:**
27 **And the rain descended, and the
floods came, and the winds blew, and
beat upon that house; and it fell: and
great was the fall of it.**
28 And it came to pass, when Jesus had
ended these sayings, the people were astonished at his doctrine:
29 For he taught them as one having
authority, and not as the scribes.

7:15 In Deuteronomy 18:20–22, the Bible proclaims capital punishment for a prophet who wasn't one hundred percent correct. Many think that the 16th-century astrologer Nostradamus was a prophet from God. However, only those who are ignorant of Bible prophecy will be impressed with the prophecies of Nostradamus. He was a false prophet who read the Bible in secret, stole its prophecies, and claimed them as his own.

7:22,23 These are perhaps the most frightening verses in the Bible. Vast multitudes of professing Christians fit into the category spoken of here. They call Jesus "Lord," but they practice lawlessness. They profess faith in Jesus, but have no regard for the divine Law. They tell "fibs" or "white" lies, take things that belong to others, have a roaming eye for the opposite sex, etc. They are liars, thieves, and adulterers at heart, who will be cast from the gates of heaven into the jaws of hell.

7:26 False converts. The foolish man was the one who heard the sayings of Jesus, but did not obey them. It's not the world that hears the sayings of Jesus and doesn't obey them. Most know only the "Golden Rule" and "Judge not," and even then their understanding is darkened. However, the Church is filled with false converts who sit among God's people and hear His words, but don't obey them. They build their house on sand rather than on the firm foundation of Jesus Christ and His words. *A. W. Tozer* said, "It is my opinion that tens of thousands of people, if not millions, have been brought into some kind of religious experience by accepting Christ, and they have not been saved." See Matthew 13:24–30 footnote.

CHAPTER 8

WHEN he was come down from the
mountain, great multitudes followed him.
2 And, behold, there came a leper and
worshipped him, saying, Lord, if you
will, you can make me clean.
3 And Jesus put forth his hand, and
touched him, saying, I will; be clean. And
immediately his leprosy was cleansed.
4 And Jesus said to him, See you tell no
man; but go your way, show yourself to
the priest, and offer the gift that Moses
commanded, for a testimony to them.
5 And when Jesus was entered into Capernaum, there came to him a centurion,
beseeching him,
6 And saying, Lord, my servant lies at
home sick of the palsy, grievously tormented.
7 And Jesus said to him, I will come and
heal him.
8 The centurion answered and said, Lord,
I am not worthy that you should come
under my roof: but speak the word only,
and my servant shall be healed.
9 For I am a man under authority, having soldiers under me: and I say to this
man, Go, and he goes; and to another,
Come, and he comes; and to my servant,
Do this, and he does it.
10 When Jesus heard it, he marveled,
and said to them that followed, Verily I
say to you, I have not found so great faith,
no, not in Israel.
11 And I say to you, That many shall
come from the east and west, and shall sit
down with Abraham, and Isaac, and Jacob, in the kingdom of heaven.
12 But the children of the kingdom shall
be cast out into outer darkness: there shall
be weeping and gnashing of teeth.
13 And Jesus said to the centurion, Go
your way; and as you have believed, so be
it done to you. And his servant was healed
in the selfsame hour.
14 And when Jesus was come into Peter's house, he saw his wife's mother laid,
and sick of a fever.
15 And he touched her hand, and the fever left her: and she arose, and ministered
to them.
16 When the even was come, they
brought to him many that were possessed
with devils: and he cast out the spirits with
his word, and healed all that were sick:
17 That it might be fulfilled which was
spoken by Isaiah the prophet, saying, Him-

8:2 Was Jesus God in human form? See John 8:58.

Jehovah's Witnesses: Was Jesus God, manifest in human form? The Bible tells us: "As Peter was coming in, Cornelius met him, and fell down at his feet, and worshipped him. But Peter took him up, saying, Stand up; I myself also am a man" (Acts 10:25,26). Peter refused worship in light of the Law that said, "You shall worship the Lord your God, and Him only you shall serve." In Revelation 19:10, when the apostle John saw an angel, he said, "I fell at his feet to worship him. And he said to me, See you do it not: I am your fellow-servant, and of your brethren that have the testimony of Jesus: worship God." Even the angel of the Lord refused to be worshipped.

However, here are many more verses showing that Jesus allowed Himself to be worshipped, simply because He was God "manifest in the flesh": "While he spoke these things to them, behold, there came a certain ruler, and worshipped him, saying, My daughter is even now dead: but come and lay your hand upon her, and she shall live" (Matthew 9:18); "Then they that were in the ship came and worshipped him, saying, Of a truth you are the Son of God" (Matthew 14:33): "Then she came and worshipped him, saying, Lord, help me" (Matthew 15:25); "And as they went to tell his disciples, behold, Jesus met them, saying, All hail. And they came and held him by the feet, and worshipped him" (Matthew 28:9); "When they saw him, they worshipped him: but some doubted" (Matthew 28:17). He received their worship because He was "the image of the invisible God" (Colossians 1:15)—"*God was manifest in the flesh*, justified in the Spirit, seen of angels, preached to the Gentiles, believed on in the world, received up into glory" (1 Timothy 3:16, emphasis added). See also chart "The Deity of Jesus" at John 10:36.

QUESTIONS & OBJECTIONS

8:14 ***"How should I witness to someone who belongs to a denomination, who I suspect isn't trusting the Savior?"***

The most effective way to speak about the issues of eternity to a religious person is not to get sidetracked from the essentials of salvation. Upon hearing a person's background, we may feel an obligation to speak to issues such as infant baptism, transubstantiation, etc. However, it is wise rather to build on the points of agreement between the Bible and the person's denomination, such as the virgin birth, the cross, and so on.

One point of agreement will almost certainly be the Ten Commandments. They are the key to bringing any religious person to a saving knowledge of the gospel. After someone is converted to Jesus Christ, the Bible will come alive and he will be led into all truth by the indwelling Holy Spirit. God's Word will then give him light, and he will forsake religious tradition as he is led by God.

While there are strong biblical arguments that may convince unregenerate people that their church's traditions contradict Holy Scripture, there is a difficulty. Some religious people hold the teachings of their church to be on a par with, or of greater authority than, Holy Scripture. It is therefore often futile to try to convince them intellectually that their trust should be in the person of Jesus Christ, rather than in their own righteousness or in their church traditions. For this reason we should aim at the conscience, rather than the intellect. Take them through the Law of God (the Commandments) to show that they are condemned despite their works, and strongly emphasize that we are saved by grace, and grace alone, rather than by trusting in our own righteousness or religious traditions.

If they are open to the gospel, and are interested in what God's Word says in reference to their church's teachings, they will listen to Scripture. For example, in Matthew 8:14 we see that Peter (whom the Roman Catholic church maintains was the first pope) was married, as were many of the other apostles (see 1 Corinthians 9:5).

self took our infirmities, and bare our sicknesses.
18 Now when Jesus saw great multitudes about him, he gave commandment to depart to the other side.
19 And a certain scribe came, and said to him, Master, I will follow you wherever you go.
20 And Jesus said to him, The foxes have holes, and the birds of the air have nests; but the Son of man has no where to lay his head.
21 **And another of his disciples said to him, Lord, suffer me first to go and bury my father.**
22 **But Jesus said to him, Follow me; and let the dead bury their dead.**
23 And when he was entered into a ship, his disciples followed him.
24 And, behold, there arose a great tempest in the sea, insomuch that the ship was covered with the waves: but he was asleep.
25 And his disciples came to him, and awoke him, saying, Lord, save us: we perish.
26 And he said to them, Why are you fearful, O you of little faith? Then he arose, and rebuked the winds and the sea; and there was a great calm.
27 But the men marveled, saying, What manner of man is this, that even the winds and the sea obey him!
28 And when he was come to the other side into the country of the Gergesenes, there met him two possessed with devils, coming out of the tombs, exceeding fierce, so that no man might pass by that way.
29 And, behold, they cried out, saying, What have we to do with you, Jesus, you Son of God? are you come here to torment us before the time?

30 And there was a good way off from
them an herd of many swine feeding.
31 So the devils besought him, saying,
If you cast us out, suffer us to go away
into the herd of swine.
32 And he said to them, Go. And when
they were come out, they went into the
herd of swine: and, behold, the whole
herd of swine ran violently down a steep
place into the sea, and perished in the
waters.
33 And they that kept them fled, and
went their ways into the city, and told
every thing, and what was befallen to the
possessed of the devils.
34 And, behold, the whole city came
out to meet Jesus: and when they saw
him, they besought him that he would
depart out of their coasts.

· · · · · ·

Learn how to prove God's existence. See Romans 1:20 footnote.

· · · · · ·

CHAPTER 9

AND he entered into a ship, and passed
over, and came into his own city.
2 And, behold, they brought to him a
man sick of the palsy, lying on a bed: and
Jesus seeing their faith said to the sick of
the palsy; Son, be of good cheer; your
sins be forgiven you.
3 And, behold, certain of the scribes said
within themselves, This man blasphemes.
4 And Jesus knowing their thoughts said,
Why do you think evil in your hearts?
5 For whether is easier, to say, Your sins
be forgiven you; or to say, Arise, and walk?
6 But that you may know that **the Son of
man has power on earth to forgive sins,**
(then said he to the sick of the palsy,)
Arise, take up your bed, and go to your
house.
7 And he arose, and departed to his house.
8 But when the multitudes saw it, they
marveled, and glorified God, which had
given such power to men.
9 And as Jesus passed forth from thence,

THE FUNCTION OF THE LAW

9:12 "Sinners that think they need no physician will not endure the healer's hand. The Law is therefore necessary to give knowledge of sin, so that proud man, who thought he was whole, may be humbled by the discovery of his own great wickedness, and sigh and pant after the grace that is set forth in Christ." *Martin Luther*

he saw a man, named Matthew, sitting at
the receipt of custom: and he said to him,
Follow me. And he arose, and followed
him.
10 And it came to pass, as Jesus sat at
meat in the house, behold, many publicans and sinners came and sat down with
him and his disciples.
11 And when the Pharisees saw it, they
said to his disciples, Why does your Master eat with publicans and sinners?
12 But when Jesus heard that, he said
to them, They that be whole need not a
physician, but they that are sick.
13 But go and learn what that means, I
will have mercy, and not sacrifice: for **I
am not come to call the righteous, but
sinners to repentance.**
14 Then came to him the disciples of
John, saying, Why do we and the Pharisees fast oft, but your disciples fast not?
15 And Jesus said to them, Can the children of the bridechamber mourn, as long
as the bridegroom is with them? but the
days will come, when the bridegroom
shall be taken from them, and then shall
they fast.
16 No man puts a piece of new cloth to
an old garment, for that which is put in
to fill it up takes from the garment, and
the rent is made worse.
17 Neither do men put new wine into
old bottles: else the bottles break, and
the wine runs out, and the bottles perish: but they put new wine into new bottles, and both are preserved.
18 While he spoke these things to them,
behold, there came a certain ruler, and

worshipped him, saying, My daughter is
even now dead: but come and lay your
hand upon her, and she shall live.
19 And Jesus arose, and followed him,
and so did his disciples.
20 And, behold, a woman, which was
diseased with an issue of blood twelve
years, came behind him, and touched the
hem of his garment:
21 For she said within herself, If I may
but touch his garment, I shall be whole.
22 But Jesus turned him about, and when
he saw her, he said, Daughter, be of good
comfort; your faith has made you whole.
And the woman was made whole from
that hour.
23 And when Jesus came into the ruler's house, and saw the minstrels and the
people making a noise,
24 He said to them, Give place: for the
maid is not dead, but sleeps. And they
laughed him to scorn.
25 But when the people were put forth,
he went in, and took her by the hand, and
the maid arose.
26 And the fame hereof went abroad into all that land.
27 And when Jesus departed thence, two
blind men followed him, crying, and saying, You Son of David, have mercy on us.
28 And when he was come into the
house, the blind men came to him: and
Jesus said to them, Do you believe that I
am able to do this? They said to him, Yes,
Lord.
29 Then touched he their eyes, saying,
According to your faith be it to you.
30 And their eyes were opened; and Jesus
straitly charged them, saying, See that no
man know it.
31 But they, when they were departed,
spread abroad his fame in all that country.
32 As they went out, behold, they brought
to him a dumb man possessed with a
devil.
33 And when the devil was cast out, the
dumb spoke: and the multitudes marveled,
saying, It was never so seen in Israel.
34 But the Pharisees said, He casts out
devils through the prince of the devils.
35 And Jesus went about all the cities and
villages, teaching in their synagogues,
and preaching the gospel of the kingdom,
and healing every sickness and every disease among the people.
36 But when he saw the multitudes, he
was moved with compassion on them, because they fainted, and were scattered
abroad, as sheep having no shepherd.
37 *Then said he to his disciples, The harvest
truly is plenteous, but the laborers are few;*
38 *Pray therefore the Lord of the harvest,
that he will send forth laborers into his
harvest.*

9:20 Evolution and blood. "Platelets" play an important role in preventing the loss of blood by beginning a chain reaction that results in blood clotting. As blood begins to flow from a cut or scratch, platelets respond to help the blood clot and to stop the bleeding after a short time.

Platelets promote the clotting process by clumping together and forming a plug at the site of a wound and then releasing proteins called "clotting factors." These proteins start a series of chemical reactions that are extremely complicated. Every step of the clotting must go smoothly if a clot is to form. If one of the clotting factors is missing or defective, the clotting process does not work. A serious genetic disorder known as "hemophilia" results from a defect in one of the clotting factor genes. Because they lack one of the clotting factors, hemophilia sufferers may bleed uncontrollably from even small cuts or scrapes.

To form a blood clot there must be twelve specific individual chemical reactions in our blood. If evolution is true, and if this 12-step process didn't happen in the first generation (i.e., if any one of these specific reactions failed to operate in their exact reaction and order), no creatures would have survived. They all would have bled to death!

9:38 If we are not laborers, we won't obey this command, because our conscience will condemn us. The devil therefore gets two victories: not only does the professing Christian not labor in the harvest fields, but neither does he pray for laborers.

"It is true that [many] are praying for worldwide revival. But it would be more timely, and more scriptural, for prayer to be made to the Lord of the harvest, that He would raise up and thrust forth laborers who would fearlessly and faithfully preach those truths which are calculated to bring about a revival."

A. W. Pink

CHAPTER 10

AND when he had called to him his twelve disciples, he gave them power against unclean spirits, to cast them out, and to heal all manner of sickness and all manner of disease.

2 Now the names of the twelve apostles are these; The first, Simon, who is called Peter, and Andrew his brother; James the son of Zebedee, and John his brother;

3 Philip, and Bartholomew; Thomas, and Matthew the publican; James the son of Alphaeus, and Lebbaeus, whose surname was Thaddaeus;

4 Simon the Canaanite, and Judas Iscariot, who also betrayed him.

5 These twelve Jesus sent forth, and commanded them, saying, Go not into the way of the Gentiles, and into any city of the Samaritans enter not:

6 But go rather to the lost sheep of the house of Israel.

7 *And as you go, preach, saying, The kingdom of heaven is at hand.*

8 *Heal the sick, cleanse the lepers, raise the dead, cast out devils: freely you have received, freely give.*

9 *Provide neither gold, nor silver, nor brass in your purses,*

10 *Nor scrip for your journey, neither two coats, neither shoes, nor yet staves: for the workman is worthy of his meat.*

11 *And into whatsoever city or town you shall enter, inquire who in it is worthy; and there abide till you go thence.*

12 *And when you come into an house, salute it.*

13 *And if the house be worthy, let your peace come upon it: but if it be not worthy, let your peace return to you.*

14 *And whosoever shall not receive you, nor hear your words, when you depart out of that house or city, shake off the dust of your feet.*

15 Verily I say to you, It shall be more tolerable for the land of Sodom and Gomorrha in the day of judgment, than for that city.

16 Behold, I send you forth as sheep in the midst of wolves: be therefore wise as serpents, and harmless as doves.

17 But beware of men: for they will deliver you up to the councils, and they will scourge you in their synagogues;

18 And you shall be brought before governors and kings for my sake, for a testimony against them and the Gentiles.

19 But when they deliver you up, take no thought how or what you shall speak: for it shall be given you in that same hour what you shall speak.

10:16 These verses contradict the "God loves you and has a wonderful plan for your life" promise of modern evangelism. It promises a life of roses without thorns. In reality, Jesus told His disciples that He was sending them among sharp thorns. Their own families would betray them and have them put to death for their faith (v. 21). This is the life Jesus promised believers: we would be hated for His name's sake and would be persecuted. See also John 15:18–21 footnote.

10:22 *God's Love: The Biblical Presentation*

The modern message of the gospel is "God loves you and has a wonderful plan for your life." However, our idea of "wonderful" and the world's may be a little different. Take a sinner through the pages of the Book of Acts and show him the terrifying scene of boulders breaking the bones of Stephen. Then smile and whisper, "*Wonderful*..." Listen together to the sound of a cat-o'-nine-tails as it rips the flesh off the back of the apostle Paul. Follow together the word "suffering" through the Epistles, and see if you can get the world to whisper, "Wonderful!" After such a ride down Honesty Road, they may think the pleasures of sin are a little more attractive than the call to "suffer affliction with the people of God." *John MacArthur* said, "We need to adjust our presentation of the gospel. We cannot dismiss the fact that God hates sin and punishes sinners with eternal torment. How can we begin a gospel presentation by telling people on their way to hell that God has a wonderful plan for their lives?"

Who in the world is going to listen if we are so blatantly honest about the Christian life? Perhaps not as many as are attracted by the talk of a wonderful plan. However, the answer to our dilemma is to make the issue one of righteousness, rather than happiness. This is what Jesus did. He used the Ten Commandments to show sinners the righteous standard of God (Luke 10:25,26; 18:18–20). Once the world sees the perfect standard by which they will be judged, they will begin to fear God, and through the fear of the Lord, men depart from sin (Proverbs 16:6). They will begin to hunger and thirst after the righteousness that is in Jesus Christ alone.

If you study the New Testament you will see that God's love is almost always given in direct correlation to the cross: herein is love, for God so loved, God commended His love, etc. (See John 3:16; Romans 5:5,6,8; Galatians 2:20; Ephesians 2:4,5; 5:2,25; 1 John 3:16; 4:10; and Revelation 1:5, among others.) The cross is the focal point of God's love for the world. How can we point to the cross without making reference to sin? How can we refer to sin without the Law (Romans 7:7)? The biblical way to express God's love to a sinner is to show him how great his sin is (using the Law—see Romans 7:13; Galatians 3:24), and then give him the incredible grace of God in Christ. This was the key to reaching so many on the Day of Pentecost. They were "devout" Jews who knew the Law and its holy demands, and therefore readily accepted the mercy of God in Christ to escape its fearful wrath.

When you use the Law to show the world their true state, get ready for sinners to thank you. For the first time in their lives, they will see the Christian message as an expression of love and concern for their eternal welfare, rather than of merely proselytizing for a better lifestyle while on this earth.

20 For it is not you that speak, but the
Spirit of your Father which speaks in you.
21 And the brother shall deliver up the
brother to death, and the father the child:
and the children shall rise up against their
parents, and cause them to be put to death.
22 And you shall be hated of all men for
my name's sake: but he that endures to
the end shall be saved.
23 But when they persecute you in this
city, flee into another: for verily I say to
you, You shall not have gone over the
cities of Israel, till the Son of man be come.
24 The disciple is not above his master,
nor the servant above his lord.
25 It is enough for the disciple that he

10:23 Don't wait around to be martyred. Leave when trouble brews. Paul once left a potential explosive situation by being lowered down a wall in a basket. Sometimes backing off can be humbling, but wise.

be as his master, and the servant as his
lord. If they have called the master of the
house Beelzebub, how much more shall
they call them of his household?
26 *Fear them not therefore: for there is
nothing covered, that shall not be revealed;
and hid, that shall not be known.*
27 *What I tell you in darkness, that speak
in light: and what you hear in the ear, that
preach upon the housetops.*
28 *And fear not them which kill the body,
but are not able to kill the soul: but rather
fear him which is able to destroy both soul
and body in hell.*
29 Are not two sparrows sold for a farthing? and one of them shall not fall on
the ground without your Father.
30 But the very hairs of your head are
all numbered.
31 Fear not therefore, you are of more
value than many sparrows.
32 **Whosoever therefore shall confess
me before men, him will I confess also
before my Father which is in heaven.**
33 **But whosoever shall deny me before
men, him will I also deny before my Father which is in heaven.**
34 Think not that I am come to send
peace on earth: I came not to send peace,
but a sword.
35 For I am come to set a man at variance
against his father, and the daughter against
her mother, and the daughter in law
against her mother in law.
36 And a man's foes shall be they of his
own household.
**37 He that loves father or mother more
than me is not worthy of me: and he that
loves son or daughter more than me is
not worthy of me.**
38 **And he that takes not his cross, and
follows after me, is not worthy of me.**
39 He that finds his life shall lose it:
and he that loses his life for my sake
shall find it.
40 He that receives you receives me, and
he that receives me receives him that sent
me.
41 He that receives a prophet in the name
of a prophet shall receive a prophet's reward; and he that receives a righteous man
in the name of a righteous man shall receive a righteous man's reward.
42 And whosoever shall give to drink to
one of these little ones a cup of cold water only in the name of a disciple, verily I
say to you, he shall in no wise lose his
reward.

10:23 Did Jesus say that He would return during the lifetime of His disciples? "Another alternative is to take the promise literally and immediately and to interpret the phrase 'before the Son of Man comes' as a reference to the fact that Jesus rejoined the disciples after their mission. This view may be supported by several facts. First, the phrase 'before the Son of Man comes' is never used by Matthew to describe the Second Coming. Second, it fits with a literal understanding of the first part of the verse. The disciples went literally and immediately into 'the cities of Israel' to preach, and Jesus literally and immediately rejoined them after their itinerant ministry." *Norman Geisler* and *Thomas Howe, When Critics Ask*

10:27,28 Faithful, not fearful, witnesses. We are to be faithful witnesses for Jesus. When it comes to preaching the gospel, we are to fear only God.

If you are fearful when it comes to witnessing, here's something you can do that doesn't take much courage. Go into a phone booth. Open the phone book to the Yellow Pages. Find "Abortion" and slip a tract in the page. Then look for the category "Escorts" and slip a tract in there. Many phone booths have a door, so you can go in, close the door and do this without fear of being seen. You are not breaking the law, and simply leaving a gospel tract in those two places may not only keep someone from making a terrible life-changing decision, but it may bring them to faith in the Savior.

10:28 Hell: For verses warning of its reality, see Matthew 18:9.

10:37 "People, who need people to walk with God, don't walk with God. They walk with people." *Emeal Zwayne*

"We must all mutually share in the knowledge that our existence only attains its true value when we have experienced in ourselves the truth of the declaration: 'He who loses his life shall find it.'"

Albert Schweitzer

CHAPTER 11

AND it came to pass, when Jesus had made an end of commanding his twelve disciples, he departed thence to teach and to preach in their cities.
2 Now when John had heard in the prison the works of Christ, he sent two of his disciples,
3 And said to him, are you he that should come, or do we look for another?
4 Jesus answered and said to them, Go and show John again those things which you do hear and see:
5 The blind receive their sight, and the lame walk, the lepers are cleansed, and the deaf hear, the dead are raised up, and the poor have the gospel preached to them.
6 **And blessed is he, whosoever shall not be offended in me.**
7 And as they departed, Jesus began to say to the multitudes concerning John, What did you go out into the wilderness to see? A reed shaken with the wind?
8 But what did you go out for to see? A man clothed in soft raiment? behold, they that wear soft clothing are in kings' houses.
9 But what did you go out for to see? A prophet? yea, I say to you, and more than a prophet.
10 For this is he, of whom it is written, Behold, I send my messenger before your face, which shall prepare your way before you.
11 Verily I say to you, Among them that are born of women there has not risen a greater than John the Baptist: notwithstanding he that is least in the kingdom of heaven is greater than he.
12 And from the days of John the Baptist until now the kingdom of heaven suffers violence, and the violent take it by force.
13 For all the prophets and the law prophesied until John.
14 And if you will receive it, this is Elijah, which was for to come.
15 He that has ears to hear, let him hear.
16 But whereunto shall I liken this generation? It is like unto children sitting in the markets, and calling to their fellows,

11:11 "If God has called you to be a missionary, your Father would be grieved for you to shrivel down into a king." *Charles Spurgeon*

11:12,13 The Law and the prophets were doing their job in Israel. The prophets established the inspiration of Holy Scripture, while the Law brought the knowledge of sin. When John began to preach that Israel should repent, they flocked to him for the baptism of repentance because the Law convinced them of sin. Just as a drowning man may become "violent" to be saved (and at times have to be knocked out by a lifeguard), so the Law makes a man *desperate* to be saved. It makes him take hold of the kingdom of God "by force."

11:14 This verse is often used to try and justify belief in reincarnation. However, Elijah wasn't reincarnated as John the Baptist. John merely came in the "spirit and power of Elijah" (Luke 1:17). It is appointed unto man *once* to die (see Hebrews 9:27).

QUESTIONS & OBJECTIONS

11:24

"God is unfair in that Hitler and a dear old lady (who never accepted Jesus) will both go to hell."

Sinners often accuse God of being unjust, because they assume that everyone will receive the same punishment in hell. God's judgment, however, will be according to righteousness (Acts 17:31). This verse shows that there will be *degrees* of punishment. See also Mark 6:11.

17 And saying, We have piped to you, and you have not danced; we have mourned to you, and you have not lamented.

18 For John came neither eating nor drinking, and they said, He has a devil.

19 The Son of man came eating and drinking, and they said, Behold a man gluttonous, and a winebibber, a friend of publicans and sinners. But wisdom is justified of her children.

20 Then began he to upbraid the cities wherein most of his mighty works were done, because they repented not:

21 Woe to you, Chorazin! woe to you, Bethsaida! for if the mighty works, which were done in you, had been done in Tyre and Sidon, they would have repented long ago in sackcloth and ashes.

22 But I say to you, It shall be more tolerable for Tyre and Sidon at the day of judgment, than for you.

23 And you, Capernaum, which are exalted to heaven, shall be brought down to hell: for if the mighty works, which have been done in you, had been done in Sodom, it would have remained until this day.

24 But I say to you, That it shall be more tolerable for the land of Sodom in the day of judgment, than for you.

25 **At that time Jesus answered and said, I thank you, O Father, Lord of heaven and earth, because you have hid these things from the wise and prudent, and have revealed them to babes.**

26 **Even so, Father: for so it seemed good in your sight.**

27 All things are delivered to me of my Father: and no man knows the Son, but the Father; neither knows any man the Father, save the Son, and he to whomsoever the Son will reveal him.

28 **Come to me, all you that labor and are heavy laden, and I will give you rest.**

29 **Take my yoke upon you, and learn of me; for I am meek and lowly in heart: and you shall find rest to your souls.**

30 **For my yoke is easy, and my burden is light.**

CHAPTER 12

AT that time Jesus went on the sabbath day through the corn; and his disciples were an hungered, and began to pluck the ears of corn, and to eat.

2 But when the Pharisees saw it, they said to him, Behold, your disciples do that which is not lawful to do upon the sabbath day.

3 But he said to them, Have you not read what David did, when he was an hungered, and they that were with him;

4 How he entered into the house of God, and did eat the shewbread, which was not lawful for him to eat, neither for them which were with him, but only for the priests?

5 Or have you not read in the law, how that on the sabbath days the priests in the temple profane the sabbath, and are blameless?

6 But I say to you, That in this place is one greater than the temple.

7 But if you had known what this means, I will have mercy, and not sacrifice, you would not have condemned the guiltless.

8 For the Son of man is Lord even of the sabbath day.

9 And when he was departed thence, he
went into their synagogue:
10 And, behold, there was a man which
had his hand withered. And they asked
him, saying, Is it lawful to heal on the sabbath days? that they might accuse him.
11 And he said to them, What man shall
there be among you, that shall have one
sheep, and if it fall into a pit on the sabbath day, will he not lay hold on it, and
lift it out?
12 How much then is a man better than
a sheep? Wherefore it is lawful to do well
on the sabbath days.

> Mass crusades, to which I have committed my life, will never finish the job; but one to one will.
>
> **BILLY GRAHAM**

13 Then said he to the man, Stretch forth
your hand. And he stretched it forth; and
it was restored whole, like as the other.
14 Then the Pharisees went out, and held
a council against him, how they might destroy him.
15 But when Jesus knew it, he withdrew
himself from thence: and great multitudes
followed him, and he healed them all;
16 And charged them that they should
not make him known:
17 That it might be fulfilled which was
spoken by Isaiah the prophet, saying,
18 Behold my servant, whom I have
chosen; my beloved, in whom my soul is
well pleased: I will put my Spirit upon
him, and he shall show judgment to the
Gentiles.
19 He shall not strive, nor cry; neither
shall any man hear his voice in the streets.
20 A bruised reed shall he not break,
and smoking flax shall he not quench, till
he send forth judgment to victory.
21 And in his name shall the Gentiles
trust.
22 Then was brought to him one possessed with a devil, blind, and dumb:
and he healed him, insomuch that the
blind and dumb both spoke and saw.
23 And all the people were amazed, and
said, Is not this the son of David?
24 But when the Pharisees heard it, they
said, This fellow does not cast out devils,
but by Beelzebub the prince of the devils.
25 And Jesus knew their thoughts, and
said to them, Every kingdom divided
against itself is brought to desolation; and
every city or house divided against itself
shall not stand:
26 And if Satan cast out Satan, he is divided against himself; how shall then his
kingdom stand?
27 And if I by Beelzebub cast out devils, by whom do your children cast them
out? therefore they shall be your judges.
28 But if I cast out devils by the Spirit of
God, then the kingdom of God is come
to you.
29 Or else how can one enter into a
strong man's house, and spoil his goods,
except he first bind the strong man? and
then he will spoil his house.
30 He that is not with me is against me;
and he that gathers not with me scatters
abroad.
31 Wherefore I say to you, All manner
of sin and blasphemy shall be forgiven to
men: but the blasphemy against the Holy
Spirit shall not be forgiven to men.
32 And whosoever speaks a word against
the Son of man, it shall be forgiven him:
but whosoever speaks against the Holy
Spirit, it shall not be forgiven him, neither
in this world, neither in the world to come.
33 Either make the tree good, and his
fruit good; or else make the tree corrupt,
and his fruit corrupt: for the tree is known
by his fruit.
34 O generation of vipers, how can you,
being evil, speak good things? for out of
the abundance of the heart the mouth
speaks.
35 A good man out of the good treasure
of the heart brings forth good things:
and an evil man out of the evil treasure
brings forth evil things.
36 But I say to you, That every idle
word that men shall speak, they shall

Questions & Objections

12:39 *"If God gives me some 'sign,' then I will believe."*

The unsaved often want a "sign" from God. This is in spite of the testimony of creation, their conscience, the Bible, and the Christian. The cross is the only thing that can truly convince a sinner of the reality of who Jesus is. Once they understand that the holes in His hands and His feet are there because of their own sin, they will fall at His feet and cry, "My Lord and my God!"

give account thereof in the day of judgment.
37 For by your words you shall be justified, and by your words you shall be condemned.
38 Then certain of the scribes and of the Pharisees answered, saying, Master, we would see a sign from you.
39 But he answered and said to them, An evil and adulterous generation seeks after a sign; and there shall no sign be given to it, but the sign of the prophet Jonah:
40 For as Jonah was three days and three nights in the whale's belly; so shall the Son of man be three days and three nights in the heart of the earth.
41 The men of Nineveh shall rise in judgment with this generation, and shall condemn it: because they repented at the preaching of Jonah; and, behold, a greater than Jonah is here.
42 The queen of the south shall rise up in the judgment with this generation, and shall condemn it: for she came from the uttermost parts of the earth to hear the wisdom of Solomon; and, behold, a greater than Solomon is here.
43 When the unclean spirit is gone out of a man, he walks through dry places, seeking rest, and finds none.
44 Then he says, I will return into my house from whence I came out; and when he is come, he finds it empty, swept, and garnished.
45 Then goes he, and takes with himself seven other spirits more wicked than himself, and they enter in and dwell there: and the last state of that man is worse than the first. Even so shall it be also to this wicked generation.

12:36 Idle words divide the body. In 1 Kings 3:16–27, the Bible tells of two harlots claiming to be the mother of one child. Solomon revealed his God-given wisdom by suggesting that the child be cut in two, thus exposing the true mother. The false mother preferred to divide the body rather than back down from her claim.

It is interesting to note that both women dwelt in the same house, just as both the wheat and the tares sit alongside each other in the House of God (Matthew 13:24–30,38). Each of the women called Solomon "lord," and both the wheat and tares call Jesus "Lord" (Matthew 7:21). It is not always easy to discern the wheat from the tares because it takes the wisdom of Solomon to do so. Here is wisdom—*the false convert will show his spirit by, without hesitation, dividing the Body of Christ in two, rather than gracefully making a withdrawal*. He will cut a body of believers in half with vicious gossip. He sows discord among the brethren. He is a slave to his tongue, which is a "world of iniquity…set on fire of hell" (James 3:6).

However, the true convert sets a watch at the door of his mouth, and will immediately back away from words that would divide a local church. He knows that "the beginning of strife is as when one lets out water" (Proverbs 17:14). He doesn't become involved in idle talk. He is a peacemaker, a child of God. The fear of God is his guide. He knows that there is not a word on his tongue that God doesn't know, and that on Judgment Day he will give an account for every idle word he speaks.

12:40 How long was Jesus in the tomb? To first-century Jews, any part of a day could be counted as if it were a full day, just as a child born December 31 at 11:59 p.m. is deductible for income-tax purposes for the full year. "Three days and three nights" may simply refer to three twenty-four-hour days (sunset-to-sunset periods), and Jesus was in fact in the tomb during part of three different days.

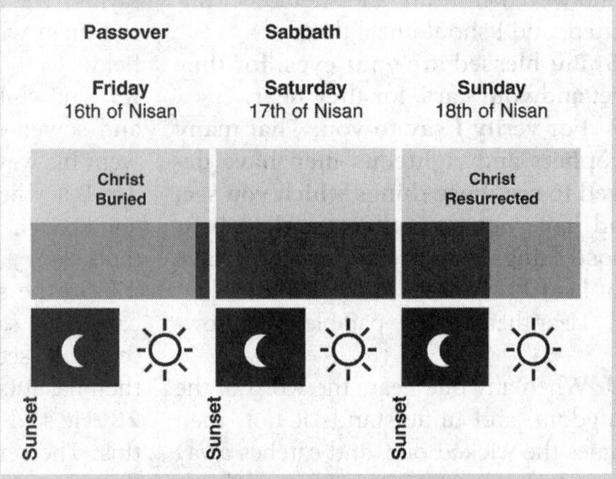

46 While he yet talked to the people, behold, his mother and his brethren stood without, desiring to speak with him.

47 Then one said to him, Behold, your mother and your brethren stand without, desiring to speak with you.

48 But he answered and said to him that told him, Who is my mother? and who are my brethren?

49 And he stretched forth his hand toward his disciples, and said, Behold my mother and my brethren!

50 For whosoever shall do the will of my Father which is in heaven, the same is my brother, and sister, and mother.

CHAPTER 13

THE same day went Jesus out of the house, and sat by the sea side.

2 And great multitudes were gathered together to him, so that he went into a ship, and sat; and the whole multitude stood on the shore.

3 And he spoke many things to them in parables, saying, Behold, a sower went forth to sow;

4 And when he sowed, some seeds fell by the way side, and the fowls came and devoured them up:

5 Some fell upon stony places, where they had not much earth: and forthwith they sprung up, because they had no deepness of earth:

6 And when the sun was up, they were scorched; and because they had no root, they withered away.

7 And some fell among thorns; and the thorns sprung up, and choked them:

8 But other fell into good ground, and brought forth fruit, some an hundredfold, some sixtyfold, some thirtyfold.

9 Who has ears to hear, let him hear.

10 And the disciples came, and said to him, Why do you speak to them in parables?

11 He answered and said to them, Because it is given to you to know the mysteries of the kingdom of heaven, but to them it is not given.

12 For whosoever has, to him shall be given, and he shall have more abundance: but whosoever has not, from him shall be taken away even that he has.

13 Therefore speak I to them in parables: because they seeing see not; and hearing they hear not, neither do they understand.

14 And in them is fulfilled the prophecy of Isaiah, which says, By hearing you shall hear, and shall not understand; and seeing you shall see, and shall not perceive:

15 For this people's heart is waxed gross, and their ears are dull of hearing, and their eyes they have closed; lest at any time they should see with their eyes, and hear with their ears, and should under-

stand with their heart, and should be converted, and I should heal them.
**16 But blessed are your eyes, for they
see: and your ears, for they hear.**
17 **For verily I say to you, That many
prophets and righteous men have desired to see those things which you see,
and have not seen them; and to hear
those things which you hear, and have
not heard them.**
18 Hear therefore the parable of the sower.
19 When any one hears the word of the
kingdom, and understands it not, then
comes the wicked one, and catches away
that which was sown in his heart. This is
he which received seed by the way side.
20 But he that received the seed into
stony places, the same is he that hears
the word, and anon with joy receives it;
21 Yet has he not root in himself, but
endures for a while: for when tribulation
or persecution arises because of the word,
by and by he is offended.
22 He also that received seed among
the thorns is he that hears the word; and
the care of this world, and the deceitfulness of riches, choke the word, and he
becomes unfruitful.
23 But he that received seed into the
good ground is he that hears the word,
and understands it; which also bears fruit,
and brings forth, some an hundredfold,
some sixty, some thirty.
24 Another parable put he forth to them,
saying, The kingdom of heaven is likened
to a man which sowed good seed in his
field:
25 But while men slept, his enemy came
and sowed tares among the wheat, and
went his way.
26 But when the blade was sprung up,
and brought forth fruit, then appeared the
tares also.
27 So the servants of the householder
came and said to him, Sir, did not you
sow good seed in your field? from whence
then has it tares?
28 He said to them, An enemy has done
this. The servants said to him, Will you
then that we go and gather them up?
29 But he said, Nay; lest while you gather up the tares, you root up also the wheat
with them.
30 Let both grow together until the harvest: and in the time of harvest I will say
to the reapers, Gather together first the
tares, and bind them in bundles to burn
them: but gather the wheat into my barn.
31 Another parable put he forth to them,
saying, The kingdom of heaven is like to
a grain of mustard seed, which a man
took, and sowed in his field:
32 Which indeed is the least of all seeds:
but when it is grown, it is the greatest
among herbs, and becomes a tree, so that
the birds of the air come and lodge in the
branches thereof.
33 Another parable spoke he to them;
The kingdom of heaven is like to leaven,

13:16 These are not the words of merely a "great teacher." These are the words of God in human form. He was speaking of Himself—blessed are those who see Him and hear His words. He was either the greatest egotist who ever lived, or He was the source of life in the flesh.

13:19 The key difference between the "wayside" hearer in this verse and the "good soil" hearer in verse 19 is understanding. This is why we must use the Law as a "schoolmaster" to bring the knowledge of sin (Galatians 3:24; Romans 3:20). Unless there is understanding as to his true plight, the sinner will not flee to the Savior.

"I had rather be fully understood by ten than admired by ten thousand." *Jonathan Edwards*

13:24–30 The wheat and the tares are the true and the false converts sitting alongside each other until the time of harvest. (See vv. 37–43.) For more on true and false converts, see Matthew 25:12 footnote.

"There are probably more unsaved church people than we can begin to imagine." *Gary Labro*

which a woman took, and hid in three measures of meal, till the whole was leavened.
34 All these things spoke Jesus to the multitude in parables; and without a parable spoke he not to them:
35 That it might be fulfilled which was spoken by the prophet, saying, I will open my mouth in parables; I will utter things which have been kept secret from the foundation of the world.
36 Then Jesus sent the multitude away, and went into the house: and his disciples came to him, saying, Declare to us the parable of the tares of the field.
37 He answered and said to them, He that sows the good seed is the Son of man;
38 The field is the world; the good seed are the children of the kingdom; but the tares are the children of the wicked one;
39 The enemy that sowed them is the devil; the harvest is the end of the world; and the reapers are the angels.
40 As therefore the tares are gathered and burned in the fire; so shall it be in the end of this world.
41 The Son of man shall send forth his angels, and they shall gather out of his kingdom all things that offend, and them which do iniquity;
42 And shall cast them into a furnace of fire: there shall be wailing and gnashing of teeth.
43 Then shall the righteous shine forth as the sun in the kingdom of their Father. Who has ears to hear, let him hear.
44 Again, the kingdom of heaven is like to treasure hid in a field; the which when a man has found, he hides, and for joy thereof goes and sells all that he has, and buys that field.
45 Again, the kingdom of heaven is like to a merchant man, seeking goodly pearls:
46 Who, when he had found one pearl of great price, went and sold all that he had, and bought it.
47 Again, the kingdom of heaven is like to a net, that was cast into the sea, and gathered of every kind:
48 Which, when it was full, they drew to shore, and sat down, and gathered the good into vessels, but cast the bad away.
49 So shall it be at the end of the world: the angels shall come forth, and sever the wicked from among the just,
50 And shall cast them into the furnace of fire: there shall be wailing and gnashing of teeth.
51 Jesus said to them, Have you understood all these things? They said to him, Yea, Lord.
52 Then said he to them, Therefore every scribe which is instructed to the kingdom of heaven is like to a man that is an householder, which brings forth out of his treasure things new and old.
53 And it came to pass, that when Jesus had finished these parables, he departed thence.
54 And when he was come into his own country, he taught them in their synagogue, insomuch that they were astonished, and said, Whence has this man this wisdom, and these mighty works?
55 Is not this the carpenter's son? is not his mother called Mary? and his brethren, James, and Joses, and Simon, and Judas?
56 And his sisters, are they not all with us? Whence then has this man all these things?
57 And they were offended in him. But Jesus said to them, A prophet is not without honor, save in his own country, and in his own house.
58 And he did not many mighty works there because of their unbelief.

CHAPTER 14

AT that time Herod the tetrarch heard of the fame of Jesus,
2 And said to his servants, This is John the Baptist; he is risen from the dead;

13:34,35 Messianic prophecy fulfilled: "I will open my mouth in a parable: I will utter dark sayings of old" (Psalm 78:2). See Matthew 26:15 footnote.

and therefore mighty works do show
forth themselves in him.
3 For Herod had laid hold on John, and
bound him, and put him in prison for
Herodias' sake, his brother Philip's wife.
4 For John said to him, It is not lawful
for you to have her.
5 And when he would have put him to
death, he feared the multitude, because
they counted him as a prophet.
6 But when Herod's birthday was kept,
the daughter of Herodias danced before
them, and pleased Herod.
7 Whereupon he promised with an oath
to give her whatsoever she would ask.
8 And she, being before instructed of her
mother, said, Give me here John Baptist's
head in a charger.
9 And the king was sorry: nevertheless
for the oath's sake, and them which sat
with him at meat, he commanded it to
be given her.
10 And he sent, and beheaded John in
the prison.
11 And his head was brought in a charger, and given to the damsel: and she
brought it to her mother.
12 And his disciples came, and took up
the body, and buried it, and went and told
Jesus.
13 When Jesus heard of it, he departed
thence by ship into a desert place apart:
and when the people had heard thereof,
they followed him on foot out of the cities.
14 And Jesus went forth, and saw a great
multitude, and was moved with compassion toward them, and he healed their
sick.
15 And when it was evening, his disciples came to him, saying, This is a desert
place, and the time is now past; send the
multitude away, that they may go into the
villages, and buy themselves victuals.
16 But Jesus said to them, They need not
depart; you give them to eat.
17 And they said to him, We have here
but five loaves, and two fishes.
18 He said, Bring them here to me.
19 And he commanded the multitude
to sit down on the grass, and took the five
loaves, and the two fishes, and looking
up to heaven, he blessed, and broke, and
gave the loaves to his disciples, and the
disciples to the multitude.
20 And they did all eat, and were filled:
and they took up of the fragments that
remained twelve baskets full.
21 And they that had eaten were about
five thousand men, beside women and
children.
22 And straightway Jesus constrained his
disciples to get into a ship, and to go before him to the other side, while he sent
the multitudes away.
23 And when he had sent the multitudes away, he went up into a mountain
apart to pray: and when the evening was
come, he was there alone.
24 But the ship was now in the midst of
the sea, tossed with waves: for the wind
was contrary.
25 And in the fourth watch of the night
Jesus went to them, walking on the sea.
26 And when the disciples saw him walk-

14:15–21 Sharing the Bread of Life. Compare this incident with 2 Kings 4:42–44, in which one hundred men were fed twenty loaves of barley bread. The Lord instructed Elisha, "Give unto the people, that they may eat…They shall eat, and shall leave thereof." In both incidents, the people were given bread to eat and had some left over. We have eaten from the Bread of Life, and now we must take that Bread to a starving world.

"The disciples watched miraculous healings for hours and then approached the Master and told Him three things: 1) the hour was late; 2) they were in a 'deserted place'; and 3) the multitude needed to eat. Jesus told His disciples that they should be the source of the multitude being fed. The boy's lunch (John 6:9) was the best they could bring, and Jesus did a miracle when they brought the best they had. Then He had them pick up what remained. There were twelve baskets, for twelve disciples. I believe Jesus was saying: 'Now that I showed you how, go feed your own multitude.'" *Mike Smalley*

ing on the sea, they were troubled, saying,
It is a spirit; and they cried out for fear.
27 But straightway Jesus spoke to them,
saying, Be of good cheer; it is I; be not
afraid.
28 And Peter answered him and said,
Lord, if it be you, bid me come to you on
the water.
29 And he said, Come. And when Peter
was come down out of the ship, he walked
on the water, to go to Jesus.
30 But when he saw the wind boister-
ous, he was afraid; and beginning to sink,
he cried, saying, Lord, save me.
31 And immediately Jesus stretched forth
his hand, and caught him, and said to him,
O you of little faith, wherefore did you
doubt?
32 And when they were come into the
ship, the wind ceased.
33 Then they that were in the ship came
and worshipped him, saying, Of a truth
you are the Son of God.
34 And when they were gone over, they
came into the land of Gennesaret.
35 And when the men of that place had
knowledge of him, they sent out into all
that country round about, and brought
to him all that were diseased;
36 And besought him that they might
only touch the hem of his garment: and
as many as touched were made perfectly
whole.

CHAPTER 15

THEN came to Jesus scribes and Pharisees, which were of Jerusalem, saying,
2 Why do your disciples transgress the
tradition of the elders? for they wash not
their hands when they eat bread.
3 But he answered and said to them, Why
do you also transgress the commandment
of God by your tradition?
4 For God commanded, saying, Honor
your father and mother: and, He that curses father or mother, let him die the death.
5 But you say, Whosoever shall say to
his father or his mother, It is a gift, by
whatsoever you might be profited by me;
6 And honor not his father or his mother, he shall be free. Thus have you made
the commandment of God of none effect
by your tradition.

> Save some, O Christians! By all means, save some. From yonder flames and outer darkness, and the weeping, wailing, and gnashing of teeth, seek to save some! Let this, as in the case of the apostle, be your great, ruling object in life, that by all means you might save some.
>
> **CHARLES SPURGEON**

7 You hypocrites, well did Isaiah prophesy of you, saying,
8 This people draws near to me with their
mouth, and honors me with their lips;
but their heart is far from me.
9 But in vain they do worship me, teaching for doctrines the commandments of
men.
10 And he called the multitude, and said
to them, Hear, and understand:
11 Not that which goes into the mouth
defiles a man; but that which comes out
of the mouth, this defiles a man.
12 Then came his disciples, and said to
him, Do you know that the Pharisees were
offended, after they heard this saying?
13 But he answered and said, Every plant,

14:28 Peter said, "Lord, if it be you, bid me come to you on the water." Peter had the concept, and Jesus put His blessing on Peter's idea. Peter knew Jesus intimately—he knew the mind of the Master. He knew that his desire wasn't an impertinent presumption, but just a longing to follow the Lord into the realm of the supernatural. Jesus said, "If any man serve me, let him follow me; and where I am, there shall also my servant be: if any man serve me, him will my Father honor" (John 12:26).

which my heavenly Father has not planted, shall be rooted up.
14 Let them alone: they be blind leaders of the blind. And if the blind lead the blind, both shall fall into the ditch.
15 Then answered Peter and said to him, Declare to us this parable.
16 And Jesus said, Are you also yet without understanding?
17 Do not you yet understand, that whatsoever enters in at the mouth goes into the belly, and is cast out into the draught?
18 But those things which proceed out of the mouth come forth from the heart; and they defile the man.
19 For out of the heart proceed evil thoughts, murders, adulteries, fornications, thefts, false witness, blasphemies:
20 **These are the things which defile a man: but to eat with unwashed hands defiles not a man.**
21 Then Jesus went thence, and departed into the coasts of Tyre and Sidon.
22 And, behold, a woman of Canaan came out of the same coasts, and cried to him, saying, Have mercy on me, O Lord, you Son of David; my daughter is grievously vexed with a devil.
23 But he answered her not a word. And his disciples came and besought him, saying, Send her away; for she cries after us.
24 But he answered and said, I am not sent but to the lost sheep of the house of Israel.
25 Then came she and worshipped him, saying, Lord, help me.
26 But he answered and said, It is not meet to take the children's bread, and to cast it to dogs.
27 And she said, Truth, Lord: yet the dogs eat of the crumbs which fall from their masters' table.
28 Then Jesus answered and said to her, O woman, great is your faith: be it to you even as you will. And her daughter was made whole from that very hour.
29 And Jesus departed from thence, and came near to the sea of Galilee; and went up into a mountain, and sat down there.
30 And great multitudes came to him, having with them those that were lame, blind, dumb, maimed, and many others, and cast them down at Jesus' feet; and he healed them:
31 Insomuch that the multitude wondered, when they saw the dumb to speak, the maimed to be whole, the lame to walk, and the blind to see: and they glorified the God of Israel.
32 Then Jesus called his disciples to him, and said, I have compassion on the multitude, because they continue with me now three days, and have nothing to eat: and I will not send them away fasting, lest they faint in the way.
33 And his disciples said to him, Whence should we have so much bread in the wilderness, as to fill so great a multitude?
34 And Jesus said to them, How many loaves have you? And they said, Seven, and a few little fishes.

15:19 The spiritual nature of the Law. Notice how the sins named are transgressions of the Moral Law—the Ten Commandments. If civil law can prove that you are planning to assassinate the president, you can be prosecuted and severely punished. That law, however, is limited in its search for evidence—it can't see what a man thinks. Not so with the all-seeing eye of our Creator. His Law searches the heart. He sees "evil thoughts," and requires truth in the inward parts (Psalm 51:6). To *think* hatred is to commit murder (1 John 3:15) and transgress the Sixth Commandment. To *think* lustfully is to commit adultery (Matthew 5:27,28) and transgress the Seventh. Fornication breaks the same Commandment (Galatians 5:19). Then Jesus names theft (Eighth Commandment), false witness (Ninth), and blasphemies (Third). A person cannot lust without breaking the Tenth, and by their nature, these sins transgress the remaining four Commandments. All sin traces in some way back to the Moral Law, for sin is transgression of the Law (1 John 3:4). This is why the Law must be used to bring the knowledge of sin to religious people who are trusting in their own righteous deeds for their salvation.

35 And he commanded the multitude
to sit down on the ground.
36 And he took the seven loaves and the
fishes, and gave thanks, and broke them,
and gave to his disciples, and the disciples
to the multitude.
37 And they did all eat, and were filled:
and they took up of the broken meat that
was left seven baskets full.
38 And they that did eat were four thousand men, beside women and children.
39 And he sent away the multitude, and
took ship, and came into the coasts of
Magdala.

CHAPTER 16

THE Pharisees also with the Sadducees came, and tempting desired him
that he would show them a sign from
heaven.
2 He answered and said to them, When it
is evening, you say, It will be fair weather: for the sky is red.
3 And in the morning, It will be foul
weather to day: for the sky is red and low-
ring. O you hypocrites, you can discern
the face of the sky; but can you not discern the signs of the times?
4 A wicked and adulterous generation
seeks after a sign; and there shall no sign
be given to it, but the sign of the prophet
Jonah. And he left them, and departed.
5 And when his disciples were come to
the other side, they had forgotten to take
bread.
6 Then Jesus said to them, Take heed
and beware of the leaven of the Pharisees
and of the Sadducees.
7 And they reasoned among themselves,
saying, It is because we have taken no
bread.
8 Which when Jesus perceived, he said
to them, O you of little faith, why reason
among yourselves, because you have
brought no bread?
9 Do you not yet understand, neither remember the five loaves of the five thousand, and how many baskets you took up?
10 Neither the seven loaves of the four
thousand, and how many baskets you took
up?
11 How is it that you do not understand
that I spoke it not to you concerning bread,
that you should beware of the leaven of
the Pharisees and of the Sadducees?
12 Then understood they how that he
bade them not beware of the leaven of
bread, but of the doctrine of the Pharisees
and of the Sadducees.
13 When Jesus came into the coasts of
Caesarea Philippi, he asked his disciples,
saying, Whom do men say that I the Son
of man am?
14 And they said, Some say that you are
John the Baptist: some, Elijah; and others, Jeremias, or one of the prophets.
15 **He said to them, But who do you
say that I am?**
16 **And Simon Peter answered and
said, You are the Christ, the Son of the
living God.**
**17 And Jesus answered and said to
him, Blessed are you, Simon Barjona:
for flesh and blood has not revealed it
to you, but my Father which is in heav-
en.**
**18 And I say also to you, That you are
Peter, and upon this rock I will build
my church; and the gates of hell shall
not prevail against it.**

16:17 Don't see it as your job to convince a Muslim, Mormon, or other unbeliever that Jesus is God. That's the Father's job. Our part is to share the simple message of the gospel.

16:18 Jesus is not saying that Peter is the "rock" upon which He will build His Church. That would contradict Scripture. First Corinthians 3:11 makes it clear that Jesus is the only foundation, and the "rock" is the revelation that He is the Christ, the Son of the Living God. See Romans 9:33.

16:18 "Give me one hundred preachers who fear nothing but sin and desire nothing but God, and I care not a straw whether they be clergymen or laymen, such alone will shake the gates of hell and set up the kingdom of God upon earth." *John Wesley*

Springboards for Preaching and Witnessing

16:26

Money or Water?

If you were offered a handful of $1,000 bills or a glass of cool water, which would you choose? The $1,000 bills, of course—*anyone in his right mind would.* However, if you were crawling through a desert, dying of thirst, and you were offered a glass of water or a handful of $1,000 bills, which would you take? The water, of course—*anyone in his right mind would.* That's called "circumstantial priorities." Your priorities change according to your circumstances.

If there were a way to find *everlasting* life, would you want to know about it? The answer is "yes," of course—*anyone in his right mind would.* What the Bible contains may surprise you. The Scriptures speak of riches beyond our wildest dreams—the "riches" of everlasting life—and they are offered in the form of cool, clear water: "Let him that is athirst come. And whosoever will, let him take the water of life freely" (Revelation 22:17). At the moment, you may not be interested in the offer, but on Judgment Day your circumstances will radically change. Then it will be too late.

19 And I will give to you the keys of the
kingdom of heaven: and whatsoever you
shall bind on earth shall be bound in
heaven: and whatsoever you shall loose
on earth shall be loosed in heaven.
20 Then charged he his disciples that
they should tell no man that he was Jesus
the Christ.
21 From that time forth began Jesus to
show to his disciples, how that he must
go to Jerusalem, and suffer many things
of the elders and chief priests and scribes,
and be killed, and be raised again the third
day.
22 Then Peter took him, and began to rebuke him, saying, Be it far from you,
Lord: this shall not be to you.
23 But he turned, and said to Peter, Get
you behind me, Satan: you are an offence
to me: for you savour not the things that
be of God, but those that be of men.
24 **Then said Jesus to his disciples, If
any man will come after me, let him
deny himself, and take up his cross,
and follow me.**
25 **For whosoever will save his life
shall lose it: and whosoever will lose
his life for my sake shall find it.**
**26 For what is a man profited, if he
shall gain the whole world, and lose his
own soul? or what shall a man give in
exchange for his soul?**
27 For the Son of man shall come in the
glory of his Father with his angels; and
then he shall reward every man according
to his works.
28 Verily I say to you, There be some
standing here, which shall not taste of
death, till they see the Son of man coming in his kingdom.

CHAPTER 17

AND after six days Jesus took Peter,
James, and John his brother, and
brought them up into an high mountain
apart,

16:23 If you are going to do something in the area of evangelism, be sure you set your face like a "flint" to do so (Isaiah 50:7). A flint is a very hard stone that produces sparks when struck. That's what Peter found when he tried to deter Jesus from doing God's will. The enemy will try to discourage you, and where you least expect it.

16:27 Second coming of Jesus: See Matthew 24:27.

17:1–8 The new birth is a Mount of Transfiguration experience. It is divine revelation as to who Jesus is: He is the One to whom the Law (Moses) and the prophets (Elijah) testify. Those who hear the voice of the Father hear the voice of the Son. They fall on their faces before Jesus and see no one but Him.

2 And was transfigured before them: and
his face did shine as the sun, and his raiment was white as the light.
3 And, behold, there appeared to them
Moses and Elijah talking with him.
4 Then answered Peter, and said to Jesus,
Lord, it is good for us to be here: if you
will, let us make here three tabernacles;
one for you, and one for Moses, and one
for Elijah.
5 While he yet spoke, behold, a bright
cloud overshadowed them: and behold a
voice out of the cloud, which said, This
is my beloved Son, in whom I am well
pleased; hear him.
6 And when the disciples heard it, they
fell on their face, and were sore afraid.
7 And Jesus came and touched them,
and said, Arise, and be not afraid.
8 And when they had lifted up their
eyes, they saw no man, save Jesus only.
9 And as they came down from the
mountain, Jesus charged them, saying,
Tell the vision to no man, until the Son
of man be risen again from the dead.
10 And his disciples asked him, saying,
Why then say the scribes that Elijah must
first come?
11 And Jesus answered and said to them,
Elijah truly shall first come, and restore all
things.
12 But I say to you, That Elijah is come
already, and they knew him not, but have
done to him whatsoever they listed. Likewise shall also the Son of man suffer of
them.
13 Then the disciples understood that
he spoke to them of John the Baptist.
14 And when they were come to the
multitude, there came to him a certain
man, kneeling down to him, and saying,
15 Lord, have mercy on my son: for he
is lunatic, and sore vexed: for often he
falls into the fire, and oft into the water.
16 And I brought him to your disciples,
and they could not cure him.
17 Then Jesus answered and said, O
faithless and perverse generation, how
long shall I be with you? how long shall
I suffer you? bring him here to me.
18 And Jesus rebuked the devil; and he
departed out of him: and the child was
cured from that very hour.
19 Then came the disciples to Jesus apart,
and said, Why could not we cast him out?
20 And Jesus said to them, Because of
your unbelief: for verily I say to you, If
you have faith as a grain of mustard seed,
you shall say to this mountain, Remove
hence to yonder place; and it shall remove; and nothing shall be impossible to
you.
21 Howbeit this kind goes not out but
by prayer and fasting.

"God loves with a great love the man whose heart is bursting with a passion for the impossible."

William Booth

17:10 See Matthew 11:13 footnote.

17:20 "The prayer power has never been tried to its full capacity. If we want to see mighty works of Divine power and grace wrought in the place of weakness, failure and disappointment, let us answer God's standing challenge, 'Call to me, and I will answer you, and show you great and mighty things, which you do not know' [Jeremiah 33:3]." *Hudson Taylor*

QUESTIONS & OBJECTIONS

18:9 *"My God would never create hell."*

Those who say that are right: their "god" would never create hell, because he *couldn't*. He doesn't exist. He is a figment of their imagination, a god they have created to suit themselves. It's called "idolatry," and it's the oldest sin in the Book. Idolaters will not inherit the kingdom of God. The one true God, however, could and did create hell for those who reject His mercy. They will reap His just wrath. (For the reasonableness of hell, see Psalm 55:15 footnote.)

22 And while they abode in Galilee, Jesus said to them, The Son of man shall be betrayed into the hands of men:
23 And they shall kill him, and the third day he shall be raised again. And they were exceeding sorry.
24 And when they were come to Capernaum, they that received tribute money came to Peter, and said, Does not your master pay tribute?
25 He said, Yes. And when he was come into the house, Jesus prevented him, saying, What do you think, Simon? of whom do the kings of the earth take custom or tribute? of their own children, or of strangers?
26 Peter said to him, Of strangers. Jesus said to him, Then are the children free.
27 Notwithstanding, lest we should offend them, go to the sea, and cast an hook, and take up the fish that first comes up; and when you have opened his mouth, you shall find a piece of money: that take, and give to them for me and you.

CHAPTER 18

AT the same time came the disciples to Jesus, saying, Who is the greatest in the kingdom of heaven?
2 **And Jesus called a little child to him, and set him in the midst of them,**
3 **And said, Verily I say to you, Except you be converted, and become as little children, you shall not enter into the kingdom of heaven.**
4 Whosoever therefore shall humble himself as this little child, the same is greatest in the kingdom of heaven.
5 And whoso shall receive one such little child in my name receives me.
6 But whoso shall offend one of these little ones which believe in me, it were better for him that a millstone were hanged about his neck, and that he were drowned in the depth of the sea.
7 Woe to the world because of offences! for it must needs be that offences come; but woe to that man by whom the offence comes!
8 **Wherefore if your hand or your foot offend you, cut them off, and cast them from you: it is better for you to enter into life halt or maimed, rather than having two hands or two feet to be cast into everlasting fire.**
9 And if your eye offend you, pluck it out, and cast it from you: it is better for you to enter into life with one eye, rather than having two eyes to be cast into hell fire.
10 Take heed that you despise not one of these little ones; for I say to you, That in heaven their angels do always behold the face of my Father which is in heaven.
11 For the Son of man is come to save that which was lost.
12 *How do you think? if a man has an hundred sheep, and one of them be gone astray, does he not leave the ninety and nine, and go into the mountains, and seek*

18:9 Hell: For verses warning of its reality, see Matthew 23:33.

that which is gone astray?
13 *And if so be that he find it, verily I say to you, he rejoices more of that sheep, than of the ninety and nine which went not astray.*
14 *Even so it is not the will of your Father which is in heaven, that one of these little ones should perish.*
15 Moreover if your brother shall trespass against you, go and tell him his fault between you and him alone: if he shall hear you, you have gained your brother.
16 But if he will not hear you, then take with you one or two more, that in the mouth of two or three witnesses every word may be established.
17 And if he shall neglect to hear them, tell it to the church: but if he neglect to hear the church, let him be to you as an heathen man and a publican.
18 Verily I say to you, Whatsoever you shall bind on earth shall be bound in heaven: and whatsoever you shall loose on earth shall be loosed in heaven.
19 Again I say to you, That if two of you shall agree on earth as touching any thing that they shall ask, it shall be done for them of my Father which is in heaven.
20 For where two or three are gathered together in my name, there am I in the midst of them.
21 Then came Peter to him, and said, Lord, how oft shall my brother sin against me, and I forgive him? till seven times?
22 Jesus said to him, I say not to you, Until seven times: but, Until seventy times seven.
23 Therefore is the kingdom of heaven likened to a certain king, which would take account of his servants.
24 And when he had begun to reckon, one was brought to him, which owed him ten thousand talents.
25 But forasmuch as he had not to pay, his lord commanded him to be sold, and his wife, and children, and all that he had, and payment to be made.
26 The servant therefore fell down, and worshipped him, saying, Lord, have patience with me, and I will pay you all.
27 Then the lord of that servant was moved with compassion, and loosed him, and forgave him the debt.
28 But the same servant went out, and found one of his fellow-servants, which owed him an hundred pence: and he laid hands on him, and took him by the throat, saying, Pay me that you owe.
29 And his fellow-servant fell down at his feet, and besought him, saying, Have patience with me, and I will pay you all.
30 And he would not: but went and cast him into prison, till he should pay the debt.
31 So when his fellow-servants saw what was done, they were very sorry, and came and told to their lord all that was done.
32 Then his lord, after that he had called him, said to him, O you wicked servant, I forgave you all that debt, because you desired me:
33 Should not you also have had compassion on your fellow-servant, even as I had pity on you?
34 And his lord was wroth, and delivered him to the tormentors, till he should pay all that was due to him.
35 So likewise shall my heavenly Father do also to you, if you from your hearts forgive not every one his brother their trespasses.

CHAPTER 19

AND it came to pass, that when Jesus had finished these sayings, he departed from Galilee, and came into the coasts of Judea beyond Jordan;
2 And great multitudes followed him; and he healed them there.

18:11 "We would not see nor realize it (what a distressing and horrible fall in which we lie), if it were not for the Law, and we would have to remain forever lost, if we were not again helped out of it through Christ. Therefore the Law and the gospel are given to the end that we may learn to know both how guilty we are and to what we should again return." *Martin Luther*

QUESTIONS & OBJECTIONS

19:16 "I need to get my life cleaned up first."

Those who think that they can clean up their lives don't see their true plight. They are standing guilty before a wrath-filled God. They have been condemned by His Law (John 3:18; Romans 3:19). If a man commits rape and murder and admits to the judge that he is guilty, will the judge let him go just because the man says he will clean up his life? He is in debt to the law and must be punished. We may be able to clean up our lives in the sight of man, but not in the sight of God. The only way we can be cleansed is to repent and trust in the Savior.

3 The Pharisees also came to him, tempting him, and saying to him, Is it lawful
for a man to put away his wife for every
cause?
4 And he answered and said to them,
Have you not read, that he who made
them at the beginning made them male
and female,
5 And said, For this cause shall a man
leave father and mother, and shall cleave
to his wife: and they twain shall be one
flesh?
6 Wherefore they are no more twain, but
one flesh. What therefore God has joined
together, let not man put asunder.
7 They said to him, Why did Moses then
command to give a writing of divorcement, and to put her away?
8 He said to them, Moses because of the
hardness of your hearts suffered you to
put away your wives: but from the beginning it was not so.
9 And I say to you, Whosoever shall put
away his wife, except it be for fornication,
and shall marry another, commits adultery: and whoso marries her which is put
away does commit adultery.
10 His disciples said to him, If the case
of the man be so with his wife, it is not
good to marry.
11 But he said to them, All men cannot
receive this saying, save they to whom it
is given.
12 For there are some eunuchs, which
were so born from their mother's womb:
and there are some eunuchs, which were
made eunuchs of men: and there be eunuchs, which have made themselves eunuchs for the kingdom of heaven's sake.
He that is able to receive it, let him re-

19:3–6 Jesus confirmed that the creation of Adam and Eve was a real historical event when He quoted Genesis 1:27 and 2:24 in His teaching. Genesis is quoted more than sixty times in seventeen books of the New Testament. See also Mark 10:6–9 and 2 Corinthians 11:3 footnotes.

19:4 Evolution—the origin of sexes. Almost all forms of complex life have both male and female—horses, dogs, humans, moths, monkeys, fish, elephants, birds, etc. The male needs the female to reproduce, and the female needs the male to reproduce. *One cannot carry on life without the other.* Which then came first according to the evolutionary theory? If a male came into being before a female, how did the male of each species reproduce *without* females? How is it possible that a male and a female each spontaneously came into being, yet they have complex, complementary reproductive systems? If each sex was able to reproduce without the other, why (and how) would they have developed a reproductive system that requires both sexes in order for the species to survive? See Psalm 139:14 and Mark 10:6 footnotes.

"I myself am convinced that the theory of evolution, especially the extent to which it has been applied, will be one of the great jokes in the history books of the future. Posterity will marvel that so flimsy and dubious an hypothesis could be accepted with the incredible credulity that it has."
Malcolm Muggeridge, British journalist and philosopher

ceive it.
13 Then were there brought to him little children, that he should put his hands
on them, and pray: and the disciples rebuked them.
14 But Jesus said, Suffer little children,
and forbid them not, to come to me: for
of such is the kingdom of heaven.
15 And he laid his hands on them, and
departed thence.
**16 And, behold, one came and said to
him, Good Master, what good thing
shall I do, that I may have eternal life?
17 And he said to him, Why do you call
me good? there is none good but one,
that is, God: but if you will enter into
life, keep the commandments.
18 He said to him, Which? Jesus said,
You shall do no murder, You shall not
commit adultery, You shall not steal,
You shall not bear false witness,
19 Honor your father and your mother: and, You shall love your neighbour
as yourself.
20 The young man said to him, All
these things have I kept from my youth
up: what lack I yet?
21 Jesus said to him, If you will be perfect, go and sell what you have, and give
to the poor, and you shall have treasure
in heaven: and come and follow me.
22 But when the young man heard that
saying, he went away sorrowful: for he
had great possessions.**
23 **Then said Jesus to his disciples, Verily I say to you, That a rich man shall
hardly enter into the kingdom of heav-
en.
24 And again I say to you, It is easier
for a camel to go through the eye of a
needle, than for a rich man to enter into the kingdom of God.**
25 When his disciples heard it, they were
exceedingly amazed, saying, Who then can
be saved?
26 But Jesus beheld them, and said to
them, With men this is impossible; but
with God all things are possible.
27 Then answered Peter and said to him,
Behold, we have forsaken all, and followed you; what shall we have therefore?
28 And Jesus said to them, Verily I say
to you, That you which have followed me,
in the regeneration when the Son of man
shall sit in the throne of his glory, you
also shall sit upon twelve thrones, judging the twelve tribes of Israel.

USING THE LAW IN EVANGELISM

19:17–22 Here is the Master Evangelist showing us how to deal with a proud, self-righteous person—a typical sinner. This is noticeably different from the approach of modern evangelism. When the man asked how he could obtain eternal life, Jesus did not ask, "Would you like to have the assurance that if you died tonight you would go straight to heaven? You can have that confidence right now simply by acknowledging that you have sinned against God, and by trusting in the finished work of Calvary's cross. Would you like me to lead you in prayer right now so that you can have that assurance?" Instead, Jesus pointed him to the Law so that he could recognize his sin. Biblical evangelism is always "Law to the proud, grace to the humble." *John Newton* said, "My grand point in preaching is to break the hard heart and to heal the broken one."

This young man is a prime example of an unregenerate person. He had no understanding of the word "good." Jesus reproved him, then gently gave him five horizontal Commandments—those dealing with his fellow man. When the man revealed his self-righteousness, Jesus showed him that in his vertical relationship with God he had transgressed the First of the Ten Commandments. God wasn't foremost in his life. The rich young man loved his money, and the Scriptures make it clear that we cannot serve God and mammon (money). The Law brought him "the knowledge of sin."

In light of the way most Christians share the gospel, Jesus failed because He didn't get a "decision." However, heaven doesn't rejoice over "decisions." It reserves its rejoicing for repentance, and there can be no repentance without a God-given knowledge of sin—and that, according to Scripture, can come only by the Law (Romans 7:7). See Mark 10:17 and John 4:7 comments.

29 And every one that has forsaken houses, or brethren, or sisters, or father, or mother, or wife, or children, or lands, for my name's sake, shall receive an hundredfold, and shall inherit everlasting life.

30 But many that are first shall be last; and the last shall be first.

CHAPTER 20

FOR the kingdom of heaven is like to a man that is an householder, which went out early in the morning to hire laborers into his vineyard.

2 And when he had agreed with the laborers for a penny a day, he sent them into his vineyard.

3 And he went out about the third hour, and saw others standing idle in the marketplace,

4 And said to them; Go also into the vineyard, and whatsoever is right I will give you. And they went their way.

5 Again he went out about the sixth and ninth hour, and did likewise.

6 And about the eleventh hour he went out, and found others standing idle, and said to them, Why do you stand here all the day idle?

7 They said to him, Because no man has hired us. He said to them, Go also into the vineyard; and whatsoever is right, that shall you receive.

8 So when even was come, the lord of the vineyard said to his steward, Call the laborers, and give them their hire, beginning from the last to the first.

9 And when they came that were hired about the eleventh hour, they received every man a penny.

10 But when the first came, they supposed that they should have received more; and they likewise received every man a penny.

11 And when they had received it, they murmured against the goodman of the house,

12 Saying, These last have wrought but one hour, and you have made them equal to us, which have borne the burden and heat of the day.

13 But he answered one of them, and said, Friend, I do you no wrong: did not you agree with me for a penny?

14 Take what is yours, and go your way: I will give to this last, even as to you.

15 Is it not lawful for me to do what I will with mine own? Is your eye evil, because I am good?

16 So the last shall be first, and the first last: for many be called, but few chosen.

17 And Jesus going up to Jerusalem took the twelve disciples apart in the way, and said to them,

18 Behold, we go up to Jerusalem; and the Son of man shall be betrayed to the chief priests and to the scribes, and they shall condemn him to death,

19 And shall deliver him to the Gentiles to mock, and to scourge, and to crucify him: and the third day he shall rise again.

20 Then came to him the mother of Zebedee's children with her sons, worship-

19:24 The eye of a needle. A common interpretation is that Jerusalem had a main gate, beside which was a smaller gate called "the eye of a needle." When the main gate was closed, a camel had to forsake its load, then get on its knees and crawl through the smaller gate to enter the city. This is what a rich man must do to enter the celestial city. He must forsake his riches and humble himself to enter. Interesting though it may sound, it is unlikely that this is correct, because of the response of both the disciples and Jesus. If that's what Jesus was saying, the disciples would have more than likely responded with something like, "That makes sense." Instead, they were "exceedingly amazed." What Jesus had said *astonished* them. He didn't then respond to their astonishment by saying that it was "difficult" for a camel to get through the eye of the needle. Rather, He used the word "impossible." It would seem therefore that the analogy was to a literal camel and a literal needle.

"The gate of heaven, though it is so wide that the greatest sinner may enter, is nevertheless so low that pride can never pass through it." *Charles Spurgeon*

ping him, and desiring a certain thing of him.
21 And he said to her, What do you want? She said to him, Grant that these my two sons may sit, the one on your right hand, and the other on the left, in your kingdom.
22 But Jesus answered and said, You know not what you ask. Are you able to drink of the cup that I shall drink of, and to be baptized with the baptism that I am baptized with? They said to him, We are able.
23 And he said to them, You shall drink indeed of my cup, and be baptized with the baptism that I am baptized with: but to sit on my right hand, and on my left, is not mine to give, but it shall be given to them for whom it is prepared of my Father.
24 And when the ten heard it, they were moved with indignation against the two brethren.
25 But Jesus called them to him, and said, You know that the princes of the Gentiles exercise dominion over them, and they that are great exercise authority upon them.
26 But it shall not be so among you: but whosoever will be great among you, let him be your minister;
27 And whosoever will be chief among you, let him be your servant:
28 Even as the Son of man came not to be ministered unto, but to minister, and to give his life a ransom for many.
29 And as they departed from Jericho, a great multitude followed him.
30 And, behold, two blind men sitting by the way side, when they heard that Jesus passed by, cried out, saying, Have mercy on us, O Lord, you Son of David.
31 And the multitude rebuked them, because they should hold their peace: but they cried the more, saying, Have mercy on us, O Lord, you Son of David.
32 And Jesus stood still, and called them, and said, What will you that I shall do to you?
33 They said to him, Lord, that our eyes may be opened.
34 So Jesus had compassion on them, and touched their eyes: and immediately their eyes received sight, and they followed him.

· · · · ·

For the Bible's uniqueness, see Psalm 119:105 footnote.

· · · · ·

CHAPTER 21

AND when they drew near to Jerusalem, and were come to Bethphage, to the mount of Olives, then sent Jesus two disciples,
2 Saying to them, Go into the village over against you, and straightway you shall find an ass tied, and a colt with her: loose them, and bring them to me.
3 And if any man says anything to you, you shall say, The Lord has need of them; and straightway he will send them.
4 All this was done, that it might be fulfilled which was spoken by the prophet, saying,
5 Tell the daughter of Zion, Behold, your King comes to you, meek, and sitting upon an ass, and a colt the foal of an ass.
6 And the disciples went, and did as Jesus commanded them,
7 And brought the ass, and the colt, and put on them their clothes, and they set

20:28 "If the sinless Christ, who is literally God in human flesh and Lord of all, would so humble Himself for us, we dare not denigrate humility or aspire to self-esteem instead of lowliness... Do you want to be blessed? Develop a servant's heart. If Jesus can step down from His glorious equality with God to become a man, and then further humble Himself to be a servant and wash the feet of twelve undeserving sinners—then humble Himself to die so horribly on our behalf, surely we ought to be willing to suffer any indignity to serve Him." *John MacArthur*, "Humility," *Moody Magazine*

him thereon.
8 And a very great multitude spread their
garments in the way; others cut down
branches from the trees, and strawed them
in the way.
9 And the multitudes that went before,
and that followed, cried, saying, Hosanna to the Son of David: Blessed is he that
comes in the name of the Lord; Hosanna
in the highest.
10 And when he was come into Jerusalem, all the city was moved, saying, Who
is this?
11 And the multitude said, This is Jesus
the prophet of Nazareth of Galilee.
12 And Jesus went into the temple of
God, and cast out all them that sold and
bought in the temple, and overthrew the
tables of the moneychangers, and the
seats of them that sold doves,
13 And said to them, It is written, My
house shall be called the house of prayer;
but you have made it a den of thieves.
14 And the blind and the lame came to
him in the temple; and he healed them.
15 And when the chief priests and scribes
saw the wonderful things that he did, and
the children crying in the temple, and
saying, Hosanna to the Son of David; they
were sore displeased,
16 And said to him, Hear what these say?
And Jesus said to them, Yea; have you
never read, Out of the mouth of babes
and sucklings you have perfected praise?
17 And he left them, and went out of the
city into Bethany; and he lodged there.
18 Now in the morning as he returned
into the city, he hungered.
19 And when he saw a fig tree in the
way, he came to it, and found nothing
thereon, but leaves only, and said to it,
Let no fruit grow on you henceforward
for ever. And presently the fig tree withered away.
20 And when the disciples saw it, they
marveled, saying, How soon is the fig tree
withered away!
21 Jesus answered and said to them,
Verily I say to you, If you have faith, and
doubt not, you shall not only do this
which is done to the fig tree, but also if
you shall say to this mountain, Be removed, and be cast into the sea; it shall
be done.
22 And all things, whatsoever you shall
ask in prayer, believing, you shall receive.
23 And when he was come into the temple, the chief priests and the elders of the
people came to him as he was teaching,
and said, By what authority do you do
these things? and who gave you this authority?
24 And Jesus answered and said to them,
I also will ask you one thing, which if
you tell me, I in like wise will tell you by
what authority I do these things.
25 The baptism of John, whence was it?
from heaven, or of men? And they reasoned with themselves, saying, If we shall
say, From heaven; he will say to us, Why
did you not then believe him?
26 But if we shall say, Of men; we fear
the people; for all hold John as a prophet.
27 And they answered Jesus, and said,
We cannot tell. And he said to them,
Neither tell I you by what authority I do
these things.
28 But what do you think? A certain man
had two sons; and he came to the first, and
said, Son, go work to day in my vineyard.
29 He answered and said, I will not: but
afterward he repented, and went.
30 And he came to the second, and said
likewise. And he answered and said, I

21:12,13 See Mark 11:15 footnote. "Genuine outrage is not just a permissible reaction to the hard-pressed Christian; God himself feels it, and so should the Christian in the presence of pain, cruelty, violence, and injustice. God, who is the Father of Jesus Christ, is neither impersonal nor beyond good and evil. By the absolute immutability of His character, He is implacably opposed to evil and outraged by it." *Os Guinness*

"Tolerance is a virtue for those who have no convictions." *G. K. Chesterton*

go, sir: and went not.
31 Which of the two did the will of his
father? They said to him, The first. Jesus
said to them, Verily I say to you, That the
publicans and the harlots go into the kingdom of God before you.
32 For John came to you in the way of
righteousness, and you believed him not:
but the publicans and the harlots believed
him: and you, when you had seen it, repented not afterward, that you might believe him.

> Preaching the gospel is to us a matter of life and death; we throw our whole soul into it. We live and are happy if you believe in Jesus and are saved. But we are almost ready to die if you refuse the gospel of Christ.
>
> **CHARLES SPURGEON**

33 Hear another parable: There was a
certain householder, which planted a vineyard, and hedged it round about, and dug
a winepress in it, and built a tower, and
let it out to husbandmen, and went into
a far country:
34 And when the time of the fruit drew
near, he sent his servants to the husbandmen, that they might receive the fruits of
it.
35 And the husbandmen took his servants, and beat one, and killed another,
and stoned another.
36 Again, he sent other servants more
than the first: and they did to them likewise.
37 But last of all he sent to them his son,
saying, They will reverence my son.
38 But when the husbandmen saw the
son, they said among themselves, This is
the heir; come, let us kill him, and let us
seize on his inheritance.
39 And they caught him, and cast him
out of the vineyard, and slew him.
40 When the lord therefore of the vineyard comes, what will he do to those husbandmen?
41 They said to him, He will miserably
destroy those wicked men, and will let
out his vineyard to other husbandmen,
which shall render him the fruits in their
seasons.
42 Jesus said to them, Did you never
read in the scriptures, The stone which
the builders rejected, the same is become
the head of the corner: this is the Lord's
doing, and it is marvelous in our eyes?
43 Therefore say I to you, The kingdom
of God shall be taken from you, and given
to a nation bringing forth the fruits thereof.
44 And whosoever shall fall on this stone
shall be broken: but on whomsoever it
shall fall, it will grind him to powder.
45 And when the chief priests and Pharisees had heard his parables, they perceived that he spoke of them.
46 But when they sought to lay hands
on him, they feared the multitude, because they took him for a prophet.

CHAPTER 22

AND Jesus answered and spoke to
them again by parables, and said,
2 The kingdom of heaven is like to a certain king, which made a marriage for his
son,
3 And sent forth his servants to call them
that were bidden to the wedding: and they
would not come.
4 Again, he sent forth other servants, saying, Tell them which are bidden, Behold,
I have prepared my dinner: my oxen and

21:44 Those who fall upon the stone of Jesus Christ are broken. He will not despise a broken and contrite heart. However, when Jesus comes in flaming fire, taking vengeance on those who do not know God (2 Thessalonians 1:8), His judgment will "grind them to powder." When you grind something to powder, you do a thorough job. He will judge right down to the thoughts and intents of the heart.

my fatlings are killed, and all things are
ready: come to the marriage.
5 But they made light of it, and went their
ways, one to his farm, another to his merchandise:
6 And the remnant took his servants, and
entreated them spitefully, and slew them.
7 But when the king heard thereof, he
was wroth: and he sent forth his armies,
and destroyed those murderers, and burned
up their city.
8 Then said he to his servants, The wedding is ready, but they which were bidden were not worthy.
9 Go therefore into the highways, and as
many as you shall find, bid to the marriage.
10 So those servants went out into the
highways, and gathered together all as
many as they found, both bad and good:
and the wedding was furnished with
guests.
11 And when the king came in to see the
guests, he saw there a man which had not
on a wedding garment:
12 And he said to him, Friend, how did
you come in here not having a wedding
garment? And he was speechless.
13 Then said the king to the servants,
Bind him hand and foot, and take him
away, and cast him into outer darkness;
there shall be weeping and gnashing of
teeth.
14 For many are called, but few are chosen.
15 Then went the Pharisees, and took
counsel how they might entangle him in
his talk.
16 And they sent out to him their disciples with the Herodians, saying, Master,
we know that you are true, and teach the
way of God in truth, neither care you for
any man: for you regard not the person of
men.
17 Tell us therefore, What do you think?
Is it lawful to give tribute to Caesar, or not?
18 But Jesus perceived their wickedness,
and said, Why tempt me, you hypocrites?
19 Show me the tribute money. And
they brought to him a penny.
20 And he said to them, Whose is this
image and superscription?
21 They said to him, Caesar's. Then said
he to them, Render therefore to Caesar the
things which are Caesar's; and to God the
things that are God's.
22 When they had heard these words,
they marveled, and left him, and went
their way.
23 The same day came to him the Sadducees, which say that there is no resurrection, and asked him,

Believe what you do believe, or else you will never persuade anybody else to believe it.

CHARLES SPURGEON

24 Saying, Master, Moses said, If a man
die, having no children, his brother shall
marry his wife, and raise up seed to his
brother.
25 Now there were with us seven brethren: and the first, when he had married a
wife, deceased, and, having no issue, left
his wife to his brother:
26 Likewise the second also, and the
third, to the seventh.
27 And last of all the woman died also.
28 Therefore in the resurrection whose
wife shall she be of the seven? for they all
had her.
29 Jesus answered and said to them, You
do err, not knowing the scriptures, nor
the power of God.
30 For in the resurrection they neither
marry, nor are given in marriage, but are
as the angels of God in heaven.
31 But as touching the resurrection of
the dead, have you not read that which

22:29 This is the error of the ungodly. They are ignorant of Holy Scripture and they have a darkened understanding of the power of God.

was spoken to you by God, saying,
32 I am the God of Abraham, and the God of Isaac, and the God of Jacob? God is not the God of the dead, but of the living.
33 And when the multitude heard this, they were astonished at his doctrine.
34 But when the Pharisees had heard that he had put the Sadducees to silence, they were gathered together.
35 Then one of them, which was a lawyer, asked him a question, tempting him, and saying,
36 Master, which is the great commandment in the law?
37 Jesus said to him, You shall love the Lord your God with all your heart, and with all your soul, and with all your mind.
38 This is the first and great commandment.
39 And the second is like it, You shall love your neighbour as yourself.
40 On these two commandments hang all the law and the prophets.
41 While the Pharisees were gathered together, Jesus asked them,
42 Saying, What do you think of Christ? whose son is he? They said to him, The Son of David.
43 He said to them, How then does David in spirit call him Lord, saying,
44 The LORD said to my Lord, Sit on my right hand, till I make your enemies your footstool?
45 If David then called him Lord, how is he his son?
46 And no man was able to answer him a word, neither dared any man from that day forth ask him any more questions.

CHAPTER 23

THEN spoke Jesus to the multitude, and to his disciples,
2 Saying, The scribes and the Pharisees sit in Moses' seat:
3 All therefore whatsoever they bid you observe, that observe and do; but do not after their works: for they said, and do not.
4 For they bind heavy burdens and grievous to be borne, and lay them on men's shoulders; but they themselves will not move them with one of their fingers.
5 But all their works they do for to be seen of men: they make broad their phylacteries, and enlarge the borders of their garments,
6 And love the uppermost rooms at feasts, and the chief seats in the synagogues,
7 And greetings in the markets, and to be called of men, Rabbi, Rabbi.
8 But be not called Rabbi: for one is your Master, even Christ; and all you are brethren.
9 And call no man your father upon the earth: for one is your Father, which is in heaven.
10 Neither be called masters: for one is

22:36–40 At war with the Law. "There is a war between you and God's Law. The Ten Commandments are against you. The first comes forward and says, 'Let him be cursed. For he denies Me. He has another god beside Me. His god is his belly and he yields his homage to his lust.' All the Ten Commandments, like ten great cannons, are pointed at you today. For you have broken all of God's statutes and lived in daily neglect of all His commands.

"Soul, thou wilt find it a hard thing to go at war with the Law. When the Law came in peace, Sinai was altogether on a smoke and even Moses said, 'I exceeding fear and quake!' What will you do when the Law of God comes in terror; when the trumpet of the archangel shall tear you from your grave; when the eyes of God shall burn their way into your guilty soul; when the great books shall be opened and all your sin and shame shall be punished... Can you stand against an angry Law in that Day?" *Charles Spurgeon*

23:9 Jesus commanded His followers not to call any man "father." The Pharisees loved to be seen and praised by men. They cherished their titles—Rabbi (Matthew 23:8) and Father (Acts 7:2; 22:1). Jesus condemned these titles because of their hypocrisy. Paul used them rightly in reference to those whom he had begotten through the gospel (1 Corinthians 4:15).

QUESTIONS & OBJECTIONS

23:13–16 ***"You shouldn't talk about sin because Jesus didn't condemn anybody. He was always loving and kind."***

Jesus did indeed condemn some people for their sin. In Matthew 23 He called the religious leaders "hypocrites" seven times. He told them that they were "blind fools," children of hell, full of hypocrisy and sin. He climaxed His sermon by saying, "You serpents, you generation of vipers, how shall you escape the damnation of hell?" (v. 33). He then warned that He would say to the wicked, "Depart from Me, you cursed, into everlasting fire, prepared for the devil and his angels" (Matthew 25:41).

your Master, even Christ.

11 But he that is greatest among you shall be your servant.

12 And whosoever shall exalt himself shall be abased; and he that shall humble himself shall be exalted.

13 But woe to you, scribes and Pharisees, hypocrites! for you shut up the kingdom of heaven against men: for you neither go in yourselves, neither suffer them that are entering to go in.

14 Woe to you, scribes and Pharisees, hypocrites! for you devour widows' houses, and for a pretence make long prayer: therefore you shall receive the greater damnation.

15 Woe to you, scribes and Pharisees, hypocrites! for you compass sea and land to make one proselyte, and when he is made, you make him twofold more the child of hell than yourselves.

16 Woe to you, you blind guides, which say, Whosoever shall swear by the temple, it is nothing; but whosoever shall swear by the gold of the temple, he is a debtor!

17 You fools and blind: for whether is greater, the gold, or the temple that sanctifies the gold?

18 And, Whosoever shall swear by the altar, it is nothing; but whosoever swears by the gift that is upon it, he is guilty.

19 You fools and blind: for whether is greater, the gift, or the altar that sanctifies the gift?

20 Whoso therefore shall swear by the altar, swears by it, and by all things thereon.

21 And whoso shall swear by the temple, swears by it, and by him that dwells therein.

22 And he that shall swear by heaven, swears by the throne of God, and by him that sits thereon.

23 Woe to you, scribes and Pharisees, hypocrites! for you pay tithe of mint and anise and cummin, and have omitted the weightier matters of the law, judgment, mercy, and faith: these ought you to have done, and not to leave the other undone.

24 You blind guides, which strain at a gnat, and swallow a camel.

25 Woe to you, scribes and Pharisees, hypocrites! for you make clean the outside of the cup and of the platter, but within they are full of extortion and excess.

26 You blind Pharisee, cleanse first that which is within the cup and platter, that the outside of them may be clean also.

27 Woe to you, scribes and Pharisees, hypocrites! for you are like whited sepulchres, which indeed appear beautiful outward, but are within full of dead men's bones, and of all uncleanness.

28 Even so you also outwardly appear righteous to men, but within you are full of hypocrisy and iniquity.

29 Woe to you, scribes and Pharisees, hypocrites! because you build the tombs of the prophets, and garnish the sepulchres of the righteous,

30 And say, If we had been in the days of our fathers, we would not have been partakers with them in the blood of the prophets.

31 Wherefore be witnesses to yourselves,
that you are the children of them which
killed the prophets.
32 Fill up then the measure of your fathers.
33 You serpents, you generation of vipers,
how can you escape the damnation of hell?
34 Wherefore, behold, I send to you
prophets, and wise men, and scribes: and
some of them you shall kill and crucify;
and some of them shall you scourge in
your synagogues, and persecute them from
city to city:
35 That upon you may come all the righteous blood shed upon the earth, from
the blood of righteous Abel to the blood
of Zacharias son of Barachias, whom you
slew between the temple and the altar.
36 Verily I say to you, All these things
shall come upon this generation.
37 O Jerusalem, Jerusalem, you that kill
the prophets, and stone them which are
sent to you, how often would I have gathered your children together, even as a hen
gathers her chickens under her wings,
and you would not!
38 Behold, your house is left to you desolate.
39 For I say to you, You shall not see me
henceforth, till you shall say, Blessed is
he that comes in the name of the Lord.

CHAPTER 24

AND Jesus went out, and departed
from the temple: and his disciples
came to him for to show him the buildings of the temple.
2 And Jesus said to them, Do you not see
all these things? verily I say to you, There
shall not be left here one stone upon another, that shall not be thrown down.
3 And as he sat upon the mount of Olives, the disciples came to him privately,
saying, Tell us, when shall these things
be? and what shall be the sign of your
coming, and of the end of the world?
4 And Jesus answered and said to them,
Take heed that no man deceive you.
5 For many shall come in my name, saying, I am Christ; and shall deceive many.
6 And you shall hear of wars and rumors
of wars: see that you be not troubled: for
all these things must come to pass, but
the end is not yet.
7 For nation shall rise against nation,
and kingdom against kingdom: and there
shall be famines, and pestilences, and
earthquakes, in divers places.
8 All these are the beginning of sorrows.
9 Then shall they deliver you up to be
afflicted, and shall kill you: and you shall
be hated of all nations for my name's sake.
10 And then shall many be offended, and
shall betray one another, and shall hate
one another.
11 And many false prophets shall rise,
and shall deceive many.
12 And because iniquity shall abound,
the love of many shall wax cold.
13 But he that shall endure to the end,
the same shall be saved.
14 And this gospel of the kingdom shall
be preached in all the world for a witness to all nations; and then shall the end

---

23:33 Hell: For verses warning of its reality, see Matthew 25:41.

24:2 Historian Josephus wrote of the temple's destruction by Romans in A.D. 70: "They carried away every stone of the sacred temple, partially in a frenzied search for every last piece of the gold ornamentation melted in the awful heat of the fire. They then plowed the ground level, and since it had already been sown with its defenders' blood, they sowed it with salt" (*Wars of the Jews*). See also Mark 13:2.

24:3 For more signs of the end times, see Mark 13:4.

24:7 The Bible informs us that in the last days there will be earthquakes in different places. This was stated 2,000 years ago, and there is little historical data regarding the size, frequency, and location of earthquakes. One thing is certain: earthquakes in different places are a sign of these times.

come.
15 When you therefore shall see the
abomination of desolation, spoken of by
Daniel the prophet, stand in the holy
place, (whoso reads, let him understand:)
16 Then let them which be in Judea flee
into the mountains:
17 Let him which is on the housetop
not come down to take any thing out of
his house:
18 Neither let him which is in the field
return back to take his clothes.
19 And woe to them that are with child,
and to them that give suck in those days!
20 But pray that your flight be not in
the winter, neither on the sabbath day:
21 For then shall be great tribulation,
such as was not since the beginning of
the world to this time, no, nor ever shall
be.
22 And except those days should be
shortened, there should no flesh be saved:
but for the elect's sake those days shall
be shortened.
23 Then if any man shall say to you, Lo,
here is Christ, or there; believe it not.
24 For there shall arise false Christs,
and false prophets, and shall show great
signs and wonders; insomuch that, if it
were possible, they shall deceive the very
elect.
25 Behold, I have told you before.
26 Wherefore if they shall say to you,
Behold, he is in the desert; go not forth:
behold, he is in the secret chambers; believe it not.
27 For as the lightning comes out of the
east, and shines even to the west; so shall
also the coming of the Son of man be.
28 For wherever the carcass is, there will
the eagles be gathered together.
29 Immediately after the tribulation of
those days shall the sun be darkened, and
the moon shall not give her light, and
the stars shall fall from heaven, and the
powers of the heavens shall be shaken:
30 And then shall appear the sign of the
Son of man in heaven: and then shall all
the tribes of the earth mourn, and they
shall see the Son of man coming in the
clouds of heaven with power and great
glory.
31 And he shall send his angels with a
great sound of a trumpet, and they shall
gather together his elect from the four
winds, from one end of heaven to the
other.
32 Now learn a parable of the fig tree;
When his branch is yet tender, and puts
forth leaves, you know that summer is
near:
33 So likewise you, when you shall see
all these things, know that it is near, even
at the doors.
34 Verily I say to you, This generation
shall not pass, till all these things be fulfilled.
35 Heaven and earth shall pass away,
but my words shall not pass away.
36 But of that day and hour knows no
man, no, not the angels of heaven, but
my Father only.
37 But as the days of Noah were, so shall
also the coming of the Son of man be.
38 For as in the days that were before
the flood they were eating and drinking,
marrying and giving in marriage, until
the day that Noah entered into the ark,
39 And knew not until the flood came,
and took them all away; so shall also the

24:14 "No one is beyond the reach of God to present the gospel to them." *Garry T. Ansdell, D.D.*

24:27 Second coming of Jesus: See Matthew 24:39.

24:35 God is able to ensure that His written Word, the Bible, will endure. See Psalm 119:105 footnote.

24:37–39 Jesus referred to Noah as an actual historical person, and the Flood as a bona fide historical event.

24:39 Second coming of Jesus: See Matthew 25:31.

24:38,39 *Points to Ponder About the Flood and Noah's Ark*

By Dr. Kent Hovind

Second Peter 3:3–8 tells us that people who scoff at the Bible are "willingly ignorant" of the Creation and the Flood. In order to understand science and the Bible, we must not be ignorant of those two great events in Earth's history.

1. Over 500 Flood legends from all parts of the world have been found. Most have similarities to the Genesis account.

2. Noah's ark was built only to float, not to sail anywhere. Many ark scholars believe that the ark was a "barge" shape, not a pointed "boat" shape. This would greatly increase the cargo capacity. Scoffers have pointed out that the largest sailing ships were less than 300 feet because of the problem of twisting and flexing the boat. These ships had giant masts and sails to catch the wind. Noah's ark needed neither of those and therefore had far less torsional stress.

3. Even using the small 18-inch cubit (my height is 6'1" and I have a 21-inch cubit), the ark was large enough to hold all the required animals, people, and food with room to spare.

4. The length-to-width ratio of 6 to 1 is what shipbuilders today often use. This is the best ratio for stability in stormy weather.

5. The ark may have had a "moon-pool" in the center. The larger ships would have a hole in the center of the bottom of the boat with walls extending up into the ship. There are several reasons for this feature:

a) It allowed water to go up into the hole as the ship crested waves. This would be needed to relieve strain on longer ships.

b) The rising and lowering water acted as a piston to pump fresh air in and out of the ship. This would prevent the buildup of dangerous gasses from all the animals on board.

c) The hole was a great place to dump waste into the ocean without going outside.

6. The ark may have had large drogue (anchor) stones suspended over the sides to keep it more stable in rough weather. Many of these stones have been found in the region where the ark landed.

7. Noah lived for 950 years. Many Bible scholars believe the pre-Flood people were much larger than modern man. Skeletons over 11 feet tall have been found. If Noah were taller, his cubit (elbow to fingertip) would have been much larger also. This would make the ark larger by the same ratio.

8. God told Noah to bring two of each kind (seven of some), not of each species or variety. Noah had only two of the dog kind, which would include the wolves, coyotes, foxes, mutts, etc. The "kind" grouping is probably closer to our modern family division in taxonomy, and would greatly reduce the number of animals on the ark. Animals have diversified into many varieties in the last 4,400 years since the Flood. This diversification is not anything similar to great claims that the evolutionists teach.

9. Noah did not have to get the animals. God brought them to him (Genesis 6:20, "shall come to thee").

10. Only land-dwelling, air-breathing animals had to be included on the ark ("in which is the breath of life," Genesis 7:15,22).

11. Many animals sleep, hibernate, or become very inactive during bad weather.

12. All animals (and people) were vegetarian before and during the Flood according to Genesis 1:20–30 with Genesis 9:3.

13. The pre-Flood people were probably much smarter and more advanced than people today. The longer life spans, Adam's direct contact with God, and the fact that they could glean the wisdom of many generations that were still alive would greatly expand their knowledge base.

14. The Bible says that the highest mountains were covered by 15 cubits [20 feet] of water (Genesis 7:20). This is half the height of the ark. The ark was safe from scraping bottom at all times.

15. The large mountains, as we have them

(continued on next page)

(24:38,39 continued)
today, did not exist until after the Flood when "the mountains arose and the valleys sank down" (Psalm 104:5–9; Genesis 8:3–8).

16. There is enough water in the oceans right now to cover the earth 8,000 feet deep if the surface of the earth were smooth.

17. Many claim to have seen the ark in recent times in the area in which the Bible says it landed. There are two primary schools of thought about the actual site of the ark. Much energy and time have been expended to prove both views. Some believe the ark is on Mt. Ararat, covered by snow (CBS showed a one-hour special in 1993 about this site). Others believe the ark is seventeen miles south of Mt. Ararat in a valley called "the valley of eight" (eight souls on the ark). The Bible says the ark landed in the "mountains" of Ararat, not necessarily on the mountain itself.

18. The continents were not separated until 100–300 years after the Flood (Genesis 10:25). The people and animals had time to migrate anywhere on earth by then.

19. The top 3,000 feet of Mount Everest (26,000–29,000 feet) is made up of sedimentary rock packed with seashells and other ocean-dwelling animals.

20. Sedimentary rock is found all over the world. Sedimentary rock is formed in water.

21. Petrified clams in the closed position (found all over the world) testify to their rapid burial while they were still alive, even on top of Mount Everest.

22. Bent rock layers, fossil graveyards, and polystrata fossils are best explained by a Flood.

23. People choose to not believe in the Flood because it speaks of the judgment of God on sin (2 Peter 3:3–8).

coming of the Son of man be.
40 Then shall two be in the field; the one shall be taken, and the other left.
41 Two women shall be grinding at the mill; the one shall be taken, and the other left.
42 Watch therefore: for you know not what hour your Lord does come.
43 But know this, that if the goodman of the house had known in what watch the thief would come, he would have watched, and would not have suffered his house to be broken up.
44 Therefore be also ready: for in such an hour as you think not the Son of man comes.
45 Who then is a faithful and wise servant, whom his lord has made ruler over his household, to give them meat in due season?
46 Blessed is that servant, whom his lord when he comes shall find so doing.
47 Verily I say to you, That he shall make him ruler over all his goods.
48 But and if that evil servant shall say in his heart, My lord delays his coming;
49 And shall begin to smite his fellowservants, and to eat and drink with the drunken;
50 The lord of that servant shall come in a day when he looks not for him, and in an hour that he is not aware of,
51 And shall cut him asunder, and appoint him his portion with the hypocrites: there shall be weeping and gnashing of teeth.

CHAPTER 25

THEN shall the kingdom of heaven be likened to ten virgins, which took their lamps, and went forth to meet the bridegroom.
2 And five of them were wise, and five were foolish.
3 They that were foolish took their lamps, and took no oil with them:
4 But the wise took oil in their vessels with their lamps.
5 While the bridegroom tarried, they all slumbered and slept.
6 And at midnight there was a cry made, Behold, the bridegroom comes; go out to meet him.
7 Then all those virgins arose, and trimmed their lamps.
8 And the foolish said to the wise, Give us of your oil; for our lamps are gone out.
9 But the wise answered, saying, Not so;

lest there be not enough for us and you: but go rather to them that sell, and buy for yourselves.
10 And while they went to buy, the bridegroom came; and they that were ready went in with him to the marriage: and the door was shut.
11 Afterward came also the other virgins, saying, Lord, Lord, open to us.
12 But he answered and said, Verily I say to you, I know you not.
13 Watch therefore, for you know neither the day nor the hour wherein the Son of man comes.
14 For the kingdom of heaven is as a man traveling into a far country, who called his own servants, and delivered to them his goods.
15 And to one he gave five talents, to another two, and to another one; to every man according to his several ability; and straightway took his journey.
16 Then he that had received the five talents went and traded with the same, and made them another five talents.
17 And likewise he that had received two, he also gained another two.
18 But he that had received one went and dug in the earth, and hid his lord's money.
19 After a long time the lord of those servants came, and reckoned with them.
20 And so he that had received five talents came and brought other five talents, saying, Lord, you delivered to me five talents: behold, I have gained beside them five talents more.
21 His lord said to him, Well done, you good and faithful servant: you have been faithful over a few things, I will make you ruler over many things: enter into the joy of your lord.
22 He also that had received two talents came and said, Lord, you delivered to me two talents: behold, I have gained two other talents beside them.
23 His lord said to him, Well done, good and faithful servant; you have been faithful over a few things, I will make you ruler over many things: enter into the joy of your lord.
24 Then he which had received the one talent came and said, Lord, I knew you that you are an hard man, reaping where you have not sown, and gathering where you have not strawed:
25 And I was afraid, and went and hid your talent in the earth: lo, there you have what is yours.
26 His lord answered and said to him, You wicked and slothful servant, you knew that I reap where I sowed not, and gather where I have not strawed:
27 You ought therefore to have put my money to the exchangers, and then at my coming I should have received mine own with usury.
28 Take therefore the talent from him, and give it to him which has ten talents.
29 For to every one that has shall be given, and he shall have abundance: but from him that has not shall be taken away even that which he has.
30 And cast the unprofitable servant into outer darkness: there shall be weeping

25:12 False converts. The foolish virgins called Him "Lord," but He said, "I know you not." They were false converts. Jesus warned, "Not every one that says to me, Lord, Lord, shall enter the kingdom of heaven, but he that does the will of my Father which is in heaven. Many will say to me in that day, Lord, Lord, have we not prophesied in your name? and in your name have cast out devils? and in your name done many wonderful works? And then will I profess to them, I never knew you: depart from me, you that work iniquity" (Matthew 7:21–23). This is why we must forsake traditional quick-fix evangelism and do all things according to the pattern given to us in Scripture. For the key to biblical evangelism, see Luke 11:52 footnote.

"The vast majority of people who are members of churches in America today are not Christians. I say that without the slightest fear of contradiction. I base it on empirical evidence of twenty-four years of examining thousands of people." *Dr. D. James Kennedy*

and gnashing of teeth.
31 When the Son of man shall come in
his glory, and all the holy angels with
him, then shall he sit upon the throne of
his glory:
32 And before him shall be gathered all
nations: and he shall separate them one
from another, as a shepherd divides his
sheep from the goats:
33 And he shall set the sheep on his
right hand, but the goats on the left.
34 Then shall the King say to them on
his right hand, Come, you blessed of my
Father, inherit the kingdom prepared for
you from the foundation of the world:
35 For I was an hungered, and you gave
me meat: I was thirsty, and you gave me
drink: I was a stranger, and you took me
in:
36 Naked, and you clothed me: I was
sick, and you visited me: I was in prison,
and you came to me.
37 Then shall the righteous answer him,
saying, Lord, when did we see you an
hungered, and fed you? or thirsty, and
gave you drink?
38 When did we see you a stranger, and
took you in? or naked, and clothed you?
39 Or when did we see you sick, or in
prison, and came to you?
40 And the King shall answer and say
to them, Verily I say to you, Inasmuch as
you have done it to one of the least of
these my brethren, you have done it to
me.
41 Then shall he say also to them on the
left hand, Depart from me, you cursed, into everlasting fire, prepared for the devil
and his angels:
42 For I was an hungered, and you gave
me no meat: I was thirsty, and you gave
me no drink:
43 I was a stranger, and you took me not
in: naked, and you clothed me not: sick,
and in prison, and you visited me not.
44 Then shall they also answer him, saying, Lord, when saw we you an hungered,
or athirst, or a stranger, or naked, or sick,
or in prison, and did not minister to you?
45 Then shall he answer them, saying,
Verily I say to you, Inasmuch as you did
it not to one of the least of these, you did
it not to me.
46 And these shall go away into everlasting punishment: but the righteous into life eternal.

> I desire to have both heaven and hell in my eye.
>
> **JOHN WESLEY**

CHAPTER 26

AND it came to pass, when Jesus had
finished all these sayings, he said to
his disciples,
2 You know that after two days is the
feast of the passover, and the Son of man
is betrayed to be crucified.
3 Then assembled together the chief
priests, and the scribes, and the elders of
the people, to the palace of the high priest,
who was called Caiaphas,
4 And consulted that they might take
Jesus by subtlety, and kill him.
5 But they said, Not on the feast day,
lest there be an uproar among the people.
6 Now when Jesus was in Bethany, in
the house of Simon the leper,
7 There came to him a woman having
an alabaster box of very precious ointment, and poured it on his head, as he
sat at meat.
8 But when his disciples saw it, they had
indignation, saying, To what purpose is
this waste?

25:31 Second coming of Jesus: See Matthew 26:64.
25:32 Judgment Day: For verses that warn of its reality, see John 5:28,29.
25:41 Hell: For verses warning of its reality, see Mark 9:43–48.

9 For this ointment might have been
sold for much, and given to the poor.
10 When Jesus understood it, he said to
them, Why trouble the woman? for she
has wrought a good work upon me.
11 For you have the poor always with
you; but me you have not always.
12 For in that she has poured this ointment on my body, she did it for my burial.
13 Verily I say to you, Wherever this
gospel shall be preached in the whole
world, there shall also this, that this woman has done, be told for a memorial of
her.
14 Then one of the twelve, called Judas
Iscariot, went to the chief priests,
15 And said to them, What will you give
me, and I will deliver him to you? And
they covenanted with him for thirty pieces
of silver.
16 And from that time he sought opportunity to betray him.
17 Now the first day of the feast of unleavened bread the disciples came to Jesus,
saying to him, Where will you that we
prepare for you to eat the passover?
18 And he said, Go into the city to such
a man, and say to him, The Master says,
My time is at hand; I will keep the passover at your house with my disciples.
19 And the disciples did as Jesus had
appointed them; and they made ready
the passover.
20 Now when the even was come, he sat
down with the twelve.
21 And as they did eat, he said, Verily I
say to you, that one of you shall betray
me.
22 And they were exceeding sorrowful,
and began every one of them to say to him,
Lord, is it I?
23 And he answered and said, He that
dips his hand with me in the dish, the
same shall betray me.
24 The Son of man goes as it is written
of him: but woe to that man by whom
the Son of man is betrayed! it had been
good for that man if he had not been born.
25 Then Judas, which betrayed him, answered and said, Master, is it I? He said
to him, You have said.
26 And as they were eating, Jesus took
bread, and blessed it, and broke it, and
gave it to the disciples, and said, Take, eat;
this is my body.
27 And he took the cup, and gave thanks,
and gave it to them, saying, Drink all of it;
28 For this is my blood of the new testament, which is shed for many for the
remission of sins.
29 But I say to you, I will not drink
henceforth of this fruit of the vine, until
that day when I drink it new with you in
my Father's kingdom.
30 And when they had sung a hymn,
they went out into the mount of Olives.
31 Then said Jesus to them, All you shall
be offended because of me this night: for
it is written, I will smite the shepherd,
and the sheep of the flock shall be scattered abroad.
32 But after I am risen again, I will go before you into Galilee.
33 Peter answered and said to him,
Though all men shall be offended because
of you, yet will I never be offended.
34 Jesus said to him, Verily I say to you,

26:15 Messianic prophecy fulfilled: "And I said unto them, If you think good, give me my price; and if not, forbear. So they weighed for my price thirty pieces of silver" (Zechariah 11:12). See Matthew 26:60 footnote.

26:26 This can only have been a *symbolic* statement. The bread was obviously not His *physical* body, as He was standing in front of them.

26:27,28 This could not have been Jesus' literal blood, because He was present with them. His words were *spiritual*. After Jesus told His disciples that they must eat of His flesh and drink of His blood, He said that the words that He spoke were spirit and life (John 6:63). When we are born of the Spirit (John 3:3–7), we "taste and see that the Lord is good" (Psalm 34:8).

That this night, before the cock crow, you
shall deny me thrice.
35 Peter said to him, Though I should die
with you, yet will I not deny you. Likewise
also said all the disciples.
36 Then came Jesus with them to a place
called Gethsemane, and said to the disciples, Sit here, while I go and pray yonder.
37 And he took with him Peter and the
two sons of Zebedee, and began to be
sorrowful and very heavy.
38 Then said he to them, My soul is exceeding sorrowful, even to death: tarry
here, and watch with me.
39 And he went a little further, and fell
on his face, and prayed, saying, O my
Father, if it be possible, let this cup pass
from me: nevertheless not as I will, but
as you will.
40 And he came to the disciples, and
found them asleep, and said to Peter,
What, could you not watch with me one
hour?
41 Watch and pray, that you enter not
into temptation: the spirit indeed is willing, but the flesh is weak.
42 He went away again the second time,
and prayed, saying, O my Father, if this
cup may not pass away from me, except
I drink it, your will be done.
43 And he came and found them asleep
again: for their eyes were heavy.
44 And he left them, and went away
again, and prayed the third time, saying
the same words.
45 Then came he to his disciples, and
said to them, Sleep on now, and take your
rest: behold, the hour is at hand, and the
Son of man is betrayed into the hands of
sinners.
46 Rise, let us be going: behold, he is at
hand that does betray me.
47 And while he yet spoke, lo, Judas,
one of the twelve, came, and with him a
great multitude with swords and staves,
from the chief priests and elders of the
people.
48 Now he that betrayed him gave them
a sign, saying, Whomsoever I shall kiss,
that same is he: hold him fast.
49 And forthwith he came to Jesus, and
said, Hail, master; and kissed him.
50 And Jesus said to him, Friend, wherefore are you come? Then came they, and
laid hands on Jesus, and took him.
51 And, behold, one of them which
were with Jesus stretched out his hand,
and drew his sword, and struck a servant
of the high priest's, and smote off his
ear.
52 Then said Jesus to him, Put up again
your sword into his place: for all they that
take the sword shall perish with the sword.
53 Think that I cannot now pray to my
Father, and he shall presently give me
more than twelve legions of angels?
54 But how then shall the scriptures be
fulfilled, that thus it must be?
55 In that same hour said Jesus to the
multitudes, Are you come out as against
a thief with swords and staves for to take
me? I sat daily with you teaching in the
temple, and you laid no hold on me.
56 But all this was done, that the scriptures of the prophets might be fulfilled.
Then all the disciples forsook him, and
fled.
57 And they that had laid hold on Jesus
led him away to Caiaphas the high priest,
where the scribes and the elders were assembled.
58 But Peter followed him afar off to

26:41 Watch and pray. "Real praying is a costly exercise but it pays far more than it costs. It is not easy work but it is most profitable of all work. We can accomplish more by time and strength put into prayer than we can by putting the same amount of time and strength into anything else." *R. A. Torrey, The Power of Prayer*

"Do you ever get that wistful feeling that there are other things more effective, even more desirable, than prayer? This explains why far too many of us are busy in attempting great things for God, rather than expecting great things from God in a humble attitude of prayer." *Robert Foster*

the high priest's palace, and went in, and
sat with the servants, to see the end.
59 Now the chief priests, and elders,
and all the council, sought false witness
against Jesus, to put him to death;
60 But found none: yea, though many
false witnesses came, yet found they none.
At the last came two false witnesses,
61 And said, This fellow said, I am able
to destroy the temple of God, and to build
it in three days.
62 And the high priest arose, and said
to him, Do you answer nothing? what is
it which these witness against you?
63 But Jesus held his peace. And the
high priest answered and said to him, I
adjure you by the living God, that you
tell us whether you be the Christ, the
Son of God.
64 Jesus said to him, You have said:
nevertheless I say to you, Hereafter shall
you see the Son of man sitting on the
right hand of power, and coming in the
clouds of heaven.
65 Then the high priest tore his clothes,
saying, He has spoken blasphemy; what
further need have we of witnesses? behold,
now you have heard his blasphemy.
66 What do you think? They answered
and said, He is guilty of death.
67 Then did they spit in his face, and
buffeted him; and others smote him with
the palms of their hands,
68 Saying, Prophesy to us, you Christ,
Who is he that smote you?
69 Now Peter sat without in the palace:
and a damsel came to him, saying, You
also were with Jesus of Galilee.
70 But he denied before them all, saying,
I know not what you say.
71 And when he was gone out into the
porch, another maid saw him, and said
to them that were there, This fellow was
also with Jesus of Nazareth.
72 And again he denied with an oath, I
do not know the man.
73 And after a while came to him they
that stood by, and said to Peter, Surely
you also are one of them; for your speech
betrays you.

26:54 Archaeology confirms the Bible. The Scriptures make more than 40 references to the great Hittite Empire. However, until one hundred years ago there was no archaeological evidence to substantiate the biblical claim that the Hittites existed. Skeptics claimed that the Bible was in error, until their mouths were suddenly stopped. In 1906, Hugo Winckler uncovered a huge library of 10,000 clay tablets, which completely documented the lost Hittite Empire. We now know that at its height, the Hittite civilization rivaled Egypt and Assyria in its glory and power. See Luke 1:27 footnote.

"It may be stated categorically that no archaeological discovery has ever controverted a Biblical reference. Scores of archaeological findings have been made which confirm in clear outline or exact detail historical statements in the Bible. And, by the same token, proper evaluation of Biblical descriptions has often led to amazing discoveries." *Dr. Nelson Glueck*

"Archaeology has confirmed countless passages which have been rejected by critics as unhistorical or contradictory to known facts...Yet archaeological discoveries have shown that these critical charges...are wrong and that the Bible is trustworthy in the very statements which have been set aside as untrustworthy...We do not know of any cases where the Bible has been proved wrong." *Dr. Joseph P. Free*

26:60 Messianic prophecy fulfilled: "Deliver me not over unto the will of mine enemies: for false witnesses are risen up against me, and such as breathe out cruelty" (Psalm 27:12). See Matthew 26:62,63 footnote.

26:62,63 Messianic prophecy fulfilled: "He was oppressed, and he was afflicted, yet he opened not his mouth: he is brought as a lamb to the slaughter, and as a sheep before her shearers is dumb, so he opened not his mouth" (Isaiah 53:7). See Matthew 27:39–44 footnote.

26:64 Second coming of Jesus: See Mark 8:38.

74 Then began he to curse and to swear,
saying, I know not the man. And immediately the cock crew.
75 And Peter remembered the word of
Jesus, which said to him, Before the cock
crow, you shall deny me thrice. And he
went out, and wept bitterly.

CHAPTER 27

WHEN the morning was come, all
the chief priests and elders of the
people took counsel against Jesus to put
him to death:
2 And when they had bound him, they
led him away, and delivered him to Pontius Pilate the governor.
3 Then Judas, which had betrayed him,
when he saw that he was condemned,
repented himself, and brought again the
thirty pieces of silver to the chief priests
and elders,
4 Saying, I have sinned in that I have
betrayed the innocent blood. And they
said, What is that to us? You see to that.
5 And he cast down the pieces of silver
in the temple, and departed, and went
and hanged himself.
6 And the chief priests took the silver
pieces, and said, It is not lawful for to put
them into the treasury, because it is the
price of blood.
7 And they took counsel, and bought
with them the potter's field, to bury strangers in.
8 Wherefore that field was called, The
field of blood, to this day.
9 Then was fulfilled that which was spoken by Jeremiah the prophet, saying, And
they took the thirty pieces of silver, the
price of him that was valued, whom they
of the children of Israel did value;
10 And gave them for the potter's field,
as the Lord appointed me.
11 And Jesus stood before the governor: and the governor asked him, saying,
are you the King of the Jews? And Jesus
said to him, It is as you say.
12 And when he was accused of the chief
priests and elders, he answered nothing.
13 Then said Pilate to him, Hear not how
many things they witness against you?
14 And he answered him to never a word;
insomuch that the governor marveled
greatly.
15 Now at that feast the governor was
accustomed to release to the people a prisoner, whom they would.
16 And they had then a notable prisoner, called Barabbas.
17 Therefore when they were gathered
together, Pilate said to them, Whom will
you that I release to you? Barabbas, or
Jesus which is called Christ?
18 For he knew that for envy they had
delivered him.
19 When he was set down on the judgment seat, his wife sent to him, saying,
Have nothing to do with that just man:
for I have suffered many things this day
in a dream because of him.
20 But the chief priests and elders persuaded the multitude that they should
ask Barabbas, and destroy Jesus.
21 The governor answered and said to
them, Which of the two will you that I
release to you? They said, Barabbas.
22 Pilate said to them, What shall I do
then with Jesus which is called Christ?
They all say to him, Let him be crucified.
23 And the governor said, Why, what
evil has he done? But they cried out the
more, saying, Let him be crucified.
24 When Pilate saw that he could prevail nothing, but that rather a tumult was

27:5 "I have had few difficulties, many friends, great success; I have gone from wife to wife, and from house to house, visited great countries of the world, but I am fed up with inventing devices to fill up 24 hours of the day." Suicide note of cartoonist *Ralph Barton*

27:9,10 Notice that Scripture doesn't say "that which was *written in* Jeremiah." This was "spoken" by Jeremiah the prophet, but it was not recorded in the Book of Jeremiah. A similar prophecy was given in Zechariah 11:12,13.

made, he took water, and washed his
hands before the multitude, saying, I am
innocent of the blood of this just person:
you see to it.
25 Then answered all the people, and
said, His blood be on us, and on our children.
26 Then released he Barabbas to them:
and when he had scourged Jesus, he delivered him to be crucified.
27 Then the soldiers of the governor
took Jesus into the common hall, and
gathered to him the whole band of soldiers.
28 And they stripped him, and put on
him a scarlet robe.
29 And when they had platted a crown
of thorns, they put it upon his head, and
a reed in his right hand: and they bowed
the knee before him, and mocked him,
saying, Hail, King of the Jews!
30 And they spit upon him, and took
the reed, and smote him on the head.
31 And after that they had mocked him,
they took the robe off from him, and put
his own raiment on him, and led him
away to crucify him.
32 And as they came out, they found a
man of Cyrene, Simon by name: him they
compelled to bear his cross.
33 And when they were come to a place
called Golgotha, that is to say, a place of a
skull,
34 They gave him vinegar to drink mingled with gall: and when he had tasted
thereof, he would not drink.
35 And they crucified him, and parted
his garments, casting lots: that it might be
fulfilled which was spoken by the prophet, They parted my garments among them,
and upon my vesture did they cast lots.
36 And sitting down they watched him
there;
37 And set up over his head his accusation written, THIS IS JESUS THE KING
OF THE JEWS.
38 Then were there two thieves crucified with him, one on the right hand, and
another on the left.
39 And they that passed by reviled him,
wagging their heads,
40 And saying, You that destroy the
temple, and build it in three days, save
yourself. If you be the Son of God, come
down from the cross.
41 Likewise also the chief priests mocking him, with the scribes and elders, said,
42 He saved others; himself he cannot
save. If he be the King of Israel, let him
now come down from the cross, and we
will believe him.
43 He trusted in God; let him deliver
him now, if he will have him: for he said,
I am the Son of God.
44 The thieves also, which were crucified with him, cast the same in his teeth.
45 Now from the sixth hour there was
darkness over all the land to the ninth
hour.
46 And about the ninth hour Jesus cried
with a loud voice, saying, Eli, Eli, lama
sabachthani? that is to say, My God, my
God, why have you forsaken me?
47 Some of them that stood there, when
they heard that, said, This man calls for
Elijah.

27:26–29 Paintings of a "suffering Savior" on the cross can never do justice to the agonies He suffered for us. Isaiah 52:14 tells us "His visage was so marred more than any man, and His form more than the sons of men."

27:39–44 Messianic prophecy fulfilled: "But I am a worm, and no man; a reproach of men, and despised of the people. All they that see me laugh me to scorn: they shoot out the lip, they shake the head, saying, He trusted on the LORD that he would deliver him: let him deliver him, seeing he delighted in him!" (Psalm 22:6–8). See Mark 14:10 footnote.

27:46 "The pain was absolutely unbearable. In fact, it was literally beyond words to describe; they had to invent a new word: *excruciating*. Literally, excruciating means 'out of the cross.'" *Alexander Metherell, M.D., Ph.D.* (quoted in *The Case for Christ* by *Lee Strobel*)

48 And straightway one of them ran, and took a sponge, and filled it with vinegar, and put it on a reed, and gave him to drink.

49 The rest said, Let be, let us see whether Elijah will come to save him.

50 Jesus, when he had cried again with a loud voice, yielded up the ghost.

51 And, behold, the veil of the temple was rent in twain from the top to the bottom; and the earth did quake, and the rocks rent;

52 And the graves were opened; and many bodies of the saints which slept arose,

> She is a traitor to the Master who sent her if she is so beguiled by the beauties of taste and art as to forget that to "preach Christ...and Him crucified" is the only object for which she exists among the sons of men. The business of the Church is salvation of souls.
>
> **CHARLES SPURGEON**

53 And came out of the graves after his resurrection, and went into the holy city, and appeared to many.

54 Now when the centurion, and they that were with him, watching Jesus, saw the earthquake, and those things that were done, they feared greatly, saying, Truly this was the Son of God.

55 And many women were there beholding afar off, which followed Jesus from Galilee, ministering to him:

56 Among which was Mary Magdalene, and Mary the mother of James and Joses, and the mother of Zebedee's children.

57 When the even was come, there came a rich man of Arimathaea, named Joseph, who also himself was Jesus' disciple:

58 He went to Pilate, and begged the body of Jesus. Then Pilate commanded the body to be delivered.

59 And when Joseph had taken the body, he wrapped it in a clean linen cloth,

60 And laid it in his own new tomb, which he had hewn out in the rock: and he rolled a great stone to the door of the sepulchre, and departed.

61 And there was Mary Magdalene, and the other Mary, sitting over against the sepulchre.

62 Now the next day, that followed the day of the preparation, the chief priests and Pharisees came together to Pilate,

63 Saying, Sir, we remember that that deceiver said, while he was yet alive, After three days I will rise again.

64 Command therefore that the sepulchre be made sure until the third day, lest his disciples come by night, and steal him away, and say to the people, He is risen from the dead: so the last error shall be worse than the first.

65 Pilate said to them, You have a watch: go your way, make it as sure as you can.

66 So they went, and made the sepulchre sure, sealing the stone, and setting a watch.

CHAPTER 28

IN the end of the sabbath, as it began to dawn toward the first day of the week, came Mary Magdalene and the other Mary to see the sepulchre.

2 And, behold, there was a great earthquake: for the angel of the Lord descended from heaven, and came and rolled back the stone from the door, and sat upon it.

3 His countenance was like lightning, and his raiment white as snow:

4 And for fear of him the keepers did shake, and became as dead men.

5 And the angel answered and said to the women, Fear not: for I know that you seek Jesus, which was crucified.

6 He is not here: for he is risen, as he said. Come, see the place where the Lord lay.

7 And go quickly, and tell his disciples that he is risen from the dead; and, behold, he goes before you into Galilee; there shall you see him: lo, I have told you.

8 And they departed quickly from the

QUESTIONS & OBJECTIONS

Q 28:9

"There are contradictions in the resurrection accounts. Did Christ appear first to the women or to His disciples?"

Both Matthew and Mark list women as the first to see the resurrected Christ. Mark says, "He appeared first to Mary Magdalene" (16:9). But Paul lists Peter (Cephas) as the first one to see Christ after His resurrection (1 Corinthians 15:5).

Jesus appeared first to Mary Magdalene, then to the other women, and then to Peter. Paul was not giving a complete list, but only the important one for his purpose. Since only men's testimony was considered legal or official in the first century, it is understandable that the apostle would not list the women as witnesses in his defense of the resurrection here.

The order of the appearances of Christ is as follows:

CHRIST'S RESURRECTION APPEARANCES

APPEARED TO:	REFERENCES:
1. Mary	John 20:10–18
2. Mary and women	Matthew 28:1–10
3. Peter	1 Corinthians 15:5
4. Two disciples	Luke 24:13–35
5. Ten apostles	Luke 24:36–49; John 20:19–23
6. Eleven apostles	John 20:24–31
7. Seven apostles	John 21
8. All apostles	Matthew 28:16–20; Mark 16:14–18
9. 500 brethren	1 Corinthians 15:6
10. James	1 Corinthians 15:7
11. All apostles	Acts 1:4–8
12. Paul	Acts 9:1–9; 1 Corinthians 15:8

sepulchre with fear and great joy; and
did run to bring his disciples word.
9 And as they went to tell his disciples,
behold, Jesus met them, saying, All hail.
And they came and held him by the feet,
and worshipped him.
10 Then said Jesus to them, Be not afraid:
go tell my brethren that they go into Galilee,
and there shall they see me.
11 Now when they were going, behold,
some of the watch came into the city,
and showed to the chief priests all the
things that were done.
12 And when they were assembled with
the elders, and had taken counsel, they
gave large money to the soldiers,
13 Saying, Say, His disciples came by
night, and stole him away while we slept.
14 And if this come to the governor's
ears, we will persuade him, and secure
you.
15 So they took the money, and did as
they were taught: and this saying is commonly
reported among the Jews until this

28:9 If Jesus was not God, He would have been transgressing the Law of God by receiving their worship.

POINTS FOR OPEN-AIR PREACHING

28:19,20

Make the Bullet Hit the Target

It is obvious from Scripture that God requires us not only to preach to sinners, but also to teach them. The servant of the Lord must be "able to teach, patient, in meekness instructing" those who oppose them (2 Timothy 2:24,25). For a long while I thought I was to leap among sinners, scatter the seed, then leave. But our responsibility goes further. We are to bring the sinner to a point of understanding his need before God. Psalm 25:8 says, "Good and upright is the LORD: therefore will he teach sinners in the way." Psalm 51:13 adds, "Then will I teach transgressors your ways; and sinners shall be converted to you." The Great Commission is to teach sinners: "teach all nations...teaching them to observe all things" (Matthew 28:19,20). The disciples obeyed the command "daily in the temple, and in every house, they ceased not to *teach* and preach Jesus Christ" (Acts 5:42, emphasis added).

The "good-soil" hearer is he who "hears...and *understands*" (Matthew 13:23). Philip the evangelist saw fit to ask his potential convert, the Ethiopian, "Do you understand what you are reading?" Some preachers are like a loud gun that misses the target. It may sound effective, but if the bullet misses the target, the exercise is in vain. He may be the largest-lunged, chandelier-swinging, pulpit-pounding preacher this side of the Book of Acts. He may have great teaching on faith, and everyone he touches may fall over, but if the sinner leaves the meeting failing to understand his desperate need of God's forgiveness, then the preacher has failed. He has missed the target, which is the understanding of the sinner. This is why the Law of God must be used in preaching. It is a "schoolmaster" to bring "the knowledge of sin." It teaches and instructs. A sinner will come to "know His will, and approve the things that are more excellent," if he is "instructed out of the Law" (Romans 2:18). See Acts 20:21 footnote.

day.
16 Then the eleven disciples went away into Galilee, into a mountain where Jesus had appointed them.
17 And when they saw him, they worshipped him: but some doubted.
18 *And Jesus came and spoke to them, saying, All power is given to me in heaven and in earth.*
19 *Go therefore, and teach all nations, baptizing them in the name of the Father, and of the Son, and of the Holy Spirit:*
20 *Teaching them to observe all things whatsoever I have commanded you: and, lo, I am with you alway, even to the end of the world. Amen.*

28:19 "We cannot pick and choose which commands of our Lord we will follow. Jesus Christ's last command to the Christian community was, 'You are to go into all the world and preach the Good News to everyone, everywhere' (Mark 16:15, TLB). This command, which the Church calls the Great Commission, was not intended merely for the eleven remaining disciples, or just for the apostles or for those in present times who may have the gift of evangelism. This command is the duty of every man and woman who confesses Christ as Lord." *Dr. Bill Bright*

"Men are mirrors, or 'carriers' of Christ to other men. Usually it is those who know Him who bring Him to others. That's why the Church, the whole body of Christians showing Him to one another, is so important. It is so easy to think that the Church has a lot of different objects—education, building, missions, holding services...The Church exists for no other purpose but to draw men into Christ, to make them little Christs. If they are not doing that, all the cathedrals, clergy, missions, sermons, even the Bible itself, are simply a waste of time. God became man for no other purpose. It is even doubtful, you know, whether the whole universe was created for any other reason." *C. S. Lewis*

Mark

CHAPTER 1

THE beginning of the gospel of Jesus
Christ, the Son of God;
2 As it is written in the prophets, Behold, I send my messenger before your
face, which shall prepare your way before you.
3 The voice of one crying in the wilderness, Prepare the way of the Lord, make
his paths straight.
4 John did baptize in the wilderness, and
preach the baptism of repentance for the
remission of sins.
5 And there went out to him all the land
of Judea, and they of Jerusalem, and were
all baptized of him in the river of Jordan,
confessing their sins.
6 And John was clothed with camel's hair,
and with a girdle of a skin about his loins;
and he did eat locusts and wild honey;
7 And preached, saying, There comes
one mightier than I after me, the latchet of
whose shoes I am not worthy to stoop
down and unloose.
8 I indeed have baptized you with water:
but he shall baptize you with the Holy
Spirit.
9 And it came to pass in those days, that
Jesus came from Nazareth of Galilee, and
was baptized of John in Jordan.
10 And straightway coming up out of the
water, he saw the heavens opened, and the
Spirit like a dove descending upon him:
11 And there came a voice from heaven,
saying, You are my beloved Son, in whom
I am well pleased.
12 And immediately the Spirit drove him
into the wilderness.
13 And he was there in the wilderness
forty days, tempted of Satan; and was with
the wild beasts; and the angels ministered
to him.
14 Now after that John was put in prison, Jesus came into Galilee, preaching the
gospel of the kingdom of God,
**15 And saying, The time is fulfilled,
and the kingdom of God is at hand: repent, and believe the gospel.**

THE FUNCTION OF THE LAW

1:3 Commenting on the Law's capacity to bring the knowledge of sin, Bible commentator *Matthew Henry* said, "Of this excellent use is the Law: it converts the soul, opens the eyes, prepares the way of the Lord in the desert, rends the rocks, levels the mountains, makes a people prepared for the Lord."

1:15 Jesus preached repentance because His hearers knew the Law. Since He was sent to "the lost sheep of the house of Israel" (Matthew 15:24), His ministry was originally confined to Jews. The Scriptures often use the phrase "to the Jew first." Romans 3:1,2 tells us that Jews had the advantage of having the Law of God. They knew what sin was, and therefore understood their need for repentance. Those without a knowledge of sin (which only the Law can bring—see Romans 7:7) need to hear the message of the Law before they are able (with God's help) to repent.

QUESTIONS & OBJECTIONS

1:4,5

"Is water baptism essential to salvation?"

While we should preach that all men are commanded to repent and be baptized (Acts 2:38), adding any other requirement to salvation by grace becomes "works" in disguise. Even though numerous Scriptures speak of the importance of water baptism, adding *anything* to the work of the cross demeans the sacrifice of the Savior. It implies that His finished work wasn't enough. But the Bible makes clear that we are saved by grace, and grace alone (Ephesians 2:8,9). Baptism is simply a step of obedience to the Lord following our repentance and confession of sin. Our obedience—water baptism, prayer, good works, fellowship, witnessing, etc.—issues from our faith in Christ. Salvation is not what we do, but Who we have: "He that has the Son has life" (1 John 5:12). See Acts 2:38 footnotes.

16 Now as he walked by the sea of Galilee, he saw Simon and Andrew his brother casting a net into the sea: for they were
fishers.
17 *And Jesus said to them, Come after me,
and I will make you to become fishers of
men.*
18 And straightway they forsook their
nets, and followed him.
19 And when he had gone a little further
thence, he saw James the son of Zebedee,
and John his brother, who also were in
the ship mending their nets.
20 And straightway he called them: and
they left their father Zebedee in the ship
with the hired servants, and went after
him.
21 And they went into Capernaum; and
straightway on the sabbath day he entered
into the synagogue, and taught.
22 And they were astonished at his doctrine: for he taught them as one that had
authority, and not as the scribes.
23 And there was in their synagogue a
man with an unclean spirit; and he cried
out,
24 Saying, Let us alone; what have we to
do with you, you Jesus of Nazareth? are
you come to destroy us? I know you who
you are, the Holy One of God.
25 And Jesus rebuked him, saying, Hold
your peace, and come out of him.
26 And when the unclean spirit had torn
him, and cried with a loud voice, he came
out of him.
27 And they were all amazed, insomuch
that they questioned among themselves,
saying, What thing is this? what new doctrine is this? for with authority commands
he even the unclean spirits, and they do
obey him.
28 And immediately his fame spread
abroad throughout all the region round
about Galilee.
29 And forthwith, when they were come
out of the synagogue, they entered into the
house of Simon and Andrew, with James
and John.
30 But Simon's wife's mother lay sick of
a fever, and anon they tell him of her.
31 And he came and took her by the
hand, and lifted her up; and immediately
the fever left her, and she ministered to
them.
32 And at even, when the sun did set,
they brought to him all that were diseased,
and them that were possessed with devils.
33 And all the city was gathered together
at the door.
34 And he healed many that were sick of
divers diseases, and cast out many devils;
and suffered not the devils to speak, because they knew him.
35 And in the morning, rising up a great
while before day, he went out, and departed into a solitary place, and there prayed.
36 And Simon and they that were with
him followed after him.

1:17 The Parable of the Fishless Fishermen

Fellowship. They were surrounded by streams and lakes full of hungry fish. They met regularly to discuss the call to fish, the abundance of fish, and the thrill of catching fish. They got excited about fishing!

Someone suggested that they needed a philosophy of fishing, so they carefully defined and redefined fishing, and the purpose of fishing. They developed fishing strategies and tactics. Then they realized that they had been going at it backwards. They had approached fishing from the point of view of the fisherman, and not from the point of view of the fish. How do fish view the world? How does the fisherman appear to the fish? What do fish eat, and when? These are all good things to know. So they began research studies, and attended conferences on fishing. Some traveled to faraway places to study different kinds of fish with different habits. Some got doctorates in fishology. But no one had yet gone fishing.

So a committee was formed to send out fishermen. As prospective fishing places outnumbered fishermen, the committee needed to determine priorities. A priority list of fishing places was posted on bulletin boards in all of the fellowship halls. But still, no one was fishing. A survey was launched to find out why. Most did not answer the survey, but from those who did, it was discovered that some felt called to study fish, a few to furnish fishing equipment, and several to go around encouraging the fishermen. What with meetings, conferences, and seminars, they just simply didn't have time to fish.

Now, Jake was a newcomer to the Fisherman's Fellowship. After one stirring meeting of the Fellowship, he went fishing and caught a large fish. At the next meeting, he told his story and was honored for his catch. He was told that he had a special "gift of fishing." He was then scheduled to speak at all the Fellowship chapters and tell how he did it.

With all the speaking invitations and his election to the board of directors of the Fisherman's Fellowship, Jake no longer had time to go fishing. But soon he began to feel restless and empty. He longed to feel the tug on the line once again. So he cut the speaking, he resigned from the board, and he said to a friend, "Let's go fishing." They did, just the two of them, and they caught fish. The members of the Fisherman's Fellowship were many, the fish were plentiful, but the fishers were few! *Anonymous*

37 And when they had found him, they
said to him, All men seek for you.
38 And he said to them, Let us go into
the next towns, that I may preach there
also: for therefore came I forth.
39 And he preached in their synagogues
throughout all Galilee, and cast out devils.
40 And there came a leper to him, beseeching him, and kneeling down to him,
and saying to him, If you will, you can
make me clean.
41 And Jesus, moved with compassion,
put forth his hand, and touched him, and
said to him, I will; be clean.
42 And as soon as he had spoken, immediately the leprosy departed from him,
and he was cleansed.
43 And he straitly charged him, and forthwith sent him away;
44 And said to him, See you say nothing

1:35 Prayer—the secret weapon: See Mark 6:46. There are some days in which we think we are too busy to take time for prayer. But the busier our schedules become, the more we need to ask God to order our day and invite Him to work through us to accomplish His will. "I have so much to do [today] that I should spend the first three hours in prayer." *Martin Luther*

"I have been driven many times upon my knees by the overwhelming conviction that I had nowhere else to go. My own wisdom, and that of all about me, seemed insufficient for that day." *Abraham Lincoln*

to any man: but go your way, show yourself to the priest, and offer for your cleansing those things which Moses commanded, for a testimony to them.
45 But he went out, and began to publish it much, and to blaze abroad the matter, insomuch that Jesus could no more
openly enter into the city, but was without in desert places: and they came to him
from every quarter.

CHAPTER 2

AND again he entered into Capernaum, after some days; and it was
noised that he was in the house.
2 And straightway many were gathered
together, insomuch that there was no
room to receive them, no, not so much as
about the door: and he preached the word
to them.
3 And they come to him, bringing one
sick of the palsy, which was borne of four.
4 And when they could not come near
to him for the press, they uncovered the
roof where he was: and when they had
broken it up, they let down the bed wherein the sick of the palsy lay.
5 When Jesus saw their faith, he said to
the sick of the palsy, Son, your sins be forgiven you.
6 But there were certain of the scribes
sitting there, and reasoning in their hearts,
7 Why does this man thus speak blasphemies? who can forgive sins but God
only?
8 And immediately when Jesus perceived
in his spirit that they so reasoned within
themselves, he said to them, Why reason
these things in your hearts?
9 Whether is it easier to say to the sick
of the palsy, Your sins be forgiven you;
or to say, Arise, and take up your bed, and
walk?
10 **But that you may know that the**
Son of man has power on earth to for-
give sins, (he said to the sick of the palsy,)
11 I say to you, Arise, and take up your
bed, and go your way into your house.
12 And immediately he arose, took up
the bed, and went forth before them all;
insomuch that they were all amazed, and
glorified God, saying, We never saw it on
this fashion.
13 And he went forth again by the sea
side; and all the multitude resorted to him,
and he taught them.
14 And as he passed by, he saw Levi the
son of Alphaeus sitting at the receipt of
custom, and said to him, Follow me. And
he arose and followed him.
15 And it came to pass, that, as Jesus sat
at meat in his house, many publicans
and sinners sat also together with Jesus
and his disciples: for there were many,
and they followed him.
16 And when the scribes and Pharisees
saw him eat with publicans and sinners,
they said to his disciples, How is it that
he eats and drinks with publicans and
sinners?
17 When Jesus heard it, he said to them,
They that are whole have no need of
the physician, but they that are sick: I
came not to call the righteous, but sin-
ners to repentance.
18 And the disciples of John and of the
Pharisees used to fast: and they come and
said to him, Why do the disciples of John
and of the Pharisees fast, but your disciples fast not?
19 And Jesus said to them, Can the children of the bridechamber fast, while the
bridegroom is with them? as long as they
have the bridegroom with them, they
cannot fast.
20 But the days will come, when the
bridegroom shall be taken away from
them, and then shall they fast in those

2:2 "In my preaching of the Word, I took special notice of this one thing, namely, that the Lord did lead me to begin where His Word begins with sinners; that is, to condemn all flesh, and to open and allege that the curse of God, by the Law, doth belong to and lay hold on all men as they come into the world, because of sin." *John Bunyan*

days.
21 No man also sews a piece of new cloth
on an old garment: else the new piece that
filled it up takes away from the old, and
the rent is made worse.
22 And no man puts new wine into old
bottles: else the new wine does burst the
bottles, and the wine is spilled, and the
bottles will be marred: but new wine must
be put into new bottles.
23 And it came to pass, that he went
through the corn fields on the sabbath
day; and his disciples began, as they went,
to pluck the ears of corn.
24 And the Pharisees said to him, Behold,
why do they do on the sabbath day that
which is not lawful?
25 And he said to them, Have you never
read what David did, when he had need,
and was an hungered, he, and they that
were with him?
26 How he went into the house of God
in the days of Abiathar the high priest,
and did eat the shewbread, which is not
lawful to eat but for the priests, and gave
also to them which were with him?
27 And he said to them, The sabbath was
made for man, and not man for the sabbath:
28 Therefore the Son of man is Lord also
of the sabbath.

CHAPTER 3

AND he entered again into the synagogue; and there was a man there
which had a withered hand.
2 And they watched him, whether he
would heal him on the sabbath day; that
they might accuse him.
3 And he said to the man which had the
withered hand, Stand forth.
4 And he said to them, Is it lawful to do
good on the sabbath days, or to do evil?
to save life, or to kill? But they held their
peace.
5 And when he had looked round about
on them with anger, being grieved for the
hardness of their hearts, he said to the man,
Stretch forth your hand. And he stretched
it out: and his hand was restored whole

"In every true searcher of Nature there is a kind of religious reverence, for he finds it impossible to imagine that he is the first to have thought out the exceedingly delicate threads that connect his perceptions."

Albert Einstein

as the other.
6 And the Pharisees went forth, and
straightway took counsel with the Herodians against him, how they might destroy him.
7 But Jesus withdrew himself with his
disciples to the sea: and a great multitude
from Galilee followed him, and from Judea,
8 And from Jerusalem, and from Idumaea,
and from beyond Jordan; and they about
Tyre and Sidon, a great multitude, when
they had heard what great things he did,
came to him.
9 And he spoke to his disciples, that a
small ship should wait on him because
of the multitude, lest they should throng
him.
10 For he had healed many; insomuch
that they pressed upon him for to touch
him, as many as had plagues.
11 And unclean spirits, when they saw
him, fell down before him, and cried, saying, You are the Son of God.
12 And he straitly charged them that they
should not make him known.
13 And he went up into a mountain, and

called to him whom he would: and they
came to him.
14 And he ordained twelve, that they
should be with him, and that he might
send them forth to preach,
15 And to have power to heal sicknesses, and to cast out devils:
16 And Simon he surnamed Peter;
17 And James the son of Zebedee, and
John the brother of James; and he surnamed them Boanerges, which is, The
sons of thunder:
18 And Andrew, and Philip, and Bartholomew, and Matthew, and Thomas, and
James the son of Alphaeus, and Thaddaeus, and Simon the Canaanite,
19 And Judas Iscariot, which also betrayed him: and they went into an house.
20 And the multitude came together
again, so that they could not so much as
eat bread.
21 And when his friends heard of it, they
went out to lay hold on him: for they said,
He is beside himself.
22 And the scribes which came down
from Jerusalem said, He has Beelzebub,
and by the prince of the devils casts he
out devils.
23 And he called them to him, and said
to them in parables, How can Satan cast
out Satan?
24 And if a kingdom be divided against
itself, that kingdom cannot stand.
25 And if a house be divided against itself, that house cannot stand.
26 And if Satan rise up against himself,
and be divided, he cannot stand, but has
an end.
27 No man can enter into a strong man's
house, and spoil his goods, except he will
first bind the strong man; and then he will
spoil his house.
28 Verily I say to you, All sins shall be
forgiven to the sons of men, and blasphemies wherewith soever they shall blaspheme:
29 But he that shall blaspheme against
the Holy Spirit has never forgiveness, but
is in danger of eternal damnation:
30 Because they said, He has an unclean
spirit.
31 There came then his brethren and his
mother, and, standing without, sent to
him, calling him.
32 And the multitude sat about him, and
they said to him, Behold, your mother and
your brethren without seek for you.
33 And he answered them, saying, Who
is my mother, or my brethren?
34 And he looked round about on them
which sat about him, and said, Behold my
mother and my brethren!
35 For whosoever shall do the will of
God, the same is my brother, and my sister, and mother.

CHAPTER 4

AND he began again to teach by the
sea side: and there was gathered to
him a great multitude, so that he entered
into a ship, and sat in the sea; and the
whole multitude was by the sea on the
land.
2 And he taught them many things by

3:29 The unpardonable sin. It is often maintained that the "unpardonable sin" is when someone "rejects Jesus Christ as Lord and Savior." However, verse 30 defines exactly what the sin is. The scribes said that Jesus did His miracles by an "unclean spirit," attributing the work of the Holy Spirit to Satan's power. If sinners do not acknowledge the Holy Spirit's work in their lives as being from God, they cannot be saved.

It is only by the Holy Spirit that men are convicted of their sin (John 16:8) and can understand the salvation God offers (1 Corinthians 2:12–14). Those who are "stiffnecked and uncircumcised in heart and... always resist the Holy Ghost" (Acts 7:51) will therefore die in their sins. Anyone who rejects the Holy Spirit's convicting influence and does not repent will not be forgiven, "neither in this world, neither in the world to come" (Matthew 12:32).

3:31–35 Jesus here affords Mary with no more honor than any believer. See also Luke 8:20,21; 11:27,28.

parables, and said to them in his doctrine,
3 Hearken; Behold, there went out a sower to sow:
4 And it came to pass, as he sowed, some
fell by the way side, and the fowls of the
air came and devoured it up.
5 And some fell on stony ground, where
it had not much earth; and immediately
it sprang up, because it had no depth of
earth:
6 But when the sun was up, it was
scorched; and because it had no root, it
withered away.

> That is the reason we have so many "mushroom" converts, because their stony ground is not plowed up; they have not got a conviction of the Law; they are stony-ground hearers.
>
> **GEORGE WHITEFIELD**

7 And some fell among thorns, and the
thorns grew up, and choked it, and it
yielded no fruit.
8 And other fell on good ground, and did
yield fruit that sprang up and increased;
and brought forth, some thirty, and some
sixty, and some an hundred.
9 And he said to them, He that has ears
to hear, let him hear.
10 And when he was alone, they that
were about him with the twelve asked of
him the parable.
11 And he said to them, to you it is giv-
en to know the mystery of the kingdom
of God: but to them that are without, all
these things are done in parables:
12 That seeing they may see, and not
perceive; and hearing they may hear, and
not understand; lest at any time they
should be converted, and their sins should
be forgiven them.
13 And he said to them, Do you not
know this parable? and how then will you
know all parables?
14 The sower sows the word.
15 And these are they by the way side,
where the word is sown; but when they
have heard, Satan comes immediately, and
takes away the word that was sown in
their hearts.
16 And these are they likewise which
are sown on stony ground; who, when
they have heard the word, immediately
receive it with gladness;
17 And have no root in themselves, and
so endure but for a time: afterward, when
affliction or persecution arises for the
word's sake, immediately they are offended.
18 And these are they which are sown
among thorns; such as hear the word,
19 And the cares of this world, and the

4:13 The key to the parables. The parable of the sower is the key to unlock the mysteries of all the other parables. If we understand this parable (that when the gospel is preached there are true and false conversions), then all the parables Jesus told will make sense: the foolish virgins (false) and the wise virgins (genuine), the good and bad fish, the wheat and tares, etc. See also John 1:13 and 3:16 footnotes.

4:14 Sowing the seed of the gospel. A student at Jacksonville University in Florida was given a tract. The student crumpled the pamphlet up and tossed it into a trash bin in his dorm. Later, his dorm mate picked it out of the trash, read it, and was soundly saved. He is now a pastor of a church in Florida.

"A Christian I met in a home group said his job was raking litter off the Avon River. It was dull, boring work and he often wondered what life was all about. One day he raked a soggy piece of paper off the water and decided it was interesting enough to keep, so he carefully placed it in his bag and took it home. That evening he dried the paper in front of a heater and carefully unfolded it, then he read it... it was a gospel tract. He became a Christian that evening." *Richard Gunther*

"Nothing surpasses a tract for sowing the seed of the Good News." *Billy Graham*

See next page for ideas on where to distribute tracts. See also 1 Corinthians 9:22 and Revelation 22:2 footnotes.

Where to Leave Tracts

- At pay phones
- In shopping carts
- In clothes pockets in stores
- In letters to loved ones
- With a generous tip
- On seats in restaurant lobbies
- With fast-food employees, cashiers, flight attendants, cab drivers, and gas station workers
- In restrooms
- At rest areas
- On ATM machines and bank counters
- In envelopes with bill payments
- In elevators
- On hotel dressers for the maid
- On ice machines
- On newspaper racks
- In waiting rooms of doctors' offices and hospitals
- On seats at airports, subways, and bus stations
- In plane seat pockets
- Inside magazines
- In cabs
- In laundromats

deceitfulness of riches, and the lusts of other things entering in, choke the word, and it becomes unfruitful.

20 And these are they which are sown on good ground; such as hear the word, and receive it, and bring forth fruit, some thirtyfold, some sixty, and some an hundred.

21 And he said to them, Is a candle brought to be put under a bushel, or under a bed? and not to be set on a candlestick?

22 For there is nothing hid, which shall not be manifested; neither was any thing kept secret, but that it should come abroad.

23 If any man have ears to hear, let him hear.

24 And he said to them, Take heed what you hear: with what measure you mete, it shall be measured to you: and to you that hear shall more be given.

25 For he that has, to him shall be given: and he that has not, from him shall be taken even that which he has.

26 And he said, So is the kingdom of God, as if a man should cast seed into the ground;

27 And should sleep, and rise night and day, and the seed should spring and grow up, he knows not how.

28 For the earth brings forth fruit of herself; first the blade, then the ear, after that the full corn in the ear.

29 But when the fruit is brought forth, immediately he puts in the sickle, because the harvest is come.

30 And he said, Whereunto shall we liken the kingdom of God? or with what comparison shall we compare it?

31 It is like a grain of mustard seed, which, when it is sown in the earth, is less than all the seeds that be in the earth:

32 But when it is sown, it grows up, and becomes greater than all herbs, and shoots out great branches; so that the fowls of the air may lodge under the shadow of it.

33 And with many such parables spoke he the word to them, as they were able to hear it.

34 But without a parable spoke he not to them: and when they were alone, he expounded all things to his disciples.

35 And the same day, when the even was come, he said to them, Let us pass over to the other side.

36 And when they had sent away the multitude, they took him even as he was in the ship. And there were also with him

4:31 Skeptics claim that this verse is an error: "The mustard seed average size is approximately 1.0 millimeter in diameter. The basil seed average is .5 millimeter, the daisy seed is .4 millimeter, the lavender seed is .35 millimeter. Obviously these three seeds are smaller than the mustard seed." However, the mustard seed in Israel was less than .35 millimeters. We can know this as absolute fact, because here we have the Maker of the mustard seed telling us so. See John 1:3.

other little ships.
37 And there arose a great storm of wind,
and the waves beat into the ship, so that
it was now full.
38 And he was in the hinder part of the
ship, asleep on a pillow: and they awake
him, and say to him, Master, care not that
we perish?
39 And he arose, and rebuked the wind,
and said to the sea, Peace, be still. And the
wind ceased, and there was a great calm.
40 And he said to them, Why are you so
fearful? how is it that you have no faith?
41 And they feared exceedingly, and said
one to another, What manner of man is
this, that even the wind and the sea obey
him?

. . . . . .

For the Holy Spirit's role in salvation, see John 16:8–11 footnote.

. . . . . .

CHAPTER 5

AND they came over to the other side
of the sea, into the country of the
Gadarenes.
2 And when he was come out of the ship,
immediately there met him out of the
tombs a man with an unclean spirit,
3 Who had his dwelling among the
tombs; and no man could bind him, no,
not with chains:
4 Because that he had been often bound
with fetters and chains, and the chains
had been plucked asunder by him, and
the fetters broken in pieces: neither could
any man tame him.
5 And always, night and day, he was in
the mountains, and in the tombs, crying,
and cutting himself with stones.
6 But when he saw Jesus afar off, he ran
and worshipped him,
7 And cried with a loud voice, and said,
What have I to do with you, Jesus, you
Son of the most high God? I adjure you
by God, that you torment me not.
8 For he said to him, Come out of the
man, you unclean spirit.
9 And he asked him, What is your name?
And he answered, saying, My name is
Legion: for we are many.
10 And he besought him much that he
would not send them away out of the
country.
11 Now there was there near to the
mountains a great herd of swine feeding.
12 And all the devils besought him, saying,
Send us into the swine, that we may
enter into them.
13 And forthwith Jesus gave them leave.
And the unclean spirits went out, and
entered into the swine: and the herd ran
violently down a steep place into the sea,
(they were about two thousand;) and were
choked in the sea.
14 And they that fed the swine fled, and
told it in the city, and in the country. And
they went out to see what it was that was
done.
15 And they come to Jesus, and see him
that was possessed with the devil, and
had the legion, sitting, and clothed, and
in his right mind: and they were afraid.
16 And they that saw it told them how
it befell to him that was possessed with
the devil, and also concerning the swine.
17 And they began to pray him to depart
out of their coasts.
18 And when he was come into the ship,
he that had been possessed with the devil
prayed him that he might be with him.
19 Howbeit Jesus suffered him not, but
said to him, Go home to your friends, and
tell them how great things the Lord has
done for you, and has had compassion on
you.
20 And he departed, and began to publish
in Decapolis how great things Jesus
had done for him: and all men did marvel.
21 And when Jesus was passed over again
by ship to the other side, much people
gathered to him: and he was near to the
sea.
22 And, behold, there came one of the
rulers of the synagogue, Jairus by name;
and when he saw him, he fell at his feet,
23 And besought him greatly, saying,
My little daughter lies at the point of death:

I pray you, come and lay your hands on
her, that she may be healed; and she shall
live.
24 And Jesus went with him; and much
people followed him, and thronged him.
25 And a certain woman, which had an
issue of blood twelve years,
26 And had suffered many things of
many physicians, and had spent all that
she had, and was nothing bettered, but
rather grew worse,
27 When she had heard of Jesus, came in
the press behind, and touched his garment.
28 For she said, If I may touch but his
clothes, I shall be whole.
29 And straightway the fountain of her
blood was dried up; and she felt in her
body that she was healed of that plague.
30 And Jesus, immediately knowing in
himself that virtue had gone out of him,
turned him about in the press, and said,
Who touched my clothes?
31 And his disciples said to him, You see
the multitude thronging you, and you say,
Who touched me?
32 And he looked round about to see her
that had done this thing.
33 But the woman fearing and trembling,
knowing what was done in her, came and
fell down before him, and told him all the
truth.
34 And he said to her, Daughter, your
faith has made you whole; go in peace,
and be whole of your plague.
35 While he yet spoke, there came from
the ruler of the synagogue's house certain
which said, Your daughter is dead: why
trouble the Master any further?
36 As soon as Jesus heard the word that
was spoken, he said to the ruler of the
synagogue, Be not afraid, only believe.
37 And he suffered no man to follow
him, save Peter, and James, and John the
brother of James.
38 And he came to the house of the ruler of the synagogue, and saw the tumult,
and them that wept and wailed greatly.
39 And when he was come in, he said
to them, Why make this ado, and weep?
the damsel is not dead, but sleeps.
40 And they laughed him to scorn. But
when he had put them all out, he took
the father and the mother of the damsel,
and them that were with him, and entered in where the damsel was lying.
41 And he took the damsel by the hand,
and said to her, Talitha cumi; which is, being interpreted, Damsel, I say to you, arise.
42 And straightway the damsel arose, and
walked; for she was of the age of twelve
years. And they were astonished with a
great astonishment.
43 And he charged them straitly that no
man should know it; and commanded
that something should be given her to eat.

CHAPTER 6

AND he went out from thence, and
came into his own country; and his
disciples follow him.
2 And when the sabbath day was come,
he began to teach in the synagogue: and
many hearing him were astonished, saying, From whence has this man these
things? and what wisdom is this which is
given to him, that even such mighty works
are wrought by his hands?
3 Is not this the carpenter, the son of
Mary, the brother of James, and Joses, and
of Juda, and Simon? and are not his sisters

6:3 Jesus' siblings. Jesus had four brothers and at least two sisters. Therefore Mary was no longer a virgin *after* she gave birth to Jesus. The Greek word used here is *adelphos*—brother (not half-brother). It is also unlikely that these were the cousins of Jesus or Jewish brethren. These children were spoken of as being with Mary, without a shadow of a hint that they were not her children. The word "mother" is mentioned at the same time (Mark 3:31; Luke 8:19; John 2:12; Acts 1:14). Likewise, Matthew 1:25 does not say that Mary remained a virgin for life, but that she had no physical union with her husband *until* Jesus was born.

"By a Carpenter mankind was made, and only by that Carpenter can mankind be remade."
Deriderius Erasmas

here with us? And they were offended at
him.
4 But Jesus said to them, A prophet is
not without honor, but in his own country, and among his own kin, and in his
own house.
5 And he could there do no mighty work,
save that he laid his hands upon a few sick
folk, and healed them.
6 And he marveled because of their unbelief. And he went round about the villages,
teaching.
7 And he called to him the twelve, and
began to send them forth by two and two;
and gave them power over unclean spirits;
8 And commanded them that they should
take nothing for their journey, save a staff
only; no scrip, no bread, no money in their
purse:
9 But be shod with sandals; and not put
on two coats.
10 And he said to them, In what place soever you enter into an house, there abide
till you depart from that place.
11 And whosoever shall not receive you,
nor hear you, when you depart thence,
shake off the dust under your feet for a
testimony against them. Verily I say to you,
It shall be more tolerable for Sodom and
Gomorrha in the day of judgment, than
for that city.
12 And they went out, and preached that
men should repent.
13 And they cast out many devils, and
anointed with oil many that were sick,
and healed them.
14 And king Herod heard of him; (for
his name was spread abroad:) and he said,
That John the Baptist was risen from the
dead, and therefore mighty works do show
forth themselves in him.
15 Others said, That it is Elijah. And others said, That it is a prophet, or as one of
the prophets.
16 But when Herod heard thereof, he
said, It is John, whom I beheaded: he is
risen from the dead.
17 For Herod himself had sent forth
and laid hold upon John, and bound him
in prison for Herodias' sake, his brother
Philip's wife: for he had married her.
18 For John had said to Herod, It is not
lawful for you to have your brother's wife.

> You and I must continue to drive at men's hearts till they are broken. Then we must keep on preaching Christ crucified until their hearts are bound up.
>
> **CHARLES SPURGEON**

19 Therefore Herodias had a quarrel
against him, and would have killed him;
but she could not:
20 For Herod feared John, knowing that
he was a just man and an holy, and observed him; and when he heard him, he
did many things, and heard him gladly.
21 And when a convenient day was
come, that Herod on his birthday made a
supper to his lords, high captains, and
chief estates of Galilee;
22 And when the daughter of the said
Herodias came in, and danced, and pleased
Herod and them that sat with him, the
king said to the damsel, Ask of me whatsoever you will, and I will give it you.
23 And he sware to her, Whatsoever you
shall ask of me, I will give it you, to the
half of my kingdom.

6:23 The power of lust. Lust blinds a man to reason (v. 22), leading him to yield up to "half his kingdom." He will abandon his wife, his children, his home, and his reputation, and run off with another woman. Herod feared John the Baptist because he knew that John was a just and holy man. He even protected him and heard him gladly, yet because of Herod's sinful eye he further violated the Law of God and had John murdered. Herod feared man more than he feared God (v. 26).

Those who don't fear God will lie to you, steal from you, and even kill you if they think they can get away with it. In truth, lust doesn't want half of your kingdom, it wants your head on a plate. See James 1:15.

24 And she went forth, and said to her
mother, What shall I ask? And she said,
The head of John the Baptist.
25 And she came in straightway with
haste to the king, and asked, saying, I will
that you give me by and by in a charger
the head of John the Baptist.
26 And the king was exceeding sorry;
yet for his oath's sake, and for their sakes
which sat with him, he would not reject
her.
27 And immediately the king sent an
executioner, and commanded his head to
be brought: and he went and beheaded
him in the prison,
28 And brought his head in a charger,
and gave it to the damsel: and the damsel
gave it to her mother.
29 And when his disciples heard of it,
they came and took up his corpse, and laid
it in a tomb.
30 And the apostles gathered themselves
together to Jesus, and told him all things,
both what they had done, and what they
had taught.
31 And he said to them, Come yourselves
apart into a desert place, and rest a while:
for there were many coming and going,
and they had no leisure so much as to eat.
32 And they departed into a desert place
by ship privately.
33 And the people saw them departing,
and many knew him, and ran afoot there
out of all cities, and outwent them, and
came together to him.
34 And Jesus, when he came out, saw
much people, and was moved with compassion toward them, because they were
as sheep not having a shepherd: and he
began to teach them many things.
35 And when the day was now far spent,
his disciples came to him, and said, This
is a desert place, and now the time is far
passed:
36 Send them away, that they may go into the country round about, and into the
villages, and buy themselves bread: for
they have nothing to eat.
37 He answered and said to them, You
give them to eat. And they said to him,
Shall we go and buy two hundred pennyworth of bread, and give them to eat?
38 He said to them, How many loaves
have you? Go and see. And when they
knew, they said, Five, and two fishes.
39 And he commanded them to make all
sit down by companies upon the green
grass.
40 And they sat down in ranks, by hundreds, and by fifties.
41 And when he had taken the five loaves
and the two fishes, he looked up to heav-
en, and blessed, and broke the loaves,
and gave them to his disciples to set before them; and the two fishes divided he
among them all.
42 And they did all eat, and were filled.
43 And they took up twelve baskets full
of the fragments, and of the fishes.
44 And they that did eat of the loaves
were about five thousand men.
45 And straightway he constrained his
disciples to get into the ship, and to go to
the other side before to Bethsaida, while
he sent away the people.
46 And when he had sent them away,
he departed into a mountain to pray.
47 And when even was come, the ship
was in the midst of the sea, and he alone
on the land.
48 And he saw them toiling in rowing;
for the wind was contrary to them: and
about the fourth watch of the night he
came to them, walking upon the sea, and
would have passed by them.
49 But when they saw him walking upon the sea, they supposed it had been a
spirit, and cried out:
50 For they all saw him, and were troubled. And immediately he talked with
them, and said to them, Be of good cheer:
it is I; be not afraid.
51 And he went up to them into the
ship; and the wind ceased: and they were

6:46 Prayer—the secret weapon: See Luke 5:16.

sore amazed in themselves beyond measure, and wondered.
52 For they considered not the miracle of
the loaves: for their heart was hardened.
53 And when they had passed over, they
came into the land of Gennesaret, and
drew to the shore.
54 And when they were come out of the
ship, straightway they knew him,
55 And ran through that whole region
round about, and began to carry about in
beds those that were sick, where they
heard he was.
56 And wherever he entered, into villages, or cities, or country, they laid the
sick in the streets, and besought him that
they might touch if it were but the border
of his garment: and as many as touched
him were made whole.

CHAPTER 7

THEN came together to him the Pharisees, and certain of the scribes, which
came from Jerusalem.
2 And when they saw some of his disciples eat bread with defiled, that is to say,
with unwashed, hands, they found fault.
3 For the Pharisees, and all the Jews, except they wash their hands oft, eat not,
holding the tradition of the elders.
4 And when they come from the market,
except they wash, they eat not. And many
other things there be, which they have
received to hold, as the washing of cups,
and pots, brazen vessels, and of tables.
5 Then the Pharisees and scribes asked
him, Why walk not your disciples according to the tradition of the elders, but
eat bread with unwashed hands?
6 He answered and said to them, Well
has Isaiah prophesied of you hypocrites,
as it is written, This people honors me
with their lips, but their heart is far from
me.
7 Howbeit in vain do they worship me,
teaching for doctrines the commandments
of men.
8 For laying aside the commandment of
God, you hold the tradition of men, as
the washing of pots and cups: and many
other such like things you do.
9 And he said to them, Full well you reject the commandment of God, that you
may keep your own tradition.
10 For Moses said, Honor your father
and your mother; and, Whoso curses father or mother, let him die the death:
11 But you say, If a man shall say to his
father or mother, It is Corban, that is to
say, a gift, by whatsoever you might be
profited by me; he shall be free.
12 And you suffer him no more to do
anything for his father or his mother;
13 Making the word of God of none effect through your tradition, which you
have delivered: and many such like things
do you.
14 And when he had called all the people to him, he said to them, Hearken to
me every one of you, and understand:
15 There is nothing from without a man,
that entering into him can defile him: but
the things which come out of him, those
are they that defile the man.
16 If any man have ears to hear, let him
hear.
17 And when he was entered into the
house from the people, his disciples asked
him concerning the parable.
18 And he said to them, Are you so without understanding also? Do you not perceive, that whatsoever thing from without enters into the man, it cannot defile
him;
19 Because it enters not into his heart,
but into the belly, and goes out into the

7:5–13 The Bible says that the Messiah would magnify the Law and make it honorable (Isaiah 42:21). Jesus did this many times, particularly in the Sermon on the Mount. The Pharisees had dishonored the Law by merely giving God lip service. They made the Commandment void through their tradition, teaching for doctrines the commandments of men. The Savior brought honor back to the Law by teaching that the Law was spiritual by nature, and that outward observance was not enough. God required truth in the inward parts (the thought-life, intent, and motives).

THE FUNCTION OF THE LAW

7:21 "Now, if you have your hearts broken up by the Law, you will find the heart is more deceitful than the devil. I can say this myself, I am very much afraid of mine, it is so bad. The heart is like a dark cellar, full of lizards, cockroaches, beetles, and all kinds of reptiles and insects, which in the dark we see not, but the Law takes down the shutters and lets in the light, and so we see the evil. Thus sin becoming apparent by the Law, it is written the Law makes the offense to abound." *Charles Spurgeon*

draught, purging all meats?
20 And he said, That which comes out
of the man, that defiles the man.
21 For from within, out of the heart of
men, proceed evil thoughts, adulteries,
fornications, murders,
22 Thefts, covetousness, wickedness,
deceit, lasciviousness, an evil eye, blas-
phemy, pride, foolishness:
23 All these evil things come from
within, and defile the man.
24 And from thence he arose, and went
into the borders of Tyre and Sidon, and
entered into an house, and would have
no man know it: but he could not be
hid.
25 For a certain woman, whose young
daughter had an unclean spirit, heard of
him, and came and fell at his feet:
26 The woman was a Greek, a Syrophe-
nician by nation; and she besought him
that he would cast forth the devil out of
her daughter.
27 But Jesus said to her, Let the children
first be filled: for it is not meet to take the
children's bread, and to cast it to the dogs.
28 And she answered and said to him,
Yes, Lord: yet the dogs under the table
eat of the children's crumbs.
29 And he said to her, For this saying go
your way; the devil is gone out of your
daughter.
30 And when she was come to her house,
she found the devil gone out, and her
daughter laid upon the bed.
31 And again, departing from the coasts
of Tyre and Sidon, he came to the sea of
Galilee, through the midst of the coasts of
Decapolis.
32 And they bring to him one that was
deaf, and had an impediment in his speech;
and they beseech him to put his hand
upon him.
33 And he took him aside from the
multitude, and put his fingers into his
ears, and he spit, and touched his tongue;
34 And looking up to heaven, he sighed,
and said to him, Ephphatha, that is, Be
opened.
35 And straightway his ears were opened,
and the string of his tongue was loosed,
and he spoke plain.
36 And he charged them that they should
tell no man: but the more he charged
them, so much the more a great deal they
published it;
37 And were beyond measure astonished, saying, He has done all things well:
he makes both the deaf to hear, and the
dumb to speak.

CHAPTER 8

IN those days the multitude being very
great, and having nothing to eat, Jesus
called his disciples to him, and said to

7:20–23 Man's heart is sinful. Jeremiah 17:9 affirms the condition of man's heart: "The heart is deceitful above all things, and desperately wicked: who can know it?" Verse 10 then warns us that God not only knows the secret things of the heart but will reward us accordingly: "I the Lord search the heart, I try the reins, even to give every man according to his ways, and according to the fruit of his doings." See Mark 12:29–31 footnote.

7:21,22 Notice that what defiles a man is directly referenced to the Moral Law (the Ten Commandments): adulteries (Seventh), fornications (Seventh), murders (Sixth), thefts (Eighth), covetousness (Tenth), blasphemy (Third). Sin is transgression of the Law (1 John 3:4).

them,
2 I have compassion on the multitude,
because they have now been with me
three days, and have nothing to eat:
3 And if I send them away fasting to
their own houses, they will faint by the
way: for divers of them came from far.
4 And his disciples answered him, From
whence can a man satisfy these men with
bread here in the wilderness?
5 And he asked them, How many loaves
have you? And they said, Seven.
6 And he commanded the people to sit
down on the ground: and he took the sev-
en loaves, and gave thanks, and broke,
and gave to his disciples to set before
them; and they did set them before the
people.
7 And they had a few small fishes: and
he blessed, and commanded to set them
also before them.
8 So they did eat, and were filled: and
they took up of the broken meat that was
left seven baskets.
9 And they that had eaten were about
four thousand: and he sent them away.
10 And straightway he entered into a
ship with his disciples, and came into the
parts of Dalmanutha.
11 And the Pharisees came forth, and began to question with him, seeking of him
a sign from heaven, tempting him.
12 And he sighed deeply in his spirit,
and said, Why does this generation seek
after a sign? verily I say to you, There
shall no sign be given to this generation.
13 And he left them, and entering into
the ship again departed to the other side.
14 Now the disciples had forgotten to
take bread, neither had they in the ship
with them more than one loaf.
15 And he charged them, saying, Take
heed, beware of the leaven of the Pharisees, and of the leaven of Herod.
16 And they reasoned among themselves,
saying, It is because we have no bread.
17 And when Jesus knew it, he said to
them, Why do you reason, because you
have no bread? Do you not yet perceive,
neither understand? have you your heart
yet hardened?
18 Having eyes, do you not see? and having ears, do you not hear? and do you not
remember?
19 When I broke the five loaves among
five thousand, how many baskets full of
fragments did you take up? They said to
him, Twelve.
20 And when the seven among four
thousand, how many baskets full of fragments did you take up? And they said,
Seven.
21 And he said to them, How is it that
you do not understand?

> “As the fisherman longs to take the fish in his net, as the hunter pants to bear home his spoil, as the mother pines to clasp her lost child to her bosom, so do we faint for the salvation of souls.”
>
> **CHARLES SPURGEON**

22 And he came to Bethsaida; and they
brought a blind man to him, and besought him to touch him.
23 And he took the blind man by the
hand, and led him out of the town; and
when he had spit on his eyes, and put
his hands upon him, he asked him if he
saw anything.
24 And he looked up, and said, I see men
as trees, walking.
25 After that he put his hands again upon his eyes, and made him look up: and he
was restored, and saw every man clearly.
26 And he sent him away to his house,
saying, Neither go into the town, nor tell
it to any in the town.
27 And Jesus went out, and his disciples, into the towns of Caesarea Philippi:
and by the way he asked his disciples,
saying to them, Whom do men say that I
am?
28 And they answered, John the Baptist:
but some say, Elijah; and others, One of
the prophets.
29 And he said to them, But whom do
you say that I am? And Peter answered

and said to him, You are the Christ.
30 And he charged them that they should
tell no man of him.
31 And he began to teach them, that the
Son of man must suffer many things, and
be rejected of the elders, and of the chief
priests, and scribes, and be killed, and after
three days rise again.
32 And he spoke that saying openly.
And Peter took him, and began to rebuke
him.
33 But when he had turned about and
looked on his disciples, he rebuked Peter,
saying, Get behind me, Satan: for you savour not the things that be of God, but
the things that be of men.
34 And when he had called the people
to him with his disciples also, he said to
them, **Whosoever will come after me,
let him deny himself, and take up his
cross, and follow me.**

. . . . . .

For the biblical way to confront sinners, see Psalm 41:4 footnote.

. . . . . .

35 **For whosoever will save his life
shall lose it; but whosoever shall lose
his life for my sake and the gospel's, the
same shall save it.**
36 **For what shall it profit a man, if
he shall gain the whole world, and lose
his own soul?**
37 **Or what shall a man give in exchange for his soul?**
**38 Whosoever therefore shall be
ashamed of me and of my words in this
adulterous and sinful generation; of him
also shall the Son of man be ashamed,
when he comes in the glory of his Father with the holy angels.**

CHAPTER 9

AND he said to them, Verily I say to
you, That there be some of them
that stand here, which shall not taste of
death, till they have seen the kingdom of
God come with power.
2 And after six days Jesus took with him
Peter, and James, and John, and led them
up into an high mountain apart by themselves: and he was transfigured before
them.
3 And his raiment became shining, exceeding white as snow; so as no fuller on
earth can white them.
4 And there appeared to them Elijah with
Moses: and they were talking with Jesus.
5 And Peter answered and said to Jesus,
Master, it is good for us to be here: and
let us make three tabernacles; one for you,
and one for Moses, and one for Elijah.
6 For he knew not what to say; for they
were sore afraid.
7 And there was a cloud that overshadowed them: and a voice came out of the
cloud, saying, This is my beloved Son:
hear him.
8 And suddenly, when they had looked
round about, they saw no man any more,
save Jesus only with themselves.
9 And as they came down from the
mountain, he charged them that they
should tell no man what things they had
seen, till the Son of man were risen from
the dead.

8:33 If you are going to do anything for the kingdom of God, be ready for unexpected discouragement. This may come through a Christian brother or sister—the place least expected. Satan spoke directly through Peter in an attempt to stop Jesus from doing the will of the Father. It was David's elder brother who tried to discourage him from slaying Goliath. See 1 Samuel 17:28.

8:38 Here's an effective way to unashamedly share your faith and show that you care about strangers: When you're eating in a restaurant, tell the waiter, "We're going to be asking the blessing for our food in a minute, and wanted to know if there's anything you'd like us to pray for?"

8:38 Second coming of Jesus: See Luke 12:40.

9:4 See Luke 9:30 footnote.

10 And they kept that saying with themselves, questioning one with another what
the rising from the dead should mean.
11 And they asked him, saying, Why say
the scribes that Elijah must first come?
12 And he answered and told them, Elijah verily comes first, and restores all
things; and how it is written of the Son
of man, that he must suffer many things,
and be set at nought.
13 But I say to you, That Elijah is indeed
come, and they have done to him whatsoever they listed, as it is written of him.
14 And when he came to his disciples,
he saw a great multitude about them,
and the scribes questioning with them.
15 And straightway all the people, when
they beheld him, were greatly amazed,
and running to him saluted him.
16 And he asked the scribes, What do
you question with them?
17 And one of the multitude answered
and said, Master, I have brought to you
my son, which has a dumb spirit;
18 And wherever he takes him, he tears
him: and he foams, and gnashes with his
teeth, and pines away: and I spoke to
your disciples that they should cast him
out; and they could not.
19 He answered him, and said, O faithless generation, how long shall I be with
you? how long shall I suffer you? bring
him to me.
20 And they brought him to him: and
when he saw him, straightway the spirit
tare him; and he fell on the ground, and
wallowed foaming.
21 And he asked his father, How long is
it ago since this came to him? And he
said, Of a child.
22 And often it has cast him into the
fire, and into the waters, to destroy him:
but if you can do any thing, have compassion on us, and help us.
23 Jesus said to him, If you can believe,
all things are possible to him that believes.
24 And straightway the father of the child
cried out, and said with tears, Lord, I believe; help mine unbelief.

"Most people are bothered by those passages of Scriptures they don't understand, but for me I have always noticed that the passages that bother me are those I do understand."

Mark Twain

25 When Jesus saw that the people came
running together, he rebuked the foul
spirit, saying to him, You dumb and deaf
spirit, I charge you, come out of him, and
enter no more into him.
26 And the spirit cried, and rent him
sore, and came out of him: and he was as
one dead; insomuch that many said, He
is dead.
27 But Jesus took him by the hand, and
lifted him up; and he arose.
28 And when he was come into the
house, his disciples asked him privately,
Why could not we cast him out?
29 And he said to them, This kind can
come forth by nothing, but by prayer and
fasting.
30 And they departed thence, and passed
through Galilee; and he would not that
any man should know it.
31 For he taught his disciples, and said
to them, The Son of man is delivered into the hands of men, and they shall kill
him; and after that he is killed, he shall
rise the third day.
32 But they understood not that saying,

QUESTIONS & OBJECTIONS

9:47 ***"Hell isn't a place. This life is hell."***

Skeptics who say this are trying to dismiss the reality of hell. They might like to think that life as we know it couldn't get any worse, but the sufferings in this life will be heaven compared to the suffering in the next life—for those who die in their sins. This life is the closest thing to hell that Christians will ever know, and the closest thing to heaven that sinners will ever know.

For a biblical description of hell, see Revelation 1:18 footnote.

and were afraid to ask him.
33 And he came to Capernaum: and
being in the house he asked them, What
was it that you disputed among yourselves by the way?
34 But they held their peace: for by the
way they had disputed among themselves, who should be the greatest.
35 And he sat down, and called the
twelve, and said to them, If any man desire to be first, the same shall be last of
all, and servant of all.
36 And he took a child, and set him in
the midst of them: and when he had
taken him in his arms, he said to them,
37 Whosoever shall receive one of such
children in my name, receives me: and
whosoever shall receive me, receives not
me, but him that sent me.
38 And John answered him, saying, Master, we saw one casting out devils in your
name, and he followed not us: and we
forbad him, because he followed not us.
39 But Jesus said, Forbid him not: for
there is no man which shall do a miracle
in my name, that can lightly speak evil of
me.
40 For he that is not against us is on our
part.
41 For whosoever shall give you a cup
of water to drink in my name, because you
belong to Christ, verily I say to you, he
shall not lose his reward.
42 And whosoever shall offend one of
these little ones that believe in me, it is
better for him that a millstone were hanged
about his neck, and he were cast into the
sea.
43 And if your hand offends you, cut
it off: it is better for you to enter into
life maimed, than having two hands to
go into hell, into the fire that never
shall be quenched:
44 Where their worm dies not, and
the fire is not quenched.
45 And if your foot offends you, cut
it off: it is better for you to enter halt
into life, than having two feet to be cast
into hell, into the fire that never shall
be quenched:
46 Where their worm dies not, and the
fire is not quenched.
47 And if your eye offends you, pluck
it out: it is better for you to enter into
the kingdom of God with one eye, than
having two eyes to be cast into hell fire:
48 Where their worm dies not, and the
fire is not quenched.
49 For every one shall be salted with fire,
and every sacrifice shall be salted with
salt.
50 Salt is good: but if the salt has lost

9:34,35 "Not everybody could be famous, but everybody can be great because greatness is determined by service." *Martin Luther King, Jr.*

9:43–48 Hell: For verses warning of its reality, see Luke 16:23.

"There is a dreadful hell, and everlasting pains; where sinners must with devils dwell, in darkness, fire, and chains." *Isaac Watts*

his saltiness, wherewith will you season
it? Have salt in yourselves, and have peace
one with another.

CHAPTER 10

AND he arose from thence, and came
into the coasts of Judea by the farther
side of Jordan: and the people resort to
him again; and, as he was wont, he taught
them again.
2 And the Pharisees came to him, and
asked him, Is it lawful for a man to put
away his wife? tempting him.
3 And he answered and said to them,
What did Moses command you?
4 And they said, Moses suffered to write
a bill of divorcement, and to put her away.
5 And Jesus answered and said to them,
For the hardness of your heart he wrote
you this precept.
6 But from the beginning of the creation
God made them male and female.
7 For this cause shall a man leave his father and mother, and cleave to his wife;
8 And they twain shall be one flesh: so
then they are no more twain, but one flesh.
9 What therefore God has joined together, let not man put asunder.
10 And in the house his disciples asked
him again of the same matter.
11 And he said to them, Whosoever shall
put away his wife, and marry another,
commits adultery against her.
12 And if a woman shall put away her
husband, and be married to another, she
commits adultery.
13 And they brought young children to
him, that he should touch them: and his
disciples rebuked those that brought them.
14 But when Jesus saw it, he was much
displeased, and said to them, Suffer the
little children to come to me, and forbid

9:50 Salty Christians. "Salvation is a radical thing. It is a call to all that Christ has demanded us to do. Real Christianity will make a salty difference, in our family, in our waking up, in our work, in our relationships, in the way we spend our money, and in the way we spend our leisure time. Real Christianity is not casual. It is dynamic. It goes beyond mere intellectual assent to correct doctrine.

"Real Christians who want to know real Christianity, who are not content with games and masks and only images of the truth, must rise from our comfortable pews and leave our 'one-stop Christian service centers' and go out into the world and make a salty difference!" *Guy Rice Doud, Joy in the Journey*

10:6 God made them male and female. If every creature "evolved" with no Creator, there are numerous problems. Take for instance the first bird. Was it male or female? Let's say it was a male. How did it produce offspring without a mate? If a female evolved, why did it evolve with differing reproductive organs? Did it evolve by chance, or did it evolve because it knew that it was needed by the male of the species? How did it know what needed to be evolved if its brain hadn't yet evolved? Did the bird breathe? Did it breathe before it evolved lungs? How did it do this? Why did it evolve lungs if it was happily surviving without them? Did the bird have a mouth? How did it eat before it had evolved a mouth? Where did the mouth send the food before a stomach evolved? How did the bird have energy if it didn't eat (because it didn't yet have a mouth)? How did the bird see what there was to eat before its eyes evolved? Evolution is intellectual suicide. It is an embarrassment. (See Romans 1:21,22.)

"Evolution is a fairy tale for grown-ups. This theory has helped nothing in the progress of science. It is useless." *Professor Louis Bounoure*, Director of Research, National Center of Scientific Research

"Scientists who go about teaching that evolution is a fact of life are great con-men, and the story they are telling may be the greatest hoax ever. In explaining evolution, we do not have one iota of fact." *Dr. T. N. Tahmisian*, Atomic Energy Commission

10:6–9 By quoting from both chapters 1 and 2 of Genesis, Jesus shows that these chapters are not contradictory, as some claim. Chapter 2 merely gives the details of chapter 1. A sports commentator is not in error when (after a game) he gives in-depth analysis and fails to repeat every detail in chronological order. He is merely reviewing the completed game by mentioning the highlights.

QUESTIONS & OBJECTIONS

10:18 *"I'm as good as any Christian!"*

A Christian, by himself, isn't good. Jesus said that only God is good. The only "goodness," or righteousness, that the believer has comes from Christ (2 Corinthians 5:21; Philippians 3:9). The Bible tells us that, without Christ, man is corrupt and filthy; "there is none that does good, no, not one" (Psalm 14:3). See also Romans 3:9 footnote.

them not: for of such is the kingdom of
God.
15 Verily I say to you, Whosoever shall
not receive the kingdom of God as a little child, he shall not enter therein.
16 And he took them up in his arms,
put his hands upon them, and blessed
them.
17 And when he was gone forth into
the way, there came one running, and
kneeled to him, and asked him, Good
Master, what shall I do that I may inherit
eternal life?

USING THE LAW IN EVANGELISM

10:17 This man came running and fell to his knees before Jesus. His earnest and humble heart would seem to make him a prime candidate as a potential convert. Yet, instead of giving him the message of God's grace, Jesus used the Law to expose the man's hidden sin. This man was a transgressor of the First of the Ten Commandments. His money was his god, and one cannot serve God and mammon. Verse 21 reveals that it was love that motivated the Savior to speak in this way to this rich young man. Love will be concerned with the desire for a genuine conversion, rather than a sense of accomplishment in leading someone in a sinner's prayer whose heart isn't right with God. (See also Matthew 19:17–22.)

18 And Jesus said to him, Why do you
call me good? there is none good but
one, that is, God.
19 You know the commandments, Do
not commit adultery, Do not kill, Do not
steal, Do not bear false witness, Defraud
not, Honor your father and mother.
20 And he answered and said to him,
Master, all these have I observed from
my youth.
21 Then Jesus beholding him loved him,
and said to him, One thing you lack: go
your way, sell whatsoever you have, and
give to the poor, and you shall have treasure in heaven: and come, take up the
cross, and follow me.
22 And he was sad at that saying, and
went away grieved: for he had great possessions.
23 And Jesus looked round about, and
said to his disciples, How hardly shall they
that have riches enter into the kingdom
of God!
24 And the disciples were astonished at
his words. But Jesus answered again, and
said to them, Children, how hard is it for
them that trust in riches to enter into the
kingdom of God!
25 **It is easier for a camel to go through
the eye of a needle, than for a rich man
to enter into the kingdom of God.**
26 And they were astonished out of
measure, saying among themselves, Who

10:21 "Christianity has always insisted that the cross we bear precedes the crown we wear." *Martin Luther King, Jr.*

"No pain, no palm; no thorns, no throne; no gall, no glory; no cross, no crown…" *William Penn*

then can be saved?
27 And Jesus looking upon them said,
With men it is impossible, but not with
God: for with God all things are possible.
28 Then Peter began to say to him, Lo,
we have left all, and have followed you.
29 And Jesus answered and said, Verily
I say to you, There is no man that has left
house, or brethren, or sisters, or father, or
mother, or wife, or children, or lands, for
my sake, and the gospel's,
30 But he shall receive an hundredfold
now in this time, houses, and brethren,
and sisters, and mothers, and children,
and lands, with persecutions; and in the
world to come eternal life.

> The diver plunges deep to find pearls, and we must accept any labor or hazard to win a soul.
>
> **CHARLES SPURGEON**

31 But many that are first shall be last;
and the last first.
32 And they were in the way going up
to Jerusalem; and Jesus went before them:
and they were amazed; and as they followed, they were afraid. And he took again
the twelve, and began to tell them what
things should happen to him,
33 Saying, Behold, we go up to Jerusalem; and the Son of man shall be delivered to the chief priests, and to the scribes;
and they shall condemn him to death,
and shall deliver him to the Gentiles:
34 And they shall mock him, and shall
scourge him, and shall spit upon him,
and shall kill him: and the third day he
shall rise again.
35 And James and John, the sons of Zebedee, come to him, saying, Master, we
would that you should do for us whatsoever we shall desire.
36 And he said to them, What would
you that I should do for you?
37 They said to him, Grant to us that we
may sit, one on your right hand, and the
other on your left hand, in your glory.
38 But Jesus said to them, You know
not what you ask: can you drink of the
cup that I drink of? and be baptized with
the baptism that I am baptized with?
39 And they said to him, We can. And
Jesus said to them, You shall indeed drink
of the cup that I drink of; and with the
baptism that I am baptized withal shall you
be baptized:
40 But to sit on my right hand and on my
left hand is not mine to give; but it shall
be given to them for whom it is prepared.
41 And when the ten heard it, they began to be much displeased with James
and John.
42 But Jesus called them to him, and
said to them, You know that they which
are accounted to rule over the Gentiles
exercise lordship over them; and their
great ones exercise authority upon them.
43 But so shall it not be among you:
but whosoever will be great among you,
shall be your minister:
44 And whosoever of you will be the
chiefest, shall be servant of all.
45 For even the Son of man came not to
be ministered unto, but to minister, and
to give his life a ransom for many.
46 And they came to Jericho: and as he
went out of Jericho with his disciples and
a great number of people, blind Bartimae-
us, the son of Timaeus, sat by the highway side begging.
47 And when he heard that it was Jesus
of Nazareth, he began to cry out, and say,
Jesus, you Son of David, have mercy on
me.
48 And many charged him that he should
hold his peace: but he cried the more a
great deal, You Son of David, have mercy
on me.
49 And Jesus stood still, and commanded him to be called. And they called the

10:44 "A Christian man is the most free lord of all, subject to no one. A Christian man is the dutiful servant of all, subject to everyone." *Martin Luther*

QUESTIONS & OBJECTIONS

11:15 ***"Jesus wasn't sinless—He became angry when He cleared the temple."***

The temple of God was filled with the day's equivalent of money-grabbing televangelists. Jesus called it a "den of thieves" (v. 17), because the moneychangers were not interested in God but in taking financial advantage of those who came to worship. Anger at hypocrisy isn't a sin—it's a virtue.

blind man, saying to him, Be of good comfort, rise; he calls you.
50 And he, casting away his garment, rose, and came to Jesus.
51 And Jesus answered and said to him, What will you that I should do to you? The blind man said to him, Lord, that I might receive my sight.
52 And Jesus said to him, Go your way; your faith has made you whole. And immediately he received his sight, and followed Jesus in the way.

CHAPTER 11

AND when they came near to Jerusalem, to Bethphage and Bethany, at the mount of Olives, he sent forth two of his disciples,
2 And said to them, Go your way into the village over against you: and as soon as you enter into it, you shall find a colt tied, whereon never a man sat; loose him, and bring him.
3 And if any man say to you, Why are you doing this? say that the Lord has need of him; and straightway he will send him here.
4 And they went their way, and found the colt tied by the door without in a place where two ways met; and they loosened him.
5 And certain of them that stood there said to them, What are you doing, loosing the colt?
6 And they said to them even as Jesus had commanded: and they let them go.
7 And they brought the colt to Jesus, and cast their garments on him; and he sat upon him.
8 And many spread their garments in the way: and others cut down branches off the trees, and strawed them in the way.
9 And they that went before, and they that followed, cried, saying, Hosanna; Blessed is he that comes in the name of the Lord:
10 Blessed be the kingdom of our father David, that comes in the name of the Lord: Hosanna in the highest.
11 And Jesus entered into Jerusalem, and into the temple: and when he had looked round about upon all things, and now the eventide was come, he went out to Bethany with the twelve.
12 And on the morrow, when they were come from Bethany, he was hungry:
13 And seeing a fig tree afar off having leaves, he came, if haply he might find any thing thereon: and when he came to it, he found nothing but leaves; for the time of figs was not yet.
14 And Jesus answered and said to it, No man eat fruit of you hereafter for ever. And his disciples heard it.
15 And they come to Jerusalem: and Jesus went into the temple, and began to cast out them that sold and bought in the temple, and overthrew the tables of the moneychangers, and the seats of them that sold doves;
16 And would not suffer that any man should carry any vessel through the temple.
17 And he taught, saying to them, Is it not written, My house shall be called of all nations the house of prayer? but you have made it a den of thieves.
18 And the scribes and chief priests heard

it, and sought how they might destroy
him: for they feared him, because all the
people were astonished at his doctrine.
19 And when even was come, he went
out of the city.
20 And in the morning, as they passed
by, they saw the fig tree dried up from the
roots.
21 And Peter calling to remembrance
said to him, Master, behold, the fig tree
which you cursed is withered away.
22 And Jesus answering said to them,
Have faith in God.
23 For verily I say to you, That whosoever shall say to this mountain, Be removed, and be cast into the sea; and shall
not doubt in his heart, but shall believe
that those things which he said shall come
to pass; he shall have whatsoever he says.
24 Therefore I say to you, What things
soever you desire, when you pray, believe that you receive them, and you shall
have them.
25 And when you stand praying, forgive,
if you have anything against any: that your
Father also which is in heaven may forgive you your trespasses.
26 But if you do not forgive, neither will
your Father which is in heaven forgive
your trespasses.
27 And they came again to Jerusalem:
and as he was walking in the temple, there
came to him the chief priests, and the
scribes, and the elders,
28 And said to him, By what authority
do you these things? and who gave you
this authority to do these things?
29 And Jesus answered and said to them,
I will also ask of you one question, and
answer me, and I will tell you by what
authority I do these things.
30 The baptism of John, was it from
heaven, or of men? answer me.
31 And they reasoned with themselves,
saying, If we shall say, From heaven; he
will say, Why then did you not believe
him?
32 But if we shall say, Of men; they
feared the people: for all men counted
John, that he was a prophet indeed.
33 And they answered and said to Jesus,
We cannot tell. And Jesus answering said
to them, Neither do I tell you by what authority I do these things.

CHAPTER 12

AND he began to speak to them by
parables. A certain man planted a
vineyard, and set an hedge about it, and
dug a place for the winefat, and built a
tower, and let it out to husbandmen, and
went into a far country.
2 And at the season he sent to the husbandmen a servant, that he might receive
from the husbandmen of the fruit of the
vineyard.
3 And they caught him, and beat him,
and sent him away empty.
4 And again he sent to them another servant; and at him they cast stones, and
wounded him in the head, and sent him
away shamefully handled.
5 And again he sent another; and him
they killed, and many others; beating
some, and killing some.
6 Having yet therefore one son, his wellbeloved, he sent him also last to them,
saying, They will reverence my son.
7 But those husbandmen said among
themselves, This is the heir; come, let us
kill him, and the inheritance shall be ours.
8 And they took him, and killed him,
and cast him out of the vineyard.
9 What shall therefore the lord of the

11:22 Faith in God. It's amazing how many people find it difficult to have faith in a perfect God, but they trust their lives without question to fallible men—the eighth leading cause of death in the U.S. is 'medical mistakes'" (*ABC News*, November 30, 1999).

11:23 Prayer—the secret weapon: This is an open invitation for Christians to beseech God for genuine revival. We should never be satisfied until every living human being is safe in Christ: "Show me a thoroughly satisfied man and I will show you a failure." *Thomas Edison*

11:25 *How to Witness to Mormons*

There are at least two approaches to use in witnessing to Mormons. We can either debate the doctrines of Mormonism (baptism for the dead, "burning" in the bosom, Joseph Smith as a prophet of God, the validity of the *Book of Mormon*, the Trinity, "God was once a man," "protective" underwear, etc.), or we can present the gospel biblically. One creates an atmosphere of contention and often leaves the Christian feeling frustrated, while the other creates an atmosphere of concern for the eternal welfare of the Mormon. Our goal should be to win a soul to Christ rather than merely win a doctrinal argument.

One point of frustration for the Christian is that Mormons often agree when they hear words such as "salvation," or Jesus as "Savior." The problem is that *their* understanding of the words differs from the biblical revelation of the words. "Salvation" for a Mormon can mean the salvation of all humanity—when the "Savior" will eventually raise everyone from the dead.

Rather than speak of "going to heaven," the Christian should ask what the Mormon has to do to be at peace with the "heavenly Father." This is language they can understand, and will reveal the basis for their salvation. Are they trusting in self-righteousness, or solely in the righteousness of Christ?

Mark J. Cares writes: "Although Mormons commonly appear self-assured and self-righteous, many are undergoing great stress. This is because Mormonism holds up perfection as an attainable goal. The one Bible passage the Mormon church constantly holds up before its membership is Matthew 5:48: 'Be ye therefore perfect, even as your Father which is in heaven is perfect.' They then expound on it with numerous exhortations to strive for perfection. Spencer W. Kimball, for example, wrote: 'Being perfect means to triumph over sin. This is a mandate from the Lord. He is just and wise and kind. He would never require anything from his children which was not for their benefit and which was not attainable. Perfection therefore is an achievable goal' (*Life and Teachings of Jesus and His Apostles*, Church of Jesus Christ of Latter-day Saints).

"This emphasis on perfection permeates every aspect of a Mormon's life. Its most common form is the unending demand on them to be 'worthy.' Every privilege in Mormonism is conditioned on a person's worthiness. Kimball wrote: 'All blessings are conditional. I know of none that are not' (*Remember Me*, Church of Jesus Christ of Latter-day Saints).

"Christians need to recognize that this constant striving for perfection—and the resultant stress it produces—offers an excellent opening to talk to Mormons about Jesus and the imputed perfection we receive through Him.

"**Reinforce their predicament.** Average hard-working Mormons view this striving for perfection as a heavy but manageable burden. They can cultivate illusions of perfection because the Mormon church has greatly watered down the concept of sin. Consequently, the Christian witness needs to show Mormons both the severity of their predicament and the impossibility of their becoming perfect. In other words, they need to have a face-to-face confrontation with the stern message of God's Law, because 'through the Law we become conscious of sin' (Romans 3:21).

"The Law must first convince Mormons of the severity of their predicament. The best way to accomplish this is to tell them, lovingly but firmly, that they are going to 'outer darkness.' (Outer darkness is the closest concept in Mormonism to an eternal hell.) Most Mormons have never been told this, nor have they ever considered that possibility for themselves, since Mormonism teaches that nearly everyone will enter one of Mormonism's three kingdoms of heaven. Therefore, until you introduce the thought of eternal suffering, they will not feel any real urgency to take your witness to heart. On the contrary, most, if they are willing to talk at all, will view any religious conversation as nothing more than an interesting intellectual discussion.

"Christians often hesitate to be this blunt. They feel that if anything will turn Mormons off, telling them that they are going to outer darkness surely will. I shared that fear when I began using this approach. To my amazement, however, rejection wasn't the reaction I

(continued)

(11:25 continued)
received. Most have been shocked, but they were also eager to know why I would say such a thing. The key is to speak this truth *with love*, in such a way that our concern for their souls is readily apparent.

"Alerting Mormons to the very real danger of their going to outer darkness opens the door to telling them the *basis* for that judgment—which is, they are not meeting God's requirement for living with Him (they are not *presently* perfect). The key to explaining this is the present imperative, *be perfect*, in Matthew 5:48."

See Luke 18:20 footnote for how to go through the Law, and 1 Corinthians 15:58 footnote on how not to be discouraged in witnessing.

vineyard do? he will come and destroy the
husbandmen, and will give the vineyard
to others.
10 And have you not read this scripture;
The stone which the builders rejected is
become the head of the corner:
11 This was the Lord's doing, and it is
marvelous in our eyes?
12 And they sought to lay hold on him,
but feared the people: for they knew that
he had spoken the parable against them:
and they left him, and went their way.
13 And they sent to him certain of the
Pharisees and of the Herodians, to catch
him in his words.
14 And when they were come, they said
to him, Master, we know that you are
true, and care for no man: for you regard
not the person of men, but teach the way
of God in truth: Is it lawful to give tribute to Caesar, or not?
15 Shall we give, or shall we not give?
But he, knowing their hypocrisy, said to
them, Why tempt me? bring me a penny,
that I may see it.
16 And they brought it. And he said to
them, Whose is this image and superscription? And they said to him, Caesar's.
17 And Jesus answering said to them,
Render to Caesar the things that are Caesar's, and to God the things that are God's.
And they marveled at him.
18 Then came to him the Sadducees,
which say there is no resurrection; and
they asked him, saying,
19 Master, Moses wrote to us, If a man's
brother die, and leave his wife behind him,
and leave no children, that his brother
should take his wife, and raise up seed to
his brother.
20 Now there were seven brethren: and
the first took a wife, and dying left no seed.
21 And the second took her, and died,
neither left he any seed: and the third
likewise.
22 And the seven had her, and left no
seed: last of all the woman died also.
23 In the resurrection therefore, when
they shall rise, whose wife shall she be of
them? for the seven had her to wife.
24 And Jesus answering said to them, Do
you not therefore err, because you know
not the scriptures, neither the power of
God?
25 For when they shall rise from the
dead, they neither marry, nor are given in
marriage; but are as the angels which are
in heaven.
26 And as touching the dead, that they
rise: have you not read in the book of
Moses, how in the bush God spoke to
him, saying, I am the God of Abraham,
and the God of Isaac, and the God of Jacob?
27 He is not the God of the dead, but the
God of the living: you therefore do greatly err.
28 And one of the scribes came, and having heard them reasoning together, and
perceiving that he had answered them
well, asked him, Which is the first commandment of all?
29 And Jesus answered him, The first
of all the commandments is, Hear, O
Israel; The Lord our God is one Lord:
30 And you shall love the Lord your
God with all your heart, and with all
your soul, and with all your mind, and

PRINCIPLES OF GROWTH FOR THE NEW AND GROWING CHRISTIAN

12:41–44 *Tithing—The Final Frontier*

It has been said that the wallet is the "final frontier." It is the final area to be conquered—the last thing that comes to God in surrender. Jesus spoke much about money. He said that we cannot serve God and mammon (Matthew 6:24). "Mammon" was the common Aramaic word for riches, which is related to a Hebrew word signifying "that which is to be trusted." In other words, we cannot trust God and money. Either money is our source of joy, our great love, our sense of security, the supplier of our needs—or God is.

When you open your purse or wallet, give generously and regularly to your local church. A guide of how much you should give can be found in the "tithe" of the Old Testament: 10 percent of your income. Whatever amount you give, make sure you give *something* to the work of God (see Malachi 3:8–11). Give because you *want* to, not because you *have* to. God loves a cheerful giver (2 Corinthians 9:6,7), so learn to hold your money with a loose hand.

with all your strength: this is the first commandment.

31 And the second is like, namely this, You shall love your neighbour as yourself. There is none other commandment greater than these.

32 And the scribe said to him, Well, Master, you have said the truth: for there is one God; and there is none other but he:

33 And to love him with all the heart, and with all the understanding, and with all the soul, and with all the strength, and to love his neighbour as himself, is more than all whole burnt offerings and sacrifices.

34 And when Jesus saw that he answered discreetly, he said to him, You are not far from the kingdom of God. And no man after that dared ask him any question.

35 And Jesus answered and said, while he taught in the temple, How say the scribes that Christ is the Son of David?

36 For David himself said by the Holy Spirit, The Lord said to my Lord, Sit on my right hand, till I make your enemies your footstool.

37 David therefore himself calls him Lord; and whence is he then his son? And the common people heard him gladly.

38 And he said to them in his doctrine, Beware of the scribes, which love to go in long clothing, and love salutations in the marketplaces,

39 And the chief seats in the synagogues, and the uppermost rooms at feasts:

40 Which devour widows' houses, and for a pretence make long prayers: these shall receive greater damnation.

41 And Jesus sat over against the treasury, and beheld how the people cast money into the treasury: and many that were rich cast in much.

42 And there came a certain poor widow, and she threw in two mites, which make a farthing.

43 And he called to him his disciples, and said to them, Verily I say to you, That this poor widow has cast more in, than all they which have cast into the treasury:

44 For all they did cast in of their abundance; but she of her want did cast in all that she had, even all her living.

12:29–31 No one has ever kept the Commandments: "The Lord looked down from heaven upon the children of men, to see if there were any that did understand, and seek God. They are all gone aside, they are all together become filthy: there is no one that does good, no, not one" (Psalm 14:2,3). See Romans 2:15,16 footnote.

12:34 It is understanding of the Law that brings a sinner closer to the kingdom of God.

CHAPTER 13

AND as he went out of the temple,
one of his disciples said to him, Master, see what manner of stones and what
buildings are here!
2 And Jesus answering said to him, See
these great buildings? There shall not be
left one stone upon another, that shall
not be thrown down.
3 And as he sat upon the mount of Olives over against the temple, Peter and
James and John and Andrew asked him
privately,
4 Tell us, when shall these things be?
and what shall be the sign when all these
things shall be fulfilled?
5 And Jesus answering them began to
say, Take heed lest any man deceive you:
6 For many shall come in my name, saying, I am Christ; and shall deceive many.
7 And when you shall hear of wars and
rumours of wars, be not troubled: for such
things must needs be; but the end shall
not be yet.
8 For nation shall rise against nation,
and kingdom against kingdom: and there
shall be earthquakes in divers places, and
there shall be famines and troubles: these
are the beginnings of sorrows.
9 But take heed to yourselves: for they
shall deliver you up to councils; and in
the synagogues you shall be beaten: and
you shall be brought before rulers and
kings for my sake, for a testimony against
them.
10 And the gospel must first be published among all nations.
11 But when they shall lead you, and
deliver you up, take no thought beforehand what you shall speak, neither pre-
meditate: but whatsoever shall be given
you in that hour, that speak: for it is not
you that speak, but the Holy Spirit.
12 Now the brother shall betray the
brother to death, and the father the son;
and children shall rise up against their
parents, and shall cause them to be put
to death.
13 And you shall be hated of all men
for my name's sake: but he that shall endure to the end, the same shall be saved.
14 But when you shall see the abomination of desolation, spoken of by Daniel
the prophet, standing where it ought not,
(let him that reads understand,) then let
them that be in Judea flee to the mountains:
15 And let him that is on the housetop
not go down into the house, neither enter
therein, to take any thing out of his house:
16 And let him that is in the field not
turn back again for to take up his garment.
17 But woe to them that are with child,
and to them that give suck in those days!

13:2 Fulfilled prophecy. This prophecy was fulfilled in A.D. 70 when Titus destroyed Jerusalem. "Now the outward face of the temple in its front wanted nothing that was likely to surprise either men's minds or their eyes; for it was covered all over with plates of gold of great weight, and, at the first rising of the sun, reflected back a very fiery splendor, and made those who forced themselves to look upon it to turn their eyes away, just as they would have done at the sun's own rays. But this temple appeared to strangers, when they were coming to it at a distance, like a mountain covered with snow; for as to those parts of it that were not gilt, they were exceeding white. On its top it had spikes with sharp points, to prevent any pollution of it by birds sitting upon it. Of its stones, some of them were forty-five cubits in length, five in height, and six in breadth." (*The History of the Destruction of Jerusalem, The Works of Flavius Josephus*)

"[The wall] was so thoroughly laid even with the ground by those that dug it up to the foundation, that there was left nothing to make those that came thither believe it had ever been inhabited." *Josephus, The Wars of the Jews* (See also Matthew 24:2.)

13:4 For more signs of the end times, see Luke 21:7.

13:10 "The world can be witnessed to in a single generation. We can welcome Him back with our present of the finished task set by Him so long ago when He said, 'This gospel of the kingdom must be preached for a witness to all nations; then shall the end come.'" *Winkie Pratney*

18 And pray that your flight be not in the winter.
19 For in those days shall be affliction, such as was not from the beginning of the creation which God created to this time, neither shall be.
20 And except that the Lord had shortened those days, no flesh should be saved: but for the elect's sake, whom he has chosen, he has shortened the days.
21 And then if any man shall say to you, Lo, here is Christ; or, lo, he is there; believe him not:
22 For false Christs and false prophets shall rise, and shall show signs and wonders, to seduce, if it were possible, even the elect.
23 But take heed: behold, I have foretold you all things.
24 But in those days, after that tribulation, the sun shall be darkened, and the moon shall not give her light,
25 And the stars of heaven shall fall, and the powers that are in heaven shall be shaken.
26 And then shall they see the Son of man coming in the clouds with great power and glory.
27 And then shall he send his angels, and shall gather together his elect from the four winds, from the uttermost part of the earth to the uttermost part of heaven.
28 Now learn a parable of the fig tree; When her branch is yet tender, and puts forth leaves, you know that summer is near:
29 So you in like manner, when you shall see these things come to pass, know that it is near, even at the doors.
30 Verily I say to you, that this generation shall not pass, till all these things be done.
31 Heaven and earth shall pass away: but my words shall not pass away.
32 But of that day and that hour knows no man, no, not the angels which are in heaven, neither the Son, but the Father.
33 Take heed, watch and pray: for you know not when the time is.
34 For the Son of man is as a man taking a far journey, who left his house, and gave authority to his servants, and to every man his work, and commanded the porter to watch.
35 Watch therefore: for you know not when the master of the house comes, at even, or at midnight, or at the cockcrowing, or in the morning:
36 Lest coming suddenly he find you sleeping.
37 And what I say to you I say to all, Watch.

· · · · · ·

For how to use the Ten Commandments in witnessing, see Psalm 51:6 footnote.

· · · · · ·

CHAPTER 14

AFTER two days was the feast of the passover, and of unleavened bread: and the chief priests and the scribes sought how they might take him by craft, and put him to death.
2 But they said, Not on the feast day, lest there be an uproar of the people.
3 And being in Bethany in the house of Simon the leper, as he sat at meat, there came a woman having an alabaster box of ointment of spikenard very precious; and she broke the box, and poured it on his head.
4 And there were some that had indignation within themselves, and said, Why was this waste of the ointment made?
5 For it might have been sold for more than three hundred pence, and have been given to the poor. And they murmured against her.
6 And Jesus said, Let her alone; why trouble her? she has wrought a good work on me.
7 For you have the poor with you always, and whenever you will you may do them good: but me you have not always.
8 She has done what she could: she is come beforehand to anoint my body to the burying.

9 Verily I say to you, Wherever this gospel shall be preached throughout the whole world, this also that she has done shall be spoken of for a memorial of her.

10 And Judas Iscariot, one of the twelve, went to the chief priests, to betray him to them.

11 And when they heard it, they were glad, and promised to give him money. And he sought how he might conveniently betray him.

12 And the first day of unleavened bread, when they killed the passover, his disciples said to him, Where will you that we go and prepare that you may eat the passover?

13 And he sent forth two of his disciples, and said to them, Go into the city, and there shall meet you a man bearing a pitcher of water: follow him.

14 And wherever he shall go in, say to the goodman of the house, The Master says, Where is the guestchamber, where I shall eat the passover with my disciples?

15 And he will show you a large upper room furnished and prepared: there make ready for us.

16 And his disciples went forth, and came into the city, and found as he had said to them: and they made ready the passover.

17 And in the evening he came with the twelve.

18 And as they sat and did eat, Jesus said, Verily I say to you, One of you which eats with me shall betray me.

19 And they began to be sorrowful, and to say to him one by one, Is it I? and another said, Is it I?

20 And he answered and said to them, It is one of the twelve, that dips with me in the dish.

21 The Son of man indeed goes, as it is written of him: but woe to that man by whom the Son of man is betrayed! good were it for that man if he had never been born.

22 And as they did eat, Jesus took bread, and blessed, and broke it, and gave to them, and said, Take, eat: this is my body.

23 And he took the cup, and when he had given thanks, he gave it to them: and they all drank of it.

24 And he said to them, This is my blood of the new testament, which is shed for many.

25 Verily I say to you, I will drink no more of the fruit of the vine, until that day that I drink it new in the kingdom of God.

26 And when they had sung a hymn, they went out into the mount of Olives.

27 And Jesus said to them, All you shall be offended because of me this night: for it is written, I will smite the shepherd, and the sheep shall be scattered.

28 But after that I am risen, I will go before you into Galilee.

29 But Peter said to him, Although all shall be offended, yet will not I.

30 And Jesus said to him, Verily I say to you, That this day, even in this night, before the cock crow twice, you shall deny me thrice.

31 But he spoke the more vehemently, If I should die with you, I will not deny you in any wise. Likewise also said they all.

32 And they came to a place which was named Gethsemane: and he said to his disciples, Sit here, while I shall pray.

33 And he took with him Peter and James and John, and began to be sore amazed, and to be very heavy;

34 And said to them, My soul is exceeding sorrowful to death: tarry here, and watch.

35 And he went forward a little, and fell

14:10 Messianic prophecy fulfilled: "Yea, mine own familiar friend, in whom I trusted, which did eat of my bread, has lifted up his heel against me" (Psalm 41:9). See Mark 14:65 footnote.

14:24 The wine wasn't His literal blood, which was still in His body. He was referring to it as being *symbolic* of His blood.

on the ground, and prayed that, if it were
possible, the hour might pass from him.
36 And he said, Abba, Father, all things
are possible to you; take away this cup
from me: nevertheless not what I will,
but what you will.
37 And he came, and found them sleeping, and said to Peter, Simon, do you
sleep? Couldn't you watch one hour?
38 Watch and pray, lest you enter into
temptation. The spirit truly is ready, but
the flesh is weak.
39 And again he went away, and prayed,
and spoke the same words.
40 And when he returned, he found them
asleep again, (for their eyes were heavy,)
neither did they know what to answer
him.
41 And he came the third time, and said
to them, Sleep on now, and take your
rest: it is enough, the hour is come; behold, the Son of man is betrayed into the
hands of sinners.
42 Rise up, let us go; lo, he that betrays
me is at hand.
43 And immediately, while he yet spoke,
came Judas, one of the twelve, and with
him a great multitude with swords and
staves, from the chief priests and the
scribes and the elders.
44 And he that betrayed him had given
them a token, saying, Whomsoever I shall
kiss, that same is he; take him, and lead
him away safely.
45 And as soon as he was come, he went
straightway to him, and said, Master, master; and kissed him.
46 And they laid their hands on him, and
took him.
47 And one of them that stood by drew
a sword, and smote a servant of the high
priest, and cut off his ear.
48 And Jesus answered and said to them,
Are you come out, as against a thief, with
swords and with staves to take me?
49 I was daily with you in the temple
teaching, and you took me not: but the
scriptures must be fulfilled.
50 And they all forsook him, and fled.
51 And there followed him a certain
young man, having a linen cloth cast about
his naked body; and the young men laid
hold on him:
52 And he left the linen cloth, and fled
from them naked.
53 And they led Jesus away to the high
priest: and with him were assembled all
the chief priests and the elders and the
scribes.
54 And Peter followed him afar off, even
into the palace of the high priest: and he
sat with the servants, and warmed himself at the fire.

> If you are saved, the work is only half done until you are employed to bring others to Christ.
>
> **CHARLES SPURGEON**

55 And the chief priests and all the council sought for witness against Jesus to
put him to death; and found none.
56 For many bare false witness against
him, but their witness agreed not together.
57 And there arose certain, and bare false
witness against him, saying,
58 We heard him say, I will destroy this
temple that is made with hands, and within three days I will build another made
without hands.
59 But neither so did their witness agree
together.
60 And the high priest stood up in the
midst, and asked Jesus, saying, Do you
answer nothing? what is it which these
witness against you?
61 But he held his peace, and answered
nothing. Again the high priest asked him,

14:38 "The reason why many fail in battle is because they wait until the hour of battle. The reason why others succeed is because they have gained their victory on their knees long before the battle came... Anticipate your battles; fight them on your knees before temptation comes, and you will always have victory." *R. A. Torrey*

and said to him, are you the Christ, the
Son of the Blessed?
62 And Jesus said, I am: and you shall
see the Son of man sitting on the right
hand of power, and coming in the clouds
of heaven.
63 Then the high priest rent his clothes,
and said, What need we any further witnesses?
64 You have heard the blasphemy: what
do you think? And they all condemned
him to be guilty of death.
65 And some began to spit on him, and
to cover his face, and to buffet him, and
to say to him, Prophesy: and the servants
did strike him with the palms of their
hands.
66 And as Peter was beneath in the palace, there came one of the maids of the
high priest:
67 And when she saw Peter warming
himself, she looked upon him, and said,
And you also were with Jesus of Nazareth.
68 But he denied, saying, I know not,
neither understand I what you say. And
he went out into the porch; and the cock
crew.
69 And a maid saw him again, and began
to say to them that stood by, This is one
of them.
70 And he denied it again. And a little
after, they that stood by said again to Peter,
Surely you are one of them: for you are a
Galilaean, and your speech agrees thereto.
71 But he began to curse and to swear,
saying, I know not this man of whom you
speak.
72 And the second time the cock crew.
And Peter called to mind the word that
Jesus said to him, Before the cock crow
twice, you shall deny me thrice. And when
he thought thereon, he wept.

CHAPTER 15

AND straightway in the morning the
chief priests held a consultation with
the elders and scribes and the whole council, and bound Jesus, and carried him
away, and delivered him to Pilate.
2 And Pilate asked him, Are you the King
of the Jews? And he answering said to him,
It is as you say.
3 And the chief priests accused him of
many things: but he answered nothing.
4 And Pilate asked him again, saying,
Do you answer nothing? behold how
many things they witness against you.
5 But Jesus yet answered nothing; so
that Pilate marveled.
6 Now at that feast he released to them
one prisoner, whomsoever they desired.
7 And there was one named Barabbas,
which lay bound with them that had made
insurrection with him, who had committed murder in the insurrection.
8 And the multitude crying aloud began
to desire him to do as he had ever done to
them.
9 But Pilate answered them, saying, Will
you that I release to you the King of the
Jews?
10 For he knew that the chief priests had
delivered him for envy.
11 But the chief priests moved the people, that he should rather release Barabbas
to them.
12 And Pilate answered and said again
to them, What will you then that I shall
do to him whom you call the King of the
Jews?
13 And they cried out again, Crucify him.
14 Then Pilate said to them, Why, what
evil has he done? And they cried out the
more exceedingly, Crucify him.
15 And so Pilate, willing to content the
people, released Barabbas to them, and

14:65 Messianic prophecy fulfilled: "I gave my back to those who struck me, and my cheeks to those who plucked out the beard; I did not hide my face from shame and spitting" (Isaiah 50:6). See Mark 15:24 footnote.

15:12 "Public opinion is held in reverence. It settles everything. Some think it is the voice of God." *Mark Twain* delivered Jesus, when he had scourged him, to be crucified.

16 And the soldiers led him away into the hall, called Praetorium; and they called together the whole band.

17 And they clothed him with purple, and platted a crown of thorns, and put it about his head,

18 And began to salute him, Hail, King of the Jews!

19 And they smote him on the head with a reed, and did spit upon him, and bowing their knees worshipped him.

20 And when they had mocked him, they took off the purple from him, and put his own clothes on him, and led him out to crucify him.

21 And they compelled one Simon a Cyrenian, who passed by, coming out of the country, the father of Alexander and Rufus, to bear his cross.

22 And they brought him to the place Golgotha, which is, being interpreted, The place of a skull.

23 And they gave him to drink wine mingled with myrrh: but he received it not.

24 And when they had crucified him, they parted his garments, casting lots upon them, what every man should take.

25 And it was the third hour, and they crucified him.

26 And the superscription of his accusation was written over, THE KING OF THE JEWS.

27 And with him they crucified two thieves; the one on his right hand, and the other on his left.

28 And the scripture was fulfilled, which says, And he was numbered with the transgressors.

29 And they that passed by railed on him, wagging their heads, and saying, Ah, you that destroy the temple, and build it in three days,

30 Save yourself, and come down from the cross.

31 Likewise also the chief priests mocking said among themselves with the scribes, He saved others; himself he cannot save.

32 Let Christ the King of Israel descend now from the cross, that we may see and believe. And they that were crucified with him reviled him.

33 And when the sixth hour was come, there was darkness over the whole land until the ninth hour.

34 And at the ninth hour Jesus cried with a loud voice, saying, Eloi, Eloi, lama sabachthani? which is, being interpreted, My God, my God, why have you forsaken me?

35 And some of them that stood by, when they heard it, said, Behold, he calls Elijah.

36 And one ran and filled a sponge full of vinegar, and put it on a reed, and gave him to drink, saying, Let alone; let us see whether Elijah will come to take him down.

37 And Jesus cried with a loud voice, and gave up the ghost.

38 And the veil of the temple was rent in twain from the top to the bottom.

39 And when the centurion, which stood over against him, saw that he so cried out, and gave up the ghost, he said, Truly this man was the Son of God.

40 There were also women looking on afar off: among whom was Mary Magdalene, and Mary the mother of James the less and of Joses, and Salome;

41 (Who also, when he was in Galilee, followed him, and ministered to him;) and many other women which came up with him to Jerusalem.

42 And now when the even was come, because it was the preparation, that is, the day before the sabbath,

43 Joseph of Arimathaea, an honorable counsellor, which also waited for the kingdom of God, came, and went in boldly

15:24 Messianic prophecy fulfilled: "They part my garments among them, and cast lots upon my vesture" (Psalm 22:18). See Luke 1:32,33 footnote.

15:26 *Contradictions in the Bible—Why Are They There?*

The Bible has many *seeming* contradictions within its pages. For example, the four Gospels give four differing accounts as to what was written on the sign that hung on the cross. Matthew said, "This is Jesus the King of the Jews" (27:37). However, Mark contradicts that with "The King of the Jews" (15:26). Luke says something different: "This is the King of the Jews" (23:38), and John maintains that the sign said "Jesus of Nazareth the King of the Jews" (19:19). Those who are *looking* for contradictions may therefore say, "See—the Bible is *full* of mistakes!" and choose to reject it entirely as being untrustworthy.

However, those who trust God have no problem harmonizing the Gospels. There is no contradiction if the sign simply said, "This is Jesus of Nazareth the King of the Jews." The godly base their confidence on two truths: 1) "all Scripture is given by inspiration of God" (2 Timothy 3:16); and 2) an elementary rule of Scripture is that God has deliberately included *seeming* contradictions in His Word to "snare" the proud. He has "hidden" things from the "wise and prudent" and "revealed them to babes" (Luke 10:21), purposely choosing foolish things to confound the wise (1 Corinthians 1:27).

If an ungodly man refuses to humble himself and obey the gospel, and instead desires to build a case against the Bible, God gives him enough material to build his own gallows.

This incredible principle is clearly illustrated in the account of the capture of Zedekiah, king of Judah. Jeremiah the prophet told Zedekiah that God would judge him. He was informed that he would be "delivered into the hand of the king of Babylon" (Jeremiah 32:4). This is confirmed in Jeremiah 39:5–7 where we are told that he was captured and brought to King Nebuchadnezzar, then they "bound him with chains, to carry him to Babylon." However, in Ezekiel 12:13, God Himself warned, "I will bring him to Babylon . . . *yet he shall not see it*, though he shall die there" (emphasis added). Here is material to build a case against the Bible! It is an *obvious* mistake. Three Bible verses say that the king would go to Babylon, and yet the Bible in another place says that he would not see Babylon. How can someone be taken somewhere and not see it? It makes no sense at all—unless Zedekiah was *blinded*. And that is precisely what happened. Zedekiah saw Nebuchadnezzar face to face, saw his sons killed before his eyes, then "the king of Babylon . . . put out Zedekiah's eyes" before taking him to Babylon (Jeremiah 39:6,7). This is the underlying principle behind the many "contradictions" of Holy Scripture (such as how many horses David had, who was the first to arrive at the tomb after the resurrection of Jesus, etc.).

God has turned the tables on proud, arrogant, self-righteous man. When he proudly stands outside of the kingdom of God, and seeks to justify his sinfulness through evidence he thinks discredits the Bible, he doesn't realize that God has simply lowered the door of life, so that only those who are prepared to exercise faith, and bow in humility may enter.

It is interesting to note that the *seeming* contradictions in the four Gospels attest to the fact that there was no corroboration between the writers.

to Pilate, and craved the body of Jesus.
44 And Pilate marveled if he were already dead: and calling to him the centurion, he asked him whether he had been any while dead.
45 And when he knew it of the centurion, he gave the body to Joseph.
46 And he bought fine linen, and took him down, and wrapped him in the linen, and laid him in a sepulchre which was hewn out of a rock, and rolled a stone to the door of the sepulchre.
47 And Mary Magdalene and Mary the mother of Joses beheld where he was laid.

CHAPTER 16

AND when the sabbath was past, Mary Magdalene, and Mary the mother of James, and Salome, had bought sweet spices, that they might come and anoint him.
2 And very early in the morning the first

15:39 *The Witness (An interesting insight into what may have been…)*

By Danny Hotea

As was my custom, I rose early that day to pay homage to the gods by prayers and burnt offerings. To which I vowed my obedience on that fateful morning, I cannot now remember. There were so many.

Leaving the place of worship, I endeavored to sit quietly and read the creeds of Rome as written by the emperor himself. It was my duty not only as a centurion, but as a Roman citizen, to understand the purpose of almighty Caesar and Rome. However, just as I began pouring over the open scroll, a nameless messenger came panting with word from Pontius Pilate, governor of Judea, ordering my garrison to his palace immediately.

I arrived with three hundred men as if by flight. The sun had hardly risen, and the air held an unseen weight, as if to distinguish this day from all others. The men, all clad in leather and metal with swords swaying from their belts and spears stabbing at the sky in protest of their unusually early arousal, wobbled restlessly in rigid formation, awaiting my command. The sound of spiked sandals scraping the stone palace floor echoed down the long, stone hallway adding tension to mystery. They undoubtedly supposed that I knew the reason for it all. But I didn't—until another messenger came with another scroll describing our purpose exactly.

Jerusalem was a place known for its concentrated reserve of mindless zealots. And I had experience in stamping out the feeble efforts of disorderly vagrants and disorganized militias meant to unshackle the Jews from Rome's iron grip. One in particular came to mind as I read the final sentence of that day's orders. It was the most recent and pathetic uprising. A small army of poorly armed religious rebels managed to assassinate an insignificant gatekeeper in the governor's palace. The idea that a handful of superstitious peasants could overthrow Rome was ridiculous and, if it weren't so sad, it would be laughable. Their leader had been a thin, sweaty man with hardly any beard, balding head and shifting eyes. A Jew. A brainless dreamer suffering from resentment. His name was Barabbas. He was hardly a match for Rome. I caught him in the streets attempting to hide beneath a vendor's blankets after his pitiful militia had been butchered and left for the dogs. I was his judge and jury. And since only Romans have the right to a trial, I stuffed him in a smaller-than-usual cell after the garrison had their day's exercise of beating him with rods and slapping him with gloved fists.

That day had another experience for me altogether.

As we pushed our way into the Praetorium hauling the scourged offender to the platform, where another Man stood, the mob sang out in a chorus of hatred, "Crucify Him!" The governor addressed the riotous masses with careful words, offering them a choice between the bloodied and uncondemned Man now occupying the platform with him, or the pathetic zealot, Barabbas, who had failed an attempt to destroy Rome. Immediately they sent out blood-curdling screams consenting to the murder of the One and the release of the other. It was apparent, by their screams, that this Man had not offended Rome. He had offended the Jews.

A messenger interrupted the procedure, which was doubtlessly an urgent matter, after which I was signaled to bring Him into the governor's inner court.

The conversation that took place proved this Man's character. He spoke only when questioned and claimed that the governor's authority was given to him by the Offender's Father, which made little sense to me at the time. When He said He was a King, I wondered whether Barabbas, the sweaty zealot, had similar thoughts. But, all in all, this Man had authority incomparable to any I had seen before. This fact was startling considering I had seen the Caesar and all his delegates more often than Pontius himself.

What seemed like moments later, my garrison had elbowed their way through the riotous crowds to the place of execution, hauling two offenders of Rome and One offender of the Jews.

His head had been crowned with thorns, no doubt a torturous invention of the guiltless soldiers in my garrison. His beard replaced with bleeding flesh. His back opened wide by a

Roman scourge to an infectious environment full of illness bred in the hearts of vehement enemies. Yet, it seemed that these were the slightest of His pains judging by the weight of grief He bore on His countenance. His visage carried an eternal load of unfamiliar burdens.

As was my custom, I drove the first nail into the left wrist of each offender inaugurating their torturous departure from this world and instructing my garrison how to proceed with the crucifixion. The two vagrants wrestled pathetically against the soldier's grip that held their filthy arms against the knotted wood, spitting out blasphemies against the gods of Rome and sprinkling our faces with bloody specs of mucus. But they could do little more than wiggle their palms and claw at my wrists with their broken nails until the iron spike impaled the wrist and its owner's arm was pinned against the wood, twitching like a wounded animal. I often delighted in the sound of their ear-splitting screams and hellish moans that filled the air and the sight of their epileptic convulsions of agony as their crosses were set upright. It became somewhat of a drama to which I looked forward with secret pleasure, even more than the gladiators and the chariot races where countless men had lost their lives to entertain Rome. I could hardly keep from smiling, at times.

But this Man, although He was innocent, displayed no reluctance in placing His arm against the wood. His eyes fastened on the soldier holding His arm and on me, His sadistic executioner. I expected the typical reaction as the iron penetrated His skin. But this Man was not typical in any sense of the word. Instead of spraying my face with spittle, He groaned and looked away, scrapping His thorny crown against the lumber behind His head. Unlike the other two, this Man did not moan in melodies of agony as the cross sat upright, disjointing its resident. Tears ran down His scabbed face as He viewed the masses streaming past the foot of His cross. Their venomous words struck the air like frothy waves pounding some seaside cliff. And, unlike the other two, whose hoarse-voiced cursing baptized each passerby with vulgar threats and swollen words of every sort, He spoke kindly to a few standing at the foot of His cross. Had He not been a Jew, I would have been compelled to defend His dying reputation for sheer sympathy's sake.

At the instant before He died, the sky blackened as if it had been split open like a carcass and all its guilt bled out onto the clouds. The earth convulsed, shaking and tossing my men and I like mere toys. At that instant I knew this Man was no mere Man.

He wielded an exclusive power. The image of Rome, as if it were a colossal statue carved of iron, lay in heaps beneath His cross as a mound of chaff vulnerable to the slightest breath of wind. The sight of His emaciated corpse stabbed at my conscience. Had I done wrong? If not, then why such agony of heart? I was bleeding now and my zeal for Rome poured from the bowels of my heart like the streamlets coursing from His side and brow. He had slain me; not I Him. His naked body, reduced to shards of stinking flesh hanging lifelessly on the cross, seemed more alive than I did standing with my hand-polished helmet and Roman embroidery hanging like empirical curtains from my shoulders. I was ashamed of myself.

I turned away to prevent my tears from being noticed. Regret welled up in my soul and poured out onto my cheeks with burning tears. I tried desperately to compose myself to no avail. Once more, I turned to look at Him, and my knees betrayed me to the ground beneath. My forehead kissed the ground in an unguarded slump. I gritted my teeth and formed the words, "Truly, this was the Son of God!"

I have never been the same since.

day of the week, they came to the sepulchre at the rising of the sun.
3 And they said among themselves, Who shall roll away the stone from the door of the sepulchre?
4 And when they looked, they saw that the stone was rolled away: for it was very great.
5 And entering into the sepulchre, they saw a young man sitting on the right side, clothed in a long white garment; and they were fearful.
6 And he said to them, Be not fearful: You seek Jesus of Nazareth, which was crucified: he is risen; he is not here: behold the place where they laid him.
7 But go your way, tell his disciples and Peter that he goes before you into Galilee:

QUESTIONS & OBJECTIONS

16:6 ***"How many angels were at the tomb—one or two?"***

The question has arisen simply because Matthew and Mark mention one angel, whereas Luke and John refer to two. There is no conflict if there were two angels but Matthew and Mark quote the one who was a spokesperson.

there shall you see him, as he said to you.
8 And they went out quickly, and fled
from the sepulchre; for they trembled
and were amazed: neither said they any
thing to any man; for they were afraid.
9 Now when Jesus was risen early the
first day of the week, he appeared first to
Mary Magdalene, out of whom he had
cast seven devils.
10 And she went and told them that had
been with him, as they mourned and wept.
11 And they, when they had heard that
he was alive, and had been seen of her,
believed not.
12 After that he appeared in another form
to two of them, as they walked, and went
into the country.
13 And they went and told it to the residue: neither believed they them.
14 Afterward he appeared to the eleven
as they sat at meat, and upbraided them
with their unbelief and hardness of heart,
because they believed not them which
had seen him after he was risen.
15 And he said to them, Go into all the
world, and preach the gospel to every
creature.
16 He that believes and is baptized shall
be saved; but he that believes not shall
be damned.
17 And these signs shall follow them that
believe; In my name shall they cast out
devils; they shall speak with new tongues;
18 They shall take up serpents; and if
they drink any deadly thing, it shall not
hurt them; they shall lay hands on the
sick, and they shall recover.
19 So then after the Lord had spoken to
them, he was received up into heaven,
and sat on the right hand of God.
20 And they went forth, and preached
everywhere, the Lord working with them,
and confirming the word with signs following. Amen.

16:15 Here is a fascinating thing. The original Greek meaning of "Go into all the world, and preach the gospel to every creature" opens up some interesting thoughts. The word for "go" is very captivating. It is *poreuomai*, meaning "go." The word "all" also carries with it gripping connotations. It is *hapas*, and actually means "all." And if that doesn't rivet you, look closely at the word "every." It is *pas*, and literally means "every." So when Jesus commanded us, "Go into all the world, and preach the gospel to every creature," to be true and faithful to the original text, what He was actually saying was, "Go into all the world, and preach the gospel to every creature." We are so fortunate to have access to knowledge like this.

"Here is our commissioning and sending. There are no exceptions—every Christian is commanded to go!" *Trevor Yaxley*

If the command to "preach the gospel to every creature" were given only to the eleven disciples, preaching of the gospel would have stopped when they died. *Every* Christian is a "disciple." The word in Greek is *mathetes* and simply means "a learner." It is used in reference to the eleven, as well as to believers such as Joseph of Arimathea (Matthew 27:57), Ananias (Acts 9:10), and others (Acts 9:36; 16:1; 21:16). In Luke 14:26,27 Jesus used the term in reference to *any* who would believe in Him.

16:17,18 In reference to true converts, Jesus said, "By their *fruits* you shall know them" (Matthew 7:20), not by their gifts. Many false converts have had "power" gifts. See Matthew 7:21–23.

Luke

CHAPTER 1

FORASMUCH as many have taken in hand to set forth in order a declaration of those things which are most surely believed among us,

2 Even as they delivered them to us, which from the beginning were eyewitnesses, and ministers of the word;

3 It seemed good to me also, having had perfect understanding of all things from the very first, to write to you in order, most excellent Theophilus,

4 That you might know the certainty of those things, wherein you have been instructed.

5 There was in the days of Herod, the king of Judea, a certain priest named Zacharias, of the course of Abia: and his wife was of the daughters of Aaron, and her name was Elizabeth.

6 And they were both righteous before God, walking in all the commandments and ordinances of the Lord blameless.

7 And they had no child, because that Elizabeth was barren, and they both were now well stricken in years.

8 And it came to pass, that while he executed the priest's office before God in the order of his course,

9 According to the custom of the priest's office, his lot was to burn incense when he went into the temple of the Lord.

10 And the whole multitude of the people were praying without at the time of incense.

11 And there appeared to him an angel of the Lord standing on the right side of the altar of incense.

12 And when Zacharias saw him, he was troubled, and fear fell upon him.

13 But the angel said to him, Fear not, Zacharias: for your prayer is heard; and your wife Elizabeth shall bear you a son, and you shall call his name John.

14 And you shall have joy and gladness; and many shall rejoice at his birth.

15 For he shall be great in the sight of the Lord, and shall drink neither wine nor strong drink; and he shall be filled with the Holy Spirit, even from his mother's womb.

16 And many of the children of Israel shall he turn to the Lord their God.

17 And he shall go before him in the spirit and power of Elijah, to turn the hearts of the fathers to the children, and the disobedient to the wisdom of the just; to make ready a people prepared for the Lord.

18 And Zacharias said to the angel, Whereby shall I know this? for I am an old man, and my wife well stricken in years.

1:3 Historical accuracy. "Given the large portion of the New Testament written by him, it's extremely significant that Luke has been established to be a scrupulously accurate historian, even in the smallest details. One prominent archaeologist carefully examined Luke's references to thirty-two countries, fifty-four cities, and nine islands, finding not a single mistake." *John McRay*

19 And the angel answering said to him,
I am Gabriel, that stands in the presence
of God; and am sent to speak to you, and
to show you these glad tidings.
20 And, behold, you shall be dumb,
and not able to speak, until the day that
these things shall be performed, because
you believe not my words, which shall
be fulfilled in their season.
21 And the people waited for Zacharias,
and marveled that he tarried so long in the
temple.
22 And when he came out, he could not
speak to them: and they perceived that
he had seen a vision in the temple: for he
beckoned to them, and remained speechless.
23 And it came to pass, that, as soon as
the days of his ministration were accomplished, he departed to his own house.
24 And after those days his wife Elizabeth
conceived, and hid herself five months,
saying,
25 Thus has the Lord dealt with me in
the days wherein he looked on me, to take
away my reproach among men.
26 And in the sixth month the angel
Gabriel was sent from God to a city of Galilee, named Nazareth,
27 To a virgin espoused to a man whose
name was Joseph, of the house of David;
and the virgin's name was Mary.
28 And the angel came in to her, and
said, Hail, you that are highly favored, the
Lord is with you: blessed are you among
women.
29 And when she saw him, she was
troubled at his saying, and cast in her mind
what manner of salutation this should be.
30 And the angel said to her, Fear not,
Mary: for you have found favor with God.
31 And, behold, you shall conceive in
your womb, and bring forth a son, and
shall call his name JESUS.
32 He shall be great, and shall be called
the Son of the Highest: and the Lord God
shall give to him the throne of his father
David:
33 And he shall reign over the house of
Jacob for ever; and of his kingdom there
shall be no end.
34 Then said Mary to the angel, How
shall this be, seeing I know not a man?
35 And the angel answered and said to
her, The Holy Spirit shall come upon you,
and the power of the Highest shall over-
shadow you: therefore also that holy thing
which shall be born of you shall be called
the Son of God.
36 And, behold, your cousin Elizabeth,
she has also conceived a son in her old
age: and this is the sixth month with her,
who was called barren.
37 For with God nothing shall be impossible.
38 And Mary said, Behold the handmaid
of the Lord; be it to me according to your
word. And the angel departed from her.
39 And Mary arose in those days, and
went into the hill country with haste, into

1:27 Archaeology confirms the Bible. Following the 1993 discovery in Israel of a stone containing the inscriptions "House of David" and "King of Israel," *Time* magazine stated, "This writing—dated to the 9th century B.C., only a century after David's reign—described a victory by a neighboring king over the Israelites... The skeptics' claim that David never existed is now hard to defend." *Time*, December 18, 1995

"In extraordinary ways, modern archeology is affirming the historical core of the Old and New Testaments, supporting key portions of crucial biblical stories." *Jeffery L. Sheler*, "Is the Bible True?" *Reader's Digest*, June 2000 (See also Matthew 26:54 footnote.)

1:31–35 See Matthew 1:20–23 footnote.

1:32,33 Messianic prophecy fulfilled: "Of the increase of his government and peace there shall be no end, upon the throne of David, and upon his kingdom, to order it, and to establish it with judgment and with justice from henceforth, even for ever. The zeal of the LORD of hosts will perform this" (Isaiah 9:7). See Luke 3:33 footnote.

a city of Juda;
40 And entered into the house of Zacharias, and saluted Elizabeth.
41 And it came to pass, that, when Elizabeth heard the salutation of Mary, the babe
leaped in her womb; and Elizabeth was
filled with the Holy Spirit:
42 And she spoke out with a loud voice,
and said, Blessed are you among women,
and blessed is the fruit of your womb.
43 And whence is this to me, that the
mother of my Lord should come to me?
44 For, lo, as soon as the voice of your
salutation sounded in mine ears, the babe
leaped in my womb for joy.
45 And blessed is she that believed: for
there shall be a performance of those things
which were told her from the Lord.
46 And Mary said, My soul does magnify the Lord,
47 And my spirit has rejoiced in God my
Savior.
48 For he has regarded the low estate of
his handmaiden: for, behold, from henceforth all generations shall call me blessed.
49 For he that is mighty has done to me
great things; and holy is his name.
50 And his mercy is on them that fear
him from generation to generation.
51 He has showed strength with his arm;
he has scattered the proud in the imagination of their hearts.
52 He has put down the mighty from
their seats, and exalted them of low degree.
53 He has filled the hungry with good
things; and the rich he has sent empty
away.
54 He has helped his servant Israel, in
remembrance of his mercy;
55 As he spoke to our fathers, to Abraham, and to his seed for ever.
56 And Mary abode with her about three
months, and returned to her own house.
57 Now Elizabeth's full time came that
she should be delivered; and she brought
forth a son.
58 And her neighbours and her cousins
heard how the Lord had showed great
mercy upon her; and they rejoiced with
her.
59 And it came to pass, that on the eighth
day they came to circumcise the child;
and they called him Zacharias, after the
name of his father.
60 And his mother answered and said,
Not so; but he shall be called John.
61 And they said to her, There is none of
your kindred that is called by this name.
62 And they made signs to his father,
how he would have him called.
63 And he asked for a writing table, and
wrote, saying, His name is John. And
they marveled all.
64 And his mouth was opened immediately, and his tongue loosed, and he spoke,
and praised God.

> I trust that you will find no rest for your feet till you have been the means of leading many to that blessed Savior who is your confidence and hope.
>
> **CHARLES SPURGEON**

65 And fear came on all that dwelt round
about them: and all these sayings were
noised abroad throughout all the hill
country of Judea.
66 And all they that heard them laid
them up in their hearts, saying, What
manner of child shall this be! And the
hand of the Lord was with him.
67 And his father Zacharias was filled
with the Holy Spirit, and prophesied, saying,
68 Blessed be the Lord God of Israel;
for he has visited and redeemed his people,
69 And has raised up an horn of salvation for us in the house of his servant
David;
70 As he spoke by the mouth of his holy
prophets, which have been since the world
began:
71 That we should be saved from our
enemies, and from the hand of all that hate
us;
72 To perform the mercy promised to
our fathers, and to remember his holy cov-

enant;
73 The oath which he sware to our father Abraham,
74 That he would grant to us, that we being delivered out of the hand of our enemies might serve him without fear,
75 In holiness and righteousness before him, all the days of our life.
76 And you, child, shall be called the prophet of the Highest: for you shall go before the face of the Lord to prepare his ways;
77 To give knowledge of salvation to his people by the remission of their sins,
78 Through the tender mercy of our God; whereby the dayspring from on high has visited us,
79 To give light to them that sit in darkness and in the shadow of death, to guide our feet into the way of peace.
80 And the child grew, and waxed strong in spirit, and was in the deserts till the day of his showing to Israel.

CHAPTER 2

AND it came to pass in those days, that there went out a decree from Caesar Augustus, that all the world should be taxed.
2 (And this taxing was first made when Cyrenius was governor of Syria.)
3 And all went to be taxed, every one into his own city.
4 And Joseph also went up from Galilee, out of the city of Nazareth, into Judea, to the city of David, which is called Bethlehem; (because he was of the house and lineage of David:)
5 To be taxed with Mary his espoused wife, being great with child.
6 And so it was, that, while they were there, the days were accomplished that she should be delivered.
7 And she brought forth her firstborn son, and wrapped him in swaddling clothes, and laid him in a manger; because there was no room for them in the inn.
8 And there were in the same country shepherds abiding in the field, keeping watch over their flock by night.
9 And, lo, the angel of the Lord came upon them, and the glory of the Lord shone round about them: and they were sore afraid.
10 And the angel said to them, Fear not: for, behold, I bring you good tidings of great joy, which shall be to all people.
11 For to you is born this day in the city of David a Savior, which is Christ the Lord.
12 And this shall be a sign to you; You shall find the babe wrapped in swaddling clothes, lying in a manger.
13 And suddenly there was with the angel a multitude of the heavenly host praising God, and saying,
14 Glory to God in the highest, and on earth peace, good will toward men.
15 And it came to pass, as the angels were gone away from them into heaven, the shepherds said one to another, Let us now go even to Bethlehem, and see this thing which is come to pass, which the Lord has made known to us.
16 And they came with haste, and found Mary, and Joseph, and the babe lying in a manger.
17 And when they had seen it, they made known abroad the saying which was told them concerning this child.
18 And all they that heard it wondered at those things which were told them by the shepherds.

1:74 Fear of man. When God commissioned Moses to go speak to Pharaoh, Moses revealed that he had a problem. His seeming humility ("Who am I . . . ?") was actually the fear of man (Exodus 3:11; 4:1). Although he argued with God that he wasn't eloquent, God promised to be with him and teach him what to say (Exodus 4:10–14). Likewise, we have no excuse for entertaining the fear of man when it comes to seeking the lost, because we are not called to use eloquent speech. We have the indwelling Christ, and through Him and His strength we can "do all things" (Philippians 4:13).

1:79 See Psalm 23:4 footnote.

19 But Mary kept all these things, and
pondered them in her heart.
20 And the shepherds returned, glorifying and praising God for all the things that
they had heard and seen, as it was told to
them.
21 And when eight days were accomplished for the circumcising of the child,
his name was called JESUS, which was so
named of the angel before he was conceived in the womb.
22 And when the days of her purification according to the law of Moses were
accomplished, they brought him to Jerusalem, to present him to the Lord;
23 (As it is written in the law of the
Lord, Every male that opens the womb
shall be called holy to the Lord;)
24 And to offer a sacrifice according to
that which is said in the law of the Lord,
A pair of turtledoves, or two young pi-
geons.
25 And, behold, there was a man in Jerusalem, whose name was Simeon; and the
same man was just and devout, waiting for
the consolation of Israel: and the Holy
Spirit was upon him.
26 And it was revealed to him by the
Holy Spirit, that he should not see death,
before he had seen the Lord's Christ.
27 And he came by the Spirit into the
temple: and when the parents brought in
the child Jesus, to do for him after the
custom of the law,
28 Then took he him up in his arms,
and blessed God, and said,
29 Lord, now let you your servant depart in peace, according to your word:
30 For mine eyes have seen your salvation,
31 Which you have prepared before the
face of all people;
32 A light to lighten the Gentiles, and
the glory of your people Israel.
33 And Joseph and his mother marveled
at those things which were spoken of
him.
34 And Simeon blessed them, and said
to Mary his mother, Behold, this child is
set for the fall and rising again of many
in Israel; and for a sign which shall be
spoken against;
35 (Yea, a sword shall pierce through
your own soul also,) that the thoughts of
many hearts may be revealed.
36 And there was one Anna, a prophetess, the daughter of Phanuel, of the tribe
of Aser: she was of a great age, and had
lived with an husband seven years from
her virginity;
37 And she was a widow of about fourscore and four years, which departed not
from the temple, but served God with
fastings and prayers night and day.
38 And she coming in that instant gave
thanks likewise to the Lord, and spoke of
him to all them that looked for redemption in Jerusalem.
39 And when they had performed all
things according to the law of the Lord,
they returned into Galilee, to their own
city Nazareth.
40 And the child grew, and waxed strong
in spirit, filled with wisdom: and the grace
of God was upon him.
41 Now his parents went to Jerusalem
every year at the feast of the passover.
42 And when he was twelve years old,
they went up to Jerusalem after the custom of the feast.
43 And when they had fulfilled the days,
as they returned, the child Jesus tarried
behind in Jerusalem; and Joseph and his
mother knew not of it.
44 But they, supposing him to have been
in the company, went a day's journey; and
they sought him among their kinsfolk
and acquaintance.
45 And when they found him not, they
turned back again to Jerusalem, seeking
him.
46 And it came to pass, that after three

2:46 Jesus was not disobedient to Joseph and Mary as some assert. If anything, they were irresponsible in assuming (for a whole day) that their twelve-year-old son was with the company when He was not (v. 44).

days they found him in the temple, sitting in the midst of the doctors, both hearing them, and asking them questions.

47 And all that heard him were astonished at his understanding and answers.

48 And when they saw him, they were amazed: and his mother said to him, Son, why have you thus dealt with us? behold, your father and I have sought you sorrowing.

49 And he said to them, How is it that you sought me? Did you not know that I must be about my Father's business?

50 And they understood not the saying which he spoke to them.

51 And he went down with them, and came to Nazareth, and was subject to them: but his mother kept all these sayings in her heart.

52 And Jesus increased in wisdom and stature, and in favor with God and man.

CHAPTER 3

NOW in the fifteenth year of the reign of Tiberius Caesar, Pontius Pilate being governor of Judea, and Herod being tetrarch of Galilee, and his brother Philip tetrarch of Ituraea and of the region of Trachonitis, and Lysanias the tetrarch of Abilene,

2 Annas and Caiaphas being the high priests, the word of God came to John the son of Zacharias in the wilderness.

3 And he came into all the country about Jordan, preaching the baptism of repentance for the remission of sins;

4 As it is written in the book of the words of Isaiah the prophet, saying, The voice of one crying in the wilderness, Prepare the way of the Lord, make his paths straight.

5 Every valley shall be filled, and every mountain and hill shall be brought low; and the crooked shall be made straight, and the rough ways shall be made smooth;

6 And all flesh shall see the salvation of God.

7 Then said he to the multitude that came forth to be baptized of him, O generation of vipers, who has warned you to flee from the wrath to come?

8 Bring forth therefore fruits worthy of repentance, and begin not to say within yourselves, We have Abraham to our father: for I say to you, That God is able of these stones to raise up children to Abraham.

9 And now also the axe is laid to the root of the trees: every tree therefore which brings not forth good fruit is hewn down, and cast into the fire.

10 And the people asked him, saying, What shall we do then?

11 He answered and said to them, He that has two coats, let him impart to him that has none; and he that has meat, let him do likewise.

THE FUNCTION OF THE LAW

3:4 "Ever more the Law *must* prepare the way for the gospel. To overlook this in instructing souls is almost certain to result in false hope, the introduction of a false standard of Christian experience, and to fill the Church with false converts...Time will make this plain." *Charles Finney*

3:1,2 Archaeology confirms the Bible. A hidden burial chamber, dating to the first century, was discovered in 1990 two miles from the Temple Mount. One bore the bones of a man in his 60s, with the inscription "Yehosef bar Qayafa" —meaning "Joseph, son of Caiaphas." Experts believe this was Caiaphas, the high priest of Jerusalem, who was involved in the arrest of Jesus, interrogated him, and handed Him over to Pontius Pilate for execution.

A few decades earlier, excavations at Caesarea Maritama, the ancient seat of Roman government in Judea, uncovered a stone slab whose complete inscription may have read: "Pontius Pilate, the prefect of Judea, has dedicated to the people of Caesarea a temple in honor of Tiberius."

The discovery is truly significant, establishing that the man depicted in the Gospels as Judea's Roman governor had the authority ascribed to him by the Gospel writers. *Jeffery L. Sheler*, "Is the Bible True?" *Reader's Digest*, June 2000

Questions & Objections

3:7–9 *"Jews don't need to be 'saved'; they're already God's chosen people. Even the New Testament says 'so all Israel shall be saved.'"*

The gospel was first preached to the Jews. They were commanded to repent and trust the Savior (Acts 2:38), and warned that if they didn't repent, they would perish (Luke 13:3). John the Baptist preached fearful words to those who, simply because they were Jews, thought that they need not repent. The Bible says, "Then said he to the multitude that came forth to be baptized of him, O generation of vipers, who has warned you to flee from the wrath to come? Bring forth therefore fruits worthy of repentance, and begin not to say within yourselves, We have Abraham to our father: for I say to you, That God is able of these stones to raise up children to Abraham. And now also the axe is laid to the root of the trees: every tree therefore which brings not forth good fruit is hewn down, and cast into the fire" (Luke 3:7–9).

12 Then came also publicans to be baptized, and said to him, Master, what shall we do?
13 And he said to them, Exact no more than that which is appointed you.
14 And the soldiers likewise demanded of him, saying, And what shall we do? And he said to them, Do violence to no man, neither accuse any falsely; and be content with your wages.
15 And as the people were in expectation, and all men mused in their hearts of John, whether he were the Christ, or not;
16 John answered, saying to them all, I indeed baptize you with water; but one mightier than I comes, the latchet of whose shoes I am not worthy to unloose: he shall baptize you with the Holy Spirit and with fire:
17 Whose fan is in his hand, and he will thoroughly purge his floor, and will gather the wheat into his garner; but the chaff he will burn with fire unquenchable.
18 And many other things in his exhortation preached he to the people.
19 But Herod the tetrarch, being reproved by him for Herodias his brother Philip's wife, and for all the evils which Herod had done,
20 Added yet this above all, that he shut up John in prison.
21 Now when all the people were baptized, it came to pass, that Jesus also being baptized, and praying, the heaven was opened,
22 And the Holy Spirit descended in a bodily shape like a dove upon him, and a voice came from heaven, which said, You are my beloved Son; in you I am well pleased.
23 And Jesus himself began to be about thirty years of age, being (as was supposed) the son of Joseph, which was the son of Heli,
24 Which was the son of Matthat, which was the son of Levi, which was the son of Melchi, which was the son of Janna, which was the son of Joseph,
25 Which was the son of Mattathias, which was the son of Amos, which was

3:21 "More than twenty times the Gospels call attention to Jesus' practice of prayer. It is given special mention during events of momentous decision in His life—His baptism (Luke 3:21); the selection of the twelve apostles (Luke 6:12); on the Mount of Transfiguration (Luke 9:29); the Last Supper (Matthew 26:27); in Gethsemane (Luke 22:39–46); and on the cross (Luke 23:46)." *Robert E. Coleman*

3:23 Some point to the different genealogies of Jesus as "errors" in the Bible. However, Luke gives the maternal genealogy of the Messiah (through His mother) and Matthew (1:1) gives His paternal genealogy (through His legal father).

the son of Naum, which was the son of
Esli, which was the son of Nagge,
26 Which was the son of Maath, which
was the son of Mattathias, which was the
son of Semei, which was the son of Joseph, which was the son of Juda,
27 Which was the son of Joanna, which
was the son of Rhesa, which was the son
of Zorobabel, which was the son of Salathiel, which was the son of Neri,
28 Which was the son of Melchi, which
was the son of Addi, which was the son
of Cosam, which was the son of Elmo-
dam, which was the son of Er,
29 Which was the son of Jose, which
was the son of Eliezer, which was the son
of Jorim, which was the son of Matthat,
which was the son of Levi,
30 Which was the son of Simeon, which
was the son of Juda, which was the son
of Joseph, which was the son of Jonan,
which was the son of Eliakim,
31 Which was the son of Melea, which
was the son of Menan, which was the son
of Mattatha, which was the son of Nathan, which was the son of David,
32 Which was the son of Jesse, which
was the son of Obed, which was the son
of Booz, which was the son of Salmon,
which was the son of Naasson,
33 Which was the son of Aminadab,
which was the son of Aram, which was
the son of Esrom, which was the son of
Phares, which was the son of Juda,
34 Which was the son of Jacob, which
was the son of Isaac, which was the son
of Abraham, which was the son of Thara,
which was the son of Nachor,
35 Which was the son of Saruch, which
was the son of Ragau, which was the son
of Phalec, which was the son of Heber,
which was the son of Sala,
36 Which was the son of Cainan, which
was the son of Arphaxad, which was the
son of Sem, which was the son of Noah,
which was the son of Lamech,
37 Which was the son of Mathusala,
which was the son of Enoch, which was
the son of Jared, which was the son of
Maleleel, which was the son of Cainan,
38 Which was the son of Enos, which
was the son of Seth, which was the son
of Adam, which was the son of God.

CHAPTER 4

AND Jesus being full of the Holy Spirit
returned from Jordan, and was led
by the Spirit into the wilderness,
2 Being forty days tempted of the devil.
And in those days he did eat nothing: and
when they were ended, he afterward hungered.
3 And the devil said to him, If you be the
Son of God, command this stone that it
be made bread.
4 And Jesus answered him, saying, It is
written, That man shall not live by bread
alone, but by every word of God.
5 And the devil, taking him up into an
high mountain, showed to him all the
kingdoms of the world in a moment of
time.
6 And the devil said to him, All this power will I give you, and the glory of them:
for that is delivered to me; and to whomsoever I will I give it.
7 If you therefore will worship me, all
shall be yours.
8 And Jesus answered and said to him,
Get behind me, Satan: for it is written,
You shall worship the Lord your God,
and him only shall you serve.
9 And he brought him to Jerusalem, and
set him on a pinnacle of the temple, and

3:33 Messianic prophecy fulfilled: "The scepter shall not depart from Judah, nor a lawgiver from between his feet, until Shiloh come; and to him shall the gathering of the people be" (Genesis 49:10). See Luke 23:32–34 footnote.

4:4 "If you wish to know God, you must know His Word. If you wish to perceive His power, you must see how He works by His Word. If you wish to know His purpose before it comes to pass, you can only discover it by His Word." *Charles Spurgeon*

said to him, If you be the Son of God, cast
yourself down from hence:
10 For it is written, He shall give his angels charge over you, to keep you:
11 And in their hands they shall bear you
up, lest at any time you dash your foot
against a stone.
12 And Jesus answering said to him, It is
said, You shall not tempt the Lord your
God.
13 And when the devil had ended all the
temptation, he departed from him for a
season.
14 And Jesus returned in the power of
the Spirit into Galilee: and there went out
a fame of him through all the region round
about.
15 And he taught in their synagogues,
being glorified of all.
16 And he came to Nazareth, where he
had been brought up: and, as his custom
was, he went into the synagogue on the
sabbath day, and stood up for to read.
17 And there was delivered to him the
book of the prophet Isaiah. And when
he had opened the book, he found the
place where it was written,
18 The Spirit of the Lord is upon me,
because he has anointed me to preach
the gospel to the poor; he has sent me
to heal the brokenhearted, to preach de-
liverance to the captives, and recover-
ing of sight to the blind, to set at liberty
them that are bruised,
19 **To preach the acceptable year of the**
Lord.
20 And he closed the book, and he gave
it again to the minister, and sat down. And
the eyes of all them that were in the synagogue were fastened on him.
21 And he began to say to them, This
day is this scripture fulfilled in your ears.
22 And all bare him witness, and wondered at the gracious words which pro-

4:8 To worship is to change. "Just as worship begins in holy expectancy, it ends in holy obedience. If worship does not propel us into greater obedience, it has not been worship. To stand before the Holy One of eternity is to change...In worship an increased power steals into the heart sanctuary, an increased compassion grows in the soul." *Richard J. Foster, Celebration of Discipline*

4:10,11 When Jesus was being tempted, the devil quoted Scripture but twisted its meaning. Jesus responded by countering with the true application of God's Word (vv. 4–13). We must know the truth in order to counter error, or we will be misled by those who take Scripture out of context and misinterpret it. That's why we should not "live by bread alone, but by every word of God" (v. 4).

4:18 Who is the gospel for? Jesus gives us a summation of who the gospel is for: the poor, the brokenhearted, the captives, the blind, the bruised (oppressed). Jesus is not referring to those who lack financial resources when He speaks of the *poor*. The word means "meek, humble, lowly" and refers to the "poor in spirit" (Matthew 5:3)—the blessed ones to whom the kingdom of God belongs. The poor are those who know that they are destitute of righteousness.

The *brokenhearted* refers not to unhappy people who have been jilted by a sweetheart, but to those who, like Peter and Isaiah, are contrite and sorrowing for their sin. *Matthew Henry* wrote of Jesus, "For He was sent to heal the brokenhearted, to give peace to those that were troubled and humbled for sins, and to bring them to rest who were weary and heavy-laden, under the burden of guilt and corruption."

The *captives* are those "taken captive by [the devil] at his will" (2 Timothy 2:26).

The *blind* are those whom "the god of this world has blinded...[to] the light of the glorious gospel of Christ" (2 Corinthians 4:4).

The *oppressed* are those who are "oppressed of the devil" (Acts 10:38).

The gospel of grace is for the humble, not the proud. God resists the proud, but gives grace to the humble (James 4:6). The Scriptures tell us, "Every one that is proud in heart is an abomination to the Lord" (Proverbs 16:5). He sets on high those who are lowly, and those who mourn are lifted to safety (Job 5:11). God looks on the man who is poor and of a contrite spirit, and who trembles at His Word (Isaiah 66:2). Only the sick need a physician, and only those who are convinced of the disease of sin will appreciate and appropriate the cure of the gospel.

ceeded out of his mouth. And they said,
Is not this Joseph's son?
23 And he said to them, You will surely
say to me this proverb, Physician, heal
yourself: whatsoever we have heard done
in Capernaum, do also here in your country.
24 And he said, Verily I say to you, No
prophet is accepted in his own country.
25 But I tell you of a truth, many widows were in Israel in the days of Elijah,
when the heaven was shut up three years
and six months, when great famine was
throughout all the land;
26 But to none of them was Elisha sent,
save to Sarepta, a city of Sidon, to a woman that was a widow.
27 And many lepers were in Israel in the
time of Elijah the prophet; and none of
them was cleansed, saving Naaman the
Syrian.
28 And all they in the synagogue, when
they heard these things, were filled with
wrath,
29 And rose up, and thrust him out of
the city, and led him to the brow of the
hill whereon their city was built, that
they might cast him down headlong.
30 But he passing through the midst of
them went his way,
31 And came down to Capernaum, a city
of Galilee, and taught them on the sabbath
days.
32 And they were astonished at his doctrine: for his word was with power.
33 And in the synagogue there was a
man, which had a spirit of an unclean devil, and cried out with a loud voice,
34 Saying, Let us alone; what have we
to do with you, Jesus of Nazareth? are you
come to destroy us? I know you who you
are; the Holy One of God.
35 And Jesus rebuked him, saying, Hold
your peace, and come out of him. And
when the devil had thrown him in the
midst, he came out of him, and hurt him
not.
36 And they were all amazed, and spoke
among themselves, saying, What a word
is this! for with authority and power he
commands the unclean spirits, and they
come out.
37 And the fame of him went out into
every place of the country round about.

. . . . . .

For evidence of the Bible's reliability, see Matthew 4:4 footnote.

. . . . . .

38 And he arose out of the synagogue,
and entered into Simon's house. And Simon's wife's mother was taken with a
great fever; and they besought him for
her.
39 And he stood over her, and rebuked
the fever; and it left her: and immediately she arose and ministered to them.
40 Now when the sun was setting, all
they that had any sick with divers diseases
brought them to him; and he laid his
hands on every one of them, and healed
them.
41 And devils also came out of many,
crying out, and saying, You are Christ the
Son of God. And he rebuking them suffered them not to speak: for they knew

4:40 Scientific facts in the Bible. For ages, scientists believed in a geocentric view of the universe. The differences between night and day were believed to be caused by the sun revolving around the earth. Today, we know that the earth's rotation on its axis is responsible for the sun's rising and setting. But 4,000 or more years ago, it was written, "Have you commanded the morning since your days; and caused the day spring [dawn] to know his place?...It [the earth] is turned as clay to the seal" (Job 38:12,14). The picture here is of a clay vessel being turned or rotated upon the potter's wheel—an accurate analogy of the earth's rotation. See also Hebrews 11:3 footnote.

"The study of the Book of Job and its comparison with the latest scientific discoveries has brought me to the matured conviction that the Bible is an inspired book and was written by the One who made the stars." *Charles Burckhalter*, Chabot Observatory

that he was Christ.
42 And when it was day, he departed and went into a desert place: and the people sought him, and came to him, and stayed him, that he should not depart from them.
43 And he said to them, I must preach the kingdom of God to other cities also: for therefore am I sent.
44 And he preached in the synagogues of Galilee.

CHAPTER 5

AND it came to pass, that, as the people pressed upon him to hear the word of God, he stood by the lake of Gennesaret,
2 And saw two ships standing by the lake: but the fishermen were gone out of them, and were washing their nets.
3 And he entered into one of the ships, which was Simon's, and prayed him that he would thrust out a little from the land. And he sat down, and taught the people out of the ship.
4 Now when he had left speaking, he said to Simon, Launch out into the deep, and let down your nets for a draught.
5 And Simon answering said to him, Master, we have toiled all the night, and have taken nothing: nevertheless at your word I will let down the net.
6 And when they had this done, they enclosed a great multitude of fishes: and their net broke.
7 And they beckoned to their partners, which were in the other ship, that they should come and help them. And they came, and filled both the ships, so that they began to sink.
8 When Simon Peter saw it, he fell down at Jesus' knees, saying, Depart from me; for I am a sinful man, O Lord.
9 For he was astonished, and all that were with him, at the draught of the fishes which they had taken:
10 *And so was also James, and John, the sons of Zebedee, which were partners with Simon. And Jesus said to Simon, Fear not; from henceforth you shall catch men.*
11 And when they had brought their ships to land, they forsook all, and followed him.
12 And it came to pass, when he was in a certain city, behold a man full of leprosy: who seeing Jesus fell on his face, and besought him, saying, Lord, if you will, you can make me clean.
13 And he put forth his hand, and touched him, saying, I will: be clean. And immediately the leprosy departed from him.
14 And he charged him to tell no man: but go, and show yourself to the priest, and offer for your cleansing, according as Moses commanded, for a testimony to them.
15 But so much the more went there a fame abroad of him: and great multitudes came together to hear, and to be healed by him of their infirmities.
16 And he withdrew himself into the wilderness, and prayed.
17 And it came to pass on a certain day, as he was teaching, that there were Pharisees and doctors of the law sitting by, which were come out of every town of Galilee, and Judea, and Jerusalem: and the power of the Lord was present to heal

5:16 Prayer—the secret weapon: Prayer was the ignition to every revival fire in history. Prayer was the key to the doorway of ministry for every preacher used by God in the past. For the soldier of Christ, true prayer should be a way of life, not just a call for help in the heat of battle.

A man was once cutting a tree stump with an obviously blunt axe. He was only bruising the bark as sweat poured from his beaded brow. Someone suggested that he stop for a moment and sharpen the axe, to which he replied, "I'm too busy chopping the tree to stop for anything." If he would only stop for a moment and sharpen the axe, he would slice through the tree with far greater ease.

Stop at the beginning of each day, and "sharpen the axe" through prayer. Seek first the kingdom of God and you will slice through that day with far greater ease. See Luke 6:12.

them.
18 And, behold, men brought in a bed
a man which was taken with a palsy: and
they sought means to bring him in, and
to lay him before him.
19 And when they could not find by
what way they might bring him in because of the multitude, they went upon
the housetop, and let him down through
the tiling with his couch into the midst
before Jesus.
20 And when he saw their faith, he said
to him, Man, your sins are forgiven you.
21 And the scribes and the Pharisees began to reason, saying, Who is this which
speaks blasphemies? Who can forgive sins,
but God alone?
22 But when Jesus perceived their
thoughts, he answering said to them,
What do you reason in your hearts?
23 Whether is easier, to say, Your sins be
forgiven you; or to say, Rise up and walk?
24 **But that you may know that the Son
of man has power upon earth to forgive
sins, (he said to the sick of the palsy,)
I say to you, Arise, and take up your
couch, and go into your house.**
25 And immediately he rose up before
them, and took up that whereon he lay,
and departed to his own house, glorifying God.
26 And they were all amazed, and they
glorified God, and were filled with fear,
saying, We have seen strange things to
day.
27 And after these things he went forth,
and saw a publican, named Levi, sitting
at the receipt of custom: and he said to
him, Follow me.
28 And he left all, rose up, and followed
him.
29 And Levi made him a great feast in his
own house: and there was a great company of publicans and of others that sat
down with them.
30 But their scribes and Pharisees murmured against his disciples, saying, Why
do you eat and drink with publicans and
sinners?
31 And Jesus answering said to them,
They that are whole need not a physician;
but they that are sick.
32 I came not to call the righteous, but
sinners to repentance.
33 And they said to him, Why do the
disciples of John fast often, and make
prayers, and likewise the disciples of the
Pharisees; but yours eat and drink?
34 And he said to them, Can you make
the children of the bridechamber fast,
while the bridegroom is with them?
35 But the days will come, when the
bridegroom shall be taken away from
them, and then shall they fast in those
days.
36 And he spoke also a parable to them;
No man puts a piece of a new garment
upon an old; if otherwise, then both the
new makes a rent, and the piece that was
taken out of the new agrees not with the
old.
37 And no man puts new wine into old
bottles; else the new wine will burst the
bottles, and be spilled, and the bottles
shall perish.
38 But new wine must be put into new
bottles; and both are preserved.
39 No man also having drunk old wine
straightway desires new: for he says, The
old is better.

CHAPTER 6

AND it came to pass on the second
sabbath after the first, that he went
through the corn fields; and his disciples
plucked the ears of corn, and did eat, rub-
bing them in their hands.
2 And certain of the Pharisees said to
them, Why do you that which is not lawful to do on the sabbath days?
3 And Jesus answering them said, Have
you not read so much as this, what David did, when himself was an hungered,
and they which were with him;

5:32 Repentance—its necessity for salvation. See Luke 13:2.

4 How he went into the house of God, and did take and eat the shewbread, and gave also to them that were with him; which it is not lawful to eat but for the priests alone?

5 And he said to them, That the Son of man is Lord also of the sabbath.

6 And it came to pass also on another sabbath, that he entered into the synagogue and taught: and there was a man whose right hand was withered.

7 And the scribes and Pharisees watched him, whether he would heal on the sabbath day; that they might find an accusation against him.

8 But he knew their thoughts, and said to the man which had the withered hand, Rise up, and stand forth in the midst. And he arose and stood forth.

9 Then said Jesus to them, I will ask you one thing; Is it lawful on the sabbath days to do good, or to do evil? to save life, or to destroy it?

10 And looking round about upon them all, he said to the man, Stretch forth your hand. And he did so: and his hand was restored whole as the other.

11 And they were filled with madness; and communed one with another what they might do to Jesus.

12 And it came to pass in those days, that he went out into a mountain to pray, and continued all night in prayer to God.

13 And when it was day, he called to him his disciples: and of them he chose twelve, whom also he named apostles;

14 Simon, (whom he also named Peter,) and Andrew his brother, James and John, Philip and Bartholomew,

15 Matthew and Thomas, James the son of Alphaeus, and Simon called Zelotes,

16 And Judas the brother of James, and Judas Iscariot, which also was the traitor.

17 And he came down with them, and stood in the plain, and the company of his disciples, and a great multitude of people out of all Judea and Jerusalem, and from the sea coast of Tyre and Sidon, which came to hear him, and to be healed of their diseases;

18 And they that were vexed with unclean spirits: and they were healed.

19 And the whole multitude sought to touch him: for there went virtue out of him, and healed them all.

20 And he lifted up his eyes on his disciples, and said, Blessed be you poor: for yours is the kingdom of God.

21 Blessed are you that hunger now: for you shall be filled. Blessed are you that weep now: for you shall laugh.

22 Blessed are you, when men shall hate you, and when they shall separate you from their company, and shall reproach you, and cast out your name as evil, for the Son of man's sake.

"[The Bible] is a Book worth more than all the other books which were ever printed."

Patrick Henry

6:12 Prayer—the secret weapon: See Luke 22:41. "The one concern of the devil is to keep Christians from praying. He fears nothing from prayerless studies, prayerless works, and prayerless religion. He laughs at our toil, mocks at our wisdom, but trembles when we pray." *Samuel Chadwick*

QUESTIONS & OBJECTIONS

6:27

"Religion has caused more wars than anything else in history."

It is true that man has used religion for political gain. Nazi Germany had "God with us" engraved in German on the belts of Nazi soldiers. America said, "Praise the Lord and pass the ammunition." The law may even allow you to start the Christian Nazi Party, if you so desire. You can become a "reverend" for a few dollars through the tabloid classifieds and then further your political agenda with the world's blessing, no matter how much it smears the name of Christ.

Jesus tells us in John 16:2,3 that there will be some who, in their error, commit atrocities and murder in the name of God: "The time is coming that whosoever kills you will think that he does God service." However, He informs us that these are not true believers: "And these things will they do to you, because they have not known the Father, nor me." (See also 1 John 3:15.)

Jesus told His followers to love their enemies. So if a man puts a knife into someone's back in the name of Christianity, something obviously isn't right. If we human beings can detect it, how much more will God? He will deal with it on Judgment Day.

"I know that the Lord is always on the side of right. But it is my constant anxiety and prayer that I—and this nation—should be on the Lord's side." *Abraham Lincoln*

23 Rejoice in that day, and leap for joy: for, behold, your reward is great in heaven: for in the like manner did their fathers to the prophets.
24 But woe to you that are rich! for you have received your consolation.
25 Woe to you that are full! for you shall hunger. Woe to you that laugh now! for you shall mourn and weep.
26 Woe to you, when all men shall speak well of you! for so did their fathers to the false prophets.
27 But I say to you which hear, Love your enemies, do good to them which hate you,
28 Bless them that curse you, and pray for them which despitefully use you.
29 And to him that smites you on the one cheek offer also the other; and him that takes away your cloak forbid not to take your coat also.
30 Give to every man that asks of you; and of him that takes away your goods ask them not again.
31 And as you would that men should do to you, do you also to them likewise.
32 For if you love them which love you, what thanks do you have? for sinners also love those that love them.

6:26 A soft gospel. Those who speak about "the love of Jesus," but refuse to preach the gospel of love revealed in the bloodied cross, *will* have the smile of the world. Their listeners have itching ears and they are more than pleased to have them scratched with a soft gospel. They are of the world; they speak of the world and the world gladly hears them. Jesus gave warning to those who fall into this subtle trap: "Woe to you, when all men shall speak well of you!"

The cross is the only God-given means of salvation from death, and we will bear reproach as long as we cling to its frame. It is only for a season—some day we will exchange it for a crown. In the meantime, let our faith in Jesus be spoken of throughout the whole world whether it be with a smile or a frown. The praise of men is a volatile minefield of pleasant flowers. In a moment it can swing from a fragrant "Hosanna!" to an explosive "Crucify Him!" Ask any baseball hero who has had a bad season. God's approval, however, is eternal.

6:27 The Church is commanded to love her enemies, just as Israel was instructed to do in Exodus 23:4,5.

6:28 This is the spirit in which we should share our faith. See Colossians 4:5,6.

QUESTIONS & OBJECTIONS

6:37 ***"Judge not lest you be judged. You therefore have no right to judge me when it comes to my sins!"***

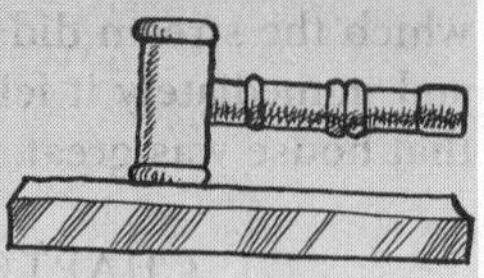

The world often takes this verse out of context and uses it to accuse Christians of being "judgmental" when they speak of sin. In the context of the verse Jesus is telling His disciples not to judge one another, something the Bible condemns (Romans 14:10; James 4:11). In Luke 6:41,42 He speaks of seeing a speck in a *brother's* eye. In John 7:24 He said, "Judge not according to the appearance, but judge righteous judgment." If someone steals, lies, commits adultery or murder, etc., the Christian can make a (righteous) moral judgment and say that the actions were morally wrong, and that these sins will have eternal consequences. *Chuck Colson* said, "True tolerance is not a total lack of judgment. It's knowing what should be tolerated—and refusing to tolerate that which shouldn't."

33 And if you do good to them which do
good to you, what thank have you? for
sinners also do even the same.
34 And if you lend to them of whom you
hope to receive, what thank have you? for
sinners also lend to sinners, to receive as
much again.
35 But love your enemies, and do good,
and lend, hoping for nothing again; and
your reward shall be great, and you shall
be the children of the Highest: for he is
kind to the unthankful and to the evil.
36 Be therefore merciful, as your Father
also is merciful.
37 Judge not, and you shall not be judged:
condemn not, and you shall not be condemned: forgive, and you shall be forgiven:
38 Give, and it shall be given to you;
good measure, pressed down, and shak-
en together, and running over, shall men
give into your bosom. For with the same
measure that you mete withal it shall be
measured to you again.
39 And he spoke a parable to them, Can
the blind lead the blind? shall they not
both fall into the ditch?
40 The disciple is not above his master:
but every one that is perfect shall be as
his master.
41 And why behold the mote that is in
your brother's eye, but perceive not the
beam that is in your own eye?
42 Either how can you say to your brother, Brother, let me pull out the mote that
is in your eye, when you yourself behold
not the beam that is in your own eye?
You hypocrite, cast out first the beam out
of your own eye, and then shall you see
clearly to pull out the mote that is in your
brother's eye.
43 For a good tree brings not forth corrupt fruit; neither does a corrupt tree bring
forth good fruit.
44 For every tree is known by his own
fruit. For of thorns men do not gather figs,
nor of a bramble bush gather they grapes.
45 A good man out of the good treasure
of his heart brings forth that which is
good; and an evil man out of the evil treasure of his heart brings forth that which
is evil: for of the abundance of the heart
his mouth speaks.
46 And why do you call me, Lord,
Lord, and do not the things which I say?
47 **Whosoever comes to me, and hears**
my sayings, and does them, I will show
you to whom he is like:
48 **He is like a man which built an**
house, and dug deep, and laid the foun-
dation on a rock: and when the flood
arose, the stream beat vehemently up-

6:38 "You gain by giving that which you can't buy with money." *Dr. Edwin Cole*

on that house, and could not shake it: for it was founded upon a rock.

49 **But he that hears, and does not, is like a man that without a foundation built an house upon the earth; against which the stream did beat vehemently, and immediately it fell; and the ruin of that house was great.**

CHAPTER 7

NOW when he had ended all his sayings in the audience of the people, he entered into Capernaum.

2 And a certain centurion's servant, who was dear to him, was sick, and ready to die.

3 And when he heard of Jesus, he sent to him the elders of the Jews, beseeching him that he would come and heal his servant.

4 And when they came to Jesus, they besought him instantly, saying, That he was worthy for whom he should do this:

5 For he loves our nation, and he has built us a synagogue.

6 Then Jesus went with them. And when he was now not far from the house, the centurion sent friends to him, saying to him, Lord, trouble not yourself: for I am not worthy that you should enter under my roof:

7 Wherefore neither thought I myself worthy to come to you: but say in a word, and my servant shall be healed.

8 For I also am a man set under authority, having under me soldiers, and I say to one, Go, and he goes; and to another, Come, and he comes; and to my servant, Do this, and he does it.

9 When Jesus heard these things, he marveled at him, and turned him about, and said to the people that followed him, I say to you, I have not found so great faith, no, not in Israel.

10 And they that were sent, returning to the house, found the servant whole that had been sick.

11 And it came to pass the day after, that he went into a city called Nain; and many of his disciples went with him, and much people.

12 Now when he came near to the gate of the city, behold, there was a dead man carried out, the only son of his mother, and she was a widow: and much people of the city was with her.

13 And when the Lord saw her, he had compassion on her, and said to her, Weep not.

14 And he came and touched the coffin: and they that bare him stood still. And he said, Young man, I say to you, Arise.

15 And he that was dead sat up, and began to speak. And he delivered him to his mother.

16 And there came a fear on all: and they glorified God, saying, That a great prophet is risen up among us; and, That God has visited his people.

17 And this rumour of him went forth throughout all Judea, and throughout all the region round about.

18 And the disciples of John showed him of all these things.

19 And John calling to him two of his disciples sent them to Jesus, saying, are you he that should come? or look we for another?

20 When the men were come to him, they said, John Baptist has sent us to you, saying, are you he that should come? or look we for another?

21 And in that same hour he cured many of their infirmities and plagues, and of evil spirits; and to many that were blind he gave sight.

22 Then Jesus answering said to them, Go your way, and tell John what things you have seen and heard; how that the blind see, the lame walk, the lepers are cleansed, the deaf hear, the dead are raised, to the poor the gospel is preached.

6:46 "You cannot say, 'No, Lord,' and mean both words; one annuls the other. If you say no to Him, then He is not your Lord." *D. James Kennedy*

23 **And blessed is he, whosoever shall
not be offended in me.**
24 And when the messengers of John
were departed, he began to speak to the
people concerning John, What went you
out into the wilderness for to see? A reed
shaken with the wind?
25 But what went you out for to see? A
man clothed in soft raiment? Behold, they
which are gorgeously appareled, and live
delicately, are in kings' courts.
26 But what went you out for to see? A
prophet? Yea, I say to you, and much more
than a prophet.
27 This is he, of whom it is written, Behold, I send my messenger before your
face, which shall prepare your way before you.
28 For I say to you, Among those that
are born of women there is not a greater
prophet than John the Baptist: but he that
is least in the kingdom of God is greater
than he.
29 And all the people that heard him,
and the publicans, justified God, being
baptized with the baptism of John.
30 But the Pharisees and lawyers rejected the counsel of God against themselves,
being not baptized of him.
31 And the Lord said, Whereunto then
shall I liken the men of this generation?
and to what are they like?
32 They are like children sitting in the
marketplace, and calling one to another,
and saying, We have piped to you, and
you have not danced; we have mourned
to you, and you have not wept.
33 For John the Baptist came neither
eating bread nor drinking wine; and you
say, He has a devil.
34 The Son of man is come eating and
drinking; and you say, Behold a gluttonous man, and a winebibber, a friend of
publicans and sinners!
35 But wisdom is justified of all her children.
36 And one of the Pharisees desired him
that he would eat with him. And he went
into the Pharisee's house, and sat down to
meat.
37 And, behold, a woman in the city,
which was a sinner, when she knew that
Jesus sat at meat in the Pharisee's house,
brought an alabaster box of ointment,
38 And stood at his feet behind him
weeping, and began to wash his feet with
tears, and did wipe them with the hairs
of her head, and kissed his feet, and
anointed them with the ointment.
39 Now when the Pharisee which had
bidden him saw it, he spoke within himself, saying, This man, if he were a prophet, would have known who and what
manner of woman this is that touches
him: for she is a sinner.

> You can be forgiven all your sin in half the tick of a clock, and pass from death to life more swiftly than I can utter the words.
>
> **CHARLES SPURGEON**

40 And Jesus answering said to him, Simon, I have somewhat to say to you. And
he says, Master, say on.
41 There was a certain creditor which
had two debtors: the one owed five hundred pence, and the other fifty.
42 And when they had nothing to pay,
he frankly forgave them both. Tell me
therefore, which of them will love him
most?
43 Simon answered and said, I suppose
that he, to whom he forgave most. And
he said to him, You have rightly judged.
44 And he turned to the woman, and
said to Simon, See this woman? I entered
into your house, you gave me no water
for my feet: but she has washed my feet
with tears, and wiped them with the hairs
of her head.
45 You gave me no kiss: but this woman
since the time I came in has not ceased
to kiss my feet.
46 My head with oil you did not anoint:
but this woman has anointed my feet with
ointment.
47 Wherefore I say to you, Her sins,
which are many, are forgiven; for she loved

much: but to whom little is forgiven, the same loves little.

48 And he said to her, Your sins are forgiven.

49 And they that sat at meat with him began to say within themselves, Who is this that forgives sins also?

50 And he said to the woman, Your faith has saved you; go in peace.

• • • • • •

For the differences between humans and animals, see Psalm 32:9 footnote.

• • • • • •

CHAPTER 8

AND it came to pass afterward, that he went throughout every city and village, preaching and showing the glad tidings of the kingdom of God: and the twelve were with him,

2 And certain women, which had been healed of evil spirits and infirmities, Mary called Magdalene, out of whom went seven devils,

3 And Joanna the wife of Chuza Herod's steward, and Susanna, and many others, which ministered to him of their substance.

4 And when much people were gathered together, and were come to him out of every city, he spoke by a parable:

5 A sower went out to sow his seed: and as he sowed, some fell by the way side; and it was trodden down, and the fowls of the air devoured it.

6 And some fell upon a rock; and as soon as it was sprung up, it withered away, because it lacked moisture.

7 And some fell among thorns; and the thorns sprang up with it, and choked it.

8 And other fell on good ground, and sprang up, and bare fruit an hundredfold. And when he had said these things, he cried, He that has ears to hear, let him hear.

9 And his disciples asked him, saying, What might this parable be?

10 And he said, to you it is given to know the mysteries of the kingdom of God: but to others in parables; that seeing they might not see, and hearing they might not understand.

11 Now the parable is this: The seed is the word of God.

12 Those by the way side are they that hear; then comes the devil, and takes away the word out of their hearts, lest they should believe and be saved.

13 They on the rock are they, which, when they hear, receive the word with joy; and these have no root, which for a while believe, and in time of temptation fall away.

14 And that which fell among thorns are they, which, when they have heard, go forth, and are choked with cares and riches and pleasures of this life, and bring no fruit to perfection.

15 But that on the good ground are they, which in an honest and good heart, having heard the word, keep it, and bring forth fruit with patience.

16 No man, when he has lighted a candle, covers it with a vessel, or puts it under a bed; but sets it on a candlestick, that they which enter in may see the light.

17 For nothing is secret, that shall not be made manifest; neither any thing hid, that shall not be known and come abroad.

18 Take heed therefore how you hear: for whosoever has, to him shall be given; and whosoever has not, from him shall be taken even that which he seems to have.

19 Then came to him his mother and his brethren, and could not come at him for the press.

20 And it was told him by certain which said, Your mother and your brethren stand

8:20,21 This was an opportunity for Jesus to exalt His mother above the rest of humanity. Blessed though she was in bearing Him, He gave her no more honor than any of the common people who heard the Word of God and obeyed it. See Luke 11:27,28 footnote.

without, desiring to see you.
21 And he answered and said to them,
My mother and my brethren are these
which hear the word of God, and do it.
22 Now it came to pass on a certain day,
that he went into a ship with his disciples:
and he said to them, Let us go over to the
other side of the lake. And they launched
forth.
23 But as they sailed he fell asleep: and
there came down a storm of wind on the
lake; and they were filled with water, and
were in jeopardy.
24 And they came to him, and awoke
him, saying, Master, master, we perish.
Then he arose, and rebuked the wind and
the raging of the water: and they ceased,
and there was a calm.
25 And he said to them, Where is your
faith? **And they being afraid wondered,
saying one to another, What manner of
man is this! for he commands even the
winds and water, and they obey him.**

> One of the earliest things a minister should do when he leaves college and settles in a country town or village is to begin open-air speaking.
>
> **CHARLES SPURGEON**

26 And they arrived at the country of the
Gadarenes, which is over against Galilee.
27 And when he went forth to land, there
met him out of the city a certain man,
which had devils long time, and ware no
clothes, neither abode in any house, but
in the tombs.
28 When he saw Jesus, he cried out,
and fell down before him, and with a loud
voice said, What have I to do with you,
Jesus, you Son of God most high? I beseech you, torment me not.
29 (For he had commanded the unclean
spirit to come out of the man. For oftentimes it had caught him: and he was kept
bound with chains and in fetters; and he
broke the bands, and was driven of the
devil into the wilderness.)
30 And Jesus asked him, saying, What
is your name? And he said, Legion: because many devils were entered into him.
31 And they besought him that he would
not command them to go out into the
deep.
32 And there was there an herd of many
swine feeding on the mountain: and they
besought him that he would suffer them
to enter into them. And he suffered them.
33 Then went the devils out of the man,
and entered into the swine: and the herd
ran violently down a steep place into the
lake, and were choked.
34 When they that fed them saw what
was done, they fled, and went and told it
in the city and in the country.
35 Then they went out to see what was
done; and came to Jesus, and found the
man, out of whom the devils were departed, sitting at the feet of Jesus, clothed, and
in his right mind: and they were afraid.
36 They also which saw it told them by
what means he that was possessed of the
devils was healed.
37 Then the whole multitude of the country of the Gadarenes round about besought him to depart from them; for they
were taken with great fear: and he went
up into the ship, and returned back again.
38 Now the man out of whom the devils were departed besought him that he
might be with him: but Jesus sent him
away, saying,
39 Return to your own house, and show
how great things God has done to you.
And he went his way, and published
throughout the whole city how great
things Jesus had done to him.
40 And it came to pass, that, when Jesus
was returned, the people gladly received
him: for they were all waiting for him.
41 And, behold, there came a man named
Jairus, and he was a ruler of the synagogue: and he fell down at Jesus' feet, and
besought him that he would come into
his house:
42 For he had one only daughter, about
twelve years of age, and she lay a dying.
But as he went the people thronged him.

43 And a woman having an issue of
blood twelve years, which had spent all
her living upon physicians, neither could
be healed of any,
44 Came behind him, and touched the
border of his garment: and immediately
her issue of blood stopped.
45 And Jesus said, Who touched me?
When all denied, Peter and they that were
with him said, Master, the multitude
throng you and press you, and you say,
Who touched me?
46 And Jesus said, Somebody has touched
me: for I perceive that virtue is gone out
of me.
47 And when the woman saw that she
was not hid, she came trembling, and
falling down before him, she declared to
him before all the people for what cause
she had touched him and how she was
healed immediately.
48 And he said to her, Daughter, be of
good comfort: your faith has made you
whole; go in peace.
49 While he yet spoke, there came one
from the ruler of the synagogue's house,
saying to him, Your daughter is dead;
trouble not the Master.
50 But when Jesus heard it, he answered
him, saying, Fear not: believe only, and
she shall be made whole.
51 And when he came into the house,
he suffered no man to go in, save Peter,
and James, and John, and the father and
the mother of the maiden.
52 And all wept, and bewailed her: but
he said, Weep not; she is not dead, but
sleeps.
53 And they laughed him to scorn, knowing that she was dead.
54 And he put them all out, and took her
by the hand, and called, saying, Maid,
arise.
55 And her spirit came again, and she
arose straightway: and he commanded to
give her meat.
56 And her parents were astonished: but
he charged them that they should tell no
man what was done.

CHAPTER 9

THEN he called his twelve disciples together, and gave them power and authority over all devils, and to cure dis-

8:39 How to witness to family members. Here's some advice that may save you a great deal of grief. As a new Christian, I did almost irreparable damage by acting like a wild bull in a crystal showroom. I bullied my mom, my dad, and many of my friends into making a "decision for Christ." I was sincere, zealous, loving, kind, and stupid. I didn't understand that salvation doesn't come through making a "decision," but through *repentance*, and repentance is God-given (2 Timothy 2:25). The Bible teaches that no one can come to the Son unless the Father "draws" him (John 6:44). If you are able to get a "decision" but the person has no conviction of sin, you will almost certainly end up with a stillborn on your hands.

In my "zeal without knowledge" I actually inoculated the very ones I was so desperately trying to reach. There is nothing more important to you than the salvation of your loved ones, and you don't want to blow it. If you do, you may find that you don't have a second chance. Fervently pray for them, thanking God for their salvation. Let them *see* your faith. Let them *feel* your kindness, your genuine love, and your gentleness. Buy gifts for no reason. Do chores when you are not asked to. Go the extra mile. Put yourself in their position. You know that you have found everlasting life—*death has lost its sting!* Your joy is unspeakable. But as far as they are concerned, you've been brainwashed and have become part of a weird sect. So your loving actions will speak more loudly than ten thousand eloquent sermons.

For this reason you should avoid *verbal* confrontation until you have knowledge that will guide your zeal. Pray for wisdom and sensitivity to God's timing. You may have only one shot, so make it count. Keep your cool. If you don't, you may end up with a lifetime of regret. *Believe* me. It is better to hear a loved one or a close friend say, "Tell me about your faith in Jesus Christ," rather than you saying, "Sit down. I want to talk to you." Continue to persevere in prayer for them, that God would open their eyes to the truth.

eases.
2 And he sent them to preach the kingdom of God, and to heal the sick.
3 And he said to them, Take nothing for
your journey, neither staves, nor scrip,
neither bread, neither money; neither
have two coats apiece.
4 And whatsoever house you enter into,
there abide, and thence depart.
5 And whosoever will not receive you,
when you go out of that city, shake off
the very dust from your feet for a testimony against them.
6 And they departed, and went through
the towns, preaching the gospel, and
healing every where.
7 Now Herod the tetrarch heard of all
that was done by him: and he was perplexed, because that it was said of some,
that John was risen from the dead;
8 And of some, that Elijah had appeared;
and of others, that one of the old prophets was risen again.
9 And Herod said, John have I beheaded: but who is this, of whom I hear such
things? And he desired to see him.
10 And the apostles, when they were
returned, told him all that they had done.
And he took them, and went aside privately into a desert place belonging to the
city called Bethsaida.
11 And the people, when they knew it,
followed him: and he received them, and
spoke to them of the kingdom of God, and
healed them that had need of healing.
12 And when the day began to wear
away, then came the twelve, and said to
him, Send the multitude away, that they
may go into the towns and country round
about, and lodge, and get victuals: for we
are here in a desert place.
13 But he said to them, You give them to
eat. And they said, We have no more but
five loaves and two fishes; except we
should go and buy meat for all this people.
14 For they were about five thousand
men. And he said to his disciples, Make
them sit down by fifties in a company.
15 And they did so, and made them all
sit down.
16 Then he took the five loaves and the
two fishes, and looking up to heaven, he
blessed them, and broke, and gave to the
disciples to set before the multitude.
17 And they did eat, and were all filled:
and there was taken up of fragments that
remained to them twelve baskets.
18 And it came to pass, as he was alone
praying, his disciples were with him: and
he asked them, saying, Whom say the
people that I am?
19 They answering said, John the Baptist; but some say, Elijah; and others say,
that one of the old prophets is risen again.
20 He said to them, But whom say you
that I am? Peter answering said, The Christ
of God.
21 And he straitly charged them, and
commanded them to tell no man that
thing;

> No sort of defense is needed for preaching out of doors; but it would need very potent arguments to prove that a man had done his duty who has never preached beyond the walls of his meeting place.
>
> **CHARLES SPURGEON**

22 Saying, The Son of man must suffer
many things, and be rejected of the elders and chief priests and scribes, and be
slain, and be raised the third day.
23 **And he said to them all, If any man
will come after me, let him deny himself, and take up his cross daily, and follow me.**
24 **For whosoever will save his life
shall lose it: but whosoever will lose his
life for my sake, the same shall save it.**
**25 For what is a man advantaged, if
he gain the whole world, and lose himself, or be cast away?**
26 **For whosoever shall be ashamed
of me and of my words, of him shall
the Son of man be ashamed, when he
shall come in his own glory, and in his
Father's, and of the holy angels.**

27 But I tell you of a truth, there be some
standing here, which shall not taste of
death, till they see the kingdom of God.
28 And it came to pass about an eight
days after these sayings, he took Peter
and John and James, and went up into a
mountain to pray.
29 And as he prayed, the fashion of his
countenance was altered, and his raiment
was white and glistering.
30 And, behold, there talked with him
two men, which were Moses and Elijah:
31 Who appeared in glory, and spoke
of his decease which he should accomplish at Jerusalem.
32 But Peter and they that were with
him were heavy with sleep: and when
they were awake, they saw his glory, and
the two men that stood with him.
33 And it came to pass, as they departed from him, Peter said to Jesus, Master,
it is good for us to be here: and let us
make three tabernacles; one for you, and
one for Moses, and one for Elijah: not
knowing what he said.
34 While he thus spoke, there came a
cloud, and overshadowed them: and they
feared as they entered into the cloud.
35 And there came a voice out of the
cloud, saying, This is my beloved Son:
hear him.
36 And when the voice was past, Jesus
was found alone. And they kept it close,
and told no man in those days any of
those things which they had seen.
37 And it came to pass, that on the next
day, when they were come down from
the hill, much people met him.
38 And, behold, a man of the company
cried out, saying, Master, I beseech you,
look upon my son: for he is mine only
child.
39 And, lo, a spirit takes him, and he
suddenly cries out; and it tears him that
he foams again, and bruising him hardly
departs from him.
40 And I besought your disciples to cast
him out; and they could not.

9:25 "[A] watchful eye must be kept on ourselves lest, while we are building great monuments of renown and bliss here, we neglect to have our names enrolled in the Annals of Heaven." *James Madison*

9:30 The Mount of Transfiguration. When Jesus was transfigured on the Holy Mountain, Moses and Elijah appeared in a vision and communed with Him. Moses represented the Law and Elijah represented the prophets.

Scripture gives us insight into what they spoke about: they communed about the cross (vv. 30,31). When Peter suggested paying homage to Moses, Elijah, and Jesus, it seems God wasn't impressed with the proposal. He spoke from heaven, telling the disciples to listen to Jesus. Then Moses and Elijah disappeared, and Jesus was left alone with the disciples.

When a person hears from the Father and understands who Jesus is, Moses and Elijah disappear. We see only Jesus. He is the Alpha and Omega, the Beginning and the End, the Author and Finisher of our faith. He is the only One to whom we bow the knee. Too many who profess to have heard the Father's voice spend too much time at the feet of Moses, bowing their knee to the Law. They are legalists who have no zeal for the lost. Their only concern is "touch not, taste not, handle not" (Colossians 2:21).

Many also spend too much time bowing down to Elijah. Prophecy is their joy. Prophecy shouldn't have us gazing into the future—it should have us gazing at the Savior and His will for the lost.

Charles Spurgeon said, "Here is another who spent all his time in interpreting the prophecies, so that everything he reads of in the newspapers he could see in Daniel or Revelation. Some say he is wise, but I would rather spend my time in winning souls. I would sooner bring one sinner to Jesus than unravel all the mysteries of the divine Word, for salvation is the one thing we are to live for."

The death and resurrection of the Savior didn't occur so that we could dabble in the future, but to open the door of salvation to hell-bound sinners. Those who hear the Father's voice hear the Son. They walk in His steps. They come down from the mountain to continue His work on earth: to seek and save that which is lost.

41 And Jesus answering said, O faithless and perverse generation, how long shall I be with you, and suffer you? Bring your son here.

42 And as he was yet a coming, the devil threw him down, and tare him. And Jesus rebuked the unclean spirit, and healed the child, and delivered him again to his father.

43 And they were all amazed at the mighty power of God. But while they wondered every one at all things which Jesus did, he said to his disciples,

44 Let these sayings sink down into your ears: for the Son of man shall be delivered into the hands of men.

45 But they understood not this saying, and it was hid from them, that they perceived it not: and they feared to ask him of that saying.

46 Then there arose a reasoning among them, which of them should be greatest.

47 And Jesus, perceiving the thought of their heart, took a child, and set him by him,

48 And said to them, Whosoever shall receive this child in my name receives me: and whosoever shall receive me receives him that sent me: for he that is least among you all, the same shall be great.

49 And John answered and said, Master, we saw one casting out devils in your name; and we forbad him, because he followed not with us.

50 And Jesus said to him, Forbid him not: for he that is not against us is for us.

51 And it came to pass, when the time was come that he should be received up, he steadfastly set his face to go to Jerusalem,

52 And sent messengers before his face: and they went, and entered into a village of the Samaritans, to make ready for him.

53 And they did not receive him, because his face was as though he would go to Jerusalem.

54 And when his disciples James and John saw this, they said, Lord, will you that we command fire to come down from heaven, and consume them, even as Elijah did?

55 But he turned, and rebuked them, and said, You know not what manner of spirit you are of.

56 For the Son of man is not come to destroy men's lives, but to save them. And they went to another village.

57 And it came to pass, that, as they went in the way, a certain man said to him, Lord, I will follow you wherever you go.

58 And Jesus said to him, Foxes have holes, and birds of the air have nests; but the Son of man has not where to lay his head.

59 *And he said to another, Follow me. But he said, Lord, suffer me first to go and bury my father.*

60 *Jesus said to him, Let the dead bury their dead: but you go and preach the kingdom of God.*

61 And another also said, Lord, I will follow you; but let me first go bid them farewell, which are at home at my house.

62 And Jesus said to him, **No man, hav-**

9:62 "Backsliders"—who are they? It is fairly common to hear someone give a testimony by saying something like: "I gave my heart to Jesus when I was a child. Then I fell away from the Lord and became involved in drugs, robbery, rape, murder, pornography, gambling, adultery, extortion, and other things I would rather not mention. All this time I still knew the Lord. Then I came back to Him when I was thirty years old."

These words usually come from those who don't understand that the Bible speaks many times of true and false conversion. Almost all of those we place in the category of "backsliders" are not backsliders. They never slid forward in the first place. They are false converts—"stony-ground" or "thorny-ground" hearers (Mark 4:16–19), who fall away in a time of temptation, tribulation, or persecution. The true convert puts his hand to the plow and doesn't look back, because he is fit for the kingdom. "Backsliders" don't just *look* back, they actually *go* back, showing that something was radically wrong.

ing put his hand to the plough, and looking back, is fit for the kingdom of God.

CHAPTER 10

AFTER these things the Lord appointed other seventy also, and sent them two and two before his face into every city and place, where he himself would come.

2 *Therefore said he to them, The harvest truly is great, but the laborers are few: pray therefore the Lord of the harvest, that he would send forth laborers into his harvest.*

3 Go your ways: behold, I send you forth as lambs among wolves.

4 Carry neither purse, nor scrip, nor shoes: and salute no man by the way.

5 And into whatsoever house you enter, first say, Peace be to this house.

6 And if the son of peace be there, your peace shall rest upon it: if not, it shall turn to you again.

7 And in the same house remain, eating and drinking such things as they give: for the laborer is worthy of his hire. Go not from house to house.

8 And into whatsoever city you enter, and they receive you, eat such things as are set before you:

9 And heal the sick that are therein, and say to them, The kingdom of God is come near to you.

10 But into whatsoever city you enter, and they receive you not, go your ways out into the streets of the same, and say,

11 Even the very dust of your city, which cleaves on us, we do wipe off against you: notwithstanding be sure of this, that the kingdom of God is come near to you.

12 But I say to you, that it shall be more tolerable in that day for Sodom, than for that city.

13 Woe to you, Chorazin! woe to you, Bethsaida! for if the mighty works had been done in Tyre and Sidon, which have been done in you, they had a great while ago repented, sitting in sackcloth and ashes.

14 But it shall be more tolerable for Tyre and Sidon at the judgment, than for you.

15 And you, Capernaum, which are exalted to heaven, shall be thrust down to hell.

16 He that hears you hears me; and he that despises you despises me; and he that despises me despises him that sent me.

17 And the seventy returned again with joy, saying, Lord, even the devils are subject to us through your name.

18 And he said to them, I beheld Satan as lightning fall from heaven.

19 Behold, I give to you power to tread on serpents and scorpions, and over all the power of the enemy: and nothing shall by any means hurt you.

20 Notwithstanding in this rejoice not, that the spirits are subject to you; but rather rejoice, because your names are written in heaven.

21 **In that hour Jesus rejoiced in spirit, and said, I thank you, O Father, Lord of heaven and earth, that you have hid these things from the wise and prudent, and have revealed them to babes: even so, Father; for so it seemed good in your sight.**

22 All things are delivered to me of my Father: and no man knows who the Son is, but the Father; and who the Father is, but the Son, and he to whom the Son will reveal him.

10:14 The world often mocks the thought of hell, by saying that God is unjust in sending all sinners there regardless of whether their sins are menial or heinous. God's punishment, however, will be according to righteousness. Here we see that the more sinful cities of Chorazin and Bethsaida will receive a more harsh judgment than Tyre and Sidon. For a description of hell, see Revelation 1:18 footnote.

10:20 "The joy of heaven will arm us against the assaults of our spiritual enemies and put our mouths out of taste for those pleasures with which the tempter baits his hooks." *Matthew Henry*

PRINCIPLES OF GROWTH FOR THE NEW AND GROWING CHRISTIAN

10:2

Evangelism—Our Most Sobering Task

Late in December 1996, a large family gathered for a joyous Christmas. There were so many gathered that night, five of the children slept in the converted garage, kept warm during the night by an electric heater placed near the door.

During the early hours of the morning, the heater suddenly burst into flames, blocking the doorway. In seconds the room became a blazing inferno. The frantic 911 call revealed the unspeakable terror as one of the children could be heard screaming, *"I'm on fire!"* The distraught father rushed into the flames to try to save his beloved children, receiving burns to 50% of his body. Tragically, all five children burned to death. They died because steel bars on the windows thwarted their escape. There was only one door, and it was blocked by the flames.

Imagine you're back in time, just minutes before the heater burst into flames. You peer through the darkness at the peaceful sight of five sleeping youngsters, knowing that at any moment the room will erupt into an inferno and burn the flesh of horrified children. *Can you in good conscience walk away?* No! You *must* awaken them and warn them to run from that death trap!

The world sleeps peacefully in the darkness of ignorance. There is only one Door by which they may escape death. The steel bars of sin prevent their salvation, and at the same time call for the flames of Eternal Justice. What a fearful thing Judgment Day will be! The fires of the wrath of Almighty God will burn for eternity. The Church has been entrusted with the task of awakening them before it's too late. We cannot turn our backs and walk away in complacency. *Think of how the father ran into the flames.* His love knew no bounds. Our devotion to the sober task God has given us will be in direct proportion to our love for the lost. There are only a few who run headlong into the flames to warn them to flee (Luke 10:2). *Please* be one of them. We really have no choice. The apostle Paul said, "Woe is to me, if I preach not the gospel!" (1 Corinthians 9:16).

The "Prince of Preachers," *Charles Spurgeon*, said, "We need to be ashamed at the bare suspicion of unconcern." A Christian *cannot* be apathetic about the salvation of the world. The love of God in him will motivate him to seek and save that which is lost.

You probably have a limited amount of time after your conversion to impact your unsaved friends and family with the gospel. After their initial shock, they will put you in a neat little ribbon-tied box, and keep you at arm's length. So it's important that you take advantage of the short time you have while you still have their ears. For advice on how to do this, see Luke 8:39 footnote.

It is important to realize that we should share our faith with others *whenever* we can. The Bible says that there are only two times we should do this: "in season, and out of season" (2 Timothy 4:2). The apostle Paul *pleaded* for prayer for his own personal witness. He said, "[Pray] for me, that utterance may be given to me, that I may open my mouth boldly, to make known the mystery of the gospel, for which I am an ambassador in bonds: that therein I may speak boldly, as I ought to speak" (Ephesians 6:19,20).

Remember that you have the sobering responsibility of speaking to other peoples' loved ones. Perhaps another Christian has prayed earnestly that God would use a faithful witness to speak to his beloved mom or dad, and *you* are the answer to that prayer. You are the true and faithful witness God wants to use.

Keep the fate of the ungodly before your eyes. Too many of us settle down on a padded pew and become introverted. Our world becomes a monastery without walls. Our friends are confined solely to those *within* the Church, when Jesus was the "friend of sinners." So take the time to deliberately befriend the lost for the sake of their salvation. Remember that each and every person who dies in his sins has an appointment with the Judge of the Universe. Hell opens wide its terrible jaws. There is no more sobering task than to be entrusted with the gospel of salvation—working with God for the eternal well-being of dying humanity.

For the next principle of growth, see Hebrews 6:18 footnote.

23 And he turned him to his disciples,
and said privately, Blessed are the eyes
which see the things that you see:
24 For I tell you, that many prophets and
kings have desired to see those things
which you see, and have not seen them;
and to hear those things which you hear,
and have not heard them.
25 And, behold, a certain lawyer stood
up, and tempted him, saying, Master, what
shall I do to inherit eternal life?
26 He said to him, What is written in the
law? how do you read it?
**27 And he answering said, You shall
love the Lord your God with all your
heart, and with all your soul, and with
all your strength, and with all your
mind; and your neighbour as yourself.**
28 And he said to him, You have answered right: this do, and you shall live.
29 But he, willing to justify himself, said
to Jesus, And who is my neighbour?
30 And Jesus answering said, A certain
man went down from Jerusalem to Jericho, and fell among thieves, which stripped
him of his raiment, and wounded him,
and departed, leaving him half dead.
31 And by chance there came down a
certain priest that way: and when he saw
him, he passed by on the other side.
32 And likewise a Levite, when he was
at the place, came and looked on him,
and passed by on the other side.
33 But a certain Samaritan, as he journeyed, came where he was: and when he
saw him, he had compassion on him,
34 And went to him, and bound up his
wounds, pouring in oil and wine, and
set him on his own beast, and brought
him to an inn, and took care of him.
35 And on the morrow when he departed, he took out two pence, and gave
them to the host, and said to him, Take
care of him; and whatsoever you spend
more, when I come again, I will repay you.
36 Which now of these three, do you
think, was neighbour to him that fell
among the thieves?
37 And he said, He that showed mercy
on him. Then said Jesus to him, Go, and
do likewise.
38 Now it came to pass, as they went,
that he entered into a certain village: and
a certain woman named Martha received
him into her house.
39 And she had a sister called Mary,
which also sat at Jesus' feet, and heard his
word.
40 But Martha was cumbered about
much serving, and came to him, and said,
Lord, do you not care that my sister has
left me to serve alone? bid her therefore
that she help me.
41 And Jesus answered and said to her,

10:26 This man was proud and self-righteous. He "stood up" and tested Jesus. He needed the Law to humble him and bring him the knowledge of sin. When the Law accused him, he tried to justify his guilt—"But he, willing to justify himself, said to Jesus, And who is my neighbor?" Jesus then explained the spiritual nature of the Commandments to show the man how far he had fallen short of the glory of God that is revealed in the Law (vv. 30–37).

10:27 Love God with the whole heart. Three children were watching a new television set their father had just purchased for them. When their dad arrived home, they didn't even get up and greet him at the door. Instead, they were watching TV. The father walked over to it, turned it off and said, "Kids, I purchased that television set because I love you and want you to be happy. But if it comes between you and your love for me, I am going to sell it, because you are loving the gift more than the giver."

If we love anything more than God (our mother, father, brother, sister, spouse, children, job, sports, or even our own life), we are loving the gift more than the Giver. This is called "inordinate affection." To love anything more than we love God is to transgress the First Commandment. See Luke 12:46 footnote.

10:34 "When you see that men have been wounded by the Law, then it is time to pour in the gospel oil." *Samuel Bolton*

Martha, Martha, you are careful and troubled about many things:

42 But one thing is needful: and Mary has chosen that good part, which shall not be taken away from her.

CHAPTER 11

AND it came to pass, that, as he was praying in a certain place, when he ceased, one of his disciples said to him, Lord, teach us to pray, as John also taught his disciples.

2 And he said to them, When you pray, say, Our Father which art in heaven, Hallowed be your name. Your kingdom come. Your will be done, as in heaven, so in earth.

3 Give us day by day our daily bread.

4 And forgive us our sins; for we also forgive every one that is indebted to us. And lead us not into temptation; but deliver us from evil.

5 And he said to them, Which of you shall have a friend, and shall go to him at midnight, and say to him, Friend, lend me three loaves;

6 For a friend of mine in his journey is come to me, and I have nothing to set before him?

7 And he from within shall answer and say, Trouble me not: the door is now shut, and my children are with me in bed; I cannot rise and give you.

8 I say to you, Though he will not rise and give him, because he is his friend, yet because of his importunity he will rise and give him as many as he needs.

9 And I say to you, Ask, and it shall be given you; seek, and you shall find; knock, and it shall be opened to you.

10 For every one that asks receives; and he that seeks finds; and to him that knocks it shall be opened.

11 If a son shall ask bread of any of you that is a father, will he give him a stone? or if he ask a fish, will he for a fish give him a serpent?

12 Or if he shall ask an egg, will he offer him a scorpion?

13 If you then, being evil, know how to give good gifts to your children: how much more shall your heavenly Father give the Holy Spirit to them that ask him?

14 And he was casting out a devil, and it was dumb. And it came to pass, when the devil was gone out, the dumb spoke; and the people wondered.

15 But some of them said, He casts out devils through Beelzebub the chief of the devils.

16 And others, tempting him, sought of him a sign from heaven.

17 But he, knowing their thoughts, said to them, Every kingdom divided against itself is brought to desolation; and a house divided against a house falls.

18 If Satan also be divided against himself, how shall his kingdom stand? because you say that I cast out devils through Beelzebub.

19 And if I by Beelzebub cast out devils, by whom do your sons cast them out? therefore shall they be your judges.

20 But if I with the finger of God cast out devils, no doubt the kingdom of God is come upon you.

21 When a strong man armed keeps his palace, his goods are in peace:

22 But when a stronger than he shall come upon him, and overcome him, he takes from him all his armor wherein he trusted, and divides his spoils.

23 He that is not with me is against me: and he that gathers not with me scatters.

24 When the unclean spirit is gone out of a man, he walks through dry places, seeking rest; and finding none, he says, I will return to my house whence I came

11:2 Prayer. "Prayer is the open admission that without Christ we can do nothing. And prayer is the turning away from ourselves to God in the confidence that He will provide the help we need. Prayer humbles *us* as needy and exalts *God* as all-sufficient." *John Piper*

"Prayer doesn't get man's will done in heaven; it gets God's will done on earth." *Ronald Dunn*

SPRINGBOARDS FOR PREACHING AND WITNESSING

11:39

Sting Operation

Some years ago, Southern California police carried out an interesting "sting" operation. They had a list of thousands of wanted criminals who had somehow evaded jail. Instead of risking their lives by going and attempting to arrest each one, they sent all the criminals a letter telling them they had won a large amount of money in a drawing.

The police put signs and banners on a building, and placed balloons and even a clown on the outside to create a festive atmosphere to welcome the "winners." As each criminal entered the building, he heard music and celebration. He was then ushered into a room where he smiled as his hand was shaken. The facial expression changed from one of joy to unbelief as each was told, "Congratulations—you have just won time in prison!" Dozens of criminals made their way through the main doors, were arrested and ushered out the back door. It was interesting that many of these lawbreakers declared, "I *thought* it was a sting operation!" but their greed wouldn't let them stay away.

out.

25 And when he comes, he finds it swept and garnished.

26 Then he goes, and takes to him seven other spirits more wicked than himself; and they enter in, and dwell there: and the last state of that man is worse than the first.

27 And it came to pass, as he spoke these things, a certain woman of the company lifted up her voice, and said to him, Blessed is the womb that bare you, and the paps which you have sucked.

28 But he said, Yes rather, blessed are they that hear the word of God, and keep it.

29 And when the people were gathered thick together, he began to say, This is an evil generation: they seek a sign; and there shall no sign be given it, but the sign of Jonah the prophet.

30 For as Jonah was a sign to the Ninevites, so shall also the Son of man be to this generation.

31 The queen of the south shall rise up in the judgment with the men of this generation, and condemn them: for she came from the utmost parts of the earth to hear the wisdom of Solomon; and, behold, a greater than Solomon is here.

32 The men of Nineveh shall rise up in the judgment with this generation, and shall condemn it: for they repented at the preaching of Jonah; and, behold, a greater than Jonah is here.

33 No man, when he has lighted a candle, puts it in a secret place, neither under a bushel, but on a candlestick, that they which come in may see the light.

34 The light of the body is the eye: therefore when your eye is single, your whole body also is full of light; but when your eye is evil, your body also is full of darkness.

35 Take heed therefore that the light which is in you be not darkness.

36 If your whole body therefore be full of light, having no part dark, the whole shall be full of light, as when the bright shining of a candle does give you light.

37 And as he spoke, a certain Pharisee besought him to dine with him: and he went in, and sat down to meat.

38 And when the Pharisee saw it, he marveled that he had not first washed before dinner.

39 And the Lord said to him, Now do you Pharisees make clean the outside of the cup and the platter; but your inward part is full of ravening and wickedness.

11:27,28 Rather than exalting Mary above the rest of the common people, Jesus said that the greater blessing belongs to those who hear the Word of God and obey it.

40 You fools, did not he that made that which is without make that which is within also?
41 But rather give alms of such things as you have; and, behold, all things are clean to you.
42 But woe to you, Pharisees! for you tithe the mint and rue and all manner of herbs, and pass over judgment and the love of God: these ought you to have done, and not to leave the other undone.
43 Woe to you, Pharisees! for you love the uppermost seats in the synagogues, and greetings in the markets.
44 Woe to you, scribes and Pharisees, hypocrites! for you are as graves which appear not, and the men that walk over them are not aware of them.
45 Then answered one of the lawyers, and said to him, Master, thus saying you reproach us also.
46 And he said, Woe to you also, you lawyers! for you load men with burdens grievous to be borne, and you yourselves touch not the burdens with one of your fingers.
47 Woe to you! for you build the sepulchres of the prophets, and your fathers killed them.
48 Truly you bear witness that you allow the deeds of your fathers: for they indeed killed them, and you build their sepulchres.
49 Therefore also said the wisdom of God, I will send them prophets and apostles, and some of them they shall slay and persecute:
50 That the blood of all the prophets, which was shed from the foundation of the world, may be required of this generation;
51 From the blood of Abel to the blood of Zacharias, which perished between the altar and the temple: verily I say to you, It shall be required of this generation.
52 Woe to you, lawyers! for you have taken away the key of knowledge: you entered not in yourselves, and them that were entering in you hindered.
53 And as he said these things to them, the scribes and the Pharisees began to urge him vehemently, and to provoke him to speak of many things:
54 Laying wait for him, and seeking to catch something out of his mouth, that they might accuse him.

CHAPTER 12

IN the mean time, when there were gathered together an innumerable multitude of people, insomuch that they trode one upon another, he began to say to his disciples first of all, Beware of the leaven of the Pharisees, which is hypocrisy.
2 **For there is nothing covered, that shall not be revealed; neither hid, that shall not be known.**
3 Therefore whatsoever you have spoken in darkness shall be heard in the light; and that which you have spoken in the ear in closets shall be proclaimed upon the housetops.
4 **And I say to you my friends, Be not afraid of them that kill the body, and after that have no more that they can do.**
5 But I will forewarn you whom you shall fear: Fear him, which after he has killed has power to cast into hell; yea, I say to you, Fear him.
6 Are not five sparrows sold for two far-

12:5 "People will never set their faces decidedly towards heaven, and live like pilgrims, until they really feel that they are in danger of hell...Let us expound and beat out the Ten Commandments, and show the length, and breadth, and depth, and height of their requirements. This is the way of our Lord in the Sermon on the Mount [Matthew 5:30]. We cannot do better than follow His plan. We may depend on it: men will never come to Jesus, and stay with Jesus, and live for Jesus, unless they really know why they are to come, and what is their need. Those whom the Spirit draws to Jesus are those whom the Spirit has convinced of sin. Without thorough conviction of sin, men may seem to come to Jesus and follow Him for a season, but they will soon fall away and return to the world." *J. C. Ryle, Holiness*

11:52 *The Key to Reaching the Lost*

Have you ever thought, "There must be a key to reaching the lost"? There is—and it's rusty through lack of use. The Bible does actually call it "the key," and its purpose is to bring us to Christ, to unlock the Door of the Savior (John 10:9).

Much of the Church still doesn't even know it exists. Not only is it biblical, but it can be shown through history that the Church used it to unlock the doors of revival. The problem is that it was lost around the turn of the twentieth century. Keys have a way of getting lost.

Jesus used it. So did Paul (Romans 3:19,20), Timothy (1 Timothy 1:8–11), and James (James 2:10). Stephen used it when he preached (Acts 7:53). Peter found that it had been used to open the door to release 3,000 imprisoned souls on the Day of Pentecost. Jesus said that the lawyers had "taken away" the key, and even refused to use it to let people enter into the kingdom of God.

The Pharisees didn't take it away. Instead, they bent it out of shape so that it wouldn't do its work (Mark 7:8). Jesus returned it to its true shape, just as the Scriptures prophesied that He would do (Isaiah 42:21).

Satan has tried to prejudice the modern Church against the key. He has maligned it, misused it, twisted it, and, of course, hidden it—he hates it because of what it does. Perhaps you are wondering what this key is. I will tell you. All I ask is that you set aside your traditions and prejudices and look at what God's Word says on the subject.

In Acts 28:23 the Bible tells us that Paul sought to persuade his hearers "concerning Jesus, both out of the law of Moses, and out of the prophets." Here we have two effective means of persuading the unsaved "concerning Jesus."

Let's first look at how the prophets can help persuade sinners concerning Jesus. Fulfilled prophecy *proves* the inspiration of Scripture. The predictions of the prophets present a powerful case for the inspiration of the Bible. Any skeptic who reads the prophetic words of Isaiah, Ezekiel, Joel, etc., or the words of Jesus in Matthew 24 cannot but be challenged that this is no ordinary book.

The other means by which Paul persuaded sinners concerning Jesus was "out of the law of Moses." The Bible tells us that the Law of Moses is good if it is used lawfully (1 Timothy 1:8). It was given by God as a "schoolmaster" to bring us to Christ (Galatians 3:24). Paul wrote that he "had not known sin, but by the law" (Romans 7:7). The Law of God (the Ten Commandments) is evidently the "key of knowledge" Jesus spoke of in Luke 11:52. He was speaking to "lawyers"—those who should have been teaching God's Law so that sinners would receive the "knowledge of sin," and thus recognize their need of the Savior.

Prophecy speaks to the *intellect* of the sinner, while the Law speaks to his *conscience*. One produces *faith* in the Word of God; the other brings *knowledge* of sin in the heart of the sinner. The Law is the God-given "key" to unlock the Door of salvation. See Matthew 19:17–22 footnote and Romans 3:19,20.

"I do not believe that any man can preach the gospel who does not preach the Law. The Law is the needle, and you cannot draw the silken thread of the gospel through a man's heart unless you first send the needle of the Law to make way for it." *Charles Spurgeon*

things, and not one of them is forgotten before God?
7 But even the very hairs of your head are all numbered. Fear not therefore: you are of more value than many sparrows.
8 Also I say to you, Whosoever shall confess me before men, him shall the Son of man also confess before the angels of God:
9 **But he that denies me before men shall be denied before the angels of God.**
10 And whosoever shall speak a word

12:8 "Our Lord needs no secret agents! Those who are not willing to confess Christ publicly are not willing to confess Christ. Perhaps acceptance of Christ begins as a very personal and private experience, but it can never stay that way." *Guy Rice Doud, Joy in the Journey*

QUESTIONS & OBJECTIONS

12:20

"I'll wait until I am old, then I'll get right with God."

You may not get the chance. God may just lose patience with you and end your life. Perhaps you don't think He would do such a thing. Then read Genesis 38:7 to see how God killed a man who was wicked. Jesus told of a man who boasted that he had so many goods that he would have to build bigger barns. God called the man a fool and took his life that night.

Those who say they will repent in their own time lack the fear of God. Their understanding of His nature is erroneous. If they caught a glimpse of His holiness, His righteousness, and His consuming justice, they wouldn't trifle with His mercy. Such arrogance needs to be confronted with the thunders of Mount Sinai. He is not wise who thinks he can outwit his Creator, enjoy a lifetime of sin, and repent at the last minute. Deathbed repentance is very rare. God killed a husband and wife because they told a lie (Acts 5:1–10). He lost patience with them. Most people think that God's patience is eternal. It evidently is not. The Bible says that it is through the fear of the Lord that men depart from sin (Proverbs 16:6). If they don't fear God, they will be complacent about their eternal salvation (Matthew 10:28).

against the Son of man, it shall be forgiven him: but to him that blasphemes against the Holy Spirit it shall not be forgiven.
11 *And when they bring you to the synagogues, and to magistrates, and powers, take no thought how or what thing you shall answer, or what you shall say:*
12 *For the Holy Spirit shall teach you in the same hour what you ought to say.*
13 And one of the company said to him, Master, speak to my brother, that he divide the inheritance with me.
14 And he said to him, Man, who made me a judge or a divider over you?
15 **And he said to them, Take heed, and beware of covetousness: for a man's life consists not in the abundance of the things which he possesses.**
16 **And he spoke a parable to them, saying, The ground of a certain rich man brought forth plentifully:**
17 **And he thought within himself, saying, What shall I do, because I have no room where to bestow my fruits?**
18 **And he said, This will I do: I will pull down my barns, and build greater; and there will I bestow all my fruits and my goods.**
19 **And I will say to my soul, Soul, you have much goods laid up for many years; take your ease, eat, drink, and be merry.**
20 **But God said to him, You fool, this night your soul shall be required of you: then whose shall those things be, which you have provided?**
21 **So is he that lays up treasure for himself, and is not rich toward God.**
22 And he said to his disciples, Therefore I say to you, Take no thought for your life, what you shall eat; neither for the body, what you shall put on.
23 The life is more than meat, and the body is more than raiment.
24 Consider the ravens: for they neither sow nor reap; which neither have storehouse nor barn; and God feeds them: how much more are you better than the fowls?
25 And which of you with taking thought can add to his stature one cubit?
26 If you then be not able to do that thing which is least, why take thought for the rest?
27 Consider the lilies how they grow: they toil not, they spin not; and yet I say to you, that Solomon in all his glory was not arrayed like one of these.
28 If then God so clothe the grass, which is to day in the field, and tomorrow is cast into the oven; how much more will he

clothe you, O you of little faith?

29 And seek not what you shall eat, or what you shall drink, neither be of doubtful mind.

30 For all these things do the nations of the world seek after: and your Father knows that you have need of these things.

31 But rather seek the kingdom of God; and all these things shall be added to you.

32 Fear not, little flock; for it is your Father's good pleasure to give you the kingdom.

33 Sell what you have, and give alms; provide yourselves bags which wax not old, a treasure in the heavens that fails not, where no thief approaches, neither moth corrupts.

34 For where your treasure is, there will your heart be also.

35 *Let your loins be girded about, and your lights burning;*

36 *And you yourselves like to men that wait for their lord, when he will return from the wedding; that when he comes and knocks, they may open to him immediately.*

37 Blessed are those servants, whom the lord when he comes shall find watching: verily I say to you, that he shall gird himself, and make them to sit down to meat, and will come forth and serve them.

38 And if he shall come in the second watch, or come in the third watch, and find them so, blessed are those servants.

39 And this know, that if the goodman of the house had known what hour the thief would come, he would have watched, and not have suffered his house to be broken through.

40 Be therefore ready also: for the Son of man comes at an hour when you think not.

41 Then Peter said to him, Lord, speak you this parable to us, or even to all?

42 And the Lord said, Who then is that faithful and wise steward, whom his lord shall make ruler over his household, to give them their portion of meat in due season?

43 Blessed is that servant, whom his lord when he comes shall find so doing.

44 Of a truth I say to you, that he will make him ruler over all that he has.

45 But and if that servant say in his heart, My lord delays his coming; and shall begin to beat the menservants and maidens, and to eat and drink, and to be drunken;

46 The lord of that servant will come in a day when he looks not for him, and at an hour when he is not aware, and will cut him in sunder, and will appoint him his portion with the unbelievers.

47 And that servant, which knew his lord's will, and prepared not himself, neither did according to his will, shall be beaten with many stripes.

48 But he that knew not, and did commit things worthy of stripes, shall be beaten with few stripes. For to whomsoever much is given, of him shall be much required: and to whom men have committed much, of him they will ask the more.

49 I am come to send fire on the earth; and what will I if it be already kindled?

50 But I have a baptism to be baptized with; and how am I straitened till it be accomplished!

51 Suppose that I am come to give peace on earth? I tell you, Nay; but rather division:

52 For from henceforth there shall be five in one house divided, three against two, and two against three.

53 The father shall be divided against the son, and the son against the father; the mother against the daughter, and the daughter against the mother; the mother in law against her daughter in law, and the daughter in law against her mother in law.

54 And he said also to the people, When you see a cloud rise out of the west, straightway you say, There comes a shower; and so it is.

12:40 Second coming of Jesus: See Luke 21:27.

55 And when you see the south wind
blow, you say, There will be heat; and it
comes to pass.
56 You hypocrites, you can discern the
face of the sky and of the earth; but how
is it that you do not discern this time?
57 Yea, and why even of yourselves judge
you not what is right?
58 When you go with your adversary to
the magistrate, as you are in the way, give
diligence that you may be delivered from
him; lest he hale you to the judge, and the
judge deliver you to the officer, and the
officer cast you into prison.
59 I tell you, you shall not depart thence,
till you have paid the very last mite.

• • • • • •

Does God really expect us to be perfect? See Matthew 5:48 footnote.

• • • • • •

CHAPTER 13

THERE were present at that season some that told him of the Galilaeans, whose blood Pilate had mingled with their sacrifices.
2 And Jesus answering said to them, Sup-
pose that these Galilaeans were sinners
above all the Galilaeans, because they suffered such things?
**3 I tell you, Nay: but, except you re-
pent, you shall all likewise perish.**
4 Or those eighteen, upon whom the
tower in Siloam fell, and slew them, do
you think that they were sinners above
all men that dwelt in Jerusalem?
5 **I tell you, Nay: but, except you repent, you shall all likewise perish.**
6 He spoke also this parable; A certain
man had a fig tree planted in his vineyard;
and he came and sought fruit thereon,
and found none.
7 Then said he to the dresser of his vineyard, Behold, these three years I come
seeking fruit on this fig tree, and find none:
cut it down; why does it cumber the
ground?
8 And he answering said to him, Lord,
let it alone this year also, till I shall dig
about it, and dung it:
9 And if it bear fruit, well: and if not, then
after that you shall cut it down.
10 And he was teaching in one of the
synagogues on the sabbath.
11 And, behold, there was a woman
which had a spirit of infirmity eighteen
years, and was bowed together, and could
in no wise lift up herself.
12 And when Jesus saw her, he called her
to him, and said to her, Woman, you are
loosed from your infirmity.
13 And he laid his hands on her: and
immediately she was made straight, and
glorified God.
14 And the ruler of the synagogue answered with indignation, because that Jesus
had healed on the sabbath day, and said to
the people, There are six days in which
men ought to work: in them therefore
come and be healed, and not on the sabbath day.
15 The Lord then answered him, and
said, You hypocrite, does not each one of
you on the sabbath loose his ox or his ass
from the stall, and lead him away to wa-
tering?

13:2 Repentance—its necessity for salvation. See Luke 24:47.

13:3 Hosea 4:6 tells us why sinners will perish. "My people are destroyed for lack of knowledge: because you have rejected knowledge, I will also reject you . . . : seeing you have forgotten the law of your God, I will also forget your children." The reason God's people were destroyed was a lack of knowledge *of God's Law.* A sinner who is ignorant of the Moral Law has no understanding of the nature of sin (Romans 7:7–9). If he doesn't understand what sin is, he will not repent; and if he fails to repent, he will perish. He perishes through lack of knowledge of the Law.

"The gospel has not been clearly preached if the hearer doesn't know that not to make a decision is a decision." *Dan Arnold*

16 And ought not this woman, being a daughter of Abraham, whom Satan has bound, lo, these eighteen years, be loosed from this bond on the sabbath day?

17 And when he had said these things, all his adversaries were ashamed: and all the people rejoiced for all the glorious things that were done by him.

18 Then said he, to what is the kingdom of God like? and whereunto shall I resemble it?

19 It is like a grain of mustard seed, which a man took, and cast into his garden; and it grew, and waxed a great tree; and the fowls of the air lodged in the branches of it.

20 And again he said, Whereunto shall I liken the kingdom of God?

21 It is like leaven, which a woman took and hid in three measures of meal, till the whole was leavened.

22 And he went through the cities and villages, teaching, and journeying toward Jerusalem.

23 **Then said one to him, Lord, are there few that be saved? And he said to them,**

24 **Strive to enter in at the strait gate: for many, I say to you, will seek to enter in, and shall not be able.**

25 When once the master of the house is risen up, and has shut to the door, and you begin to stand without, and to knock at the door, saying, Lord, Lord, open to us; and he shall answer and say to you, I know not from where you are:

26 Then shall you begin to say, We have eaten and drunk in your presence, and you have taught in our streets.

27 But he shall say, I tell you, I know not from where you are; depart from me, all you workers of iniquity.

28 There shall be weeping and gnashing of teeth, when you shall see Abraham, and Isaac, and Jacob, and all the prophets, in the kingdom of God, and you yourselves thrust out.

29 And they shall come from the east, and from the west, and from the north, and from the south, and shall sit down in the kingdom of God.

30 And, behold, there are last which shall be first, and there are first which shall be last.

31 The same day there came certain of the Pharisees, saying to him, Get out, and depart hence: for Herod will kill you.

32 And he said to them, Go, and tell that fox, Behold, I cast out devils, and I do cures to day and tomorrow, and the third day I shall be perfected.

33 Nevertheless I must walk to day, and tomorrow, and the day following: for it cannot be that a prophet perish out of Jerusalem.

34 O Jerusalem, Jerusalem, which kills the prophets, and stones them that are sent to you; how often would I have gathered your children together, as a hen does gather her brood under her wings, and you would not!

35 Behold, your house is left to you desolate: and verily I say to you, You shall not see me, until the time come when you shall say, Blessed is he that comes in the name of the Lord.

CHAPTER 14

AND it came to pass, as he went into the house of one of the chief Pharisees to eat bread on the sabbath day, that they watched him.

2 And, behold, there was a certain man before him which had the dropsy.

3 And Jesus answering spoke to the lawyers and Pharisees, saying, Is it lawful to heal on the sabbath day?

4 And they held their peace. And he took him, and healed him, and let him go;

5 And answered them, saying, Which of

13:20,21 This is a picture of the false convert in the midst of God's people: "This shall have its accomplishment in the destruction of the corrupt and hypocritical part of the Church." *Matthew Henry*

QUESTIONS & OBJECTIONS

14:26 ***"Jesus taught hatred by saying that a Christian should 'hate' his father and mother."***

This is called "hyperbole"—a statement of extremes, contrasting love with hate for emphasis' sake. The Bible often does this (Proverbs 13:24; 29:24). Jesus tells us that the first and greatest Commandment is to love God with all of our heart, soul, and mind (Matthew 22:37,38). As much as we treasure our spouse and family, and even our own life, there should be no one whom we love and value more than God, no one who takes precedence in our life. To place love for another (including ourself) above God is idolatry.

you shall have an ass or an ox fallen into
a pit, and will not straightway pull him
out on the sabbath day?
6 And they could not answer him again
to these things.
7 And he put forth a parable to those
which were bidden, when he marked how
they chose out the chief rooms; saying to
them,
8 When you are bidden of any man to a
wedding, sit not down in the highest
room; lest a more honorable man than you
be bidden of him;
9 And he that bade you and him come
and say to you, Give this man place; and
you begin with shame to take the lowest
room.
10 But when you are bidden, go and sit
down in the lowest room; that when he
that bade you comes, he may say to you,
Friend, go up higher: then shall you have
worship in the presence of them that sit
at meat with you.
11 **For whosoever exalts himself shall
be abased; and he that humbles himself
shall be exalted.**
12 Then said he also to him that bade
him, When you make a dinner or a supper, call not your friends, nor your brethren, neither your kinsmen, nor your rich
neighbours; lest they also bid you again,
and a recompense be made you.
13 But when you make a feast, call the
poor, the maimed, the lame, the blind:
14 And you shall be blessed; for they
cannot recompense you: for you shall be
recompensed at the resurrection of the just.
15 And when one of them that sat at
meat with him heard these things, he said
to him, Blessed is he that shall eat bread in
the kingdom of God.
16 Then said he to him, A certain man
made a great supper, and bade many:
17 And sent his servant at supper time
to say to them that were bidden, Come;
for all things are now ready.
18 And they all with one consent began
to make excuse. The first said to him, I
have bought a piece of ground, and I must
needs go and see it: I pray you have me
excused.
19 And another said, I have bought five
yoke of oxen, and I go to prove them: I
pray you have me excused.
20 And another said, I have married a
wife, and therefore I cannot come.
21 So that servant came, and showed his
lord these things. Then the master of the
house being angry said to his servant, Go
out quickly into the streets and lanes of
the city, and bring in here the poor, and
the maimed, and the halt, and the blind.
22 And the servant said, Lord, it is done
as you have commanded, and yet there
is room.
23 *And the lord said to the servant, Go
out into the highways and hedges, and compel them to come in, that my house may be
filled.*
24 *For I say to you, That none of those
men which were bidden shall taste of my
supper.*
25 And there went great multitudes with
him: and he turned, and said to them,
**26 If any man come to me, and hate not
his father, and mother, and wife, and**

children, and brethren, and sisters, yea, and his own life also, he cannot be my disciple.

27 **And whosoever does not bear his cross, and come after me, cannot be my disciple.**

28 **For which of you, intending to build a tower, sits not down first, and counts the cost, whether he has sufficient to finish it?**

29 **Lest haply, after he has laid the foundation, and is not able to finish it, all that behold it begin to mock him,**

30 **Saying, This man began to build, and was not able to finish.**

31 **Or what king, going to make war against another king, sits not down first, and consults whether he be able with ten thousand to meet him that comes against him with twenty thousand?**

32 **Or else, while the other is yet a great way off, he sends an ambassage, and desires conditions of peace.**

33 **So likewise, whosoever he be of you that forsakes not all that he has, he cannot be my disciple.**

34 Salt is good: but if the salt have lost his savour, wherewith shall it be seasoned?

35 It is neither fit for the land, nor yet for the dunghill; but men cast it out. He that has ears to hear, let him hear.

CHAPTER 15

THEN drew near to him all the publicans and sinners for to hear him.

2 And the Pharisees and scribes murmured, saying, This man receives sinners, and eats with them.

3 **And he spoke this parable to them, saying,**

4 **What man of you, having an hundred sheep, if he lose one of them, does not leave the ninety and nine in the wilderness, and go after that which is lost, until he find it?**

5 **And when he has found it, he lays it**

"The salvation of a single soul is more important than the production or preservation of all the epics and tragedies in the world."

on his shoulders, rejoicing.

6 **And when he comes home, he calls together his friends and neighbours, saying to them, Rejoice with me; for I have found my sheep which was lost.**

7 **I say to you, that likewise joy shall be in heaven over one sinner that repents, more than over ninety and nine just persons, which need no repentance.**

8 **Either what woman having ten pieces of silver, if she lose one piece, does not light a candle, and sweep the house, and seek diligently till she find it?**

9 **And when she has found it, she calls her friends and her neighbours together, saying, Rejoice with me; for I have found the piece which I had lost.**

10 **Likewise, I say to you, there is joy in the presence of the angels of God over one sinner that repents.**

11 **And he said, A certain man had two sons:**

12 **And the younger of them said to his father, Father, give me the portion**

15:10 Heaven doesn't rejoice over those who make "decisions." It reserves its rejoicing for sinners who repent.

of goods that falls to me. And he divided to them his living.

13 **And not many days after the younger son gathered all together, and took his journey into a far country, and there wasted his substance with riotous living.**

14 **And when he had spent all, there arose a mighty famine in that land; and he began to be in want.**

15 **And he went and joined himself to a citizen of that country; and he sent him into his fields to feed swine.**

16 **And he would fain have filled his belly with the husks that the swine did eat: and no man gave to him.**

17 **And when he came to himself, he said, How many hired servants of my father's have bread enough and to spare, and I perish with hunger!**

18 **I will arise and go to my father, and will say to him, Father, I have sinned against heaven, and before you,**

19 **And am no more worthy to be called your son: make me as one of your hired servants.**

20 **And he arose, and came to his father. But when he was yet a great way off, his father saw him, and had compassion, and ran, and fell on his neck, and kissed him.**

21 And the son said to him, Father, I have sinned against heaven, and in your sight, and am no more worthy to be called your son.

22 **But the father said to his servants, Bring forth the best robe, and put it on him; and put a ring on his hand, and shoes on his feet:**

23 **And bring here the fatted calf, and kill it; and let us eat, and be merry:**

24 **For this my son was dead, and is alive again; he was lost, and is found. And they began to be merry.**

25 Now his elder son was in the field: and as he came and drew near to the house, he heard music and dancing.

26 And he called one of the servants, and asked what these things meant.

27 And he said to him, Your brother is come; and your father has killed the fatted calf, because he has received him safe and sound.

28 And he was angry, and would not go in: therefore came his father out, and entreated him.

29 And he answering said to his father, Lo, these many years do I serve you, neither transgressed I at any time your commandment: and yet you never gave me a kid, that I might make merry with my friends:

30 But as soon as this your son was come, which has devoured your living with harlots, you have killed for him the fatted calf.

31 And he said to him, Son, you are ever with me, and all that I have is yours.

32 It was meet that we should make merry, and be glad: for this your brother was dead, and is alive again; and was lost, and is found.

CHAPTER 16

AND he said also to his disciples, There was a certain rich man, which had a steward; and the same was accused to him that he had wasted his goods.

15:21 All sin is against God. Often sinners will try to justify their vices because there is no "victim" involved (such as in adult pornography). However, *all* sin is an offense against God. When Joseph was sexually propositioned by Potiphar's wife, he spoke of it as being a sin against God (Genesis 39:9). When David sinned with Bathsheba, he acknowledged that he had sinned against the LORD (2 Samuel 12:13). The prodigal son recognized that he had sinned against heaven (Luke 15:21). God is always the offended Party when someone commits sin. However, the real victim of sin will be the sinner. His sin will damn him, because he is a victim of his own foolishness.

15:32 "The evangelist who preaches for eternity is never great on numbers. He is not apt to count hundreds of converts where there is no restitution, no confession, and no glad cry which proclaims, "The lost is found, the dead is made alive again!" *E. M. Bounds*

2 And he called him, and said to him, How is it that I hear this of you? give an account of your stewardship; for you may be no longer steward.
3 Then the steward said within himself, What shall I do? for my lord takes away from me the stewardship: I cannot dig; to beg I am ashamed.
4 I am resolved what to do, that, when I am put out of the stewardship, they may receive me into their houses.
5 So he called every one of his lord's debtors to him, and said to the first, How much do you owe to my lord?
6 And he said, An hundred measures of oil. And he said to him, Take your bill, and sit down quickly, and write fifty.
7 Then said he to another, And how much do you owe? And he said, An hundred measures of wheat. And he said to him, Take your bill, and write fourscore.
8 And the lord commended the unjust steward, because he had done wisely: for the children of this world are in their generation wiser than the children of light.
9 And I say to you, Make to yourselves friends of the mammon of unrighteousness; that, when you fail, they may receive you into everlasting habitations.
10 He that is faithful in that which is least is faithful also in much: and he that is unjust in the least is unjust also in much.
11 If therefore you have not been faithful in the unrighteous mammon, who will commit to your trust the true riches?
12 And if you have not been faithful in that which is another man's, who shall give you that which is your own?
13 No servant can serve two masters: for either he will hate the one, and love the other; or else he will hold to the one, and despise the other. You cannot serve God and mammon.
14 And the Pharisees also, who were covetous, heard all these things: and they derided him.
15 And he said to them, You are they which justify yourselves before men; but God knows your hearts: for that which is highly esteemed among men is abomination in the sight of God.
16 The law and the prophets were until John: since that time the kingdom of God is preached, and every man presses into it.
17 And it is easier for heaven and earth to pass, than one tittle of the law to fail.
18 Whosoever puts away his wife, and marries another, commits adultery: and whosoever marries her that is put away from her husband commits adultery.
19 There was a certain rich man, which was clothed in purple and fine linen, and fared sumptuously every day:
20 And there was a certain beggar named Lazarus, which was laid at his gate, full of sores,
21 And desiring to be fed with the crumbs which fell from the rich man's table: moreover the dogs came and licked his sores.
22 And it came to pass, that the beggar died, and was carried by the angels into Abraham's bosom: the rich man also died, and was buried;
23 And in hell he lift up his eyes, being in torments, and saw Abraham afar off, and Lazarus in his bosom.
24 And he cried and said, Father Abraham, have mercy on me, and send Laza-

16:10 If I am not a straight-shooter with a pistol, He won't let me near the cannon.

16:13 If you were given $1,000 every time you witnessed to someone, would you be more zealous in your evangelism? If so, you are serving money rather than God.

16:15 A little girl was once looking at a sheep as it ate green grass. She thought to herself how nice and white the sheep looked against the green grass. Then it began to snow. The little girl then thought how dirty the sheep looked against the white snow. It was the same sheep, but with a different background. When we compare ourselves to the background of man's standards, we come up reasonably clean. However, when we compare ourselves to the snow-white righteousness of the Law of God, we see that we are all as an unclean thing, and our righteous deeds are as filthy rags (Isaiah 64:6).

SPRINGBOARDS FOR PREACHING AND WITNESSING

The Rush

16:17 You've always wanted to skydive, but the thought scared you too much to try it. That is, until you met someone who had made over 100 jumps. He talked you into it by explaining how safe it was. His enthusiasm was contagious. He spoke of the freedom of falling through the air...the adrenaline rush...the unspeakable exhilaration.

Now you are standing on the edge of a plane, looking down on the earth far, far below. Everything has been checked. *Double*-checked. This is safer than driving on the freeway—a thought that helps you deal with the fear. Modern parachutes are state-of-the-art. Besides, there is a backup chute. Still, your heart is beating with apprehension.

Suddenly, you *jump!* You have trained so much for this moment, you instinctively spread your hands and legs. The speed is unbelievable. The power of the air forcing itself against your body is incredible. It's like a dream. You are defying the law of gravity, racing through the air at more than 120 mph!

The earth is coming closer. All normal sense of time lost. Speed, thrust of air, unspeakable joy. You glance at the altimeter on your wrist. Only another ten seconds and you will pull the rip cord and feel the jolt of the parachute opening. All that you had been told was true. The adrenaline rush is like nothing you have experienced. If only it could last a little longer. Reluctantly, you pull the cord. It opens, *but there is no jolt!*

You tilt your head back to see a horrifying sight: the parachute has twisted and is trailing like a flapping streamer. Your heart races with fear, pounding in your chest. Your eyes bulge in terror. Your chest heaves as you gasp for air. You try to keep a clear mind and remember your training...pull the second cord. *Nothing happens!* You pull again. Again! Harder. *Harder!* Nothing. Your throat lets out a scream, a groan of panic. Your heart is pounding so hard you think your chest will burst. Sweat breaks through your skin. A thousand thoughts speed through your mind. Your family! Your fate!...Safer than driving on the freeway! You whisper, "What a fool I was...to think that I could defy the law of gravity." Now a merciless law waits for the moment of impact. The ground accelerates toward you. No words can describe the terror gripping your mind. A voice is speaking to you. It is the voice of good sense. It is the voice you ignored so often: "You have played the fool. You have given up your life, your most precious possession, for a cheap thrill. You have exchanged your loved ones for a rush of adrenaline. What a fool...*what a fool!*"

One word stands alone to describe how you feel about what you've done. One word screams within the corridors of your terrified mind as the earth races toward you, as death readies to embrace you. One word, a word that you have never understood fully until this moment. That terrible word is *remorse!*

The world, the flesh, and the devil whisper to you about how pleasurable sin is. That God isn't angry at sin. God is love. It is safe to jump into the arms of iniquity and abandon yourself to a free fall through its vast domain.

You go where angels fear to tread. But it is worth it. The rush is everything sin promised. You drink in iniquity like water. You love the darkness. Conscience speaks again and again, but you ignore its warning. You are defying the Moral Law and loving every minute.

Now you stand before the Judge on Judgment Day. You pull your first line by telling God what a good person you are. Nothing happens. The Moral Law rushes at you. In panic, you pull the second line and tell God that you believed in Him. *Again, nothing happens*. It is no use. Your mouth is stopped. The Moral Law accelerates toward you even faster, promising to so impact you that it will "grind you to powder" (Luke 20:18). Death and hell wait to embrace you. Unspeakable terror fills your heart. Conscience speaks so clearly now: "What a fool you have been. You rejected the mercy of God in Jesus Christ. You have given up your loved ones in exchange for the joys of a sinful lifestyle. You relinquished your most precious possession, *your very life*, for the cheap thrill of sin. What a fool! What a fool!" One word will stay with you for eternity. One

(continued on next page)

(16:17 continued)
word alone will echo forever within your tormented mind. Remorse! You whisper the word, "Remorse...*remorse*."

Suddenly you are staring at the ceiling of your bedroom, still mouthing the word through dry lips. *Remorse!* The sheets are soaked with sweat. *It was just a dream.* You look out the window and see the sun breaking through the green trees. It was just a dream! It's morning now. A peaceful new day. Today's the day you go skydiving. It will be your first time.

rus, that he may dip the tip of his finger in water, and cool my tongue; for I am tormented in this flame.
25 But Abraham said, Son, remember that you in your lifetime received your good things, and likewise Lazarus evil things: but now he is comforted, and you are tormented.
26 And beside all this, between us and you there is a great gulf fixed: so that they which would pass from here to you cannot; neither can they pass to us, that would come from thence.
27 Then he said, I pray you therefore, father, that you would send him to my father's house:
28 For I have five brethren; that he may testify to them, lest they also come into this place of torment.
29 Abraham said to him, They have Moses and the prophets; let them hear them.
30 And he said, Nay, father Abraham: but if one went to them from the dead, they will repent.
31 And he said to him, If they hear not Moses and the prophets, neither will they be persuaded, though one rose from the dead.

CHAPTER 17

THEN said he to the disciples, It is impossible but that offences will come: but woe to him, through whom they come!
2 It were better for him that a millstone were hanged about his neck, and he cast into the sea, than that he should offend one of these little ones.
3 Take heed to yourselves: If your brother trespass against you, rebuke him; and if he repent, forgive him.
4 And if he trespass against you seven times in a day, and seven times in a day turn again to you, saying, I repent; you shall forgive him.
5 And the apostles said to the Lord, Increase our faith.
6 And the Lord said, If you had faith as a grain of mustard seed, you might say to this sycamine tree, Be plucked up by the root, and be planted in the sea; and it should obey you.
7 But which of you, having a servant plowing or feeding cattle, will say to him by and by, when he is come from the field, Go and sit down to meat?
8 And will not rather say to him, Make ready wherewith I may sup, and gird yourself, and serve me, till I have eaten and drunken; and afterward you shall eat and drink?
9 Does he thank that servant because he did the things that were commanded him? I think not.
10 So likewise, when you shall have done all those things which are commanded you, say, We are unprofitable servants: we have done that which was our duty to do.
11 And it came to pass, as he went to Jerusalem, that he passed through the midst of Samaria and Galilee.

16:23 Hell: For verses warning of its reality, see Revelation 20:15.

16:24 "Love your fellowmen, and cry about them if you cannot bring them to Christ. If you cannot save them, you can weep over them. If you cannot give them a drop of water in hell, you can give them your heart's tears while they are still in this body." *Charles Spurgeon*

17:4 "Forgiveness is not just an occasional act: it is a permanent attitude." *Martin Luther King, Jr.*

12 And as he entered into a certain village, there met him ten men that were
lepers, which stood afar off:
13 And they lifted up their voices, and
said, Jesus, Master, have mercy on us.
14 And when he saw them, he said to
them, Go show yourselves to the priests.
And it came to pass, that, as they went,
they were cleansed.
15 And one of them, when he saw that
he was healed, turned back, and with a
loud voice glorified God,
16 And fell down on his face at his feet,
giving him thanks: and he was a Samaritan.
17 And Jesus answering said, Were there
not ten cleansed? but where are the nine?
18 There are not found that returned to
give glory to God, save this stranger.
19 And he said to him, Arise, go your
way: your faith has made you whole.
20 And when he was demanded of the
Pharisees, when the kingdom of God
should come, he answered them and said,
The kingdom of God comes not with ob-
servation:
21 Neither shall they say, Lo here! or, lo
there! for, behold, the kingdom of God
is within you.
22 And he said to the disciples, The days
will come, when you shall desire to see
one of the days of the Son of man, and
you shall not see it.
23 And they shall say to you, See here;
or, see there: go not after them, nor follow
them.
24 For as the lightning, that lightens out
of the one part under heaven, shines to
the other part under heaven; so shall
also the Son of man be in his day.
25 But first must he suffer many things,
and be rejected of this generation.
26 And as it was in the days of Noah,
so shall it be also in the days of the Son
of man.
27 They did eat, they drank, they married wives, they were given in marriage,
until the day that Noah entered into the
ark, and the flood came, and destroyed
them all.
28 Likewise also as it was in the days of
Lot; they did eat, they drank, they bought,
they sold, they planted, they built;
29 But the same day that Lot went out
of Sodom it rained fire and brimstone
from heaven, and destroyed them all.

> The conscience of a man, when he is really quickened and awakened by the Holy Spirit, speaks the truth. It rings the great alarm bell. And if he turns over in his bed, that great alarm bell rings out again and again, "The wrath to come! The wrath to come! The wrath to come."
>
> **CHARLES SPURGEON**

30 Even thus shall it be in the day when
the Son of man is revealed.
31 In that day, he which shall be upon
the housetop, and his stuff in the house,
let him not come down to take it away:
and he that is in the field, let him likewise
not return back.
32 Remember Lot's wife.
33 **Whosoever shall seek to save his**
life shall lose it; and whosoever shall
lose his life shall preserve it.
34 I tell you, in that night there shall be
two men in one bed; the one shall be
taken, and the other shall be left.
35 Two women shall be grinding together; the one shall be taken, and the
other left.
36 Two men shall be in the field; the
one shall be taken, and the other left.
37 And they answered and said to him,

17:26,27 Jesus referred to Noah as an actual historical person, and the Flood as a bona fide historical event. See Matthew 24:38,39 for details on the Flood.

17:32 Some dismiss the Book of Genesis as just an allegory, but Jesus believed the Genesis account of Lot's wife.

Where, Lord? And he said to them, Wherever the body is, there will the eagles be gathered together.

CHAPTER 18

AND he spoke a parable to them to this end, that men ought always to pray, and not to faint;
2 Saying, There was in a city a judge, which feared not God, neither regarded man:
3 And there was a widow in that city; and she came to him, saying, Avenge me of mine adversary.
4 And he would not for a while: but afterward he said within himself, Though I fear not God, nor regard man;
5 Yet because this widow troubles me, I will avenge her, lest by her continual coming she weary me.
6 And the Lord said, Hear what the unjust judge says.
7 And shall not God avenge his own elect, which cry day and night to him, though he bear long with them?
8 I tell you that he will avenge them speedily. Nevertheless when the Son of man comes, shall he find faith on the earth?
9 **And he spoke this parable to certain which trusted in themselves that they were righteous, and despised others:**
10 **Two men went up into the temple to pray; the one a Pharisee, and the other a publican.**
11 **The Pharisee stood and prayed thus with himself, God, I thank you, that I am not as other men are, extortioners, unjust, adulterers, or even as this publican.**
12 **I fast twice in the week, I give tithes of all that I possess.**

"To be a Christian without prayer is no more possible than to be alive without breathing."

Martin Luther

13 **And the publican, standing afar off, would not lift up so much as his eyes to heaven, but smote upon his breast, saying, God be merciful to me a sinner.**
14 **I tell you, this man went down to his house justified rather than the other: for every one that exalts himself shall be abased; and he that humbles himself shall be exalted.**
15 **And they brought to him also infants, that he would touch them: but when his disciples saw it, they rebuked them.**
16 **But Jesus called them to him, and said, Suffer little children to come to me, and forbid them not: for of such is the kingdom of God.**
17 **Verily I say to you, Whosoever shall not receive the kingdom of God as a lit-**

18:1 Prayerlessness. "Prayerlessness is an insult to God. Every prayerless day is a statement by a helpless individual, 'I do not need God today.' Failing to pray reflects idolatry—a trust in substitutes for God. We rely on our money instead of God's provision. We rest on our own flawed thinking rather than on God's perfect wisdom. We take charge of our lives rather than trusting God. Prayerlessness short-circuits the working of God. Neglecting prayer, therefore, is not a weakness; it is a sinful choice." *Ben Jennings, The Arena of Prayer*

QUESTIONS & OBJECTIONS

18:21 ***"What if someone says they've never lied, stolen, lusted, blasphemed—if they deny having any sin at all?"***

Ask the person if he has kept the First of the Ten Commandments. Has he always loved God above all else—with all of his heart, soul, mind, and strength (Mark 12:30)? If he says that he has, gently say, "The Bible says that 'there is none that seeks after God' (Romans 3:11). *Nobody* (except Jesus Christ) has kept the First of the Ten Commandments. One of you is lying—either you or God—and the Bible says that it is *impossible* for God to lie" (Hebrews 6:18; Titus 1:2).

tle child shall in no wise enter therein.
18 And a certain ruler asked him, saying, Good Master, what shall I do to inherit eternal life?
19 And Jesus said to him, Why call me good? none is good, save one, that is, God.
20 You know the commandments, Do not commit adultery, Do not kill, Do not steal, Do not bear false witness, Honor your father and your mother.
21 And he said, All these have I kept from my youth up.
22 Now when Jesus heard these things, he said to him, Yet you lack one thing: sell all that you have, and distribute to the poor, and you shall have treasure in heaven: and come, follow me.
23 And when he heard this, he was very sorrowful: for he was very rich.
24 And when Jesus saw that he was very sorrowful, he said, How hardly shall they that have riches enter into the kingdom of God!
25 For it is easier for a camel to go through a needle's eye, than for a rich man to enter into the kingdom of God.
26 And they that heard it said, Who then can be saved?
27 And he said, The things which are impossible with men are possible with God.
28 Then Peter said, Lo, we have left all, and followed you.
29 And he said to them, Verily I say to you, There is no man that has left house, or parents, or brethren, or wife, or children, for the kingdom of God's sake,
30 Who shall not receive manifold more in this present time, and in the world to come life everlasting.
31 Then he took to him the twelve, and said to them, Behold, we go up to Jerusalem, and all things that are written by the prophets concerning the Son of man shall be accomplished.
32 For he shall be delivered to the Gentiles, and shall be mocked, and spitefully entreated, and spitted on:
33 And they shall scourge him, and put him to death: and the third day he shall rise again.
34 And they understood none of these things: and this saying was hid from them, neither knew they the things which were spoken.
35 And it came to pass, that as he was come near to Jericho, a certain blind man sat by the way side begging:
36 And hearing the multitude pass by, he asked what it meant.
37 And they told him, that Jesus of Nazareth passes by.

18:20 Jesus gave him five "horizontal" Commandments having to do with his fellow man. When he said that he had kept them, Jesus then used the First of the Ten Commandments to show this man that his god was his money, and you cannot serve God and money.

18:24,25 There is hope for the rich: see Luke 19:2.

38 And he cried, saying, Jesus, you Son
of David, have mercy on me.
39 And they which went before rebuked
him, that he should hold his peace: but
he cried so much the more, You Son of
David, have mercy on me.
40 And Jesus stood, and commanded
him to be brought to him: and when he
was come near, he asked him,
41 Saying, What will you that I shall do
to you? And he said, Lord, that I may receive my sight.
42 And Jesus said to him, Receive your
sight: your faith has saved you.
43 And immediately he received his sight,
and followed him, glorifying God: and all
the people, when they saw it, gave praise
to God.

CHAPTER 19

AND Jesus entered and passed through
Jericho.
2 And, behold, there was a man named
Zacchaeus, which was the chief among
the publicans, and he was rich.
3 And he sought to see Jesus who he
was; and could not for the press, because
he was little of stature.
4 And he ran before, and climbed up into a sycamore tree to see him: for he was
to pass that way.
5 And when Jesus came to the place, he
looked up, and saw him, and said to him,
Zacchaeus, make haste, and come down;
for to day I must abide at your house.
6 And he made haste, and came down,
and received him joyfully.
7 And when they saw it, they all murmured, saying, That he was gone to be
guest with a man that is a sinner.
8 And Zacchaeus stood, and said to the
Lord; Behold, Lord, the half of my goods
I give to the poor; and if I have taken any
thing from any man by false accusation,
I restore him fourfold.
9 And Jesus said to him, This day is salvation come to this house, forasmuch as
he also is a son of Abraham.
**10 For the Son of man is come to seek
and to save that which was lost.**
11 And as they heard these things, he
added and spoke a parable, because he
was near to Jerusalem, and because they
thought that the kingdom of God should
immediately appear.
12 He said therefore, A certain nobleman
went into a far country to receive for himself a kingdom, and to return.
13 And he called his ten servants, and
delivered them ten pounds, and said to
them, Occupy till I come.
14 But his citizens hated him, and sent
a message after him, saying, We will not
have this man to reign over us.
15 And it came to pass, that when he
was returned, having received the kingdom, then he commanded these servants
to be called to him, to whom he had giv-
en the money, that he might know how
much every man had gained by trading.
16 Then came the first, saying, Lord,
your pound has gained ten pounds.
17 And he said to him, Well, you good
servant: because you have been faithful
in a very little, have authority over ten
cities.
18 And the second came, saying, Lord,
your pound has gained five pounds.
19 And he said likewise to him, Be also
over five cities.

19:10 "Christ said, 'I came into this world for one reason—to reach and save lost souls!' Yet, this was not only Jesus' mission. He made it our mission as well: 'And he said unto them, Go ye into all the world, and preach the gospel to every creature'" (Mark 16:15). *David Wilkerson*

19:17 "Dietrich Bonhoeffer wrote that 'only he who believes is obedient, and only he who is obedient believes.' Neither proposition can stand alone. Christians often think we are doing the Lord's work when we are not. Jesus himself warned us about this. We cannot serve two masters. The one we choose will determine whether at our death we hear, 'Well done, good and faithful servant,' or 'I never knew you.'" *Daniel L. Weiss*

20 And another came, saying, Lord, behold, here is your pound, which I have kept laid up in a napkin:
21 For I feared you, because you are an austere man: you take up that you laid not down, and reap that you did not sow.
22 And he said to him, Out of your own mouth will I judge you, you wicked servant. You knew that I was an austere man, taking up that I laid not down, and reaping that I did not sow:
23 Why didn't you then give my money into the bank, that at my coming I might have required mine own with usury?
24 And he said to them that stood by, Take from him the pound, and give it to him that has ten pounds.
25 (And they said to him, Lord, he has ten pounds.)
26 For I say to you, That to every one which has shall be given; and from him that has not, even that he has shall be taken away from him.

> He that pleads for Christ should himself be moved with the prospect of Judgment Day.
>
> **CHARLES SPURGEON**

27 But those mine enemies, which would not that I should reign over them, bring here, and slay them before me.
28 And when he had thus spoken, he went before, ascending up to Jerusalem.
29 And it came to pass, when he was come near to Bethphage and Bethany, at the mount called the mount of Olives, he sent two of his disciples,
30 Saying, Go into the village over against you; in the which at your entering you shall find a colt tied, whereon yet never man sat: loose him, and bring him here.
31 And if any man ask you, Why do you loose him? thus shall you say to him, Because the Lord has need of him.
32 And they that were sent went their way, and found even as he had said to them.
33 And as they were loosing the colt, the owners thereof said to them, Why do you loose the colt?
34 And they said, The Lord has need of him.
35 And they brought him to Jesus: and they cast their garments upon the colt, and they set Jesus thereon.
36 And as he went, they spread their clothes in the way.
37 And when he was come near, even now at the descent of the mount of Olives, the whole multitude of the disciples began to rejoice and praise God with a loud voice for all the mighty works that they had seen;
38 Saying, Blessed be the King that comes in the name of the Lord: peace in heaven, and glory in the highest.
39 And some of the Pharisees from among the multitude said to him, Master, rebuke your disciples.
40 And he answered and said to them, I tell you that, if these should hold their peace, the stones would immediately cry out.
41 And when he was come near, he beheld the city, and wept over it,
42 Saying, If you had known, even you, at least in this your day, the things which belong to your peace! but now they are hid from your eyes.
43 For the days shall come upon you, that your enemies shall cast a trench about you, and compass you round, and keep you in on every side,
44 And shall lay you even with the ground, and your children within you; and they shall not leave in you one stone upon another; because you knew not the time of your visitation.
45 And he went into the temple, and began to cast out them that sold therein, and them that bought;
46 Saying to them, It is written, My house is the house of prayer: but you have made it a den of thieves.
47 And he taught daily in the temple. But the chief priests and the scribes and the chief of the people sought to destroy

him,
48 And could not find what they might
do: for all the people were very attentive
to hear him.

CHAPTER 20

AND it came to pass, that on one of
those days, as he taught the people
in the temple, and preached the gospel,
the chief priests and the scribes came
upon him with the elders,
2 And spoke to him, saying, Tell us, by
what authority do you these things? or
who is he that gave you this authority?
3 And he answered and said to them, I
will also ask you one thing; and answer
me:
4 The baptism of John, was it from heav-
en, or of men?
5 And they reasoned with themselves,
saying, If we shall say, From heaven; he
will say, Why then did you not believe
him?
6 But and if we say, Of men; all the people will stone us: for they are persuaded
that John was a prophet.
7 And they answered, that they could not
tell whence it was.
8 And Jesus said to them, Neither tell I
you by what authority I do these things.
9 Then began he to speak to the people
this parable; A certain man planted a vineyard, and let it forth to husbandmen, and
went into a far country for a long time.
10 And at the season he sent a servant
to the husbandmen, that they should give
him of the fruit of the vineyard: but the
husbandmen beat him, and sent him away
empty.
11 And again he sent another servant:
and they beat him also, and entreated him
shamefully, and sent him away empty.
12 And again he sent a third: and they
wounded him also, and cast him out.
13 Then said the lord of the vineyard,
What shall I do? I will send my beloved
son: it may be they will reverence him
when they see him.
14 But when the husbandmen saw him,
they reasoned among themselves, saying,
This is the heir: come, let us kill him, that
the inheritance may be ours.
15 So they cast him out of the vineyard,
and killed him. What therefore shall the
lord of the vineyard do to them?
16 He shall come and destroy these husbandmen, and shall give the vineyard to
others. And when they heard it, they said,
God forbid.
17 And he beheld them, and said, What
is this then that is written, The stone
which the builders rejected, the same is
become the head of the corner?
18 **Whosoever shall fall upon that stone
shall be broken; but on whomsoever it
shall fall, it will grind him to powder.**
19 And the chief priests and the scribes
the same hour sought to lay hands on
him; and they feared the people: for they
perceived that he had spoken this parable against them.

> I would freely give my eyes if you might but see Christ, and I would willingly give my hands if you might but lay hold on Him.
>
> **CHARLES SPURGEON**

20 And they watched him, and sent forth
spies, which should feign themselves just
men, that they might take hold of his
words, that so they might deliver him to
the power and authority of the governor.
21 And they asked him, saying, Master,
we know that you say and teach rightly,
neither accept you the person of any, but
teach the way of God truly:
22 Is it lawful for us to give tribute to
Caesar, or no?
23 But he perceived their craftiness, and
said to them, Why tempt me?
24 Show me a penny. Whose image and
superscription has it? They answered and
said, Caesar's.
25 And he said to them, Render therefore
to Caesar the things which be Caesar's,
and to God the things which be God's.
26 And they could not take hold of his
words before the people: and they mar-

veled at his answer, and held their peace.
27 Then came to him certain of the Sadducees, which deny that there is any resurrection; and they asked him,
28 Saying, Master, Moses wrote to us, If
any man's brother die, having a wife, and
he die without children, that his brother
should take his wife, and raise up seed to
his brother.
29 There were therefore seven brethren:
and the first took a wife, and died without children.
30 And the second took her to wife, and
he died childless.
31 And the third took her; and in like
manner the seven also: and they left no
children, and died.
32 Last of all the woman died also.
33 Therefore in the resurrection whose
wife of them is she? for seven had her to
wife.
34 And Jesus answering said to them,
The children of this world marry, and are
given in marriage:
35 But they which shall be accounted
worthy to obtain that world, and the resurrection from the dead, neither marry, nor
are given in marriage:
36 Neither can they die any more: for
they are equal to the angels; and are the
children of God, being the children of the
resurrection.
37 Now that the dead are raised, even
Moses showed at the bush, when he calls
the Lord the God of Abraham, and the
God of Isaac, and the God of Jacob.
38 For he is not a God of the dead, but
of the living: for all live to him.
39 Then certain of the scribes answering
said, Master, you have well said.
40 And after that they dared not ask him
any question at all.
41 And he said to them, How say they
that Christ is David's son?
42 And David himself said in the book of
Psalms, The LORD said to my Lord, Sit you
on my right hand,
43 Till I make your enemies your footstool.
44 David therefore calls him Lord, how
is he then his son?
45 Then in the audience of all the people
he said to his disciples,
46 Beware of the scribes, which desire
to walk in long robes, and love greetings
in the markets, and the highest seats in
the synagogues, and the chief rooms at
feasts;
47 Which devour widows' houses, and
for a show make long prayers: the same
shall receive greater damnation.

CHAPTER 21

AND he looked up, and saw the rich
men casting their gifts into the treasury.
2 And he saw also a certain poor widow
casting in there two mites.
3 And he said, Of a truth I say to you,
that this poor widow has cast in more
than they all:
4 For all these have of their abundance
cast in to the offerings of God: but she of
her penury has cast in all the living that
she had.
5 And as some spoke of the temple, how
it was adorned with goodly stones and
gifts, he said,
6 As for these things which you behold,
the days will come, in the which there
shall not be left one stone upon another,
that shall not be thrown down.
7 And they asked him, saying, Master,
but when shall these things be? and what
sign will there be when these things shall
come to pass?
8 And he said, Take heed that you be
not deceived: for many shall come in my
name, saying, I am Christ; and the time
draws near: go not therefore after them.
9 But when you shall hear of wars and
commotions, be not terrified: for these

20:47 See Matthew 11:24 footnote.

21:7 For more signs of the end times, see 1 Timothy 4:1.

Questions & Objections

21:24

"If the Jews are God's 'chosen people,' why have they been so oppressed?"

Israel's blessings were dependent upon her obedience. If the nation sinned, it would be chastened. This is God's warning to the Jews, followed by His promised restoration: "The Lord shall scatter you among all people, from the one end of the earth to the other, and there you shall serve other gods, which neither you nor your fathers have known, even wood and stone. And among these nations shall you find no ease, neither shall the sole of your foot have rest: but the Lord shall give you there a trembling heart, and failing eyes, and sorrow of mind" (Deuteronomy 28:64,65).

"In the latter years you shall come into the land that is brought back from the sword, and is gathered out of many people, against the mountains of Israel, which have been always waste: but it is brought forth out of the nations, and they shall dwell safely all of them" (Ezekiel 38:8).

things must first come to pass; but the end
is not by and by.
10 Then said he to them, Nation shall rise
against nation, and kingdom against kingdom:
11 And great earthquakes shall be in divers places, and famines, and pestilences;
and fearful sights and great signs shall
there be from heaven.
12 But before all these, they shall lay
their hands on you, and persecute you,
delivering you up to the synagogues, and
into prisons, being brought before kings
and rulers for my name's sake.
13 And it shall turn to you for a testimony.
14 Settle it therefore in your hearts, not
to meditate before what you shall answer:
15 For I will give you a mouth and wisdom, which all your adversaries shall not
be able to gainsay nor resist.
16 And you shall be betrayed both by
parents, and brethren, and kinsfolks, and
friends; and some of you shall they cause
to be put to death.
17 And you shall be hated of all men for
my name's sake.
18 But there shall not an hair of your
head perish.
19 In your patience possess your souls.
20 And when you shall see Jerusalem
compassed with armies, then know that
the desolation thereof is near.
21 Then let them which are in Judea flee
to the mountains; and let them which
are in the midst of it depart out; and let
not them that are in the countries enter
therein.
22 For these be the days of vengeance,
that all things which are written may be
fulfilled.
23 But woe to them that are with child,
and to them that give suck, in those days!
for there shall be great distress in the
land, and wrath upon this people.
24 And they shall fall by the edge of the
sword, and shall be led away captive into
all nations: and Jerusalem shall be trodden down of the Gentiles, until the times
of the Gentiles be fulfilled.
25 And there shall be signs in the sun,
and in the moon, and in the stars; and upon the earth distress of nations, with per-
plexity; the sea and the waves roaring;
26 Men's hearts failing them for fear,
and for looking after those things which

21:26 It has been said that there are three types of people in this world: those who are fearful, those who don't know enough to be fearful, and those who know their Bibles.

are coming on the earth: for the powers
of heaven shall be shaken.
27 And then shall they see the Son of
man coming in a cloud with power and
great glory.
28 And when these things begin to come
to pass, then look up, and lift up your
heads; for your redemption draws near.
29 And he spoke to them a parable; Behold the fig tree, and all the trees;
30 When they now shoot forth, you see
and know of your own selves that summer
is now near at hand.
31 So you likewise, when you see these
things come to pass, know that the kingdom of God is near at hand.
32 Verily I say to you, This generation
shall not pass away, till all be fulfilled.
33 Heaven and earth shall pass away:
but my words shall not pass away.
34 And take heed to yourselves, lest at
any time your hearts be overcharged with
surfeiting, and drunkenness, and cares of
this life, and so that day come upon you
unawares.
35 For as a snare shall it come on all
them that dwell on the face of the whole
earth.
36 Watch therefore, and pray always, that
you may be accounted worthy to escape
all these things that shall come to pass, and
to stand before the Son of man.
37 And in the day time he was teaching
in the temple; and at night he went out,
and abode in the mount that is called the
mount of Olives.
38 And all the people came early in the
morning to him in the temple, for to hear
him.

CHAPTER 22

NOW the feast of unleavened bread
drew near, which is called the Passover.

21:26 Russia and Israel. A number of books of the Bible speak of future events. Ezekiel 38 (written approximately 600 B.C.) prophesies that in these times ("the latter days," v. 16), Russia (referred to as the "Prince of Rosh," see *Smith's Bible Dictionary*, p. 584) will combine with Iran, Libya (in Hebrew called "Put"), and communistic Ethiopia (in Hebrew called "Cush") and attack Israel (vv. 5–8). This will take place after an Israeli peace initiative has been successful (v. 11). The Bible even gives the Russian reasoning for and the direction of the attack (vv. 10–15), as well as the location of the battle (Armageddon—Revelation 16:16). This is generally interpreted as meaning "the mountain of Megiddo," which is located on the north side of the plains of Jezreel. Russia has had a foothold in the Middle East for many years: "The Soviets are entrenched around the rim of the Middle East heartland, in Afghanistan, South Yemen, Ethiopia, and Libya" ("Countdown in the Middle East," *Reader's Digest*, May 1982).

Israel will never have lasting peace until she obeys God. If she will obey His statutes and keep His commandments, He will give her rain in due season, an abundance of food, freedom from fear, victory over the enemy, and peace within the land (Leviticus 26:1–13). Sadly, from what we see of the Scriptures, Israel will only seek God as a last resort, when she sees that she cannot prevail against the might and power of the Russian invasion (Joel 2:12–20). Deuteronomy 4:30 gives warning that it would take tribulation to turn Israel to God in the latter days. When Israel finally turns to God in true repentance, He will take pity on His people and remove far from them the "northern army" (Joel 2:20).

Another sign of the latter days will be a clear understanding of the judgments and the will of God. No other generation has seen Russia mustering forces against Israel, the Arab-Israeli conflict in the Middle East and the Jews in Jerusalem. No other generation has had the scientific knowledge to help it understand "strange" Scriptures, nor have they had access to the Bible as we have. We can understand perfectly the times in which we live: "The anger of the Lord shall not return, until he have executed, and till he have performed the thoughts of his heart: in the latter days you shall consider it perfectly" (Jeremiah 23:20). Keep one eye on the Middle East—and the other toward the heavens. See also Revelation 9:9 and 16:16 footnotes.

21:27 Second coming of Jesus: See Acts 1:11.

2 And the chief priests and scribes sought
how they might kill him; for they feared
the people.
3 Then entered Satan into Judas surnamed
Iscariot, being of the number of the twelve.
4 And he went his way, and communed
with the chief priests and captains, how he
might betray him to them.
5 And they were glad, and covenanted
to give him money.
6 And he promised, and sought opportunity to betray him to them in the absence of the multitude.
7 Then came the day of unleavened bread,
when the passover must be killed.
8 And he sent Peter and John, saying, Go
and prepare us the passover, that we may
eat.
9 And they said to him, Where will you
that we prepare?
10 And he said to them, Behold, when
you are entered into the city, there shall
a man meet you, bearing a pitcher of water; follow him into the house where he
enters in.
11 And you shall say to the goodman of
the house, The Master said to you, Where
is the guestchamber, where I shall eat the
passover with my disciples?
12 And he shall show you a large upper
room furnished: there make ready.
13 And they went, and found as he had
said to them: and they made ready the
passover.
14 And when the hour was come, he sat
down, and the twelve apostles with him.
15 And he said to them, With desire I
have desired to eat this passover with you
before I suffer:
16 For I say to you, I will not any more
eat thereof, until it be fulfilled in the kingdom of God.
17 And he took the cup, and gave thanks,
and said, Take this, and divide it among
yourselves:
18 For I say to you, I will not drink of the
fruit of the vine, until the kingdom of God
shall come.
19 And he took bread, and gave thanks,
and broke it, and gave to them, saying,
This is my body which is given for you:
this do in remembrance of me.
20 Likewise also the cup after supper,
saying, This cup is the new testament in
my blood, which is shed for you.
21 But, behold, the hand of him that betrays me is with me on the table.
22 And truly the Son of man goes, as it
was determined: but woe to that man by
whom he is betrayed!
23 And they began to inquire among
themselves, which of them it was that
should do this thing.
24 And there was also a strife among
them, which of them should be accounted
the greatest.
25 And he said to them, The kings of the
Gentiles exercise lordship over them; and
they that exercise authority upon them
are called benefactors.
26 But you shall not be so: but he that
is greatest among you, let him be as the
younger; and he that is chief, as he that
does serve.
27 For whether is greater, he that sits at
meat, or he that serves? is not he that sits
at meat? but I am among you as he that
serves.
28 You are they which have continued
with me in my temptations.
29 And I appoint to you a kingdom, as
my Father has appointed to me;
30 That you may eat and drink at my
table in my kingdom, and sit on thrones
judging the twelve tribes of Israel.
31 And the Lord said, Simon, Simon, behold, Satan has desired to have you, that
he may sift you as wheat:
32 But I have prayed for you, that your
faith fail not: and when you are converted, strengthen your brethren.
33 And he said to him, Lord, I am ready
to go with you, both into prison, and to
death.
34 And he said, I tell you, Peter, the cock
shall not crow this day, before that you
shall thrice deny that you know me.
35 And he said to them, When I sent
you without purse, and scrip, and shoes,
did you lack any thing? And they said,

Nothing.
36 Then said he to them, But now, he
that has a purse, let him take it, and likewise his scrip: and he that has no sword,
let him sell his garment, and buy one.
37 For I say to you, that this that is written must yet be accomplished in me,
And he was reckoned among the transgressors: for the things concerning me
have an end.
38 And they said, Lord, behold, here are
two swords. And he said to them, It is
enough.
39 And he came out, and went, as he
was wont, to the mount of Olives; and his
disciples also followed him.
40 And when he was at the place, he said
to them, Pray that you enter not into temptation.
41 And he was withdrawn from them
about a stone's cast, and kneeled down,
and prayed,
42 Saying, Father, if you be willing, remove this cup from me: nevertheless not
my will, but yours, be done.
43 And there appeared an angel to him
from heaven, strengthening him.
44 And being in an agony he prayed
more earnestly: and his sweat was as it
were great drops of blood falling down to
the ground.

"He who kneels the most, stands best."

D. L. Moody

45 And when he rose up from prayer,
and was come to his disciples, he found
them sleeping for sorrow,
46 And said to them, Why do you sleep?
rise and pray, lest you enter into temptation.
47 And while he yet spoke, behold a
multitude, and he that was called Judas,
one of the twelve, went before them, and
drew near to Jesus to kiss him.

22:31,32 The purpose of sifting. "In Luke 22:31, the word *sift* is translated from the Greek *siniazo*, meaning 'to sift, shake in a sieve; by inward agitation to try one's faith to the verge of overthrow.'

"Jesus did not pray that Simon Peter would escape this intense shaking. He prayed that his faith would not fail in the process…Satan had requested permission to shake Simon Peter so severely that he would lose his faith, but God had a different purpose for the shaking. He allowed the enemy to shake everything in Simon Peter that *needed* to be shaken.

"There are five purposes for shaking an object: 1) to bring it closer to its foundation; 2) to remove what is dead; 3) to harvest what is ripe; 4) to awaken it; and 5) to unify or mix together so it can no longer be separated. As a result of this tremendous shaking, all of Simon Peter's self-confidence would be gone, and all that would remain was God's sure foundation. He would be awakened to his true condition, the dead would be removed and the ripe fruit harvested, bringing him closer to his true foundation. He would no longer function independently but would be interdependent on the Lord." *John Bevere, The Bait of Satan*

22:41 Prayer—the secret weapon: See Acts 1:14.

22:44 This is not just hyperbole like "sweating bullets," but is an actual medical condition known as *hematidrosis*.

48 But Jesus said to him, Judas, do you betray the Son of man with a kiss?
49 When they which were about him saw what would follow, they said to him, Lord, shall we smite with the sword?
50 And one of them smote the servant of the high priest, and cut off his right ear.
51 And Jesus answered and said, Suffer you thus far. And he touched his ear, and healed him.
52 Then Jesus said to the chief priests, and captains of the temple, and the elders, which were come to him, Have you come out, as against a thief, with swords and staves?
53 When I was daily with you in the temple, you stretched forth no hands against me: but this is your hour, and the power of darkness.
54 Then took they him, and led him, and brought him into the high priest's house. And Peter followed afar off.
55 And when they had kindled a fire in the midst of the hall, and were set down together, Peter sat down among them.
56 But a certain maid beheld him as he sat by the fire, and earnestly looked upon him, and said, This man was also with him.
57 And he denied him, saying, Woman, I know him not.
58 And after a little while another saw him, and said, You are also of them. And Peter said, Man, I am not.
59 And about the space of one hour after another confidently affirmed, saying, Of a truth this fellow also was with him: for he is a Galilaean.
60 And Peter said, Man, I know not what you say. And immediately, while he yet spoke, the cock crew.
61 And the Lord turned, and looked upon Peter. And Peter remembered the word of the Lord, how he had said to him, Before the cock crow, you shall deny me thrice.
62 And Peter went out, and wept bitterly.
63 And the men that held Jesus mocked him, and smote him.
64 And when they had blindfolded him, they struck him on the face, and asked him, saying, Prophesy, who is it that smote you?
65 And many other things blasphemously spoke they against him.
66 And as soon as it was day, the elders of the people and the chief priests and the scribes came together, and led him into their council, saying,
67 Are you the Christ? tell us. And he said to them, If I tell you, you will not believe:
68 And if I also ask you, you will not answer me, nor let me go.
69 Hereafter shall the Son of man sit on the right hand of the power of God.
70 Then said they all, are you then the Son of God? And he said to them, You say that I am.
71 And they said, What need we any further witness? for we ourselves have heard of his own mouth.

22:47 Modern evangelism. The Bible tells us that Judas led a "multitude" to Jesus. His motive, however, wasn't to bring them to the Savior for salvation. Modern evangelism is also bringing "multitudes" to Jesus. Their motive may be different from Judas's, but the end result is the same. Just as the multitudes that Judas directed to Christ fell back from the Son of God, statistics show that up to 90% of those coming to Christ under the methods of modern evangelism fall away from the faith. Their latter end becomes worse than the first. They openly crucify the Son of God afresh.

In their zeal without knowledge, those who prefer the ease of modern evangelism to biblical evangelism betray the cause of the gospel with a kiss. What may look like love for the sinner's welfare is in truth eternally detrimental to him.

Like Peter (v. 51), our zeal without knowledge is actually cutting off the ears of sinners. Those we erroneously call "backsliders" won't listen to our reasonings. As far as they are concerned, they have tried it once, and it didn't work. What a victory for the prince of darkness, and what an unspeakable tragedy for the Church!

CHAPTER 23

AND the whole multitude of them
arose, and led him to Pilate.
2 And they began to accuse him, saying,
We found this fellow perverting the nation, and forbidding to give tribute to Caesar, saying that he himself is Christ a King.
3 And Pilate asked him, saying, are you
the King of the Jews? And he answered
him and said, You say it.
4 Then said Pilate to the chief priests and
to the people, I find no fault in this man.
5 And they were the more fierce, saying,
He stirs up the people, teaching throughout all Jewry, beginning from Galilee to
this place.
6 When Pilate heard of Galilee, he asked
whether the man were a Galilaean.
7 And as soon as he knew that he belonged to Herod's jurisdiction, he sent
him to Herod, who himself also was at
Jerusalem at that time.
8 And when Herod saw Jesus, he was exceeding glad: for he was desirous to see
him of a long season, because he had
heard many things of him; and he hoped
to have seen some miracle done by him.
9 Then he questioned with him in many
words; but he answered him nothing.
10 And the chief priests and scribes stood
and vehemently accused him.
11 And Herod with his men of war set
him at nought, and mocked him, and arrayed him in a gorgeous robe, and sent
him again to Pilate.
12 And the same day Pilate and Herod
were made friends together: for before
they were at enmity between themselves.
13 And Pilate, when he had called together the chief priests and the rulers and the
people,
14 Said to them, You have brought this
man to me, as one that perverts the people: and, behold, I, having examined him
before you, have found no fault in this
man touching those things whereof you
accuse him:
15 No, nor yet Herod: for I sent you to
him; and, lo, nothing worthy of death is
done to him.
16 I will therefore chastise him, and release him.
17 (For of necessity he must release one
to them at the feast.)
18 And they cried out all at once, saying,
Away with this man, and release to us Barabbas:
19 (Who for a certain sedition made in
the city, and for murder, was cast into prison.)
20 Pilate therefore, willing to release
Jesus, spoke again to them.
21 But they cried, saying, Crucify him,
crucify him.
22 And he said to them the third time,
Why, what evil has he done? I have found
no cause of death in him: I will therefore
chastise him, and let him go.
23 And they were instant with loud voices, requiring that he might be crucified.
And the voices of them and of the chief
priests prevailed.
24 And Pilate gave sentence that it should
be as they required.
25 And he released to them him that for
sedition and murder was cast into prison,
whom they had desired; but he delivered
Jesus to their will.
26 And as they led him away, they laid
hold upon one Simon, a Cyrenian, coming out of the country, and on him they
laid the cross, that he might bear it after
Jesus.
27 And there followed him a great company of people, and of women, which also
bewailed and lamented him.
28 But Jesus turning to them said, Daughters of Jerusalem, weep not for me, but
weep for yourselves, and for your children.
29 For, behold, the days are coming, in
the which they shall say, Blessed are the
barren, and the wombs that never bare,
and the paps which never gave suck.
30 Then shall they begin to say to the
mountains, Fall on us; and to the hills,
Cover us.
31 For if they do these things in a green
tree, what shall be done in the dry?
32 And there were also two other, malefactors, led with him to be put to death.

33 And when they were come to the
place, which is called Calvary, there they
crucified him, and the malefactors, one on
the right hand, and the other on the left.
34 Then said Jesus, Father, forgive them;
for they know not what they do. And they
parted his raiment, and cast lots.
35 And the people stood beholding. And
the rulers also with them derided him,
saying, He saved others; let him save himself, if he be Christ, the chosen of God.
36 And the soldiers also mocked him,
coming to him, and offering him vinegar,
37 And saying, If you be the king of the
Jews, save yourself.
38 And a superscription also was written over him in letters of Greek, and Latin, and Hebrew, THIS IS THE KING OF
THE JEWS.
39 And one of the malefactors which
were hanged railed on him, saying, If you
be Christ, save yourself and us.
40 But the other answering rebuked him,
saying, Do you not fear God, seeing you
are in the same condemnation?
41 And we indeed justly; for we receive
the due reward of our deeds: but this man
has done nothing amiss.
42 And he said to Jesus, Lord, remember
me when you come into your kingdom.
43 And Jesus said to him, Verily I say to
you, To day shall you be with me in paradise.
44 And it was about the sixth hour, and
there was a darkness over all the earth
until the ninth hour.
45 And the sun was darkened, and the
veil of the temple was rent in the midst.
46 And when Jesus had cried with a loud
voice, he said, Father, into your hands I
commend my spirit: and having said thus,
he gave up the ghost.
47 Now when the centurion saw what
was done, he glorified God, saying, Certainly this was a righteous man.
48 And all the people that came together to that sight, beholding the things which
were done, smote their breasts, and returned.
49 And all his acquaintance, and the women that followed him from Galilee, stood
afar off, beholding these things.
50 And, behold, there was a man named
Joseph, a counsellor; and he was a good
man, and a just:
51 (The same had not consented to the
counsel and deed of them;) he was of Arimathaea, a city of the Jews: who also himself waited for the kingdom of God.
52 This man went to Pilate, and begged
the body of Jesus.
53 And he took it down, and wrapped it
in linen, and laid it in a sepulchre that was
hewn in stone, wherein never man before
was laid.
54 And that day was the preparation,
and the sabbath drew on.
55 And the women also, which came with
him from Galilee, followed after, and beheld the sepulchre, and how his body was
laid.
56 And they returned, and prepared
spices and ointments; and rested the sabbath day according to the commandment.

CHAPTER 24

NOW upon the first day of the week,
very early in the morning, they came
to the sepulchre, bringing the spices which
they had prepared, and certain others with
them.
2 And they found the stone rolled away
from the sepulchre.
3 And they entered in, and found not
the body of the Lord Jesus.
4 And it came to pass, as they were
much perplexed thereabout, behold, two
men stood by them in shining garments:
5 **And as they were afraid, and bowed
down their faces to the earth, they said**

23:32–34 Messianic prophecy fulfilled: "He has poured out his soul unto death: and he was numbered with the transgressors, and he bare the sin of many, and made intercession for the transgressors" (Isaiah 53:12). See Luke 24:39 footnote.

23:53 *The Hands of the Carpenter*

It was Joseph of Arimathaea who had the honor of taking the body of Jesus down from the cross. Think what it would be like to have to pull the cold and lifeless hands of the Son of God from the thick, barbed Roman nails. These were carpenter's hands, which once held nails and wood, now being held by nails and wood. These were the hands that broke bread and fed multitudes, now being broken to feed multitudes. They once applied clay to a blind man's eyes, touched lepers, healed the sick, washed the disciple's feet, and took children in His arms. These were the hands that, more than once, loosed the cold hand of death, now held firmly by its icy grip.

These were the fingers that wrote in the sand when the adulterous woman was cast at His feet, and for the love of God, fashioned a whip that purged His Father's house. These were the same fingers that took bread and dipped it in a dish, and gave it to Judas as a gesture of deep love and friendship. Here was the Bread of Life itself, being dipped in the cup of suffering, as the ultimate gesture of God's love for the evil world that Judas represented.

Joseph's shame, that he had been afraid to own the Savior, sickened him as he tore the blood-sodden feet from the six-inch cold steel spikes that fastened them to the cross. These were the "beautiful feet" of Him that preached the gospel of peace, that Mary washed with her hair, that walked upon the Sea of Galilee, now crimson with a sea of blood.

As Joseph reached out his arms to get Him down from the cross, perhaps he stared for an instant at the inanimate face of the Son of God. His heart wrenched as he looked upon Him whom they had pierced. This face, which once radiated with the glory of God on the Mount of Transfiguration, which so many had looked upon with such veneration, was now blood-stained from the needle-sharp crown of thorns, deathly pale and twisted from unspeakable suffering as the sin of the world was laid upon Him.

His eyes, which once sparkled with the life of God, now stared at nothingness, as He was brought into the dust of death. His lips, which spoke such gracious words and calmed the fears of so many, were swollen and bruised from the beating given to Him by the hardened fists of cruel soldiers.

As it is written, "His visage was so marred more than any man" (Isaiah 52:14).

Nicodemus may have reached up to help Joseph with the body. As the cold blood of the Lamb of God covered his hand he was reminded of the blood of the Passover lamb he had seen shed so many times. The death of each spotless animal had been so quick and merciful, but this death had been unspeakably cruel, vicious, inhumane, and brutal. It seemed that all the hatred that sin-loving humanity had for the Light formed itself into a dark and evil spear, and was thrust with cruel delight into the perfect Lamb of God.

Perhaps as he carefully pried the crown from His head, looked at the gaping hole in His side, the deep mass of abrasions upon His back, and the mutilated wounds in His hands and feet, a sense of outrage engrossed him, that this could happen to such a Man as this. But the words of the prophet Isaiah rang within his heart:

> "He was wounded for our transgressions, he was bruised for our iniquities ...the Lord has laid on him the iniquity of us all...as a lamb to the slaughter ...for the transgression of my people he was stricken...yet it pleased the Lord to bruise him...by his knowledge shall my righteous servant justify many" (Isaiah 53:5–11).

Jesus of Nazareth was stripped of His robe, that we might be robed in pure righteousness. He suffered a deathly thirst, that our thirst for life might be quenched. He agonized under the curse of the Law, that we might relish the blessing of the gospel. He took upon Himself the hatred of the world, so that we could experience the love of God. Hell was let loose upon Him so that heaven could be let loose upon us. Jesus of Nazareth tasted the bitterness of death, so that we might taste the sweetness of life everlasting. The Son of God willingly passed over His life, that death might freely pass over the sons and daughters of Adam.

(continued on next page)

(23:53 continued)

May Calvary's cross be as real to us as it was to those who stood on its bloody soil on that terrible day. May we also gaze upon the face of the crucified Son of God, and may shame grip our hearts if ever the fear of man comes near our souls. May we identify with the apostle Paul, who could have gloried in his dramatic and miraculous experience on the road to Damascus. Instead, he whispered in awe of God's great love:

> "God forbid that I should glory, save in the cross of our Lord Jesus Christ, by whom the world is crucified unto me, and I unto the world" (Galatians 6:14).

to them, Why do you seek the living among the dead?
6 **He is not here, but is risen: remember how he spoke to you when he was yet in Galilee,**
7 **Saying, The Son of man must be delivered into the hands of sinful men, and be crucified, and the third day rise again.**
8 And they remembered his words,
9 And returned from the sepulchre, and told all these things to the eleven, and to all the rest.
10 It was Mary Magdalene, and Joanna, and Mary the mother of James, and other women that were with them, which told these things to the apostles.
11 And their words seemed to them as idle tales, and they believed them not.
12 Then arose Peter, and ran to the sepulchre; and stooping down, he beheld the linen clothes laid by themselves, and departed, wondering in himself at that which was come to pass.
13 And, behold, two of them went that same day to a village called Emmaus, which was from Jerusalem about threescore furlongs.
14 And they talked together of all these things which had happened.
15 And it came to pass, that, while they communed together and reasoned, Jesus himself drew near, and went with them.
16 But their eyes were withheld that they should not know him.
17 And he said to them, What manner of communications are these that you have one to another, as you walk, and are sad?
18 And the one of them, whose name was Cleopas, answering said to him, are you only a stranger in Jerusalem, and have not known the things which are come to pass therein these days?
19 And he said to them, What things? And they said to him, Concerning Jesus of Nazareth, which was a prophet mighty in deed and word before God and all the people:
20 And how the chief priests and our rulers delivered him to be condemned to death, and have crucified him.
21 But we trusted that it had been he which should have redeemed Israel: and beside all this, to day is the third day since these things were done.
22 Yea, and certain women also of our company made us astonished, which were early at the sepulchre;
23 And when they found not his body, they came, saying, that they had also seen a vision of angels, which said that he was alive.
24 And certain of them which were with us went to the sepulchre, and found it even so as the women had said: but him

24:1 Who arrived at the tomb first? There seems to be a contradiction as to who arrived at the tomb. However, there is no contradiction when the Gospels are read in harmony. When the women arrived at the edge of the garden, they looked and saw that the stone had been rolled back from the tomb. Mary concluded that the body had been stolen, and ran back to Peter and John in Jerusalem. The other women continued to the tomb, and went on inside where they encountered the angels.

they saw not.
25 Then he said to them, O fools, and slow of heart to believe all that the prophets have spoken:
26 **Ought not Christ to have suffered these things, and to enter into his glory?**
27 And beginning at Moses and all the prophets, he expounded to them in all the scriptures the things concerning himself.
28 And they drew near to the village, where they went: and he made as though he would have gone further.
29 But they constrained him, saying, Abide with us: for it is toward evening, and the day is far spent. And he went in to tarry with them.
30 And it came to pass, as he sat at meat with them, he took bread, and blessed it, and broke, and gave to them.
31 And their eyes were opened, and they knew him; and he vanished out of their sight.
32 And they said one to another, Did not our heart burn within us, while he talked with us by the way, and while he opened to us the scriptures?
33 And they rose up the same hour, and returned to Jerusalem, and found the eleven gathered together, and them that were with them,
34 Saying, The Lord is risen indeed, and has appeared to Simon.
35 And they told what things were done in the way, and how he was known of them in breaking of bread.
36 And as they thus spoke, Jesus himself stood in the midst of them, and said to them, Peace be to you.
37 But they were terrified and fearful, and supposed that they had seen a spirit.
38 And he said to them, Why are you troubled? and why do thoughts arise in your hearts?
39 Behold my hands and my feet, that it is I myself: handle me, and see; for a spirit has not flesh and bones, as you see me have.

> Let eloquence be flung to the dogs rather than souls be lost. What we want is to win souls. They are not won by flowery speeches.
>
> **CHARLES SPURGEON**

40 And when he had thus spoken, he showed them his hands and his feet.
41 And while they yet believed not for joy, and wondered, he said to them, Have you here any meat?
42 And they gave him a piece of a broiled fish, and of an honeycomb.
43 And he took it, and did eat before them.
44 And he said to them, These are the words which I spoke to you, while I was yet with you, that all things must be ful-

---

24:25 "About this time there lived Jesus, a wise man, if indeed one ought to call him a man. For he was one who wrought surprising feats and was a teacher of such people as accepted the truth gladly. He won over many Jews and many Greeks. He was the Christ. When Pilate, upon hearing him accused by men of the highest standing among us, had condemned him to be crucified, those who had in the first place come to love him did not give up their affection for him. On the third day he appeared to them restored to life, for the prophets of God had prophesied these and countless other marvelous things about him. And the tribe of Christians, so called after him, has still to this day not disappeared." *Josephus, Testimonium Flavianum*

24:39 Messianic prophecy fulfilled: "For dogs have compassed me: the assembly of the wicked have enclosed me: they pierced my hands and my feet" (Psalm 22:16). See John 1:11 footnote.

24:43 Jesus' resurrected body was physical. He was visible, could be touched, and could eat food. He was not a spirit, but had flesh and bones. Our resurrected bodies will also be physical; see Romans 8:23.

QUESTIONS & OBJECTIONS

24:44,45 ***"What if someone claims to have read the Bible and says it's just a book of fairy tales?"***

Call his bluff. Gently ask, "What is the thread of continuity that runs through the Bible—the consistent theme from the Old Testament through the New Testament?" More than likely he won't know. So say, "The Old Testament was God's promise that He would destroy death. The New Testament tells how He did it." Then appeal directly to the conscience by asking if he has kept the Ten Commandments. See John 4:7–26 and 2 Timothy 3:16 footnotes.

filled, which were written in the law of
Moses, and in the prophets, and in the
psalms, concerning me.
45 Then opened he their understanding,
that they might understand the scriptures,
46 *And said to them, Thus it is written, and
thus it behoved Christ to suffer, and to rise
from the dead the third day:*
47 *And that repentance and remission of
sins should be preached in his name among
all nations, beginning at Jerusalem.*
48 *And you are witnesses of these things.*
49 And, behold, I send the promise of
my Father upon you: but tarry in the city
of Jerusalem, until you be endued with
power from on high.
50 And he led them out as far as to Bethany, and he lifted up his hands, and blessed
them.
51 And it came to pass, while he blessed
them, he was parted from them, and carried up into heaven.
52 And they worshipped him, and returned to Jerusalem with great joy:
53 And were continually in the temple,
praising and blessing God. Amen.

24:47 Repentance—its necessity for salvation. See Acts 2:38.

"There are many who speak only of the forgiveness of sin, but who say little or nothing about repentance. If there is nevertheless no forgiveness of sins without repentance, so also forgiveness of sins cannot be understood without repentance. Therefore, if forgiveness of sins is preached without repentance, it follows that the people imagine they have already received the forgiveness of sins, and thereby they become cocksure and fearless, which is then greater error and sin than all the error that preceded our time." *Melanchthon*

John

CHAPTER 1

IN the beginning was the Word, and
the Word was with God, and the Word
was God.
2 The same was in the beginning with
God.
3 All things were made by him; and without him was not any thing made that was
made.
4 In him was life; and the life was the
light of men.
5 And the light shines in darkness; and
the darkness comprehended it not.
6 There was a man sent from God, whose
name was John.
7 The same came for a witness, to bear
witness of the Light, that all men through
him might believe.
8 He was not that Light, but was sent to
bear witness of that Light.
9 That was the true Light, which lights
every man that comes into the world.
10 He was in the world, and the world
was made by him, and the world knew
him not.
11 He came to his own, and his own received him not.
12 **But as many as received him, to
them gave he power to become the sons
of God, even to them that believe on his
name:**
**13 Which were born, not of blood, nor
of the will of the flesh, nor of the will
of man, but of God.**
14 And the Word was made flesh, and
dwelt among us, (and we beheld his glory,
the glory as of the only begotten of the Father,) full of grace and truth.

1:3,4 Rejection of the Bible's account of creation as given in the Book of Genesis could rightly be called "Genecide," because it eradicated man's purpose of existence and left a whole generation with no certainty as to its beginning. Consequently, theories and tales of our origin have crept like primeval slime from the minds of those who don't know God. This intellectual genocide has given the godless a temporary license to labor to the extremes of their imagination, giving birth to painful conjecture of human beginnings. They speak in *speculation*, the uncertain language of those who drift aimlessly across the endless sea of secular philosophy.

The Scriptures, on the other hand, deal only with truth and certainty. They talk of fact, reality, and purpose for man's existence. The darkness of the raging sea of futility retreats where the lighthouse of Genesis begins.

1:9 On the Day of Judgment no one can plead ignorance. God has given light to every man. (See also 2 Corinthians 4:6.)

1:11 Messianic prophecy fulfilled: "He is despised and rejected of men; a man of sorrows, and acquainted with grief: and we hid as it were our faces from him; he was despised, and we esteemed him not" (Isaiah 53:3). See John 1:32 comment.

1:13 New birth—its necessity for salvation: See John 3:7.

1:13 *The "Sinner's Prayer"—To Pray or Not To Pray?*

The question often arises about what a Christian should do if someone is repentant. Should we lead him in what's commonly called a "sinner's prayer" or simply instruct him to seek after God? Perhaps the answer comes by looking to the natural realm. As long as there are no complications when a child is born, all the doctor needs to do is *guide the head*. The same applies spiritually. When someone is "born of God," all we need to do is guide the head—make sure that they *understand* what they are doing.

Philip the evangelist did this with the Ethiopian eunuch. He asked him, "Do you understand what you read?" (Acts 8:30). In the parable of the sower, the true convert (the "good soil" hearer) is he who hears "and understands." This understanding comes by the Law in the hand of the Spirit (Romans 7:7). If a sinner is ready for the Savior, it is because he has been drawn by the Holy Spirit (John 6:44). This is why we must be careful to allow the Holy Spirit to do His work and not rush in where angels fear to tread. Praying a sinner's prayer with someone who isn't genuinely repentant may leave you with a stillborn in your hands. Therefore, rather than *lead* him in a prayer of repentance, it is wise to encourage him to pray himself.

When Nathan confronted David about his sin, he didn't lead the king in a prayer of repentance. If a man committed adultery, and his wife is willing to take him back, should you have to write out an apology for him to read to her? No. Sorrow for his betrayal of her trust should spill from his lips. She doesn't want eloquent words, but simply sorrow of heart. The same applies to a prayer of repentance. The words aren't as important as the presence of "godly sorrow." The sinner should be told to repent—to confess and forsake his sins. He could do this as a whispered prayer, then you could pray for him. If he's not sure what to say, perhaps David's prayer of repentance (Psalm 51) could be used as a model, but his own words are more desirable.

15 John bare witness of him, and cried, saying, This was he of whom I spoke, He that comes after me is preferred before me: for he was before me.
16 And of his fulness have all we received, and grace for grace.
17 For the law was given by Moses, but grace and truth came by Jesus Christ.
18 No man has seen God at any time; the only begotten Son, which is in the bosom of the Father, he has declared him.
19 And this is the record of John, when the Jews sent priests and Levites from Jerusalem to ask him, Who are you?
20 And he confessed, and denied not; but confessed, I am not the Christ.
21 And they asked him, What then? are you Elijah? And he said, I am not. Are you that prophet? And he answered, No.
22 Then said they to him, Who are you?

1:13 How to get false converts. Our aim should be to ensure that sinners are born of the Spirit—of the will of God and not of the will of man. Too many of our "decisions" are not a work of the Spirit, but a work of our sincere but manipulative practices. It is simple to secure a decision for Jesus by using this popular method: "Do you know whether you are going to heaven when you die? God wants you to have that assurance. All you need to do is: 1) realize that you are a sinner ('All have sinned, and come short of the glory of God'), and 2) believe that Jesus died on the cross for you. Would you like me to pray with you right now so that you can give your heart to Jesus? Then you will have the assurance that you are going to heaven when you die." For the *biblical* way to present the gospel, see John 4:7–26 comment. For more on false converts, see Matthew 25:12 comment.

1:17 "A wrong understanding of the harmony between Law and grace would produce 'error on the left and the right hand.'" *John Newton*

Questions & Objections

1:18

"I will believe if God will appear to me."

A proud and ignorant sinner who says this has no understanding of the nature of His Creator. No man has ever seen the essence of God. (When God "appeared" to certain men in the Old Testament, He manifested Himself in other forms, such as a burning bush or "the Angel of the Lord.") When Moses asked to see God's glory, God told him, "I will make all my goodness pass before you,…[but] you cannot see my face: for there shall no man see me, and live" (Exodus 33:18–23). If all of God's "goodness" were shown to a sinner, he would instantly die. God's "goodness" would just spill wrath upon evil man.

However, the Lord told Moses, "It shall come to pass, while my glory passes by, that I will put you in a cleft of the rock, and will cover you with My hand while I pass by." The only way a sinner can live in the presence of a holy God is to be hidden in the Rock of Jesus Christ (1 Corinthians 10:4).

that we may give an answer to them that
sent us. What do you say of yourself?
23 He said, I am the voice of one crying
in the wilderness, Make straight the way
of the Lord, as said the prophet Isaiah.
24 And they which were sent were of
the Pharisees.
25 And they asked him, and said to him,
Why do you baptize then, if you be not
that Christ, nor Elijah, neither that prophet?
26 John answered them, saying, I baptize
with water: but there stands one among
you, whom you know not;
27 He it is, who coming after me is preferred before me, whose shoe's latchet I
am not worthy to unloose.
28 These things were done in Bethabara
beyond Jordan, where John was baptizing.
29 **The next day John saw Jesus coming to him, and said, Behold the Lamb of
God, which takes away the sin of the
world.**
30 This is he of whom I said, After me
comes a man which is preferred before
me: for he was before me.
31 And I knew him not: but that he
should be made manifest to Israel, therefore am I come baptizing with water.
32 And John bare record, saying, I saw
the Spirit descending from heaven like a
dove, and it abode upon him.
33 And I knew him not: but he that sent
me to baptize with water, the same said to
me, Upon whom you shall see the Spirit
descending, and remaining on him, the
same is he which baptizes with the Holy
Spirit.
34 And I saw, and bare record that this
is the Son of God.
35 Again the next day after John stood,
and two of his disciples;
36 And looking upon Jesus as he walked,
he said, Behold the Lamb of God!
37 And the two disciples heard him
speak, and they followed Jesus.
38 Then Jesus turned, and saw them following, and said to them, What do you
seek? They said to him, Rabbi, (which is
to say, being interpreted, Master,) where
do you dwell?
39 He said to them, Come and see. They
came and saw where he dwelt, and abode
with him that day: for it was about the
tenth hour.
40 One of the two which heard John

1:32 Messianic prophecy fulfilled: "And the spirit of the LORD shall rest upon him, the spirit of wisdom and understanding, the spirit of counsel and might, the spirit of knowledge and of the fear of the LORD" (Isaiah 11:2). See John 6:14 comment.

"I believe that lack of efficient personal work is one of the failures of the Church today. The people of the Church are like squirrels in a cage. Lots of activity, but accomplishing nothing. It doesn't require a Christian life to sell oyster soup or run a bazaar or a rummage sale…"

Billy Sunday

speak, and followed him, was Andrew,
Simon Peter's brother.
41 He first found his own brother Simon, and said to him, We have found the
Messiah, which is, being interpreted, the
Christ.
42 And he brought him to Jesus. And
when Jesus beheld him, he said, You are
Simon the son of Jonah: you shall be called
Cephas, which is by interpretation, A
stone.
43 The day following Jesus went forth into Galilee, and found Philip, and said to
him, Follow me.
44 Now Philip was of Bethsaida, the city
of Andrew and Peter.
45 Philip found Nathanael, and said to
him, We have found him, of whom Moses in the law, and the prophets, did write,
Jesus of Nazareth, the son of Joseph.
46 And Nathanael said to him, Can there
any good thing come out of Nazareth?
Philip said to him, Come and see.
47 Jesus saw Nathanael coming to him,
and said of him, Behold an Israelite indeed, in whom is no guile!
48 Nathanael said to him, Where do you
know me from? Jesus answered and said
to him, Before that Philip called you, when
you were under the fig tree, I saw you.
49 Nathanael answered and said to him,
Rabbi, you are the Son of God; you are the
King of Israel.
50 Jesus answered and said to him, Be-

1:41 After we have found the Messiah, we are to tell others about Him. The only "failure" when it comes to reaching out to the lost is not to be doing it.

"Many churches report no new members on confession of faith. Why these meager results with this tremendous expenditure of energy and money? Why are so few people coming into the Kingdom? I will tell you—there is not a definite effort put forth to persuade a definite person to receive a definite Savior at a definite time, and that definite time is now." *Billy Sunday*

"Our forefathers must be asking, 'How is it that we did so much with so little, and you do so little with so much?'" *R. Albert Mohler Jr.*

1:46 Come and see. Jesus called Philip to follow Him, then Philip immediately found Nathanael and told him about the Savior. Nathanael's question is a typical reaction of the contemporary world to those who follow the Savior. To the cynical, Christians are intellectual wimps, prudes, rejects—unlearned cripples who need some sort of crutch to get them through life. So it is understandable for them to ask, "Can any good thing come out of Christianity?" Down through the ages, its good name has been tainted with the stained brush of hypocrisy, dead religion, and more recently, fanatical sects and televangelism.

Philip merely answered Nathanael's cynicism with the same thing Jesus said to Andrew—"Come and see." Skeptic, come and see. Atheist, come and see. Intellectual, come and see. Just come with a humble and teachable heart, and you who are sightless *will* see and know that this Man from Nazareth is the Son of God.

cause I said to you, I saw you under the fig
tree, do you believe? you shall see greater
things than these.
51 And he said to him, Verily, verily, I
say to you, Hereafter you shall see heaven
open, and the angels of God ascending
and descending upon the Son of man.

CHAPTER 2

AND the third day there was a marriage in Cana of Galilee; and the
mother of Jesus was there:
2 And both Jesus was called, and his disciples, to the marriage.
3 And when they wanted wine, the mother of Jesus said to him, They have no wine.
4 Jesus said to her, Woman, what have
I to do with you? mine hour is not yet
come.
5 **His mother said to the servants,
Whatsoever he says to you, do it.**
6 And there were set there six waterpots
of stone, after the manner of the purifying
of the Jews, containing two or three fir-
kins apiece.
7 Jesus said to them, Fill the waterpots
with water. And they filled them up to the
brim.
8 And he said to them, Draw out now,
and bear to the governor of the feast. And
they bare it.
9 When the ruler of the feast had tasted
the water that was made wine, and knew
not whence it was: (but the servants which
drew the water knew;) the governor of the
feast called the bridegroom,
10 And said to him, Every man at the
beginning does set forth good wine; and
when men have well drunk, then that
which is worse: but you have kept the
good wine until now.
11 This beginning of miracles did Jesus
in Cana of Galilee, and manifested forth
his glory; and his disciples believed on
him.
12 After this he went down to Capernaum, he, and his mother, and his brethren, and his disciples: and they continued
there not many days.
13 And the Jews' passover was at hand,
and Jesus went up to Jerusalem,
14 And found in the temple those that
sold oxen and sheep and doves, and the
changers of money sitting:
15 And when he had made a scourge of
small cords, he drove them all out of the
temple, and the sheep, and the oxen; and
poured out the changers' money, and over-

1:47 Nathanael was "an Israelite indeed, in whom is no guile." He was a Jew in *deed*, not just in *word*. As an honest Jew he didn't twist the Law, as did the Pharisees. He read it in truth. The Law and the prophets had pointed him to Jesus and he was therefore ready to come to the Savior.

2:13–17 Cleansing the temple. When Jesus went to the temple, He found it to be filled with those buying and selling merchandise. According to the Jewish historian Josephus, at each Passover, over 250,000 animals were sacrificed. The priests sold licenses to the dealers and therefore would have had a great source of income from the Passover. When the Bible called them "changers of money," it was an appropriate term.

There is, however, another theft going on in another temple. Mankind was made as a dwelling place for his Creator. God made him a little lower than the angels, crowned him with glory and honor, and set him over the works of His hands (Hebrews 2:7), yet sin has given the dwelling place to the devil. The thief, who came to steal, kill, and destroy, is making merchandise out of mankind. Instead of the heart of man being a temple of the Living God (2 Corinthians 6:16)—a house of prayer—iniquity has made it a den of thieves.

When someone repents and calls upon the name of Jesus Christ, He turns the tables on the devil. The ten stinging cords of the Ten Commandments in the hand of the Savior cleanse the temple of sin. *Charles Spurgeon* had a resolute grasp of the Law. In preaching to sinners, he said, "I would that this whip would fall upon your backs, that you might be flogged out of your self-righteousness and made to fly to Jesus Christ and find shelter there."

2:15 This is the Lord's righteous indignation at Israel's equivalent of money-hungry televangelists.

2:6–11 *The Significance of the First Miracle*

1. The turning of water into blood was the first of the public miracles that Moses did in Egypt (Exodus 7:20), and the water into wine was the first of the public miracles that Jesus did in the world (John 2:11).

2. The signs that God gave to Egypt in the Old Testament were plagues, destruction, and death, and the signs that Jesus did in the world in the New Testament were healings, blessings, and life.

3. The turning of water to blood initiated Moses (a type of the Savior—Deuteronomy 18:15) leading his people out of the bondage of Egypt into an earthly liberty; the turning of water into wine initiated Jesus taking His people out of the bondage of the corruption of the world into the glorious liberty of the children of God (Romans 8:21).

4. The turning of water to blood culminated in the firstborn in Egypt being delivered to death, while turning the water into wine culminated in the life of the Firstborn being delivered from death (Colossians 1:18).

5. The Law was a ministration of death, the gospel a ministration of life. One was written on cold tablets of stone, the other on the warm fleshly tablets of the heart. One was a ministration of sin unto condemnation and bondage, the other a ministration of righteousness unto life and liberty (2 Corinthians 3:7–9).

6. When Moses changed the water into blood, we are told that all the fish in the river died. When Jesus initiated the new covenant, the catch of the fish are made alive in the net of the kingdom of God (Matthew 4:19).

7. The river of blood was symbolic of death for Egypt, but the water into wine is symbolic of life for the world. The letter of the Law kills, but the Spirit makes alive (2 Corinthians 3:6).

8. When Moses turned the waters of Egypt into blood, the river reeked and made the Egyptians search for another source of water supply (Exodus 7:21,24). When the Law of Moses does its work in the sinner, it makes life odious for him. The weight of sin on his back becomes unbearable as he begins to labor and be heavy laden under its weight. Like the Egyptians, he begins to search for another spring of water; he begins to "thirst for righteousness," because he knows that without a right standing with God, he will perish.

9. Moses turned water into blood, and Jesus' blood turned into water (1 John 5:6). They both poured from His side (John 19:34), perhaps signifying that both Law and grace found harmony in the Savior's death—"Mercy and truth are met together; righteousness and peace have kissed each other" (Psalm 85:10).

10. The water of the old covenant ran out. It could do nothing but leave the sinner with a thirst for righteousness. But as with the wine at Cana, God saved the best until last. The new wine given on the Day of Pentecost (Acts 2:13; Ephesians 5:18) was the Bridegroom giving us the new and "better" covenant (Hebrews 8:5,6).

threw the tables;
16 And said to them that sold doves,
Take these things hence; make not my
Father's house an house of merchandise.
17 And his disciples remembered that it
was written, The zeal of your house has
eaten me up.
18 Then answered the Jews and said to
him, What sign do you show to us, seeing that you do these things?
19 **Jesus answered and said to them,
Destroy this temple, and in three days
I will raise it up.**
20 Then said the Jews, Forty and six
years was this temple in building, and
will you rear it up in three days?
21 But he spoke of the temple of his
body.
22 When therefore he was risen from the
dead, his disciples remembered that he
had said this to them; and they believed
the scripture, and the word which Jesus
had said.
23 Now when he was in Jerusalem at
the passover, in the feast day, many believed in his name, when they saw the

QUESTIONS & OBJECTIONS

3:3

"I have been born again many times."

Like Nicodemus, many people have no concept of what it means to be born again. He thought Jesus was speaking of a physical rebirth. Others see the experience as being a spiritual "tingle" when they think of God or a warm fuzzy feeling when they enter a building they erroneously call a "Church." Or maybe they are of the impression that one is born again when one is "christened" or "confirmed." However, the new birth spoken of by Jesus is absolutely essential for sinners to enter heaven. If they are not born again, they will not enter the kingdom of God. Therefore it is necessary to establish the fact that one becomes a Christian by being born again, pointing out that Jesus Himself said that the experience was crucial. The difference between *believing* in Jesus and being born again is like believing in a parachute, and putting one on. The difference will be seen when you jump. (See Romans 13:14.)

How is one born again? Simply through repentance toward God and faith in the Lord Jesus Christ. Confess and forsake your sins, and trust in Jesus alone for your eternal salvation. When you do, you receive spiritual life through the Holy Spirit who comes to live within you. See Ephesians 4:18 and 1 Peter 1:23 comments.

miracles which he did.
24 But Jesus did not commit himself to
them, because he knew all men,
25 And needed not that any should testify of man: for he knew what was in man.

CHAPTER 3

**THERE was a man of the Pharisees,
named Nicodemus, a ruler of the
Jews:**
**2 The same came to Jesus by night, and
said to him, Rabbi, we know that you are
a teacher come from God: for no man
can do these miracles that you do, except God be with him.**
**3 Jesus answered and said to him, Ver-
ily, verily, I say to you, Except a man be
born again, he cannot see the kingdom
of God.**
4 **Nicodemus said to him, How can a
man be born when he is old? can he enter the second time into his mother's
womb, and be born?**
**5 Jesus answered, Verily, verily, I say
to you, Except a man be born of water
and of the Spirit, he cannot enter into
the kingdom of God.**
**6 That which is born of the flesh is
flesh; and that which is born of the
Spirit is spirit.**
**7 Marvel not that I said to you, You
must be born again.**
8 The wind blows where it lists, and
you hear the sound thereof, but can not

2:24,25 "We may deceive all the people sometimes; we may deceive some of the people all the time, but not all the people all the time, and not God at any time." *Abraham Lincoln*

"Character is what you are in the dark." *D. L. Moody*

3:2 Grace to the humble. Nicodemus was a humble Jew (he acknowledged the deity of the Son of God), and he knew the Law (he was a "master of Israel," v. 10); therefore, Jesus gave him the good news of the gospel. He was convinced of the disease of sin and consequently ready to hear of the cure.

3:3 "These verses aren't necessarily about what Nicodemus asked Jesus; they are about what Jesus knew. The last verse of the previous chapter said that He knew what was in man. Jesus knew what was in the heart of Nicodemus: he was a Law-breaker, and he needed to be born again." *Garry T. Ansdell, D.D.*

USING THE LAW IN EVANGELISM

3:16

"If I had my way, I would declare a moratorium on public preaching of 'the plan of salvation' in America for one to two years. Then I would call on everyone who has use of the airwaves and the pulpits to preach the holiness of God, the righteousness of God, and the Law of God, until sinners would cry out, 'What must we do to be saved?' Then I would take them off in a corner and whisper the gospel to them. Don't use John 3:16. Such drastic action is needed because we have gospel-hardened a generation of sinners by telling them how to be saved before they have any understanding why they need to be saved."
Paris Reidhead

tell whence it comes, and where it goes:
so is every one that is born of the Spirit.
9 Nicodemus answered and said to him,
How can these things be?
10 Jesus answered and said to him, Are
you a master of Israel, and know not these
things?
11 Verily, verily, I say to you, We speak
that we do know, and testify that we have
seen; and you receive not our witness.
12 If I have told you earthly things, and
you believe not, how shall you believe, if
I tell you of heavenly things?
13 And no man has ascended up to heaven,
but he that came down from heaven,
even the Son of man which is in heaven.
14 And as Moses lifted up the serpent
in the wilderness, even so must the Son
of man be lifted up:
15 That whosoever believes in him should
not perish, but have eternal life.
16 For God so loved the world, that he

3:7 New birth—its necessity for salvation. This is a fulfillment of Ezekiel 36:26: "A new heart also will I give you, and a new spirit will I put within you: and I will take away the stony heart out of your flesh, and I will give you an heart of flesh." Man cannot enter heaven in his spiritually dead state; he must be born again to have spiritual life. Jesus said that He is life (John 14:6; John 11:25,26), and that we must come to Him to have life (John 5:39,40; 1 John 5:11,12). Those who trust in Christ are "born again, not of corruptible seed, but of incorruptible, by the word of God, which lives and abides for ever" (1 Peter 1:23). See 2 Corinthians 5:17.

"Ever since Adam sinned, the earth has been the land of the walking dead—spiritually dead. What is the disease that killed man? 'The wages of sin is death.' So from God's point of view, salvation involves the raising of spiritually dead men to life. But before God could give life to the dead, He had to totally eradicate the fatal disease that killed men—sin. So the cross was God's method of dealing with the disease called sin, and the resurrection of Christ was and is God's method of giving life to the dead!" *Bob George, Classic Christianity*

3:14,15 When fiery serpents were sent among Israel, they caused the Israelites to admit that they had sinned. The means of their salvation was to look up to a bronze serpent that Moses had placed on a pole. Those who had been bitten and were doomed to die could look at the bronze serpent and live (Numbers 21:6–9). In John 3:14,15, Jesus specifically cited this Old Testament passage in reference to salvation from sin.

The Ten Commandments are like ten biting serpents that carry with them the venomous curse of the Law. They drive sinners to look to the One lifted up on a cross, and those who look to Him will live. It was the Law of Moses that put Jesus on the cross. The Messiah became a curse for us, and redeemed us from the curse of the Law.

3:16,17 Salvation is possible for every person. See John 4:14.

3:16,17 God Himself provided our way of escape: "But God commends his love toward us, in that, while we were yet sinners, Christ died for us" (Romans 5:8). "For he has made him to be sin for us, who knew no sin; that we might be made the righteousness of God in him" (2 Corinthians 5:21). "But he was wounded for our transgressions, he was bruised for our iniquities: the chastisement of our peace was upon him; and with his stripes we are healed. All we like sheep have gone astray; we have turned every one to his own way; and the Lord has laid on him the iniquity of us all" (Isaiah 53:5,6). See Romans 10:9 comment.

3:16 *Is Repentance Necessary for Salvation?*

It is true that numerous Bible verses speak of the promise of salvation with no mention of repentance. These verses merely say to "believe" on Jesus Christ and you shall be saved (Acts 16:31; Romans 10:9). However, the Bible makes it clear that God is holy and man is sinful, and that sin makes a separation between the two (Isaiah 59:1,2). Without repentance from sin, wicked men cannot have fellowship with a holy God. We are *dead* in our trespasses and sins (Ephesians 2:1) and until we forsake them through repentance, we cannot be made alive in Christ. The Scriptures speak of "repentance unto life" (Acts 11:18). We turn *from* sin *to* the Savior. This is why Paul preached "repentance toward God, and faith toward our Lord Jesus Christ" (Acts 20:21).

The first public word Jesus preached was "repent" (Matthew 4:17). John the Baptist began his ministry the same way (Matthew 3:2). Jesus told His hearers that without repentance, they would perish (Luke 13:3). If belief is all that is necessary for salvation, then the logical conclusion is that one need never repent. However, the Bible tells us that a false convert "believes" and yet is not saved (Luke 8:13); he remains a "worker of iniquity." Look at the warning of Scripture: "If we say that we have fellowship with him, and walk in darkness, we lie, and do not the truth" (1 John 1:6). The Scriptures also say, "He that covers his sins shall not prosper, but whoso confesses and forsakes them [repentance] shall have mercy" (Proverbs 28:13). Jesus said that there was joy in heaven over one sinner who "repents" (Luke 15:10). If there is no repentance, there is no joy because there is no salvation.

As Peter preached on the Day of Pentecost, he commanded his hearers to repent "for the remission of sins" (Acts 2:38). Without repentance, there is no remission of sins; we are still under God's wrath. Peter further said, "Repent...and be converted, that your sins may be blotted out" (Acts 3:19). We cannot be "converted" unless we repent. God Himself "commands *all* men *everywhere* [leaving no exceptions] to repent" (Acts 17:30). Peter said a similar thing at Pentecost: "Repent, and be baptized *every one* of you" (Acts 2:38).

If repentance wasn't necessary for salvation, why then did Jesus command that *repentance* be preached to all nations (Luke 24:47)? With so many Scriptures speaking of the necessity of repentance for salvation, one can only suspect that those who preach salvation without repentance are strangers to repentance themselves, and thus strangers to true conversion.

gave his only begotten Son, that whoso-
ever believes in him should not perish,
but have everlasting life.
17 For God sent not his Son into the
world to condemn the world; but that
the world through him might be saved.
18 **He that believes on him is not con-**
demned: but he that believes not is con-
demned already, because he has not be-
lieved in the name of the only begotten
Son of God.
19 And this is the condemnation, that
light is come into the world, and men
loved darkness rather than light, be-
cause their deeds were evil.
20 For every one that does evil hates
the light, neither comes to the light, lest
his deeds should be reproved.
21 **But he that does truth comes to the**
light, that his deeds may be made man-

3:19 Jesus said that we loved the darkness of sin rather than the light of righteousness, because the human heart finds pleasure in sin. If you don't believe it, visit the "adult" section of your local video store. Look at the covers to see the type of entertainment the hearts of men and women crave—unspeakable violence, inconceivable horror, and unending sexual perversion.

ifest, that they are wrought in God.
22 After these things came Jesus and his
disciples into the land of Judea; and there
he tarried with them, and baptized.
23 And John also was baptizing in Aenon
near to Salim, because there was much
water there: and they came, and were baptized.
24 For John was not yet cast into prison.
25 Then there arose a question between
some of John's disciples and the Jews
about purifying.

> Sin and hell are married unless repentance proclaims the divorce.
>
> **CHARLES SPURGEON**

26 And they came to John, and said to
him, Rabbi, he that was with you beyond Jordan, to whom you bare witness,
behold, the same baptizes, and all men
come to him.
27 John answered and said, A man can
receive nothing, except it be given him
from heaven.
28 You yourselves bear me witness, that
I said, I am not the Christ, but that I am
sent before him.
29 He that has the bride is the bridegroom: but the friend of the bridegroom,
which stands and hears him, rejoices greatly because of the bridegroom's voice: this
my joy therefore is fulfilled.
30 He must increase, but I must decrease.
31 He that comes from above is above all:
he that is of the earth is earthly, and speaks
of the earth: he that comes from heaven
is above all.
32 And what he has seen and heard, that
he testifies; and no man receives his testimony.
33 He that has received his testimony has
set to his seal that God is true.
34 For he whom God has sent speaks the
words of God: for God gives not the Spirit
by measure to him.
35 The Father loves the Son, and has giv-
en all things into his hand.
36 He that believes on the Son has ever-
lasting life: and he that believes not the
Son shall not see life; but the wrath of
God abides on him.

CHAPTER 4

WHEN therefore the Lord knew how
the Pharisees had heard that Jesus
made and baptized more disciples than
John,
2 (Though Jesus himself baptized not,
but his disciples,)
3 He left Judea, and departed again into
Galilee.

3:19,20 The same sunlight that melts wax also hardens clay. As God's light shines on man, the sinner's heart determines his response. One whose heart is tender will respond to God; one whose heart is bent on evil will harden his heart further against God and will remain in darkness. Sinners should note: After Pharaoh repeatedly hardened his heart against God (Exodus 8:15,32), God then hardened Pharaoh's heart (Exodus 10:27). Those who continually reject God will be given up to "uncleanness, vile affections, and a reprobate mind" (Romans 1:24,26,28).

3:36 The Greek word used here for the first occurrence of "believes" is *pisteuo*—which means "to trust." However, in the second occurrence in this verse ("he that believes not the Son shall not see life; but the wrath of God abides on him"), the word used for "believes" is *apeitheo*—which means "disobedient." The disobedient will not see the salvation of God, no matter what prayer they have prayed, because they refuse to surrender their will to the Lordship of Jesus Christ. He is coming "in flaming fire taking vengeance on them that know not God, and that *obey not the gospel of our Lord Jesus Christ*" (2 Thessalonians 1:8, emphasis added).

3:36 Those without Christ are dead in their sins, separated from the life of God, and will not have spiritual life unless they trust in Jesus Christ. Their sin makes them objects of God's wrath.

Somehow we think that time forgives sin. This is not so. The more we sin, the more we store up God's wrath. See Romans 2:5.

4 And he must needs go through Samaria.
5 Then came he to a city of Samaria,
which is called Sychar, near to the parcel
of ground that Jacob gave to his son Joseph.
6 Now Jacob's well was there. Jesus therefore, being wearied with his journey, sat
thus on the well: and it was about the sixth
hour.
7 There came a woman of Samaria to
draw water: Jesus said to her, Give me to
drink.
8 (For his disciples were gone away to the
city to buy meat.)
9 Then said the woman of Samaria to
him, How is it that you, being a Jew, ask
drink of me, which am a woman of Samaria? for the Jews have no dealings with the
Samaritans.
10 Jesus answered and said to her, If you
knew the gift of God, and who it is that
said to you, Give me to drink; you would
have asked of him, and he would have
given you living water.
11 The woman said to him, Sir, you have
nothing to draw with, and the well is deep:
from whence then have you that living

4:7 *Personal Witnessing—How Jesus Did It*

How to address the sinner's conscience and speak with someone who doesn't believe in hell

Verses 7–26 give us the Master's example of how to share our faith. Notice that Jesus spoke to the woman at the well when she was alone. We will often find that people are more open and honest when they are alone. So, if possible, pick a person who is sitting by himself. From these verses, we can see four clear principles to follow.

First: Jesus began in the natural realm (v. 7). This woman was unregenerate, and the Bible tells us "the natural man receives not the things of the Spirit of God" (1 Corinthians 2:14). He therefore spoke of something she could relate to—water. Most of us can strike up a conversation with a stranger in the natural realm. It may be a friendly "How are you doing?" or a warm "Good morning!" If the person responds with a sense of warmth, we may then ask, "Do you live around here?" and from there develop a conversation.

Second: Jesus swung the conversation to the spiritual realm (v. 10). He simply mentioned the things of God. This will take courage. We may say something like, "Did you go to church on Sunday?" or "Did you see that Christian TV program last week?" If the person responds positively, the question "Do you have a Christian background?" will probe his background. He may answer, "I went to church when I was a child, but I drifted away from it."

Another simple way to swing to the spiritual is to offer the person a gospel tract and ask, "Did you get one of these?" When he takes it, simply say, "It's a gospel tract. Do you come from a Christian background?"

Third: Jesus brought conviction using the Law of God (vv. 16–18). Jesus gently spoke to her conscience by alluding to the fact that she had transgressed the Seventh of the Ten Commandments. He used the Law to bring "the knowledge of sin" (see Romans 3:19,20). We can do the same by asking, "Do you think that you have kept the Ten Commandments?" Most people think they have, so quickly follow with, "Have you ever told a lie?" This *is* confrontational, but if it's asked in a spirit of love and gentleness, there won't be any offense. Remember that the "work of the Law [is] written in their hearts" and that the conscience will bear "witness" (Romans 2:15). Jesus confronted the rich young ruler in Luke 18:18–21 with five of the Ten Commandments and there was no offense. Have confidence that the conscience will do its work and affirm the truth of each Commandment. Don't be afraid to gently ask, "Have you ever stolen something, even if it's small?" Learn how to open up the spirituality of the Law and show how God considers lust to be the same as adultery (Matthew 5:27,28) and hatred the same as murder (1 John 3:15). Make sure you get an admission of guilt.

(continued on next page)

(4:7 continued)

Ask the person, "If God judges you by the Ten Commandments on Judgment Day, do you think you will be innocent or guilty?" If he says he will be innocent, ask, "Why is that?" If he admits his guilt, ask, "Do you think you will go to heaven or hell?"

From there the conversation may go one of three ways:

1. *He may confidently say, "I don't believe in hell."* Gently respond, "That doesn't matter. You still have to face God on Judgment Day *whether you believe in it or not.* If I step onto the freeway when a massive truck is heading for me and I say, 'I don't believe in trucks,' my lack of belief isn't going to change reality."

Then tenderly tell him he has *already* admitted to you that he has lied, stolen, and committed adultery in his heart, and that God gave him a conscience so that he would know right from wrong. His conscience and the conviction of the Holy Spirit will do the rest.

That's why it is essential to draw out an admission of guilt *before* you mention Judgment Day or the existence of hell.

2. *He may say that he's guilty, but that he will go to heaven.* This is usually because he thinks that God is "good," and that He will, therefore, overlook sin in his case. Point out that if a judge in a criminal case has a guilty murderer standing before him, the judge, if he is a good man, can't just let him go. He must ensure that the guilty man is punished. If God is good, He must (by nature) punish murderers, rapists, thieves, liars, adulterers, fornicators, and those who have lived in rebellion to the inner light that God has given to every man.

3. *He may admit that he is guilty and therefore going to hell.* Ask him if that concerns him. Speak to him about how much he values his eyes and how much more therefore he should value the salvation of his soul. (For the biblical description of hell, see Revelation 1:18 comment.) If possible, take the person through the linked verses in this Bible, beginning at the Matthew 5:21,22 comment.

Fourth: Jesus revealed Himself to her (v. 26). Once the Law has humbled the person, he is ready for grace. Remember, the Bible says that God resists the proud and gives grace to the humble (James 4:6). The gospel is for the humble (see Luke 4:18 comment). Only the sick need a physician, and only those who will admit that they have the disease of sin will truly embrace the cure of the gospel.

Learn how to present the work of the cross —that God sent His Son to suffer and die in our place. Tell the sinner of the love of God in Christ; that Jesus rose from the dead and defeated death. Take him back to civil law and say, "It's as simple as this: We broke God's Law, and Jesus paid our fine. If you will repent and trust in the Savior, God will forgive your sins and dismiss your case." Ask him if he understands what you have told him. If he is willing to confess and forsake his sins, and trust the Savior with his eternal salvation, have him pray and ask God to forgive him. Then pray for him. Get him a Bible. Instruct him to read it daily and obey what he reads, and encourage him to get into a Bible-believing, Christ-preaching church.

water?
12 Are you greater than our father Jacob, which gave us the well, and drank thereof himself, and his children, and his cattle?
13 **Jesus answered and said to her, Whosoever drinks of this water shall thirst again:**
14 But whosoever drinks of the water that I shall give him shall never thirst; but the water that I shall give him shall be in him a well of water springing up into everlasting life.
15 The woman said to him, Sir, give me this water, that I thirst not, neither come here to draw.
16 Jesus said to her, Go, call your husband, and come here.
17 The woman answered and said, I have no husband. Jesus said to her, You have well said, I have no husband:
18 For you have had five husbands; and he whom you now have is not your husband: in that you said truly.
19 The woman said to him, Sir, I per-

4:14 Salvation is possible for every person. See John 6:51.

ceive that you are a prophet.
20 Our fathers worshipped in this mountain; and you say, that in Jerusalem is the
place where men ought to worship.
21 Jesus said to her, Woman, believe me,
the hour comes, when you shall neither in
this mountain, nor yet at Jerusalem, worship the Father.
22 You worship you know not what: we
know what we worship: for salvation is of
the Jews.
23 But the hour comes, and now is, when
the true worshippers shall worship the
Father in spirit and in truth: for the Father
seeks such to worship him.
24 God is a Spirit: and they that worship
him must worship him in spirit and in
truth.
25 The woman said to him, I know that
Messiah comes, which is called Christ:
when he is come, he will tell us all things.
26 Jesus said to her, I that speak to you
am he.
27 And upon this came his disciples, and
marveled that he talked with the woman:
yet no man said, What do you seek? or,
Why do you talk with her?
28 The woman then left her waterpot,
and went her way into the city, and said
to the men,
29 Come, see a man, which told me all
things that ever I did: is not this the Christ?
30 Then they went out of the city, and
came to him.
31 In the mean while his disciples prayed
him, saying, Master, eat.
32 But he said to them, I have meat to eat
that you know not of.
33 Therefore said the disciples one to another, has any man brought him anything
to eat?
34 *Jesus said to them, My meat is to do
the will of him that sent me, and to finish
his work.*
35 *Do you not say, There are yet four
months, and then comes harvest? behold, I
say to you, Lift up your eyes, and look on the
fields; for they are white already to harvest.*
36 *And he that reaps receives wages, and
gathers fruit to life eternal: that both he that
sows and he that reaps may rejoice together.*
37 *And herein is that saying true, One
sows, and another reaps.*
38 *I sent you to reap that whereon you bestowed no labour: other men laboured, and
you are entered into their labours.*
39 And many of the Samaritans of that
city believed on him for the saying of the
woman, which testified, He told me all
that ever I did.
40 So when the Samaritans were come
to him, they besought him that he would
tarry with them: and he abode there two
days.
41 And many more believed because of
his own word;
42 And said to the woman, Now we believe, not because of your saying: for we
have heard him ourselves, and know that
this is indeed the Christ, the Savior of the
world.

4:34 The "meat" that nourished the Savior was to carry out the work of evangelism—to seek and to save that which was lost.

4:36 "I would think it a greater happiness to gain one soul to Christ than mountains of silver and gold to myself." *Matthew Henry*

4:37,38 **The measure of success.** Don't be tempted to measure evangelistic "success" by the number of "decisions" obtained. We tend to rejoice over decisions, when heaven reserves its rejoicing for repentance—"There is joy in the presence of the angels of God over one sinner that repents" (Luke 15:10). It is easy to get "decisions for Jesus" using the modern method of well-chosen words and psychological manipulation. Rather, see success as having the opportunity to sow the seed of God's Word into the hearts of your hearers. If you faithfully sow, someone else will reap. If you have the privilege of reaping, then someone has faithfully sown before you. One sows, another reaps, but it is God who gives the increase. See 1 Corinthians 3:6,7.

43 Now after two days he departed thence, and went into Galilee.

44 For Jesus himself testified, that a prophet has no honor in his own country.

45 Then when he was come into Galilee, the Galilaeans received him, having seen all the things that he did at Jerusalem at the feast: for they also went to the feast.

46 So Jesus came again into Cana of Galilee, where he made the water wine. And there was a certain nobleman, whose son was sick at Capernaum.

47 When he heard that Jesus was come out of Judea into Galilee, he went to him, and besought him that he would come down, and heal his son: for he was at the point of death.

48 Then said Jesus to him, Except you see signs and wonders, you will not believe.

49 The nobleman said to him, Sir, come down ere my child die.

50 Jesus said to him, Go your way; your son lives. And the man believed the word that Jesus had spoken to him, and he went his way.

51 And as he was now going down, his servants met him, and told him, saying, Your son lives.

52 Then inquired he of them the hour when he began to amend. And they said to him, Yesterday at the seventh hour the fever left him.

53 So the father knew that it was at the same hour, in the which Jesus said to him, Your son lives: and himself believed, and his whole house.

54 This is again the second miracle that Jesus did, when he was come out of Judea into Galilee.

CHAPTER 5

AFTER this there was a feast of the Jews; and Jesus went up to Jerusalem.

2 Now there is at Jerusalem by the sheep market a pool, which is called in the Hebrew tongue Bethesda, having five porches.

3 In these lay a great multitude of impotent folk, of blind, halt, withered, waiting for the moving of the water.

4 For an angel went down at a certain season into the pool, and troubled the water: whosoever then first after the troubling of the water stepped in was made whole of whatsoever disease he had.

5 And a certain man was there, which had an infirmity thirty and eight years.

6 When Jesus saw him lie, and knew that he had been now a long time in that case, he said to him, Will you be made whole?

7 The impotent man answered him, Sir, I have no man, when the water is troubled, to put me into the pool: but while I am coming, another steps down before me.

When your will is God's will, you will have your will.

CHARLES SPURGEON

8 Jesus said to him, Rise, take up your bed, and walk.

9 And immediately the man was made whole, and took up his bed, and walked: and on the same day was the sabbath.

10 The Jews therefore said to him that was cured, It is the sabbath day: it is not lawful for you to carry your bed.

11 He answered them, He that made me whole, the same said to me, Take up your bed, and walk.

12 Then asked they him, What man is that which said to you, Take up your bed, and walk?

13 And he that was healed did not know who it was: for Jesus had conveyed himself away, a multitude being in that place.

14 Afterward Jesus found him in the temple, and said to him, Behold, you are made whole: sin no more, lest a worse thing come to you.

15 The man departed, and told the Jews that it was Jesus, which had made him whole.

16 And therefore did the Jews persecute Jesus, and sought to slay him, because he had done these things on the sabbath day.

17 But Jesus answered them, My Father works hitherto, and I work.

18 Therefore the Jews sought the more to kill him, because he not only had broken the sabbath, but said also that God was his Father, making himself equal with God.

19 Then answered Jesus and said to them, Verily, verily, I say to you, The Son can do nothing of himself, but what he sees the Father do: for what things soever he does, these also does the Son likewise.

20 For the Father loves the Son, and shows him all things that himself does: and he will show him greater works than these, that you may marvel.

21 For as the Father raises up the dead, and quickens them; even so the Son quickens whom he will.

22 For the Father judges no man, but has committed all judgment to the Son:

23 That all men should honor the Son, even as they honor the Father. He that honors not the Son honors not the Father which has sent him.

24 **Verily, verily, I say to you, He that hears my word, and believes on him that sent me, has everlasting life, and shall not come into condemnation; but is passed from death to life.**

25 Verily, verily, I say to you, The hour is coming, and now is, when the dead shall hear the voice of the Son of God: and they that hear shall live.

26 For as the Father has life in himself; so has he given to the Son to have life in himself;

27 And has given him authority to execute judgment also, because he is the Son of man.

28 Marvel not at this: for the hour is coming, in the which all that are in the graves shall hear his voice,

29 And shall come forth; they that have

5:14 We once lay as feeble, fragile, and frail folk, helpless and hopeless, pathetically paralyzed by the devil—"taken captive to do his will" until Jesus spoke a word to us. We were on a deathbed of sin with no one able to help us, but we heard the voice of the Word of God saying: "Arise from the dead, and Christ shall give you light" (Ephesians 5:14).

Now a thankful heart for the unspeakable gift makes us want to be always in the presence of God. Unlike the healed man, however, we need not go to the temple to thank the Father, for He now abides in the heart of the believer. The work of Calvary has made the believer the temple of the Living God. See 2 Corinthians 6:16.

5:17 Jesus' claims. Jesus was either God in human form, or a crackpot. There is no middle ground. In verses 17–29 He said:

- Whatever He saw the Father do, He did.
- God showed Jesus everything He did and He had even greater things to show Him, which would cause the people to be astonished.
- Just as God raised the dead and gave life to them, so Jesus gives life to whoever He would.
- God Himself had appointed Jesus of Nazareth as the Judge of all mankind.
- Humanity should honor Jesus as much as they honor the Father.
- Those who didn't honor Jesus didn't honor God.
- All who heard His words and trusted in the Father escape the wrath of the Law.
- All who trusted Him passed from death to life.
- The hour would come when *everyone* in their graves would hear the voice of Jesus, and be raised from the dead.
- As God is the source of all life, so He has given Jesus life in Himself.

5:28 Jesus' unique words: Jesus is saying that His voice will raise *billions* who have died. Psalm 29:3–9 describes the powerful voice of God. See John 6:38 comment.

5:28,29 Judgment Day: For verses that warn of its reality, see Acts 17:31.

**done good, to the resurrection of life;
and they that have done evil, to the resurrection of damnation.**
30 I can of mine own self do nothing: as
I hear, I judge: and my judgment is just;
because I seek not mine own will, but the
will of the Father which has sent me.
31 If I bear witness of myself, my witness
is not true.
32 There is another that bears witness
of me; and I know that the witness which
he witnesses of me is true.
33 You sent to John, and he bare witness
to the truth.
34 But I receive not testimony from man:
but these things I say, that you might be
saved.
35 He was a burning and a shining light:
and you were willing for a season to rejoice in his light.
36 But I have greater witness than that
of John: for the works which the Father
has given me to finish, the same works
that I do, bear witness of me, that the Father has sent me.
37 And the Father himself, which has
sent me, has borne witness of me. You
have neither heard his voice at any time,
nor seen his shape.
38 And you have not his word abiding
in you: for whom he has sent, him you
believe not.
39 Search the scriptures; for in them you
think you have eternal life: and they are
they which testify of me.
40 And you will not come to me, that
you might have life.
41 I receive not honor from men.
42 But I know you, that you have not
the love of God in you.
43 I am come in my Father's name, and
you receive me not: if another shall come
in his own name, him you will receive.
44 How can you believe, which receive
honor one of another, and seek not the
honor that comes from God only?
45 Do not think that I will accuse you
to the Father: there is one that accuses
you, even Moses, in whom you trust.
46 For had you believed Moses, you
would have believed me: for he wrote of
me.
47 But if you believe not his writings,
how shall you believe my words?

*For the Bible's inspiration,
see 2 Timothy 3:16 comment.*

CHAPTER 6

AFTER these things Jesus went over
the sea of Galilee, which is the sea
of Tiberias.
2 And a great multitude followed him,
because they saw his miracles which he
did on them that were diseased.
3 And Jesus went up into a mountain,
and there he sat with his disciples.
4 And the passover, a feast of the Jews,
was nigh.
5 When Jesus then lifted up his eyes, and
saw a great company come to him, he
said to Philip, Whence shall we buy bread,
that these may eat?
6 And this he said to prove him: for he
himself knew what he would do.
7 Philip answered him, Two hundred
pennyworth of bread is not sufficient for
them, that every one of them may take a
little.
8 One of his disciples, Andrew, Simon
Peter's brother, said to him,
9 There is a lad here, which has five barley loaves, and two small fishes: but what
are they among so many?
10 And Jesus said, Make the men sit
down. Now there was much grass in the
place. So the men sat down, in number
about five thousand.
11 And Jesus took the loaves; and when

5:39,40 To see why sinners need to come to Jesus to have life, see John 3:7 comment and Ephesians 4:18 "Questions & Objections."

he had given thanks, he distributed to
the disciples, and the disciples to them
that were set down; and likewise of the
fishes as much as they would.
12 When they were filled, he said to his
disciples, Gather up the fragments that
remain, that nothing be lost.
13 Therefore they gathered them together, and filled twelve baskets with the
fragments of the five barley loaves, which
remained over and above to them that
had eaten.
14 Then those men, when they had seen
the miracle that Jesus did, said, This is of
a truth that prophet that should come into the world.
15 When Jesus therefore perceived that
they would come and take him by force,
to make him a king, he departed again into a mountain himself alone.
16 And when even was now come, his
disciples went down to the sea,
17 And entered into a ship, and went
over the sea toward Capernaum. And it
was now dark, and Jesus was not come
to them.
18 And the sea arose by reason of a great
wind that blew.
19 So when they had rowed about five
and twenty or thirty furlongs, they see
Jesus walking on the sea, and drawing
near to the ship: and they were afraid.
20 But he said to them, It is I; be not
afraid.
21 Then they willingly received him into the ship: and immediately the ship was
at the land where they went.
22 The day following, when the people
which stood on the other side of the sea
saw that there was none other boat there,
save that one whereinto his disciples were
entered, and that Jesus went not with his
disciples into the boat, but that his disciples were gone away alone;
23 (Howbeit there came other boats from
Tiberias near to the place where they did
eat bread, after that the Lord had given
thanks:)
24 When the people therefore saw that
Jesus was not there, neither his disciples,
they also took shipping, and came to Capernaum, seeking for Jesus.
25 And when they had found him on
the other side of the sea, they said to him,
Rabbi, when did you come here?
26 Jesus answered them and said, Verily, verily, I say to you, You seek me, not
because you saw the miracles, but because you did eat of the loaves, and were
filled.
27 **Labour not for the meat which perishes, but for that meat which endures
to everlasting life, which the Son of man
shall give to you: for him has God the
Father sealed.**
28 Then said they to him, What shall we
do, that we might work the works of God?
29 Jesus answered and said to them, This
is the work of God, that you believe on
him whom he has sent.
30 They said therefore to him, What sign
do you show then, that we may see, and
believe you? what do you work?
31 Our fathers did eat manna in the desert; as it is written, He gave them bread
from heaven to eat.
32 Then Jesus said to them, Verily, verily, I say to you, Moses gave you not that
bread from heaven; but my Father gives
you the true bread from heaven.
33 For the bread of God is he which
came down from heaven, and gives life to
the world.
34 Then said they to him, Lord, evermore
give us this bread.
35 **And Jesus said to them, I am the**

6:14 Messianic prophecy fulfilled: "The LORD your God will raise up to you a Prophet from your midst, of your brethren, like unto me; to him you shall hearken" (Deuteronomy 18:15). See John 19:29 comment.

6:28,29 Most religions teach that certain works are required in order to be saved. Here God tells us the only "work" He considers: "believe on him whom he has sent."

bread of life: he that comes to me shall never hunger; and he that believes on me shall never thirst.
36 But I said to you, That you also have seen me, and believe not.
37 **All that the Father gives me shall come to me; and him that comes to me I will in no wise cast out.**
38 For I came down from heaven, not to do mine own will, but the will of him that sent me.
39 And this is the Father's will which has sent me, that of all which he has given me I should lose nothing, but should raise it up again at the last day.
40 And this is the will of him that sent me, that every one which sees the Son, and believes on him, may have everlasting life: and I will raise him up at the last day.
41 The Jews then murmured at him, because he said, I am the bread which came down from heaven.
42 And they said, Is not this Jesus, the son of Joseph, whose father and mother we know? how is it then that he says, I came down from heaven?
43 Jesus therefore answered and said to them, Murmur not among yourselves.
44 **No man can come to me, except the Father which has sent me draw him: and I will raise him up at the last day.**
45 It is written in the prophets, And they shall be all taught of God. Every man therefore that has heard, and has learned of the Father, comes to me.
46 Not that any man has seen the Father, save he which is of God, he has seen the Father.
47 Verily, verily, I say to you, He that believes on me has everlasting life.
48 I am that bread of life.
49 Your fathers did eat manna in the wilderness, and are dead.
50 This is the bread which came down from heaven, that a man may eat thereof, and not die.
51 I am the living bread which came down from heaven: if any man eat of this bread, he shall live for ever: and the bread that I will give is my flesh, which I will give for the life of the world.
52 The Jews therefore strove among themselves, saying, How can this man give us his flesh to eat?
53 Then Jesus said to them, Verily, verily, I say to you, Except you eat the flesh of the Son of man, and drink his blood, you have no life in you.
54 Whoso eats my flesh, and drinks my blood, has eternal life; and I will raise him up at the last day.

6:38 Jesus' unique words: Jesus said that He "came down" from heaven, that He was pre-existent. He says elsewhere: "I am from above...I am not of this world" (8:23), and "I proceeded forth and came from God" (8:42). For more on His pre-existence, see John 17:5. See also John 6:47 comment.

6:45 Taught by God. "Read and read again, and do not despair of help to understand the will and mind of God though you think they are fast locked up from you. Neither trouble your heads though you have not commentaries and exposition. Pray and read, read and pray; for a little from God is better than a great deal from men. Also, what is from men is uncertain, and is often lost and tumbled over by men; but what is from God is fixed as a nail in a sure place. There is nothing that so abides with us as what we receive from God; and the reason why the Christians in this day are at such a loss as to some things is that they are contented with what comes from men's mouths, without searching and kneeling before God to know of Him the truth of things. Things we receive at God's hands come to us as truths from the minting house, though old in themselves, yet new to us. Old truths are always new to us if they come with the smell of heaven upon them." *John Bunyan*

6:47 Jesus' unique words: He was saying that He had the authority to grant *everlasting life* to all who trust in Him. See John 6:53,54 comment.

6:51 Salvation is possible for every person. See John 7:37.

Halloween—an incredible opportunity for sharing the gospel. See 1 Timothy 4:1 comment.

55 For my flesh is meat indeed, and my
blood is drink indeed.
56 He that eats my flesh, and drinks my
blood, dwells in me, and I in him.
57 As the living Father has sent me, and
I live by the Father: so he that eats me,
even he shall live by me.
58 This is that bread which came down
from heaven: not as your fathers did eat
manna, and are dead: he that eats of this
bread shall live for ever.
59 These things said he in the synagogue,
as he taught in Capernaum.
60 Many therefore of his disciples, when
they had heard this, said, This is an hard
saying; who can hear it?
61 When Jesus knew in himself that his
disciples murmured at it, he said to them,
Does this offend you?
62 What and if you shall see the Son of
man ascend up where he was before?
63 It is the spirit that quickens; the flesh
profits nothing: the words that I speak to
you, they are spirit, and they are life.
64 But there are some of you that believe
not. For Jesus knew from the beginning
who they were that believed not, and
who should betray him.
65 And he said, Therefore said I to you,
that no man can come to me, except it
were given to him of my Father.
66 From that time many of his disciples
went back, and walked no more with him.
67 Then said Jesus to the twelve, Will
you also go away?
68 Then Simon Peter answered him,
Lord, to whom shall we go? you have
the words of eternal life.
69 And we believe and are sure that you
are that Christ, the Son of the living God.
70 Jesus answered them, Have not I chosen you twelve, and one of you is a devil?
71 He spoke of Judas Iscariot the son of
Simon: for he it was that should betray
him, being one of the twelve.

CHAPTER 7

AFTER these things Jesus walked in Galilee: for he would not walk in Jewry, because the Jews sought to kill him.

6:53,54 Jesus' unique words: These are the words of a madman . . . or God in human form. He was not advocating cannibalism, but was speaking in a spiritual sense. Just as we need to eat and drink in order to live, so we must "eat" the Bread of Life (John 6:48,51) and "drink" His "blood, which is shed for you" (Luke 22:20) in order to have spiritual life. Unless we trust in Christ, relying on Him daily for our life-sustaining nourishment, we have no life in us and remain dead in our sins. (See Ephesians 2:1 comment.) See also John 8:51 comment.

6:65 "The impulse to pursue God originates with God." *A. W. Tozer*

6:68 The uniqueness of Jesus. "This Jesus of Nazareth, without money and arms, conquered more millions than Alexander, Caesar, Mohammed, and Napoleon; without science and learning, He shed more light on things human and divine than all philosophers and scholars combined; without the eloquence of schools, He spoke such words of life as were never spoken before or since, and produced effects which lie beyond the reach of orator or poet; without writing a single line, He set more pens in motion, and furnished themes for more sermons, orations, discussions, learned volumes, works of art, and songs of praise than the whole army of great men of ancient and modern times." *Philip Schaff, The Person of Christ*

2 Now the Jews' feast of tabernacles was at hand.
3 His brethren therefore said to him, Depart hence, and go into Judea, that your disciples also may see the works that you do.
4 For there is no man that does any thing in secret, and he himself seeks to be known openly. If you do these things, show yourself to the world.
5 For neither did his brethren believe in him.
6 Then Jesus said to them, My time is not yet come: but your time is always ready.
7 The world cannot hate you; but me it hates, because I testify of it, that the works thereof are evil.
8 Go up to this feast: I go not up yet to this feast; for my time is not yet full come.
9 When he had said these words to them, he abode still in Galilee.
10 But when his brethren were gone up, then went he also up to the feast, not openly, but as it were in secret.
11 Then the Jews sought him at the feast, and said, Where is he?
12 And there was much murmuring among the people concerning him: for some said, He is a good man: others said, Nay; but he deceives the people.
13 Howbeit no man spoke openly of him for fear of the Jews.
14 Now about the midst of the feast Jesus went up into the temple, and taught.
15 And the Jews marveled, saying, How knows this man letters, having never learned?
16 Jesus answered them, and said, My doctrine is not mine, but his that sent me.
17 If any man will do his will, he shall know of the doctrine, whether it be of God, or whether I speak of myself.
18 He that speaks of himself seeks his own glory: but he that seeks his glory that sent him, the same is true, and no unrighteousness is in him.
19 Did not Moses give you the law, and yet none of you keeps the law? Why do you go about to kill me?
20 The people answered and said, You have a devil: who goes about to kill you?
21 Jesus answered and said to them, I have done one work, and you all marvel.
22 Moses therefore gave to you circumcision; (not because it is of Moses, but of the fathers;) and you on the sabbath day circumcise a man.
23 If a man on the sabbath day receive circumcision, that the law of Moses should not be broken; are you angry at me, because I have made a man every whit whole on the sabbath day?
24 Judge not according to the appearance, but judge righteous judgment.
25 Then said some of them of Jerusalem, Is not this he, whom they seek to kill?
26 But, lo, he speaks boldly, and they say nothing to him. Do the rulers know indeed that this is the very Christ?
27 Howbeit we know this man whence he is: but when Christ comes, no man knows whence he is.
28 Then cried Jesus in the temple as he taught, saying, You both know me, and you know whence I am: and I am not come of myself, but he that sent me is true, whom you know not.
29 But I know him: for I am from him,

7:17 In reference to creation, respected Bible teacher *Derek Prince* said, "I am simple-minded enough to believe that it happened the way the Bible described it. I have been a professor at Britain's largest university [Cambridge] for nine years. I hold various degrees and academic distinctions, and I feel in many ways I am quite sophisticated intellectually, but I don't feel in any way intellectually inferior when I say that I believe the Bible record of creation. Prior to believing the Bible I have studied many other attempts to explain man's origin and found them all unsatisfying and in many cases self-contradictory. I turned to study the Bible as a professional philosopher—not as a believer—and I commented to myself, 'At least it can't be any sillier than some of the other things I've heard,' and to my astonishment, I discovered it had the answer."

and he has sent me.
30 Then they sought to take him: but no
man laid hands on him, because his hour
was not yet come.
31 And many of the people believed on
him, and said, When Christ comes, will he
do more miracles than these which this
man has done?
32 The Pharisees heard that the people
murmured such things concerning him;
and the Pharisees and the chief priests
sent officers to take him.
33 Then said Jesus to them, Yet a little
while am I with you, and then I go to him
that sent me.
34 You shall seek me, and shall not find
me: and where I am, there you cannot
come.
35 Then said the Jews among themselves,
Where will he go, that we shall not find
him? will he go to the dispersed among
the Gentiles, and teach the Gentiles?
36 What manner of saying is this that he
said, You shall seek me, and shall not find
me: and where I am, there you cannot
come?
37 In the last day, that great day of the
feast, Jesus stood and cried, saying, If
any man thirst, let him come to me, and
drink.
38 **He that believes on me, as the scrip-**
ture has said, out of his belly shall flow
rivers of living water.
39 (But this spoke he of the Spirit, which
they that believe on him should receive:
for the Holy Spirit was not yet given; because that Jesus was not yet glorified.)
40 Many of the people therefore, when
they heard this saying, said, Of a truth
this is the Prophet.
41 Others said, This is the Christ. But

"I know men and I tell you that Jesus Christ is no mere man..." (See what Napolean had to say about Jesus in John 7:46.)

Napolean Bonaparte

some said, Shall Christ come out of Galilee?
42 Has not the scripture said, That Christ
comes of the seed of David, and out of the
town of Bethlehem, where David was?
43 So there was a division among the
people because of him.
44 And some of them would have taken
him; but no man laid hands on him.
45 Then came the officers to the chief
priests and Pharisees; and they said to
them, Why have you not brought him?
46 The officers answered, Never man
spoke like this man.
47 Then answered them the Pharisees,
Are you also deceived?
48 Have any of the rulers or of the Pharisees believed on him?

7:37 Salvation is possible for every person. See Acts 2:21.

7:46 The uniqueness of Jesus. "I know men and I tell you that Jesus Christ is no mere man. Between Him and every other person in the world there is no possible term of comparison. Alexander, Caesar, Charlemagne, and I have founded empires. But on what did we rest the creations of our genius? Upon force. Jesus Christ founded His empire upon love; and at this hour millions of men would die for Him." *Napoleon Bonaparte* (quoted in *Evidence That Demands a Verdict* by *Josh McDowell*)

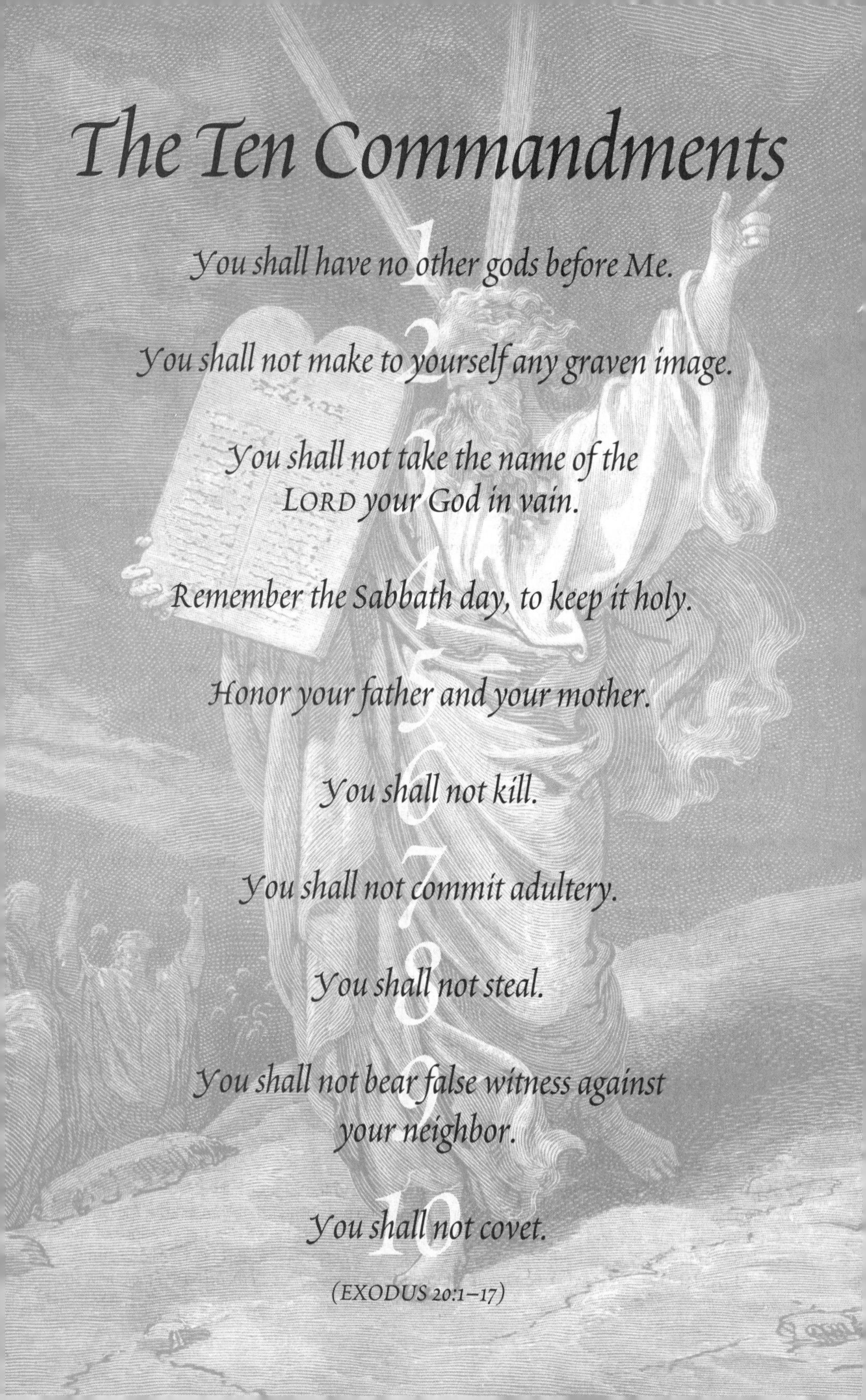

The Ten Commandments

1. *You shall have no other gods before Me.*

2. *You shall not make to yourself any graven image.*

3. *You shall not take the name of the LORD your God in vain.*

4. *Remember the Sabbath day, to keep it holy.*

5. *Honor your father and your mother.*

6. *You shall not kill.*

7. *You shall not commit adultery.*

8. *You shall not steal.*

9. *You shall not bear false witness against your neighbor.*

10. *You shall not covet.*

(EXODUS 20:1–17)

QUESTIONS & OBJECTIONS

8:9 ***"You are trying to make me feel guilty by quoting the Ten Commandments."***

Ask the person which one of the Ten Commandments makes him feel guilty. Simply state, "The Bible says, 'You shall not steal.' If you feel guilty when you hear that, why do you think that is? Could it be because you *are* guilty?" God gave us our conscience so we would know when we break His Law; the guilt we feel when we do something wrong tells us that we need to repent. (See also Romans 2:15 comment.)

49 But this people who knows not the
law are cursed.
50 Nicodemus said to them, (he that
came to Jesus by night, being one of them,)
51 Does our law judge any man, before
it hear him, and know what he does?
52 They answered and said to him, are
you also of Galilee? Search, and look: for
out of Galilee arises no prophet.
53 And every man went to his own
house.

CHAPTER 8

JESUS went to the mount of Olives.
2 And early in the morning he came
again into the temple, and all the people
came to him; and he sat down, and taught
them.
3 And the scribes and Pharisees brought
to him a woman taken in adultery; and
when they had set her in the midst,
4 They said to him, Master, this woman
was taken in adultery, in the very act.
5 Now Moses in the law commanded
us, that such should be stoned: but what
do you say?
6 This they said, tempting him, that they
might have to accuse him. But Jesus
stooped down, and with his finger wrote
on the ground, as though he heard them
not.
7 So when they continued asking him,
he lifted up himself, and said to them, He
that is without sin among you, let him first
cast a stone at her.
8 And again he stooped down, and wrote
on the ground.
9 And they which heard it, being convicted by their own conscience, went out
one by one, beginning at the eldest, even
to the last: and Jesus was left alone, and
the woman standing in the midst.
10 When Jesus had lifted up himself,
and saw none but the woman, he said to
her, Woman, where are those your accus-

USING THE LAW IN EVANGELISM

8:4,5 The wrath of the Law brought this woman to the feet of the Savior. That's the function of the Law: to condemn. Some may say that we shouldn't *condemn* anyone, when all the Law does is reveal to the sinner that he is "condemned already" (John 3:18). The Law shows him his danger and therefore his desperate need for the Savior. See Galatians 3:19 comment.

7:52 This showed their ignorance of Scripture (see Isaiah 9:1,2), and of the fact that Jesus was born in Bethlehem.

8:6 It is likely that Jesus wrote the Ten Commandments on the ground. They had been talking about the Law, and each of the men were convicted by their conscience (v. 9), which is the effect of the Law (Romans 2:15). The Law was written in stone (uncompromising), this was written in sand (removable)—*besides, what else does God write with His finger?* See Exodus 31:18.

QUESTIONS & OBJECTIONS

8:11 ***"Jesus didn't condemn the woman caught in the act of adultery, but condemned those who judged her. Therefore you shouldn't judge others."***

The Christian is not "judging others" but simply telling the world of *God's* judgment—that God (not the Christian) has judged all the world as being guilty before Him (Romans 3:19,23). Jesus was able to offer that woman forgiveness for her sin, because He was on His way to die on the cross for her. She acknowledged Him as "Lord," but He still told her, "Go, and sin no more." If she didn't repent, she would perish.

ers? has no man condemned you?
11 She said, No man, Lord. And Jesus
said to her, Neither do I condemn you:
go, and sin no more.
12 Then spoke Jesus again to them,
saying, I am the light of the world: he
that follows me shall not walk in dark-
ness, but shall have the light of life.
13 The Pharisees therefore said to him,
You bear record of yourself; your record
is not true.
14 Jesus answered and said to them,
Though I bear record of myself, yet my
record is true: for I know whence I came,
and where I go; but you cannot tell whence
I come, and where I go.
15 You judge after the flesh; I judge no
man.
16 And yet if I judge, my judgment is
true: for I am not alone, but I and the Father that sent me.
17 It is also written in your law, that the
testimony of two men is true.
18 I am one that bears witness of myself,
and the Father that sent me bears witness of me.
19 Then said they to him, Where is your
Father? Jesus answered, You neither know
me, nor my Father: if you had known me,
you should have known my Father also.
20 These words spoke Jesus in the treasury, as he taught in the temple: and no
man laid hands on him; for his hour was
not yet come.
21 Then said Jesus again to them, I go
my way, and you shall seek me, and shall
die in your sins: where I go, you cannot
come.
22 Then said the Jews, Will he kill himself? because he says, Where I go, you cannot come.
23 And he said to them, You are from
beneath; I am from above: you are of this
world; I am not of this world.
24 I said therefore to you, that you shall
die in your sins: for if you believe not that
I am he, you shall die in your sins.
25 Then said they to him, Who are thou?
And Jesus said to them, Even the same
that I said to you from the beginning.
26 I have many things to say and to
judge of you: but he that sent me is true;

8:10–12 What a fearful thing it is when we face God's Law. The very stones call for our blood. The Law cries out for justice; it has no mercy. It demands, "The soul that sins shall die!" But the Judge who rules can, at His own discretion, administer the *spirit* of the Law, and its spirit says that mercy rejoices over judgment—God is rich in mercy to all who call upon Him.

The letter kills, but the Spirit brings life. God is not willing that the wrath of the Law fall upon guilty sinners, because He would rather acquit the criminal from the courtroom... and He can do so because of Calvary.

A. N. Martin said, "The moment God's Law ceases to be the most powerful factor in influencing the moral sensitivity of any individual or nation, there will be indifference to Divine wrath, and when indifference comes in it always brings in its train indifference to salvation."

and I speak to the world those things
which I have heard of him.
27 They understood not that he spoke
to them of the Father.
28 Then said Jesus to them, When you
have lifted up the Son of man, then shall
you know that I am he, and that I do nothing of myself; but as my Father has taught
me, I speak these things.
29 And he that sent me is with me: the
Father has not left me alone; for I do always those things that please him.
30 As he spoke these words, many believed on him.
31 **Then said Jesus to those Jews which
believed on him, If you continue in my
word, then are you my disciples indeed;**
32 **And you shall know the truth, and
the truth shall make you free.**
33 They answered him, We are Abraham's seed, and were never in bondage
to any man: how do you say, You shall
be made free?
34 Jesus answered them, Verily, verily,
I say to you, Whosoever commits sin is
the servant of sin.
35 And the servant abides not in the
house for ever: but the Son abides ever.
36 If the Son therefore shall make you
free, you shall be free indeed.
37 I know that you are Abraham's seed;
but you seek to kill me, because my word
has no place in you.
38 I speak that which I have seen with
my Father: and you do that which you
have seen with your father.
39 They answered and said to him, Abraham is our father. Jesus said to them, If
you were Abraham's children, you would
do the works of Abraham.
40 But now you seek to kill me, a man
that has told you the truth, which I have
heard of God: this did not Abraham.
41 You do the deeds of your father. Then
said they to him, We are not born of fornication; we have one Father, even God.
42 Jesus said to them, If God were your
Father, you would love me: for I proceeded forth and came from God; neither
came I of myself, but he sent me.
43 Why do you not understand my
speech? even because you cannot hear
my word.
**44 You are of your father the devil,
and the lusts of your father you will do.
He was a murderer from the beginning,
and abode not in the truth, because there
is no truth in him. When he speaks a
lie, he speaks of his own: for he is a
liar, and the father of it.**
45 And because I tell you the truth, you
believe me not.
46 Which of you convinces me of sin?
And if I say the truth, why do you not
believe me?
47 He that is of God hears God's words:
you therefore hear them not, because you
are not of God.
48 Then answered the Jews, and said to
him, Say we not well that you are a Samaritan, and have a devil?
49 Jesus answered, I have not a devil; but
I honor my Father, and you do dishonor
me.
50 And I seek not mine own glory: there
is one that seeks and judges.
51 Verily, verily, I say to you, If a man
keep my saying, he shall never see death.

8:44 Names of the enemy. The devil is called the god and prince of this world, and the ruler of darkness (2 Corinthians 4:4; John 12:31; Acts 26:18; Ephesians 6:12). He seeks to hinder the work of God and suppress God's Word (Matthew 13:38,39; 1 Thessalonians 2:18). He is a liar, the father of lies, and a murderer (John 8:44). The devil is your adversary and a devourer (1 Peter 5:8). He is the promoter of pride (Genesis 3:5; 1 Timothy 3:6), the stimulator of lust (Ephesians 2:2,3), and the tempter (Luke 4:1–13).

8:51 Jesus' unique words: *Anyone* who obeys Him would not die. This is not advocating works as a means of salvation, but obedience as a *sign* of our salvation. We keep His word because we love Him (John 14:23). See 1 John 2:17 and John 8:58 comment.

52 Then said the Jews to him, Now we
know that you have a devil. Abraham is
dead, and the prophets; and you say, If a
man keep my saying, he shall never taste
of death.
53 Are you greater than our father Abraham, which is dead? and the prophets are
dead: whom do you make yourself?
54 Jesus answered, If I honor myself,
my honor is nothing: it is my Father that
honors me; of whom you say, that he is
your God:
55 Yet you have not known him; but I
know him: and if I should say, I know
him not, I shall be a liar like you: but I
know him, and keep his saying.
56 Your father Abraham rejoiced to see
my day: and he saw it, and was glad.
57 Then said the Jews to him, You are
not yet fifty years old, and have you seen
Abraham?
**58 Jesus said to them, Verily, verily, I
say to you, Before Abraham was, I am.**
59 Then took they up stones to cast at
him: but Jesus hid himself, and went out
of the temple, going through the midst
of them, and so passed by.

CHAPTER 9

AND as Jesus passed by, he saw a man
which was blind from his birth.
2 And his disciples asked him, saying,
Master, who did sin, this man, or his parents, that he was born blind?
3 Jesus answered, Neither has this man
sinned, nor his parents: but that the works
of God should be made manifest in him.
4 I must work the works of him that sent
me, while it is day: the night comes, when
no man can work.
5 As long as I am in the world, I am the
light of the world.
6 When he had thus spoken, he spat on
the ground, and made clay of the spittle,
and he anointed the eyes of the blind man
with the clay,
7 And said to him, Go, wash in the pool
of Siloam, (which is by interpretation,
Sent.) He went his way therefore, and
washed, and came seeing.
8 The neighbours therefore, and they
which before had seen him that he was
blind, said, Is not this he that sat and
begged?
9 Some said, This is he: others said, He

8:58 Jesus' unique words: Jesus was affirming that He was God manifest in the flesh. He is the Great "I AM"—the Eternal One who revealed Himself to Moses in the burning bush (Exodus 3:14). See John 11:25 comment.

8:58 Was Jesus God in human form? If I give you a small slice of cheese from a large block (the taste being constant throughout the whole block), and you spit out the cheese saying you hate the taste, then you reject the whole block. Jesus was God manifest in human form. If the Jews rejected Him, they rejected the Father also—he who is of God hears God's words. John later stated in his epistle, "Whosoever denies the Son, the same has not the Father: (but) he that acknowledges the Son has the Father also" (1 John 2:23). See John 10:30.

9:4 *John Wesley* was asked what he would do with his life if he knew that he would die at midnight the next day. His answer was something like this: "I would just carry on with what I am doing. I will arise at 5:00 a.m. for prayer, then take a house meeting at 6.00 a.m. At 12 noon, I will be preaching at an open-air. At 3:00 p.m. I have another meeting in another town. At 6:00 p.m. I have a house meeting; at 10:00 p.m. I have a prayer meeting and at 12:00 midnight, I would go to be with my Lord."

If we knew we were to die at 12 o'clock tomorrow night, would we have to step up our evangelistic efforts, or could we in all good conscience carry on just as we are?

"The evangelistic harvest is always urgent. The destiny of men and of nations is always being decided. Every generation is strategic. We are not responsible for the past generation, and we cannot bear the full responsibility for the next one; but we do have our generation. God will hold us responsible as to how well we fulfill our responsibilities to this age and take advantage of our opportunities." *Billy Graham*

The Function of the Law

9:7 When we apply the tablets of the Law to the eyes of sinners, it causes them to have reason to go to the cleansing pool of the gospel. This man would not have had a *reason* to go to the pool, until he perceived that he was unclean. That's the function of the Law—to convince a man he is unclean (Romans 7:13). *Charles Spurgeon* said, "No man will ever put on the robe of Christ's righteousness till he is stripped of his fig leaves, nor will he wash in the fount of mercy till he perceives his filthiness. Therefore, my brethren, we must not cease to declare the Law, its demands, its threatenings, and the sinner's multiplied breaches of it."

is like him: but he said, I am he.
10 Therefore said they to him, How were
your eyes opened?
11 He answered and said, A man that is
called Jesus made clay, and anointed mine
eyes, and said to me, Go to the pool of Siloam, and wash: and I went and washed,
and I received sight.
12 Then said they to him, Where is he?
He said, I know not.
13 They brought to the Pharisees him
that beforetime was blind.
14 And it was the sabbath day when
Jesus made the clay, and opened his eyes.
15 Then again the Pharisees also asked
him how he had received his sight. He
said to them, He put clay upon mine eyes,
and I washed, and do see.
16 Therefore said some of the Pharisees, This man is not of God, because he
keeps not the sabbath day. Others said,
How can a man that is a sinner do such
miracles? And there was a division among
them.
17 They said to the blind man again,
What do you say of him, that he has
opened your eyes? He said, He is a prophet.
18 But the Jews did not believe concerning him, that he had been blind, and
received his sight, until they called the
parents of him that had received his sight.
19 And they asked them, saying, Is this
your son, who you say was born blind?
how then does he now see?
20 His parents answered them and said,
We know that this is our son, and that
he was born blind:
21 But by what means he now sees, we
know not; or who has opened his eyes, we
know not: he is of age; ask him: he shall
speak for himself.
22 These words spoke his parents, because they feared the Jews: for the Jews
had agreed already, that if any man did
confess that he was Christ, he should be
put out of the synagogue.
23 Therefore said his parents, He is of
age; ask him.
24 Then again called they the man that
was blind, and said to him, Give God the
praise: we know that this man is a sinner.
25 He answered and said, Whether he
be a sinner or no, I know not: one thing
I know, that, whereas I was blind, now I
see.
26 Then said they to him again, What
did he to you? how opened he your eyes?
27 He answered them, I have told you
already, and you did not hear: wherefore
would you hear it again? will you also be
his disciples?
28 Then they reviled him, and said, You
are his disciple; but we are Moses' disciples.
29 We know that God spoke to Moses: as
for this fellow, we know not from whence
he is.
30 The man answered and said to them,
Why herein is a marvelous thing, that
you know not from whence he is, and yet

9:25 This is the testimony of the newly saved. There are many questions for which they have no answers. But one thing they do know: "Whereas I was blind, now I see." It has been well said that the man with an experience is not at the mercy of a man with an argument.

he has opened mine eyes.

31 Now we know that God hears not sinners: but if any man be a worshipper of God, and does his will, him he hears.

32 Since the world began was it not heard that any man opened the eyes of one that was born blind.

33 If this man were not of God, he could do nothing.

34 They answered and said to him, You were altogether born in sins, and do you teach us? And they cast him out.

35 Jesus heard that they had cast him out; and when he had found him, he said to him, Do you believe on the Son of God?

36 He answered and said, Who is he, Lord, that I might believe on him?

37 And Jesus said to him, You have both seen him, and it is he that talks with you.

38 And he said, Lord, I believe. And he worshipped him.

39 And Jesus said, For judgment I am come into this world, that they which see not might see; and that they which see might be made blind.

40 And some of the Pharisees which were with him heard these words, and said to him, Are we blind also?

41 Jesus said to them, If you were blind, you should have no sin: but now you say, We see; therefore your sin remains.

CHAPTER 10

VERILY, verily, I say to you, He that enters not by the door into the sheepfold, but climbs up some other way, the same is a thief and a robber.

2 But he that enters in by the door is the shepherd of the sheep.

3 To him the porter opens; and the sheep hear his voice: and he calls his own sheep by name, and leads them out.

4 And when he puts forth his own sheep, he goes before them, and the sheep follow him: for they know his voice.

5 And a stranger will they not follow, but will flee from him: for they know not the voice of strangers.

6 This parable spoke Jesus to them: but they understood not what things they were which he spoke to them.

7 **Then said Jesus to them again, Verily, verily, I say to you, I am the door of the sheep.**

8 **All that ever came before me are thieves and robbers: but the sheep did not hear them.**

9 I am the door: by me if any man enter in, he shall be saved, and shall go in and out, and find pasture.

10 The thief comes not, but for to steal, and to kill, and to destroy: I am come that they might have life, and that they

10:2 True believers are likened to sheep, which: know the voice of their shepherd; are easily led (they submit without resistance); flock together (in unity); need a shepherd (or they stray); were a type of Israel (Matthew 10:6); imitate one another; are productive (wool, leather, meat, and milk); were a sign of God's blessing (see Deuteronomy 7:13); will be divided from the "goats" at the Judgment; were offered in sacrifice.

10:9 A Hebrew servant who was given his freedom had the option to stay with a master he loved. If he chose to give up his freedom, his master took him to the doorpost and pierced his ear with an awl, "and he shall serve him forever" (Exodus 21:5,6). In the same way, the sinner, upon conversion, is given freedom from sin and becomes a servant of Jesus Christ (1 Corinthians 7:22), to serve Him forever. He presents his body as a living sacrifice. His ear is forever open to the Door of the Savior (John 10:9).

10:10 "Evangelism is about experiencing God. If you choose to be obedient, He will take you on a journey so exciting that your life will never be the same." *Bill Fay, Share Jesus Without Fear*

"Evangelism is the cure to the disease of church boredom." *Todd P. McCollum*

"I can tell you that there is no greater joy than leading someone to faith in Jesus Christ. Even if they reject your message, it still feels great to obey Christ. Yet regardless of how we feel, we need to remember this is what He has commanded." *D. James Kennedy*

might have it more abundantly.
11 I am the good shepherd: the good
shepherd gives his life for the sheep.
12 But he that is an hireling, and not
the shepherd, whose own the sheep are
not, sees the wolf coming, and leaves the
sheep, and flees: and the wolf catches
them, and scatters the sheep.
13 The hireling flees, because he is an
hireling, and cares not for the sheep.
14 I am the good shepherd, and know
my sheep, and am known of mine.
15 As the Father knows me, even so
know I the Father: and I lay down my life
for the sheep.
16 And other sheep I have, which are not
of this fold: them also I must bring, and
they shall hear my voice; and there shall
be one fold, and one shepherd.
17 Therefore does my Father love me,
because I lay down my life, that I might
take it again.
18 **No man takes it from me, but I lay**
it down of myself. I have power to lay
it down, and I have power to take it
again. This commandment have I re-
ceived of my Father.
19 There was a division therefore again
among the Jews for these sayings.
20 And many of them said, He has a devil, and is mad; why do you hear him?
21 Others said, These are not the words
of him that has a devil. Can a devil open
the eyes of the blind?
22 And it was at Jerusalem the feast of
the dedication, and it was winter.
23 And Jesus walked in the temple in
Solomon's porch.
24 Then came the Jews round about
him, and said to him, How long do you
make us to doubt? If you be the Christ,
tell us plainly.
25 Jesus answered them, I told you, and
you believed not: the works that I do in
my Father's name, they bear witness of
me.

The Bible is unique and proves itself to be supernatural in origin. See Psalm 119:105 comment.

26 But you believe not, because you are
not of my sheep, as I said to you.
27 My sheep hear my voice, and I know
them, and they follow me:
28 And I give to them eternal life; and
they shall never perish, neither shall any
man pluck them out of my hand.
29 My Father, which gave them me, is
greater than all; and no man is able to
pluck them out of my Father's hand.
30 I and my Father are one.

10:11 Hundreds of years earlier, David had written that the Lord was his shepherd, and now that Shepherd had become flesh. Here is a continuance of the most famous of psalms, Psalm 23. This was the "Great Shepherd" Himself (Hebrews 13:20), the One who takes away the "want" of the covetous human heart. He was the path of righteousness, who brought light to the valley of the shadow of death. Here was the Bread of Life, placed by God on a table in the presence of our enemies. Heaven's cup "ran over," and brought the Father's goodness and mercy to us, so that we might dwell in the House of the Lord forever.

10:16 The Mormons misrepresent this verse. It is an obvious reference to the Gentiles. See John 11:52; Romans 15:9–12; Ephesians 2:11–18.

10:27 See 2 Timothy 2:19 comment.

10:30 **Was Jesus God in human form?** See John 10:38.

31 Then the Jews took up stones again to stone him.
32 Jesus answered them, Many good works have I showed you from my Father; for which of those works do you stone me?
33 The Jews answered him, saying, For a good work we stone you not; but for blasphemy; and because that you, being a man, make yourself God.
34 Jesus answered them, Is it not written in your law, I said, You are gods?
35 If he called them gods, to whom the word of God came, and the scripture cannot be broken;
36 Do you say of him, whom the Father has sanctified, and sent into the world, You blaspheme; because I said, I am the Son of God?

> Preach Christ or nothing: don't dispute or discuss except with your eye on the cross.
>
> **CHARLES SPURGEON**

37 If I do not the works of my Father, believe me not.
38 But if I do, though you believe not me, believe the works: that you may know, and believe, that the Father is in me, and I in him.
39 Therefore they sought again to take him: but he escaped out of their hand,
40 And went away again beyond Jordan into the place where John at first baptized; and there he abode.
41 And many resorted to him, and said, John did no miracle: but all things that John spoke of this man were true.
42 And many believed on him there.

CHAPTER 11

NOW a certain man was sick, named Lazarus, of Bethany, the town of Mary and her sister Martha.
2 (It was that Mary which anointed the Lord with ointment, and wiped his feet with her hair, whose brother Lazarus was sick.)
3 Therefore his sisters sent to him, saying, Lord, behold, he whom you love is sick.
4 When Jesus heard that, he said, This sickness is not to death, but for the glory of God, that the Son of God might be glorified thereby.
5 Now Jesus loved Martha, and her sister, and Lazarus.
6 When he had heard therefore that he was sick, he abode two days still in the same place where he was.
7 Then after that said he to his disciples, Let us go into Judea again.
8 His disciples said to him, Master, the Jews of late sought to stone you; and you go there again?
9 Jesus answered, Are there not twelve hours in the day? If any man walk in the day, he stumbles not, because he sees the light of this world.
10 But if a man walk in the night, he stumbles, because there is no light in him.
11 These things said he: and after that he said to them, Our friend Lazarus sleeps; but I go, that I may awake him out of sleep.
12 Then said his disciples, Lord, if he sleep, he shall do well.

10:38 Was Jesus God in human form? See John 14:10.

11:6 God's ways are distinctively and consistently different from ours. God did not rescue Daniel out of the lion's den as we would have. He didn't turn off the fiery furnace into which Shadrach, Meshach, and Abed-Nego were cast, as we would. He didn't kill Pharaoh and save the Israelites from the Red Sea; instead He worked His wondrous purposes *in* the lion's den, *in* the furnace, and *in* the Red Sea. Lion's teeth, fire, and water are no big deal to the God who created them. Death, at the presence of the Light of the world, is but a shadow that quickly dissipates like a frightened and sickly child.

10:36 *The Deity of Jesus*

From *Christ Before the Manger* by *Ron Rhodes*

A strong argument for the deity of Christ is the fact that many of the names, titles, and attributes ascribed to Yahweh are also ascribed to Jesus Christ.

DESCRIPTION	FATHER	JESUS
Yahweh ("I AM")	Exodus 3:14 Deuteronomy 32:39 Isaiah 43:10	John 8:24 John 8:58 John 18:4–6
God	Genesis 1:1 Deuteronomy 6:4 Psalm 45:6,7	Isaiah 7:14 Isaiah 9:6 John 1:1,14 John 20:28 Titus 2:13 Hebrews 1:8 2 Peter 1:1 Matthew 1:23 1 John 5:20
Alpha and Omega (First and Last)	Isaiah 41:4 Isaiah 48:12 Revelation 1:8	Revelation 1:17,18 Revelation 2:8 Revelation 22:12–16
Lord	Isaiah 45:23	Matthew 12:8 Acts 7:59,60 Acts 10:36 Romans 10:12 1 Corinthians 2:8 1 Corinthians 12:3 Philippians 2:10,11
Savior	Isaiah 43:3 Isaiah 43:11 Isaiah 49:26 Isaiah 63:8 Luke 1:47 1 Timothy 4:10	Matthew 1:21 Luke 2:11 John 1:29 John 4:42 2 Timothy 1:10 Titus 2:13 Hebrews 5:9
King	Psalm 95:3 Isaiah 43:15 1 Timothy 6:14–16	Revelation 17:14 Revelation 19:16
Judge	Genesis 18:25 Deuteronomy 32:36 Psalm 50:4,6 Psalm 58:11 Psalm 75:7 Psalm 96:13	John 5:22 2 Corinthians 5:10 2 Timothy 4:1
Light	2 Samuel 22:29 Psalm 27:1	John 1:4,9 John 3:19 John 8:12 John 9:5

(continued)

(10:36 continued)

DESCRIPTION	FATHER	JESUS
Rock	Deuteronomy 32:3,4 2 Samuel 22:32 Psalm 89:26	Romans 9:33 1 Corinthians 10:3,4 1 Peter 2:4–8
Redeemer	Psalm 130:7,8 Isaiah 43:1 Isaiah 48:17 Isaiah 49:26 Isaiah 54:5	Acts 20:28 Ephesians 1:7 Hebrews 9:12
Our Righteousness	Isaiah 45:24	Jeremiah 23:6 Romans 3:21,22
Husband	Isaiah 54:5 Hosea 2:16	Matthew 25:1 Mark 2:18,19 2 Corinthians 11:2 Ephesians 5:25–32 Revelation 21:2,9
Shepherd	Genesis 49:24 Psalm 23:1 Psalm 80:1	John 10:11,16 Hebrews 13:20 1 Peter 2:25 1 Peter 5:4
Creator	Genesis 1:1 Job 33:4 Psalm 95:5,6 Psalm 102:24,25 Isaiah 40:28 Isaiah 43:1 Acts 4:24	John 1:2,3,10 Colossians 1:15–18 Hebrews 1:1–3,10
Giver of Life	Genesis 2:7 Deuteronomy 32:39 1 Samuel 2:6 Psalm 36:9	John 5:21 John 10:28 John 11:25
Forgiver of Sin	Exodus 34:6,7 Nehemiah 9:17 Daniel 9:9 Jonah 4:2	Matthew 9:2 Mark 2:1–12 Acts 26:18 Colossians 2:13 Colossians 3:13
Lord our Healer	Exodus 15:26	Acts 9:34
Omnipresent	Psalm 139:7–12 Proverbs 15:3	Matthew 18:20 Matthew 28:20 Ephesians 3:17 Ephesians 4:10
Omniscient	1 Kings 8:39 Jeremiah 17:10,16	Matthew 9:4 Matthew 11:27 Luke 5:4–6 John 2:25 John 16:30 John 21:17 Acts 1:24

(continued)

(10:36 continued)

DESCRIPTION	FATHER	JESUS
Omnipotent	Isaiah 40:10–31 Isaiah 45:5–13 Revelation 19:6	Matthew 28:18 Mark 1:29–34 John 10:18 Jude 24
Preexistent	Genesis 1:1	John 1:15,30 John 3:13,31,32 John 6:62 John 16:28 John 17:5
Eternal	Psalm 102:26,27 Habakkuk 3:6	Isaiah 9:6 Micah 5:2 John 8:58
Immutable	Malachi 3:6 James 1:17	Hebrews 13:8
Receiver of worship	Matthew 4:10 John 4:24 Revelation 5:14 Revelation 7:11 Revelation 11:16 Revelation 19:4,10	Matthew 2:8,11 Matthew 14:33 Matthew 28:9 John 9:38 Philippians 2:10,11 Hebrews 1:6
Hope	Jeremiah 17:7	1 Timothy 1:1
Speaker with divine authority	"Thus saith the Lord . . ." —used hundreds of times	Matthew 23:34–37 John 3:5 John 7:46 "Truly, truly, I say . . ."
Who raised Jesus from the dead?	Acts 2:24,32 Romans 8:11 1 Corinthians 6:14	John 2:19–22 John 10:17,18 Matthew 27:40
Who gets the glory?	Isaiah 42:8 Isaiah 48:11	Hebrews 13:21 John 17:5

13 Howbeit Jesus spoke of his death: but
they thought that he had spoken of taking of rest in sleep.
14 Then said Jesus to them plainly, Lazarus is dead.
15 And I am glad for your sakes that I
was not there, to the intent you may believe; nevertheless let us go to him.
16 Then said Thomas, which is called
Didymus, to his fellow-disciples, Let us also go, that we may die with him.
17 Then when Jesus came, he found that
he had lain in the grave four days already.
18 Now Bethany was near to Jerusalem,
about fifteen furlongs off:
19 And many of the Jews came to Martha
and Mary, to comfort them concerning their brother.
20 Then Martha, as soon as she heard
that Jesus was coming, went and met him: but Mary sat still in the house.
21 Then said Martha to Jesus, Lord, if
you had been here, my brother had not died.
22 But I know, that even now, whatsoever you will ask of God, God will give it you.
23 Jesus said to her, Your brother shall

11:14 How to Preach at a Funeral for Someone You Suspect Died Unsaved

By Mike Smalley

1. Start in the natural realm and swing to the spiritual.

2. Say something positive about the person who has died—either personally, or their marriage, kids, work ethic, their generation, etc. This should build rapport with the audience. Use a humorous story that relates to the above.

3. Don't feel pressured to mention where the deceased may have gone after death (God is the only One who truly knows).

4. Never insinuate that he went to heaven.

5. Use this as a springboard: "Good friends often remind us of things that we don't want to deal with, but that are very important. Bob, today, reminds us that we *all* must die."

6. Use anecdotes that convey eternal truths.

7. Go quickly but thoroughly through each of the Ten Commandments.

8. Warn briefly about sin, death, judgment, and eternity.

9. Give a clear gospel presentation.

10. Appeal to the audience to repent today.

"When anyone dies, I ask myself, 'Was I faithful?' Did I speak all the truth? And did I speak it from my very soul every time I preached?" *Charles Spurgeon*

rise again.
24 Martha said to him, I know that he
shall rise again in the resurrection at the
last day.
25 Jesus said to her, I am the resurrec-
tion, and the life: he that believes in me,
though he were dead, yet shall he live:
26 **And whosoever lives and believes in**
me shall never die. Do you believe this?
27 She said to him, Yea, Lord: I believe
that you are the Christ, the Son of God,
which should come into the world.
28 And when she had so said, she went
her way, and called Mary her sister secretly, saying, The Master is come, and
calls for you.
29 As soon as she heard that, she arose
quickly, and came to him.
30 Now Jesus was not yet come into the
town, but was in that place where Martha
met him.
31 The Jews then which were with her
in the house, and comforted her, when
they saw Mary, that she rose up hastily and
went out, followed her, saying, She goes
to the grave to weep there.
32 Then when Mary was come where
Jesus was, and saw him, she fell down at
his feet, saying to him, Lord, if you had
been here, my brother had not died.
33 When Jesus therefore saw her weeping, and the Jews also weeping which
came with her, he groaned in the spirit,
and was troubled,
34 And said, Where have you laid him?
They said to him, Lord, come and see.
35 Jesus wept.
36 Then said the Jews, Behold how he
loved him!
37 And some of them said, Could not this
man, which opened the eyes of the blind,
have caused that even this man should

11:25 The uniqueness of Jesus. "A man who was merely a man and said the sort of things Jesus said wouldn't be a great moral teacher. He'd either be a lunatic—on a level with the man who says he's a poached egg—or else he'd be the Devil of Hell. You must make your choice. Either this man was, and is, the Son of God: or else a madman or something worse. You can shut Him up for a fool, you can spit at Him and kill Him as a demon; or you can fall at His feet and call Him Lord and God. But don't let us come with any patronizing nonsense about His being a great human teacher. He hasn't left that open to us. He didn't intend to." *C. S. Lewis, The Case for Christianity*

11:25 Jesus' unique words: See John 14:6 comment.

not have died?
38 Jesus therefore again groaning in himself came to the grave. It was a cave, and a stone lay upon it.
39 Jesus said, Take away the stone. Martha, the sister of him that was dead, said to him, Lord, by this time he stinks: for he has been dead four days.
40 Jesus said to her, Said I not to you, that, if you would believe, you should see the glory of God?
41 Then they took away the stone from the place where the dead was laid. And Jesus lifted up his eyes, and said, Father, I thank you that you have heard me.
42 And I knew that you hear me always: but because of the people which stand by I said it, that they may believe that you have sent me.
43 And when he thus had spoken, he cried with a loud voice, Lazarus, come forth.
44 And he that was dead came forth, bound hand and foot with graveclothes: and his face was bound about with a napkin. Jesus said to them, Loose him, and let him go.
45 Then many of the Jews which came to Mary, and had seen the things which Jesus did, believed on him.
46 But some of them went their ways to the Pharisees, and told them what things Jesus had done.
47 Then gathered the chief priests and the Pharisees a council, and said, What do we? for this man does many miracles.
48 If we let him thus alone, all men will believe on him: and the Romans shall come and take away both our place and nation.
49 And one of them, named Caiaphas, being the high priest that same year, said to them, You know nothing at all,
50 Nor consider that it is expedient for us, that one man should die for the people, and that the whole nation perish not.
51 And this spoke he not of himself: but being high priest that year, he prophe-

11:35 In one sense, this verse is a mystery because Jesus knew what He was about to do. He was about to give Mary and Martha the greatest gift, outside of salvation, that they could ever hope for. Yet, He wept.

The prophets tell us that the Messiah would be a "man of sorrows, and acquainted with grief" (Isaiah 53:3). He was moved with compassion for the multitudes, wept over Jerusalem, and knew what it was to "weep with those who weep." Even though we have heaven before us, it pains the Head of the Body when the foot hurts. Jesus is a High Priest who is "touched with the feeling of our infirmities" (Hebrews 4:15).

11:43,44 The words of Jesus cut through the icy grip of death like a white-hot blade through soft powdered snow. The same Word that brought life in the beginning breathed life into the decomposing corpse of Lazarus. Suddenly, from the blackened shadow of the tomb appeared a figure, wrapped in grave clothes. As he stood at the entrance of the tomb (for tombs didn't need an exit until that day), his face and body were covered with grave clothes. God took him by the hand and led him to the light.

What a picture of what is before us! The hour is coming when all who are in their graves will hear His voice. The victory Lazarus had over death was bad news for the devil and the undertaker, but it was only a temporary triumph, for the undertaker would eventually get his deathly fee. Lazarus would ultimately depart from this earth, but the time is coming when death shall be no more. On that day, we will exchange these vile, perishing bodies for incorruptible bodies that will never feel pain, disease, or death:

> "So when this corruptible shall have put on incorruption, and this mortal shall have put on immortality, then shall be brought to pass the saying that is written, Death is swallowed up in victory" (1 Corinthians 15:54).

For those who trust in Jesus, this body is but a chrysalis, which may become wrinkled and crusty with age, but it is just a shell that will be dropped off as the new butterfly emerges.

sied that Jesus should die for that nation;
52 And not for that nation only, but that
also he should gather together in one the
children of God that were scattered abroad.
53 Then from that day forth they took
counsel together for to put him to death.
54 Jesus therefore walked no more openly among the Jews; but went thence to a
country near to the wilderness, into a city
called Ephraim, and there continued with
his disciples.
55 And the Jews' passover was near at
hand: and many went out of the country
up to Jerusalem before the passover, to
purify themselves.
56 Then sought they for Jesus, and spoke
among themselves, as they stood in the
temple, What do you think, that he will
not come to the feast?
57 Now both the chief priests and the
Pharisees had given a commandment,
that, if any man knew where he were, he
should show it, that they might take him.

CHAPTER 12

THEN Jesus six days before the passover came to Bethany, where Lazarus
was which had been dead, whom he raised
from the dead.
2 There they made him a supper; and
Martha served: but Lazarus was one of
them that sat at the table with him.
3 Then took Mary a pound of ointment
of spikenard, very costly, and anointed
the feet of Jesus, and wiped his feet with
her hair: and the house was filled with
the odor of the ointment.
4 Then said one of his disciples, Judas Iscariot, Simon's son, which should betray
him,
5 Why was not this ointment sold for
three hundred pence, and given to the
poor?
6 This he said, not that he cared for the
poor; but because he was a thief, and had
the bag, and bare what was put therein.
7 Then said Jesus, Let her alone: against
the day of my burying has she kept this.
8 For the poor always you have with
you; but me you have not always.

> Men have been helped to live by remembering that they must die.
>
> **CHARLES SPURGEON**

9 Much people of the Jews therefore
knew that he was there: and they came
not for Jesus' sake only, but that they
might see Lazarus also, whom he had
raised from the dead.
10 But the chief priests consulted that
they might put Lazarus also to death;
11 Because that by reason of him many
of the Jews went away, and believed on
Jesus.
12 On the next day much people that
were come to the feast, when they heard
that Jesus was coming to Jerusalem,
13 Took branches of palm trees, and
went forth to meet him, and cried, Hosanna: Blessed is the King of Israel that comes

12:9 The undertaker's nightmare. The Son of God created havoc for undertakers by speaking to their frigid merchandise. His voice was supernatural. A mere "Lazarus, come forth," spoken to a corpse meant a nightmarish dilemma for the Bethany funeral director, because he was left with no body to deal with. Up until that moment, his business was mortally secure. Four days after the death, he had everything wrapped up, when suddenly, three words unraveled his inanimate toil. Reimbursement of all funeral expenses was just the beginning of the bad dream. Death was his living, and if this stranger from Nazareth continued to speak around graves, his business itself would soon be terminal. Jesus Christ was the undertaker's nightmare because death bowed its vile knee to His voice, and the day is promised when all undertakers will hit the unemployment line!

The raising of Lazarus snatched the profit from the undertaker; but the incident happened *for* the inestimable profit of humanity. It was the long-awaited fulfillment of what was spoken of by the prophets of old. It was a beam of wondrous and glistening light in the most hopeless and darkest of all caves.

in the name of the Lord.
14 And Jesus, when he had found a
young ass, sat thereon; as it is written,
15 Fear not, daughter of Zion: behold,
your King comes, sitting on an ass's colt.
16 These things understood not his disciples at the first: but when Jesus was
glorified, then remembered they that these
things were written of him, and that they
had done these things to him.
17 The people therefore that was with
him when he called Lazarus out of his
grave, and raised him from the dead, bare
record.
18 For this cause the people also met
him, for that they heard that he had done
this miracle.
19 The Pharisees therefore said among
themselves, Perceive how you prevail
nothing? behold, the world is gone after
him.
20 And there were certain Greeks among
them that came up to worship at the feast:
21 The same came therefore to Philip,
which was of Bethsaida of Galilee, and desired him, saying, Sir, we would see Jesus.
22 Philip came and told Andrew: and
again Andrew and Philip tell Jesus.
23 And Jesus answered them, saying,
The hour is come, that the Son of man
should be glorified.
24 Verily, verily, I say to you, Except a
corn of wheat fall into the ground and
die, it abides alone: but if it die, it brings
forth much fruit.
**25 He that loves his life shall lose it;
and he that hates his life in this world
shall keep it to life eternal.**
26 *If any man serve me, let him follow me;
and where I am, there shall also my servant
be: if any man serve me, him will my Father honor.*
27 Now is my soul troubled; and what
shall I say? Father, save me from this hour:
but for this cause came I to this hour.
28 Father, glorify your name. Then came
there a voice from heaven, saying, I have
both glorified it, and will glorify it again.
29 The people therefore, that stood by,
and heard it, said that it thundered: others said, An angel spoke to him.
30 Jesus answered and said, This voice
came not because of me, but for your
sakes.
31 Now is the judgment of this world:
now shall the prince of this world be cast
out.
32 **And I, if I be lifted up from the
earth, will draw all men to me.**
33 This he said, signifying what death
he should die.
34 The people answered him, We have
heard out of the law that Christ abides for
ever: and how do you say, The Son of
man must be lifted up? who is this Son of
man?
35 Then Jesus said to them, Yet a little
while is the light with you. Walk while
you have the light, lest darkness come
upon you: for he that walks in darkness
knows not where he goes.
36 While you have light, believe in the
light, that you may be the children of light.
These things spoke Jesus, and departed,
and did hide himself from them.
37 But though he had done so many
miracles before them, yet they believed
not on him:
38 That the saying of Isaiah the prophet
might be fulfilled, which he spoke, Lord,

12:14 Instead of riding triumphantly through the streets of Jerusalem on a kingly white stallion, He chose to ride on a young donkey, a lowly beast of burden. Imagine how humbling it would be for the president of the United States to ride through New York on the back of a donkey. But this is what the King of kings did. This time He came in lowliness, humbling Himself and becoming obedient to the death of the cross. The next time He will come in flaming fire, on a white horse with ten thousands of His saints.

12:25 "The greatest proof of Christianity for others is not how far a man can logically analyze his reasons for believing, but how far in practice he will stake his life on his belief." *T. S. Eliot*

who has believed our report? and to whom
has the arm of the Lord been revealed?
39 Therefore they could not believe, because that Isaiah said again,
40 He has blinded their eyes, and hardened their heart; that they should not see
with their eyes, nor understand with their
heart, and be converted, and I should heal
them.
41 These things said Isaiah, when he saw
his glory, and spoke of him.
42 Nevertheless among the chief rulers
also many believed on him; but because of
the Pharisees they did not confess him, lest
they should be put out of the synagogue:
43 For they loved the praise of men more
than the praise of God.
44 **Jesus cried and said, He that believes on me, believes not on me, but on
him that sent me.**
45 **And he that sees me sees him that
sent me.**
46 **I am come a light into the world,
that whosoever believes on me should
not abide in darkness.**
47 And if any man hear my words, and
believe not, I judge him not: for I came
not to judge the world, but to save the
world.
48 He that rejects me, and receives not
my words, has one that judges him: the
word that I have spoken, the same shall
judge him in the last day.
49 **For I have not spoken of myself; but
the Father which sent me, he gave me a
commandment, what I should say, and
what I should speak.**
50 **And I know that his commandment
is life everlasting: whatsoever I speak
therefore, even as the Father said to me,
so I speak.**

CHAPTER 13

NOW before the feast of the passover,
when Jesus knew that his hour was
come that he should depart out of this
world to the Father, having loved his own
which were in the world, he loved them
to the end.
2 And supper being ended, the devil having now put into the heart of Judas Iscariot, Simon's son, to betray him;
3 Jesus knowing that the Father had
given all things into his hands, and that
he was come from God, and went to God;
4 He rose from supper, and laid aside his
garments; and took a towel, and girded
himself.
5 After that he poured water into a basin,
and began to wash the disciples' feet, and
to wipe them with the towel wherewith
he was girded.
6 Then came he to Simon Peter: and Peter
said to him, Lord, do you wash my feet?
7 Jesus answered and said to him, What
I do you know not now; but you shall
know hereafter.
8 Peter said to him, You shall never wash
my feet. Jesus answered him, If I wash you
not, you have no part with me.
9 Simon Peter said to him, Lord, not my
feet only, but also my hands and my head.
10 Jesus said to him, He that is washed
needs not save to wash his feet, but is
clean every whit: and you are clean, but
not all.
11 For he knew who should betray him;
therefore said he, You are not all clean.

12:38 One would think that a terminally ill world would gladly embrace the cure of the gospel, but few, so few believe our report.

13:2 While "the devil made me do it" will not be a valid defense on Judgment Day, if more people would believe that the devil is at work in their lives, our prisons would be less full and human suffering would be much less.

So often we hear of people feeling "compelled" to kill, and thinking the impulses were their own. If potential homosexuals understood the influence of unclean spirits, they would be less likely to follow every grimy impulse that comes into their minds. Those who believe that our battle is not against flesh and blood, but demonic personalities, will then be less prone to be tools of darkness.

12 So after he had washed their feet,
and had taken his garments, and was set
down again, he said to them, Do you
know what I have done to you?
13 You call me Master and Lord: and
you say well; for so I am.
14 If I then, your Lord and Master, have
washed your feet; you also ought to wash
one another's feet.

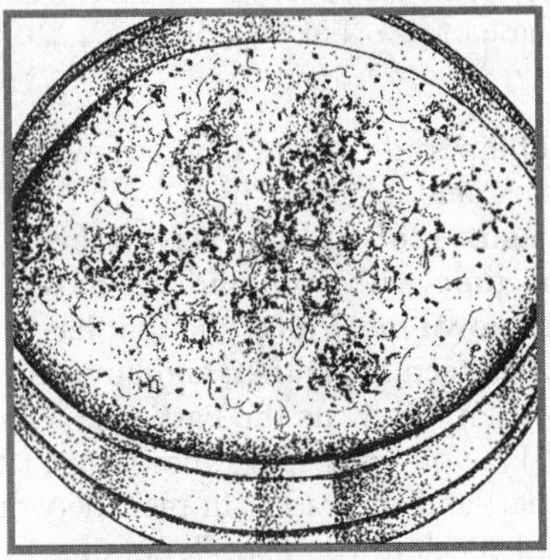

The Bible gives instructions on how to avoid diseases, thousands of years before man discovered their cause. See Hebrews 11:3 comment.

15 For I have given you an example,
that you should do as I have done to you.
16 Verily, verily, I say to you, The servant is not greater than his lord; neither he
that is sent greater than he that sent him.
17 If you know these things, happy are
you if you do them.
18 I speak not of you all: I know whom
I have chosen: but that the scripture may
be fulfilled, He that eats bread with me
has lifted up his heel against me.
19 Now I tell you before it come, that,
when it is come to pass, you may believe
that I am he.
20 Verily, verily, I say to you, He that receives whomsoever I send receives me;
and he that receives me receives him that
sent me.
21 When Jesus had thus said, he was
troubled in spirit, and testified, and said,
Verily, verily, I say to you, that one of you
shall betray me.
22 Then the disciples looked one on another, doubting of whom he spoke.
23 Now there was leaning on Jesus' bosom one of his disciples, whom Jesus loved.
24 Simon Peter therefore beckoned to
him, that he should ask who it should be
of whom he spoke.
25 He then lying on Jesus' breast said to
him, Lord, who is it?
26 Jesus answered, He it is, to whom I
shall give a sop, when I have dipped it.
And when he had dipped the sop, he gave
it to Judas Iscariot, the son of Simon.
27 And after the sop Satan entered into
him. Then said Jesus to him, That you do,
do quickly.
28 Now no man at the table knew for
what intent he spoke this to him.
29 For some of them thought, because
Judas had the bag, that Jesus had said to
him, Buy those things that we have need
of against the feast; or, that he should give
something to the poor.
30 He then having received the sop went
immediately out: and it was night.
31 Therefore, when he was gone out,
Jesus said, Now is the Son of man glorified, and God is glorified in him.
32 If God be glorified in him, God shall
also glorify him in himself, and shall
straightway glorify him.
33 Little children, yet a little while I am
with you. You shall seek me: and as I said
to the Jews, Where I go, you cannot come;
so now I say to you.
34 A new commandment I give to you,
That you love one another; as I have loved
you, that you also love one another.
35 By this shall all men know that you
are my disciples, if you have love one to
another.
36 Simon Peter said to him, Lord, where
are you going? Jesus answered him, Where
I go, you can not follow me now; but you
shall follow me afterwards.
37 Peter said to him, Lord, why cannot
I follow you now? I will lay down my life
for your sake.
38 Jesus answered him, Will you lay
down your life for my sake? Verily, verily,

QUESTIONS & OBJECTIONS

14:6

"It's intolerant to say that Jesus is the only way to God!"

Jesus is the One who said that He is the only way to the Father. For Christians to say that there are other ways to find peace with God is to bear false testimony. In one sweeping statement, Jesus discards all other religions as a means of finding forgiveness of sins. This agrees with other Scriptures: "Neither is there salvation in any other: for there is no other name under heaven given among men, whereby we must be saved" (Acts 4:12), and "For there is one God, and one mediator between God and men, the man Christ Jesus" (1 Timothy 2:5).

I say to you, The cock shall not crow, till you have denied me thrice.

CHAPTER 14

LET not your heart be troubled: you believe in God, believe also in me.
2 In my Father's house are many mansions: if it were not so, I would have told you. I go to prepare a place for you.
3 And if I go and prepare a place for you, I will come again, and receive you to myself; that where I am, there you may be also.
4 And where I go you know, and the way you know.
5 Thomas said to him, Lord, we know not where you go; and how can we know the way?
6 Jesus said to him, I am the way, the truth, and the life: no man comes to the Father, but by me.
7 If you had known me, you should have known my Father also: and from henceforth you know him, and have seen him.
8 Philip said to him, Lord, show us the Father, and it suffices us.
9 Jesus said to him, Have I been so long time with you, and yet have you not known me, Philip? he that has seen me has seen the Father; and how do you say then, Show us the Father?
10 Do you not believe that I am in the Father, and the Father in me? the words that I speak to you I speak not of myself: but the Father that dwells in me, he does the works.
11 Believe me that I am in the Father, and the Father in me: or else believe me for the very works' sake.
12 *Verily, verily, I say to you, He that believes on me, the works that I do shall he do also; and greater works than these shall he do; because I go to my Father.*
13 And whatsoever you shall ask in my name, that will I do, that the Father may be glorified in the Son.
14 If you shall ask any thing in my name, I will do it.

14:2 Faith in God clears the muddy waters of fear. The Christian who has confidence in Jesus Christ knows that his eternal footsteps have been ordered by the Lord, and that there is a mansion prepared for him that his wildest imaginations could not conceive. If these things weren't so, Jesus would have told us. *He is not a liar*. His word is sure and steadfast, a mooring for the soul, and those who come into the harbor of a calm faith in God have perfect peace in the troubled storms of this world.

14:6 Jesus' unique words: *Paige Patterson* stated, "It comes down to a question of truth. Every false religious expression is a religion of darkness. That doesn't mean there are no good things in that faith. But if Jesus is to be taken seriously when He says, 'No one comes to the Father but through Me,' every other proposal is one of darkness." See John 14:21 comment.

14:10 Was Jesus God in human form? See John 17:22.

QUESTIONS & OBJECTIONS

14:21

"I made a commitment, but nothing happened."

Some people don't get past "square one" because they trust in their feelings rather than God. His promises are true, despite our feelings. If I make a promise to my wife, that promise is true whether she is feeling happy or sad. If she doubts my word, then she brings a slur to my integrity.

Anyone who genuinely repents and trusts in Christ will be saved. The Bible makes this promise: "He that has my commandments, and keeps them, he it is that loves me: and he that loves me shall be loved of my Father, and I will love him, and will manifest myself to him" [John 14:21]. There's the promise, and there's the condition. Any person who loves and obeys Jesus will begin a supernatural relationship with Him and the Father. He said, "And this is life eternal, that they might know you the only true God, and Jesus Christ, whom you have sent" (John 17:3). That doesn't mean you will hear voices or see visions. God will instead make you a new person from within. He will send His Spirit to live within you. You will have a new heart with new desires. You will suddenly become conscious of God and His creation. The Bible will open up to you and become a living Word, and you will have an inner witness that you are saved, that your name is written in heaven, and that death has lost its sting (1 John 5:10–12).

15 If you love me, keep my commandments.
16 And I will pray the Father, and he shall give you another Comforter, that he may abide with you for ever;
17 Even the Spirit of truth; whom the world cannot receive, because it sees him not, neither knows him: but you know him; for he dwells with you, and shall be in you.
18 I will not leave you comfortless: I will come to you.
19 Yet a little while, and the world sees me no more; but you see me: because I live, you shall live also.
20 At that day you shall know that I am in my Father, and you in me, and I in you.
21 He that has my commandments, and keeps them, he it is that loves me: and he that loves me shall be loved of my Father, and I will love him, and will manifest myself to him.
22 Judas said to him, not Iscariot, Lord, how is it that you will manifest yourself to us, and not to the world?
23 Jesus answered and said to him, If a man love me, he will keep my words: and my Father will love him, and we will come to him, and make our abode with him.
24 He that loves me not keeps not my sayings: and the word which you hear is not mine, but the Father's which sent me.
25 These things have I spoken to you,

14:14 In 1 Kings 3:5, the LORD appeared to Solomon in a dream by night, and said, "Ask! What shall I give you?" God asks us the same question. Be like Solomon and ask for wisdom. God promises to give it liberally (James 1:5). He who gets wisdom loves his own soul (Proverbs 19:8). If you have wisdom, you will think right, do right, and speak right. Remember: He who wins souls is wise (Proverbs 11:30).

14:15 We show our love for God by our obedience. If we do not obey, we do not truly love Him (see vv. 23,24). There are many who call Him "Lord, Lord," but do not do what He says. Matthew 7:21–23 tells us their fearful fate.

14:21 Jesus' unique words: Jesus promises that He and the Father will reveal themselves to all who love and obey Him. This is the ultimate challenge to any skeptic. See John 17:5 comment.

SPRINGBOARDS FOR PREACHING AND WITNESSING

15:13

Revolting Natives

An African chief got wind of a mutiny being planned in his tribe. In an effort to quash the revolt, he called the tribe together and said that *anyone* caught in rebellion would be given one hundred lashes, *without mercy*.

A short time later, to the chief's dismay he found that his own brother was behind the revolt. He was trying to overthrow him so he could be head of the tribe. Everyone thought the chief would break his word. But being a just man, he had his brother tied to a tree. Then he had himself tied next to him, *and he took those one hundred lashes across his own bare flesh, in his brother's place*. In doing so, he not only kept his word (justice was done), but he also demonstrated his great love and forgiveness toward his brother.

being yet present with you.
26 But the Comforter, which is the Holy
Spirit, whom the Father will send in my
name, he shall teach you all things, and
bring all things to your remembrance,
whatsoever I have said to you.
27 Peace I leave with you, my peace I
give to you: not as the world gives, give I
to you. Let not your heart be troubled,
neither let it be afraid.
28 You have heard how I said to you, I
go away, and come again to you. If you
loved me, you would rejoice, because I
said, I go to the Father: for my Father is
greater than I.
29 And now I have told you before it
come to pass, that, when it is come to
pass, you might believe.
30 Hereafter I will not talk much with
you: for the prince of this world comes,
and has nothing in me.
31 But that the world may know that I
love the Father; and as the Father gave
me commandment, even so I do. Arise, let
us go hence.

CHAPTER 15

I AM the true vine, and my Father is
the husbandman.
2 Every branch in me that bears not fruit
he takes away: and every branch that bears
fruit, he purges it, that it may bring forth
more fruit.
3 Now you are clean through the word
which I have spoken to you.
4 Abide in me, and I in you. As the
branch cannot bear fruit of itself, except
it abide in the vine; no more can you,
except you abide in me.
5 I am the vine, you are the branches:
He that abides in me, and I in him, the
same brings forth much fruit: for without
me you can do nothing.
6 If a man abide not in me, he is cast
forth as a branch, and is withered; and
men gather them, and cast them into the
fire, and they are burned.
7 If you abide in me, and my words
abide in you, you shall ask what you
will, and it shall be done to you.
8 Herein is my Father glorified, that you
bear much fruit; so shall you be my disciples.
9 As the Father has loved me, so have I
loved you: continue in my love.
10 If you keep my commandments, you
shall abide in my love; even as I have
kept my Father's commandments, and
abide in his love.
11 These things have I spoken to you,
that my joy might remain in you, and
that your joy might be full.
12 This is my commandment, That you
love one another, as I have loved you.
13 Greater love has no man than this,
that a man lay down his life for his
friends.
14 **You are my friends, if you do whatsoever I command you.**
15 Henceforth I call you not servants;
for the servant knows not what his lord
does: but I have called you friends; for

all things that I have heard of my Father I have made known to you.
16 You have not chosen me, but I have chosen you, and ordained you, that you should go and bring forth fruit, and that your fruit should remain: that whatsoever you shall ask of the Father in my name, he may give it you.
17 These things I command you, that you love one another.
18 If the world hate you, you know that it hated me before it hated you.
19 If you were of the world, the world would love his own: but because you are not of the world, but I have chosen you out of the world, therefore the world hates you.

> There must be true and deep conviction of sin. This the preacher must labor to produce, for where this is not felt, the new birth has not taken place.
>
> **CHARLES SPURGEON**

20 Remember the word that I said to you, The servant is not greater than his lord. If they have persecuted me, they will also persecute you; if they have kept my saying, they will keep yours also.
21 But all these things will they do to you for my name's sake, because they know not him that sent me.
22 If I had not come and spoken to them, they had not had sin: but now they have no cloak for their sin.
23 He that hates me hates my Father also.
24 If I had not done among them the works which none other man did, they had not had sin: but now have they both seen and hated both me and my Father.
25 But this comes to pass, that the word might be fulfilled that is written in their law, They hated me without a cause.
26 But when the Comforter is come, whom I will send to you from the Father, even the Spirit of truth, which proceeds from the Father, he shall testify of me:
27 And you also shall bear witness, because you have been with me from the beginning.

CHAPTER 16

THESE things have I spoken to you,
that you should not be offended.
2 They shall put you out of the synagogues: yea, the time comes, that whosoever kills you will think that he does God service.
3 And these things will they do to you, because they have not known the Father, nor me.
4 But these things have I told you, that when the time shall come, you may remember that I told you of them. And these things I said not to you at the beginning, because I was with you.
5 But now I go my way to him that sent me; and none of you asks me, Where are you going?
6 But because I have said these things to you, sorrow has filled your heart.
7 Nevertheless I tell you the truth; It is expedient for you that I go away: for if I go not away, the Comforter will not come to you; but if I depart, I will send him to you.
8 And when he is come, he will reprove the world of sin, and of righteousness, and of judgment:
9 Of sin, because they believe not on me;
10 Of righteousness, because I go to my Father, and you see me no more;
11 Of judgment, because the prince of this world is judged.
12 I have yet many things to say to you,

15:18–21 Some preachers promise a life of peace and happiness, but the Bible promises something else: *"all* that will live godly in Christ Jesus *shall* suffer persecution" (2 Timothy 3:12). See Matthew 10:16 and Philippians 1:29 comments.

but you cannot bear them now.
13 Howbeit when he, the Spirit of truth,
is come, he will guide you into all truth:
for he shall not speak of himself; but
whatsoever he shall hear, that shall he
speak: and he will show you things to
come.
14 He shall glorify me: for he shall receive of mine, and shall show it to you.
15 All things that the Father has are
mine: therefore said I, that he shall take
of mine, and shall show it to you.
16 A little while, and you shall not see
me: and again, a little while, and you
shall see me, because I go to the Father.
17 Then said some of his disciples among
themselves, What is this that he said to
us, A little while, and you shall not see
me: and again, a little while, and you shall
see me: and, Because I go to the Father?
18 They said therefore, What is this that
he says, A little while? we cannot tell what
he says.
19 Now Jesus knew that they were desirous to ask him, and said to them, Do
you inquire among yourselves of that I
said, A little while, and you shall not see
me: and again, a little while, and you shall
see me?
20 Verily, verily, I say to you, That you
shall weep and lament, but the world shall
rejoice: and you shall be sorrowful, but
your sorrow shall be turned into joy.
21 A woman when she is in travail has
sorrow, because her hour is come: but as
soon as she is delivered of the child, she
remembers no more the anguish, for joy
that a man is born into the world.
22 And you now therefore have sorrow:
but I will see you again, and your heart

16:8–11 The Holy Spirit's role in salvation. The question may arise about the Holy Spirit's role in the salvation of sinners. The answer is clear from Scripture. We are drawn by, convicted by, born of, and kept by the Holy Spirit. Why then do we need to use the Law when witnessing? Why don't we just leave the salvation of sinners up to the Holy Spirit? Simply because, just as God has condescended to choose the foolishness of preaching to save those who believe, so He has chosen the Moral Law to bring the knowledge of sin.

Jesus Himself tells us how the Holy Spirit works in the salvation of the lost. He said that when the Holy Spirit comes "he will reprove the world of sin [which is *transgression* of the Law—1 John 3:4], and of righteousness [which is *of* the Law—Romans 8:4], and of judgment [which is *by* the Law—Romans 2:12]. So when we use the Law to bring the knowledge of sin to the lost, we simply become instruments the Holy Spirit uses to lead sinners to the Savior.

"When 100 years ago earnest scholars decreed that the Law had no relationship to the preaching of the gospel, they deprived the Holy Spirit in the area where their influence prevailed of the only instrument with which He had ever armed Himself to prepare sinners for grace." *Paris Reidhead*

"The Holy Spirit convicts us…He shows us the Ten Commandments; the Law is the schoolmaster that leads us to Christ. We look in the mirror of the Ten Commandments, and we see ourselves in that mirror." *Billy Graham*

16:9 Why will sinners go to hell? Much damage has been done to the cause of the gospel by telling the world that they will go to hell "because they don't believe in Jesus." This makes no sense to the ungodly. It seems unreasonable that God would eternally damn them for not believing something. However, the verse can be explained this way: If a man jumps out of a plane without a parachute, he will perish because he transgressed the law of gravity. Had he put on a parachute, he would have been saved. In one sense, he perished because he didn't put on the parachute. But the primary reason he died was because he broke the law of gravity.

If a sinner refuses to trust in Jesus Christ when he passes through the door of death, he will perish. This isn't because he refused to trust the Savior, but because he transgressed the Law of God. Had he "put on the Lord Jesus Christ" (Romans 13:14), he would have been saved; but because he refused to repent, he will suffer the full consequences of his sin. Sin is not "failing to believe in Jesus." Sin is "transgression of the Law" (1 John 3:4).

QUESTIONS & OBJECTIONS

17:3 ***"I don't believe that God is knowable."***

It is amazing how it's human nature to assume that because we believe or don't believe something, that makes it true. Some may not believe in the law of gravity, and may feel thay have "evidence" to back up their belief. However, gravity exists whether they believe in it or not. The truth is, God is knowable. Jesus testified, "And this is life eternal, that they might know you the only true God, and Jesus Christ, whom you have sent" (John 17:3). We not only have the testimony of the Scriptures to tell us this, but we have the testimony of multitudes of Christians who know the Lord personally. It is more truthful to say, "I don't *want* to know God." Sinful man runs from Him as did Adam in the garden of Eden.

shall rejoice, and your joy no man takes from you.

23 And in that day you shall ask me nothing. Verily, verily, I say to you, Whatsoever you shall ask the Father in my name, he will give it you.

24 Hitherto have you asked nothing in my name: ask, and you shall receive, that your joy may be full.

25 These things have I spoken to you in proverbs: but the time comes, when I shall no more speak to you in proverbs, but I shall show you plainly of the Father.

26 At that day you shall ask in my name: and I say not to you, that I will pray the Father for you:

27 For the Father himself loves you, because you have loved me, and have believed that I came out from God.

28 I came forth from the Father, and am come into the world: again, I leave the world, and go to the Father.

29 His disciples said to him, Lo, now you speak plainly, and speak no proverb.

30 Now are we sure that you know all things, and need not that any man should ask you; by this we believe that you came forth from God.

31 Jesus answered them, Do you now believe?

32 Behold, the hour comes, yea, is now come, that you shall be scattered, every man to his own, and shall leave me alone: and yet I am not alone, because the Father is with me.

33 These things I have spoken to you, that in me you might have peace. In the world you shall have tribulation: but be of good cheer; I have overcome the world.

. . . .

For what great leaders have said about the Bible, see page 570.

. . . .

CHAPTER 17

THESE words spoke Jesus, and lifted up his eyes to heaven, and said, Father, the hour is come; glorify your Son, that your Son also may glorify you:

2 As you have given him power over all flesh, that he should give eternal life to as many as you have given him.

3 And this is life eternal, that they might know you the only true God, and Jesus Christ, whom you have sent.

4 I have glorified you on the earth: I have finished the work which you gave me to do.

5 And now, O Father, glorify me with your own self with the glory which I had with you before the world was.

6 I have manifested your name to the men which you gave me out of the world: yours they were, and you gave them me; and they have kept your word.

7 Now they have known that all things whatsoever you have given me are of you.

8 For I have given to them the words

SPRINGBOARDS FOR PREACHING AND WITNESSING

17:3

Experiential Faith

Our faith isn't intellectual; it is experiential. We don't know *about* God, we know *Him*. At the University of Chicago Divinity School, each year they have what is called "Baptist Day." It is a day when the school invites all the Baptists in the area to the school because they want the Baptist dollars to keep coming in.

On this day each one is to bring a lunch to be eaten outdoors in a grassy picnic area. Every "Baptist Day" the school would invite one of the greatest minds to lecture in the theological education center. One year they invited Dr. Paul Tillich. Dr. Tillich spoke for two-and-a-half hours proving that the resurrection of Jesus was false. He quoted scholar after scholar and book after book. He concluded that since there was no such thing as the historical resurrection, the religious tradition of the Church was groundless, emotional mumbo-jumbo, because it was based on a relationship with a risen Jesus, who, in fact, never rose from the dead in any literal sense. He then asked if there were any questions.

After about 30 seconds, an old preacher with a head of short-cropped, woolly white hair stood up in the back of the auditorium. "Docta Tillich, I got one question," he said as all eyes turned toward him. He reached into his lunch sack and pulled out an apple and began eating it. "Docta Tillich *(crunch, munch)*, my question is a simple one *(crunch, munch)*. Now, I ain't never read them books you read *(crunch, munch)*, and I can't recite the Scriptures in the original Greek *(crunch, munch)*. I don't know nothin' about Niebuhr and Heidegger *(crunch, munch)*." He finished the apple. "All I wanna know is: This apple I just ate—was it bitter or sweet?"

Dr. Tillich paused for a moment and answered in exemplary scholarly fashion: "I cannot possibly answer that question, for I haven't tasted your apple." The white-haired preacher dropped the apple core into his crumpled paper bag, looked up at Dr. Tillich and said calmly, "Neither have you tasted my Jesus."

The 1,000-plus in attendance could not contain themselves. The auditorium erupted with applause and cheers. Dr. Tillich thanked his audience and promptly left the platform.

"Taste and see that the Lord is good: blessed is the man that trusts in him" (Psalm 34:8). It has been well said, "The man with an experience is not at the mercy of a man with an argument."

which you gave me; and they have received them, and have known surely that I came out from you, and they have believed that you did send me.
9 I pray for them: I pray not for the world, but for them which you have given me; for they are yours.
10 And all mine are yours, and yours are mine; and I am glorified in them.
11 And now I am no more in the world, but these are in the world, and I come to you. Holy Father, keep through your own name those whom you have given me, that they may be one, as we are.
12 While I was with them in the world, I kept them in your name: those that you gave me I have kept, and none of them is lost, but the son of perdition; that the scripture might be fulfilled.
13 And now come I to you; and these things I speak in the world, that they might have my joy fulfilled in themselves.
14 I have given them your word; and the world has hated them, because they are not of the world, even as I am not of the world.
15 I pray not that you should take them out of the world, but that you should keep

17:5 Jesus' unique words: Jesus declared that He was with the Father before the world came into existence, and that the Father loved Him before the foundation of the world (v. 24). Hebrews 7:3 tells us that He had no beginning. He not only existed before Abraham (John 8:58), He existed before the creation of the world (John 1:1–3).

them from the evil.
16 They are not of the world, even as I am not of the world.
17 Sanctify them through your truth: your word is truth.
18 As you have sent me into the world, even so have I also sent them into the world.
19 And for their sakes I sanctify myself, that they also might be sanctified through the truth.
20 Neither pray I for these alone, but for them also which shall believe on me through their word;
21 That they all may be one; as you, Father, are in me, and I in you, that they also may be one in us: that the world may believe that you have sent me.
22 And the glory which you gave me I have given them; that they may be one, even as we are one:
23 I in them, and you in me, that they may be made perfect in one; and that the world may know that you have sent me, and have loved them, as you have loved me.

"Let men of science and learning expound their knowledge and prize and probe with their researches every detail of the records which have been preserved to us from those dim ages. All they will do is fortify the grand simplicity and essential accuracy of the recorded truths which have lighted so far the pilgrimage of men."

Winston Churchill

17:14 Do you feel discouraged by negative reactions to the gospel? You shouldn't. According to the Gospels, the religious leaders tried to kill Jesus ten times. Let's look to Scripture and see what happened when Paul preached the biblical gospel:

Acts 13:45: The crowd began "contradicting and blaspheming."

Acts 13:50: Paul and Barnabas were persecuted and thrown out of the region.

Acts 14:5: The crowd plotted to stone them, forcing them to flee.

Acts 14:19: Paul was stoned and left for dead.

Acts 16:23: Both Paul and Silas were beaten with "many stripes" and thrown in prison.

Acts 18:6: Paul's hearers "opposed themselves, and blasphemed."

Acts 19:26–28: His hearers were "full of wrath" and seized Paul's companions.

Acts 20:23: The Holy Spirit warned Paul that bonds and afflictions awaited him wherever he preached the gospel.

Acts 22:21,22: His listeners called for his death.

Acts 23:1,2: As soon as he began to speak, he was smacked in the mouth.

Acts 23:10. After Paul spoke there was "great dissension" in the crowd and he was nearly "pulled in pieces."

Acts 23:12,13: More than forty Jews conspired to murder him.

Acts 24:5: He is called a "pestilent fellow," a "mover of sedition," and a "ringleader" of a "sect."

17:22 Was Jesus God in human form? See Colossians 1:15,16.

24 Father, I will that they also, whom you have given me, be with me where I am; that they may behold my glory, which you have given me: for you loved me before the foundation of the world.
25 O righteous Father, the world has not known you: but I have known you, and these have known that you have sent me.
26 And I have declared to them your name, and will declare it: that the love wherewith you have loved me may be in them, and I in them.

CHAPTER 18

WHEN Jesus had spoken these words, he went forth with his disciples over the brook Cedron, where was a garden, into the which he entered, and his disciples.
2 And Judas also, which betrayed him, knew the place: for Jesus often resorted there with his disciples.
3 Judas then, having received a band of men and officers from the chief priests and Pharisees, came there with lanterns and torches and weapons.
4 Jesus therefore, knowing all things that should come upon him, went forth, and said to them, Whom do you seek?
5 They answered him, Jesus of Nazareth. Jesus said to them, I am he. And Judas also, which betrayed him, stood with them.
6 As soon then as he had said to them, I am he, they went backward, and fell to the ground.
7 Then asked he them again, Whom do you seek? And they said, Jesus of Nazareth.
8 Jesus answered, I have told you that I am he: if therefore you seek me, let these go their way:
9 That the saying might be fulfilled, which he spoke, Of them which you gave me have I lost none.
10 Then Simon Peter having a sword drew it, and smote the high priest's servant, and cut off his right ear. The servant's name was Malchus.
11 Then said Jesus to Peter, Put up your sword into the sheath: the cup which my Father has given me, shall I not drink it?
12 Then the band and the captain and officers of the Jews took Jesus, and bound him,
13 And led him away to Annas first; for he was father in law to Caiaphas, which was the high priest that same year.
14 Now Caiaphas was he, which gave counsel to the Jews, that it was expedient that one man should die for the people.
15 And Simon Peter followed Jesus, and so did another disciple: that disciple was known to the high priest, and went in with Jesus into the palace of the high priest.
16 But Peter stood at the door without. Then went out that other disciple, which was known to the high priest, and spoke to her that kept the door, and brought in Peter.
17 Then said the damsel that kept the door to Peter, are you not also one of this man's disciples? He said, I am not.
18 And the servants and officers stood there, who had made a fire of coals; for it was cold: and they warmed themselves: and Peter stood with them, and warmed himself
19 The high priest then asked Jesus of his disciples, and of his doctrine.
20 Jesus answered him, I spoke openly to the world; I ever taught in the synagogue, and in the temple, where the Jews always resort; and in secret have I said nothing.
21 Why do you ask me? ask them which heard me, what I have said to them: behold, they know what I said.
22 And when he had thus spoken, one of the officers which stood by struck Jesus

18:17 Who of us who know the Lord cannot identify with Peter? We have felt the paralyzing power of the fear of man grip our hearts and fasten our lips. Peter stood by the fire and warmed his cold body, but what he really needed was a fiery coal from the altar of God to touch his frozen lips.

with the palm of his hand, saying, Do you
answer the high priest so?
23 Jesus answered him, If I have spoken
evil, bear witness of the evil: but if well,
why do you smite me?
24 Now Annas had sent him bound to
Caiaphas the high priest.
25 And Simon Peter stood and warmed
himself. They said therefore to him, are
not you also one of his disciples? He denied it, and said, I am not.
26 One of the servants of the high priest,
being his kinsman whose ear Peter cut off,
said, Did not I see you in the garden with
him?
27 Peter then denied again: and immediately the cock crew.
28 Then led they Jesus from Caiaphas to
the hall of judgment: and it was early; and
they themselves went not into the judgment hall, lest they should be defiled; but
that they might eat the passover.
29 Pilate then went out to them, and
said, What accusation do you bring against
this man?
30 They answered and said to him, If he
were not a malefactor, we would not have
delivered him up to you.
31 Then said Pilate to them, You take
him, and judge him according to your law.
The Jews therefore said to him, It is not
lawful for us to put any man to death:
32 That the saying of Jesus might be fulfilled, which he spoke, signifying what
death he should die.
33 Then Pilate entered into the judgment
hall again, and called Jesus, and said to
him, Are you the King of the Jews?
34 Jesus answered him, Do you say this
thing of yourself, or did others tell it of
me?
35 Pilate answered, Am I a Jew? Your
own nation and the chief priests have delivered you to me: what have you done?
36 Jesus answered, My kingdom is not
of this world: if my kingdom were of this
world, then would my servants fight, that
I should not be delivered to the Jews: but
now is my kingdom not from hence.
37 Pilate therefore said to him, Are you
a king then? Jesus answered, You say that
I am a king. To this end was I born, and
for this cause came I into the world, that
I should bear witness to the truth. Every
one that is of the truth hears my voice.
38 Pilate said to him, What is truth? And
when he had said this, he went out again
to the Jews, and said to them, I find in him
no fault at all.
39 But you have a custom, that I should
release to you one at the passover: will
you therefore that I release to you the King
of the Jews?
40 Then cried they all again, saying, Not
this man, but Barabbas. Now Barabbas was
a robber.

• • • • • •

For witnessing to those who don't speak English, see page 671 for the entire gospel in picture form.

• • • • • •

CHAPTER 19

THEN Pilate therefore took Jesus, and
scourged him.
2 And the soldiers platted a crown of
thorns, and put it on his head, and they
put on him a purple robe,
3 And said, Hail, King of the Jews! and
they smote him with their hands.
4 Pilate therefore went forth again, and
said to them, Behold, I bring him forth

19:1,2 It was plain that the direction this Pilate was taking was not a good one, and he knew it. He could see that it was going to land him on ground he preferred not to touch. He tried vainly to alter his course by having Jesus scourged, in the hope that it would appease the Jews. After the whipping, the twisted soldiers twisted a crown of thorns and put it on His head. This was perhaps symbolic of the Messiah taking upon Himself the curse placed upon creation when Adam sinned (Genesis 3:18).

to you, that you may know that I find no
fault in him.
5 Then came Jesus forth, wearing the
crown of thorns, and the purple robe. And
Pilate said to them, Behold the man!
6 When the chief priests therefore and
officers saw him, they cried out, saying,
Crucify him, crucify him. Pilate said to
them, You take him, and crucify him: for
I find no fault in him.
7 The Jews answered him, We have a
law, and by our law he ought to die, because he made himself the Son of God.
8 When Pilate therefore heard that saying, he was the more afraid;

> We must school and train ourselves to deal personally with the unconverted. We must not excuse ourselves, but force ourselves to the irksome task until it becomes easy.
>
> **CHARLES SPURGEON**

9 And went again into the judgment hall,
and said to Jesus, Where are you from?
But Jesus gave him no answer.
10 Then said Pilate to him, Do you not
speak to me? Do you not know that I have
power to crucify you, and have power to
release you?
11 Jesus answered, You could have no
power at all against me, except it were giv-
en you from above: therefore he that delivered me to you has the greater sin.
12 And from thenceforth Pilate sought to
release him: but the Jews cried out, saying, If you let this man go, you are not
Caesar's friend: whosoever makes himself
a king speaks against Caesar.
13 When Pilate therefore heard that saying, he brought Jesus forth, and sat down
in the judgment seat in a place that is
called the Pavement, but in the Hebrew,
Gabbatha.
14 And it was the preparation of the
passover, and about the sixth hour: and
he said to the Jews, Behold your King!
15 But they cried out, Away with him,
away with him, crucify him. Pilate said to
them, Shall I crucify your King? The chief
priest answered, We have no king but
Caesar.
16 Then delivered he him therefore to
them to be crucified. And they took Jesus,
and led him away.
17 And he bearing his cross went forth
into a place called the place of a skull,
which is called in the Hebrew Golgotha:
18 Where they crucified him, and two
other with him, on either side one, and
Jesus in the midst.
19 And Pilate wrote a title, and put it on
the cross. And the writing was, JESUS
OF NAZARETH THE KING OF THE
JEWS.
20 This title then read many of the Jews:
for the place where Jesus was crucified
was near to the city: and it was written in
Hebrew, and Greek, and Latin.
21 Then said the chief priests of the Jews
to Pilate, Write not, The King of the Jews;
but that he said, I am King of the Jews.
22 Pilate answered, What I have written
I have written.
23 Then the soldiers, when they had
crucified Jesus, took his garments, and
made four parts, to every soldier a part;
and also his coat: now the coat was without seam, woven from the top throughout.
24 They said therefore among themselves, Let us not rend it, but cast lots for
it, whose it shall be: that the scripture
might be fulfilled, which says, They parted my raiment among them, and for my
vesture they did cast lots. These things
therefore the soldiers did.
25 Now there stood by the cross of Jesus
his mother, and his mother's sister, Mary
the wife of Cleophas, and Mary Magdalene.
26 When Jesus therefore saw his mother, and the disciple standing by, whom
he loved, he said to his mother, Woman,
behold your son!
27 Then said he to the disciple, Behold
your mother! And from that hour that disciple took her to his own home.
28 After this, Jesus knowing that all

Questions & Objections

19:33,34 *"Is it possible that Jesus simply fainted on the cross, and revived while He was in the tomb?"*

Jesus had been whipped and beaten, and was bleeding from His head, back, hands, and feet for at least six hours. While he was on the cross, a soldier pierced His side with a spear and blood and water gushed out. Professional soldiers would certainly have completed their assigned task and ensured his death.

"It is impossible that a being who had stolen half-dead out of the sepulcher, who crept about weak and ill, wanting medical treatment, who required bandaging, strengthening, and indulgence, and who still at last yielded to his sufferings, could have given to the disciples the impression that he was a conqueror over death and the grave, the Prince of Life: an impression which lay at the bottom of their future ministry. Such a resuscitation could only have weakened the impression which he had made upon them in life and in death, at the most could only have given it an elegiac voice, but could by no possibility have changed their sorrow into enthusiasm, have elevated their reverence into worship." *Strauss, New Life of Jesus* (quoted in *Who Moved the Stone?* by *Frank Morison*)

things were now accomplished, that the
scripture might be fulfilled, said, I thirst.
29 Now there was set a vessel full of
vinegar: and they filled a sponge with
vinegar, and put it upon hyssop, and put
it to his mouth.
30 When Jesus therefore had received
the vinegar, he said, It is finished: and he
bowed his head, and gave up the ghost.
31 The Jews therefore, because it was
the preparation, that the bodies should
not remain upon the cross on the sabbath
day, (for that sabbath day was an
high day,) besought Pilate that their legs
might be broken, and that they might be
taken away.
32 Then came the soldiers, and broke
the legs of the first, and of the other which
was crucified with him.
33 But when they came to Jesus, and
saw that he was dead already, they broke
not his legs:
34 But one of the soldiers with a spear
pierced his side, and forthwith came there
out blood and water.
35 And he that saw it bare record, and
his record is true: and he knows what he
said is true, that you might believe.

19:29 Messianic prophecy fulfilled: "They gave me also gall for my meat; and in my thirst they gave me vinegar to drink" (Psalm 69:21). See John 19:33,36 comment.

19:31,32 Archaeology confirms the Bible. "During the past four decades, spectacular discoveries have produced data corroborating the historical backdrop of the Gospels. In 1968, for example, the skeletal remains of a crucified man were found in a burial cave in northern Jerusalem ...There was evidence that his wrists may have been pierced with nails. The knees had been doubled up and turned sideways and an iron nail (still lodged in the heel bone of one foot) driven through both heels. The shinbones appeared to have been broken, perhaps corroborating the Gospel of John." *Jeffery L. Sheler*, "Is the Bible True?" *Reader's Digest*, June 2000

19:33,34 "Clearly the weight of historical and medical evidence indicates that Jesus was dead before the wound to His side was inflicted and supports the traditional view that the spear, thrust between his right rib, probably perforated not only the right lung but also the pericardium and heart and thereby ensured His death. Accordingly, interpretations based on the assumption that Jesus did not die on the cross appear to be at odds with modern medical knowledge." *Journal of the American Medical Society*, March 21, 1986

36 For these things were done, that the
scripture should be fulfilled, A bone of
him shall not be broken.
37 And again another scripture says, They
shall look on him whom they pierced.
38 And after this Joseph of Arimathaea,
being a disciple of Jesus, but secretly for
fear of the Jews, besought Pilate that he
might take away the body of Jesus: and
Pilate gave him leave. He came therefore,
and took the body of Jesus.
39 And there came also Nicodemus,
which at the first came to Jesus by night,
and brought a mixture of myrrh and
aloes, about an hundred pound weight.
40 Then took they the body of Jesus,
and wound it in linen clothes with the
spices, as the manner of the Jews is to
bury.
41 Now in the place where he was crucified there was a garden; and in the garden a new sepulchre, wherein was never
man yet laid.
42 There laid they Jesus therefore because of the Jews' preparation day; for the
sepulchre was near at hand.

CHAPTER 20

THE first day of the week came Mary
Magdalene early, when it was yet
dark, to the sepulchre, and saw the stone
taken away from the sepulchre.
2 Then she ran, and came to Simon Peter,
and to the other disciple, whom Jesus
loved, and said to them, They have taken
away the Lord out of the sepulchre, and
we know not where they have laid him.
3 Peter therefore went forth, and that
other disciple, and came to the sepulchre.
4 So they ran both together: and the
other disciple did outrun Peter, and came
first to the sepulchre.
5 And he stooping down, and looking in,
saw the linen clothes lying; yet went he
not in.
6 Then came Simon Peter following him,
and went into the sepulchre, and saw the
linen clothes lie,
7 And the napkin, that was about his
head, not lying with the linen clothes, but
wrapped together in a place by itself.
8 Then went in also that other disciple,
which came first to the sepulchre, and he
saw, and believed.
9 For as yet they knew not the scripture,
that he must rise again from the dead.
10 Then the disciples went away again
to their own home.
11 But Mary stood without at the sepulchre weeping: and as she wept, she stooped
down, and looked into the sepulchre,
12 And saw two angels in white sitting,
the one at the head, and the other at the
feet, where the body of Jesus had lain.
13 And they said to her, Woman, why
are you weeping? She said to them, Because they have taken away my Lord,
and I know not where they have laid him.
14 And when she had thus said, she
turned herself back, and saw Jesus standing, and knew not that it was Jesus.
15 Jesus said to her, Woman, why are
you weeping? whom do you seek? She,
supposing him to be the gardener, said
to him, Sir, if you have borne him hence,
tell me where you have laid him, and I
will take him away.
16 Jesus said to her, Mary. She turned
herself, and said to him, Rabboni; which
is to say, Master.
17 Jesus said to her, Touch me not; for
I am not yet ascended to my Father: but
go to my brethren, and say to them, I ascend to my Father, and your Father; and
to my God, and your God.
18 Mary Magdalene came and told the

19:33,36 Messianic prophecy fulfilled: As Exodus 12:46 instructs, none of the Passover lamb's bones were to be broken. When Jesus, our Passover Lamb, was sacrificed for our sins, none of His bones were broken. See Acts 2:31 comment.

20:18 The first evangelist was a woman. She took the good news of the resurrection to the men, who were hiding behind locked doors.

Questions & Objections

20:25

"Seeing is believing. If I can't see it, I don't believe it exists."

We believe in many things that we can't see. (See Optical Illusions on page 590.) Ask a skeptic if he has ever seen the wind. Has he seen history? Has he ever seen his brain? We see the *effects* of the wind, but the wind is invisible. We have records of history, but it is by "faith" that we believe certain historical events happened. Television waves are invisible, but an antenna and a receiver can detect their presence. The unregenerate man likewise has a "receiver." However, the receiver (his spirit) is dead because of sin (Ephesians 2:1). He needs to be plugged into the life of God; then he will come alive and be aware of the invisible spiritual realm.

disciples that she had seen the Lord, and
that he had spoken these things to her.
19 Then the same day at evening, being
the first day of the week, when the doors
were shut where the disciples were assembled for fear of the Jews, came Jesus
and stood in the midst, and said to them,
Peace be to you.
20 And when he had so said, he showed
to them his hands and his side. Then were
the disciples glad, when they saw the
Lord.
21 Then said Jesus to them again, Peace
be to you: as my Father has sent me, even
so send I you.
22 And when he had said this, he
breathed on them, and said to them, Receive the Holy Spirit:
23 Whose soever sins you remit, they are
remitted to them; and whose soever sins
you retain, they are retained.
24 But Thomas, one of the twelve, called
Didymus, was not with them when Jesus
came.
25 The other disciples therefore said to
him, We have seen the Lord. But he said
to them, Except I shall see in his hands
the print of the nails, and put my finger
into the print of the nails, and thrust my
hand into his side, I will not believe.
26 And after eight days again his disciples were within, and Thomas with them:
then came Jesus, the doors being shut,
and stood in the midst, and said, Peace
be to you.
27 Then said he to Thomas, reach here
your finger, and behold my hands; and
reach here your hand, and thrust it into

20:22 Why did Jesus breathe on His disciples and say, "Receive the Holy Spirit," when He had already told them that the Holy Spirit could come only after His ascension (John 16:7)? Perhaps it was at that moment that the Body of Christ on earth was conceived within the womb. Perhaps it was then that He *planted* the seed of the life of the Church, but after the gestation period, on the Day of Pentecost, the Body of Christ was then *birthed* on earth.

The first seed of Adam's race began with the breath of God (Genesis 2:7), but the "last Adam" began with the breath of God in Christ. The first man had been formed from the dust of the ground, and when the Lord God breathed into his nostrils the breath of life, he became a "living soul," but Christ was made a "quickening spirit" (1 Corinthians 15:45).

Jesus picked up fallen dust from the ground of Israel, shaped them for three years, and now He breathed life into them, as He did in Genesis with the dust He had formed into Adam's body. It was but a gentle breath at conception, which became a rushing mighty wind on the Day of Pentecost (Acts 2:2), and caused the living Body of Christ to stand on its feet on earth.

20:23 If someone has turned from sin and is trusting in Jesus Christ alone for his eternal salvation, every believer has power to inform him that his sin is forgiven, based on his professed faith in the Savior.

my side: and be not faithless, but believing.
28 **And Thomas answered and said to him, My Lord and my God.**
29 **Jesus said to him, Thomas, because you have seen me, you have believed: blessed are they that have not seen, and yet have believed.**
30 And many other signs truly did Jesus in the presence of his disciples, which are not written in this book:
31 But these are written, that you might believe that Jesus is the Christ, the Son of God; and that believing you might have life through his name.

CHAPTER 21

AFTER these things Jesus showed himself again to the disciples at the sea of Tiberias; and on this wise showed he himself.
2 There were together Simon Peter, and Thomas called Didymus, and Nathanael of Cana in Galilee, and the sons of Zebedee, and two other of his disciples.
3 Simon Peter said to them, I go a fishing. They said to him, We also go with you. They went forth, and entered into a ship immediately; and that night they caught nothing.
4 But when the morning was now come, Jesus stood on the shore: but the disciples knew not that it was Jesus.
5 Then Jesus said to them, Children, have you any meat? They answered him, No.
6 And he said to them, Cast the net on the right side of the ship, and you shall find. They cast therefore, and now they were not able to draw it for the multitude of fishes.
7 Therefore that disciple whom Jesus loved said to Peter, It is the Lord. Now when Simon Peter heard that it was the Lord, he girt his fisher's coat to him, (for he was naked,) and did cast himself into the sea.

> "A dead calm is our enemy, a storm may prove our helper. Controversy may arouse thought, and through thought may come the Divine change."
>
> **CHARLES SPURGEON**

8 And the other disciples came in a little ship; (for they were not far from land, but as it were two hundred cubits,) dragging the net with fishes.
9 As soon then as they were come to land, they saw a fire of coals there, and fish laid thereon, and bread.
10 Jesus said to them, Bring of the fish which you have now caught.
11 Simon Peter went up, and drew the net to land full of great fishes, an hundred and fifty and three: and for all there were so many, yet was not the net broken.

20:26 Scientific facts in the Bible. Babies are circumcised on the eighth day because this is the day that the coagulating factor in the blood, called prothrombin, is the highest. Medical science has discovered that this is when the human body's immune system is at its peak.

Just as the eighth day was the God-given timing for circumcision (Genesis 17:12), there is a God-given timing for every person who is "circumcised with the circumcision made without hands" (Colossians 2:11). Jesus appeared to Thomas on the eighth day. What Thomas saw cut away the flesh of his unbelieving heart. He became a Jew inwardly as his circumcision became "that of the heart, in the spirit, and not in the letter" (Romans 2:29). Thomas bowed his heart to Jesus of Nazareth as his Lord and his God. He needed a miracle, and God graciously gave it to him.

Each of us is dealt with individually by God; some get incredible spiritual manifestations at conversion. Others quietly trust the promises of God, and God reveals Himself to them through faith rather than feelings of great joy. What matters is not *how* each of us came to Christ, but that we became new creatures in Christ, because that is the *real* miracle that proves the reality of salvation. This is what Paul meant when he wrote, "For in Christ Jesus neither circumcision avails anything, nor uncircumcision, but a new creature" (Galatians 6:15).

"God, if you are there, strike me dead!"
(See Proverbs 3:34 comment.)

12 Jesus said to them, Come and dine.
And none of the disciples dared ask him,
Who are you? knowing that it was the
Lord.
13 Jesus then came, and took bread, and
gave, and fish likewise.
14 This is now the third time that Jesus
showed himself to his disciples, after that
he was risen from the dead.
15 So when they had dined, Jesus said
to Simon Peter, Simon, son of Jonah, do
you love me more than these? He said to
him, Yea, Lord; you know that I love you.
He said to him, Feed my lambs.
16 He said to him again the second time,
Simon, son of Jonah, do you love me? He
said to him, Yea, Lord; you know that I
love you. He said to him, Feed my sheep.
17 He said to him the third time, Simon,
son of Jonah, do you love me? Peter was
grieved because he said to him the third
time, Do you love me? And he said to
him, Lord, you know all things; you know
that I love you. Jesus said to him, Feed
my sheep.
18 Verily, verily, I say to you, When you
were young, you girded yourself, and
walked where you would: but when you
shall be old, you shall stretch forth your
hands, and another shall gird you, and
carry you where you would not.
19 This spoke he, signifying by what
death he should glorify God. And when
he had spoken this, he said to him, Follow me.
20 Then Peter, turning about, saw the
disciple whom Jesus loved following;
which also leaned on his breast at supper,
and said, Lord, which is he that betrays
you?
21 Peter seeing him said to Jesus, Lord,
and what shall this man do?
22 Jesus said to him, If I will that he tarry
till I come, what is that to you? You follow me.
23 Then went this saying abroad among
the brethren, that that disciple should
not die: yet Jesus said not to him, He shall
not die; but, If I will that he tarry till I
come, what is that to you?
24 This is the disciple which testifies of
these things, and wrote these things: and
we know that his testimony is true.
25 And there are also many other things
which Jesus did, the which, if they should
be written every one, I suppose that even
the world itself could not contain the
books that should be written. Amen.

Islam

OFFICIAL NAME: Islam

KEY FIGURE IN HISTORY: Muhammad (A.D. 570–632)

DATE OF ITS ESTABLISHMENT: A.D. 622

ADHERENTS: Worldwide: Estimated 800 million to 1 billion; 58 percent live in South and Southeast Asia; 28 percent in Africa; 9 percent in Near and Middle East; 5 percent other. U.S.: Estimated 6.5 to 8 million.

WHAT IS ISLAM?

Islam is the world's youngest major world religion. It claims to be the restoration of original monotheism and truth and thus supersedes both Judaism and Christianity. It stresses submission to *Allah*, the Arabic name for God, and conformity to the "five pillars" or disciplines of that religion as essential for salvation. From its inception, Islam was an aggressively missionary-oriented religion. Within one century of its formation, and often using military force, Islam had spread across the Middle East, most of North Africa, and as far east as India. While God is, in the understanding of most Muslims, unknowable personally, His will is believed to be perfectly revealed in the holy book, the *Qur'an*. The Qur'an is to be followed completely and its teaching forms a complete guide for life and society.

WHO WAS MUHAMMAD?

Muhammad is believed by Muslims to be the last and greatest prophet of God—"the seal of the prophets." It was through him that the Qur'an was dictated, thus according him the supreme place among the seers of God. A native of Mecca, Muhammad was forced to flee that city in A.D. 622 after preaching vigorously against the paganism of the city. Having secured his leadership in Medina, and with several military victories to his credit, Muhammad returned in triumph to Mecca in A.D. 630. There, he established Islam as the religion of all Arabia.

WHAT IS THE QUR'AN?

The Qur'an is the sacred book of Islam and the perfect word of God for the Muslim. It is claimed that the Qur'an was dictated in Arabic by the angel Gabriel to Muhammad and were God's precise words. As such, it had preexisted from eternity in heaven with God as the "Mother of the Book" and was in that form uncreated and co-eternal with God. Islam teaches that it contains the total and perfect revelation and will of God. The Qur'an is about four-fifths the length of the New Testament and is divided into 114 *surahs* or chapters. While Islam respects the Torah, the psalms of David, and the four Gospels, the Qur'an stands alone in its authority and absoluteness. It is believed to be most perfectly understood in Arabic and it is a religious obligation to seek to read and quote it in the original language.

WHAT ARE THE "FIVE PILLARS"?

They are the framework for the Muslims' life and discipline. Successful and satisfactory adherence to the pillars satisfies the will of Allah. They form the basis for the Muslim's hope for salvation along with faith and belief in Allah's existence, the authority of Muhammad as a prophet, and the finality and perfection of the Qur'an. The five pillars are:

The confession of Faith or *Shahada*: It is the declaration that there is no god but Allah and Muhammad is his prophet. Sincerity in the voicing of the confession is necessary for it to be valid. It must be held until death, and repudiation of the *Shahada* nullifies hope for salvation.

Prayer of *Salat*: Five times a day, preceded by ceremonial washing, the Muslim is required to pray facing Mecca. Specific formulas recited from the Qur'an (in Arabic), along with prostrations, are included. Prayer is, in this sense, an expression of submission to the will of Allah. While most of Islam has no hierarchical priesthood, prayers are led in mosques by respected lay leaders. The five times of prayer are before sunrise, noon, midafternoon, sunset, and prior to sleep.

Almsgiving or *Zakat*: The Qur'an teaches the giving of two-and-a-half percent of one's capital wealth to the poor and/or for the propagation of Islam. By doing so, the Muslim's remaining wealth is purified.

The Fast or *Sawm*: during the course of the lunar month of Ramadan, a fast is to be observed by every Muslim from sunrise to sunset. Nothing is to pass over the lips during this time, and they should refrain from sexual relations. After sunset, feasting and other celebrations often occur. The daylight hours are set aside for self-purification. The month is used to remember the giving of the Qur'an to Muhammad.

Pilgrimage or *Hajj*: All Muslims who are economically and physically able are required to journey to Mecca at least once in their lifetime. The required simple pilgrim's dress stresses the notion of equality before God. Another element of the Hajj is the mandatory walk of each pilgrim seven times around the *Kaabah*—the shrine of the black rock, the holiest site of Islam. Muhammad taught that the Kaabah was the original place of worship for Adam and later for Abraham. The Kaabah is thus venerated as the site of true religion, the absolute monotheism of Islam.

THE DOCTRINES OF ISLAM

God: He is numerically and absolutely one. Allah is beyond the understanding of man so that only his will may be revealed and known. He is confessed as the "merciful and compassionate one."

Sin: The most serious sin that can be ascribed to people is that of *shirk* or considering god as more than one. Original sin is viewed as a "lapse" by Adam. Humankind is considered weak and forgetful but not as fallen.

Angels: Islam affirms the reality of angels as messengers and agents of god. Evil spirits or *Jinn* also exist. Satan is a fallen angel. Angels perform important functions for Allah both now and at the end of time.

Final Judgment: The world will be judged at the end of time by Allah. The good deeds and obedience of all people to the five pillars and the Qur'an will serve as the basis of judgment.

Salvation: It is determined by faith, as defined by Islam, as well as by compiling good deeds primarily in conformity to the five pillars.

Marriage: Muslims uphold marriage as honorable and condemn adultery. While many Muslim marriages are monogamous, Islamic states allow as many as four wives. Men consider a woman as less than an equal, and while a man has the right to divorce his wife, the wife has no similar power (see Surah 2:228, 4:34). Nonetheless, the female has a right to own and dispose of property. Modesty in dress is encouraged for both men and women.

War: The term *jihad* or "struggle" is often considered as both external and internal, both a physical and spiritual struggle. The enemies of Islam or "idolaters," states the Qur'an, may be slain "wherever you find them" (Surah:5). (See Surah 47:4). Paradise is promised for those who die fighting in the cause of Islam (see Surah 3:195, 2:224). Moderate Muslims emphasize the spiritual dimension of Jihad and not its political element.

ANSWERING MUSLIM OBJECTIONS TO CHRISTIANITY

Christians and Jews are acknowledged as "people of the book," although their failure to conform to the confession of Islam labels them as unbelievers. Following are several questions that Muslims have about Christianity.

Is the Trinity a belief in three gods?

Christians are monotheistic and believe that God is one. But both in His work in accomplishing salvation through the person of Jesus Christ and through biblical study it has become clear that His oneness in fact comprises three persons—Father, Son (Jesus Christ), and the third person of the Godhead, the Holy Spirit. Mary is not part of the Godhead. The notion of God, who is three-in-one, is part of both the mystery and greatness of God. God is in essence one while in persons three. This truth helps us understand God as truly personal and having the capacity to relate to other persons. As well, Christians confirm the holiness, sovereignty, and greatness of God.

How can Jesus be the Son of God?

Scripture affirms that Jesus was conceived supernaturally by the Holy Spirit and was born of the Virgin Mary. It does not in any way claim that Jesus was directly God the Father's biological and physical son. It rejects the notion of the Arabic word for son, *walad*, meaning physical son, for the word *ibin*, which is the title of relationship. Jesus is the Son in a symbolic manner designating that He was God the Word who became man in order to save humankind from its sin. The virgin birth was supernatural as God the Holy Spirit conceived in Mary, without physical relations, Jesus the Messiah. In this manner even the Qur'an affirms the miraculous birth of

Christ (see Surah 19:16–21). Jesus was in this sense "God's unique Son." During His earthly ministry He carried out the will of the Father. Notably the Qur'an affirms Jesus' supernatural birth, life of miracles, His compassion, and ascension to heaven (see Surah 19:16–21,29–31, 3:37–47, 5:110).

How could Jesus have died on the cross especially if He's God's son?

The testimony of history and the *Injil,* or the four Gospels, is that Jesus died on the cross. If it is understood that God is love, and that humankind is lost in sin, then is it not likely that God would have provided a sacrifice for sin? Jesus is God's sacrifice for all the sins of the world and is a bridge from a holy God to fallen and sinful humans.

This truth is revealed in the Injil, John 3:16. Even the Qur'an states in Surah 3:55 that "Allah said: O Isa [Jesus], I am going to terminate [to put to death] the period of your stay (on earth) and cause you to ascend unto Me." What other way could this concept have any meaning apart from Jesus' death for sin and His subsequent resurrection?

Muslims believe that God took Jesus from the cross and substituted Judas in His place, or at least someone who looked like Jesus. He was then taken to heaven where He is alive and from where one day He will return.

ANSWERING MUSLIMS' QUESTIONS TO CHRISTIANS ABOUT ISLAM

What do you think about the prophet Muhammad?

Muhammad was apparently a well-meaning man who sought to oppose paganism and evil in his day. While he succeeded in uniting the Arabian Peninsula and upheld several important virtues, we do not believe he received a fresh revelation from God. Jesus Christ fulfilled not only the final prophetic role from God, but He is the Savior or the world and God the Son. While Islam believes that some Bible passages refer to Muhammad (see Deut. 18:18–19; John 14:16; 15:26; 16:7), that is clearly not the meaning of the texts. Other passages may help in understanding and interpreting the previous texts (see Matthew 21:11; Luke 24:19; John 6;14; 7:40; Acts 1:8–16; 7:37).

What is your opinion of the Qur'an?

It is a greatly valued book for the Muslim. It is not received or believed to be a divine book by the Christian. The statements of the Qur'an are accepted only where they agree with the Bible.

What is your opinion about the five pillars?

Salvation is from God and comes only through the saving work of Jesus Christ. When we put our faith in Him, we may be saved (see John 3:16–21,31–36).

WITNESSING TO MUSLIMS

- Be courteous and loving.
- Reflect interest in their beliefs. Allow them time to articulate their views.
- Be acquainted with their basic beliefs.
- Be willing to examine passages of the Qur'an concerning their beliefs.
- Stick to the cardinal doctrines of the Christian faith but also take time to respond to all sincere questions.
- Point out the centrality of the person and work of Jesus Christ for salvation.
- Stress that because of Jesus, His cross, and resurrection, one may have the full assurance of salvation, both now and for eternity (see 1 John 5:13).
- Share the plan of salvation with the Muslim. Point out that salvation is a gift and not to be earned.
- Pray for the fullness of the Holy Spirit. Trust Him to provide wisdom and grace.
- Be willing to become a friend and a personal evangelist to Muslims.

Acts

CHAPTER 1

THE former treatise have I made, O Theophilus, of all that Jesus began both to do and teach,
2 Until the day in which he was taken up, after that he through the Holy Spirit had given commandments to the apostles whom he had chosen:
3 To whom also he showed himself alive after his passion by many infallible proofs, being seen of them forty days, and speaking of the things pertaining to the kingdom of God:
4 And, being assembled together with them, commanded them that they should not depart from Jerusalem, but wait for the promise of the Father, which, said he, you have heard of me.
5 For John truly baptized with water; but you shall be baptized with the Holy Spirit not many days hence.
6 When they therefore were come together, they asked of him, saying, Lord, will you at this time restore again the kingdom to Israel?
7 And he said to them, It is not for you to know the times or the seasons, which the Father has put in his own power.
8 *But you shall receive power, after that the Holy Spirit is come upon you: and you shall be witnesses to me both in Jerusalem, and in all Judea, and in Samaria, and to the uttermost part of the earth.*
9 And when he had spoken these things, while they beheld, he was taken up; and a cloud received him out of their sight.
10 And while they looked steadfastly toward heaven as he went up, behold, two men stood by them in white apparel;
11 *Which also said, You men of Galilee, why do you stand gazing up into heaven? this same Jesus, which is taken up from you into heaven, shall so come in like manner as you have seen him go into heaven.*

1:5 Water baptism doesn't save us. In Acts 2:38, Peter's hearers repented and believed the gospel *before* they were baptized. In Acts 10:47, those who believed the gospel received the Holy Spirit (they passed from death to life) *before* they were baptized.

1:8 "Oh my friends, we are loaded down with countless church activities, while the *real* work of the church, that of evangelizing the world and winning the lost, is almost entirely neglected!" *Oswald J. Smith*

1:10,11 The inference is, "Don't stand here gazing up into the heavens. God has granted everlasting life to sinful humanity. Go and wait for the power to take the gospel to the world." We haven't been saved to gaze up to heaven, but to take the light to those who sit in the dark shadow of death. How can any person, who professes to have the love of God in him, sit passively while sinners die daily and go to hell? Paul said, "Woe is to me, if I preach not the gospel!" (1 Corinthians 9:16).

1:11 **Second coming of Jesus:** See 1 Corinthians 4:5.

12 Then returned they to Jerusalem from
the mount called Olivet, which is from
Jerusalem a sabbath day's journey.
13 And when they were come in, they
went up into an upper room, where abode
both Peter, and James, and John, and Andrew, Philip, and Thomas, Bartholomew,
and Matthew, James the son of Alphaeus,
and Simon Zelotes, and Judas the brother of James.
14 These all continued with one accord
in prayer and supplication, with the women, and Mary the mother of Jesus, and
with his brethren.
15 And in those days Peter stood up in
the midst of the disciples, and said, (the
number of names together were about an
hundred and twenty,)
16 Men and brethren, this scripture must
needs have been fulfilled, which the Holy
Spirit by the mouth of David spoke before
concerning Judas, which was guide to
them that took Jesus.
17 For he was numbered with us, and
had obtained part of this ministry.
18 Now this man purchased a field with
the reward of iniquity; and falling headlong, he burst asunder in the midst, and
all his bowels gushed out.
19 And it was known to all the dwellers
at Jerusalem; insomuch as that field is
called in their proper tongue, Akeldama,
that is to say, The field of blood.
20 For it is written in the book of Psalms,
Let his habitation be desolate, and let no
man dwell therein: and his bishopric let
another take.
21 Wherefore of these men which have
companied with us all the time that the
Lord Jesus went in and out among us,
22 Beginning from the baptism of John,
to that same day that he was taken up
from us, must one be ordained to be a
witness with us of his resurrection.
23 And they appointed two, Joseph called
Barsabas, who was surnamed Justus, and
Matthias.
24 And they prayed, and said, You, Lord,
which know the hearts of all men, show
whether of these two you have chosen,
25 That he may take part of this ministry and apostleship, from which Judas by
transgression fell, that he might go to his
own place.
26 And they gave forth their lots; and the
lot fell upon Matthias; and he was numbered with the eleven apostles.

CHAPTER 2

AND when the day of Pentecost was
fully come, they were all with one accord in one place.
2 And suddenly there came a sound from
heaven as of a rushing mighty wind, and it
filled all the house where they were sitting.
3 And there appeared to them cloven
tongues like as of fire, and it sat upon each
of them.
4 And they were all filled with the Holy
Spirit, and began to speak with other
tongues, as the Spirit gave them utterance.
5 And there were dwelling at Jerusalem
Jews, devout men, out of every nation under heaven.
6 Now when this was noised abroad, the
multitude came together, and were confounded, because that every man heard
them speak in his own language.
7 And they were all amazed and marveled, saying one to another, Behold, are
not all these which speak Galilaeans?
8 And how hear we every man in our
own tongue, wherein we were born?
9 Parthians, and Medes, and Elamites, and

1:14 Prayer—the secret weapon: See Acts 4:24.

1:18 When a hanging body decomposes, this will be the grisly result.

1:21–26 As Israel crossed over the Jordan on dry ground, God instructed them to place twelve stones as immovable witnesses—a memorial to tell the Israelite children what God had done for them (Joshua 4:1–7). Likewise, the Church was established with twelve witnesses so that we would know and tell what God has done for us through Christ.

POINTS FOR OPEN-AIR PREACHING

2:14

How to Draw a Crowd

One of the most difficult things to do is draw a crowd to hear the gospel. Today's society has been programmed to want immediate action, and open-air preaching isn't too attractive to guilty sinners. Therefore we have to be as wise as serpents and as gentle as doves. A serpent gets its heart's desire subtly. Our desire is for sinners to gather under the sound of the gospel.

Ask people passing by what they think is the greatest killer of drivers in the U.S. This stirs their curiosity. Some begin calling out "Alcohol!" or "Falling asleep at the wheel!" Tell them it's not and repeat the question a few more times, saying that you will give a dollar to the person who gets the answer. Tell them that they will never guess what it is that kills more drivers than anything else in America. A few more shouts emit from the crowd. People are now waiting around for the answer. What is it that kills more drivers than anything else in the United States? What is it that could be the death of you and me? You won't believe this, but it is "trees." Millions of them line our highways, waiting for a driver to kill. When one is struck, the tree stays still, sending the driver into eternity.

Then tell the crowd that you have another question for them. Ask what they think is the most common food on which people choke to death in U.S. restaurants. Over the next few minutes, go through the same scenario. People call out "Steak!" "Chicken bones!" Believe it or not, the answer is "hard-boiled egg yoke."

By now you have a crowd that is enjoying what is going on. Ask them what they think is the most dangerous job in America. Someone calls out "cop." It's not. Someone else may name another dangerous profession like "fire fighter." Say, "Good one... but wrong." Give a suggestion by saying, "Why doesn't someone say 'electrician'?" Someone takes the suggestion and says, "Electrician!" Say, "Sorry, it's not electrician." The most dangerous job in the United States... is to be the president. Out of forty or so, four have been murdered while on the job.

Then tell the crowd you have another question. "Does anyone in the crowd consider himself to be a "good person"? By now you will have noted who in the crowd has the self-confidence to speak out. Point to one or two and ask, "Sir, do you consider yourself to be a good person?" The Bible tells us that "every man will proclaim his own goodness" (Proverbs 20:6), and he does. He smiles and says, "Yes, I do consider myself to be a good person." Ask him if he has ever told a lie. Has he stolen, lusted, blasphemed, etc.? That's when all heaven breaks loose. There is conviction of sin. Sinners hear the gospel, and angels rejoice.

MORE QUESTIONS FOR CROWD DRAWING

- Who wrote, "Ask not what your country can do for you. Ask what you can do for your country"? *(President Kennedy's speechwriter)*
- What is the only fish that can blink with both eyes? *(A shark)*
- Who was John Lennon's first girlfriend? *(Thelma Pickles)*
- How long does it take the average person to fall asleep: 2 minutes, 7 minutes, or 4 hours? *(7 minutes)*
- How long is a goldfish's memory span: 3 seconds, 3 minutes, or 3 hours? *(3 seconds)*
- How many muscles does a cat have in each ear: 2, 32, or 426? *(32)*

the dwellers in Mesopotamia, and in Judea, and Cappadocia, in Pontus, and Asia,
10 Phrygia, and Pamphylia, in Egypt, and
in the parts of Libya about Cyrene, and
strangers of Rome, Jews and proselytes,
11 Cretes and Arabians, we do hear them
speak in our tongues the wonderful works
of God.
12 And they were all amazed, and were
in doubt, saying one to another, What
means this?
13 Others mocking said, These men are
full of new wine.
14 But Peter, standing up with the elev-

en, lifted up his voice, and said to them,
You men of Judea, and all you that dwell
at Jerusalem, be this known to you, and
hearken to my words:
15 For these are not drunken, as you
suppose, seeing it is but the third hour of
the day.
16 But this is that which was spoken by
the prophet Joel;
17 And it shall come to pass in the last
days, said God, I will pour out of my Spirit upon all flesh: and your sons and your
daughters shall prophesy, and your young
men shall see visions, and your old men
shall dream dreams:
18 And on my servants and on my hand-
maidens I will pour out in those days of
my Spirit; and they shall prophesy:
19 And I will show wonders in heaven
above, and signs in the earth beneath;
blood, and fire, and vapor of smoke:
20 The sun shall be turned into darkness, and the moon into blood, before that
great and notable day of the Lord come:
**21 And it shall come to pass, that who-
soever shall call on the name of the
Lord shall be saved.**
22 You men of Israel, hear these words;
Jesus of Nazareth, a man approved of God
among you by miracles and wonders and
signs, which God did by him in the midst
of you, as you yourselves also know:
23 Him, being delivered by the determi-
nate counsel and foreknowledge of God,
you have taken, and by wicked hands have
crucified and slain:
24 Whom God has raised up, having
loosed the pains of death: because it was
not possible that he should be held by it.
25 For David speaks concerning him, I
foresaw the Lord always before my face,
for he is on my right hand, that I should
not be moved:
26 Therefore did my heart rejoice, and
my tongue was glad; moreover also my
flesh shall rest in hope:
27 Because you will not leave my soul
in hell, neither will you suffer your Holy
One to see corruption.
28 You have made known to me the
ways of life; you shall make me full of joy
with your countenance.
29 Men and brethren, let me freely speak
to you of the patriarch David, that he is
both dead and buried, and his sepulchre is
with us to this day.
30 Therefore being a prophet, and knowing that God had sworn with an oath to
him, that of the fruit of his loins, according to the flesh, he would raise up Christ
to sit on his throne;
31 He, seeing this before spoke of the
resurrection of Christ, that his soul was
not left in hell, neither his flesh did see
corruption.
32 This Jesus has God raised up, whereof we all are witnesses.
33 Therefore being by the right hand of
God exalted, and having received of the
Father the promise of the Holy Spirit, he
has shed forth this, which you now see
and hear.
34 For David is not ascended into the
heavens: but he said himself, The LORD
said to my Lord, Sit on my right hand,
35 Until I make your foes your footstool.
36 Therefore let all the house of Israel
know assuredly, that God has made that
same Jesus, whom you have crucified,
both Lord and Christ.
37 Now when they heard this, they were
pricked in their heart, and said to Peter
and to the rest of the apostles, Men and
brethren, what shall we do?
**38 Then Peter said to them, Repent,
and be baptized every one of you in the
name of Jesus Christ for the remission**

2:21 Salvation is possible for every person. See Romans 10:13.

2:31 Messianic prophecy fulfilled: "For thou wilt not leave my soul in hell; neither wilt thou suffer thine Holy One to see corruption" (Psalm 16:10). See 1 Peter 2:24 comment.

2:38 Repentance—its necessity for salvation. See Acts 3:19.

PRINCIPLES OF GROWTH FOR THE NEW AND GROWING CHRISTIAN

2:38

Water Baptism—Sprinkle or Immerse?

The Bible says, "Repent, and be baptized every one of you in the name of Jesus Christ for the remission of sins..." (Acts 2:38). There is no question about whether you *should* be baptized. The questions are how, when, and by whom?

It would seem clear from Scripture that those who were baptized were fully immersed in water. Here's one reason why: "John also was baptizing in Aenon near to Salim, because there was much water there" (John 3:23). If John were merely sprinkling believers, he would have needed only a cupful of water. Baptism by immersion also pictures our death to sin, burial, and resurrection to new life in Christ. (See Romans 6:4; Colossians 2:12.)

The Philippian jailer and his family were baptized at midnight, the same hour they believed (Acts 16:30–33). The Ethiopian eunuch was baptized as soon as he believed (Acts 8:35–37), as was Paul (Acts 9:17,18). Baptism is a step of obedience, and God blesses our obedience. So what are you waiting for?

Who should baptize you? It is clear from Scripture that other believers had the privilege, but check with your pastor; he may want the honor himself.

For the next principle of growth, see Mark 12:41–44 comment.

of sins, and you shall receive the gift of
the Holy Spirit.
39 **For the promise is to you, and to**
your children, and to all that are afar
off, even as many as the Lord our God
shall call.
40 **And with many other words did he**
testify and exhort, saying, Save your-
selves from this untoward generation.
41 Then they that gladly received his
word were baptized: and the same day
there were added to them about three
thousand souls.
42 And they continued steadfastly in the
apostles' doctrine and fellowship, and in
breaking of bread, and in prayers.
43 And fear came upon every soul: and
many wonders and signs were done by
the apostles.
44 And all that believed were together,
and had all things common;
45 And sold their possessions and goods,
and parted them to all men, as every man
had need.
46 And they, continuing daily with one
accord in the temple, and breaking bread
from house to house, did eat their meat
with gladness and singleness of heart,
47 Praising God, and having favor with
all the people. And the Lord added to the
church daily such as should be saved.

USING THE LAW IN EVANGELISM

2:37

Peter's audience was composed of "devout men" (v. 2) who were gathered at Pentecost to celebrate the giving of God's Law on Mount Sinai. Even though these were godly Jews, Peter told them that they were "lawless"—that they had violated God's Law by murdering Jesus (v. 23). He drove home that fact by saying, "Therefore let all the house of Israel know assuredly, that God has made that same Jesus, *whom you have crucified*, both Lord and Christ" (v. 36, emphasis added). It was then that they saw that their sin was personal. They were "pricked in their heart" and cried out for help. Only after the Law convicted them of their guilt did Peter tell his hearers the good news of the fine being paid for them in Christ (v. 38).

CHAPTER 3

NOW Peter and John went up together into the temple at the hour of
prayer, being the ninth hour.
2 And a certain man lame from his mother's womb was carried, whom they laid
daily at the gate of the temple which is
called Beautiful, to ask alms of them that

POINTS FOR OPEN-AIR PREACHING

3:4

Crowd Etiquette

If you have other Christians with you, have them form an audience and look as though they are listening to your preaching. This will encourage others to stop and listen. Tell the Christians to never stand with their back to the preacher. I have seen open-air meetings when a fellow laborer is preaching for the first time, and what are the Christians doing? They are talking among themselves. Why then should anyone stop and listen if those in front of the speaker aren't even attentive? It is so easy to chat with friends when you've heard the gospel a million times before. I have found myself doing it, but it is so disheartening for the preacher to speak to the backs of a crowd.

Also, instruct Christians not to argue with hecklers. That will ruin an open-air meeting. I have seen an old lady hit a heckler with her umbrella and turn the crowd from listening to the gospel to watching the fight she has just started. Who can blame them? Remember, the enemy will do everything he can to distract your listeners. Don't let him. See 2 Timothy 2:24–26 comment.

entered into the temple;
3 Who seeing Peter and John about to go
into the temple asked an alms.
4 And Peter, fastening his eyes upon him
with John, said, Look on us.
5 And he gave heed to them, expecting to
receive something of them.
6 Then Peter said, Silver and gold have I
none; but such as I have give I you: In the
name of Jesus Christ of Nazareth rise up
and walk.
7 And he took him by the right hand,
and lifted him up: and immediately his
feet and ankle bones received strength.
8 And he leaping up stood, and walked,
and entered with them into the temple,
walking, and leaping, and praising God.
9 And all the people saw him walking
and praising God:
10 And they knew that it was he which
sat for alms at the Beautiful gate of the
temple: and they were filled with wonder and amazement at that which had
happened to him.
11 And as the lame man which was
healed held Peter and John, all the people ran together to them in the porch
that is called Solomon's, greatly wondering.
12 And when Peter saw it, he answered
to the people, You men of Israel, why do
you marvel at this? or why do you look
so earnestly on us, as though by our own
power or holiness we had made this man
to walk?
13 The God of Abraham, and of Isaac,
and of Jacob, the God of our fathers, has
glorified his Son Jesus; whom you delivered up, and denied him in the presence
of Pilate, when he was determined to let

2:44–46 The need for church. "None of us is self-sufficient in our spiritual lives. We need God, and we need each other. A lot of people go to church because they think God takes roll. For them, the important thing is to make sure their name gets checked off every Sunday on the heavenly roster. But that's not the way it works. Church is not some kind of moral obligation, some habit or tradition that is 'the right thing to do.' Church is a place where we worship God, share our faith with the community of believers, build each other up, and get empowered to go out into the world and *live out our faith!*

"Similarly, some people think of their spiritual life as if they were one person in a telephone booth, talking to God on a private line. They don't want to be bothered by the demands of 'organized religion' and don't think they need anyone else. 'Oh yeah, I'm spiritual,' they say, 'I just don't like church.' To those folks I say: You cannot grow spiritually in isolation." *Rich DeVos, Hope From My Heart: Ten Lessons for Life*

him go.
14 But you denied the Holy One and the
Just, and desired a murderer to be granted
to you;
15 And killed the Prince of life, whom
God has raised from the dead; whereof we
are witnesses.
16 And his name through faith in his
name has made this man strong, whom
you see and know: yes, the faith which is
by him has given him this perfect soundness in the presence of you all.
17 And now, brethren, I realize that
through ignorance you did it, as did also
your rulers.
18 But those things, which God before
had showed by the mouth of all his prophets, that Christ should suffer, he has so
fulfilled.

> The open-air speaker's calling is as honorable as it is arduous, as useful as it is laborious. God alone can sustain you in it, but with Him at your side you will have nothing to fear.
>
> **CHARLES SPURGEON**

19 Repent therefore, and be converted,
that your sins may be blotted out, when
the times of refreshing shall come from
the presence of the Lord;
20 **And he shall send Jesus Christ,**
which before was preached to you:
21 **Whom the heaven must receive un-**
til the times of restitution of all things,
which God has spoken by the mouth of
all his holy prophets since the world be-
gan.
22 For Moses truly said to the fathers, A
prophet shall the Lord your God raise up
to you of your brethren, like to me; him
shall you hear in all things whatsoever he
shall say to you.
23 And it shall come to pass, that every
soul, which will not hear that prophet,
shall be destroyed from among the people.
24 Yes, and all the prophets from Samuel
and those that follow after, as many as have
spoken, have likewise foretold of these
days.
25 You are the children of the prophets,
and of the covenant which God made with
our fathers, saying to Abraham, And in
your seed shall all the kindreds of the earth
be blessed.
26 To you first God, having raised up his
Son Jesus, sent him to bless you, in turning
away every one of you from his iniquities.

CHAPTER 4

AND as they spoke to the people, the
priests, and the captain of the temple,
and the Sadducees, came upon them,
2 Being grieved that they taught the people, and preached through Jesus the resurrection from the dead.
3 And they laid hands on them, and put
them in hold to the next day: for it was
now eventide.
4 Howbeit many of them which heard
the word believed; and the number of
the men was about five thousand.
5 And it came to pass on the morrow,
that their rulers, and elders, and scribes,
6 And Annas the high priest, and Caiaphas, and John, and Alexander, and as
many as were of the kindred of the high
priest, were gathered together at Jerusalem.
7 And when they had set them in the
midst, they asked, By what power, or by
what name, have you done this?
8 Then Peter, filled with the Holy Spirit,
said to them, You rulers of the people, and
elders of Israel,
9 If we this day be examined of the good
deed done to the impotent man, by what
means he is made whole;
10 Be it known to you all, and to all the
people of Israel, that by the name of Jesus
Christ of Nazareth, whom you crucified,
whom God raised from the dead, even by

3:19 Repentance—its necessity for salvation. See Acts 17:30.

4:12 Is Suffering the Entrance to Heaven?

In January 2000, a well-known ex-televangelist said on a worldwide TV talk show, "I believe that every person who died in the Holocaust went to heaven." He was very sincere, and if he was seeking the commendation of the world, he surely got it with that statement. Who wouldn't consider what he said to be utterly compassionate? However, let's look at the implications of his heartfelt beliefs. His statement seemed to limit salvation to the *Jews* who died in the Holocaust, because he added that "their blood laid a foundation for the nation of Israel." If the slaughtered Jews made it to heaven, did the many *Gypsies* who died in the Holocaust also obtain eternal salvation? If his statement includes Gentiles, is the salvation he spoke of limited to those who died at the hands of Nazis? Did the many *Frenchmen* who met their death at the hands of cruel Nazis go to heaven also?

Perhaps he was saying that the death of Jesus on the cross covered *all* of humanity, and that all will eventually be saved—something called "universalism." This means that salvation will also come to Hitler and the Nazis who killed the Jews. However, I doubt if he was saying that. Such a statement would have brought the scorn of his Jewish host, and of the world whose compassion has definite limits.

If pressed, he probably didn't mean that only the Jews in the camps went to heaven, because that smacks of *racism*. He was likely saying that those who died were saved because they died in such *tragic circumstances*. Then Jesus was lying when He said, "I am the way, the truth, and the life: no man comes to the Father, but by me" (John 14:6). There is another way to heaven—death in a Nazi concentration camp. Does that mean that the many Jews who died under *communism* went to heaven? Or is salvation limited to *German* concentration camps?

If their salvation came because of the grim circumstances surrounding their death, does a Jew therefore enter heaven after suffering for hours before dying in a car wreck...if he was killed by a drunk driver who happened to be German? Bear in mind that his suffering may have been much greater than someone who died within minutes in a Nazi gas chamber.

Many unsaved think we *can* merit entrance into heaven by our suffering. Their error was confirmed by this sincere, compassionate man of God. They may now disregard the truth, "Neither is there salvation in any other: for there is no other name under heaven given among men, whereby we must be saved" (Acts 4:12). They can now save themselves by the means of their own death...if they suffer enough.

The ex-televangelist was concerned that his indiscretions of the 1980s brought discredit to the kingdom of God. However, those actions fade into history compared to the damage done by saying that there is another means of salvation outside of Jesus Christ, on a program watched by untold millions around the world. Who on earth needs to repent and trust in Jesus, if millions entered the kingdom without being born again? No one.

him does this man stand here before you whole.
11 This is the stone which was set at nought of you builders, which is become the head of the corner.
12 Neither is there salvation in any other: for there is no other name under heaven given among men, whereby we must be saved.
13 Now when they saw the boldness of Peter and John, and perceived that they were unlearned and ignorant men, they marveled; and they took knowledge of them, that they had been with Jesus.
14 And beholding the man which was healed standing with them, they could say nothing against it.
15 But when they had commanded them to go aside out of the council, they conferred among themselves,
16 Saying, What shall we do to these men? for that indeed a notable miracle has been done by them is manifest to all them that dwell in Jerusalem; and we cannot deny it.
17 But that it spread no further among

the people, let us straitly threaten them,
that they speak henceforth to no man in
this name.
18 And they called them, and commanded them not to speak at all nor teach in
the name of Jesus.
19 But Peter and John answered and said
to them, Whether it be right in the sight
of God to hearken to you more than to
God, you judge.
20 *For we cannot but speak the things
which we have seen and heard.*
21 So when they had further threatened
them, they let them go, finding nothing
how they might punish them, because of
the people: for all men glorified God for
that which was done.
22 For the man was above forty years
old, on whom this miracle of healing was
showed.
23 And being let go, they went to their
own company, and reported all that the
chief priests and elders had said to them.
24 And when they heard that, they lifted up their voice to God with one accord,
and said, Lord, you are God, which have
made heaven, and earth, and the sea, and
all that in them is:
25 Who by the mouth of your servant
David have said, Why did the heathen
rage, and the people imagine vain things?
26 The kings of the earth stood up, and
the rulers were gathered together against
the Lord, and against his Christ.
27 For of a truth against your holy child
Jesus, whom you have anointed, both
Herod, and Pontius Pilate, with the Gentiles, and the people of Israel, were gathered together,
28 For to do whatsoever your hand and
your counsel determined before to be
done.
29 And now, Lord, behold their threatenings: and grant to your servants, that
with all boldness they may speak your
word,
30 By stretching forth your hand to heal;
and that signs and wonders may be done
by the name of your holy child Jesus.
31 *And when they had prayed, the place
was shaken where they were assembled together; and they were all filled with the
Holy Spirit, and they spoke the word of God
with boldness.*
32 And the multitude of them that believed were of one heart and of one soul:
neither said any of them that anything of
the things which he possessed was his
own; but they had all things common.
33 And with great power gave the apostles witness of the resurrection of the Lord
Jesus: and great grace was upon them all.
34 Neither was there any among them
that lacked: for as many as were posses-
sors of lands or houses sold them, and
brought the prices of the things that were
sold,
35 And laid them down at the apostles'
feet: and distribution was made to every
man according as he had need.
36 And Joses, who by the apostles was
surnamed Barnabas, (which is, being interpreted, The son of consolation,) a Levite, and of the country of Cyprus,
37 Having land, sold it, and brought the
money, and laid it at the apostles' feet.

4:24 Prayer—the secret weapon: See Acts 12:12.

4:24 Fossil evidence points to creation. "The creation account in Genesis and the theory of evolution could not be reconciled. One must be right and the other wrong. The story of the fossils agrees with the account of Genesis. In the oldest rocks we did not find a series of fossils covering the gradual changes from the most primitive creatures to developed forms but rather, in the oldest rocks, developed species suddenly appeared. Between every species there was a complete absence of intermediate fossils." *D. B. Gower* (biochemist), "Scientist Rejects Evolution," *Kentish Times*

4:29 When we are afraid to witness to sinners, we can stand firmly upon the wonderful promise of God given in Isaiah 41:10. We need not fear or be dismayed because He is with us. He will strengthen, help, and uphold us with His righteous right hand.

CHAPTER 5

BUT a certain man named Ananias,
with Sapphira his wife, sold a possession,
2 And kept back part of the price, his
wife also being privy to it, and brought a
certain part, and laid it at the apostles' feet.
3 But Peter said, Ananias, why has Satan
filled your heart to lie to the Holy Spirit,
and to keep back part of the price of the
land?
4 Whiles it remained, was it not your
own? and after it was sold, was it not in
your own power? why have you conceived
this thing in your heart? you have not lied
to men, but to God.
5 And Ananias hearing these words fell
down, and gave up the ghost: and great
fear came on all them that heard these
things.
6 And the young men arose, wound him
up, and carried him out, and buried him.
7 And it was about the space of three
hours after, when his wife, not knowing
what was done, came in.
8 And Peter answered to her, Tell me
whether you sold the land for so much?
And she said, Yes, for so much.
9 Then Peter said to her, How is it that
you have agreed together to tempt the
Spirit of the Lord? behold, the feet of
them which have buried your husband
are at the door, and shall carry you out.
10 Then fell she down straightway at his
feet, and yielded up the ghost: and the
young men came in, and found her dead,
and, carrying her forth, buried her by her
husband.
11 And great fear came upon all the
church, and upon as many as heard these
things.
12 And by the hands of the apostles were
many signs and wonders wrought among
the people; (and they were all with one
accord in Solomon's porch.
13 And of the rest no man dared join
himself to them: but the people magnified
them.
14 And believers were the more added to
the Lord, multitudes both of men and wo-

"We have been assured, Sir, in the Sacred Writings, that 'except the Lord build the house, they labor in vain that build it.' I firmly believe this; and I also believe that without his concurring aid we shall succeed in this political building no better than the builders of Babel."

Benjamin Franklin

men.)
15 Insomuch that they brought forth
the sick into the streets, and laid them on
beds and couches, that at the least the
shadow of Peter passing by might over-
shadow some of them.
16 There came also a multitude out of the
cities round about to Jerusalem, bringing
sick folks, and them which were vexed
with unclean spirits: and they were healed
every one.
17 Then the high priest rose up, and all
they that were with him, (which is the
sect of the Sadducees,) and were filled
with indignation,
18 And laid their hands on the apostles,
and put them in the common prison.
19 But the angel of the Lord by night
opened the prison doors, and brought
them forth, and said,
20 Go, stand and speak in the temple to
the people all the words of this life.
21 And when they heard that, they entered into the temple early in the morn-

ing, and taught. But the high priest came,
and they that were with him, and called
the council together, and all the senate
of the children of Israel and sent to the
prison to have them brought.
22 But when the officers came, and found
them not in the prison, they returned, and
told,
23 Saying, The prison truly found we
shut with all safety, and the keepers standing without before the doors: but when
we had opened, we found no man within.
24 Now when the high priest and the
captain of the temple and the chief priests
heard these things, they doubted of them
whereunto this would grow.
25 Then came one and told them, saying,
Behold, the men whom you put in prison
are standing in the temple, and teaching
the people.
26 Then went the captain with the officers, and brought them without violence:
for they feared the people, lest they should
have been stoned.
27 And when they had brought them,
they set them before the council: and the
high priest asked them,
28 Saying, Did not we straitly command
you that you should not teach in this
name? and, behold, you have filled Jerusalem with your doctrine, and intend to
bring this man's blood upon us.
29 Then Peter and the other apostles
answered and said, We ought to obey God
rather than men.
30 The God of our fathers raised up
Jesus, whom you slew and hanged on a
tree.
31 Him has God exalted with his right
hand to be a Prince and a Savior, for to
give repentance to Israel, and forgiveness
of sins.
32 And we are his witnesses of these
things; and so is also the Holy Spirit, whom
God has given to them that obey him.
33 When they heard that, they were cut
to the heart, and took counsel to slay them.
34 Then stood there up one in the council, a Pharisee, named Gamaliel, a doctor
of the law, had in reputation among all
the people, and commanded to put the
apostles forth a little space;
35 And said to them, You men of Israel,
take heed to yourselves what you intend
to do as touching these men.
36 For before these days rose up Theu-
das, boasting himself to be somebody; to
whom a number of men, about four hundred, joined themselves: who was slain;
and all, as many as obeyed him, were scattered, and brought to nought.
37 After this man rose up Judas of Galilee in the days of the taxing, and drew
away much people after him: he also perished; and all, even as many as obeyed
him, were dispersed.
38 And now I say to you, Refrain from
these men, and let them alone: for if this
counsel or this work be of men, it will
come to nought:
39 But if it be of God, you cannot overthrow it; lest haply you be found even to
fight against God.
40 And to him they agreed: and when
they had called the apostles, and beaten
them, they commanded that they should
not speak in the name of Jesus, and let
them go.
41 And they departed from the presence
of the council, rejoicing that they were
counted worthy to suffer shame for his
name.
42 And daily in the temple, and in every
house, they ceased not to teach and preach
Jesus Christ.

. . . . . .

For how to witness to Jews, see Romans 3:1 comment.

. . . . . .

CHAPTER 6

AND in those days, when the number of the disciples was multiplied,
there arose a murmuring of the Grecians
against the Hebrews, because their widows were neglected in the daily ministration.
2 Then the twelve called the multitude

of the disciples to them, and said, It is not reason that we should leave the word of God, and serve tables.

3 Wherefore, brethren, look out among you seven men of honest report, full of the Holy Spirit and wisdom, whom we may appoint over this business.

4 But we will give ourselves continually to prayer, and to the ministry of the word.

5 And the saying pleased the whole multitude: and they chose Stephen, a man full of faith and of the Holy Spirit, and Philip, and Prochorus, and Nicanor, and Timon, and Parmenas, and Nicolas a proselyte of Antioch:

6 Whom they set before the apostles: and when they had prayed, they laid their hands on them.

7 And the word of God increased; and the number of the disciples multiplied in Jerusalem greatly; and a great company of the priests were obedient to the faith.

8 *And Stephen, full of faith and power, did great wonders and miracles among the people.*

9 Then there arose certain of the synagogue, which is called the synagogue of the Libertines, and Cyrenians, and Alexandrians, and of them of Cilicia and of Asia, disputing with Stephen.

10 And they were not able to resist the wisdom and the spirit by which he spoke.

11 Then they suborned men, which said, We have heard him speak blasphemous words against Moses, and against God.

12 And they stirred up the people, and the elders, and the scribes, and came upon him, and caught him, and brought him to the council,

13 And set up false witnesses, which said, This man ceases not to speak blasphemous words against this holy place, and the law:

14 For we have heard him say, that this Jesus of Nazareth shall destroy this place, and shall change the customs which Moses delivered us.

15 And all that sat in the council, looking steadfastly on him, saw his face as it had been the face of an angel.

CHAPTER 7

THEN said the high priest, Are these things so?

2 And he said, Men, brethren, and fathers, hearken; The God of glory appeared to our father Abraham, when he was in Mesopotamia, before he dwelt in Haran,

3 And said to him, Get you out of your country, and from your kindred, and come into the land which I shall show you.

4 Then came he out of the land of the Chaldaeans, and dwelt in Charran: and from thence, when his father was dead, he removed him into this land, wherein you now dwell.

5 And he gave him none inheritance in it, no, not so much as to set his foot on: yet he promised that he would give it to him for a possession, and to his seed after him, when as yet he had no child.

6 And God spoke on this wise, That his seed should sojourn in a strange land; and that they should bring them into bondage, and entreat them evil four hundred years.

7 And the nation to whom they shall be in bondage will I judge, said God: and after that shall they come forth, and serve me in this place.

8 And he gave him the covenant of circumcision: and so Abraham begat Isaac, and circumcised him the eighth day; and

7:5 The Bible's fascinating facts. In the Book of Beginnings, in Genesis 16:12, God said that Ishmael (the progenitor of the Arab race, see *Time*, April 4, 1988) would be a "wild man...and every man's hand [will be] against him; and he shall dwell in the presence of all his brethren." Almost four thousand years later, who could deny that this prophecy is being fulfilled in the Arab race? The Arabs and the Jews are "brethren" having Abraham as their ancestor. The whole Middle East conflict is caused by their dwelling together.

Isaac begat Jacob; and Jacob begat the twelve patriarchs.
9 And the patriarchs, moved with envy, sold Joseph into Egypt: but God was with him,
10 And delivered him out of all his afflictions, and gave him favor and wisdom in the sight of Pharaoh king of Egypt; and he made him governor over Egypt and all his house.
11 Now there came a dearth over all the land of Egypt and Canaan, and great affliction: and our fathers found no sustenance.
12 But when Jacob heard that there was corn in Egypt, he sent out our fathers first.
13 And at the second time Joseph was made known to his brethren; and Joseph's kindred was made known to Pharaoh.
14 Then sent Joseph, and called his father Jacob to him, and all his kindred, threescore and fifteen souls.
15 So Jacob went down into Egypt, and died, he, and our fathers,
16 And were carried over into Sychem, and laid in the sepulchre that Abraham bought for a sum of money of the sons of Emmor the father of Sychem.
17 But when the time of the promise drew nigh, which God had sworn to Abraham, the people grew and multiplied in Egypt,
18 Till another king arose, which knew not Joseph.
19 The same dealt subtly with our kindred, and evil entreated our fathers, so that they cast out their young children, to the end they might not live.
20 In which time Moses was born, and was exceeding fair, and nourished up in his father's house three months:
21 And when he was cast out, Pharaoh's daughter took him up, and nourished him for her own son.
22 And Moses was learned in all the wisdom of the Egyptians, and was mighty in words and in deeds.
23 And when he was full forty years old, it came into his heart to visit his brethren the children of Israel.
24 And seeing one of them suffer wrong, he defended him, and avenged him that was oppressed, and smote the Egyptian:
25 For he supposed his brethren would have understood how that God by his hand would deliver them: but they understood not.
26 And the next day he showed himself to them as they strove, and would have set them at one again, saying, Sirs, you are brethren; why do you wrong one to another?
27 But he that did his neighbour wrong thrust him away, saying, Who made you a ruler and a judge over us?
28 Will you kill me, as you did the Egyptian yesterday?
29 Then fled Moses at this saying, and was a stranger in the land of Madian,

7:22 Don't be concerned that you aren't "gifted" as a speaker when it comes to reaching the lost. Moses "was learned in all the wisdom of the Egyptians, and was mighty in words and in deeds," yet God didn't use him to deliver Israel until 40 years later. It took all that time of tending sheep to produce in him a meekness of character. We are told, "The meek will he guide in judgment: and the meek will he teach his way" (Psalm 25:9). The "wisdom" that Moses gained in Egypt was not wisdom from above. When he saw injustice, he took the law into his own hands and committed murder. God doesn't need the wisdom of this world. He merely desires a pure, humble, peace-loving, compassionate soul to use as a mouthpiece for the gospel. He wants us to be a lighthouse of His love. The moment we receive the Spirit of Christ, we receive the gift of those virtues. We don't need to tend sheep for 40 years when we have the character of the Good Shepherd manifesting through us.

7:26 "We do wrong, we think wrong, and our efforts to deal with wrong are themselves corrupted by wrong." *Chuck Colson*

where he begat two sons.
30 And when forty years were expired,
there appeared to him in the wilderness
of mount Sinai an angel of the Lord in a
flame of fire in a bush.
31 When Moses saw it, he wondered at
the sight: and as he drew near to behold
it, the voice of the Lord came to him,
32 Saying, I am the God of your fathers,
the God of Abraham, and the God of Isaac,
and the God of Jacob. Then Moses trembled, and dared not behold.
33 Then said the Lord to him, Put off
your shoes from your feet: for the place
where you stand is holy ground.
34 I have seen, I have seen the affliction
of my people which is in Egypt, and I have
heard their groaning, and am come down
to deliver them. And now come, I will
send you into Egypt.
35 This Moses whom they refused, saying, Who made you a ruler and a judge?
the same did God send to be a ruler and
a deliverer by the hand of the angel which
appeared to him in the bush.
36 He brought them out, after that he
had showed wonders and signs in the land
of Egypt, and in the Red sea, and in the
wilderness forty years.
37 This is that Moses, which said to the
children of Israel, A prophet shall the Lord
your God raise up to you of your brethren, like to me; him shall you hear.
38 This is he, that was in the church in
the wilderness with the angel which spoke
to him in the mount Sinai, and with our
fathers: who received the lively oracles to
give to us:
39 To whom our fathers would not obey,
but thrust him from them, and in their
hearts turned back again into Egypt,
40 Saying to Aaron, Make us gods to go
before us: for as for this Moses, which
brought us out of the land of Egypt, we
know not what is become of him.
41 And they made a calf in those days,
and offered sacrifice to the idol, and rejoiced in the works of their own hands.
42 Then God turned, and gave them up
to worship the host of heaven; as it is
written in the book of the prophets, O
you house of Israel, have you offered to
me slain beasts and sacrifices by the space
of forty years in the wilderness?
43 Yes, you took up the tabernacle of
Moloch, and the star of your god Rem-
phan, figures which you made to worship
them: and I will carry you away beyond
Babylon.
44 Our fathers had the tabernacle of witness in the wilderness, as he had appointed, speaking to Moses, that he should
make it according to the fashion that he
had seen.
45 Which also our fathers that came after
brought in with Jesus into the possession
of the Gentiles, whom God drove out before the face of our fathers, to the days of
David;
46 Who found favor before God, and desired to find a tabernacle for the God of
Jacob.
47 But Solomon built him an house.
48 Howbeit the most High dwells not
in temples made with hands; as said the
prophet,
49 Heaven is my throne, and earth is
my footstool: what house will you build
me? said the Lord: or what is the place of
my rest?
50 Has not my hand made all these
things?
51 You stiff-necked and uncircumcised
in heart and ears, you do always resist the
Holy Spirit: as your fathers did, so do you.
52 Which of the prophets have not your

7:33 Moses was told to remove his sandals because by God's presence even the ground on which he stood was made holy. Through faith in Christ, the believer himself is made holy. Now his feet are shod with the gospel of peace (Ephesians 6:15), to take the word of salvation to those who stand on unholy ground.

7:39 When you turn your back on God, any way you go is a wrong direction.

History reveals the fate of the apostles:

PHILIP: Stoned to death, Phrygia, A.D. 54
BARNABAS: Burned to death, Cyprus, A.D. 64
PETER: Crucified, Rome, A.D. 69
PAUL: Beheaded, Rome, A.D. 69
ANDREW: Crucified, Achaia, A.D. 70
MATTHEW: Beheaded, Ethiopia, A.D. 70
LUKE: Hanged, Greece, A.D. 93
THOMAS: Speared to death, Calamino, A.D. 70
MARK: Dragged to death, Alexandria, A.D. 64
JAMES (THE LESS): Clubbed to death, Jerusalem, A.D. 63
JOHN: Abandoned, Isle of Patmos, A.D. 63

fathers persecuted? and they have slain
them which showed before of the coming
of the Just One; of whom you have been
now the betrayers and murderers:
53 Who have received the law by the dis-
position of angels, and have not kept it.
54 When they heard these things, they
were cut to the heart, and they gnashed
on him with their teeth.
55 But he, being full of the Holy Spirit,
looked up steadfastly into heaven, and
saw the glory of God, and Jesus standing

7:55 Honesty Road. As I was open-air preaching one day, a man looked to the heavens not to see the glory of God, but to shout obscenities at Jesus Christ that would make your hair curl in tight knots. He concluded his conversation by telling the Lord to strike him dead. He then turned to me and screamed, "Nothing happened!" I said, "Yes, it did. You have just stored up wrath for yourself, which will be revealed on the Day of Wrath."

Why would a man lack *any* fear of God? I believe it's because we insist on telling a sinful world that God loves them and has a wonderful plan for their lives. This is the gospel according to the contemporary Church. We give the world a choice: Do they choose God's wonderful plan, or is their own life's plan more wonderful? For the answer to this dilemma and the biblical way to witness, see Matthew 10:22 comment.

on the right hand of God,
56 And said, Behold, I see the heavens
opened, and the Son of man standing on
the right hand of God.
57 Then they cried out with a loud voice,
and stopped their ears, and ran upon him
with one accord,
58 And cast him out of the city, and
stoned him: and the witnesses laid down
their clothes at a young man's feet, whose
name was Saul.
59 And they stoned Stephen, calling upon God, and saying, Lord Jesus, receive
my spirit.
60 And he kneeled down, and cried with
a loud voice, Lord, lay not this sin to their
charge. And when he had said this, he
fell asleep.

CHAPTER 8

AND Saul was consenting to his death.
And at that time there was a great
persecution against the church which was
at Jerusalem; and they were all scattered
abroad throughout the regions of Judea
and Samaria, except the apostles.
2 And devout men carried Stephen to his
burial, and made great lamentation over
him.
3 As for Saul, he made havoc of the
church, entering into every house, and
haling men and women committed them
to prison.
4 *Therefore they that were scattered abroad*
went every where preaching the word.
5 Then Philip went down to the city of
Samaria, and preached Christ to them.
6 And the people with one accord gave
heed to those things which Philip spoke,
hearing and seeing the miracles which
he did.
7 For unclean spirits, crying with loud
voice, came out of many that were possessed with them: and many taken with
palsies, and that were lame, were healed.
8 And there was great joy in that city.
9 But there was a certain man, called Simon, which beforetime in the same city
used sorcery, and bewitched the people
of Samaria, giving out that himself was
some great one:
10 To whom they all gave heed, from the
least to the greatest, saying, This man is
the great power of God.
11 And to him they had regard, because
for a long time he had bewitched them
with sorceries.
12 But when they believed Philip preaching the things concerning the kingdom
of God, and the name of Jesus Christ, they
were baptized, both men and women.
13 Then Simon himself believed also:
and when he was baptized, he continued
with Philip, and wondered, beholding the
miracles and signs which were done.
14 Now when the apostles which were
at Jerusalem heard that Samaria had received the word of God, they sent to them
Peter and John:
15 Who, when they were come down,
prayed for them, that they might receive
the Holy Spirit:
16 (For as yet he was fallen upon none
of them: only they were baptized in the
name of the Lord Jesus.)
17 Then laid they their hands on them,
and they received the Holy Spirit.
18 And when Simon saw that through
laying on of the apostles' hands the Holy
Spirit was given, he offered them money,
19 Saying, Give me also this power, that
on whomsoever I lay hands, he may receive the Holy Spirit.
20 But Peter said to him, Your money
perish with you, because you have thought
that the gift of God may be purchased with

7:59 "You can kill us, but you cannot do us any real harm." *Justin Martyr* (martyred A.D. 165)

8:19 Using God's power. "Waste of power is a tragedy. God does not waste the great power of his Spirit on those who want it simply for their own sake, to be more holy, or good, or gifted. His great task is to carry on the work for which Jesus sacrificed his throne and his life—the redemption of fallen humanity." *Alan Redpath, The Life of Victory*

money.
21 You have neither part nor lot in this
matter: for your heart is not right in the
sight of God.
22 Repent therefore of this your wickedness, and pray God, if perhaps the thought
of your heart may be forgiven you.
23 For I perceive that you are in the gall
of bitterness, and in the bond of iniquity.
24 Then answered Simon, and said, Pray
to the Lord for me, that none of these
things which you have spoken come upon me.
25 And they, when they had testified and
preached the word of the Lord, returned
to Jerusalem, and preached the gospel in
many villages of the Samaritans.
26 And the angel of the Lord spoke to
Philip, saying, Arise, and go toward the
south to the way that goes down from Jerusalem to Gaza, which is desert.
27 And he arose and went: and, behold,
a man of Ethiopia, an eunuch of great authority under Candace queen of the Ethi-
opians, who had the charge of all her treasure, and had come to Jerusalem for to
worship,
28 Was returning, and sitting in his chariot read Isaiah the prophet.
29 Then the Spirit said to Philip, Go near,
and join yourself to this chariot.
30 And Philip ran there to him, and heard
him read the prophet Isaiah, and said,
Do you understand what you read?
31 And he said, How can I, except some
man should guide me? And he desired
Philip that he would come up and sit with
him.
32 The place of the scripture which he
read was this, He was led as a sheep to the
slaughter; and like a lamb dumb before
his shearer, so opened he not his mouth:
33 In his humiliation his judgment was
taken away: and who shall declare his generation? for his life is taken from the earth.
34 And the eunuch answered Philip, and
said, I pray you, of whom does the prophet speak? of himself, or of some other man?

> No man who preaches the gospel without zeal is sent from God to preach at all.
>
> **CHARLES SPURGEON**

35 Then Philip opened his mouth, and
began at the same scripture, and preached
to him Jesus.
36 **And as they went on their way, they
came to a certain water: and the eunuch
said, See, here is water; what does hinder me to be baptized?**
37 **And Philip said, If you believe with
all your heart, you may. And he answered and said, I believe that Jesus
Christ is the Son of God.**
38 And he commanded the chariot to
stand still: and they went down both into

8:26,27 "God has placed you where He has placed no one else. No one else in the world has the same relationships you have. No one will stand in the same grocery store line at exactly the same moment you do. No one else will come across a hungering diplomat in the desert at exactly the same time you do. God hasn't put you in those places merely to model the truth. Listen for the voice of the Spirit to whisper in your ear. Watch for the stranger on the road. And be aware of your opportunities to go where He would send you." *Chuck Swindoll*

8:35 Wisdom in witnessing. The Scriptures tell us, "He who wins souls is wise" (Proverbs 11:30). If we are wise, we will discern the condition of a person's heart. If he is a sincere Nicodemus, tell him the good news; if he is like the arrogant lawyer (Luke 10:25–29) who has no understanding of sin, righteousness, and judgment, use the Law to stir his conscience and will. If he is not conscious of his sin, use the Law to convict him. If he has a knowledge of sin, give him the gospel. (See Matthew 19:17–22 comment.)

When the fruit is ripe, it should practically fall off the tree, as with the Ethiopian eunuch. God led Philip to a soul that was ripe for salvation! If you have to twist and pull an apple off a branch, you will probably find it to be sour.

the water, both Philip and the eunuch; and he baptized him.
39 And when they were come up out of the water, the Spirit of the Lord caught away Philip, that the eunuch saw him no more: and he went on his way rejoicing.
40 But Philip was found at Azotus: and passing through he preached in all the cities, till he came to Caesarea.

CHAPTER 9

AND Saul, yet breathing out threatenings and slaughter against the disciples of the Lord, went to the high priest,
2 And desired of him letters to Damascus to the synagogues, that if he found any of this way, whether they were men or women, he might bring them bound to Jerusalem.
3 And as he journeyed, he came near Damascus: and suddenly there shined round about him a light from heaven:
4 And he fell to the earth, and heard a voice saying to him, Saul, Saul, why do you persecute me?
5 And he said, Who are you, Lord? And the Lord said, I am Jesus whom you persecute: it is hard for you to kick against the pricks.
6 And he trembling and astonished said, Lord, what will you have me to do? And the Lord said to him, Arise, and go into the city, and it shall be told you what you must do.
7 And the men which journeyed with him stood speechless, hearing a voice, but seeing no man.
8 And Saul arose from the earth; and when his eyes were opened, he saw no man: but they led him by the hand, and brought him into Damascus.
9 And he was three days without sight, and neither did eat nor drink.
10 And there was a certain disciple at Damascus, named Ananias; and to him said the Lord in a vision, Ananias. And he said, Behold, I am here, Lord.
11 And the Lord said to him, Arise, and go into the street which is called Straight, and inquire in the house of Judas for one called Saul, of Tarsus: for, behold, he prays,
12 And has seen in a vision a man named Ananias coming in, and putting his hand on him, that he might receive his sight.
13 Then Ananias answered, Lord, I have heard by many of this man, how much evil he has done to your saints at Jerusalem:
14 And here he has authority from the chief priests to bind all that call on your name.
15 But the Lord said to him, Go your way: for he is a chosen vessel to me, to bear my name before the Gentiles, and kings, and the children of Israel:
16 For I will show him how great things he must suffer for my name's sake.
17 And Ananias went his way, and entered into the house; and putting his hands on him said, Brother Saul, the Lord, even

---

8:39 God does the "follow-up." The exciting thing about true conversion is that there will be little need for what is commonly called "follow-up." A true convert will not need to be followed. He will put his hand to the plow and not look back (Luke 9:62). Of course, he will have to be fed, discipled, and nurtured. These things are biblical and most necessary. This can be done simply by encouraging him to read the Bible daily, answering questions he may have, and teaching him principles of fellowship, prayer, evangelism, etc.

Sometimes there is confusion between "follow-up" (we need to follow the new convert because he will fall away if we don't) and discipleship (instructing him to continue in the word of Christ—John 8:31). Look what happened after the Ethiopian eunuch was saved—he was left without follow-up. The Spirit of God transported Philip away and left the new convert in the wilderness. This is because his salvation wasn't dependent on Philip, but upon his relationship with the indwelling Lord. Those whom God saves, He keeps. If He is the author of their faith, He will be the finisher. If He has begun a good work in them, He will complete it. He is able to keep them from falling and present them faultless before the presence of His glory with exceeding joy.

Jesus, that appeared to you in the way as
you came, has sent me, that you might receive your sight, and be filled with the
Holy Spirit.
18 And immediately there fell from his
eyes as it had been scales: and he received sight forthwith, and arose, and
was baptized.

The Buddhist seeks salvation by works.
For how to witness to him,
see page 628.

19 And when he had received meat, he
was strengthened. Then was Saul certain
days with the disciples which were at
Damascus.
20 And straightway he preached Christ
in the synagogues, that he is the Son of
God.
21 But all that heard him were amazed,
and said; Is not this he that destroyed them
which called on this name in Jerusalem,
and came here for that intent, that he
might bring them bound to the chief
priests?
22 But Saul increased the more in
strength, and confounded the Jews which
dwelt at Damascus, proving that this is
very Christ.
23 And after that many days were fulfilled, the Jews took counsel to kill him:
24 But their laying await was known of
Saul. And they watched the gates day and
night to kill him.
25 Then the disciples took him by night,
and let him down by the wall in a basket.
26 And when Saul was come to Jerusalem, he assayed to join himself to the disciples: but they were all afraid of him,
and believed not that he was a disciple.
27 But Barnabas took him, and brought
him to the apostles, and declared to them
how he had seen the Lord in the way,
and that he had spoken to him, and how
he had preached boldly at Damascus in
the name of Jesus.
28 And he was with them coming in and
going out at Jerusalem.
29 And he spoke boldly in the name of
the Lord Jesus, and disputed against the
Grecians: but they went about to slay him.
30 Which when the brethren knew, they
brought him down to Caesarea, and sent
him forth to Tarsus.
31 Then had the churches rest throughout all Judea and Galilee and Samaria, and
were edified; and walking in the fear of
the Lord, and in the comfort of the Holy
Spirit, were multiplied.
32 And it came to pass, as Peter passed
throughout all quarters, he came down
also to the saints which dwelt at Lydda.
33 And there he found a certain man
named Aeneas, which had kept his bed

9:22 Don't be discouraged if, as a new Christian you feel inadequate to share your faith. The very fact that you were once enjoying the pleasures of sin and are now walking that path of righteousness is a testimony that Jesus is the Christ. Many no doubt heard of the conversion of Saul of Tarsus without hearing him preach. A changed life is a testimony in itself.

9:31 Fear of the Lord. "The fear of the Lord involves a sober awareness of what He loves, of what He despises, and of the consequences of disobedience and rebellion against Him. It leads to a sincere desire to please Him, heartfelt gratefulness for His mercy, and unending delight in His loving presence. So when we choose to 'fear the Lord' we will heed Romans 12:9, 'Abhor what is evil. Cling to what is good.'" *Berit Kjos*

QUESTIONS & OBJECTIONS

9:37

"What should I say to someone who has lost a loved one through cancer?"

Be very careful not to give the impression that God was punishing the person for his sins. Instead, speak about the fact that all around us we can see the evidence of a "fallen creation." Explain how in the beginning there was no disease, pain, suffering, or death. But when sin entered the world, it brought suffering with it. Then gently turn the conversation away from the person who died to the person who is still living. Ask if he has been thinking about God, and if he has kept the Ten Commandments. Then take the opportunity to go through the spiritual nature of God's Law. Someone who has lost a loved one often begins to ask soul-searching questions about God, death, and eternity. Many people are so hard-hearted that it takes a tragedy to make them receptive to God.

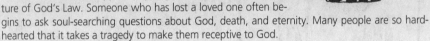

eight years, and was sick of the palsy.
34 And Peter said to him, Aeneas, Jesus
Christ makes you whole: arise, and make
your bed. And he arose immediately.
35 And all that dwelt at Lydda and Saron
saw him, and turned to the Lord.
36 Now there was at Joppa a certain disciple named Tabitha, which by interpretation is called Dorcas: this woman was
full of good works and almsdeeds which
she did.
37 And it came to pass in those days, that
she was sick, and died: whom when they
had washed, they laid her in an upper
chamber.
38 And forasmuch as Lydda was near to
Joppa, and the disciples had heard that
Peter was there, they sent to him two men,
desiring him that he would not delay to
come to them.
39 Then Peter arose and went with them.
When he was come, they brought him into the upper chamber: and all the widows
stood by him weeping, and showing the
coats and garments which Dorcas made,
while she was with them.
40 But Peter put them all forth, and
kneeled down, and prayed; and turning
him to the body said, Tabitha, arise. And
she opened her eyes: and when she saw
Peter, she sat up.
41 And he gave her his hand, and lifted
her up, and when he had called the saints
and widows, presented her alive.
42 And it was known throughout all Joppa; and many believed in the Lord.
43 And it came to pass, that he tarried
many days in Joppa with one Simon a tanner.

CHAPTER 10

THERE was a certain man in Caesarea
called Cornelius, a centurion of the
band called the Italian band,
2 A devout man, and one that feared
God with all his house, which gave many
alms to the people, and prayed to God always.
3 He saw in a vision evidently about the
ninth hour of the day an angel of God
coming in to him, and saying to him,
Cornelius.
4 And when he looked on him, he was
afraid, and said, What is it, Lord? And he
said to him, Your prayers and your alms
are come up for a memorial before God.
5 And now send men to Joppa, and call
for one Simon, whose surname is Peter:
6 He lodges with one Simon a tanner,
whose house is by the sea side: he shall
tell you what you ought to do.
7 And when the angel which spoke to
Cornelius was departed, he called two of
his household servants, and a devout sol-

dier of them that waited on him continually;
8 And when he had declared all these things to them, he sent them to Joppa.
9 On the morrow, as they went on their journey, and drew near to the city, Peter went up upon the housetop to pray about the sixth hour:
10 And he became very hungry, and would have eaten: but while they made ready, he fell into a trance,
11 And saw heaven opened, and a certain vessel descending to him, as it had been a great sheet knit at the four corners, and let down to the earth:
12 Wherein were all manner of four-footed beasts of the earth, and wild beasts, and creeping things, and fowls of the air.
13 And there came a voice to him, Rise, Peter; kill, and eat.
14 But Peter said, Not so, Lord; for I have never eaten any thing that is common or unclean.
15 And the voice spoke to him again the second time, What God has cleansed, that call not common.
16 This was done thrice: and the vessel was received up again into heaven.
17 Now while Peter doubted in himself what this vision which he had seen should mean, behold, the men which were sent from Cornelius had made inquiry for Simon's house, and stood before the gate,
18 And called, and asked whether Simon, which was surnamed Peter, were lodged there.
19 While Peter thought on the vision, the Spirit said to him, Behold, three men seek you.
20 Arise therefore, and get down, and go with them, doubting nothing: for I have sent them.
21 Then Peter went down to the men which were sent to him from Cornelius; and said, Behold, I am he whom you seek: what is the cause wherefore you are come?
22 And they said, Cornelius the centurion, a just man, and one that fears God, and of good report among all the nation of the Jews, was warned from God by an holy angel to send for you into his house, and to hear words of you.
23 Then called he them in, and lodged them. And on the morrow Peter went away with them, and certain brethren from Joppa accompanied him.
24 And the morrow after they entered into Caesarea. And Cornelius waited for them, and had called together his kinsmen and near friends.
25 And as Peter was coming in, Cornelius met him, and fell down at his feet, and worshipped him.
26 But Peter took him up, saying, Stand up; I myself also am a man.

> If people are to be saved by a message, it must contain at least some measure of knowledge. There must be light as well as fire.
>
> **CHARLES SPURGEON**

27 And as he talked with him, he went in, and found many that were come together.
28 And he said to them, You know how that it is an unlawful thing for a man that is a Jew to keep company, or come to one of another nation; but God has showed me that I should not call any man common or unclean.
29 Therefore came I to you without gainsaying, as soon as I was sent for: I ask therefore for what intent you have sent for me?
30 And Cornelius said, Four days ago I was fasting until this hour; and at the ninth hour I prayed in my house, and, behold, a man stood before me in bright clothing,
31 And said, Cornelius, your prayer is heard, and your alms are had in remembrance in the sight of God.
32 Send therefore to Joppa, and call here Simon, whose surname is Peter; he is lodged in the house of one Simon a tanner by the sea side: who, when he comes, shall speak to you.
33 Immediately therefore I sent to you;

and you have well done that you are come. Now therefore are we all here present before God, to hear all things that are commanded you of God.
34 Then Peter opened his mouth, and said, Of a truth I perceive that God is no respecter of persons:
35 But in every nation he that fears him, and works righteousness, is accepted with him.
36 The word which God sent to the children of Israel, preaching peace by Jesus Christ: (he is Lord of all:)
37 That word, I say, you know, which was published throughout all Judea, and began from Galilee, after the baptism which John preached;
38 How God anointed Jesus of Nazareth with the Holy Spirit and with power: who went about doing good, and healing all that were oppressed of the devil; for God was with him.
39 And we are witnesses of all things which he did both in the land of the Jews, and in Jerusalem; whom they slew and hanged on a tree:
40 Him God raised up the third day, and showed him openly;
41 Not to all the people, but to witnesses chosen before of God, even to us, who did eat and drink with him after he rose from the dead.
42 And he commanded us to preach to the people, and to testify that it is he which was ordained of God to be the Judge of quick and dead.
43 To him give all the prophets witness, that through his name whosoever believes in him shall receive remission of sins.
44 While Peter yet spoke these words, the Holy Spirit fell on all them which heard the word.
45 And they of the circumcision which believed were astonished, as many as came with Peter, because that on the Gentiles also was poured out the gift of the Holy Spirit.
46 For they heard them speak with tongues, and magnify God. Then answered Peter,
47 Can any man forbid water, that these should not be baptized, which have received the Holy Spirit as well as we?
48 And he commanded them to be baptized in the name of the Lord. Then prayed they him to tarry certain days.

10:38 The Trinity at work in redemption. "In every major phase of the redemption, each Person of the Godhead is directly involved. Their involvement in each successive phase may be set out as follows:

1. *Incarnation*. The Father incarnated the Son in the womb of Mary by the Holy Spirit (see Luke 1:35).
2. *Baptism in the Jordan River*. The Spirit descended on the Son, and the Father spoke His approval from heaven (see Matthew 3:14–17).
3. *Public ministry*. The Father anointed the Son with the Spirit (see Acts 10:38).
4. *The crucifixion*. Jesus offered Himself to the Father through the Spirit (see Hebrews 9:14).
5. *The resurrection*. The Father resurrected the Son by the Spirit (see Acts 2:32; Romans 1:4).
6. *Pentecost*. From the Father the Son received the Spirit, whom He then poured out on His disciples (see Acts 2:33).

Each Person of the Godhead—and I mean this reverently—was jealous to be included in the process of redeeming humanity." *Derek Prince, Atonement*

10:47 Baptism. If we are saved by being water baptized (as certain Scriptures *seem* to imply), then we are saved by works and not grace. The Holy Spirit fell on the Gentiles *before* they were baptized. This means they were saved (by God's grace) *before* they went near water. Paul said that Christ sent him not to baptize, but to preach (1 Corinthians 1:17). That's because it is the gospel that saves us, not our works in response to it. As this verse shows, baptism is an act of obedience *after* salvation.

CHAPTER 11

AND the apostles and brethren that
were in Judea heard that the Gentiles
had also received the word of God.
2 And when Peter was come up to Jerusalem, they that were of the circumcision
contended with him,
3 Saying, You went in to men uncircumcised, and did eat with them.
4 But Peter rehearsed the matter from the
beginning, and expounded it by order to
them, saying,
5 I was in the city of Joppa praying: and
in a trance I saw a vision, A certain vessel descend, as it had been a great sheet,
let down from heaven by four corners;
and it came even to me:
6 Upon the which when I had fastened
mine eyes, I considered, and saw four-
footed beasts of the earth, and wild beasts,
and creeping things, and fowls of the air.
7 And I heard a voice saying to me, Arise,
Peter; slay and eat.
8 But I said, Not so, Lord: for nothing
common or unclean has at any time entered into my mouth.
9 But the voice answered me again from
heaven, What God has cleansed, that call
not common.
10 And this was done three times: and
all were drawn up again into heaven.
11 And, behold, immediately there were
three men already come to the house
where I was, sent from Caesarea to me.
12 And the spirit bade me go with them,
nothing doubting. Moreover these six
brethren accompanied me, and we entered
into the man's house:
13 And he showed us how he had seen
an angel in his house, which stood and
said to him, Send men to Joppa, and call
for Simon, whose surname is Peter;
14 Who shall tell you words, whereby
you and all your house shall be saved.
15 And as I began to speak, the Holy Spirit fell on them, as on us at the beginning.
16 Then remembered I the word of the
Lord, how that he said, John indeed baptized with water; but you shall be baptized with the Holy Spirit.
17 Forasmuch then as God gave them
the like gift as he did to us, who believed
on the Lord Jesus Christ; what was I, that
I could withstand God?
18 When they heard these things, they
held their peace, and glorified God, saying,
Then has God also to the Gentiles granted repentance to life.
19 Now they which were scattered abroad
upon the persecution that arose about
Stephen traveled as far as Phenice, and
Cyprus, and Antioch, preaching the word
to none but to the Jews only.
20 And some of them were men of Cyprus and Cyrene, which, when they were
come to Antioch, spoke to the Grecians,
preaching the Lord Jesus.
21 And the hand of the Lord was with
them: and a great number believed, and
turned to the Lord.

Each individual is unique from the moment of conception. For how we are fearfully and wonderfully made, see Psalm 139:14 comment.

22 Then tidings of these things came to
the ears of the church which was in Jerusalem: and they sent forth Barnabas, that
he should go as far as Antioch.
23 Who, when he came, and had seen
the grace of God, was glad, and exhorted
them all, that with purpose of heart they
would cleave to the Lord.
24 For he was a good man, and full of
the Holy Spirit and of faith: and much
people was added to the Lord.

25 Then departed Barnabas to Tarsus, for
to seek Saul:
26 And when he had found him, he
brought him to Antioch. And it came to
pass, that a whole year they assembled
themselves with the church, and taught
much people. And the disciples were
called Christians first in Antioch.
27 And in these days came prophets from
Jerusalem to Antioch.
28 And there stood up one of them
named Agabus, and signified by the spirit
that there should be great dearth throughout all the world: which came to pass in
the days of Claudius Caesar.
29 Then the disciples, every man according to his ability, determined to send relief to the brethren which dwelt in Judea:
30 Which also they did, and sent it to the
elders by the hands of Barnabas and Saul.

CHAPTER 12

NOW about that time Herod the king
stretched forth his hands to vex certain of the church.
2 And he killed James the brother of John
with the sword.
3 And because he saw it pleased the Jews,
he proceeded further to take Peter also.
(Then were the days of unleavened bread.)
4 And when he had apprehended him, he
put him in prison, and delivered him to
four quaternions of soldiers to keep him;
intending after Easter to bring him forth to
the people.
5 Peter therefore was kept in prison: but
prayer was made without ceasing of the
church to God for him.
6 And when Herod would have brought
him forth, the same night Peter was sleeping between two soldiers, bound with two
chains: and the keepers before the door
kept the prison.
7 And, behold, the angel of the Lord
came upon him, and a light shined in the
prison: and he smote Peter on the side,
and raised him up, saying, Arise up quickly. And his chains fell off from his hands.
8 And the angel said to him, Gird your-

THE FUNCTION OF THE LAW

12:7 "The very first end of the Law [is], namely, convicting men of sin; awakening those who are still asleep on the brink of hell...The ordinary method of God is to convict sinners by the Law, and that only. The gospel is not the means which God hath ordained, or which our Lord Himself used, for this end." *John Wesley*

"Few, very few, are ever awakened or convinced by the encouragements and promises of the gospel, but almost all by the denunciations of the law." *Timothy Dwight*

12:6 The chains of sin and death. Peter lay soundly asleep in Herod's prison. This is faith in action: Faith snoozes, even in a storm. Stephen had been stoned, James had just been killed with a sword,...and Peter sleeps like a parishioner in the back row of a dead church. He was bound with chains between two soldiers. More guards stood before the door of the prison. Suddenly an angel of the Lord appeared and stood by him, "and a light shined in the prison." There is a strong inference that the light didn't awaken Peter from his sleep, because the Scriptures then tell us that the angel struck him on the side. As he arose, his chains fell off, he girded himself, tied on his shoes, put on his garment, and followed the angel. After that, the iron gate leading to the city opened of its own accord, and Peter was free.

The sinner is in the prison of his sins. He is taken captive by the devil. He is bound by the chains of sin, under the sentence of death. He is asleep in his sins. He lives in a dream world. But it isn't the gospel light that will awaken him. How can "Good News" alarm a sinner? Rather, the Law must strike him. He needs to be struck with the lightning of Sinai and awakened by its thunderings. That will rouse him to his plight of being on the threshold of death. Then he will arise and the gospel will remove the chains of sin and death. It will be "the power of God unto salvation." Then he will gird himself with truth, tie on his gospel shoes, put on his garment of righteousness, follow the Lord, and the iron gate of the Celestial City will open of its own accord.

self, and bind on your sandals. And so he
did. And he said to him, Cast your garment about you, and follow me.
9 And he went out, and followed him;
and did not know that it was true which
was done by the angel; but thought he
saw a vision.
10 When they were past the first and
the second ward, they came to the iron
gate that leads to the city; which opened
to them of his own accord: and they went
out, and passed on through one street; and
forthwith the angel departed from him.
11 And when Peter was come to himself, he said, Now I know of a surety, that
the Lord has sent his angel, and has delivered me out of the hand of Herod, and
from all the expectation of the people of
the Jews.
12 And when he had considered the
thing, he came to the house of Mary the
mother of John, whose surname was Mark;
where many were gathered together praying.
13 And as Peter knocked at the door of
the gate, a damsel came to hearken, named
Rhoda.
14 And when she knew Peter's voice, she
opened not the gate for gladness, but ran
in, and told how Peter stood before the
gate.
15 And they said to her, You are mad.
But she constantly affirmed that it was
even so. Then said they, It is his angel.
16 But Peter continued knocking: and
when they had opened the door, and saw
him, they were astonished.
17 But he, beckoning to them with the
hand to hold their peace, declared to them
how the Lord had brought him out of the
prison. And he said, Go show these things
to James, and to the brethren. And he departed, and went into another place.
18 Now as soon as it was day, there was
no small stir among the soldiers, what
was become of Peter.
19 And when Herod had sought for him,
and found him not, he examined the
keepers, and commanded that they should
be put to death. And he went down from
Judea to Caesarea, and there abode.
20 And Herod was highly displeased with
them of Tyre and Sidon: but they came
with one accord to him, and, having made
Blastus the king's chamberlain their friend,
desired peace; because their country was
nourished by the king's country.
21 And upon a set day Herod, arrayed in
royal apparel, sat upon his throne, and
made an oration to them.
22 And the people gave a shout, saying,
It is the voice of a god, and not of a man.
23 And immediately the angel of the Lord
smote him, because he gave not God the
glory: and he was eaten of worms, and
gave up the ghost.
24 But the word of God grew and multiplied.
25 And Barnabas and Saul returned from
Jerusalem, when they had fulfilled their
ministry, and took with them John, whose
surname was Mark.

For questions to ask evolutionists, see Proverbs 3:19 comment.

CHAPTER 13

NOW there were in the church that
was at Antioch certain prophets and
teachers; as Barnabas, and Simeon that
was called Niger, and Lucius of Cyrene,
and Manaen, which had been brought
up with Herod the tetrarch, and Saul.
2 As they ministered to the Lord, and
fasted, the Holy Spirit said, Separate me
Barnabas and Saul for the work whereunto I have called them.
3 And when they had fasted and prayed,
and laid their hands on them, they sent
them away.
4 So they, being sent forth by the Holy

12:12 Prayer—the secret weapon: See Acts 21:5.

Spirit, departed to Seleucia; and from
thence they sailed to Cyprus.
5 And when they were at Salamis, they
preached the word of God in the synagogues of the Jews: and they had also John
as their minister.
6 And when they had gone through the
isle to Paphos, they found a certain sorcerer, a false prophet, a Jew, whose name was
Bar-jesus:
7 Which was with the deputy of the
country, Sergius Paulus, a prudent man;
who called for Barnabas and Saul, and desired to hear the word of God.
8 But Elymas the sorcerer (for so is his
name by interpretation) withstood them,
seeking to turn away the deputy from the
faith.
9 Then Saul, (who also is called Paul,)
filled with the Holy Spirit, set his eyes on
him,
10 And said, O full of all subtlety and all
mischief, you child of the devil, you enemy of all righteousness, will you not cease
to pervert the right ways of the Lord?
11 And now, behold, the hand of the
Lord is upon you, and you shall be blind,
not seeing the sun for a season. And immediately there fell on him a mist and a
darkness; and he went about seeking some
to lead him by the hand.
12 Then the deputy, when he saw what
was done, believed, being astonished at
the doctrine of the Lord.
13 Now when Paul and his company
loosed from Paphos, they came to Perga
in Pamphylia: and John departing from
them returned to Jerusalem.
14 But when they departed from Perga,
they came to Antioch in Pisidia, and went
into the synagogue on the sabbath day,
and sat down.
15 And after the reading of the law and
the prophets the rulers of the synagogue
sent to them, saying, You men and brethren, if you have any word of exhortation
for the people, say on.
16 Then Paul stood up, and beckoning
with his hand said, Men of Israel, and you
that fear God, give audience.
17 The God of this people of Israel chose
our fathers, and exalted the people when
they dwelt as strangers in the land of
Egypt, and with an high arm brought he
them out of it.
18 And about the time of forty years suffered he their manners in the wilderness.
19 And when he had destroyed seven nations in the land of Canaan, he divided
their land to them by lot.
20 And after that he gave to them judges
about the space of four hundred and fifty
years, until Samuel the prophet.
21 And afterward they desired a king:
and God gave to them Saul the son of Cis,
a man of the tribe of Benjamin, by the
space of forty years.
22 And when he had removed him, he
raised up to them David to be their king;
to whom also he gave testimony, and said,
I have found David the son of Jesse, a man
after mine own heart, which shall fulfil all
my will.
23 Of this man's seed has God according
to his promise raised to Israel a Savior,
Jesus:
24 When John had first preached before
his coming the baptism of repentance to
all the people of Israel.
25 And as John fulfilled his course, he
said, Whom do you think that I am? I am
not he. But, behold, there comes one after
me, whose shoes of his feet I am not
worthy to loose.
26 Men and brethren, children of the
stock of Abraham, and whosoever among
you fears God, to you is the word of this
salvation sent.

13:22 The psalms reveal that David was sometimes vindictive and even hateful in prayer. However, he proved to be "a man after [God's] own heart" in his dealings with King Saul. He was full of mercy and grace in the face of murderous hostility. This may be because he had the good sense to pour his heart out to God, dealing with his anger in the privacy of prayer.

27 For they that dwell at Jerusalem, and their rulers, because they knew him not, nor yet the voices of the prophets which are read every sabbath day, they have fulfilled them in condemning him.
28 And though they found no cause of death in him, yet desired they Pilate that he should be slain.
29 And when they had fulfilled all that was written of him, they took him down from the tree, and laid him in a sepulchre.
30 But God raised him from the dead:
31 And he was seen many days of them which came up with him from Galilee to Jerusalem, who are his witnesses to the people.
32 And we declare to you glad tidings, how that the promise which was made to the fathers,
33 God has fulfilled the same to us their children, in that he has raised up Jesus again; as it is also written in the second psalm, You are my Son, this day have I begotten you.
34 And as concerning that he raised him up from the dead, now no more to return to corruption, he said on this wise, I will give you the sure mercies of David.
35 Wherefore he said also in another psalm, You shall not suffer your Holy One to see corruption.
36 For David, after he had served his own generation by the will of God, fell on sleep, and was laid to his fathers, and saw corruption:
37 But he, whom God raised again, saw no corruption.
38 Be it known to you therefore, men and brethren, that through this man is preached to you the forgiveness of sins:
39 And by him all that believe are justified from all things, from which you could not be justified by the law of Moses.
40 Beware therefore, lest that come upon you, which is spoken of in the prophets;
41 Behold, you despisers, and wonder, and perish: for I work a work in your days, a work which you shall in no wise believe, though a man declare it to you.

> Some have used the terrors of the Lord to terrify, but Paul used them to persuade.
>
> **CHARLES SPURGEON**

42 And when the Jews were gone out of the synagogue, the Gentiles besought that these words might be preached to them the next sabbath.
43 Now when the congregation was broken up, many of the Jews and religious proselytes followed Paul and Barnabas: who, speaking to them, persuaded them to continue in the grace of God.
44 And the next sabbath day came almost the whole city together to hear the word of God.
45 But when the Jews saw the multitudes, they were filled with envy, and spoke against those things which were spoken by Paul, contradicting and blaspheming.
46 Then Paul and Barnabas waxed bold, and said, It was necessary that the word of God should first have been spoken to you: but seeing you put it from you, and

13:38,39 Notice to whom Paul was speaking. This was to Jews who knew the Law (v. 15). He therefore preached the gospel of grace—Christ crucified and risen from the dead.

13:39 Justification. "[Justification] is the judicial act of God, by which He pardons all the sins of those who believe in Christ, and accounts, accepts, and treats them as righteous in the eye of the Law, i.e., as conformed to all its demands. In addition to the pardon of sin, justification declares that all the claims of the Law are satisfied in respect of the justified. It is the act of a judge and not of a sovereign. The Law is not relaxed or set aside, but is declared to be fulfilled in the strictest sense; and so the person justified is declared to be entitled to all the advantages and rewards arising from perfect obedience to the Law." *Easton Bible Dictionary*

QUESTIONS & OBJECTIONS

13:47 ***"If I submit to God, I'll just become a puppet!"***

"A brilliant young man questioned Dr. Henrietta Mears about surrendering his life to God. He was convinced that becoming a Christian would mean the destruction of his personality, that he'd be altered in some strange way, and that he'd lose control of his own mind. He feared becoming a mere puppet in God's hands.

"So Miss Mears asked him to watch as she turned on a lamp. One moment it was dark, then she turned on the switch. She explained, 'The lamp surrendered itself to the electric current and light has filled the room. The lamp didn't destroy its personality when it surrendered to the current. On the contrary—the very thing happened for which the lamp was created: it gave light.'"

Vonette Bright, Renew a Steadfast Spirit Within Me

judge yourselves unworthy of everlasting life, lo, we turn to the Gentiles.

47 For so has the Lord commanded us, saying, I have set you to be a light of the Gentiles, that you should be for salvation to the ends of the earth.

48 And when the Gentiles heard this, they were glad, and glorified the word of the Lord: and as many as were ordained to eternal life believed.

49 And the word of the Lord was published throughout all the region.

50 But the Jews stirred up the devout and honorable women, and the chief men of the city, and raised persecution against Paul and Barnabas, and expelled them out of their coasts.

51 But they shook off the dust of their feet against them, and came to Iconium.

52 And the disciples were filled with joy, and with the Holy Spirit.

CHAPTER 14

AND it came to pass in Iconium, that they went both together into the synagogue of the Jews, and so spoke, that a great multitude both of the Jews and also of the Greeks believed.

2 But the unbelieving Jews stirred up the Gentiles, and made their minds evil affected against the brethren.

3 Long time therefore abode they speaking boldly in the Lord, which gave testimony to the word of his grace, and granted signs and wonders to be done by their hands.

4 But the multitude of the city was divided: and part held with the Jews, and part with the apostles.

5 And when there was an assault made both of the Gentiles, and also of the Jews with their rulers, to use them despitefully, and to stone them,

6 They were ware of it, and fled to Lystra and Derbe, cities of Lycaonia, and to the region that lies round about:

7 And there they preached the gospel.

8 And there sat a certain man at Lystra, impotent in his feet, being a cripple from his mother's womb, who never had walked:

9 The same heard Paul speak: who steadfastly beholding him, and perceiving that he had faith to be healed,

10 Said with a loud voice, Stand upright on your feet. And he leaped and walked.

11 And when the people saw what Paul had done, they lifted up their voices, saying in the speech of Lycaonia, The gods are come down to us in the likeness of men.

12 And they called Barnabas, Jupiter; and Paul, Mercurius, because he was the chief speaker.

13 Then the priest of Jupiter, which was before their city, brought oxen and garlands to the gates, and would have done sacrifice with the people.

14 Which when the apostles, Barnabas

14:15 "Missing Link" Still Missing

"Did dinos soar? Imaginations certainly took flight over *Archaeoraptor Liaoningensis*, a birdlike fossil with a meat-eater's tail that was spirited out of northeastern China, 'discovered' at a Tucson, Arizona, gem and mineral show last year, and displayed at the National Geographic Society in Washington, D.C. Some 110,000 visitors saw the exhibit, which closed January 17; millions more read about the find in November's *National Geographic*. Now, paleontologists are eating crow. Instead of 'a true missing link' connecting dinosaurs to birds, the specimen appears to be a composite, its unusual appendage likely tacked on by a Chinese farmer, not evolution.

"*Archaeoraptor* is hardly the first 'missing link' to snap under scrutiny. In 1912, fossil remains of an ancient hominid were found in England's Piltdown quarries and quickly dubbed man's apelike ancestor. It took decades to reveal the hoax." *U.S. News & World Report*, February 14, 2000

"Darwin admitted that millions of 'missing links,' transitional life forms, would have to be discovered in the fossil record to prove the accuracy of his theory that all species had gradually evolved by chance mutation into new species. [See next page.] Unfortunately for his theory, despite hundreds of millions spent on searching for fossils worldwide for more than a century, the scientists have failed to locate *a single missing link* out of the millions that must exist if their theory of evolution is to be vindicated." *Grant R. Jeffery, The Signature of God*

"There are gaps in the fossil graveyard, places where there should be intermediate forms, but where there is nothing whatsoever instead. No paleontologist...denies that this is so. It is simply a fact. Darwin's theory and the fossil record are in conflict." *David Berlinsky*

"Scientists concede that their most cherished theories are based on embarrassingly few fossil fragments and that huge gaps exist in the fossil record." *Time* magazine, Nov. 7, 1977

"The evolutionists seem to know everything about the missing link except the fact that it is missing." *G. K. Chesterton*

and Paul, heard of, they rent their clothes,
and ran in among the people, crying out,
15 And saying, Sirs, why do you these
things? We also are men of like passions
with you, and preach to you that you
should turn from these vanities to the living God, which made heaven, and earth,
and the sea, and all things that are therein:
16 Who in times past suffered all nations
to walk in their own ways.
17 Nevertheless he left not himself with-

14:15 Evolutionary fraud. "Charles Dawson, a British lawyer and amateur geologist, announced in 1912 his discovery of pieces of a human skull and an apelike jaw in a gravel pit near the town of Piltdown, England...Dawson's announcement stopped the scorn cold. Experts instantly declared Piltdown Man (estimated to be 300,000 to one million years old) the evolutionary find of the century. Darwin's missing link had been identified.

"Or so it seemed for the next 40 or so years. Then, in the early fifties...scientists began to suspect misattribution. In 1953, that suspicion gave way to a full-blown scandal: Piltdown Man was a hoax. Radiocarbon tests proved that its skull belonged to a 600-year old woman, and its jaw to a 500-year old orangutan from the East Indies." *Our Times: The Illustrated History of the 20th Century*

The Piltdown Man fraud wasn't an isolated incident. The famed Nebraska Man was derived from a single tooth, which was later found to be from an extinct pig. Java Man, found in the early 20th century, was nothing more than a piece of skull, a fragment of a thigh bone, and three molar teeth. The rest came from the deeply fertile imaginations of plaster of Paris workers. Java Man is now regarded as fully human. Heidelberg Man came from a jawbone, a large chin section, and a few teeth. Most scientists reject the jawbone because it's similar to that of modern man. Still, many evolutionists believe that he's 250,000 years old. No doubt they pinpointed *(continued on next page)*

out witness, in that he did good, and gave
us rain from heaven, and fruitful seasons,
filling our hearts with food and gladness.
18 And with these sayings scarce restrained they the people, that they had
not done sacrifice to them.
19 And there came there certain Jews
from Antioch and Iconium, who persuaded the people, and, having stoned Paul,
drew him out of the city, supposing he
had been dead.
20 Howbeit, as the disciples stood round
about him, he rose up, and came into the
city: and the next day he departed with
Barnabas to Derbe.
21 And when they had preached the gospel to that city, and had taught many, they
returned again to Lystra, and to Iconium,
and Antioch,
22 Confirming the souls of the disciples,
and exhorting them to continue in the
faith, and that we must through much
tribulation enter into the kingdom of God.
23 And when they had ordained them

"As by this theory innumerable transitional forms must have existed, why do we not find them embedded in countless numbers in the crust of the earth? The number of intermediate links between all living and extinct species must have been inconceivably great!"

Charles Darwin

(14:15 continued) his birthday with carbon dating. However, *Time* magazine (June 11, 1990) published a science article subtitled, "Geologists show that carbon dating can be way off." And don't look to Neanderthal Man for any evidence of evolution. He died of exposure. His skull was exposed as being fully human, not ape. Not only was his stooped posture found to be caused by disease, but he spoke and was artistic and religious.

"Shells from *living* snails were carbon dated as being 27,000 years old." *Science* magazine, vol. 224, 1984 (emphasis added)

14:17 Scientific facts in the Bible. Job stated, "[God] made a decree for the rain, and a way for the lightning of the thunder" (Job 28:26). Centuries later, scientists began to discern the "decrees [rules] for the rain." Rainfall is part of a process called the "water cycle." The sun evaporates water from the ocean. The water vapor then rises and becomes clouds. This water in the clouds falls back to earth as rain, and collects in streams and rivers, then makes its way back to the ocean. That process repeats itself again and again. About 300 years ago, Galileo discovered this cycle. But amazingly the Scriptures described it centuries before. The prophet Amos (9:6) wrote that God "calls for the water of the sea, and pours them out upon the face of the earth." Scientists are just beginning to fully understand God's "decrees for the rain."

14:19 Open-air preaching. "The [street] preachers needed to have faces set like flints, and so indeed they had. John Furz says, 'As soon as I began to preach, a man came forward and presented a gun at my face; swearing that he would blow my brains out if I spoke another word. However, I continued speaking and he continued swearing, sometimes putting the muzzle of the gun to my mouth, sometimes against my ear. While we were singing the last hymn, he got behind me, fired the gun, and burned off part of my hair.'

"After this, my brethren, we ought never to speak of petty interruptions or annoyances. The proximity of a blunderbuss in the hands of a son of Belial is not very conducive to collected thought and clear utterance." *Charles Spurgeon*

elders in every church, and had prayed
with fasting, they commended them to
the Lord, on whom they believed.
24 And after they had passed throughout Pisidia, they came to Pamphylia.
25 And when they had preached the
word in Perga, they went down into At-
talia:
26 And thence sailed to Antioch, from
whence they had been recommended to
the grace of God for the work which they
fulfilled.
27 And when they were come, and had
gathered the church together, they rehearsed all that God had done with them,
and how he had opened the door of faith
to the Gentiles.
28 And there they abode long time with
the disciples.

CHAPTER 15

AND certain men which came down
from Judea taught the brethren, and
said, Except you be circumcised after the
manner of Moses, you cannot be saved.
2 When therefore Paul and Barnabas
had no small dissension and disputation
with them, they determined that Paul
and Barnabas, and certain other of them,
should go up to Jerusalem to the apostles and elders about this question.
3 And being brought on their way by
the church, they passed through Phenice
and Samaria, declaring the conversion of
the Gentiles: and they caused great joy
to all the brethren.
4 And when they were come to Jerusalem, they were received of the church, and
of the apostles and elders, and they declared all things that God had done with
them.
5 But there rose up certain of the sect of
the Pharisees which believed, saying, That
it was needful to circumcise them, and to
command them to keep the law of Moses.
6 And the apostles and elders came together for to consider of this matter.
7 And when there had been much disputing, Peter rose up, and said to them,
Men and brethren, you know how that a
good while ago God made choice among
us, that the Gentiles by my mouth should
hear the word of the gospel, and believe.
8 And God, which knows the hearts,
bare them witness, giving them the Holy
Spirit, even as he did to us;
9 And put no difference between us and
them, purifying their hearts by faith.
10 Now therefore why do you tempt
God, to put a yoke upon the neck of the
disciples, which neither our fathers nor
we were able to bear?
11 But we believe that through the grace
of the Lord Jesus Christ we shall be saved,
even as they.
12 Then all the multitude kept silence,
and gave audience to Barnabas and Paul,
declaring what miracles and wonders God
had wrought among the Gentiles by them.
13 And after they had held their peace,
James answered, saying, Men and brethren, hearken to me:
14 Simeon has declared how God at the
first did visit the Gentiles, to take out of
them a people for his name.
15 And to this agree the words of the
prophets; as it is written,
16 After this I will return, and will build
again the tabernacle of David, which is fallen down; and I will build again the ruins
thereof, and I will set it up:
17 That the residue of men might seek
after the Lord, and all the Gentiles, upon
whom my name is called, said the Lord,
who does all these things.
18 Known to God are all his works from
the beginning of the world.
19 Wherefore my sentence is, that we

15:18 God doesn't think as we do. He is omniscient—He knows all things. That means He never has an idea. If a concept suddenly came to Him, then He would be ignorant of the thought before it formed in His mind. However, God doesn't have thoughts "come to His mind." Because He is omniscient, His mind has all thoughts resident.

trouble not them, which from among the Gentiles are turned to God:
20 But that we write to them, that they abstain from pollutions of idols, and from fornication, and from things strangled, and from blood.
21 For Moses of old time has in every city them that preach him, being read in the synagogues every sabbath day.
22 Then pleased it the apostles and elders, with the whole church, to send chosen men of their own company to Antioch with Paul and Barnabas; namely, Judas surnamed Barsabas, and Silas, chief men among the brethren:

> My main business is the saving of souls. This one thing I do.
>
> **CHARLES SPURGEON**

23 And they wrote letters by them after this manner; The apostles and elders and brethren send greeting to the brethren which are of the Gentiles in Antioch and Syria and Cilicia:
24 Forasmuch as we have heard, that certain which went out from us have troubled you with words, subverting your souls, saying, You must be circumcised, and keep the law: to whom we gave no such commandment:
25 It seemed good to us, being assembled with one accord, to send chosen men to you with our beloved Barnabas and Paul,
26 Men that have hazarded their lives for the name of our Lord Jesus Christ.
27 We have sent therefore Judas and Silas, who shall also tell you the same things by mouth.
28 For it seemed good to the Holy Spirit, and to us, to lay upon you no greater burden than these necessary things;
29 That you abstain from meats offered to idols, and from blood, and from things strangled, and from fornication: from which if you keep yourselves, you shall do well. Fare you well.
30 So when they were dismissed, they came to Antioch: and when they had gathered the multitude together, they delivered the epistle:
31 Which when they had read, they rejoiced for the consolation.
32 And Judas and Silas, being prophets also themselves, exhorted the brethren with many words, and confirmed them.
33 And after they had tarried there a space, they were let go in peace from the brethren to the apostles.
34 Notwithstanding it pleased Silas to abide there still.
35 Paul also and Barnabas continued in Antioch, teaching and preaching the word of the Lord, with many others also.
36 And some days after Paul said to Barnabas, Let us go again and visit our brethren in every city where we have preached the word of the Lord, and see how they do.
37 And Barnabas determined to take with them John, whose surname was Mark.
38 But Paul thought it not good to take him with them, who departed from them from Pamphylia, and went not with them to the work.
39 And the contention was so sharp between them, that they departed asunder one from the other: and so Barnabas took Mark, and sailed to Cyprus;
40 And Paul chose Silas, and departed, being recommended by the brethren to the grace of God.
41 And he went through Syria and Cilicia, confirming the churches.

CHAPTER 16

THEN came he to Derbe and Lystra: and, behold, a certain disciple was there, named Timotheus, the son of a certain woman, which was a Jewess, and believed; but his father was a Greek:
2 Which was well reported of by the brethren that were at Lystra and Iconium.
3 Him would Paul have to go forth with him; and took and circumcised him because of the Jews which were in those quarters: for they knew all that his father was a Greek.

4 And as they went through the cities, they delivered them the decrees for to keep, that were ordained of the apostles and elders which were at Jerusalem.
5 And so were the churches established in the faith, and increased in number daily.
6 Now when they had gone throughout Phrygia and the region of Galatia, and were forbidden of the Holy Spirit to preach the word in Asia,
7 After they were come to Mysia, they assayed to go into Bithynia: but the Spirit suffered them not.
8 And they passing by Mysia came down to Troas.
9 And a vision appeared to Paul in the night; There stood a man of Macedonia, and prayed him, saying, Come over into Macedonia, and help us.
10 And after he had seen the vision, immediately we endeavored to go into Macedonia, assuredly gathering that the Lord had called us for to preach the gospel to them.
11 Therefore loosing from Troas, we came with a straight course to Samothracia, and the next day to Neapolis;
12 And from thence to Philippi, which is the chief city of that part of Macedonia, and a colony: and we were in that city abiding certain days.
13 And on the sabbath we went out of the city by a river side, where prayer was wont to be made; and we sat down, and spoke to the women which resorted there.
14 And a certain woman named Lydia, a seller of purple, of the city of Thyatira, which worshipped God, heard us: whose heart the Lord opened, that she attended to the things which were spoken of Paul.
15 And when she was baptized, and her household, she besought us, saying, If you have judged me to be faithful to the Lord, come into my house, and abide there. And she constrained us.
16 And it came to pass, as we went to prayer, a certain damsel possessed with a spirit of divination met us, which brought her masters much gain by soothsaying:

16:6 "I think a good rule of thumb to follow would be to presume the Lord wants you to share the gospel with everyone unless He leads you not to." *Danny Lehmann*

16:16 Those who think they are contacting their dead loved ones through the occult are actually contacting "familiar spirits" (demons), a forbidden practice (Leviticus 19:31; 20:6; Deuteronomy 18:10–12).

16:16–18 The woman (or the demon) was speaking the truth. These men *were* servants of the Most High God, and they *were* showing the way of salvation. Why then was Paul grieved? Satan is very subtle. Rather than openly oppose the truth, he will often attempt to conceal it by maintaining that the occult and God are compatible. If you are open-air preaching, don't be surprised to have someone who is obviously demonically controlled loudly agree with you, so that it looks to the crowd that you are both preaching the same message. This *is* very frustrating.

For two years I was heckled almost daily by a woman named Petra. She dressed in black, carried a wooden staff, and said she was a prophet to the nation. As in the days of Noah, only eight would be saved. She maintained that she was one of them, and that she determined who the other seven would be. She also claimed that my spirit visited her spirit in the night (it did not!). My problem was that she would "Amen" much of what I preached, adding her thoughts at the points I made. She would do this at the top of her very loud voice. It must have appeared to newcomers to the crowd that we were a team, preaching the same thing. This was why I was delighted when (every now and then) she would get angry with something I said and let out a string of cuss words, revealing to the crowd that we were *not* on the same side.

The question arises as to whether Paul did the right thing by casting out the demon. I'm not sure he did. If the woman wasn't repentant, she may have received seven more demons (Matthew 12:43–45). After his action, great persecution came against the disciples, but God in His goodness worked it out for their good, and for the good of the Philippian jailer and his family (see vv. 24–34).

17 The same followed Paul and us, and
cried, saying, These men are the servants
of the most high God, which show to us
the way of salvation.
18 And this did she many days. But Paul,
being grieved, turned and said to the spirit, I command you in the name of Jesus
Christ to come out of her. And he came
out the same hour.
19 And when her masters saw that the
hope of their gains was gone, they caught
Paul and Silas, and drew them into the
marketplace to the rulers,
20 And brought them to the magistrates,
saying, These men, being Jews, do exceedingly trouble our city,
21 And teach customs, which are not
lawful for us to receive, neither to observe,
being Romans.
22 And the multitude rose up together
against them: and the magistrates tore
off their clothes, and commanded to beat
them.
23 And when they had laid many stripes
upon them, they cast them into prison,
charging the jailor to keep them safely:
24 Who, having received such a charge,
thrust them into the inner prison, and
made their feet fast in the stocks.
25 And at midnight Paul and Silas prayed,
and sang praises to God: and the prisoners heard them.
26 And suddenly there was a great earthquake, so that the foundations of the prison were shaken: and immediately all the
doors were opened, and every one's bands
were loosed.
27 And the keeper of the prison awaking
out of his sleep, and seeing the prison
doors open, he drew out his sword, and
would have killed himself, supposing that
the prisoners had been fled.
28 But Paul cried with a loud voice, saying, Do yourself no harm: for we are all
here.
29 Then he called for a light, and sprang
in, and came trembling, and fell down before Paul and Silas,
30 **And brought them out, and said,
Sirs, what must I do to be saved?**
31 **And they said, Believe on the Lord
Jesus Christ, and you shall be saved, and
your house.**
32 And they spoke to him the word of
the Lord, and to all that were in his house.
33 And he took them the same hour of
the night, and washed their stripes; and
was baptized, he and all his, straightway.
34 And when he had brought them into
his house, he set meat before them, and rejoiced, believing in God with all his house.
35 And when it was day, the magistrates

16:25 Ira Sankey, before he became D. L. Moody's famous song leader (and a powerful preacher himself), was assigned to night duty in the American Civil War. While he was on duty, he lifted his eyes toward heaven and began to sing, praising the Lord while he was alone. At least, he thought he was alone.

Years later, after the war had ended, Sankey was on a ship traveling across the Atlantic Ocean. Since he was now a famous singer, a crowd of people approached him and asked him to sing. He lifted his eyes toward heaven and sang a beautiful hymn.

After his song, a man from the crowd asked him if, on a certain night during the Civil War, he had performed night duty for a certain infantry unit. "Yes, I did," was his reply.

The man continued, "I was on the opposite side of the war, and I was hiding in a bush near your camp. With my rifle aimed at your head, I was about to shoot you when you looked toward heaven and began to sing. I thought, 'Well, I like music, and this guy has a nice voice. I'll sit here, let him sing the song,...and then shoot him. He's not going anywhere.' But then I realized what you were singing. It was the same hymn my mother used to sing at my bedside when I was a child. And it's the same hymn you sang tonight! I tried, but that night during the Civil War, I was powerless to shoot you."

Ira Sankey pointed that man to Christ. He and thousands of others were saved under Sankey's ministry. All this stemmed from the fact that Sankey praised the Lord at all times.

QUESTIONS & OBJECTIONS

17:2

"Christians can't use 'circular reasoning' by trying to prove the Bible by quoting from the Bible!"

The "circular reasoning" argument is absurd. That's like saying you can't prove that the President lives in the White House by *looking into* the White House. It is looking into the White House that will provide the necessary proof. The fulfilled prophecies, the amazing consistency, and the many scientific statements of the Bible prove it to be the Word of God. They provide evidence that it is supernatural in origin.

See also Psalm 119:105 comment.

sent the serjeants, saying, Let those men
go.
36 And the keeper of the prison told this
saying to Paul, The magistrates have sent
to let you go: now therefore depart, and
go in peace.
37 But Paul said to them, They have beaten us openly uncondemned, being Romans, and have cast us into prison; and
now do they thrust us out privately? nay
verily; but let them come themselves and
fetch us out.
38 And the serjeants told these words to
the magistrates: and they feared, when
they heard that they were Romans.
39 And they came and besought them,
and brought them out, and desired them
to depart out of the city.
40 And they went out of the prison, and
entered into the house of Lydia and when
they had seen the brethren, they comforted them, and departed.

CHAPTER 17

NOW when they had passed through Amphipolis and Apollonia, they came to Thessalonica, where was a synagogue of the Jews:
2 And Paul, as his manner was, went in
to them, and three sabbath days reasoned
with them out of the scriptures,
3 Opening and alleging, that Christ must
needs have suffered, and risen again from
the dead; and that this Jesus, whom I
preach to you, is Christ.
4 And some of them believed, and consorted with Paul and Silas; and of the devout Greeks a great multitude, and of
the chief women not a few.
5 But the Jews which believed not, moved
with envy, took to them certain lewd fellows of the baser sort, and gathered a
company, and set all the city on an uproar,
and assaulted the house of Jason, and
sought to bring them out to the people.
6 And when they found them not, they
drew Jason and certain brethren to the
rulers of the city, crying, These that have
turned the world upside down are come
here also;
7 Whom Jason has received: and these all
do contrary to the decrees of Caesar, saying that there is another king, one Jesus.
8 And they troubled the people and the
rulers of the city, when they heard these
things.
9 And when they had taken security of
Jason, and of the others, they let them go.
10 And the brethren immediately sent
away Paul and Silas by night to Berea: who
coming there went into the synagogue of
the Jews.
11 **These were more noble than those
in Thessalonica, in that they received
the word with all readiness of mind, and
searched the scriptures daily, whether
those things were so.**
12 Therefore many of them believed; also
of honorable women which were Greeks,
and of men, not a few.
13 But when the Jews of Thessalonica
had knowledge that the word of God was
preached of Paul at Berea, they came there
also, and stirred up the people.

POINTS FOR OPEN-AIR PREACHING

17:22

Give Yourself a Lift

If you are going to preach in the open-air, elevate yourself. For eighteen months, I preached without any elevation and hardly attracted any listeners. As soon as I did it "soapbox" style, people stopped to listen. Their attitude was "What has this guy got to say?" They had an excuse to stop.

Also, elevation will give you protection. I was once almost eaten by an angry 6'6" gentleman who kept fuming, "God is love!" We were eye to eye...while I was elevated. On another occasion, a very heavy gentleman who had a mean countenance placed it about 6" from mine and whispered, "Jesus said to love your enemies." I nodded in agreement. Then he asked in a deep voice, "Who is your enemy?" I shrugged. His voice deepened and spilled forth in a chilling tone, *"Lucifer!"* I was standing beside my stepladder at the time so he pushed me backwards with his stomach. He kept doing so until I was moved back about 20 feet. I prayed, "Wisdom, Lord," then said, "You are either going to hit me or hug me." He hugged me and walked off. That wouldn't have happened if I had been elevated.

Elevation will also give you added authority. Often hecklers will walk right up to you and ask questions quietly. This is an attempt to stifle the preaching, and it will work if you are not higher than your heckler. If they come too close to me, I talk over their heads and tell them to go back to the heckler's gallery. They actually obey me because they get the impression I am bigger than they are.

When Ezra preached the Law, he was elevated (Nehemiah 8:4,5). John Wesley used elevation to preach. Jesus preached the greatest sermon ever on a mount (Matthew 5–7), and Paul went up Mars' Hill to preach (Acts 17:22). So if you can't find a hilltop to preach from, use a soapbox or a stepladder. See Acts 3:4 comment.

14 And then immediately the brethren
sent away Paul to go as it were to the sea:
but Silas and Timotheus abode there still.
15 And they that conducted Paul brought
him to Athens: and receiving a commandment
to Silas and Timotheus for to come
to him with all speed, they departed.
16 *Now while Paul waited for them at
Athens, his spirit was stirred in him, when
he saw the city wholly given to idolatry.*
17 *Therefore disputed he in the synagogue
with the Jews, and with the devout persons,
and in the market daily with them that met
with him.*
18 Then certain philosophers of the Epicureans,
and of the Stoicks, encountered
him. And some said, What will this babbler
say? other some, He seems to be a
setter forth of strange gods: because he
preached to them Jesus, and the resurrection.
19 And they took him, and brought him
to Areopagus, saying, May we know what
this new doctrine, whereof you speak, is?
20 For you bring certain strange things
to our ears: we would know therefore
what these things mean.
21 (For all the Athenians and strangers
which were there spent their time in
nothing else, but either to tell, or to hear
some new thing.)
22 Then Paul stood in the midst of Mars'
hill, and said, You men of Athens, I perceive
that in all things you are too superstitious.
23 For as I passed by, and beheld your
devotions, I found an altar with this inscription,
TO THE UNKNOWN GOD.
Whom therefore you ignorantly worship,
him declare I to you.
24 God that made the world and all
things therein, seeing that he is Lord of
heaven and earth, dwells not in temples
made with hands;
25 Neither is worshipped with men's
hands, as though he needed any thing,

17:22 *How to Witness to Muslims*

In Acts 17:22–31 the apostle Paul built on areas of "common ground" as he prepared his listeners for the good news of the gospel. Even though he was addressing Gentiles whose beliefs were erroneous, he didn't rebuke them for having a doctrine of devils—"The things which the Gentiles sacrifice, they sacrifice to devils, and not to God" (1 Corinthians 10:20). Neither did he present the great truth that Jesus of Nazareth was Almighty God manifest in human form. This may have initially offended his hearers and closed the door to the particular knowledge he wanted to convey. Instead, he built on what they already knew. He first established that there is a Creator who made all things. He then exposed their sin of transgression of the First and Second of the Ten Commandments. Then he preached future punishment for sin.

There are three main areas of common ground upon which Christians may stand with Muslims. First, that there is one God—the Creator of all things. The second area is the fact that Jesus of Nazareth was a prophet of God. The Bible makes this clear: "And He shall send Jesus Christ, ... For Moses truly said to the fathers, A prophet shall the Lord your God raise up to you of your brethren, like to me; him shall you hear in all things whatsoever he shall say to you" (Acts 3:20–22).

The Qur'an (Koran) says: "Behold! The angel said 'O Mary! Allah giveth you Glad Tidings of a word from Him. His name will be (Christ Jesus) the son of Mary, held in honor in this world and the hereafter and of (the company of) those nearest to Allah'" (Surah 3:45). In Surah 19:19, the angel said to Mary, "I am only a messenger of thy Lord to announce to you a gift of a holy son." Surah 3:55 says, "Allah said: 'O Jesus! I will take you and raise you to Myself."

It is because of these and other references to Jesus in the Qur'an that a Muslim will not object when you establish that Jesus was a prophet from God.

This brings us to the third area of common ground. Muslims also respect Moses as a prophet of God. Therefore, there should be little contention when Christians speak of God (as Creator), Jesus the prophet, and the Law of the prophet Moses.

Most Muslims do have some knowledge of their sinfulness, but few see sin in its true light. It is therefore essential to take them through the spiritual nature of the Ten Commandments. While it is true that the Law of Moses begins with, "I am the Lord your God, you shall have no other gods before Me," it may be unwise to tell a Muslim, at that point, that Allah is a false god. Such talk may close the door before you are able to speak to his conscience. It is wise rather to present the Law in a similar order in which Jesus gave it in Luke 18:20. He addressed the man's sins of the flesh. He spoke directly to sins that have to do with his fellow man. Therefore, ask your hearer if he has ever told a lie. When (if) he admits that he has, ask him what that makes him. Don't call him a liar. Instead, gently press him to tell you what someone is called who has lied. Try to get him to say that he is a "liar."

Then ask him if he has ever stolen something, even if it's small. If he has, ask what that makes him (a thief). Then quote from the Prophet Jesus: "Whosoever looks on a woman to lust after her has committed adultery with her already in his heart" (Matthew 5:27). Ask if he has ever looked at a woman with lust. If he is reasonable, he will admit that he has sinned in that area. Then gently tell him that, *by his own admission*, he is a "lying, thieving adulterer-at-heart." Say, "If God judges you by the Law of Moses on Judgment Day, will you be innocent or guilty?"

At this point, he will more than likely say that he will be innocent, because he confesses his sins to God. However, the Qur'an says: "Every soul that has sinned, if it possessed all that is on earth, would fain give it in ransom" (Surah 10:54). In other words, if he possessed the *whole world* and offered it to God as a sacrifice for his sins, it wouldn't be enough to provide atonement for his sins.

Imagine that a criminal is facing a $50,000 fine. He is penniless, so he sincerely tells the judge that he is sorry for a crime and vows never to do it again. The judge won't let him go on the basis of his sorrow, or his vow never to commit the crime again. Of course, he

(continued on next page)

(17:22 continued)
should be sorry for what he has done, and of course, he shouldn't break the law again. The judge will, however, let him go if someone else pays the fine for him.

Now tell him that Moses gave instructions to Israel to shed the blood of a spotless lamb to provide a temporary atonement for their sin; and that Jesus was the Lamb that God provided to make atonement for the sins of the world. Through faith in Jesus, he can have atonement with God. All his sin can be washed away—once and for all. God can grant him the gift of everlasting life through faith in Jesus Christ on the basis of His death and resurrection.

The uniqueness of Jesus of Nazareth was that He claimed He had power on earth to forgive sins (Matthew 9:2–6). No other prophet of any of the great religions made this claim. Only Jesus can provide peace with God. This is why He said, "I am the way, the truth, and the life: no man comes to the Father, but by me" (John 14:6). God commands sinners to repent and trust in Jesus as Lord and Savior, or they will perish.

To try to justify himself, your listener may say something like, "The Bible has changed. It has been altered. There are many different versions, but the Koran has never changed." Explain to him that there are many different versions, printed in different languages and in modern English, to help people understand the Bible, but the content of the Scriptures remains the same. The Dead Sea Scrolls prove that God has preserved the Scriptures. Tell him that the 100% accurate prophecies of Matthew 24, Luke 21, and 2 Timothy 3 prove that this is the Book of the Creator.

Your task is to present the truth of the gospel. It is God who makes it come alive (1 Corinthians 3:6,7). It is God who brings conviction of sin (John 16:7,8). It is God who reveals who Jesus is (Matthew 16:16,17). All God requires is your faithful presentation of the truth (Matthew 25:21).

seeing he gives to all life, and breath, and
all things;
26 And has made of one blood all nations of men for to dwell on all the face of
the earth, and has determined the times
before appointed, and the bounds of their
habitation;
27 That they should seek the Lord, if
haply they might feel after him, and find
him, though he be not far from every one
of us:
28 For in him we live, and move, and
have our being; as certain also of your own
poets have said, For we are also his offspring.
29 Forasmuch then as we are the offspring of God, we ought not to think that
the Godhead is like to gold, or silver, or

17:24 Evolution should not be taught. *Dr. Colin Patterson*, senior paleontologist, British Museum of Natural History, gave a keynote address at the American Museum of Natural History, New York City, in 1981. In it, he explained his sudden "anti-evolutionary" view: "One morning I woke up and...it struck me that I had been working on this stuff for twenty years and there was not one thing I knew about it. That's quite a shock to learn that one can be misled so long...I've tried putting a simple question to various people: 'Can you tell me anything you know about evolution, any one thing, any one thing that is true?' I tried that question on the geology staff at the Field Museum of Natural History and the only answer I got was silence. I tried it on the members of the Evolutionary Morphology Seminar in the University of Chicago, a very prestigious body of evolutionists, and all I got there was silence for a long time and eventually one person said, 'I do know one thing—it ought not to be taught in high school.'"

17:26 Mormons believe that God cursed Cain with black skin and a flat nose. However, the "mark" was set upon Cain *before* the Flood. In that Flood all flesh perished except for Noah, his wife, his three sons, and their wives. If the curse upon Cain was dark skin, the only way the race could have survived was for Noah to be a direct descendent of Cain. However, Noah's genealogy didn't come from Cain, but from Seth (Genesis 5:3,6–32).

Questions & Objections

17:26 "Where do all the races come from?"

Some have wondered, if we are all descendents of Adam and Eve, why are there so many races? The Bible informed us 2,000 years ago that God has made all nations from "one blood." We are all of the same race—the "human race," descendents of Adam and Eve, something science is slowly coming to realize.

Reuters news service reported the following article by Maggie Fox:

> Science may have caught up with the Bible, which says that Adam and Eve are the ancestors of all humans alive today.
>
> Peter Underhill of Stanford University in California remarked on findings published in the November 2000 issue of the journal *Nature Genetics*... Geneticists have long agreed there is no genetic basis to race—only to ethnic and geographic groups.
>
> "People look at a very conspicuous trait like skin color and they say, 'Well, this person's so different'... but that's only skin deep," Underhill said. "When you look at the level of the Y chromosome you find that, gee, there is very little difference between them. And skin color differences are strictly a consequence of climate."

stone, graven by art and man's device.
30 And the times of this ignorance God
winked at; but now commands all men
every where to repent:
31 Because he has appointed a day, in
the which he will judge the world in
righteousness by that man whom he
has ordained; whereof he has given as-
surance to all men, in that he has raised
him from the dead.
32 And when they heard of the resurrection of the dead, some mocked: and others
said, We will hear you again of this matter.
33 So Paul departed from among them.
34 Howbeit certain men clave to him,
and believed: among the which was Dio-
nysius the Areopagite, and a woman
named Damaris, and others with them.

Using the Law in Evangelism

17:29 Paul was preaching the essence of the First and Second Commandments to show his hearers that they were idolaters. See Acts 28:23 comment.

17:30 Repentance—its necessity for salvation. See Acts 20:21.

"If my six-year-old daughter was out on the road playing in front of my house and I saw a huge truck barreling around the corner, what would I do in that moment? Out of my love for my daughter I would not gently invite her to step away from the street. I would *command* her to change her direction, and get off the road! Why? Because of my love for her. I know that the truck would not be able to stop in time and it would run her over and kill her. The same is true of the Father's love for us. Out of His love, he commands us to repent, because at any moment the truck of sin and death could run us over for playing on the road of rebellion!" *Rob Price*

17:31 Judgment Day: For verses that warn of its reality, see Romans 2:16. We preach Christ and Him crucified for the sins of the world, seeking to warn every man of the great and coming Day of the Lord, in which God will judge the world in righteousness. The standard of judgment will be a perfect Law (Psalm 19:7), and those who fail to meet its perfect requirements will come under its terrible wrath. See also Acts 18:9 comment.

CHAPTER 18

AFTER these things Paul departed
from Athens, and came to Corinth;
2 And found a certain Jew named Aquila,
born in Pontus, lately come from Italy,
with his wife Priscilla; (because that Claudius had commanded all Jews to depart
from Rome:) and came to them.
3 And because he was of the same craft,
he abode with them, and wrought: for by
their occupation they were tentmakers.
4 And he reasoned in the synagogue every
sabbath, and persuaded the Jews and the
Greeks.
5 And when Silas and Timotheus were
come from Macedonia, Paul was pressed
in the spirit, and testified to the Jews that
Jesus was Christ.
6 And when they opposed themselves,
and blasphemed, he shook his raiment,
and said to them, Your blood be upon
your own heads; I am clean: from henceforth I will go to the Gentiles.
7 And he departed thence, and entered
into a certain man's house, named Justus,
one that worshipped God, whose house
joined hard to the synagogue.
8 And Crispus, the chief ruler of the synagogue, believed on the Lord with all his
house; and many of the Corinthians hearing believed, and were baptized.
9 Then spoke the Lord to Paul in the
night by a vision, Be not afraid, but speak,
and hold not your peace:
10 For I am with you, and no man shall
set on you to hurt you: for I have much
people in this city.
11 And he continued there a year and
six months, teaching the word of God
among them.
12 And when Gallio was the deputy of
Achaia, the Jews made insurrection with
one accord against Paul, and brought him
to the judgment seat,

18:4 Paul did not go to the synagogue to keep the Sabbath holy. He went there to *reason* with the Jews about Christ. His manner was to become like a Jew to the Jews. His heart's desire was to reach his own nation with the gospel. See 1 Corinthians 9:20–22.

18:9 "God [has] appointed a day in which He will judge the world, and we sigh and cry until it shall end the reign of wickedness, and give rest to the oppressed. Brethren, we must preach the coming of the Lord, and preach it somewhat more than we have done, *because it is the driving power of the gospel*. Too many have kept back these truths, and thus the bone has been taken out of the arm of the gospel. Its point has been broken; its edge has been blunted. The doctrine of judgment to come is the power by which men are to be aroused. There is another life; the Lord will come a second time; judgment will arrive; the wrath of God will be revealed. *Where this is not preached, I am bold to say the gospel is not preached.*

"It is absolutely necessary to the preaching of the gospel of Christ that men be warned as to what will happen if they continue in their sins. Ho, ho sir surgeon, you are too delicate to tell the man that he is ill! You hope to heal the sick without their knowing it. You therefore flatter them; and what happens? They laugh at you; they dance upon their own graves. At last they die! Your delicacy is cruelty; your flatteries are poisons; *you are a murderer*. Shall we keep men in a fool's paradise? Shall we lull them into soft slumbers from which they will awake in hell? Are we to become helpers of their damnation by our smooth speeches? In the name of God we will not." *Charles Spurgeon*

18:10 Never be discouraged by thinking that you are the only one God can use to reach the lost. Elijah, fearing that all the other prophets had been killed, said, "I, even I only, am left; and they seek my life, to take it away" (1 Kings 19:10). Yet God had reserved 7,000 faithful followers who hadn't bowed their knee to worship Baal (v. 18). Because God has His laborers, we need never panic when it comes to our loved ones being reached with the gospel. If we faithfully reach out and touch the lives of other peoples' loved ones, God (in His perfect timing) can use others to touch the lives of the ones we love so dearly. Claim your family in prayer, then thank God for His faithfulness in answering those prayers.

13 Saying, This fellow persuades men to worship God contrary to the law.
14 And when Paul was now about to open his mouth, Gallio said to the Jews, If it were a matter of wrong or wicked lewdness, O you Jews, reason would that I should bear with you:
15 But if it be a question of words and names, and of your law, you look to it; for I will be no judge of such matters.
16 And he drove them from the judgment seat.
17 Then all the Greeks took Sosthenes, the chief ruler of the synagogue, and beat him before the judgment seat. And Gallio cared for none of those things.

> The great benefit of open-air preaching is that we get so many new comers to hear the gospel who otherwise would never hear it.
>
> **CHARLES SPURGEON**

18 And Paul after this tarried there yet a good while, and then took his leave of the brethren, and sailed thence into Syria, and with him Priscilla and Aquila; having shorn his head in Cenchrea: for he had a vow.
19 And he came to Ephesus, and left them there: but he himself entered into the synagogue, and reasoned with the Jews.
20 When they desired him to tarry longer time with them, he consented not;
21 But bade them farewell, saying, I must by all means keep this feast that comes in Jerusalem: but I will return again to you, if God will. And he sailed from Ephesus.
22 And when he had landed at Caesarea, and gone up, and saluted the church, he went down to Antioch.
23 And after he had spent some time there, he departed, and went over all the country of Galatia and Phrygia in order, strengthening all the disciples.
24 And a certain Jew named Apollos, born at Alexandria, an eloquent man, and mighty in the scriptures, came to Ephesus.
25 This man was instructed in the way of the Lord; and being fervent in the spirit, he spoke and taught diligently the things of the Lord, knowing only the baptism of John.
26 And he began to speak boldly in the synagogue: whom when Aquila and Priscilla had heard, they took him to them, and expounded to him the way of God more perfectly.
27 And when he was disposed to pass into Achaia, the brethren wrote, exhorting the disciples to receive him: who, when he was come, helped them much which had believed through grace:
28 For he mightily convinced the Jews, and that publicly, showing by the scriptures that Jesus was Christ.

CHAPTER 19

AND it came to pass, that, while Apollos was at Corinth, Paul having passed through the upper coasts came to Ephesus: and finding certain disciples,
2 He said to them, Have you received the Holy Spirit since you believed? And they said to him, We have not so much as heard whether there be any Holy Spirit.
3 And he said to them, to what then were you baptized? And they said, to John's

18:19 "The proper goal in apologetics is not to force someone to admit that we have proved our position, but simply to remove objections so that a nonbeliever cannot hide behind intellectual objections." *John S. Hammett*

18:26 "It is better to be divided by truth than united in error; it is better to speak truth that hurts and then heals than to speak a lie; it is better to be hated for telling the truth than to be loved for telling a lie; it is better to stand alone with truth than to be wrong with the multitude…The religion of today is 'get-along-ism.' It is time for men and women of God to stand, [even] if they have to stand alone." *Adrian Rogers*

I Have a Problem

"FATHER, I HAVE a problem. It's weighing heavy on me. It's all I can think about, night and day. Before I bring it to you in prayer, I suppose I should pray for those who are less fortunate than me—those in this world who have hardly enough food for this day, and for those who don't have a roof over their heads at night. I also pray for families who have lost loved ones in sudden death, for parents whose children have leukemia, for the many people who are dying of brain tumors, for the hundreds of thousands who are laid waste with other terrible cancers, for people whose bodies have been suddenly shattered in car wrecks, for those who are lying in hospitals with agonizing burns over their bodies, whose faces have been burned beyond recognition. I pray for people with emphysema, whose eyes fill with terror as they struggle for every breath merely to live, for those who are tormented beyond words by irrational fears, for the elderly who are wracked with the pains of aging, whose only 'escape' is death.

"I pray for people who are watching their loved ones fade before their eyes through the grief of Alzheimer's disease, for the many thousands who are suffering the agony of AIDS, for those who are in such despair that they are contemplating suicide, for people who are tormented by the demons of alcoholism and drug addiction. I pray for children who have been abandoned by their parents, for those who are sexually abused, for wives held in quiet despair, beaten and abused by cruel drunken husbands, for people whose minds have been destroyed by mental disorders, for those who have lost everything in floods, tornadoes, hurricanes, and earthquakes. I pray for the blind, who never see the faces of the ones they love or the beauty of a sunrise, for those whose bodies are deformed by painful arthritis, for the many whose lives will be taken from them today by murderers, for those wasting away on their deathbeds in hospitals.

"Most of all, I cry out for the millions who don't know the forgiveness that is in Jesus Christ...for those who in a moment of time will be swept into hell by the cold hand of death, and find to their utter horror the unspeakable vengeance of eternal fire. They will be eternally damned to everlasting punishment. O God, I pray for them.

"Strange. I can't seem to remember what my problem was. In Jesus' name I pray. Amen."

baptism.
4 Then said Paul, John verily baptized
with the baptism of repentance, saying to
the people, that they should believe on
him which should come after him, that is,
on Christ Jesus.
5 When they heard this, they were baptized in the name of the Lord Jesus.
6 And when Paul had laid his hands upon them, the Holy Spirit came on them;
and they spoke with tongues, and prophesied.
7 And all the men were about twelve.
8 And he went into the synagogue, and
spoke boldly for the space of three months,
disputing and persuading the things concerning the kingdom of God.
9 But when divers were hardened, and
believed not, but spoke evil of that way
before the multitude, he departed from
them, and separated the disciples, disputing daily in the school of one Tyrannus.
10 And this continued by the space of
two years; so that all they which dwelt in
Asia heard the word of the Lord Jesus,
both Jews and Greeks.
11 And God wrought special miracles by
the hands of Paul:
12 So that from his body were brought
to the sick handkerchiefs or aprons, and
the diseases departed from them, and the
evil spirits went out of them.
13 Then certain of the vagabond Jews,
exorcists, took upon them to call over
them which had evil spirits the name of
the Lord Jesus, saying, We adjure you by
Jesus whom Paul preaches.
14 And there were seven sons of one Sce-
va, a Jew, and chief of the priests, which
did so.
15 And the evil spirit answered and said,
Jesus I know, and Paul I know; but who
are you?
16 And the man in whom the evil spirit
was leaped on them, and overcame them,
and prevailed against them, so that they
fled out of that house naked and wounded.
17 And this was known to all the Jews
and Greeks also dwelling at Ephesus; and
fear fell on them all, and the name of the
Lord Jesus was magnified.
18 And many that believed came, and
confessed, and showed their deeds.
19 Many of them also which used curi-
ous arts brought their books together, and
burned them before all men: and they
counted the price of them, and found it
fifty thousand pieces of silver.
20 So mightily grew the word of God
and prevailed.

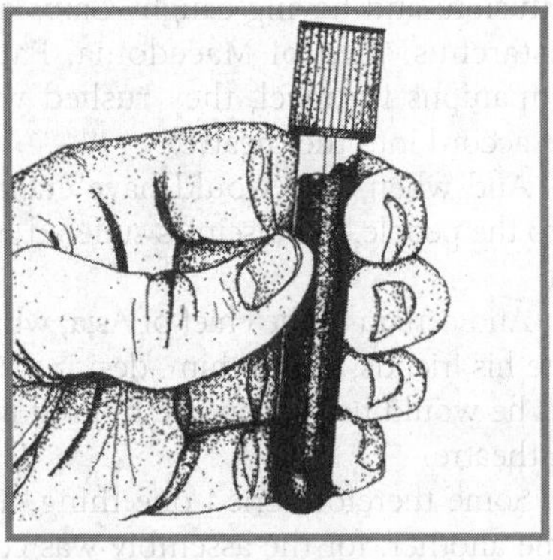

The platelets in blood reveal the folly of evolution. See Matthew 9:20 comment.

21 After these things were ended, Paul
purposed in the spirit, when he had
passed through Macedonia and Achaia,
to go to Jerusalem, saying, After I have
been there, I must also see Rome.
22 So he sent into Macedonia two of
them that ministered to him, Timotheus
and Erastus; but he himself stayed in Asia
for a season.
23 And the same time there arose no
small stir about that way.
24 For a certain man named Demetrius,
a silversmith, which made silver shrines
for Diana, brought no small gain to the
craftsmen;
25 Whom he called together with the
workmen of like occupation, and said,
Sirs, you know that by this craft we have
our wealth.
26 Moreover you see and hear, that not
alone at Ephesus, but almost throughout
all Asia, this Paul has persuaded and

turned away much people, saying that they
be no gods, which are made with hands:
27 So that not only this our craft is in
danger to be set at nought; but also that
the temple of the great goddess Diana
should be despised, and her magnificence
should be destroyed, whom all Asia and
the world worships.
28 And when they heard these sayings,
they were full of wrath, and cried out, saying, Great is Diana of the Ephesians.
29 And the whole city was filled with
confusion: and having caught Gaius and
Aristarchus, men of Macedonia, Paul's
companions in travel, they rushed with
one accord into the theatre.
30 And when Paul would have entered
in to the people, the disciples suffered him
not.
31 And certain of the chief of Asia, which
were his friends, sent to him, desiring him
that he would not adventure himself into
the theatre.
32 Some therefore cried one thing, and
some another: for the assembly was confused; and the more part knew not wherefore they were come together.
33 And they drew Alexander out of the
multitude, the Jews putting him forward.
And Alexander beckoned with the hand,
and would have made his defence to the
people.
34 But when they knew that he was a
Jew, all with one voice about the space of
two hours cried out, Great is Diana of the
Ephesians.
35 And when the town clerk had ap-
peased the people, he said, You men of
Ephesus, what man is there that knows
not how that the city of the Ephesians is
a worshipper of the great goddess Diana,
and of the image which fell down from
Jupiter?
36 Seeing then that these things cannot
be spoken against, you ought to be quiet,
and to do nothing rashly.
37 For you have brought here these men,
which are neither robbers of churches, nor
yet blasphemers of your goddess.
38 Wherefore if Demetrius, and the craftsmen which are with him, have a matter
against any man, the law is open, and
there are deputies: let them implead one
another.
39 But if you inquire any thing concerning other matters, it shall be determined
in a lawful assembly.
40 For we are in danger to be called in
question for this day's uproar, there being
no cause whereby we may give an account of this concourse.
41 And when he had thus spoken, he
dismissed the assembly.

· · · · · ·

For the key to reaching the lost, see Luke 11:32 comment.

· · · · · ·

CHAPTER 20

AND after the uproar was ceased, Paul
called to him the disciples, and embraced them, and departed for to go into
Macedonia.
2 And when he had gone over those
parts, and had given them much exhortation, he came into Greece,
3 And there abode three months. And
when the Jews laid wait for him, as he was
about to sail into Syria, he purposed to return through Macedonia.
4 And there accompanied him into Asia
Sopater of Berea; and of the Thessalonians, Aristarchus and Secundus; and Gaius
of Derbe, and Timotheus; and of Asia,
Tychicus and Trophimus.
5 These going before tarried for us at
Troas.
6 And we sailed away from Philippi after
the days of unleavened bread, and came
to them to Troas in five days; where we
abode seven days.
7 And upon the first day of the week,
when the disciples came together to break
bread, Paul preached to them, ready to depart on the morrow; and continued his
speech until midnight.
8 And there were many lights in the upper chamber, where they were gathered

together.
9 And there sat in a window a certain
young man named Eutychus, being fall-
en into a deep sleep: and as Paul was long
preaching, he sunk down with sleep, and
fell down from the third loft, and was
taken up dead.
10 And Paul went down, and fell on him,
and embracing him said, Trouble not
yourselves; for his life is in him.
11 When he therefore was come up
again, and had broken bread, and eaten,
and talked a long while, even till break
of day, so he departed.
12 And they brought the young man
alive, and were not a little comforted.

> That sin must die, or you will perish by it. Depend on it, that sin which you would save from the slaughter will slaughter you.
>
> CHARLES SPURGEON

13 And we went before to ship, and
sailed to Assos, there intending to take in
Paul: for so had he appointed, minding
himself to go afoot.
14 And when he met with us at Assos,
we took him in, and came to Mitylene.
15 And we sailed thence, and came the
next day over against Chios; and the next
day we arrived at Samos, and tarried at
Trogyllium; and the next day we came to
Miletus.
16 For Paul had determined to sail by
Ephesus, because he would not spend
the time in Asia: for he hasted, if it were
possible for him, to be at Jerusalem the
day of Pentecost.
17 And from Miletus he sent to Ephesus, and called the elders of the church.
18 And when they were come to him,
he said to them, You know, from the first
day that I came into Asia, after what manner I have been with you at all seasons,
19 Serving the Lord with all humility of
mind, and with many tears, and temptations, which befell me by the lying in
wait of the Jews:
20 **And how I kept back nothing that
was profitable to you, but have showed
you, and have taught you publicly, and
from house to house,**
**21 Testifying both to the Jews, and also
to the Greeks, repentance toward God,
and faith toward our Lord Jesus Christ.**
22 And now, behold, I go bound in the
spirit to Jerusalem, not knowing the things
that shall befall me there:
23 Save that the Holy Spirit witnesses in
every city, saying that bonds and afflictions abide me.
24 *But none of these things move me, neither count I my life dear to myself, so that I
might finish my course with joy, and the
ministry, which I have received of the Lord
Jesus, to testify the gospel of the grace of
God.*
25 And now, behold, I know that you
all, among whom I have gone preaching

20:9 Eutychus had some good excuses for dozing off:

- Paul's sermon was long.
- The many lights no doubt made the room hot.
- He was a young man staying up until midnight.
- He was "overcome" by sleep.

It is the midnight hour. We sit on the window of eternity. We can fall into eternity in a heartbeat. If the stale air of this world's influence makes us sink into a sleep of apathy, we must seek refreshing from the presence of the Lord. When our Christian life seems to be a dry and lifeless sermon without end, and the joy of feeding on God's Word is no longer in our hearts, we must get on our knees and return to our first love.

20:21 Repentance—its necessity for salvation. See 2 Peter 3:9.

POINTS FOR OPEN-AIR PREACHING

20:21

Aim for Repentance Rather Than a Decision

As you witness, divorce yourself from the thought that you are merely seeking "decisions for Christ." What we should be seeking is repentance within the heart. This is the purpose of the Law, to bring the knowledge of sin. How can a man repent if he doesn't know what sin is? If there is no repentance, there is no salvation. Jesus said, "Unless you repent, you shall all likewise perish" (Luke 13:3). God is not willing that any should perish, but that all should come to repentance (2 Peter 3:9).

Many don't understand that the salvation of a soul is not a resolution to change a way of life, but "repentance toward God, and faith toward our Lord Jesus Christ." The modern concept of success in evangelism is to relate how many people were "saved" (that is, how many prayed the "sinner's prayer"). This produces a "no decisions, no success" mentality. This shouldn't be, because Christians who seek decisions in evangelism become discouraged after a time of witnessing if "no one came to the Lord." The Bible tells us that as we sow the good seed of the gospel, one sows and another reaps. If you faithfully sow the seed, someone will reap. If you reap, it is because someone has sown in the past, but it is God who causes the seed to grow. If His hand is not on the person you are leading in a prayer of committal, if there is not *God-given* repentance, then you will end up with a stillbirth on your hands, and that is nothing to rejoice about. We should measure our success by how faithfully we sowed the seed. In that way, we will avoid becoming discouraged.

"If you have not repented, you will not see the inside of the kingdom of God." *Billy Graham*

the kingdom of God, shall see my face no more.
26 *Wherefore I take you to record this day, that I am pure from the blood of all men.*
27 *For I have not shunned to declare to you all the counsel of God.*
28 Take heed therefore to yourselves, and to all the flock, over the which the Holy Spirit has made you overseers, to feed the church of God, which he has purchased with his own blood.
29 For I know this, that after my departing shall grievous wolves enter in among you, not sparing the flock.
30 Also of your own selves shall men arise, speaking perverse things, to draw away disciples after them.
31 Therefore watch, and remember, that by the space of three years I ceased not to warn every one night and day with tears.
32 And now, brethren, I commend you to God, and to the word of his grace, which is able to build you up, and to give you an inheritance among all them which are sanctified.
33 I have coveted no man's silver, or gold, or apparel.
34 Yes, you yourselves know, that these hands have ministered to my necessities, and to them that were with me.
35 I have showed you all things, how that so laboring you ought to support the weak, and to remember the words of the Lord Jesus, how he said, It is more blessed to give than to receive.
36 And when he had thus spoken, he

20:24 A missionary society wrote to *David Livingstone* and suggested that if he could ensure them of safe roads, they would send him some help. He responded with the following note: "If you have men who will only come if they have a good road, I don't want them. I want men who will come if there is no road at all."

20:26 "My anxious desire in that every time I preach, I may clear myself of blood of all men; that if I step from this platform to my coffin, I may have told out all I knew of the way of salvation." *Charles Spurgeon*

kneeled down, and prayed with them all.
37 And they all wept sore, and fell on
Paul's neck, and kissed him,
38 Sorrowing most of all for the words
which he spoke, that they should see his
face no more. And they accompanied him
to the ship.

CHAPTER 21

AND it came to pass, that after we were
gotten from them, and had launched,
we came with a straight course to Coos,
and the day following to Rhodes, and from
thence to Patara:
2 And finding a ship sailing over to Phe-
nicia, we went aboard, and set forth.
3 Now when we had discovered Cyprus,
we left it on the left hand, and sailed into
Syria, and landed at Tyre: for there the
ship was to unload her burden.
4 And finding disciples, we tarried there
seven days: who said to Paul through the
Spirit, that he should not go up to Jerusalem.
5 And when we had accomplished those
days, we departed and went our way;
and they all brought us on our way, with
wives and children, till we were out of the
city: and we kneeled down on the shore,
and prayed.
6 And when we had taken our leave one
of another, we took ship; and they returned home again.
7 And when we had finished our course
from Tyre, we came to Ptolemais, and saluted the brethren, and abode with them
one day.
8 And the next day we that were of Paul's
company departed, and came to Caesarea:
and we entered into the house of Philip
the evangelist, which was one of the sev-
en; and abode with him.
9 And the same man had four daughters, virgins, which did prophesy.
10 And as we tarried there many days,
there came down from Judea a certain
prophet, named Agabus.
11 And when he was come to us, he
took Paul's girdle, and bound his own
hands and feet, and said, Thus says the
Holy Spirit, So shall the Jews at Jerusalem
bind the man that owns this girdle, and
shall deliver him into the hands of the
Gentiles.
12 And when we heard these things, both
we, and they of that place, besought him
not to go up to Jerusalem.
13 *Then Paul answered, Why do you weep
and break my heart? for I am ready not to
be bound only, but also to die at Jerusalem
for the name of the Lord Jesus.*
14 And when he would not be persuaded, we ceased, saying, The will of the Lord
be done.
15 And after those days we took up our
carriages, and went up to Jerusalem.
16 There went with us also certain of the
disciples of Caesarea, and brought with

20:27 How to witness. Here is a suggested structure of a gospel message:

Begin in the natural realm if you are not in a normal church setting. Perhaps you could springboard off some well-publicized tragedy, then ask if your hearers ever wonder how they are going to die. Say that we will all die because we have broken an eternal law—the Law of God, often referred to as the Ten Commandments. Then open up each Commandment, emphasizing its spiritual nature (lust is seen by God as adultery, hatred is murder—that God sees man's thoughts, and nothing is hidden from His eyes).

Stress the fact of Judgment Day—that God is holy and will bring every work into judgment, including every secret thing whether it is good or evil. Don't be afraid to use the word "hell." Tell them that it is God's place of punishment for sin. Emphasize that He doesn't want them to go there, that He has made provision for their forgiveness. Then preach Christ and Him crucified, risen from the dead. Thoroughly lace the message with God's Word—verbally quote relevant Scriptures. Then preach the necessity of repentance (that it's *commanded*), and the importance of faith in and obedience *to* God's Word. See Acts 20:21 comment.

21:5 Prayer—the secret weapon: See Mark 11:23.

Points for Open-air Preaching

21:30

Raw Nerves

When you're preaching open-air, don't let angry reactions from the crowd concern you. A dentist knows where to work on a patient when he touches a raw nerve. When you touch a raw nerve in the heart of the sinner, it means that you are in business. Anger is a thousand times better than apathy. Anger is a sign of conviction. If I have an argument with my wife and suddenly realize that I am in the wrong, I can come to her in a repentant attitude and apologize, or I can save face by lashing out in anger.

Read Acts 19 and see how Paul was a dentist with an eye for decay. He probed raw nerves wherever he went. At one point, he had to be carried shoulder height by soldiers because of the "violence of the people" (Acts 21:36). Now there's a successful preacher! He didn't seek the praise of men. John Wesley told his evangelist trainees that when they preached, people should either get angry or get converted. No doubt, he wasn't speaking about the "Jesus loves you" gospel, but about sin, Law, righteousness, judgment, and hell. See Matthew 28:19,20 comment.

them one Mnason of Cyprus, an old disciple, with whom we should lodge.
17 And when we were come to Jerusalem, the brethren received us gladly.
18 And the day following Paul went in with us to James; and all the elders were present.
19 And when he had saluted them, he declared particularly what things God had wrought among the Gentiles by his ministry.
20 And when they heard it, they glorified the Lord, and said to him, You see, brother, how many thousands of Jews there are which believe; and they are all zealous of the law:
21 And they are informed of you, that you teach all the Jews which are among the Gentiles to forsake Moses, saying that they ought not to circumcise their children, neither to walk after the customs.
22 What is it therefore? the multitude must needs come together: for they will hear that you are come.
23 Do therefore this that we say to you: We have four men which have a vow on them;
24 Them take, and purify yourself with them, and be at charges with them, that they may shave their heads: and all may know that those things, whereof they were informed concerning you, are nothing; but that you yourself also walk orderly, and keep the law.
25 As touching the Gentiles which believe, we have written and concluded that they observe no such thing, save only that they keep themselves from things offered to idols, and from blood, and from strangled, and from fornication.
26 Then Paul took the men, and the next day purifying himself with them entered into the temple, to signify the accomplishment of the days of purification, until that an offering should be offered for every one of them.
27 And when the seven days were almost ended, the Jews which were of Asia, when they saw him in the temple, stirred up all the people, and laid hands on him,
28 Crying out, Men of Israel, help: This is the man, that teaches all men every where against the people, and the law, and this place: and further brought Greeks also into the temple, and has polluted this holy place.
29 (For they had seen before with him in the city Trophimus an Ephesian, whom they supposed that Paul had brought into the temple.)
30 And all the city was moved, and the people ran together: and they took Paul, and drew him out of the temple: and forthwith the doors were shut.
31 And as they went about to kill him, tidings came to the chief captain of the

band, that all Jerusalem was in an uproar.
32 Who immediately took soldiers and centurions, and ran down to them: and when they saw the chief captain and the soldiers, they left beating of Paul.
33 Then the chief captain came near, and took him, and commanded him to be bound with two chains; and demanded who he was, and what he had done.
34 And some cried one thing, some another, among the multitude: and when he could not know the certainty for the tumult, he commanded him to be carried into the castle.
35 And when he came upon the stairs, so it was, that he was borne of the soldiers for the violence of the people.
36 For the multitude of the people followed after, crying, Away with him.
37 And as Paul was to be led into the castle, he said to the chief captain, May I speak to you? Who said, Can you speak Greek?
38 Are you not that Egyptian, which before these days made an uproar, and lead out into the wilderness four thousand men that were murderers?
39 But Paul said, I am a man which am a Jew of Tarsus, a city in Cilicia, a citizen of no mean city: and, I beseech you, suffer me to speak to the people.
40 And when he had given him license, Paul stood on the stairs, and beckoned with the hand to the people. And when there was made a great silence, he spoke to them in the Hebrew tongue, saying,

CHAPTER 22

MEN, brethren, and fathers, hear my defence which I make now to you.
2 (And when they heard that he spoke in the Hebrew tongue to them, they kept the more silence: and he said,)
3 I am verily a man which am a Jew, born in Tarsus, a city in Cilicia, yet brought up in this city at the feet of Gamaliel, and taught according to the perfect manner of the law of the fathers, and was zealous toward God, as you all are this day.
4 And I persecuted this way to the death, binding and delivering into prisons both men and women.
5 As also the high priest does bear me witness, and all the estate of the elders: from whom also I received letters to the brethren, and went to Damascus, to bring them which were there bound to Jerusalem, for to be punished.

> "The greatest enemy to human souls is the self-righteous spirit which makes men look to themselves for salvation."
>
> **CHARLES SPURGEON**

6 And it came to pass, that, as I made my journey, and was come near to Damascus about noon, suddenly there shone from heaven a great light round about me.
7 And I fell to the ground, and heard a voice saying to me, Saul, Saul, why do you persecute me?
8 And I answered, Who are you, Lord? And he said to me, I am Jesus of Nazareth, whom you persecute.
9 And they that were with me saw indeed the light, and were afraid; but they heard not the voice of him that spoke to me.
10 And I said, What shall I do, Lord? And the Lord said to me, Arise, and go into Damascus; and there it shall be told you of all things which are appointed for you to do.
11 And when I could not see for the glory

22:9 Contradiction in the Bible? Some may think that this is a mistake in the Scriptures, because in Acts 9:7 Paul said that those who were with him *heard* the voice. However, John 12:29 gives us insight into what God's voice sounds like. People *heard* His voice but thought that it thundered (see also 2 Samuel 22:14; Job 37:4,5; 40:9). They obviously heard it but the words were not coherent to them.

"Labor to keep alive in your breast that spark of celestial fire called conscience."

George Washington

of that light, being led by the hand of
them that were with me, I came into Damascus.
12 And one Ananias, a devout man according to the law, having a good report
of all the Jews which dwelt there,
13 Came to me, and stood, and said to
me, Brother Saul, receive your sight. And
the same hour I looked up upon him.
14 And he said, The God of our fathers
has chosen you, that you should know his
will, and see that Just One, and should
hear the voice of his mouth.
15 For you shall be his witness to all
men of what you have seen and heard.
16 And now why do you tarry? arise, and
be baptized, and wash away your sins,
calling on the name of the Lord.
17 And it came to pass, that, when I was
come again to Jerusalem, even while I
prayed in the temple, I was in a trance;
18 And saw him saying to me, Make
haste, and get quickly out of Jerusalem:
for they will not receive your testimony
concerning me.
19 And I said, Lord, they know that I
imprisoned and beat in every synagogue
them that believed on you:
20 And when the blood of your martyr
Stephen was shed, I also was standing
by, and consenting to his death, and
kept the raiment of them that slew him.
21 And he said to me, Depart: for I will
send you far hence to the Gentiles.
22 And they gave him audience to this
word, and then lifted up their voices,
and said, Away with such a fellow from
the earth: for it is not fit that he should
live.
23 And as they cried out, and cast off
their clothes, and threw dust into the air,
24 The chief captain commanded him
to be brought into the castle, and bade
that he should be examined by scourging; that he might know wherefore they
cried so against him.
25 And as they bound him with thongs,
Paul said to the centurion that stood by,
Is it lawful for you to scourge a man that
is a Roman, and uncondemned?
26 When the centurion heard that, he
went and told the chief captain, saying,
Take heed what you do: for this man is a
Roman.
27 Then the chief captain came, and said
to him, Tell me, are you a Roman? He
said, Yes.
28 And the chief captain answered, With
a great sum obtained I this freedom. And
Paul said, But I was free born.
29 Then straightway they departed from
him which should have examined him:
and the chief captain also was afraid, after
he knew that he was a Roman, and because he had bound him.
30 On the morrow, because he would
have known the certainty wherefore he
was accused of the Jews, he loosed him
from his bands, and commanded the chief
priests and all their council to appear,
and brought Paul down, and set him before them.

CHAPTER 23

AND Paul, earnestly beholding the
council, said, Men and brethren, I
have lived in all good conscience before
God until this day.

2 And the high priest Ananias commanded them that stood by him to smite him on the mouth.
3 Then said Paul to him, God shall smite you, you whited wall: for you sit to judge me after the law, and command me to be smitten contrary to the law?
4 And they that stood by said, Do you revile God's high priest?
5 Then said Paul, I knew not, brethren, that he was the high priest: for it is written, You shall not speak evil of the ruler of your people.
6 But when Paul perceived that the one part were Sadducees, and the other Pharisees, he cried out in the council, Men and brethren, I am a Pharisee, the son of a Pharisee: of the hope and resurrection of the dead I am called in question.
7 And when he had so said, there arose a dissension between the Pharisees and the Sadducees: and the multitude was divided.
8 For the Sadducees say that there is no resurrection, neither angel, nor spirit: but the Pharisees confess both.
9 And there arose a great cry: and the scribes that were of the Pharisees' part arose, and strove, saying, We find no evil in this man: but if a spirit or an angel has spoken to him, let us not fight against God.
10 And when there arose a great dissension, the chief captain, fearing lest Paul should have been pulled in pieces of them, commanded the soldiers to go down, and to take him by force from among them, and to bring him into the castle.
11 And the night following the Lord stood by him, and said, Be of good cheer, Paul: for as you have testified of me in Jerusalem, so must you bear witness also at Rome.
12 And when it was day, certain of the Jews banded together, and bound themselves under a curse, saying that they would neither eat nor drink till they had killed Paul.
13 And they were more than forty which had made this conspiracy.
14 And they came to the chief priests and elders, and said, We have bound ourselves under a great curse, that we will eat nothing until we have slain Paul.
15 Now therefore you with the council signify to the chief captain that he bring him down to you tomorrow, as though you would inquire something more perfectly concerning him: and we, or ever he come near, are ready to kill him.
16 And when Paul's sister's son heard of their lying in wait, he went and entered into the castle, and told Paul.

> I have known what it is to use up all my ammunition, and then I have, as it were, rammed myself into the great gospel gun and fired myself at the hearers—all my experience of God's goodness, all my consciousness of sin, and all my sense of the power of the gospel.
>
> **CHARLES SPURGEON**

17 Then Paul called one of the centurions to him, and said, Bring this young man to the chief captain: for he has a certain thing to tell him.
18 So he took him, and brought him to the chief captain, and said, Paul the prisoner called me to him, and prayed me to bring this young man to you, who has something to say to you.
19 Then the chief captain took him by the hand, and went with him aside privately, and asked him, What is that you have to tell me?
20 And he said, The Jews have agreed to desire you that you would bring down Paul tomorrow into the council, as though they would inquire somewhat of him more perfectly.
21 But do not yield to them: for there lie in wait for him of them more than forty men, which have bound themselves with an oath, that they will neither eat nor drink till they have killed him: and now are they ready, looking for a promise from

you.
22 So the chief captain then let the young man depart, and charged him, See you tell no man that you have showed these things to me.
23 And he called to him two centurions, saying, Make ready two hundred soldiers to go to Caesarea, and horsemen threescore and ten, and spearmen two hundred, at the third hour of the night;
24 And provide them beasts, that they may set Paul on, and bring him safe to Felix the governor.
25 And he wrote a letter after this manner:
26 Claudius Lysias to the most excellent governor Felix sends greeting.
27 This man was taken of the Jews, and should have been killed of them: then came I with an army, and rescued him, having understood that he was a Roman.
28 And when I would have known the cause wherefore they accused him, I brought him forth into their council:
29 Whom I perceived to be accused of questions of their law, but to have nothing laid to his charge worthy of death or of bonds.
30 And when it was told me how that the Jews laid wait for the man, I sent straightway to you, and gave commandment to his accusers also to say before you what they had against him. Farewell.
31 Then the soldiers, as it was commanded them, took Paul, and brought him by night to Antipatris.
32 On the morrow they left the horsemen to go with him, and returned to the castle:
33 Who, when they came to Caesarea, and delivered the epistle to the governor, presented Paul also before him.
34 And when the governor had read the letter, he asked of what province he was. And when he understood that he was of Cilicia;
35 I will hear you, said he, when your accusers are also come. And he commanded him to be kept in Herod's judgment hall.

CHAPTER 24

AND after five days Ananias the high priest descended with the elders, and with a certain orator named Tertullus, who informed the governor against Paul.
2 And when he was called forth, Tertullus began to accuse him, saying, Seeing that by you we enjoy great quietness, and that very worthy deeds are done to this nation by your providence,
3 We accept it always, and in all places, most noble Felix, with all thankfulness.
4 Notwithstanding, that I be not further tedious to you, I pray you that you would hear us of your clemency a few words.
5 For we have found this man a pestilent fellow, and a mover of sedition among all the Jews throughout the world, and a ringleader of the sect of the Nazarenes:
6 Who also has gone about to profane the temple: whom we took, and would have judged according to our law.
7 But the chief captain Lysias came upon us, and with great violence took him away out of our hands,
8 Commanding his accusers to come to you: by examining of whom yourself may take knowledge of all these things, whereof we accuse him.
9 And the Jews also assented, saying that these things were so.
10 Then Paul, after that the governor had beckoned to him to speak, answered, Forasmuch as I know that you have been of many years a judge to this nation, I do the more cheerfully answer for myself:
11 Because that you may understand, that there are yet but twelve days since I went up to Jerusalem for to worship.

24:5 The apostle Paul was called a "pestilent fellow," a "mover of sedition," and a "ringleader" of a "sect." The prophet Elijah was called a "troubler of Israel" (1 Kings 18:17). Those who stand for righteousness will be considered troublemakers in the world's eyes.

QUESTIONS & OBJECTIONS

24:25 *"Is 'hell-fire' preaching effective?"*

Preaching the reality of hell, without using the Law to bring the knowledge of sin, can do a great deal of damage to the cause of the gospel. A sinner cannot conceive of the thought that God would send anyone to hell, as long as he is deceived into thinking that God's standard of righteousness is the same as his. Paul "reasoned" with Felix regarding righteousness, temperance, and judgment to come (Acts 24:25). This is the righteousness that is of the Law and judgment by the Law. Felix "trembled" because he suddenly understood that his intemperance made him a guilty sinner in the sight of a holy God. The reality of hell suddenly became *reasonable* to him when the Law was used to bring the knowledge of sin.

Imagine if the police burst into your home, arrested you, and shouted, "You are going away for a long time!" Such conduct would probably leave you bewildered and angry. What they have done seems unreasonable.

However, imagine if the law burst into your home and instead told you specifically why you were in trouble: "We have discovered 10,000 marijuana plants growing in your back yard. You are going away for a long time!" At least then you would understand *why* you are in trouble. Knowledge of the law you have transgressed furnished you with that understanding. It makes judgment *reasonable*. Hell-fire preaching without use of the Law to show the sinner why God is angry with him will more than likely leave him bewildered and angry—for what he considers *unreasonable* punishment.

12 And they neither found me in the temple disputing with any man, neither raising up the people, neither in the synagogues, nor in the city:

13 Neither can they prove the things whereof they now accuse me.

14 But this I confess to you, that after the way which they call heresy, so worship I the God of my fathers, believing all things which are written in the law and in the prophets:

15 And have hope toward God, which they themselves also allow, that there shall be a resurrection of the dead, both of the just and unjust.

16 And herein do I exercise myself, to have always a conscience void of offence toward God, and toward men.

17 Now after many years I came to bring alms to my nation, and offerings.

18 Whereupon certain Jews from Asia found me purified in the temple, neither with multitude, nor with tumult.

19 Who ought to have been here before you, and object, if they had anything against me.

20 Or else let these same here say, if they have found any evil doing in me, while I stood before the council,

21 Except it be for this one voice, that I cried standing among them, Touching the resurrection of the dead I am called in question by you this day.

22 And when Felix heard these things, having more perfect knowledge of that way, he deferred them, and said, When Lysias the chief captain shall come down, I will know the uttermost of your matter.

23 And he commanded a centurion to keep Paul, and to let him have liberty, and that he should forbid none of his acquaintance to minister or come to him.

24 And after certain days, when Felix came with his wife Drusilla, which was a Jewess, he sent for Paul, and heard him concerning the faith in Christ.

25 And as he reasoned of righteousness, temperance, and judgment to come Felix trembled, and answered, Go your way for this time; when I have a convenient season, I will call for you.

26 He hoped also that money should

have been given him of Paul, that he might
loose him: wherefore he sent for him the
oftener, and communed with him.
27 But after two years Porcius Festus
came into Felix' room: and Felix, willing to
show the Jews a pleasure, left Paul bound.

CHAPTER 25

NOW when Festus was come into the
province, after three days he ascended from Caesarea to Jerusalem.
2 Then the high priest and the chief of
the Jews informed him against Paul, and
besought him,
3 And desired favor against him, that he
would send for him to Jerusalem, laying
wait in the way to kill him.
4 But Festus answered, that Paul should
be kept at Caesarea, and that he himself
would depart shortly there.
5 Let them therefore, said he, which
among you are able, go down with me,
and accuse this man, if there be any wickedness in him.
6 And when he had tarried among them
more than ten days, he went down to Caesarea; and the next day sitting on the judgment seat commanded Paul to be brought.
7 And when he was come, the Jews
which came down from Jerusalem stood
round about, and laid many and grievous
complaints against Paul, which they could
not prove.
8 While he answered for himself, Neither against the law of the Jews, neither
against the temple, nor yet against Caesar, have I offended any thing at all.
9 But Festus, willing to do the Jews a
pleasure, answered Paul, and said, Will
you go up to Jerusalem, and there be
judged of these things before me?
10 Then said Paul, I stand at Caesar's
judgment seat, where I ought to be judged:
to the Jews have I done no wrong, as you
very well know.
11 For if I be an offender, or have committed any thing worthy of death, I refuse
not to die: but if there be none of these
things whereof these accuse me, no man
may deliver me to them. I appeal to Caesar.
12 Then Festus, when he had conferred
with the council, answered, have you appealed to Caesar? to Caesar shall you go.
13 And after certain days king Agrippa
and Bernice came to Caesarea to salute
Festus.
14 And when they had been there many
days, Festus declared Paul's cause to the
king, saying, There is a certain man left in
bonds by Felix:
15 About whom, when I was at Jerusalem, the chief priests and the elders of the
Jews informed me, desiring to have judgment against him.
16 To whom I answered, It is not the
manner of the Romans to deliver any man
to die, before that he which is accused
have the accusers face to face, and have
license to answer for himself concerning
the crime laid against him.
17 Therefore, when they were come here,
without any delay on the morrow I sat on
the judgment seat, and commanded the
man to be brought forth.
18 Against whom when the accusers
stood up, they brought none accusation
of such things as I supposed:
19 But had certain questions against him
of their own superstition, and of one Jesus,
which was dead, whom Paul affirmed to
be alive.
20 And because I doubted of such manner of questions, I asked him whether he
would go to Jerusalem, and there be
judged of these matters.
21 But when Paul had appealed to be reserved to the hearing of Augustus, I commanded him to be kept till I might send
him to Caesar.
22 Then Agrippa said to Festus, I would

24:25 "What we think about God influences our friendship with him . . . The Bible is our only safe source of knowledge about God—and it requires thinking. God's persistent invitation in every age remains: '"Come now, let us *reason* together," says the Lord' (Isaiah 1:18)." *Joni Eareckson Tada*

also hear the man myself. Tomorrow, said
he, you shall hear him.
23 And on the morrow, when Agrippa
was come, and Bernice, with great pomp,
and was entered into the place of hearing,
with the chief captains, and principal men
of the city, at Festus' commandment Paul
was brought forth.
24 And Festus said, King Agrippa, and
all men which are here present with us,
you see this man, about whom all the
multitude of the Jews have dealt with me,
both at Jerusalem, and also here, crying
that he ought not to live any longer.
25 But when I found that he had committed nothing worthy of death, and that
he himself has appealed to Augustus, I
have determined to send him.
26 Of whom I have no certain thing to
write to my lord. Wherefore I have brought
him forth before you, and specially before you, O king Agrippa, that, after examination had, I might have somewhat
to write.
27 For it seems to me unreasonable to
send a prisoner, and not withal to signify
the crimes laid against him.

CHAPTER 26

THEN Agrippa said to Paul, You are permitted to speak for yourself. Then Paul stretched forth the hand, and answered for himself:
2 I think myself happy, king Agrippa, because I shall answer for myself this day
before you touching all the things whereof I am accused of the Jews:
3 Especially because I know you to be
expert in all customs and questions which
are among the Jews: wherefore I beseech
you to hear me patiently.
4 My manner of life from my youth,
which was at the first among mine own
nation at Jerusalem, know all the Jews;
5 Which knew me from the beginning,
if they would testify, that after the most
strait sect of our religion I lived a Pharisee.
6 And now I stand and am judged for
the hope of the promise made of God to
our fathers:
7 To which promise our twelve tribes, instantly serving God day and night, hope to
come. For which hope's sake, king Agrippa, I am accused of the Jews.
8 Why should it be thought a thing incredible with you, that God should raise
the dead?
9 I verily thought with myself, that I
ought to do many things contrary to the
name of Jesus of Nazareth.
10 Which thing I also did in Jerusalem:
and many of the saints did I shut up in
prison, having received authority from the
chief priests; and when they were put to
death, I gave my voice against them.
11 And I punished them oft in every
synagogue, and compelled them to blaspheme; and being exceedingly mad against
them, I persecuted them even to strange
cities.

> The early disciples were fishers of men —while modern disciples are often little more than aquarium keepers.
>
> **UNKNOWN**

12 Whereupon as I went to Damascus
with authority and commission from the
chief priests,
13 At midday, O king, I saw in the way
a light from heaven, above the brightness
of the sun, shining round about me and
them which journeyed with me.
14 And when we were all fallen to the
earth, I heard a voice speaking to me, and
saying in the Hebrew tongue, Saul, Saul,
why do you persecute me? it is hard for
you to kick against the pricks.
15 And I said, Who are you, Lord? And
he said, I am Jesus whom you persecute.
16 But rise, and stand upon your feet:
for I have appeared to you for this purpose, to make you a minister and a witness both of these things which you have
seen, and of those things in the which I
will appear to you;
17 *Delivering you from the people, and
from the Gentiles, to whom now I send you,*
18 *To open their eyes, and to turn them*

from darkness to light, and from the power
of Satan to God, that they may receive for-
giveness of sins, and inheritance among them
which are sanctified by faith that is in me.
19 Whereupon, O king Agrippa, I was
not disobedient to the heavenly vision:
20 But showed first to them of Damascus, and at Jerusalem, and throughout
all the coasts of Judea, and then to the
Gentiles, that they should repent and turn
to God, and do works meet for repentance.
21 For these causes the Jews caught me
in the temple, and went about to kill me.
22 Having therefore obtained help of
God, I continue to this day, witnessing
both to small and great, saying none other
things than those which the prophets and
Moses did say should come:
23 That Christ should suffer, and that
he should be the first that should rise from
the dead, and should show light to the
people, and to the Gentiles.
24 And as he thus spoke for himself,
Festus said with a loud voice, Paul, you
are beside yourself; much learning does
make you mad.
25 But he said, I am not mad, most noble
Festus; but speak forth the words of truth
and soberness.
26 For the king knows of these things,
before whom also I speak freely: for I am
persuaded that none of these things are
hidden from him; for this thing was not
done in a corner.
27 **King Agrippa, do you believe the**
prophets? I know that you believe.
28 Then Agrippa said to Paul, You al-
most persuade me to be a Christian.
29 **And Paul said, I would to God, that**
not only you, but also all that hear me
this day, were both almost, and alto-
gether such as I am, except these bonds.
30 And when he had thus spoken, the
king rose up, and the governor, and Bernice, and they that sat with them:
31 And when they were gone aside, they
talked between themselves, saying, This
man does nothing worthy of death or of
bonds.
32 Then said Agrippa to Festus, This man
might have been set at liberty, if he had
not appealed to Caesar.

CHAPTER 27

AND when it was determined that we
should sail into Italy, they delivered
Paul and certain other prisoners to one
named Julius, a centurion of Augustus'
band.
2 And entering into a ship of Adramytti-
um, we launched, meaning to sail by the
coasts of Asia; one Aristarchus, a Mace-
donian of Thessalonica, being with us.
3 And the next day we touched at Sidon.
And Julius courteously entreated Paul,
and gave him liberty to go to his friends
to refresh himself.
4 And when we had launched from
thence, we sailed under Cyprus, because
the winds were contrary.
5 And when we had sailed over the sea of

26:20 The problem with modern evangelism. Many Christian obtain "decisions" by using the following method: "Do you know that you are going to heaven when you die?" Most will say, "I *hope* so." The Christian then says, "You can *know* so. The Bible says 'All have sinned.' Jesus died on the cross for our sins, and if you give your heart to Him today, you can know for sure that you are going to heaven. Would you like to have that assurance that you will go to heaven when you die?" He will almost always say, "Yes." The person is then led in what is commonly called a "sinner's prayer."

There are a few difficulties with the popular approach: 1) There is no mention of Judgment Day—the very *reason* men are commanded to repent; 2) There is no mention of hell; and 3) The Law isn't used to bring the knowledge of sin. The apostle Paul said that the Law was the *only* means by which he came to know what sin was (Romans 7:7). The modern approach may get a decision or gain a church member, but if there is no biblical repentance, there will be a false conversion. See John 4:7–26 comment.

QUESTIONS & OBJECTIONS

26:28

"What should I say to someone who acknowledges his sins, but says, 'I just hope God is forgiving'?"

These people could be referred to as "awakened, but not alarmed." Explain that God *is* forgiving—but only to those who repent of their sins. Ask him, "If you died right now, where would you go?" If he says, "Hell," ask if that concerns him. If it does concern him, ask, "What are you going to do?" Then tell him that God *commands* him to repent and trust the Savior. If it doesn't concern him, speak of the value of his life, the threat of *eternal* damnation, and the biblical description of hell. Caution him that he doesn't have the promise of tomorrow, and plead with him to come to his senses.

Cilicia and Pamphylia, we came to Myra, a city of Lycia.
6 And there the centurion found a ship of Alexandria sailing into Italy; and he put us therein.
7 And when we had sailed slowly many days, and scarce were come over against Cnidus, the wind not suffering us, we sailed under Crete, over against Salmone;
8 And, hardly passing it, came to a place which is called The fair havens; near whereunto was the city of Lasea.
9 Now when much time was spent, and when sailing was now dangerous, because the fast was now already past, Paul admonished them,
10 And said to them, Sirs, I perceive that this voyage will be with hurt and much damage, not only of the lading and ship, but also of our lives.
11 Nevertheless the centurion believed the master and the owner of the ship, more than those things which were spoken by Paul.
12 And because the haven was not commodious to winter in, the more part advised to depart thence also, if by any means they might attain to Phenice, and there to winter; which is an haven of Crete, and lies toward the south west and north west.
13 And when the south wind blew softly, supposing that they had obtained their purpose, loosing thence, they sailed close by Crete.
14 But not long after there arose against it a tempestuous wind, called Euroclydon.
15 And when the ship was caught, and could not bear up into the wind, we let her drive.
16 And running under a certain island which is called Clauda, we had much work to come by the boat:
17 Which when they had taken up, they used helps, undergirding the ship; and, fearing lest they should fall into the quicksands, strake sail, and so were driven.
18 And we being exceedingly tossed with a tempest, the next day they lightened the ship;
19 And the third day we cast out with our own hands the tackling of the ship.
20 And when neither sun nor stars in many days appeared, and no small tempest lay on us, all hope that we should be saved was then taken away.
21 But after long abstinence Paul stood forth in the midst of them, and said, Sirs, you should have hearkened to me, and not have loosed from Crete, and to have gained this harm and loss.
22 And now I exhort you to be of good cheer: for there shall be no loss of any man's life among you, but of the ship.
23 For there stood by me this night the angel of God, whose I am, and whom I serve,
24 Saying, Fear not, Paul; you must be brought before Caesar: and, lo, God has given you all them that sail with you.

25 Wherefore, sirs, be of good cheer: for I believe God, that it shall be even as it was told me.
26 Howbeit we must be cast upon a certain island.
27 But when the fourteenth night was come, as we were driven up and down in Adria, about midnight the shipmen deemed that they drew near to some country;
28 And sounded, and found it twenty fathoms: and when they had gone a little further, they sounded again, and found it fifteen fathoms.

> What comes into our minds when we think about God is the most important thing about us.
>
> **A. W. TOZER**

29 Then fearing lest we should have fallen upon rocks, they cast four anchors out of the stern, and wished for the day.
30 And as the shipmen were about to flee out of the ship, when they had let down the boat into the sea, under colour as though they would have cast anchors out of the foreship,
31 Paul said to the centurion and to the soldiers, Except these abide in the ship, you cannot be saved.
32 Then the soldiers cut off the ropes of the boat, and let her fall off.
33 And while the day was coming on, Paul besought them all to take meat, saying, This day is the fourteenth day that you have tarried and continued fasting, having taken nothing.
34 Wherefore I pray you to take some meat: for this is for your health: for there shall not an hair fall from the head of any of you.
35 And when he had thus spoken, he took bread, and gave thanks to God in presence of them all: and when he had broken it, he began to eat.
36 Then were they all of good cheer, and they also took some meat.
37 And we were in all in the ship two hundred threescore and sixteen souls.
38 And when they had eaten enough, they lightened the ship, and cast out the wheat into the sea.
39 And when it was day, they knew not the land: but they discovered a certain creek with a shore, into the which they were minded, if it were possible, to thrust in the ship.
40 And when they had taken up the anchors, they committed themselves to the sea, and loosed the rudder bands, and hoisted up the mainsail to the wind, and made toward shore.
41 And falling into a place where two seas met, they ran the ship aground; and the forepart stuck fast, and remained unmoveable, but the hinder part was broken with the violence of the waves.
42 And the soldiers' counsel was to kill the prisoners, lest any of them should swim out, and escape.
43 But the centurion, willing to save Paul, kept them from their purpose; and commanded that they which could swim should cast themselves first into the sea, and get to land:
44 And the rest, some on boards, and some on broken pieces of the ship. And so it came to pass, that they escaped all safe to land.

CHAPTER 28

AND when they were escaped, then they knew that the island was called Melita.
2 And the barbarous people showed us no little kindness: for they kindled a fire, and received us every one, because of the present rain, and because of the cold.
3 And when Paul had gathered a bundle of sticks, and laid them on the fire, there came a viper out of the heat, and fastened on his hand.
4 And when the barbarians saw the venomous beast hang on his hand, they said among themselves, No doubt this man is a murderer, whom, though he has escaped the sea, yet vengeance suffers not to

live.
5 And he shook off the beast into the
fire, and felt no harm.
6 Howbeit they looked when he should
have swollen, or fallen down dead suddenly: but after they had looked a great
while, and saw no harm come to him,
they changed their minds, and said that
he was a god.
7 In the same quarters were possessions
of the chief man of the island, whose
name was Publius; who received us, and
lodged us three days courteously.
8 And it came to pass, that the father of
Publius lay sick of a fever and of a bloody
flux: to whom Paul entered in, and prayed,
and laid his hands on him, and healed
him.
9 So when this was done, others also,
which had diseases in the island, came,
and were healed:
10 Who also honored us with many honors; and when we departed, they laded us
with such things as were necessary.
11 And after three months we departed
in a ship of Alexandria, which had win-
tered in the isle, whose sign was Castor
and Pollux.
12 And landing at Syracuse, we tarried
there three days.
13 And from thence we fetched a compass, and came to Rhegium: and after one
day the south wind blew, and we came
the next day to Puteoli:
14 Where we found brethren, and were
desired to tarry with them seven days:
and so we went toward Rome.
15 And from thence, when the brethren
heard of us, they came to meet us as far
as Appiiforum, and The three taverns:
whom when Paul saw, he thanked God,
and took courage.
16 And when we came to Rome, the
centurion delivered the prisoners to the
captain of the guard: but Paul was suffered
to dwell by himself with a soldier that

USING THE LAW IN EVANGELISM

28:23 Notice that Paul used *both* prophecy and the Law of Moses in his evangelism. Prophecy appeals to a man's intellect and creates faith in the Word of God. As he realizes that the Bible is no ordinary book—that it contains numerous indisputable prophecies that prove its supernatural origin—he begins to give Scripture credibility. However, the Law of Moses appeals to a man's conscience and brings conviction of sin. A "decision" for Jesus purely in the realm of the intellect—with no biblical knowledge of sin, which comes only by the Law (Romans 7:7)—will almost certainly produce a false convert. See Romans 2:21 comment.

kept him.
17 And it came to pass, that after three
days Paul called the chief of the Jews together: and when they were come together, he said to them, Men and brethren,
though I have committed nothing against
the people, or customs of our fathers, yet
was I delivered prisoner from Jerusalem
into the hands of the Romans.
18 Who, when they had examined me,
would have let me go, because there was
no cause of death in me.
19 But when the Jews spoke against it, I
was constrained to appeal to Caesar; not
that I had anything to accuse my nation of.
20 For this cause therefore have I called
for you, to see you, and to speak with you:
because that for the hope of Israel I am
bound with this chain.
21 And they said to him, We neither received letters out of Judea concerning
you, neither any of the brethren that came
showed or spoke any harm of you.
22 But we desire to hear of you what you
think: for as concerning this sect, we know
that every where it is spoken against.
23 And when they had appointed him
a day, there came many to him into his

28:23 The goal of evangelism is to persuade people concerning Jesus. He is the way, the truth, and the life. There is salvation in no other name.

THE FUNCTION OF THE LAW

28:23 "The Law's part in transformation is to make a person aware of his sin and of his need for divine forgiveness and redemption and to set the standard of acceptable morality.

"Until a person acknowledges his basic sinfulness and inability to perfectly fulfill the demands of God's Law, he will not come repentantly to seek salvation. Until he despairs of himself and his own sinfulness, he will not come in humble faith to be filled with Christ's righteousness. A person who says he wants salvation but refuses to recognize and repent of his sin deceives himself.

"Grace means nothing to a person who does not know he is sinful and that such sinfulness means he is separated from God and damned. It is therefore pointless to preach grace until the impossible demands of the Law and the reality of guilt before God are preached." *John MacArthur*

lodging; to whom he expounded and testified the kingdom of God, persuading them concerning Jesus, both out of the law of Moses, and out of the prophets, from morning till evening.
24 And some believed the things which were spoken, and some believed not.
25 And when they agreed not among themselves, they departed, after that Paul had spoken one word, Well spoke the Holy Spirit by Isaiah the prophet to our fathers,
26 Saying, Go to this people, and say, Hearing you shall hear, and shall not understand; and seeing you shall see, and not perceive:
27 For the heart of this people is waxed gross, and their ears are dull of hearing, and their eyes have they closed; lest they should see with their eyes, and hear with their ears, and understand with their heart, and should be converted, and I should heal them.
28 Be it known therefore to you, that the salvation of God is sent to the Gentiles, and that they will hear it.
29 And when he had said these words, the Jews departed, and had great reasoning among themselves.
30 And Paul dwelt two whole years in his own hired house, and received all that came in to him,
31 Preaching the kingdom of God, and teaching those things which concern the Lord Jesus Christ, with all confidence, no man forbidding him.

"The great of the kingdom have been those who loved God more than others did."

A. W. TOZER

Romans

CHAPTER 1

PAUL, a servant of Jesus Christ, called to be an apostle, separated to the gospel of God,
2 (Which he had promised before by his prophets in the holy scriptures,)
3 Concerning his Son Jesus Christ our Lord, which was made of the seed of David according to the flesh;
4 And declared to be the Son of God with power, according to the spirit of holiness, by the resurrection from the dead:
5 By whom we have received grace and apostleship, for obedience to the faith among all nations, for his name:
6 Among whom are you also the called of Jesus Christ:
7 To all that be in Rome, beloved of God, called to be saints: Grace to you and peace from God our Father, and the Lord Jesus Christ.
8 *First, I thank my God through Jesus Christ for you all, that your faith is spoken of throughout the whole world.*
9 For God is my witness, whom I serve with my spirit in the gospel of his Son, that without ceasing I make mention of you always in my prayers;
10 Making request, if by any means now at length I might have a prosperous journey by the will of God to come to you.
11 For I long to see you, that I may impart to you some spiritual gift, to the end you may be established;
12 That is, that I may be comforted together with you by the mutual faith both of you and me.
13 Now I would not have you ignorant, brethren, that oftentimes I purposed to come to you, (but was let hitherto,) that I might have some fruit among you also, even as among other Gentiles.
14 *I am debtor both to the Greeks, and to the Barbarians; both to the wise, and to the unwise.*
15 *So, as much as in me is, I am ready to preach the gospel to you that are at Rome also.*
16 *For I am not ashamed of the gospel of Christ: for it is the power of God to salvation to every one that believes; to the Jew first, and also to the Greek.*
17 For therein is the righteousness of God revealed from faith to faith: as it is written, The just shall live by faith.
18 For the wrath of God is revealed from heaven against all ungodliness and unrighteousness of men, who hold the truth in unrighteousness;
19 Because that which may be known of God is manifest in them; for God has showed it to them.
20 For the invisible things of him from the creation of the world are clearly seen, being understood by the things that are made, even his eternal power and God-

1:14 "So long as there is a human being who does not know Jesus Christ, I am his debtor to serve him until he does." *Oswald Chambers*

head; so that they are without excuse:
21 Because that, when they knew God,
they glorified him not as God, neither
were thankful; but became vain in their
imaginations, and their foolish heart was
darkened.
22 Professing themselves to be wise, they
became fools,
23 And changed the glory of the uncor-
ruptible God into an image made like to
corruptible man, and to birds, and four-
footed beasts, and creeping things.
24 Wherefore God also gave them up to
uncleanness through the lusts of their
own hearts, to dishonor their own bodies between themselves:
25 Who changed the truth of God into
a lie, and worshipped and served the
creature more than the Creator, who is
blessed for ever. Amen.
26 For this cause God gave them up to
vile affections: for even their women did
change the natural use into that which is
against nature:
27 And likewise also the men, leaving
the natural use of the woman, burned in
their lust one toward another; men with
men working that which is unseemly,
and receiving in themselves that recompense of their error which was meet.
28 And even as they did not like to retain God in their knowledge, God gave
them over to a reprobate mind, to do
those things which are not convenient;
29 Being filled with all unrighteousness,
fornication, wickedness, covetousness,
maliciousness; full of envy, murder, debate, deceit, malignity; whisperers,
30 Backbiters, haters of God, despiteful,
proud, boasters, inventors of evil things,
disobedient to parents,
31 Without understanding, covenant-

1:20 Faith in God is not "blind faith"; it is based on the fact of God's existence seen clearly through creation.

"This most beautiful system of the sun, planets, and comets could only proceed from the counsel and dominion of an intelligent and powerful Being." *Sir Isaac Newton*

"The more I study nature, the more I stand amazed at the work of the Creator." *Louis Pasteur*

1:20 How to prove God's existence. When I look at a building, how do I know that there was a builder? I can't see him, hear him, touch, taste, or smell him. Of course, the build*ing* is proof that there was a build*er*. In fact, I couldn't want better evidence that there was a builder than to have the building in front of me. I don't need "faith" to know that there was a builder. All I need is eyes that can see and a brain that works.

Likewise, when I look at a painting, how can I know that there was a painter? Again, the paint*ing* is proof positive that there was a paint*er*. I don't need "faith" to believe in a painter because I can see the clear evidence.

The same principle applies with the existence of God. When I look at creation, how can I *know* that there was a Creator? I can't see Him, hear Him, touch Him, taste Him, or smell Him. How can I know that He exists? Why, creation shows me that there is a Creator. *I couldn't want better proof that a Creator exists than to have the creation in front of me.* I don't need faith to believe in a Creator; all I need is eyes that can see and a brain that works: "For the invisible things of Him from the creation of the world are clearly seen, being understood by the things that are made, even His eternal power and Godhead; so that they are without excuse" (Romans 1:20).

If, however, I want the builder to *do* something for me, *then* I need to have faith in him. The same applies to God: "Without faith it is impossible to please Him: for He that comes to God must believe that He is, and that He is a rewarder of them that diligently seek Him" (Hebrews 11:6).

1:27 Homosexuality. Despite claims to the contrary, no scientific evidence has been found that homosexuals are "born that way." In fact, God's Word is clear that sexual activity is to be only within the bounds of marriage, between one man and one woman. Homosexuality goes against God's created order and expressed will. If a homosexual claims to be born that way, gently explain that all people are born with a sin nature, but that our nature makes us children of wrath. (See Jude 7 comment.) See also 1 Timothy 1:8–10 comment.

QUESTIONS & OBJECTIONS

2:12 ***"Will people who have never heard the gospel all go to hell because they haven't heard about Jesus Christ?"***

No one will go to hell because they haven't heard of Jesus Christ. The heathen will go to hell for murder, rape, adultery, lust, theft, lying, etc. Sin is not *failing to hear the gospel.* Rather, "sin is the transgression of the Law" (1 John 3:4). If we really care about the lost, we will become missionaries and take the good news of God's forgiveness in Christ to them. See John 16:9 comment.

breakers, without natural affection, implacable, unmerciful:
32 Who knowing the judgment of God, that they which commit such things are worthy of death, not only do the same, but have pleasure in them that do them.

CHAPTER 2

THEREFORE you are inexcusable, O man, whosoever you are that judge: for wherein you judge another, you condemn yourself; for you that judge do the same things.
2 But we are sure that the judgment of God is according to truth against them which commit such things.
3 And do you think this, O man, that judge them which do such things, and do the same, that you shall escape the judgment of God?
4 Or do you despise the riches of his goodness and forbearance and longsuffering; not knowing that the goodness of God leads you to repentance?
5 But after your hardness and impenitent heart you treasure up to yourself wrath against the day of wrath and revelation of the righteous judgment of God;
6 Who will render to every man according to his deeds:
7 To them who by patient continuance in well doing seek for glory and honor and immortality, eternal life:
8 But to them that are contentious, and do not obey the truth, but obey unrighteousness, indignation and wrath,
9 Tribulation and anguish, upon every soul of man that does evil, of the Jew first, and also of the Gentile;
10 But glory, honor, and peace, to every man that works good, to the Jew first, and also to the Gentile:
11 For there is no respect of persons with God.
12 For as many as have sinned without law shall also perish without law: and as many as have sinned in the law shall be judged by the law;
13 (For not the hearers of the law are just before God, but the doers of the law shall be justified.
14 For when the Gentiles, which have not the law, do by nature the things contained in the law, these, having not the law, are a law to themselves:
15 Which show the work of the law written in their hearts, their conscience also bearing witness, and their thoughts

---

2:4 This verse is sandwiched between statements of God's judgment and wrath. If Paul was saying that we should speak only of God's goodness to sinners, he wasn't practicing what he preached.

"I never knew but one person in the whole course of my ministry who acknowledged that the first motions of religion in his own heart arose from a sense of the goodness of God, 'What shall I render to the Lord, who has dealt so bountifully with me?' But I think all besides who have come within my notice have rather been first awakened to fly from the wrath to come by the passion of fear." *Isaac Watts*

2:15 "Conscience is the internal perception of God's moral Law." *Oswald Chambers*

USING THE LAW IN EVANGELISM

2:21 Here Paul uses the Law to bring "the knowledge of sin." *Dr. J Gresham Machen* said, "A new and more powerful proclamation of [the] Law is perhaps the most pressing need of the hour; men would have little difficulty with the gospel if they had only learned the lesson of the Law." See James 2:8 comment.

the mean while accusing or else excusing
one another;)
16 In the day when God shall judge the
secrets of men by Jesus Christ according
to my gospel.
17 Behold, you are called a Jew, and rest
in the law, and make your boast of God,
18 And know his will, and approve the
things that are more excellent, being instructed out of the law;
19 And are confident that you yourself
are a guide of the blind, a light of them
which are in darkness,
20 An instructor of the foolish, a teacher
of babes, which have the form of knowledge and of the truth in the law.
21 You therefore which teach another, do
you not teach yourself? you that preach a
man should not steal, do you steal?
22 You that say a man should not commit adultery, do you commit adultery?
you that abhor idols, do you commit sac-
rilege?
23 You that make your boast of the law,
through breaking the law do you dishonor God?
24 For the name of God is blasphemed
among the Gentiles through you, as it is
written.
25 For circumcision verily profits, if you
keep the law: but if you be a breaker of
the law, your circumcision is made uncircumcision.
26 Therefore if the uncircumcision keep
the righteousness of the law, shall not
his uncircumcision be counted for circumcision?
27 And shall not uncircumcision which
is by nature, if it fulfil the law, judge you,
who by the letter and circumcision do
transgress the law?
28 For he is not a Jew, which is one
outwardly; neither is that circumcision,
which is outward in the flesh:
29 But he is a Jew, which is one inwardly; and circumcision is that of the
heart, in the spirit, and not in the letter;
whose praise is not of men, but of God.

. . . . . .

How did the apostles die?
See Acts 17:55.

. . . . . .

CHAPTER 3

WHAT advantage then has the Jew?
or what profit is there of circumcision?
2 Much every way: chiefly, because that
to them were committed the oracles of
God.
3 For what if some did not believe? shall
their unbelief make the faith of God without effect?
4 God forbid: yea, let God be true, but
every man a liar; as it is written, That you

2:15 The sinner's conscience. God has given light to every man. The word "con-science" means "with knowledge." The conscience is the headline warning of sin; the Scriptures give the fine print. No man can say he doesn't know that it's wrong to murder or commit adultery. That knowledge is written in bold print on his heart. However, in the Scriptures we see the true nature of sin: that God requires truth even in the inward parts (Psalm 51:6). The fine print reveals that lust is adultery of the heart, hatred is murder of the heart, etc.

2:15,16 There are two witnesses to our crimes: Our conscience and God Himself accuse us. See 1 Corinthians 6:9,10 comment.

2:16 Judgment Day: For verses that warn of its reality, see Romans 14:10.

Questions & Objections

3:1 "How should I witness to a Jew?"

Sadly, many of today's Jews profess godliness but don't embrace the Scriptures as we presume they do. Therefore, it is often difficult to reason with them about Jesus being the Messiah. This is why it is imperative to ask a Jew if he has kept the Law of Moses—to "shut" him up under the Law (Galatians 3:23) and strip him of his self-righteousness. The Law will show him his need of a Savior and become a "schoolmaster" to bring him to Christ (Galatians 3:24), as happened to Paul, Nicodemus, and Nathaniel. It was the Law that brought 3,000 Jews to the foot of the cross on the Day of Pentecost. Without it they would not have known that they had sinned (Romans 7:7), and therefore would not have seen their need of the Savior. See Luke 18:20 comment for how to use the Law in evangelism.

might be justified in your sayings, and
might overcome when you are judged.
5 But if our unrighteousness commend
the righteousness of God, what shall we
say? Is God unrighteous who takes vengeance? (I speak as a man)
6 God forbid: for then how shall God
judge the world?
7 For if the truth of God has more
abounded through my lie to his glory;
why yet am I also judged as a sinner?
8 And not rather, (as we be slanderous-
ly reported, and as some affirm that we
say,) Let us do evil, that good may come?
whose damnation is just.
9 What then? are we better than they?
No, in no wise: for we have before proved
both Jews and Gentiles, that they are all
under sin;
10 **As it is written, There is none righteous, no, not one:**
11 **There is none that understands,
there is none that seeks after God.**
12 **They are all gone out of the way,
they are together become unprofitable;
there is none that does good, no, not
one.**
13 **Their throat is an open sepulchre;
with their tongues they have used deceit; the poison of asps is under their
lips:**
14 **Whose mouth is full of cursing and
bitterness:**
15 **Their feet are swift to shed blood:**
16 **Destruction and misery are in their
ways:**
17 **And the way of peace have they not
known:**
18 **There is no fear of God before their
eyes.**
19 Now we know that what things soever the law says, it says to them who
are under the law: that every mouth may
be stopped, and all the world may become guilty before God.

The Function of the Law

3:19 The purpose of the Law is to stop the sinner's mouth of justification. The Law tells him what sin is (see 1 John 3:4) and stops him proclaiming his own goodness. Its intent is to drive him to the cross. *John Wesley* said, "The first use of [the Law], without question, is to convince the world of sin. By this is the sinner discovered to himself. All his fig-leaves are torn away, and he sees that he is 'wretched and poor and miserable, blind and naked.' The Law flashes conviction on every side. He feels himself a mere sinner. He has nothing to pay. His 'mouth is stopped' and he stands 'guilty before God.'"

"Ask Paul why [the Law] was given. Here is his answer, 'That every mouth may be stopped, and all the world may become guilty before God' (Romans 3:19). The Law stops every man's mouth. I can always tell a man who is near the kingdom of God; his mouth is stopped. This, then, is why God gives us the Law—to show us ourselves in our true colors." *D. L. Moody*

Questions & Objections

3:9

"Do you think that Christians are better than non-Christians?"

The Christian is no better than a non-Christian, but he is infinitely *better off*. It is like two men on a plane, one of whom is wearing a parachute while the other is not. Neither is better than the other, but the man with the parachute is certainly better off than the man who is not wearing a parachute. The difference will be seen when they jump from the plane at 20,000 feet. Jesus warned that if we "jump" into death without Him, we would perish.

Even harsher than the law of gravity is the Law of an infinitely holy and just Creator. Scripture states that sinners are God's enemy (Romans 5:10) and that "it is a fearful thing to fall into the hands of the living God (Hebrews 10:31).

20 Therefore by the deeds of the law
there shall no flesh be justified in his
sight: for by the law is the knowledge of
sin.
21 But now the righteousness of God
without the law is manifested, being witnessed by the law and the prophets;
22 Even the righteousness of God which
is by faith of Jesus Christ to all and upon
all them that believe: for there is no difference:
23 **For all have sinned, and come short
of the glory of God;**
24 Being justified freely by his grace
through the redemption that is in Christ
Jesus:
25 Whom God has set forth to be a propitiation through faith in his blood, to
declare his righteousness for the remission of sins that are past, through the forbearance of God;
26 To declare, I say, at this time his
righteousness: that he might be just, and
the justifier of him which believes in
Jesus.
27 Where is boasting then? It is excluded. By what law? of works? Nay: but by
the law of faith.
28 Therefore we conclude that a man is
justified by faith without the deeds of
the law.
29 Is he the God of the Jews only? is he
not also of the Gentiles? Yes, of the Gentiles also:

The Function of the Law

3:20

Sin is like smog—it is not visible while you are in its midst. The Law takes the sinner above the smog of his own perspective and shows him heaven's viewpoint. It gives the sinner knowledge of his sin. *John Bunyan* stated, "The man who does not know the nature of the Law cannot know the nature of sin."

"The trouble with people who are not seeking for a Savior, and for salvation, is that they do not understand the nature of sin. It is the peculiar function of the Law to bring such an understanding to a man's mind and conscience. That is why great evangelical preachers 300 years ago in the time of the Puritans, and 200 years ago in the time of Whitefield and others, always engaged in what they called a preliminary 'Law work.'" *Martyn Lloyd-Jones*

"The first duty of the gospel preacher is to declare God's Law and show the nature of sin." *Martin Luther*

3:19 "Every unredeemed human being, Jew or Gentile, is under the Law of God and accountable to God. The final verdict, then, is that unredeemed mankind has no defense whatever and is guilty of all charges. The defense must rest, as it were, before it has opportunity to say anything, because the omniscient and all-wise God has infallibly demonstrated the impossibility of any grounds of acquittal. Absolute silence is the only possible response." *John MacArthur*

30 Seeing it is one God, which shall justify the circumcision by faith, and uncircumcision through faith.
31 Do we then make void the law
through faith? God forbid: yea, we establish the law.

CHAPTER 4

WHAT shall we say then that Abraham our father, as pertaining to
the flesh, has found?
2 For if Abraham were justified by works,
he has whereof to glory; but not before
God.
3 For what do the Scriptures say? Abraham believed God, and it was counted to
him for righteousness.
4 Now to him that works is the reward
not reckoned of grace, but of debt.
5 But to him that works not, but believes on him that justifies the ungodly,
his faith is counted for righteousness.
6 Even as David also describes the blessedness of the man, to whom God imputes
righteousness without works,
7 **Saying, Blessed are they whose iniquities are forgiven, and whose sins are
covered.**
8 Blessed is the man to whom the Lord
will not impute sin.
9 Came this blessedness then upon the
circumcision only, or upon the uncircumcision also? for we say that faith was
reckoned to Abraham for righteousness.
10 How was it then reckoned? when he
was in circumcision, or in uncircumcision? Not in circumcision, but in uncircumcision.
11 And he received the sign of circumcision, a seal of the righteousness of the
faith which he had yet being uncircumcised: that he might be the father of all
them that believe, though they be not
circumcised; that righteousness might be
imputed to them also:
12 And the father of circumcision to
them who are not of the circumcision
only, but who also walk in the steps of
that faith of our father Abraham, which
he had being yet uncircumcised.
13 For the promise, that he should be
the heir of the world, was not to Abraham, or to his seed, through the law, but
through the righteousness of faith.
14 For if they which are of the law be
heirs, faith is made void, and the promise made of no effect:

> I would sooner bring one sinner to Jesus than unravel all the mysteries of the Word, for salvation is the thing we are to live for.
>
> **CHARLES SPURGEON**

15 Because the law works wrath: for
where no law is, there is no transgression.
16 Therefore it is of faith, that it might
be by grace; to the end the promise
might be sure to all the seed; not to that
only which is of the law, but to that also
which is of the faith of Abraham; who is
the father of us all,
17 (As it is written, I have made you a
father of many nations,) before him
whom he believed, even God, who quickens the dead, and calls those things which
be not as though they were.
18 Who against hope believed in hope,
that he might become the father of many
nations; according to that which was
spoken, So shall your seed be.
19 And being not weak in faith, he considered not his own body now dead,
when he was about an hundred years old,
neither yet the deadness of Sara's womb:
20 He staggered not at the promise of
God through unbelief; but was strong in

4:20 There is a wise saying: "If it sounds too good to be true, it probably is." That is solid advice when you are dealing with sinful mankind. But the promises of God—of forgiveness of sin, of peace with God through trusting in the Savior, of a new heaven and a new earth—come from a faithful Creator, and there is no greater insult to God than not to believe His promises.

faith, giving glory to God;
21 And being fully persuaded that, what
he had promised, he was able also to
perform.
22 And therefore it was imputed to him
for righteousness.
23 Now it was not written for his sake
alone, that it was imputed to him;
24 But for us also, to whom it shall be
imputed, if we believe on him that raised
up Jesus our Lord from the dead;
25 Who was delivered for our offences,
and was raised again for our justification.

CHAPTER 5

THEREFORE being justified by faith,
we have peace with God through
our Lord Jesus Christ:
2 By whom also we have access by faith
into this grace wherein we stand, and rejoice in hope of the glory of God.
3 And not only so, but we glory in tribulations also: knowing that tribulation
works patience;
4 And patience, experience; and experience, hope:
5 And hope makes not ashamed; because the love of God is shed abroad in
our hearts by the Holy Spirit which is giv-
en to us.
6 **For when we were yet without
strength, in due time Christ died for
the ungodly.**
7 **For scarcely for a righteous man will
one die: yet peradventure for a good
man some would even dare to die.**
**8 But God commends his love toward
us, in that, while we were yet sinners,
Christ died for us.**
9 **Much more then, being now justified
by his blood, we shall be saved from
wrath through him.**
10 For if, when we were enemies, we
were reconciled to God by the death of
his Son, much more, being reconciled,
we shall be saved by his life.
11 And not only so, but we also joy in
God through our Lord Jesus Christ, by
whom we have now received the atonement.
**12 Wherefore, as by one man sin en-
tered into the world, and death by sin;
and so death passed upon all men, for
that all have sinned:**
13 (For until the law sin was in the
world: but sin is not imputed when there
is no law.
14 Nevertheless death reigned from Adam
to Moses, even over them that had not
sinned after the similitude of Adam's transgression, who is the figure of him that
was to come.
15 But not as the offence, so also is the
free gift. For if through the offence of
one many be dead, much more the grace
of God, and the gift by grace, which is
by one man, Jesus Christ, has abounded
to many.
16 And not as it was by one that sinned,
so is the gift: for the judgment was by

5:8 "God proved His love on the cross. When Christ hung, and bled, and died, it was God saying to the world, 'I love you.'" *Billy Graham*

5:14 Many years ago, a man jumped off a high bridge in an effort to end his life. Fortunately, he lived through the ordeal but broke his back as a result of the fall, and ended up in a wheelchair. His attempt to take his life caused a great deal of distress, to those in control of the bridge, to paramedics, to traffic, and especially to his family. Authorities wanted to press charges against him but they couldn't; since this was the city's first suicide attempt, they had no law forbidding such an act. He escaped the consequences of the law of man, but suffered the painful consequences of breaking another law, the law of gravity.

In the same way, every person in Adam still sinned and therefore suffered the consequences of breaking the then unwritten moral Law—"the soul that sins, it shall die" (Ezekiel 18:4). Death reigned as king, with a dominion from Adam to Moses. They didn't partake from the Tree of Knowledge of Good and Evil as did Adam, but they still sinned against God.

QUESTIONS & OBJECTIONS

5:12

"Why is there suffering? That proves there is no 'loving' God."

Study the soil for a moment. It naturally produces weeds. No one plants them; no one waters them. They even stubbornly push through cracks of a dry sidewalk. Millions of useless weeds sprout like there's no tomorrow, strangling our crops and ruining our lawns. Pull them out by the roots, and there will be more tomorrow. They are nothing but a curse!

Consider how much of the earth is uninhabitable. There are millions of square miles of barren deserts in Africa and other parts of the world. Most of Australia is nothing but miles and miles of useless desolate land.

Not only that, but the earth is constantly shaken with massive earthquakes. Its shores are lashed with hurricanes; tornadoes rip through creation with incredible fury; devastating floods soak the land; and terrible droughts parch the soil. Sharks, tigers, lions, snakes, spiders, and disease-carrying mosquitoes attack humanity and suck its life's blood. The earth's inhabitants are afflicted with disease, pain, suffering, and death.

Think of how many people are plagued with cancer, Alzheimer's, multiple sclerosis, heart disease, emphysema, Parkinson's, and a number of other debilitating illnesses. Consider all the children with leukemia, or people born with crippling diseases or without the mental capability to even feed themselves. All these things should convince thinking minds that something is radically wrong.

Did God blow it when He created humanity? What sort of tyrant must our Creator be if this was His master plan?

Sadly, many use the issue of suffering as an excuse to reject any thought of God, when its existence is the *very reason* we should accept Him. Suffering stands as terrible testimony to the truth of the explanation given by the Word of God.

But how can we know that the Bible is true? Simply by studying the prophecies of Matthew 24, Luke 21, and 2 Timothy 3. A few minutes of openhearted inspection will convince any honest skeptic that this is no ordinary book. It is the supernatural testament of our Creator about why there is suffering... and what we can do about it.

The Bible tells us that God cursed the earth because of Adam's transgression. Weeds *are* a curse. So is disease. Sin and suffering cannot be separated. The Scriptures inform us that we live in a *fallen* creation. In the beginning, God created man perfect, and he lived in a perfect world without suffering. *It was heaven on earth.* When sin came into the world, death and misery came with it.

Those who understand the message of Holy Scripture eagerly await a new heaven and a new earth "wherein dwells righteousness." In that coming Kingdom there will be no more pain, suffering, disease, or death. We are told that no eye has ever seen, nor has any ear heard, neither has any man's mind ever imagined the wonderful things that God has in store for those who love Him (1 Corinthians 2:9). Think for a moment what it would be like if food grew with the fervor of weeds. Consider how wonderful it would be if the deserts became incredibly fertile, if creation stopped devouring humanity. Imagine if the weather worked *for* us instead of against us, if disease completely disappeared, if pain was a thing of the past, if death was no more.

The dilemma is that we are like a child whose insatiable appetite for chocolate has caused his face to break out with ugly sores. He looks in the mirror and sees a sight that makes him depressed. But instead of giving up his beloved chocolate, he consoles himself by stuffing more into his mouth. Yet, the source of his pleasure is actually the *cause* of his suffering.

The whole face of the earth is nothing but ugly sores of suffering. Everywhere we look we see unspeakable pain. But instead of believing God's explanation and asking Him to forgive us and change our appetite, we run deeper into sin's sweet embrace. There we find solace in its temporal pleasures, thus intensifying our pain, both in this life and in the life to come.

one to condemnation, but the free gift is of many offences to justification.

17 For if by one man's offence death reigned by one; much more they which receive abundance of grace and of the gift of righteousness shall reign in life by one, Jesus Christ.)

18 Therefore as by the offence of one judgment came upon all men to condemnation; even so by the righteousness of one the free gift came upon all men to justification of life.

19 For as by one man's disobedience many were made sinners, so by the obedience of one shall many be made righteous.

20 Moreover the law entered, that the offence might abound. But where sin abounded, grace did much more abound:

21 That as sin has reigned to death, even so might grace reign through righteousness to eternal life by Jesus Christ our Lord.

CHAPTER 6

WHAT shall we say then? Shall we continue in sin, that grace may abound?

2 God forbid. How shall we, that are dead to sin, live any longer therein?

3 Do you not know, that so many of us as were baptized into Jesus Christ were baptized into his death?

4 Therefore we are buried with him by baptism into death: that like as Christ was raised up from the dead by the glory of the Father, even so we also should walk in newness of life.

5 For if we have been planted together in the likeness of his death, we shall be also in the likeness of his resurrection:

6 Knowing this, that our old man is crucified with him, that the body of sin might be destroyed, that henceforth we should not serve sin.

7 For he that is dead is freed from sin.

8 Now if we be dead with Christ, we believe that we shall also live with him:

9 Knowing that Christ being raised from the dead dies no more; death has no more dominion over him.

10 For in that he died, he died to sin once: but in that he lives, he lives to God.

11 Likewise reckon you also yourselves to be dead indeed to sin, but alive to God through Jesus Christ our Lord.

12 Let not sin therefore reign in your mortal body, that you should obey it in the lusts thereof.

13 Neither yield your members as instruments of unrighteousness to sin: but yield yourselves to God, as those that are alive from the dead, and your members as instruments of righteousness to God.

14 For sin shall not have dominion over you: for you are not under the law, but under grace.

15 What then? shall we sin, because we are not under the law, but under grace? God forbid.

16 Do you not know, that to whom you yield yourselves servants to obey, his servants you are to whom you obey; whether of sin to death, or of obedience to righteousness?

5:20 "God's grace cannot be faithfully preached to unbelievers until His Law is preached and man's corrupt nature is exposed. It is impossible for a person to fully realize his need for God's grace until he sees how terribly he has failed the standards of God's Law. It is impossible for him to realize his need for mercy until he realizes the magnitude of his guilt." *John MacArthur*

6:6 See 1 John 2:1 comment.

6:14 In Christ we are sheltered under the umbrella of grace from the rain of the wrath of the Law. Paul is not saying that the Law has been done away with. Jesus Himself said that He hadn't come to do away with the Law. We "establish" the Law in Christ (Romans 3:31). We corroborate it. It still remains as the standard of God's righteousness, and it will be the means by which He will judge the world.

17 But God be thanked, that you were
the servants of sin, but you have obeyed
from the heart that form of doctrine which
was delivered you.
18 Being then made free from sin, you
became the servants of righteousness.
19 I speak after the manner of men because of the infirmity of your flesh: for as
you have yielded your members servants
to uncleanness and to iniquity to iniquity; even so now yield your members servants to righteousness to holiness.
20 For when you were the servants of
sin, you were free from righteousness.
21 What fruit had you then in those
things whereof you are now ashamed?
for the end of those things is death.
22 But now being made free from sin,
and become servants to God, you have
your fruit to holiness, and the end everlasting life.
23 **For the wages of sin is death; but
the gift of God is eternal life through
Jesus Christ our Lord.**

CHAPTER 7

DO you not know, brethren, (for I
speak to them that know the law,)
how that the law has dominion over a
man as long as he lives?
2 For the woman which has an husband is bound by the law to her husband so long as he lives; but if the husband be dead, she is loosed from the law
of her husband.
3 So then if, while her husband lives,
she be married to another man, she shall
be called an adulteress: but if her husband be dead, she is free from that law;
so that she is no adulteress, though she
be married to another man.
4 Wherefore, my brethren, you also are
become dead to the law by the body of
Christ; that you should be married to
another, even to him who is raised from
the dead, that we should bring forth fruit
to God.
5 For when we were in the flesh, the
motions of sins, which were by the law,
did work in our members to bring forth
fruit to death.
6 But now we are delivered from the
law, that being dead wherein we were
held; that we should serve in newness of
spirit, and not in the oldness of the letter.
7 What shall we say then? Is the law
sin? God forbid. Nay, I had not known
sin, but by the law: for I had not known
lust, except the law had said, You shall
not covet.
8 But sin, taking occasion by the commandment, wrought in me all manner of
concupiscence. For without the law sin
was dead.
9 For I was alive without the law once:
but when the commandment came, sin
revived, and I died.
10 And the commandment, which was

7:7 "Even with the light of nature, and the light of conscience, and the light of tradition, there are some things we should never have believed to be sins had we not been taught so by the Law." *Charles Spurgeon*

7:9 "It is right for a preacher of the gospel first, by a revelation of the Law and of sin, to rebuke everything and make sin of everything that is not the living fruit of the Spirit and faith in Christ, so that men may be led to know themselves and their own wretchedness, and become humble and ask for help.

"No one knows that lime has heat until he pours water upon it. Then the heat has occasion to show itself. The water did not create the heat in the lime, but it has made itself manifest. It is similar to the will of man and the Law.

"'I was alive without the law once: but when the commandment came, sin revived' (Romans 7:9). So it is with the work-righteous and the proud unbelievers. Because they do not know the Law of God, which is directed against them, it is impossible for them to know their sin. Therefore also they are not amenable to instruction. If they would know the Law, they would also know their sin; and sin to which they are now dead would become alive in them." *Martin Luther*

The Function of the Law

7:11 "To slay the sinner is then the first use of the Law, to destroy the life and strength wherein he trusts and convince him that he is dead while he lives; not only under the sentence of death, but actually dead to God, void of all spiritual life, dead in trespasses and sins." *John Wesley*

ordained to life, I found to be to death.
11 For sin, taking occasion by the commandment, deceived me, and by it slew
me.
12 Wherefore the law is holy, and the
commandment holy, and just, and good.
13 Was then that which is good made
death to me? God forbid. But sin, that it
might appear sin, working death in me
by that which is good; that sin by the
commandment might become exceeding
sinful.
14 For we know that the law is spiritual:
but I am carnal, sold under sin.
15 For that which I do I allow not: for
what I would, that do I not; but what I
hate, that do I.
16 If then I do that which I would not,
I consent to the law that it is good.
17 Now then it is no more I that do it,
but sin that dwells in me.
18 For I know that in me (that is, in my
flesh,) dwells no good thing: for to will
is present with me; but how to perform
that which is good I find not.
19 For the good that I would I do not:
but the evil which I would not, that I do.
20 Now if I do that I would not, it is no
more I that do it, but sin that dwells in me.

. . . . . .

For last words of famous people, see 1 Corinthians 15:55 comment.

. . . . . .

21 I find then a law, that, when I would
do good, evil is present with me.
22 For I delight in the law of God after
the inward man:
23 But I see another law in my members, warring against the law of my mind,
and bringing me into captivity to the law
of sin which is in my members.

7:10 "The Law is not in fault, but our evil and wicked nature; even as a heap of lime is still and quiet until water be poured thereon, but then it begins to smoke and burn, not from the fault of the water, but from the nature and kind of the lime which will not endure it." *Augustine*

7:18,19 There is disagreement about whether Paul is speaking of his pre-conversion experience or the battle the Christian has with sin. It would seem that both interpretations may be applied. God bless the Christian who is able to obtain "sinless perfection." He is a better man than most Christians. Rather, the majority of believers can identify with *George Whitefield*:

> After we are renewed, yet we are renewed but in part, indwelling sin continues in us, there is a mixture of corruption in every one of our duties; so that after we are converted, were Jesus Christ only to accept us according to our works, our works would damn us, for we cannot put up a prayer but it is far from that perfection which the moral Law requireth. I do not know what you may think, but I can say that I cannot pray but I sin—cannot preach to you or others but I sin—I can do nothing without sin; and, as one expresseth it, my repentance wants to be repented of, and my tears to be washed in the precious blood of my dear Redeemer.

7:22 "Never, never let us despise [the Law]. It is the symptom of an ignorant ministry, and unhealthy state of religion, when the Law is reckoned unimportant. The true Christian delights in God's Law." *J. C. Ryle*

In speaking of the Christian's attitude to the Law, John Wesley said, "Yea, love and value it for the sake of Him from whom it came, and of Him to whom it leads. Let it be thy glory and joy, next to the cross of Christ. Declare its praise, and make it honorable before all men."

(Can Hinduism provide deliverance from sin? See Romans 7:24,25 comment.)

Mahatma Ghandi

24 O wretched man that I am! who
shall deliver me from the body of this
death?
25 I thank God through Jesus Christ
our Lord. So then with the mind I myself
serve the law of God; but with the flesh
the law of sin.

CHAPTER 8

THERE is therefore now no condemnation to them which are in Christ
Jesus, who walk not after the flesh, but
after the Spirit.
2 For the law of the Spirit of life in Christ
Jesus has made me free from the law of
sin and death.
3 For what the law could not do, in that
it was weak through the flesh, God sending his own Son in the likeness of sinful
flesh, and for sin, condemned sin in the
flesh:
4 That the righteousness of the law
might be fulfilled in us, who walk not
after the flesh, but after the Spirit.
5 For they that are after the flesh do
mind the things of the flesh; but they that
are after the Spirit the things of the Spirit.
6 For to be carnally minded is death;
but to be spiritually minded is life and
peace.
7 Because the carnal mind is enmity
against God: for it is not subject to the
law of God, neither indeed can be.
8 So then they that are in the flesh cannot please God.
9 But you are not in the flesh, but in the
Spirit, if so be that the Spirit of God dwell
in you. Now if any man have not the
Spirit of Christ, he is none of his.
10 And if Christ be in you, the body is
dead because of sin; but the Spirit is life
because of righteousness.
11 But if the Spirit of him that raised up
Jesus from the dead dwell in you, he that
raised up Christ from the dead shall also
quicken your mortal bodies by his Spirit

7:24,25 Mahatma Ghandi acknowledged the inability of his religion to atone for sin. Despite his moral lifestyle and good works, he admitted, "It is a constant torture to me that I am still so far from Him whom I know to be my very life and being. I know it is my own wretchedness and wickedness that keeps me from Him." All works-based religions lead to futility and death. It is only in Jesus Christ that sinners can find forgiveness for their sins and deliverance from death and hell.

8:2 A higher Law. One hundred fifty years ago it would have been thought insane that a jumbo jet, filled with people, could fly. The law of gravity made it impossible for even a feather to remain in the air. Yet, we know that when a certain object moves at a particular speed, it moves out of the law of gravity into a higher law—the law of aerodynamics—even though the law of gravity still remains. The world thinks the Christian is insane to live for Jesus Christ. But we know that, even though there is the law of sin and death, we live in a higher law—the law of the Spirit of life in Christ Jesus.

8:6 "Let no man think of fighting hell's legions if he is still fighting an internal warfare. Carnage without will sicken him if he has carnality within. It is the man who has surrendered to the Lord who will never surrender to his enemies." *Leonard Ravenhill*

QUESTIONS & OBJECTIONS

8:22 *"Mother Nature sure blew it..."*

Hurricanes, tornadoes, floods, droughts, and earthquakes kill tens of thousands of people each year. Multitudes endure crippling diseases, endless suffering, and unspeakable pain (see Romans 5:12 comment). Many non-Christians credit a heartless Mother Nature for giving us all this grief. They fail to consider that "Mother Nature" has a Senior Partner—Father God.

However, if God is responsible for all this heartache, that presents an interesting dilemma. If God is an "all-loving" Father figure, as we are told, we seem to have three choices: 1) God blew it when He made everything (He's creative but incompetent); 2) God is a tyrant, who gets His kicks from seeing kids die of leukemia; 3) something between God and man is radically wrong. These are our choices...and those who take time to consider the evidence will lean toward number three. Something between man and God *is* radically wrong, and the Bible tells us what it is.

There is a war going on. We are told that mankind is an enemy of God in his mind through wicked works (Colossians 1:21). That's not too hard to see. Man is continually committing violent acts such as murder and rape, lying, stealing, etc., as the daily news confirms. He uses God's name as a curse word, while Mother Nature gets the glory for His creation—unless there's a horrible disaster; then man calls that "an act of God."

An applicable acronym for WAR is We Are Right. Any country going to war does so because it has the conviction that it is in the right. However, a quick look at God's Law shows us who is right and who is wrong. We, not God, are the guilty party. If we want His blessing back on our nation and in our lives, we must make peace with Him, and that is possible only through faith in Jesus Christ.

that dwells in you.
12 Therefore, brethren, we are debtors,
not to the flesh, to live after the flesh.
13 For if you live after the flesh, you
shall die: but if you through the Spirit do
mortify the deeds of the body, you shall
live.
14 For as many as are led by the Spirit
of God, they are the sons of God.
15 For you have not received the spirit
of bondage again to fear; but you have
received the Spirit of adoption, whereby
we cry, Abba, Father.
16 The Spirit itself bears witness with our
spirit, that we are the children of God:
17 And if children, then heirs; heirs of
God, and joint-heirs with Christ; if so be
that we suffer with him, that we may be
also glorified together.
18 For I reckon that the sufferings of
this present time are not worthy to be
compared with the glory which shall be
revealed in us.
19 For the earnest expectation of the
creature waits for the manifestation of
the sons of God.
20 For the creature was made subject to
vanity, not willingly, but by reason of
him who has subjected the same in hope,
21 Because the creature itself also shall
be delivered from the bondage of corruption
into the glorious liberty of the
children of God.
22 For we know that the whole creation
groans and travails in pain together until
now.
23 And not only they, but ourselves also,
which have the firstfruits of the Spirit,
even we ourselves groan within ourselves,
waiting for the adoption, to wit, the redemption
of our body.
24 For we are saved by hope: but hope
that is seen is not hope: for what a man
sees, why does he yet hope for?
25 But if we hope for that we see not,
then do we with patience wait for it.
26 Likewise the Spirit also helps our infirmities:
for we know not what we should

pray for as we ought: but the Spirit itself
makes intercession for us with groanings
which cannot be uttered.
27 And he that searches the hearts knows
what is the mind of the Spirit, because
he makes intercession for the saints according to the will of God.
28 And we know that all things work
together for good to them that love God,
to them who are the called according to
his purpose.
29 For whom he did foreknow, he also
did predestinate to be conformed to the
image of his Son, that he might be the
firstborn among many brethren.

> The gospel isn't a treasure to be hoarded; it's a gift to be shared.
>
> **GREG LAURIE**

30 Moreover whom he did predestinate,
them he also called: and whom he called,
them he also justified: and whom he justified, them he also glorified.
31 What shall we then say to these things?
If God be for us, who can be against us?
32 He that spared not his own Son, but
delivered him up for us all, how shall he
not with him also freely give us all things?
33 Who shall lay any thing to the charge
of God's elect? It is God that justifies.
34 Who is he that condemns? It is Christ
that died, yes rather, that is risen again,
who is even at the right hand of God,
who also makes intercession for us.
35 Who shall separate us from the love
of Christ? shall tribulation, or distress, or
persecution, or famine, or nakedness, or
peril, or sword?
36 As it is written, For your sake we are
killed all the day long; we are accounted
as sheep for the slaughter.
37 Nay, in all these things we are more
than conquerors through him that loved
us.
38 For I am persuaded, that neither
death, nor life, nor angels, nor principalities, nor powers, nor things present, nor
things to come,
39 Nor height, nor depth, nor any other
creature, shall be able to separate us from
the love of God, which is in Christ Jesus
our Lord.

CHAPTER 9

I SAY the truth in Christ, I lie not, my
conscience also bearing me witness in
the Holy Spirit,
2 That I have great heaviness and continual sorrow in my heart.
3 For I could wish that myself were accursed from Christ for my brethren, my
kinsmen according to the flesh:
4 Who are Israelites; to whom pertain
the adoption, and the glory, and the covenants, and the giving of the law, and the
service of God, and the promises;
5 Whose are the fathers, and of whom as
concerning the flesh Christ came, who is

8:39 The cost of our redemption was the blood of God's Son. The Father's love for us was and is so great, He didn't hesitate for a moment, but delivered Him up freely for us like a lamb for the slaughter. If that is the case, then what good thing will He hold back from those who walk uprightly in Christ! What demon can make one peep, or mutter an accusation against us, when we have such evidence of God's love set before our eyes? What trial could ever separate us from the devotion of God in Christ?

Shall the Shepherd, who put His life in great jeopardy by climbing down a precipice to rescue a lost sheep, carry it back carelessly? Will He now let it starve after He risked His very life to rescue it? Will He now stand by idly and let wolves devour the sheep? The Chief Shepherd descended into death itself to deliver us. He has already proven His great love by willingly giving His life for the sheep, so no tribulation, distress, persecution, famine, or even sharp sword will cut us off from such love.

9:1 "When a man calls himself an atheist, he is not attacking God; he is attacking his own conscience." *Michael Pearl*

over all, God blessed for ever. Amen.
6 Not as though the word of God has
taken none effect. For they are not all
Israel, which are of Israel:
7 Neither, because they are the seed of
Abraham, are they all children: but, In
Isaac shall your seed be called.
8 That is, they which are the children of
the flesh, these are not the children of
God: but the children of the promise are
counted for the seed.
9 For this is the word of promise, At
this time will I come, and Sara shall have
a son.
10 And not only this; but when Rebecca
also had conceived by one, even by our
father Isaac;
11 (For the children being not yet born,
neither having done any good or evil,
that the purpose of God according to
election might stand, not of works, but
of him that calls;)
12 It was said to her, The elder shall
serve the younger.
13 As it is written, Jacob have I loved,
but Esau have I hated.
14 What shall we say then? Is there unrighteousness with God? God forbid.
15 For he said to Moses, I will have
mercy on whom I will have mercy, and I
will have compassion on whom I will
have compassion.
16 So then it is not of him that wills, nor
of him that runs, but of God that shows
mercy.
17 For the scripture said to Pharaoh,
Even for this same purpose have I raised
you up, that I might show my power in
you, and that my name might be declared
throughout all the earth.
18 Therefore has he mercy on whom he
will have mercy, and whom he will he
hardens.
19 You will say then to me, Why does
he yet find fault? For who has resisted
his will?
20 Nay but, O man, who are you that
reply against God? Shall the thing formed
say to him that formed it, Why have you
made me thus?
21 Has not the potter power over the
clay, of the same lump to make one vessel to honor, and another to dishonor?
22 What if God, willing to show his
wrath, and to make his power known,
endured with much longsuffering the
vessels of wrath fitted to destruction:
23 And that he might make known the
riches of his glory on the vessels of mercy,
which he had before prepared to glory,
24 Even us, whom he has called, not of
the Jews only, but also of the Gentiles?

9:2,3 A letter from an atheist:
"You are really convinced that you've got all the answers. You've really got yourself tricked into believing that you're 100% right. Well, let me tell you just one thing. Do you consider yourself to be compassionate of other humans? If you're right about God, as you say you are, and you believe that, then how can you sleep at night? When you speak with me, you are speaking with someone who you believe is walking directly into eternal damnation, into an endless onslaught of horrendous pain which your 'loving' god created, yet you stand by and do nothing.

"If you believed one bit that thousands every day were falling into an eternal and unchangeable fate, you should be running the streets mad with rage at their blindness. That's equivalent to standing on a street corner and watching every person that passes you walk blindly directly into the path of a bus and die, yet you stand idly by and do nothing. You're just twiddling your thumbs, happy in the knowledge that one day that 'Walk' signal will shine your way across the road.

"Think about it. Imagine the horrors hell must have in store if the Bible is true. You're just going to allow that to happen and not care about saving anyone but yourself? If you're right, then you're an uncaring, unemotional and purely selfish (expletive) that has no right to talk about subjects such as love and caring."

If we have great heaviness and sorrow in *our* heart for the lost, we'll warn them of the reality of hell (see 2 Thessalonians 1:8,9 comment) and how to avoid it. See John 4:1 comment for witnessing tips.

QUESTIONS & OBJECTIONS

10:3 *"Why are there so many different religions?"*

It has been well said that "religion" is man's way of trying to deal with his guilt. Different religions have different ways of attempting to rid their adherants of sin and its consequences. They fast, pray, deny themselves legitimate pleasures, or chasten themselves, often to a point of inflicting pain. They do this because they have a concept of what they think God (or "the gods") is like, so they seek to establish their own righteousness, being "ignorant of God's righteousness."

The Good News of the Christian faith is that no one need suffer the pains of religious works. Christ's blood can cleanse our conscience from the "dead works" of religion (Hebrews 9:14). Jesus took our punishment upon Himself, and He is the only One who can save us from sin and death. See Acts 4:12 and John 14:6.

25 As he said also in Hosea, I will call them my people, which were not my people; and her beloved, which was not beloved.
26 And it shall come to pass, that in the place where it was said to them, You are not my people; there shall they be called the children of the living God.
27 Isaiah also cries concerning Israel, Though the number of the children of Israel be as the sand of the sea, a remnant shall be saved:
28 For he will finish the work, and cut it short in righteousness: because a short work will the Lord make upon the earth.
29 And as Isaiah said before, Except the Lord of Sabaoth had left us a seed, we had been as Sodom, and been made like to Gomorrah.
30 What shall we say then? That the Gentiles, which followed not after righteousness, have attained to righteousness, even the righteousness which is of faith.
31 But Israel, which followed after the law of righteousness, has not attained to the law of righteousness.
32 Wherefore? Because they sought it not by faith, but as it were by the works of the law. For they stumbled at that stumblingstone;
33 As it is written, Behold, I lay in Zion a stumblingstone and rock of offence: and whosoever believes on him shall not be ashamed.

CHAPTER 10

BRETHREN, my heart's desire and prayer to God for Israel is, that they might be saved.
2 For I bear them record that they have a zeal of God, but not according to knowledge.
3 For they being ignorant of God's righteousness, and going about to establish their own righteousness, have not submitted themselves to the righteousness of God.
4 For Christ is the end of the law for righteousness to every one that believes.
5 For Moses describes the righteousness which is of the law, That the man which does those things shall live by them.
6 But the righteousness which is of faith speaks on this wise, Say not in your heart,

9:32 For those who are trusting in good works, see Ephesians 2:8,9 and Titus 3:5.

10:1 The heart of a person who is close to God must be consumed with prayer for the salvation of the world. The theme will permeate his prayers.

Who shall ascend into heaven? (that is, to bring Christ down from above:)
7 Or, Who shall descend into the deep? (that is, to bring up Christ again from the dead.)
8 **But what said it? The word is near you, even in your mouth, and in your heart: that is, the word of faith, which we preach;**
9 That if you shall confess with your mouth the Lord Jesus, and shall believe in your heart that God has raised him from the dead, you shall be saved.
10 **For with the heart man believes to righteousness; and with the mouth confession is made to salvation.**
11 **For the scripture says, Whosoever believes on him shall not be ashamed.**
12 For there is no difference between the Jew and the Greek: for the same Lord over all is rich to all that call upon him.
13 For whosoever shall call upon the name of the Lord shall be saved.
14 *How then shall they call on him in whom they have not believed? and how shall they believe in him of whom they have not heard? and how shall they hear without a preacher?*
15 *And how shall they preach, except they be sent? as it is written, How beautiful are the feet of them that preach the gospel of peace, and bring glad tidings of good things!*
16 But they have not all obeyed the gospel. For Isaiah says, Lord, who has believed our report?
17 So then faith comes by hearing, and hearing by the word of God.
18 But I say, Have they not heard? Yes verily, their sound went into all the earth, and their words to the ends of the world.
19 But I say, Did not Israel know? First Moses says, I will provoke you to jealousy by them that are no people, and by a foolish nation I will anger you.
20 But Isaiah is very bold, and says, I was found of them that sought me not; I was made manifest to them that asked not after me.
21 But to Israel he says, All day long I have stretched forth my hands to a disobedient and gainsaying people.

CHAPTER 11

I SAY then, has God cast away his people? God forbid. For I also am an Israelite, of the seed of Abraham, of the tribe of Benjamin.

10:9 We must confess and forsake our sins to receive God's mercy: Here is a model prayer of repentance, from Psalm 51: "Have mercy upon me, O God, according to your lovingkindness: according to the multitude of Your tender mercies blot out my transgressions. Wash me thoroughly from my iniquity, and cleanse me from my sin. For I acknowledge my transgressions, and my sin is ever before me. Against You, You only, have I sinned, and done this evil in Your sight. I believe that Jesus suffered and died in my place. I believe that He rose from the dead. I put my trust in Him this day as my Lord and my Savior. I will read Your Word daily and obey what I read. In Jesus' name I pray. Amen."

10:12 Here are God's promises to those who call upon Him: "If we confess our sins, He is faithful and just to forgive us our sins, and to cleanse us from all unrighteousness" (1 John 1:9). "He who believes in the Son of God has the witness in himself; he who does not believe God has made Him a liar, because he has not believed the testimony that God has given of His Son. And this is the testimony: that God has given us eternal life, and this life is in His Son. He who has the Son has life; he who does not have the Son of God does not have life. These things I have written to you who believe in the name of the Son of God, that you may know that you have eternal life, and that you may continue to believe in the name of the Son of God" (1 John 5:10–13).

10:13 Salvation is possible for every person. See also 1 Timothy 2:4.

10:15 If we take the gospel to a world that desperately needs to hear it, God considers even the lowest part of us to be beautiful.

2 God has not cast away his people which he foreknew. Do you not know what the scripture said of Elijah? how he makes intercession to God against Israel, saying,

3 Lord, they have killed your prophets, and dug down your altars; and I am left alone, and they seek my life.

4 But what said the answer of God to him? I have reserved to myself seven thousand men, who have not bowed the knee to the image of Baal.

5 Even so then at this present time also there is a remnant according to the election of grace.

6 And if by grace, then is it no more of works: otherwise grace is no more grace. But if it be of works, then is it no more grace: otherwise work is no more work.

7 What then? Israel has not obtained that which he seeks for; but the election has obtained it, and the rest were blinded

8 (According as it is written, God has given them the spirit of slumber, eyes that they should not see, and ears that they should not hear;) to this day.

9 And David said, Let their table be made a snare, and a trap, and a stumbling block, and a recompense to them:

10 Let their eyes be darkened, that they may not see, and bow down their back always.

11 I say then, Have they stumbled that they should fall? God forbid: but rather through their fall salvation is come to the Gentiles, for to provoke them to jealousy.

12 Now if the fall of them be the riches of the world, and the diminishing of them the riches of the Gentiles; how much more their fulness?

13 For I speak to you Gentiles, inasmuch as I am the apostle of the Gentiles, I magnify mine office:

14 If by any means I may provoke to emulation them which are my flesh, and might save some of them.

15 For if the casting away of them be the reconciling of the world, what shall the receiving of them be, but life from the dead?

16 For if the firstfruit be holy, the lump is also holy: and if the root be holy, so are the branches.

17 And if some of the branches be broken off, and you, being a wild olive tree, were grafted in among them, and with them partake of the root and fatness of the olive tree;

18 Boast not against the branches. But if you boast, you bear not the root, but the root you.

19 You will say then, The branches were broken off, that I might be grafted in.

20 Well; because of unbelief they were broken off, and you stand by faith. Be not high-minded, but fear:

> God, send me anywhere, only go with me. Lay any burden on me, only sustain me. And sever any tie in my heart except the tie that binds my heart to Yours.
>
> **DAVID LIVINGSTONE**

21 For if God spared not the natural branches, take heed lest he also spare not you.

22 Behold therefore the goodness and severity of God: on them which fell, severity; but toward you, goodness, if you continue in his goodness: otherwise you also shall be cut off.

23 And they also, if they abide not still in unbelief, shall be grafted in: for God is able to graft them in again.

24 For if you were cut out of the olive tree which is wild by nature, and were grafted contrary to nature into a good olive tree: how much more shall these, which be the natural branches, be grafted into their own olive tree?

25 For I would not, brethren, that you should be ignorant of this mystery, lest you should be wise in your own conceits; that blindness in part is happened to Israel, until the fulness of the Gentiles be come in.

26 And so all Israel shall be saved: as it is written, There shall come out of Zion

the Deliverer, and shall turn away ungodliness from Jacob:

27 For this is my covenant to them, when I shall take away their sins.

28 As concerning the gospel, they are enemies for your sakes: but as touching the election, they are beloved for the fathers' sakes.

29 For the gifts and calling of God are without repentance.

30 For as you in times past have not believed God, yet have now obtained mercy through their unbelief:

31 Even so have these also now not believed, that through your mercy they also may obtain mercy.

32 For God has concluded them all in unbelief, that he might have mercy upon all.

33 O the depth of the riches both of the wisdom and knowledge of God! how unsearchable are his judgments, and his ways past finding out!

34 For who has known the mind of the Lord? or who has been his counsellor?

35 Or who has first given to him, and it shall be recompensed to him again?

36 For of him, and through him, and to him, are all things: to whom be glory for ever. Amen.

CHAPTER 12

I BESEECH you therefore, brethren, by the mercies of God, that you present your bodies a living sacrifice, holy, acceptable to God, which is your reasonable service.

2 And be not conformed to this world: but be transformed by the renewing of your mind, that you may prove what is that good, and acceptable, and perfect, will of God.

3 For I say, through the grace given to me, to every man that is among you, not to think of himself more highly than he ought to think; but to think soberly, according as God has dealt to every man the measure of faith.

4 For as we have many members in one body, and all members have not the same office:

5 So we, being many, are one body in Christ, and every one members one of another.

6 Having then gifts differing according to the grace that is given to us, whether prophecy, let us prophesy according to the proportion of faith;

7 Or ministry, let us wait on our ministering: or he that teaches, on teaching;

8 Or he that exhorts, on exhortation: he that gives, let him do it with simplicity; he that rules, with diligence; he that shows mercy, with cheerfulness.

9 Let love be without dissimulation. Abhor that which is evil; cleave to that which is good.

10 Be kindly affectionate one to another with brotherly love; in honor preferring one another;

11 Not slothful in business; fervent in spirit; serving the Lord;

12 Rejoicing in hope; patient in tribulation; continuing instant in prayer;

13 Distributing to the necessity of saints; given to hospitality.

14 Bless them which persecute you: bless, and curse not.

15 Rejoice with them that do rejoice, and weep with them that weep.

16 Be of the same mind one toward another. Mind not high things, but condescend to men of low estate. Be not wise in your own conceits.

17 Recompense to no man evil for evil. Provide things honest in the sight of all men.

18 If it be possible, as much as lies in you, live peaceably with all men.

19 Dearly beloved, avenge not yourselves, but rather give place to wrath: for it is written, Vengeance is mine; I will repay, says the Lord.

12:1 "If Jesus Christ be God and died for me, no sacrifice I make can be too great for Him." *C. T. Studd*

"I was honored today with having a few stones, dirt, rotten eggs, and pieces of dead cats thrown at me."

George Whitefield

20 Therefore if your enemy hunger, feed
him; if he thirst, give him drink: for in so
doing you shall heap coals of fire on his
head.
21 Be not overcome of evil, but overcome evil with good.

. . . . . .

Are there contradictions in the Bible? See Mark 15:26 comment.

. . . . . .

CHAPTER 13

LET every soul be subject to the higher powers. For there is no power but
of God: the powers that be are ordained
of God.
2 Whosoever therefore resists the power,
resists the ordinance of God: and they
that resist shall receive to themselves
damnation.
3 For rulers are not a terror to good
works, but to the evil. Will you then not
be afraid of the power? do that which is
good, and you shall have praise of the
same:
4 For he is the minister of God to you
for good. But if you do that which is evil,
be afraid; for he bears not the sword in
vain: for he is the minister of God, a revenger to execute wrath upon him that
does evil.
5 Wherefore you must needs be subject,
not only for wrath, but also for conscience sake.
6 For for this cause you pay tribute also:
for they are God's ministers, attending
continually upon this very thing.
7 Render therefore to all their dues: tribute to whom tribute is due; custom to
whom custom; fear to whom fear; honor
to whom honor.
8 Owe no man any thing, but to love one
another: for he that loves another has
fulfilled the law.
9 For this, You shall not commit adultery, You shall not kill, You shall not
steal, You shall not bear false witness,
You shall not covet; and if there be any
other commandment, it is briefly comprehended in this saying, namely, You
shall love your neighbor as yourself.
10 Love works no ill to his neighbor:
therefore love is the fulfilling of the law.
11 *And that, knowing the time, that now
it is high time to awake out of sleep: for now
is our salvation nearer than when we believed.*
12 *The night is far spent, the day is at
hand: let us therefore cast off the works of
darkness, and let us put on the armor of
light.*
13 Let us walk honestly, as in the day;
not in rioting and drunkenness, not in
chambering and wantonness, not in strife

QUESTIONS & OBJECTIONS

Q 14:12 ***"How do I witness to someone I know?"***

For most of us, it is far easier to witness to a stranger than to someone we know and respect. An effective way to soften the message without compromise is to speak in the "first person" or in testimonial form. Say something like, "I didn't realize that the Bible warns that for every idle word I have spoken, I will have to give an account on Judgment Day. I thought that as long as I believed in God and tried to live a good life, I would go to heaven when I died. I was so wrong. Jesus said that if I as much as looked with lust, I had committed adultery in my heart, and that there was nothing I could do to wash away my sins. I knew that if God judged me by the Ten Commandments on Judgment Day, I would end up guilty, and go to hell.

"It was when I acknowledged my sins that I began to understand why Jesus died. It was to take the punishment for my sins, and the sins of the world." Then, depending on the person's openness, you may ask, "How do you think you will do on Judgment Day, if God judges you by the Ten Commandments?"

and envying.
14 But put on the Lord Jesus Christ, and
make not provision for the flesh, to fulfil
the lusts thereof.

CHAPTER 14

HIM that is weak in the faith receive,
but not to doubtful disputations.
2 For one believes that he may eat all
things: another, who is weak, eats herbs.
3 Let not him that eats despise him that
eats not; and let not him which eats not
judge him that eats: for God has received
him.
4 Who are you that judge another man's
servant? to his own master he stands or
falls. Yes, he shall be held up: for God is
able to make him stand.
5 One man esteems one day above another: another esteems every day alike.
Let every man be fully persuaded in his
own mind.
6 He that regards the day, regards it to
the Lord; and he that regards not the day,
to the Lord he does not regard it. He that
eats, eats to the Lord, for he gives God
thanks; and he that eats not, to the Lord
he eats not, and gives God thanks.
7 For none of us lives to himself, and
no man dies to himself.
8 For whether we live, we live to the
Lord; and whether we die, we die to the
Lord: whether we live therefore, or die,
we are the Lord's.
9 For to this end Christ both died, and
rose, and revived, that he might be Lord
both of the dead and living.
10 But why do you judge your brother?
or why do you set at nought your brother? for we shall all stand before the judgment seat of Christ.
11 For it is written, As I live, says the
Lord, every knee shall bow to me, and
every tongue shall confess to God.
12 So then every one of us shall give account of himself to God.
13 Let us not therefore judge one another any more: but judge this rather, that
no man put a stumblingblock or an occasion to fall in his brother's way.

13:14 Salvation comes through trusting Jesus Christ in the same way you trust a parachute. You don't just "believe" in it, you *put it on*. See Galatians 3:27.

14:2 Vegetarianism. See 1 Timothy 4:3 comment.

14:10 Judgment Day: For verses that warn of its reality, see 2 Corinthians 5:10.

14 I know, and am persuaded by the
Lord Jesus, that there is nothing unclean
of itself: but to him that esteems any
thing to be unclean, to him it is unclean.
15 But if your brother be grieved with
your meat, now you do not walk charita-
bly. Destroy not him with your meat, for
whom Christ died.
16 Let not then your good be evil spoken of:
17 For the kingdom of God is not meat
and drink; but righteousness, and peace,
and joy in the Holy Spirit.
18 For he that in these things serves
Christ is acceptable to God, and approved
of men.
19 Let us therefore follow after the things
which make for peace, and things wherewith one may edify another.
20 For meat destroy not the work of
God. All things indeed are pure; but it is
evil for that man who eats with offence.
21 It is good neither to eat flesh, nor to
drink wine, nor any thing whereby your
brother stumbles, or is offended, or is
made weak.
22 Do you have faith? have it to yourself
before God. Happy is he that condemns
not himself in that thing which he allows.
23 And he that doubts is damned if he
eat, because he eats not of faith: for whatsoever is not of faith is sin.

CHAPTER 15

WE then that are strong ought to
bear the infirmities of the weak,
and not to please ourselves.
2 Let every one of us please his neighbor for his good to edification.
3 For even Christ pleased not himself;
but, as it is written, The reproaches of
them that reproached you fell on me.
4 For whatsoever things were written
beforetime were written for our learning,
that we through patience and comfort of
the scriptures might have hope.
5 Now the God of patience and consolation grant you to be likeminded one
toward another according to Christ Jesus:
6 That you may with one mind and one
mouth glorify God, even the Father of
our Lord Jesus Christ.
7 Wherefore receive one another, as
Christ also received us to the glory of God.
8 Now I say that Jesus Christ was a minister of the circumcision for the truth of
God, to confirm the promises made to
the fathers:
9 And that the Gentiles might glorify
God for his mercy; as it is written, For
this cause I will confess to you among
the Gentiles, and sing to your name.

> No pursuit of mortal men is to be compared with that of soul-winning.
>
> **CHARLES SPURGEON**

10 And again he says, Rejoice, you Gentiles, with his people.
11 And again, Praise the Lord, all you
Gentiles; and laud him, all you people.
12 And again, Isaiah says, There shall be
a root of Jesse, and he that shall rise to
reign over the Gentiles; in him shall the
Gentiles trust.
13 Now the God of hope fill you with
all joy and peace in believing, that you
may abound in hope, through the power
of the Holy Spirit.
14 And I myself also am persuaded of
you, my brethren, that you also are full
of goodness, filled with all knowledge,
able also to admonish one another.
15 Nevertheless, brethren, I have written the more boldly to you in some sort,
as putting you in mind, because of the
grace that is given to me of God,
16 That I should be the minister of Jesus
Christ to the Gentiles, ministering the
gospel of God, that the offering up of the
Gentiles might be acceptable, being sanc-

15:16 "Consider as sin any minute of life spent on something other than saving souls for eternity from this world doomed to destruction." *Richard Wurmbrand*

Memorize the Ten Commandments

Memorize the Ten Commandments using these special picture figures. Then test your memory, and grade yourself. Put each picture in your mind, and it will remind you of each commandment.

1. "You shall have no other gods before Me"
(God should be Number One)

2. "You shall not make yourself any graven image"
(Don't bow down to anything but God)

3. "You shall not take the name of the Lord your God in vain"
(Don't use your lips to dishonor God)

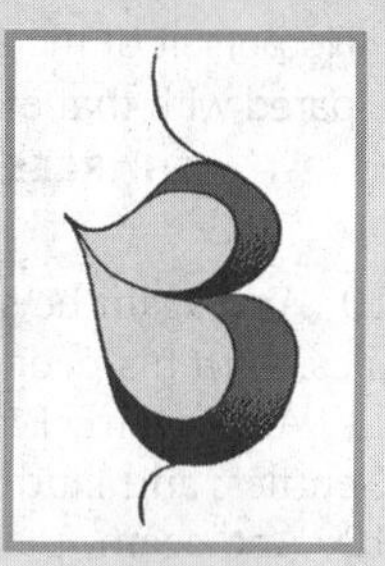

4. "Remember the Sabbath Day to keep it holy"
(Don't neglect the things of God)

5. "Honor your Father and your Mother"

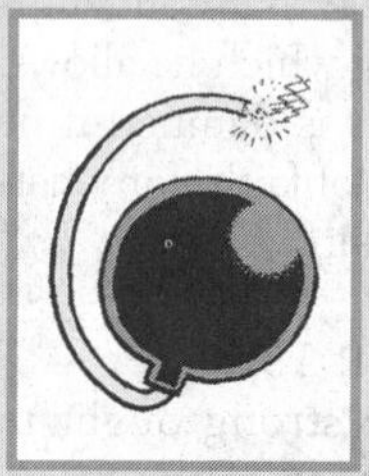

6. "You shall not kill"

7. "You shall not commit adultery"
(Adultery leaves a heart broken)

8. "You shall not steal"

9. "You shall not lie"
(a "lying" nine)

10. "You shall not covet"
(want what others have)

tified by the Holy Spirit.
17 I have therefore whereof I may glory
through Jesus Christ in those things which
pertain to God.
18 For I will not dare to speak of any of
those things which Christ has not wrought
by me, to make the Gentiles obedient, by
word and deed,
19 **Through mighty signs and wonders,
by the power of the Spirit of God; so
that from Jerusalem, and round about
to Illyricum, I have fully preached the
gospel of Christ.**
20 Yea, so have I strived to preach the
gospel, not where Christ was named, lest
I should build upon another man's foundation:
21 But as it is written, To whom he was
not spoken of, they shall see: and they
that have not heard shall understand.
22 For which cause also I have been
much hindered from coming to you.
23 But now having no more place in
these parts, and having a great desire these
many years to come to you;
24 Whenever I take my journey into
Spain, I will come to you: for I trust to
see you in my journey, and to be brought
on my way thitherward by you, if first I
be somewhat filled with your company.
25 But now I go to Jerusalem to minister to the saints.
26 For it has pleased them of Macedonia
and Achaia to make a certain contribu-
tion for the poor saints which are at Jerusalem.
27 It has pleased them verily; and their
debtors they are. For if the Gentiles have
been made partakers of their spiritual
things, their duty is also to minister to
them in carnal things.
28 When therefore I have performed this,
and have sealed to them this fruit, I will
come by you into Spain.
29 And I am sure that, when I come to
you, I shall come in the fulness of the
blessing of the gospel of Christ.
30 Now I beseech you, brethren, for the
Lord Jesus Christ's sake, and for the love
of the Spirit, that you strive together with
me in your prayers to God for me;
31 That I may be delivered from them
that do not believe in Judea; and that my
service which I have for Jerusalem may
be accepted of the saints;
32 That I may come to you with joy by
the will of God, and may with you be refreshed.
33 Now the God of peace be with you
all. Amen.

CHAPTER 16

I COMMEND to you Phebe our sister,
which is a servant of the church which
is at Cenchrea:
2 That you receive her in the Lord, as
becomes saints, and that you assist her
in whatsoever business she has need of
you: for she has been a succourer of many,
and of myself also.
3 Greet Priscilla and Aquila my helpers
in Christ Jesus:
4 Who have for my life laid down their
own necks: to whom not only I give
thanks, but also all the churches of the
Gentiles.
5 Likewise greet the church that is in
their house. Salute my wellbeloved Epae-
netus, who is the firstfruits of Achaia to
Christ.
6 Greet Mary, who bestowed much labor
on us.
7 Salute Andronicus and Junia, my kinsmen, and my fellow-prisoners, who are
of note among the apostles, who also
were in Christ before me.
8 Greet Amplias my beloved in the Lord.
9 Salute Urbane, our helper in Christ,

16:5 Believers in many countries today must meet secretly in homes to worship. These "house churches" follow the New Testament model for fellowship, prayer, and study of the Scriptures better than do many modern churches that have the finest facilities. The true *Church* is actually the body of believers, and can worship the Lord with or without a building.

and Stachys my beloved.
10 Salute Apelles approved in Christ. Salute them which are of Aristobulus' household.
11 Salute Herodion my kinsman. Greet them that be of the household of Narcissus, which are in the Lord.
12 Salute Tryphena and Tryphosa, who labor in the Lord. Salute the beloved Persis, which labored much in the Lord.
13 Salute Rufus chosen in the Lord, and his mother and mine.
14 Salute Asyncritus, Phlegon, Hermas, Patrobas, Hermes, and the brethren which are with them.
15 Salute Philologus, and Julia, Nereus, and his sister, and Olympas, and all the saints which are with them.
16 Salute one another with an holy kiss. The churches of Christ salute you.
17 Now I beseech you, brethren, mark them which cause divisions and offences contrary to the doctrine which you have learned; and avoid them.
18 For they that are such serve not our Lord Jesus Christ, but their own belly; and by good words and fair speeches deceive the hearts of the simple.
19 For your obedience is come abroad to all men. I am glad therefore on your behalf: but yet I would have you wise to that which is good, and simple concerning evil.
20 And the God of peace shall bruise Satan under your feet shortly. The grace of our Lord Jesus Christ be with you. Amen.
21 Timotheus my workfellow, and Lucius, and Jason, and Sosipater, my kinsmen, salute you.
22 I Tertius, who wrote this epistle, salute you in the Lord.
23 Gaius mine host, and of the whole church, salutes you. Erastus the chamberlain of the city salutes you, and Quartus a brother.
24 The grace of our Lord Jesus Christ be with you all. Amen.
25 Now to him that is of power to stablish you according to my gospel, and the preaching of Jesus Christ, according to the revelation of the mystery, which was kept secret since the world began,
26 But now is made manifest, and by the scriptures of the prophets, according to the commandment of the everlasting God, made known to all nations for the obedience of faith:
27 To God only wise, be glory through Jesus Christ for ever. Amen.

"To God only wise, be the glory forever through Jesus Christ. Amen."

ROMANS 16:27

1 Corinthians

CHAPTER 1

PAUL, called to be an apostle of Jesus
Christ through the will of God, and
Sosthenes our brother,
2 To the church of God which is at Corinth, to them that are sanctified in Christ
Jesus, called to be saints, with all that in
every place call upon the name of Jesus
Christ our Lord, both theirs and ours:
3 Grace be to you, and peace, from God
our Father, and from the Lord Jesus
Christ.
4 I thank my God always on your behalf, for the grace of God which is given
you by Jesus Christ;
5 That in every thing you are enriched
by him, in all utterance, and in all knowledge;
6 Even as the testimony of Christ was
confirmed in you:
7 So that you come behind in no gift;
waiting for the coming of our Lord Jesus
Christ:
8 Who shall also confirm you to the
end, that you may be blameless in the
day of our Lord Jesus Christ.
9 God is faithful, by whom you were
called to the fellowship of his Son Jesus
Christ our Lord.
10 Now I beseech you, brethren, by the
name of our Lord Jesus Christ, that you
all speak the same thing, and that there
be no divisions among you; but that you
be perfectly joined together in the same
mind and in the same judgment.
11 For it has been declared to me of
you, my brethren, by them which are of
the house of Chloe, that there are contentions among you.
12 Now this I say, that every one of you
says, I am of Paul; and I of Apollos; and I
of Cephas; and I of Christ.
13 Is Christ divided? was Paul crucified
for you? or were you baptized in the name
of Paul?
14 I thank God that I baptized none of
you, but Crispus and Gaius;
15 Lest any should say that I had baptized in mine own name.
16 And I baptized also the household of
Stephanas: besides, I know not whether
I baptized any other.
17 For Christ sent me not to baptize, but
to preach the gospel: not with wisdom of
words, lest the cross of Christ should be
made of none effect.
18 For the preaching of the cross is
to them that perish foolishness; but to
us which are saved it is the power of
God.
19 For it is written, I will destroy the
wisdom of the wise, and will bring to
nothing the understanding of the prudent.

1:18 "To convince the world of the truth of Christianity, it must first be convinced of sin. It is only sin that renders Christ intelligible." *Andrew Murray, The Spirit of Christ*

SPRINGBOARDS FOR PREACHING AND WITNESSING

1:18

The Sinking Ship

Imagine for a moment that you are standing on the seashore gazing at a large ocean liner. The sun is shining. There is no wind and the sea is calm. To your amazement, about thirty people suddenly dive off the end of the ship and cling to a lifeboat.

You shake your head in disbelief at their foolishness. Then without warning, the great ocean liner strikes an iceberg and suddenly sinks, taking all on board with it.

Those who *looked* like fools in abandoning the ship were actually wise, and those who seemed wise by staying on board were, in truth, fools.

The world scoffs at those who abandon the ship of this world and cling to the lifeboat of the Savior. But Christians know that this great pleasure-cruiser will eventually come into contact with the immovable iceberg of the Law of God, sink into hell...and take all those on board with it.

20 Where is the wise? where is the scribe? where is the disputer of this world? has not God made foolish the wisdom of this world?

21 For after that in the wisdom of God the world by wisdom knew not God, it pleased God by the foolishness of preaching to save them that believe.

22 For the Jews require a sign, and the Greeks seek after wisdom:

23 But we preach Christ crucified, to the Jews a stumblingblock, and to the Greeks foolishness;

24 But to them which are called, both Jews and Greeks, Christ the power of God, and the wisdom of God.

25 Because the foolishness of God is wiser than men; and the weakness of God is stronger than men.

26 For you see your calling, brethren, how that not many wise men after the flesh, not many mighty, not many noble, are called:

27 But God has chosen the foolish things of the world to confound the wise; and God has chosen the weak things of the world to confound the things which are mighty;

1:23 There were some in John Wesley's day who refused to preach the Law to bring the knowledge of sin. They justified their method by saying that they preached "Christ and Him crucified." So Wesley points to Paul's method of preaching Christ crucified:

"...when Felix sent for Paul, on purpose that he might 'hear him concerning the faith in Christ;' instead of preaching Christ in *your* sense (which would probably have caused the Governor, either to mock or to contradict and blaspheme,) 'he reasoned of righteousness, temperance, and judgment to come,' till Felix (hardened as he was) 'trembled,' (Acts 24:24,25). Go thou and tread in his steps. Preach Christ to the careless sinner, by reasoning 'of righteousness, temperance, and judgment to come!'" *John Wesley*

1:25 "Everything that can be invented has been invented." *Charles H. Duell*, Commissioner, U.S. Office of Patents, 1899

1:27,28 Many years ago, I ran a children's club. At the end of the club I told about one hundred kids to line up for some candy. There was an immediate rush, and the line sorted itself into what I saw as being a line of greed. The bigger, selfish kids were at the front, and the small and timid ones were at the back. I then did something that gave me great satisfaction. I told them to turn about face. Everyone did. Then I said to stay where they were, and I took great delight in going to the other end of the line and giving the candy to the smaller, timid kids first.

In a world where the rich get richer and the poor get stomped on, we are informed that God

POINTS FOR OPEN-AIR PREACHING

2:4

Watch for "Red Herrings" or "Rabbit Trails"

The Bible warns us to avoid foolish questions because they start arguments (2 Timothy 2:23). Most of us have fallen into the trap of jumping at every objection to the gospel. However, these questions can often be arguments in disguise to sidetrack you from the "weightier matters of the Law." While apologetics (arguments for God's existence, creation vs. evolution, etc.) are legitimate in evangelism, they should merely be "bait," with the Law of God being the "hook" that brings the conviction of sin. Those who witness solely in the realm of apologetical argument may just get an intellectual decision rather than a repentant conversion. The sinner may come to a point of acknowledging that the Bible is the Word of God, and Jesus is Lord—but even the devil knows that.

Always pull the sinner back to his responsibility before God on Judgment Day, as Jesus did in Luke 13:1–5. Whenever you are in an open-air situation, be wary of so-called Christians who are intent on distracting workers from witnessing. They argue about prophecy, of how much water one should baptize with, or in whose name they should be baptized. It is grievous to see five or six Christians standing around arguing with some sectarian nitpicker, while sinners are sinking into hell. See Acts 21:30 comment.

28 And base things of the world, and
things which are despised, has God chosen, yes, and things which are not, to
bring to nothing things that are:
29 That no flesh should glory in his
presence.
30 But of him are you in Christ Jesus,
who of God is made to us wisdom, and
righteousness, and sanctification, and redemption:
31 That, according as it is written, He
that glories, let him glory in the Lord.

CHAPTER 2

*AND I, brethren, when I came to you,
came not with excellency of speech or
of wisdom, declaring to you the testimony
of God.*
2 *For I determined not to know any thing
among you, save Jesus Christ, and him crucified.*
3 *And I was with you in weakness, and in
fear, and in much trembling.*
4 *And my speech and my preaching was
not with enticing words of man's wisdom,*

has gone to the other end of the line with the message of everlasting life. How has He done that? Simply by choosing that which is weak, base, and despised. You can see this by asking a skeptic, "Do you believe that the following biblical accounts actually happened?"

> Adam and Eve, Noah's ark, Jonah and the whale, Joshua and the walls of Jericho, Samson and his long hair, Daniel and the lion's den, Moses and the Red Sea

Of course he doesn't. To say that he believed such fantastic stories would mean that he would have to surrender his intellectual dignity. Who in their right mind would ever do that? The answer is simply *those who understand that God has chosen foolish, base, weak, and despised things of the world to confound those who think they are wise.*

2:1–4 Qualifications for Evangelism:

1. A witness need not have "excellency of speech or of wisdom." He should simply declare what he has seen and heard.
2. He must not get sidetracked with unnecessary details, but focus on the essentials of Christ's death on the cross.
3. He must have "weakness" (not trusting in his own strength or ability).
4. He must have "fear" (in Greek, *phobos*, "that which is caused by being scared").
5. He must have "much trembling" (awareness of his insufficiency).

Do you meet these qualifications?

QUESTIONS & OBJECTIONS

2:14

"I've tried to read the Bible, but I can't understand it."

The Scriptures tell us that the "natural man" cannot understand the things of the Spirit of God. Most Americans would find it difficult to understand the Chinese language. However, a child who is *born* into a Chinese family can understand every word. That's why you must be born again with God's Spirit living within you (John 3:3). The moment you become part of God's family, the Bible will begin to make sense.

but in demonstration of the Spirit and of power:
5 *That your faith should not stand in the wisdom of men, but in the power of God.*
6 Howbeit we speak wisdom among them that are perfect: yet not the wisdom of this world, nor of the princes of this world, that come to nothing:
7 But we speak the wisdom of God in a mystery, even the hidden wisdom, which God ordained before the world to our glory:
8 Which none of the princes of this world knew: for had they known it, they would not have crucified the Lord of glory.
9 But as it is written, Eye has not seen, nor ear heard, neither have entered into the heart of man, the things which God has prepared for them that love him.
10 But God has revealed them to us by his Spirit: for the Spirit searches all things, yes, the deep things of God.
11 For what man knows the things of a man, save the spirit of man which is in him? even so the things of God knows no man, but the Spirit of God.
12 Now we have received, not the spirit of the world, but the spirit which is of God; that we might know the things that are freely given to us of God.
13 Which things also we speak, not in the words which man's wisdom teaches, but which the Holy Spirit teaches; comparing spiritual things with spiritual.
14 But the natural man receives not the things of the Spirit of God: for they are foolishness to him: neither can he know them, because they are spiritually discerned.
15 But he that is spiritual judges all things, yet he himself is judged of no man.
16 For who has known the mind of the Lord, that he may instruct him? But we

2:5 If someone has been converted to the Christian faith by the wisdom of men, all it would take is the wisdom of *un*converted men to talk him out of his faith. However, if he is transformed by the power of God, he is not solely motivated to Christianity by his intellect. The Holy Spirit has convicted him of sin, righteousness, and judgment. The motivation is the Law of God working upon his conscience. That has given him the knowledge that he has offended a holy God. His repentance is therefore directed at God, who responds in mercy. Those who are converted by God cannot be *talked out* of their faith because they were not *talked into* it.

2:11 "Groanings which cannot be uttered are often prayers which cannot be refused." *Spurgeon*

2:16 The Mind of God. We can get a glimpse of the incredible mind of God simply by looking at His creation. Take one (very) small part—the mind of man: The brain is a soft lump of tissue weighing about 3 pounds. It is one of the most watery organs of the body, its outer tissue being 85% water. There is very little relationship between brain size and intelligence. Some very bright people have smaller brains than those who are less intelligent. The brain feels no pain because it has no pain receptors. It floats in fluid inside the skull, and the fluid (derived from blood) acts as a shock absorber. The brain stops growing in size at about age 15. *(continued on next page)* have the mind of Christ.

CHAPTER 3

AND I, brethren, could not speak to
you as to spiritual, but as to carnal,
even as to babes in Christ.
2 I have fed you with milk, and not with
meat: for hitherto you were not able to
bear it, neither yet now are you able.
3 For you are yet carnal: for whereas
there is among you envying, and strife,
and divisions, are you not carnal, and
walk as men?
4 For while one says, I am of Paul; and
another, I am of Apollos; are you not
carnal?
5 Who then is Paul, and who is Apollos,
but ministers by whom you believed,
even as the Lord gave to every man?
6 I have planted, Apollos watered; but
God gave the increase.
7 *So then neither is he that plants any
thing, neither he that waters; but God that
gives the increase.*
8 *Now he that plants and he that waters
are one: and every man shall receive his
own reward according to his own labor.*
9 For we are laborers together with God:
you are God's husbandry, you are God's
building.
10 According to the grace of God which
is given to me, as a wise masterbuilder, I
have laid the foundation, and another
built thereon. But let every man take
heed how he build thereupon.
**11 For other foundation can no man
lay than that is laid, which is Jesus
Christ.**
12 Now if any man build upon this
foundation gold, silver, precious stones,
wood, hay, stubble;
13 Every man's work shall be made
manifest: for the day shall declare it, because it shall be revealed by fire; and the
fire shall try every man's work of what
sort it is.
14 If any man's work abide which he
has built thereupon, he shall receive a

Its surface is covered with folds. If it were laid out flat, the brain surface would cover two average student desks. The brain has four times as many nerve cells as there are people on Earth. With its 10 billion neurons, it can record 86 million bits of information each day of our lives. Supporting, protecting, and nourishing these 10 billion neurons are 100 billion glia cells, which make up half the mass of the brain.

The brain continues sending out electrical wave signals as long as 37 hours after death. Since nerve cells can't reproduce, you have fewer of them as you get older. Persons of 70 or 80 may have only 75% of the nerve cells they were born with. Nerve impulses travel more quickly than cars do, with some up to 250 miles per hour. If all the nerves were laid end to end, they would stretch almost 45 miles. If all the nerve cell connections—axons and dendrites—from a human brain could be placed end to end, they would encircle the earth many times. The dendrites alone could stretch an estimated 100,000 miles.

Let's now look to the heavens: "They defined the exact shape of the closest major galaxy, a beautiful spiral named Andromeda, containing more than 300 billion stars. The nearest of these is (an incredible) thirteen quintillion (13,000,000,000,000,000,000) miles, or 2.2 million light-years, beyond the Milky Way, a distance calculated by comparing the star's apparent brightness with a star of similar brightness and known distance from Earth. And beyond Andromeda lay billions of other galaxies." *Solar System* (Time-Life Books)

The incredible complexity of the human brain and the vastness of the heavens speak of the awesome power of the Creator's mind, and together "declare the glory of God" (Psalm 19:1).

2:16 Evolutionist *Stephen Hawking* wrote, "It would be very difficult to explain why the universe should have begun in just this way, except as the act of a God who intended to create beings like us" *(A Brief History of Time)*. He also stated: "Then we shall…be able to take part in the discussion of the question of why it is that we and the universe exist. If we find the answer to that, it would be the ultimate triumph of human reason—for then we would know the mind of God."

3:6,7 See John 4:37,38 comment.

Questions & Objections

3:17 "Does someone go to hell for committing suicide?"

Those who are adamant that a person who takes his life is committing a mortal sin, and will go to hell, are basing their belief on church doctrine rather than on the Bible. Scripture is silent on the subject. There are no verses that say "He who takes his own life shall be damned." According to Scripture, only *one* sin does not have forgiveness, and that is blasphemy of the Holy Spirit (see Mark 3:29 comment). That means there *is* forgiveness for every other sin.

Some quote 1 Corinthians 3:17, which says that God will destroy someone who "defiles" the temple of the Holy Spirit. Yet, there is disagreement about what it means to *defile* the temple. Does this include suicide? Does it include illicit drug abuse (slow suicide), prescription drug abuse, cigarettes (deliberately breathing in poisons that will eventually kill), tattoos, over-eating (digging a grave with your spoon), or alcohol abuse?

God forbid that we add to the pain of someone who has lost a loved one through the tragedy of suicide, by making a judgment about their eternal destiny. God is the ultimate Judge, and we should therefore leave the issue in His hands. It would be wise to follow the biblical example and not come to any verdict in the case of suicide.

reward.
15 If any man's work shall be burned, he shall suffer loss: but he himself shall be saved; yet so as by fire.
16 Do you not know that you are the temple of God, and that the Spirit of God dwells in you?
17 If any man defile the temple of God, him shall God destroy; for the temple of God is holy, which temple you are.
18 Let no man deceive himself. If any man among you seems to be wise in this world, let him become a fool, that he may be wise.
19 For the wisdom of this world is foolishness with God. For it is written, He takes the wise in their own craftiness.
20 And again, The Lord knows the thoughts of the wise, that they are vain.
21 Therefore let no man glory in men. For all things are yours;
22 Whether Paul, or Apollos, or Cephas, or the world, or life, or death, or things present, or things to come; all are yours;

3:13,14 "If we work on marble, it will perish; if on brass, time will efface it; if we rear up temples, they will crumble into dust; but if we work on immortal minds and imbue them with principles, with the just fear of God and the love of our fellow men, we engrave on those tablets something that will brighten to all eternity." *Daniel Webster*

3:19 The World's Ignorant Maxims:
1. *"All good things must come to an end."* This isn't true for the Christian; see Ephesians 2:4–7. **2.** *"Which came first, the chicken or the egg?"* The chicken; see Genesis 1:20. **3.** *"There's no such thing as a free lunch."* See Matthew 14:19. **4.** *"You can't take it with you."* The Christian's works "follow" him; see Revelation 14:13. **5.** *"There are only two things in life that are sure—death and taxes."* Plenty of people avoid taxes; none avoid death. See Hebrews 9:27. **6.** *"Crime doesn't pay."* It *does*...up until Judgment Day; see Romans 2:6. **7.** *"As miserable as sin."* Sin gives pleasure; see Hebrews 11:25. **8.** *"That's impossible!"* With God, *nothing* is impossible; see Mark 10:27. **9.** *"No one knows!" God* does; see 1 John 3:20. **10.** *"It's the perfect crime."* Judgment Day will prove that there is no such thing as a crime that escapes justice; see Hebrews 4:13. **11.** *"Seeing is believing."* Any magician knows that isn't true. The eyes are easily fooled; see Proverbs 28:26. **12.** *"God helps those who help themselves."* God helps those who *cannot* help themselves; see Romans 5:6.

The Bible tells us that it is the Law of the Lord that make wise the simple. (See Psalm 19:7 comment.)

23 And you are Christ's; and Christ is God's.

CHAPTER 4

LET a man so account of us, as of the ministers of Christ, and stewards of the mysteries of God.
2 Moreover it is required in stewards, that a man be found faithful.
3 But with me it is a very small thing that I should be judged of you, or of man's judgment: yes, I judge not mine own self.
4 For I know nothing by myself; yet am I not hereby justified: but he that judges me is the Lord.
5 Therefore judge nothing before the time, until the Lord come, who both will bring to light the hidden things of darkness, and will make manifest the counsels of the hearts: and then shall every man have praise of God.
6 And these things, brethren, I have in a figure transferred to myself and to Apollos for your sakes; that you might learn in us not to think of men above that which is written, that no one of you be puffed up for one against another.
7 For who makes you to differ from another? and what have you that you did not receive? now if you did receive it, why do you glory, as if you had not received it?
8 Now you are full, now you are rich, you have reigned as kings without us: and I would to God you did reign, that we also might reign with you.
9 For I think that God has set forth us the apostles last, as it were appointed to death: for we are made a spectacle to the world, and to angels, and to men.
10 *We are fools for Christ's sake, but you are wise in Christ; we are weak, but you are strong; you are honorable, but we are despised.*
11 Even to this present hour we both hunger, and thirst, and are naked, and are buffeted, and have no certain dwellingplace;
12 *And labor, working with our own hands: being reviled, we bless; being persecuted, we suffer it:*
13 *Being defamed, we entreat: we are made as the filth of the world, and are the offscouring of all things to this day.*
14 I write not these things to shame you, but as my beloved sons I warn you.
15 For though you have ten thousand instructors in Christ, yet you do not have many fathers: for in Christ Jesus I have begotten you through the gospel.
16 Wherefore I beseech you, be followers of me.
17 For this cause have I sent to you Timotheus, who is my beloved son, and faithful in the Lord, who shall bring you

---

4:5 Second coming of Jesus: See Philippians 4:5.

4:15 See Matthew 23:9 comment.

4:16 Pastors often ask me how they can be more effective in reaching their city. This is what I tell them. Ask your congregation how many are concerned for their city. There will be a forest of hands. As how many are praying daily for the city. Many hands will appear. Then ask how many are sharing their faith on a regular basis. Give a gauge by asking how many have verbally spoken of the way of salvation to twelve people in the preceding twelve months. About 5 percent will raise their hands.

I once attended an interdenominational prayer meeting, where I could tell who attended a particular church simply by the way they prayed. I could recognize phrases of their pastors in their prayers. It confirmed that congregations imitate their pastor. This is why I would advise a pastor to join a secular health club, or a golf club, or somewhere where he will rub shoulders with the ungodly. I encourage him to regularly tell his congregation of his witnessing experiences and to share his fears—to show not only that he "condescends" to witness to the unsaved, but that he has the same fears they have. In this way he can "lead the flock of God," and it won't be long before they imitate him.

into remembrance of my ways which be in Christ, as I teach every where in every church.

18 Now some are puffed up, as though I would not come to you.

19 But I will come to you shortly, if the Lord will, and will know, not the speech of them which are puffed up, but the power.

20 For the kingdom of God is not in word, but in power.

21 What do you want? shall I come to you with a rod, or in love, and in the spirit of meekness?

> In many ministries, there is not enough of probing the heart and arousing the conscience by the revelation of man's alienation from God, and by the declaration of the selfishness and the wickedness of such a state.
>
> **CHARLES SPURGEON**

CHAPTER 5

IT is reported commonly that there is fornication among you, and such fornication as is not so much as named among the Gentiles, that one should have his father's wife.

2 And you are puffed up, and have not rather mourned, that he that has done this deed might be taken away from among you.

3 For I verily, as absent in body, but present in spirit, have judged already, as though I were present, concerning him that has so done this deed,

4 In the name of our Lord Jesus Christ, when you are gathered together, and my spirit, with the power of our Lord Jesus Christ,

5 To deliver such an one to Satan for the destruction of the flesh, that the spirit may be saved in the day of the Lord Jesus.

6 Your glorying is not good. Do you not know that a little leaven leavens the whole lump?

7 Purge out therefore the old leaven, that you may be a new lump, as you are unleavened. For even Christ our passover is sacrificed for us:

8 Therefore let us keep the feast, not with old leaven, neither with the leaven of malice and wickedness; but with the unleavened bread of sincerity and truth.

9 *I wrote to you in an epistle not to company with fornicators:*

10 *Yet not altogether with the fornicators of this world, or with the covetous, or extortioners, or with idolaters; for then you would need to go out of the world.*

11 But now I have written to you not to keep company, if any man that is called a brother be a fornicator, or covetous, or an idolater, or a railer, or a drunkard, or an extortioner; with such an one no not to eat.

12 For what have I to do to judge them also that are without? do you not judge them that are within?

13 But them that are without God judges. Therefore put away from among yourselves that wicked person.

CHAPTER 6

DARE any of you, having a matter against another, go to law before the unjust, and not before the saints?

2 Do you not know that the saints shall judge the world? and if the world shall be judged by you, are you unworthy to judge the smallest matters?

3 Do you not know that we shall judge angels? how much more things that pertain to this life?

4 If then you have judgments of things pertaining to this life, set them to judge who are least esteemed in the church.

5 I speak to your shame. Is it so, that there is not a wise man among you? no, not one that shall be able to judge between his brethren?

6 But brother goes to law with brother, and that before the unbelievers.

7 Now therefore there is utterly a fault among you, because you go to law one with another. Why do you not rather take wrong? why do you not rather suf-

fer yourselves to be defrauded?

8 Nay, you do wrong, and defraud, and that your brethren.

9 Do you not know that the unrighteous shall not inherit the kingdom of God? Be not deceived: neither fornicators, nor idolaters, nor adulterers, nor effeminate, nor abusers of themselves with mankind,

10 Nor thieves, nor covetous, nor drunkards, nor revilers, nor extortioners, shall inherit the kingdom of God.

11 And such were some of you: but you are washed, but you are sanctified, but you are justified in the name of the Lord Jesus, and by the Spirit of our God.

12 All things are lawful to me, but all things are not expedient: all things are lawful for me, but I will not be brought under the power of any.

13 Meats for the belly, and the belly for meats: but God shall destroy both it and them. Now the body is not for fornication, but for the Lord; and the Lord for the body.

14 And God has both raised up the Lord, and will also raise up us by his own power.

15 Do you not know that your bodies are the members of Christ? shall I then take the members of Christ, and make them the members of an harlot? God forbid.

16 What? Do you not know that he which is joined to an harlot is one body? for two, said he, shall be one flesh.

17 But he that is joined to the Lord is one spirit.

18 Flee fornication. Every sin that a man does is without the body; but he that commits fornication sins against his own body.

19 What? Do you not know that your body is the temple of the Holy Spirit which is in you, which you have of God, and you are not your own?

20 For you are bought with a price: therefore glorify God in your body, and in your spirit, which are God's.

CHAPTER 7

NOW concerning the things whereof you wrote to me: It is good for a man not to touch a woman.

2 Nevertheless, to avoid fornication, let every man have his own wife, and let every woman have her own husband.

3 Let the husband render to the wife due benevolence: and likewise also the wife to the husband.

4 The wife has not power of her own body, but the husband: and likewise also the husband has not power of his own body, but the wife.

5 Defraud not one the other, except it be with consent for a time, that you may give yourselves to fasting and prayer; and come together again, that Satan tempt you not for your incontinency.

6 But I speak this by permission, and not of commandment.

7 For I would that all men were even as

6:9,10 Sinners will not enter the kingdom of God: "Who can say, I have made my heart clean, I am pure from my sin?" (Proverbs 20:9). "For there is not a just man on earth who does good and does not sin" (Ecclesiastes 7:20). "If we say that we have no sin, we deceive ourselves, and the truth is not in us" (1 John 1:8). "For all have sinned, and come short of the glory of God" (Romans 3:23). See Revelation 21:8 comment.

6:9–11 Homosexuals are deceived if they think they find in Scripture that their lifestyle is okay with God, and that they cannot change. This list of sins (which encompass most, if not all, of the Ten Commandments) makes it clear who will not be included in the kingdom of God. However, Paul says to those who are now believers, "And such were some of you" (v. 11). No matter what their sins, God can wash sinners clean and make them righteous in His sight. See Jude 7 comment.

6:19 "Coming under the loving Lordship of Jesus Christ means an end to our 'rights' as well as to our wrongs. It means the end of life on our own terms." *Larry Tomczak*

I myself. But every man has his proper
gift of God, one after this manner, and
another after that.
8 I say therefore to the unmarried and
widows, It is good for them if they abide
even as I.
9 But if they cannot contain, let them
marry: for it is better to marry than to
burn.
10 And to the married I command, yet
not I, but the Lord, Let not the wife depart from her husband:
11 But and if she depart, let her remain
unmarried, or be reconciled to her husband: and let not the husband put away
his wife.
12 But to the rest speak I, not the Lord:
If any brother has a wife that believes
not, and she be pleased to dwell with
him, let him not put her away.
13 And the woman which has an husband that believes not, and if he be
pleased to dwell with her, let her not
leave him.
14 For the unbelieving husband is sanctified by the wife, and the unbelieving
wife is sanctified by the husband: else
were your children unclean; but now are
they holy.
15 But if the unbelieving depart, let
him depart. A brother or a sister is not
under bondage in such cases: but God
has called us to peace.
16 For how do you know, O wife,
whether you shall save your husband? or
how do you know, O man, whether you
shall save your wife?
17 But as God has distributed to every
man, as the Lord has called every one, so
let him walk. And so ordain I in all
churches.
18 Is any man called being circumcised?
let him not become uncircumcised. Is
any called in uncircumcision? let him
not be circumcised.
19 Circumcision is nothing, and uncircumcision is nothing, but the keeping of
the commandments of God.
20 Let every man abide in the same
calling wherein he was called.
21 Are you called being a servant? care
not for it: but if you may be made free,
use it rather.
22 For he that is called in the Lord, being a servant, is the Lord's freeman: likewise also he that is called, being free, is
Christ's servant.
23 You are bought with a price; be not
the servants of men.
24 Brethren, let every man, wherein he
is called, therein abide with God.
25 Now concerning virgins I have no
commandment of the Lord: yet I give my
judgment, as one that has obtained mercy

7:2–5 Biblical sexuality. The gift of sex came from God; it didn't come about through an evolutionary process. It was given by God for procreation and pleasure. Scripture says that the only time a husband and wife should refrain from the joys of sex is when they are praying and fasting. The Bible also says that a man should be ravished (enraptured) always with her love (Proverbs 5:18–20). The only stipulation is that it is his wife he is to be enraptured with—not the woman down the street.

Those who forsake marriage thinking that they can enjoy sex outside the bonds of the institution risk getting AIDS and numerous other sexually transmitted diseases—several of which are incurable. It is interesting to note that a man and a woman can engage in sex ten thousand times within marriage and never even once risk contracting any sexually transmitted disease.

One who commits fornication (from the Greek *Porneia*, "illicit sexual intercourse") takes what could lawfully be his as a gift from God, and corrupts it. He is like a child who one night steals a crisp, new twenty-dollar bill from his father's wallet, not realizing that his father intended to give it to him as a gift in the morning.

The fornicator not only sins against God and incurs the wrath of eternal justice, but he sins against his conscience, and his own body (1 Corinthians 6:18). Fornicators will not inherit the kingdom of God (1 Corinthians 6:9).

of the Lord to be faithful.
26 I suppose therefore that this is good
for the present distress, I say, that it is
good for a man so to be.
27 Are you bound to a wife? seek not to
be loosed. are you loosed from a wife?
seek not a wife.
28 But and if you marry, you have not
sinned; and if a virgin marry, she has not
sinned. Nevertheless such shall have
trouble in the flesh: but I spare you.
29 *But this I say, brethren, the time is*
short: it remains, that both they that have
wives be as though they had none;
30 *And they that weep, as though they*
wept not; and they that rejoice, as though
they rejoiced not; and they that buy, as
though they possessed not;
31 *And they that use this world, as not*
abusing it: for the fashion of this world pass-
es away.
32 But I would have you without carefulness. He that is unmarried cares for
the things that belong to the Lord, how
he may please the Lord:
33 But he that is married cares for the
things that are of the world, how he may
please his wife.
34 There is difference also between a
wife and a virgin. The unmarried woman
cares for the things of the Lord, that she
may be holy both in body and in spirit:
but she that is married cares for the things
of the world, how she may please her
husband.
35 And this I speak for your own profit;
not that I may cast a snare upon you, but
for that which is comely, and that you
may attend upon the Lord without dis-
traction.
36 But if any man think that he behaves
himself uncomely toward his virgin, if
she pass the flower of her age, and need
so require, let him do what he will, he
sins not: let them marry.
37 Nevertheless he that stands steadfast
in his heart, having no necessity, but has
power over his own will, and has so decreed in his heart that he will keep his
virgin, does well.
38 So then he that gives her in marriage
does well; but he that gives her not in
marriage does better.
39 The wife is bound by the law as long
as her husband lives; but if her husband
be dead, she is at liberty to be married to
whom she will; only in the Lord.
40 But she is happier if she so abide,
after my judgment: and I think also that
I have the Spirit of God.

· · · · · ·

For how to speak with someone who doesn't believe in the afterlife, see Psalm 49:15 comment.

· · · · · ·

CHAPTER 8

NOW as touching things offered to
idols, we know that we all have
knowledge. Knowledge puffs up, but
charity edifies.
2 And if any man think that he knows
anything, he knows nothing yet as he
ought to know.
3 But if any man love God, the same is
known of him.
4 As concerning therefore the eating of
those things that are offered in sacrifice
to idols, we know that an idol is nothing
in the world, and that there is none other
God but one.
5 For though there be that are called
gods, whether in heaven or in earth, (as
there be gods many, and lords many,)
6 But to us there is but one God, the
Father, of whom are all things, and we
in him; and one Lord Jesus Christ, by
whom are all things, and we by him.
7 Howbeit there is not in every man that
knowledge: for some with conscience of
the idol to this hour eat it as a thing offered to an idol; and their conscience be-

8:4 See Psalm 115:4–9 comment.

ing weak is defiled.
8 But meat commends us not to God: for neither, if we eat, are we the better; neither, if we eat not, are we the worse.
9 But take heed lest by any means this liberty of yours become a stumbling-block to them that are weak.
10 For if any man see you which have knowledge sit at meat in the idol's temple, shall not the conscience of him which is weak be emboldened to eat those things which are offered to idols;
11 And through your knowledge shall the weak brother perish, for whom Christ died?
12 But when you sin so against the brethren, and wound their weak conscience, you sin against Christ.
13 Wherefore, if meat make my brother to offend, I will eat no flesh while the world stands, lest I make my brother to offend.

CHAPTER 9

AM I not an apostle? am I not free? have I not seen Jesus Christ our Lord? are not you my work in the Lord?
2 If I be not an apostle to others, yet doubtless I am to you: for the seal of mine apostleship are you in the Lord.
3 Mine answer to them that do examine me is this,
4 Have we not power to eat and to drink?
5 Have we not power to lead about a sister, a wife, as well as other apostles, and as the brethren of the Lord, and Cephas?
6 Or I only and Barnabas, have not we power to forbear working?
7 Who goes a warfare any time at his own charges? who plants a vineyard, and eats not of the fruit thereof? or who feeds a flock, and eats not of the milk of the flock?
8 Say I these things as a man? or said not the law the same also?
9 For it is written in the law of Moses, You shall not muzzle the mouth of the ox that treads out the corn. Does God take care for oxen?
10 Or said he it altogether for our sakes? For our sakes, no doubt, this is written: that he that plows should plow in hope; and that he that threshes in hope should be partaker of his hope.
11 If we have sown to you spiritual things, is it a great thing if we shall reap your carnal things?
12 If others be partakers of this power over you, are not we rather? Nevertheless we have not used this power; but suffer all things, lest we should hinder the gospel of Christ.
13 Do you not know that they which minister about holy things live of the things of the temple? and they which wait at the alter are partakers with the alter?
14 *Even so has the Lord ordained that they which preach the gospel should live of the gospel.*
15 But I have used none of these things: neither have I written these things, that it should be so done to me: for it were better for me to die, than that any man should make my glorying void.

8:9 Although we have incredible liberty as Christians, we are servants of all. If something we are at liberty to do offends an unsaved person, we must stop doing it, for the sake of the gospel. It has been well said that if Paul saw a Jew, he would hide his ham sandwich behind his back. We need to walk in that same spirit.

9:16 Second Kings 7:9 tells of lepers who had seen a great victory and initially kept the good news to themselves. But their consciences spoke to them of their moral obligation to not remain silent: "Then they said one to another, We do not well: this day is a day of good tidings, and we hold our peace." How much more should we feel an obligation to take the Good News of everlasting life to a dying world? We must speak about what we have seen and heard. Like Paul, we are a "debtor" to those who haven't heard the gospel (Romans 1:14). "Woe" to us if we do not preach the gospel.

16 *For though I preach the gospel, I have nothing to glory of: for necessity is laid upon me; yes, woe is to me, if I preach not the gospel!*
17 For if I do this thing willingly, I have a reward: but if against my will, a dispensation of the gospel is committed to me.
18 What is my reward then? Verily that, when I preach the gospel, I may make the gospel of Christ without charge, that I abuse not my power in the gospel.
19 *For though I be free from all men, yet have I made myself servant to all, that I might gain the more.*
20 *And to the Jews I became as a Jew, that I might gain the Jews; to them that are under the law, as under the law, that I might gain them that are under the law;*
21 *To them that are without law, as without law, (being not without law to God, but under the law to Christ,) that I might gain them that are without law.*
22 *To the weak became I as weak, that I might gain the weak: I am made all things to all men, that I might by all means save some.*
23 *And this I do for the gospel's sake, that I might be partaker thereof with you.*
24 Do you not know that they which run in a race run all, but one receives the prize? So run, that you may obtain.
25 And every man that strives for the mastery is temperate in all things. Now they do it to obtain a corruptible crown; but we an incorruptible.
26 I therefore so run, not as uncertainly; so fight I, not as one that beats the air:
27 But I keep under my body, and bring it into subjection: lest that by any means, when I have preached to others, I myself should be a castaway.

9:22 Gospel tracts—how to use them. If Paul meant "by all means," he no doubt would have used gospel tracts as a means to reach the lost. A Christian book relates the true story of a diver who saw a piece of paper clutched in the shell of an oyster. The man grabbed it, found that it was a gospel tract and said, "I can't hold out any longer. His mercy is so great that He has caused His Word to follow me even to the bottom of the ocean." God used a tract to save the man.

Why should a Christian use tracts? Simply because *God* uses them. He used a tract to save the great missionary Hudson Taylor, as well as innumerable others. That fact alone should be enough incentive for a Christian to always use tracts to reach the lost, but there are even more reasons why we should use them. Here are a few:

- Tracts can provide an opening for us to share our faith. We can watch people's reaction as we give them a tract, and see if they are open to listening to spiritual things.
- They can do the witnessing for us. If we are too timid to speak to someone about the things of God, we can at least give them a tract, or leave it lying around so that someone will pick it up.
- They speak to the individuals when they are ready—they don't read it until they want to.
- They can find their way into people's homes when we can't.
- They don't get into arguments; they just state their case.

Dr. Oswald J. Smith said, "The only way to carry out the Great Commission will be by the means of the printed page." *Charles Spurgeon* stated, "When preaching and private talk are not available, you need to have a tract ready... Get good striking tracts, or none at all. But a touching gospel tract may be the seed of eternal life. Therefore, do not go out without your tracts."

If you want people to accept your literature, try to greet them before offering them a tract. If you can get them to respond to a warm "Good morning," or "How are you doing?" that will almost always break the ice and they will take it. After the greeting, don't ask, "Would you like this?" They will probably respond, "What is it?" Instead, say, "Did you get one of these?" That question has a twofold effect. You stir their curiosity and make them ask, "One of what?" That's when you hand it to them. It also makes them feel as though they are missing out on something. So they are.

(continued on next page)

CHAPTER 10

MOREOVER, brethren, I would not that you should be ignorant, how
that all our fathers were under the cloud,
and all passed through the sea;
2 And were all baptized unto Moses in
the cloud and in the sea;
3 And did all eat the same spiritual meat;
4 And did all drink the same spiritual
drink: for they drank of that spiritual
Rock that followed them: and that Rock
was Christ.
5 But with many of them God was not
well pleased: for they were overthrown
in the wilderness.
6 Now these things were our examples,
to the intent we should not lust after evil
things, as they also lusted.
7 Neither be idolaters, as were some of
them; as it is written, The people sat
down to eat and drink, and rose up to
play.
8 Neither let us commit fornication, as
some of them committed, and fell in one
day three and twenty thousand.
9 Neither let us tempt Christ, as some
of them also tempted, and were destroyed of serpents.
10 Neither murmur, as some of them
also murmured, and were destroyed of the
destroyer.
11 Now all these things happened to
them for ensamples: and they are written
for our admonition, upon whom the ends
of the world are come.
12 Wherefore let him that thinks he

(9:22 continued) Perhaps you almost pass out at the thought of passing out a tract. Don't worry; you are not alone. We *all* battle fear. The answer to fear is found in the prayer closet. Ask God to give you a compassion that will swallow your fears. Meditate on the fate of the ungodly. Give hell some deep thought. Confront what it is that makes you fearful.

Do you like roller coasters? Some Christians want to try bungee-jumping or sky diving. Isn't it strange? We are prepared to risk our lives for the love of fear—and yet we are willing to let a sinner go to hell for fear of giving out a tract. Ask yourself how many piles of bloodied stones you can find where Christians have been stoned to death for preaching the gospel. How much singed soil can you find where they have been burned at the stake? Part of our fear is a fear of rejection. We are fearful of looking foolish. That's a subtle form of pride. The other part of our battle with fear comes directly from the enemy. He knows that fear paralyzes. We must resist the devil and his lies. If God is with us, nothing can be against us.

Never underestimate the power of a gospel tract. After *George Whitefield* read one called "The Life of God in the Soul of a Man," he said, "God showed me I must be born again or be damned." He went on to pray, "Lord, if I am not a Christian, or if I am not a real one, for Jesus Christ's sake show me what Christianity is, that I may not be damned at last!" Then his journal tells us "from that moment... did I know that I must become a new creature."

If you have never given out tracts, why not begin today? Leave them in a shopping cart, or put them in the mail when you pay bills. Then each night as you shut your eyes to go to sleep, you will have something very special to pray about—that God will use the tract you put somewhere. You will also have a deep sense of satisfaction that you played a small part in carrying out the Great Commission to reach this dying world with the gospel of everlasting life. Don't waste your life. Do something for the kingdom of God while you are able to. Always remember: treat every day as though it were your last—one day you will be right. See also Mark 4:14 and Revelation 22:2 comments.

10:1 This chapter shows how subtle idolatry can be. If we create an idol of God in our minds, that idol will not speak to us when we fall into the sin of lust. However, if we keep before us the true revelation of God's omniscient holiness, when Potiphar's wife calls we will flee from sexual sin. Despite our protests that lust easily overcomes our weak wills, verse 13 leaves each of us without excuse. See how that verse is linked to verse 14.

10:4 Just as Moses struck the rock to bring forth life-sustaining water for the Israelites in the desert (Exodus 17:6), it was Moses' Law that came down upon the Rock (Christ) at the cross.

QUESTIONS & OBJECTIONS

10:20

"Why is Christianity better than other religions?"

In all major religions, the followers strive to rid themselves of sin through various practices. They may pray in a prescribed way, do various good works, deny themselves legitimate sexual pleasure, follow dietary restrictions, lie on beds of nails, etc. The uniqueness of Jesus is shown in His statement, "The Son of Man has power on earth to forgive sins." No other religious leader has ever made this claim. Jesus Christ alone can wash away every sin anyone has ever committed, because of what He did on the cross. By paying the penalty for our sin, He can release us from the torture of guilt. We cannot do anything in the way of religious works to wash away our sins. Forgiveness is a free gift of God (Ephesians 2:8,9). To see what "religion" does (or rather doesn't do), see what Mahatma Ghandi has to say in Romans 7:24,25.

stands take heed lest he fall.
13 There has no temptation taken you
but such as is common to man: but God
is faithful, who will not suffer you to be
tempted above that you are able; but will
with the temptation also make a way to
escape, that you may be able to bear it.
14 Wherefore, my dearly beloved, flee
from idolatry.
15 I speak as to wise men; judge what I
say.
16 The cup of blessing which we bless,
is it not the communion of the blood of
Christ? The bread which we break, is it
not the communion of the body of Christ?
17 For we being many are one bread,
and one body: for we are all partakers of
that one bread.
18 Behold Israel after the flesh: are not
they which eat of the sacrifices partakers
of the alter?
19 What say I then? that the idol is any
thing, or that which is offered in sacrifice
to idols is any thing?
20 But I say, that the things which the
Gentiles sacrifice, they sacrifice to devils,
and not to God: and I would not that
you should have fellowship with devils.
21 You cannot drink the cup of the Lord,
and the cup of devils: you cannot be par-

10:14 Idolatry. Those who deny the fact that God is angry at sin insinuate that sinful man (with his measure of desire to see justice) is more just than God. This is an incredible affront to the integrity of God. The following *Time* magazine letter to the editor epitomizes idolatry (the oldest sin in the Book):

> "Excellent topic! I truly enjoyed reading 'Does Heaven Exist?' I am a devout Christian, and I don't give much thought to heaven. My spirituality isn't based on an anthropomorphic, kick-butt God who will throw four generations of children into eternal damnation because some distant forefather ticked him off [see Proverbs 28:5]. Heaven is the flip side of the absolutely barbaric notion of hell that evolved under that kick-butt mindset…To me, God is a symbol for something unfathomable, an utter mystery that fills my heart with joy and my spirit with song."

10:20 To many, Eastern religions have a sense of romantic mysticism. It must therefore be a surprise to find that India has 220 million cows that are worshiped as the supreme givers of life (God). The cow's hooves are bathed in religious ceremonies. Their urine is considered holy and is used to anoint believers. The animal's dung is also applied to the skin of the faithful in religious rituals. They believe that all the gods inhabit some part of the cow's body. A Christian revival in India would not only provide eternal salvation for the country, but would also release enough meat to feed their hungry population.

takers of the Lord's table, and of the table
of devils.
22 Do we provoke the Lord to jealousy?
are we stronger than he?
23 All things are lawful for me, but all
things are not expedient: all things are
lawful for me, but all things edify not.
24 Let no man seek his own, but every
man another's wealth.
25 Whatsoever is sold in the shambles,
that eat, asking no question for conscience sake:
26 For the earth is the Lord's, and the
fulness thereof.
27 If any of them that believe not bid
you to a feast, and you be disposed to
go; whatsoever is set before you, eat, asking no question for conscience sake.
28 But if any man say to you, This is offered in sacrifice to idols, eat not for his
sake that showed it, and for conscience
sake: for the earth is the Lord's, and the
fulness thereof:
29 Conscience, I say, not your own, but
of the other: for why is my liberty judged
of another man's conscience?
30 For if I by grace be a partaker, why
am I evil spoken of for that for which I
give thanks?
31 Whether therefore you eat, or drink,
or whatsoever you do, do all to the glory
of God.
32 Give none offence, neither to the Jews,
nor to the Gentiles, nor to the church of
God:
33 Even as I please all men in all things,
not seeking mine own profit, but the
profit of many, that they may be saved.

CHAPTER 11

*BE followers of me, even as I also am of
Christ.*
2 Now I praise you, brethren, that you
remember me in all things, and keep the
ordinances, as I delivered them to you.
3 But I would have you know, that the
head of every man is Christ; and the
head of the woman is the man; and the
head of Christ is God.
4 Every man praying or prophesying,
having his head covered, dishonors his
head.
5 But every woman that prays or prophesies with her head uncovered dishonors
her head: for that is even all one as if she
were shaven.

> If any man's life at home is unworthy, he should go several miles away before he stands up to preach. When he stands up, he should say nothing.
>
> **CHARLES SPURGEON**

6 For if the woman be not covered, let
her also be shorn: but if it be a shame for
a woman to be shorn or shaven, let her
be covered.
7 For a man indeed ought not to cover
his head, forasmuch as he is the image
and glory of God: but the woman is the
glory of the man.
8 For the man is not of the woman; but
the woman of the man.
9 Neither was the man created for the
woman; but the woman for the man.
10 For this cause ought the woman to
have power on her head because of the
angels.
11 Nevertheless neither is the man without the woman, neither the woman without the man, in the Lord.
12 For as the woman is of the man, even
so is the man also by the woman; but all
things of God.
13 Judge in yourselves: is it comely that
a woman pray to God uncovered?
14 Does not even nature itself teach you,
that, if a man have long hair, it is a shame
to him?
15 But if a woman have long hair, it is a
glory to her: for her hair is given her for

11:8 It has been well said that woman was made from Adam's rib—close to his heart, under his protective arm (Genesis 2:21,22).

a covering.
16 But if any man seem to be contentious, we have no such custom, neither the churches of God.
17 Now in this that I declare to you I praise you not, that you come together not for the better, but for the worse.
18 For first of all, when you come together in the church, I hear that there be divisions among you; and I partly believe it.
19 For there must be also heresies among you, that they which are approved may be made manifest among you.
20 When you come together therefore into one place, this is not to eat the Lord's supper.
21 For in eating every one takes before other his own supper: and one is hungry, and another is drunken.
22 What? have you not houses to eat and to drink in? or do you despise the church of God, and shame them that have not? What shall I say to you? shall I praise you in this? I praise you not.
23 For I have received of the Lord that which also I delivered to you, That the Lord Jesus the same night in which he was betrayed took bread:
24 And when he had given thanks, he broke it, and said, Take, eat: this is my body, which is broken for you: this do in remembrance of me.
25 After the same manner also he took the cup, when he had supped, saying, This cup is the new testament in my blood: this do, as oft as you drink it, in remembrance of me.
26 For as often as you eat this bread, and drink this cup, you do show the Lord's death till he come.
27 Wherefore whosoever shall eat this bread, and drink this cup of the Lord, unworthily, shall be guilty of the body and blood of the Lord.
28 But let a man examine himself, and so let him eat of that bread, and drink of that cup.
29 For he that eats and drinks unworthily, eats and drinks damnation to himself, not discerning the Lord's body.
30 For this cause many are weak and sickly among you, and many sleep.
31 For if we would judge ourselves, we should not be judged.
32 But when we are judged, we are chastened of the Lord, that we should not be condemned with the world.
33 Wherefore, my brethren, when you come together to eat, tarry one for an-

11:9 Earth's population refutes evolution. "The evolutionary scientists who believe that man existed for over a million years have an almost insurmountable problem. Using the assumption of forty-three years for an average human generation, the population growth over a million years would produce 23,256 consecutive generations. We calculate the expected population by starting with one couple one million years ago and use the same assumptions of a forty-three-year generation and 2.5 children per family... The evolutionary theory of a million years of growth would produce trillions × trillions × trillions × trillions of people that should be alive today on our planet. To put this in perspective, this number is vastly greater than the total number of atoms in our vast universe. If mankind had lived on earth for a million years, we would all be standing on enormously high mountains of bones from the trillions of skeletons of those who had died in past generations. However, despite the tremendous archeological and scientific investigation in the last two centuries, the scientists have not found a fraction of the trillions of skeletons predicted by the theory of evolutionary scientists." *Grant R. Jeffery, The Signature of God*

One common ancestor. "Researchers suggest that virtually all modern men—99% of them, says one scientist—are closely related genetically and share genes with one male ancestor, dubbed 'Y-chromosome Adam.'

We are finding that humans have very, very shallow genetic roots which go back very recently to one ancestor... That indicates that there was an origin in a specific location on the globe, and then it spread out from there." *U.S. News & World Report*, December 4, 1995

other.
34 And if any man hunger, let him eat at home; that you come not together to condemnation. And the rest will I set in order when I come.

CHAPTER 12

NOW concerning spiritual gifts, brethren, I would not have you ignorant.
2 You know that you were Gentiles, carried away to these dumb idols, even as you were led.
3 Wherefore I give you to understand, that no man speaking by the Spirit of God calls Jesus accursed: and that no man can say that Jesus is the Lord, but by the Holy Spirit.
4 Now there are diversities of gifts, but the same Spirit.
5 And there are differences of administrations, but the same Lord.
6 And there are diversities of operations, but it is the same God which works all in all.
7 But the manifestation of the Spirit is given to every man to profit withal.
8 For to one is given by the Spirit the word of wisdom; to another the word of knowledge by the same Spirit;
9 To another faith by the same Spirit; to another the gifts of healing by the same Spirit;
10 To another the working of miracles; to another prophecy; to another discerning of spirits; to another divers kinds of tongues; to another the interpretation of tongues:
11 But all these work that one and the selfsame Spirit, dividing to every man severally as he will.
12 For as the body is one, and has many members, and all the members of that one body, being many, are one body: so also is Christ.
13 For by one Spirit are we all baptized into one body, whether we be Jews or Gentiles, whether we be bond or free; and have been all made to drink into one Spirit.
14 For the body is not one member, but many.
15 If the foot shall say, Because I am not the hand, I am not of the body; is it therefore not of the body?
16 And if the ear shall say, Because I am not the eye, I am not of the body; is it therefore not of the body?
17 If the whole body were an eye, where were the hearing? If the whole were hearing, where were the smelling?
18 But now has God set the members every one of them in the body, as it has pleased him.
19 And if they were all one member, where were the body?
20 But now are they many members, yet but one body.
21 And the eye cannot say to the hand, I have no need of you: nor again the head to the feet, I have no need of you.
22 Nay, much more those members of the body, which seem to be more feeble, are necessary:
23 And those members of the body, which we think to be less honorable, upon these we bestow more abundant honor; and our uncomely parts have more abundant comeliness.
24 For our comely parts have no need: but God has tempered the body together, having given more abundant honor to that part which lacked:
25 That there should be no schism in the body; but that the members should have the same care one for another.
26 And whether one member suffer, all the members suffer with it; or one member be honored, all the members rejoice with it.
27 Now you are the body of Christ, and members in particular.
28 And God has set some in the church,

12:25 "Satan always hates Christian fellowship; it is his policy to keep Christians apart. Anything which can divide saints from one another he delights in." *Charles Spurgeon*

13:2 *Speaking the Truth in Love to Jehovah's Witnesses*

By Clint DeBoer

I was raised as a Jehovah's Witness and remained one until age 11. Coming out of this cult, I entered my teenage years as a bitter atheist where I remained until I graduated from college. Through God's amazing grace I was saved in 1994 after reading the Bible and realizing that it was indeed the true Word of God.

Repeatedly God has blessed me with the passion and privilege to witness to the Jehovah's Witnesses. You've almost certainly had them come knocking on your door on a Saturday afternoon and you may have even engaged a Jehovah's Witness in a theological discussion. In talking to other Christians I find that when presented with a face-to-face encounter with a Jehovah's Witness there are usually two responses:

1) A "frontal assault" via debate or heated discussion; or

2) A polite "no thanks, I'm already a Christian" followed by an all too abrupt closing of the door.

For the mature Christian, what's usually missing is the realization that this is a true witnessing opportunity—one that has arrived right at your doorstep.

In my earliest attempts at grabbing the proverbial bull by the horns, I tried engaging them in direct debates, often quoting from several texts I had studied regarding the cultic practices of the Jehovah's Witnesses. After several failed "conversion" attempts, often ending with thoroughly frustrated Jehovah's Witnesses unwilling to ever return to my residence, I arrived at a startling realization: Jehovah's Witnesses are real people, with real needs and real feelings. They can feel frustration, anger, fear, and confusion. I then realized that the reason my frontal assaults on the Jehovah's Witnesses never seemed to work was because I had not put myself in their place and taken their feelings into account.

A wise man once said, "When you want to get someone's attention, you don't shine a flashlight in their eyes." In presenting my arguments and facts without giving them time to prepare, I had forgotten that they were human beings searching for the truth. I had not been speaking this truth in love.

Months later, when I was again presented with an opportunity to speak with Jehovah's Witnesses at my door, I engaged them in conversation, and agreed to do a weekly Bible study with them in order to further discuss what exactly they believed. They agreed, with the understanding that along the way I would ask questions whenever we arrived at a topic or subject with which I disagreed or failed to understand. The amazing difference was that instead of blindsiding them with questions and points of contention, I was giving them an opportunity to prepare themselves for a topic of discussion.

More importantly, though, I began to care about them personally and yearn for their salvation.

In this way, I am able to meet with Witnesses on a weekly basis and take them off the streets, focusing on critical topics such as the requirement that one be born again to enter the kingdom of God, the unbiblical theology of a two-class system of believers, and the true identity of Jesus Christ.

first apostles, secondarily prophets, thirdly teachers, after that miracles, then gifts of healings, helps, governments, diversities of tongues.
29 Are all apostles? are all prophets? are
all teachers? are all workers of miracles?
30 Have all the gifts of healing? do all
speak with tongues? do all interpret?
31 But covet earnestly the best gifts: and
yet show I to you a more excellent way.

CHAPTER 13

THOUGH I speak with the tongues of men and of angels, and have not charity, I am become as sounding brass, or a tinkling cymbal.
2 And though I have the gift of prophe-
cy, and understand all mysteries, and all knowledge; and though I have all faith, so that I could remove mountains, and have not charity, I am nothing.

3 And though I bestow all my goods to feed the poor, and though I give my body to be burned, and have not charity, it profits me nothing.

4 Charity suffers long, and is kind; charity envies not; charity vaunts not itself, is not puffed up,

5 Does not behave itself unseemly, seeks not her own, is not easily provoked, thinks no evil;

6 Rejoice not in iniquity, but rejoices in the truth;

7 Bears all things, believes all things, hope all things, endures all things.

8 Charity never fails: but whether there be prophecies, they shall fail; whether there be tongues, they shall cease; whether there be knowledge, it shall vanish away.

9 For we know in part, and we prophesy in part.

10 But when that which is perfect is come, then that which is in part shall be done away.

11 When I was a child, I spoke as a child, I understood as a child, I thought as a child: but when I became a man, I put away childish things.

12 For now we see through a glass, darkly; but then face to face: now I know in part; but then shall I know even as also I am known.

13 And now abides faith, hope, charity, these three; but the greatest of these is charity.

CHAPTER 14

FOLLOW after charity, and desire spiritual gifts, but rather that you may prophesy.

2 For he that speaks in an unknown tongue speaks not to men, but to God: for no man understands him; howbeit in the spirit he speaks mysteries.

3 But he that prophesies speaks to men to edification, and exhortation, and comfort.

4 He that speaks in an unknown tongue edifies himself; but he that prophesies edifies the church.

5 I would that you all spoke with tongues, but rather that you prophesied: for greater is he that prophesies than he that speaks with tongues, except he interpret, that the church may receive edifying.

6 Now, brethren, if I come to you speaking with tongues, what shall I profit you, except I shall speak to you either by revelation, or by knowledge, or by prophesying, or by doctrine?

> Love will find a way. Indifference will find an excuse.
>
> **ANONYMOUS**

7 And even things without life giving sound, whether pipe or harp, except they give a distinction in the sounds, how shall it be known what is piped or harped?

8 For if the trumpet give an uncertain sound, who shall prepare himself to the battle?

9 So likewise you, except you utter by the tongue words easy to be understood, how shall it be known what is spoken? for you shall speak into the air.

10 There are, it may be, so many kinds of voices in the world, and none of them is without signification.

11 Therefore if I know not the meaning of the voice, I shall be to him that speaks a barbarian, and he that speaks shall be a barbarian to me.

12 Even so you, forasmuch as you are zealous of spiritual gifts, seek that you may excel to the edifying of the church.

13 Wherefore let him that speaks in an unknown tongue pray that he may interpret.

14 For if I pray in an unknown tongue, my spirit prays, but my understanding is unfruitful.

15 What is it then? I will pray with the spirit, and I will pray with the understanding also: I will sing with the spirit, and I will sing with the understanding also.

16 Else when you shall bless with the

spirit, how shall he that occupies the
room of the unlearned say Amen at your
giving of thanks, seeing he understands
not what you say?
17 For you verily give thanks well, but
the other is not edified.
18 I thank my God, I speak with tongues
more than you all:
19 Yet in the church I had rather speak
five words with my understanding, that
by my voice I might teach others also,
than ten thousand words in an unknown
tongue.
20 Brethren, be not children in understanding: howbeit in malice be children,
but in understanding be men.
21 In the law it is written, With men of
other tongues and other lips will I speak
to this people; and yet for all that will
they not hear me, says the Lord.
22 Wherefore tongues are for a sign,
not to them that believe, but to them
that believe not: but prophesying serves
not for them that believe not, but for
them which believe.
23 If therefore the whole church be come
together into one place, and all speak with
tongues, and there come in those that
are unlearned, or unbelievers, will they
not say that you are mad?
24 But if all prophesy, and there come
in one that believes not, or one unlearned,
he is convinced of all, he is judged of all:
25 And thus are the secrets of his heart
made manifest; and so falling down on
his face he will worship God, and report
that God is in you of a truth.
26 How is it then, brethren? when you
come together, everyone of you has a
psalm, has a doctrine, has a tongue, has
a revelation, has an interpretation. Let all
things be done to edifying.
27 If any man speak in an unknown
tongue, let it be by two, or at the most
by three, and that by course; and let one
interpret.
28 But if there be no interpreter, let him
keep silence in the church; and let him
speak to himself, and to God.
29 Let the prophets speak two or three,

"We do not know one-millionth of one percent about anything." (See 1 Corinthians 8:2.)

Thomas Edison

and let the other judge.
30 If any thing be revealed to another
that sits by, let the first hold his peace.
31 For you may all prophesy one by
one, that all may learn, and all may be
comforted.
32 And the spirits of the prophets are
subject to the prophets.
33 For God is not the author of confusion, but of peace, as in all churches of
the saints.
34 Let your women keep silence in the
churches: for it is not permitted to them
to speak; but they are commanded to be
under obedience, as also says the law.
35 And if they will learn any thing, let
them ask their husbands at home: for it
is a shame for women to speak in the
church.
36 What? came the word of God out
from you? or came it to you only?
37 If any man think himself to be a
prophet, or spiritual, let him acknowledge that the things that I write to you
are the commandments of the Lord.
38 But if any man be ignorant, let him
be ignorant.

39 Wherefore, brethren, covet to prophesy, and forbid not to speak with tongues.
40 Let all things be done decently and in order.

CHAPTER 15

MOREOVER, brethren, I declare to you the gospel which I preached to you, which also you have received, and wherein you stand;
2 By which also you are saved, if you keep in memory what I preached to you, unless you have believed in vain.
3 **For I delivered to you first of all that which I also received, how that Christ died for our sins according to the scriptures;**
4 **And that he was buried, and that he rose again the third day according to the scriptures:**
5 **And that he was seen of Cephas, then of the twelve:**
6 After that, he was seen of above five hundred brethren at once; of whom the greater part remain to this present, but some are fallen asleep.
7 After that, he was seen of James; then of all the apostles.
8 And last of all he was seen of me also, as of one born out of due time.
9 For I am the least of the apostles, that am not meet to be called an apostle, because I persecuted the church of God.
10 But by the grace of God I am what I am: and his grace which was bestowed upon me was not in vain; but I labored more abundantly than they all: yet not I, but the grace of God which was with me.

> It was not the volume of sin that sent Christ to the cross; it was the fact of sin.
>
> **RAVI ZACHARIAS**

11 Therefore whether it were I or they, so we preach, and so you believed.
12 Now if Christ be preached that he rose from the dead, how say some among you that there is no resurrection of the dead?
13 But if there be no resurrection of the dead, then is Christ not risen:
14 And if Christ be not risen, then is our preaching vain, and your faith is also vain.
15 Yes, and we are found false witnesses of God; because we have testified of God that he raised up Christ: whom he

---

15:6 "The fact that Abraham Lincoln was born, became president, or was assassinated cannot be proven using scientific methods. To be 'scientific' it must be *repeatable* (as in the testing of gravity). The proofs that Lincoln did exist and was a historical figure are: 1) the written evidence; 2) eyewitness testimony; and 3) physical evidence that remains to this day—the Ford Theatre, birth records, and newspaper articles regarding his election. All these facts are acceptable in a court of law as proof to a judge and jury.

"The resurrection of Jesus Christ from the dead is "evidential": 1) the empty tomb still exists; 2) His birth record is documented all the way back to Adam and Eve; 3) the four Gospels record His death; 4) the location, and even the names of the political leaders who sentenced Him are historically recorded; 5) there were more than five hundred eyewitnesses who saw Jesus after the resurrection, recorded by the New Testament writers; 6) the very existence of the Christian faith, based on His death and resurrection; 7) the cultural and political evidence of the time, including the Roman calendar separating all of time into 'Before Christ' (B.C.) and 'in the year of our Lord' (A.D.)." *Garry T. Ansdell, D.D.*

15:10 "There is nothing but God's grace. We walk upon it; we breathe it; we live and die by it; it makes the nails and axles of the universe." *Robert Louis Stevenson*

15:14 If Jesus Christ didn't rise from the tomb, then the Bible is a fraud and any hope of resurrection is therefore in vain. However, God has given us irrefutable evidence in His Word to strengthen our faith in His promises—historical, scientific, medical, archeological, and prophetic evidence.

QUESTIONS & OBJECTIONS

15:22 ***"If God is perfect, why did He make an imperfect creation?"***

The Bible tells us that the Genesis creation was "good." There was no sin and therefore no suffering or death. Why then did God give Adam and Eve the ability to sin, knowing full well that they would sin and bring death and pain to the human race? Some believe that if Adam had been created without the ability to chose, then he would have been a "robot." A father *cannot* make his children love him. They choose to love him because they have a free will. Others point out that humanity would never have seen the depth of the love of God, as displayed in the cross, unless Adam had sinned, and that fact could be one reason why God allowed sin to enter the world.

raised not up, if so be that the dead rise
not.
16 For if the dead rise not, then is not
Christ raised:
17 And if Christ be not raised, your
faith is vain; you are yet in your sins.
18 Then they also which are fallen asleep
in Christ are perished.
19 If in this life only we have hope in
Christ, we are of all men most miserable.
20 But now is Christ risen from the dead,
and become the firstfruits of them that
slept.
21 For since by man came death, by man
came also the resurrection of the dead.
22 For as in Adam all die, even so in
Christ shall all be made alive.
23 But every man in his own order:
Christ the firstfruits; afterward they that
are Christ's at his coming.
24 Then comes the end, when he shall
have delivered up the kingdom to God,
even the Father; when he shall have put
down all rule and all authority and power.
25 For he must reign, till he has put all
enemies under his feet.
26 The last enemy that shall be destroyed is death.
27 For he has put all things under his
feet. But when he says, all things are put
under him, it is manifest that he is ex-
cepted, which did put all things under
him.
28 And when all things shall be subdued to him, then shall the Son also himself be subject to him that put all things
under him, that God may be all in all.
29 Else what shall they do which are
baptized for the dead, if the dead rise
not at all? why are they then baptized for
the dead?
30 And why stand we in jeopardy every
hour?
31 I protest by your rejoicing which I
have in Christ Jesus our Lord, I die daily.
32 If after the manner of men I have

15:17 "How can anyone lose who chooses to become a Christian? If, when he dies, there turns out to be no God and his faith was in vain, he has lost nothing—in fact, he has been happier in life than his nonbelieving friends. If, however, there is a God and a heaven and hell, then he has gained heaven and his skeptical friends will have lost everything in hell!" *Blaise Pascal*

15:29 Some believe in baptizing for the dead, which Paul mentions in these verses. Note that Paul does not say "we," but "they," thus distancing himself from the practice. See Acts 2:38 comment for the biblical basis for baptism.

15:31 "We are not merely imperfect creatures who must be improved: we are, as Newman said, rebels who must lay down our arms...To surrender a self-will inflamed and swollen with years of usurpation is a kind of death...Hence the necessity to die daily: however often we think we have broken the rebellious self, we shall still find it alive." *C. S. Lewis, The Problem of Pain*

QUESTIONS & OBJECTIONS

15:39 ***"Evolution disproves the Bible!"***

The Book of Genesis tells us that *everything* was created by God—nothing "evolved." Every creature was given the ability to reproduce *after its own kind* as is stated ten times in Genesis 1. Dogs do not produce cats. Neither do cats and dogs have a common ancestry. Dogs began as dogs and are still dogs. They vary in species from Chihuahuas to Saint Bernards, but you will not find a "dat" or a "cog" (part cat/dog) throughout God's creation. Frogs don't reproduce oysters, cows don't have lambs, and pregnant pigs don't give birth to rabbits. God made monkeys as monkeys, and man as man. Each creature brings forth after its own kind. That's no theory; that's a fact.

Why then should we believe that man comes from another species? If evolution is true, then it is proof that the Bible is false. However, the whole of creation stands in contradiction to the theory of evolution. Dr. Kent Hovind of Florida has a standing offer of $250,000 to "anyone who can give any empirical evidence (scientific proof) for evolution." Evolution—true science fiction. His website is www.drdino.com.

fought with beasts at Ephesus, what advantage is it to me, if the dead rise not?
let us eat and drink; for tomorrow we die.
33 Be not deceived: evil communications
corrupt good manners.
34 Awake to righteousness, and sin not;
for some have not the knowledge of God:
I speak this to your shame.
35 But some man will say, How are the
dead raised up? and with what body do
they come?
36 You fool, that which you sow is not
quickened, except it die:
37 And that which you sow, you sow
not that body that shall be, but bare
grain, it may chance of wheat, or of some
other grain:
38 But God gives it a body as it has
pleased him, and to every seed his own
body.
39 All flesh is not the same flesh: but
there is one kind of flesh of men, another flesh of beasts, another of fishes, and
another of birds.
40 There are also celestial bodies, and
bodies terrestrial: but the glory of the celestial is one, and the glory of the terrestrial is another.
41 There is one glory of the sun, and
another glory of the moon, and another
glory of the stars: for one star differs
from another star in glory.
42 So also is the resurrection of the dead.
It is sown in corruption; it is raised in incorruption:
43 It is sown in dishonor; it is raised in
glory: it is sown in weakness; it is raised
in power:
44 It is sown a natural body; it is raised
a spiritual body. There is a natural body,

15:34 False converts. Paul acknowledges that there were false converts in their midst; to their shame, some among them did not know God, were dead to righteousness, and were continuing to sin. We also should feel a sense of shame at the state of the lukewarm contemporary Church, where only 2 percent have any real concern for the salvation of the world.

15:39 "This notion of species as 'natural kinds' fits splendidly with creationist tenets of a pre-Darwinian age. *Louis Agassiz* even argued that species are God's individual thoughts, made incarnate so that we might perceive both His majesty and His message. Species, Agassiz wrote, are 'instituted by the Divine Intelligence as the categories of his mode of thinking.' But how could a division of the organic world into discrete entities be justified by an evolutionary theory that proclaimed ceaseless change as the fundamental fact of nature?" *Stephen J. Gould*, professor of geology and paleontology, Harvard University

QUESTIONS & OBJECTIONS

15:45

"Adam was a mythical figure who never really lived."

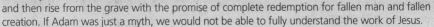

Adam is a key figure in Scripture. He is described as the "first Adam," the one who brought sin into the world. He made it necessary for Jesus, the "last Adam," to atone for all humans, and then rise from the grave with the promise of complete redemption for fallen man and fallen creation. If Adam was just a myth, we would not be able to fully understand the work of Jesus.

If Adam and Eve were not real, then we ought to doubt whether their children were real too, and their children…and then we ought to doubt the first 11 chapters of Genesis, and so on. All the genealogies accept Adam as being a literal person, so their children Cain and Abel (Genesis 4:9,10; Luke 11:50,51) must be real too. Jesus was descended from Adam, and it is impossible to be descended from a myth.

and there is a spiritual body.
45 And so it is written, The first man
Adam was made a living soul; the last
Adam was made a quickening spirit.
46 Howbeit that was not first which is
spiritual, but that which is natural; and
afterward that which is spiritual.
47 The first man is of the earth, earthy:
the second man is the Lord from heaven.
48 As is the earthy, such are they also
that are earthy: and as is the heavenly,
such are they also that are heavenly.
49 And as we have borne the image of
the earthy, we shall also bear the image
of the heavenly.
50 Now this I say, brethren, that flesh
and blood cannot inherit the kingdom of
God; neither does corruption inherit incorruption.
51 **Behold, I show you a mystery; We
shall not all sleep, but we shall all be
changed,**
52 **In a moment, in the twinkling of
an eye, at the last trump: for the trumpet shall sound, and the dead shall be
raised incorruptible, and we shall be
changed.**
53 **For this corruptible must put on
incorruption, and this mortal must
put on immortality.**
54 **So when this corruptible shall have
put on incorruption, and this mortal
shall have put on immortality, then
shall be brought to pass the saying that
is written, Death is swallowed up in
victory.**
**55 O death, where is your sting? O
grave, where is your victory?**
56 **The sting of death is sin; and the
strength of sin is the law.**
57 **But thanks be to God, who gives
us the victory through our Lord Jesus
Christ.**
58 *Therefore, my beloved brethren, be
steadfast, unmoveable, always abounding
in the work of the Lord, forasmuch as you
know that your labor is not in vain in the
Lord.*

CHAPTER 16

NOW concerning the collection for
the saints, as I have given order to
the churches of Galatia, even so do.
2 Upon the first day of the week let
every one of you lay by him in store, as
God has prospered him, that there be no
gatherings when I come.
3 And when I come, whomsoever you
shall approve by your letters, them will I
send to bring your liberality to Jerusalem.
4 And if it be meet that I go also, they
shall go with me.
5 Now I will come to you, when I shall
pass through Macedonia: for I do pass
through Macedonia.
6 And it may be that I will abide, yes,
and winter with you, that you may bring

15:55 Last Words of Famous People

Fearful Last Words:

Cardinal Borgia: "I have provided in the course of my life for everything except death, and now, alas, I am to die unprepared."

Elizabeth the First: "All my possessions for one moment of time."

Kurt Cobain (suicide note): "Frances and Courtney, I'll be at your altar. Please keep going Courtney, for Frances. For her life will be so much happier without me. I love you. *I love you.*"

Ludwig van Beethoven: "Too bad, too bad! It's too late!"

Thomas Hobbs: "I am about to take my last voyage, a great leap in the dark."

Anne Boleyn: "O God, have pity on my soul. O God, have pity on my soul."

Prince Henry of Wales: "Tie a rope round my body, pull me out of bed, and lay me in ashes, that I may die with repentant prayers to an offended God. O! I in vain wish for that time I lost with you and others in vain recreations."

Socrates: "All of the wisdom of this world is but a tiny raft upon which we must set sail when we leave this earth. If only there was a firmer foundation upon which to sail, perhaps some divine word."

Sigmund Freud: "The meager satisfaction that man can extract from reality leaves him starving."

Tony Hancock (British comedian): "Nobody will ever know I existed. Nothing to leave behind me. Nothing to pass on. Nobody to mourn me. That's the bitterest blow of all."

Phillip III, King of France: "What an account I shall have to give to God! How I should like to live otherwise than I have lived."

Luther Burbank: "I don't feel good."

Voltaire (skeptic): "I am abandoned by God and man! I will give you half of what I am worth if you will give me six months' life. Then I shall go to hell; and you will go with me. O Christ! O Jesus Christ!" (The talented French writer once said of Jesus, "Curse the wretch!" He stated, "Every sensible man, every honorable man, must hold the Christian sect in horror... Christianity is the most ridiculous, the most absurd and bloody religion that has ever infected the world.")

He also boasted, "In twenty years Christianity will be no more. My single hand shall destroy the edifice it took twelve apostles to rear." Some years later, Voltaire's house was used by the Geneva Bible Society to print Bibles.

Philosophical Last Words:

Aldus Huxley (humanist): "It is a bit embarrassing to have been concerned with the human problem all one's life and find at the end that one has no more to offer by way of advice than 'Try and be a little kinder.'"

Karl Marx: "Go on, get out! Last words are for fools who haven't said enough!"

Napoleon: "I marvel that where the ambitious dreams of myself and of Alexander and of Caesar should have vanished into thin air, a Judean peasant—Jesus—should be able to stretch his hands across the centuries, and control the destinies of men and nations."

Leonardo da Vinci: "I have offended God and mankind because my work did not reach the quality it should have."

Tolstoy: "Even in the valley of the shadow of death, two and two do not make six."

Benjamin Franklin: "A dying man can do nothing easy."

Grotius: "I have lived my life in a laborious doing of nothing."

Unexpected Demise:

H. G. Wells: "Go away: I'm alright."

General John Sedgwick (during the heat of battle in 1864): "They couldn't hit an elephant at this dist——!"

Bing Crosby: "That was a great game of golf."

Mahatma Ghandi: "I am late by ten minutes. I hate being late. I like to be at the prayer punctually at the stroke of five."

Diana (Spencer), Princess of Wales: "My God. What's happened?" (per police files)

Douglas Fairbanks, Sr.: "Never felt better."

Franklin D. Roosevelt: "I have a terrific headache."

Sal Mineo: (stabbed through the heart): "Oh God! No! Help! Someone help!"

Jesse James: "It's awfully hot today."

Lee Harvey Oswald: "I will be glad to discuss this proposition with my attorney, and that after I talk with one, we could either discuss it with him or discuss it with my attorney, if the attorney thinks it is a wise thing to do, but at the present time I have nothing more to say to you."

Unusual Last Words:

Vincent Van Gogh: "I shall never get rid of this depression."

James Dean: "My fun days are over."

Oscar Wilde: "My wallpaper and I are fighting a duel to the death. One or the other of us has to go..."

W. C. Fields: "I'm looking for a loophole."

Louis XVII: "I have something to tell you..."

Assurance of Salvation:

Jonathan Edwards: "Trust in God and you shall have nothing to fear."

Patrick Henry: "Doctor, I wish you to observe how real and beneficial the religion of Christ is to a man about to die..." In his will he wrote: "This is all the inheritance I give to my dear family. The religion of Christ which will give them one which will make them rich indeed."

John Owen: "I am going to Him whom my soul loveth, or rather who has loved me with an everlasting love, which is the sole ground of all my consolation."

D. L. Moody: "I see earth receding; heaven is opening. God is calling me."

Lew Wallace (author of *Ben Hur*): "Thy will be done."

Alexander Hamilton: "I have a tender reliance on the mercy of the Almighty, through the merits of the Lord Jesus Christ. I am a sinner. I look to Him for mercy."

William Shakespeare: "I commend my soul into the hands of God my Creator, hoping and assuredly believing, through the only merits of Jesus Christ my Savior, to be made partaker of life everlasting; and my body to the earth, whereof it was made."

Martin Luther: "Into Thy hands I commend my spirit! Thou hast redeemed me, O God of truth."

John Milton (British poet): "Death is the great key that opens the palace of Eternity."

Sir Walter Raleigh (at his execution): "So the heart be right, it is no matter which way the head lieth."

Daniel Webster (just before his death): "The great mystery is Jesus Christ—the gospel. What would the condition of any of us be if we had not the hope of immortality?...Thank God, the gospel of Jesus Christ brought life and immortality to light." His last words were: "I still live."

General William Booth (to his son): "And the homeless children, Bramwell, look after the homeless. Promise me..."

David Livingstone: "Build me a hut to die in. I am going home."

Charles Dickens: "I commit my soul to the mercy of God, through our Lord and Savior Jesus Christ, and I exhort my dear children humbly to try and guide themselves by the teaching of the New Testament."

Andrew Jackson: "My dear children, do not grieve for me...I am my God's. I belong to Him. I go but a short time before you, and...I hope and trust to meet you all in heaven."

Isaac Watts (hymn-writer): "It is a great mercy that I have no manner of fear or dread of death. I could, if God please, lay my head back and die without terror this afternoon."

me on my journey wherever I go.
7 For I will not see you now by the way;
but I trust to tarry a while with you, if
the Lord permit.
8 But I will tarry at Ephesus until Pentecost.
9 For a great door and effectual is opened
to me, and there are many adversaries.

10 Now if Timotheus come, see that he
may be with you without fear: for he
works the work of the Lord, as I also do.
11 Let no man therefore despise him:
but conduct him forth in peace, that he
may come to me: for I look for him with
the brethren.
12 As touching our brother Apollos, I
greatly desired him to come to you with
the brethren: but his will was not at all
to come at this time; but he will come
when he shall have convenient time.
13 Watch, stand fast in the faith, quit
you like men, be strong.
14 Let all your things be done with charity.
15 I beseech you, brethren, (you know
the house of Stephanas, that it is the firstfruits of Achaia, and that they have ad-
dicted themselves to the ministry of the
saints,)
16 That you submit yourselves to such,
and to every one that helps with us, and
labors.
17 I am glad of the coming of Stephanas and Fortunatus and Achaicus: for that
which was lacking on your part they
have supplied.
18 For they have refreshed my spirit
and yours: therefore acknowledge them
that are such.
19 The churches of Asia salute you.
Aquila and Priscilla salute you much in
the Lord, with the church that is in their
house.
20 All the brethren greet you. Greet one
another with an holy kiss.
21 The salutation of me Paul with mine
own hand.
22 If any man love not the Lord Jesus
Christ, let him be Anathema Maranatha.
23 The grace of our Lord Jesus Christ
be with you.
24 My love be with you all in Christ
Jesus. Amen.

"Grace is love that cares and stoops and rescues."

JOHN R. W. STOTT

15:58 Discouragement in witnessing. It is easy to become discouraged after trying to reason with sinners. But to do so is to demean the influence of the Holy Spirit in our witness. If the salvation of a single soul depended solely upon us, we *should* be depressed if we see little visible and immediate fruit for our labors. However, the Bible tells us that "salvation is of the Lord." We *do* play a part as a co-laborer with Christ—He may instruct us to roll the stone away, but it is the Lord alone who calls the sinner from the tomb of his deathly state. He gives us opportunity, but He opens the heart of the sinner, and it is Him alone that makes the sinner come to life.

Our confidence should then be in *Him.* Jesus said, "With God, nothing shall be impossible." We therefore can *always* abound in the Lord, knowing that our labors (even with cults) are not in vain. His Word cannot return void. Our part is simply to be true and faithful in our witness, then to stand back and watch the miracle work of our God. Who knows, perhaps the words we placed in the heart of the person may bear fruit years after they were spoken, and we will have the joy of unwrapping the grave clothes when God, in His time, calls them.

2 Corinthians

CHAPTER 1

PAUL, an apostle of Jesus Christ by
the will of God, and Timothy our
brother, to the church of God which is at
Corinth, with all the saints which are in
all Achaia:
2 Grace be to you and peace from God
our Father, and from the Lord Jesus
Christ.
3 Blessed be God, even the Father of
our Lord Jesus Christ, the Father of mercies, and the God of all comfort;
4 Who comforts us in all our tribulation, that we may be able to comfort them
which are in any trouble, by the comfort
wherewith we ourselves are comforted of
God.
5 For as the sufferings of Christ abound
in us, so our consolation also abounds
by Christ.
6 And whether we be afflicted, it is for
your consolation and salvation, which is
effectual in the enduring of the same sufferings which we also suffer: or whether
we be comforted, it is for your consolation and salvation.
7 And our hope of you is steadfast, knowing, that as you are partakers of the sufferings, so shall you be also of the consolation.
8 For we would not, brethren, have you
ignorant of our trouble which came to us
in Asia, that we were pressed out of measure, above strength, insomuch that we
despaired even of life:
9 But we had the sentence of death in
ourselves, that we should not trust in
ourselves, but in God which raises the
dead:
10 Who delivered us from so great a
death, and does deliver: in whom we
trust that he will yet deliver us;
11 You also helping together by prayer
for us, that for the gift bestowed upon us
by the means of many persons thanks
may be given by many on our behalf.
12 For our rejoicing is this, the testimony of our conscience, that in simplicity
and godly sincerity, not with fleshly wisdom, but by the grace of God, we have
had our conversation in the world, and
more abundantly toward you.
13 For we write none other things to
you, than what you read or acknowledge;
and I trust you shall acknowledge even
to the end;
14 As also you have acknowledged us
in part, that we are your rejoicing, even
as you also are ours in the day of the
Lord Jesus.
15 And in this confidence I was minded
to come to you before, that you might

1:4,5 This chapter is in direct conflict with the message of modern evangelism, which promises a life of happiness, joy, peace, and fulfillment. The truth is that the Christian life is flavored with trials that keep us on our knees.

have a second benefit;
16 And to pass by you into Macedonia, and to come again out of Macedonia to you, and of you to be brought on my way toward Judea.
17 When I therefore was thus minded, did I use lightness? or the things that I purpose, do I purpose according to the flesh, that with me there should be yes yes, and no no?
18 But as God is true, our word toward you was not yes and no.
19 For the Son of God, Jesus Christ, who was preached among you by us, even by me and Silvanus and Timotheus, was not yes and no, but in him was yes.
20 For all the promises of God in him are yes, and in him Amen, to the glory of God by us.
21 Now he which stablishes us with you in Christ, and has anointed us, is God;
22 Who has also sealed us, and given the earnest of the Spirit in our hearts.
23 Moreover I call God for a record upon my soul, that to spare you I came not as yet to Corinth.
24 Not for that we have dominion over your faith, but are helpers of your joy: for by faith you stand.

CHAPTER 2

BUT I determined this with myself, that I would not come again to you in heaviness.
2 For if I make you sorry, who is he then that makes me glad, but the same which is made sorry by me?
3 And I wrote this same to you, lest, when I came, I should have sorrow from them of whom I ought to rejoice; having confidence in you all, that my joy is the joy of you all.
4 For out of much affliction and anguish of heart I wrote to you with many tears; not that you should be grieved, but that you might know the love which I have more abundantly to you.
5 But if any have caused grief, he has not grieved me, but in part: that I may not overcharge you all.
6 Sufficient to such a man is this punishment, which was inflicted of many.
7 So that contrariwise you ought rather to forgive him, and comfort him, lest perhaps such a one should be swallowed up with overmuch sorrow.
8 Wherefore I beseech you that you would confirm your love toward him.
9 For to this end also did I write, that I might know the proof of you, whether you be obedient in all things.
10 To whom you forgive any thing, I forgive also: for if I forgave any thing, to whom I forgave it, for your sakes forgave I it in the person of Christ;
11 Lest Satan should get an advantage of us: for we are not ignorant of his devices.
12 Furthermore, when I came to Troas to preach Christ's gospel, and a door was opened to me of the Lord,
13 I had no rest in my spirit, because I found not Titus my brother: but taking my leave of them, I went from thence into Macedonia.
14 Now thanks be to God, which always causes us to triumph in Christ, and makes manifest the savour of his knowledge by us in every place.
15 *For we are to God a sweet savour of Christ, in them that are saved, and in them that perish:*
16 *To the one we are the savour of death to death; and to the other the savour of life to life. And who is sufficient for these things?*
17 *For we are not as many, which corrupt the word of God: but as of sincerity, but as of God, in the sight of God speak we in Christ.*

2:17 Opticians now offer glasses with titanium frames. Titanium twists and bends but retains its integrity. It always goes back to its original shape. That's what a Christian should be like. We bend; we are flexible on certain issues. However, we always retain our integrity. We refuse to compromise the truth of God's Word. See also 2 Corinthians 4:2.

2:17 *The Gospel: Why not preach that Jesus gives happiness, peace, and joy?*

Two men are seated on a plane. The first is given a parachute and told to put it on as it would improve his flight. He's a little skeptical at first, since he can't see how wearing a parachute on a plane could possibly improve his flight.

He decides to experiment and see if the claims are true. As he puts it on, he notices the weight of it upon his shoulders and he finds he has difficulty in sitting upright. However, he consoles himself with the fact he was told that the parachute would improve his flight. So he decides to give it a little time.

As he waits he notices that some of the other passengers are laughing at him for wearing a parachute on a plane. He begins to feel somewhat humiliated. As they continue to point and laugh at him, he can stand it no longer. He slinks in his seat, unstraps the parachute and throws it to the floor. Disillusionment and bitterness fill his heart, because as far as he was concerned he was told an outright lie.

The second man is given a parachute, *but listen to what he is told*. He's told to put it on because at any moment he'll be jumping 25,000 feet out of the plane. He gratefully puts the parachute on. He doesn't notice the weight of it upon his shoulders, nor that he can't sit upright. His mind is consumed with the thought of what would happen to him if he jumped without the parachute.

Let's now analyze the motive and the result of each passenger's experience. The first man's motive for putting the parachute on was solely to improve his flight. The result of his experience was that he was humiliated by the passengers, disillusioned, and somewhat embittered against those who gave him the parachute. As far as he's concerned, it will be a long time before anyone gets one of those things on his back again.

The second man put the parachute on solely to escape the jump to come. And because of his knowledge of what would happen to him if he jumped without it, he has a deep-rooted joy and peace in his heart knowing that he's saved from sure death. This knowledge gives him the ability to withstand the mockery of the other passengers. His attitude toward those who gave him the parachute is one of heartfelt gratitude.

Now listen to what the modern gospel says: "Put on the Lord Jesus Christ. He'll give you love, joy, peace, fulfillment, and lasting happiness." In other words, Jesus will improve your flight. The sinner responds, and in an experimental fashion puts on the Savior to see if the claims are true. And what does he get? The promised temptation, tribulation, and persecution—the other "passengers" mock him. So what does he do? He takes off the Lord Jesus Christ; he's offended for the Word's sake; he's disillusioned and somewhat embittered . . . and quite rightly so.

He was promised peace, joy, love, and fulfillment, and all he got were trials and humiliation. His bitterness is directed at those who gave him the so-called "good news." His latter end becomes worse than the first, and he's another inoculated and bitter "backslider."

Instead of preaching that Jesus improves the flight, we should be warning sinners that they have to jump out of a plane. That it's appointed for man to die once and then face judgment (Hebrews 9:27). When a sinner understands the horrific consequences of breaking the Law of God, he will flee to the Savior, solely to escape the wrath that's to come. If we are true and faithful witnesses, that's what we'll be preaching—that there is wrath to come—that God "commands all men every where to repent: *because* he has appointed a day in which he will judge the world in righteousness" (Acts 17:30,31).

The issue isn't one of happiness, but one of righteousness. It doesn't matter how happy a sinner is, or how much he is enjoying the pleasures of sin for a season, without the righteousness of Christ, he will perish on the day of wrath. Proverbs 11:4 says, "Riches profit not in the day of wrath: but righteousness delivers from death." Peace and joy are legitimate *fruits* of salvation, but it's not legitimate to use these fruits as a drawing card for

(continued on next page)

(2:17 continued)
salvation. If we continue to do so, the sinner will respond with an impure motive, lacking repentance.

Can you remember why the *second* passenger had joy and peace in his heart? It was because he knew that the parachute was going to save him from sure death. In the same way, as believers we have joy and peace in believing because we know that the righteousness of Christ is going to deliver us from the wrath that is to come.

With that thought in mind, let's take a close look at an incident aboard the plane. We have a brand-new flight attendant. It's her first day. She's carrying a tray of boiling hot coffee. She wants to leave an impression upon the passengers and she certainly does! As she's walking down the aisle she trips over someone's foot and slops the hot coffee all over the lap of our second passenger. What's his reaction as that boiling liquid hits his tender flesh? Does he go, "Man that hurt!"? Yes, he does. But then does he rip the parachute from his shoulders, throw it to the floor, and say, "The stupid parachute!"? No, why should he? He didn't put the parachute on for a better flight. He put it on to save him from the jump to come. If anything, the hot coffee incident causes him to cling tighter to the parachute and even look forward to the jump.

If we have put on the Lord Jesus Christ for the right motive—to flee from the wrath that's to come—when tribulation strikes, when the flight gets bumpy, we won't get angry at God, and we won't lose our joy and peace. Why should we? We didn't come to Christ for a better lifestyle, but to flee from the wrath. to come

If anything, tribulation drives the true believer *closer* to the Savior. Sadly, we have multitudes of professing Christians who lose their joy and peace when the flight gets bumpy. Why? They are the product of a man-centered gospel. They came lacking repentance, without which they cannot be saved.

CHAPTER 3

DO we begin again to commend ourselves? or need we, as some others,
epistles of commendation to you, or letters of commendation from you?
2 You are our epistle written in our
hearts, known and read of all men:
3 Forasmuch as you are manifestly declared to be the epistle of Christ ministered by us, written not with ink, but
with the Spirit of the living God; not in
tables of stone, but in fleshy tables of the
heart.
4 And such trust have we through Christ
to God-ward:

THE FUNCTION OF THE LAW

3:5,6 "God be thanked when the Law so works as to take off the sinner from all confidence in himself! To make the leper confess that he is incurable is going a great way toward compelling him to go to that divine Savior, who alone is able to heal him. This is the whole end of the Law toward men whom God will save." *Charles Spurgeon*

5 Not that we are sufficient of ourselves
to think any thing as of ourselves; but
our sufficiency is of God;
6 Who also has made us able ministers
of the new testament; not of the letter,
but of the spirit: for the letter kills, but
the spirit gives life.
7 But if the ministration of death, written and engraven in stones, was glorious,
so that the children of Israel could not
steadfastly behold the face of Moses for
the glory of his countenance; which glory
was to be done away:
8 How shall not the ministration of the
spirit be rather glorious?
9 For if the ministration of condemnation be glory, much more does the ministration of righteousness exceed in glory.
10 For even that which was made glorious had no glory in this respect, by reason of the glory that excels.
11 For if that which is done away was
glorious, much more that which remains
is glorious.
12 Seeing then that we have such hope,
we use great plainness of speech:
13 And not as Moses, which put a veil

over his face, that the children of Israel
could not steadfastly look to the end of
that which is abolished:
14 But their minds were blinded: for
until this day remains the same veil un-
taken away in the reading of the old testament; which veil is done away in Christ.
15 But even to this day, when Moses is
read, the veil is upon their heart.
16 Nevertheless when it shall turn to
the Lord, the veil shall be taken away.
17 Now the Lord is that Spirit: and where
the Spirit of the Lord is, there is liberty.
18 But we all, with open face beholding
as in a glass the glory of the Lord, are
changed into the same image from glory
to glory, even as by the Spirit of the Lord.

CHAPTER 4

THEREFORE seeing we have this min-
istry, as we have received mercy, we
faint not;
2 *But have renounced the hidden things of*
dishonesty, not walking in craftiness, nor
handling the word of God deceitfully; but
by manifestation of the truth commending
ourselves to every man's conscience in the
sight of God.
3 **But if our gospel be hid, it is hid to**
them that are lost:
4 In whom the god of this world has
blinded the minds of them which be-
lieve not, lest the light of the glorious
gospel of Christ, who is the image of
God, should shine to them.
5 **For we preach not ourselves, but**
Christ Jesus the Lord; and ourselves
your servants for Jesus' sake.
6 For God, who commanded the light
to shine out of darkness, has shined in
our hearts, to give the light of the knowledge of the glory of God in the face of
Jesus Christ.
7 But we have this treasure in earthen
vessels, that the excellency of the power
may be of God, and not of us.
8 We are troubled on every side, yet not
distressed; we are perplexed, but not in
despair;
9 Persecuted, but not forsaken; cast down,
but not destroyed;
10 Always bearing about in the body
the dying of the Lord Jesus, that the life
also of Jesus might be made manifest in
our body.
11 For we which live are always deliv-

3:12 "The big problem is that many Christians speak with forked tongues. They speak a strange lingo called the 'language of Zion' and can only be understood by using a special unscrambler, which most [people] do not possess. So we have to learn to speak plainly and not in code." *Dan Wooding*

3:14–16 "Be cold, sober, wise, circumspect. Keep yourself low by the ground avoiding high questions. Expound the Law truly and open the veil of Moses to condemn all flesh and prove all men sinners, and set at broach the mercy of our Lord Jesus, and let wounded consciences drink of Him." *William Tyndale*

3:18 We often delight in sifting gnats, making issues out of things that aren't important. If someone becomes a Christian, some in the Church seem intent on shaping him to be conformed to their own image, rather than the image of Christ. They feel that he should dress, look, believe, speak, eat, and breathe just as they do.

When someone comes to the Lord, he may not look as we think he should. His hair may be long, his clothes may be radical, he may have an earring in his ear, but if these things are wrong God will speak in his ear. In the meantime, He may be ministering to him about the need to return stolen goods, or about seeking forgiveness from those he has wronged in the past. Those are the things that matter to God.

4:2 "I believe in preaching without compromise against sin." *Franklin Graham*
"Some evangelists are prepared to be anything to anybody as long as they get somebody at the altar for something." *Leonard Ravenhill*

PRINCIPLES OF GROWTH FOR THE NEW AND GROWING CHRISTIAN

4:4

Warfare—Praise the Lord and Pass the Ammunition

Before you became a Christian, you floated downstream with the other dead fish. But now, God has put His life within you, and you will find yourself swimming against a threefold current: the world, the devil, and the flesh. Let's look at these three resistant enemies.

Our first enemy is the world, which refers to the sinful, rebellious, world system. The world loves the darkness and hates the light (John 3:20), and is governed by the "prince of the power of the air" (Ephesians 2:2). The Bible says the Christian has escaped the corruption that is in the world through lust. "Lust" is unlawful desire, and is the life's blood of the world—whether it be the lust for sexual sin, for power, for money, for material things. Lust is a monster that will never be gratified, so don't feed it. It will grow bigger and bigger until it weighs heavy upon your back, and will be the death of you (James 1:15).

There is nothing wrong with sex, power, money, or material things, but when desire for these becomes predominant, it becomes idolatry. We are told, "Love not the world, neither the things that are in the world. If any man love the world, the love of the Father is not in him"; whoever is "a friend of the world is the enemy of God" (1 John 2:15; James 4:4).

The second enemy is the devil, who is the "god of this world" (2 Corinthians 4:4). He was your spiritual father before you joined the family of God (John 8:44; Ephesians 2:2). Jesus called the devil a thief who came to steal, kill, and destroy (John 10:10).

The way to overcome him and his demons is to make sure you are outfitted with the spiritual armor of God (Ephesians 6:10–20). Become intimately familiar with it. Sleep in it. Never take it off. Bind the sword to your hand so you never lose its grip. The reason for this brings us to the third enemy.

The third enemy is what the Bible calls the "flesh." This is your sinful nature. The domain for the battle is your mind.

If you have a mind to, you *will* be attracted to the world and all its sin. The mind is the control panel for the eyes and the ears, the center of your appetites. All sin begins in the "heart" (Proverbs 4:23; Matthew 15:19). We think of sin before we commit it. James 1:15 warns that lust brings forth sin, and sin when it's conceived brings forth death. Every day of life, we have a choice. To sin or not to sin—that is the question. The answer is the fear of God. If you don't fear God, you will sin to your sinful heart's delight.

Did you know that God kills people? He killed a man for what he did sexually (Genesis 38:9,10), killed another man for being greedy (Luke 12:15–21), and killed a husband and wife for lying (Acts 5:1–10). Knowledge of God's goodness—His righteous judgments against evil—should put the fear of God in us and help us not to indulge in sin.

If we know that the eye of the Lord is in every place beholding the evil and the good, and that He will bring every work to judgment, we will live accordingly. Such weighty thoughts are valuable, for "by the fear of the Lord men depart from evil" (Proverbs 16:6).

For the next principle of growth, see Hebrews 10:25 comment.

ered to death for Jesus' sake, that the life
also of Jesus might be made manifest in
our mortal flesh.
12 So then death works in us, but life
in you.
13 *We having the same spirit of faith, according as it is written, I believed, and therefore have I spoken; we also believe, and therefore speak;*
14 Knowing that he which raised up

4:6 Just as in the beginning the earth was without form and void, and in darkness (Genesis 1:2), the understanding of unregenerate man is darkened (Ephesians 4:18). It is without form and void until God says, "Let there be light."

QUESTIONS & OBJECTIONS

5:14,15 ***"Because Jesus died on the cross, we are all forgiven of every sin."***

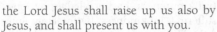

The forgiveness that is in Jesus Christ is conditional upon "repentance toward God, and faith toward our Lord Jesus Christ" (Acts 20:21). It is a gift that God offers to everyone, but individuals must receive it by repenting and trusting in Christ, or they will remain dead in their sins.

No one has biblical grounds to continue in sin, assuming that they are safe just because Jesus died on the cross. See 1 John 3:4–6.

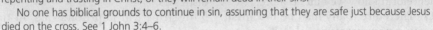

the Lord Jesus shall raise up us also by
Jesus, and shall present us with you.
15 For all things are for your sakes, that
the abundant grace might through the
thanksgiving of many redound to the
glory of God.
16 For which cause we faint not; but
though our outward man perish, yet the
inward man is renewed day by day.
17 For our light affliction, which is but
for a moment, works for us a far more
exceeding and eternal weight of glory;
18 While we look not at the things
which are seen, but at the things which
are not seen: for the things which are
seen are temporal; but the things which
are not seen are eternal.

CHAPTER 5

FOR we know that if our earthly
house of this tabernacle were dissolved, we have a building of God, an
house not made with hands, eternal in
the heavens.
2 For in this we groan, earnestly desiring to be clothed upon with our house
which is from heaven:
3 If so be that being clothed we shall
not be found naked.
4 For we that are in this tabernacle do
groan, being burdened: not for that we
would be unclothed, but clothed upon,
that mortality might be swallowed up of
life.
5 Now he that has wrought us for the
selfsame thing is God, who also has
given to us the earnest of the Spirit.
6 Therefore we are always confident,
knowing that, whilst we are at home in
the body, we are absent from the Lord:
7 (For we walk by faith, not by sight:)
8 We are confident, I say, and willing
rather to be absent from the body, and
to be present with the Lord.
9 Wherefore we labor, that, whether
present or absent, we may be accepted of
him.
10 For we must all appear before the
judgment seat of Christ; that every one
may receive the things done in his body,
according to that he has done, whether it
be good or bad.
11 *Knowing therefore the terror of the
Lord, we persuade men; but we are made
manifest to God; and I trust also are made
manifest in your consciences.*
12 For we commend not ourselves again
to you, but give you occasion to glory on
our behalf, that you may have somewhat
to answer them which glory in appearance, and not in heart.
13 For whether we be beside ourselves,
it is to God: or whether we be sober, it is
for your cause.
14 For the love of Christ constrains us;
because we thus judge, that if one died

5:10 Judgment Day: For verses that warn of its reality, see 2 Thessalonians 1:7–9.

5:11 "We fear men so much because we fear God so little. One fear causes another. When man's terror scares you, turn your thoughts to the wrath of God." *William Gurnall* for all, then were all dead:

15 And that he died for all, that they which live should not henceforth live to themselves, but to him which died for them, and rose again.

16 Wherefore henceforth know we no man after the flesh: yes, though we have known Christ after the flesh, yet now henceforth know we him no more.

17 Therefore if any man be in Christ, he is a new creature: old things are passed away; behold, all things are become new.

18 And all things are of God, who has reconciled us to himself by Jesus Christ, and has given to us the ministry of reconciliation;

19 *To wit, that God was in Christ, reconciling the world to himself, not imputing their trespasses to them; and has committed to us the word of reconciliation.*

20 **Now then we are ambassadors for Christ, as though God did beseech you by us: we pray you in Christ's stead, be reconciled to God.**

21 For he has made him to be sin for us, who knew no sin; that we might be made the righteousness of God in him.

CHAPTER 6

WE then, as workers together with him, beseech you also that you receive not the grace of God in vain.

2 (For he says, I have heard you in a time accepted, and in the day of salvation have I succoured you: behold, now is the accepted time; **behold, now is the day of salvation**.)

3 Giving no offence in any thing, that the ministry be not blamed:

4 But in all things approving ourselves as the ministers of God, in much patience, in afflictions, in necessities, in distresses,

5 In stripes, in imprisonments, in tumults, in labors, in watchings, in fastings;

6 By pureness, by knowledge, by longsuffering, by kindness, by the Holy Spirit, by love unfeigned,

7 By the word of truth, by the power of God, by the armor of righteousness on the right hand and on the left,

8 By honor and dishonor, by evil report and good report: as deceivers, and yet true;

9 As unknown, and yet well known; as dying, and, behold, we live; as chastened, and not killed;

10 As sorrowful, yet always rejoicing; as poor, yet making many rich; as having nothing, and yet possessing all things.

11 O you Corinthians, our mouth is open to you, our heart is enlarged.

12 You are not straitened in us, but you are straitened in your own bowels.

13 Now for a recompense in the same, (I speak as to my children,) be you also enlarged.

14 Be not unequally yoked together with

5:17 New birth—its necessity for salvation. See Titus 3:5. "It is easier to denature plutonium than to denature the evil spirit of man." *Albert Einstein*

5:21 "Christians are continually trying to *change* their lives; but God calls us to experience the *exchanged* life. Christianity is not a self-improvement program. It isn't a reformation project. It is resurrection! It is new life! And it is expressed in terms of a total exchange of identity. Jesus Christ identified Himself with us in our death in order that we might be identified with Him in His resurrection. We give Christ all that we were—spiritually dead, guilty sinners—and Christ gives us all that He is—resurrected life, forgiveness, righteousness, acceptance." *Bob George, Classic Christianity* (See Galatians 2:20.)

6:1 "It's very sobering to find how many people whom I would presume to be saved feel little or no urgency regarding their spiritual condition, the condition of the church, or that of our nation ...Whereas I once thought the battlefield was 'out there' among those rejecting Christ, I see things differently now...The front-line of the battle is in the hearts of God's people." *Rob Cummins* (quoted in *The Transforming Power of Fasting and Prayer* by *Bill Bright*)

SPRINGBOARDS FOR PREACHING AND WITNESSING

6:2

The Olympic High Diver

An Olympic gold-medalist high-diving champion was once plagued with insomnia. As he tossed and turned upon his bed, he began thinking deeply about the success he had attained in his field. He meditated on the gold medals he had won. To his dismay he realized that his success had not achieved what he had hoped. The excitement of winning, the photographers, the medals, and the fame had given him some sense of pleasure, but the fact of death awaiting him left him with a complete sense of futility.

He rose from the bed and made his way to his diving pool. Because of a full moon, he didn't even bother to turn the lights on. As he climbed the high diving board, he watched his shadow cast by the moonlight on the far wall. The routine had become so commonplace to him that he could confidently walk that board in the semi-darkness.

At the end of the diving board, he prepared for the dive. He placed his feet together, then pulled his arms up to a horizontal position. As he did so, his eyes caught a glimpse of his shadow on the far wall. All he could see was a perfect cross. His mind immediately raced back to his Sunday school days: "God commends his love toward us, in that, while we were yet sinners, Christ died for us" (Romans 5:8). All of a sudden he felt unclean as he considered the Commandments he had broken. The sinless Son of God had come to pay the penalty for his sins. With tears in his eyes, the great athlete turned around, slowly made his way down to the bottom of the diving board, fell to his knees, and yielded his life to Jesus Christ. He was able to go back to bed and sleep peacefully.

In the morning he arose with a new sense of forgiveness of his sins. He made his way back to the pool, but to his utter astonishment, *it was completely empty*. The previous evening, the caretaker had emptied it and was just beginning the process of refilling.

unbelievers: for what fellowship has righteousness with unrighteousness? and what communion has light with darkness?

15 And what concord has Christ with Belial? or what part has he that believes with an infidel?

16 And what agreement has the temple of God with idols? for you are the temple of the living God; as God has said, I will dwell in them, and walk in them; and I will be their God, and they shall be my people.

17 **Wherefore come out from among them, and be separate, says the Lord, and touch not the unclean thing; and I will receive you,**

18 **And will be a Father to you, and you shall be my sons and daughters, said the Lord Almighty.**

CHAPTER 7

HAVING therefore these promises, dearly beloved, let us cleanse ourselves from all filthiness of the flesh and spirit, perfecting holiness in the fear of God.

2 Receive us; we have wronged no man, we have corrupted no man, we have defrauded no man.

3 I speak not this to condemn you: for I have said before, that you are in our hearts to die and live with you.

4 Great is my boldness of speech toward you, great is my glorying of you: I am filled with comfort, I am exceeding joyful in all our tribulation.

5 For, when we were come into Mace-

7:4 "Receive every inward and outward trouble, every disappointment, pain, uneasiness, temptation, darkness and desolation with both hands, as to a true opportunity and blessed occasion of dying to self and entering into a fuller fellowship with thy self-denying, suffering Savior." *John Wesley*

donia, our flesh had no rest, but we were
troubled on every side; without were
fightings, within were fears.
6 Nevertheless God, that comforts those
that are cast down, comforted us by the
coming of Titus;
7 And not by his coming only, but by
the consolation wherewith he was comforted in you, when he told us your
earnest desire, your mourning, your fervent mind toward me; so that I rejoiced
the more.

> You must have, more or less, a distinct sense of the dreadful wrath of God and of the terrors of the judgment to come, or you will lack energy in your work and so lack one of the essentials of success.
>
> **CHARLES SPURGEON**

8 For though I made you sorry with a
letter, I do not repent, though I did repent: for I perceive that the same epistle
has made you sorry, though it were but
for a season.
9 Now I rejoice, not that you were made
sorry, but that you sorrowed to repentance: for you were made sorry after a
godly manner, that you might receive
damage by us in nothing.
10 For godly sorrow works repentance
to salvation not to be repented of: but
the sorrow of the world works death.
11 For behold this selfsame thing, that
you sorrowed after a godly sort, what
carefulness it wrought in you, yes, what
clearing of yourselves, yes, what indignation, yes, what fear, yes, what vehement
desire, yes, what zeal, yes, what revenge!
In all things you have approved yourselves to be clear in this matter.
12 Wherefore, though I wrote to you, I
did it not for his cause that had done the
wrong, nor for his cause that suffered
wrong, but that our care for you in the
sight of God might appear to you.
13 Therefore we were comforted in your
comfort: yes, and exceedingly the more
joyed we for the joy of Titus, because his
spirit was refreshed by you all.
14 For if I have boasted any thing to
him of you, I am not ashamed; but as we
spoke all things to you in truth, even so
our boasting, which I made before Titus,
is found a truth.
15 And his inward affection is more
abundant toward you, whilst he remembered the obedience of you all, how with
fear and trembling you received him.
16 I rejoice therefore that I have confidence in you in all things.

CHAPTER 8

MOREOVER, brethren, we make
known to you the grace of God
bestowed on the churches of Macedonia;

7:10 Godly sorrow. A pastor was once approached by his six-year-old son who said he wanted to "ask Jesus into his heart." The father, suspecting that the child lacked the knowledge of sin, told him that he could do so when he was older, then sent him off to bed.

A short time later, the boy got out of bed and asked his father if he could give his life to the Savior. The father still wasn't persuaded of the son's understanding, so, not wanting the child's salvation to be spurious, he sent him back to his room.

A third time the son returned. This time the father questioned him about whether he had broken any of the Ten Commandments. The young boy didn't think he had. When asked if he was a liar, the child said he wasn't. The father thought for a moment, then asked him how many lies he had to tell to be a liar. When it was established that one lie made a person a liar, the child thought for a moment, realized he had lied, and broke down in uncontrollable tears. When the father then asked if he wanted to "ask Jesus into his heart," the child *cringed* and shook his head. He was fearful because now he knew that he had sinned against God. At this point, he could do more than experimentally "ask Jesus into his heart." He could find a place of godly sorrow, repentance toward God, and faith toward our Lord Jesus Christ (Acts 20:21).

"If your sorrow is because of certain consequences which have come on your family because of your sin, this is remorse, not true repentance. If, on the other hand, you are grieved because you also sinned against God and His holy laws, then you are on the right road." *(See 2 Corinthians 7:10.)*

Billy Graham

2 How that in a great trial of affliction
the abundance of their joy and their
deep poverty abounded to the riches of
their liberality.
3 For to their power, I bear record, yes,
and beyond their power they were willing of themselves;
4 Praying us with much entreaty that
we would receive the gift, and take upon
us the fellowship of the ministering to
the saints.
5 And this they did, not as we hoped,
but first gave their own selves to the Lord,
and to us by the will of God.
6 Insomuch that we desired Titus, that
as he had begun, so he would also finish
in you the same grace also.
7 Therefore, as you abound in every
thing, in faith, and utterance, and knowledge, and in all diligence, and in your
love to us, see that you abound in this
grace also.
8 I speak not by commandment, but by
occasion of the forwardness of others,
and to prove the sincerity of your love.
9 For you know the grace of our Lord
Jesus Christ, that, though he was rich,
yet for your sakes he became poor, that
you through his poverty might be rich.
10 And herein I give my advice: for this
is expedient for you, who have begun
before, not only to do, but also to be forward a year ago.
11 Now therefore perform the doing of
it; that as there was a readiness to will,
so there may be a performance also out
of that which you have.
12 For if there be first a willing mind, it
is accepted according to that a man has,
and not according to that he has not.
13 For I mean not that other men be
eased, and you burdened:
14 But by an equality, that now at this
time your abundance may be a supply
for their want, that their abundance also
may be a supply for your want: that there
may be equality:
15 As it is written, He that had gathered
much had nothing over; and he that had
gathered little had no lack.
16 But thanks be to God, which put the
same earnest care into the heart of Titus
for you.
17 For indeed he accepted the exhortation; but being more forward, of his own
accord he went to you.
18 And we have sent with him the brother, whose praise is in the gospel throughout all the churches;
19 And not that only, but who was also
chosen of the churches to travel with us
with this grace, which is administered by
us to the glory of the same Lord, and declaration of your ready mind:
20 Avoiding this, that no man should
blame us in this abundance which is administered by us:
21 Providing for honest things, not only
in the sight of the Lord, but also in the
sight of men.
22 And we have sent with them our
brother, whom we have oftentimes proved

diligent in many things, but now much
more diligent, upon the great confidence
which I have in you.
23 Whether any do inquire of Titus, he
is my partner and fellow-helper concerning you: or our brethren be inquired of,
they are the messengers of the churches,
and the glory of Christ.
24 Wherefore show to them, and before
the churches, the proof of your love, and
of our boasting on your behalf.

CHAPTER 9

FOR as touching the ministering to
the saints, it is superfluous for me to
write to you:
2 For I know the forwardness of your
mind, for which I boast of you to them
of Macedonia, that Achaia was ready a
year ago; and your zeal has provoked
very many.
3 Yet have I sent the brethren, lest our
boasting of you should be in vain in this
behalf; that, as I said, you may be ready:
4 Lest haply if they of Macedonia come
with me, and find you unprepared, we
(that we say not, you) should be ashamed
in this same confident boasting.
5 Therefore I thought it necessary to exhort the brethren, that they would go
before to you, and make up beforehand
your bounty, whereof you had notice before, that the same might be ready, as a
matter of bounty, and not as of covetousness.
6 But this I say, He which sows sparingly shall reap also sparingly; and he which
sows bountifully shall reap also bountifully.
7 Every man according as he purposes
in his heart, so let him give; not grudg-
ingly, or of necessity: for God loves a
cheerful giver.
8 And God is able to make all grace
abound toward you; that you always
having all sufficiency in all things, may
abound to every good work:
9 (As it is written, He has dispersed
abroad; he has given to the poor: his
righteousness remains for ever.
10 Now he that ministers seed to the
sower both minister bread for your food,
and multiply your seed sown, and increase the fruits of your righteousness;)
11 Being enriched in every thing to all
bountifulness, which causes through us
thanksgiving to God.
12 For the administration of this service
not only supplies the want of the saints,
but is abundant also by many thanksgiv-
ings to God;
13 Whiles by the experiment of this
ministration they glorify God for your professed subjection to the gospel of Christ,
and for your liberal distribution to them,
and to all men;
14 And by their prayer for you, which
long after you for the exceeding grace of
God in you.
15 Thanks be to God for his unspeakable gift.

CHAPTER 10

NOW I Paul myself beseech you by
the meekness and gentleness of
Christ, who in presence am base among
you, but being absent am bold toward
you:
2 But I beseech you, that I may not be
bold when I am present with that confidence, wherewith I think to be bold
against some, which think of us as if we
walked according to the flesh.
3 For though we walk in the flesh, we

9:2 "If you never have sleepless hours, if you never have weeping eyes, if your hearts never swell as if they would burst, you need not anticipate that you will be called zealous. You do not know the beginning of true zeal, for the foundation of Christian zeal lies in the heart. The heart must be heavy with grief and yet must beat high with holy ardor. The heart must be vehement in desire, panting continually for God's glory, or else we shall never attain to anything like the zeal which God would have us know." *Charles Spurgeon*

do not war after the flesh:
4 (For the weapons of our warfare are
not carnal, but mighty through God to
the pulling down of strong holds;)
5 Casting down imaginations, and every
high thing that exalts itself against the
knowledge of God, and bringing into captivity every thought to the obedience of
Christ;
6 And having in a readiness to revenge
all disobedience, when your obedience is
fulfilled.
7 Do you look on things after the outward appearance? If any man trust to himself that he is Christ's, let him of himself
think this again, that, as he is Christ's,
even so are we Christ's.
8 For though I should boast somewhat
more of our authority, which the Lord has
given us for edification, and not for your
destruction, I should not be ashamed:
9 That I may not seem as if I would terrify you by letters.
10 For his letters, say they, are weighty
and powerful; but his bodily presence is
weak, and his speech contemptible.
11 Let such an one think this, that, such
as we are in word by letters when we are
absent, such will we be also in deed when
we are present.
12 For we dare not make ourselves of
the number, or compare ourselves with
some that commend themselves: but they
measuring themselves by themselves,
and comparing themselves among themselves, are not wise.
13 But we will not boast of things without our measure, but according to the
measure of the rule which God has distributed to us, a measure to reach even
to you.
14 For we stretch not ourselves beyond
our measure, as though we reached not
to you: for we are come as far as to you
also in preaching the gospel of Christ:
15 Not boasting of things without our
measure, that is, of other men's labors;
but having hope, when your faith is increased, that we shall be enlarged by you
according to our rule abundantly,
16 To preach the gospel in the regions
beyond you, and not to boast in another
man's line of things made ready to our
hand.
17 But he that glories, let him glory in
the Lord.
18 For not he that commends himself is
approved, but whom the Lord commends.

CHAPTER 11

WOULD to God you could bear with
me a little in my folly: and indeed
bear with me.
2 For I am jealous over you with godly
jealousy: for I have espoused you to one
husband, that I may present you as a
chaste virgin to Christ.
3 But I fear, lest by any means, as the
serpent beguiled Eve through his subtlety, so your minds should be corrupted
from the simplicity that is in Christ.
4 For if he that comes preaches another
Jesus, whom we have not preached, or if
you receive another spirit, which you have
not received, or another gospel, which
you have not accepted, you might well
bear with him.
5 For I suppose I was not a whit behind

11:3 Notice that Paul believed the Genesis account of the Fall. See 2 Peter 3:6 comment.

11:3 When the serpent deceived Eve, he cast doubt on God's Word, causing her to mistrust God Himself (Genesis 3:1–5). God said, "You shall surely die," but Eve chose to believe that God was deceitful. To partake of the fruit was an act of rebellion against the God who had not only given Adam and Eve life but had lavished His goodness upon them.

We must remember that Satan is the father of lies (John 8:44), and he usually uses enough of the truth to make the lie believable. Here Paul cautions believers to reject any message that differs from the true gospel as revealed in the Word of God. See Ephesians 4:18 and Luke 4:1–13 comments.

the very chiefest apostles.
6 But though I be rude in speech, yet
not in knowledge; but we have been
thoroughly made manifest among you in
all things.
7 Have I committed an offence in abas-
ing myself that you might be exalted, because I have preached to you the gospel
of God freely?
8 I robbed other churches, taking wages
of them, to do you service.
9 And when I was present with you,
and wanted, I was chargeable to no man:
for that which was lacking to me the
brethren which came from Macedonia
supplied: and in all things I have kept
myself from being burdensome to you,
and so will I keep myself.
10 As the truth of Christ is in me, no
man shall stop me of this boasting in the
regions of Achaia.
11 Wherefore? because I love you not?
God knows.
12 But what I do, that I will do, that I
may cut off occasion from them which
desire occasion; that wherein they glory,
they may be found even as we.
13 For such are false apostles, deceitful
workers, transforming themselves into
the apostles of Christ.
14 And no marvel; for Satan himself is
transformed into an angel of light.
15 Therefore it is no great thing if his
ministers also be transformed as the
ministers of righteousness; whose end
shall be according to their works.
16 I say again, Let no man think me a
fool; if otherwise, yet as a fool receive
me, that I may boast myself a little.
17 That which I speak, I speak it not
after the Lord, but as it were foolishly, in
this confidence of boasting.
18 Seeing that many glory after the flesh,
I will glory also.
19 For you suffer fools gladly, seeing
you yourselves are wise.
20 For you suffer, if a man bring you
into bondage, if a man devour you, if a
man take of you, if a man exalt himself,
if a man smite you on the face.

"Thrice was I beaten with rods,
once was I stoned, thrice I suffered
shipwreck, a night and a day I
have been in the deep . . ." (v. 25).

For other trials and tribulations Paul suffered for preaching the gospel, see John 17:14.

21 I speak as concerning reproach, as
though we had been weak. Howbeit
whereinsoever any is bold, (I speak foolishly,) I am bold also.
22 Are they Hebrews? so am I. Are they
Israelites? so am I. Are they the seed of
Abraham? so am I.
23 Are they ministers of Christ? (I speak
as a fool) I am more; in labors more
abundant, in stripes above measure, in
prisons more frequent, in deaths oft.
24 Of the Jews five times received I forty
stripes save one.
25 Thrice was I beaten with rods, once
was I stoned, thrice I suffered shipwreck,
a night and a day I have been in the deep;
26 In journeyings often, in perils of waters, in perils of robbers, in perils by mine
own countrymen, in perils by the heathen, in perils in the city, in perils in the
wilderness, in perils in the sea, in perils
among false brethren;
27 In weariness and painfulness, in
watchings often, in hunger and thirst, in
fastings often, in cold and nakedness.
28 Beside those things that are without,
that which comes upon me daily, the
care of all the churches.
29 Who is weak, and I am not weak?
who is offended, and I burn not?
30 If I must needs glory, I will glory of
the things which concern mine infirmities.

31 The God and Father of our Lord Jesus
Christ, which is blessed for evermore,
knows that I lie not.
32 In Damascus the governor under
Aretas the king kept the city of the Dama-
scenes with a garrison, desirous to apprehend me:
33 And through a window in a basket
was I let down by the wall, and escaped
his hands.

CHAPTER 12

IT is not expedient for me doubtless to
glory. I will come to visions and revelations of the Lord.
2 I knew a man in Christ above fourteen years ago, (whether in the body, I
cannot tell; or whether out of the body, I
cannot tell: God knows;) such an one
caught up to the third heaven.
3 And I knew such a man, (whether in
the body, or out of the body, I cannot
tell: God knows;)
4 How that he was caught up into paradise, and heard unspeakable words,
which it is not lawful for a man to utter.
5 Of such an one will I glory: yet of myself I will not glory, but in mine infirmities.
6 For though I would desire to glory, I
shall not be a fool; for I will say the
truth: but now I forbear, lest any man
should think of me above that which he
sees me to be, or that he hears of me.
7 And lest I should be exalted above
measure through the abundance of the
revelations, there was given to me a thorn
in the flesh, the messenger of Satan to
buffet me, lest I should be exalted above
measure.
8 For this thing I besought the Lord
thrice, that it might depart from me.
9 And he said to me, My grace is sufficient for you: for my strength is made
perfect in weakness. Most gladly therefore will I rather glory in my infirmities,
that the power of Christ may rest upon
me.
10 Therefore I take pleasure in infirmities, in reproaches, in necessities, in persecutions, in distresses for Christ's sake:
for when I am weak, then am I strong.
11 I am become a fool in glorying; you
have compelled me: for I ought to have
been commended of you: for in nothing
am I behind the very chiefest apostles,
though I be nothing.
12 Truly the signs of an apostle were
wrought among you in all patience, in
signs, and wonders, and mighty deeds.

> We spend our entire lives acting out our concept of God.
>
> **JACK TAYLOR**

13 For what is it wherein you were inferior to other churches, except it be that
I myself was not burdensome to you?
forgive me this wrong.
14 Behold, the third time I am ready to
come to you; and I will not be burdensome to you: for I seek not yours, but
you: for the children ought not to lay up
for the parents, but the parents for the
children.
15 And I will very gladly spend and be
spent for you; though the more abundantly I love you, the less I be loved.
16 But be it so, I did not burden you:
nevertheless, being crafty, I caught you
with guile.
17 Did I make a gain of you by any of
them whom I sent to you?

12:9 "God whispers to us in our pleasures, speaks to us in our conscience, but shouts in our pains: It is His megaphone to rouse a deaf world." *C. S. Lewis, The Problem of Pain*

12:11 "God creates out of nothing. Therefore until man is nothing, God can make nothing out of him." *Martin Luther*

12:15 "You have nothing to do but to save souls. Therefore spend and be spent in this work." *John Wesley*

18 I desired Titus, and with him I sent
a brother. Did Titus make a gain of you?
walked we not in the same spirit? walked
we not in the same steps?
19 Again, do you think that we excuse
ourselves to you? we speak before God
in Christ: but we do all things, dearly
beloved, for your edifying.
20 For I fear, lest, when I come, I shall
not find you such as I would, and that I
shall be found to you such as you would
not: lest there be debates, envyings,
wraths, strifes, backbitings, whisperings,
swellings, tumults:
21 And lest, when I come again, my
God will humble me among you, and
that I shall bewail many which have
sinned already, and have not repented of
the uncleanness and fornication and lasciviousness which they have committed.

. . . . . .

To find out where the races came from, see Acts 17:26 comment.

. . . . . .

CHAPTER 13

THIS is the third time I am coming to
you. In the mouth of two or three
witnesses shall every word be established.
2 I told you before, and foretell you, as
if I were present, the second time; and
being absent now I write to them which
heretofore have sinned, and to all other,
that, if I come again, I will not spare:
3 Since you seek a proof of Christ speaking in me, which toward you is not weak,
but is mighty in you.
4 For though he was crucified through
weakness, yet he lives by the power of
God. For we also are weak in him, but
we shall live with him by the power of
God toward you.
5 Examine yourselves, whether you be
in the faith; prove your own selves. Do
you not know your own selves, how that
Jesus Christ is in you, except you be reprobates?
6 But I trust that you shall know that
we are not reprobates.
7 Now I pray to God that you do no evil;
not that we should appear approved, but
that you should do that which is honest,
though we be as reprobates.
8 For we can do nothing against the
truth, but for the truth.
9 For we are glad, when we are weak,
and you are strong: and this also we
wish, even your perfection.
10 Therefore I write these things being
absent, lest being present I should use
sharpness, according to the power which
the Lord has given me to edification, and
not to destruction.
11 Finally, brethren, farewell. Be perfect, be of good comfort, be of one mind,
live in peace; and the God of love and
peace shall be with you.
12 Greet one another with an holy kiss.
13 All the saints salute you.
14 The grace of the Lord Jesus Christ,
and the love of God, and the communion
of the Holy Spirit, be with you all. Amen.

13:3 The Christian life. "The Christian life is more than difficult; it is humanly impossible to live. Only Jesus Christ can live it through you as He dwells within you. The Christian life is not a person trying to imitate Christ; rather, it is Christ imparting His life to and living His life through the person. The Christian life is not what you do for Him; it is what He does for and through you. He wants to think with your mind, express Himself through your emotions, and speak through your voice, though you may be unconscious of it." *Dr. Bill Bright*

13:5 See 1 John 4:8 comment.

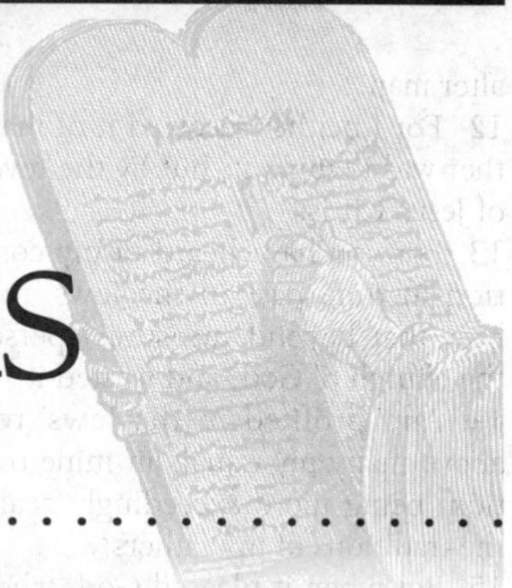

Galatians

CHAPTER 1

PAUL, an apostle, (not of men, neither by man, but by Jesus Christ,
and God the Father, who raised him
from the dead;)
2 And all the brethren which are with
me, to the churches of Galatia:
3 Grace be to you and peace from God
the Father, and from our Lord Jesus
Christ,
4 Who gave himself for our sins, that he
might deliver us from this present evil
world, according to the will of God and
our Father:
5 To whom be glory for ever and ever.
Amen.
6 I marvel that you are so soon removed
from him that called you into the grace
of Christ to another gospel:
7 Which is not another; but there be
some that trouble you, and would pervert the gospel of Christ.
8 But though we, or an angel from heav-
en, preach any other gospel to you than
that which we have preached to you, let
him be accursed.
9 As we said before, so say I now again,
If any man preach any other gospel to
you than that you have received, let him
be accursed.
10 For do I now persuade men, or God?
or do I seek to please men? for if I yet
pleased men, I should not be the servant
of Christ.
11 But I certify you, brethren, that the
gospel which was preached of me is not

1:3 Many who don't know the Savior claim to have made their "peace with God." But there is no peace with God without accepting the grace of God, which is given only to those who repent.

1:4 Jesus willingly "gave" Himself for the sins of the world. No one took His life from Him.

1:6 These are strong words from the same apostle who wrote the "love chapter" of 1 Corinthians 13. His words reveal his passion for the truth and his knowledge of the consequences of preaching "a different gospel." This should make the gospel preacher strive to make sure his hearers understand that salvation is by grace alone. Any message saying that we must add anything to the work of the cross to be saved is another gospel.

"Satan, the God of all dissension, stirreth up daily new sects, and last of all, which of all other I should never have foreseen or once suspected, he has raised up a sect such as teach…that men should not be terrified by the Law, but gently exhorted by the preaching of the grace of Christ." *Martin Luther*

1:8 "Avoid a sugared gospel as you would shun sugar of lead. Seek that gospel which rips up and tears and cuts and wounds and hacks and even kills, for that is the gospel that makes alive again. And when you have found it, give good heed to it. Let it enter into your inmost being. As the rains soaks into the ground, so pray the Lord to let His gospel soak into your soul." *Charles Spurgeon*

after man.
12 For I neither received it of man, neither was I taught it, but by the revelation
of Jesus Christ.
13 For you have heard of my conversation in time past in the Jews' religion,
how that beyond measure I persecuted
the church of God, and wasted it:
14 And profited in the Jews' religion
above many my equals in mine own nation, being more exceedingly zealous of
the traditions of my fathers.
15 But when it pleased God, who separated me from my mother's womb, and
called me by his grace,

. . . . . .

Does God "hate the sin but love the sinner"? See 1 Timothy 1:8–10 "Questions & Objections."

. . . . . .

16 To reveal his Son in me, that I might
preach him among the heathen; immediately I conferred not with flesh and blood:
17 Neither went I up to Jerusalem to
them which were apostles before me; but
I went into Arabia, and returned again to
Damascus.
18 Then after three years I went up to
Jerusalem to see Peter, and abode with
him fifteen days.
19 But other of the apostles saw I none,
save James the Lord's brother.
20 Now the things which I write to you,
behold, before God, I lie not.
21 Afterwards I came into the regions
of Syria and Cilicia;
22 And was unknown by face to the
churches of Judea which were in Christ:
23 But they had heard only, That he
which persecuted us in times past now
preaches the faith which once he destroyed.
24 And they glorified God in me.

CHAPTER 2

THEN fourteen years after I went up
again to Jerusalem with Barnabas,
and took Titus with me also.
2 And I went up by revelation, and
communicated to them that gospel which
I preach among the Gentiles, but privately to them which were of reputation, lest
by any means I should run, or had run,
in vain.
3 But neither Titus, who was with me,
being a Greek, was compelled to be circumcised:
4 And that because of false brethren unawares brought in, who came in privately to spy out our liberty which we have
in Christ Jesus, that they might bring us
into bondage:
5 To whom we gave place by subjection, no, not for an hour; that the truth
of the gospel might continue with you.
6 But of these who seemed to be somewhat, (whatsoever they were, it makes
no matter to me: God accepts no man's
person:) for they who seemed to be somewhat in conference added nothing to me:
7 But contrariwise, when they saw that
the gospel of the uncircumcision was
committed to me, as the gospel of the
circumcision was to Peter;
8 (For he that wrought effectually in
Peter to the apostleship of the circumcision, the same was mighty in me toward
the Gentiles:)
9 And when James, Cephas, and John,
who seemed to be pillars, perceived the
grace that was given to me, they gave to
me and Barnabas the right hands of fellowship; that we should go to the heathen, and they to the circumcision.
10 Only they would that we should re-

1:16 God also wants to reveal His Son in us. We can do this by following in Paul's steps and preaching Jesus Christ and Him crucified.

2:4 The Bible speaks of false brethren, false apostles, false prophets, false teachers, and false conversion (Mark 4:3–20).

member the poor; the same which I also
was forward to do.
11 But when Peter was come to Antioch, I withstood him to the face, because
he was to be blamed.
12 For before that certain came from
James, he did eat with the Gentiles: but
when they were come, he withdrew and
separated himself, fearing them which
were of the circumcision.
13 And the other Jews dissembled likewise with him; insomuch that Barnabas
also was carried away with their dissimulation.
14 But when I saw that they walked not
uprightly according to the truth of the
gospel, I said to Peter before them all, If
you, being a Jew, live after the manner of
Gentiles, and not as do the Jews, why
compel the Gentiles to live as do the Jews?
15 We who are Jews by nature, and not
sinners of the Gentiles,
16 Knowing that a man is not justified
by the works of the law, but by the faith
of Jesus Christ, even we have believed in
Jesus Christ, that we might be justified
by the faith of Christ, and not by the
works of the law: for by the works of the
law shall no flesh be justified.
17 But if, while we seek to be justified
by Christ, we ourselves also are found
sinners, is therefore Christ the minister
of sin? God forbid.
18 For if I build again the things which
I destroyed, I make myself a transgressor.

THE FUNCTION OF THE LAW

2:19 The Law's function is to bring death to the sinner in the same way civil law brings capital punishment to a guilty murderer. However, our offense was paid for by the Savior, leaving us free to receive the pardon of the gospel. The Law has no demand on the Christian.

19 For I through the law am dead to
the law, that I might live to God.
20 I am crucified with Christ: nevertheless I live; yet not I, but Christ lives in
me: and the life which I now live in the
flesh I live by the faith of the Son of God,
who loved me, and gave himself for me.
21 I do not frustrate the grace of God:
for if righteousness come by the law, then
Christ is dead in vain.

CHAPTER 3

O FOOLISH Galatians, who has bewitched you, that you should not
obey the truth, before whose eyes Jesus
Christ has been evidently set forth, crucified among you?
2 This only would I learn of you, Did
you receive the Spirit by the works of
the law, or by the hearing of faith?
3 Are you so foolish? having begun in
the Spirit, are you now made perfect by
the flesh?
4 Have you suffered so many things in
vain? if it be yet in vain.

2:10 Good works are a legitimate form of evangelism. When the Salvation Army first began, their message was "soap, soup, and salvation." See Titus 3:8.

2:16 For those trusting in good works, see Galatians 3:11. "Neither the Jewish Law of ten commands nor its law of ceremonies was ever intended to save anybody. By a set of pictures it set forth the way of salvation, but it was not itself the way. It was a map, not a country; a model of the road, not the road itself." *Charles Spurgeon*

2:20 Dying to self. "The path toward humility is death to self. When self is dead, humility has been perfected. Jesus humbled Himself unto death, and by His example the way is opened for us to follow. A dead man or woman does not react to an offense. The truth is, if we become offended by the words of others, then death to self has not been finished. When we humble ourselves despite injustice and there is perfect peace of heart, then death to self is complete. Death is the seed, while humility is the ripened fruit." *Alice Smith, Beyond the Veil: God's Call to Intimate Intercession* (See also Galatians 5:24.)

5 He therefore that ministers to you the
Spirit, and works miracles among you,
does he do it by the works of the law, or
by the hearing of faith?
6 Even as Abraham believed God, and it
was accounted to him for righteousness.
7 Know therefore that they which are of
faith, the same are the children of Abraham.
8 And the scripture, foreseeing that God
would justify the heathen through faith,
preached before the gospel to Abraham,
saying, In you shall all nations be blessed.
9 So then they which be of faith are
blessed with faithful Abraham.
**10 For as many as are of the works of
the law are under the curse: for it is
written, Cursed is every one that continues not in all things which are written in the book of the law to do them.**
**11 But that no man is justified by the
law in the sight of God, it is evident:
for, The just shall live by faith.**
12 And the law is not of faith: but, The
man that does them shall live in them.
13 **Christ has redeemed us from the
curse of the law, being made a curse for
us: for it is written, Cursed is every one
that hangs on a tree:**
14 That the blessing of Abraham might
come on the Gentiles through Jesus Christ;
that we might receive the promise of the
Spirit through faith.
15 Brethren, I speak after the manner of
men; Though it be but a man's covenant,
yet if it be confirmed, no man disannuls,
or adds thereto.
16 Now to Abraham and his seed were
the promises made. He said not, And to
seeds, as of many; but as of one, And to
your seed, which is Christ.
17 And this I say, that the covenant, that
was confirmed before of God in Christ,
the law, which was four hundred and
thirty years after, cannot disannul, that it
should make the promise of none effect.
18 For if the inheritance be of the law,
it is no more of promise: but God gave it
to Abraham by promise.
19 Wherefore then serves the law? It
was added because of transgressions, till
the seed should come to whom the promise was made; and it was ordained by angels in the hand of a mediator.
20 Now a mediator is not a mediator of
one, but God is one.
21 Is the law then against the promises
of God? God forbid: for if there had been
a law given which could have given life,
verily righteousness should have been by
the law.
22 But the scripture has concluded all
under sin, that the promise by faith of
Jesus Christ might be given to them that
believe.
23 But before faith came, we were kept
under the law, shut up to the faith which
should afterwards be revealed.
24 Wherefore the law was our schoolmaster to bring us to Christ, that we might
be justified by faith.
25 But after that faith is come, we are
no longer under a schoolmaster.
26 For you are all the children of God
by faith in Christ Jesus.
27 For as many of you as have been
baptized into Christ have put on Christ.
28 There is neither Jew nor Greek, there
is neither bond nor free, there is neither
male nor female: for you are all one in
Christ Jesus.
29 And if you be Christ's, then are you
Abraham's seed, and heirs according to
the promise.

3:10 Those who try to keep the Law are usually ignorant of its holy demands. It requires perfection in thought, word, and deed. The proclamation of the spiritual nature of the Law (that God requires truth in the inward parts) strips a sinner of self-righteousness. See James 2:10 comment.

3:11 No one will earn their way into heaven by keeping the Ten Commandments. They were not given for that purpose. The Law is like a mirror. All it can do is reflect what we are in truth—unclean and desperately in need of cleansing. For those trusting in good works, see Ephesians 2:8,9.

3:19 *What is the Purpose of the Law?*

By Charles Spurgeon

"Beloved, the Law is a great deluge which would have drowned the world with worse than the water of Noah's flood; it is a great fire which would have burned the earth with a destruction worse than that which fell on Sodom; it is a stern angel with a sword, athirst for blood, and winged to slay; it is a great destroyer sweeping down the nations; it is the great messenger of God's vengeance sent into the world. Apart from the gospel of Jesus Christ, the Law is nothing but the condemning voice of God thundering against mankind. 'Wherefore then serveth the Law?' seems a very natural question. Can the Law be of any benefit to man? Can the Judge who puts on a black cap and condemns us all, this Lord Chief Justice Law, can he help in salvation? Yes, he can; and you shall see how he does it, if God shall help us while we preach.

"Now, if you are unrepentant, you have never obeyed your Maker. Every step you have taken has added to your crimes. When God has fanned your heaving lungs, you have breathed out your poisonous breath in rebellion against Him. How should God feel toward you? You have walked over the principles of righteousness with your unsanctified feet. You have lifted up your hands, filled with poisoned weapons, against the throne of the Almighty. You have spurned every principle of right, of love and of happiness. You are the enemy of God, the foe of man and a child of the devil in league with hell. Ought not God hate you with all His heart?

"Yet, in the midst of your rebellion He has borne with you. All this you have done, and He has kept silent. Dare you think that He will never reprove?

"Lo, I see, the Law given upon Mount Sinai. The very hill doth quake with fear. Lightnings and thunders are the attendants of those dreadful syllables which make the hearts of Israel to melt. Sinai seemeth altogether on the smoke. The Lord came from Paran, and the Holy One from Mount Sinai; 'He came with ten thousands of his saints.' Out of His mouth went a fiery Law for them. It was a dread Law even when it was given, and since then from that Mount of Sinai an awful lava of vengeance has run down, to deluge, to destroy, to burn, and to consume the whole human race, if it had not been that Jesus Christ had stemmed its awful torrent and bidden its waves of fire be still. If you could see the world without Christ in it, simply under the Law, you would see a world in ruins, a world with God's black seal put upon it, stamped and sealed for condemnation; you would see men, who, if they knew their condition, would have their hands on their loins and be groaning all their days—you would see men and women condemned, lost, and ruined; and in the uttermost regions you would see the pit that is digged for the wicked, into which the whole earth must have been cast if the Law had its way, apart from the gospel of Jesus Christ our Redeemer.

"My hearer, does not the Law of God convince you of sin? Under the hand of God's Spirit does it not make you feel that you have been guilty, that you deserve to be lost, that you have incurred the fierce anger of God? Look here: have you not broken these Ten Commandments; even in the letter, have you not broken them? Who is there among you who has always honored his mother and father? Who is there among you who has always spoken the truth? Have we not sometimes borne false witness against our neighbors? Is there one person here who has not made to himself another god, and loved himself, or his business, or his friends, more than he has Jehovah, the God of the whole earth? Which of you has not coveted his neighbor's house, or his manservant, or his ox, or his donkey? We are all guilty with regard to every letter of the Law; we have all of us transgressed the Commandments.

"And if we really understood these Commandments, and felt that they condemned us, they would have this useful influence on us of showing us our danger, and so leading us to fly to Christ. But, my hearers, does not this Law condemn you, because even if you should say you have not broken the letter of it, yet you have violated the spirit of it. What, though you have never killed, yet we are told, he that is angry with his brother is a murderer.

(continued on next page)

(3:19 continued)

"This Law does not only mean what it says in words, but it has deep things hidden in its bowels. It says, 'Thou shall not commit adultery,' but it means as Jesus has it, 'He that looketh on a woman to lust after her has committed adultery with her already in his heart.' It says, 'Thou shall not take the name of the Lord thy God in vain.' It meaneth that we should reverence God in every place, and have His fear before our eyes, and should always pay respect to His ordinances and evermore walk in His fear and love. My brethren, surely there is not one here so foolhardy in self-righteousness as to say, 'I am innocent.' The spirit of the Law condemns us. And this is its useful property; it humbles us, makes us know we are guilty, and so we are led to receive the Savior."

THE FUNCTION OF THE LAW

3:24 "Lower the Law and you dim the light by which man perceives his guilt; this is a very serious loss to the sinner rather than a gain; for it lessens the likelihood of his conviction and conversion. I say you have deprived the gospel of its ablest auxiliary [its most powerful weapon] when you have set aside the Law. You have taken away from it the schoolmaster that is to bring men to Christ... *They will never accept grace till they tremble before a just and holy Law.* Therefore the Law serves a most necessary purpose, and it must not be removed from its place." *Charles Spurgeon*

CHAPTER 4

NOW I say, That the heir, as long as
he is a child, differs nothing from a
servant, though he be lord of all;
2 But is under tutors and governors
until the time appointed of the father.
3 Even so we, when we were children,
were in bondage under the elements of
the world:
4 But when the fulness of the time was
come, God sent forth his Son, made of a
woman, made under the law,
5 To redeem them that were under the
law, that we might receive the adoption
of sons.
6 And because you are sons, God has
sent forth the Spirit of his Son into your
hearts, crying, Abba, Father.
7 Wherefore you are no more a servant,
but a son; and if a son, then an heir of
God through Christ.
8 Howbeit then, when you knew not
God, you did service to them which by
nature are no gods.
9 But now, after that you have known
God, or rather are known of God, how
can you turn again to the weak and beggarly elements, whereunto you desire
again to be in bondage?
10 You observe days, and months, and
times, and years.
11 I am afraid of you, lest I have bestowed upon you labor in vain.
12 Brethren, I beseech you, be as I am;
for I am as you are: you have not injured
me at all.
13 You know how through infirmity of
the flesh I preached the gospel to you at

3:21 "Although the Law disclosed and increases sin, it is still not against the promises of God but is, in fact, for them. For in its true and proper work and purpose it humbles a man and prepares him—if he uses the Law correctly—to yearn and seek for grace." *Martin Luther*

4:5 There is no difference between Jew and Gentile. Both must be put "under the Law" first, before the gospel can redeem them. Why would any sinner see any need to be redeemed, if he didn't first see himself as a lawbreaker? Until each Commandment is applied to the conscience, sinners will not see sin as being "exceedingly sinful." The Law must also be preached in conjunction with future punishment. It has been well observed that "Law without consequence is nothing but good advice." The world must be made to understand that God is going to judge the world "in righteousness."

QUESTIONS & OBJECTIONS

4:6

"How can you know that you are saved?"

A two-year-old boy was once staring at a heater, fascinated by its bright orange glow. His father saw him and warned, "Don't touch that heater, son. It may look pretty, but it's hot." The little boy believed him, and moved away from the heater.

Some time later, after his father had left the room, the boy thought, "I wonder if it really is hot." He then reached out to touch it and see for himself. The second his flesh burned, he stopped *believing* it was hot; he now *knew* it was hot! He had moved out of the realm of *belief* into the realm of *experience*.

Christians believed in God's existence before their conversion. However, when they obeyed the Word of God, turned from their sins, and embraced Jesus Christ, they stopped merely believing. The moment they reached out and touched the heater bar of God's mercy, they moved out of *belief* into the realm of *experience*. This experience is so radical, Jesus referred to it as being "born again."

The Bible says that those who don't know God are spiritually dead (Ephesians 2:1; 4:18). We are born with physical life, but not spiritual life. Picture unbelievers as corpses walking around who, by repenting and placing their faith in Christ, receive His very life. There is a radical difference between a corpse and a living, breathing human, just as there is when sinners pass from spiritual death to life. The apostle Paul said if you are "in Christ," you are a brand new creature (2 Corinthians 5:17).

Those who now have God's Spirit living in them will love what He loves and desire to do His will; they will have a hunger for His Word, a love for other believers, and a burden for the lost. The Holy Spirit also confirms in their spirit that they are now children of God (Romans 8:16). Those who believe on the name of the Son of God can *know* that they have eternal life (1 John 5:12,13).

Paul wrote to the church at Corinth, "My speech and my preaching were not with enticing words of man's wisdom, but in demonstration of the Spirit and of power: that your faith should not stand in the wisdom of men, but in the power of God" (1 Corinthians 2:4,5). What Paul was saying was, "I deliberately didn't talk you into your faith, but I let God's power transform you." He didn't reach them through an intellectual assent, but through the realm of personal experience.

Suppose two people—a heater manufacturer and a skin specialist—walked into the room just after that child had burned his hand on the heater. Both assured the boy that he couldn't possibly have been burned. But all the experts, theories, and arguments in the world will not dissuade that boy, because of his experience.

Those who have been transformed by God's power need never fear scientific or other arguments, because the man with an experience is not at the mercy of a man with an argument. "For our gospel came not to you in word only, but also in power, and in the Holy Spirit, and in much assurance..." (1 Thessalonians 1:5).

the first.
14 And my temptation which was in my flesh you despised not, nor rejected; but received me as an angel of God, even as Christ Jesus.
15 Where is then the blessedness you spoke of? for I bear you record, that, if it had been possible, you would have plucked out your own eyes, and have given them to me.
16 Am I therefore become your enemy, because I tell you the truth?
17 They zealously affect you, but not well; yes, they would exclude you, that you might affect them.
18 But it is good to be zealously affect-

ed always in a good thing, and not only
when I am present with you.
19 My little children, of whom I travail in
birth again until Christ be formed in you,
20 I desire to be present with you now,
and to change my voice; for I stand in
doubt of you.
21 Tell me, you that desire to be under
the law, do you not hear the law?
22 For it is written, that Abraham had
two sons, the one by a bondmaid, the
other by a freewoman.

> The preacher's work is to throw sinners down in utter helplessness, so that they may be compelled to look up to Him who alone can help them.
>
> **CHARLES SPURGEON**

23 But he who was of the bondwoman
was born after the flesh; but he of the
freewoman was by promise.
24 Which things are an allegory: for
these are the two covenants; the one from
the mount Sinai, which genders to bondage, which is Agar.
25 For this Agar is mount Sinai in Arabia, and answers to Jerusalem which now
is, and is in bondage with her children.
26 But Jerusalem which is above is free,
which is the mother of us all.
27 For it is written, Rejoice, you barren
that bear not; break forth and cry, you
that travail not: for the desolate has many
more children than she which has an
husband.
28 Now we, brethren, as Isaac was, are
the children of promise.
29 But as then he that was born after
the flesh persecuted him that was born
after the Spirit, even so it is now.
30 Nevertheless what do the Scriptures
say? Cast out the bondwoman and her
son: for the son of the bondwoman shall
not be heir with the son of the freewoman.
31 So then, brethren, we are not children of the bondwoman, but of the free.

CHAPTER 5

STAND fast therefore in the liberty
wherewith Christ has made us free,
and be not entangled again with the yoke
of bondage.
2 Behold, I Paul say to you, that if you
be circumcised, Christ shall profit you
nothing.
3 For I testify again to every man that is
circumcised, that he is a debtor to do the
whole law.
4 Christ is become of no effect to you,
whosoever of you are justified by the
law; you are fallen from grace.
5 For we through the Spirit wait for the
hope of righteousness by faith.
6 For in Jesus Christ neither circumcision avails anything, nor uncircumcision; but faith which works by love.
7 You did run well; who did hinder you
that you should not obey the truth?
8 This persuasion comes not of him that
calls you.
9 A little leaven leavens the whole lump.
10 I have confidence in you through
the Lord, that you will be none otherwise minded: but he that troubles you
shall bear his judgment, whosoever he be.
11 And I, brethren, if I yet preach circumcision, why do I yet suffer persecution? then is the offence of the cross
ceased.
12 I would they were even cut off which
trouble you.
13 For, brethren, you have been called
to liberty; only use not liberty for an occasion to the flesh, but by love serve one
another.
14 For all the law is fulfilled in one word,
even in this; You shall love your neighbour as yourself.
15 But if you bite and devour one an-

5:11 The cross will cause offense to the proud and self-righteous—those whose understanding is darkened. To those who understand their need of grace (the humble), it is a tree of life.

QUESTIONS & OBJECTIONS

5:14

"I believe I will go to heaven because I live by the Golden Rule."

Much of the world knows the Golden Rule simply as "do unto others as you would have them do unto you" (see Luke 6:31). According to this verse, if we can live by this rule and love our neighbor as much as we love ourselves, we fulfill the Law. Ask those who claim to do this if they have ever lied, stolen, hated, or looked with lust. If they have broken any of these Commandments, then they haven't loved those they have lied to, stolen from, etc. This will show them that they have *violated* the Golden Rule. They are under God's wrath (John 3:36), desperately needing the Savior's cleansing blood.

other, take heed that you be not consumed one of another.
16 This I say then, Walk in the Spirit,
and you shall not fulfill the lust of the
flesh.
17 For the flesh lusts against the Spirit,
and the Spirit against the flesh: and these
are contrary the one to the other: so that
you cannot do the things that you would.
18 But if you be led of the Spirit, you
are not under the law.
19 Now the works of the flesh are manifest, which are these; Adultery, fornication, uncleanness, lasciviousness,
20 Idolatry, witchcraft, hatred, variance,
emulations, wrath, strife, seditions, heresies,
21 Envyings, murders, drunkenness,
revellings, and such like: of the which I
tell you before, as I have also told you in
time past, that they which do such things
shall not inherit the kingdom of God.

5:16

Ten Ways to Break the Stronghold of Pornography

1 Would you ever take pornography to church and look at it during worship? You may as well, because God is just as present in your bedroom as He is in the church building.

2 Face the fact that you may not be saved. Examine yourself to ensure that Christ is living in you (2 Corinthians 13:5). See Romans 6:11–22; 8:1–14; Ephesians 5:3–8.

3 Realize that when you give yourself to pornography, you are committing adultery (Matthew 5:27,28).

4 Grasp the serious nature of your sin. Jesus said that it would be better for you to be blind and go to heaven, than for your eye to cause you to sin and end up in hell (Matthew 5:29).

5 Those who profess to be Christians yet give themselves to pornographic material evidently lack the fear of God (Proverbs 16:6). Cultivate the fear of God by reading Proverbs 2:1–5.

6 Read Psalm 51 and make it your own prayer.

7 Memorize James 1:14,15 and 1 Corinthians 10:13. Follow Jesus' example (Matthew 4:3–11) and quote the Word of God when you are tempted (see Ephesians 6:12–20).

8 Make no provision for your flesh (Romans 13:14; 1 Peter 2:11). Get rid of every access to pornographic material—the Internet, printed literature, TV, videos, and movies. Stop feeding the fire.

9 Guard your heart with all diligence (Proverbs 4:23). Don't let the demonic realm have access to your thought-life. If you give yourself to it, you will become its slave (Romans 6:16). Read the Bible daily, without fail. As you submit to God, the devil will flee (James 4:7,8).

10 The next time temptation comes, do fifty push-ups, then fifty sit-ups. If you are still burning, repeat the process (see 1 Corinthians 9:27).

22 But the fruit of the Spirit is love, joy, peace, longsuffering, gentleness, goodness, faith,
23 Meekness, temperance: against such there is no law.
24 And they that are Christ's have crucified the flesh with the affections and lusts.
25 If we live in the Spirit, let us also walk in the Spirit.
26 Let us not be desirous of vain glory, provoking one another, envying one another.

CHAPTER 6

BRETHREN, if a man be overtaken in a fault, you which are spiritual, restore such an one in the spirit of meekness; considering yourself, lest you also be tempted.
2 Bear one another's burdens, and so fulfil the law of Christ.
3 For if a man think himself to be something, when he is nothing, he deceives himself.
4 But let every man prove his own work, and then shall he have rejoicing in himself alone, and not in another.
5 For every man shall bear his own burden.
6 Let him that is taught in the word communicate to him that teaches in all good things.
7 Be not deceived; God is not mocked: for whatsoever a man sows, that shall he also reap.
8 For he that sows to his flesh shall of the flesh reap corruption; but he that sows to the Spirit shall of the Spirit reap life everlasting.
9 And let us not be weary in well doing: for in due season we shall reap, if we faint not.
10 As we have therefore opportunity, let us do good to all men, especially to them who are of the household of faith.
11 You see how large a letter I have written to you with mine own hand.
12 As many as desire to make a fair show in the flesh, they constrain you to be circumcised; only lest they should suffer persecution for the cross of Christ.
13 For neither they themselves who are circumcised keep the law; but desire to have you circumcised, that they may glory in your flesh.
14 But God forbid that I should glory, save in the cross of our Lord Jesus Christ, by whom the world is crucified to me, and I to the world.
15 For in Christ Jesus neither circumcision avails anything, nor uncircumcision, but a new creature.
16 And as many as walk according to this rule, peace be on them, and mercy, and upon the Israel of God.
17 From henceforth let no man trouble me: for I bear in my body the marks of the Lord Jesus.
18 Brethren, the grace of our Lord Jesus Christ be with your spirit. Amen.

5:19 Men will often deceive themselves by believing that the Ten Commandments condemn only adultery, leaving them free to have sex outside the bonds of marriage. However, the Law condemns all unlawful sex. First Timothy 1:8–10 tells us that the Law was also made for fornicators (whoremongers).

6:7 "Many people think they can break the Ten Commandments right and left and get by with it. That reminds me of the whimsical story of the man who jumped off the Empire State Building in New York City. As he went sailing by the fiftieth floor, a man looked out the window and said to him, 'Well, how is it?' The falling man replied, 'So far, so good.' That is not where the law of gravity enforces itself. Fifty more floors down and the man will find out, 'So far, not so good.' The interesting thing is that a law must be enforced to be a law and therefore God says in Ezekiel 18:4, 'The soul that sins, it shall die.' The Law must be enforced and the breaker of the Law must pay the penalty." *J. Vernon McGee*

6:14 "All heaven is interested in the cross of Christ, all hell terribly afraid of it, while men are the only beings who more or less ignore its meaning." *Oswald Chambers*

Ephesians

CHAPTER 1

PAUL, an apostle of Jesus Christ by
the will of God, to the saints which
are at Ephesus, and to the faithful in
Christ Jesus:
2 Grace be to you, and peace, from God
our Father, and from the Lord Jesus
Christ.
3 Blessed be the God and Father of our
Lord Jesus Christ, who has blessed us
with all spiritual blessings in heavenly
places in Christ:
4 According as he has chosen us in him
before the foundation of the world, that
we should be holy and without blame
before him in love:
5 Having predestinated us to the adoption of children by Jesus Christ to himself, according to the good pleasure of
his will,
6 To the praise of the glory of his grace,
wherein he has made us accepted in the
beloved.
7 In whom we have redemption through
his blood, the forgiveness of sins, according to the riches of his grace;
8 Wherein he has abounded toward us
in all wisdom and prudence;
9 Having made known to us the mystery of his will, according to his good
pleasure which he has purposed in himself:
10 That in the dispensation of the fulness of times he might gather together in
one all things in Christ, both which are
in heaven, and which are on earth; even
in him:
11 In whom also we have obtained an in-

1:1 Sainthood. There are those who believe that someone must be dead for many years, and have performed miracles, before he can be "exalted" to sainthood. Not so. Paul is writing to *living* people and, as he often begins his letters, he refers to them as "saints." The word "saint" comes from the same Hebrew root as "sanctified" and "holy," which mean "set apart." The moment we are born again, God sets us apart from the world (sanctifies us) for His use. In addressing the Corinthian church, Paul writes: "to them that are *sanctified* in Christ Jesus, called to be *saints*, with *all* that in every place call upon the name of Jesus Christ our Lord" (1 Corinthians 1:2). A saint is not someone who has lived a "holy" life, but a forgiven sinner who has called upon the name of Jesus and been made righteous by the grace of God.

1:9 The will of God is no longer a mystery ("having *made* known..."). The next verse makes His will clear: He wants to gather the redeemed together. We can work within His will by seeking to save that which is lost. He is not willing that *any* perish, but that *all* come to repentance. He has commanded us to "Go." We don't need to wait for another moment. To wait upon God for His will, when it is so plainly given, is to sit in disobedience. If you are paralyzed by fear, leave a gospel tract in a shopping cart. Crawl before you walk. Do *something* to bring the message of eternal salvation to a dying world.

QUESTIONS & OBJECTIONS

1:7 *"I know I'm a sinner, but I confess my sins to God daily. I tell Him that I'm sorry and I won't sin again."*

If you find yourself in court with a $50,000 fine, will a judge let you go simply because you say you're sorry and you won't commit the crime again? Of course not. You *should* be sorry for breaking the law and, of course, you shouldn't commit the crime again. But only when someone pays your $50,000 fine will you be free from the demands of the law.

God will not forgive a sinner on the basis that he is sorry. Of course we should be sorry for sin—we have a conscience to tell us that adultery, rape, lust, murder, hatred, lying, stealing, etc., are wrong. And of course we shouldn't sin again. However, God will only release us from the demands for eternal justice on the basis that someone else paid our fine. Two thousand years ago, Jesus Christ died on the cross to pay for the sins of the world. His words on the cross were, "It is finished!" In other words, the debt has been paid in full. All who repent and trust in Him receive forgiveness of sins. Their case is dismissed on the basis of His suffering death.

heritance, being predestinated according to the purpose of him who works all things after the counsel of his own will:

12 That we should be to the praise of his glory, who first trusted in Christ.

13 In whom you also trusted, after that you heard the word of truth, the gospel of your salvation: in whom also after that you believed, you were sealed with that holy Spirit of promise,

14 Which is the earnest of our inheritance until the redemption of the purchased possession, to the praise of his glory.

15 Wherefore I also, after I heard of your faith in the Lord Jesus, and love to all the saints,

16 Cease not to give thanks for you, making mention of you in my prayers;

17 That the God of our Lord Jesus Christ, the Father of glory, may give to you the spirit of wisdom and revelation in the knowledge of him:

18 The eyes of your understanding being enlightened; that you may know what is the hope of his calling, and what the riches of the glory of his inheritance in the saints,

19 And what is the exceeding greatness of his power toward us who believe, according to the working of his mighty power,

20 Which he wrought in Christ, when he raised him from the dead, and set him at his own right hand in the heavenly places,

---

1:13 Many think that to "believe" in Jesus is merely an intellectual assent. However, when the Bible speaks of believing in Jesus Christ, it means to *trust* in Him in the same way you trust yourself to an elevator. It is more than a mere acknowledgment of its ability to transport.

1:19 Our God's power is so great that He could easily turn 800 billion enemy tanks into fine powder with the flutter of an eyelash. Never, never lose sight of the victory! Don't let the lies of enemy propaganda penetrate your mind. Remember the command, "Fear not; for I am with you: be not dismayed; for I am your God: I will strengthen you;...yes, I will uphold you with the right hand of my righteousness" (Isaiah 41:10).

To be discouraged is to dishonor God. If He is with us we must never lose courage. A blind, anemic, weak-kneed flea on crutches would have a greater chance of defeating a herd of a thousand wild stampeding elephants than the enemy has of defeating God!

SPRINGBOARDS FOR PREACHING AND WITNESSING

2:4,5

The Love of God

Imagine a place on the earth that never saw the sun. Day in, day out, it is covered with thick clouds. From the time a person was born until the time he died he never saw even a glimpse of the sun. Suppose you visited this place and tried to convince the inhabitants of the reality, the beauty, and the power of the sun. "Where I come from," you say, "a huge yellow ball rises up over the sea each day and floats across the sky, no strings attached, giving warmth and light to those upon the earth. The reason you don't experience it is because you are cut off from it by the clouds." Although the thought may seem fantastic to those people, the fact that they don't believe in it does not change the reality that it exists.

21 Far above all principality, and power, and might, and dominion, and every name that is named, not only in this world, but also in that which is to come:
22 And has put all things under his feet, and gave him to be the head over all things to the church,
23 Which is his body, the fulness of him that fills all in all.

CHAPTER 2

AND you has he quickened, who were dead in trespasses and sins;
2 Wherein in time past you walked according to the course of this world, according to the prince of the power of the air, the spirit that now works in the children of disobedience:
3 Among whom also we all had our conversation in times past in the lusts of our flesh, fulfilling the desires of the flesh and of the mind; and were by nature the children of wrath, even as others.
4 But God, who is rich in mercy, for his great love wherewith he loved us,
5 Even when we were dead in sins, has quickened us together with Christ, (by grace you are saved;)
6 And has raised us up together, and made us sit together in heavenly places in Christ Jesus:
7 That in the ages to come he might show the exceeding riches of his grace in his kindness toward us through Christ Jesus.
8 For by grace are you saved through faith; and that not of yourselves: it is the gift of God:
9 Not of works, lest any man should boast.
10 For we are his workmanship, created in Christ Jesus to good works, which God has before ordained that we should walk in them.
11 Wherefore remember, that you being in time past Gentiles in the flesh, who are called Uncircumcision by that which is called the Circumcision in the flesh made by hands;
12 That at that time you were without Christ, being aliens from the commonwealth of Israel, and strangers from the covenants of promise, having no hope, and without God in the world:

2:3 Unsaved people often try to justify themselves when confronted with their sinfulness, by saying, "It's only *natural* that we sin." They're right—sin does come naturally to us. We naturally lie, steal, lust, etc. The lifestyles of the ungodly can be clearly seen in soap operas, movies, talk shows, and tabloids. However, because it's natural doesn't make it right. By nature we are children of wrath. See Titus 3:3 comment.

2:8,9 These verses make it clear that no one will be saved through their own goodness. Nothing we can do could ever merit everlasting life. It can come only as a gift, by the grace of God. Note that we are not saved *by* our faith—it is not faith itself that saves us. Faith is the medium God uses to extend His grace to us. For those trusting in good works, see Titus 3:5.

13 But now in Christ Jesus you who sometimes were far off are made near by the blood of Christ.
14 For he is our peace, who has made both one, and has broken down the middle wall of partition between us;
15 Having abolished in his flesh the enmity, even the law of commandments contained in ordinances; for to make in himself of twain one new man, so making peace;
16 And that he might reconcile both to God in one body by the cross, having slain the enmity thereby:
17 And came and preached peace to you which were afar off, and to them that were nigh.
18 For through him we both have access by one Spirit to the Father.
19 Now therefore you are no more strangers and foreigners, but fellowcitizens with the saints, and of the household of God;
20 And are built upon the foundation of the apostles and prophets, Jesus Christ himself being the chief corner stone;
21 In whom all the building fitly framed together grows to an holy temple in the Lord:
22 In whom you also are built together for an habitation of God through the Spirit.

. . . . . .

To read about the power of lust, see Mark 6:23 comment.

. . . . . .

CHAPTER 3

FOR this cause I Paul, the prisoner of Jesus Christ for you Gentiles,
2 If you have heard of the dispensation of the grace of God which is given me toward you:
3 How that by revelation he made known to me the mystery; (as I wrote before in few words,
4 Whereby, when you read, you may understand my knowledge in the mystery of Christ)
5 Which in other ages was not made known to the sons of men, as it is now revealed to his holy apostles and prophets by the Spirit;

> Your one business in life is to lead men to believe in Jesus Christ by the power of the Holy Spirit. Every other thing should be made subservient to this one objective.
>
> **CHARLES SPURGEON**

6 That the Gentiles should be fellowheirs, and of the same body, and partakers of his promise in Christ by the gospel:
7 Whereof I was made a minister, according to the gift of the grace of God given to me by the effectual working of his power.
8 To me, who am less than the least of all saints, is this grace given, that I should preach among the Gentiles the unsearchable riches of Christ;
9 And to make all men see what is the fellowship of the mystery, which from the beginning of the world has been hid in God, who created all things by Jesus Christ:
10 To the intent that now to the principalities and powers in heavenly places might be known by the church the manifold wisdom of God,
11 According to the eternal purpose which he purposed in Christ Jesus our Lord:

2:13 There is nothing more valuable in the universe than the precious blood of our Savior. We were separated from God and without hope, but the blood of Jesus brought us to God.

3:7 It is God's power, working in us through His Holy Spirit, that equips us to share the gospel. (See Acts 1:8.) God provides the ability; all He wants from us is our *avail*ability.

12 In whom we have boldness and access with confidence by the faith of him.
13 Wherefore I desire that you faint not
at my tribulations for you, which is your
glory.
14 For this cause I bow my knees to the
Father of our Lord Jesus Christ,
15 Of whom the whole family in heav-
en and earth is named,
16 That he would grant you, according
to the riches of his glory, to be strengthened with might by his Spirit in the inner man;
17 That Christ may dwell in your hearts
by faith; that you, being rooted and
grounded in love,
18 May be able to comprehend with all
saints what is the breadth, and length,
and depth, and height;
19 And to know the love of Christ, which
passes knowledge, that you might be
filled with all the fulness of God.
20 Now to him that is able to do exceeding abundantly above all that we ask
or think, according to the power that
works in us,
21 To him be glory in the church by
Christ Jesus throughout all ages, world
without end. Amen.

CHAPTER 4

I THEREFORE, the prisoner of the Lord,
beseech you that you walk worthy of
the vocation wherewith you are called,
2 With all lowliness and meekness, with
longsuffering, forbearing one another in
love;
3 Endeavouring to keep the unity of the
Spirit in the bond of peace.
4 There is one body, and one Spirit, even
as you are called in one hope of your calling;
5 One Lord, one faith, one baptism,
6 One God and Father of all, who is
above all, and through all, and in you all.
7 But to every one of us is given grace

3:9 Life's origins—the ever-changing mind of science. According to an NBC News report in August 1999, there was a "remarkable" discovery in Australia. They said the *Journal of Science* reported that they had found what they considered to be proof that life appeared on earth 2.7 billion years ago—a billion years earlier than previously thought. They now admit that they were wrong in their first estimate (a mere 1,000,000,000 years off), but with this discovery they are now sure that they have the truth... until their next discovery.

CBS News reported in October 1999 that discoveries were made of the bones of an unknown animal in Asia that may be as much as 40 million years old. This changed scientific minds as to *where* man first originated. Scientists once believed that primates evolved in Africa, but now they think they may be wrong, and that man's ancestors may have originated in Asia. So they believe ...until the next discovery.

USA Today (March 21, 2001) reported, "Paleontologists have discovered a new skeleton in the closet of human ancestry that is likely to force science to revise, if not scrap, current theories of human origins." *Reuters* reported that the discovery left "scientists of human evolution...*confused*," saying, "Lucy may not even be a direct human ancestor after all."

What is science? "We are invited, brethren, most earnestly to go away from the old-fashioned belief of our forefathers because of the supposed discoveries of science. What is science? The method by which man tries to hide his ignorance. It should not be so, but so it is. You are not to be dogmatical in theology, my brethren, it is wicked; but for scientific men it is the correct thing. You are never to assert anything very strongly; but scientists may boldly assert what they cannot prove, and may demand a faith far more credulous than any we possess. Forsooth, you and I are to take our Bibles and shape and mould our belief according to the ever-shifting teachings of so-called scientific men. What folly is this! Why, the march of science, falsely so called, through the world may be traced by exploded fallacies and abandoned theories. Former explorers once adored are now ridiculed; the continual wreckings of false hypotheses is a matter of universal notoriety. You may tell where the supposed learned have encamped by the debris left behind of suppositions and theories as plentiful as broken bottles." *Charles Spurgeon*

according to the measure of the gift of
Christ.
8 Wherefore he says, When he ascended up on high, he led captivity captive,
and gave gifts to men.
9 (Now that he ascended, what is it but
that he also descended first into the lower parts of the earth?
10 He that descended is the same also
that ascended up far above all heavens,
that he might fill all things.)
11 And he gave some, apostles; and
some, prophets; and some, evangelists;
and some, pastors and teachers;
12 For the perfecting of the saints, for
the work of the ministry, for the edifying
of the body of Christ:
13 Till we all come in the unity of the
faith, and of the knowledge of the Son of
God, to a perfect man, to the measure of
the stature of the fulness of Christ:
14 That we henceforth be no more children, tossed to and fro, and carried about
with every wind of doctrine, by the sleight
of men, and cunning craftiness, whereby
they lie in wait to deceive;
15 But speaking the truth in love, may
grow up into him in all things, which is
the head, even Christ:
16 From whom the whole body fitly
joined together and compacted by that
which every joint supplies, according to
the effectual working in the measure of
every part, makes increase of the body to
the edifying of itself in love.
17 This I say therefore, and testify in the
Lord, that you henceforth walk not as
other Gentiles walk, in the vanity of their
mind,
18 Having the understanding darkened,
being alienated from the life of God
through the ignorance that is in them, because of the blindness of their heart:
19 Who being past feeling have given
themselves over to lasciviousness, to work
all uncleanness with greediness.
20 But you have not so learned Christ;
21 If so be that you have heard him, and
have been taught by him, as the truth is
in Jesus:
22 That you put off concerning the former conversation the old man, which is
corrupt according to the deceitful lusts;
23 And be renewed in the spirit of your
mind;
24 And that you put on the new man,
which after God is created in righteousness and true holiness.

4:11 Often Christians pass off their responsibility to reach out to the lost by saying that it's not their "gifting." However, there is no such thing as the "gift of evangelism." That's like saying, "He has the gift of feeding starving children." It is not a gift. Rather, he has love enough to take food to the hungry. Another word for *evangelism* is "love." The Scriptures here are speaking of the God-given ability of the evangelist to equip the saints for the work of ministry.

"It occurred to me that in our work with secular organizations, the leader shapes the heart and passion of the corporate entity. In our work with non-profit organizations, we have found the same principle to be operative. When it comes to the focus of the organization, the people who serve there tend to take on many of the core personality traits of the leader toward fulfilling the mandate of the organization. If this is true, and most churches seem to lack the fervor and focus for evangelism, is it reasonable to conclude that it may be because of the lack of zeal most pastors have for identifying, befriending, loving and evangelizing non-Christian people?" *George Barna, Evangelism That Works*

4:18 When New Age followers say, "I am God," rather than revealing their delusions of grandeur, they are revealing their darkened understanding of their concept of God. The god of this world has blinded their minds. If, in their ignorance, sinners continually harden their hearts against the truth of God, they will eventually be unable to feel the Holy Spirit's conviction, and will be given over to a life of sin (Romans 1:21–24).

To reach them we must use God's Law to provide understanding (Romans 3:20). It breaks the hard heart, and reveals to the sinner that he is cut off from the life of God (Romans 7:9).

QUESTIONS & OBJECTIONS

4:18

"Adam didn't die the day God said he would!"

He certainly did. He died spiritually. The moment he sinned, he became "dead in trespasses and sins" (Ephesians 2:1). Ezekiel 18:4 says, "The soul that sins, it shall die." It is because we are born spiritually dead that Jesus came to give us spiritual life (John 5:40; 10:10; 14:6; etc.). This is why Jesus told us that we must be born again (John 3:3). When we repent of our sins and believe in Jesus Christ, the Bible tells us that we "pass from death to life" (John 5:24; Romans 6:13; 1 John 3:14).

"We are born dead in trespasses and sins, alienated, cut off, detached from the life of God. The day that man believed the devil's lie (which is sin), he forfeited the life that distinguished him from the animal kingdom—the life of God. When sin came in, the life went out." *Ian Thomas*

25 Wherefore putting away lying, speak every man truth with his neighbour: for we are members one of another.
26 Be angry, and sin not: let not the sun go down upon your wrath:
27 Neither give place to the devil.
28 Let him that stole steal no more: but rather let him labor, working with his hands the thing which is good, that he may have to give to him that needs.
29 Let no corrupt communication proceed out of your mouth, but that which is good to the use of edifying, that it may minister grace to the hearers.
30 And grieve not the holy Spirit of God, whereby you are sealed to the day of redemption.
31 Let all bitterness, and wrath, and anger, and clamour, and evil speaking, be put away from you, with all malice:
32 And be kind one to another, tenderhearted, forgiving one another, even as God for Christ's sake has forgiven you.

CHAPTER 5

BE therefore followers of God, as dear children;
2 And walk in love, as Christ also has loved us, and has given himself for us an offering and a sacrifice to God for a sweetsmelling savour.
3 But fornication, and all uncleanness, or covetousness, let it not be once named among you, as becomes saints;
4 Neither filthiness, nor foolish talking, nor jesting, which are not convenient: but rather giving of thanks.
5 For this you know, that no whoremonger, nor unclean person, nor covetous man, who is an idolater, has any inheritance in the kingdom of Christ and of God.
6 **Let no man deceive you with vain words: for because of these things comes the wrath of God upon the children of disobedience.**
7 Be not therefore partakers with them.
8 For you were sometimes darkness, but now are you light in the Lord: walk as children of light:
9 (For the fruit of the Spirit is in all goodness and righteousness and truth;)
10 Proving what is acceptable to the Lord.

4:29 If you wouldn't say it in prayer, don't say it at all.

5:5 A covetous person transgresses the Tenth, First, and Second Commandments. When he loves material things more than he loves God, he is setting his affections on the gift, rather than on the Giver. What father wouldn't be grieved if his beloved child loved his toys more than the father who gave him the toys? A child should love his father first and foremost. He should love the *giver* more than the *gift*.

PRINCIPLES OF GROWTH FOR THE NEW AND GROWING CHRISTIAN

5:20 *Thanksgiving—Do the Right Thing*

For the Christian, every day should be Thanksgiving Day. We should be thankful even in the midst of problems. The apostle Paul said, "I am exceedingly joyful in all our tribulation" (2 Corinthians 7:4). He knew that God was working all things together for his good, even his trials (Romans 8:28).

Problems *will* come your way. God will see to it personally that you grow as a Christian. He will allow storms, to send your roots deep into the soil of His Word. We also pray more in the midst of problems. It's been well said that you will see more from your knees than on your tiptoes.

A man once watched a butterfly struggling to get out of its cocoon. In an effort to help it, he took a razor blade and carefully slit the edge of the cocoon. The butterfly escaped from its problem...but immediately died. It is God's way to have the butterfly struggle. It is the struggle that causes its tiny heart to beat fast, and send the life's blood into its wings.

Trials have their purpose. They make us struggle in the cocoon in which we often find ourselves. It is there that the life's blood of faith in God helps us spread our wings.

Faith and thanksgiving are close friends. If you have faith in God, you will be thankful because you know His loving hand is upon you, even though you are in a lion's den. That will give you a deep sense of joy, which is the barometer of the depth of faith you have in God. Let me give you an example. Imagine if I said I'd give one million dollars to everyone who ripped out the last page of this book and mailed it to me. Of course, you don't believe I would do that. But imagine if you did, and that you knew 1,000 people who had sent in the page, and every one received their million dollars—no strings attached. More than that, you actually called me, and I assured you personally that I would keep my word. If you believed me, *wouldn't* you have joy? If you didn't believe me—no joy. The amount of joy you have would be a barometer of how much you believed my promise.

We have so much for which to be thankful. God has given us "exceeding great and precious promises" that are more to be desired than gold. Do yourself a big favor: believe those promises, thank God continually for them, and "let your joy be full."

For the next principle of growth, see Acts 2:38 comment.

11 And have no fellowship with the unfruitful works of darkness, but rather reprove them.
12 For it is a shame even to speak of those things which are done of them in secret.
13 But all things that are reproved are made manifest by the light: for whatsoever does make manifest is light.
14 Wherefore he says, Awake you that sleep, and arise from the dead, and Christ shall give you light.
15 See then that you walk circumspectly, not as fools, but as wise,
16 Redeeming the time, because the days are evil.
17 Wherefore be not unwise, but understanding what the will of the Lord is.
18 And be not drunk with wine, wherein is excess; but be filled with the Spirit;
19 Speaking to yourselves in psalms and hymns and spiritual songs, singing and making melody in your heart to the Lord;
20 Giving thanks always for all things to God and the Father in the name of our Lord Jesus Christ;
21 Submitting yourselves one to another in the fear of God.
22 Wives, submit yourselves to your own husbands, as to the Lord.

5:17 Those who don't understand the will of the Lord are unwise. See Ephesians 1:9 comment.

23 For the husband is the head of the
wife, even as Christ is the head of the
church: and he is the savior of the body.
24 Therefore as the church is subject to
Christ, so let the wives be to their own
husbands in every thing.
25 Husbands, love your wives, even as
Christ also loved the church, and gave
himself for it;
26 That he might sanctify and cleanse it
with the washing of water by the word,
27 That he might present it to himself a
glorious church, not having spot, or
wrinkle, or any such thing; but that it
should be holy and without blemish.

> The only real argument against the Bible is an unholy life. When a man argues against the Word of God, follow him home, and see if you cannot discover the reason of his enmity to the Word of the Lord. It lies in some sort of sin.
>
> **CHARLES SPURGEON**

28 So ought men to love their wives as
their own bodies. He that loves his wife
loves himself.
29 For no man ever yet hated his own
flesh; but nourishes and cherishes it, even
as the Lord the church:
30 For we are members of his body, of
his flesh, and of his bones.
31 For this cause shall a man leave his
father and mother, and shall be joined to
his wife, and they two shall be one flesh.
32 This is a great mystery: but I speak
concerning Christ and the church.
33 Nevertheless let every one of you in
particular so love his wife even as himself; and the wife see that she reverence
her husband.

CHAPTER 6

CHILDREN, obey your parents in the
Lord: for this is right.
2 Honor your father and mother; (which
is the first commandment with promise;)
3 That it may be well with you, and you
may live long on the earth.
4 And, you fathers, provoke not your
children to wrath: but bring them up in
the nurture and admonition of the Lord.
5 Servants, be obedient to them that are
your masters according to the flesh, with
fear and trembling, in singleness of your
heart, as to Christ;
6 Not with eye-service, as men-pleasers;
but as the servants of Christ, doing the
will of God from the heart;
7 With good will doing service, as to
the Lord, and not to men:
8 Knowing that whatsoever good thing
any man does, the same shall he receive

5:22–25 See Proverbs 31:10 comment.

6:1,2 Teaching children God's Law. Paul uses the Commandment to bring the knowledge of sin. The biblical way to bring a child to the Savior is to teach him God's Law. Immediately after Moses had read the Ten Commandments to Israel, he said that they should teach them to their children as they sit and as they walk, when they lie down and rise up. The Commandments should be placed where they can be constant reminders (see Deuteronomy 6:4–9). Why should our children be taught the Ten Commandments? Simply because they will show the child what sin is. As the child matures and discovers sin in his heart, and he begins to understand that God requires truth in the inward parts, the threat of the Law will drive him to the foot of a blood-stained cross. What child can look at Ephesians 6:1,2 and say that he is guiltless and therefore free of its warning? To help children memorize the Ten Commandments, see page 456.

6:4 "I am much afraid that schools will prove to be the great gates of hell unless they diligently labor in explaining the Holy Scriptures, engraving them in the hearts of youth. I advise no one to place his child where the Scriptures do not reign paramount. Every institution in which men are not increasingly occupied with the Word of God must become corrupt." *Martin Luther* (See also Proverbs 4:1–5 comment.)

of the Lord, whether he be bond or free.
9 And, you masters, do the same things to them, forbearing threatening: knowing that your Master also is in heaven; neither is there respect of persons with him.
10 Finally, my brethren, be strong in the Lord, and in the power of his might.
11 Put on the whole armor of God, that you may be able to stand against the wiles of the devil.
12 For we wrestle not against flesh and blood, but against principalities, against powers, against the rulers of the darkness of this world, against spiritual wickedness in high places.
13 Wherefore take to you the whole armor of God, that you may be able to withstand in the evil day, and having done all, to stand.
14 Stand therefore, having your loins girt about with truth, and having on the breastplate of righteousness;
15 And your feet shod with the preparation of the gospel of peace;
16 Above all, taking the shield of faith, wherewith you shall be able to quench all the fiery darts of the wicked.
17 And take the helmet of salvation, and the sword of the Spirit, which is the word of God:
18 Praying always with all prayer and supplication in the Spirit, and watching thereunto with all perseverance and supplication for all saints;
19 *And for me, that utterance may be given to me, that I may open my mouth boldly, to make known the mystery of the gospel,*
20 *For which I am an ambassador in bonds: that therein I may speak boldly, as I ought to speak.*
21 But that you also may know my affairs, and how I do, Tychicus, a beloved brother and faithful minister in the Lord, shall make known to you all things:
22 Whom I have sent to you for the same purpose, that you might know our affairs, and that he might comfort your hearts.
23 Peace be to the brethren, and love with faith, from God the Father and the Lord Jesus Christ.
24 Grace be with all them that love our Lord Jesus Christ in sincerity. Amen.

6:10 "Do not pray for easy lives. Pray to be stronger men. Do not pray for tasks commensurate with your strength. Pray for strength commensurate with your tasks." *Phillips Brooks*

6:15 Don't go barefoot. In verse 11 we are told to put on the *whole* armor of God. Many Christians are truthful. They have their heart free of sin, they are sure of their salvation, they rightly use the Word of God. But they are shoeless—they are not prepared to share the gospel. Those who do not advance the cause of the gospel are stationary soldiers; any evangelistic movement is too painful for them. If they are not seeking to save the lost, they are not taking ground for the kingdom of God. Paul climaxed his admonition to the Ephesians by highlighting what the battle is for. He pleads with them to pray for him to have boldness to reach out to the unsaved, citing his moral responsibility (v. 20).

6:17 "We must thrust the sword of the Spirit into the hearts of men." *Charles Spurgeon*

6:18 "Let's move from theology to kneeology! Power for victory in spiritual warfare is found in prayer." *Robert R. Lawrence*

6:19 Beware of the subtlety of passive prayer. We have been commanded to *preach* the gospel. Make sure you don't pacify a guilty conscience by simply *praying* for the salvation of the lost, but not preaching to them. It is the gospel that is the power of God unto salvation. How shall they hear without a preacher? See Romans 10:14.

Philippians

CHAPTER 1

PAUL and Timotheus, the servants of
Jesus Christ, to all the saints in Christ
Jesus which are at Philippi, with the bish-
ops and deacons:
2 Grace be to you, and peace, from God
our Father, and from the Lord Jesus
Christ.
3 I thank my God upon every remembrance of you,
4 Always in every prayer of mine for you
all making request with joy,
5 For your fellowship in the gospel from
the first day until now;
6 Being confident of this very thing,
that he which has begun a good work in
you will perform it until the day of Jesus
Christ:
7 Even as it is meet for me to think this
of you all, because I have you in my
heart; inasmuch as both in my bonds,
and in the defence and confirmation of
the gospel, you all are partakers of my
grace.
8 For God is my record, how greatly I
long after you all in the bowels of Jesus
Christ.
9 And this I pray, that your love may
abound yet more and more in knowledge and in all judgment;
10 That you may approve things that
are excellent; that you may be sincere
and without offence till the day of Christ;
11 Being filled with the fruits of righteousness, which are by Jesus Christ, to
the glory and praise of God.
12 But I would you should understand,
brethren, that the things which happened to me have fallen out rather to the
furtherance of the gospel;
13 So that my bonds in Christ are manifest in all the palace, and in all other
places;
14 And many of the brethren in the
Lord, waxing confident by my bonds,
are much more bold to speak the word

1:6 Do you ever think about how many faces there are upon the earth? As you line up in a store, do you sometimes feel like a tiny grain of sand in the massive desert? Then lift your head and look to the heavens—God Almighty is your Maker. Like a giant heavenly zoom lens, He focused in on you from eternity. He foreknew every sinew of your fearfully and wonderfully made body. He is the lover of your soul. He breathed life into your human frame, and is at work in you to will and do of His good pleasure.

His good pleasure is to conform you to the image of His Son. Never let discouragement fall upon your mind, for God will complete the good work He has begun in you. He picked you out of the ranks of the masses, called you by His Grace, justified you through faith, and glorified you in Christ.

1:14 The Church should never dread persecution, as it can work *for* rather than *against* the furtherance of the gospel. The winds of persecution only spread the flames of the gospel.

without fear.
15 Some indeed preach Christ even of envy and strife; and some also of good will:
16 The one preach Christ of contention, not sincerely, supposing to add affliction to my bonds:
17 But the other of love, knowing that I am set for the defence of the gospel.
18 What then? notwithstanding, every way, whether in pretence, or in truth, Christ is preached; and I therein do rejoice, yes, and will rejoice.
19 For I know that this shall turn to my salvation through your prayer, and the supply of the Spirit of Jesus Christ,
20 According to my earnest expectation and my hope, that in nothing I shall be ashamed, but that with all boldness, as always, so now also Christ shall be magnified in my body, whether it be by life, or by death.
21 *For to me to live is Christ, and to die is gain.*
22 But if I live in the flesh, this is the fruit of my labor: yet what I shall choose I do not know.
23 For I am in a strait betwixt two, having a desire to depart, and to be with Christ; which is far better:
24 Nevertheless to abide in the flesh is more needful for you.
25 And having this confidence, I know that I shall abide and continue with you all for your furtherance and joy of faith;
26 That your rejoicing may be more abundant in Jesus Christ for me by my coming to you again.
27 *Only let your conversation be as it becomes the gospel of Christ: that whether I come and see you, or else be absent, I may hear of your affairs, that you stand fast in one spirit, with one mind striving together for the faith of the gospel;*
28 *And in nothing terrified by your adversaries: which is to them an evident token of perdition, but to you of salvation, and that of God.*
29 For to you it is given in the behalf of Christ, not only to believe on him, but also to suffer for his sake;
30 Having the same conflict which you saw in me, and now hear to be in me.

CHAPTER 2

IF there be therefore any consolation in Christ, if any comfort of love, if any fellowship of the Spirit, if any bowels and mercies,
2 Fulfil my joy, that you be likeminded, having the same love, being of one accord, of one mind.
3 Let nothing be done through strife or vainglory; but in lowliness of mind let each esteem other better than themselves.
4 *Look not every man on his own things, but every man also on the things of others.*
5 Let this mind be in you, which was also in Christ Jesus:
6 Who, being in the form of God, thought it not robbery to be equal with God:
7 But made himself of no reputation, and took upon him the form of a ser-

1:18 Paul rejoiced even though Christ was preached from the mouth of a hypocrite. This is because the quality is in the seed, not in the sower. This gives great consolation to those of us who lack what is commonly called "ability."

1:20 Paul lived for the furtherance of the gospel. God's will was his will.

1:29 "Suffering and sacrifice are essential to the Christian life just as they were essential to Christ's life. 'When Christ calls a man,' [Dietrich] Bonhoeffer wrote, 'He bids him come and die' *(The Cost of Discipleship)*. This doesn't always—or even usually—necessitate our physical deaths, but Christ calls us first and foremost to die to sin and to ourselves. Leave your home, sell everything you own, turn the other cheek, do not store up earthly treasures, love your enemies, take up your cross and follow me. None of Christ's commands call believers to a life of comfort. All require patience, suffering, and sacrifice." *Daniel L. Weiss*

vant, and was made in the likeness of
men:
8 And being found in fashion as a man,
he humbled himself, and became obedient to death, even the death of the cross.
9 Wherefore God also has highly exalted him, and given him a name which is
above every name:
10 That at the name of Jesus every knee
should bow, of things in heaven, and
things in earth, and things under the earth;
11 And that every tongue should confess that Jesus Christ is Lord, to the glory
of God the Father.
12 Wherefore, my beloved, as you have
always obeyed, not as in my presence
only, but now much more in my absence, work out your own salvation with
fear and trembling.
13 For it is God which works in you
both to will and to do of his good pleasure.
14 *Do all things without murmurings and
disputings:*
15 *That you may be blameless and harmless, the sons of God, without rebuke, in the
midst of a crooked and perverse nation,
among whom you shine as lights in the
world;*
16 *Holding forth the word of life; that I
may rejoice in the day of Christ, that I
have not run in vain, neither labored in
vain.*
17 Yes, and if I be offered upon the sacrifice and service of your faith, I joy, and
rejoice with you all.
18 For the same cause also do you joy,
and rejoice with me.
19 But I trust in the Lord Jesus to send
Timotheus shortly to you, that I also may
be of good comfort, when I know your
state.

> Preach Christ or nothing: don't dispute or discuss except with your eye on the cross.
>
> **CHARLES SPURGEON**

20 For I have no man likeminded, who
will naturally care for your state.
21 For all seek their own, not the things
which are Jesus Christ's.
22 But you know the proof of him, that,
as a son with the father, he has served
with me in the gospel.
23 Him therefore I hope to send presently, so soon as I shall see how it will

2:8 The death of the cross. "Oh sinner, why provoke your Maker? Your judgment does not linger and your damnation does not slumber. When the Law was broken and mankind was exposed to its fearful penalty, God offered justice to the universe and mercy for sinners, which He displayed in the atonement. To make this universal offer of pardon without justice would violate His Law. A due regard for public interest forbade the Lawgiver to forgive and set aside the penalty without finding a way to secure obedience to the Law. Therefore, His compassion for mankind and His regard for the Law were so great that He was willing to suffer in the person of His Son, who became a substitute for the penalty of the Law. This was the most stupendous exhibition of self-denial that was ever made: the Father giving His only begotten and beloved Son; the Son veiling the glories of His uncreated Godhead and becoming obedient to death, even the death of the cross, that we may never die." *Charles Finney*

2:13 "I used to ask God to help me. Then I asked if I might help Him. I ended up by asking Him to do His work through me." *Hudson Taylor*

2:15 Too often the Church becomes exclusive. We fellowship only with Christians—a monastery without walls. We become salt among salt, light among light. In reality, the Church should be "in the midst…among whom…in the world." Verse 16 tells us what we should be doing "in the midst."

"I would not give much for your religion unless it can be seen. Lamps do not talk, but they do shine." *Charles Spurgeon*

go with me.
24 But I trust in the Lord that I also myself shall come shortly.
25 Yet I supposed it necessary to send
to you Epaphroditus, my brother, and
companion in labor, and fellowsoldier,
but your messenger, and he that ministered to my wants.
26 For he longed after you all, and was
full of heaviness, because that you had
heard that he had been sick.
27 For indeed he was sick near to death:
but God had mercy on him; and not on
him only, but on me also, lest I should
have sorrow upon sorrow.
28 I sent him therefore the more carefully, that, when you see him again, you
may rejoice, and that I may be the less
sorrowful.
29 Receive him therefore in the Lord
with all gladness; and hold such in reputation:
30 Because for the work of Christ he
was near to death, not regarding his life,
to supply your lack of service toward me.

· · · · · ·

For the new birth—its necessity for salvation, see John 1:13 comment.

· · · · · ·

CHAPTER 3

FINALLY, my brethren, rejoice in the
Lord. To write the same things to
you, to me indeed is not grievous, but for
you it is safe.
2 Beware of dogs, beware of evil workers, beware of the concision.
3 For we are the circumcision, which
worship God in the spirit, and rejoice in
Christ Jesus, and have no confidence in
the flesh.
4 Though I might also have confidence
in the flesh. If any other man thinks that
he has whereof he might trust in the
flesh, I more:
5 Circumcised the eighth day, of the
stock of Israel, of the tribe of Benjamin,
an Hebrew of the Hebrews; as touching
the law, a Pharisee;
6 Concerning zeal, persecuting the church;
touching the righteousness which is in
the law, blameless.
7 But what things were gain to me, those
I counted loss for Christ.
8 Yes doubtless, and I count all things
but loss for the excellency of the knowledge of Christ Jesus my Lord: for whom
I have suffered the loss of all things, and
do count them but dung, that I may win
Christ,
9 And be found in him, not having mine
own righteousness, which is of the law,
but that which is through the faith of
Christ, the righteousness which is of
God by faith:
10 That I may know him, and the power of his resurrection, and the fellowship
of his sufferings, being made conform-
able to his death;
11 If by any means I might attain to the
resurrection of the dead.
12 Not as though I had already attained,

3:8 The greatest discovery. Dr. James Simpson, born in 1811, was responsible for the discovery of chloroform's anesthetic qualities, leading to its medical use worldwide. He also laid a solid foundation for gynecology and predicted the discovery of the X-ray. Dr. Simpson was president of the Royal Medical Society and Royal Physician to the Queen, the highest medical position of his day. He once stated, "Christianity works because it is supremely true and therefore supremely livable. There is nothing incompatible between religion and science."

When asked what his greatest discovery was, Dr. Simpson replied: "It was not chloroform. It was to know I am a sinner and that I could be saved by the grace of God. A man has missed the whole meaning of life if he has not entered into an active, living relationship with God through Christ." The greatest discovery in history has not been the law of gravity, calculus, telescopes, or the telegraph. The greatest discovery an individual could ever make is finding Jesus Christ and making Him both Lord and Savior.

"Man is never so tall as when he kneels before God—never so great as when he humbles himself before God. And the man who kneels to God can stand up to anything."

Louis H. Evans

either were already perfect: but I follow
after, if that I may apprehend that for
which also I am apprehended of Christ
Jesus.
13 Brethren, I count not myself to have
apprehended: but this one thing I do,
forgetting those things which are behind,
and reaching forth to those things which
are before,
14 I press toward the mark for the prize
of the high calling of God in Christ Jesus.
15 Let us therefore, as many as be perfect, be thus minded: and if in any thing
you be otherwise minded, God shall reveal even this to you.
16 Nevertheless, whereto we have already attained, let us walk by the same
rule, let us mind the same thing.
17 Brethren, be followers together of
me, and mark them which walk so as
you have us for an ensample.
18 (For many walk, of whom I have told
you often, and now tell you even weeping, that they are the enemies of the
cross of Christ:
19 Whose end is destruction, whose God
is their belly, and whose glory is in their
shame, who mind earthly things.)
20 For our conversation is in heaven;
from whence also we look for the Savior,
the Lord Jesus Christ:
21 Who shall change our vile body, that
it may be fashioned like to his glorious
body, according to the working whereby
he is able even to subdue all things to
himself.

CHAPTER 4

THEREFORE, my brethren dearly
beloved and longed for, my joy and
crown, so stand fast in the Lord, my
dearly beloved.
2 I beseech Euodias, and beseech Syn-
tyche, that they be of the same mind in
the Lord.
3 And I entreat you also, true yokefel-
low, help those women which labored
with me in the gospel, with Clement
also, and with other my fellowlaborers,
whose names are in the book of life.
4 Rejoice in the Lord always: and again
I say, Rejoice.

3:13 "Oh God, let this horrible war quickly come to an end that we may all return home and engage in the only work that is worthwhile—and that is the salvation of men." *General "Stonewall" Jackson*

3:21 New bodies for Christians. The unsaved have no idea of our hope. They presume that when we die we will spend eternity in heaven as a spirit or an angel. In truth, God's kingdom is coming to earth, and God's will *will* be done on earth as it is in heaven. We will become neither spirits nor angels, but we will have new bodies similar to the resurrected body of the Savior, never again to be plagued by disease, decay, death, or even dandruff. See Luke 24:36–43.

4:3 True companions are those who "labor" in the gospel. These are the ones of whom Jesus said there was a great lack (Luke 10:2). The fruit of genuine converts (those whose names are in the Book of Life) is a concern for the lost. Love cannot sit in passivity while sinners sink into hell.

5 Let your moderation be known to all
men. The Lord is at hand.
6 Be careful for nothing; but in every
thing by prayer and supplication with
thanksgiving let your requests be made
known to God.
7 And the peace of God, which passes
all understanding, shall keep your hearts
and minds through Christ Jesus.
8 Finally, brethren, whatsoever things
are true, whatsoever things are honest,
whatsoever things are just, whatsoever
things are pure, whatsoever things are
lovely, whatsoever things are of good report; if there be any virtue, and if there
be any praise, think on these things.
9 Those things, which you have both
learned, and received, and heard, and
seen in me, do: and the God of peace
shall be with you.
10 But I rejoiced in the Lord greatly,
that now at the last your care of me has
flourished again; wherein you were also
careful, but you lacked opportunity.
11 Not that I speak in respect of want:
for I have learned, in whatsoever state I
am, therewith to be content.
12 I know both how to be abased, and I
know how to abound: every where and
in all things I am instructed both to be
full and to be hungry, both to abound
and to suffer need.
13 *I can do all things through Christ who
strengthens me.*
14 Notwithstanding you have well done,
that you did communicate with my affliction.
15 Now you Philippians know also, that
in the beginning of the gospel, when I departed from Macedonia, no church communicated with me as concerning giving
and receiving, but you only.
16 For even in Thessalonica you sent
once and again to my necessity.
17 Not because I desire a gift: but I desire fruit that may abound to your account.
18 But I have all, and abound: I am full,
having received of Epaphroditus the things
which were sent from you, an odor of a
sweet smell, a sacrifice acceptable, well-
pleasing to God.
19 But my God shall supply all your
need according to his riches in glory by
Christ Jesus.
20 Now to God and our Father be glory
for ever and ever. Amen.
21 Salute every saint in Christ Jesus.
The brethren which are with me greet
you.
22 All the saints salute you, chiefly they
that are of Caesar's household.
23 The grace of our Lord Jesus Christ
be with you all. Amen.

4:5 Second coming of Jesus: See 1 Thessalonians 5:2.

4:6 "Realistically, the way you regard prayer is the way you regard God, for prayer is communicating with Him. No other way exists in which to relate with Him! Put simply, low levels of prayer signal a demotion of God in our attitude. High levels of prayer indicate an expectation for a fullness of His presence and power." *Ben Jennings, The Arena of Prayer*

4:13 Although God assured the prophet Jeremiah that He formed him, knew him, sanctified and ordained him, he still was paralyzed by the fear of man (Jeremiah 1:5,6). When the fear of man seeks to paralyze us, we must stop saying "I cannot speak," and instead say, "I can do all things through Christ who strengthens me." This verse obliterates every excuse we try to offer for not preaching the gospel to every creature. It counters the fear of man, the fear of rejection, the fear of public speaking, and the fear of offering a stranger a gospel tract.

Hudson Taylor said, "All God's giants have been weak men, who did great things for God because they believed that God would be with them."

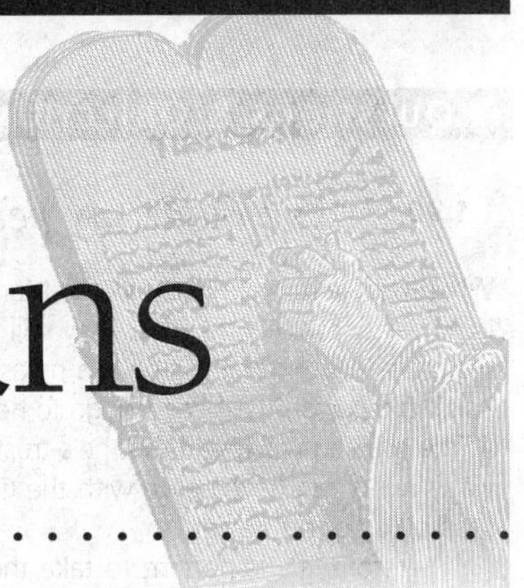

Colossians

CHAPTER 1

PAUL, an apostle of Jesus Christ by
the will of God, and Timotheus our
brother,
2 To the saints and faithful brethren in
Christ which are at Colosse: Grace be to
you, and peace, from God our Father
and the Lord Jesus Christ.
3 We give thanks to God and the Father
of our Lord Jesus Christ, praying always
for you,
4 Since we heard of your faith in Christ
Jesus, and of the love which you have to
all the saints,
5 For the hope which is laid up for you
in heaven, whereof you heard before in
the word of the truth of the gospel;
6 Which is come to you, as it is in all
the world; and brings forth fruit, as it
does also in you, since the day you heard
of it, and knew the grace of God in truth:
7 As you also learned of Epaphras our
dear fellow-servant, who is for you a
faithful minister of Christ;
8 Who also declared to us your love in
the Spirit.
9 For this cause we also, since the day
we heard it, do not cease to pray for you,
and to desire that you might be filled
with the knowledge of his will in all wisdom and spiritual understanding;
10 That you might walk worthy of the
Lord to all pleasing, being fruitful in every
good work, and increasing in the knowledge of God;
11 Strengthened with all might, according to his glorious power, to all patience
and longsuffering with joyfulness;
12 Giving thanks to the Father, which
has made us meet to be partakers of the
inheritance of the saints in light:
13 Who has delivered us from the power of darkness, and has translated us into
the kingdom of his dear Son:
14 In whom we have redemption
through his blood, even the forgiveness
of sins:
15 Who is the image of the invisible
God, the firstborn of every creature:
16 For by him were all things created,
that are in heaven, and that are in earth,
visible and invisible, whether they be
thrones, or dominions, or principalities,
or powers: all things were created by him,
and for him:
17 And he is before all things, and by

1:3,4 Some people applaud when sinners step forward to make a decision for Christ. It is more biblical to hold the applause until the genuineness of their repentance is evidenced by "fruit." See verse 6.

1:15,16 Was Jesus God in human form? The One who created all things and brought life into being is the Word of God, who became flesh in the person of Jesus of Nazareth (John 1:3,4,14). See Colossians 2:9.

QUESTIONS & OBJECTIONS

1:20 ***"I've made my peace with the 'Man upstairs.'"***

When people refer to God as "the Man upstairs," they reveal that they have no concept of (nor living relationship with) Him. They will use such words because they feel uncomfortable saying His name. Often they will have a measure of reverence for God, but not enough to obey Him. Ask if the person thinks he will go to heaven when he dies. He'll almost certainly say he will, and a little probing will reveal that he's trusting in his own goodness to save him. However, the only way sinners can have peace with the God they have offended is through the shed blood of the Savior.

Therefore, it's important to take the person through the Ten Commandments and strip him of his self-righteousness and his false sense of assurance of salvation. As you do so, you may feel bad that you are making him uncomfortable, but if you care about his eternal salvation, you must ask yourself, "Which is worse: a few moments of conviction under the sound of God's Law, or eternity in the Lake of Fire?" Unless there is a knowledge of sin (which comes by the Law—Romans 7:7), there will be no repentance.

him all things consist.
18 And he is the head of the body, the
church: who is the beginning, the firstborn from the dead; that in all things he
might have the preeminence.
19 For it pleased the Father that in him
should all fulness dwell;
20 And, having made peace through
the blood of his cross, by him to reconcile all things to himself; by him, I say,
whether they be things in earth, or things
in heaven.
21 And you, that were sometime alienated and enemies in your mind by wicked
works, yet now has he reconciled
22 In the body of his flesh through death,
to present you holy and unblameable
and unreproveable in his sight:
23 If you continue in the faith grounded and settled, and be not moved away
from the hope of the gospel, which you
have heard, and which was preached to
every creature which is under heaven;
whereof I Paul am made a minister;
24 Who now rejoice in my sufferings
for you, and fill up that which is behind
of the afflictions of Christ in my flesh for
his body's sake, which is the church:
25 Whereof I am made a minister, according to the dispensation of God which
is given to me for you, to fulfil the word
of God;
26 Even the mystery which has been
hid from ages and from generations, but
now is made manifest to his saints:
27 To whom God would make known
what is the riches of the glory of this mystery among the Gentiles; which is Christ
in you, the hope of glory:
28 *Whom we preach, warning every man,
and teaching every man in all wisdom; that
we may present every man perfect in Christ
Jesus:*
29 Whereunto I also labor, striving according to his working, which works in
me mightily.

1:21 This runs contrary to the secular concept of man's relationship to his Creator. We are alienated from God, separated from Him by our iniquities (Isaiah 59:2). We are His enemies, and our works are wicked.

1:27 Salvation doesn't come from *what* we know, but from *Who* we know. Jesus said, "This is life eternal, that they might know you the only true God, and Jesus Christ, whom you have sent" (John 17:3).

CHAPTER 2

FOR I would that you knew what
great conflict I have for you, and for
them at Laodicea, and for as many as
have not seen my face in the flesh;
2 That their hearts might be comforted,
being knit together in love, and to all
riches of the full assurance of understanding, to the acknowledgement of the mystery of God, and of the Father, and of
Christ;
3 In whom are hid all the treasures of
wisdom and knowledge.
4 And this I say, lest any man should beguile you with enticing words.
5 For though I be absent in the flesh,
yet am I with you in the spirit, joying and
beholding your order, and the stead-
fastness of your faith in Christ.
6 As you have therefore received Christ
Jesus the Lord, so walk in him:
7 Rooted and built up in him, and stab-
lished in the faith, as you have been
taught, abounding therein with thanksgiving.
8 Beware lest any man spoil you through
philosophy and vain deceit, after the tradition of men, after the rudiments of the
world, and not after Christ.
9 For in him dwells all the fulness of

1:28 Our primary task. A lighthouse keeper gained a reputation as being a very kind man. He would give free fuel to ships that miscalculated the amount of fuel needed to reach their destination port. One night during a storm, lightning struck his lighthouse and put out his light. He immediately turned on his generator, but it soon ran out of fuel, and he had given his reserves to passing ships. During the dark night, a ship struck the rocks and many lives were lost.

At his trial, the judge knew of the lighthouse keeper's reputation as a kind man and wept as he gave sentence. He accused the lighthouse keeper of neglecting his primary responsibility—to keep the light shining.

The Church can so often get caught up in legitimate acts of kindness—standing for political righteousness, feeding the hungry, etc.—but our primary task is to warn sinners of danger. We are to keep the light of the gospel shining so that sinners can avoid the jagged-edged rocks of wrath and escape being eternally damned.

My friend, I stand in judgment now,
and feel that you're to blame somehow.
On earth I walked with you by day,
and never did you show the way.
You knew the Savior in truth and glory,
But never did you tell the story.
My knowledge then was very dim.
You could have led me safe to Him.
Though we lived together, here on earth,
you never told me of the second birth.
And now I stand before eternal hell,
because of heaven's glory you did not tell!
(Anonymous)

"Each person we meet on a daily basis who does not know Christ is hell-bound. That may make some folks bristle—but it's a fact. When we refuse to warn people that their actions and lifestyles have eternal consequences, we're not doing them any favors. If everybody feels good about his or her sin, why would anyone repent?" *Franklin Graham*

"If they are breathing . . . they need Jesus." *Mark Cahill*

2:9 Was Jesus God in human form? Some may ask how Jesus could be both God and man. It has been well said that when God, the Creator and Sustainer of the universe, became a man, He didn't cease to be God. He created a body, and then filled that body as a hand fills a glove (Hebrews 10:5). See 1 Timothy 3:16.

2:16 *Freedom from Sabbath-keeping*

Some today insist that Christians must keep the Sabbath day, that those who worship on the first day of the week (Sunday) are in great error. They reason that "Sun-day" comes from the pagan worship of the Sun god, that Jesus and Paul kept the Sabbath day as an example for us to follow, and that the Roman Catholic church is responsible for the change in the day of worship. Those who continue to worship on Sunday will receive the mark of the beast.

Let's briefly look at these arguments. First, nowhere does the Fourth Commandment say that Christians are to *worship* on the Sabbath. It commands that we *rest* on that day: "Remember the Sabbath day, to keep it holy. Six days shall you labor, and do all your work: But the seventh day is the Sabbath of the LORD your God: in it you shall not do any work ...For in six days the LORD made heaven and earth, the sea, and all that in them is, and rested the seventh day: wherefore the LORD blessed the Sabbath day, and hallowed it" (Exodus 20:8–11).

Sabbath-keepers worship on Saturday. However, the word "Satur-day" comes from the Latin for "Saturn's day," a pagan day of worship of the planet Saturn (astrology).

If a Christian's salvation depends upon his keeping a certain day, surely God would have told us. At one point, the apostles gathered specifically to discuss the relationship of believers to the Law of Moses. Acts 15:5–11, 24–29 was God's opportunity to make His will clear to His children. All He had to do to save millions from damnation was say, "Remember to keep the Sabbath holy," and millions of Christ-centered, God-loving, Bible-believing Christians would have gladly kept it. Instead, the only commands the apostles gave were to "abstain from meats offered to idols, and from blood, and from things strangled, and from fornication."

There isn't even one command in the New Testament for Christians to keep the Sabbath holy. In fact, we are told not to let others judge us regarding Sabbaths (Colossian 2:16), and that man was not made for the Sabbath, but the Sabbath for man (Mark 2:27). The Sabbath was given as a sign to Israel (Exodus 31:13–17); nowhere is it given as a sign to the Church. Thousands of years after the Commandment was given we can still see the sign that separates Israel from the world—they continue to keep the Sabbath holy.

The apostles came together on the first day of the week to break bread (Acts 20:7). The collection was taken on the first day of the week (1 Corinthians 16:2). When do Sabbath-keepers gather together to break bread or take up the collection? It's not on the same day as the early Church. They tell us that the Roman Catholic church changed their day of worship from Saturday to Sunday, but what has that got to do with the disciples keeping the first day of the week? That was the Roman Catholic church in the early centuries, not the Church of the Book of Acts.

Romans 14:5–10 tells us that one man esteems one day of the week above another; another esteems every day alike. Then Scripture tells us that everyone should be fully persuaded in his own mind. We are not to judge each other regarding the day on which we worship.

Jesus did keep the Sabbath. He had to keep the whole Law to be the perfect sacrifice. The Bible makes it clear that the Law has been satisfied in Christ. The reason Paul went to the synagogue each Sabbath wasn't to keep the Law; that would have been contrary to everything he taught about being saved by grace alone (Ephesians 2:8,9). It was so he could preach the gospel to the Jews, as evident in the Book of Acts. Paul had an incredible evangelistic zeal for Israel to be saved (Romans 10:1). To the Jew he became as a Jew, that he might win the Jews (1 Corinthians 9:19,20). That meant he went to where they gathered on the day they gathered.

D. L. Moody said, "The Law can only chase a man to Calvary, no further." Christ redeemed us from the curse of the Law so we are no longer in bondage to it. If we try to keep one part of the Law (even out of love for God), we are obligated to keep the whole Law (Galatians 3:10)—all 613 precepts.

If those who insist on keeping the Sabbath were as zealous about the salvation of the lost as they are about other Christians keeping the Sabbath, we would see revival.

the Godhead bodily.
10 And you are complete in him, which
is the head of all principality and power:
11 In whom also you are circumcised
with the circumcision made without
hands, in putting off the body of the sins
of the flesh by the circumcision of Christ:
12 Buried with him in baptism, wherein also you are risen with him through
the faith of the operation of God, who
has raised him from the dead.
13 And you, being dead in your sins
and the uncircumcision of your flesh,
has he quickened together with him,
having forgiven you all trespasses;
14 Blotting out the handwriting of ordinances that was against us, which was
contrary to us, and took it out of the way,
nailing it to his cross;
15 And having spoiled principalities
and powers, he made a show of them
openly, triumphing over them in it.
16 Let no man therefore judge you in
meat, or in drink, or in respect of an holy-
day, or of the new moon, or of the sabbath days:
17 Which are a shadow of things to
come; but the body is of Christ.
18 Let no man beguile you of your reward in a voluntary humility and worshipping of angels, intruding into those
things which he has not seen, vainly
puffed up by his fleshly mind,
19 And not holding the Head, from
which all the body by joints and bands
having nourishment ministered, and knit
together, increases with the increase of
God.
20 Wherefore if you be dead with Christ
from the rudiments of the world, why, as
though living in the world, are you subject to ordinances,
21 (Touch not; taste not; handle not;
22 Which all are to perish with the using;) after the commandments and doctrines of men?
23 Which things have indeed a show of
wisdom in will worship, and humility,
and neglecting of the body; not in any
honor to the satisfying of the flesh.

CHAPTER 3

IF you then be risen with Christ, seek
those things which are above, where
Christ sits on the right hand of God.
2 Set your affection on things above,
not on things on the earth.
3 For you are dead, and your life is hid
with Christ in God.

THE FUNCTION OF THE LAW

2:21 Some may wonder whether using the Law in evangelism produces legalism. When the Law is used to show a sinner that sin is "exceedingly sinful"—that nothing can commend him to God—he clings to the cross knowing that he is saved by grace and grace alone. This knowledge gives the Christian the understanding that even after a lifetime of good works, fasting, praying, seeking the lost, etc., his "works" don't commend him to God—he is still saved by grace and grace alone.

However, when the Law *isn't* used before the cross, and a sinner simply makes a "decision for Christ," he comes with a lack of understanding about the true nature of sin. After his commitment, he thinks that his good works, his fasting, praying, evangelism, etc., commend him to God. He is the one who thinks that what he eats, what he wears, and what he does become relevant to his salvation. He is the one who is liable to say "touch not, taste not, handle not"—the one who becomes "legalistic." Using the Law in evangelism before the cross liberates a new convert from legalism.

2:16 "I am no preacher of the old legal Sabbath. I am a preacher of the gospel. The Sabbath of the Jew is to him a task; the Lord's Day of the Christian, the first day of the week, is to him a joy, a day of rest, of peace, and of thanksgiving. And if you Christian men can earnestly drive away all distractions, so that you can really rest today, it will be good for your bodies, good for your souls, good mentally, good spiritually, good temporally, and good eternally." *Charles Spurgeon*

4 When Christ, who is our life, shall appear, then shall you also appear with him
in glory.
5 Mortify therefore your members which
are upon the earth; fornication, uncleanness, inordinate affection, evil concupiscence, and covetousness, which is idolatry:
6 For which things' sake the wrath of
God comes on the children of disobedience:
7 In the which you also walked some
time, when you lived in them.
8 But now you also put off all these;
anger, wrath, malice, blasphemy, filthy
communication out of your mouth.
9 Lie not one to another, seeing that you
have put off the old man with his deeds;
10 And have put on the new man,
which is renewed in knowledge after the
image of him that created him:
11 Where there is neither Greek nor
Jew, circumcision nor uncircumcision,
Barbarian, Scythian, bond nor free: but
Christ is all, and in all.
12 Put on therefore, as the elect of God,
holy and beloved, bowels of mercies,
kindness, humbleness of mind, meekness, longsuffering;
13 Forbearing one another, and forgiving one another, if any man have a quarrel against any: even as Christ forgave
you, so also do.
14 And above all these things put on
charity, which is the bond of perfectness.
15 And let the peace of God rule in
your hearts, to the which also you are
called in one body; and be thankful.
16 Let the word of Christ dwell in you
richly in all wisdom; teaching and ad-
monishing one another in psalms and
hymns and spiritual songs, singing with
grace in your hearts to the Lord.

> I am told that Christians do not love each other. I am very sorry if that be true, but I rather doubt it, for I suspect that those who do not love each other are not Christians.
>
> **CHARLES SPURGEON**

17 And whatsoever you do in word or
deed, do all in the name of the Lord Jesus,
giving thanks to God and the Father by
him.
18 Wives, submit yourselves to your
own husbands, as it is fit in the Lord.
19 Husbands, love your wives, and be
not bitter against them.
20 Children, obey your parents in all
things: for this is well pleasing to the Lord.
21 Fathers, provoke not your children
to anger, lest they be discouraged.
22 Servants, obey in all things your masters according to the flesh; not with eye-
service, as men-pleasers; but in singleness of heart, fearing God:

3:3 "There was a day when I died, utterly died, died to George Mueller, his opinions, preferences, tastes, and will—died to the world, its approval or censure—died to the approval or blame even of my brethren and friends—and since then I have only to show myself approved to God." *George Mueller*

3:6 The Bible calls us children of disobedience. Children know naturally how to be selfish and lie. Rebellion is rooted deep in the human heart until we are born again and become children of God (John 1:12).

3:10 Feminists bristle at the Bible's statement that God made man in *His* image. This verse doesn't mean that God is a man, or that He looks like man (John 4:24). It means that when God made man and woman, He endowed them with a mind, emotions, and will. Humans are rational, moral beings with an inherent God-consciousness. However, in revealing Himself to mankind, God describes Himself in the male gender using terms such as Father, Son, Bridegroom, etc. Those who consider God to be female and call Him "Mother" are engaging in idolatry. To change who God has revealed Himself to be is to create a god in their own image.

23 And whatsoever you do, do it hearti-
ly, as to the Lord, and not to men;
24 Knowing that of the Lord you shall
receive the reward of the inheritance: for
you serve the Lord Christ.
25 But he that does wrong shall receive
for the wrong which he has done: and
there is no respect of persons.

. . . . . .

For scientific facts in the Bible, see Hebrews 11:3 comment.

. . . . . .

CHAPTER 4

MASTERS, give to your servants that
which is just and equal; knowing
that you also have a Master in heaven.
2 Continue in prayer, and watch in the
same with thanksgiving;
3 Withal praying also for us, that God
would open to us a door of utterance, to
speak the mystery of Christ, for which I
am also in bonds:
4 That I may make it manifest, as I ought
to speak.
5 Walk in wisdom toward them that are
without, redeeming the time.
6 Let your speech be always with grace,
seasoned with salt, that you may know
how you ought to answer every man.
7 All my state shall Tychicus declare to
you, who is a beloved brother, and a
faithful minister and fellow-servant in
the Lord:
8 Whom I have sent to you for the same
purpose, that he might know your estate, and comfort your hearts;
9 With Onesimus, a faithful and beloved brother, who is one of you. They
shall make known to you all things which
are done here.
10 Aristarchus my fellow-prisoner salutes you, and Marcus, sister's son to
Barnabas, (touching whom you received
commandments: if he come to you, receive him;)
11 And Jesus, which is called Justus,
who are of the circumcision. These only
are my fellow-workers to the kingdom of
God, which have been a comfort to me.

4:3,4 Paul asks the Colossian church to pray that God would open doors of opportunity for him to evangelize. Reaching out to the unsaved was the apostle's number one priority (see Romans 9:1–3). He often uses the phrase "as I ought to speak." He didn't see evangelism as a ministry only for people with a "gift" to reach the unsaved; he saw it as a moral responsibility, as each of us should. The only "gift" we need for evangelizing is the Holy Spirit, and every born-again believer has received Him.

4:4 Witnessing to telemarketers. If you are ever bugged by telemarketers, take the opportunity to share your faith. Simply say, "May I ask *you* a question?" Telemarketers will usually say yes. Ask, "Have you kept the Ten Commandments?" Then ask, "Have you ever told a lie?" Most admit to at least telling "fibs" or "white lies." When they admit it, ask what that makes them. If they refuse to call themselves a liar, say, "If *I* told a lie, what would I be called?" When they say, "Liar," ask, "Have you ever stolen something, even if it's small?" Be gentle and loving in your tone. Then say, "Jesus said that if you look with lust, you commit adultery in your heart. Have you ever looked with lust?"

Don't be afraid to inquire how they will do on Judgment Day—will they be innocent or guilty...heaven or hell? The worst thing that can happen is that they hang up in your ear. If that happens, you can rejoice that they were convicted enough to do so. You not only had the privilege of planting the seed of God's Word in the heart of a stranger, but you proved yourself to be faithful to the Lord, you conquered the fear of man, and now you can rejoice that you were rejected for the sake of righteousness. If they hang up, spend a moment in prayer for them. If they are open to hearing more, take them through the cross, repentance, and faith. Ask if they have a Bible at home, encourage them to read it daily, and then thank them for listening to you.

4:5,6 This is the spirit in which we should share our faith. See 1 Thessalonians 5:14.

"When thou prayest, rather let thy heart be without words than thy words be without heart."

John Bunyan

12 Epaphras, who is one of you, a servant of Christ, salutes you, always laboring fervently for you in prayers, that you may stand perfect and complete in all the will of God.
13 For I bear him record, that he has a great zeal for you, and them that are in Laodicea, and them in Hierapolis.
14 Luke, the beloved physician, and Demas, greet you.
15 Salute the brethren which are in Laodicea, and Nymphas, and the church which is in his house.
16 And when this epistle is read among you, cause that it be read also in the church of the Laodiceans; and that you likewise read the epistle from Laodicea.
17 And say to Archippus, Take heed to the ministry which you have received in the Lord, that you fulfil it.
18 The salutation by the hand of me Paul. Remember my bonds. Grace be with you. Amen.

4:12 Transforming prayer. "Prayer can move mountains. It can change human hearts, families, neighborhoods, cities, and nations. It's the ultimate source of power because it is, in reality, the power of Almighty God.

"Prayer can do what political action cannot, what education cannot, what military might cannot, and what planning committees cannot. All these are impotent by comparison.

"By prayer the kingdom of God is built, and by prayer the kingdom of Satan is destroyed. Where there is no prayer, there are no great works, and there is no building of the kingdom. Where there is much prayer and fervent prayer, there are great gains for the kingdom: God's rule is established, His power is directed, His will is done, society is transformed, lost persons are saved, and saints are enabled to 'stand against the devil's schemes' (Eph. 6:11). If that isn't enough to compel us to 'devote [ourselves] to prayer' and 'always [wrestle] in prayer' (Col. 4:2,12), I don't know what is!" *Alvin J. Vander Griend*, "Your Prayers Matter," *Discipleship Journal*

1 Thessalonians

CHAPTER 1

PAUL, and Silvanus, and Timotheus, to the church of the Thessalonians which is in God the Father and in the Lord Jesus Christ: Grace be to you, and peace, from God our Father, and the Lord Jesus Christ.
2 We give thanks to God always for you all, making mention of you in our prayers;
3 Remembering without ceasing your work of faith, and labor of love, and patience of hope in our Lord Jesus Christ, in the sight of God and our Father;
4 Knowing, brethren beloved, your election of God.
5 *For our gospel came not to you in word only, but also in power, and in the Holy Spirit, and in much assurance; as you know what manner of men we were among you for your sake.*
6 And you became followers of us, and of the Lord, having received the word in much affliction, with joy of the Holy Spirit:
7 So that you were ensamples to all that believe in Macedonia and Achaia.
8 For from you sounded out the word of the Lord not only in Macedonia and Achaia, but also in every place your faith to God-ward is spread abroad; so that we need not to speak any thing.
9 For they themselves show of us what manner of entering in we had to you, and how you turned to God from idols to serve the living and true God;
10 **And to wait for his Son from heaven, whom he raised from the dead, even Jesus, which delivered us from the wrath to come.**

CHAPTER 2

For yourselves, brethren, know our entrance in to you, that it was not in vain:
2 But even after that we had suffered before, and were shamefully entreated, as you know, at Philippi, we were bold in our God to speak to you the gospel of God with much contention.
3 For our exhortation was not of deceit, nor of uncleanness, nor in guile:
4 *But as we were allowed of God to be put*

1:5 God backs up His Word with power. When the unsaved ask for proof, we have it. If any person obeys the command to repent and trust Jesus Christ, he will experience the power of the gospel. God will transform him on the inside by giving him a new heart with new desires. Instead of drinking in iniquity like water, he will begin to thirst after righteousness. He will be born again. God will make him a new creature, all of which will give him "much assurance."

1:9 This reveals the essence of Paul's message to the Thessalonians. He preached against their sin of idolatry (transgression of the First and Second Commandments). This is also the essence of his message to the Athenians (see Acts 17:29).

Questions & Objections

2:13 *"There is no absolute truth. You can't be sure of anything!"*

Those who say that there are no absolutes are often very adamant about their belief. If they say that they are *absolutely* sure, then they are wrong because their own statement is an absolute. If they are not 100 percent sure, then there is a chance that they are wrong and they are risking their eternal salvation by trusting in a wrong belief. God tells us that there is an objective, absolute truth that is not subject to man's interpretations or whims, on which we can base our eternity. That truth is the Word of God (John 17:7).

in trust with the gospel, even so we speak;
not as pleasing men, but God, which tries
our hearts.
5 For neither at any time used we flattering words, as you know, nor a cloak
of covetousness; God is witness:
6 Nor of men sought we glory, neither
of you, nor yet of others, when we might
have been burdensome, as the apostles
of Christ.
7 But we were gentle among you, even
as a nurse cherishes her children:
8 So being affectionately desirous of you,
we were willing to have imparted to you,
not the gospel of God only, but also our
own souls, because you were dear to us.
9 For you remember, brethren, our labor and travail: for laboring night and
day, because we would not be chargeable to any of you, we preached to you
the gospel of God.
10 You are witnesses, and God also, how
holy and justly and unblameably we behaved ourselves among you that believe:
11 As you know how we exhorted and
comforted and charged every one of you,
as a father does his children,
12 That you would walk worthy of God,
who has called you to his kingdom and
glory.
13 For this cause also thank we God
without ceasing, because, when you received the word of God which you heard
of us, you received it not as the word of
men, but as it is in truth, the word of God,
which effectually works also in you that
believe.
14 For you, brethren, became followers
of the churches of God which in Judea
are in Christ Jesus: for you also have suffered like things of your own countrymen, even as they have of the Jews:
15 Who both killed the Lord Jesus, and
their own prophets, and have persecuted
us; and they please not God, and are
contrary to all men:
16 Forbidding us to speak to the Gentiles that they might be saved, to fill up
their sins always: for the wrath is come
upon them to the uttermost.
17 But we, brethren, being taken from
you for a short time in presence, not in
heart, endeavored the more abundantly
to see your face with great desire.
18 Wherefore we would have come to
you, even I Paul, once and again; but Satan hindered us.
19 For what is our hope, or joy, or crown

2:4 It is a great betrayal of trust to fashion our message to please men. We must never fail to call hell "hell" and sin "sin," rather than use timid clichés such as a "Christless eternity" and "indiscretions."

"Never mind *who* frowns, if God smiles." *Catherine Booth*

2:9,10 We must strive to be devout, just, and blameless in the sight of a sinful world. God forbid that any soul should stumble because they see what they perceive to be hypocrisy in our lives.

of rejoicing? Are not even you in the presence of our Lord Jesus Christ at his coming?
20 For you are our glory and joy.

. . . . . .

For how to witness to homosexuals, see 1 Timothy 1:8–10 comment.

. . . . . .

CHAPTER 3

WHEREFORE when we could no
longer forbear, we thought it
good to be left at Athens alone;
2 And sent Timotheus, our brother, and
minister of God, and our fellowlaborer
in the gospel of Christ, to establish you,
and to comfort you concerning your
faith:
3 That no man should be moved by these
afflictions: for yourselves know that we
are appointed thereunto.
4 For verily, when we were with you,
we told you before that we should suffer
tribulation; even as it came to pass, and
you know.
5 For this cause, when I could no longer
forbear, I sent to know your faith, lest by
some means the tempter have tempted
you, and our labor be in vain.
6 But now when Timotheus came from
you to us, and brought us good tidings
of your faith and charity, and that you
have good remembrance of us always,
desiring greatly to see us, as we also to
see you:
7 Therefore, brethren, we were comforted over you in all our affliction and distress by your faith:
8 For now we live, if you stand fast in
the Lord.
9 For what thanks can we render to God
again for you, for all the joy wherewith
we joy for your sakes before our God;
10 Night and day praying exceedingly
that we might see your face, and might
perfect that which is lacking in your
faith?
11 Now God himself and our Father,
and our Lord Jesus Christ, direct our way
to you.
12 And the Lord make you to increase
and abound in love one toward another,
and toward all men, even as we do toward
you:
13 To the end he may stablish your
hearts unblameable in holiness before
God, even our Father, at the coming of
our Lord Jesus Christ with all his saints.

> In proportion as a church is holy, in that proportion will its testimony for Christ be powerful.
>
> **CHARLES SPURGEON**

CHAPTER 4

FURTHERMORE then we beseech
you, brethren, and exhort you by the
Lord Jesus, that as you have received of
us how you ought to walk and to please
God, so you would abound more and
more.
2 For you know what commandments
we gave you by the Lord Jesus.
3 For this is the will of God, even your

2:16 Some lack the fear of God and believe that it is their right to suppress the truth of God's Word. However, those who hinder the progress of the gospel will come under the severe wrath of the Almighty. It would be better that a millstone be placed around their neck and they be cast into the depths of the sea, rather than hinder a single person from coming to peace with their Creator.

We can take strong consolation in the fact that God will have His way. Whoever calls upon the name of the Lord *shall* be saved and the wicked *will* be punished. He has delusions of grandeur indeed who thinks he can stop the will of God from coming to pass. Though hand join in hand, the wicked will not go unpunished (Proverbs 11:21). God will judge the world in righteousness. It would be infinitely easier to build a bacon-burger restaurant on the Temple Mount in Jerusalem than to stop God from saving those who call upon Him and from having His Day of Justice.

Two Prayers

"DEAR GOD, I have sinned against You by breaking Your Commandments. Despite the conscience You gave me, I have looked with lust and therefore committed adultery in my heart. I have lied, stolen, failed to love You, failed to love my neighbor as myself, and failed to keep the Sabbath holy. I have been covetous, harbored hatred in my heart and therefore been guilty of murder in Your sight. I have used Your holy name in vain, have made a god to suit myself, and because of the nature of my sin, I have dishonored my parents. If I stood before You in Your burning holiness on Judgment Day, if every secret sin I have committed and every idle word I have spoken came out as evidence of my crimes against You, I would be utterly guilty, and justly deserve hell. I am unspeakably thankful that Jesus took my place by suffering and dying on the cross. He was bruised for my iniquities. He paid my fine so that I could leave the courtroom. He revealed how much You love me. I believe that He then rose from the dead (according to the Scriptures). I now confess and forsake my sin and yield myself to Him to be my Lord and Savior. I will no longer live for myself. I present my body, soul, and spirit to You as a living sacrifice, to serve You in the furtherance of Your Kingdom. I will read Your Word daily and obey what I read. It is solely because of Calvary's cross that I will live forever. I am eternally Yours. In Jesus' name I pray. Amen."

"Choose you this day whom you will serve..."

"SATAN, the Bible tells me that you are the god of this world. You are the father of lies. You deceive the nations and blind the minds of those who do not believe. God warns that I cannot enter His Kingdom because I have lied, stolen, looked with lust and therefore committed adultery in my heart. I have harbored hatred, which the Bible says is the same as murder. I have blasphemed, refused to put God first, violated the Sabbath, coveted other people's goods, dishonored my parents, and have been guilty of the sin of idolatry—I even made a god to suit myself. I did all this despite the presence of my conscience. I know that it was God who gave me life. I have seen the splendor of a sunrise. I have heard the sounds of nature. I have enjoyed pleasures of an incredible array of food, all of which came from His generous hand. I realize that if I die in my sins I will never know pleasure again. I know that Jesus Christ shed His life's blood for my sins and rose again to destroy the power of death, but today I refuse to confess and forsake my sins. On the Day of Judgment, if I am cast into the Lake of Fire I will have no one to blame but myself. It is not God's will that I perish. He commended His love toward me through the death of His Son, who came to give me life. It was you who came to kill, steal, and destroy. You are my spiritual father. I choose to continue to serve you and do your will. This is because I love the darkness and hate the light. If I do not come to my senses, I will be eternally yours. Amen."

sanctification, that you should abstain
from fornication:
4 That every one of you should know
how to possess his vessel in sanctification and honor;
5 Not in the lust of concupiscence, even
as the Gentiles which know not God:
6 That no man go beyond and defraud
his brother in any matter: because that
the Lord is the avenger of all such, as we
also have forewarned you and testified.
7 For God has not called us to uncleanness, but to holiness.
8 He therefore that despises, despises
not man, but God, who has also given to
us his holy Spirit.
9 But as touching brotherly love you
need not that I write to you: for you
yourselves are taught of God to love one
another.
10 And indeed you do it toward all the
brethren which are in all Macedonia: but
we beseech you, brethren, that you increase more and more;
11 And that you study to be quiet, and
to do your own business, and to work with
your own hands, as we commanded you;
12 That you may walk honestly toward
them that are without, and that you may
have lack of nothing.
13 But I would not have you to be ignorant, brethren, concerning them which
are asleep, that you sorrow not, even as
others which have no hope.
14 For if we believe that Jesus died and
rose again, even so them also which sleep
in Jesus will God bring with him.
15 For this we say to you by the word
of the Lord, that we which are alive and
remain to the coming of the Lord shall
not prevent them which are asleep.
16 For the Lord himself shall descend
from heaven with a shout, with the voice
of the archangel, and with the trump of
God: and the dead in Christ shall rise
first:
17 Then we which are alive and remain
shall be caught up together with them in
the clouds, to meet the Lord in the air:
and so shall we ever be with the Lord.
18 Wherefore comfort one another with
these words.

The Dead Sea Scrolls confirm that the Bible hasn't changed through the years. See 1 Peter 1:25 comment.

CHAPTER 5

BUT of the times and the seasons,
brethren, you have no need that I
write to you.
2 For yourselves know perfectly that
the day of the Lord so comes as a thief in
the night.
3 For when they shall say, Peace and
safety; then sudden destruction comes
upon them, as travail upon a woman with
child; and they shall not escape.
4 But you, brethren, are not in darkness,
that that day should overtake you as a
thief.
5 You are all the children of light, and
the children of the day: we are not of the
night, nor of darkness.
6 Therefore let us not sleep, as do others; but let us watch and be sober.
7 For they that sleep sleep in the night;
and they that be drunken are drunken in
the night.
8 But let us, who are of the day, be sober, putting on the breastplate of faith

5:2 Second coming of Jesus: See Hebrews 9:28.

and love; and for an helmet, the hope of
salvation.
9 For God has not appointed us to wrath,
but to obtain salvation by our Lord Jesus
Christ,
10 Who died for us, that, whether we
wake or sleep, we should live together
with him.
11 Wherefore comfort yourselves together, and edify one another, even as
also you do.
12 And we beseech you, brethren, to
know them which labor among you, and
are over you in the Lord, and admonish
you;
13 And to esteem them very highly in
love for their work's sake. And be at peace
among yourselves.
14 Now we exhort you, brethren, warn
them that are unruly, comfort the feebleminded, support the weak, be patient
toward all men.
15 See that none render evil for evil to
any man; but ever follow that which is
good, both among yourselves, and to all
men.
16 Rejoice evermore.
17 Pray without ceasing.
18 In every thing give thanks: for this is
the will of God in Christ Jesus concerning
you.
19 Quench not the Spirit.
20 Despise not prophesyings.
21 Prove all things; hold fast that which
is good.
22 Abstain from all appearance of evil.
23 And the very God of peace sanctify
you wholly; and I pray God your whole
spirit and soul and body be preserved
blameless to the coming of our Lord Jesus
Christ.
24 Faithful is he that calls you, who also
will do it.
25 Brethren, pray for us.
26 Greet all the brethren with an holy
kiss.
27 I charge you by the Lord that this
epistle be read to all the holy brethren.
28 The grace of our Lord Jesus Christ
be with you. Amen.

5:14 This is the spirit in which we should share our faith. See 2 Timothy 2:24.

5:17 *General "Stonewall" Jackson*, one of the country's greatest generals, gives a good example of how to "pray without ceasing":

> "When we take our meals, there is the grace. When I take a draught of water, I always pause...to lift up my heart to God in thanks and prayer for the water of life. Whenever I [send] a letter...I send a petition along with it, for God's blessing upon its mission and upon the person to whom it is sent.
>
> "When I [open] a letter...I stop to pray to God that He may prepare me for its contents...When I go to my class-room and await the arrangement of the cadets in their places, that is my time to intercede with God for them."

5:17 "Prayers are not limited to place and time. If you are not in the right place to pray, you're not in the right place." *Chuck Missler*

"Prayer is the shield to the soul, a delight to God, and a scourge to Satan." *John Bunyan*

5:20 The Bible's fascinating facts. In Isaiah 66:7,8 (700 B.C.), the prophet Isaiah gives a strange prophecy: "Before she travailed, she brought forth; before her pain came, she was delivered of a man child. Who has heard such a thing? Who has seen such things? Shall the earth be made to bring forth in one day? Or shall a nation be born at once? For as soon as Zion travailed, she brought forth her children." In 1922 the League of Nations gave Great Britain the mandate (political authority) over Palestine. On May 14, 1948, Britain withdrew her mandate, and the nation of Israel was "born in a day." There are more than 25 Bible prophecies concerning Palestine that have been literally fulfilled. Probability estimations conclude that the chances of these being accidentally fulfilled are less than one chance in 33 million.

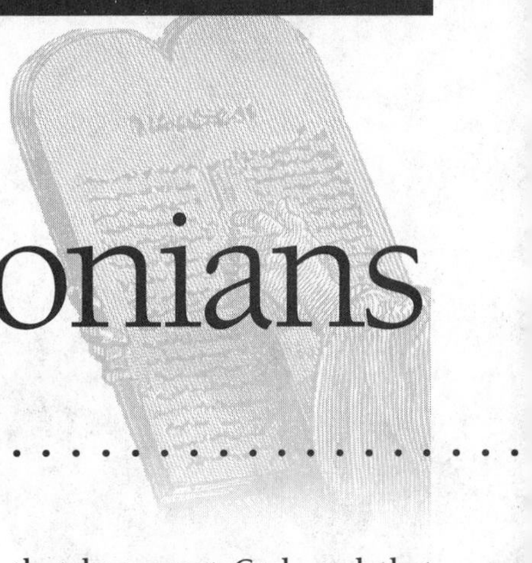

2 Thessalonians

CHAPTER 1

PAUL, and Silvanus, and Timotheus,
to the church of the Thessalonians in
God our Father and the Lord Jesus Christ:
2 Grace to you, and peace, from God
our Father and the Lord Jesus Christ.
3 We are bound to thank God always
for you, brethren, as it is meet, because
that your faith grows exceedingly, and
the charity of every one of you all toward
each other abounds;
4 So that we ourselves glory in you in
the churches of God for your patience
and faith in all your persecutions and
tribulations that you endure:
5 Which is a manifest token of the
righteous judgment of God, that you
may be counted worthy of the kingdom
of God, for which you also suffer:
6 Seeing it is a righteous thing with
God to recompense tribulation to them
that trouble you;
7 And to you who are troubled rest
with us, when the Lord Jesus shall be
revealed from heaven with his mighty
angels,
8 In flaming fire taking vengeance on
them that know not God, and that
obey not the gospel of our Lord Jesus
Christ:
9 Who shall be punished with ever-
lasting destruction from the presence
of the Lord, and from the glory of his
power;
10 When he shall come to be glorified
in his saints, and to be admired in all
them that believe (because our testimo-
ny among you was believed) in that day.
11 Wherefore also we pray always for
you, that our God would count you worthy of this calling, and fulfil all the good
pleasure of his goodness, and the work
of faith with power:
12 That the name of our Lord Jesus
Christ may be glorified in you, and you
in him, according to the grace of our
God and the Lord Jesus Christ.

CHAPTER 2

NOW we beseech you, brethren, by
the coming of our Lord Jesus Christ,
and by our gathering together to him,
2 That you be not soon shaken in mind,
or be troubled, neither by spirit, nor by

1:6 The world doesn't understand why the Christian turns the other cheek. This isn't because he is weak. Rather than take the law into his own hands, he simply commits himself to "Him who judges righteously." If God sees fit to repay, He will. The Scriptures tell us, "Vengeance is mine; I will repay, says the Lord" (Romans 12:19).

1:7–9 Judgment Day: Such a thought should stir in us a passion for evangelism. It is a fearful thing to fall into the hands of the living God. For verses that warn of its reality, see 2 Timothy 4:1.

1:10 Our beliefs govern our actions. Those who don't believe that they are in danger of God's wrath will not flee from it.

"I never thought much of the courage of a lion-tamer. Inside the cage he is at least safe from people."

George Bernard Shaw

word, nor by letter as from us, as that
the day of Christ is at hand.
3 Let no man deceive you by any means:
for that day shall not come, except there
come a falling away first, and that man
of sin be revealed, the son of perdition;
4 Who opposes and exalts himself above
all that is called God, or that is worshipped;
so that he as God sits in the
temple of God, showing himself that he
is God.
5 Do you not remember, that, when I
was yet with you, I told you these things?
6 And now you know what withholds
that he might be revealed in his time.
7 For the mystery of iniquity does already
work: only he who now lets will
let, until he be taken out of the way.
8 And then shall that Wicked be revealed,
whom the Lord shall consume
with the spirit of his mouth, and shall
destroy with the brightness of his coming:
9 Even him, whose coming is after the
working of Satan with all power and
signs and lying wonders,
10 And with all deceivableness of unrighteousness
in them that perish; because
they received not the love of the
truth, that they might be saved.
11 And for this cause God shall send
them strong delusion, that they should
believe a lie:
12 That they all might be damned who
believed not the truth, but had pleasure
in unrighteousness.
13 But we are bound to give thanks always
to God for you, brethren beloved of
the Lord, because God has from the beginning
chosen you to salvation through
sanctification of the Spirit and belief of
the truth:
14 Whereunto he called you by our gospel,
to the obtaining of the glory of our
Lord Jesus Christ.

> I further believe, although certain persons deny it, that the influence of fear is to be exercised over the minds of men, and that it ought to operate upon the mind of the preacher himself: "Noah...moved with fear, prepared an ark to the saving of his house" (Hebrews 11:7).
>
> **CHARLES SPURGEON**

15 Therefore, brethren, stand fast, and
hold the traditions which you have been
taught, whether by word, or our epistle.
16 Now our Lord Jesus Christ himself,
and God, even our Father, who has
loved us, and has given us everlasting
consolation and good hope through grace,
17 Comfort your hearts, and stablish
you in every good word and work.

2:11,12 If sinners refuse to truly embrace the gospel, God in His righteousness will give them over to "powerful delusion" and a "depraved mind" (Romans 1:28). Those who refuse to come to the light will be given over to darkness. See John 3:19,20 comment.

CHAPTER 3

FINALLY, brethren, pray for us, that the word of the Lord may have free course, and be glorified, even as it is with you:

2 And that we may be delivered from unreasonable and wicked men: for all men have not faith.

3 But the Lord is faithful, who shall stablish you, and keep you from evil.

4 And we have confidence in the Lord touching you, that you both do and will do the things which we command you.

5 And the Lord direct your hearts into the love of God, and into the patient waiting for Christ.

6 Now we command you, brethren, in the name of our Lord Jesus Christ, that you withdraw yourselves from every brother that walks disorderly, and not after the tradition which he received of us.

7 For yourselves know how you ought to follow us: for we behaved not ourselves disorderly among you;

8 Neither did we eat any man's bread for nothing; but wrought with labor and travail night and day, that we might not be chargeable to any of you:

9 Not because we have not power, but to make ourselves an ensample to you to follow us.

10 For even when we were with you, this we commanded you, that if any would not work, neither should he eat.

11 For we hear that there are some which walk among you disorderly, working not at all, but are busybodies.

12 Now them that are such we command and exhort by our Lord Jesus Christ, that with quietness they work, and eat their own bread.

13 But you, brethren, be not weary in well doing.

14 And if any man obey not our word by this epistle, note that man, and have no company with him, that he may be ashamed.

Archaeological discoveries confirm the Bible's account of historical events. See Matthew 26:54 comment.

15 Yet count him not as an enemy, but admonish him as a brother.

16 Now the Lord of peace himself give you peace always by all means. The Lord be with you all.

17 The salutation of Paul with mine own hand, which is the token in every epistle: so I write.

18 The grace of our Lord Jesus Christ be with you all. Amen.

3:1 Paul again requests prayer for the evangelistic enterprise. "The word of the Lord" refers to the salvation message. "Unreasonable and wicked men" (v. 2) continually seek to stop the gospel from having "free course."

Hinduism

ORIGIN: India, about 1500 B.C. to 2500 B.C.

FOUNDER: No single person

ADHERENTS: 1998 worldwide: 825–850 million; India 780 million; Bangladesh 20 million; Nepal 20 million; Indonesia 7 million; Sri Lanka 3 million; Pakistan 2 million. In Fiji, Guyana, Mauritius, Surinam, and Trinidad and Tobago, over 20 percent of their people practice Hinduism. A considerable number of Hindus live in Africa, Myanmar, and the United Kingdom. U.S.: Estimated 1.5 to 2 million.

SCRIPTURES: *Vedas*, *Upanishads*, *epics*, *Puranas*, and the *Bhagavad Gita* explain the essence of Hinduism. Hinduism is the world's oldest surviving organized religion. It is a complex family of sects whose copious scriptures, written over a period of almost 2,000 years (1500 B.C.–A.D. 250), allow a diverse belief system. Hinduism has no single creed and recognizes no final truth. At its core, Hinduism has a pagan background in which the forces of nature and human heroes are personified as gods and goddesses. They are worshiped with prayers and offerings. Hinduism can be divided into Popular Hinduism, characterized by the worship of gods through offerings, rituals, and prayers; and Philosophical Hinduism, the complex belief system understood by those who can study ancient texts, meditate, and practice yoga.

GOD: God (*Brahman*) is the one impersonal, ultimate, but unknowable, spiritual Reality. Sectarian Hinduism personalizes Brahman as *Brahma* (Creator, with four heads symbolizing creative energy), *Vishnu* (Preserver, the god of stability and control), and *Shiva* (Destroyer, god of endings). Most Hindus worship two of Vishnu's 10 mythical incarnations: Krishna and Rama. On special occasions, Hindus may worship other gods, as well as family and individual deities. Hindus claim that there are 330 million gods. In Hinduism, belief in astrology, evil spirits, and curses also prevails.

Christian Response: If God (Ultimate Reality) is impersonal, then the impersonal must be greater than the personal. Our life experiences reveal that the personal is of more value than the impersonal. Even Hindus treat their children as having more value than a rock in a field.

The Bible teaches that God is personal and describes Him as having personal attributes. The Bible regularly describes God in ways used to describe human personality. God talks, rebukes, feels, becomes angry, is jealous, laughs, loves, and even has a personal name (Gen. 1:3; 6:6, 12; Ex. 3:15; 16:12; 20:5; Lev. 20:23; Deut. 5:9; 1 Sam. 26:19; Ps. 2:4; 59:9; Hos. 1:8–9; Amos 9:4; Zeph. 3:17). The Bible also warns Christians to avoid all forms of idolatry (Gen. 35:2; Ex. 23:13; Josh. 23:7; Ezek. 20:7; 1 Cor. 10:20). No idol or pagan deity is a representation of the true God. They are all false deities and must be rejected.

CREATION: Hindus accept various forms of pantheism and reject the Christian doctrine of creation. According to Hinduism, Brahman alone exists; everything is ultimately an illusion (*maya*). God emanated itself to cause the illusion of creation. There is no beginning or conclusion to creation, only endless repetitions or cycles of creation and destruction. History has little value since it is based on an illusion.

Christian Response: Christianity affirms the reality of the material world and the genuineness of God's creation. The Bible declares that all is not God. God is present in His creation but He is not to be confused with it. The Bible teaches that in the beginning God created that which was not God (Gen. 1:1ff; Heb 11:3). The Bible contradicts pantheism by teaching creation rather than pantheistic emanation. The Bible issues strong warnings to those who confuse God with His creation (Rom. 1:22–23). God created the world at a definite time and will consummate His creation (2 Pet. 2:12–13). Christianity is founded upon the historical event of God's incarnation in Jesus Christ (John 1:1–14).

MAN: The eternal soul (*atman*) of man is a manifestation or "spark" of Brahman mysteriously trapped in the physical body. *Samsara*, repeated lives or reincarnations, are required before the soul can be liberated (*moksha*) from the body. An individual's present life is determined by the law of *karma* (actions, words, and thoughts in previous lifetimes). The physical body is ultimately an illusion (*maya*) with little inherent or permanent worth. Bodies generally are cremated, and the eternal soul goes to an intermediate state of punishment or reward before rebirth in another body. Rebirths are experienced until karma has been removed to allow the soul's re-absorption into Brahman.

Christian Response: People are created in God's image (Gen. 12:7). The body's physical resurrection and eternal worth are emphasized in John 2:18–22 and 1 Corinthians 15. The Bible declares, "And as it is appointed unto men once to die, but after this the judgment: so Christ was once offered to bear the sins of many" (Heb. 9:27–28, KJV). Since we die only once, reincarnation cannot be true. Instead of reincarnation, the Bible teaches resurrection (John 5:25). At death, Christians enjoy a state of conscious fellowship with Christ (Matt. 22:32; 2 Cor. 5:8; Phil. 1:23) to await the resurrection and heavenly reward. A person's eternal destiny is determined by his or her acceptance or rejection of Jesus Christ as Savior and Lord (John 3:36; Rom. 10:9–10).

SIN: Hindus have no concept of rebellion against a holy God. Ignorance of unity with Brahman, desire, and violation of *dharma* (one's social duty) are humanity's problems.

Christian Response: Sin is not ignorance of unity with Brahman, but is rather a willful act of rebellion against God and His commandments (Eccl. 7:20; Rom. 1:28–32; 2:1–16; 3:9,19; 11:32; Gal. 3:22; 1 John 1:8–10). The Bible declares, "All have sinned and fall short of the glory of God" (Rom. 3:23, NIV).

SALVATION: There is no clear concept of salvation in Hinduism. *Moksha* (freedom from infinite being and self-hood and final self-realization of the truth) is the goal of existence. *Yoga* and meditation (especially *raja-yoga*) taught by a *guru* (religious teacher) is one way to attain *moksha*. The other valid paths for *moksha* are: the way of works (*karma marga*), the way of knowledge (*jnana marga*), and the way of love and devotion (*bhakti marga*). Hindus hope to eventually get off the cycle of reincarnation. They believe the illusion of personal existence will end and they will become one with the impersonal God.

Christian Response: Salvation is a gift from God through faith in Jesus Christ (Eph. 2:8–10). Belief in reincarnation opposes the teaching of the Bible (Heb. 9:27). The Christian hope of eternal life means that all true believers in Christ will not only have personal existence but personal fellowship with God. It is impossible to earn one's salvation by good works (Titus 3:1–7). Religious deeds and exercises cannot save (Matt. 7:22–23; Rom 9:32; Gal. 2:16; Eph. 2:8–9).

WORSHIP: Hindu worship has an almost endless variety with color symbolism, offerings, fasting, and dance as integral parts. Most Hindus daily worship an image of their chosen deity, with chants (*mantras*), flowers, and incense. Worship, whether in a home or temple, is primarily individualistic rather than congregational.

HINDUS IN THE UNITED STATES

- Traditional movements include the Ramakrishna Mission and Vedanta Societies, Sri Aurobindo Society, Satya Sai Baba Movement, Self-Realization Fellowship, and International Sivananda Yoga Society.
- Hindu-based sects include the International Society for Krishna Consciousness (Hare Krishna), Transcendental Meditation, Vedanta Society, Self-Realization Fellowship, Theosophy, and Eckankar.
- Sects that have "Americanized" Hindu concepts include Church of Christ, Scientists (Christian Science); Unity School of Christianity; and several groups within the New Age Movement.

WITNESSING TO HINDUS

- Pray and trust the Holy Spirit to use the gospel message to reach the heart and mind of your Hindu friend.
- Share your personal faith in Jesus Christ as your Lord and Savior. Keep your testimony short.
- Stress the uniqueness of Jesus Christ as God's revelation of Himself.
- Stress the necessity of following Jesus to the exclusion of all other deities.
- Keep the gospel presentation Christ-centered.
- Share the assurance of salvation that God's grace gives you and about your hope in the resurrection. Make sure you communicate that your assurance is derived from God's grace and not from your good works or your ability to be spiritual (1 John 5:13).
- Give a copy of the New Testament. If a Hindu desires to study the Bible, begin with the Gospel of John. Point out passages that explain salvation.

The Great Commission

"Go into all the world, and preach the gospel to every creature" *(Mark 16:15)*.

"Have you no wish for others to be saved? Then you are not saved yourself. Be sure of that." *Charles Spurgeon*

"If you do not make it a matter of study, how you may successfully act in building up the kingdom of Christ, you are acting a very wicked and absurd part as a Christian." *Charles Finney*

"The harvest truly is plenteous, but the laborers are few; pray therefore the Lord of the harvest, that he will send forth laborers into his harvest" *(Matthew 9:37,38)*.

"Oh my friends, we are loaded down with countless church activities, while the real work of the church, that of evangelizing the world and winning the lost, is almost entirely neglected!"
Oswald J. Smith

"Why call you me, Lord, Lord, and do not the things which I say?" *(Luke 6:46)*.

(See John 4:7 comment on how to effectively share your faith.)

1 Timothy

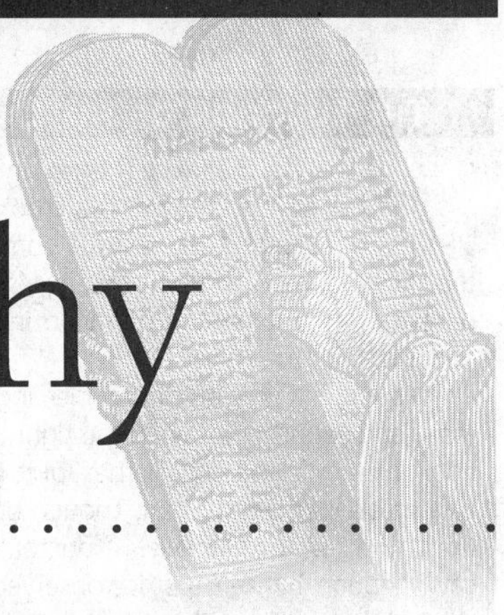

CHAPTER 1

PAUL, an apostle of Jesus Christ by
the commandment of God our Savior, and Lord Jesus Christ, which is our
hope;
2 To Timothy, my own son in the faith:
Grace, mercy, and peace, from God our
Father and Jesus Christ our Lord.
3 As I besought you to abide still at
Ephesus, when I went into Macedonia,
that you might charge some that they
teach no other doctrine,
4 Neither give heed to fables and endless genealogies, which minister questions, rather than godly edifying which is
in faith: so do.
5 Now the end of the commandment is
charity out of a pure heart, and of a good
conscience, and of faith unfeigned:
6 From which some having swerved
have turned aside to vain jangling;
7 Desiring to be teachers of the law; understanding neither what they say, nor
whereof they affirm.
8 But we know that the law is good, if a
man use it lawfully;
9 Knowing this, that the law is not made
for a righteous man, but for the lawless
and disobedient, for the ungodly and for
sinners, for unholy and profane, for murderers of fathers and murderers of mothers, for manslayers,
10 For whoremongers, for them that defile themselves with mankind, for men-
stealers, for liars, for perjured persons,
and if there be any other thing that is
contrary to sound doctrine;
11 According to the glorious gospel of
the blessed God, which was committed
to my trust.
12 And I thank Christ Jesus our Lord,
who has enabled me, for that he counted
me faithful, putting me into the ministry;
13 Who was before a blasphemer, and a
persecutor, and injurious: but I obtained
mercy, because I did it ignorantly in unbelief.
14 And the grace of our Lord was ex-

1:5 In the context of this passage (vv. 5–11), Paul is speaking of the Law of God when he refers to the "commandment." Its purpose is to bring a sinner to genuine conversion, with the evidence of the fruit of love from a pure heart, a good conscience, and true faith. The purpose of a mirror is to send us to the water that we might be made clean. The purpose of the Law is to reveal sin and send us to be washed clean by the blood of Jesus Christ.

1:8 The way to use the Law "lawfully" is to use it in evangelism as a "schoolmaster" to bring sinners to Christ (Galatians 3:24). See verses 9,10.

"I have found by long experience that the severest threatenings of the Law of God have a prominent place in leading men to Christ. They must see themselves lost before they will cry for mercy. They will not escape from danger until they see it." *A. B. Earle*

THE FUNCTION OF THE LAW

1:8 "As that which is straight discovers that which is crooked, so there is no way of coming to that knowledge of sin which is necessary to repentance, but by comparing our hearts and lives with the Law.

"Paul had a very quick and piercing judgment and yet never attained the right knowledge of indwelling sin till the Spirit by the Law made it known to him. Though brought up at the feet of Gamaliel, a doctor of the Law, though himself a strict observer of it, yet without the Law. He had the letter of the Law, but he had not the spiritual meaning of it—the shell, but not the kernel. He had the Law in his hand and in his head, but he had it not in his heart. But when the commandment came (not to his eyes only, but to his heart), sin revived, as the dust in a room rises when the sunshine is let into it. Paul then saw that in sin which he had never seen before—sin in its consequences, sin with death at the heels of it, sin and the curse entailed upon it. 'The Spirit, by the commandment, convinced me that I was in a state of sin, and in a state of death because of sin.' Of this excellent use is the Law; it is a lamp and a light; it opens the eyes, prepares the way of the Lord." *Matthew Henry*

ceeding abundant with faith and love
which is in Christ Jesus.
15 **This is a faithful saying, and worthy of all acceptation, that Christ Jesus
came into the world to save sinners; of
whom I am chief.**
16 Howbeit for this cause I obtained
mercy, that in me first Jesus Christ might
show forth all longsuffering, for a pattern to them which should hereafter believe on him to life everlasting.
17 Now to the King eternal, immortal,
invisible, the only wise God, be honor
and glory for ever and ever. Amen.
18 This charge I commit to you, son
Timothy, according to the prophecies
which went before on you, that you by
them might war a good warfare;
19 Holding faith, and a good conscience;
which some having put away concerning
faith have made shipwreck:
20 Of whom is Hymenaeus and Alexander; whom I have delivered to Satan,
that they may learn not to blaspheme.

CHAPTER 2

I EXHORT therefore, that, first of all,
supplications, prayers, intercessions,
and giving of thanks, be made for all
men;
2 For kings, and for all that are in authority; that we may lead a quiet and
peaceable life in all godliness and honesty.
3 **For this is good and acceptable in
the sight of God our Savior;**
4 **Who will have all men to be saved,
and to come to the knowledge of the**

1:12 Here are three wonderful truths for evangelism:

1. God has enabled you to be His witness (Acts 1:8).
2. God considers you faithful, entrusting you with the stewardship of the gospel (1 Corinthians 9:16,17).
3. God has placed you into the ministry (Mark 16:15).

2:1 Intercessory prayer. "God gave us intercessory prayer so we could partner with Him in transforming society, saving the lost, and establishing His kingdom. To be sure, God is perfectly capable of doing these things without us. He is all-wise, full of love, and almighty. In His wisdom He always knows what is best. In His love He always chooses what is best. And in His power He is able to do what is best. He doesn't need us. Nevertheless, in His sovereign good pleasure, He has chosen to involve us, through our prayers, in accomplishing His will. Our intercessory prayers are important to God; they should also be important to us." *Alvin J. Vander Griend*, "Your Prayers Matter," *Discipleship Journal*

2:4 Salvation is possible for every person. See 2 Peter 3:9.

QUESTIONS & OBJECTIONS

1:8–10

"How should I witness to a homosexual?"

Rather than offend homosexuals by directly confronting the issue of their sinful lifestyle, modern evangelism often tries to soften the approach by saying that "God hates the sin, but loves the sinner." This isn't a new concept. *Charles Finney* stated, "God is not angry merely against the sin abstracted from the sinner, but against the sinner himself. Some persons have labored hard to set up this ridiculous and absurd abstraction, and would fain make it appear that God is angry at sin, yet not at the sinner. He hates the theft, but loves the thief. He abhors adultery, but is pleased with the adulterer. Now this is supreme nonsense. The sin has no moral character apart from the sinner. The act is nothing apart from the actor. The very thing that God hates and disapproves is not the mere event—the thing done in distinction from the doer; but it is the *doer himself*. It grieves and displeases Him that a rational moral agent, under His government, should array himself against his own God and Father, against all that is right and just in the universe. This is the thing that offends God. The sinner himself is the direct and the only object of his anger.

"So the Bible shows. God is angry with the wicked [Psalm 7:11], not with the abstract sin. If the wicked turn not, God will whet His sword—He has bent His bow and made it ready—not to shoot at the *sin*, but the *sinner*—the wicked man who has done the abominable thing. This is the only doctrine of either the Bible or of common sense on this subject" *(The Guilt of Sin)*.

The biblical way to witness to a homosexual is not to argue with him about his lifestyle but to use the Law to bring the knowledge of sin. This will show him that he is guilty of breaking God's holy Law, and he is damned *despite* his sexual preference. The Law was made for homosexuals, as well as other lawbreakers. See Psalm 5:5 and 2 Peter 2:6–8 comments.

truth.
5 For there is one God, and one mediator between God and men, the man Christ Jesus;
6 Who gave himself a ransom for all, to be testified in due time.
7 Whereunto I am ordained a preacher, and an apostle, (I speak the truth in Christ, and lie not;) a teacher of the Gentiles in faith and verity.
8 I will therefore that men pray every where, lifting up holy hands, without wrath and doubting.
9 In like manner also, that women adorn themselves in modest apparel, with shamefacedness and sobriety; not with broided hair, or gold, or pearls, or costly array;
10 But (which becomes women professing godliness) with good works.
11 Let the woman learn in silence with all subjection.
12 But I suffer not a woman to teach, nor to usurp authority over the man, but to be in silence.

2:5 "We know God only through Jesus Christ. Without this Mediator, is taken away all communication with God; through Jesus Christ we know God. All those who have pretended to know God, and prove Him without Jesus Christ, have only impotent proofs.

"But, to prove Jesus Christ we have the prophecies which are good and valid proofs. And those prophecies, being fulfilled, and truly proved by the event, indicate the certainty of these truths, and therefore the truth of the divinity of Jesus Christ. In Him, and by Him, then, we know God. Otherwise, and without Scripture, without original sin, without a necessary Mediator, we can not absolutely prove God, nor teach a good doctrine and sound morals." *Blaise Pascal*

2:8 "The neglect of prayer is a grand hindrance to holiness." *John Wesley*

QUESTIONS & OBJECTIONS

2:14 ***"God made me like this. Sin is His fault!"***

If this won't work in a civil court, it certainly won't work on Judgment Day. Even with an expert defense lawyer, it would take a pretty inept judge to fall for the old "God made me do it" defense. We are responsible moral agents. The "buck" stopped at Adam. He tried to blame both God and Eve for his sin; Eve blamed the serpent. It is human nature to try, but it doesn't work with God.

13 For Adam was first formed, then Eve.
14 And Adam was not deceived, but the woman being deceived was in the transgression.
15 Notwithstanding she shall be saved in childbearing, if they continue in faith and charity and holiness with sobriety.

CHAPTER 3

THIS is a true saying, If a man desire the office of a bishop, he desires a good work.
2 A bishop then must be blameless, the husband of one wife, vigilant, sober, of good behavior, given to hospitality, able to teach;
3 Not given to wine, no striker, not greedy of filthy lucre; but patient, not a brawler, not covetous;
4 One that rules well his own house, having his children in subjection with all gravity;
5 (For if a man know not how to rule his own house, how shall he take care of the church of God?)
6 Not a novice, lest being lifted up with pride he fall into the condemnation of the devil.
7 Moreover he must have a good report of them which are without; lest he fall into reproach and the snare of the devil.
8 Likewise must the deacons be grave, not double-tongued, not given to much wine, not greedy of filthy lucre;
9 Holding the mystery of the faith in a pure conscience.
10 And let these also first be proved; then let them use the office of a deacon, being found blameless.
11 Even so must their wives be grave, not slanderers, sober, faithful in all things.
12 Let the deacons be the husbands of one wife, ruling their children and their own houses well.
13 For they that have used the office of a deacon well purchase to themselves a good degree, and great boldness in the faith which is in Christ Jesus.
14 These things write I to you, hoping to come to you shortly:
15 But if I tarry long, that you may know how you ought to behave yourself in the house of God, which is the church of the living God, the pillar and ground of the truth.
16 And without controversy great is the

2:14 Why God created the serpent and allowed him to tempt Eve is a great mystery. However, those who would be quick to accuse God of wrongdoing would be wise to lay a hand on their mouth. We don't have to question His integrity because we know that all of His judgments are true and altogether righteous (Psalm 19:9). See also 2 Corinthians 11:3 comment.

3:9 "Without God there is no virtue because there is no prompting of the conscience...without God there is a coarsening of the society; without God democracy will not and cannot long endure...If we ever forget that we are One Nation Under God, then we will be a nation gone under." *Ronald Reagan*

3:16 **Was Jesus God in human form?** See Hebrews 1:1–3.

3:16 *Jehovah's Witnesses: Witnessing Tips*

By David A. Reed, Ex-Jehovah's Witness elder

Encounters between Christians and Jehovah's Witnesses typically revolve around a discussion of deity. The reason for this is twofold. First, this is the area where Watchtower theology deviates most dramatically from orthodox Christianity. In contrast to the Trinitarian concept of one God in three Persons—Father, Son, and Holy Spirit—the JWs have been taught to believe that God the Father alone is "Jehovah," the only true God; that Jesus Christ is Michael the archangel, the first angelic being created by God; and that the Holy Spirit is neither God nor a person, but rather God's impersonal "active force." Second, the subject of deity is a frequent confrontational focus because *both* Jehovah's Witnesses and Christians (at least those who like to witness to JWs) feel confident and well-prepared to defend their stand and attack the opposing viewpoint.

Due to the profound theological differences, such discussions often take the form of spiritual trench warfare—a long series of arguments and counterarguments, getting nowhere and ending in mutual frustration. But this need not be the case, especially if the Christian will "become all things to all men" by taking a moment to put himself in the Witness's shoes, so to speak (see 1 Corinthians 9:22). In the JW's mind he himself is a worshiper of the true God of the Bible, while you are a lost soul who has been misled by the devil into worshiping a pagan three-headed deity. He is, no doubt, quite sincere in these beliefs and feels both threatened and offended by the doctrine of the Trinity. To give any serious consideration to your arguments in support of the Trinity is simply unthinkable to the JW; he would be sinning against Jehovah God to entertain such a thought.

So, in order to make any headway with the Witness, it is necessary to bridge the gap—to find common ground that will enable him to rethink his theology. Rather than plunging into a defense of "the doctrine of the Trinity," which can be mind-boggling even to a Christian, take things one step at a time.

A good first step would be to consider the question, "Is Jesus Christ really an angel?" It will be frightening to the Jehovah's Witness to open this cherished belief of his to critical reexamination, but not nearly as frightening as to start off discussing evidence that God is triune.

Since the Watchtower Society speaks of "Jesus Christ, whom we understand from the Scriptures to be Michael the archangel" (*The Watchtower,* February 15, 1979, p. 31), put the JW on the spot and ask him to show you "the Scriptures" that say Jesus is Michael. There are none. The Watchtower Society *New World Translation* (NWT) mentions Michael five times as: 1) "one of the foremost princes" (Dan. 10:13); 2) "the prince of [Daniel's] people" (Dan. 10:21); 3) "the great prince who is standing in behalf of the sons of [Daniel's] people" (Dan. 12:1); 4) "the archangel" who "had a difference with the devil and was disputing about Moses' body" but "did not dare to bring a judgment against him in abusive terms" (Jude 9); and 5) a participant in heavenly conflict when "Michael and his angels battled with the dragon" (Rev. 12:7).

Ask the Jehovah's Witness which one of these verses says that Michael is Jesus Christ. Help him to see that it is necessary to read Scripture *plus* a complicated Watchtower argument to reach that conclusion. Rather than being merely "*one of* the foremost princes," Jesus Christ is "Lord of lords and King of kings" (Rev. 17:14, NWT) and is "far above every government and authority and power and lordship and every name named, not only in this system of things, but also in that to come" (Ephesians 1:21, NWT). And, unlike "Michael who did not dare condemn the Devil with insulting words, but said, 'The Lord rebuke you!'" (Jude 9, *Today's English Version*), Jesus Christ displayed His authority over the devil when He freely commanded him, "Go away, Satan!" (Matthew 4:10, NWT).

In arguing that Jesus is Michael the archangel, the Watchtower Society also points to another verse that does not use the name Michael but says that "the Lord himself will descend from heaven with a commanding call, with an archangel's voice and with God's trumpet..." (1 Thessalonians 4:16, NWT).

(continued on next page)

(3:16 continued)
However, the expression "with an archangel's voice" simply means that the archangel, like God's trumpet, will herald the coming of the Lord, not that the Lord is an archangel.

Point out to the JW that none of the verses he has attempted to use as proof-texts even comes close to stating that Jesus Christ is Michael the archangel. In fact, Scripture clearly teaches the opposite: namely, that the Son of God is *superior* to the angels. The entire first chapter of Hebrews is devoted to this theme. Have the Witness read Hebrews chapter one aloud with you, and, as you do so, interrupt to point out the sharp contrast between angels and the Son of God. "For to what angel did God ever say, 'Thou are my Son...?' And again, when he brings the first-born into the world, he says, 'Let all God's angels worship him'" (vv. 5,6, *Revised Standard Version*).

Remind the JW that angels consistently refuse worship ("Be careful! Do not do that! ...Worship God," Revelation 22:8,9, NWT), but the Father's command concerning the Son is, "Let all God's angels worship him" (Hebrews 1:6). That is how the Watchtower's own *New World Translation* read for some 20 years until, in 1970, the Society changed it to read "do obeisance to him" instead of "worship him"—part of their consistent campaign to eliminate from their Bible all references to the deity of Christ. (See John 10:36 comment.)

True, you have not yet proved the "doctrine of the Trinity" in this discussion. But you have laid a good foundation by giving the Jehovah's Witness convincing evidence that Jesus Christ is not an angel (he is now faced with the question of who Jesus really is), and you have shown that the Watchtower Society has misled him, even resorting to altering Scripture to do so. Now you are in a much better position to go on to present the gospel.

mystery of godliness: God was manifest in the flesh, justified in the Spirit, seen of angels, preached to the Gentiles, believed on in the world, received up into glory.

CHAPTER 4

NOW the Spirit speaks expressly, that in the latter times some shall depart from the faith, giving heed to seducing spirits, and doctrines of devils;
2 Speaking lies in hypocrisy; having their conscience seared with a hot iron;
3 Forbidding to marry, and commanding to abstain from meats, which God has created to be received with thanksgiving of them which believe and know

4:1 For more signs of the end times, see 2 Timothy 3:1.

4:1 Halloween. The celebration can be traced back to the Druid festival of the dead. The Roman Pantheon, built by Emperor Hadrian in A.D. 100 as a temple to the goddess Cybele and other Roman gods, became the principle place of worship. In 609, Emperor Phocas seized Rome and gave the Pantheon to Pope Boniface IV. Boniface consecrated it to the Virgin Mary and kept using the temple to pray for the dead, only now it was "Christianized," as men added the unscriptural teaching of purgatory. In 834, Gregory IV extended the feast for all the church and it became known as All Saint's Day, still remembering the dead.

Samhain, a Druid god of the dead, was honored at Hallowe'en ("All Hallows Eve") in Britain, Germany, France, and the Celtic countries. Samhain called together all wicked souls who died within the past year and who were destined to inhabit animals. The Druids believed that souls of the dead came back to their homes to be entertained by those still living. Suitable food and shelter were provided for these spirits or else they would cast spells, steal infants, destroy crops, kill farm animals, and create terror as they haunted the living. This is the action that "Trick-or-Treat" copies today. The Samhain celebration used nuts, apples, skeletons, witches, and black cats. Divination and auguries were practiced as well as magic to seek answers for the future. Even today witchcraft practitioners declare October 31 as the most favorable time to practice their arts.

Many Christians use Halloween as an opportunity to reach out to the lost by giving candy and gospel tracts to those who knock on their door during Halloween. *What other day do scores of people come to your door for gospel tracts?*

Questions & Objections

4:2 "I don't feel guilty."

People often don't feel guilty when they sin because they have "seared" their conscience. They have removed the batteries from the smoke detector of their conscience, so that they can sin without interruption. The way to resurrect a deadened conscience is to go through each of the Ten Commandments, reminding the person that they know that it's wrong to lie, steal, commit adultery, etc. Always preach the Law along with future punishment, then pray that the Holy Spirit will come upon them and cause them to be convicted of sin, righteousness, and judgment to come.

the truth.
4 For every creature of God is good,
and nothing to be refused, if it be received with thanksgiving:
5 For it is sanctified by the word of God
and prayer.
6 If you put the brethren in remembrance of these things, you shall be a
good minister of Jesus Christ, nourished
up in the words of faith and of good
doctrine, whereunto you have attained.
7 But refuse profane and old wives' fables, and exercise yourself rather to godliness.
8 For bodily exercise profits little: but
godliness is profitable to all things, having promise of the life that now is, and
of that which is to come.
9 This is a faithful saying and worthy of
all acceptation.
10 For therefore we both labor and suffer reproach, because we trust in the living God, who is the Savior of all men,
specially of those that believe.
11 These things command and teach.
12 Let no man despise your youth; but
be an example of the believers, in word,
in conversation, in charity, in spirit, in
faith, in purity.
13 Till I come, give attendance to reading, to exhortation, to doctrine.

The Function of the Law

4:2 "When once God the Holy Spirit applies the Law to the conscience, secret sins are dragged to light, little sins are magnified to their true size, and things apparently harmless become exceedingly sinful. Before that dread searcher of the hearts and trier of the reins makes His entrance into the soul, it appears righteous, just, lovely, and holy; but when He reveals the hidden evils, the scene is changed. Offenses which were once styled peccadilloes, trifles, freaks of youth, follies, indulgences, little slips, etc., then appear in their true color, as breaches of the Law of God, deserving condign punishment." *Charles Spurgeon*

"The proper effect of the Law is to lead us out of our tents and tabernacles, that is to say, from the quietness and security wherein we dwell, and from trusting in ourselves, and to bring us before the presence of God, to reveal his wrath to us, and to set us before our sins." *Martin Luther*

4:3,4 Vegetarianism. One of the signs of the end of this age is that people would try to impose a vegetarian lifestyle on others, but the Scriptures tell us that *every* creature of God is good for food, and *nothing* is to be refused.

Vegetarianism is not always the blessing it is made out to be. In India in 1942, three million people died of starvation. Alongside the bodies of men, women, and children lay the carcasses of hundreds of thousands of "sacred" cows—potential beef-steaks. They were God-given protein that would have saved the lives of multitudes. See Psalm 66:15 and Revelation 22:3 comments.

14 Neglect not the gift that is in you, which was given you by prophecy, with the laying on of the hands of the presbytery.
15 Meditate upon these things; give yourself wholly to them; that your profiting may appear to all.
16 Take heed to yourself, and to the doctrine; continue in them: for in doing this you shall both save yourself, and them that hear you.

CHAPTER 5

REBUKE not an elder, but entreat him as a father; and the younger men as brethren;
2 The elder women as mothers; the younger as sisters, with all purity.
3 Honor widows that are widows indeed.
4 But if any widow have children or nephews, let them learn first to show piety at home, and to requite their parents: for that is good and acceptable before God.
5 Now she that is a widow indeed, and desolate, trusts in God, and continues in supplications and prayers night and day.
6 But she that lives in pleasure is dead while she lives.
7 And these things give in charge, that they may be blameless.
8 But if any provide not for his own, and specially for those of his own house, he has denied the faith, and is worse than an infidel.
9 Let not a widow be taken into the number under threescore years old, having been the wife of one man,
10 Well reported of for good works; if she have brought up children, if she have lodged strangers, if she have washed the saints' feet, if she have relieved the afflicted, if she have diligently followed every good work.
11 But the younger widows refuse: for when they have begun to wax wanton against Christ, they will marry;
12 Having damnation, because they have cast off their first faith.
13 And withal they learn to be idle, wandering about from house to house; and not only idle, but tattlers also and busybodies, speaking things which they ought not.

> Try after sermons to talk to strangers. The preacher may have missed the mark, but you need not miss it. Or the preacher may have struck the mark, and you can help to make the impression deeper by a kind word.
>
> **CHARLES SPURGEON**

14 I will therefore that the younger women marry, bear children, guide the house, give none occasion to the adversary to speak reproachfully.
15 For some are already turned aside after Satan.
16 If any man or woman that believes have widows, let them relieve them, and let not the church be charged; that it may relieve them that are widows indeed.
17 Let the elders that rule well be counted worthy of double honor, especially they who labor in the word and doctrine.
18 For the scripture says, You shall not muzzle the ox that treads out the corn.

4:7 The way to prevent injuries and pain is to keep yourself fit. Exercise. After warning Timothy to refuse false doctrine, Paul told him to exercise himself to godliness. Paul kept fit through exercise. He said, "Herein do I exercise myself, to have always a conscience void of offense toward God, and toward men" (Acts 24:16). Do the same. Listen to the voice of conscience. It's your friend, not your enemy.

5:5 "I have no confidence at all in polished speech or brilliant literary effort to bring about a revival, but I have all the confidence in the world in the poor saint who would weep her eyes out because people are living in sin." *Charles Spurgeon*

QUESTIONS & OBJECTIONS

Q 6:1

"Isn't it blasphemous to call the Bible 'God's Word' when it makes Him look so bad?"

I am going to tell you some things about my father that will make him look bad. He regularly left my mother to fend for herself. I was once horrified to hear that he deliberately killed a helpless animal. Not only that, but he hit me (often).

Here's the information that's missing: The reason he left my mom during the day was to work to earn money to take care of her and their children. He killed the animal because it had been run over by a car and was suffering. He regularly chastened me because he loved me enough to teach me right from wrong (I was a brat).

Portions of the Bible that "make God look bad" merely reveal that we lack understanding. I never once questioned my dad's integrity, because I trusted him (see Mark 10:15).

And, The laborer is worthy of his reward.
19 Against an elder receive not an accusation, but before two or three witnesses.
20 Them that sin rebuke before all, that
others also may fear.
21 I charge you before God, and the
Lord Jesus Christ, and the elect angels,
that you observe these things without
preferring one before another, doing nothing by partiality.
22 Lay hands suddenly on no man, neither be partaker of other men's sins: keep
yourself pure.
23 Drink no longer water, but use a little wine for your stomach's sake and your
often infirmities.
24 Some men's sins are open beforehand,
going before to judgment; and some men
they follow after.
25 Likewise also the good works of some
are manifest beforehand; and they that are
otherwise cannot be hid.

. . . . . .

For how to address the sinner's conscience, see John 4:7 comment.

. . . . . .

CHAPTER 6

LET as many servants as are under the
yoke count their own masters worthy of all honor, that the name of God
and his doctrine be not blasphemed.
2 And they that have believing masters,
let them not despise them, because they
are brethren; but rather do them service,
because they are faithful and beloved,
partakers of the benefit. These things teach
and exhort.
3 If any man teach otherwise, and consent not to wholesome words, even the
words of our Lord Jesus Christ, and to
the doctrine which is according to godliness;
4 He is proud, knowing nothing, but
doting about questions and strifes of
words, whereof comes envy, strife, rail-
ings, evil surmisings,
5 Perverse disputings of men of corrupt
minds, and destitute of the truth, supposing that gain is godliness: from such
withdraw yourself.
6 But godliness with contentment is
great gain.
7 For we brought nothing into this world,
and it is certain we can carry nothing out.
8 And having food and raiment let us
be therewith content.
9 But they that will be rich fall into
temptation and a snare, and into many
foolish and hurtful lusts, which drown
men in destruction and perdition.
10 For the love of money is the root of
all evil: which while some coveted after,
they have erred from the faith, and pierced
themselves through with many sorrows.
11 But you, O man of God, flee these
things; and follow after righteousness,
godliness, faith, love, patience, meekness.

Questions & Objections

6:20 "Didn't the Church persecute Galileo?"

Skeptics often try to demean Scripture by saying that the Christian Church persecuted Galileo when he maintained that the earth circled the sun. As a professor of astronomy at the University of Pisa, Galileo was required to teach the accepted theory of his time that the sun and all the planets revolved around the Earth. Later at the University of Padua he was exposed to a new theory, proposed by Nicolaus Copernicus, that the Earth and all the other planets revolved around the sun. Galileo's observations with his new telescope convinced him of the truth of Copernicus's sun-centered or heliocentric theory. Galileo's support for the heliocentric theory got him into trouble with the *Roman Catholic church*. In 1633 during the Inquisition he was convicted of heresy and ordered to recant (publicly withdraw) his support of Copernicus. The Roman Catholic church sentenced him to life imprisonment, but because of his advanced age allowed him to serve his term under house arrest at his villa outside of Florence, Italy. The Christian Church therefore should not be blamed for his imprisonment. It was the Roman Catholic church that persecuted Galileo.

"Under the sentence of imprisonment Galileo remained till his death in 1642. It is, however, untrue to speak of him as in any proper sense a 'prisoner.' As his Protestant biographer, von Gebler, tells us, 'One glance at the truest historical source for the famous trial would convince anyone that Galileo spent altogether twenty-two days in the buildings of the Holy Office [during the Inquisition], and even then not in a prison cell with barred windows, but in the handsome and commodious apartment of an official of the Inquisition.'" *(Catholic Encyclopedia)*

12 *Fight the good fight of faith, lay hold on eternal life, whereunto you are also called, and have professed a good profession before many witnesses.*
13 I give you charge in the sight of God, who quickens all things, and before Christ Jesus, who before Pontius Pilate witnessed a good confession;
14 That you keep this commandment without spot, unrebukeable, until the appearing of our Lord Jesus Christ:
15 Which in his times he shall show, who is the blessed and only Potentate, the King of kings, and Lord of lords;
16 Who only has immortality, dwelling in the light which no man can approach unto; whom no man has seen, nor can see: to whom be honor and power everlasting. Amen.
17 Charge them that are rich in this world, that they be not high-minded, nor trust in uncertain riches, but in the living God, who gives us richly all things to enjoy;
18 That they do good, that they be rich in good works, ready to distribute, willing to communicate;
19 Laying up in store for themselves a good foundation against the time to come, that they may lay hold on eternal life.
20 O Timothy, keep that which is committed to your trust, avoiding profane and vain babblings, and oppositions of science falsely so called:
21 Which some professing have erred concerning the faith. Grace be with you. Amen.

6:18 "Do all the good you can, by all the means you can, in all the places you can, at all the times you can, to all the people you can, as long as you ever can." *John Wesley*

2 Timothy

CHAPTER 1

PAUL, an apostle of Jesus Christ by
the will of God, according to the
promise of life which is in Christ Jesus,
2 To Timothy, my dearly beloved son:
Grace, mercy, and peace, from God the
Father and Christ Jesus our Lord.
3 I thank God, whom I serve from my
forefathers with pure conscience, that
without ceasing I have remembrance of
you in my prayers night and day;
4 Greatly desiring to see you, being
mindful of your tears, that I may be filled
with joy;
5 When I call to remembrance the unfeigned faith that is in you, which dwelt
first in your grandmother Lois, and your
mother Eunice; and I am persuaded that
in you also.
6 Wherefore I put you in remembrance
that you stir up the gift of God, which is
in you by the putting on of my hands.
7 *For God has not given us the spirit of
fear; but of power, and of love, and of a
sound mind.*
8 *Be not therefore ashamed of the testimony of our Lord, nor of me his prisoner: but
you be a partaker of the afflictions of the
gospel according to the power of God;*
9 *Who has saved us, and called us with
an holy calling, not according to our works,
but according to his own purpose and grace,
which was given us in Christ Jesus before
the world began,*
10 *But is now made manifest by the appearing of our Savior Jesus Christ, who has
abolished death, and has brought life and
immortality to light through the gospel:*
11 *Whereunto I am appointed a preacher, and an apostle, and a teacher of the
Gentiles.*
12 For the which cause I also suffer these
things: nevertheless I am not ashamed:
for I know whom I have believed, and
am persuaded that he is able to keep that
which I have committed to him against
that day.
13 Hold fast the form of sound words,
which you have heard of me, in faith
and love which is in Christ Jesus.
14 That good thing which was committed to you keep by the Holy Spirit which
dwells in us.
15 This you know, that all they which
are in Asia be turned away from me; of
whom are Phygellus and Hermogenes.
16 The Lord give mercy to the house of
Onesiphorus; for he oft refreshed me, and

1:8,9 "We want the power of God to be manifested, but sometimes we fail to seek purity on our part." Anonymous testimony (quoted in *The Transforming Power of Fasting and Prayer* by *Bill Bright*)

1:10 "Surely God would not have created such a being as man, with an ability to grasp the infinite, to exist only for a day. No, no, man was made for immortality." *Abraham Lincoln*

was not ashamed of my chain:
17 But, when he was in Rome, he sought
me out very diligently, and found me.
18 The Lord grant to him that he may
find mercy of the Lord in that day: and
in how many things he ministered to me
at Ephesus, you know very well.

CHAPTER 2

YOU therefore, my son, be strong in
the grace that is in Christ Jesus.
2 And the things that you have heard of
me among many witnesses, the same
commit to faithful men, who shall be
able to teach others also.
3 You therefore endure hardness, as a
good soldier of Jesus Christ.
4 No man that wars entangles himself
with the affairs of this life; that he may
please him who has chosen him to be a
soldier.
5 And if a man also strive for masteries,
yet is he not crowned, except he strive
lawfully.
6 The husbandman that labors must be
first partaker of the fruits.
7 Consider what I say; and the Lord
give you understanding in all things.
8 Remember that Jesus Christ of the
seed of David was raised from the dead
according to my gospel:
9 Wherein I suffer trouble, as an evil
doer, even to bonds; but the word of God
is not bound.
10 Therefore I endure all things for the
elect's sakes, that they may also obtain
the salvation which is in Christ Jesus
with eternal glory.
11 It is a faithful saying: For if we be
dead with him, we shall also live with
him:
12 **If we suffer, we shall also reign
with him: if we deny him, he also will
deny us:**
13 **If we believe not, yet he abides
faithful: he cannot deny himself.**
14 Of these things put them in remembrance, charging them before the Lord
that they strive not about words to no
profit, but to the subverting of the hearers.
15 Study to show yourself approved to
God, a workman that needs not to be
ashamed, rightly dividing the word of
truth.
16 But shun profane and vain babblings:
for they will increase to more ungodliness.
17 And their word will eat as does a
canker: of whom is Hymenaeus and Phi-
letus;
18 Who concerning the truth have erred,
saying that the resurrection is past already; and overthrow the faith of some.
19 Nevertheless the foundation of God
stands sure, having this seal, The Lord
knows them that are his. And, Let every
one that names the name of Christ depart from iniquity.
20 But in a great house there are not

2:3 "A barracks is meant to be a place where real soldiers were to be fed and equipped for war, not a place to settle down in or as a comfortable snuggery in which to enjoy ourselves. I hope that if ever they, our soldiers, do settle down God will burn their barracks over their heads!" *Catherine Booth*

2:19 True and false converts. False converts lack genuine contrition for sin. They make a profession of faith but are deficient in biblical repentance—"They profess that they know God; but in works they deny him, being abominable, and disobedient, and to every good work reprobate" (Titus 1:16). A true convert, however, has a knowledge of sin and has godly sorrow, truly repents, and produces the "things that accompany salvation" (Hebrews 6:9). This is evident by the fruit of the Spirit, the fruit of righteousness, etc. However, only God truly knows the genuine from the false.

"Our churches are full of the nicest, kindest people who have never known the despair of guilt or the breathless wonder of forgiveness." *P. T. Forsyth*

QUESTIONS & OBJECTIONS

2:19 ***"The church is full of hypocrites."***

Hypocrites may show up at a church building every Sunday, but there are no hypocrites in the Church (Christ's body). *Hypocrite* comes from the Greek word for "actor," or pretender. Hypocrisy is "the practice of professing beliefs, feelings, or virtues that one does not hold." The Church is made up of true believers; hypocrites are "pretenders" who sit among God's people. God knows those who love Him, and the Bible warns that He will sort out the true converts from the false on the Day of Judgment. All hypocrites will end up in hell (Matthew 24:51).

only vessels of gold and of silver, but
also of wood and of earth; and some to
honor, and some to dishonor.
21 If a man therefore purge himself
from these, he shall be a vessel to honor,
sanctified, and meet for the master's use,
and prepared to every good work.
22 Flee also youthful lusts: but follow
righteousness, faith, charity, peace, with
them that call on the Lord out of a pure
heart.
23 But foolish and unlearned questions
avoid, knowing that they do gender strifes.
24 And the servant of the Lord must
not strive; but be gentle to all men, able
to teach, patient,
25 In meekness instructing those that
oppose themselves; if God peradventure
will give them repentance to the acknowledging of the truth;
26 And that they may recover themselves out of the snare of the devil, who
are taken captive by him at his will.

CHAPTER 3

**This know also, that in the last days
perilous times shall come.**
2 **For men shall be lovers of their own
selves, covetous, boasters, proud, blasphemers, disobedient to parents, unthankful, unholy,**
3 **Without natural affection, trucebreakers, false accusers, incontinent,
fierce, despisers of those that are good,**
4 **Traitors, heady, high-minded, lovers
of pleasures more than lovers of God;**
**5 Having a form of godliness, but denying the power thereof: from such turn
away.**
6 For of this sort are they which creep
into houses, and lead captive silly women laden with sins, led away with divers lusts,
7 Ever learning, and never able to come
to the knowledge of the truth.
8 Now as Jannes and Jambres withstood
Moses, so do these also resist the truth:

2:21 "When you are willing, God will call you. When you are prepared, God will empower you. When you are empowered, God will test you. When you are tested, God will strengthen you. When you are strengthened, God will use you, and when you are used, God will reward you." *Ross Rhodes*

"Clay is molded into a vessel, but the ultimate use of the vessel depends on the part where nothing exists. Doors and windows are cut out of the wall of a house, but the ultimate use of the house depends on the parts where nothing exists. I wish to become such a useful nothing." *Richard Wurmbrand*

2:24 This is the spirit in which we should share our faith. It has been well said, "Never argue with a fool. Someone watching might not be able to tell the difference." As we witness, we must be kind and gentle to those who oppose us. It is not our job to convince them with brilliant arguments, but simply to share the truth, so that God may bring them to repentance. See 2 Timothy 4:2.

POINTS FOR OPEN-AIR PREACHING

2:24–26

"Watch It, Blind Man!"

There is one passage in Scripture to which I point for all those who want to witness or preach in the open-air. It is 2 Timothy 2:24–26. Memorize it. Scripture tells us that sinners are blind. They *cannot* see. What would you think if I were to stomp up to a blind man who had just stumbled, and say, "Watch where you're going, blind man!"? Such an attitude is completely unreasonable. The man *cannot* see.

The same applies to the lost—spiritual sight is beyond their ability. Look at the words used in Scripture: "Except a man be born again, he *cannot see* the kingdom of God . . . The god of this world has *blinded* the minds of them which believe not . . . But the natural man receives not the things of the Spirit of God: for they are foolishness to him: neither *can* he know them . . . Having the understanding *darkened* . . . because of the *blindness* of their heart . . . Ever learning, and *never able* to come to the knowledge of the truth."

With these thoughts in mind, read 2 Timothy 2:24–26 again and look at the adjectives used by Paul to describe the attitude we are to have with sinners: "must not strive . . . be gentle . . . patient . . . in meekness." Just as it is unreasonable to be impatient with a blind man, so it is with the sinner. See Matthew 5:10–12 comment.

men of corrupt minds, reprobate concerning the faith.
9 But they shall proceed no further: for their folly shall be manifest to all men, as theirs also was.
10 But you have fully known my doctrine, manner of life, purpose, faith, longsuffering, charity, patience,
11 Persecutions, afflictions, which came to me at Antioch, at Iconium, at Lystra;

2:26 Warning sinners of judgment. Jeremiah warned King Zedekiah repeatedly that God would judge His people. The prophet pleaded with the king, but still he would not do what Jeremiah said. One cannot but wonder what the king thought about after he was blinded and bound with chains (Jeremiah 39:6–8). Perhaps his thoughts were of the last thing he saw—the unspeakable agony of seeing his own beloved sons butchered before his eyes. Perhaps the words of Jeremiah flashed before his tormented mind, warning him that all of Israel (including his sons) could have been saved if he had obeyed the voice of the Lord. We can't begin to imagine the remorse he felt.

How this must typify the ungodly who have been bound by the bronze fetters of sin, "taken captive by [the devil] at his will." We warn that there is judgment coming (both temporal and eternal) to those who live for the devil, but most remain in unbelief. Their master is he who came "to steal, and to kill, and to destroy" (John 10:10). He blinds the minds of those who don't believe. Like Zedekiah, so many see their own sons and daughters die before their very eyes. AIDS and other sin-related diseases, as well as alcohol, drugs, and suicide, kill many before their time. Multitudes give themselves to the burning fires of sexual lust, and so the devil breaks down the walls of entire nations.

Yet, there is still time to warn them. There is still time to pray that God will open their understanding. God told Jeremiah to tell an Ethiopian named Ebedmelech that He would deliver him from judgment. He said, "For I will surely deliver you, and you shall not fall by the sword, but your life shall be for a prey to you: because you have put your trust in me, says the Lord" (Jeremiah 39:18). This is the message we are to deliver. He who keeps his life will lose it, but those who trust in the Lord will be safe on the Day of Judgment. On that Day, the sword of the Word of God will not fall upon him, because it fell on the Savior two thousand years ago.

3:1 For more signs of the end times, see 2 Peter 3:3.

3:5 "The chief danger of the 20th century will be religion without the Holy Spirit, Christianity without Christ, forgiveness without repentance, salvation without regeneration, politics without God, and heaven without hell." *General William Booth*

what persecutions I endured: but out of
them all the Lord delivered me.
12 Yes, and all that will live godly in
Christ Jesus shall suffer persecution.
13 But evil men and seducers shall wax
worse and worse, deceiving, and being
deceived.
14 But continue in the things which you
have learned and have been assured of,
knowing of whom you have learned
them;
15 And that from a child you have
known the holy scriptures, which are able
to make you wise to salvation through
faith which is in Christ Jesus.
16 All scripture is given by inspiration
of God, and is profitable for doctrine, for
reproof, for correction, for instruction in
righteousness:
17 That the man of God may be perfect,
thoroughly furnished to all good works.

CHAPTER 4

I CHARGE you therefore before God,
and the Lord Jesus Christ, who shall
judge the quick and the dead at his appearing and his kingdom;
2 *Preach the word; be instant in season,*
out of season; reprove, rebuke, exhort with
all longsuffering and doctrine.
3 For the time will come when they will
not endure sound doctrine; but after their
own lusts shall they heap to themselves
teachers, having itching ears;
4 And they shall turn away their ears
from the truth, and shall be turned to fa-

"The New Testament is the very best book that ever was or ever will be known in the world."

Charles Dickens

3:16 The Bible's Inspiration. "The authors, speaking under the inspiration of the Holy Spirit, ...wrote on hundreds of controversial subjects with absolute harmony from the beginning to the end. There is one unfolding story from Genesis to Revelation: the redemption of mankind through the Messiah—the Old Testament through the coming Messiah, the New Testament from the Messiah that has come. In Genesis, you have paradise lost, in Revelation you have paradise gained. You can't understand Revelation without understanding Genesis. It's all interwoven on hundreds of controversial subjects.

"Now here's the picture: 1,600 years, 60 generations, 40-plus authors, different walks of life, different places, different times, different moods, different continents, three languages, writing on hundreds of controversial subjects and yet when they are brought together, there is absolute harmony from beginning to end...There is no other book in history to even compare to the uniqueness of this continuity." *Josh McDowell*

"We account the Scriptures of God to be the most sublime philosophy. I find more sure marks of authenticity in the Bible than in any profane history whatsoever." *Sir Isaac Newton*

"The Bible is endorsed by the ages. Our civilization is built upon its words. In no other Book is there such a collection of inspired wisdom, reality, and hope." *Dwight D. Eisenhower*

3:16,17 What better "good work" can there be than to use the Law of God to bring sinners to repentance? For the biblical way to witness, see John 4:7–26 comment.

4:1 Judgment Day: For verses that warn of its reality, see Hebrews 9:27.

4:2 This is the spirit in which we should share our faith. See Titus 3:2,3.

bles.
5 *But watch in all things, endure afflictions, do the work of an evangelist, make full proof of your ministry.*
6 For I am now ready to be offered, and the time of my departure is at hand.
7 I have fought a good fight, I have finished my course, I have kept the faith:
8 Henceforth there is laid up for me a crown of righteousness, which the Lord, the righteous judge, shall give me at that day: and not to me only, but to all them also that love his appearing.
9 Do your diligence to come shortly to me:
10 For Demas has forsaken me, having loved this present world, and is departed to Thessalonica; Crescens to Galatia, Titus to Dalmatia.
11 Only Luke is with me. Take Mark, and bring him with you: for he is profitable to me for the ministry.
12 And Tychicus have I sent to Ephesus.
13 The cloak that I left at Troas with Carpus, when you come, bring with you, and the books, but especially the parchments.
14 Alexander the coppersmith did me much evil: the Lord reward him according to his works:
15 Of whom be ware also; for he has greatly withstood our words.
16 At my first answer no man stood with me, but all men forsook me: I pray God that it may not be laid to their charge.
17 Notwithstanding the Lord stood with me, and strengthened me; that by me the preaching might be fully known, and that all the Gentiles might hear: and I was delivered out of the mouth of the lion.

For how to use gospel tracts, see 1 Corinthians 9:22 comment.

18 And the Lord shall deliver me from every evil work, and will preserve me to his heavenly kingdom: to whom be glory for ever and ever. Amen.
19 Salute Prisca and Aquila, and the household of Onesiphorus.
20 Erastus abode at Corinth: but Trophimus have I left at Miletum sick.
21 Do your diligence to come before winter. Eubulus greets you, and Pudens, and Linus, and Claudia, and all the brethren.
22 The Lord Jesus Christ be with your spirit. Grace be with you. Amen.

4:2 When it comes to seeking and saving the lost, it's always "hunting" season. We should be ready to preach the gospel to everyone we meet.

"We want in the church of Christ a band of well-trained sharpshooters, who will pick the people out individually and be always on the watch for all who come into the place, not annoying them, but making sure that they do not go away without having had a personal warning, invitation, and exhortation to come to Christ." *Charles Spurgeon*

4:3,4 "Scratching people where they itch and addressing their 'felt needs' is a stratagem of the poor steward of the oracles of God. This was the recipe for success for the false prophets of the Old Testament." *R. C. Sproul*

Titus

CHAPTER 1

PAUL, a servant of God, and an apostle of Jesus Christ, according to the
faith of God's elect, and the acknowledging of the truth which is after godliness;
2 *In hope of eternal life, which God, that
cannot lie, promised before the world began;*
3 *But has in due times manifested his word
through preaching, which is committed to
me according to the commandment of God
our Savior;*
4 To Titus, mine own son after the common faith: Grace, mercy, and peace, from
God the Father and the Lord Jesus Christ
our Savior.
5 For this cause left I you in Crete, that
you should set in order the things that
are wanting, and ordain elders in every
city, as I had appointed you:
6 If any be blameless, the husband of
one wife, having faithful children not accused of riot or unruly.
7 For a bishop must be blameless, as
the steward of God; not self-willed, not
soon angry, not given to wine, no striker, not given to filthy lucre;
8 But a lover of hospitality, a lover of
good men, sober, just, holy, temperate;
9 *Holding fast the faithful word as he has
been taught, that he may be able by sound
doctrine both to exhort and to convince the
gainsayers.*
10 For there are many unruly and vain
talkers and deceivers, specially they of
the circumcision:
11 Whose mouths must be stopped,
who subvert whole houses, teaching things
which they ought not, for filthy lucre's
sake.
12 One of themselves, even a prophet
of their own, said, The Cretians are always liars, evil beasts, slow bellies.
13 This witness is true. Wherefore rebuke them sharply, that they may be
sound in the faith;
14 Not giving heed to Jewish fables, and
commandments of men, that turn from
the truth.
15 To the pure all things are pure: but
to them that are defiled and unbelieving
is nothing pure; but even their mind and
conscience is defiled.
16 They profess that they know God;
but in works they deny him, being abom-

1:1 The world cries out for truth. They have no idea of their origin, why they exist, or what death holds in store for them. Sin has left them lost and in darkness. The truth will set them free (John 8:31,32), but there can be no understanding of the truth without repentance and faith. It comes *after* godliness.

1:9 The steward of God is not to see himself as being above the lowly task of evangelism.

1:11 The way to "stop the mouth" is to use the Law of God. See Romans 3:19 comment.

1:15 Those who defile the conscience remove the battery from their own smoke detector.

inable, and disobedient, and to every good work reprobate.

. . . . . .

For alleged mistakes in the Bible, see Mark 15:26 comment.

. . . . . .

CHAPTER 2

BUT speak the things which become sound doctrine:

2 That the aged men be sober, grave, temperate, sound in faith, in charity, in patience.

3 The aged women likewise, that they be in behavior as becomes holiness, not false accusers, not given to much wine, teachers of good things;

4 That they may teach the young women to be sober, to love their husbands, to love their children,

5 To be discreet, chaste, keepers at home, good, obedient to their own husbands, that the word of God be not blasphemed.

6 Young men likewise exhort to be sober minded.

7 In all things showing yourself a pattern of good works: in doctrine showing uncorruptness, gravity, sincerity,

8 Sound speech, that cannot be condemned; that he that is of the contrary part may be ashamed, having no evil thing to say of you.

9 Exhort servants to be obedient to their own masters, and to please them well in all things; not answering again;

10 Not purloining, but showing all good fidelity; that they may adorn the doctrine of God our Savior in all things.

11 For the grace of God that brings salvation has appeared to all men,

12 Teaching us that, denying ungodliness and worldly lusts, we should live soberly, righteously, and godly, in this present world;

13 Looking for that blessed hope, and the glorious appearing of the great God and our Savior Jesus Christ;

14 Who gave himself for us, that he might redeem us from all iniquity, and purify to himself a peculiar people, zealous of good works.

15 These things speak, and exhort, and rebuke with all authority. Let no man despise you.

CHAPTER 3

PUT them in mind to be subject to principalities and powers, to obey magistrates, to be ready to every good work,

2 To speak evil of no man, to be no brawlers, but gentle, showing all meekness to all men.

3 For we ourselves also were sometimes foolish, disobedient, deceived, serving divers lusts and pleasures, living in mal-

---

1:16 There are many who profess to know God, but they lack the things that accompany salvation—the fruit of righteousness, holiness, repentance, good works, and the fruit of the Spirit. We must repent, turn to God, and do works befitting repentance (Acts 26:20).

2:6–8 We must be sober-minded, rich in good works, sound in doctrine, living in the fear of God and without corruption—all for the sake of our testimony.

3:2 This is the spirit in which we should share our faith. See James 3:17.

3:3 This is why we should never have a holier-than-thou attitude toward the unsaved (see also 1 Corinthians 6:9–11).

3:3 The deceitfulness of sin. Two women from Southern California were about to cross the Mexican border to return to the U.S. when they saw what looked like a very small, sick animal in the ditch beside their car. As they examined it in the darkness of the night, they saw that it was a tiny Chihuahua. There they decided to take it home with them and nurse it back to health. However, because they were afraid that they were breaking the law, they put it in the trunk of their car, and drove across the border. Once they were in the U.S., they retrieved the animal and nursed

ice and envy, hateful, and hating one another.
4 But after that the kindness and love of
God our Savior toward man appeared,
**5 Not by works of righteousness which
we have done, but according to his
mercy he saved us, by the washing of
regeneration, and renewing of the Holy
Spirit;**
6 Which he shed on us abundantly
through Jesus Christ our Savior;
7 That being justified by his grace, we
should be made heirs according to the
hope of eternal life.

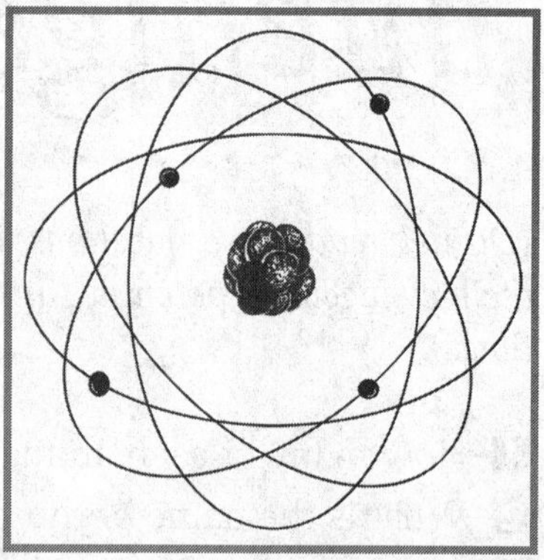

The Bible tells us that God created everything with things that are not seen. See Hebrews 11:3 comment.

> He is no Christian who does not seek to serve his God. The very motto of the Christian should be "I serve."
>
> **CHARLES SPURGEON**

8 This is a faithful saying, and these
things I will that you affirm constantly,
that they which have believed in God
might be careful to maintain good works.
These things are good and profitable to
men.
9 But avoid foolish questions, and genealogies, and contentions, and strivings
about the law; for they are unprofitable
and vain.
10 A man that is an heretic after the
first and second admonition reject;
11 Knowing that he that is such is subverted, and sins, being condemned of
himself.
12 When I shall send Artemas to you,
or Tychicus, be diligent to come to me
to Nicopolis: for I have determined there
to winter.
13 Bring Zenas the lawyer and Apollos
on their journey diligently, that nothing
be wanting to them.
14 And let ours also learn to maintain
good works for necessary uses, that they
be not unfruitful.
15 All that are with me salute you. Greet
them that love us in the faith. Grace be
with you all. Amen.

---

it until they arrived home.

One of the women was so concerned for the ailing dog that she actually took it to bed with her, and reached out several times during the night to touch the tiny animal and reassure it that she was still present.

The dog was so sick the next morning, she decided to take it to the veterinarian. That's when she found out that the animal wasn't a tiny sick dog. It was a Mexican water rat, dying of rabies.

The world, in the blackness of its ignorance, thinks that sin is a puppy to be played with. It is the light of God's Law that enlightens the sinner to the fact that he is in bed with a deadly rat.

We were once "deceived, serving divers lusts and pleasures," but now, if we are truly converted, our eyes have been opened. We see sin for the sugar-coated venom that it is.

3:5 New birth—its necessity for salvation. See 1 Peter 1:3.

3:5 For those trusting in good works, see Galatians 2:16 comment.

3:10 It is wise to avoid those brethren who only want to argue about doctrine. Rather, put your energy into reaching the lost.

Intelligence Tests

(Do not read these questions yourself. If you do, you will fail to see their evangelistic potential. Instead, have someone ask you the questions.)

1. How many of each animal did Moses take into the ark?
2. What is the name of the raised print that deaf people use?
3. Is it possible to end a sentence with the word "the"?
4. Spell the word "shop." What do you do when you come to a green light?
5. It is noon. You look at the clock. The big hand is on three. The little hand is on five. What time is it?
6. Spell the word "silk." What do cows drink?
7. Listen carefully: You are the driver of a train. There are thirty people on board. At the first stop ten people get off. At the next stop five people get on. Now for the question: What is the name of the train driver?

Answers:

1. None. It was Noah.
2. Deaf people don't use raised print.
3. The question is an example of one.
4. Go.
5. Noon.
6. Water.
7. You are the driver of the train.

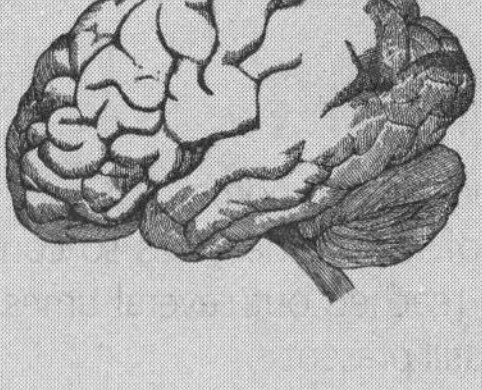

The Bible warns, "He who trusts his own heart is a fool" (Proverbs 28:26). The tests are an excellent way to humble an unsaved person and show him that he can't trust his own judgments. This may be followed with, "If you make a mistake with something as simple as this, could you be wrong in your beliefs about God, Judgment Day, the existence of hell, etc.?"

Philemon

PAUL, a prisoner of Jesus Christ, and
Timothy our brother, to Philemon
our dearly beloved, and fellow-laborer,
2 And to our beloved Apphia, and Archippus our fellow-soldier, and to the
church in your house:
3 Grace to you, and peace, from God
our Father and the Lord Jesus Christ.
4 *I thank my God, making mention of you*
always in my prayers,
5 *Hearing of your love and faith, which you*
have toward the Lord Jesus, and toward all
saints;
6 *That the communication of your faith*
may become effectual by the acknowledg-
ing of every good thing which is in you in
Christ Jesus.
7 For we have great joy and consolation
in your love, because the bowels of the
saints are refreshed by you, brother.
8 Wherefore, though I might be much
bold in Christ to enjoin you that which
is convenient,
9 Yet for love's sake I rather beseech you,
being such an one as Paul the aged, and
now also a prisoner of Jesus Christ.
10 I beseech you for my son Onesimus,
whom I have begotten in my bonds:
11 Which in time past was to you unprofitable, but now profitable to you and
to me:
12 Whom I have sent again: therefore
receive him, that is, mine own bowels:
13 Whom I would have retained with
me, that in your stead he might have
ministered to me in the bonds of the gospel:
14 But without your mind would I do
nothing; that your benefit should not be
as it were of necessity, but willingly.
15 For perhaps he therefore departed
for a season, that you should receive him
for ever;
16 Not now as a servant, but above a
servant, a brother beloved, specially to
me, but how much more to you, both in
the flesh, and in the Lord?
17 If you count me therefore a partner,
receive him as myself.
18 If he has wronged you, or owes you
anything, put that on my account;
19 I Paul have written it with mine own
hand, I will repay it: albeit I do not say
to you how you owe to me even your own

4–6 For the "communication" of our faith to be "effectual" (active, operative, and powerful), we must not confine our love to the Lord Jesus and the saints. Philemon's love went beyond the walls of the church building. He communicated his faith. This is what made Paul prayerfully thankful.

11 Now that the runaway slave was a Christian, upon return to Philemon he would be "profitable." The world gains unspeakable profit from the presence of Christians. People who once were filled with corruption, upon conversion live as law-abiding, useful members of society. Onesimus ("useful") would be a faithful servant for God's kingdom. He would work not only for his earthly master, but also for his heavenly Master, to whom he had submitted himself as a willing slave.

self besides.
20 Yes, brother, let me have joy of you in
the Lord: refresh my bowels in the Lord.
21 Having confidence in your obedience
I wrote to you, knowing that you will also do more than I say.
22 But withal prepare me also a lodging: for I trust that through your prayers
I shall be given to you.
23 There salute you Epaphras, my fellow-
prisoner in Christ Jesus;
24 Marcus, Aristarchus, Demas, Lucas,
my fellow-laborers.
25 The grace of our Lord Jesus Christ be
with your spirit. Amen.

. . . . . .

For untrue things the world says, see 1 Corinthians 3:19 comment.

. . . . . .

"The Bible is the best book in the world. It contains more than all the libraries I have seen."

John Adams

Great Leaders Speak About the Bible

"Here is a Book worth more than all the other books which were ever printed." *Patrick Henry*

"That book, Sir, is the Rock upon which our republic rests." *Andrew Jackson*

"The more profoundly we study this wonderful Book, and the more closely we observe its divine precepts, the better citizens we will become and the higher will be our destiny as a nation." *William McKinley*

"The best religion the world has ever known is the religion of the Bible. It builds up all that is good." *Rutherford B. Hayes*

"There are a good many problems before the American people today, and before me as President, but I expect to find the solution of those problems just in the proportion that I am faithful in the study of the Word of God." *Woodrow Wilson*

"The whole inspiration of our civilization springs from the teachings of Christ and the lessons of the prophets. To read the Bible for these fundamentals is a necessity of American life." *Herbert Hoover*

"I say to you, Search the Scriptures! The Bible is the book of all others, to be read at all ages, and in all conditions of human life; not to be read once or twice or thrice through, and then laid aside, but to be read in small portions of one or two chapters every day, and never to be intermitted, unless by some overruling necessity." *John Quincy Adams*

"We cannot read the history of our rise and development as a nation, without reckoning the place the Bible has occupied in shaping the advances of the Republic." *Franklin D. Roosevelt*

"Within the covers of the Bible are all the answers for all the problems men face. The Bible can touch hearts, order minds and refresh souls." *Ronald Reagan*

"In all my perplexities and distresses, the Bible has never failed to give me light and strength." *Robert E. Lee*

"I have read the Bible through many times, and now make it a practice to read it through once every year. It is a book of all others for lawyers, as well as divines; and I pity the man who cannot find in it a rich supply of thought and of rules for conduct. It fits a man for life —it prepares him for death." *Daniel Webster*

Hebrews

CHAPTER 1

GOD, who at sundry times and in divers manners spoke in time past to the fathers by the prophets,
2 Has in these last days spoken to us by his Son, whom he has appointed heir of all things, by whom also he made the worlds;
3 Who being the brightness of his glory, and the express image of his person, and upholding all things by the word of his power, when he had by himself purged our sins, sat down on the right hand of the Majesty on high;
4 Being made so much better than the angels, as he has by inheritance obtained a more excellent name than they.
5 For to which of the angels said he at any time, You are my Son, this day have I begotten you? And again, I will be to him a Father, and he shall be to me a Son?
6 And again, when he brought in the first begotten into the world, he says, And let all the angels of God worship him.
7 And of the angels he says, Who makes his angels spirits, and his ministers a flame of fire.
8 But to the Son he says, Your throne, O God, is for ever and ever: a sceptre of righteousness is the sceptre of your kingdom.
9 You have loved righteousness, and hated iniquity; therefore God, even your God, has anointed you with the oil of gladness above your fellows.
10 And, You, Lord, in the beginning have laid the foundation of the earth; and the heavens are the works of your hands:
11 They shall perish; but you remain; and

1:1 The Bible's inspiration. The Bible doesn't attempt to defend its inspiration. But here is an interesting thing: Genesis opens with the words "God said" nine times in the first chapter. The statement "Thus says the Lord" appears 23 times in the last Old Testament book, Malachi. So you have "God says" from Genesis to Malachi. "The Lord spoke" appears 560 times in the first five books of the Bible and at least 3,800 times in the whole of the Old Testament! Isaiah claims at least 40 times that his message came directly from the Lord; Ezekiel, 60 times; and Jeremiah, 100 times.

There are about 3,856 verses directly or indirectly concerned with prophecy in Scripture. God's challenge to the world is, "Prove Me now…I the LORD have spoken it: it shall come to pass" (see Malachi 3:10; Ezekiel 24:14). Mormons, Buddhists, and Muslims have their own sacred writings, but the element of proven prophecy is absent in them. The destruction of Tyre, the invasion of Jerusalem, the fall of Babylon and Rome—each event was accurately predicted in the Bible and later fulfilled to the smallest detail. See Matthew 4:4 comment.

"Defend the Bible? I would as soon defend a lion!" *Charles Spurgeon*

1:2,3 "There is a Being who made all things, who holds all things in His power, and is therefore to be feared." *Sir Isaac Newton*

1:11 See Psalm 102:25,26 comment.

they all shall wax old as does a garment;
12 And as a vesture shall you fold them
up, and they shall be changed: but you are
the same, and your years shall not fail.
13 But to which of the angels said he at
any time, Sit on my right hand, until I
make your enemies your footstool?
14 Are they not all ministering spirits,
sent forth to minister for them who shall
be heirs of salvation?

CHAPTER 2

**Therefore we ought to give the more
earnest heed to the things which we
have heard, lest at any time we should
let them slip.**
2 **For if the word spoken by angels was
steadfast, and every transgression and
disobedience received a just recompense of reward;**
3 **How shall we escape, if we neglect
so great salvation; which at the first began to be spoken by the Lord, and was
confirmed to us by them that heard him;**
4 God also bearing them witness, both
with signs and wonders, and with divers
miracles, and gifts of the Holy Spirit, according to his own will?
5 For to the angels has he not put in
subjection the world to come, whereof we
speak.
6 But one in a certain place testified, saying, What is man, that you are mindful
of him? or the son of man, that you visit
him?
7 You made him a little lower than the
angels; you crowned him with glory and
honor, and did set him over the works of
your hands:
8 You have put all things in subjection
under his feet. For in that he put all in
subjection under him, he left nothing that
is not put under him. But now we see
not yet all things put under him.
9 **But we see Jesus, who was made a
little lower than the angels for the suffering of death, crowned with glory and
honor; that he by the grace of God
should taste death for every man.**
10 For it became him, for whom are all
things, and by whom are all things, in
bringing many sons to glory, to make the
captain of their salvation perfect through
sufferings.
11 For both he that sanctifies and they
who are sanctified are all of one: for which
cause he is not ashamed to call them
brethren,
12 Saying, I will declare your name to
my brethren, in the midst of the church
will I sing praise to you.
13 And again, I will put my trust in him.
And again, Behold I and the children
which God has given me.

> No sinner looks to the Savior with a dry eye or a hard heart. Aim, therefore, at heart-breaking, at bringing home condemnation to the conscience and weaning the mind from sin. Be not content till the whole mind is deeply and vitally changed in reference to sin.
>
> **CHARLES SPURGEON**

14 **Forasmuch then as the children are
partakers of flesh and blood, he also
himself likewise took part of the same;
that through death he might destroy
him that had the power of death, that
is, the devil;**
15 **And deliver them who through fear
of death were all their lifetime subject
to bondage.**
16 For verily he took not on him the
nature of angels; but he took on him the
seed of Abraham.
17 Wherefore in all things it behoved
him to be made like to his brethren, that
he might be a merciful and faithful high
priest in things pertaining to God, to

2:6 "Young man, the secret of my success is that at an early age I discovered I was not God."
Oliver Wendell Holmes, Jr.

Springboards for Preaching and Witnessing

The Titanic

2:10

The story of the Titanic has incredibly close parallels to the biblical plan of salvation. Just as the great pleasure ship struck an iceberg and sank, this great world—with all its inhabitants—is slowly sinking into the cold grip of death. As with the Titanic, where only those passengers who believed that they were in impending danger looked to the lifeboats, so only those who believe that they are in mortal danger will look to the Lifeboat of the Savior, Jesus Christ. The great "iceberg" that will take the world to an icy grave is the Moral Law—the Ten Commandments.

Here is the evidence that we are sinking: Jesus said that if we look with lust, we commit adultery in our heart. No one who has had sex outside of marriage, or any liar, or any thief will enter heaven. The Bible says that if we hate someone, we are guilty of murder. We fail to put God first. We make a god in our image. We break all the Commandments. If we stay with the "ship," we will perish on the Day of Judgment, when all of our sins come out as evidence of our guilt. God, however, is rich in mercy and doesn't want anyone to go to hell. He made a way for us to be saved. Jesus Christ, the One whom the Bible calls the "Captain of our salvation," gave His life so that we could have a place in the lifeboat. He took our punishment upon Himself, suffering on the cross for us. We broke God's Law, but He paid our fine. Then He rose from the dead, defeating death. The moment we repent and trust in Him alone for our eternal salvation, God will forgive us and grant us the gift of eternal life.

Don't hesitate. You may wait until it's too late! It was reported that some of the lifeboats that left the Titanic early were only half full. Many more on board could have been saved, but they refused to believe that the great "unsinkable" ship was sinking. They perished because their faith was misguided. Don't be like them. Believe the gospel. Repent and trust Jesus Christ today... and God will never let you down.

make reconciliation for the sins of the people.

18 For in that he himself has suffered being tempted, he is able to succour them that are tempted.

CHAPTER 3

WHEREFORE, holy brethren, partakers of the heavenly calling, consider the Apostle and High Priest of our profession, Christ Jesus;

2 Who was faithful to him that appointed him, as also Moses was faithful in all his house.

3 For this man was counted worthy of more glory than Moses, inasmuch as he who has built the house has more honor than the house.

4 For every house is built by some man; but he that built all things is God.

5 And Moses verily was faithful in all his house, as a servant, for a testimony of those things which were to be spoken after;

6 But Christ as a son over his own house; whose house are we, if we hold fast the confidence and the rejoicing of the hope firm to the end.

7 Wherefore (as the Holy Spirit says, Today if you will hear his voice,

8 Harden not your hearts, as in the provocation, in the day of temptation in the wilderness:

9 When your fathers tempted me, proved me, and saw my works forty years.

10 Wherefore I was grieved with that generation, and said, They do always err in their heart; and they have not known my ways.

11 So I sware in my wrath, They shall not enter into my rest.)

12 Take heed, brethren, lest there be in any of you an evil heart of unbelief, in departing from the living God.

THE FUNCTION OF THE LAW

3:12 "While [every true believer] cries out, 'O what love have I unto thy Law! All the day long is my study in it;' he sees daily, in that divine mirror, more and more of his own sinfulness. He sees more and more clearly that he is fullness a sinner in all things—that neither his heart nor his ways are right before God, and that every moment sends him to Christ.

"Therefore I cannot spare the Law one moment, no more than I can spare Christ, seeing I now want it as much to keep me to Christ, as I ever wanted it to bring me to Him. Otherwise this 'evil heart of unbelief' would immediately 'depart from the living God.' Indeed each is continually sending me to the other—the Law to Christ, and Christ to the Law." *John Wesley*

13 But exhort one another daily, while
it is called Today; lest any of you be
hardened through the deceitfulness of sin.
14 For we are made partakers of Christ,
if we hold the beginning of our confidence steadfast to the end;
15 While it is said, Today if you will
hear his voice, harden not your hearts, as
in the provocation.
16 For some, when they had heard, did
provoke: howbeit not all that came out
of Egypt by Moses.
17 But with whom was he grieved forty
years? was it not with them that had
sinned, whose carcasses fell in the wilderness?
18 And to whom sware he that they
should not enter into his rest, but to them
that believed not?
19 So we see that they could not enter
in because of unbelief.

CHAPTER 4

LET us therefore fear, lest, a promise
being left us of entering into his rest,
any of you should seem to come short of
it.
2 For to us was the gospel preached, as
well as to them: but the word preached
did not profit them, not being mixed with
faith in them that heard it.
3 For we which have believed do enter
into rest, as he said, As I have sworn in
my wrath, if they shall enter into my rest:
although the works were finished from
the foundation of the world.
4 For he spoke in a certain place of the
seventh day on this wise, And God did

4:4 Creation in six days. Most theologians throughout church history agree that in using the phrase "the evening and the morning were the first day," the Scriptures are speaking of a literal 24-hour day, rather than a period of years.

"To understand the meaning of 'day' in Genesis 1, we need to determine how the Hebrew word for 'day,' *yom*, is used in the context of Scripture... A number, and the phrase 'evening and morning,' are used for each of the six days of creation (Genesis 1:5,8,13,19,23,31). Outside Genesis 1, *yom* is used with a number 410 times, and each time it means an ordinary day—why would Genesis 1 be the exception? Outside Genesis 1, *yom* is used with the word 'evening' or 'morning' 23 times. 'Evening' and 'morning' appear in association, but without *yom*, 38 times. All 61 times the text refers to an ordinary day—why would Genesis 1 be the exception? In Genesis 1:5, *yom* occurs in context with the word 'night.' Outside of Genesis 1, 'night' is used with *yom* 53 times—and each time it means an ordinary day. Why would Genesis 1 be the exception? Even the usage of the word 'light' with *yom* in this passage determines the meaning as ordinary day." *Ken Ham*, et al., *The Answers Book* (revised and expanded)

"So far as I know, there is no professor of Hebrew or Old Testament at any world-class university who does not believe that the writer(s) of Genesis 1–11 intended to convey to their readers the idea that (a) creation took place in a series of six days which were the same as the days of 24 hours we now experience; (b) the figures contained in the Genesis genealogies provided by simple addition a chronology from the beginning of the world up to later stages in the biblical story; (c) Noah's Flood was understood to be worldwide and extinguish all human and animal life except for those in the ark." *Dr. James Barr*, professor of Hebrew, Oxford University

rest the seventh day from all his works.
5 And in this place again, If they shall
enter into my rest.
6 Seeing therefore it remains that some
must enter therein, and they to whom it
was first preached entered not in because of unbelief:
7 Again, he limits a certain day, saying
in David, Today, after so long a time; as
it is said, **Today if you will hear his
voice, harden not your hearts.**
8 For if Jesus had given them rest, then
would he not afterward have spoken of
another day.
9 There remains therefore a rest to the
people of God.
10 For he that is entered into his rest,
he also has ceased from his own works,
as God did from his.
11 Let us labor therefore to enter into
that rest, lest any man fall after the same
example of unbelief.
12 For the word of God is quick, and
powerful, and sharper than any two-
edged sword, piercing even to the dividing asunder of soul and spirit, and of the
joints and marrow, and is a discerner of
the thoughts and intents of the heart.
13 **Neither is there any creature that is
not manifest in his sight: but all things
are naked and opened to the eyes of him
with whom we have to do.**
14 Seeing then that we have a great high
priest, that is passed into the heavens,
Jesus the Son of God, let us hold fast our
profession.
15 For we have not an high priest which
cannot be touched with the feeling of our
infirmities; but was in all points tempted
like as we are, yet without sin.
16 Let us therefore come boldly to the
throne of grace, that we may obtain mercy, and find grace to help in time of need.

THE FUNCTION OF THE LAW

4:12 "It is the ordinary method of the Spirit of God to convict sinners by the Law. It is this which, being set home on the conscience, generally breaketh the rocks in pieces. It is more especially this part of the Word of God which is quick and powerful, full of life and energy and sharper than any two-edged sword." *John Wesley*

"The Law cuts into the core of the evil, it reveals the seat of the malady, and informs us that the leprosy lies deep within." *Charles Spurgeon*

CHAPTER 5

FOR every high priest taken from
among men is ordained for men in

4:4 The creation days. Some of the early church fathers believed that God created everything in only one day, or in an instant. To counter this teaching, *Martin Luther* wrote: "When Moses writes that God created Heaven and Earth and whatever is in them in six days, then let this period continue to have been six days, and do not venture to devise any comment according to which six days were one day. But, if you cannot understand how this could have been done in six days, then grant the Holy Spirit the honor of being more learned than you are. For you are to deal with Scripture in such a way that you bear in mind that God Himself says what is written. But since God is speaking, it is not fitting for you to wantonly turn His Word in the direction you wish it to go."

4:7 Isaiah 55:6 exhorts the lost to "seek the Lord while He may be found, call upon Him while He is near." God's offer of grace will end, so sinners are commanded to seek the Lord "while He may be found." They must then "call" upon Him. An intellectual belief in His existence is not saving faith. Romans 10:13 says "whoever *calls* upon the name of the Lord shall be saved."

4:12 Soldier of Christ, throw away your sheath, it is not part of your armor. Strap the two-edged sword firmly in your hand. The way to keep the sword on hand is to have it in your mouth. In Jeremiah 1:7–9, God told the prophet not to be afraid to speak. God then put His words in the mouth of Jeremiah, and in chapter 5 we are given a report of his transformation: "Thus says the Lord God of hosts, Because you speak this word, behold, I will make my words in your mouth fire, and this people wood, and it shall devour them" (v. 14).

things pertaining to God, that he may offer both gifts and sacrifices for sins:
2 Who can have compassion on the ignorant, and on them that are out of the way; for that he himself also is compassed with infirmity.
3 And by reason hereof he ought, as for the people, so also for himself, to offer for sins.
4 And no man takes this honor to himself, but he that is called of God, as was Aaron.
5 So also Christ glorified not himself to be made an high priest; but he that said to him, You are my Son, today have I begotten you.
6 As he said also in another place, You are a priest for ever after the order of Melchisedec.
7 Who in the days of his flesh, when he had offered up prayers and supplications with strong crying and tears to him that was able to save him from death, and was heard in that he feared;
8 Though he were a Son, yet learned he obedience by the things which he suffered;
9 And being made perfect, he became the author of eternal salvation to all them that obey him;
10 Called of God an high priest after the order of Melchisedec.
11 Of whom we have many things to say, and hard to be uttered, seeing you are dull of hearing.
12 For when for the time you ought to be teachers, you have need that one teach you again which be the first principles of the oracles of God; and are become such as have need of milk, and not of strong meat.
13 For every one that uses milk is unskilful in the word of righteousness: for he is a babe.
14 But strong meat belongs to them that are of full age, even those who by reason of use have their senses exercised to discern both good and evil.

CHAPTER 6

THEREFORE leaving the principles of the doctrine of Christ, let us go on to perfection; not laying again the foundation of repentance from dead works, and of faith toward God,
2 Of the doctrine of baptisms, and of laying on of hands, and of resurrection of the dead, and of eternal judgment.
3 And this will we do, if God permit.
4 For it is impossible for those who were once enlightened, and have tasted of the heavenly gift, and were made partakers of the Holy Spirit,
5 And have tasted the good word of God,

4:15 Some believe that because Scripture says Jesus was "in all points tempted like as we are" that He must have struggled with temptations to lie, steal, sin sexually, etc. But Scripture explains that all the attractions of this world fit into three categories: the lust of the flesh, the lust of the eyes, and the pride of life (1 John 2:16). Jesus was tempted by the devil in these three areas and, as the "second Adam," He successfully passed the tests. These are the same tests that the first Adam underwent and failed (Genesis 3:6). Adam and Eve saw that the tree was good for food ("lust of the flesh"; compare Luke 4:3,4), was pleasant to the eyes ("lust of the eyes"; compare Luke 4:5–8), and was desirable to make one wise ("pride of life"; compare Luke 4:9–12). We will "pass the test" and not succumb to these temptations by following Jesus' example. He quoted the truths of the Word of God, using the sword of the Spirit to vanquish the lies of the enemy.

4:16 If you have a zeal for the lost, you will be a target for the enemy of your soul. He wants you to be beset by sin. His devious obsession is for iniquity to defile your conscience, and therefore take away your confidence before God. God forbid that we should allow that to happen. May each of us be so saturated in prayer and in the grace of God that we can boldly come before His throne with our head held high in faith and effectively stand in the gap for a dark and sinful world.

5:9 "I don't believe in any religion apart from doing the will of God." *Catherine Booth*

PRINCIPLES OF GROWTH FOR THE NEW AND GROWING CHRISTIAN

6:18 *Faith—Elevators Can Let You Down*

I have heard people say, "I just find it hard to have faith in God," not realizing the implications of their words. These are the same people who often accept the daily weather forecast, believe the newspapers, and trust their lives to a pilot they have never seen whenever they board a plane. We exercise faith every day. We rely on our car's brakes. We trust history books, medical journals, and elevators. Yet elevators can let us down. History books can be wrong. Planes can crash. How much more then should we trust the sure and true promises of Almighty God. He will never let us down...if we trust Him.

Cynics often argue, "You can't trust the Bible—it's full of mistakes." It is. The first mistake was when man rejected God, and the Scriptures show men and women making the same tragic mistake again and again. It's also full of what *seem to be* contradictions. For example, the Scriptures tell us "with God nothing shall be impossible" (Luke 1:37); there is nothing Almighty God can't do. Yet we are also told that it is "impossible for God to lie" (Hebrews 6:18). So there is something God cannot do! Isn't that an obvious "mistake" in the Bible? No, it isn't.

Lying, deception, bearing false witness, etc., is so repulsive to God, so disgusting to Him, so against His holy character, that the Scriptures draw on the strength of the word "impossible" to substantiate the claim. He cannot, could not, and would not lie.

That means that in a world where we are continually let down, we can totally rely on, trust in, and count on His promises. They are sure, certain, indisputable, true, trustworthy, reliable, faithful, unfailing, dependable, steadfast, and an anchor for the soul. In other words, you can truly believe them, and because of that, you can throw yourself blindfolded and without reserve, into His mighty hands. He will *never, ever* let you down. Do you believe that?

For the next principle of growth, see 1 Peter 2:2 comment.

and the powers of the world to come,
6 If they shall fall away, to renew them
again to repentance; seeing they crucify
to themselves the Son of God afresh, and
put him to an open shame.
7 For the earth which drinks in the rain
that comes oft upon it, and brings forth
herbs meet for them by whom it is
dressed, receives blessing from God:
8 But that which bears thorns and briers
is rejected, and is near to cursing; whose
end is to be burned.
9 But, beloved, we are persuaded better
things of you, and things that accompany
salvation, though we thus speak.
10 For God is not unrighteous to forget
your work and labor of love, which you
have showed toward his name, in that
you have ministered to the saints, and do
minister.
11 And we desire that every one of you
do show the same diligence to the full assurance of hope to the end:
12 That you be not slothful, but followers of them who through faith and patience inherit the promises.
13 For when God made promise to
Abraham, because he could swear by no
greater, he sware by himself,
14 Saying, Surely blessing I will bless
you, and multiplying I will multiply you.
15 And so, after he had patiently endured, he obtained the promise.
16 For men verily swear by the greater:
and an oath for confirmation is to them
an end of all strife.
17 Wherein God, willing more abundantly to show to the heirs of promise
the immutability of his counsel, confirmed
it by an oath:
18 That by two immutable things, in
which it was impossible for God to lie,
we might have a strong consolation, who
have fled for refuge to lay hold upon the
hope set before us:
19 Which hope we have as an anchor

of the soul, both sure and steadfast, and
which enters into that within the veil;
20 Whither the forerunner is for us entered, even Jesus, made an high priest for
ever after the order of Melchisedec.

. . . . . .

Check out "The Rush."
See James 4:15 comment.

. . . . . .

CHAPTER 7

FOR this Melchisedec, king of Salem,
priest of the most high God, who
met Abraham returning from the slaughter of the kings, and blessed him;
2 To whom also Abraham gave a tenth
part of all; first being by interpretation
King of righteousness, and after that also
King of Salem, which is, King of peace;
3 Without father, without mother, without descent, having neither beginning of
days, nor end of life; but made like to the
Son of God; abides as a priest continually.
4 Now consider how great this man was,
to whom even the patriarch Abraham gave
the tenth of the spoils.
5 And verily they that are of the sons of
Levi, who receive the office of the priesthood, have a commandment to take tithes
of the people according to the law, that
is, of their brethren, though they come
out of the loins of Abraham:
6 But he whose descent is not counted
from them received tithes of Abraham,
and blessed him that had the promises.
7 And without all contradiction the less
is blessed of the better.
8 And here men that die receive tithes;
but there he receives them, of whom it is
witnessed that he lives.
9 And as I may so say, Levi also, who
receives tithes, paid tithes in Abraham.
10 For he was yet in the loins of his father, when Melchisedec met him.
11 If therefore perfection were by the
Levitical priesthood, (for under it the
people received the law,) what further
need was there that another priest should
rise after the order of Melchisedec, and
not be called after the order of Aaron?
12 For the priesthood being changed,
there is made of necessity a change also
of the law.
13 For he of whom these things are
spoken pertains to another tribe, of which
no man gave attendance at the altar.
14 For it is evident that our Lord sprang
out of Judah; of which tribe Moses spoke
nothing concerning priesthood.
15 And it is yet far more evident: for
that after the similitude of Melchisedec
there arose another priest,
16 Who is made, not after the law of a
carnal commandment, but after the power
of an endless life.
17 For he testifies, You are a priest for
ever after the order of Melchisedec.
18 For there is verily a disannulling of
the commandment going before for the
weakness and unprofitableness thereof.
19 For the law made nothing perfect,
but the bringing in of a better hope did;
by the which we draw near to God.

> To be a soul winner is the happiest thing in this world. And with every soul you bring to Jesus Christ, you seem to get a new heaven here upon earth.
>
> **CHARLES SPURGEON**

20 And inasmuch as not without an
oath he was made priest:
21 (For those priests were made without an oath; but this with an oath by him
that said to him, The Lord sware and will
not repent, You are a priest for ever after
the order of Melchisedec:)
22 By so much was Jesus made a surety
of a better testament.
23 And they truly were many priests,
because they were not suffered to continue by reason of death:
24 But this man, because he continues
ever, has an unchangeable priesthood.
25 Wherefore he is able also to save
them to the uttermost that come to God
by him, seeing he ever lives to make in-

SPRINGBOARDS FOR PREACHING AND WITNESSING

8:6

Solid Ice

There once was a man who was traveling on foot through a snowstorm in a strange country. He had to get to a certain town by nightfall and was somewhat perturbed when he came to an ice-covered river. *How thick was the ice?* Could he trust it to hold him? He began crawling on the ice on his stomach, inch-by-inch, tapping with his fingers. Sweat poured from his forehead. He was filled with the fear that at any moment he could plunge to an icy death.

An hour later, he had progressed only about 40 feet. He suddenly stopped crawling. He could hear singing! He turned his head to see a horse and cart, laden with people. The driver was singing at the top of his voice as he drove his cart across the ice. The driver knew that lake was solid ice and his faith was such that he had total confidence, with not an ounce of fear. Such are the solid promises of God.

tercession for them.
26 For such an high priest became us,
who is holy, harmless, undefiled, separate from sinners, and made higher than
the heavens;
27 Who needs not daily, as those high
priests, to offer up sacrifice, first for his
own sins, and then for the people's: for
this he did once, when he offered up
himself.
28 For the law makes men high priests
which have infirmity; but the word of
the oath, which was since the law, makes
the Son, who is consecrated for evermore.

CHAPTER 8

NOW of the things which we have
spoken this is the sum: We have
such an high priest, who is set on the
right hand of the throne of the Majesty
in the heavens;
2 A minister of the sanctuary, and of the
true tabernacle, which the Lord pitched,
and not man.
3 For every high priest is ordained to
offer gifts and sacrifices: wherefore it is
of necessity that this man have somewhat
also to offer.
4 For if he were on earth, he should not
be a priest, seeing that there are priests
that offer gifts according to the law:
5 Who serve to the example and shadow of heavenly things, as Moses was admonished of God when he was about to
make the tabernacle: for, See, said he,
that you make all things according to the
pattern showed to you in the mount.
6 But now has he obtained a more excellent ministry, by how much also he is
the mediator of a better covenant, which

8:5 Following the God-given pattern. When God spoke to Moses about the tabernacle, He told him to do all things according to the pattern. He didn't say, "Do the best you can"—it had to be 100% accurate, according to the instructions God had given him. How much more then should we follow the pattern God has given us for bringing men and women into the knowledge of eternal salvation? Our failure to use the Law lawfully, as a "schoolmaster" to bring sinners to Christ (Galatians 3:24), has resulted in the ruin of millions of souls—something which will not be fully realized until Judgment Day.

The pattern of evangelistic endeavor is made plain in the Book of Romans. To obtain God's blessing, we must never deviate from the biblical paradigm set so clearly before us in the inspired words of the apostle Paul. *Winston Churchill* noted that the nose of the bulldog is slanted backward so he can continue to breathe without letting go. Get your teeth into the importance of using the Law of God to bring the knowledge of sin, and don't let it go for any reason. Let it be said of you, "The Law of his God is in his heart; none of his steps shall slide" (Psalm 37:31). See 2 Corinthians 2:17 comment.

was established upon better promises.
7 For if that first covenant had been
faultless, then should no place have been
sought for the second.
8 For finding fault with them, he says,
Behold, the days come, says the Lord,
when I will make a new covenant with
the house of Israel and with the house of
Judah:
9 Not according to the covenant that I
made with their fathers in the day when
I took them by the hand to lead them
out of the land of Egypt; because they
continued not in my covenant, and I regarded them not, says the Lord.
10 For this is the covenant that I will
make with the house of Israel after
those days, says the Lord; I will put my
laws into their mind, and write them
in their hearts: and I will be to them a
God, and they shall be to me a people:
11 **And they shall not teach every man**
his neighbour, and every man his broth-
er, saying, Know the Lord: for all shall
know me, from the least to the greatest.
12 **For I will be merciful to their un-**
righteousness, and their sins and their
iniquities will I remember no more.
13 In that he says, A new covenant, he
has made the first old. Now that which
decays and waxes old is ready to vanish
away.

CHAPTER 9

THEN verily the first covenant had
also ordinances of divine service, and
a worldly sanctuary.
2 For there was a tabernacle made; the
first, wherein was the candlestick, and
the table, and the showbread; which is
called the sanctuary.
3 And after the second veil, the tabernacle which is called the Holiest of all;

"O Lord, Almighty and everlasting God, by Thy holy Word Thou hast created the heaven, and the earth, and the sea; blessed and glorified be Thy name, and praised be Thy majesty, which hath deigned to use us, Thy humble servants, that Thy holy name may be proclaimed in this second part of the earth."

Christopher Columbus

4 Which had the golden censer, and the
ark of the covenant overlaid round about
with gold, wherein was the golden pot that
had manna, and Aaron's rod that budded,
and the tables of the covenant;
5 And over it the cherubims of glory
shadowing the mercyseat; of which we
cannot now speak particularly.
6 Now when these things were thus ordained, the priests went always into the
first tabernacle, accomplishing the service of God.
7 But into the second went the high
priest alone once every year, not without
blood, which he offered for himself, and
for the errors of the people:
8 The Holy Spirit thus signifying, that

8:10 God puts His Law into our minds, giving us a new mind—the "mind of Christ" (1 Corinthians 2:16), and renewing us in the "spirit" of our minds. He gives us a "new and living way" (Hebrews 10:20). Now God's ways are our ways and God's thoughts become our thoughts. We are led by the Spirit, walking "in his ways" (Psalm 119:3). This is the miracle of the new birth. We are completely new creatures in Christ (2 Corinthians 5:17).

the way into the holiest of all was not yet
made manifest, while as the first tabernacle was yet standing:
9 Which was a figure for the time then
present, in which were offered both gifts
and sacrifices, that could not make him
that did the service perfect, as pertaining
to the conscience;
10 Which stood only in meats and drinks,
and divers washings, and carnal ordinances, imposed on them until the time
of reformation.
11 But Christ being come an high priest
of good things to come, by a greater and
more perfect tabernacle, not made with
hands, that is to say, not of this building;
12 Neither by the blood of goats and
calves, but by his own blood he entered
in once into the holy place, having obtained eternal redemption for us.
13 For if the blood of bulls and of goats,
and the ashes of an heifer sprinkling the
unclean, sanctifies to the purifying of the
flesh:
14 How much more shall the blood of
Christ, who through the eternal Spirit offered himself without spot to God, purge
your conscience from dead works to
serve the living God?
15 And for this cause he is the mediator
of the new testament, that by means of
death, for the redemption of the transgressions that were under the first testament, they which are called might receive the promise of eternal inheritance.
16 For where a testament is, there must
also of necessity be the death of the testator.
17 For a testament is of force after men
are dead: otherwise it is of no strength at
all while the testator lives.
18 Whereupon neither the first testament was dedicated without blood.

The Function of the Law

9:14 "You understand that the work of the Law is the revealing of sin. Furthermore, when I speak of sin, I include all kinds of sin—external, internal, hypocrisy, unbelief, love of self, and contempt for or ignorance of God—which are certainly the very roots of all human works. In the justification of sinners the first work of God is to reveal our sin; to confound our conscience, make us tremble, terrify us, briefly, to condemn us.

"The beginning of repentance consists of that work of the Law by which the Spirit of God terrifies and confounds consciences… Just as the Christian life must certainly begin with the knowledge of sin, so Christian doctrine must begin with the function of the Law." *Melanchthon*

19 For when Moses had spoken every
precept to all the people according to the
law, he took the blood of calves and of
goats, with water, and scarlet wool, and
hyssop, and sprinkled both the book,
and all the people,
20 Saying, This is the blood of the testament which God has enjoined to you.
21 Moreover he sprinkled with blood
both the tabernacle, and all the vessels of
the ministry.
22 And almost all things are by the law
purged with blood; and without shedding of blood is no remission.
23 It was therefore necessary that the
patterns of things in the heavens should
be purified with these; but the heavenly
things themselves with better sacrifices
than these.
24 For Christ is not entered into the
holy places made with hands, which are
the figures of the true; but into heaven
itself, now to appear in the presence of

9:22 Forgiveness of sin requires the shedding of blood: God was the first person to kill an animal, as recorded in Genesis 3:21. As Adam and Eve sinned and lost their righteousness, God shed the blood of an innocent animal to provide a covering for them. The fig leaves of self-righteousness will not cover a sinner on the Day of Judgment. God alone can provide the covering through the shed blood of the Savior (1 John 1:7–10). See John 3:16,17 and Psalm 51:6 comments.

God for us:
25 Nor yet that he should offer himself
often, as the high priest enters into the
holy place every year with blood of others;
26 For then must he often have suffered
since the foundation of the world: but
now once in the end of the world has he
appeared to put away sin by the sacrifice
of himself.
**27 And as it is appointed to men once
to die, but after this the judgment:**
28 So Christ was once offered to bear
the sins of many; and to them that look
for him shall he appear the second time
without sin to salvation.

CHAPTER 10

FOR the law having a shadow of good things to come, and not the very image of the things, can never with those sacrifices which they offered year by year continually make the comers thereunto perfect.
2 For then would they not have ceased
to be offered? because that the worshippers once purged should have had no
more conscience of sins.
3 But in those sacrifices there is a remembrance again made of sins every year.
4 For it is not possible that the blood of
bulls and of goats should take away sins.
5 Wherefore when he came into the
world, he says, Sacrifice and offering you
would not, but a body have you prepared
me:
6 In burnt offerings and sacrifices for
sin you have had no pleasure.
7 Then said I, Lo, I come (in the volume
of the book it is written of me,) to do
your will, O God.
8 Above when he said, Sacrifice and offering and burnt offerings and offering
for sin you would not, neither had pleasure therein; which are offered by the
law;
9 Then said he, Lo, I come to do your
will, O God. He takes away the first, that
he may establish the second.
10 By the which will we are sanctified
through the offering of the body of Jesus
Christ once for all.
11 And every priest stands daily ministering and offering oftentimes the same
sacrifices, which can never take away sins:
12 But this man, after he had offered
one sacrifice for sins for ever, sat down
on the right hand of God;
13 From henceforth expecting till his
enemies be made his footstool.
14 For by one offering he has perfected
for ever them that are sanctified.
15 Whereof the Holy Spirit also is a
witness to us: for after that he had said
before,
**16 This is the covenant that I will
make with them after those days, said
the Lord, I will put my laws into their
hearts, and in their minds will I write
them;**
17 **And their sins and iniquities will I
remember no more.**

9:27 Judgment Day: For verses that warn of its reality, see 2 Peter 2:4,5,9.

9:27 Reincarnation. This verse shows that there is no such thing as reincarnation. It is merely wishful thinking for guilty sinners. Many of the world's largest religions teach their adherents that if they don't "get it right" in this lifetime, they'll have multiple opportunities in future lives. That people don't need to trust in Jesus before they die is one of Satan's greatest lies. See Psalm 49:15 comment.

9:28 Second coming of Jesus: See Hebrews 10:37.

10:16 This is the promise of the gospel of salvation. The experience of "conversion" is when God puts His Law in the heart of those who repent and trust in the Savior. He causes them to walk in His statutes (Ezekiel 36:26,27), and gives believers the desire to obey the Moral Law. The Christian no longer desires to lie, steal, covet, commit adultery, etc.; he has a new heart with new desires. He is a new creature in Christ (2 Corinthians 5:17). See Psalm 40:8,9 comment.

PRINCIPLES OF GROWTH FOR THE NEW AND GROWING CHRISTIAN

10:25 *Fellowship—Flutter by Butterfly*

Pray about where you should fellowship. Make sure your church home calls sin what it is: sin. Do they believe the promises of God? Are they loving? Does the pastor treat his wife with respect? Is he a man of the Word? Does he have a humble heart and a gentle spirit? Listen closely to his teaching. It should glorify God, magnify Jesus, and edify the believer.

One evidence that you have been truly saved is that you will have a love for other Christians (1 John 3:14). You will want to fellowship with them. The old saying that birds of a feather flock together is true of Christians. You gather together for the breaking of bread (communion), for teaching from the Word, and for fellowship. You share the same inspirations, illuminations, inclinations, temptations, aspirations, motivations, and perspirations—you are working together for the same thing: the furtherance of the kingdom of God on earth. This is why you attend church—not because you have to, but because you want to.

Don't become a "spiritual butterfly." If you are flitting from church to church, how will your pastor know what type of food you are digesting? The Bible says that your shepherd is accountable to God for you (Hebrews 13:17), so make yourself known to your pastor. Pray for him regularly. Pray also for his wife, his family, and the elders. Being a pastor is no easy task. Most people don't realize how long it takes to prepare a fresh sermon each week. They don't appreciate the time spent in prayer and in study of the Word. If the pastor repeats a joke or a story, remember, he's human. So give him a great deal of grace, and double honor. Never murmur about him. If you don't like something he has said, pray about it, then leave the issue with God. If that doesn't satisfy you, leave the church, rather than divide it through murmuring and complaining. God hates those who cause division among the brethren (Proverbs 6:16–19). See Psalm 92:13 comment.

For the next principle of growth, see Ephesians 5:20 comment.

18 Now where remission of these is, there is no more offering for sin.

19 Having therefore, brethren, boldness to enter into the holiest by the blood of Jesus,

20 By a new and living way, which he has consecrated for us, through the veil, that is to say, his flesh;

21 And having an high priest over the house of God;

22 Let us draw near with a true heart in full assurance of faith, having our hearts sprinkled from an evil conscience, and our bodies washed with pure water.

23 Let us hold fast the profession of our faith without wavering; (for he is faithful that promised;)

24 And let us consider one another to provoke to love and to good works:

25 Not forsaking the assembling of ourselves together, as the manner of some is; but exhorting one another: and so much the more, as you see the day approaching.

26 For if we sin wilfully after that we have received the knowledge of the truth, there remains no more sacrifice for sins,

27 But a certain fearful looking for of judgment and fiery indignation, which shall devour the adversaries.

10:22 The sinner's conscience. "O soul! Thou are at war with thy conscience. Thou have tried to quiet it, but it will prick you. Oh, there be some of you to whom conscience is a ghost haunting you by day and night. You know the good, though you choose the evil; you prick your fingers with the thorn of conscience when you try to pluck the rose of sin." *Charles Spurgeon*

10:23 "Never be afraid to trust an unknown future to a known God." *Corrie ten Boom*

QUESTIONS & OBJECTIONS

10:31 *"You are using scare tactics by talking about hell and Judgment Day."*

In the late 1980s, TV commercials in the U.S. asked, "What goes through the mind of a driver who is not wearing a seat belt in a head-on collision?" Then they showed a crash dummy having its head crushed by a steering wheel in a collision, and said, *"The steering wheel!"* Those were scare tactics, but no one complained because they were *legitimate* scare tactics. That's what happens in a head-on collision if you are foolish enough to not put on a seat belt.

To warn of hell is fearful, but it is *absolutely* legitimate, because the Bible says that it is a *fearful* thing for a sinner to fall into the hands of the living God.

28 He that despised Moses' law died without mercy under two or three witnesses:

29 Of how much sorer punishment, do you suppose, shall he be thought worthy, who has trodden under foot the Son of God, and has counted the blood of the covenant, wherewith he was sanctified, an unholy thing, and has done despite to the Spirit of grace?

30 For we know him that has said, Vengeance belongs to me, I will recompense, says the Lord. And again, The Lord shall judge his people.

31 It is a fearful thing to fall into the hands of the living God.

32 But call to remembrance the former days, in which, after you were illuminated, you endured a great fight of afflictions;

33 Partly, whilst you were made a gazingstock both by reproaches and afflictions; and partly, whilst you became companions of them that were so used.

34 For you had compassion of me in my bonds, and took joyfully the spoiling of your goods, knowing in yourselves that you have in heaven a better and an enduring substance.

35 Cast not away therefore your confidence, which has great recompense of reward.

36 For you have need of patience, that, after you have done the will of God, you might receive the promise.

37 For yet a little while, and he that shall come will come, and will not tarry.

38 Now the just shall live by faith: but if any man draw back, my soul shall have no pleasure in him.

39 But we are not of them who draw back to perdition; but of them that believe to the saving of the soul.

CHAPTER 11

NOW faith is the substance of things hoped for, the evidence of things not seen.

2 For by it the elders obtained a good report.

3 Through faith we understand that the worlds were framed by the word of God, so that things which are seen were not made of things which do appear.

4 By faith Abel offered to God a more excellent sacrifice than Cain, by which he obtained witness that he was righteous, God testifying of his gifts: and by it he being dead yet speaks.

5 By faith Enoch was translated that he should not see death; and was not found, because God had translated him: for before his translation he had this testimony, that he pleased God.

6 But without faith it is impossible to please him: for he that comes to God must believe that he is, and that he is a

10:37 Second coming of Jesus: See James 5:8.

11:3 *Scientific Facts in the Bible*

1. Only in recent years has science discovered that everything we see is composed of invisible atoms. Here, Scripture tells us that the "things which are seen were not made of things which do appear."

2. Medical science has only recently discovered that blood-clotting in a newborn reaches its peak on the eighth day, then drops. The Bible consistently says that a baby must be circumcised on the eighth day.

3. At a time when it was believed that the earth sat on a large animal or a giant (1500 B.C.), the Bible spoke of the earth's free float in space: "He . . . hangs the earth upon nothing" (Job 26:7).

4. The prophet Isaiah also tells us that the earth is round: "It is he that sits upon the circle of the earth" (Isaiah 40:22). This is not a reference to a flat disk, as some skeptic maintain, but to a sphere. Secular man discovered this 2,400 years later. At a time when science believed that the earth was flat, is was the Scriptures that inspired Christopher Columbus to sail around the world (see Proverbs 3:6 comment).

5. God told Job in 1500 B.C.: "Can you send lightnings, that they may go, and say to you, Here we are?" (Job 38:35). The Bible here is making what appears to be a scientifically ludicrous statement—that light can be *sent*, and then manifest itself in speech. But did you know that radio waves travel at the speed of light? This is why you can have *instantaneous* wireless communication with someone on the other side of the earth. Science didn't discover this until 1864 when "British scientist James Clerk Maxwell suggested that electricity and light waves were two forms of the same thing" (*Modern Century Illustrated Encyclopedia*).

6. Job 38:19 asks, "Where is the way where light dwells?" Modern man has only recently discovered that light (electromagnetic radiation) has a "way," traveling at 186,000 miles per second.

7. Science has discovered that stars emit radio waves, which are received on earth as a high pitch. God mentioned this in Job 38:7: "When the morning stars sang together . . ."

8. "Most cosmologists (scientists who study the structures and evolution of the universe) agree that the Genesis account of creation, in imagining an initial void, may be uncannily close to the truth" (*Time*, Dec. 1976).

9. Solomon described a "cycle" of air currents two thousand years before scientists "discovered" them. "The wind goes toward the south, and turns about unto the north; it whirls about continually, and the wind returns again according to his circuits" (Ecclesiastes 1:6).

10. Science expresses the universe in five terms: time, space, matter, power, and motion. Genesis 1:1,2 revealed such truths to the Hebrews in 1450 B.C.: "In the beginning [*time*] God created [*power*] the heaven [*space*] and the earth [*matter*] . . . And the Spirit of God moved [*motion*] upon the face of the waters." The first thing God tells man is that He controls of all aspects of the universe.

11. The great biological truth concerning the importance of blood in our body's mechanism has been fully comprehended only in recent years. Up until 120 years ago, sick people were "bled," and many died because of the practice. If you lose your blood, you lose your life. Yet Leviticus 17:11, written 3,000 years ago, declared that blood is the source of life: "For the life of the flesh is in the blood."

12. All things were made by Him (see John 1:3), including dinosaurs. Why then did the dinosaur disappear? The answer may be in Job 40:15–24. In this passage, God speaks about a great creature called "behemoth." Some commentators think this was a hippopotamus. However, the hippo's tail isn't like a large tree, but a small twig. Following are the characteristics of this huge animal: It was the largest of all the creatures God made; was plant-eating (herbivorous); had its strength in its hips and a tail like a large tree. It had very strong bones, lived among the trees, drank massive amounts of water, and was not disturbed by a raging river. He appears impervious to attack because his nose could pierce through snares, but Scripture says, "He that made him can make his sword to approach unto him." In other words, God caused this, the largest of all the

(continued on next page)

(11:3 continued)
creatures He had made, to become extinct.

13. *Encyclopedia Britannica* documents that in 1845, a young doctor in Vienna named Dr. Ignaz Semmelweis was horrified at the terrible death rate of women who gave birth in hospitals. As many as 30 percent died after giving birth. Semmelweis noted that doctors would examine the bodies of patients who died, then, without washing their hands, go straight to the next ward and examine expectant mothers. This was their normal practice, because the presence of microscopic diseases was unknown. Semmelweis insisted that doctors wash their hands before examinations, and the death rate immediately dropped to 2 percent.

Look at the specific instructions God gave His people for when they encounter disease: "And when he that has an issue is cleansed of his issue; then he shall number to himself seven days for his cleansing, and wash his clothes, and bathe his flesh in running water, and shall be clean" (Leviticus 15:13). Until recent years, doctors washed their hands in a bowl of water, leaving invisible germs on their hands. However, the Bible says specifically to wash hands under "running water."

14. Luke 17:34–36 says the Second Coming of Jesus Christ will occur while some are asleep at night and others are working at daytime activities in the field. This is a clear indication of a revolving earth, with day and night at the same time.

15. "During the devastating Black Death of the fourteenth century, patients who were sick or dead were kept in the same rooms as the rest of the family. People often wondered why the disease was affecting so many people at one time. They attributed these epidemics to 'bad air' or 'evil spirits.' However, careful attention to the medical commands of God as revealed in Leviticus would have saved untold millions of lives. Arturo Castiglione wrote about the overwhelming importance of this biblical medical law: 'The laws against leprosy in Leviticus 13 may be regarded as the first model of sanitary legislation' (*A History of Medicine*)." *Grant R. Jeffery, The Signature of God*

With all these truths revealed in Scripture, how could a thinking person deny that the Bible is supernatural in origin? There is no other book in any of the world's religions (Vedas, Bhagavad-Gita, Koran, Book of Mormon, etc.) that contains scientific truth. In fact, they contain statements that are clearly unscientific. *Hank Hanegraaff* said, "Faith in Christ is not some blind leap into a dark chasm, but a faith based on established evidence."

rewarder of them that diligently seek him.
7 By faith Noah, being warned of God of things not seen as yet, moved with fear, prepared an ark to the saving of his house; by the which he condemned the world, and became heir of the righteousness which is by faith.

11:6 The need for faith. The key that unlocks the door of salvation is faith. Without faith, we cannot please God. Try establishing any sort of friendship without faith. Walk up to a woman and introduce yourself. When she tells you her name, say, "I don't believe you." Watch her reaction. When she tells you where she works, say that you don't believe that either. Carry on like that for a while, and before long you may be nursing a black eye. Your lack of faith in her is a strong insinuation that she is a liar.

If she, a mere mortal, feels insulted by your lack of faith in her word, how much more do unbelievers insult Almighty God by refusing to believe His Word. In doing so, they are saying that God isn't worth trusting—that He is a liar and a deceiver. The Bible says, "He that believes not God has made him a liar" (1 John 5:10). It also says, "Take heed, brethren, lest there be in any of you *an evil heart of unbelief*..." (Hebrews 3:12, emphasis added). The command of the Scriptures is, "Have faith in God" (Mark 11:22). If a meaningful human relationship can't be established without faith, what sort of relationship could we expect to have with God, if by our unbelief we continue to call Him a liar?

8 By faith Abraham, when he was called
to go out into a place which he should
after receive for an inheritance, obeyed;
and he went out, not knowing where he
went.
9 By faith he sojourned in the land of
promise, as in a strange country, dwelling in tabernacles with Isaac and Jacob,
the heirs with him of the same promise:
10 For he looked for a city which has
foundations, whose builder and maker is
God.
11 Through faith also Sara herself received strength to conceive seed, and was
delivered of a child when she was past
age, because she judged him faithful who
had promised.
12 Therefore sprang there even of one,
and him as good as dead, so many as the
stars of the sky in multitude, and as the
sand which is by the sea shore innumerable.
13 These all died in faith, not having
received the promises, but having seen
them afar off, and were persuaded of them,
and embraced them, and confessed that
they were strangers and pilgrims on the
earth.
14 For they that say such things declare
plainly that they seek a country.
15 And truly, if they had been mindful
of that country from whence they came
out, they might have had opportunity to
have returned.
16 But now they desire a better country, that is, an heavenly: wherefore God
is not ashamed to be called their God:
for he has prepared for them a city.
17 By faith Abraham, when he was tried,
offered up Isaac: and he that had received
the promises offered up his only begotten son,
18 Of whom it was said, That in Isaac
shall your seed be called:
19 Accounting that God was able to
raise him up, even from the dead; from
whence also he received him in a figure.
20 By faith Isaac blessed Jacob and Esau
concerning things to come.
21 By faith Jacob, when he was dying,
blessed both the sons of Joseph; and
worshipped, leaning upon the top of his
staff.
22 By faith Joseph, when he died, made
mention of the departing of the children
of Israel; and gave commandment concerning his bones.
23 By faith Moses, when he was born,
was hid three months of his parents, because they saw he was a proper child;
and they were not afraid of the king's
commandment.
24 **By faith Moses, when he was come
to years, refused to be called the son of
Pharaoh's daughter;**
**25 Choosing rather to suffer affliction
with the people of God, than to enjoy
the pleasures of sin for a season;**
26 **Esteeming the reproach of Christ
greater riches than the treasures in
Egypt: for he had respect to the recompense of the reward.**
27 By faith he forsook Egypt, not fearing
the wrath of the king: for he endured, as

11:7 The writer of the Book of Hebrews believed the Genesis account of Noah's Flood.

11:11 Scientific facts in the Bible. Genesis 3:15 reveals that a female possesses a "seed" for childbearing. This was not the common knowledge until a few centuries ago. It was widely believed that only the male possessed the "seed of life" and that the woman was nothing more than a "glorified incubator."

11:25 As we witness, we should remember that there *is* pleasure in sin for a season. Contrary to the claims of modern evangelism, the world *can* find happiness without Jesus. The prophet Jeremiah complained to the Lord, "Why does the way of the wicked prosper? Why are those happy who deal so treacherously?" (Jeremiah 12:1). However, this sinful world cannot find *righteousness* without Jesus, and it is righteousness that they will need on the Day of Wrath (Proverbs 11:4). See Revelation 6:15 comment.

QUESTIONS & OBJECTIONS

11:25 *"I'm doing fine. I don't need God."*

Many people feel this way because of the modern gospel message. It says that Jesus will help their marriage, remove their drug problem, fill the emptiness in their heart, give them peace and joy, etc. In doing so, it restricts the gospel's field of influence. If the message of the cross is for people who have bad marriages, are lonely, and have problems, those who are happy won't see their need for the Savior.

In truth, the forgiveness of God in Jesus Christ is for people with bad marriages and people with good marriages. It is for the happy and the sad. It is for people with problems and for those without problems. It is for those who are miserable in their sins, and for those who are enjoying the pleasures of sin for a season. Those who think they are doing fine need to be confronted with a holy Law that they have violated a multitude of times. Then they will see themselves through the eyes of the Judge of the Universe and will flee to the Savior. See also Luke 4:18 comment.

seeing him who is invisible.
28 Through faith he kept the passover, and the sprinkling of blood, lest he that destroyed the firstborn should touch them.
29 By faith they passed through the Red sea as by dry land: which the Egyptians trying to do were drowned.
30 By faith the walls of Jericho fell down, after they were compassed about seven days.
31 By faith the harlot Rahab perished not with them that believed not, when she had received the spies with peace.
32 And what shall I more say? for the time would fail me to tell of Gideon, and of Barak, and of Samson, and of Jephthae; of David also, and Samuel, and of the prophets:
33 Who through faith subdued kingdoms, wrought righteousness, obtained promises, stopped the mouths of lions,
34 Quenched the violence of fire, escaped the edge of the sword, out of weakness were made strong, waxed valiant in fight, turned to flight the armies of the aliens.
35 Women received their dead raised to life again: and others were tortured, not accepting deliverance; that they might obtain a better resurrection:
36 And others had trial of cruel mockings and scourgings, yes, moreover of bonds and imprisonment:

SPRINGBOARDS FOR PREACHING AND WITNESSING

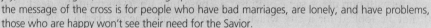

11:29 *The New Convert*

A new convert was reading his Bible when he called out, "Wow! Praise the Lord!" A liberal minister heard him, and asked him what the noise was about. The young Christian replied with great enthusiasm, "This is incredible. It says here that God performed a miracle of deliverance by opening up the Red Sea for the Jews to march through!"

The minister replied, "Owing to tidal patterns around that time of year, the Red Sea was a swamp that was only three-inches deep."

Somewhat subdued, the young man continued reading, but soon exclaimed, "Wow! Praise the Lord!" "What's the matter now?" asked the minister. To which the Christian replied, *"God has just drowned the whole Egyptian army in three inches of water!"*

Over 3,000 times, the Bible speaks of its inspiration by God. His Word is true, and you can believe every word of it.

37 They were stoned, they were sawn
asunder, were tempted, were slain with
the sword: they wandered about in sheep-
skins and goatskins; being destitute, afflicted, tormented;
38 (Of whom the world was not worthy:)
they wandered in deserts, and in mountains, and in dens and caves of the earth.
39 And these all, having obtained a good
report through faith, received not the
promise:
40 God having provided some better
thing for us, that they without us should
not be made perfect.

CHAPTER 12

WHEREFORE seeing we also are
compassed about with so great a
cloud of witnesses, let us lay aside every
weight, and the sin which does so easily
beset us, and let us run with patience the
race that is set before us,
2 Looking to Jesus the author and finisher of our faith; who for the joy that
was set before him endured the cross,
despising the shame, and is set down at
the right hand of the throne of God.
3 For consider him that endured such
contradiction of sinners against himself,
lest you be wearied and faint in your
minds.
4 You have not yet resisted to blood,
striving against sin.
5 And you have forgotten the exhortation which speaks to you as to children,
My son, despise not the chastening of the
Lord, nor faint when you are rebuked of
him:
6 For whom the Lord loves he chastens,
and scourges every son whom he receives.
7 If you endure chastening, God deals
with you as with sons; for what son is he
whom the father chastens not?
8 But if you be without chastisement,
whereof all are partakers, then are you
bastards, and not sons.
9 Furthermore we have had fathers of
our flesh which corrected us, and we gave
them reverence: shall we not much rather
be in subjection to the Father of spirits,
and live?
10 For they verily for a few days chastened us after their own pleasure; but he
for our profit, that we might be partakers
of his holiness.
11 Now no chastening for the present
seems to be joyous, but grievous: nevertheless afterward it yields the peaceable
fruit of righteousness to them which are
exercised thereby.
12 Wherefore lift up the hands which
hang down, and the feeble knees;
13 And make straight paths for your feet,
lest that which is lame be turned out of

12:3 Evangelistic discouragement. "One night when [Dwight L.] Moody was going home, it suddenly occurred to him that he had not spoken to a single person that day about accepting Christ. A day lost, he thought to himself. But as he walked up the street he saw a man by a lamp-post. He promptly walked up to the man and asked, 'Are you a Christian?'

"Nor did Moody find soul-winning easy. In fact, even Christians often criticized him for having 'zeal without knowledge.' Others called him 'Crazy Moody.' Once when he spoke to a perfect stranger about Christ, the man said, 'That is none of your business... If you were not a sort of a preacher I would knock you into the gutter for your impertinence.'

"The next day, a businessman friend sent for Moody. The businessman told Moody that the stranger he had spoken to was a friend of his. 'Moody, you've got zeal without knowledge: you insulted a friend of mine on the street last night. You went up to him, a perfect stranger, and asked him if he were a Christian.'

"Moody went out of his friend's office almost brokenhearted. For some time he worried about this. Then late one night a man pounded on the door of his home. It was the stranger he had supposedly insulted. The stranger said, 'Mr. Moody, I have not had a good night's sleep since that night you spoke to me under the lamppost, and I have come around at this unearthly hour of the night for you to tell me what I have to do to be saved.'" *Harry Albus*

Optical Illusions

Seeing is believing?

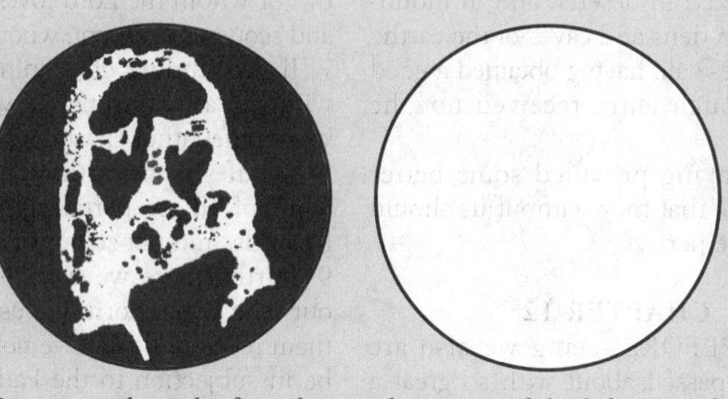

1. Stare intently at the four dots in the center of the left image for 40 seconds. Then stare at the empty circle for 30 seconds.

2. Are there dots between the white boxes?

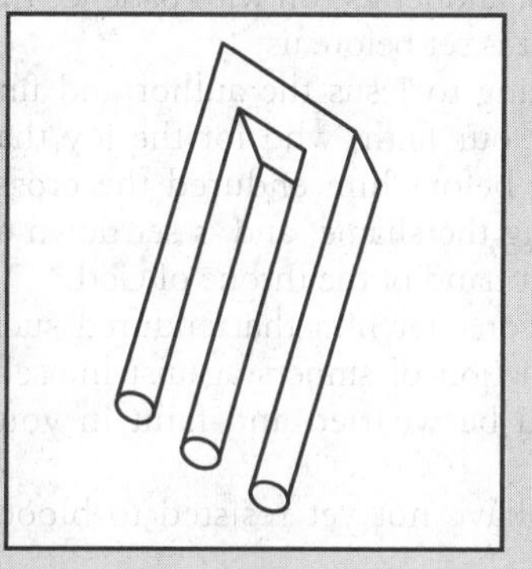

3. How many "prongs" —three or four?

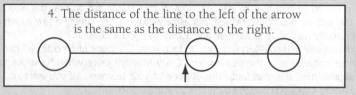

4. The distance of the line to the left of the arrow is the same as the distance to the right.

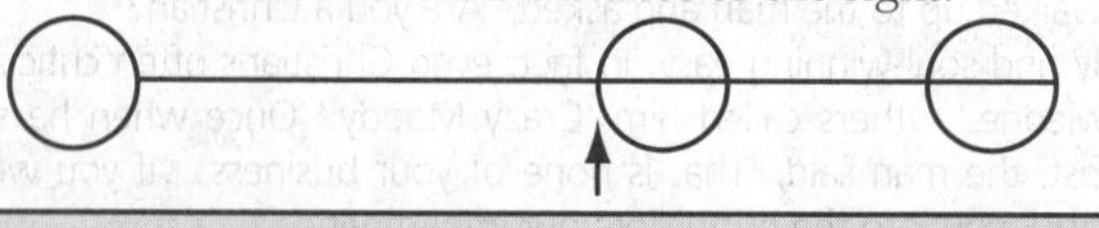

The Atheist Test: Imagine a circle represents all the knowledge in the universe (someone who had all knowledge would know every hair on every head, every thought of every heart, every grain of sand, every event in human history, etc.). Let's surmise that you know an incredible 1 percent of all knowledge. Is it possible that, in the 99 percent of the knowledge you haven't yet come across, there is ample evidence to prove that God does exist?

(See John 20:25 comment.)

the way; but let it rather be healed.
14 Follow peace with all men, and holiness, without which no man shall see the
Lord:
15 Looking diligently lest any man fail
of the grace of God; lest any root of bitterness springing up trouble you, and
thereby many be defiled;
16 Lest there be any fornicator, or profane person, as Esau, who for one morsel
of meat sold his birthright.
17 For you know how that afterward,
when he would have inherited the blessing, he was rejected: for he found no
place of repentance, though he sought it
carefully with tears.
18 For you are not come to the mount
that might be touched, and that burned
with fire, nor to blackness, and darkness,
and tempest,
19 And the sound of a trumpet, and the
voice of words; which voice they that
heard entreated that the word should
not be spoken to them any more:
20 (For they could not endure that which
was commanded, And if so much as a
beast touch the mountain, it shall be
stoned, or thrust through with a dart:
21 And so terrible was the sight, that
Moses said, I exceedingly fear and quake:)
22 But you are come to mount Zion,
and to the city of the living God, the
heavenly Jerusalem, and to an innumerable company of angels,
23 To the general assembly and church
of the firstborn, which are written in
heaven, and to God the Judge of all, and
to the spirits of just men made perfect,
24 And to Jesus the mediator of the
new covenant, and to the blood of sprinkling, that speaks better things than that
of Abel.
25 **See that you refuse not him that
speaks. For if they escaped not who refused him that spoke on earth, much
more shall not we escape, if we turn
away from him that speaks from heaven:**
26 **Whose voice then shook the earth:
but now he has promised, saying, Yet
once more I shake not the earth only,
but also heaven.**
27 And this word, Yet once more, signifies the removing of those things that are
shaken, as of things that are made, that
those things which cannot be shaken
may remain.
28 **Wherefore we receiving a kingdom
which cannot be moved, let us have
grace, whereby we may serve God ac-
ceptably with reverence and godly fear:**
29 For our God is a consuming fire.

For how to convince a sinner of the reasonableness of judgment, see Psalm 55:15 comment.

CHAPTER 13

LET brotherly love continue.
2 Be not forgetful to entertain strangers: for thereby some have entertained
angels unawares.
3 Remember them that are in bonds, as
bound with them; and them which suffer adversity, as being yourselves also in
the body.

12:29 "Our God is a consuming fire, and we try to reduce Him to something we can handle or are comfortable with... We are religious consumers. We want our religion to be convenient. It's the perpetual job of writers, preachers, the church and the gospel to help people respond to God as He reveals Himself." *Eugene Peterson*

4 **Marriage is honorable in all, and the bed undefiled: but whoremongers and adulterers God will judge.**

5 Let your conversation be without covetousness; and be content with such things as you have: for he has said, I will never leave you, nor forsake you.

6 *So that we may boldly say, The Lord is my helper, and I will not fear what man shall do to me.*

7 Remember them which have the rule over you, who have spoken to you the word of God: whose faith follow, considering the end of their conversation.

8 Jesus Christ the same yesterday, and today, and for ever.

9 Be not carried about with divers and strange doctrines. For it is a good thing that the heart be established with grace; not with meats, which have not profited them that have been occupied therein.

10 We have an altar, whereof they have no right to eat which serve the tabernacle.

11 For the bodies of those beasts, whose blood is brought into the sanctuary by the high priest for sin, are burned without the camp.

12 Wherefore Jesus also, that he might sanctify the people with his own blood, suffered without the gate.

13 Let us go forth therefore to him without the camp, bearing his reproach.

14 For here have we no continuing city, but we seek one to come.

15 By him therefore let us offer the sacrifice of praise to God continually, that is, the fruit of our lips giving thanks to his name.

16 But to do good and to communicate forget not: for with such sacrifices God is well pleased.

17 Obey them that have the rule over you, and submit yourselves: for they watch for your souls, as they that must give account, that they may do it with joy, and not with grief: for that is unprofitable for you.

18 Pray for us: for we trust we have a good conscience, in all things willing to live honestly.

19 But I beseech you the rather to do this, that I may be restored to you the sooner.

> Only by imitating the spirit and manner of the Lord Jesus shall we become wise to win souls.
>
> **CHARLES SPURGEON**

20 Now the God of peace, that brought again from the dead our Lord Jesus, that great shepherd of the sheep, through the blood of the everlasting covenant,

21 Make you perfect in every good work to do his will, working in you that which is well-pleasing in his sight, through Jesus Christ; to whom be glory for ever and ever. Amen.

22 And I beseech you, brethren, suffer the word of exhortation: for I have written a letter to you in few words.

23 Know that our brother Timothy is set at liberty; with whom, if he come shortly, I will see you.

24 Salute all them that have the rule over you, and all the saints. They of Italy salute you.

25 Grace be with you all. Amen.

13:8 Jesus has never changed. He has no variableness or shadow of turning (James 1:17). Hebrews 1:12 says of Him, "You are the same, and your years shall not fail."

James

CHAPTER 1

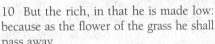

JAMES, a servant of God and of the
Lord Jesus Christ, to the twelve tribes
which are scattered abroad, greeting.
2 My brethren, count it all joy when you
fall into divers temptations;
3 Knowing this, that the trying of your
faith works patience.
4 But let patience have her perfect work,
that you may be perfect and entire, wanting nothing.
5 If any of you lack wisdom, let him ask
of God, that gives to all men liberally, and
upbraides not; and it shall be given him.
6 But let him ask in faith, nothing wavering. For he that wavers is like a wave of
the sea driven with the wind and tossed.
7 For let not that man think that he shall
receive any thing of the Lord.
8 A double minded man is unstable in
all his ways.
9 Let the brother of low degree rejoice
in that he is exalted:
10 But the rich, in that he is made low:
because as the flower of the grass he shall
pass away.
11 For the sun is no sooner risen with a
burning heat, but it withers the grass,
and the flower thereof falls, and the grace
of the fashion of it perishes: so also shall
the rich man fade away in his ways.
12 Blessed is the man that endures temptation: for when he is tried, he shall receive the crown of life, which the Lord has
promised to them that love him.
13 Let no man say when he is tempted,
I am tempted of God: for God cannot be
tempted with evil, neither tempts he any
man:
14 But every man is tempted, when he is
drawn away of his own lust, and enticed.
15 Then when lust has conceived, it
brings forth sin: and sin, when it is finished, brings forth death.
16 Do not err, my beloved brethren.
17 Every good gift and every perfect gift

1:3 Satan tempts us in order to bring out the worst in us; God tests us to bring out the best. (See verse 12.)

1:5 One mark of wisdom is the saving of souls (Proverbs 11:30). With an open-ended promise such as this, we should plead with God for wisdom (see Proverbs 2:1–7). Proverbs 19:8 tells us that he who gets wisdom loves his own soul.

1:15 The ungodly hold firmly onto the lighted stick of dynamite called "sin." They relish its flickering flame. Lust may delight the human heart, but its terrible consequences are sin, death, and hell.

"Human nature rises against restraint: 'I had not known lust except the Law had said, 'Thou shall not covet.' The depravity of man is excited to rebellion by the promulgation of laws. So evil are we, that we conceive at once the desire to commit an act, simply because it is forbidden." *Charles Spurgeon*

THE FUNCTION OF THE LAW

1:25 "God, being a perfect God, had to give a perfect Law, and the Law was given not to save men, but to measure them. I want you to understand this clearly, because I believe hundreds and thousands stumble at this point. They try to save themselves by trying to keep the Law; but it was never meant for men to save themselves by." *D. L. Moody*

is from above, and comes down from the
Father of lights, with whom is no variableness, neither shadow of turning.
18 Of his own will begat he us with the
word of truth, that we should be a kind
of firstfruits of his creatures.
19 **Wherefore, my beloved brethren, let every man be swift to hear, slow to speak, slow to wrath:**
20 **For the wrath of man works not the righteousness of God.**
21 Wherefore lay apart all filthiness and
superfluity of naughtiness, and receive
with meekness the engrafted word, which
is able to save your souls.
22 But be doers of the word, and not
hearers only, deceiving your own selves.
23 For if any be a hearer of the word, and
not a doer, he is like unto a man beholding his natural face in a glass:
24 For he beholds himself, and goes his
way, and straightway forgets what manner of man he was.
25 But whoso looks into the perfect law
of liberty, and continues therein, he being
not a forgetful hearer, but a doer of the
work, this man shall be blessed in his
deed.
26 If any man among you seem to be
religious, and bridles not his tongue, but
deceives his own heart, this man's religion is vain.
27 Pure religion and undefiled before
God and the Father is this, To visit the
fatherless and widows in their affliction,
and to keep himself unspotted from the
world.

CHAPTER 2

MY brethren, have not the faith of
our Lord Jesus Christ, the Lord of
glory, with respect of persons.
2 For if there come to your assembly a
man with a gold ring, in goodly apparel,
and there come in also a poor man in vile
raiment;
3 And you have respect to him that wears
the gay clothing, and say to him, Sit here
in a good place; and say to the poor, Stand
there, or sit here under my footstool:
4 Are you not then partial in yourselves,
and are become judges of evil thoughts?
5 Hearken, my beloved brethren, has not
God chosen the poor of this world rich in
faith, and heirs of the kingdom which he
has promised to them that love him?
6 But you have despised the poor. Do
not rich men oppress you, and draw you
before the judgment seats?
7 Do not they blaspheme that worthy
name by the which you are called?
8 If you fulfil the royal law according to
the scripture, You shall love your neighbour as yourself, you do well:
9 But if you have respect to persons, you
commit sin, and are convinced of the law
as transgressors.
10 For whosoever shall keep the whole
law, and yet offend in one point, he is
guilty of all.

1:22 This is particularly applicable to the many commands to evangelize this world.

1:23–25 The only way you and I can see ourselves in truth is to look into a mirror. Yet a mirror can only do its job and reflect truth if there is bright light. In Scripture, the Law of God is called both a mirror (James 1:23–25; 2:11,12) and light (Proverbs 6:23). Many of today's "converts" aren't shown the mirror of the Law. We think that a long look at what they are in truth will be too painful for them, so "All have sinned" is all we tell them. Without the conviction of their own sin, they are stillborn with no life in them.

The Function of the Law

2:10 "It is of great importance that the sinner should be made to feel his guilt, and not to the impression that he is unfortunate. Do not be afraid, but show him the breadth of the divine Law, and the exceeding strictness of its precepts. Make him see how it condemns his thoughts and life. By a convicted sinner, I mean one who feels himself condemned by the Law of God, as a guilty sinner.

"I remark that this [the Law] is the rule, and the only just rule by which the guilt of sin can be measured…Every man need only consult his own consciousness faithfully and he will see that it is equally affirmed by the mind's own intuition to be right." *Charles Finney*

11 For he that said, Do not commit adultery, said also, Do not kill. Now if you
commit no adultery, yet if you kill, you
are become a transgressor of the law.
12 So speak, and so do, as they that shall
be judged by the law of liberty.
13 For he shall have judgment without
mercy, that has showed no mercy; and
mercy rejoices against judgment.
14 What does it profit, my brethren,
though a man say he has faith, and have
not works? can faith save him?
15 If a brother or sister be naked, and
destitute of daily food,
16 And one of you say to them, Depart
in peace, be you warmed and filled; notwithstanding you give them not those
things which are needful to the body;
what does it profit?
17 Even so faith, if it has not works, is
dead, being alone.
18 Yes, a man may say, You have faith,
and I have works: show me your faith
without your works, and I will show you
my faith by my works.
19 **You believe that there is one God;
you do well: the devils also believe, and
tremble.**
**20 But will you know, O vain man, that
faith without works is dead?**
21 Was not Abraham our father justified by works, when he had offered Isaac
his son upon the altar?
22 See how faith wrought with his works,
and by works was faith made perfect?
23 And the scripture was fulfilled which
says, Abraham believed God, and it was
imputed to him for righteousness: and he
was called the Friend of God.
24 You see then how that by works a
man is justified, and not by faith only.
25 Likewise also was not Rahab the harlot justified by works, when she had received the messengers, and had sent them
out another way?

2:7 Witnessing to blasphemers. If you hear God's name taken in vain, don't tell the person it's offensive; use it as an opening for the gospel. Greet him, talk about something in the natural realm, then give him a gospel tract. Gently say, "I noticed that you used God's name in vain. Do you know what you're actually doing when you do that?" Most people will say no. Then say, "Instead of using a filth word to express disgust, you're putting God's name in place of that word. That's called 'blasphemy,' and the Bible says, 'The Lord will not hold him guiltless who takes His name in vain.'"

2:8 Using the Law in evangelism. In verses 8–12 James uses the Law (in conjunction with future punishment) to bring the knowledge of sin. See John 8:4,5 comment.

2:10 Galatians 3:10 warns that the sinner must continue to do "*all* things" that are written in the Law. The strict demands of the Law cannot be kept by sinful man and should send the sinner to the Savior. See Matthew 5:48 comment.

"God's Law is unified; it all hangs together and is inseparable. It is like hitting a window with a hammer. You may hit it only once, and that rather lightly, but the whole window is shattered." *John MacArthur*

2:16 "Science may have found a cure for most evils; but it has found no remedy for the worst of them all: the apathy of human beings." *Helen Keller*

26 For as the body without the spirit is dead, so faith without works is dead also.

CHAPTER 3

MY brethren, be not many masters, knowing that we shall receive the greater condemnation.
2 For in many things we offend all. If any man offend not in word, the same is a perfect man, and able also to bridle the whole body.
3 Behold, we put bits in the horses' mouths, that they may obey us; and we turn about their whole body.
4 Behold also the ships, which though they be so great, and are driven of fierce winds, yet are they turned about with a very small helm, wherever the governor lists.
5 Even so the tongue is a little member, and boasts great things. Behold, how great a matter a little fire kindles!
6 And the tongue is a fire, a world of iniquity: so is the tongue among our members, that it defiles the whole body, and sets on fire the course of nature; and it is set on fire of hell.
7 For every kind of beasts, and of birds, and of serpents, and of things in the sea, is tamed, and has been tamed of mankind:
8 But the tongue can no man tame; it is an unruly evil, full of deadly poison.
9 Therewith bless we God, even the Father; and therewith curse we men, which are made after the similitude of God.
10 Out of the same mouth proceeds blessing and cursing. My brethren, these things ought not so to be.

> What can be wiser than in the highest sense to bless our fellow men—to snatch a soul from the gulf that yawns, to lift it up to the heaven that glorifies, to deliver an immortal from the thralldom of Satan, and to bring him into the liberty of Christ?
>
> **CHARLES SPURGEON**

11 Does a fountain send forth at the same place sweet water and bitter?
12 Can the fig tree, my brethren, bear olive berries? either a vine, figs? so can no fountain both yield salt water and fresh.
13 Who is a wise man and endued with

2:17 Faith without works. A Christian farmer in western Kansas felt sure that God spoke to him to give his $40,000 hail insurance to missions. So, in faith he gave the money, trusting that God would protect his crop. Sure enough, the hail came and severely damaged all his neighbor's crops, but not his.

In contrast, there is a well-known story about a brilliant tightrope artist named Blondin, who pushed a wheelbarrow across Niagara Falls. After he had walked to the other side, the crowd roared with applause at his amazing feat.

He asked a small boy in the crowd if he believed that Blondin could walk back. The boy said, "Yes, sir!" He then asked if the boy thought he could do it with him in the wheelbarrow. The boy said he believed he could do it, to which the famous tightrope walker said, *"Good! Jump in then and I will take you!"* The boy would not get in.

Here are two different types of faith. The farmer had faith that he had heard from God; he was so sure that he was prepared to step out. But the boy's faith was (understandably) lacking; he wasn't prepared to step out, and get in. Many sincere folks have a measure of faith in Jesus, but they have never *trusted* in Him. In that sense, their faith, because it doesn't have works with it, is dead.

2:20 "What is it [evolution] based upon? Upon nothing whatever but faith, upon belief in the reality of the unseen—belief in the fossils that cannot be produced, belief in the embryological experiments that refuse to come off. It is faith unjustified by works." *Arthur N. Field*

3:6 The tongue weighs practically nothing, but so few people are able to hold it.

Here we are told that the tongue is set on fire by hell. At Pentecost, God gave man a new tongue —set on fire by heaven. The mouths of men reveal their wicked hearts. See Romans 3:13,14.

knowledge among you? let him show out of a good conversation his works with meekness of wisdom.

14 But if you have bitter envying and strife in your hearts, glory not, and lie not against the truth.

15 This wisdom descends not from above, but is earthly, sensual, devilish.

16 For where envying and strife is, there is confusion and every evil work.

17 But the wisdom that is from above is first pure, then peaceable, gentle, and easy to be entreated, full of mercy and good fruits, without partiality, and without hypocrisy.

18 And the fruit of righteousness is sown in peace of them that make peace.

CHAPTER 4

FROM whence come wars and fightings among you? come they not hence, even of your lusts that war in your members?

2 You lust, and have not: you kill, and desire to have, and cannot obtain: you fight and war, yet you have not, because you ask not.

3 You ask, and receive not, because you ask amiss, that you may consume it upon your lusts.

4 You adulterers and adulteresses, do you not know that the friendship of the world is enmity with God? whosoever therefore will be a friend of the world is the enemy of God.

5 Do you think that the scripture said in vain, The spirit that dwells in us lusts to envy?

6 But he gives more grace. Wherefore he says, God resists the proud, but gives grace to the humble.

7 **Submit yourselves therefore to God. Resist the devil, and he will flee from you.**

8 **Draw near to God, and he will draw near to you. Cleanse your hands, you sinners; and purify your hearts, you double minded.**

9 Be afflicted, and mourn, and weep: let your laughter be turned to mourning, and your joy to heaviness.

10 Humble yourselves in the sight of the Lord, and he shall lift you up.

11 Speak not evil one of another, brethren. He that speaks evil of his brother, and judges his brother, speaks evil of the law, and judges the law: but if you judge the law, you are not a doer of the law, but a judge.

12 There is one lawgiver, who is able to

3:17 This is the spirit in which we should share our faith. See Proverbs 15:1.

Beware of "religious" types. They tend to gravitate toward the evangelistic enterprise. They will contend with you about doctrine and steal your time from the work of evangelism. You will recognize them by their lack of gentleness, mercy, and willingness to yield to reason.

4:2–4 Using the Law in evangelism. James here uses the Law once again to bring the knowledge of sin—speaking of lust, adultery, murder, and covetousness.

4:6 Biblical evangelism is always "Law to the proud and grace to the humble." With the Law we break the hard heart; with the gospel we heal the broken one. See Matthew 19:17–22 comment.

4:9,10 These are the inner workings of a genuinely repentant heart—affliction, mourning, weeping (contrition), heaviness, and humility. These are the ones the Lord lifts up. See Psalm 147:6.

4:12 The idea for the American government's divided powers came directly from Scripture. Isaiah 33:22 says, "For the Lord is our Judge [the judicial branch], the Lord is our Lawgiver [the legislative branch], the Lord is our King [the executive branch]." Our Founding Fathers knew that separated powers were needed because of man's inherent sinfulness and desire for control—and what better model could there be for a government than the Lord who governs the universe!

"The teachings of the Bible are so interwoven and entwined with our whole civic and social life that it would be literally—I do not mean figuratively, I mean literally—impossible for us to figure to ourselves what life would be if these teachings were removed." *Theodore Roosevelt*

Springboards for Preaching and Witnessing

4:14

The Will to Live

Millions of people spend dozens of hours each week watching dead people on TV. From Elvis to Lucy to Jimmy Stewart, the faces of folks who no longer exist entertain us. Time not only snatched their looks, it snatched their lives. Today, good-looking Hollywood stars are making movies so that tomorrow's generation can also pass the time by watching dead people on TV.

Time makes today tomorrow's memory. Each weekend seems to pass us by like blurred telephone poles flashing past the window of the speeding train of life.

If I purchased a new car and saw in the owner's manual that it had a certain type of engine, I shouldn't be surprised to lift the hood and find the engine to be exactly as the manual stated. The maker's handbook gives me insight into the unseen workings of the vehicle. This is also true with human beings. The Maker's manual tells us how each of us thinks and why we react the way we do. It lifts the hood and reveals the inner workings of homo sapiens.

In doing so, the Bible discloses an often-overlooked tool that we can use to reach the lost. That tool is the "fear of death." For the Christian who may find such an approach to be negative, it may be looked at in a *positive* light. The tool may also be called "the will to live." Every human being in his right mind has a fear of death (Hebrews 2:15). *He doesn't want to die.* He sits wide-eyed, staring out the window of the speeding train watching life pass him by.

Here is how to use that tool when speaking to an unsaved person: "Let's assume that the average person dies at 70 years old. Then if you are 20 years old, you have just 2,500 weekends left to live. If you have turned 30, you have 2,000 weekends left until the day you die. If you are 40 years old, you have only 1,500 weekends left. If you are 50, then you have just 1,000 weekends, and if you are 60, you have a mere 500 weekends left until the day death comes to you."

Even as a Christian that thought concerns me. I somehow can relate to "weekends," while "years" puts death into the distance. It shakes me enough to ask myself, *What I am doing with my life?* It sickens me that I am doing so little to reach the lost. It also deeply concerns me that I have dry eyes when I pray. My train will take me into the presence of God. For those trusting in Jesus Christ, death has been defeated. But the train of the unregenerate will take them to horrific disaster. Their end will be eternal hell. In light of such terrible thoughts, all my activities outside of warning the world of their destination seem trivial.

It has been wisely stated that every one of us is unique...*just like everyone else.* In truth, each unique individual is uniquely predictable. Every sinner has a fear of death. No one can deny that he naturally has a will to live. Therefore, it makes sense to confront him with reality by reminding him that he has an "appointment" to keep. Bluntly tell him how many weekends he has left. Then appeal to his reason by saying, "If there was one chance in a million that Jesus Christ 'has abolished death, and has brought life and immortality to light through the gospel,' you owe it to your good sense just to look into it."

save and to destroy: who are you that
judge another?
13 **Go to now, you that say, Today or
tomorrow we will go into such a city,
and continue there a year, and buy and
sell, and get gain:**
**14 Whereas you know not what shall
be on the morrow. For what is your life?
It is even a vapor, that appears for a little time, and then vanishes away.**
15 For that you ought to say, If the Lord
will, we shall live, and do this, or that.
16 But now you rejoice in your boastings: all such rejoicing is evil.
**17 Therefore to him that knows to do
good, and does it not, to him it is sin.**

4:17 "To sin by silence when they should protest makes cowards out of men." *Abraham Lincoln*

CHAPTER 5

GO to now, you rich men, weep and howl for your miseries that shall come upon you.
2 Your riches are corrupted, and your garments are motheaten.
3 Your gold and silver is cankered; and the rust of them shall be a witness against you, and shall eat your flesh as it were fire. You have heaped treasure together for the last days.
4 Behold, the hire of the laborers who have reaped down your fields, which is of you kept back by fraud, cries: and the cries of them which have reaped are entered into the ears of the Lord of sabaoth.
5 You have lived in pleasure on the earth, and been wanton; you have nourished your hearts, as in a day of slaughter.
6 You have condemned and killed the just; and he does not resist you.
7 Be patient therefore, brethren, to the coming of the Lord. Behold, the husbandman waits for the precious fruit of the earth, and has long patience for it, until he receive the early and latter rain.
8 Be also patient; stablish your hearts: for the coming of the Lord draws nigh.
9 Grudge not one against another, brethren, lest you be condemned: behold, the judge stands before the door.
10 Take, my brethren, the prophets, who have spoken in the name of the Lord, for an example of suffering affliction, and of patience.
11 Behold, we count them happy which endure. You have heard of the patience of Job, and have seen the end of the Lord; that the Lord is very pitiful, and of tender mercy.
12 But above all things, my brethren, swear not, neither by heaven, neither by the earth, neither by any other oath: but let your yes be yes; and your no, no; lest you fall into condemnation.
13 Is any among you afflicted? let him pray. Is any merry? let him sing psalms.
14 Is any sick among you? let him call for the elders of the church; and let them pray over him, anointing him with oil in the name of the Lord:
15 And the prayer of faith shall save the sick, and the Lord shall raise him up; and if he has committed sins, they shall be forgiven him.
16 Confess your faults one to another, and pray one for another, that you may be healed. The effectual fervent prayer of a righteous man avails much.
17 Elijah was a man subject to like passions as we are, and he prayed earnestly that it might not rain: and it rained not on the earth by the space of three years and six months.
18 And he prayed again, and the heaven gave rain, and the earth brought forth her fruit.
19 *Brethren, if any of you do err from the truth, and one convert him;*
20 *Let him know, that he which converts the sinner from the error of his way shall save a soul from death, and shall hide a multitude of sins.*

5:8 Second coming of Jesus: See Jude 14.

5:16 "Prayer is the honest thoughts of the heart and mind converted into a form of communication, either verbal or mental, directed toward God." *Emeal Zwayne*

5:20 There is no higher calling than to turn a sinner from the error of his ways. A surgeon may extend someone's life, but death eventually takes the person. Our work has eternal consequences.

Mormonism

OFFICIAL NAME: Church of Jesus Christ of Latter-day Saints (LDS, Mormons)

FOUNDER: Joseph Smith Jr., on April 6, 1830

CURRENT LEADER: Gordon B. Hinckley (b. 1910)

HEADQUARTERS: Salt Lake City, Utah

MEMBERSHIP (1998): Worldwide: 10.3 million in 28,670 wards and branches in 162 countries; United States: 5.1 million in all 50 states and D.C.; Canada: 152,000.

MISSIONARIES (1998): 58,700

The Church of Jesus Christ of Latter-day Saints was founded by Joseph F. Smith Jr. (1805–1844). Smith claimed to have had a visitation from God in 1820 in which God directed him to establish the true church. Consequently he organized the Mormon Church on April 6, 1830, with six original members. Beginning with a few hundred followers the church moved to Ohio, Missouri, and Illinois before Smith's death at the hands of a mob at the Carthage, Ill., jail. Smith had been arrested for encouraging the destruction of the *Expositor*, a Nauvoo, Ill., newspaper. After Smith's death, Brigham Young was affirmed as president of the church by a majority of the church's leaders and led several thousand followers to Utah where they established Salt Lake City in 1847. Joseph Smith's widow, Emma, resided in Independence, Mo. Those who affirmed her son, Joseph Smith, as the true successor of his father and as prophet of the church helped found the Reorganized Church of Jesus Christ of Latter Day Saints, now headquartered in Independence, Mo., in 1852.

MAJOR BELIEFS OF MORMONS

ONE TRUE CHURCH: The Mormon church claims to be the only true church. In God's supposed revelation to Joseph Smith, Jesus Christ told him to join no other church for "they were all wrong . . . their creeds were an abomination . . . those professors [members] were all corrupt" (*The Pearl of Great Price*, Joseph Smith History —1:19). Mormons teach that after the New Testament all churches became heretical and no true saints existed until the "Church of the Latter-day Saints" was organized, hence their name. Non-Mormons are thus called "Gentiles." The new revelations given to Smith, the institution of the prophet and apostles in the church, the restoration of the divine priesthoods, and the temple ceremonies make the church authentic. True and full salvation or exaltation is found only in the LDS Church.

Biblical Response: The true church of Jesus Christ has had an ongoing presence and witness in the world since Pentecost. Jesus Christ promised that His church, *true* baptized and regenerate believers, would not fail (Matt. 16:17–18). The marks of a true church include faithfulness to the teaching of the first apostles (Acts 2:42)—not the creation of new doctrines.

AUTHORITY OF THE PROPHET: The *president* or *prophet* of the Church is thought to be the sole spokesman and revelator of God. Joseph Smith was the initial prophet, but each successive president holds that position. Through him God's will can be made known to the church. All revelations are made scripture and no Mormon can attain godhood without accepting Joseph Smith as a true prophet. The Mormon scriptures state that Latter-day Saints "shalt give heed unto all his [the prophet's] words and commandments . . . For his word ye shall receive as if from mine [God's] own mouth" (*Doctrine and Covenants* 21:4–5).

Biblical Response: Old and New Testament prophets were God's spokesmen. Their words were always consistent with the Bible and pointed to God's Son, Jesus Christ. A test of genuineness for prophets was that any prediction they proclaimed would come true (Deut. 18:20–22). For example, Joseph Smith predicted that the temple of the church would be built in Independence, Mo., within his lifetime (*Doctrine and Covenants* 84:2–5). No temple has yet been built there. New Testament prophets spoke, along with teachers, pastors, and evangelists, in evangelizing with and edifying the church (Eph. 4:11–13).

MORMON SCRIPTURE: Mormons accept four books as scripture and the word of God. The King James Version of the Bible is one of them, but only "as far as it is translated correctly"—seemingly allowing for possible questions about its authority. Joseph Smith made over 600 corrections to its text. Other "standard works" are the *Book of Mormon*, *Doctrine and Covenants*, and *The Pearl of Great Price*. The Bible is missing "plain and precious parts" according to the *Book of Mormon* (1 Nephi 13:26) which the other three volumes complete. The *Book of Mormon* has the "fullness of the gospel" and tells the story of a supposed migration of Israelites in 600 B.C. to the American continent. These Israelites subsequently lapsed into apostasy although their story was preserved on golden plates written in Reformed Egyptian. Joseph Smith, it is said, translated the plates by the "gift and power of God" (*Doctrine and Covenants* 135:3). Reformed Egyptian does not exist as a language. The golden plates were returned to the angel Moroni after they were transcribed and Moroni returned them to heaven. The *Book of Mormon* does not contain explicit Mormon doctrine. *Doctrine and Covenants* contains the revelations of the Mormon prophets—138 in number along with two "declarations." Here most of Mormon doctrine can be found including the priesthood, baptism for the dead, godhood, and polygamy. *The Pearl of Great Price* contains Smith's religious history, the Articles of Faith, the Book of Abraham, and the Book of Moses.

Biblical Response: The Bible explicitly warns against adding to or detracting from its teaching (Rev. 22:18; Deut. 4:2). The New Testament contains the inspired and totally accurate witness of contemporary disciples and followers of Jesus. It alone claims to be fully inspired of God and usable for the establishment of doctrine (2 Tim. 3:15–17; 2 Pet. 1:19–21).

ESTABLISHMENT OF TEMPLES: The first Mormon temple was constructed in Kirtland, Ohio, in 1836. Subsequently, a temple was constructed in Nauvoo, Ill., in 1846. Presently there are at least 53 operating temples throughout the world including the one finished in Salt Lake City in 1893. The purpose and function of temples is for the practice of eternal ordinances including primarily baptism for the dead, endowments, and celestial marriages. Baptism in the Mormon church, for both the living and the dead, is essential for the fullness of salvation. The dead often are baptized by proxy which affords them after death the opportunity to become Mormons. Celestial marriage for "time and eternity" is also a temple ordinance. It is necessary for godhood and seals the marriage forever. Temples form an essential part of Mormon salvation. Only Mormons in possession of a "temple recommend" by their bishop may enter a temple.

Biblical Response: The Temple of the Old Testament was a place of symbolic sacrifice forefiguring the sacrifice of Christ. Worship in the Jewish temple in Jerusalem was a practice of early Jewish believers (Acts 2:46). Otherwise there is no mention of any such practice in the New Testament. Never was the Jewish temple used for baptism for the dead, marriage, or other secret ceremonies. It was the place in the Old Testament where the glory of God occasionally dwelt. Today the individual believer is God's dwelling place and not a physical building (1 Cor. 3:16).

GOD IS AN EXALTED MAN: Elohim, the god of this universe, was previously a man in a prior existence. As a result of having kept the requirements of Mormonism, he was exalted to godhood and inherited his own universe. God is confined to a "body of flesh and bones" (*Doctrine and Covenants* 130:22) and yet is thought to be omniscient and omnipotent. He obviously cannot be omnipresent. There are an infinite number of gods with their own worlds—these too were previously men. The Holy Ghost, Jesus Christ, and "Heavenly Father" comprise three separate and distinct gods. Heavenly Father sires spiritual children in heaven destined for human life on earth. All humans, as well as Jesus Christ and Lucifer, are god's heavenly children. (See *Doctrine and Covenants* 130:22; God, Jesus, and the Spirit thus had beginnings.)

Biblical Response: God is Spirit and is not confined to a physical body (John 4:24). Jesus Christ was incarnated through a miraculous and non-physical conception through the Virgin Mary. He was fully God from the beginning (John 1:1). Together with the person of the Holy Spirit they form the triune (three-in-one) eternal God.

JESUS IS GOD'S "SON": Jesus was Heavenly Father's firstborn spirit child in heaven. He was begotten by God through Mary as in a "literal, full and complete sense" in the same "sense in which he is the son of Mary" (Bruce McConkie, *A New Witness for the Articles of Faith* [Salt Lake City: Deseret Book Co., 1993], 67). These two elements of Jesus being literally God's son form his uniqueness in Mormon theology. In the Garden of Gethsemane as well as on the cross Jesus atoned for Adam's sin and guaranteed all humankind resurrection and immortality. Jesus visited the Israelites or Indians of North

America after his resurrection and established the true church among them. We are the spiritual, but literal, younger brothers and sisters of Christ. Some Mormon documents claim that Jesus was married at Cana in Galilee (Mark 2) and had children himself.

Biblical Response: Jesus is viewed as God, the Word or Son, eternally existent with the Father and worthy of identity as God (John 1:1–14). He was born of the Virgin Mary who had conceived him supernaturally by the Holy Spirit. He lived a perfect life, died on the cross for the sins of the world, and was raised from the dead. He will come again and reign as Lord of lords.

HUMANS ARE GODS IN EMBRYO: Every human being has the potential of becoming a god by keeping the requirements of Mormonism. A well-known statement within Mormonism is, "As man is god once was, as god is man may become." From a prior spirit existence in heaven, humans may be born on earth in order to exercise freedom to choose good or evil and to have a body for the resurrection. Basically humans are good, but they will be punished for their sin. But by keeping Mormon teaching and obeying the church and the Prophet, after the resurrection worthy Mormon males may pass the celestial guards, bring their wives with them, and achieve a status similar to Elohim—the god of this world. The consequences of their sin are erased by their allegiance to the tenets of Mormonism. In resurrection faithful Mormons receive exaltation to godhood and will exercise dominion over their world.

Biblical Response: Human beings are God's special creation. There is no evidence from Scripture of preexistence, rather God acknowledges that it was in the womb of our mothers that He formed us (Isaiah 44:2). A sinful nature is part of humanity's experience. Liberation from the power and presence of sin is experienced as a result of faith in Christ. At that point God's image is begun to be remade in every Christian. Although the believer is being transformed to Christlikeness, the Bible does not teach literal godhood as the inheritance of the saints (Rom. 8:29; Rev. 1:5–6).

MORMON PLAN OF SALVATION: The Mormon plan of salvation is built on the idea that all people have eternal life, but only the most faithful Mormons have godhood or enter the celestial Kingdom. In order to obtain this ultimate step, Mormons must exercise faith in the God of Mormonism, its Christ, and the Church of Jesus Christ of Latter-day Saints; exercise repentance; and be baptized in the LDS Church. Additionally Mormons must keep the "Word of Wisdom" by abstaining from alcohol, tobacco, and caffeine; tithe to the church; attend weekly sacrament meetings; support the Mormon prophet; do temple works; and be active in their support of the church.

Biblical Response: Salvation, according to the Bible, is due to God's grace and love. He provided Jesus as the sacrifice for the sins of the world. It is through faith in the crucified and risen Jesus that we may be saved. Works are excluded (John 1:12; 3:16; Rom. 10:9–13; Eph. 2:8–9).

EVANGELIZING MORMONS

- Know clearly the Christian faith and the gospel.
- Be aware of the unique Mormon doctrines as presented here.
- Remember, Mormons use Christian vocabulary (gospel, atonement, god) but radically redefine their meanings. Define clearly what you mean when you use biblical words.
- Present a clear testimony of your faith in Christ alone for your salvation.
- Show your Mormon friend that the Bible teaches salvation alone through the cross of Christ (John 3:16; Rom. 10:4,10–13; Eph. 2:8–9). Emphasize that salvation is a gift to be received, not a merit to be earned.
- Warn the Mormon about trusting in feelings (i.e., the burning in the bosom) for a validation of Mormonism's truth claim. Without historical, objective verification, feelings are useless.
- When Mormons use a Bible verse, read carefully the verses before and afterward to make clear the exact meaning and purpose of the passage. Don't let them take Bible verses out of context. Read carefully the full reference in the Bible before deciding what any one verse means.
- Keep the central doctrines of the faith as the focus of your discussion.
- Do the basics: pray, trust the Holy Spirit, and be loving, patient, and steadfast.

1 Peter

CHAPTER 1

Peter, an apostle of Jesus Christ, to
the strangers scattered throughout
Pontus, Galatia, Cappadocia, Asia, and
Bithynia,
2 Elect according to the foreknowledge
of God the Father, through sanctification
of the Spirit, to obedience and sprinkling
of the blood of Jesus Christ: Grace to you,
and peace, be multiplied.
3 Blessed be the God and Father of our
Lord Jesus Christ, which according to his
abundant mercy has begotten us again to
a lively hope by the resurrection of Jesus
Christ from the dead,
4 To an inheritance incorruptible, and
undefiled, and that fades not away, reserved in heaven for you,
5 Who are kept by the power of God
through faith to salvation ready to be revealed in the last time.
6 Wherein you greatly rejoice, though
now for a season, if need be, you are in
heaviness through manifold temptations:
7 That the trial of your faith, being much
more precious than of gold that perishes
though it be tried with fire, might be found
unto praise and honor and glory at the
appearing of Jesus Christ:
8 Whom having not seen, you love; in
whom, though now you see him not, yet
believing, you rejoice with joy unspeakable and full of glory:
9 Receiving the end of your faith, even
the salvation of your souls.
10 Of which salvation the prophets have
inquired and searched diligently, who
prophesied of the grace that should come

1:3 New birth—its necessity for salvation. See 1 Peter 1:23.

1:4 The beloved son. A true story is told of a millionaire who had a portrait of his beloved son painted before the son went to war. He was tragically killed in battle, and shortly afterward, the heartbroken millionaire died.

His will stated that all his riches were to be auctioned, specifying that the painting must sell first.

Many showed up at the auction, where a mass of the rich man's wealth was displayed. When the painting was held up for sale, there were no bids made. It was an unknown painting by an unknown painter of the rich man's uncelebrated son, so sadly, there was little interest.

After a few moments, a butler who worked for the man remembered how much the millionaire loved his son, decided to bid for it, and purchased the portrait for a very low price.

Suddenly, to everyone's surprise the auctioneer brought down his gavel and declared the auction closed. The rich man's will had secretly specified that the person who cared enough to purchase the painting of his beloved son was also to be given all the riches of his will.

This is precisely what God has done through the gospel. He who accepts the beloved Son of God also receives all the riches of His will—the gift of eternal life and "pleasures for evermore." They become "joint heirs" with the Son (Romans 8:16,17).

to you:

11 Searching what, or what manner of time the Spirit of Christ which was in them did signify, when it testified beforehand the sufferings of Christ, and the glory that should follow.

12 To whom it was revealed, that not to themselves, but to us they did minister the things, which are now reported to you by them that have preached the gospel to you with the Holy Spirit sent down from heaven; which things the angels desire to look into.

13 Wherefore gird up the loins of your mind, be sober, and hope to the end for the grace that is to be brought to you at the revelation of Jesus Christ;

14 As obedient children, not fashioning yourselves according to the former lusts in your ignorance:

15 But as he which has called you is holy, so be holy in all manner of conversation;

16 Because it is written, Be holy; for I am holy.

17 And if you call on the Father, who without respect of persons judges according to every man's work, pass the time of your sojourning here in fear:

18 Forasmuch as you know that you were not redeemed with corruptible things, as silver and gold, from your vain conversation received by tradition from your fathers;

19 But with the precious blood of Christ, as of a lamb without blemish and without spot:

20 Who verily was foreordained before the foundation of the world, but was manifest in these last times for you,

21 Who by him do believe in God, that raised him up from the dead, and gave him glory; that your faith and hope might be in God.

22 Seeing you have purified your souls in obeying the truth through the Spirit to unfeigned love of the brethren, see that you love one another with a pure heart fervently:

23 Being born again, not of corruptible seed, but of incorruptible, by the word of God, which lives and abides for ever.

24 **For all flesh is as grass, and all the glory of man as the flower of grass. The grass withers, and the flower thereof falls away:**

25 But the word of the Lord endures for ever. And this is the word which by the

---

1:8 The source of joy. "Joy is not the same as pleasure or happiness. A wicked and evil man may have pleasure, while any ordinary mortal is capable of being happy. Pleasure generally comes from things, and always through the senses; happiness comes from humans through fellowship. Joy comes from loving God and neighbor. Pleasure is quick and violent, like a flash of lightning. Joy is steady and abiding, like a fixed star. Pleasure depends on external circumstances, such as money, food, travel, etc. Joy is independent of them, for it comes from a good conscience and love of God." *Fulton J. Sheen*

1:15 "To ask that God's love should be content with us as we are is to ask that God should cease to be God: because He is what He is, His love must, in the nature of things, be impeded and repelled by certain stains in our present character, and because He already loves us He must labor to make us lovable." *C. S. Lewis*

1:23 New birth—its necessity for salvation. If you speak to someone who professes to know God and you are not certain of their salvation, simply ask if they have been "born again" (see John 3:1–7). If you find that they are not sure (this is one sign that they haven't—1 John 5:10) or they say that they haven't, here is how you can bring focus to its importance. Tell them that the difference between *believing* in God and being *born again* is like the difference between *believing* in a parachute and *putting it on*. There's a big difference when you jump from the plane. Then say, "Do you know what convinced me that I had to be born again? It was the Ten Commandments." Then take them through the spiritual nature of the Law, which brings the knowledge of sin (Romans 7:7). See 1 John 5:1.

1:25 The Dead Sea Scrolls— "The greatest manuscript discovery of all times."

By William F. Albright

The discovery of the Dead Sea Scrolls (DSS) at Qumran in 1949 had significant effects in corroborating evidence for the Scriptures. The ancient texts, found hidden in pots in cliff-top caves by a monastic religious community, confirm the reliability of the Old Testament text. These texts, which were copied and studied by the Essenes, include one complete Old Testament book (Isaiah) and thousands of fragments, representing every Old Testament book except Esther.

The manuscripts date from the third century B.C. to the first century A.D. and give the earliest window found so far into the texts of the Old Testament books and their predictive prophecies. The Qumran texts have become an important witness for the divine origin of the Bible, providing further evidence against the criticism of such crucial books as Daniel and Isaiah.

Dating the Manuscripts. Carbon-14 dating is a reliable form of scientific dating when applied to uncontaminated material several thousand years old. Results indicated an age of 1917 years with a 200-year (10 percent) variant.

Paleography (ancient writing forms) and orthography (spelling) indicated that some manuscripts were inscribed before 100 B.C. Albright set the date of the complete Isaiah scroll to around 100 B.C.—"there can happily not be the slightest doubt in the world about the genuineness of the manuscript."

Archaeological Dating. Collaborative evidence for an early date came from archaeology. Pottery accompanying the manuscripts was late Hellenistic (c. 150–63 B.C.) and Early Roman (c. 63 B.C. to A.D. 100). Coins found in the monastery ruins proved by their inscriptions to have been minted between 135 B.C. and A.D. 135. The weave and pattern of the cloth supported an early date. There is no reasonable doubt that the Qumran manuscripts came from the century before Christ and the first century A.D.

Significance of the Dating. Previous to the DSS, the earliest known manuscript of the Old Testament was the Masoretic Text (A.D. 900) and two others (dating about A.D. 1000) from which, for example, the King James version of the Old Testament derived its translation. Perhaps most would have considered the Masoretic text as a very late text and therefore questioned the reliability of the Old Testament wholesale. The Dead Sea Scrolls eclipse these texts by 1,000 years and provide little reason to question their reliability, and further, present only confidence for the text. The beauty of the Dead Sea Scrolls lies in the close match they have with the Masoretic text—demonstrable evidence of reliability and preservation of the authentic text through the centuries. So the discovery of the DSS provides evidence for the following:

1) Confirmation of the Hebrew Text
2) Support for the Masoretic Text
3) Support for the Greek translation of the Hebrew Text (the Septuagint). Since the New Testament often quotes from the Greek Old Testament, the DSS furnish the reader with further confidence for the Masoretic texts in this area where it can be tested.

(Generated from *Norman Geisler*, "Dead Sea Scrolls," *Baker Encyclopedia of Christian Apologetics*)

gospel is preached to you.

CHAPTER 2

WHEREFORE laying aside all malice, and all guile, and hypocrisies, and envies, and all evil speakings,
2 As newborn babes, desire the sincere milk of the word, that you may grow thereby:
3 If so be you have tasted that the Lord is gracious.
4 To whom coming, as to a living stone,

2:2 "Had the doctrines of Jesus been preached always as pure as they came from His lips, the whole civilized world would now have been Christians." *Thomas Jefferson*

PRINCIPLES OF GROWTH FOR THE NEW AND GROWING CHRISTIAN

2:2 *Feeding on the Word—Daily Nutrition*

A healthy baby has a healthy appetite. If you have truly been "born" of the Spirit of God, you *will* have a healthy appetite. The Bible says, "As newborn babes, desire the sincere milk of the word, that you may grow thereby" (1 Peter 2:2). Feed yourself daily without fail. Job said, "I have esteemed the words of His mouth more than my necessary food" (Job 23:12). The more you eat, the quicker you will grow, and the less bruising you will have. Speed up the process and save yourself some pain—vow to read God's Word every day, *without fail*. Say to yourself, "No Bible, no breakfast. No read, no feed." Be like Job, and put your Bible *before* your belly. If you do that, God promises that you will be like a fruitful, strong, and healthy tree (Psalm 1). Each day, find somewhere quiet and thoroughly soak your soul in the Word of God.

There may be times when you read through its pages with great enthusiasm, and other times when it seems dry and even boring. But food profits your body whether you enjoy it or not. As a child, you no doubt ate desserts with great enthusiasm. Perhaps vegetables weren't so exciting. If you were a normal child, you probably had to be *encouraged* to eat them at first. Then, as you matured in life you were taught to discipline yourself to eat vegetables, because they benefit you physically even though they may not bring pleasure to your taste buds.

For the next principle of growth, see Matthew 6:9 comment.

disallowed indeed of men, but chosen of
God, and precious,
5 You also, as lively stones, are built up
a spiritual house, an holy priesthood, to
offer up spiritual sacrifices, acceptable to
God by Jesus Christ.
6 Wherefore also it is contained in the
scripture, Behold, I lay in Zion a chief corner stone, elect, precious: and he that believes on him shall not be confounded.
7 To you therefore which believe he is
precious: but to them which be disobedient, the stone which the builders disallowed, the same is made the head of the
corner,
8 And a stone of stumbling, and a rock
of offence, even to them which stumble
at the word, being disobedient: whereunto also they were appointed.
9 But you are a chosen generation, a
royal priesthood, an holy nation, a peculiar people; that you should show forth
the praises of him who has called you out
of darkness into his marvelous light:
10 Which in time past were not a people, but are now the people of God: which
had not obtained mercy, but now have
obtained mercy.
11 Dearly beloved, I beseech you as
strangers and pilgrims, abstain from fleshly lusts, which war against the soul;
12 Having your conversation honest
among the Gentiles: that, whereas they
speak against you as evildoers, they may
by your good works, which they shall behold, glorify God in the day of visitation.
13 Submit yourselves to every ordinance
of man for the Lord's sake: whether it be
to the king, as supreme;
14 Or to governors, as to them that are
sent by him for the punishment of evildoers, and for the praise of them that do well.
15 For so is the will of God, that with
well doing you may put to silence the ig-

2:7 Perhaps the number one fruit of salvation will be that Jesus will become precious to the believer. See 1 Corinthians 16:22.

2:15 Good works are a legitimate form of evangelism. Since the way to a man's heart is often through his taste buds, buying him a hamburger may reach him more effectively than an argument. "Kindness has converted more sinners than zeal, eloquence, or learning." *Frederick W. Faber*

QUESTIONS & OBJECTIONS

2:15 *"How should I witness to my coworkers?"*

When we interact with people on a daily basis, we have many opportunities for sharing our faith.

First, be sure you are respectful to your employer and set a good example in your work ethic by working "as to the Lord" (Colossians 3:23). When others around you grumble and complain, if you have a calm, forgiving, steadfast spirit, it will make an impression. As you respond in a Christlike way to angry coworkers and stressful circumstances, people will see a difference in your life.

Always be friendly and courteous, and show genuine interest in your coworkers' lives. Invite them out to lunch to get better acquainted. Share their joys and sorrows by congratulating them in their good times and offering to pray for them in their bad times. Be sure you *do* pray for them, then follow up by asking them about the situation you prayed for. They will be moved by your concern.

If coworkers are discussing what they did during the previous weekend, you can share your excitement about attending church services or a special church event. Ask others if they have any plans for celebrating Christmas or Easter; be nonjudgmental of their answer, but be ready (if asked) to explain why you celebrate as you do. Displaying a favorite Scripture or a devotional calendar, or reading your Bible during lunchtime, may prompt others to inquire about your faith.

Bringing home-baked goods or leaving a small gift with a note on a coworker's desk can sometimes have a greater impact than a thousand eloquent sermons. We can show our faith *by* our works. Others may not like a tree of righteousness, but they cannot help but like its fruit. Pray for opportunities to share the gospel, being careful not to infringe on your boss's time.

norance of foolish men:
16 As free, and not using your liberty
for a cloak of maliciousness, but as the
servants of God.
17 Honor all men. Love the brotherhood.
Fear God. Honor the king.
18 Servants, be subject to your masters
with all fear; not only to the good and
gentle, but also to the froward.
19 For this is thankworthy, if a man for
conscience toward God endure grief, suffering wrongfully.
20 For what glory is it, if, when you are
buffeted for your faults, you shall take it
patiently? but if, when you do well, and
suffer for it, you take it patiently, this is
acceptable with God.
21 For even hereunto were you called:
because Christ also suffered for us, leaving us an example, that you should follow his steps:
22 Who did no sin, neither was guile
found in his mouth:
23 Who, when he was reviled, reviled
not again; when he suffered, he threatened not; but committed himself to him
that judges righteously:
24 Who his own self bare our sins in his
own body on the tree, that we, being dead
to sins, should live to righteousness: by
whose stripes you were healed.
25 For you were as sheep going astray;
but are now returned to the Shepherd and
Bishop of your souls.

CHAPTER 3

LIKEWISE, you wives, be in subjection to your own husbands; that, if

2:24 Messianic prophecy fulfilled: "But he was wounded for our transgressions, he was bruised for our iniquities: the chastisement of our peace was upon him; and with his stripes we are healed" (Isaiah 53:5). See Matthew 13:34,35 comment.

any obey not the word, they also may
without the word be won by the conversation of the wives;
2 While they behold your chaste conversation coupled with fear.
3 Whose adorning let it not be that outward adorning of plaiting the hair, and of
wearing of gold, or of putting on of apparel;
4 But let it be the hidden man of the
heart, in that which is not corruptible,
even the ornament of a meek and quiet
spirit, which is in the sight of God of great
price.
5 For after this manner in the old time
the holy women also, who trusted in God,
adorned themselves, being in subjection
to their own husbands:
6 Even as Sara obeyed Abraham, calling
him lord: whose daughters you are, as
long as you do well, and are not afraid
with any amazement.
7 Likewise, you husbands, dwell with
them according to knowledge, giving
honor to the wife, as to the weaker vessel, and as being heirs together of the
grace of life; that your prayers be not hindered.
8 Finally, be all of one mind, having
compassion one of another, love as brethren, be pitiful, be courteous:
9 Not rendering evil for evil, or railing for
railing: but contrariwise blessing; knowing that you are thereunto called, that you
should inherit a blessing.
10 For he that will love life, and see good
days, let him refrain his tongue from evil,
and his lips that they speak no guile:
11 Let him eschew evil, and do good;
let him seek peace, and ensue it.
12 For the eyes of the Lord are over the
righteous, and his ears are open to their
prayers: but the face of the Lord is against
them that do evil.
13 And who is he that will harm you, if
you be followers of that which is good?
14 But and if you suffer for righteousness' sake, happy are you: and be not
afraid of their terror, neither be troubled;
15 But sanctify the Lord God in your
hearts: and be ready always to give an answer to every man that asks you a reason
of the hope that is in you with meekness
and fear:
16 Having a good conscience; that,
whereas they speak evil of you, as of evildoers, they may be ashamed that falsely
accuse your good conversation in Christ.
17 For it is better, if the will of God be
so, that you suffer for well doing, than for
evil doing.
18 **For Christ also has once suffered
for sins, the just for the unjust, that he
might bring us to God, being put to
death in the flesh, but quickened by the
Spirit:**
19 By which also he went and preached
to the spirits in prison;

3:1,2 Do not preach to loved ones, or express frustration or anger because they don't believe. Win them with your works rather than your words. Buy them gifts, do them favors, show them love and kindness. Make sure that you are free from the slightest hint of hypocrisy.

3:8,9 Witnessing tips. "When you approach a careless individual, be sure to treat him kindly. Let him see that you are talking with him, not because you seek a quarrel with him, but because you love his soul and desire his best good in time and eternity. If you are harsh and overbearing, you will probably drive him farther away from the way of life.

"Be serious! Avoid all lightness of manner or language. Levity will produce anything but a right impression. You ought to feel that you are engaged in a very serious work, which is going to affect the character of your friend or neighbor and probably determine his destiny for eternity. Who could trifle and use levity in such circumstances if his heart were sincere?

"Be respectful. Some think it is necessary to be abrupt, rude, and coarse in their discussions with the careless and impenitent. No mistake can be greater. The apostle Peter has given us a better rule on the subject, where he says: 'Be pitiful, be courteous: not rendering evil for evil, or railing for railing: but contrariwise blessing.'" *Charles Finney*

QUESTIONS & OBJECTIONS

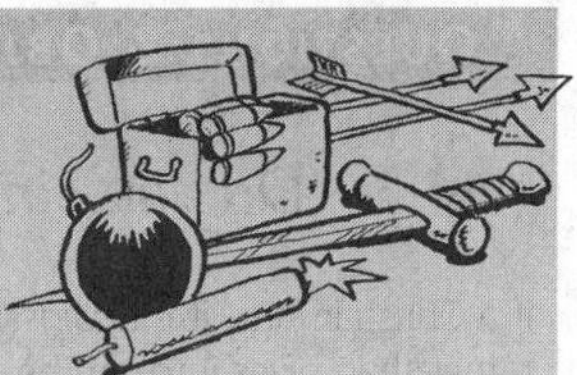

3:12 ***"If God is a God of love, why hasn't He dealt with evil?"***

In Dr. Robert Morey's book *The New Atheism and the Erosion of Freedom*, he talks with an atheist about this issue. The atheist assumes that everything is relative, and there are no absolutes (he is absolutely sure of that). Morey replies that the first thing an atheist must do is prove the existence of evil. By what process can an atheist identify evil? He must have a universal absolute to do so. Without an absolute reference point for "good" (which only God can provide), no one can identify what is good or evil. Thus without the existence of God, there is no "evil" or "good" in an absolute sense. Everything is relative. The problem of evil does not negate the existence of God. It actually requires it.

Many assume that because evil still exists today, God has not dealt with it. How can atheists assume that God has not already solved the problem of evil in such a way that neither His goodness nor omnipotence is limited? On what grounds do they limit what God can and cannot do to solve the problem? God has already solved the problem of evil. And He did it in a way in which He did not contradict His nature or the nature of man.

We assume God will solve the problem of evil in one single act. But why can't He deal with evil in a progressive way? Can't He deal with it throughout time as we know it, and then bring it to the climax on the Day of Judgment?

God sent His Son to die on the cross in order to solve the problem of evil. Christ atoned for evil and secured the eventual removal of all evil from the earth. One day evil will be quarantined in one spot called "hell." Then there will be a perfect world devoid of all evil. If God declared that all evil would, at this moment, cease to exist, you and I and all of humanity would go up in a puff of smoke. Divine judgment demands that sin be punished. *Ron Meade*

20 Which sometime were disobedient,
when once the longsuffering of God waited in the days of Noah, while the ark was
being prepared, wherein few, that is, eight
souls were saved by water.
21 The like figure whereunto even baptism does also now save us (not the putting away of the filth of the flesh, but the

3:15 Fear of questions. "In a terrible accident at a railroad crossing, a train smashed into a car and pushed it nearly four hundred yards down the track. Though no one was killed, the driver took the train company to court.

"At the trial, the engineer insisted that he had given the driver ample warning by waving his lantern back and forth for nearly a minute. He even stood and convincingly demonstrated how he'd done it. The court believed his story, and the suit was dismissed.

"'Congratulations,' the lawyer said to the engineer when it was over. 'You did superbly under cross-examination.'

"'Thanks,' he said, 'but he sure had me worried. I was afraid he was going to ask if the lantern was lit!'

"In a similar way, we often go through our lives afraid that someone will ask us a particular question. 'If someone asks me why I believe in God and not evolution, what will I say?...What if someone asks me how I can possibly believe in the resurrection?...What should I say if someone asks me why I believe the Bible truly is the Word of God, or why I believe that it teaches this or that?'

"Instead of being detrimental as in the case of the engineer above, though, such questions provide us with an opportunity to share our faith. Don't be afraid for anyone to ask!" *Alan Smith*

3:20 Peter believed the Genesis account of Noah's Flood—that is was a worldwide deluge in which only eight people were saved.

QUESTIONS & OBJECTIONS

Q 4:1 *"Do you sin, as a Christian?"*

If a Christian sins, it is *against* his will. One who is regenerate *falls* rather than *dives* into sin; he resists rather than embraces it. Any dead fish can float downstream. It takes a live one to swim against the flow. Christians still experience temptations and can sometimes fall into sin, but they are no longer slaves to sin (Romans 6:6). They have God's Holy Spirit within them to help them say no to temptation, and to convict their conscience of wrongdoing when they do sin.

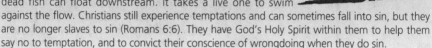

answer of a good conscience toward God,)
by the resurrection of Jesus Christ:
22 Who is gone into heaven, and is on
the right hand of God; angels and authorities and powers being made subject
to him.

CHAPTER 4

FORASMUCH then as Christ has suffered for us in the flesh, arm yourselves likewise with the same mind: for he
that has suffered in the flesh has ceased
from sin;
2 That he no longer should live the rest
of his time in the flesh to the lusts of
men, but to the will of God.
3 For the time past of our life may suf-
fice us to have wrought the will of the
Gentiles, when we walked in lasciviousness, lusts, excess of wine, revellings,
banquetings, and abominable idolatries:
4 Wherein they think it strange that you
run not with them to the same excess of
riot, speaking evil of you:
5 Who shall give account to him that is
ready to judge the quick and the dead.
6 For for this cause was the gospel
preached also to them that are dead, that
they might be judged according to men
in the flesh, but live according to God in
the spirit.
7 But the end of all things is at hand: be
therefore sober, and watch to prayer.
8 And above all things have fervent charity among yourselves: for charity shall
cover the multitude of sins.
9 Use hospitality one to another without grudging.
10 As every man has received the gift,
even so minister the same one to another,
as good stewards of the manifold grace
of God.
11 *If any man speak, let him speak as the*
oracles of God; if any man minister, let
him do it as of the ability which God gives:
that God in all things may be glorified
through Jesus Christ, to whom be praise and
dominion for ever and ever. Amen.
12 Beloved, think it not strange concerning the fiery trial which is to try you,
as though some strange thing happened
to you:
13 But rejoice, inasmuch as you are partakers of Christ's sufferings; that, when
his glory shall be revealed, you may be
glad also with exceeding joy.
14 If you are reproached for the name
of Christ, happy are you; for the spirit of
glory and of God rests upon you: on
their part he is evil spoken of, but on
your part he is glorified.
15 But let none of you suffer as a murderer, or as a thief, or as an evildoer, or
as a busybody in other men's matters.
16 Yet if any man suffer as a Christian,
let him not be ashamed; but let him glo-

4:5 *Daniel Webster* (1782–1852), politician and diplomat, is considered one of the greatest orators in American history. When asked, "What is the greatest thought that ever passed through your mind?" Webster responded, "My accountability to God."

Science Confirms the Bible

THE BIBLE *(2,000–3,000 years ago)*	SCIENCE THEN	SCIENCE NOW
The earth is a sphere (Isaiah 40:22).	The earth was a flat disk.	The earth is a sphere.
Innumerable stars (Jeremiah 33:22).	Only 1,100 stars.	Innumerable stars.
Free float of earth in space (Job 26:7).	Earth sat on a large animal.	Free float of earth in space.
Creation made of invisible elements (Hebrews 11:3).	Science was ignorant on the subject.	Creation made of invisible elements (atoms).
Each star is different (1 Corinthians 15:41).	All stars were the same.	Each star is different.
Light moves (Job 38:19,20).	Light was fixed in place.	Light moves.
Air has weight (Job 28:25).	Air was weightless.	Air has weight.
Winds blow in cyclones (Ecclesiastes 1:6).	Winds blew straight.	Winds blow in cyclones.
Blood is the source of life and health (Leviticus 17:11).	Sick people must be bled.	Blood is the source of life and health.
Ocean floor contains deep valleys and mountains (2 Samuel 22:16; Jonah 2:6).	The ocean floor was flat.	Ocean floor contains deep valleys and mountains.
Ocean contains springs (Job 38:16).	Ocean fed only by rivers and rain.	Ocean contains springs.
When dealing with disease, hands should be washed under running water (Leviticus 15:13).	Hands washed in still water.	When dealing with disease, hands should be washed under running water.

(See Hebrews 11:3 comment.)

rify God on this behalf.

17 For the time is come that judgment must begin at the house of God: and if it first begin at us, what shall the end be of them that obey not the gospel of God?

18 And if the righteous scarcely be saved, where shall the ungodly and the sinner appear?

19 Wherefore let them that suffer according to the will of God commit the keeping of their souls to him in well doing, as to a faithful Creator.

RIDDLE

RIDDLE:
Name nine people who were saved from drowning by an ark.

ANSWER:
Eight members of Noah's family were saved by an ark in the Flood (Genesis 7:13), and the infant Moses was also saved by an ark (Exodus 2:3).
(See 1 Peter 3:20.)

CHAPTER 5

THE elders which are among you I exhort, who am also an elder, and a witness of the sufferings of Christ, and also a partaker of the glory that shall be revealed:

2 Feed the flock of God which is among you, taking the oversight thereof, not by constraint, but willingly; not for filthy lucre, but of a ready mind;

3 Neither as being lords over God's heritage, but being ensamples to the flock.

4 And when the chief Shepherd shall appear, you shall receive a crown of glory that fades not away.

5 Likewise, you younger, submit yourselves to the elder. Yes, all of you be subject one to another, and be clothed with humility: for God resists the proud, and gives grace to the humble.

6 Humble yourselves therefore under the mighty hand of God, that he may exalt you in due time:

7 Casting all your care upon him; for he cares for you.

8 Be sober, be vigilant; because your adversary the devil, as a roaring lion, walks about, seeking whom he may devour:

9 Whom resist steadfast in the faith, knowing that the same afflictions are accomplished in your brethren that are in the world.

10 But the God of all grace, who has called us to his eternal glory by Christ Jesus, after that you have suffered a while, make you perfect, stablish, strengthen, settle you.

11 To him be glory and dominion for ever and ever. Amen.

12 By Silvanus, a faithful brother to you, as I suppose, I have written briefly, exhorting, and testifying that this is the true grace of God wherein you stand.

13 The church that is at Babylon, elected together with you, salutes you; and so does Marcus my son.

14 Greet one another with a kiss of charity. Peace be with you all that are in Christ Jesus. Amen.

4:14 "When we share our faith, we are in a win/win situation. If people accept what we say, we win. If we plant the seed of God's Word, we win; and even if we are rejected, we win. This is because the Bible says that when that happens, the Spirit of glory and of God rests upon us. When we contend for the faith and are rejected, we are to rejoice and leap for joy, for great is our reward in heaven (Luke 6:22,23). It is a winning situation every single time that you share your faith!"
Mark Cahill

5:3 "A message prepared in the mind reaches a mind; a message prepared in a life reaches a life."
Bill Gothard

2 Peter

CHAPTER 1

SIMON Peter, a servant and an apostle of Jesus Christ, to them that have obtained like precious faith with us through the righteousness of God and our Savior Jesus Christ:

2 Grace and peace be multiplied to you through the knowledge of God, and of Jesus our Lord,

3 According as his divine power has given to us all things that pertain to life and godliness, through the knowledge of him that has called us to glory and virtue:

4 Whereby are given to us exceeding great and precious promises: that by these you might be partakers of the divine nature, having escaped the corruption that is in the world through lust.

5 And beside this, giving all diligence, add to your faith virtue; and to virtue knowledge;

6 And to knowledge temperance; and to temperance patience; and to patience godliness;

7 And to godliness brotherly kindness; and to brotherly kindness charity.

8 For if these things be in you, and abound, they make you that you shall neither be barren nor unfruitful in the knowledge of our Lord Jesus Christ.

9 But he that lacks these things is blind, and cannot see afar off, and has forgotten that he was purged from his old sins.

10 Wherefore the rather, brethren, give diligence to make your calling and election sure: for if you do these things, you shall never fall:

11 For so an entrance shall be ministered to you abundantly into the everlasting kingdom of our Lord and Savior Jesus Christ.

12 Wherefore I will not be negligent to put you always in remembrance of these things, though you know them, and be established in the present truth.

13 Yes, I think it meet, as long as I am in this tabernacle, to stir you up by putting you in remembrance;

14 Knowing that shortly I must put off this my tabernacle, even as our Lord Jesus Christ has showed me.

15 Moreover I will endeavour that you may be able after my decease to have these things always in remembrance.

16 For we have not followed cunningly devised fables, when we made known to you the power and coming of our Lord Jesus Christ, but were eyewitnesses of his majesty.

17 For he received from God the Father honor and glory, when there came such a voice to him from the excellent glory, This is my beloved Son, in whom I am well pleased.

18 And this voice which came from heaven we heard, when we were with him in the holy mount.

19 We have also a more sure word of prophecy; whereunto you do well that you take heed, as to a light that shines in a dark place, until the day dawn, and the day star arise in your hearts:

QUESTIONS & OBJECTIONS

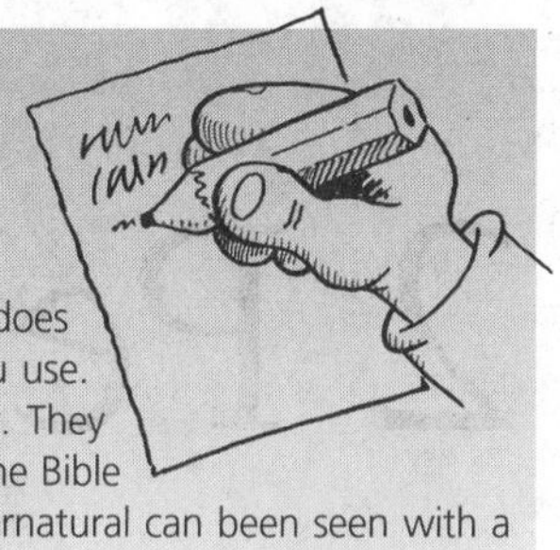

1:21 *"Didn't men write the Bible?"*

Absolutely. When you write a letter, do *you* write the letter, or does the pen? Obviously you do; the pen is merely the instrument you use. God used men as instruments to write His "letter" to humanity. They ranged from kings to common fishermen, but the 66 books of the Bible were all given by inspiration of God. Proof that this Book is supernatural can been seen with a quick study of its prophecies. See Psalm 119:105 comment.

20 Knowing this first, that no prophecy
of the scripture is of any private interpretation.
21 For the prophecy came not in old time
by the will of man: but holy men of God
spoke as they were moved by the Holy
Spirit.

CHAPTER 2

BUT there were false prophets also
among the people, even as there shall
be false teachers among you, who privately shall bring in damnable heresies,
even denying the Lord that bought them,
and bring upon themselves swift destruction.
2 And many shall follow their pernicious
ways; by reason of whom the way of truth
shall be evil spoken of.
3 And through covetousness shall they
with feigned words make merchandise of
you: whose judgment now of a long time
lingers not, and their damnation slumbers not.
4 For if God spared not the angels that
sinned, but cast them down to hell, and
delivered them into chains of darkness, to
be reserved to judgment;
5 And spared not the old world, but
saved Noah the eighth person, a preacher of righteousness, bringing in the flood
upon the world of the ungodly;
6 And turning the cities of Sodom and
Gomorrha into ashes condemned them
with an overthrow, making them an ensample to those that after should live ungodly;
7 And delivered just Lot, vexed with the

1:19 It is important to point out that it isn't the Bible that converts people. The first Christians didn't have the Bible as we know it. The New Testament hadn't been compiled, and there was no such thing as the printing press. Besides, many couldn't read. Rather, they were converted by the spoken message of the gospel. It is the gospel that is "the power of God to salvation" (Romans 1:16). Until God gives light to His Word, it will remain a dry history book to its reader.

1:21 "The idea conveyed is that just as the wind controls the sails of a boat, so also the breath of God controlled the writers of the Bible. The end result was exactly what God intended." *Josh McDowell*

2:4,5,9 Judgment Day: For verses that warn of its reality, see 2 Peter 3:7.

2:5 The Bible's fascinating facts. In Genesis 6, God gave Noah the dimensions of the 1.5 million cubic foot ark he was to build. In 1609 at Hoorn in Holland, a ship was built after that same pattern, revolutionizing shipbuilding. By 1900 every large ship on the high seas was inclined toward the proportions of the ark (as verified by "Lloyd's Register of Shipping" in the *World Almanac*).

2:6–8 Witnessing to homosexuals. I had an angry lesbian heckle me one Friday night while speaking in Santa Monica in front of a large crowd. I was so pleased to have the Law of God as a weapon. When she insisted that she was born with homosexual desires, I told her that I was too. I was born with a capacity to be a homosexual, to fornicate, commit adultery, lie, and steal. I said

filthy conversation of the wicked:
8 (For that righteous man dwelling among them, in seeing and hearing, vexed his righteous soul from day to day with their unlawful deeds;)
9 The Lord knows how to deliver the godly out of temptations, and to reserve the unjust to the day of judgment to be punished:
10 But chiefly them that walk after the flesh in the lust of uncleanness, and despise government. Presumptuous are they, self-willed, they are not afraid to speak evil of dignities.
11 Whereas angels, which are greater in power and might, bring not railing accusation against them before the Lord.
12 But these, as natural brute beasts, made to be taken and destroyed, speak evil of the things that they understand not; and shall utterly perish in their own corruption;
13 And shall receive the reward of unrighteousness, as they that count it pleasure to riot in the day time. Spots they are and blemishes, sporting themselves with their own deceivings while they feast with you;
14 Having eyes full of adultery, and that cannot cease from sin; beguiling unstable souls: an heart they have exercised with covetous practices; cursed children:
15 Which have forsaken the right way, and are gone astray, following the way of Balaam the son of Bosor, who loved the wages of unrighteousness;
16 But was rebuked for his iniquity: the dumb ass speaking with man's voice forbad the madness of the prophet.

> I believe that the most damnable thing a man can do is to preach the gospel merely as an actor and turn the worship of God into a kind of theatrical performance.
>
> **CHARLES SPURGEON**

17 These are wells without water, clouds that are carried with a tempest; to whom the mist of darkness is reserved for ever.
18 For when they speak great swelling words of vanity, they allure through the lusts of the flesh, through much wantonness, those that were clean escaped from them who live in error.
19 While they promise them liberty, they themselves are the servants of corruption: for of whom a man is overcome, of the same is he brought in bondage.
20 For if after they have escaped the pollutions of the world through the knowl-

that it was called 'sin,' and that we all had it in our nature. It diffused her intent on making me seem like a 'gay-basher.' I could see the frustration on her face when she wasn't able to take the discourse in the direction she wanted. Instead of seeming the poor victim, she found herself in the public hot-seat of having sinned against God.

The way to witness to a homosexual is simply to follow the biblical guidelines and use the Law. See Matthew 19:17–22 comment.

2:9 Using a Survey to Share Your Faith. Begin by asking: "Do you have a moment to answer a couple of quick questions for a survey?"

1) Do you believe in the existence of any type of God or Higher Power? *(Yes___ No___)*

2) If there truly was a coming Day of Judgment when God would give every person either everlasting life or everlasting punishment, do you think it would be important for people to know what they would need to do to receive everlasting life? *(Yes___ No___)*

3) If there truly was a coming Day of Judgment, do you think you would know how a person could receive everlasting life? *(Yes___ No___)* If so, how?

2:14 These workers of iniquity violate God's Law by transgressing the Seventh and Tenth Commandments.

edge of the Lord and Savior Jesus Christ,
they are again entangled therein, and overcome, the latter end is worse with them
than the beginning.
21 For it had been better for them not
to have known the way of righteousness,
than, after they have known it, to turn
from the holy commandment delivered
to them.
22 But it is happened to them according to the true proverb, The dog is turned
to his own vomit again; and the sow that
was washed to her wallowing in the mire.

CHAPTER 3

THIS second epistle, beloved, I now
write to you; in both which I stir up
your pure minds by way of remembrance:
2 That you may be mindful of the words
which were spoken before by the holy
prophets, and of the commandment of us
the apostles of the Lord and Savior:
3 Knowing this first, that there shall come
in the last days scoffers, walking after
their own lusts,
4 And saying, Where is the promise of
his coming? for since the fathers fell
asleep, all things continue as they were
from the beginning of the creation.
5 For this they willingly are ignorant of,
that by the word of God the heavens were
of old, and the earth standing out of the
water and in the water:
6 Whereby the world that then was, be-

2:21 When sinners make professions of faith and refuse to have any regard for God's Moral Law, their latter end becomes worse than the first. They fall away and become hardened (inoculated) against the truth. It would have been better for them not to have known the way of righteousness (the gospel) than, after they have known it, to turn from the "holy commandment" (the Moral Law).

The Law cannot condemn the Christian (Romans 8:1), but those who are truly converted will not transgress its precepts. Those who do, prove to be "workers of iniquity" (lawlessness). See Matthew 7:21–23. This is why we must thunder out the precepts of God's Law before we offer sinners the pardon of the gospel. If they don't see the serious nature of sin, they will still toy with its pleasures after they make a profession of faith.

2:22 Some argue that sins such as pornography are wrong because they are "harmful to society." However, you have more chance of convincing a pig that the mud in which he wallows is harmful to him. The reason he wallows is to cool his flesh. The only practical way to stop a pig wallowing in the mire is to kill him. That's the function of the Law: it nails the sin-loving sinner to the cross. It deals directly with the sinful nature. Sin is wrong not because it's harmful to society—it is wrong because God says that it's wrong.

3:3 Signs of the end times (combined from Matthew 24; Mark 13; Luke 21; 1 Timothy 4; and 2 Timothy 3): There will be false Christs; wars and rumors of wars; nation rising against nation; famines; disease (pestilence); false prophets who will deceive many; and lawlessness (forsaking of the Ten Commandments). The gospel will be preached in all the world. There will be earthquakes in various places; signs from heaven (in the sun, moon, and stars); and persecution against Christians in all nations. Men's hearts will fail them for fear of the future; they will be selfish, materialistic, arrogant, proud. Homosexuality will increase; there will be blasphemy; cold-heartedness; intemperance; brutality; rebellious youth; hatred of those who stand up for righteousness; ungodliness; pleasure-seeking; much hypocrisy. False Bible teachers will have many followers, be money-hungry, and slander the Christian faith (2 Peter 2:1–3).

Men will scoff and say that there was no such thing as the flood of Noah and that these "signs" have always been around. Their motivation for hating the truth will be their love of lust (2 Peter 3:1–7). The Scriptures tell us that they make one big mistake. Their understanding of God is erroneous. They don't understand that God's time frame is not the same as ours. They think (in their ignorance) that God's continued silence means that He doesn't see their sins. In truth, He is merely holding back His wrath, waiting for them to repent and escape the damnation of hell.

Jesus warned that the sign to look for was the repossession of Jerusalem by the Jews. That happened in 1967, after 2,000 years, bringing into culmination all the signs of the times.

QUESTIONS & OBJECTIONS

3:3–6

"The number of fossils in some areas is enormous. How could earth have supported all those creatures at the same time?"

This question shows a common false assumption that many people make. They assume the earth today is the same as it has always been. Today's earth is seventy percent under water. There are scriptural and scientific indications that the pre-Flood world had greater air pressure, higher percentages of oxygen and carbon dioxide, much more land (above sea level), less water (on the earth's surface), and a canopy of water to filter out the harmful effects of the sun. This would cause there to be many times more plants and animals on the earth than there are today. The added air pressure would diffuse more gasses into the water and support a much greater fish population. Aquatic plant life per cubic mile would multiply also.

Second Peter 3 tells us that the scoffers in the last days will be willingly ignorant of how God created the heavens and the earth. They would also be ignorant of the Flood. These two great events must be considered before making any statements about the conditions on earth today. Only about three percent of the earth today is habitable for man. The rest is under water, ice, deserts, mountains, etc. If the earth before the Flood were, say, seventy percent habitable, it could have supported a huge population. The vast amount and worldwide distribution of fossils shows that the Flood was global and that God hates sin enough to judge the entire world." *Dr. Kent Hovind*

"About 85% of the rock surface around the world is made up of sedimentary rock, indicating that at some time in the past, the world was covered by water." *Peter and Paul Lalonde, 301 Startling Proofs & Prophecies*

ing overflowed with water, perished:
7 But the heavens and the earth, which
are now, by the same word are kept in
store, reserved to fire against the day of
judgment and perdition of ungodly men.
8 But, beloved, be not ignorant of this
one thing, that one day is with the Lord
as a thousand years, and a thousand
years as one day.
9 The Lord is not slack concerning his
promise, as some men count slackness;
but is longsuffering to us-ward, not will-
ing that any should perish, but that all
should come to repentance.
10 **But the day of the Lord will come as**
a thief in the night; in the which the
heavens shall pass away with a great
noise, and the elements shall melt with
fervent heat, the earth also and the
works that are therein shall be burned
up.
11 Seeing then that all these things shall
be dissolved, what manner of persons
ought you to be in all holy conversation
and godliness,
12 Looking for and hastening to the coming of the day of God, wherein the heavens being on fire shall be dissolved, and
the elements shall melt with fervent heat?
13 Nevertheless we, according to his

3:6 Peter believed the Genesis account of Noah's Flood.

3:7 Judgment Day: For verses that warn of its reality, see Jude 14,15.

3:8 Because God is eternal and outside of the dimension of time, to Him one day is the same as a thousand years. In the same way, a person who is in space, outside of the influence of gravity, will find that one ounce is the same as a thousand pounds.

3:9 Salvation is possible for every person. See John 3:16,17.

QUESTIONS & OBJECTIONS

Q **3:9** *"Why does God allow evil?"*

Why does God allow evil men and women to live? Should He instead kill them before they do evil deeds? Should He judge murderers and rapists now? What about thieves and liars, adulterers, fornicators, those who lust, and those who hate? If God judged evil today, all unconverted men and women would perish under His wrath. Thank God that He is patiently waiting for them to turn to the Savior and be saved from His terrible wrath.

promise, look for new heavens and a new
earth, wherein dwells righteousness.
14 Wherefore, beloved, seeing that you
look for such things, be diligent that you
may be found of him in peace, without
spot, and blameless.
15 And account that the longsuffering
of our Lord is salvation; even as our beloved brother Paul also according to the
wisdom given to him has written to you;
16 As also in all his epistles, speaking in
them of these things; in which are some
things hard to be understood, which they
that are unlearned and unstable wrest, as
they do also the other scriptures, to their
own destruction.
17 You therefore, beloved, seeing you
know these things before, beware lest
you also, being led away with the error
of the wicked, fall from your own stead-
fastness.
18 But grow in grace, and in the knowledge of our Lord and Savior Jesus Christ.
To him be glory both now and for ever.
Amen.

"Bless O Lord the whole race of mankind, and let the world be filled with the knowledge of Thee and Thy Son, Jesus Christ."

GEORGE WASHINGTON

3:16 Never feel as though you have to be able to explain every Bible verse. Ever Peter admits that some things Paul wrote are hard to understand. In doing so, he also puts his seal of approval on the fact that Paul's letters were not the mere writings of a man, but "Scriptures."

1 John

CHAPTER 1

THAT which was from the beginning,
which we have heard, which we have
seen with our eyes, which we have looked
upon, and our hands have handled, of
the Word of life;
2 (For the life was manifested, and we
have seen it, and bear witness, and show
to you that eternal life, which was with
the Father, and was manifested to us;)
3 That which we have seen and heard
declare we to you, that you also may have
fellowship with us: and truly our fellowship is with the Father, and with his Son
Jesus Christ.
4 And these things write we to you, that
your joy may be full.
5 This then is the message which we
have heard of him, and declare to you, that
God is light, and in him is no darkness
at all.
6 If we say that we have fellowship with
him, and walk in darkness, we lie, and do
not the truth:
7 But if we walk in the light, as he is in
the light, we have fellowship one with
another, and the blood of Jesus Christ his
Son cleanses us from all sin.
8 **If we say that we have no sin, we deceive ourselves, and the truth is not in
us.**
**9 If we confess our sins, he is faithful
and just to forgive us our sins, and to
cleanse us from all unrighteousness.**
10 **If we say that we have not sinned,
we make him a liar, and his word is not
in us.**

CHAPTER 2

MY little children, these things write
I to you, that you sin not. And if any
man sin, we have an advocate with the
Father, Jesus Christ the righteous:
2 And he is the propitiation for our sins:
and not for ours only, but also for the
sins of the whole world.
3 **And hereby we do know that we
know him, if we keep his commandments.**
4 **He that says, I know him, and keeps**

1:9 The Christian who sins. "The great foundational truth respecting the believer in relationship to his sins is the fact that his salvation comprehends the forgiveness of all his trespasses past, present and future so far as condemnation is concerned (see Romans 8:1, Colossians 2:13; John 3:18; John 5:24). Since Christ has vicariously borne all sin and since the believer's standing in Christ is complete, he is perfected forever in Christ. When a believer sins, he is subjected to chastisement from the Father, but never to condemnation with the world (see 1 Corinthians 11:31,32). By confession the Christian is forgiven and restored to fellowship (see 1 John 1:9). It needs to be remembered that were it not for Christ's finished work on the cross and His present intercession in heaven, the least sin would result in his banishment from God's presence and eternal ruin." *Unger's Bible Dictionary*

The Function of the Law

1:7 "The Law also shows us our great need—our need of cleansing, cleansing with the water and the blood. It discovers to us our filthiness, and this naturally leads us to feel that we must be washed from it if we are ever to draw near to God. So the Law drives us to accept Christ as the only Person who can cleanse us, and make us fit to stand within the veil in the presence of the Most High.

"The Law is the surgeon's knife that cuts out the proud flesh that the wound may heal. The Law by itself only sweeps and raises the dust, but the gospel sprinkles clean water upon the dust, and all is well in the chamber of the soul. The Law kills, the gospel makes alive; the Law strips, and then Jesus Christ comes in and robes the soul in beauty and glory. All the commandments, and all the types direct us to Christ, if we will but heed their evident intent." *Charles Spurgeon*

not his commandments, is a liar, and the truth is not in him.
5 But whoso keeps his word, in him verily is the love of God perfected: hereby know we that we are in him.
6 He that said he abides in him ought himself also so to walk, even as he walked.
7 Brethren, I write no new commandment to you, but an old commandment which you had from the beginning. The old commandment is the word which you have heard from the beginning.
8 Again, a new commandment I write to you, which thing is true in him and in you: because the darkness is past, and the true light now shines.
9 He that says he is in the light, and hates his brother, is in darkness even until now.
10 He that loves his brother abides in the light, and there is none occasion of stumbling in him.
11 But he that hates his brother is in darkness, and walks in darkness, and knows not where he goes, because that darkness has blinded his eyes.
12 I write to you, little children, because your sins are forgiven you for his name's sake.
13 I write to you, fathers, because you have known him that is from the beginning. I write to you, young men, because you have overcome the wicked one. I write to you, little children, because you have known the Father.
14 I have written to you, fathers, because you have known him that is from the beginning. I have written to you, young men, because you are strong, and the word of God abides in you, and you have overcome the wicked one.
15 **Love not the world, neither the things that are in the world. If any man love the world, the love of the Father is not in him.**
16 For all that is in the world, the lust of the flesh, and the lust of the eyes, and the pride of life, is not of the Father, but is of the world.
17 And the world passes away, and the lust thereof: but he that does the will of God abides for ever.
18 Little children, it is the last time: and as you have heard that antichrist shall come, even now are there many antichrists; whereby we know that it is the last time.
19 They went out from us, but they were not of us; for if they had been of us, they would no doubt have continued with us: but they went out, that they might be made manifest that they were not all of us.

2:11 "The Incarnation is the ultimate reason why the service of God cannot be divorced from the service of man. He who says he loves God and hates his brother is a liar." *Dietrich Bonhoeffer*

2:16 See Hebrews 4:15 comment.

2:19 "I have left my religious conversion behind and settled into a comfortable state of atheism. I have come to think that religion has caused more harm than any other idea since the beginning of time." *Larry Flynt* (publisher of Hustler magazine, in his autobiography *An Unseemly Man*)

QUESTIONS & OBJECTIONS

2:19 ***"I was once a born-again Christian. Now I believe it's all rubbish!"***

When a person maintains that he was once a Christian, but came to his senses, he is saying that he once knew the Lord (see John 17:3). Ask him, "Did you know the Lord?" He will then be forced to say, "I *thought* I did!" This gives you license to gently say, "If you don't *know* so, then you probably didn't." If he didn't know the Lord, he was therefore never a Christian (1 John 5:11–13,20). Explain to him that the Bible speaks of false conversion, in which a "stony ground" hearer receives the Word with joy and gladness. Then, in a time of tribulation, temptation, and persecution, falls away. If he is open to reason, take him through the Ten Commandments, into the message of the cross, and the necessity of repentance and faith in the Savior.

20 But you have an unction from the Holy One, and you know all things.

21 I have not written to you because you know not the truth, but because you know it, and that no lie is of the truth.

22 Who is a liar but he that denies that Jesus is the Christ? He is antichrist, that denies the Father and the Son.

23 Whosoever denies the Son, the same has not the Father: (but) he that acknowledges the Son has the Father also.

> The most terrible warning to impenitent men in all the world is the death of Christ. For if God spared not His only Son, on whom was only laid imputed sin, will He spare sinners whose sins are their own?
>
> **CHARLES SPURGEON**

24 Let that therefore abide in you, which you have heard from the beginning. If that which you have heard from the beginning shall remain in you, you also shall continue in the Son, and in the Father.

25 And this is the promise that he has promised us, even eternal life.

26 These things have I written to you concerning them that seduce you.

27 But the anointing which you have received of him abides in you, and you need not that any man teach you: but as the same anointing teaches you of all things, and is truth, and is no lie, and even as it has taught you, you shall abide in him.

28 And now, little children, abide in him; that, when he shall appear, we may have confidence, and not be ashamed before him at his coming.

29 If you know that he is righteous, you know that every one that does righteousness is born of him.

CHAPTER 3

BEHOLD, what manner of love the Father has bestowed upon us, that we should be called the sons of God: therefore the world knows us not, because it knew him not.

2 Beloved, now are we the sons of God, and it does not yet appear what we shall be: but we know that, when he shall appear, we shall be like him; for we shall see him as he is.

3 And every man that has this hope in him purifies himself, even as he is pure.

4 **Whosoever commits sin transgresses also the law: for sin is the transgression of the law.**

5 And you know that he was manifested to take away our sins; and in him is no sin.

6 Whosoever abides in him sins not: whosoever sins has not seen him, neither known him.

7 Little children, let no man deceive you:

QUESTIONS & OBJECTIONS

3:12 "Where did Cain get his wife?"

Many ask this question thinking they've found a "mistake" in the Bible—that there must have been other people besides Adam and Eve. Scripture tells us that Adam is "the first man" (1 Corinthians 15:45); that there were no other humans when he was created, because God said, "It is not good that the man should be alone" (Genesis 2:18); and that Eve is "the mother of all living" (Genesis 3:20). Cain and Abel, then, must have married distant sisters. All of the first-generation siblings married each other in order to populate the earth. At that time there was no law against incest. But as the population grew large enough, and as the risk of genetic problems increased because of sin's curse, God outlawed marriage between siblings.

he that does righteousness is righteous,
even as he is righteous.
8 He that commits sin is of the devil; for
the devil sinned from the beginning. For
this purpose the Son of God was manifested, that he might destroy the works
of the devil.
9 Whosoever is born of God does not
commit sin; for his seed remains in him:
and he cannot sin, because he is born of
God.
10 In this the children of God are manifest, and the children of the devil: whosoever does not righteousness is not of
God, neither he that loves not his brother.
11 For this is the message that you heard
from the beginning, that we should love
one another.
12 Not as Cain, who was of that wicked
one, and slew his brother. And wherefore slew he him? Because his own works
were evil, and his brother's righteous.
13 Marvel not, my brethren, if the world
hate you.
14 We know that we have passed from
death to life, because we love the brethren. He that loves not his brother abides
in death.
**15 Whosoever hates his brother is a
murderer: and you know that no murderer has eternal life abiding in him.**
16 Hereby perceive we the love of God,

3:12 "The cool impudence of Cain is an indication of the state of heart which led up to his murdering his brother; and it was also a part of the result of his having committed that terrible crime. He would not have proceeded to the cruel deed of bloodshed if he had not first cast off the fear of God and been ready to defy his Maker." *Charles Spurgeon*

3:13 Hypocrisy in the Church. It's interesting to note that the world hates hypocrisy in the Church. They detest the "pretender." Does that mean that they *want* the Christian to be genuine? Do they *want* us to be true and faithful in our witness and therefore speak of sin, righteousness, and judgment? Do they want us to live in holiness rather than in compromise? Does the world really want us to speak up against pornography, greed, adultery, abortion, homosexuality, fornication, and other sins they so love? In their eyes we are damned if we do, and damned if we don't.

3:15 Always be ready to "earnestly contend for the faith" (Jude 3). Learn how to prove God's existence. Study the theory of evolution and the evidence for creation. Become proficient in presenting the spiritual nature of God's Law. Say, "I can do all things through Christ who strengthens me," and thereby walk above the snare of the fear of man.

Note that this verse is not a prescription for what is commonly called "lifestyle evangelism." We are not being told to wait until we are asked about our faith—we may be waiting for a long time. As soldiers of Christ we are not only to *defend* the faith, but we are to *advance* the cause of the gospel. The word "go" in the Great Commission, means just that—go.

because he laid down his life for us: and
we ought to lay down our lives for the
brethren.
17 But whoso has this world's good,
and sees his brother have need, and shuts
up his bowels of compassion from him,
how dwells the love of God in him?
18 My little children, let us not love in
word, neither in tongue; but in deed and
in truth.
19 And hereby we know that we are of
the truth, and shall assure our hearts before him.
20 For if our heart condemn us, God is
greater than our heart, and knows all
things.
21 Beloved, if our heart condemn us not,
then have we confidence toward God.
22 And whatsoever we ask, we receive of
him, because we keep his commandments,
and do those things that are pleasing in
his sight.
23 And this is his commandment, That
we should believe on the name of his Son
Jesus Christ, and love one another, as he
gave us commandment.
24 And he that keeps his commandments
dwells in him, and he in him. And hereby
we know that he abides in us, by the
Spirit which he has given us.

CHAPTER 4

BELOVED, believe not every spirit, but try the spirits whether they are of God: because many false prophets are gone out into the world.
2 Hereby know you the Spirit of God:
Every spirit that confesses that Jesus Christ
is come in the flesh is of God:
3 And every spirit that confesses not
that Jesus Christ is come in the flesh is not
of God: and this is that spirit of antichrist,
whereof you have heard that it should
come; and even now already is it in the
world.
4 You are of God, little children, and
have overcome them: because greater is he
that is in you, than he that is in the world.
5 They are of the world: therefore speak
they of the world, and the world hears
them.
6 *We are of God: he that knows God hears
us; he that is not of God hears not us. Hereby know we the spirit of truth, and the
spirit of error.*
7 Beloved, let us love one another: for
love is of God; and every one that loves
is born of God, and knows God.
8 He that loves not knows not God; for
God is love.
9 **In this was manifested the love of
God toward us, because that God sent
his only begotten Son into the world,
that we might live through him.**
10 **Herein is love, not that we loved
God, but that he loved us, and sent his
Son to be the propitiation for our sins.**
11 Beloved, if God so loved us, we ought
also to love one another.
12 No man has seen God at any time. If
we love one another, God dwells in us,
and his love is perfected in us.

3:16 "You are more sinful than you ever dared to believe, but you are more loved than you ever dared to hope." *Mark Liederbach*

4:4 Confidence in witnessing. "When you represent the Lord Jesus Christ as His disciple, you can be assured that you are representing the One who possesses all power, wisdom, and authority. You have everything when you have Him. Jesus said: 'I tell you the truth, anyone who has faith in me will do what I have been doing. He will do even greater things than these, because I am going to the Father' (John 14:12). No power can resist you as you go in obedience and faith as His ambassador (2 Corinthians 5:19,20). You have the promise, 'The one who is in you is greater than the one who is in the world' (1 John 4:4). Also, you are assured that even the gates of hell will not prevail against you (Matthew 16:18). The more you understand who Christ is and all that He has done and will do for you and through you, the more completely you will want to trust, obey, and serve Him." *Dr. Bill Bright*

4:8 The Firefighters

Imagine seeing a group of firefighters polishing their engine outside a burning building with people trapped at a top floor window. Obviously, there is nothing wrong with cleaning a fire-engine—*but not while people are trapped in a burning building!* Instead of ignoring their cries, the firefighters should have an overwhelming sense of urgency to rescue them. That's the spirit that should be behind the task of evangelism. But according to Dr. Bill Bright of Campus Crusade for Christ, "Only 2 percent of believers in America regularly share their faith with others." That means that 98 percent of the professing Body of Christ are "lukewarm" when it comes to obeying the Great Commission (Mark 16:15).

Oswald J. Smith said, "Oh my friends, we are loaded down with countless church activities, while the *real* work of the Church, that of evangelizing and winning the lost, is almost entirely neglected." We have polished the engines of worship, prayer, and praise and neglected the sober task given to us by God. A firefighter who ignores his responsibilities and allows people to perish in flames is not a firefighter; he is an impostor. How could we ignore our responsibility and allow the world to walk blindly into the fires of hell? If God's love dwells in us, we must warn them. The Bible tells us to "have compassion...save with fear, pulling them out of the fire; hating even the garment spotted by the flesh" (Jude 22,23). If we don't have love and compassion, then we don't know God—we are impostors (1 John 4:8).

Charles Spurgeon said, "Have you no wish for others to be saved? Then you are not saved yourself. Be sure of that." Please, examine yourself to see if you are in the faith (2 Corinthians 13:5). Don't be part of the great multitude who called Jesus "Lord," but refused to obey Him. It will be professing *believers* who will hear those fearful words, "I never knew you: depart from me" (Matthew 7:21–23).

Backward Christian Soldiers

Backward Christian soldiers, fleeing from the fight
With the cross of Jesus nearly out of sight.
Christ, our rightful master, stands against the foe
But forward into battle, we are loathe to go.

Like a mighty tortoise moves the Church of God
Brothers we are treading where we've always trod.
We are much divided, many bodies we
Having many doctrines, not much charity.

Crowns and thorns may perish, kingdoms rise and wane,
But the Church of Jesus hidden does remain.
Gates of hell should never 'gainst the Church prevail
We have Christ's own promise, but think that it will fail.

Sit here then ye people, join our useless throng
Blend with ours your voices in a feeble song.
Blessings, ease and comfort, ask from Christ the King
With our modern thinking, we don't do a thing.
(Anonymous)

If God is speaking to you about your lack of evangelistic concern, pray something like this now:

Father, please forgive me for my lack of love for this dying world. From this day forward I will strive to be a "true and faithful witness." Please give me the wisdom to know what to say to reach the lost. In Jesus' name I pray. Amen.

13 Hereby know we that we dwell in him, and he in us, because he has given us of his Spirit.

14 And we have seen and do testify that the Father sent the Son to be the Savior of the world.

QUESTIONS & OBJECTIONS

5:10 ***"I find it difficult to have faith in God."***

If you don't believe someone, it means you think that he is a liar. The Bible says that those who don't believe God accuse Him of lying. Martin Luther said, "What greater insult…can there be to God, than to not believe His promises." See Hebrews 11:6 comment.

15 Whosoever shall confess that Jesus is
the Son of God, God dwells in him, and
he in God.
16 And we have known and believed
the love that God has to us. God is love;
and he that dwells in love dwells in God,
and God in him.
17 Herein is our love made perfect, that
we may have boldness in the day of
judgment: because as he is, so are we in
this world.
18 *There is no fear in love; but perfect
love casts out fear: because fear has torment. He that fears is not made perfect in
love.*
19 We love him, because he first loved
us.
20 If a man say, I love God, and hates
his brother, he is a liar: for he that loves
not his brother whom he has seen, how
can he love God whom he has not seen?
21 And this commandment have we
from him, That he who loves God love
his brother also.

……

For two forms of the "Sinner's Prayer," see page 540.

……

CHAPTER 5

WHOSOEVER believes that Jesus is
the Christ is born of God: and
every one that loves him that begat loves
him also that is begotten of him.
2 By this we know that we love the children of God, when we love God, and keep
his commandments.
3 For this is the love of God, that we keep
his commandments: and his commandments are not grievous.
4 For whatsoever is born of God overcomes the world: and this is the victory
that overcomes the world, even our faith.
5 Who is he that overcomes the world,
but he that believes that Jesus is the Son
of God?

> The Church has developed a theology that doesn't require much repentance. We have a theology that is uncomfortable with the very term 'Jesus is Lord.'"
>
> **DR. PAUL A. CEDAR**

6 This is he that came by water and
blood, even Jesus Christ; not by water
only, but by water and blood. And it is
the Spirit that bears witness, because the
Spirit is truth.
7 For there are three that bear record in
heaven, the Father, the Word, and the
Holy Spirit: and these three are one.
8 And there are three that bear witness in
earth, the spirit, and the water, and the
blood: and these three agree in one.
9 If we receive the witness of men, the
witness of God is greater: for this is the
witness of God which he has testified of

4:20 "I really only love God as much as I love the person I love the least." *Dorothy Day*

"I shall allow no man to belittle my soul by making me hate him." *Booker T. Washington*

5:1 New birth—its necessity for salvation. See John 1:13.

QUESTIONS & OBJECTIONS

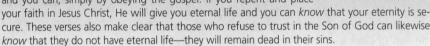

5:12,13 ***"I hope I'm going to heaven when I die."***

Of all the things that you should be sure of, it's your eternal destiny. To say "I hope I'm going to heaven" is like standing at the open door of a plane 25,000 feet in the air and, when asked "Have you got your parachute on?" answering with "I hope so." You want to *know* so—and you can, simply by obeying the gospel. If you repent and place your faith in Jesus Christ, He will give you eternal life and you can *know* that your eternity is secure. These verses also make clear that those who refuse to trust in the Son of God can likewise *know* that they do not have eternal life—they will remain dead in their sins.

his Son.
10 He that believes on the Son of God
has the witness in himself: he that be-
lieves not God has made him a liar; be-
cause he believes not the record that
God gave of his Son.
11 **And this is the record, that God has**
given to us eternal life, and this life is
in his Son.
12 He that has the Son has life; and he
that has not the Son of God has not life.
13 These things have I written to you
that believe on the name of the Son of
God; that you may know that you have
eternal life, and that you may believe
on the name of the Son of God.
14 And this is the confidence that we
have in him, that, if we ask any thing
according to his will, he hears us:
15 And if we know that he hear us,
whatsoever we ask, we know that we
have the petitions that we desired of him.
16 If any man see his brother sin a sin
which is not to death, he shall ask, and he
shall give him life for them that sin not to
death. There is a sin to death: I do not say
that he shall pray for it.
17 All unrighteousness is sin: and there
is a sin not to death.
18 We know that whosoever is born of
God sins not; but he that is begotten of
God keeps himself, and that wicked one
touches him not.
19 And we know that we are of God,
and the whole world lies in wickedness.
20 And we know that the Son of God is
come, and has given us an understanding, that we may know him that is true,
and we are in him that is true, even in
his Son Jesus Christ. This is the true God,
and eternal life.
21 Little children, keep yourselves from
idols. Amen.

5:14 Prayer begins with God. "God prompts His people to pray and then acts in response to their prayers. Things happen or don't happen because of prayer. This does not mean God can be manipulated through prayer to do what we want if what we want is contrary to His will. Instead, God reveals His will to us by His Word and works in us by His Spirit so that we know His will and pray in accord with it. Then, in responding to our prayers, He accomplishes both His will and ours, and, in the process, involves us." *Alvin J. Vander Griend*, "Your Prayers Matter," *Discipleship Journal*

2 John

THE elder to the elect lady and her
children, whom I love in the truth;
and not I only, but also all they that have
known the truth;
2 For the truth's sake, which dwells in
us, and shall be with us for ever.
3 Grace be with you, mercy, and peace,
from God the Father, and from the Lord
Jesus Christ, the Son of the Father, in
truth and love.
4 I rejoiced greatly that I found of your
children walking in truth, as we have received a commandment from the Father.
5 And now I beseech you, lady, not as
though I wrote a new commandment to
you, but that which we had from the beginning, that we love one another.
6 And this is love, that we walk after his
commandments. This is the commandment, That, as you have heard from the
beginning, you should walk in it.
7 For many deceivers are entered into
the world, who confess not that Jesus
Christ is come in the flesh. This is a deceiver and an antichrist.
8 Look to yourselves, that we lose not
those things which we have wrought,
but that we receive a full reward.
9 Whosoever transgresses, and abides
not in the doctrine of Christ, has not
God. He that abides in the doctrine of
Christ, he has both the Father and the
Son.
10 If there come any to you, and bring
not this doctrine, receive him not into
your house, neither bid him God speed:
11 For he that bids him God speed is
partaker of his evil deeds.
12 Having many things to write to you,
I would not write with paper and ink:
but I trust to come to you, and speak face
to face, that our joy may be full.
13 The children of your elect sister greet
you. Amen.

7 Religions and "Christian" sects that deny the great truth that God was manifest in the flesh are deceivers and are antichrist in spirit. See 1 John 4:2; 1 Timothy 3:16.

9 Those who object to Christianity's claim that there is only one way to God usually argue that we should be tolerant of all religions. In that case, they should practice what they preach and be tolerant of the Christian claim. Jesus is *the* way, *the* truth, and *the* life. No one comes to the Father except through Him (John 14:6). See 1 John 2:23.

Buddhism

FOUNDER: Siddhartha Gautama, a prince from northern India near modern Nepal who lived about 563–483 B.C.

SCRIPTURES: Various, but the oldest and most authoritative are compiled in the Pali Canon.

ADHERENTS: 613 million worldwide; 1 million in the United States.

GENERAL DESCRIPTION: Buddhism is the belief system of those who follow the Buddha, the Enlightened One, a title given to its founder. The religion has evolved into three main schools:

1. *Theravada* or the Doctrine of the Elders (38%) is followed in Sri Lanka (Ceylon), Myanmar (Burma), Thailand, Cambodia (Kampuchea), and Vietnam.

2. *Mahayana* or the Greater Vehicle (56%) is strong in China, Korea, and Japan.

3. *Vajrayana*, also called Tantrism or Lamaism, (6%) is rooted in Tibet, Nepal, and Mongolia. Theravada is closest to the original doctrines. It does not treat the Buddha as deity and regards the faith as a worldview—not a type of worship. Mahayana has accommodated many different beliefs and worships the Buddha as a god. Vajrayana has added elements of shamanism and the occult and includes taboo breaking (intentional immorality) as a means of spiritual enlightenment.

GROWTH IN THE UNITED STATES: Buddhists regard the United States as a prime mission field, and the number of Buddhists in this country is growing rapidly due to surges in Asian immigration, endorsement by celebrities such as Tina Turner and Richard Gere, and positive exposure in major movies such as *Siddhartha*, *The Little Buddha*, and *What's Love Got to Do with It?* Buddhism is closely related to the New Age Movement and may to some extent be driving it. Certainly Buddhist growth is benefiting from the influence of New Age thought on American life.

HISTORIC BACKGROUND: Buddhism was founded as a form of atheism that rejected more ancient beliefs in a permanent, personal, creator God (Ishvara) who controlled the eternal destiny of human souls. Siddhartha Gautama rejected more ancient theistic beliefs because of difficulty he had over reconciling the reality of suffering, judgment, and evil with the existence of a good and holy God.

CORE BELIEFS: Buddhism is an impersonal religion of self-perfection, the end of which is death (extinction)—not life. The essential elements of the Buddhist belief system are summarized in the Four Noble Truths, the Noble Eightfold Path, and several additional key doctrines. The Four Noble Truths affirm that (1) life is full of suffering (*dukkha*); (2) suffering is caused by craving (*samudaya*); (3) suffering will cease only when craving ceases (*nirodha*); and (4) this can be achieved by following the Noble Eightfold Path consisting of right views, right aspiration, right speech, right conduct, right livelihood, right effort, right mindfulness, and right contemplation. Other key doctrines include belief that nothing in life is permanent (*anicca*), that individual selves do not truly exist (*anatta*), that all is determined by an impersonal law of moral causation (*karma*), that reincarnation is an endless cycle of continuous suffering, and that the goal of life is to break out of this cycle by finally extinguishing the flame of life and entering a permanent state of pure nonexistence (*nirvana*).

BRIDGES FOR EVANGELIZING BUDDHISTS

The gospel can be appealing to Buddhists if witnessing focuses on areas of personal need where the Buddhist belief system is weak. Some major areas include:

Suffering: Buddhists are deeply concerned with overcoming suffering but must deny that suffering is real. Christ faced the reality of suffering and overcame it by solving the problem of sin, which is the real source of suffering. Now, those who trust in Christ can rise above suffering in this life because they have hope of a future life free of suffering. "We fix our eyes not on what is seen [suffering], but on what is unseen [eternal life free of suffering]. For what is seen [suffering] is temporary, but what is unseen [future good life with Christ] is eternal" (2 Cor. 4:18, NIV).

Meaningful Self: Buddhists must work to convince themselves they have no personal significance, even though they live daily as though they do. Jesus taught that each person has real significance. Each person is made in God's image with an immortal soul and an eternal destiny. Jesus demonstrated the value of people by loving us so much that He sacrificed His life in order to offer eternal future good life to anyone who trusts Him. "God demonstrates his own love for us in this: While we were still sinners, Christ died for us" (Rom. 5:8, NIV).

Future Hope: The hope of nirvana is no hope at all—only death and extinction. The hope of those who put their trust in Christ is eternal good life in a "new heaven and new earth" in which God "will wipe every tear from their eyes. There will be no more death or mourning or crying or pain, for the old order of things [suffering] has passed [will pass] away" (Rev. 21:4, NIV).

Moral Law: Because karma, the Buddhist law of moral cause and effect, is completely rigid and impersonal, life for a Buddhist is very oppressive. Under karma, there can be no appeal, no mercy, and no escape except through unceasing effort at self-perfection. Christians understand that the moral force governing the universe is a personal God who listens to those who pray, who has mercy on those who repent, and who with love personally controls for good the lives of those who follow Christ. "In all things God works for the good of those who love him" (Rom. 8:28, NIV).

Merit: Buddhists constantly struggle to earn merit by doing good deeds, hoping to collect enough to break free from the life of suffering. They also believe saints can transfer surplus merit to the undeserving. Jesus taught no one can ever collect enough merit on his own to earn everlasting freedom from suffering. Instead, Jesus Christ, who has unlimited merit (righteousness) by virtue of His sinless life, meritorious death, and resurrection, now offers His unlimited merit as a free gift to anyone who will become His disciple. "For it is by grace you have been saved, through faith—and this not from yourselves, it is the gift of God—not by works, so that no one can boast" (Eph. 2:8–9, NIV).

Desire: Buddhists live a contradiction—they seek to overcome suffering by rooting out desire, but at the same time they cultivate desire for self-control, meritorious life, and nirvana. Christians are consistent—we seek to reject evil desires and cultivate good desires according to the standard of Christ. "Flee the evil desires of youth and pursue righteousness, faith, love and peace, along with those who call on the Lord out of a pure heart" (2 Tim. 2:22, NIV).

JESUS AND THE EIGHTFOLD PATH

Because Buddhists think a good life consists of following the Eightfold Path, the stages of the path can be used to introduce them to Christ as follows:

Right views: Jesus is the way, the truth, and the life (John 14:6), and there is salvation in no one else (Acts 4:12).

Right aspiration: Fights and quarrels come from selfish desires and wrong motives (Jas. 4:1–3); right desires and motives honor God (1 Cor. 10:31).

Right speech: A day of judgment is coming when God will hold men accountable for every careless word they have spoken (Matt. 12:36).

Right conduct: The one who loves Jesus must obey Him (John 14:21), and those who live by God's wisdom will produce good acts/fruit (Jas. 3:17).

Right livelihood: God will care for those who put Him first (Matt. 6:31,33), and all work must be done for God's approval (2 Tim. 2:15).

Right effort: Like runners in a race, followers of Christ must throw off every hindrance in order to give Him their best efforts (Heb. 12:1–2).

Right mindfulness: The sinful mind cannot submit to God's law (Rom. 8:7), and disciples of Christ must orient their minds as He did (Phil. 2:5).

Right contemplation: The secret of true success, inner peace, self-control, and lasting salvation is submission to Jesus Christ as Savior and Lord and setting your heart and mind on things above where He now sits in glory waiting to bring the present order of sin and suffering to an end (Col. 3:1–4).

WHEN WITNESSING TO BUDDHISTS

1. Avoid terms such as "new birth," "rebirth," "regeneration," or "born again." Use alternatives such as "endless freedom from suffering, guilt, and sin," "new power for living a holy life," "promise of eternal good life without suffering," or "gift of unlimited merit."
2. Emphasize the uniqueness of Christ.

3. Focus on the gospel message and do not get distracted by details of Buddhist doctrine.
4. Understand Buddhist beliefs enough to discern weaknesses that can be used to make the gospel appealing (see "Bridges for Evangelizing Buddhists" and "Jesus and the Eightfold Path").
5. While using bridge concepts (see "Bridges for Evangelizing Buddhists"), be careful not to reduce Christian truth to a form of Buddhism. Buddhism has been good at accommodating other religions. Do not say "Buddhism is good, but Christianity is easier."
6. Share your own testimony, especially your freedom from guilt, assurance of heaven (no more pain), and personal relationship with Christ.
7. Prepare with prayer. Do not witness in your own strength.

Daniel R. Heimbach, Associate Professor of Christian Ethics, Southeastern Baptist Theological Seminary, Wake Forest, N.C.

Evangelistic Survey

- Where do people go to when they die?
- What do you think God is like?
- If you could ask God one thing, what would it be?
- Should God punish murderers? If so, how should He punish them?
- What do you think a person has to do to go to heaven?
- Do you consider yourself to be a "good" person?
- How many of the Ten Commandments can you name?
- Do you think you have kept the Ten Commandments?
- Where would you go if you died tonight?
- Do you believe there is such a place as hell?
- If there was a way to avoid death, would you be interested?
- Do you think the Bible's claim, that someone can know that they have everlasting life, is true?
- Who do you think Jesus was?
- What is stopping you from asking God for forgiveness and being converted right now?

3 John

THE elder to the wellbeloved Gaius,
whom I love in the truth.
2 Beloved, I wish above all things that
you may prosper and be in health, even
as your soul prospers.
3 For I rejoiced greatly, when the brethren came and testified of the truth that is
in you, even as you walk in the truth.
4 I have no greater joy than to hear that
my children walk in truth.
5 Beloved, you do faithfully whatsoever
you do to the brethren, and to strangers;
6 Which have borne witness of your
charity before the church: whom if you
bring forward on their journey after a
godly sort, you shall do well:
7 Because that for his name's sake they
went forth, taking nothing of the Gentiles.
8 We therefore ought to receive such, that
we might be fellow-helpers to the truth.
9 I wrote to the church: but Diotrephes,
who loves to have the preeminence among
them, receives us not.
10 Wherefore, if I come, I will remember his deeds which he does, prating
against us with malicious words: and not
content therewith, neither does he himself receive the brethren, and forbids them
that would, and casts them out of the
church.
11 Beloved, follow not that which is
evil, but that which is good. He that does
good is of God: but he that does evil has
not seen God.
12 Demetrius has good report of all men,
and of the truth itself: yes, and we also
bear record; and you know that our record is true.

> Satan always hates Christian fellowship; it is his policy to keep Christians apart. Anything which can divide saints from one another he delights in.
>
> **CHARLES SPURGEON**

13 I had many things to write, but I will
not with ink and pen write to you:
14 But I trust I shall shortly see you, and
we shall speak face to face. Peace be to
you. Our friends salute you. Greet the
friends by name.

9 Loving to have preeminence is not a fruit of godliness. Those who want it will manifest their unregenerate hearts with malicious words. They will divide the Body of Christ for their own ends, as did Diotrephes.

Test Your I.Q.

Read OUT LOUD the wording in the three triangles:

READ this sentence:

**FINISHED FILES ARE THE RE-
SULTS OF YEARS OF SCIEN-
TIFIC STUDY COMBINED WITH
THE EXPERIENCE OF YEARS**

Now count aloud the F's in the box. Count them only ONCE; do not look back and count them again.

Answers: The words "the" and "a" are repeated. There are six F's.

Here is another I.Q. test:

This one is more important. Answer Yes or No OUT LOUD:

1 Is there a God?

2 Does God care about right and wrong?

3 Are God's standards the same as ours?

4 Will God punish sin?

5 Is there a hell?

6 Can you avoid hell by living a good life?

Answers:

1 Yes. 2 Yes. 3 No. 4 Yes. 5 Yes. 6 No.

Jude

JUDE, the servant of Jesus Christ, and
brother of James, to them that are
sanctified by God the Father, and preserved in Jesus Christ, and called:
2 Mercy to you, and peace, and love, be
multiplied.
3 *Beloved, when I gave all diligence to write
to you of the common salvation, it was
needful for me to write to you, and exhort
you that you should earnestly contend for
the faith which was once delivered to the
saints.*
4 For there are certain men crept in unawares, who were before of old ordained
to this condemnation, ungodly men, turning the grace of our God into lasciviousness, and denying the only Lord God, and
our Lord Jesus Christ.
5 I will therefore put you in remembrance, though you once knew this, how
that the Lord, having saved the people
out of the land of Egypt, afterward destroyed them that believed not.
6 And the angels which kept not their
first estate, but left their own habitation,
he has reserved in everlasting chains
under darkness to the judgment of the
great day.
7 Even as Sodom and Gomorrha, and the
cities about them in like manner, giving
themselves over to fornication, and going
after strange flesh, are set forth for an example, suffering the vengeance of eternal
fire.
8 Likewise also these filthy dreamers
defile the flesh, despise dominion, and
speak evil of dignities.
9 Yet Michael the archangel, when con-
tending with the devil he disputed about

USING THE LAW IN EVANGELISM

3 Regarding the Law's use in evangelism, *Martin Luther* stated: "This now is the Christian teaching and preaching, which God be praised, we know and possess, and it is not necessary at present to develop it further, but only to offer the admonition that it be maintained in Christendom with all diligence. For Satan has attacked it hard and strong from the beginning until present, and gladly would he completely extinguish it and tread it under foot."

3 Never lose sight of the mandate of the Church: to contend earnestly for the faith. The battle in which we find ourselves is for the salvation of lost sinners.

"When people inquire as to the relevance of our gospel, we must not be tricked into going on the defensive. We must immediately take the offensive, for our Lord Himself has promised that the gates of hell shall not withstand the assault of His Church." *Dr. Leighton Ford*

4 False converts have "crept in unawares" and sit amid God's people. They think that salvation and sin are compatible. They are actually workers of iniquity. See Matthew 7:21–23.

QUESTIONS & OBJECTIONS

7

"God made me to be a homosexual, so He doesn't want me to change."

Homosexuals argue that they did not make a conscious decision to be that way, so it must be natural. They *are* born that way—just as all of us are born with a sin nature and sinful desires (Ephesians 2:1–3). Tell them that it *is* natural for them, and for all of us, to be tempted to do things that God says are wrong. In the same way, pedophiles and adulterers (alcoholics, drug addicts, etc.) don't make a conscious decision to "choose" that self-destructive lifestyle, they simply give in to their sinful desires. However, although sin is natural for unbelievers, that doesn't mean God wants them to remain that way. God can set them free from their sinful nature (Romans 7:23–8:2), give them new desires (Ephesians 4:22–24), and help them withstand temptations (1 Corinthians 10:13). See 1 Corinthians 6:9–11 comment.

the body of Moses, dared not bring against
him a railing accusation, but said, The
Lord rebuke you.
10 But these speak evil of those things
which they know not: but what they know
naturally, as brute beasts, in those things
they corrupt themselves.
11 Woe to them! for they have gone in
the way of Cain, and ran greedily after the
error of Balaam for reward, and perished
in the gainsaying of Core.

> Preach with this object, that men may quit their sins and fly to Christ for pardon, that by His blessed Spirit they may be renovated and become as much in love with everything that is holy as they are now in love with everything that is sinful.
>
> **CHARLES SPURGEON**

12 These are spots in your feasts of charity, when they feast with you, feeding
themselves without fear: clouds they are
without water, carried about of winds;
trees whose fruit withers, without fruit,
twice dead, plucked up by the roots;
13 Raging waves of the sea, foaming out
their own shame; wandering stars, to
whom is reserved the blackness of darkness for ever.
14 And Enoch also, the seventh from
Adam, prophesied of these, saying, Behold,
the Lord comes with ten thousands of
his saints,
15 To execute judgment upon all, and
to convince all that are ungodly among
them of all their ungodly deeds which
they have ungodly committed, and of all
their hard speeches which ungodly sinners have spoken against him.
16 These are murmurers, complainers,
walking after their own lusts; and their
mouth speaks great swelling words, having men's persons in admiration because
of advantage.
17 But, beloved, remember the words
which were spoken before of the apostles of our Lord Jesus Christ;
18 How that they told you there should
be mockers in the last time, who should
walk after their own ungodly lusts.

14 Second coming of Jesus: See Revelation 1:7.

15 With the help of God, we are to convince the ungodly that their deeds and their speech are offensive to their Creator, and will bring swift judgment upon them.

19 These be they who separate themselves, sensual, having not the Spirit.
20 But you, beloved, building up yourselves on your most holy faith, praying in the Holy Spirit,
21 Keep yourselves in the love of God, looking for the mercy of our Lord Jesus Christ to eternal life.
22 And of some have compassion, making a difference:
23 And others save with fear, pulling them out of the fire; hating even the garment spotted by the flesh.
24 Now to him that is able to keep you from falling, and to present you faultless before the presence of his glory with exceeding joy,
25 To the only wise God our Savior, be glory and majesty, dominion and power, both now and ever. Amen.

"Before I can preach love, mercy, and grace, I must preach sin, Law, and judgment."

John Wesley

18,19 A failure to preach the Commandments of God has left an entire generation without the fear of God. They are mockers in these last days. Scripture sheds light on their secret sins—lust and sensuality.

20 "What is the reason that some believers are so much brighter and holier than others? I believe the difference, in nineteen cases out of twenty, arises from different habits about private prayer. I believe that those who are not eminently holy pray little, and those who are eminently holy pray much." *J. C. Ryle*

23 "The world says you can't confront people with Jesus; you'll run them off. Where are you going to run them to? Hell number 2?" *Darrell Robinson*

Evolution: True Science Fiction

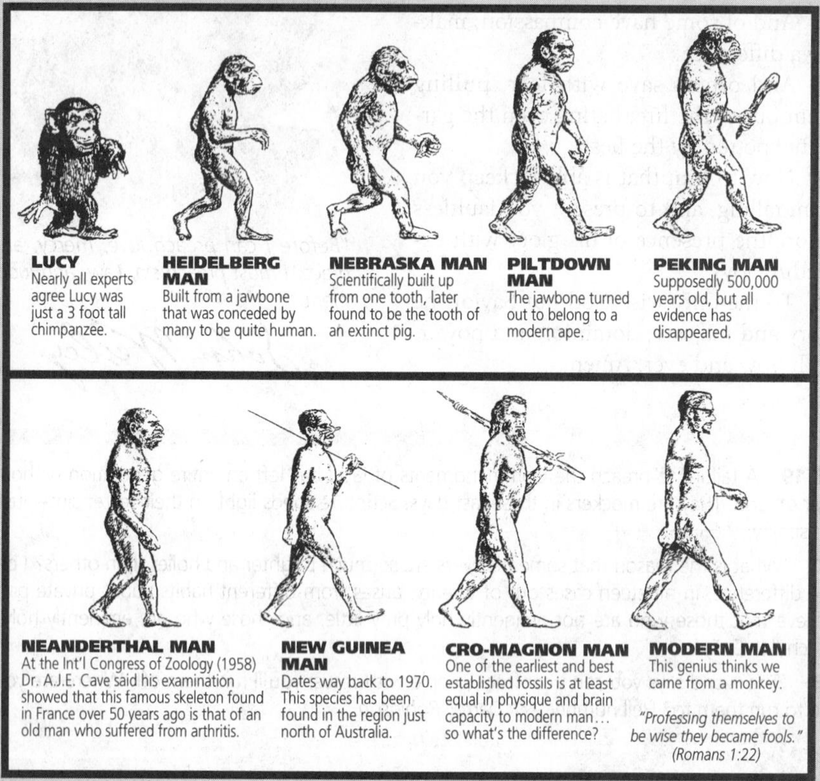

LUCY
Nearly all experts agree Lucy was just a 3 foot tall chimpanzee.
HEIDELBERG MAN
Built from a jawbone that was conceded by many to be quite human.
NEBRASKA MAN
Scientifically built up from one tooth, later found to be the tooth of an extinct pig.
PILTDOWN MAN
The jawbone turned out to belong to a modern ape.
PEKING MAN
Supposedly 500,000 years old, but all evidence has disappeared.
NEANDERTHAL MAN
At the Int'l Congress of Zoology (1958) Dr. A.J.E. Cave said his examination showed that this famous skeleton found in France over 50 years ago is that of an old man who suffered from arthritis.
NEW GUINEA MAN
Dates way back to 1970. This species has been found in the region just north of Australia.
CRO-MAGNON MAN
One of the earliest and best established fossils is at least equal in physique and brain capacity to modern man… so what's the difference?
MODERN MAN
This genius thinks we came from a monkey.
"Professing themselves to be wise they became fools." (Romans 1:22)

$250,000 REWARD

Offered by Dr. Kent Hovind to:

"Anyone who can give any empirical evidence (scientific proof) for evolution."

(See www.drdino.com/Articles/Article1.htm.)

Revelation

CHAPTER 1

THE Revelation of Jesus Christ, which God gave to him, to show to his servants things which must shortly come to pass; and he sent and signified it by his angel to his servant John:

2 Who bare record of the word of God, and of the testimony of Jesus Christ, and of all things that he saw.

3 Blessed is he that reads, and they that hear the words of this prophecy, and keep those things which are written therein: for the time is at hand.

4 John to the seven churches which are in Asia: Grace be to you, and peace, from him which is, and which was, and which is to come; and from the seven Spirits which are before his throne;

5 And from Jesus Christ, who is the faithful witness, and the first begotten of the dead, and the prince of the kings of the earth. To him that loved us, and washed us from our sins in his own blood,

6 And has made us kings and priests to God and his Father; to him be glory and dominion for ever and ever. Amen.

7 Behold, he comes with clouds; and every eye shall see him, and they also which pierced him: and all kindreds of the earth shall wail because of him. Even so, Amen.

8 I am Alpha and Omega, the beginning and the ending, says the Lord, which is, and which was, and which is to come, the Almighty.

9 I John, who also am your brother, and companion in tribulation, and in the kingdom and patience of Jesus Christ, was in the isle that is called Patmos, for the word of God, and for the testimony of Jesus Christ.

10 I was in the Spirit on the Lord's day, and heard behind me a great voice, as of a trumpet,

11 Saying, I am Alpha and Omega, the first and the last: and, What you see, write in a book, and send it to the seven churches which are in Asia; to Ephesus, and to Smyrna, and to Pergamos, and to Thyatira, and to Sardis, and to Philadelphia, and to Laodicea.

12 And I turned to see the voice that spoke with me. And being turned, I saw seven golden candlesticks;

13 And in the midst of the seven candlesticks one like to the Son of man, clothed with a garment down to the foot, and girt about the paps with a golden girdle.

14 His head and his hairs were white like wool, as white as snow; and his eyes were as a flame of fire;

15 And his feet like to fine brass, as if they burned in a furnace; and his voice as the sound of many waters.

16 And he had in his right hand seven stars: and out of his mouth went a sharp

1:7 Second coming of Jesus: See Revelation 3:11.

QUESTIONS & OBJECTIONS

1:7 ***"The Bible teaches that the earth is flat."***

This is often claimed because the Bible says said that every eye will see Jesus at His Second Coming. However, it would seem that His coming will envelop the entire earth. (See Hebrews 11:3 comment.)

two-edged sword: and his countenance
was as the sun shines in his strength.
17 And when I saw him, I fell at his feet
as dead. And he laid his right hand upon
me, saying to me, Fear not; I am the first
and the last:
**18 I am he that lives, and was dead;
and, behold, I am alive for evermore,
Amen; and have the keys of hell and of
death.**
19 Write the things which you have seen,
and the things which are, and the things
which shall be hereafter;
20 The mystery of the seven stars which
you saw in my right hand, and the seven
golden candlesticks. The seven stars are
the angels of the seven churches: and the
seven candlesticks which you saw are
the seven churches.

CHAPTER 2

TO the angel of the church of Ephesus write; These things says he that
holds the seven stars in his right hand,
who walks in the midst of the seven
golden candlesticks;
2 I know your works, and your labor,
and your patience, and how you can not
bear them which are evil: and you have
tried them which say they are apostles,
and are not, and have found them liars:
3 And have borne, and have patience,
and for my name's sake have labored,
and have not fainted.
4 Nevertheless I have somewhat against
you, because you have left your first love.
5 Remember therefore from whence you
are fallen, and repent, and do the first
works; or else I will come to you quickly,
and will remove your candlestick out of
his place, except you repent.
6 But this you have, that you hate the
deeds of the Nicolaitans, which I also hate.
7 He that has an ear, let him hear what
the Spirit says to the churches; To him that
overcomes will I give to eat of the tree of
life, which is in the midst of the paradise
of God.
8 And to the angel of the church in Smyrna write; These things says the first and
the last, which was dead, and is alive;
9 I know your works, and tribulation,
and poverty, (but you are rich) and I know
the blasphemy of them which say they are
Jews, and are not, but are the synagogue
of Satan.

1:17 Perfection of mercy and love. "If you have studied the matchless purity of [Jesus'] character with adoring admiration, you must have been amazed at the absolute perfection of his manhood, and the glory of his moral and spiritual character. At such times, if you have had a true sense of your own position, you have been ready to sink into the dust, and you have exclaimed, 'Shall he wash my feet? Shall he give himself for me? Can it be that he could have loved one so stained and polluted, so mean and so beggarly, so altogether unworthy even to live, much less to be loved by such an altogether lovely one?'

"But I pray you always to remember, when you think of his perfection, that he has perfection of mercy as well as of holiness, and perfection of love to sinners as well as perfection of hatred of sin; and that, guilty as you are, you must never doubt his affection, for he has pledged you in his heart's blood, and proved his love by his death." *Charles Spurgeon*

Questions & Objections

1:18

"Hell is just a metaphor for the grave."

There are three words translated "hell" in Scripture:

Gehenna (Greek): The place of punishment (Matthew 5:22,29; 10:28; and James 3:6)

Hades (Greek): The abode of the dead (Matthew 11:23; 16:18, Luke 16:23; Acts 2:27)

Sheol (Hebrew): The grave (Psalm 9:17; 16:10)

There are those who accept that hell is a place of punishment, but believe that the punishment is to be annihilated—to cease conscious existence. They can't conceive that the punishment of the wicked will be conscious and *eternal*. If they are correct, then a man like Adolph Hitler, who was responsible for the deaths of millions, is being "punished" merely with eternal sleep. His fate is simply to return to the non-existent state he was in before he was born, where he doesn't even know that he is being punished.

However, Scripture paints a different story. The rich man who found himself in hell (Luke 16:19–31) was conscious. He was able to feel pain, to thirst, and to experience remorse. He wasn't asleep in the grave; he was in a place of "torment."

If hell is a place of knowing nothing or a reference to the grave into which we go at death, Jesus's statements about hell make no sense. He said that if your hand, foot, or eye causes you to sin, it would be better to remove it than to "go into hell, into the fire that never shall be quenched: where their worm dies not, and the fire is not quenched" (Mark 9:43–48).

The Bible refers to the fate of the unsaved with such fearful words as the following:

"Shame and everlasting contempt" (Daniel 12:2)

"Everlasting punishment" (Mathew 25:46)

"Weeping and gnashing of teeth" (Matthew 24:51)

"Fire unquenchable" (Luke 3:17)

"Indignation and wrath, tribulation and anguish" (Romans 2:8,9)

"Everlasting destruction from the presence of the Lord" (2 Thessalonians 1:9)

"Eternal fire... the blackness of darkness for ever" (Jude 7,13)

Revelation 14:10,11 tells us the final, eternal destiny of the sinner: "He shall be tormented with fire and brimstone... the smoke of their torment ascended up for ever and ever: and they have no rest day or night."

10 Fear none of those things which you
shall suffer: behold, the devil shall cast
some of you into prison, that you may
be tried; and you shall have tribulation
ten days: be faithful to death, and I will
give you a crown of life.
11 He that has an ear, let him hear what
the Spirit says to the churches; He that
overcomes shall not be hurt of the second death.
12 And to the angel of the church in Pergamos write; These things says he which
has the sharp sword with two edges;
13 I know your works, and where you
dwell, even where Satan's seat is: and
you hold fast my name, and have not denied my faith, even in those days wherein Antipas was my faithful martyr, who
was slain among you, where Satan dwells.
14 But I have a few things against you,
because you have there them that hold
the doctrine of Balaam, who taught Balak to cast a stumblingblock before the
children of Israel, to eat things sacrificed
to idols, and to commit fornication.
15 So have you also them that hold the
doctrine of the Nicolaitans, which thing
I hate.

Hitler's Nazi Germany had "God with us" engraved on the belts of Nazi soldiers. See Luke 6:27 comment.

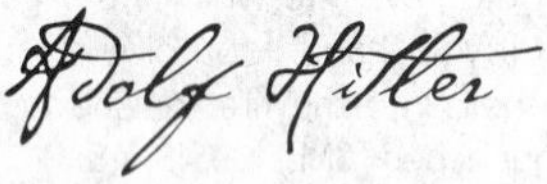

16 Repent; or else I will come to you quickly, and will fight against them with the sword of my mouth.

17 He that has an ear, let him hear what the Spirit says to the churches; To him that overcomes will I give to eat of the hidden manna, and will give him a white stone, and in the stone a new name written, which no man knows saving he that receives it.

18 And to the angel of the church in Thyatira write; These things says the Son of God, who has his eyes like to a flame of fire, and his feet are like fine brass;

19 I know your works, and charity, and service, and faith, and your patience, and your works; and the last to be more than the first.

20 Notwithstanding I have a few things against you, because you suffer that woman Jezebel, which calls herself a prophetess, to teach and to seduce my servants to commit fornication, and to eat things sacrificed to idols.

21 And I gave her space to repent of her fornication; and she repented not.

22 Behold, I will cast her into a bed, and them that commit adultery with her into great tribulation, except they repent of their deeds.

23 And I will kill her children with death; and all the churches shall know that I am he which searches the reins and hearts: and I will give to every one of you according to your works.

24 But to you I say, and to the rest in Thyatira, as many as have not this doctrine, and which have not known the depths of Satan, as they speak; I will put upon you none other burden.

25 But that which you have already hold fast till I come.

26 And he that overcomes, and keeps my works to the end, to him will I give power over the nations:

27 And he shall rule them with a rod of iron; as the vessels of a potter shall they be broken to shivers: even as I received of my Father.

28 And I will give him the morning star.

29 He that has an ear, let him hear what the Spirit says to the churches.

CHAPTER 3

AND to the angel of the church in Sardis write; These things says he that has the seven Spirits of God, and the seven stars; I know your works, that you have a name that you live, and are dead.

2 Be watchful, and strengthen the things which remain, that are ready to die: for I have not found your works perfect before God.

3 Remember therefore how you have received and heard, and hold fast, and repent. If therefore you shall not watch, I will come on you as a thief, and you shall not know what hour I will come upon you.

4 You have a few names even in Sardis which have not defiled their garments; and they shall walk with me in white: for they are worthy.

5 He that overcomes, the same shall be clothed in white raiment; and I will not blot out his name out of the book of life, but I will confess his name before my

Father, and before his angels.
6 He that has an ear, let him hear what
the Spirit says to the churches.
7 And to the angel of the church in Philadelphia write; These things says he that
is holy, he that is true, he that has the key
of David, he that opens, and no man shuts;
and shuts, and no man opens;
8 I know your works: behold, I have set
before you an open door, and no man can
shut it: for you have a little strength, and
have kept my word, and have not denied
my name.
9 Behold, I will make them of the synagogue of Satan, which say they are Jews,
and are not, but do lie; behold, I will make
them to come and worship before your
feet, and to know that I have loved you.
10 Because you have kept the word of
my patience, I also will keep you from
the hour of temptation, which shall come
upon all the world, to try them that dwell
upon the earth.
11 Behold, I come quickly: hold that fast
which you have, that no man take your
crown.
12 Him that overcomes will I make a
pillar in the temple of my God, and he
shall go no more out: and I will write
upon him the name of my God, and the
name of the city of my God, which is
new Jerusalem, which comes down out
of heaven from my God: and I will write
upon him my new name.
13 He that has an ear, let him hear what
the Spirit says to the churches.
14 And to the angel of the church of the
Laodiceans write; These things says the
Amen, the faithful and true witness, the
beginning of the creation of God;
15 *I know your works, that you are nei-*
ther cold nor hot: I would you were cold or
hot.
16 *So then because you are lukewarm,*
and neither cold nor hot, I will spue you
out of my mouth.
17 Because you say, I am rich, and increased with goods, and have need of nothing; and know not that you are wretched,
and miserable, and poor, and blind, and
naked:
18 I counsel you to buy of me gold tried
in the fire, that you may be rich; and
white raiment, that you may be clothed,
and that the shame of your nakedness do
not appear; and anoint your eyes with
eyesalve, that you may see.
19 As many as I love, I rebuke and chasten: be zealous therefore, and repent.
20 **Behold, I stand at the door, and**
knock: if any man hear my voice, and
open the door, I will come in to him,
and will sup with him, and he with me.
21 To him that overcomes will I grant to
sit with me in my throne, even as I also
overcame, and am set down with my
Father in his throne.
22 He that has an ear, let him hear what
the Spirit says to the churches.

CHAPTER 4

AFTER this I looked, and, behold, a
door was opened in heaven: and the
first voice which I heard was as it were
of a trumpet talking with me; which said,
Come up here, and I will show you things

3:11 Second coming of Jesus: See Revelation 16:15.

3:14–19 Here is a perfect description of the contemporary Church, especially in America, with its beautiful facilities, the finest music, and state-of-the-art technology. It has busied itself in everything but the will of God—to seek and save the lost. The word "evangelism" has as much attraction for the modern Church as the word "righteousness" has for the world.

3:16 "The Christian world is in a deep sleep; nothing but a loud shout can awaken them out of it!" *George Whitefield*

"We are not a generation marked by passion. Passion can be lost in programs and progress reports and institutions and calendars. In doing what is good, we may fail to do what is best." *R. Albert Mohler Jr.*

which must be hereafter.
2 And immediately I was in the spirit:
and, behold, a throne was set in heaven,
and one sat on the throne.
3 And he that sat was to look upon like
a jasper and a sardine stone: and there
was a rainbow round about the throne,
in sight like to an emerald.
4 And round about the throne were four
and twenty seats: and upon the seats I
saw four and twenty elders sitting, clothed
in white raiment; and they had on their
heads crowns of gold.
5 And out of the throne proceeded lightnings and thunderings and voices: and
there were seven lamps of fire burning before the throne, which are the seven Spirits of God.
6 And before the throne there was a sea
of glass like to crystal: and in the midst of
the throne, and round about the throne,
were four beasts full of eyes before and
behind.
7 And the first beast was like a lion, and
the second beast like a calf, and the third
beast had a face as a man, and the fourth
beast was like a flying eagle.
8 And the four beasts had each of them
six wings about him; and they were full
of eyes within: and they rest not day and
night, saying, Holy, holy, holy, Lord God
Almighty, which was, and is, and is to
come.
9 And when those beasts give glory and
honor and thanks to him that sat on the
throne, who lives for ever and ever,
10 The four and twenty elders fall down
before him that sat on the throne, and
worship him that lives for ever and ever,
and cast their crowns before the throne,
saying,
11 You are worthy, O Lord, to receive
glory and honor and power: for you have
created all things, and for your pleasure
they are and were created.

CHAPTER 5

AND I saw in the right hand of him
that sat on the throne a book written within and on the backside, sealed
with seven seals.
2 And I saw a strong angel proclaiming
with a loud voice, Who is worthy to open
the book, and to loose the seals thereof?
3 And no man in heaven, nor in earth,
neither under the earth, was able to open
the book, neither to look thereon.
4 And I wept much, because no man was
found worthy to open and to read the
book, neither to look thereon.
5 And one of the elders said to me, Weep
not: behold, the Lion of the tribe of Judah, the Root of David, has prevailed to
open the book, and to loose the seven
seals thereof.
6 And I beheld, and, lo, in the midst of
the throne and of the four beasts, and in
the midst of the elders, stood a Lamb as
it had been slain, having seven horns and
seven eyes, which are the seven Spirits of
God sent forth into all the earth.
7 And he came and took the book out
of the right hand of him that sat upon
the throne.
8 And when he had taken the book, the
four beasts and four and twenty elders
fell down before the Lamb, having every
one of them harps, and golden vials full
of odors, which are the prayers of saints.
9 And they sung a new song, saying,
You are worthy to take the book, and to
open the seals thereof: for you were slain,
and have redeemed us to God by your
blood out of every kindred, and tongue,
and people, and nation;
10 And have made us to our God kings
and priests: and we shall reign on the
earth.

4:11 This is the reason for our existence on earth. The entire creation was made for the pleasure of God. That doesn't mean that we are "God's toys" as some would suggest. Just as a father is pleased when he sees that his children have pleasure, so our pleasure is God's pleasure. Those who love God will have "pleasures for evermore" (Psalm 16:11).

11 And I beheld, and I heard the voice
of many angels round about the throne
and the beasts and the elders: and the
number of them was ten thousand times
ten thousand, and thousands of thousands;
12 Saying with a loud voice, Worthy is
the Lamb that was slain to receive power,
and riches, and wisdom, and strength,
and honor, and glory, and blessing.
13 And every creature which is in heav-
en, and on the earth, and under the earth,
and such as are in the sea, and all that
are in them, heard I saying, Blessing, and
honor, and glory, and power, be to him
that sits upon the throne, and to the Lamb
for ever and ever.
14 And the four beasts said, Amen. And
the four and twenty elders fell down and
worshipped him that lives for ever and
ever.

CHAPTER 6

AND I saw when the Lamb opened
one of the seals, and I heard, as it
were the noise of thunder, one of the four
beasts saying, Come and see.
2 And I saw, and behold a white horse:
and he that sat on him had a bow; and a
crown was given to him: and he went
forth conquering, and to conquer.
3 And when he had opened the second
seal, I heard the second beast say, Come
and see.
4 And there went out another horse
that was red: and power was given to
him that sat thereon to take peace from
the earth, and that they should kill one
another: and there was given to him a
great sword.
5 And when he had opened the third
seal, I heard the third beast say, Come
and see. And I beheld, and lo a black
horse; and he that sat on him had a pair
of balances in his hand.
6 And I heard a voice in the midst of the
four beasts say, A measure of wheat for a
penny, and three measures of barley for
a penny; and see you hurt not the oil
and the wine.
7 And when he had opened the fourth
seal, I heard the voice of the fourth beast
say, Come and see.
8 And I looked, and behold a pale horse:
and his name that sat on him was Death,
and Hell followed with him. And power
was given to them over the fourth part of
the earth, to kill with sword, and with
hunger, and with death, and with the
beasts of the earth.
9 And when he had opened the fifth seal,
I saw under the altar the souls of them
that were slain for the word of God, and
for the testimony which they held:
10 And they cried with a loud voice,
saying, How long, O Lord, holy and true,
do you not judge and avenge our blood
on them that dwell on the earth?
11 And white robes were given to every
one of them; and it was said to them,
that they should rest yet for a little season, until their fellow-servants also and
their brethren, that should be killed as
they were, should be fulfilled.
12 And I beheld when he had opened
the sixth seal, and, lo, there was a great
earthquake; and the sun became black as
sackcloth of hair, and the moon became
as blood;
13 And the stars of heaven fell to the
earth, even as a fig tree casts her untimely figs, when she is shaken of a mighty
wind.
14 **And the heaven departed as a scroll
when it is rolled together; and every
mountain and island were moved out**

6:10,11 Never fear the thought that you are causing sinners to fear by referring to the Judgment. Judgment Day is the climax of the ages. It is an event for which the very creation cries out (Romans 8:21,22). It has done so from the blood of Abel to the last injustice of this age.

With God, justice delayed is not justice denied. Every transgression against the Moral Law will receive just recompense—in His time. God loves justice . . . and He will have it.

of their places.
15 And the kings of the earth, and the
great men, and the rich men, and the
chief captains, and the mighty men, and
every bondman, and every free man, hid
themselves in the dens and in the rocks
of the mountains;
16 And said to the mountains and
rocks, Fall on us, and hide us from the
face of him that sits on the throne, and
from the wrath of the Lamb:
17 For the great day of his wrath is
come; and who shall be able to stand?

CHAPTER 7

AND after these things I saw four angels standing on the four corners of
the earth, holding the four winds of the
earth, that the wind should not blow on
the earth, nor on the sea, nor on any tree.
2 And I saw another angel ascending
from the east, having the seal of the living God: and he cried with a loud voice
to the four angels, to whom it was given
to hurt the earth and the sea,
3 Saying, Hurt not the earth, neither the
sea, nor the trees, till we have sealed the
servants of our God in their foreheads.
4 And I heard the number of them which
were sealed: and there were sealed an
hundred and forty and four thousand of
all the tribes of the children of Israel.
5 Of the tribe of Judah were sealed twelve
thousand. Of the tribe of Reuben were
sealed twelve thousand. Of the tribe of
Gad were sealed twelve thousand.
6 Of the tribe of Aser were sealed twelve
thousand. Of the tribe of Nepthalim were
sealed twelve thousand. Of the tribe of
Manasses were sealed twelve thousand.
7 Of the tribe of Simeon were sealed
twelve thousand. Of the tribe of Levi were
sealed twelve thousand. Of the tribe of
Issachar were sealed twelve thousand.
8 Of the tribe of Zabulon were sealed
twelve thousand. Of the tribe of Joseph
were sealed twelve thousand. Of the tribe
of Benjamin were sealed twelve thousand.
9 After this I beheld, and, lo, a great multitude, which no man could number, of
all nations, and kindreds, and people, and
tongues, stood before the throne, and before the Lamb, clothed with white robes,
and palms in their hands;
10 And cried with a loud voice, saying,
Salvation to our God which sits upon the
throne, and to the Lamb.
11 And all the angels stood round about
the throne, and about the elders and the
four beasts, and fell before the throne on
their faces, and worshipped God,
12 Saying, Amen: Blessing, and glory,
and wisdom, and thanksgiving, and hon-
or, and power, and might, be to our God
for ever and ever. Amen.
13 And one of the elders answered, saying to me, What are these which are arrayed in white robes? and whence came
they?
14 And I said to him, Sir, you know. And
he said to me, These are they which came
out of great tribulation, and have washed

6:15 Note the truth of Proverbs 11:4: "Riches profit not in the day of wrath: but righteousness delivers from death." Those who are unrighteous—no matter how wealthy or prominent, great or mighty—all will be cowering in fear of a holy God's wrath.

6:16,17 Concern for the lost. The very thought of this terrible day should motivate the hardest heart into urgent evangelism.

"You blame me for weeping; but how can I help it when you will not weep for yourselves, although your own immortal souls are on the verge of destruction, and ought I know, you are hearing your last sermon, and may never have opportunity to have Christ offered to you." *George Whitefield*

"If you haven't got tears in your eyes, let them hear tears in your voice!" *Catherine Booth*

7:4–8 These are not Jehovah's Witnesses who have been born again, as the Jehovah's Witnesses claim. The 144,000 are from the twelve tribes of Israel.

QUESTIONS & OBJECTIONS

8:11 ***"God told Joshua to kill every man, woman, and child, and He killed masses of people in Revelation. If that's your 'God of love,' I want nothing to do with Him!"***

God didn't confine His wrath to the Canaanites, or to those mentioned in Revelation. He proclaimed the death sentence upon the *whole* of humanity. We will all die because we have broken God's Law. Every one of us is waiting on death row. Instead of standing in moral judgment over Almighty God, we need to judge ourselves according to the Law of God. We will find that we have a multitude of sins and therefore are deserving of punishment. Yet God, out of love, paid the penalty for our sin so we would not have to.

their robes, and made them white in the
blood of the Lamb.
15 Therefore are they before the throne
of God, and serve him day and night in
his temple: and he that sits on the throne
shall dwell among them.
16 They shall hunger no more, neither
thirst any more; neither shall the sun light
on them, nor any heat.
17 For the Lamb which is in the midst
of the throne shall feed them, and shall
lead them to living fountains of waters:
and God shall wipe away all tears from
their eyes.

CHAPTER 8

AND when he had opened the seventh seal, there was silence in heav-
en about the space of half an hour.
2 And I saw the seven angels which stood
before God; and to them were given seven
trumpets.
3 And another angel came and stood at
the altar, having a golden censer; and there
was given to him much incense, that he
should offer it with the prayers of all saints
upon the golden altar which was before
the throne.
4 And the smoke of the incense, which
came with the prayers of the saints, ascended up before God out of the angel's
hand.
5 And the angel took the censer, and
filled it with fire of the altar, and cast it
into the earth: and there were voices, and
thunderings, and lightnings, and an earthquake.
6 And the seven angels which had the
seven trumpets prepared themselves to
sound.
7 The first angel sounded, and there followed hail and fire mingled with blood,
and they were cast upon the earth: and
the third part of trees was burnt up, and
all green grass was burnt up.
8 And the second angel sounded, and
as it were a great mountain burning with
fire was cast into the sea: and the third
part of the sea became blood;
9 And the third part of the creatures
which were in the sea, and had life, died;
and the third part of the ships were destroyed.
10 And the third angel sounded, and
there fell a great star from heaven, burning as it were a lamp, and it fell upon the
third part of the rivers, and upon the fountains of waters;
11 And the name of the star is called
Wormwood: and the third part of the waters became wormwood; and many men
died of the waters, because they were
made bitter.
12 And the fourth angel sounded, and

7:17 How we long for this day, and how the world will eternally regret beyond words its rejection of the gospel.

the third part of the sun was smitten, and
the third part of the moon, and the third
part of the stars; so as the third part of
them was darkened, and the day shone
not for a third part of it, and the night
likewise.
13 And I beheld, and heard an angel
flying through the midst of heaven, saying with a loud voice, Woe, woe, woe, to
the inhabiters of the earth by reason of
the other voices of the trumpet of the three
angels, which are yet to sound!

CHAPTER 9

AND the fifth angel sounded, and I saw
a star fall from heaven to the earth:
and to him was given the key of the bottomless pit.
2 And he opened the bottomless pit; and
there arose a smoke out of the pit, as the
smoke of a great furnace; and the sun and
the air were darkened by reason of the
smoke of the pit.
3 And there came out of the smoke locusts upon the earth: and to them was giv-
en power, as the scorpions of the earth
have power.
4 And it was commanded them that they
should not hurt the grass of the earth, neither any green thing, neither any tree;
but only those men which have not the
seal of God in their foreheads.
5 And to them it was given that they
should not kill them, but that they should
be tormented five months: and their torment was as the torment of a scorpion,
when he strikes a man.
6 And in those days shall men seek death,
and shall not find it; and shall desire to
die, and death shall flee from them.
7 And the shapes of the locusts were like
to horses prepared to battle; and on their
heads were as it were crowns like gold,
and their faces were as the faces of men.
8 And they had hair as the hair of women, and their teeth were as the teeth of
lions.
9 And they had breastplates, as it were
breastplates of iron; and the sound of their
wings was as the sound of chariots of
many horses running to battle.
10 And they had tails like to scorpions,
and there were stings in their tails: and
their power was to hurt men five months.
11 And they had a king over them, which
is the angel of the bottomless pit, whose
name in the Hebrew tongue is Abaddon,
but in the Greek tongue has his name
Apollyon.
12 One woe is past; and, behold, there
come two woes more hereafter.
13 And the sixth angel sounded, and I
heard a voice from the four horns of the
golden altar which is before God,
14 Saying to the sixth angel which had
the trumpet, Loose the four angels which
are bound in the great river Euphrates.
15 And the four angels were loosed,
which were prepared for an hour, and a
day, and a month, and a year, for to slay
the third part of men.
16 And the number of the army of the
horsemen were two hundred thousand
thousand: and I heard the number of
them.
17 And thus I saw the horses in the vision, and them that sat on them, having
breastplates of fire, and of jacinth, and
brimstone: and the heads of the horses
were as the heads of lions; and out of their

9:9 Joel 2:1–10 relates a striking account of the coming Battle of Armageddon, the greatest of all battles. As this vision (which seems to entail flame-throwing tank warfare) was given to him approximately 2,800 years ago, the prophet relates it to the only thing he has seen in battle—horse-drawn chariots. Think of modern warfare and compare: fire goes before them (v. 3); they burn what is behind them (v. 3); they destroy everything in their path (v. 3); they move at the speed of a horse (30–40 mph, v. 4); their rumbling sounds like the noise of many chariots and the roar of a fire (v. 5); they climb over walls (v. 7); they don't break ranks (v. 7); the sword can't stop them (v. 8); they climb into houses (v. 9); they make the earth quake (v. 10).

mouths issued fire and smoke and brimstone.
18 By these three was the third part of
men killed, by the fire, and by the smoke,
and by the brimstone, which issued out
of their mouths.
19 For their power is in their mouth,
and in their tails: for their tails were like
to serpents, and had heads, and with them
they do hurt.
20 And the rest of the men which were
not killed by these plagues yet repented
not of the works of their hands, that they
should not worship devils, and idols of
gold, and silver, and brass, and stone, and
of wood: which neither can see, nor hear,
nor walk:
21 Neither repented they of their murders, nor of their sorceries, nor of their fornication, nor of their thefts.

. . . . . .

Why not preach that Jesus gives happiness?
See 2 Corinthians 2:17 comment.

. . . . . .

CHAPTER 10

AND I saw another mighty angel come
down from heaven, clothed with a
cloud: and a rainbow was upon his head,
and his face was as it were the sun, and
his feet as pillars of fire:
2 And he had in his hand a little book
open: and he set his right foot upon the
sea, and his left foot on the earth,
3 And cried with a loud voice, as when
a lion roars: and when he had cried,
seven thunders uttered their voices.
4 And when the seven thunders had uttered their voices, I was about to write:
and I heard a voice from heaven saying to
me, Seal up those things which the seven
thunders uttered, and write them not.
5 And the angel which I saw stand upon the sea and upon the earth lifted up
his hand to heaven,
6 And sware by him that lives for ever
and ever, who created heaven, and the
things that therein are, and the earth, and
the things that therein are, and the sea,
and the things which are therein, that
there should be time no longer:
7 But in the days of the voice of the seventh angel, when he shall begin to sound,
the mystery of God should be finished, as
he has declared to his servants the prophets.
8 And the voice which I heard from heav-
en spoke to me again, and said, Go and
take the little book which is open in the
hand of the angel which stands upon the
sea and upon the earth.
9 And I went to the angel, and said to
him, Give me the little book. And he said
to me, Take it, and eat it up; and it shall
make your belly bitter, but it shall be in
your mouth sweet as honey.
10 And I took the little book out of the
angel's hand, and ate it up; and it was in
my mouth sweet as honey: and as soon
as I had eaten it, my belly was bitter.
11 And he said to me, You must prophesy again before many peoples, and nations, and tongues, and kings.

CHAPTER 11

AND there was given me a reed like to
a rod: and the angel stood, saying,
Rise, and measure the temple of God, and
the altar, and them that worship therein.
2 But the court which is without the
temple leave out, and measure it not; for
it is given to the Gentiles: and the holy
city shall they tread under foot forty and
two months.
3 And I will give power to my two witnesses, and they shall prophesy a thousand two hundred and threescore days,
clothed in sackcloth.
4 These are the two olive trees, and the
two candlesticks standing before the God
of the earth.
5 And if any man will hurt them, fire
proceeds out of their mouth, and devours
their enemies: and if any man will hurt
them, he must in this manner be killed.
6 These have power to shut heaven, that
it rain not in the days of their prophecy:

and have power over waters to turn them
to blood, and to smite the earth with all
plagues, as often as they will.
7 And when they shall have finished
their testimony, the beast that ascended
out of the bottomless pit shall make war
against them, and shall overcome them,
and kill them.
8 And their dead bodies shall lie in the
street of the great city, which spiritually
is called Sodom and Egypt, where also our
Lord was crucified.
9 And they of the people and kindreds
and tongues and nations shall see their
dead bodies three days and an half, and
shall not suffer their dead bodies to be
put in graves.
10 And they that dwell upon the earth
shall rejoice over them, and make merry,
and shall send gifts one to another; because these two prophets tormented them
that dwelt on the earth.
11 And after three days and an half the
Spirit of life from God entered into them,
and they stood upon their feet; and great
fear fell upon them which saw them.
12 And they heard a great voice from
heaven saying to them, Come up here. And
they ascended up to heaven in a cloud;
and their enemies beheld them.
13 And the same hour was there a great
earthquake, and the tenth part of the city
fell, and in the earthquake were slain of
men seven thousand: and the remnant
were fearful, and gave glory to the God
of heaven.
14 The second woe is past; and, behold,
the third woe comes quickly.
15 And the seventh angel sounded; and
there were great voices in heaven, saying, The kingdoms of this world are become the kingdoms of our Lord, and of
his Christ; and he shall reign for ever
and ever.
16 And the four and twenty elders, which
sat before God on their seats, fell upon
their faces, and worshipped God,
17 Saying, We give you thanks, O Lord
God Almighty, which are, and was, and
are to come; because you have taken to
you your great power, and have reigned.
18 And the nations were angry, and
your wrath is come, and the time of the
dead, that they should be judged, and
that you should give reward to your servants the prophets, and to the saints, and
them that fear your name, small and
great; and should destroy them which
destroy the earth.
19 And the temple of God was opened
in heaven, and there was seen in his
temple the ark of his testament: and there
were lightnings, and voices, and thunderings, and an earthquake, and great hail.

CHAPTER 12

AND there appeared a great wonder in
heaven; a woman clothed with the
sun, and the moon under her feet, and
upon her head a crown of twelve stars:
2 And she being with child cried, travail-
ing in birth, and pained to be delivered.
3 And there appeared another wonder
in heaven; and behold a great red dragon,
having seven heads and ten horns, and
seven crowns upon his heads.
4 And his tail drew the third part of the
stars of heaven, and did cast them to the
earth: and the dragon stood before the woman which was ready to be delivered, for
to devour her child as soon as it was born.
5 And she brought forth a man child,
who was to rule all nations with a rod of
iron: and her child was caught up to God,
and to his throne.
6 And the woman fled into the wilder-

11:18 These days, some would have us believe that those who "destroy the earth" are people who are not environmentally conscious. There are many who worship "Mother Earth" and think that those who harvest forests, utilize fossil fuels, and don't recycle should be punished. God has made us stewards of His creation, but we are to worship only Him, the Creator. Sinners who refuse to acknowledge Almighty God are the objects of wrath spoken of here.

They loved not their lives unto death:

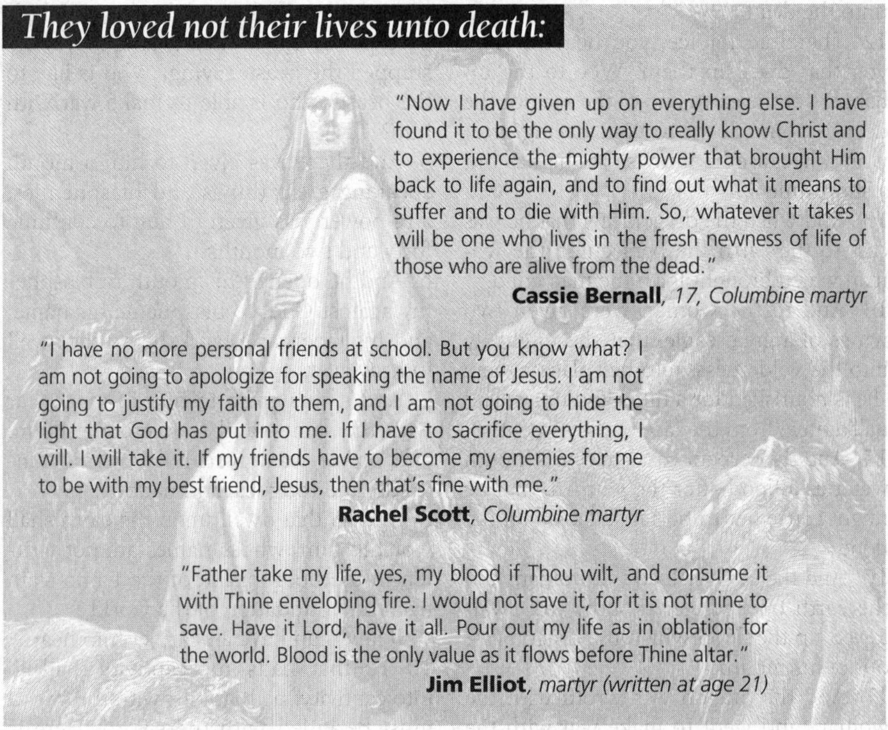

"Now I have given up on everything else. I have found it to be the only way to really know Christ and to experience the mighty power that brought Him back to life again, and to find out what it means to suffer and to die with Him. So, whatever it takes I will be one who lives in the fresh newness of life of those who are alive from the dead."

Cassie Bernall, *17, Columbine martyr*

"I have no more personal friends at school. But you know what? I am not going to apologize for speaking the name of Jesus. I am not going to justify my faith to them, and I am not going to hide the light that God has put into me. If I have to sacrifice everything, I will. I will take it. If my friends have to become my enemies for me to be with my best friend, Jesus, then that's fine with me."

Rachel Scott, *Columbine martyr*

"Father take my life, yes, my blood if Thou wilt, and consume it with Thine enveloping fire. I would not save it, for it is not mine to save. Have it Lord, have it all. Pour out my life as in oblation for the world. Blood is the only value as it flows before Thine altar."

Jim Elliot, *martyr (written at age 21)*

ness, where she has a place prepared of
God, that they should feed her there a
thousand two hundred and threescore
days.
7 And there was war in heaven: Michael
and his angels fought against the dragon;
and the dragon fought and his angels,
8 And prevailed not; neither was their
place found any more in heaven.
9 And the great dragon was cast out,
that old serpent, called the Devil, and Satan, which deceives the whole world: he
was cast out into the earth, and his angels were cast out with him.
10 And I heard a loud voice saying in
heaven, Now is come salvation, and
strength, and the kingdom of our God,
and the power of his Christ: for the accuser of our brethren is cast down, which
accused them before our God day and
night.
11 And they overcame him by the blood
of the Lamb, and by the word of their
testimony; and they loved not their lives

12:9 The god of this world blinds the minds of those who do not believe (2 Corinthians 4:4). If they would *believe*, they would see their danger, and therefore obey the command to repent and be saved.

12:11 Here are the keys to victory in the Christian life:

1) Trust in the blood of Jesus. If sin enters our heart, we must confess it and the blood of Jesus Christ will cleanse us from all sin (1 John 1:7–9). If we do that, then the accuser will have nothing for which to accuse us before the throne of God (v. 10).
2) Our testimony is that Jesus Christ died for our sins and rose again, defeating the grave. Satan has been stripped of the power of death (Hebrews 2:14).
3) We don't live to ourselves, but for the will of God. We love Jesus more than our life (Luke 14:26).

unto the death.

12 Therefore rejoice, you heavens, and you that dwell in them. Woe to the inhabiters of the earth and of the sea! for the devil is come down to you, having great wrath, because he knows that he has but a short time.

13 And when the dragon saw that he was cast to the earth, he persecuted the woman which brought forth the man child.

14 And to the woman were given two wings of a great eagle, that she might fly into the wilderness, into her place, where she is nourished for a time, and times, and half a time, from the face of the serpent.

15 And the serpent cast out of his mouth water as a flood after the woman, that he might cause her to be carried away of the flood.

16 And the earth helped the woman, and the earth opened her mouth, and swallowed up the flood which the dragon cast out of his mouth.

17 And the dragon was wroth with the woman, and went to make war with the remnant of her seed, which keep the commandments of God, and have the testimony of Jesus Christ.

. . . . . .

For evolution and its clash with the Bible, see 1 Corinthians 15:39 comment.

. . . . . .

CHAPTER 13

AND I stood upon the sand of the sea, and saw a beast rise up out of the sea, having seven heads and ten horns, and upon his horns ten crowns, and upon his heads the name of blasphemy.

2 And the beast which I saw was like to a leopard, and his feet were as the feet of a bear, and his mouth as the mouth of a lion: and the dragon gave him his power, and his seat, and great authority.

3 And I saw one of his heads as it were wounded to death; and his deadly wound was healed: and all the world wondered after the beast.

4 And they worshipped the dragon which gave power to the beast: and they worshipped the beast, saying, Who is like to the beast? who is able to make war with him?

5 And there was given to him a mouth speaking great things and blasphemies; and power was given to him to continue forty and two months.

6 And he opened his mouth in blasphemy against God, to blaspheme his name, and his tabernacle, and them that dwell in heaven.

7 And it was given to him to make war with the saints, and to overcome them: and power was given him over all kindreds, and tongues, and nations.

8 And all that dwell upon the earth shall worship him, whose names are not written in the book of life of the Lamb slain from the foundation of the world.

9 If any man have an ear, let him hear.

10 He that leads into captivity shall go into captivity: he that kills with the sword must be killed with the sword. Here is the patience and the faith of the saints.

11 And I beheld another beast coming up out of the earth; and he had two horns like a lamb, and he spoke as a dragon.

12 And he exercises all the power of the first beast before him, and causes the earth and them which dwell therein to worship the first beast, whose deadly wound was healed.

13 And he does great wonders, so that he makes fire come down from heaven on the earth in the sight of men,

14 And deceives them that dwell on the earth by the means of those miracles which he had power to do in the sight of the beast; saying to them that dwell on the earth, that they should make an image to the beast, which had the wound by a sword, and did live.

15 And he had power to give life to the image of the beast, that the image of the beast should both speak, and cause that as many as would not worship the image of the beast should be killed.

16 And he causes all, both small and

great, rich and poor, free and bond, to receive a mark in their right hand, or in their
foreheads:
17 And that no man might buy or sell,
save he that had the mark, or the name of
the beast, or the number of his name.
18 Here is wisdom. Let him that has
understanding count the number of the
beast: for it is the number of a man; and
his number is Six hundred threescore and
six.

CHAPTER 14

AND I looked, and, lo, a Lamb stood
on the mount Zion, and with him an
hundred forty and four thousand, having
his Father's name written in their foreheads.
2 And I heard a voice from heaven, as the
voice of many waters, and as the voice of
a great thunder: and I heard the voice of
harpers harping with their harps:
3 And they sung as it were a new song
before the throne, and before the four
beasts, and the elders: and no man could
learn that song but the hundred and forty
and four thousand, which were redeemed
from the earth.
4 These are they which were not defiled
with women; for they are virgins. These
are they which follow the Lamb wherever he goes. These were redeemed from
among men, being the firstfruits to God
and to the Lamb.
5 And in their mouth was found no guile:
for they are without fault before the throne
of God.
6 And I saw another angel fly in the midst
of heaven, having the everlasting gospel
to preach to them that dwell on the earth,
and to every nation, and kindred, and
tongue, and people,
7 Saying with a loud voice, Fear God,
and give glory to him; for the hour of his
judgment is come: and worship him that
made heaven, and earth, and the sea, and
the fountains of waters.
8 And there followed another angel, saying, Babylon is fallen, is fallen, that great
city, because she made all nations drink of
the wine of the wrath of her fornication.
9 And the third angel followed them,
saying with a loud voice, If any man worship the beast and his image, and receive
his mark in his forehead, or in his hand,
10 The same shall drink of the wine of
the wrath of God, which is poured out
without mixture into the cup of his indig-

14:6 We have the great honor of preaching "the everlasting gospel," which is for *all* who dwell on the earth.

14:7 Law of probabilities refutes evolution. "The chance that higher life forms might have emerged in this way is comparable to the chance that a tornado sweeping through a junkyard might assemble a Boeing 747 from the materials therein." *Sir Fred Hoyle*, professor of astronomy, Cambridge University

"The likelihood of the formation of life from inanimate matter is one out of $10^{40,000}$... It is big enough to bury Darwin and the whole theory of evolution. There was no primeval soup, neither on this planet nor on any other, and if the beginnings of life were not random, they must therefore have been the product of purposeful intelligence." *Sir Fred Hoyle, Evolution from Space*

"I believe that Darwin's mechanism for evolution doesn't explain much of what is seen under a microscope. Cells are simply too complex to have evolved randomly. Intelligence was required to produce them." *Michael J. Behe*

"Evolution is unproved and unprovable. We believe it only because the only alternative is special creation, and that is unthinkable" *Sir Arthur Keith* (author of Foreword to *The Origin of Species*, 100th edition)

"In fact, evolution became in a sense a scientific religion; almost all scientists have accepted it and many are prepared to 'bend' their observations to fit in with it." *H. S. Lipson*, professor of physics, University of Manchester, UK

nation; and he shall be tormented with
fire and brimstone in the presence of the
holy angels, and in the presence of the
Lamb:
11 And the smoke of their torment ascended up for ever and ever: and they
have no rest day nor night, who worship
the beast and his image, and whosoever
receives the mark of his name.
12 Here is the patience of the saints: here
are they that keep the commandments of
God, and the faith of Jesus.
13 And I heard a voice from heaven saying to me, Write, Blessed are the dead
which die in the Lord from henceforth:
Yes, says the Spirit, that they may rest
from their labors; and their works do follow them.
14 And I looked, and behold a white
cloud, and upon the cloud one sat like to
the Son of man, having on his head a gold-
en crown, and in his hand a sharp sickle.

> If persecution should arise, you should be willing to part with all that you possess—with your liberty, with your life itself, for Christ—or you cannot be His disciple.
>
> **CHARLES SPURGEON**

15 And another angel came out of the
temple, crying with a loud voice to him
that sat on the cloud, Thrust in your sickle, and reap: for the time is come for you
to reap; for the harvest of the earth is ripe.
16 And he that sat on the cloud thrust
in his sickle on the earth; and the earth
was reaped.
17 And another angel came out of the
temple which is in heaven, he also having a sharp sickle.
18 And another angel came out from
the altar, which had power over fire; and
cried with a loud cry to him that had the
sharp sickle, saying, Thrust in your sharp
sickle, and gather the clusters of the vine
of the earth; for her grapes are fully ripe.
19 And the angel thrust in his sickle into the earth, and gathered the vine of the
earth, and cast it into the great winepress
of the wrath of God.
20 And the winepress was trodden without the city, and blood came out of the
winepress, even to the horse bridles, by
the space of a thousand and six hundred
furlongs.

CHAPTER 15

AND I saw another sign in heaven,
great and marvelous, seven angels
having the seven last plagues; for in them
is filled up the wrath of God.
2 And I saw as it were a sea of glass
mingled with fire: and them that had gotten the victory over the beast, and over
his image, and over his mark, and over
the number of his name, stand on the sea
of glass, having the harps of God.
3 And they sing the song of Moses the
servant of God, and the song of the Lamb,
saying, Great and marvelous are your
works, Lord God Almighty; just and true
are your ways, you King of saints.
4 Who shall not fear you, O Lord, and
glorify your name? for you only are holy:
for all nations shall come and worship
before you; for your judgments are made
manifest.
5 And after that I looked, and, behold, the
temple of the tabernacle of the testimony
in heaven was opened:
6 And the seven angels came out of the
temple, having the seven plagues, clothed
in pure and white linen, and having their
breasts girded with golden girdles.
7 And one of the four beasts gave to the
seven angels seven golden vials full of the
wrath of God, who lives for ever and ever.
8 And the temple was filled with smoke
from the glory of God, and from his power; and no man was able to enter into the
temple, till the seven plagues of the seven
angels were fulfilled.

14:13 If we die in the Lord, our works follow us. No good deed will be forgotten by God.

CHAPTER 16

AND I heard a great voice out of the
temple saying to the seven angels,
Go your ways, and pour out the vials of
the wrath of God upon the earth.
2 And the first went, and poured out his
vial upon the earth; and there fell a noisome and grievous sore upon the men
which had the mark of the beast, and upon them which worshipped his image.
3 And the second angel poured out his
vial upon the sea; and it became as the
blood of a dead man: and every living soul
died in the sea.
4 And the third angel poured out his
vial upon the rivers and fountains of waters; and they became blood.
5 And I heard the angel of the waters
say, You are righteous, O Lord, which are,
and was, and shall be, because you have
judged thus.
6 For they have shed the blood of saints
and prophets, and you have given them
blood to drink; for they are worthy.
7 And I heard another out of the altar
say, Even so, Lord God Almighty, true and
righteous are your judgments.
8 And the fourth angel poured out his
vial upon the sun; and power was given
to him to scorch men with fire.
9 And men were scorched with great
heat, and blasphemed the name of God,
which has power over these plagues: and
they repented not to give him glory.
10 And the fifth angel poured out his
vial upon the seat of the beast; and his
kingdom was full of darkness; and they
gnawed their tongues for pain,
11 And blasphemed the God of heaven
because of their pains and their sores, and
repented not of their deeds.
12 And the sixth angel poured out his
vial upon the great river Euphrates; and
the water thereof was dried up, that the
way of the kings of the east might be prepared.
13 And I saw three unclean spirits like
frogs come out of the mouth of the dragon, and out of the mouth of the beast, and
out of the mouth of the false prophet.
14 For they are the spirits of devils, working miracles, which go forth to the kings
of the earth and of the whole world, to
gather them to the battle of that great day
of God Almighty.
15 Behold, I come as a thief. Blessed is he
that watches, and keeps his garments, lest
he walk naked, and they see his shame.
16 And he gathered them together into
a place called in the Hebrew tongue Armageddon.
17 And the seventh angel poured out his
vial into the air; and there came a great
voice out of the temple of heaven, from

16:15 Second coming of Jesus: See Revelation 22:20.

16:16 Ezekiel 39, written over 2,500 years ago, speaks of God's judgment upon the enemies of Israel. Verses 12–15 describe what will happen after what many see as the Battle of Armageddon:

> And seven months shall the house of Israel be burying of them, that they may cleanse the land. . . And they shall sever out men of continual employment, passing through the land to bury with the passengers those that remain upon the face of the earth, to cleanse it: after the end of seven months shall they search. And the passengers that pass through the land, when any sees a man's bone, then shall he set up a sign by it, till the buriers have buried it in the valley of Hamongog.

Before the days of nuclear warfare, this portion of the Bible would have made no sense to the reader. We are told that even the weapons left by the enemy will have to be burned (Ezekiel 39:9). So many will die that it will take those specially employed for the purpose seven months to bury the dead (v. 14). The Scriptures are very specific about the method of burial. When even a bone is found by searchers, a special marker is to be placed near the bone until the buriers have buried it. This would seem to be a clear reference to radioactive contamination after nuclear war. This thought is confirmed in Joel 2:30, which speaks of "pillars of smoke."

Did the Church persecute Galileo?
See 1 Timothy 6:20 comment.

Galileo

the throne, saying, It is done.
18 And there were voices, and thunders,
and lightnings; and there was a great
earthquake, such as was not since men
were upon the earth, so mighty an earthquake, and so great.
19 And the great city was divided into
three parts, and the cities of the nations
fell: and great Babylon came in remembrance before God, to give to her the cup
of the wine of the fierceness of his wrath.
20 And every island fled away, and the
mountains were not found.
21 And there fell upon men a great hail
out of heaven, every stone about the weight
of a talent: and men blasphemed God
because of the plague of the hail; for the
plague thereof was exceeding great.

CHAPTER 17

AND there came one of the seven angels which had the seven vials, and
talked with me, saying to me, Come here;
I will show to you the judgment of the
great whore that sits upon many waters:
2 With whom the kings of the earth have
committed fornication, and the inhabitants
of the earth have been made drunk with
the wine of her fornication.
3 So he carried me away in the spirit into the wilderness: and I saw a woman sit
upon a scarlet colored beast, full of names
of blasphemy, having seven heads and
ten horns.
4 And the woman was arrayed in purple
and scarlet color, and decked with gold
and precious stones and pearls, having a
golden cup in her hand full of abominations and filthiness of her fornication:
5 And upon her forehead was a name
written, MYSTERY, BABYLON THE
GREAT, THE MOTHER OF HARLOTS
AND ABOMINATIONS OF THE EARTH.
6 And I saw the woman drunken with
the blood of the saints, and with the blood
of the martyrs of Jesus: and when I saw
her, I wondered with great admiration.
7 And the angel said to me, Wherefore
did you marvel? I will tell you the mystery of the woman, and of the beast that
carried her, which has the seven heads
and ten horns.
8 The beast that you saw was, and is
not; and shall ascend out of the bottomless pit, and go into perdition: and they
that dwell on the earth shall wonder,
whose names were not written in the book
of life from the foundation of the world,
when they behold the beast that was,
and is not, and yet is.
9 And here is the mind which has wisdom. The seven heads are seven mountains, on which the woman sits.
10 And there are seven kings: five are
fallen, and one is, and the other is not yet
come; and when he comes, he must continue a short space.
11 And the beast that was, and is not,
even he is the eighth, and is of the seven,
and goes into perdition.
12 And the ten horns which you saw
are ten kings, which have received no
kingdom as yet; but receive power as
kings one hour with the beast.
13 These have one mind, and shall give
their power and strength to the beast.
14 These shall make war with the Lamb,
and the Lamb shall overcome them: for

he is Lord of lords, and King of kings: and
they that are with him are called, and
chosen, and faithful.
15 And he said to me, The waters which
you saw, where the whore sits, are peoples,
and multitudes, and nations, and tongues.
16 And the ten horns which you saw upon the beast, these shall hate the whore,
and shall make her desolate and naked,
and shall eat her flesh, and burn her with
fire.
17 For God has put in their hearts to fulfil his will, and to agree, and give their
kingdom to the beast, until the words of
God shall be fulfilled.
18 And the woman which you saw is that
great city, which reigns over the kings of
the earth.

CHAPTER 18

AND after these things I saw another
angel come down from heaven, having great power; and the earth was lightened with his glory.
2 And he cried mightily with a strong
voice, saying, Babylon the great is fallen,
is fallen, and is become the habitation of
devils, and the hold of every foul spirit, and
a cage of every unclean and hateful bird.
3 For all nations have drunk of the wine
of the wrath of her fornication, and the
kings of the earth have committed fornication with her, and the merchants of the
earth are waxed rich through the abundance of her delicacies.
4 And I heard another voice from heav-
en, saying, Come out of her, my people,
that you be not partakers of her sins, and
that you receive not of her plagues.
5 For her sins have reached to heaven,
and God has remembered her iniquities.
6 Reward her even as she rewarded you,
and double to her double according to
her works: in the cup which she has filled
fill to her double.
7 How much she has glorified herself,
and lived deliciously, so much torment
and sorrow give her: for she said in her
heart, I sit a queen, and am no widow, and
shall see no sorrow.
8 Therefore shall her plagues come in
one day, death, and mourning, and famine; and she shall be utterly burned with
fire: for strong is the Lord God who judges
her.
9 And the kings of the earth, who have
committed fornication and lived deliciously with her, shall bewail her, and lament
for her, when they shall see the smoke of
her burning,
10 Standing afar off for the fear of her
torment, saying, Alas, alas, that great city
Babylon, that mighty city! for in one hour
is your judgment come.
11 And the merchants of the earth shall
weep and mourn over her; for no man
buys their merchandise any more:
12 The merchandise of gold, and silver,
and precious stones, and of pearls, and
fine linen, and purple, and silk, and scarlet, and all thyine wood, and all manner
vessels of ivory, and all manner vessels of
most precious wood, and of brass, and
iron, and marble,
13 And cinnamon, and odors, and ointments, and frankincense, and wine, and
oil, and fine flour, and wheat, and beasts,
and sheep, and horses, and chariots, and
slaves, and souls of men.
14 And the fruits that your soul lusted
after are departed from you, and all things
which were dainty and goodly are departed from you, and you shall find them
no more at all.
15 The merchants of these things, which
were made rich by her, shall stand afar off
for the fear of her torment, weeping and
wailing,
16 And saying, Alas, alas, that great city,
that was clothed in fine linen, and purple, and scarlet, and decked with gold,
and precious stones, and pearls!
17 For in one hour so great riches is
come to nothing. And every shipmaster,
and all the company in ships, and sailors,
and as many as trade by sea, stood afar off,
18 And cried when they saw the smoke
of her burning, saying, What city is like
to this great city!
19 And they cast dust on their heads,

The Resurrection:

Does Circumstantial Evidence Confirm It?

Timothy McVeigh, the man behind the Oklahoma City bombing, has a date with death. He'll receive a lethal injection for killing 168 innocent people, even though no one saw him commit this heinous crime. All the evidence against McVeigh was circumstantial.

Indirect testimony: That's what circumstantial evidence is. It's an accumulation of facts from which one can draw intelligent conclusions.

As a newspaper reporter covering the courts, former journalist Lee Strobel saw how circumstantial evidence is used to expose what really happened during a crime. So, in the midst of a spiritual quest, Strobel began to wonder: Could circumstantial evidence verify that the resurrection of Christ really happened?

Well, he took his question to philosopher J. P. Moreland. In a challenging voice, Strobel asked Moreland: "Can you give me five pieces of solid circumstantial evidence that convince you Jesus rose from the dead?"

Certainly, Moreland responded. **First**, there's the evidence of the skeptics. Some of those who were most hostile to Jesus prior to his death became his most ardent supporters afterwards.

Second, the ancient Jews had a number of immensely important religious rituals. These included the offering of animal sacrifices, obeying the Mosaic law, and keeping the Sabbath. But within five weeks of Jesus' death, more than 10,000 Jews had suddenly altered or abandoned these rituals. Moreland asked: Why would they relinquish rites that had long given them their national identity? The implication is that something enormously significant had occurred.

Third, we see the emergence of new rituals: the sacraments of Communion and Baptism. The early Jews baptized in the name of the Father, the Son, and the Holy Spirit, "which," Moreland said, "meant they had elevated Jesus to the full status of God."

Fourth, we see the rapid rise of a new church, beginning shortly after the death of Jesus. Within twenty years this new church (begun by the companions of a dead carpenter) had reached Caesar's palace in Rome, and eventually spread throughout the Roman empire.

And **fifth**, Moreland said, there's the most convincing circumstantial evidence of all: the fact that every one of Jesus' disciples was willing to suffer and die for his beliefs. These men spent the rest of their lives witnessing about Christ. They frequently went without food; they were mocked, beaten, and thrown into prison. In the end, all but one died a painful martyr's death.

Would they have done this for a lie? Of course not. They did it because they were convinced beyond a doubt that they had seen the risen Christ.

Even if we doubted 2,000-year-old evidence, we have all the circumstantial evidence we could possibly want—right in front of us. It is, Moreland said, "the ongoing encounter with the resurrected Christ that happens all over the world, in every culture, to people from all kinds of backgrounds and personalities. They all will testify that more than any single thing in their lives, Jesus Christ has changed them."

Circumstantial evidence earned Timothy McVeigh a death sentence. But sacred circumstantial evidence about the resurrection of Jesus Christ can lead all of us, including McVeigh, to a much better verdict: everlasting life in the presence of God.

From "BreakPoint with Charles Colson," April 19, 2001, reprinted with permission of Prison Fellowship, PO Box 17500, Washington, DC 20041-7500, www.pfm.org.

and cried, weeping and wailing, saying,
Alas, alas, that great city, wherein were
made rich all that had ships in the sea by
reason of her costliness! for in one hour
is she made desolate.
20 Rejoice over her, you heaven, and you
holy apostles and prophets; for God has
avenged you on her.
21 And a mighty angel took up a stone
like a great millstone, and cast it into the
sea, saying, Thus with violence shall that
great city Babylon be thrown down, and
shall be found no more at all.
22 And the voice of harpers, and musi-
cians, and of pipers, and trumpeters, shall
be heard no more at all in you; and no
craftsman, of whatsoever craft he be, shall
be found any more in you; and the sound
of a millstone shall be heard no more at
all in you;
23 And the light of a candle shall shine
no more at all in you; and the voice of
the bridegroom and of the bride shall be
heard no more at all in you: for your merchants were the great men of the earth;
for by your sorceries were all nations deceived.
24 And in her was found the blood of
prophets, and of saints, and of all that were
slain upon the earth.

CHAPTER 19

AND after these things I heard a great
voice of much people in heaven,
saying, Alleluia; Salvation, and glory, and
honor, and power, to the Lord our God:
2 For true and righteous are his judgments: for he has judged the great whore,
which did corrupt the earth with her fornication, and has avenged the blood of his
servants at her hand.
3 And again they said, Alleluia. And her
smoke rose up for ever and ever.
4 And the four and twenty elders and
the four beasts fell down and worshipped
God that sat on the throne, saying, Amen;
Alleluia.
5 And a voice came out of the throne,
saying, Praise our God, all you his servants, and you that fear him, both small
and great.
6 And I heard as it were the voice of a
great multitude, and as the voice of many
waters, and as the voice of mighty thunderings, saying, Alleluia: for the Lord God
omnipotent reigns.
7 Let us be glad and rejoice, and give
honor to him: for the marriage of the Lamb
is come, and his wife has made herself
ready.
8 And to her was granted that she should
be arrayed in fine linen, clean and white:
for the fine linen is the righteousness of
saints.
9 And he said to me, Write, Blessed are
they which are called to the marriage supper of the Lamb. And he said to me, These
are the true sayings of God.
10 And I fell at his feet to worship him.
And he said to me, See you do it not: I am
your fellow-servant, and of your brethren
that have the testimony of Jesus: worship
God: for the testimony of Jesus is the
spirit of prophecy.
11 And I saw heaven opened, and behold a white horse; and he that sat upon
him was called Faithful and True, and in
righteousness he does judge and make
war.
12 His eyes were as a flame of fire, and
on his head were many crowns; and he
had a name written, that no man knew,
but he himself.
13 And he was clothed with a vesture
dipped in blood: and his name is called
The Word of God.
14 And the armies which were in heaven
followed him upon white horses, clothed
in fine linen, white and clean.
15 And out of his mouth goes a sharp
sword, that with it he should smite the
nations: and he shall rule them with a
rod of iron: and he treads the winepress of
the fierceness and wrath of Almighty God.
16 And he has on his vesture and on his
thigh a name written, KING OF KINGS,
AND LORD OF LORDS.
17 And I saw an angel standing in the
sun; and he cried with a loud voice, saying to all the fowls that fly in the midst

of heaven, Come and gather yourselves
together to the supper of the great God;
18 That you may eat the flesh of kings,
and the flesh of captains, and the flesh of
mighty men, and the flesh of horses, and
of them that sit on them, and the flesh of
all men, both free and bond, both small
and great.
19 And I saw the beast, and the kings of
the earth, and their armies, gathered together to make war against him that sat on
the horse, and against his army.
20 And the beast was taken, and with
him the false prophet that wrought miracles before him, with which he deceived
them that had received the mark of the
beast, and them that worshipped his
image. These both were cast alive into a
lake of fire burning with brimstone.
21 And the remnant were slain with the
sword of him that sat upon the horse,
which sword proceeded out of his mouth:
and all the fowls were filled with their
flesh.

CHAPTER 20

AND I saw an angel come down from
heaven, having the key of the bottomless pit and a great chain in his hand.
2 And he laid hold on the dragon, that
old serpent, which is the Devil, and Satan, and bound him a thousand years,
3 And cast him into the bottomless pit,
and shut him up, and set a seal upon
him, that he should deceive the nations
no more, till the thousand years should
be fulfilled: and after that he must be
loosed a little season.
4 And I saw thrones, and they sat upon
them, and judgment was given to them:
and I saw the souls of them that were
beheaded for the witness of Jesus, and
for the word of God, and which had not
worshipped the beast, neither his image,
neither had received his mark upon their
foreheads, or in their hands; and they
lived and reigned with Christ a thousand
years.
5 But the rest of the dead lived not again
until the thousand years were finished.
This is the first resurrection.
6 Blessed and holy is he that has part in
the first resurrection: on such the second
death has no power, but they shall be
priests of God and of Christ, and shall
reign with him a thousand years.
7 And when the thousand years are expired, Satan shall be loosed out of his
prison,
8 And shall go out to deceive the nations which are in the four quarters of the
earth, Gog and Magog, to gather them
together to battle: the number of whom
is as the sand of the sea.
9 And they went up on the breadth of
the earth, and compassed the camp of the
saints about, and the beloved city: and
fire came down from God out of heaven,
and devoured them.
10 And the devil that deceived them was
cast into the lake of fire and brimstone,
where the beast and the false prophet are,
and shall be tormented day and night for
ever and ever.
11 And I saw a great white throne, and
him that sat on it, from whose face the

20:11 No hiding from God. "Whither can the enemies of God flee? If up to heaven their high-flown impudence could carry them, His right hand of holiness would hurl them thence, or, if under hell's profoundest wave they dive, to seek a sheltering grave, His left hand would pluck them out of the fire, to expose them to the fiercer light of His countenance. Nowhere is there a refuge from the Most High. The morning beams cannot convey the fugitive so swiftly as the almighty Pursuer would follow him; neither can the mysterious lightning flash, which annihilates time and space, journey so rapidly as to escape His far-reaching hand. 'If I mount up to heaven, thou art there; if I make my bed in hell, thou art there.'

"It was said of the Roman Empire under the Caesars that the whole world was only one great prison for Caesar, for if any man offended the emperor it was impossible for him to escape. If he crossed the Alps, could not Caesar find him out in Gaul? If he sought to hide himself in the Indies,

QUESTIONS & OBJECTIONS

21:4 ***"How can people be happy in heaven, knowing that their unsaved loved ones are suffering in hell?"***

Those who ask such questions fall into the category of those who asked Jesus a similar question. The Pharisees said that a certain woman had seven consecutive husbands, so whose wife will she be in heaven (Mark 12:23)? Jesus answered by saying that they neither knew the Scriptures nor the power of God. The unregenerate mind has no concept of God's mind or His infinite power. If God can speak the sun into existence; if He can see every thought of every human heart at the same time; if He can create the human eye with its 137,000,000 light-sensitive cells, then He can handle the minor details of our eternal salvation.

John writes that in heaven "we shall be like him; for we shall see him as he is" (1 John 3:2), so perhaps we will be fully satisfied that God is perfectly just and merciful, and that He gave every individual the opportunity to accept or reject Him. However He works it out, God promises that there will not be sorrow or crying in heaven. Our focus in heaven won't be on our loss, but on our gain.

earth and the heaven fled away; and
there was found no place for them.
12 **And I saw the dead, small and great,**
stand before God; and the books were
opened: and another book was opened,
which is the book of life: and the dead
were judged out of those things which
were written in the books, according to
their works.
13 **And the sea gave up the dead which**
were in it; and death and hell deliv-
ered up the dead which were in them:
and they were judged every man ac-
cording to their works.
14 **And death and hell were cast into**
the lake of fire. This is the second death.
15 And whosoever was not found writ-
ten in the book of life was cast into
the lake of fire.

CHAPTER 21

AND I saw a new heaven and a new
earth: for the first heaven and the
first earth were passed away; and there was
no more sea.
2 And I John saw the holy city, new Jerusalem, coming down from God out of
heaven, prepared as a bride adorned for
her husband.
3 And I heard a great voice out of heav-
en saying, Behold, the tabernacle of God
is with men, and he will dwell with them,
and they shall be his people, and God
himself shall be with them, and be their
God.
4 And God shall wipe away all tears

even the swarthy monarchs there knew the power of the Roman arms, so that they would give no shelter to a man who had incurred imperial vengeance. And yet, perhaps, a fugitive from Rome might have prolonged his miserable life by hiding in the dens and caves of the earth.

"But oh! sinner, there is no hiding from God. The mountains cannot cover you from Him, even if they would, neither can the rocks conceal you. See, then, at the very outset how this throne should awe our minds with terror. Founded in right, sustained by might, and universal in its dominion, look ye and see the throne which John of old beheld." *Charles Spurgeon*

20:15 Hell: It should be grievous for any Christian to make light of or joke about hell. This verse should break our hearts, drive us to weep for the unsaved, and then motivate us to put legs to our prayers and plead with sinners to turn to the Savior. For verses warning of its reality, see Revelation 21:8.

from their eyes; and there shall be no more death, neither sorrow, nor crying, neither shall there be any more pain: for the former things are passed away.

5 **And he that sat upon the throne said, Behold, I make all things new. And he said to me, Write: for these words are true and faithful.**

6 **And he said to me, It is done. I am Alpha and Omega, the beginning and the end. I will give to him that is athirst of the fountain of the water of life freely.**

7 He that overcomes shall inherit all things; and I will be his God, and he shall be my son.

8 But the fearful, and unbelieving, and the abominable, and murderers, and whoremongers, and sorcerers, and idolaters, and all liars, shall have their part in the lake which burns with fire and brimstone: which is the second death.

> Young men and old men, and sisters of all ages, if you love the Lord, get a passion for souls. Do you not see them? They are going down to hell by the thousands.
>
> **CHARLES SPURGEON**

9 And there came to me one of the seven angels which had the seven vials full of the seven last plagues, and talked with me, saying, Come here, I will show you the bride, the Lamb's wife.

10 And he carried me away in the spirit to a great and high mountain, and showed me that great city, the holy Jerusalem, descending out of heaven from God,

11 Having the glory of God: and her light was like to a stone most precious, even like a jasper stone, clear as crystal;

12 And had a wall great and high, and had twelve gates, and at the gates twelve angels, and names written thereon, which are the names of the twelve tribes of the children of Israel:

13 On the east three gates; on the north three gates; on the south three gates; and on the west three gates.

14 And the wall of the city had twelve foundations, and in them the names of the twelve apostles of the Lamb.

15 And he that talked with me had a golden reed to measure the city, and the gates thereof, and the wall thereof.

16 And the city lies foursquare, and the length is as large as the breadth: and he measured the city with the reed, twelve thousand furlongs. The length and the breadth and the height of it are equal.

17 And he measured the wall thereof, an hundred and forty and four cubits, according to the measure of a man, that is, of the angel.

18 And the building of the wall of it was of jasper: and the city was pure gold, like to clear glass.

19 And the foundations of the wall of the city were garnished with all manner of precious stones. The first foundation was jasper; the second, sapphire; the third, a chalcedony; the fourth, an emerald;

20 The fifth, sardonyx; the sixth, sardius; the seventh, chrysolite; the eighth, beryl; the ninth, a topaz; the tenth, a chrysoprasus; the eleventh, a jacinth; the twelfth, an amethyst.

21 And the twelve gates were twelve pearls; every several gate was of one pearl: and the street of the city was pure gold, as it were transparent glass.

22 And I saw no temple therein: for the Lord God Almighty and the Lamb are the temple of it.

21:8 Hell: For verses warning of its reality, see Matthew 5:22.

God isn't willing that any perish. "Behold, the LORD's hand is not shortened, that it cannot save; neither his ear heavy, that it cannot hear: but your iniquities have separated between you and your God, and your sins have hid his face from you, that he will not hear" (Isaiah 59:1,2). See Hebrews 9:22 comment.

23 And the city had no need of the sun,
neither of the moon, to shine in it: for the
glory of God did lighten it, and the Lamb
is the light thereof.
24 And the nations of them which are
saved shall walk in the light of it: and the
kings of the earth do bring their glory and
honor into it.
25 And the gates of it shall not be shut
at all by day: for there shall be no night
there.
26 And they shall bring the glory and
honor of the nations into it.
27 **And there shall in no wise enter into it any thing that defiles, neither whatsoever works abomination, or makes a lie: but they which are written in the Lamb's book of life.**

CHAPTER 22

AND he showed me a pure river of water of life, clear as crystal, proceeding out of the throne of God and of the Lamb.
2 In the midst of the street of it, and on
either side of the river, was there the tree
of life, which bare twelve manner of fruits,
and yielded her fruit every month: and
the leaves of the tree were for the healing
of the nations.
3 And there shall be no more curse: but
the throne of God and of the Lamb shall
be in it; and his servants shall serve him:
4 And they shall see his face; and his
name shall be in their foreheads.
5 And there shall be no night there; and
they need no candle, neither light of the
sun; for the Lord God gives them light:
and they shall reign for ever and ever.
6 And he said to me, These sayings are
faithful and true: and the Lord God of
the holy prophets sent his angel to show
to his servants the things which must
shortly be done.
7 Behold, I come quickly: blessed is he
that keeps the sayings of the prophecy of
this book.
8 And I John saw these things, and heard
them. And when I had heard and seen, I
fell down to worship before the feet of
the angel which showed me these things.
9 Then said he to me, See you do it not:

22:2 Charles Spurgeon on Tracts:
"I well remember distributing them in a town in England where tracts had never been distributed before, and going from house to house, and telling in humble language the things of the kingdom of God. I might have done nothing, if I had not been encouraged by finding myself able to do something...[Tracts are] adapted to those persons who have but little power and little ability, but nevertheless, wish to do something for Christ. They have not the tongue of the eloquent, but they may have the hand of the diligent. They cannot stand and preach, but they can stand and distribute here and there these silent preachers...They may buy their thousand tracts, and these they can distribute broadcast.

"I look upon the giving away of a religious tract as only the first step for action not to be compared with many another deed done for Christ; but were it not for the first step we might never reach to the second, but that first attained, we are encouraged to take another, and so at the last...There is a real service of Christ in the distribution of the gospel in its printed form, a service the result of which heaven alone shall disclose, and the judgment day alone discover. How many thousands have been carried to heaven instrumentally upon the wings of these tracts, none can tell.

"I might say, if it were right to quote such a Scripture, 'The leaves were for the healing of the nations'—verily they are so. Scattered where the whole tree could scarcely be carried, the very leaves have had a medicinal and a healing virtue in them and the real word of truth, the simple statement of a Savior crucified and of a sinner who shall be saved by simply trusting in the Savior, has been greatly blessed, and many thousand souls have been led into the kingdom of heaven by this simple means. *Let each one of us, if we have done nothing for Christ, begin to do something now. The distribution of tracts is the first thing.*"

See also Mark 4:14 and 1 Corinthians 9:22 comments.

for I am your fellow-servant, and of your
brethren the prophets, and of them which
keep the sayings of this book: worship
God.
10 And he said to me, Seal not the sayings of the prophecy of this book: for the
time is at hand.
11 He that is unjust, let him be unjust
still: and he which is filthy, let him be
filthy still: and he that is righteous, let him
be righteous still: and he that is holy, let
him be holy still.
12 And, behold, I come quickly; and my
reward is with me, to give every man according as his work shall be.
13 I am Alpha and Omega, the beginning
and the end, the first and the last.
14 Blessed are they that do his commandments, that they may have right to the tree
of life, and may enter in through the gates
into the city.
15 **For without are dogs, and sorcerers,
and whoremongers, and murderers, and
idolaters, and whosoever loves and
makes a lie.**
16 I Jesus have sent mine angel to testify to you these things in the churches. I
am the root and the offspring of David,
and the bright and morning star.
17 **And the Spirit and the bride say,
Come. And let him that hears say,
Come. And let him that is athirst come.
And whosoever will, let him take the
water of life freely.**
18 For I testify to every man that hears
the words of the prophecy of this book,
If any man shall add to these things, God
shall add to him the plagues that are written in this book:
19 And if any man shall take away from
the words of the book of this prophecy,
God shall take away his part out of the
book of life, and out of the holy city, and
from the things which are written in this
book.
20 He which testifies these things says,
Surely I come quickly. Amen. Even so,
come, Lord Jesus.

22:3 A magnificent doe stands with its foal and drinks in the cool water from a mountain stream. The sun sparkles off the dew on deep green leaves of native tree branches. The mother gently caresses her offspring as it begins to also drink from the brook. The scene is one of incredible serenity…the picture of innocence. What more could optimize the beauty of God's creation?

Suddenly a mountain lion leaps from a tree and digs its sharp claws deeply into the mother's neck, dragging the helpless creature to the ground. As it holds its terrified prey in a death grip, its powerful jaws bite into the jugular vein, turning the mountain stream crimson with the creature's blood.

It is a strong consolation to know that this isn't the way God planned it in the beginning. Animals were not created to devour each other; they were created to be vegetarian (Genesis 1:29,30). The original creation was "good" and was not filled with violence and bloodshed. We live in a *fallen* creation (Romans 8:20–23). As a result of Adam's sin, the perfect creation was cursed and death was introduced into the world (Romans 5:12). The day will come when the entire creation will be delivered from the "bondage of corruption" and there will be no more curse. In the new heaven and new earth, "the wolf and the lamb shall feed together, and the lion shall eat straw like the bullock…They shall not hurt nor destroy in all my holy mountain" (Isaiah 65:25). See also Isaiah 11:6–9.

Closing Words of Comfort

RARELY DO I become involved in counseling; I leave that to the expertise of the local pastor. However, I was awakened one morning by my wife, Sue. She said, "There is someone in the living room and he desperately wants to talk to you." I protested, "But it's not even 7 A.M.... and I don't do counseling!"

Nevertheless, I made my way into the living room and found a man whose eyes flashed with despair. I had met him a few months earlier when he purchased a series of our tapes, but this day he looked like a different man. It turned out that his whole life seemed to be falling to pieces. There were terrible problems at work, at home, and even in his church. Everything had suddenly gone wrong. I looked him in the eye and asked, "You didn't pray that God would 'break' you, did you?" He looked back at me and said, "I asked God to break me and grind me to powder..."

Make sure you realize what you are saying at church when you sing words like "Refiner's fire, my heart's one desire, is to be holy." I hum the song. Let me tell you why.

We may think that we are asking God for the "warm fuzzies," but the refining fire is what Job went through, and God may just give you your heart's one desire if you keep asking Him. After the service, you find that someone has just crashed into your new car. That week you discover that God has let the devil get at you and your house has burned to the ground, your spouse and children have been killed, and someone forgot to pay the insurance premium.

The loss of your family, car, and home and financial collapse give you a complete nervous breakdown. Well, rejoice—because you are getting your heart's one desire. Read the Book of Job. I've been through the Refiner's fire and I never want to go through it again. My prayer is, "If it is possible, let this cup pass from me." Jesus had to suffer; there was no alternative for Him. But there is an alternative for us. If we chasten ourselves, perhaps we will not be chastened by God. Instead of praying that God will break me, I say, "Please, Lord, be gentle on your servant. 'Neither chasten me in your hot displeasure' [Psalm 38:1]. Help me to see the areas that I need to change."

If we discipline ourselves to pray and read the Word, we may avoid the Refiner's fire. If we draw close to Him, we won't need a lion's den to bring us to our knees. If we scatter abroad, preaching the Word everywhere, we may not need a Saul of Tarsus to breathe out slaughter against us. If we cut off unfruitful branches, we won't feel the pain of the Husbandman's sharp pruning sheers. Read the last chapters of Job and learn the lesson, so that you won't have to go through the earlier chapters. Scripture was written for our instruction. Lay your hand on your mouth and quickly bow to the sovereignty of God.

THE FIERY TRIAL

Let me share something very personal. In June 1985, I had just finished preaching in a small country church when a lean-looking young man approached me and said, "I wish I was like you." I managed a smile, but held onto the words that came to mind. *You don't know what you are saying.* Little did he know that at that moment I was going through sheer terror. I had been praying earlier that day when suddenly it seemed that all hell was let loose in my mind. It was as though God had removed every hedge of protection from me and a thousand spirits of terror invaded my thoughts. I fell upon the floor. I wept. I cried out to God. I exorcised myself, to no avail. There is no way I can describe the experience of the following months other than to say that it was like being held over a black pit of insanity by a spider's web.

When I arrived home from that series of meetings, Sue asked how they went. I said, "The meetings were fine," then broke down. I felt so crushed within my mind that I was unable to have family devotions, or even eat a meal at the table with my family for over twelve months.

I diagnosed myself as having a "wounded spirit." Before God could use me, I needed to have a broken spirit:

> But this is the man to whom I will look and have regard: he who is humble and of a broken or wounded spirit, and who trembles at My word and reveres My commands (Isaiah 66:2, *Amplified Bible*).

It was A. W. Tozer who said, "Before God uses a man, God will break the man."

It took years to overcome that experience. At one point, I couldn't even gather enough courage to go to my home church. I wanted to, but irrational fear was paralyzing me. The first Sunday after the initial experience, I was in my bedroom trying to gather strength to go with my family to church. The fear was so strong, I would actually lose my breath even while I lay in bed. My son, who was seven at the time, came into the bedroom and handed me a note. He had written out a few Scriptures he thought I should read, although he had no idea what I was going through. These were the verses:

> The Lord is my helper, and I will not fear what man shall do to me (Hebrews 13:6).
>
> But the path of the just is as the shining light, that shines more and more unto the perfect day (Proverbs 4:18).
>
> Greater is he that is in you, than he that is in the world (1 John 4:4).

Then he had written the words, "I love you, Dad!"

HOW TO SPEED UP THE PROCESS

If there is a cry in your heart to be used by God, then you may go through a similar experience. I don't want to unnecessarily alarm you, but if you understand why it is happening and what you can do to speed up the process, it will help. If God in His great wisdom sees fit to use the Refiner's fire (if He takes you through a fiery trial), then it is only "if need be" (1 Peter 1:6). Pray that you may avoid it, but this is often normal procedure in being prepared for ministry. A wild horse is no good to a rider. It can't be trusted. It needs its spirit broken so that it will willingly yield to the desire of the rider. So, let me share with you a few words of comfort, so that if you find yourself hanging over a dark chasm of insanity by the spider web of faith, you will know why, and realize that the web is unbreakable.

You are asleep in bed, when suddenly a creak of the floor causes you to open your eyes in the semi-dark room. Towering over you stands the ugly sight of a huge man, wearing a stocking over his face, with a gun pointed at your head.

Suddenly, your heart races with fear. Your mouth becomes dry. Terror paralyzes you. You can see his evil lips smile in delight at having another human being under his power. Time stands still. Your racing heart is taking too much blood into your brain, feeding it an oversupply of oxygen, making your mind go blank. This inability to respond, even mentally, brings a panic that causes your breathing to become erratic. The over-action of the heart has also speedily lifted your body temperature to a point where cold sweat is forming on your brow, back, and legs.

With malicious intent, the intruder slowly moves the gun to the temple of your moistened brow. You can feel its cold barrel against your warm skin. The reality of what is happening tells you that this is no mere nightmare.

Adrenalin is being pumped throughout your body. Your mind is instinctively screaming *Run!* and yet you know that if you move, you are dead. With both hands on the gun, the cruel intruder slowly cocks the weapon. You see his white teeth grit in perverted delight. *You are going to die!* Unspeakable terror grips your mind. Perspiration pours out of your flesh. Your mouth is totally dry. It's as though your heart is pounding through your chest. Your breath seems to have drained from your lungs and you can feel your eyes bulge with overwhelming dread…

That's what an attack of irrational fear feels like. There is no intruder, no gun, and no threat of death. Yet there are those same, very real, worse-than-nightmarish symptoms.

According to estimates, three million people in the U.S. have panic attacks. These are characterized by rapid heartbeat, dizziness, shortness of breath, and fear of losing control, going crazy, or dying.

The unsaved who experience panic attacks are often driven to drugs, alcohol, despair, or insanity. The Christian who suffers doesn't do so in vain, but there is a sense of guilt on top of the fear. The experience doesn't seem to match the Bible's description of a faith-filled Christian. He says, "I *will not* fear"…*and yet he still fears.* His will is incapacitated.

For those who have prayed, and prayed, and prayed for deliverance, and still find themselves in such a predicament, there are strong consolations.

The apostle Paul was no stranger to fear. He said, "For, when we were come into Macedonia, our flesh had no rest, but we were troubled on every side; without were fightings, *within were fears*" (2 Corinthians 7:5, emphasis added).

Look at these verses from 2 Corinthians 12:7–9:

> And lest I should be exalted above measure through the abundance of the revelations, there was given to me a thorn in the flesh, the messenger of Satan to buffet me, lest I should be exalted above measure. For this thing I besought the Lord thrice, that it might depart from me. And he said to me, My grace is sufficient for you: for my strength is made perfect in weakness. Most gladly therefore will I rather glory in my infirmities, that the power of Christ may rest upon me.

Paul asked for deliverance from this demonic attack three times. Yet God chose to leave him with it. Some say it was a sickness, but that doesn't seem to be what the Bible teaches. It says it was a "messenger of Satan" (a demon) that buffeted him.

Why then did God allow demonic oppression to come against His apostle? He wanted to use Paul, but He didn't want him to fall through pride and fail in his calling. The demonic oppression was to keep him humble as God gave him an abundance of revelations. He had to remain small in his own eyes. The Greek word for "buffet" is *kolaphizo*, which means to "rap with the fist." Its root word is *kolos*, which means "dwarf."

Satan fires arrows only at those who have potential for the kingdom of God. You have great potential to be used by God in these last days. Instead of saying, "But God can't use me when I am paralyzed by fear," say, "Because His strength is made perfect in my weakness, God can use me for His glory *because the fear I am plagued by actually keeps me in weakness.*"

EXAMINE YOURSELF

Today, there are many who name the name of Christ, but who never "depart from iniquity." They are false converts who "ask Jesus into their heart," but are actually unconverted because they have never truly repented. So it is important that you examine yourself to see if you are in the faith (2 Corinthians 13:5). Those who allow sin in their lives are actually opening themselves up to demonic influence. The Bible instructs us to "neither give place to the devil" (Ephesians 4:27).

Afflictions only work together for our good, if we are "called according to [God's] purpose" (Romans 8:28). Therefore, the following are questions each of us need to ask ourselves:

> Do I honor my parents? Do I value them implicitly? God commands that we honor our parents, then Scripture warns, "that it may be well with you, and you may live long on the earth" (Ephesians 6:3). In other words, if you don't value your parents, all will not be well with you. I have found that many people have demonic problems because they *hate* their parents.
>
> Is there any unconfessed sin in my life? Is there any bitterness, resentment, or jealousy? Have I been hurt by someone in the past whom I can't find it within my heart to forgive? Then I am giving place to the devil. If I won't forgive and forget, I'm like a man who is stung to death by one bee. You could understand someone being stung to death by a *swarm* of bees, but we can do something about one bee. The sad thing about someone who becomes bitter is that all they need to do to deal with their problem is to swat the thing through repentance. God says He will not forgive us if we will not forgive from our heart (Matthew 6:15).
>
> Has there been any occult activity in my life in the past? Do I have idols (even as souvenirs) in my home? Is there any pornography? I need to prayerfully walk around in the house and ask God if there is anything that is unpleasing to Him. Then I must consider the same thing within the temple of my own body. Am I a glutton? Do I feed filth into my mind through my eyes or through my ears? Do my hands touch only what is pleasing in His sight? Are my words kind and loving? Are the meditations of my mind pleasing to God?
>
> The only way to know if you are a Christian is by your fruit. There are a number of fruits in Scripture: the fruit of praise, the fruit of thanksgiving, the fruit of holiness, the fruit of repentance, the fruit of righteousness, and the fruit of the Spirit—love, joy, peace, patience, goodness, gentleness, faith, meekness, and temperance.

A key to overcoming trials is to understand that they are *relative*. The next time Satan tries to make you feel sorry for yourself in the midst of a trial, ask yourself, "Would I like to trade places with someone who has a horrible terminal disease? Would I like to trade places with a burn victim who has been burned over 90% of his body?" We can't imagine the agonies those in such a predicament go through. Have you ever burned yourself on a toaster? Think what it must be like for those poor people. Such sober thoughts bring our problem into perspective, and should make us want to thank God for His many blessings. Not only for what we have, but also for those things we don't have—like unspeakable pain.

The fruit of thanksgiving should be evident in the Christian, not only for temporal blessings, but for the cross. Paul was persecuted beyond measure, merely for his faith in God, yet he said, "Thanks be to God for his unspeakable gift" (2 Corinthians 9:15).

As Christians, we should have the fruit of holiness. We should be separated from this world, with all of its corruption, to God. We should have evidence of our repentance. If we have stolen, we will return what isn't ours. We will set right (where possible) that which we have wronged. Lastly, we will possess the fruit of the Spirit. If we are rooted and grounded in Him, we will have the fruits of His character hanging from the branches of our lives. Do we have love that cares for others? Do we care enough about the salvation of sinners to put feet to our prayers and take the gospel to them? Love is not passive. It will not be self-indulgent while others suffer. It is empathetic.

GOOD REASON

If we haven't given place to the devil, what is he doing in our lives? There must be good reason for him to be there. The only reasonable conclusion is that God has given permission. This happened in the Book of Job. God allowed Satan to buffet Job so that he would grow in his faith in God. As I have said before, God has given us the Book of Job for our admonition and instruction.

Study the following verse from the *Amplified Bible:*

> It is God who is all the while effectually at work in you [energizing and creating in you the power and desire], both to will and to work for His good pleasure and satisfaction and delight (Philippians 2:13).

We have established that God is at work in you. You have this demonic "buffeting" from which God will not presently deliver you because He is doing a good work in you. Therefore, what should be your attitude to this good work He is doing? It should be one of joy—*because your joy is evidence of how much you trust God.* If you trust Him, then you will rejoice for His goodness, and that joy will be strength to you.

Take for instance a world champion boxer. His coach loves him to a point where he wants him above all things to be a winner. So what does the coach do —buy him a sofa, a TV, and potato chips? No. Instead, he place weights on his shoulders and resistance against his arms. He will even look around for the toughest sparring partner he can find. If the boxer doesn't understand what his trainer is doing, if he doesn't have faith in his methods, he will get depressed and lose heart. But if he knows what's going on, he will rejoice now in the trials because he sees, through the eyes of faith, the finished product.

That's why God is letting the devil loose on you: to make you strong. Paul says,

> For our light affliction, which is but for a moment [in the light of eternity], works for us a far more exceeding and eternal weight of glory (2 Corinthians 4:17).

Afflictions work *for* us, not against us, if we are in God's will. How is your joy when the Trainer brings the resistance your way? How much faith do you have in Him? The joy you have will be your measuring rod.

> For you, O God, have proved us: you have tried us, as silver is tried. You have caused men to ride over

> our heads; we went through fire and through water: but you brought us out into a wealthy place (Psalm 66:10,12).

God takes us through the fires of persecution, tribulation, and temptation to purify us, not to burn us. He takes us through water to cleanse us, not to drown us. Look at the reason God chastens His children, given in Hebrews 12:9–15:

> Furthermore we have had fathers of our flesh which corrected us, and we gave them reverence: shall we not much rather be in subjection to the Father of spirits, and live? For they verily for a few days chastened us after their own pleasure; but he for our profit, that we might be partakers of his holiness. Now no chastening for the present seems to be joyous, but grievous: nevertheless afterward it yields the peaceable fruit of righteousness to them which are exercised thereby.
>
> Wherefore lift up the hands which hang down, and the feeble knees; and make straight paths for your feet, lest that which is lame be turned out of the way; but let it rather be healed. Follow peace with all men, and holiness, without which no man shall see the Lord: looking diligently lest any man fail of the grace of God; lest any root of bitterness springing up trouble you, and thereby many be defiled.

In other words, get it together. Don't fall into discouragement, which is essentially a lack of faith in God. If you let your arms hang down in depression instead of rejoicing that God is working all things out for your good, you are saying that God isn't faithful, that His promises aren't worth believing, that He is actually a liar. There is no greater insult to God than to not believe His promises. The result of unbelief will be depression, discouragement, self-pity, resentment, then bitterness, which you will end up spreading to others.

If you have never thanked God for His promises, for His faithfulness, for the fact that He is working with you, in you, and for you—if you have been joyless, or even despised what has been happening to you and moved into bitterness—then repent of the sin of mistrust. How insulted you would be if you were a faithful and loving trainer, and your boxer, for whose good you are laboring, began to despise you for what you were doing.

On the other hand, if you are "exercised thereby," the result will be the "peaceable fruit of righteousness." In other words, you will end up living a life that is in complete righteousness, and bring a smile to the heart of your heavenly Father.

Look at Hebrews 12:11. Notice the word "afterward." That one word was my light in the dark tunnel. It meant there was an end to my terror, a light at the end of the tunnel that wasn't a train heading for me. Write down the word "afterward," and put it somewhere where you will be reminded that you have hope—and "hope never disappoints or deludes or shames us" (Romans 5:5, *Amplified*).

Guard against condemnation. You are no "less spiritual" than those who seem to have complete victory. If you don't believe it, think of the experience of Oswald Chambers, author of the mega-bestselling devotional *My Utmost For His Highest*. Now there's a man whose life and words have been an inspiration to millions. He was "spiritual" in the truest sense of the word. However, the great author had four years in his life of which he said, "God used me during those years for the conversion of souls, but I had no conscious communion with Him. The Bible was the dullest, most uninteresting book in existence" (*Oswald Chambers: Abandoned to God*). He described those four years as "hell on earth." However, he found that there was an "afterward," saying,

> But those of you who know the experience know very well how God brings one to the point of utter despair, and I got to the place where I did not care whether everyone knew how bad I was, I cared not for another on earth, saving to get out of my present condition (ibid).

If you have panic attacks or agoraphobia (fear of open spaces), don't fall into the deep pit of self-pity, because it has ugly bedfellows—discouragement, joylessness, condemnation, despair, and hopelessness. The sides of the pit of self-pity are very slippery, but there is one firm foothold. It is the uplifting stairs of thanksgiving. Let me explain how you can get your foot into it.

AN ATTITUDE OF THANKSGIVING

Sue and I were visiting an elderly lady named Helen, a 93-year-old who had broken her hip. She was unhappy because the food in the convalescent home wasn't very good. One day Mary walked into Helen's room. Mary was in her late seventies and had to be permanently fed through a tube that ran from a bottle directly into her stomach. Mary never tasted food or drink, and barring a miracle from God, she would never taste food or liquid again. Mary's condition made Helen thankful that at least she could have the pleasure of food and drink, even if it wasn't up to standard.

Then there was Robert. Robert had a good clear brain, but he had chronic emphysema. He couldn't breathe. Whenever she looked into his room, he was sitting on his bed, leaning over with his hand on his forehead. He gasped for every breath, twenty-four hours a day. Robert's problem made Mary thankful that at least she could breathe.

The point is that, despite your tormenting fears, you won't have to look too far for people who are suffering so badly that their problems dwarf yours. If you don't believe me, try being Robert for two minutes. Pinch your nose with one hand, then with the other one hold your lips together so that a meager amount of air gets into your mouth. Don't cheat. Do that for 120 long seconds. Feel the sweat break out on your forehead. Feel the panic. After two minutes of gasping for your breath, when you let go you will begin to thank God that you can breathe, and that will bring your problems into perspective. I'm not demeaning your fears. I'm offering you a way to lift yourself out of the pit of pity.

So next time you are attacked in some way, pull yourself together with a prayer of heartfelt thanksgiving, and say,

> Father I thank You that all things work together for my good; that it is You who are at work in me to will and do of Your good pleasure. Your strength is made perfect in my weakness. I will not let this attack discourage me because Your grace is sufficient for me. You will help me through it. When I think of the sufferings of many, many others, I feel ashamed for having any self-pity. I will therefore rejoice in the God of my salvation and give You thanks in and for everything. In Jesus' name I pray. Amen.

Your constant battle with trials will make you no stranger to them. Like a tree that is constantly beaten about by the wind, your roots will be deep. You will find, if you have an acquaintance with fear, etc., that you can live with it where others can't. You will be able to do things that others can't. The roots of your faith in God will be deeper than the roots of those who have never been ravaged by the winds of terror. Affliction works *for* us. God doesn't let the wind blow to destroy, but to strengthen. You will be able to go places and do things that others would fear to do, because those things that should (rationally) produce fear pale in significance compared to the average attack of irrational fear.

Again, do you believe God is at work in you to will and do of His good pleasure? Then rejoice, and let the joy of the Lord be your strength. There is a world weighed in the balance and found wanting. Don't fiddle while Rome burns. Your problems and fears are nothing compared to the terrible plight of the sinner. Eternal hell is his destiny. Lift up hands that hang down, lift up your heart through faith, then lift up your voice like a trumpet and show this people their transgression.

The Wordless Gospel

The following is a presentation of the gospel in picture form, so you can present it to someone who doesn't speak English. At the conclusion is John 3:16 in twenty-seven major languages.

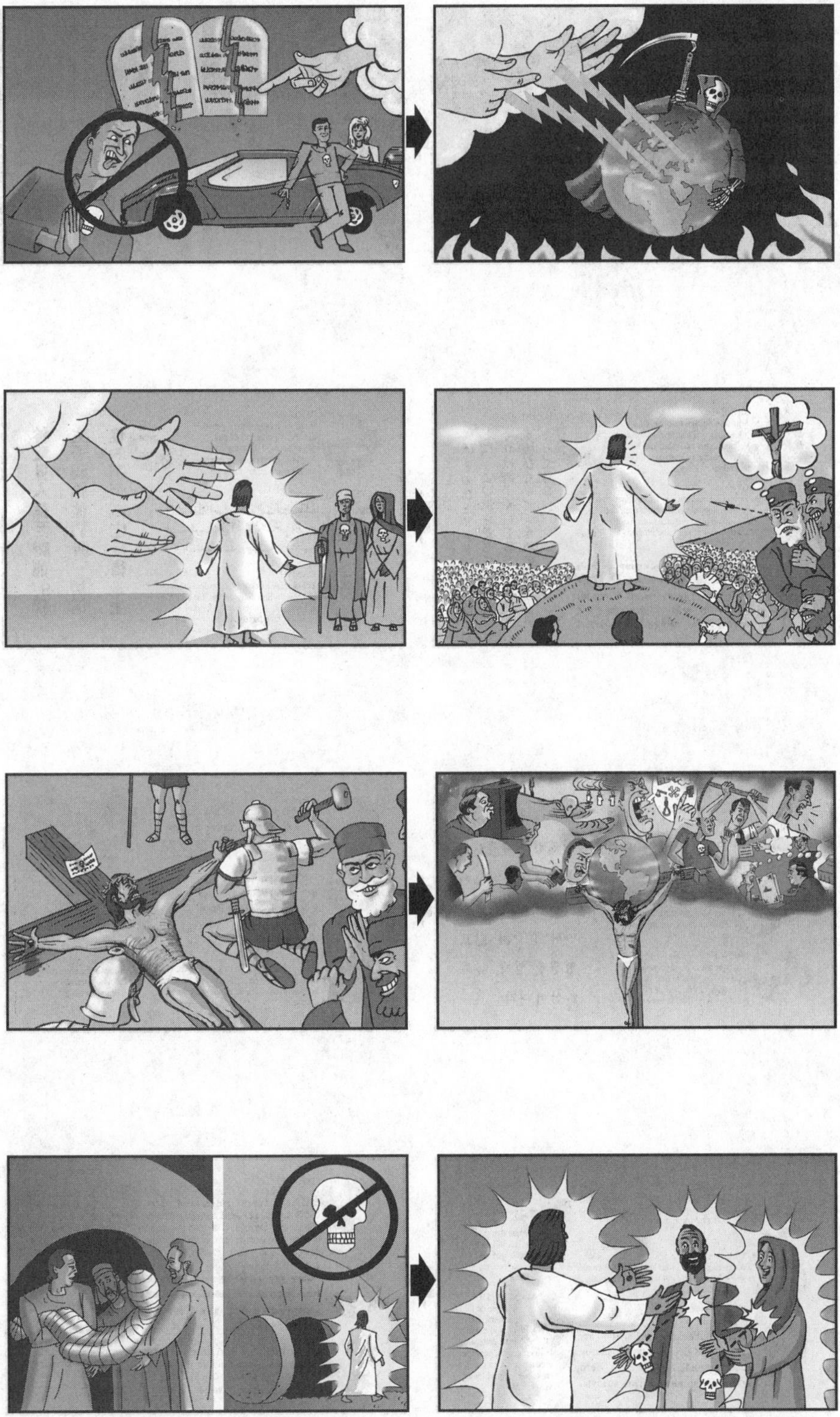

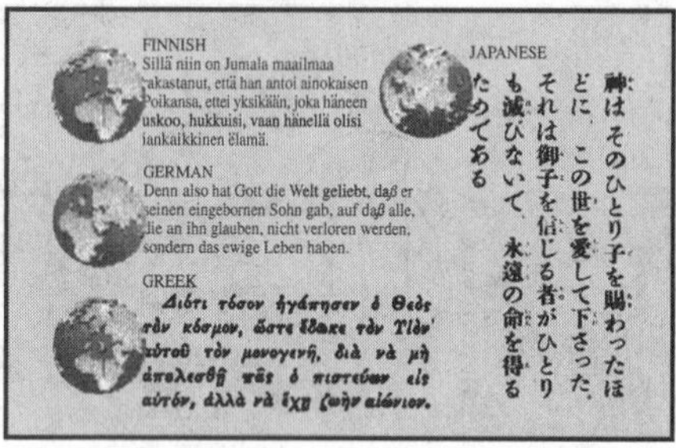
FINNISH
Sillä niin on Jumala maailmaa rakastanut, että han antoi ainokaisen Poikansa, ettei yksikään, joka häneen uskoo, hukkuisi, vaan hänellä olisi iankaikkinen elämä.
GERMAN
Denn also hat Gott die Welt geliebt, daß er seinen eingebornen Sohn gab, auf daß alle, die an ihn glauben, nicht verloren werden, sondern das ewige Leben haben.
GREEK
Διότι τόσον ἠγάπησεν ὁ Θεὸς τὸν κόσμον, ὥστε ἔδωκε τὸν Υἱὸν αὐτοῦ τὸν μονογενῆ, διὰ νὰ μὴ ἀπολεσθῇ πᾶς ὁ πιστεύων εἰς αὐτόν, ἀλλὰ νὰ ἔχῃ ζωὴν αἰώνιον.
JAPANESE
神はそのひとり子を賜わったほどに、この世を愛して下さった。それは御子を信じる者がひとりも滅びないで、永遠の命を得るためである。

AFRIKAANS
Want so lief die wêreld gehad, dat Hy sy eniggebore Seun gegee het, sodat elkeen wat in Hom glo, nie verlore mag gaan nie, maar die ewige lewe kan hê.
ARABIC
لأنه هكذا أحب الله العالم حتى بذل ابنه الوحيد لكي لا يهلك كل من يؤمن به بل تكون له الحياة الأبدية
DANISH
Thi således elskede Gud verden, at hangav sin Søn den enbårne, for at enhver, som tror på ham, ikke skal fortabes, men have evigt liv.
CHINESE
神爱世人、甚至將他的獨生子賜給他們、叫一切信他的、不至滅亡、反得永生，

DUTCH
Want alzo lief heeft God de wereld gehad, dat Hij zijn eniggeboren Zoon gegeven heeft, opdat een ieder, die in Hem gelooft, niet verloren ga, maar eeuwig leven hebbe.
ENGLISH
For God so loved the world, that He gave His only begotten Son, that whosoever believes in Him should not perish, but have everlasting life.
FRENCH
Car Dieu a tant aimé le monde qu'il a donné son Fils unique, afin que quiconque croit en lui ne périsse point, mais qu'il ait la vie éternelle.
KOREAN
하나님이 세상을 이처럼 사랑하사 독생자를 주셨으니 이는 저를 믿는 자 마다 멸망치 않고 영생을 얻게 하려 하심이니라

HEBREW
כִּי־כָכָה אָהַב הָאֱלֹהִים אֶת־הָעוֹלָם עַד־אֲשֶׁר נָתַן אֶת־בְּנוֹ אֶת־יְחִידוֹ לְמַעַן לֹא־יֹאבַד כָּל־הַמַּאֲמִין בּוֹ כִּי אִם־יִחְיֶה חַיֵּי עוֹלָמִים׃
HINDI
क्योंकि परमेश्वर ने संसार से ऐसा प्रेम रखा कि अपना एकलौता पुत्र दे दिया कि जो कोई उस पर विश्वास करे, नष्ट न हो परन्तु शाश्वत जीवन पाए।
TURKISH
Çünkü Tanrı dünyayi o kadar çok sevdi ki, biricik Oğlunu verdi. Öyle ki, O'na iman edenlerin hiçbiri mahvolmasin, ama hepsi sonsuz yaşama kavuşsun.
ICELANDIC
Því að svo elskaði Guð heiminn, að hann gaf son sinn eingetinn, til þess að hver, sem á hann trúir, glatist ekki, heldur hafi eilíft líf.
ITALIAN
Poichè Iddio ha tanto amato il mondo, che ha dato il suo unigenito Figliuolo, affinchè chiunque crede in lui non perisca, ma abbia vita eterna.

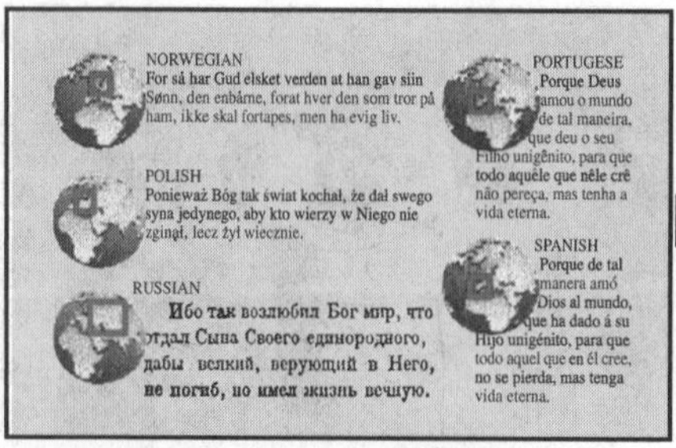
NORWEGIAN
For så har Gud elsket verden at han gav sin Sønn, den enbårne, forat hver den som tror på ham, ikke skal fortapes, men ha evig liv.
POLISH
Ponieważ Bóg tak świat kochał, że dał swego syna jedynego, aby kto wierzy w Niego nie zginął, lecz żył wiecznie.
RUSSIAN
Ибо так возлюбил Бог мир, что отдал Сына Своего единородного, дабы всякий, верующий в Него, не погиб, но имел жизнь вечную.
PORTUGESE
Porque Deus amou o mundo de tal maneira, que deu o seu Filho unigênito, para que todo aquêle que nêle crê não pereça, mas tenha a vida eterna.
SPANISH
Porque de tal manera amó Dios al mundo, que ha dado a su Hijo unigénito, para que todo aquel que en él cree, no se pierda, mas tenga vida eterna.

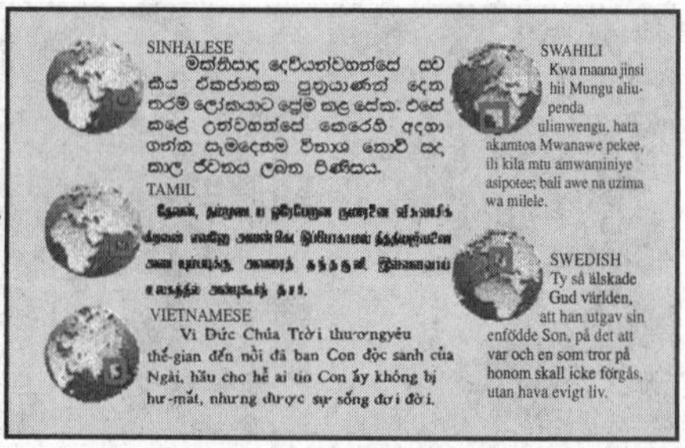
SINHALESE
TAMIL
VIETNAMESE
Vì Đức Chúa Trời thương yêu thế-gian đến nỗi đã ban Con độc sanh của Ngài, hầu cho hễ ai tin Con ấy không bị hư-mất, nhưng được sự sống đời đời.
SWAHILI
Kwa maana jinsi hii Mungu aliupenda ulimwengu, hata akamtoa Mwanawe pekee, ili kila mtu amwaminiye asipotee; bali awe na uzima wa milele.
SWEDISH
Ty så älskade Gud världen, att han utgav sin enfödde Son, på det att var och en som tror på honom skall icke förgås, utan hava evigt liv.

Index

RAY COMFORT has spoken in approximately 700 churches from almost every denomination. Dr. D. James Kennedy, Bill Gothard, David Wilkerson, and many other Christian leaders have commended his ministry. He has written extensively on evangelism, including writing for Billy Graham's *Decision* magazine. The Moody Bible Institute, Leighton Ford Ministries, Institute in Basic Life Principles, and the Institute for Scientific & Biblical Research use his literature. He has written more than 35 books and is a regular platform speaker at the Southern Baptist State Conferences. His videos have been seen by more than 30,000 pastors.